The Complete Works..

Luther A. Johnson.
1894.

The "Arundel Poets"

THE COMPLETE WORKS

OF

WILLIAM SHAKESPEARE

ARRANGED IN THEIR CHRONOLOGICAL ORDER

EDITED BY

Wᵐ G. CLARK AND Wᵐ ALDIS WRIGHT

WITH AN INTRODUCTION TO EACH PLAY, ADAPTED FROM THE SHAKESPEAREAN PRIMER OF

PROFESSOR *Edward* DOWDEN

VOL. II.

Illustrated

CHICAGO
W. B. CONKEY COMPANY.
1894.

CONTENTS.

VOL. II.

KING HENRY IV. PART I.

(WRITTEN ABOUT 1597–98.)

INTRODUCTION.

The two parts of *King Henry IV* may be considered as one play in ten acts. It is probable that Shakespeare went on with little or no delay from the first part to its continuation in the second. Both were written before the entry of the first in the Stationers' register, Feb 25, 1597–98, for the entry shows that the name of the fat knight, who originally appeared in both parts under the name of Oldcastle, had been already altered to Falstaff. Meres makes mention of *Henry IV*, and Ben Jonson, in *Every Man Out of His Humour* (1599), alludes to Justice Silence, one of the characters of the Second Part of Shakespeare's play. The materials upon which Shakespeare worked in *Henry IV* and *Henry V*, were obtained from Holinshed, and from an old play, full of vulgar mirth, and acted before 1588, *The Famous Victories of Henry V*. Both parts of *Henry IV* consist of a comedy and a history fused together. The hero of the one is the royal Bolingbroke, the hero of the other is Falstaff, while Prince Henry passes to and fro between the history and the comedy, serving as the bond which unites the two. Henry IV. is the same Bolingbroke who had been so greatly conceived in *Richard II*, only he is no longer in the full force of his manhood. He is worn by care and toil, harassed by revolts and conspiracies, yet still resolved to hold firmly what he has forcibly attained. There is a pathetic power in the figure of this weary ambitious man, who can take no rest until the rest of death comes upon him. Hotspur, who, to bring him into contrast with the Prince, is made much younger than the Harry Percy of history, is as ardent in the pursuit of glory as the Prince seems to be indifferent to it. To his hot temper and quick sense of personal honor small matters are great, he does not see things in their true proportions; he lacks self-control, he has no easiness of nature. Yet he is gallant, chivalrous, not devoid of generosity nor of quick affections, though never in a high sense disinterested. Prince Hal, whom Shakespeare admires and loves more than any other person in English history, afterwards to become Shakespeare's ideal king of England, cares little for mere reputation. He does not think much of himself and of his own honor, and while there is nothing to do, and his great father holds all power in his own right hand, he escapes from the cold proprieties of the court to the boisterous life and mirth of the tavern. He is, however, only waiting for a call to action, and Shakespeare declares that from the first he was conscious of his great destiny, and while seeming to scatter his force in frivolity, was holding his true self, well-guarded, in reserve. Falstaff is everything in little, or rather everything in *much*, for is he not a tun of flesh? English literature knows no numerous creation to set beside Falstaff, and to find his equal—yet his opposite—we must turn to the gaunt figure of the romantic knight of La Mancha, in whose person Cervantes smiled away pathetically the chivalry of the Middle Ages from out our modern world. Falstaff exercises upon the reader of these plays much the same fascination which he exercised upon the Prince. We know him to be a gross-bodied, self-indulgent old sinner, devoid of moral sense and of self-respect, and yet we cannot part with him. We cannot live in this world withe it humor, and Falstaff is humor maintaining its mastery against all antagonisms. We admit, however, the necessity of his utter banishment from Henry, when Henry enters upon the grave responsibilities of kingship. Still we have a tender thought for Sir John in his exile from London taverns. And at the last, when he fumbles with the sheets and plays with flowers, when "a' went away, an it had been any christom child," we bid him adieu with a tear that does not forbid a smile. The historical period represented by 1 *Henry IV*. dates from the battle of Holmedon Hill, Sept. 14 1402, to the battle of Shrewsbury, July 21, 1403. 2 *Henry IV*. continues the history to the king's death and the accession of Henry V., 1413.

DRAMATIS PERSONÆ.

KING HENRY the Fourth.
HENRY, Prince of Wales, } sons to the King.
JOHN of Lancaster,
EARL OF WESTMORELAND.
SIR WALTER BLUNT.
THOMAS PERCY, Earl of Worcester
HENRY PERCY, Earl of Northumberland.

HENRY PERCY, surnamed HOTSPUR, his son
EDMUND MORTIMER, Earl of March
RICHARD SCROOP, Archbishop of York.
ARCHIBALD, Earl of DOUGLAS.
OWEN GLENDOWER.
SIR RICHARD VERNON.
SIR JOHN FALSTAFF.

(383)

SIR MICHAEL, a friend to the Archbishop of York.
POINS.
GADSHILL.
PETO.
BARDOLPH.

LADY PERCY, wife to Hotspur, and sister to Mortimer.

LADY MORTIMER, daughter to Glendower, and wife to Mortimer.
MISTRESS QUICKLY, hostess of a tavern in Eastcheap.

Lords, Officers, Sheriff, Vintner, Chamberlain, Drawers, two Carriers, Travellers, and Attendants.

SCENE : *England.*

ACT I.

SCENE I. *London. The palace.*

Enter KING HENRY, LORD JOHN OF LANCASTER, *the* EARL OF WESTMORELAND, SIR WALTER BLUNT, *and others.*

  King. So shaken as we are, so wan with care,
Find we a time for frighted peace to pant,
And breathe short-winded accents of new broils
To be commenced in strands afar remote.
†No more the thirsty entrance of this soil
Shall daub her lips with her own children's blood ;
Nor more shall trenching war channel her fields,
Nor bruise her flowerets with the armed hoofs
Of hostile paces : those opposed eyes,
Which, like the meteors of a troubled heaven,
All of one nature, of one substance bred,   11
Did lately meet in the intestine shock
And furious close of civil butchery
Shall now, in mutual well-beseeming ranks,
March all one way and be no more opposed
Against acquaintance, kindred and allies :
The edge of war, like an ill-sheathed knife,
No more shall cut his master. Therefore, friends,
As far as to the sepulchre of Christ,
Whose soldier now, under whose blessed cross
We are impressed and engaged to fight,   21
Forthwith a power of English shall we levy ;
Whose arms were moulded in their mothers' womb
To chase these pagans in those holy fields
Over whose acres walk'd those blessed feet
Which fourteen hundred years ago were nail'd
For our advantage on the bitter cross.
But this our purpose now is twelve month old,
And bootless 'tis to tell you we will go :
Therefore we meet not now. Then let me hear
Of you, my gentle cousin Westmoreland,   31
What yesternight our council did decree
In forwarding this dear expedience.
  West. My liege, this haste was hot in question,
And many limits of the charge set down
But yesternight : when all athwart there came
A post from Wales loaden with heavy news ;
Whose worst was, that the noble Mortimer,
Leading the men of Herefordshire to fight
Against the irregular and wild Glendower,   40

Was by the rude hands of that Welshman taken,
A thousand of his people butchered ;
Upon whose dead corpse there was such misuse,
Such beastly shameless transformation,
By those Welshwomen done as may not be
Without much shame retold or spoken of.
  King. It seems then that the tidings of this broil
Brake off our business for the Holy Land.
  West. This match'd with other did, my gracious lord ;
For more uneven and unwelcome news   50
Came from the north and thus it did import :
On Holy-rood day, the gallant Hotspur there,
Young Harry Percy and brave Archibald,
That ever-valiant and approved Scot,
At Holmedon met,
Where they did spend a sad and bloody hour,
As by discharge of their artillery,
And shape of likelihood, the news was told ;
For he that brought them, in the very heat
And pride of their contention did take horse,
Uncertain of the issue any way.   61
  King. Here is a dear, a true industrious friend,
Sir Walter Blunt, new lighted from his horse,
Stain'd with the variation of each soil
Betwixt that Holmedon and this seat of ours ;
And he hath brought us smooth and welcome news.
The Earl of Douglas is discomfited :
Ten thousand bold Scots, two and twenty knights,
Balk'd in their own blood did Sir Walter see
On Holmedon's plains. Of prisoners, Hotspur took   70
Mordake the Earl of Fife, and eldest son
To beaten Douglas ; and the Earl of Athol,
Of Murray, Angus, and Menteith :
And is not this an honorable spoil ?
A gallant prize ? ha, cousin, is it not ?
  West. In faith,
It is a conquest for a prince to boast of.
  King. Yea, there thou makest me sad and makest me sin
In envy that my Lord Northumberland
Should be the father to so blest a son,   80
A son who is the theme of honor's tongue ;
Amongst a grove, the very straightest plant ;
Who is sweet Fortune's minion and her pride :
Whilst I, by looking on the praise of him,
See riot and dishonor stain the brow

Of my young Harry. O that it could be proved
That some night-tripping fairy had exchanged
In cradle-clothes our children where they lay,
And call'd mine Percy, his Plantagenet!
Then would I have his Harry, and he mine. 90
But let him from my thoughts. What think
    you, coz,
Of this young Percy's pride? the prisoners,
Which he in this adventure hath surprised,
To his own use he keeps; and sends me word,
I shall have none but Mordake Earl of Fife.

West. This is his uncle's teaching; this is
    Worcester,
Malevolent to you in all aspects;
Which makes him prune himself, and bristle
    up
The crest of youth against your dignity.

King. But I have sent for him to answer
    this; 100
And for this cause awhile we must neglect
Our holy purpose to Jerusalem.
Cousin, on Wednesday next our council we
Will hold at Windsor; so inform the lords:
But come yourself with speed to us again;
For more is to be said and to be done
Than out of anger can be uttered.

West. I will, my liege.   [*Exeunt.*

SCENE II. *London. An apartment of the
Prince's.*

Enter the PRINCE OF WALES *and* FALSTAFF.

Fal. Now, Hal, what time of day is it, lad?

Prince. Thou art so fat-witted, with drinking of old sack and unbuttoning thee after supper and sleeping upon benches after noon, that thou hast forgotten to demand that truly which thou wouldst truly know. What a devil hast thou to do with the time of the day? Unless hours were cups of sack and minutes capons and clocks the tongues of bawds and dials the signs of leaping-houses and the blessed sun himself a fair hot wench in flame-colored taffeta, I see no reason why thou shouldst be so superfluous to demand the time of the day.

Fal. Indeed, you come near me now, Hal; for we that take purses go by the moon and the seven stars, and not by Phœbus, he, 'that wandering knight so fair.' And, I prithee, sweet wag, when thou art king, as, God save thy grace,—majesty I should say, for grace thou wilt have none,— 20

Prince. What, none?

Fal. No, by my troth, not so much as will serve to be prologue to an egg and butter.

Prince. Well, how then? come, roundly, roundly.

Fal. Marry, then, sweet wag, when thou art king, let not us that are squires of the night's body be called thieves of the day's beauty: let us be Diana's foresters, gentlemen of the shade, minions of the moon; and let men say we be men of good government, being governed, as the sea is, by our noble and chaste mistress the moon, under whose countenance we steal.

Prince. Thou sayest well, and it holds well too; for the fortune of us that are the moon's men doth ebb and flow like the sea, being governed, as the sea is, by the moon. As, for proof, now: a purse of gold most resolutely snatched on Monday night and most dissolutely spent on Tuesday morning; got with swearing 'Lay by' and spent with crying 'Bring in;' now in as low an ebb as the foot of the ladder and by and by in as high a flow as the ridge of the gallows.

Fal. By the Lord, thou sayest true, lad. And is not my hostess of the tavern a most sweet wench?

Prince. As the honey of Hybla, my old lad of the castle. And is not a buff jerkin a most sweet robe of durance? 49

Fal. How now, how now, mad wag! what, in thy quips and thy quiddities? what a plague have I to do with a buff jerkin?

Prince. Why, what a pox have I to do with my hostess of the tavern?

Fal. Well, thou hast called her to a reckoning many a time and oft.

Prince. Did I ever call for thee to pay thy part?

Fal. No; I'll give thee thy due, thou hast paid all there. 60

Prince. Yea, and elsewhere, so far as my coin would stretch; and where it would not, I have used my credit.

Fal. Yea, and so used it that, were it not here apparent that thou art heir apparent— But, I prithee, sweet wag, shall there be gallows standing in England when thou art king? and resolution thus fobbed as it is with the rusty curb of old father antic the law? Do not thou, when thou art king, hang a thief. 70

Prince. No; thou shalt.

Fal. Shall I? O rare! By the Lord, I'll be a brave judge.

Prince. Thou judgest false already: I mean, thou shalt have the hanging of the thieves and so become a rare hangman.

Fal. Well, Hal, well; and in some sort it jumps with my humor as well as waiting in the court, I can tell you.

Prince. For obtaining of suits? 80

Fal. Yea, for obtaining of suits, whereof the hangman hath no lean wardrobe. 'Sblood, I am as melancholy as a gib cat or a lugged bear.

Prince. Or an old lion, or a lover's lute.

Fal. Yea, or the drone of a Lincolnshire bagpipe.

Prince. What sayest thou to a hare, or the melancholy of Moor-ditch?

Fal. Thou hast the most unsavory similes and art indeed the most comparative, rascalliest, sweet young prince. But, Hal, I prithee, trouble me no more with vanity. I would to God thou and I knew where a commodity of good names were to be bought. An old lord of the council rated me the other day in the street about you, sir, but I marked him not; and yet he talked very wisely, but I regarded

25

him not ; and yet he talked wisely, and in the street too.

Prince. Thou didst well ; for wisdom cries out in the streets, and no man regards it   190

Fal. O, thou hast damnable iteration and art indeed able to corrupt a saint   Thou hast done much harm upon me, Hal , God forgive thee for it ! Before I knew thee, Hal, I knew nothing ; and now am I, if a man should speak truly, little better than one of the wicked   I must give over this life, and I will give it over by the Lord, and I do not, I am a villain   I'll be damned for never a king's son in Christendom

Prince. Where shall we take a purse tomorrow, Jack ?   111

Fal. 'Zounds, where thou wilt, lad , I'll make one , an I do not, call me villain and baffle me.

Prince. I see a good amendment of life in thee ; from praying to purse-taking

Fal. Why, Hal, 'tis my vocation, Hal ; 'tis no sin for a man to labor in his vocation.

Enter POINS.

Poins ! Now shall we know if Gadshill have set a match   O, if men were to be saved by merit, what hole in hell were hot enough for him ?   This is the most omnipotent villain that ever cried ' Stand ' to a true man.

Prince. Good morrow, Ned.

Poins Good morrow, sweet Hal. What says Monsieur Remorse ? what says Sir John Sack and Sugar ? Jack ! how agrees the devil and thee about thy soul, that thou soldest him on Good-Friday last for a cup of Madeira and a cold capon's leg ?   129

Prince Sir John stands to his word, the devil shall have his bargain , for he was never yet a breaker of proverbs : he will give the devil his due

Poins. Then art thou damned for keeping thy word with the devil

Prince Else he had been damned for cozening the devil

Poins But, my lads, my lads, to-morrow morning, by four o'clock, early at Gadshill ! there are pilgrims going to Canterbury with rich offerings, and traders riding to London with fat purses   I have vizards for you all , you have horses for yourselves   Gadshill lies tonight in Rochester . I have bespoke supper tomorrow night in Eastcheap ; we may do it as secure as sleep   If you will go, I will stuff your purses full of crowns , if you will not, tarry at home and be hanged

Fal. Hear ye, Yedward , if I tarry at home and go not, I'll hang you for going   150

Poins. You will, chops ?

Fal. Hal, wilt thou make one ?

Prince Who, I rob ? I a thief ? not I, by my faith

Fal. There's neither honesty, manhood, nor good fellowship in thee, nor thou camest not of the blood royal, if thou darest not stand for ten shillings

Prince. Well then, once in my days I'll be a madcap   160

Fal. Why, that's well said.

Prince. Well, come what will, I'll tarry at home

Fal By the Lord, I'll be a traitor then, when thou art king.

Prince I care not.

Poins Sir John, I prithee, leave the prince and me alone · I will lay him down such reasons for this adventure that he shall go   169

Fal Well, God give thee the spirit of persuasion and him the ears of profiting, that what thou speakest may move and what he hears may be believed, that the true prince may, for recreation sake, prove a false thief ; for the poor abuses of the time want countenance. Farewell · you shall find me in Eastcheap

Prince. Farewell, thou latter spring ! farewell, All-hallown summer !   [*Exit Falstaff* ·

Poins Now, my good sweet honey lord, ride with us to-morrow   I have a jest to execute that I cannot manage alone   Falstaff, Bardolph, Peto and Gadshill shall rob those men that we have already waylaid   yourself and I will not be there , and when they have the booty, if you and I do not rob them, cut this head off from my shoulders

Prince. How shall we part with them in setting forth ?

Poins Why, we will set forth before or after them, and appoint them a place of meeting, wherein it is at our pleasure to fail, and then will they adventure upon the exploit themselves , which they shall have no sooner achieved, but we'll set upon them.

Prince Yea, but 'tis like that they will know us by our horses, by our habits and by every other appointment, to be ourselves

Poins Tut ! our horses they shall not see: I'll tie them in the wood , our vizards we will change after we leave them · and, sirrah I have cases of buckram for the nonce, to immask our noted outward garments.

Prince. Yea, but I doubt they will be too hard for us.

Poins Well, for two of them, I know them to be as true-bred cowards as ever turned back, and for the third, if he fight longer than he sees reason, I'll forswear arms   The virtue of this jest will be, the incomprehensible lies that this same fat rogue will tell us when we meet at supper.. how thirty, at least, he fought with ; what wards, what blows, what extremities he endured , and in the reproof of this lies the jest.

Prince Well, I'll go with thee . provide us all things necessary and meet me to-morrow night in Eastcheap ; there I'll sup. Farewell.

Poins Farewell, my lord.   [*Exit*

Prince I know you all, and will awhile uphold

The unyoked humor of your idleness :   220

Yet herein will I imitate the sun,

Who doth permit the base contagious clouds

To smother up his beauty from the world,
That, when he please again to be himself,
Being wanted, he may be more wonder'd at,
By breaking through the foul and ugly mists
Of vapors that did seem to strangle him.
If all the year were playing holidays,
To sport would be as tedious as to work ;
But when they seldom come, they wish'd for
  come,   230
And nothing pleaseth but rare accidents.
So, when this loose behavior I throw off
And pay the debt I never promised,
By how much better than my word I am,
By so much shall I falsify men's hopes,
And like bright metal on a sullen ground,
My reformation, glittering o'er my fault,
Shall show more goodly and attract more
  eyes
Than that which hath no foil to set it off.
I'll so offend, to make offence a skill ,   240
Redeeming time when men think least I will
                             [*Exit.*

SCENE III. *London   The palace*

Enter the KING, NORTHUMBERLAND. WOR-
CESTER, HOTSPUR, SIR WALTER BLUNT,
with others.

King. My blood hath been too cold and
  temperate,
Unapt to stir at these indignities,
And you have found me , for accordingly
  ou tread upon my patience   but be sure
I will from henceforth rather be myself,
Mighty and to be fear'd, than my condition ,
Which hath been smooth as oil, soft as young
  down,
And therefore lost that title of respect
Which the proud soul ne'er pays but to the
  proud
  Wor   Our house, my sovereign liege, little
  deserves   10
The scourge of greatness to be used on it ;
And that same greatness too which our own
  hands
Have holp to make so portly.
  North.   My lord,—
  King   Worcester, get thee gone , for I do
  see
Danger and disobedience in thine eye ·
O, sir, your presence is too bold and peremp-
  tory,
And majesty might never yet endure
The moody frontier of a servant brow
You have good leave to leave us . when we
  need   20
Your use and counsel, we shall send for you.
                         [*Exit Wor.*
You were about to speak   [*To North.*
  North.   Yea, my good lord
Those prisoners in your highness' name de-
  manded,
Which Harry Percy here at Holmedon took,
Were, as he says, not with such strength de-
  nied
As is deliver'd to your majesty:

Either envy, therefore, or misprision
Is guilty of this fault and not my son
  Hot   My liege, I did deny no prisoners,
But I remember, when the fight was done, 30
When I was dry with rage and extreme toil,
Breathless and faint, leaning upon my sword,
Came there a certain lord, neat, and trimly
  dress'd,
Fresh as a bridegroom , and his chin new
  reap'd
Show'd like a stubble-land at harvest-home ,
He was perfumed like a milliner ,
And 'twixt his finger and his thumb he held
A pouncet-box, which ever and anon
He gave his nose and took't away again ,
Who therewith angry, when it next came
  there,   40
Took it in snuff ; and still he smiled and
  talk'd,
And as the soldiers bore dead bodies by,
He call'd them untaught knaves, unmannerly,
To bring a slovenly unhandsome corse
Betwixt the wind and his nobility.
With many holiday and lady terms
He question'd me , amongst the rest, de-
  manded
My prisoners in your majesty's behalf
I then, all smarting with my wounds being
  cold,
To be so pester'd with a popinjay,   50
Out of my grief and my impatience,
Answer'd neglectingly I know not what,
He should or he should not , for he made me
  mad
To see him shine so brisk and smell so sweet
And talk so like a waiting-gentlewoman
Of guns and drums and wounds,—God save
  the mark '—
And telling me the sovereign'st thing on earth
Was parmaceti for an inward bruise,
And that it was great pity, so it was,
This villanous salt-petre should be digg'd 60
Out of the bowels of the harmless earth,
Which many a good tall fellow had destroy'd
So cowardly , and but for these vile guns,
He would himself have been a soldier
This bald unjointed chat of his, my lord,
I answer'd indirectly, as I said ;
And I beseech you, let not his report
Come current for an accusation
Betwixt my love and your high majesty
  Blunt.   The circumstance consider'd, good
  my lord,   70
Whate'er Lord Harry Percy then had said
To such a person and in such a place,
At such a time, with all the rest retold,
May reasonably die and never rise
To do him wrong or any way impeach
What then he said, so he unsay it now
  King   Why, yet he doth deny his prisoners,
But with proviso and exception,
That we at our own charge shall ransom
  straight
His brother-in-law, the foolish Mortimer ;   80
Who, on my soul, hath wilfully betray'd
The lives of those that he did lead to fight

Against that great magician, damn'd Glen-
    dower,
Whose daughter, as we hear, the Earl of
    March
Hath lately married. Shall our coffers, then,
Be emptied to redeem a traitor home ?
Shall we buy treason ? and indent with fears,
When they have lost and forfeited themselves ?
No, on the barren mountains let him starve ;
For I shall never hold that man my friend   90
Whose tongue shall ask me for one penny cost
To ransom home revolted Mortimer.
   Hot. Revolted Mortimer !
He never did fall off, my sovereign liege,
But by the chance of war : to prove that true
Needs no more but one tongue for all those
    wounds,
Those mouthed wounds, which valiantly he
    took,
When on the gentle Severn's sedgy bank,
In single opposition, hand to hand,
He did confound the best part of an hour   100
In changing hardiment with great Glendower :
Three times they breathed and three times did
    they drink,
Upon agreement, of swift Severn's flood ;   -
Who then, affrighted with their bloody looks,
Ran fearfully among the trembling reeds,
And hid his crisp head in the hollow bank
Bloodstained with these valiant combatants.
Never did base and rotten policy
Color her working with such deadly wounds ;
Nor never could the noble Mortimer   110
Receive so many, and all willingly :
Then let not him be slander'd with revolt.
   King. Thou dost belie him, Percy, thou
    dost belie him ;
He never did encounter with Glendower :
I tell thee,
He durst as well have met the devil alone
As Owen Glendower for an enemy.
Art thou not ashamed ? But, sirrah, hence-
    forth
Let me not hear you speak of Mortimer :
Send me your prisoners with the speediest
    means,   120
Or you shall hear in such a kind from me
As will displease you. My Lord Northumber-
    land,
We license your departure with your son.
Send us your prisoners, or you will hear of it.
     [*Exeunt King Henry, Blunt, and train.*
   Hot. An if the devil come and roar for
    them,
I will not send them : I will after straight
And tell him so ; for I will ease my heart,
Albeit I make a hazard of my head.
   North. What, drunk with choler ? stay and
    pause awhile :
Here comes your uncle.

        Re-enter WORCESTER.

   Hot.   Speak of Mortimer !   130
'Zounds, I will speak of him ; and let my
    soul
Want mercy, if I do not join with him :

Yea, on his part I'll empty all these veins,
And shed my dear blood drop by drop in the
    dust,
But I will lift the down-trod Mortimer
As high in the air as this unthankful king,
As this ingrate and canker'd Bolingbroke.
   North. Brother, the king hath made your
    nephew mad.
   Wor. Who struck this heat up after I was
    gone ?
   Hot. He will, forsooth, have all my prisoners ;
And when I urged the ransom once again   44l
Of my wife's brother, then his cheek look'd
    pale,
And on my face he turn'd an eye of death,
Trembling even at the name of Mortimer.
   Wor. I cannot blame him : was not he pro-
    claim'd
By Richard that dead is the next of blood ?.
   North. He was ; I heard the proclama-
    tion :
And then it was when the unhappy king,—
Whose wrongs in us God pardon !—did set
    forth
Upon his Irish expedition ;   150
From whence he intercepted did return
To be deposed and shortly murdered.
   Wor. And for whose death we in the world's
    wide mouth
Live scandalized and foully spoken of.
   Hot. But, soft, I pray you ; did King Rich-
    ard then
Proclaim my brother Edmund Mortimer
Heir to the crown ?
   North.   He did ; myself did hear it
   Hot. Nay, then I cannot blame his cousin
    king,
That wished him on the barren mountains
    starve.
But shall it be that you, that set the crown 160
Upon the head of this forgetful man
And for his sake wear the detested blot
Of murderous subornation, shall it be,
That you a world of curses undergo,
Being the agents, or base second means,
The cords, the ladder, or the hangman rather ?
O, pardon me that I descend so low,
To show the line and the predicament
Wherein you range under this subtle king ;
Shall it for shame be spoken in these days, 170
Or fill up chronicles in time to come,
That men of your nobility and power
Did gage them both in an unjust behalf,
As both of you—God pardon it !—have done,
To put down Richard, that sweet lovely rose,
And plant this thorn, this canker, Boling-
    broke ?
And shall it in more shame be further spoken,
That you are fool'd, discarded and shook off
By him for whom these shames ye under-
    went ?   179
No ; yet time serves wherein you may redeem
Your banish'd honors and restore yourselves
Into the good thoughts of the world again,
Revenge the jeering and disdain'd contempt
Of this proud king, who studies day and night

To answer all the debt he owes to you
Even with the bloody payment of your deaths:
Therefore, I say,—
   Wor.   Peace, cousin, say no more :
And now I will unclasp a secret book,
And to your quick-conceiving discontents
I'll read you matter deep and dangerous,   190
As full of peril and adventurous spirit
As to o'er-walk a current roaring loud
On the unsteadfast footing of a spear.
   Hot. If he fall in, good night ! or sink or
      swim :
Send danger from the east unto the west,
So honor cross it from the north to south,
And let them grapple : O, the blood more stirs
To rouse a lion than to start a hare !
   North. Imagination of some great exploit
Drives him beyond the bounds of patience. 200
   Hot. By heaven, methinks it were an easy
      leap,
To pluck bright honor from the pale-faced
      moon,
Or dive into the bottom of the deep,
Where fathom-line could never touch the
      ground,
And pluck up drowned honor by the locks ;
So he that doth redeem her thence might wear
Without corrival, all her dignities :
But out upon this half-faced fellowship !
   Wor. He apprehends a world of figures
      here,
But not the form of what he should attend.
Good cousin, give me audience for a while. 211
   Hot. I cry you mercy.
   Wor.   Those same noble Scots
That are your prisoners,—
   Hot.   I'll keep them all ;
By God, he shall not have a Scot of them ;
No, if a Scot would save his soul, he shall not :
I'll keep them, by this hand.
   Wor.   You start away
And lend no ear unto my purposes.
Those prisoners you shall keep.
   Hot.   Nay, I will ; that's flat :
He said he would not ransom Mortimer ;
Forbad my tongue to speak of Mortimer ; 220
But I will find him when he lies asleep,
And in his ear I'll holla ' Mortimer !'
Nay,
I'll have a starling shall be taught to speak
Nothing but ' Mortimer,' and give it him
To keep his anger still in motion.
   Wor. Hear you, cousin, a word.
   Hot. All studies here I solemnly defy,
Save how to gall and pinch this Bolingbroke :
And that same sword-and-buckler Prince of
      Wales,   230
But that I think his father loves him not
And would be glad he met with some mis-
      chance,
I would have him poison'd with a pot of ale.
   Wor. Farewell, kinsman : I'll talk to you
When you are better temper'd to attend.
   North. Why, what a wasp-stung and im-
      patient fool
Art thou to break into this woman's mood,

Tying thine ear to no tongue but thine own !
   Hot. Why, look you, I am whipp'd and
      scourged with rods,
Nettled and stung with pismires, when I hear
Of this vile politician, Bolingbroke.   241
In Richard's time,—what do you call the
      place ?—
A plague upon it, it is in Gloucestershire ;
'Twas where the madcap duke his uncle kept,
His uncle York ; where I first bow'd my knee
Unto this king of smiles, this Bolingbroke,—
'Sblood !—
When you and he came back from Ravens-
      purgh.
   North. At Berkley castle.
   Hot. You say true :   250
Why, what a candy deal of courtesy
This fawning greyhound then did proffer me !
Look, ' when his infant fortune came to age,'
And ' gentle Harry Percy,' and ' kind cousin;'
O, the devil take such cozeners ! God forgive
      me !
Good uncle, tell your tale ; I have done.
   Wor. Nay, if you have not, to it again ;
We will stay your leisure.
   Hot.   I have done, i' faith.
   Wor. Then once more to your Scottish pris-
      oners.   259
Deliver them up without their ransom straight,
And make the Douglas' son your only mean
For powers in Scotland ; which, for divers
      reasons
Which I shall send you written, be assured,
Will easily be granted. You, my lord,
           [*To Northumberland.*
Your son in Scotland being thus employ'd,
Shall secretly into the bosom creep
Of that same noble prelate, well beloved,
The archbishop.
   Hot. Of York, is it not ?
   Wor. True ; who bears hard   270
His brother's death at Bristol, the Lord
      Scroop.
I speak not this in estimation,
As what I think might be, but what I know
Is ruminated, plotted and set down,
And only stays but to behold the face
Of that occasion that shall bring it on.
   Hot. I smell it : upon my life, it will do
      well.
   North. Before the game is afoot, thou still
      let'st slip.
   Hot. Why, it cannot choose but be a noble
      plot ;
And then the power of Scotland and of York,
To join with Mortimer, ha ?   281
   Wor.   And so they shall.
   Hot. In faith, it is exceedingly well aim'd.
   Wor. And 'tis no little reason bids us
      speed,
To save our heads by raising of a head ;
For, bear ourselves as even as we can,
The king will always think him in our debt,
And think we think ourselves unsatisfied,
Till he hath found a time to pay us home :
And see already how he doth begin

To make us strangers to his looks of love. 290

Hot. He does, he does : we'll be revenged
    on him.   [this

Wor. Cousin, farewell : no further go in
Than I by letters shall direct your course.
When time is ripe, which will be suddenly,
I'll steal to Glendower and Lord Mortimer ;
Where you and Douglas and our powers at
    once,
As I will fashion it, shall happily meet,
To bear our fortunes in our own strong arms,
Which now we hold at much uncertainty.

North. Farewell, good brother : we shall
    thrive, I trust.   300

Hot. Uncle, adieu : O, let the hours be
    short
Till fields and blows and groans applaud our
    sport !   [*Exeunt.*

ACT II.

SCENE I. *Rochester. An inn yard.*

Enter a Carrier *with a lantern in his hand.*

First Car. Heigh-ho ! an it be not four by
the day, I'll be hanged : Charles' wain is over
the new chimney, and yet our horse not
packed. What, ostler !

Ost. [*Within*] Anon, anon.

First Car. I prithee, Tom, beat Cut's saddle, put a few flocks in the point ; poor jade,
is wrung in the withers out of all cess.

Enter another Carrier.

Sec. Car. Peas and beans are as dank here
as a dog, and that is the next way to give poor
jades the bots : this house is turned upside
down since Robin Ostler died.

First Car. Poor fellow, never joyed since
the price of oats rose ; it was the death of
him.

Sec. Car. I think this be the most villanous
house in all London road for fleas : I am stung
like a tench.

First Car. Like a tench ! by the mass,
there is ne'er a king christen could be better
bit than I have been since the first cock.   20

Sec. Car. Why, they will allow us ne'er a
jordan, and then we leak in your chimney ;
and your chamber-lie breeds fleas like a loach.

First Car. What, ostler ! come away and
be hanged ! come away.

Sec. Car. I have a gammon of bacon and
two razes of ginger, to be delivered as far as
Charing-cross.

First Car. God's body ! the turkeys in my
pannier are quite starved. What, ostler ! A
plague on thee ! hast thou never an eye in
thy head ? canst not hear ? An 'twere not as
good deed as drink, to break the pate on thee,
I am a very villain. Come, and be hanged !
hast no faith in thee ?

Enter GADSHILL.

Gads. Good morrow, carriers. What's
o'clock ?

First Car. I think it be two o'clock.

Gads. I pray thee lend me thy lantern, to
see my gelding in the stable.

First Car. Nay, by God, soft ; I know a
trick worth two of that, i' faith.   41

Gads. I pray thee, lend me thine.

Sec. Car. Ay, when ? can'st tell ? Lend
me thy lantern, quoth he ? marry, I'll see thee
hanged first.

Gads. Sirrah carrier, what time do you
mean to come to London ?

Sec. Car. Time enough to go to bed with a
candle, I warrant thee. Come, neighbor
Mugs, we'll call up the gentlemen : they will
along with company, for they have great
charge.   [*Exeunt carriers.* 51

Gads. What, ho ! chamberlain !

Cham. [*Within*] At hand, quoth pick-purse.

Gads. That's even as fair as—at hand,
quoth the chamberlain ; for thou variest no
more from picking of purses than giving direction doth from laboring ; thou layest the
plot how.

Enter Chamberlain.

Cham. Good morrow, Master Gadshill. It
holds current that I told you yesternight :
there's a franklin in the wild of Kent hath
brought three hundred marks with him in
gold : I heard him tell it to one of his company last night at supper ; a kind of auditor ;
one that hath abundance of charge too, God
knows what. They are up already, and call
for eggs and butter ; they will away presently.

Gads. Sirrah, if they meet not with Saint
Nicholas' clerks, I'll give thee this neck.

Cham. No, I'll none of it : I pray thee,
keep that for the hangman ; for I know thou
worshippest St. Nicholas as truly as a man of
falsehood may.

Gads. What talkest thou to me of the
hangman ? if I hang, I'll make a fat pair of
gallows ; for if I hang, old Sir John hangs with
me, and thou knowest he is no starveling.
Tut ! there are other Trojans that thou dream-
est not of, the which for sport sake are content to do the profession some grace ; that
would, if matters should be looked into, for
their own credit sake, make all whole. I am
joined with no foot-land rakers, no long-staff
sixpenny strikers, none of these mad mus-
tachio purple-hued malt-worms ; but with nobility and tranquillity, burgomasters and great
oneyers, such as can hold in, such as will
strike sooner than speak, and speak sooner
than drink, and drink sooner than pray : and
yet, 'zounds, I lie ; for they pray continually
to their saint, the commonwealth ; or rather,
not pray to her, but prey on her, for they ride
up and down on her and make her their
boots.   91

Cham. What, the commonwealth their
boots ? will she hold out water in foul way ?

Gads. She will, she will ; justice hath li-
quored her. We steal as in a castle, cock-

sure; we have the receipt of fern-seed, we walk invisible.

Cham. Nay, by my faith, I think you are more beholding to the night than to fern-seed for your walking invisible.

Gads. Give me thy hand: thou shalt have a share in our purchase, as I am a true man.

Cham. Nay, rather let me have it, as you are a false thief.

Gads. Go to; 'homo' is a common name to all men. Bid the ostler bring my gelding out of the stable. Farewell, you muddy knave.

[*Exeunt.*

SCENE II. *The highway, near Gadshill.*

Enter PRINCE HENRY *and* POINS.

Poins. Come, shelter, shelter: I have removed Falstaff's horse, and he frets like a gummed velvet.

Prince. Stand close.

Enter FALSTAFF.

Fal. Poins! Poins, and be hanged! Poins!

Prince. Peace, ye fat-kidneyed rascal! what a brawling dost thou keep!

Fal. Where's Poins, Hal?

Prince. He is walked up to the top of the hill: I'll go seek him.   9

Fal. I am accursed to rob in that thief's company: the rascal hath removed my horse, and tied him I know not where. If I travel but four foot by the squier further afoot, I shall break my wind. Well, I doubt not but to die a fair death for all this,·if I 'scape hanging for killing that rogue. I have forsworn his company hourly any time this two and twenty years, and yet I am bewitched with the rogue's company. If the rascal hath not given me medicines to make me love him, I'll be hanged; it could not be else; I have drunk medicines. Poins! Hal! a plague upon you both! Bardolph! Peto! I'll starve ere I'll rob a foot further. An 'twere not as good a deed as drink, to turn true man and to leave these rogues, I am the veriest varlet that ever chewed with a tooth. Eight yards of uneven ground is threescore and ten miles afoot with me; and the stony-hearted villains know it well enough: a plague upon it. when thieves cannot be true one to another! [*They whistle.*] Whew! A plague upon you all! Give me my horse, you rogues; give me my horse, and be hanged!

Prince. Peace, ye fat-guts! lie down; lay thine ear close to the ground and list if thou canst hear the tread of travellers.

Fal. Have you any levers to lift me up again, being down? 'Sblood, I'll not bear mine own flesh so far afoot again for all the coin in thy father's exchequer. What a plague mean ye to colt me thus?   40

Prince. Thou liest; thou art not colted, thou art uncolted.

Fal. I prithee, good Prince Hal, help me to my horse, good king's son.

Prince. Out, ye rogue! shall I be your ostler?

Fal. Go, hang thyself in thine own heir-apparent garters! If I be ta'en, I'll peach for this. An I have not ballads made on you all and sung to filthy tunes, let a cup of sack be my poison: when a jest is so forward, and afoot too! I hate it.

Enter GADSHILL, BARDOLPH *and* PETO *with him.*

Gads. Stand.

Fal. So I do, against my will.

Poins. O, 'tis our setter: I know his voice. Bardolph, what news?

Bard. Case ye, case ye; on with your vizards: there's money of the king's coming down the hill; 'tis going to the king's exchequer.

Fal. You lie, ye rogue; 'tis going to the king's tavern.

Gads. There's enough to make us all.   60

Fal. To be hanged.

Prince. Sirs, you four shall front them in the narrow lane; Ned Poins and I will walk lower: if they 'scape from your encounter, then they light on us.

Peto. How many be there of them?

Gads. Some eight or ten.

Fal. 'Zounds, will they not rob us?

Prince. What, a coward, Sir John Paunch?

Fal. Indeed, I am not John of Gaunt, your grandfather; but yet no coward, Hal.   71

Prince. Well, we leave that to the proof.

Poins. Sirrah Jack, thy horse stands behind the hedge: when thou needest him, there thou shalt find him. Farewell, and stand fast.

Fal. Now cannot I strike him, if I should be hanged.

Prince. Ned, where are our disguises?

Poins. Here, hard by: stand close.

[*Exeunt Prince and Poins.*

Fal. Now, my masters, happy man be his dole, say I: every man to his business.

Enter the Travellers.

First Trav. Come, neighbor: the boy shall lead our horses down the hill; we'll walk afoot awhile, and ease our legs.

Thieves. Stand!

Travellers. Jesus bless us!

Fal. Strike; down with them; cut the villains' throats: ah! whoreson caterpillars! bacon-fed knaves! they hate us youth: down with them: fleece them.   90

Travellers. O, we are undone, both we and ours for ever!

Fal. Hang ye, gorbellied knaves, are ye undone? No, ye fat chuffs; I would your store were here! On, bacons, on! What, ye knaves! young men must live. You are grand jurors, are ye? we'll jure ye, 'faith.

[*Here they rob them and bind them. Exeunt.*

Re-enter PRINCE HENRY *and* POINS.

Prince. The thieves have bound the true men. Now could thou and I rob the thieves and go merrily to London, it would be argument for a week, laughter for a month and a good jest for ever.

Poins. Stand close ; I hear them coming.

Enter the Thieves again.

Fal. Come, my masters, let us share, and then to horse before day. An the Prince and Poins be not two arrant cowards, there's no equity stirring : there's no more valor in that Poins than in a wild-duck.

Prince. Your money !

Poins. Villains !　　　　　　　　　　　110

[*As they are sharing, the Prince and Poins set upon them ; they all run away ; and Falstaff, after a blow or two, runs away too, leaving the booty behind them.*]

Prince. Got with much ease. Now merrily to horse :
The thieves are all scatter'd and possess'd with fear
So strongly that they dare not meet each other;
Each takes his fellow for an officer.
Away, good Ned. Falstaff sweats to death,
And lards the lean earth as he walks along :
Were 't not for laughing, I should pity him.

Poins. How the rogue roar'd !　　　　[*Exeunt.*

SCENE III. *Warkworth castle.*

Enter HOTSPUR, *solus, reading a letter.*

Hot. 'But for mine own part, my lord, I could be well contented to be there, in respect of the love I bear your house.' He could be contented : why is he not, then ? In respect of the love he bears our house : he shows in this, he loves his own barn better than he loves our house. Let me see some more. 'The purpose you undertake is dangerous ;'—why, that's certain : 'tis dangerous to take a cold, to sleep, to drink ; but I tell you, my lord fool, out of this nettle, danger, we pluck this flower, safety. 'The purpose you undertake is dangerous ; the friends you have named uncertain ; the time itself unsorted ; and your whole plot too light for the counterpoise of so great an opposition.' Say you so, say you so? I say unto you again, you are a shallow cowardly hind, and you lie. What a lackbrain is this ! By the Lord, our plot is a good plot as ever was laid ; our friends true and constant : a good plot, good friends, and full of expectation ; an excellent plot, very good friends. What a frosty-spirited rogue is this ! Why, my lord of York commends the plot and the general course of the action. 'Zounds, an I were now by this rascal, I could brain him' with his lady's fan. Is there not my father, my uncle and myself ? lord Edmund Mortimer, my lord of York and Owen Glendower? is there not besides the Douglas ? have I not all their letters to meet us in arms by the ninth of the next month ? and are they not some of them set forward already? What a pagan rascal is this! an infidel ! Ha! you shall see now in very sincerity of fear and cold heart.

will he to the king and lay open all our proceedings. O, I could divide myself and go to buffets, for moving such a dish of skim milk with so honorable an action ! Hang him ! let him tell the king : we are prepared. I will set forward to-night.

Enter LADY PERCY.

How now, Kate ! I must leave you within these two hours.

Lady. O, my good lord, why are you thus alone ?　　　　　　　　　　　　　　40
For what offence have I this fortnight been
A banish'd woman from my Harry's bed ?
Tell me, sweet lord, what is't that takes from thee
Thy stomach, pleasure and thy golden sleep ?
Why dost thou bend thine eyes upon the earth,
And start so often when thou sit'st alone?
Why hast thou lost the fresh blood in thy cheeks ;
And given my treasures and my rights of thee
To thick-eyed musing and cursed melancholy?
In thy faint slumbers I by thee have watch'd,
And heard thee murmur tales of iron wars ;
Speak terms of manage to thy bounding steed;
Cry 'Courage ! to the field !' And thou hast talk'd
Of sallies and retires, of trenches, tents,
Of palisadoes, frontiers, parapets,
Of basilisks, of cannon, culverin,
Of prisoners' ransom and of soldiers slain,
And all the currents of a heady fight.
Thy spirit within thee hath been so at war　59
And thus hath so bestirr'd thee in thy sleep,
That beads of sweat have stood upon thy brow
Like bubbles in a late-disturbed stream ;
And in thy face strange motions have appear'd,
Such as we see when men restrain their breath
On some great sudden hest. O, what portents are these ?
Some heavy business hath my lord in hand,
And I must know it, else he loves me not.

Hot. What, ho !

Enter Servant.

Hot. Is Gilliams with the packet gone ?

Serv. He is, my lord, an hour ago.

Hot. Hath Butler brought those horses from the sheriff ?　　　　　　　　　　70

Serv. One horse, my lord, he brought even now.

Hot. What horse ? a roan, a crop-ear, is it not ?

Serv. It is, my lord.

Hot.　　　　　That roan shall by my throne.
Well, I will back him straight : O esperance !
Bid Butler lead him forth into the park.
　　　　　　　　　　　　　　[*Exit Servant.*

Lady. But hear you, my lord.

Hot. What say'st thou, my lady ?

Lady. What is it carries you away ?

Hot. Why, my horse, my love, my horse.

Lady. Out, you mad-headed ape !　　　80
A weasel hath not such a deal of spleen
As you are toss'd with. In faith,
I'll know your business, Harry, that I will.

I fear my brother Mortimer doth stir
About his title, and hath sent for you
To line his enterprize but if you go,—
  Hot. So far afoot, I shall be weary, love.
  Lady Come, come, you paraquito, answer
      me
Directly unto this question that I ask :
In faith, I'll break thy little finger, Harry, 90
An if thou wilt not tell me all things true.
  Hot Away,
Away, you trifler ! Love ! I love thee not,
I care not for thee, Kate this is no world
To play with mammets and to tilt with lips
We must have bloody noses and crack'd crowns,
And pass them current too God's me, my
      horse !
What say'st thou, Kate ? what would'st thou
      have with me ?
  Lady Do you not love me ? do you not,
      indeed ? 99
Well, do not then , for since you love me not,
I will not love myself Do you not love me ?
Nay, tell me if you speak in jest or no ?
  Hot Come, wilt thou see me ride ?
And when I am o' horseback, I will swear
I love thee infinitely But hark you, Kate ,
I must not have you henceforth question me
Whither I go, nor reason whereabout
Whither I must, I must ; and, to conclude,
This evening must I leave you, gentle Kate
I know you wise, but yet no farther wise 110
Than Harry Percy's wife constant you are,
But yet a woman and for secrecy,
No lady closer for I well believe
Thou wilt not utter what thou dost not know ,
And so far will I trust thee, gentle Kate
  Lady How ! so far ?
  Hot Not an inch further But hark you,
      Kate
Whither I go, thither shall you go too ,
To-day will I set forth, to-morrow you
Will this content you, Kate ?
  Lady It must of force   [*Exeunt* 120

SCENE IV. *The Boar's-Head Tavern,*
            Eastcheap

Enter the PRINCE, *and* POINS.

  Prince Ned, prithee, come out of that fat
room, and lend me thy hand to laugh a little
  Poins. Where hast been, Hal ?
  Prince. With three or four loggerheads
amongst three or four score hogsheads I have
sounded the very base-string of humility
Sirrah, I am sworn brother to a leash of drawers ; and can call them all by their christen
names, as Tom, Dick, and Francis They take
it already upon their salvation, that though I be
but Prince of Wales, yet I am the king of
courtesy ; and tell me flatly I am no proud
Jack, like Falstaff, but a Corinthian, a lad of
mettle, a good boy, by the Lord, so they call
me, and when I am king of England, I shall
command all the good lads in Eastcheap They
call drinking deep, dyeing scarlet , and when
you breathe in your watering, they cry ' hem !'

and bid you play it off To conclude, I am so
good a proficient in one quarter of an hour,
that I can drink with any tinker in his own
language during my life I tell thee, Ned,
thou hast lost much honor, that thou wert not
with me in this action But, sweet Ned,—to
sweeten which name of Ned, I give thee this
pennyworth of sugar, clapped even now into
my hand by an under-skinker, one that never
spake other English in his life than ' Eight
shillings and sixpence,' and ' You are welcome,'
with this shrill addition, ' Anon, anon, sir '
Score a pint of bastard in the Half-moon ' or
so But, Ned, to drive away the time till Falstaff come, I prithee, do thou stand in some
by-room, while I question my puny drawer to
what end he gave me the sugar ; and do thou
never leave calling ' Francis,' that his tale to
me may be nothing but ' Anon ' Step aside,
and I'll show thee a precedent
  Poins Francis '
  Prince Thou art perfect
  Poins Francis!   [*Exit Poins*]

Enter FRANCIS

  Fran Anon, anon, sir Look down into
the Pomgarnet, Ralph
  Prince Come hither, Francis
  Fran. My lord ?
  Prince. How long hast thou to serve, Francis ?
  Fran Forsooth, five years, and as much
as to—
  Poins [*Within*] Francis '
  Fran Anon, anon, sir   40
  Prince Five year ' by'r lady, a long lease
for the clinking of pewter But, Francis,
darest thou be so valiant as to play the coward
with thy indenture and show it a fair pair
of heels and run from it ?
  Fran O Lord, sir, I'll be sworn upon all
the books in England, I could find in my
heart
  Poins [*Within*] Francis '
  Fran Anon, sir
  Prince How old art thou, Francis ?
  Fran Let me see—about Michaelmas next
I shall be—   61
  Poins [*Within*] Francis '
  Fran Anon, sir Pray stay a little, my
lord.
  Prince Nay, but hark you, Francis . for
the sugar thou gavest me, 'twas a pennyworth, wast not ?
  Fran O Lord, I would it had been two !
  Prince I will give thee for it a thousand
pound ask me when thou wilt, and thou
shalt have it   70
  Poins [*Within*] Francis '
  Fran Anon, anon
  Prince Anon, Francis ? No, Francis . but
to-morrow, Francis , or, Francis, o' Thursday , or indeed, Francis, when thou wilt
But, Francis '
  Fran My lord ?
  Prince Wilt thou rob this leathern jerkin,

crystal-button, not-pated, agate-ring, puke-stocking, caddis-garter, smooth-tongue, Spanish-pouch,—   80

Fran. O Lord, sir, who do you mean ?

Prince. Why, then, your brown bastard is your only drink ; for look you, Francis, your white canvas doublet will sully : in Barbary, sir, it cannot come to so much.

Fran. What, sir ?

Poins. [*Within*] Francis !

Prince. Away, you rogue ! dost thou not hear them call ?

[*Here they both call him ; the drawer stands amazed, not knowing which way to go.*

Enter Vintner

Vint. What, standest thou still, and hearest such a calling ? Look to the guests within. [*Exit Francis.*] My lord, old Sir John, with half-a-dozen more, are at the door : shall I let them in ?

Prince. Let them alone awhile, and then open the door. [*Exit Vintner.*] Poins !

Re-enter POINS.

Poins. Anon, anon, sir.

Prince. Sirrah, Falstaff and the rest of the thieves are at the door : shall we be merry ?

Poins. As merry as crickets, my lad. But hark ye ; what cunning match have you made with this jest of the drawer ? come, what's the issue ?

Prince. I am now of all humors that have showed themselves humors since the old days of goodman Adam to the pupil age of this present twelve o'clock at midnight.

Re-enter FRANCIS.

What's o'clock, Francis ?

Fran. Anon, anon, sir.   [*Exit.* 109

Prince. That ever this fellow should have fewer words than a parrot, and yet the son of a woman ! His industry is up-stairs and down-stairs ; his eloquence the parcel of a reckoning. I am not yet of Percy's mind, the Hotspur of the north ;—he that kills me some six or seven dozen of Scots at a breakfast, washes his hands, and says to his wife ' Fie upon this quiet life ! I want work.' ' O my sweet Harry,' says she, ' how many hast thou killed to-day ?' ' Give my roan horse a drench,' says he ; and answers ' Some fourteen,' an hour after.; ' a trifle, a trifle.' I prithee, call in Falstaff : I'll play Percy, and that damned brawn shall play Dame Mortimer his wife. ' Rivo !' says the drunkard. Call in ribs, call in tallow.

Enter FALSTAFF, GADSHILL, BARDOLPH, *and* PETO ; FRANCIS *following with wine.*

Poins. Welcome, Jack : where hast thou been?

Fal. A plague of all cowards, I say, and a vengeance too ! marry, and amen ! Give me a cup of sack, boy. Ere I lead this life long, I'll sew nether stocks and mend them and foot them too. A plague of all cowards ! Give

me a cup of sack, rogue. Is there no virtue extant ?   [*He drinks.*

Prince. Didst thou never see Titan kiss a dish of butter ? pitiful-hearted Titan, that melted at the sweet tale of the sun's ! if thou didst, then behold that compound.

Fal. You rogue, here's lime in this sack too : there is nothing but roguery to be found in villanous man : yet a coward is worse than a cup of sack with lime in it. A villanous coward ! Go thy ways, old Jack ; die when thou wilt, if manhood, good manhood, be not forgot upon the face of the earth, then am I a shotten herring. There live not three good men unhanged in England ; and one of them is fat and grows old : God help the while ! a bad world, I say. I would I were a weaver ; I could sing psalms or any thing. A plague of all cowards, I say still.

Prince. How now, wool-sack ! what mutter you ?   149

Fal. A king's son ! If I do not beat thee out of thy kingdom with a dagger of lath, and drive all thy subjects afore thee like a flock of wild-geese, I'll never wear hair on my face more. You Prince of Wales !

Prince. Why, you whoreson round man, what's the matter ?

Fal. Are not you a coward ? answer me to that : and Poins there?

Poins. 'Zounds, ye fat paunch, an ye call me coward, by the Lord, I'll stab thee.   160

Fal. I call thee coward ! I'll see thee damned ere I call thee coward : but I would give a thousand pound I could run as fast as thou canst. You are straight enough in the shoulders, you care not who sees your back : call you that backing of your friends ? A plague upon such backing ! give me them that will face me. Give me a cup of sack : I am a rogue, if I drunk to-day.

Prince. O villain ! thy lips are scarce wiped since thou drunkest last.   171

Fal. All's one for that. [*He drinks.*] A plague of all cowards, still say I.

Prince. What's the matter?

Fal. What's the matter ! there be four of us here have ta'en a thousand pound this day morning.

Prince. Where is it, Jack ? where is it ?

Fal. Where is it ! taken from us it is : a hundred upon poor four of us.   180

Prince. What, a hundred, man ?

Fal. I am a rogue, if I were not at half-sword with a dozen of them two hours together. I have 'scaped by miracle. I am eight times thrust through the doublet, four through the hose ; my buckler cut through and through ; my sword hacked like a hand-saw—ecce signum ! I never dealt better since I was a man : all would not do. A plague of all cowards ! Let them speak : if they speak more or less than truth, they are villains and the sons of darkness.   191

Prince. Speak, sirs ; how was it ?

Gads. We four set upon some dozen—

Fal. Sixteen at least, my lord.

Gads. And bound them.

Peto. No, no, they were not bound.

Fal. You rogue, they were bound, every man of them ; or I am a Jew else, an Ebrew Jew.

Gads. As we were sharing, some six or seven fresh men set upon us—　　　　　200

Fal. And unbound the rest, and then come in the other.

Prince. What, fought you with them all ?

Fal. All ! I know not what you call all ; but if I fought not with fifty of them, I am a bunch of radish : if there were not two or three and fifty upon poor old Jack, then am I no two-legged creature.

Prince. Pray God you have not murdered some of them.　　　　　　210

Fal. Nay, that's past praying for : I have peppered two of them ; two I am sure I have paid, two rogues in buckram suits. I tell thee what, Hal, if I tell thee a lie, spit in my face, call me horse. Thou knowest my old ward ; here I lay, and thus I bore my point. Four rogues in buckram let drive at me—

Prince. What, four ? thou saidst but two even now.

Fal. Four, Hal ; I told thee four.　　220

Poins. Ay, ay, he said four.

Fal. These four came all a-front, and mainly thrust at me. I made me no more ado but took all their seven points in my target, thus.

Prince. Seven ? why, there were but four even now.

Fal. In buckram ?

Poins. Ay, four, in buckram suits.

Fal. Seven, by these hilts, or I am a villain else.　　　　　　　　　230

Prince. Prithee, let him alone ; we shall have more anon.

Fal. Dost thou hear me, Hal ?

Prince. Ay, and mark thee too. Jack.

Fal. Do so, for it is worth the listening to. These nine in buckram that I told thee of—

Prince. So, two more already.

Fal. Their points being broken,—

Poins. Down fell their hose.　　　239

Fal. Began to give me ground : but I followed me close, came in foot and hand ; and with a thought seven of the eleven I paid.

Prince. O monstrous! eleven buckram men grown out of two !

Fal. But, as the devil would have it, three misbegotten knaves in Kendal green came at my back and let drive at me ; for it was so dark, Hal, that thou couldst not see thy hand.

Prince. These lies are like their father that begets them ; gross as a mountain, open, palpable. Why, thou clay-brained guts, thou knotty-pated fool, thou whoreson, obscene, greasy tallow-catch,—

Fal. What, art thou mad ? art thou mad ? is not the truth the truth ?

Prince. Why, how couldst thou know these men in Kendal green, when it was so dark thou couldst not see thy hand ? come, tell us your reason : what sayest thou to this ?　　　　　　　　253

Poins. Come, your reason, Jack, your reason.

Fal. What, upon compulsion ? 'Zounds, an I were at the strappado, or all the racks in the world, I would not tell you on compulsion. Give you a reason on compulsion ! if reasons were as plentiful as blackberries, I would give no man a reason upon compulsion, I.

Prince. I'll be no longer guilty of this sin ; this sanguine coward, this bed-presser, this horseback-breaker, this huge hill of flesh,—

Fal. 'Sblood, you starveling, you elf-skin, you dried neat's tongue, you bull's pizzle, you stock-fish ! O for breath to utter what is like thee ! you tailor's-yard, you sheath, you bow-case, you vile standing-tuck,—

Prince. Well, breathe awhile, and then to it again : and when thou hast tired thyself in base comparisons, hear me speak but this.

Poins. Mark, Jack.

Prince. We two saw you four set on four and bound them, and were masters of their wealth. Mark now, how a plain tale shall put you down. Then did we two set on you four ; and, with a word, out-faced you from your prize, and have it ; yea, and can show it you here in the house : and, Falstaff, you carried your guts away as nimbly, with as quick dexterity, and roared for mercy and still run and roared, as ever I heard bull-calf. What a slave art thou, to hack thy sword as thou hast done, and then say it was in fight ! What trick, what device, what starting-hole, canst thou now find out to hide thee from this open and apparent shame ?

Poins. Come, let's hear, Jack ; what trick hast thou now ?

Fal. By the Lord, I knew ye as well as he that made ye. Why, hear you, my masters : was it for me to kill the heir-apparent ? should I turn upon the true prince ? why, thou knowest I am as valiant as Hercules : but beware instinct ; the lion will not touch the true prince. Instinct is a great matter ; I was now a coward on instinct. I shall think the better of myself and thee during my life ; I for a valiant lion, and thou for a true prince. But, by the Lord, lads, I am glad you have the money. Hostess, clap to the doors : watch to-night, pray to-morrow. Gallants, lads, boys, hearts of gold, all the titles of good fellowship come to you ! What, shall we be merry ? shall we have a play extempore ?

Prince. Content ; and the argument shall be thy running away.　　　　　311

Fal. Ah, no more of that, Hal, an thou lovest me !

Enter Hostess.

Host. O Jesu, my lord the prince !

Prince. How now, my lady the hostess ! what sayest thou to me ?

Host. Marry, my lord, there is a nobleman of the court at door would speak with you: he says he comes from your father.   319

Prince. Give him as much as will make him a royal man, and send him back again to my mother.

Fal. What manner of man is he?

Host. An old man.

Fal. What doth gravity out of his bed at midnight? Shall I give him his answer?

Prince. Prithee, do, Jack.

Fal. 'Faith, and I'll send him packing.

                                [*Exit.*

Prince. Now, sirs: by'r lady, you fought fair; so did you, Peto; so did you, Bardolph: you are lions too, you ran away upon instinct, you will not touch the true prince; no, fie!

Bard. 'Faith, I ran when I saw others run.

Prince. 'Faith, tell me now in earnest, how came Falstaff's sword so hacked?

Peto. Why, he hacked it with his dagger, and said he would swear truth out of England but he would make you believe it was done in fight, and persuaded us to do the like.   339

Bard. Yea, and to tickle our noses with spear-grass to make them bleed, and then to beslubber our garments with it and swear it was the blood of true men. I did that I did not this seven year before, I blushed to hear his monstrous devices.

Prince. O villain, thou stolest a cup of sack eighteen years ago, and wert taken with the manner, and ever since thou hast blushed extempore. Thou hadst fire and sword on thy side, and yet thou rannest away: what instinct hadst thou for it?   350

Bard. My lord, do you see these meteors? do you behold these exhalations?

Prince. I do.

Bard. What think you they portend?

Prince. Hot livers and cold purses.

Bard. Choler, my lord, if rightly taken.

Prince. No, if rightly taken, halter.

Re-enter FALSTAFF.

Here comes lean Jack, here comes bare-bone. How now, my sweet creature of bombast! How long is't ago, Jack, since thou sawest thine own knee?   361

Fal. My own knee! when I was about thy years, Hal, I was not an eagle's talon in the waist; I could have crept into any alderman's thumb-ring: a plague of sighing and grief! it blows a man up like a bladder. There's villanous news abroad: here was Sir John Bracy from your father; you must to the court in the morning. That same mad fellow of the north, Percy, and he of Wales, that gave Amamon the bastinado and made Lucifer cuckold and swore the devil his true liegeman upon the cross of a Welsh hook—what a plague call you him?

Poins. O, Glendower.

Fal. Owen, Owen, the same: and his son-in-law Mortimer, and old Northumberland, and that sprightly Scot of Scots, Douglas,

that runs o' horseback up a hill perpendicular,—

Prince. He that rides at high speed and with his pistol kills a sparrow flying.   380

Fal. You have hit it.

Prince. So did he never the sparrow.

Fal. Well, that rascal hath good mettle in him; he will not run.

Prince. Why, what a rascal art thou then, to praise him so for running!

Fal. O' horseback, ye cuckoo; but afoot he will not budge a foot.

Prince. Yes, Jack, upon instinct.   389

Fal. I grant ye, upon instinct. Well, he is there too, and one Mordake, and a thousand blue-caps more: Worcester is stolen away to-night; thy father's beard is turned white with the news: you may buy land now as cheap as stinking mackerel.

Prince. Why, then, it is like, if there come a hot June and this civil buffeting hold, we shall buy maidenheads as they buy hob-nails, by the hundreds.   399

Fal. By the mass, lad, thou sayest true; it is like we shall have good trading that way. But tell me, Hal, art not thou horrible afeard? thou being heir-apparent, could the world pick thee out three such enemies again as that fiend Douglas, that spirit Percy, and that devil Glendower? Art thou not horribly afraid? doth not thy blood thrill at it?

Prince. Not a whit, i' faith; I lack some of thy instinct.   409

Fal. Well, thou wilt be horribly chid to-morrow when thou comest to thy father: if thou love me, practise an answer.

Prince. Do thou stand for my father, and examine me upon the particulars of my life.

Fal. Shall I? content: this chair shall be my state, this dagger my sceptre, and this cushion my crown.

Prince. Thy state is taken for a joined-stool, thy golden sceptre for a leaden dagger, and thy precious rich crown for a pitiful bald crown!   420

Fal. Well, an the fire of grace be not quite out of thee, now shalt thou be moved. Give me a cup of sack to make my eyes look red, that it may be thought I have wept; for I must speak in passion, and I will do it in King Cambyses' vein.

Prince. Well, here is my leg.

Fal. And here is my speech. Stand aside, nobility.   429

Host. O Jesu, this is excellent sport, i' faith!

Fal. Weep not, sweet queen; for trickling tears are vain.

Host. O, the father, how he holds his countenance!

Fal. For God's sake, lords, convey my tristful queen;

For tears do stop the flood-gates of her eyes.

Host. O Jesu, he doth it as like one of these harlotry players as ever I see!

Fal. Peace, good pint-pot; peace, good

tickle-brain. Harry, I do not only marvel where thou spendest thy time, but also how thou art accompanied : for though the camomile, the more it is trodden on the faster it grows, yet youth, the more it is wasted the sooner it wears. That thou art my son, I have partly thy mother's word, partly my own opinion, but chiefly a villanous trick of thine eye and a foolish hanging of thy nether lip, that doth warrant me. If then thou be son to me, here lies the point ; why, being son to me, art thou so pointed at? Shall the blessed sun of heaven prove a micher and eat blackberries ? a question not to be asked Shall the son of England prove a thief and take purses ? a question to be asked. There is a thing, Harry, which thou hast often heard of and it is known to many in our land by the name of pitch : this pitch, as ancient writers do report, doth defile ; so doth the company thou keepest : for, Harry, now I do not speak to thee in drink but in tears, not in pleasure but in passion, not in words only, but in woes also : and yet there is a virtuous man whom I have often noted in thy company, but I know not his name.   461

Prince. What manner of man, an it like your majesty ?

Fal. A goodly portly man, i' faith, and a corpulent ; of a cheerful look, a pleasing eye and a most noble carriage ; and, as I think, his age some fifty, or, by'r lady, inclining to three score ; and now I remember me, his name is Falstaff : if that man should be lewdly given, he deceiveth me ; for, Harry, I see virtue in his looks. If then the tree may be known by the fruit, as the fruit by the tree, then, peremptorily I speak it, there is virtue in that Falstaff : him keep with, the rest banish. And tell me now, thou naughty varlet, tell me, where hast thou been this month ?

Prince. Dost thou speak like a king ? Do thou stand for me, and I'll play my father.

Fal. Depose me ? if thou dost it half so gravely, so majestically, both in word and matter, hang me up by the heels for a rabbit-sucker or a poulter's hare.   481

Prince. Well, here I am set.

Fal. And here I stand : judge, my masters.

Prince. Now, Harry, whence come you ?

Fal. My noble lord, from Eastcheap.

Prince. The complaints I hear of thee are grievous.

Fal. 'Sblood, my lord, they are false : nay, I'll tickle ye for a young prince, i' faith.   489

Prince. Swearest thou, ungracious boy? henceforth ne'er look on me. Thou art violently carried away from grace : there is a devil haunts thee in the likeness of an old fat man ; a tun of man is thy companion. Why dost thou converse with that trunk of humors, that bolting-hutch of beastliness, that swollen parcel of dropsies, that huge bombard of sack, that stuffed cloak-bag of guts, that roasted Manningtree ox with the pudding in his belly, that reverend vice, that grey iniquity, that

father ruffian, that vanity in years ? Wherein is he good, but to taste sack and drink it ? wherein neat and cleanly, but to carve a capon and eat it ? wherein cunning, but in craft ? wherein crafty, but in villany ? wherein villanous, but in all things ? wherein worthy, but in nothing ?

Fal. I would your grace would take me with you : whom means your grace ?

Prince. That villanous abominable misleader of youth, Falstaff, that old white-bearded Satan.

Fal. My lord, the man I know.   510

Prince. I know thou dost.

Fal. But to say I know more harm in him than in myself, were to say more than I know. That he is old, the more the pity, his white hairs do witness it ; but that he is, saving your reverence, a whoremaster, that I utterly deny. If sack and sugar be a fault, God help the wicked ! if to be old and merry be a sin, then many an old host that I know is damned : if to be fat be to be hated, then Pharaoh's lean kine are to be loved. No, my good lord ; banish Peto, banish Bardolph, banish Poins : but for sweet Jack Falstaff, kind Jack Falstaff, true Jack Falstaff, valiant Jack Falstaff, and therefore more valiant, being, as he is, old Jack Falstaff, banish not him thy Harry's company, banish not him thy Harry's company : banish plump Jack, and banish all the world.

Prince. I do, I will.   [*A knocking heard.*
[*Exeunt Hostess, Francis, and Bardolph.*

Re-enter BARDOLPH, *running.*

Bard. O, my lord, my lord ! the sheriff with a most monstrous watch is at the door.

Fal. Out, ye rogue ! Play out the play : I have much to say in the behalf of that Falstaff.

Re-enter the Hostess.

Host. O Jesu, my lord, my lord !

Prince. Heigh, heigh ! the devil rides upon a fiddlestick : what's the matter ?

Host. The sheriff and all the watch are at the door : they are come to search the house. Shall I let them in ?

Fal. Dost thou hear, Hal ? never call a true piece of gold a counterfeit : thou art essentially mad, without seeming so.   541

Prince. And thou a natural coward, without instinct.

Fal. I deny your major : if you will deny the sheriff, so ; if not, let him enter : if I become not a cart as well as another man, a plague on my bringing up ! I hope I shall as soon be strangled with a halter as another.

Prince. Go, hide thee behind the arras the rest walk up above. Now, my master for a true face and good conscience.   550

Fal. Both which I have had : but their date is out, and therefore I'll hide me.

Prince. Call in the sheriff.
[*Exeunt all except the Prince and Peto.*

Enter Sheriff *and the* Carrier.

Now, master sheriff, what is your will with
  me ?
Sher. First, pardon me, my lord. A hue
  and cry
Hath follow'd certain men unto this house
Prince What men ?
Sher. One of them is well known, my
  gracious lord,
A gross fat man
Car.   As fat as butter.   560
Prince The man, I do assure you, is not
  here ;
For I myself at this time have employ'd him
And, sheriff, I will engage my word to thee
That I will, by to-morrow dinner-time,
Send him to answer thee, or any man,
For any thing he shall be charged withal ·
And so let me entreat you leave the house
Sher. I will, my lord. There are two gen-
  tlemen   [marks
Have in this robbery lost three hundred
Prince It may be so . if he have robb'd
  these men,   570
He shall be answerable , and so farewell.
Sher Good night, my noble lord
Prince I think it is good morrow, is it
  not ?
Sher Indeed, my lord. I think it be two
  o'clock.   [*Exeunt Sheriff and Carrier*
Prince This oily rascal is known as well as
Paul's   Go, call him forth
Peto Falstaff !—Fast asleep behind the arras,
and snorting like a horse
Prince Hark, how hard he fetches breath.
Search his pockets. [*He searcheth his pockets,
and findeth certain papers*] What hast thou
found ?
Peto. Nothing but papers, my lord
Prince Let's see what they be. read them
Peto. [*Reads*] Item, A capon, . . 2s. 2d
      Item, Sauce,   . .   4d
      Item, Sack, two gallons, 5s 8d
      Item, Anchovies and sack
          after supper, . 2s. 6d
      Item, Bread, . .   ob
Prince. O monstrous ' but one half-penny-
worth of bread to this intolerable deal of sack!
What there is else, keep close , we'll read it at
more advantage . there let him sleep till day.
I'll to the court in the morning We must all
to the wars, and thy place shall be honorable
I'll procure this fat rogue a charge of foot ,
and I know his death will be a march of
twelve-score The money shall be paid back
again with advantage. Be with me betimes in
the morning , and so, good morrow, Peto. 601
                    [*Exeunt.*
Peto. Good morrow, good my lord.

ACT III.

SCENE I   *Bangor. The Archdeacon's house*
Enter HOTSPUR, WORCESTER, MORTIMER, *and*
    GLENDOWER.

Mort. These promises are fair, the parties
  sure,
And our induction full of prosperous hope.
Hot. Lord Mortimer, and cousin Glen-
  dower,
Will you sit down ?
And uncle Worcester : a plague upon it !
I have forgot the map.
Glend   No, here it is
Sit, cousin Percy ; sit, good cousin Hotspur,
For by that name as oft as Lancaster
Doth speak of you, his cheek looks pale and
  with
A rising sigh he wisheth you in heaven   10
Hot And you in hell, as oft as he hears
Owen Glendower spoke of
Glend I cannot blame him at my nativity
The front of heaven was full of fiery shapes,
Of burning cressets ; and at my birth
The frame and huge foundation of the earth
Shaked like a coward
Hot Why, so it would have done at the
same season, if your mother's cat had but kit-
tened, though yourself had never been born
Glend. I say the earth did shake when I
  was born.   21
Hot. And I say the earth was not of my
  mind,
If you suppose as fearing you it shook.
Glend The heavens were all on fire, the
  earth did tremble.
Hot. O, then the earth shook to see the
  heavens on fire,
And not in fear of your nativity.
Diseased nature oftentimes breaks forth
In strange eruptions , oft the teeming earth
Is with a kind of colic pinch'd and vex'd
By the imprisoning of unruly wind   30
Within her womb ; which, for enlargement
  striving,
Shakes the old beldam earth and topples
  down
Steeples and moss-grown towers At your
  birth
Our grandam earth, having this distempera-
  ture,
In passion shook
Glend.   Cousin, of many men
I do not bear these crossings. Give me leave
To tell you once again that at my birth
The front of heaven was full of fiery shapes,
The goats ran from the mountains, and the
  herds
Were strangely clamorous to the frighted
  fields   40
These signs have mark'd me extraordinary ;
And all the courses of my life do show
I am not in the roll of common men
Where is he living, clipp'd in with the sea
That chides the banks of England, Scotland,
  Wales,
Which calls me pupil, or hath read to me ?
And bring him out that is but woman's son
Can trace me in the tedious ways of art
And hold me pace in deep experiments.
Hot. I think there's no man speaks better

Welsh. I'll to dinner   50
Mort. Peace, cousin Percy ; you will make
  him mad.
  Glend. I can call spirits from the vasty
    deep
  Hot. Why, so can I, or so can any man ;
But will they come when you do call for
    them ?
  Glend Why, I can teach you, cousin, to
    command
The devil.
  Hot. And I can teach thee, coz, to shame
    the devil
By telling truth . tell truth and shame the
    devil
If thou have power to raise him, bring him
    hither,   60
And I'll be sworn I have power to shame him
    hence.
O, while you live, tell truth and shame the
    devil !
  Mort Come, come, no more of this unprofit-
    able chat
  Glend. Three times hath Henry Bolingbroke
    made head
Against my power ; thrice from the banks of
    Wye
And sandy-bottom'd Severn have I sent him
Bootless home and weather-beaten back.
  Hot. Home without boots, and in foul
    weather too !
How 'scapes he agues, in the devil's name ?
  Glend. Come, here's the map . shall we di-
    vide our right   70
According to our threefold order ta'en ?
  Mort The archdeacon hath divided it
Into three limits very equally
England, from Trent and Severn hitherto,
By south and east is to my part assign'd .
All westward, Wales beyond the Severn shore,
And all the fertile land within that bound.
To Owen Glendower. and, dear coz, to you
The remnant northward, lying off from Trent.
And our indentures tripartite are drawn,   80
Which being sealed interchangeably,
A business that this night may execute,
To-morrow, cousin Percy, you and I
And my good Lord of Worcester will set forth
To meet your father and the Scottish power,
As is appointed us, at Shrewsbury
My father Glendower is not ready yet.
Nor shall we need his help these fourteen
    days.
Within that space you may have drawn to-
    gether
Your tenants, friends and neighboring gentle-
    men   90
  Glend. A shorter time shall send me to you,
    lords:
And in my conduct shall your ladies come;
From whom you now must steal and take no
    leave,
For there will be a world of water shed
Upon the parting of your wives and you.
  Hot Methinks my moiety, north from Bur-
    ton here,

In quantity equals not one of yours .
See how this river comes me cranking in,
And cuts me from the best of all my land
A huge half-moon, a monstrous cantle out   100
I'll have the current in this place damm'd up,
And here the smug and silver Trent shall run
In a new channel, fair and evenly ,
It shall not wind with such a deep indent,
To rob me of so rich a bottom here   .
  Glend Not wind ? it shall, it must ; you
    see it doth
  Mort Yea, but
Mark how he bears his course, and runs me
    up
With like advantage on the other side ,
Gelding the opposed continent as much .   110
As on the other side it takes from you
  Wor Yea, but a little charge will trench
    him here
And on this north side win this cape of land ,
And then he runs straight and even
  Hot I'll have it so a little charge will do
    it
  Glend I'll not have it alter'd
  Hot   Will not you?
  Glend No, nor you shall not
  Hot   Who shall say me nay ?
  Glend Why, that will I
  Hot. Let me not understand you, then ;
speak it in Welsh.   120
  Glend I can speak English, lord, as well as
    you ,
For I was train'd up in the English court :
Where, being but young, I framed to the harp
Many an English ditty lovely well
And gave the tongue a helpful ornament,
A virtue that was never seen in you.
  Hot. Marry,
And I am glad of it with all my heart :
I had rather be a kitten and cry mew
Than one of these same metre ballad-mongers,
I had rather hear a brazen canstick turn'd, 131
Or a dry wheel grate on the axle-tree ,
And that would set my teeth nothing on edge,
Nothing so much as mincing poetry
'Tis like the forced gait of a shuffling nag
  Glend Come, you shall have Trent turn'd.
  Hot I do not care I'll give thrice so much
    land
To any well-deserving friend ,
But in the way of bargain, mark ye me,
I'll cavil on the ninth part of a hair.   140
Are the indentures drawn ? shall we be gone?
  Glend The moon shines fair , you may
    away by night :
I'll haste the writer and withal
Break with your wives of your departure
    hence
I am afraid my daughter will run mad,
So much she doteth on her Mortimer. [*Exit.*
  Mort. Fie, cousin Percy ' how you cross my
    father !
  Hot I cannot choose : sometime he angers
    me
With telling me of the moldwarp and the ant,
Of the dreamer Merlin and his prophecies, 150

And of a dragon and a finless fish,
A clip-wing'd griffin and a moulten raven,
A couching lion and a ramping cat,
And such a deal of skimble-skamble stuff
As puts me from my faith. I tell you what ,
He held me last night at least nine hours
In reckoning up the several devils' names
That were his lackeys . I cried 'hum,' and
   'well, go to,'
But mark'd him not a word   O, he is as tedi-
   ous
As a tired horse, a railing wife ,   160
Worse than a smoky house   I had rather live
With cheese and garlic in a windmill, far,
Than feed on cates and have him talk to me
In any summer-house in Christendom.
   Mort. In faith, he is a worthy gentleman,
Exceedingly well read, and profited
In strange concealments, valiant as a lion
And wondrous affable and as bountiful
As mines of India   Shall I tell you, cousin ?
He holds your temper in a high respect   170
And curbs himself even of his natural scope
When you come 'cross his humor ; faith, he
   does .
I warrant you, that man is not alive
Might so have tempted him as you have done,
Without the taste of danger and reproof .
But do not use it oft, let me entreat you
   Wor   In faith, my lord, you are too wilful-
   blame ,
And since your coming hither have done
   enough
To put him quite beside his patience.
You must needs learn, lord, to amend this
   fault ·   180
Though sometimes it show greatness, courage,
   blood,—
And that's the dearest grace it renders you,—
Yet oftentimes it doth present harsh rage,
Defect of manners, want of government,
Pride, haughtiness, opinion and disdain
The least of which haunting a nobleman
Loseth men's hearts and leaves behind a stain
Upon the beauty of all parts besides,
Beguiling them of commendation
   Hot   Well, I am school'd · good manners
   be your speed !   190
Here come our wives, and let us take our
   leave

Re-enter GLENDOWER *with the ladies*

   Mort   This is the deadly spite that angers
   me ;
My wife can speak no English, I no Welsh.
   Glend   My daughter weeps   she will not
   part with you ,
She'll be a soldier too, she'll to the wars
   Mort   Good father, tell her that she and my
   aunt Percy
Shall follow in your conduct speedily.
   [*Glendower speaks to her in Welsh, and she
           answers him in the same.*
   Glend.   She is desperate here , a peevish
self-will'd harlotry, one that no persuasion can
do good upon.   [*The lady speaks in Welsh*

   Mort   I understand thy looks . that pretty
   Welsh   201
Which thou pour'st down from these swelling
   heavens
I am too perfect in , and, but for shame,
In such a parley should I answer thee   ·
       [*The lady speaks again in Welsh.*
I understand thy kisses and thou mine,
And that's a feeling disputation :
But I will never be a truant, love,
Till I have learned thy language ; for thy
   tongue
Makes Welsh as sweet as ditties highly penn'd,
Sung by a fair queen in a summer's bower,   210
With ravishing division, to her lute.
   Glend   Nay, if you melt, then will she run
   mad.   [*The lady speaks again in Welsh.*
   Mort   O, I am ignorance itself in this !
   Glend   She bids you on the wanton rushes
   lay you down
And rest your gentle head upon her lap,
And she will sing the song that pleaseth you
And on your eyelids crown the god of sleep,
Charming your blood with pleasing heaviness,
Making such difference 'twixt wake and sleep
As is the difference betwixt day and night   220
The hour before the heavenly-harness'd team
Begins his golden progress in the east
   Mort   With all my heart I'll sit and hear
   her sing :
By that time will our book, I think, be drawn.
   Glend.   Do so ,
And those musicians that shall play to you
Hang in the air a thousand leagues from hence,
And straight they shall be here   sit, and at-
   tend
   Hot   Come, Kate, thou art perfect in lying
down   come, quick, quick, that I may lay my
head in thy lap.   231
   Lady P   Go, ye giddy goose
           [*The music plays.*
   Hot.   Now I perceive the devil understands
   Welsh ,
And 'tis no marvel he is so humorous
By'r lady, he is a good musician
   Lady P   Then should you be nothing but
musical for you are altogether governed by
humors   Lie still, ye thief, and hear the lady
sing in Welsh
   Hot.   I had rather hear Lady, my brach,
howl in Irish   241
   Lady P.   Wouldst thou have thy head
   broken ?
   Hot   No
   Lady P   Then be still
   Hot   Neither ; 'tis a woman's fault
   Lady P   Now God help thee !
   Hot.   To the Welsh lady's bed
   Lady P.   What's that ?
   Hot   Peace ! she sings.
       [*Here the lady sings a Welsh song.*
   Hot.   Come, Kate, I'll have your song too
   Lady P   Not mine, in good sooth   251
   Hot.   Not yours, in good sooth ! Heart !
you swear like a comfit-maker's wife . ' Not
you, in good sooth,' and ' as true as I live,' and

'as God shall mend me,' and 'as sure as day,'
And givest such sarcenet surety for thy oaths,
As if thou never walk'st further than Fins-
bury.
Swear me, Kate, like a lady as thou art,
A good mouth-filling oath, and leave ' in sooth,'
And such protest of pepper-gingerbread, 260
To velvet-guards and Sunday-citizens.
Come, sing.
  Lady P. I will not sing.
  Hot. 'Tis the next way to turn tailor, or
be red-breast teacher. An the indentures be
drawn, I'll away within these two hours ; and
so, come in when ye will. [*Exit.*
  Glend. Come, come, Lord Mortimer ; you
are as slow
As hot Lord Percy is on fire to go.
By this our book is drawn ; we'll but seal, 270
And then to horse immediately.
  Mort. With all my heart. [*Exeunt.*

SCENE II. *London. The palace.*

Enter the KING, PRINCE OF WALES, *and others.*

  King. Lords, give us leave ; the Prince of
Wales and I
Must have some private conference : but be
near at hand,
For we shall presently have need of you.
                          [*Exeunt Lords.*
I know not whether God will have it so,
For some displeasing service I have done,
That, in his secret doom, out of my blood
He'll breed revengement and a scourge for me ;
But thou dost in thy passages of life
Make me believe that thou art only mark'd
For the hot vengeance and the rod of heaven
To punish my mistreadings. Tell me else, 11
Could such inordinate and low desires,
Such poor, such bare, such lewd, such mean
attempts,
Such barren pleasures, rude society,
As thou art match'd withal and grafted to,
Accompany the greatness of thy blood .
And hold their level with thy princely heart?
  Prince. So please your majesty, I would I
could
Quit all offences with as clear excuse
As well as I am doubtless I can purge   20
Myself of many I am charged withal :
Yet such extenuation let me beg,
As, in reproof of many tales devised,
Which oft the ear of greatness needs must
hear,
By smiling pick-thanks and base newsmongers,
I may, for some things true, wherein my youth
Hath faulty wander'd and irregular,
Find pardon on my true submission.
  King. God pardon thee ! yet let me won-
der, Harry,
At thy affections, which do hold a wing   30
Quite from the flight of all thy ancestors.
Thy place in council thou hast rudely lost,
Which by thy younger brother is supplied,
And art almost an alien to the hearts
Of all the court and princes of my blood :

The hope and expectation of thy time
Is ruin'd, and the soul of every man
Prophetically doth forethink thy fall.
Had I so lavish of my presence been,
So common-hackney'd in the eyes of men, 40
So stale and cheap to vulgar company,
Opinion, that did help me to the crown,
Had still kept loyal to possession
And left me in reputeless banishment,
A fellow of no mark nor likelihood.
By being seldom seen, I could not stir
But like a comet I was wonder'd at ;
That men would tell their children ' This is he ;'
Others would say 'Where, which is Boling-
broke ?'
And then I stole all courtesy from heaven, 50
And dress'd myself in such humility
That I did pluck allegiance from men's hearts,
Loud shouts and salutations from their mouths,
Even in the presence of the crowned king.
Thus did I keep my person fresh and new ;
My presence, like a robe pontifical,
Ne'er seen but wonder'd at : and so my state,
Seldom but sumptuous, showed like a feast
And won by rareness such solemnity.
The skipping king, he ambled up and down 60
With shallow jesters and rash bavin wits,
Soon kindled and soon burnt ; carded his state,
Mingled his royalty with capering fools,
Had his great name profaned with their scorns
And gave his countenance, against his name,
To laugh at gibing boys and stand the push
Of every beardless vain comparative,
Grew a companion to the common streets,
Enfeoff'd himself to popularity ;
That, being daily swallow'd by men's eyes, 70
They surfeited with honey and began
To loathe the taste of sweetness, whereof a
little
More than a little is by much too much.
So when he had occasion to be seen,
He was but as the cuckoo is in June,
Heard, not regarded ; seen, but with such eyes
As, sick and blunted with community,
Afford no extraordinary gaze,
Such as is bent on sun-like majesty
When it shines seldom in admiring eyes ;   80
But rather drowzed and hung their eyelids
down,
Slept in his face and render'd such aspect
As cloudy men use to their adversaries, ·
Being with his presence glutted, gorged and
full.
And in that very line, Harry, standest thou ;
For thou hast lost thy princely privilege
With vile participation : not an eye
But is a-weary of thy common sight,
Save mine, which hath desired to see thee
more ;
Which now doth that I would not have it do,
Make blind itself with foolish tenderness.   91
  Prince. I shall hereafter, my thrice gra-
cious lord,
Be more myself.
  King.   For all the world
As thou art to this hour was Richard then

26

When I from France set foot at Ravenspurgh,
And even as I was then is Percy now.
Now, by my sceptre and my soul to boot,
He hath more worthy interest to the state
Than thou the shadow of succession ;
For of no right, nor color like to right,   100
He doth fill fields with harness in the realm,
Turns head against the lion's armed jaws,
And, being no more in debt to years than thou,
Leads ancient lords and reverend bishops on
To bloody battles and to bruising arms.
What never-dying honor hath he got
Against renowned Douglas ! whose high deeds,
Whose hot incursions and great name in arms
Holds from all soldiers chief majority
And military title capital   110
Through all the kingdoms that acknowledge
        Christ :
Thrice hath this Hotspur, Mars in swathling
        clothes,
This infant warrior, in his enterprizes
Discomfited great Douglas, ta'en him once,
Enlarged him and made a friend of him,
To fill the mouth of deep defiance up
And shake the peace and safety of our throne.
And what say you to this ? Percy, Northumber-
        land,
The Archbishop's grace of York, Douglas, Mor-
        timer,
Capitulate against us and are up.   120
But wherefore do I tell these news to thee ?
Why, Harry, do I tell thee of my foes,
Which art my near'st and dearest enemy ?
Thou that art like enough, through vassal fear,
Base inclination and the start of spleen,
To fight against me under Percy's pay,
To dog his heels and curtsy at his frowns,
To show how much thou art degenerate.
    Prince. Do not think so; you shall not find
        it so :
And God forgive them that so much have
        sway'd   130
Your majesty's good thoughts away from me!
I will redeem all this on Percy's head .
And in the closing of some glorious day
Be bold to tell you that I am your son ;
When I will wear a garment all of blood
And stain my favors in a bloody mask,
Which, wash'd away, shall scour my shame
        with it :
And that shall be the day, whene'er it lights,
That this same child of honor and renown,
This gallant Hotspur, this all-praised knight,
And your unthought-of Harry chance to meet.
For every honor sitting on his helm,
Would they were multitudes, and on my head
My shames redoubled ! for the time will come,
That I shall make this northern youth ex-
        change
His glorious deeds for my indignities.
Percy is but my factor, good my lord,
To engross up glorious deeds on my behalf ;
And I will call him to so strict account,
That he shall render every glory up,   150
Yea, even the slightest worship of his time,
Or I will tear the reckoning from his heart.

This, in the name of God, I promise here :
The which if He be pleased I shall perform,
I do beseech your majesty may salve
The long-grown wounds of my intemperance:
If not, the end of life cancels all bands ;
And I will die a hundred thousand deaths
Ere break the smallest parcel of this vow.
    King. A hundred thousand rebels die in
        this :   160
Thou shalt have charge and sovereign trust
        herein.

Enter BLUNT.

How now, good Blunt ? thy looks are full of
        speed.
    Blunt. So hath the business that I come to
        speak of.
Lord Mortimer of Scotland hath sent word
That Douglas and the English rebels met
The eleventh of this month at Shrewsbury:
A mighty and a fearful head they are,
If promises be kept on every hand,
As ever offer'd foul play in a state.
    King. The Earl of Westmoreland set forth
        to-day;   170
With him my son, Lord John of Lancaster;
For this advertisement is five days old :
On Wednesday next, Harry, you shall set for-
        ward;
On Thursday we ourselves will march: our
        meeting
Is Bridgenorth: and, Harry, you shall march
Through Gloucestershire; by which account,
Our business valued, some twelve days hence
Our general forces at Bridgenorth shall meet.
Our hands are full of business: let's away;
Advantage feeds him fat, while men delay.   180
        [*Exeunt.*

SCENE III.   *Eastcheap.   The Boar's-Head
                Tavern.*

Enter FALSTAFF *and* BARDOLPH.

    Fal. Bardolph, am I not fallen away vilely
since this last action ? do I not bate ? do I not
dwindle ? Why, my skin hangs about me like
an old lady's loose gown ; I am withered like
an old apple-john. Well, I'll repent, and that
suddenly, while I am in some liking ; I shall
be out of heart shortly, and then I shall have
no strength to repent. An I have not forgotten
what the inside of a church is made of, I am a
peppercorn, a brewer's horse : the inside of a
church ! Company, villanous company, hath
been the spoil of me.
    Bard. Sir John, you are so fretful, you
cannot live long.
    Fal. Why, there is it : come sing me a
bawdy song ; make me merry. I was as virtuously given as a gentleman need to be ; virtuous enough ; swore little ; diced not above
seven times a week ; went to a bawdy-house
not above once in a quarter—of an hour ; paid
money that I borrowed, three or four times ;
lived well and in good compass : and now I live
out of all order, out of all compass.

Bard. Why, you are so fat, Sir John, that you must needs be out of all compass, out of all reasonable compass, Sir John.

Fal. Do thou amend thy face, and I'll amend my life : thou art our admiral, thou bearest the lantern in the poop, but 'tis in the nose of thee ; thou art the Knight of the Burning Lamp.   30

Bard. Why, Sir John, my face does you no harm.

Fal. No, I'll be sworn ; I make as good use of it as many a man doth of a Death's-head or a memento mori : I never see thy face but I think upon hell-fire and Dives that lived in purple ; for there he is in his robes, burning, burning. If thou wert any way given to virtue, I would swear by thy face ; my oath should be ' By this fire, that's God's angel :' but thou art altogether given over ; and wert indeed, but for the light in thy face, the son of utter darkness. When thou rannest up Gadshill in the night to catch my horse, if I did not think thou hadst been an ignis fatuus or a ball of wildfire, there's no purchase in money. O, thou art a perpetual triumph, an everlasting bonfire-light ! Thou hast saved me a thousand marks in links and torches, walking with thee in the night betwixt tavern and tavern ; but the sack that thou hast drunk me would have bought me lights as good cheap at the dearest chandler's in Europe. I have maintained that salamander of yours with fire any time this two and thirty years ; God reward me for it !

Bard. 'Sblood, I would my face were in your belly !

Fal. God-a-mercy ! so should I be sure to be heart-burned.

Enter HOSTESS.

How now, Dame Partlet the hen ! have you inquired yet who picked my pocket ?   61

Host. Why, Sir John, what do you think, Sir John ? do you think I keep thieves in my house ? I have searched, I have inquired, so has my husband, man by man, boy by boy, servant by servant : the tithe of a hair was never lost in my house before.

Fal. Ye lie, hostess : Bardolph was shaved and lost many a hair ; and I'll be sworn my pocket was picked. Go to, you are a woman, go.

Host. Who, I ? no ; I defy thee : God's light, I was never called so in mine own house before.

Fal. Go to, I know you well enough.

Host. No, Sir John ; you do not know me, Sir John. I know you, Sir John : you owe me money, Sir John ; and now you pick a quarrel to beguile me of it : I bought you a dozen of shirts to your back.

Fal. Dowlas, filthy dowlas : I have given them away to bakers' wives, and they have made bolters of them.   81

Host. Now, as I am a true woman, holland of eight shillings an ell. You owe money here besides, Sir John, for your diet and by-drinkings, and money lent you, four and twenty pound.

Fal. He had his part of it ; let him pay.

Host. He ? alas, he is poor ; he hath nothing.

Fal. How ! poor ? look upon his face ; what call you rich ? let them coin his nose, let them coin his cheeks : I'll not pay a denier. What, will you make a younker of me ? shall I not take mine ease in mine inn but I shall have my pocket picked ? I have lost a seal-ring of my grandfather's worth forty mark.

Host. O Jesu, I have heard the prince tell him, I know not how oft, that that ring was copper !

Fal. How ! the prince is a Jack, a sneak-cup : 'sblood, an he were here, I would cudgel him like a dog, if he would say so.   101

Enter the PRINCE *and* PETO, *marching, and* FALSTAFF *meets them playing on his truncheon like a fife.*

How now, lad ! is the wind in that door, i' faith ? must we all march ?

Bard. Yea, two and two, Newgate fashion.

Host. My lord, I pray you, hear me.

Prince. What sayest thou, Mistress Quickly ? How doth thy husband ? I love him well ; he is an honest man.

Host. Good my lord, hear me.

Fal. Prithee, let her alone, and list to me.

Prince. What sayest thou, Jack ?   111

Fal. The other night I fell asleep here behind the arras and had my pocket picked : this house is turned bawdy-house ; they pick pockets.

Prince. What didst thou lose, Jack ?

Fal. Wilt thou believe me, Hal ? three or four bonds of forty pound a-piece, and a seal-ring of my grandfather's.

Prince. A trifle, some eight-penny matter.

Host. So I told him, my lord ; and I said I heard your grace say so : and, my lord, he speaks most vilely of you, like a foul-mouthed man as he is ; and said he would cudgel you.

Prince. What ! he did not ?

Host. There's neither faith, truth, nor womanhood in me else.

Fal. There's no more faith in thee than in a stewed prune ; nor no more truth in thee than in a drawn fox ; and for womanhood, Maid Marian may be the deputy's wife of the ward to thee. Go, you thing, go.   131

Host. Say, what thing ? what thing ?

Fal. What thing ! why, a thing to thank God on.

Host. I am no thing to thank God on, I would thou shouldst know it ; I am an honest man's wife : and, setting thy knighthood aside, thou art a knave to call me so.

Fal. Setting thy womanhood aside, thou art a beast to say otherwise.   140

Host. Say, what beast, thou knave, thou ?

Fal. What beast ! why, an otter.

Prince. An otter, Sir John ! why an otter?

Fal. Why, she's neither fish nor flesh; a man knows not where to have her.

Host. Thou art an unjust man in saying so: thou or any man knows where to have me, thou knave, thou!

Prince. Thou sayest true, hostess; and he slanders thee most grossly. 150

Host. So he doth you, my lord; and said this other day you ought him a thousand pound.

Prince. Sirrah, do I owe you a thousand pound?

Fal. A thousand pound, Hal! a million: thy love is worth a million: thou owest me thy love.

Host. Nay, my lord, he called you Jack, and said he would cudgel you.

Fal. Did I, Bardolph? 160

Bard. Indeed, Sir John, you said so.

Fal. Yea, if he said my ring was copper.

Prince. I say 'tis copper: darest thou be as good as thy word now?

Fal. Why, Hal, thou knowest, as thou art but man, I dare: but as thou art prince, I fear thee as I fear the roaring of the lion's whelp.

Prince. And why not as the lion?

Fal. The king himself is to be feared as the lion: dost thou think I'll fear thee as I fear thy father? nay, an I do, I pray God my girdle break.

Prince. O, if it should, how would thy guts fall about thy knees! But, sirrah, there's no room for faith, truth, nor honesty in this bosom of thine; it is all filled up with guts and midriff. Charge an honest woman with picking thy pocket! why, thou whoreson, impudent, embossed rascal, if there were anything in thy pocket but tavern-reckonings, memorandums of bawdy-houses, and one poor penny-worth of sugar-candy to make thee long-winded, if thy pocket were enriched with any other injuries but these, I am a villain: and yet you will stand to it; you will not pocket up wrong: art thou not ashamed?

Fal. Dost thou hear, Hal? thou knowest in the state of innocency Adam fell; and what should poor Jack Falstaff do in the days of villany? Thou seest I have more flesh than another man, and therefore more frailty. You confess then, you picked my pocket? 190

Prince. It appears so by the story.

Fal. Hostess, I forgive thee: go, make ready breakfast; love thy husband, look to thy servants, cherish thy guests: thou shalt find me tractable to any honest reason: thou seest I am pacified still. Nay, prithee, be gone. [*Exit Hostess.*] Now, Hal, to the news at court: for the robbery, lad, how is that answered?

Prince. O, my sweet beef, I must still be good angel to thee: the money is paid back again. 200

Fal. O, I do not like that paying back; 'tis a double labor.

Prince. I am good friends with my father and may do any thing.

Fal. Rob me the exchequer the first thing thou doest, and do it with unwashed hands too.

Bard. Do, my lord.

Prince. I have procured thee, Jack, a charge of foot. 208

Fal. I would it had been of horse. Where shall I find one that can steal well? O for a fine thief, of the age of two and twenty or thereabouts! I am heinously unprovided. Well, God be thanked for these rebels, they offend none but the virtuous: I laud them, I praise them.

Prince. Bardolph!

Bard. My lord?

Prince. Go bear this letter to Lord John of Lancaster, to my brother John; this to my Lord of Westmoreland. [*Exit Bardolph.*] Go, Peto, to horse, to horse; for thou and I have thirty miles to ride yet ere dinner time. [*Exit Peto.*] Jack, meet me to-morrow in the temple hall at two o'clock in the afternoon. There shalt thou know thy charge; and there receive

Money and order for their furniture.
The land is burning; Percy stands on high;
And either we or they must lower lie. [*Exit.*

Fal. Rare words! brave world! Hostess, my breakfast, come! 229
O, I could wish this tavern were my drum!
[*Exit.*

ACT IV.

SCENE I. *The rebel camp near Shrewsbury.*

Enter HOTSPUR, WORCESTER, *and* DOUGLAS.

Hot. Well said, my noble Scot: if speaking truth
In this fine age were not thought flattery,
Such attribution should the Douglas have,
As not a soldier of this season's stamp
Should go so general current through the world.
By God, I cannot flatter; I do defy
The tongues of soothers; but a braver place
In my heart's love hath no man than yourself:
Nay, task me to my word; approve me, lord.

Doug. Thou art the king of honor: 10
No man so potent breathes upon the ground
But I will beard him.

Hot.   Do so, and 'tis well.

Enter a Messenger *with letters.*

What letters hast thou there?—I can but thank you.

Mess. These letters come from your father.

Hot. Letters from him! why comes he not himself?

Mess. He cannot come, my lord; he is grievous sick.

Hot. 'Zounds! how has he the leisure to be sick
In such a justling time? Who leads his power?
Under whose government come they along?

Mess. His letters bear his mind, not I, my
   lord.   20
Wor. I prithee, tell me, doth he keep his
   bed?
Mess. He did, my lord, four days ere I set
   forth;
And at the time of my departure thence
He was much fear'd by his physicians.
Wor. I would the state of time had first
   been whole
Ere he by sickness had been visited:
His health was never better worth than now.
Hot. Sick now! droop now! this sickness
   doth infect
The very life-blood of our enterprise;
'Tis catching hither, even to our camp.   30
†He writes me here, that inward sickness—
And that his friends by deputation could not
So soon be drawn, nor did he think it meet
To lay so dangerous and dear a trust
On any soul removed but on his own.
Yet doth he give us bold advertisement,
That with our small conjunction we should on,
To see how fortune is disposed to us;
For, as he writes, there is no quailing now,
Because the king is certainly possess'd   40
Of all our purposes. What say you to it?
Wor. Your father's sickness is a maim to
   us.
Hot. A perilous gash, a very limb lopp'd
   off:
And yet, in faith, it is not; his present want
Seems more than we shall find it: were it
   good
To set the exact wealth of all our states
All at one cast? to set so rich a main
On the nice hazard of one doubtful hour?
It were not good; †for therein should we read
The very bottom and the soul of hope,   50
The very list, the very utmost bound
Of all our fortunes.
Doug.   . 'Faith, and so we should;
Where now remains a sweet reversion:
†We may boldly spend upon the hope of what
Is to come in:
A comfort of retirement lives in this.
Hot. A rendezvous, a home to fly unto,
If that the devil and mischance look big
Upon the maidenhead of our affairs.
Wor. But yet I would your father had been
   here.   60
The quality and hair of our attempt
Brooks no division: it will be thought
By some, that know not why he is away,
That wisdom, loyalty and mere dislike
Of our proceedings kept the earl from hence:
And think how such an apprehension
May turn the tide of fearful faction
And breed a kind of question in our cause;
For well you know we of the offering side
Must keep aloof from strict arbitrement,   70
And stop all sight-holes, every loop from
   whence
The eye of reason may pry in upon us:
This absence of your father's draws a curtain,
That shows the ignorant a kind of fear

Before not dreamt of.
Hot.   You strain too far.
I rather of his absence make this use:
It lends a lustre and more great opinion,
A larger dare to our great enterprise,
Than if the earl were here; for men must think
If we without his help can make a head   80
To push against a kingdom, with his help
We shall o'erturn it topsy-turvy down.
Yet all goes well, yet all our joints are whole.
Doug. As heart can think: there is not such
   a word
Spoke of in Scotland as this term of fear.

Enter Sir RICHARD VERNON.

Hot. My cousin Vernon, welcome, by my
   soul.
Ver. Pray God my news be worth a wel-
   come, lord.
The Earl of Westmoreland, seven thousand
   strong,
Is marching hitherwards; with him Prince
   John.
Hot. No harm: what more?
Ver.   And further, I have learn'd,   90
The king himself in person is set forth,
Or hitherwards intended speedily,
With strong and mighty preparation.
Hot. He shall be welcome too. Where is
   his son,
The nimble-footed madcap Prince of Wales,
And his comrades, that daff'd the world aside,
And bid it pass?
Ver.   All furnish'd, all in arms;
†All plumed like estridges that with the wind
Baited like eagles having lately bathed;
Glittering in golden coats, like images;   100
As full of spirit as the month of May,
And gorgeous as the sun at midsummer;
Wanton as youthful goats, wild as young bulls.
I saw young Harry, with his beaver on,
His cuisses on his thighs gallantly arm'd,
Rise from the ground like feather'd Mercury,
And vaulted with such ease into his seat,
As if an angel dropp'd down from the clouds,
To turn and wind a fiery Pegasus
And witch the world with noble horsemanship.
Hot. No more, no more: worse than the sun
   in March,   111
This praise doth nourish agues. Let them
   come;
They come like sacrifices in their trim,
And to the fire-eyed maid of smoky war
All hot and bleeding will we offer them
The mailed Mars shall on his altar sit
Up to the ears in blood. I am on fire
To hear this rich reprisal is so nigh
And yet not ours. Come, let me taste my
   horse,
Who is to bear me like a thunderbolt   120
Against the bosom of the Prince of Wales:
Harry to Harry shall, hot horse to horse,
Meet and ne'er part till one drop down a corse.
O that Glendower were come!
Ver.   There is more news:
I learn'd in Worcester, as I rode along,

He cannot draw his power this fourteen days.

Doug. That's the worst tidings that I hear
of yet.

Wor. Ay, by my faith, that bears a frosty
sound.

Hot. What may the king's whole battle
reach unto ?

Ver. To thirty thousand.

Hot.   Forty let it be : 130
My father and Glendower being both away,
The powers of us may serve so great a day.
Come, let us take a muster speedily :
Doomsday is near ; die all, die merrily.

Doug. Talk not of dying : I am out of fear
Of death or death's hand for this one-half
    year.   [*Exeunt.*

SCENE II. *A public road near Coventry.*

Enter FALSTAFF *and* BARDOLPH.

Fal. Bardolph, get thee before to Coventry;
fill me a bottle of sack : our soldiers shall
march through ; we'll to Sutton Co'fil' to-
night.

Bard. Will you give me money, captain ?

Fal. Lay out, lay out.

Bard. This bottle makes an angel.

Fal. An if it do, take it for thy labor ; and
if it make twenty, take them all ; I'll answer
the coinage. Bid my lieutenant Peto meet me
at town's end.   10

Bard. I will, captain : farewell.   [*Exit.*

Fal. If I be not ashamed of my soldiers, I
am a soused gurnet. I have misused the king's
press damnably. I have got, in exchange of a
hundred and fifty soldiers, three hundred and
odd pounds. I press me none but good house-
holders, yeoman's sons ; inquire me out contracted bachelors, such as had been asked
twice on the banns ; such a commodity of warm
slaves, as had as lieve hear the devil as a drum;
such as fear the report of a caliver worse than
a struck fowl or a hurt wild-duck. I pressed
me none but such toasts-and-butter, with
hearts in their bellies no bigger than pins'
heads, and they have bought out their services ; and now my whole charge consists of
ancients, corporals, lieutenants, gentlemen of
companies, slaves as ragged as Lazarus in the
painted cloth, where the glutton's dogs licked
his sores ; and such as indeed were never soldiers, but discarded unjust serving-men,
younger sons to younger brothers, revolted
tapsters and ostlers trade-fallen, the cankers
of a calm world and a long peace, ten times
more dishonorable ragged than an old faced
ancient ; and such have I, to fill up the rooms
of them that have bought out their services,
that you would think that I had a hundred
and fifty tattered prodigals lately come from
swine-keeping, from eating draff and husks.
A mad fellow met me on the way and told me
I had unloaded all the gibbets and pressed the
dead bodies. No eye hath seen such scare-
crows. I'll not march through Coventry with
them, that's flat : nay, and the villains march

wide betwixt the legs, as if they had gyves on;
for indeed I had the most of them out of prison. There's but a shirt and a half in all my
company ; and the half shirt is two napkins
tacked together and thrown over the shoulders
like an herald's coat without sleeves ; and the
shirt, to say the truth, stolen from my host at
Saint Alban's, or the red-nose innkeeper of
Daventry. But that's all one ; they'll find
linen enough on every hedge.

Enter the PRINCE *and* WESTMORELAND.

Prince. How now, blown Jack ! how now,
quilt !

Fal. What, Hal ! how now, mad wag !
what a devil dost thou in Warwickshire ? My
good Lord of Westmoreland, I cry you mercy :
I thought your honor had already been at
Shrewsbury.   59

West. Faith, Sir John, 'tis more than time
that I were there, and you too ; but my powers
are there already. The king, I can tell you
looks for us all : we must away all night.

Fal. Tut, never fear me : I am as vigilant
as a cat to steal cream.

Prince. I think, to steal cream indeed, for
thy theft hath already made thee butter. But
tell me, Jack, whose fellows are these that
come after ?

Fal. Mine, Hal, mine.   69

Prince. I did never see such pitiful rascals.

Fal. Tut, tut ; good enough to toss ; food
for powder, food for powder ; they'll fill a pit
as well as better : tush, man, mortal men, mortal men.

West. Ay, but, Sir John, methinks they are
exceeding poor and bare, too beggarly.

Fal. 'Faith, for their poverty, I know not
where they had that ; and for their bareness,
I am sure they never learned that of me.

Prince. No, I'll be sworn ; unless you call
three fingers on the ribs bare. But, sirrah,
make haste : Percy is already in the field. 81

Fal. What, is the king encamped ?

West. He is, Sir John : I fear we shall stay
    too long.

Fal. Well,
To the latter end of a fray and the beginning
    of a feast   85
Fits a dull fighter and a keen guest.
                    [*Exeunt.*

SCENE III. *The rebel camp near Shrewsbury.*
Enter HOTSPUR, WORCESTER, DOUGLAS, *and*
        VERNON.

Hot. We'll fight with him to-night.

Wor.   It may not be.

Doug. You give him then advantage.

Ver.   Not a whit.

Hot. Why say you so ? looks he not for
    supply ?

Ver. So do we.

Hot.   His is certain, ours is doubtful.

Wor. Good cousin, be advised ; stir not to-
    night.

Ver. Do not, my lord.

Doug.   You do not counsel well :
You speak it out of fear and cold heart.
  Ver.   Do me no slander, Douglas : by. my
    life,
And I dare well maintain it with my life,
If well-respected honor bid me on,   10
I hold as little counsel with weak fear
As you, my lord, or any Scot that this day
    lives :
Let it be seen to-morrow in the battle
Which of us fears.
  Doug.   Yea, or to-night.
  Ver.   Content.
  Hot. To-night, say I.
  Ver. Come, come, it may not be. I wonder
    much,
Being men of such great leading as you are,
That you foresee not what impediments
Drag back our expedition : certain horse
Of my cousin Vernon's are not yet come up :
Your uncle Worcester's horse came but to-
    day ;   21
And now their pride and mettle is asleep,
Their courage with hard labor tame and dull,
That not a horse is half the half of himself.
  Hot. So are the horses of the enemy
In general, journey-bated and brought low :
The better part of ours are full of rest.
  Wor. The number of the king exceedeth
    ours :
For God's sake, cousin, stay till all come in.
            [*The trumpet sounds a parley.*

        Enter SIR WALTER BLUNT.

  Blunt. I come with gracious offers from
    · the king,   30
If you vouchsafe me hearing and respect.
  Hot. Welcome, Sir Walter Blunt ; and
    would to God
You were of our determination !
Some of us love you well ; and even those
    some
Envy your great deservings and good name,
Because you are not of our quality,
But stand against us like an enemy.
  Blunt. And God defend but still I should
    stand so,
So long as out of limit and true rule
You stand against anointed majesty.   40
But to my charge. The king hath sent to know
The nature of your griefs, and whereupon
You conjure from the breast of civil peace
Such bold hostility, teaching his duteous land
Audacious cruelty. If that the king
Have any way your good deserts forgot,
Which he confesseth to be manifold,
He bids you name your griefs ; and with all
    speed
You shall have your desires with interest
And pardon absolute for yourself and these 50
Herein misled by your suggestion.
  Hot. The king is kind ; and well we know
    the king
Knows at what time to promise, when to pay.
My father and my uncle and myself
Did give him that same royalty he wears ;

And when he was not six and twenty strong,
Sick in the world's regard, wretched and low,
A poor unminded outlaw sneaking home,
My father gave him welcome to the shore ;
And when he heard him swear and vow to God
He came but to be Duke of Lancaster,   61
To sue his livery and beg his peace,
With tears of innocency and terms of zeal,
My father, in kind heart and pity moved,
Swore him assistance and perform'd it too.
Now when the lords and barons of the realm
Perceived Northumberland did lean to him,
The more and less came in with cap and knee;
Met him in boroughs, cities, villages,
Attended him on bridges, stood in lanes,   70
Laid gifts before him, proffer'd him their oaths,
Gave him their heirs, as pages follow'd him
Even at the heels in golden multitudes.
He presently, as greatness knows itself,
Steps me a little higher than his vow
Made to my father, while his blood was poor,
Upon the naked shore at Ravenspurgh ;
And now, forsooth, takes on him to reform
Some certain edicts and some strait decrees
That lie too heavy on the commonwealth,   80
Cries out upon abuses, seems to weep
Over his country's wrongs ; and by this face,
This seeming brow of justice, did he win
The hearts of all that he did angle for ;
Proceeded further ; cut me off the heads
Of all the favorites that the absent king
In deputation left behind him here,
When he was personal in the Irish war.
  Blunt. Tut, I came not to hear this.
  Hot.   Then to the point.
In short time after, he deposed the king ;   90
Soon after that, deprived him of his life ;
And in the neck of that, task'd the whole state:
To make that worse, suffer'd his kinsman
    March,
Who is, if every owner were well placed,
Indeed his king, to be engaged in Wales
There without ransom to lie forfeited ;
Disgraced me in my happy victories,
Sought to entrap me by intelligence ;
Rated mine uncle from the council-board ;
In rage dismiss'd my father from the court ;
Broke oath on oath, committed wrong on
    wrong,   101
And in conclusion drove us to seek out
This head of safety ; and withal to pry
Into his title, the which we find
Too indirect for long continuance.
  Blunt. Shall I return this answer to the
    king ?
  Hot. Not so, Sir Walter : we'll withdraw
    awhile.
Go to the king ; and let there be impawn'd
Some surety for a safe return again,
And in the morning early shall my uncle   110
Bring him our purposes : and so farewell.
  Blunt. I would you would accept of grace
    and love.
  Hot. And may be so we shall.
  Blunt.   Pray God you do.
                                    [*Exeunt.*

SCENE IV. *York. The* ARCHBISHOP'S *palace.*

Enter the ARCHBISHOP OF YORK *and* SIR
MICHAEL.

Arch. Hie, good Sir Michael ; bear this
  sealed brief
With winged haste to the lord marshal ;
This to my cousin Scroop, and all the rest
To whom they are directed. If you knew
How much they do import, you would make
  haste.
Sir M. My good lord,
I guess their tenor.
Arch.   Like enough you do.
To-morrow, good Sir Michael, is a day
Wherein the fortune of ten thousand men
Must bide the touch ; for, sir, at Shrewsbury,
As I am truly given to understand,   11
The king with mighty and quick-raised power
Meets with Lord Harry : and, I fear, Sir
  Michael,
What with the sickness of Northumberland,
Whose power was in the first proportion,
And what with Owen Glendower's absence
  thence,
Who with them was a rated sinew too
And comes not in, o'er-ruled by prophecies,
I fear the power of Percy is too weak
To wage an instant trial with the king.   20
Sir M. Why, my good lord, you need not
  fear ;
There is Douglas and Lord Mortimer.
Arch. No, Mortimer is not there.
Sir M. But there is Mordake, Vernon, Lord
  Harry Percy,
And there is my Lord of Worcester and a head
Of gallant warriors, noble gentlemen.
Arch. And so there is : but yet the king
  hath drawn
The special head of all the land together :
The Prince of Wales, Lord John of Lancaster,
The noble Westmoreland and warlike Blunt ;
And many moe corrivals and dear men   31
Of estimation and command in arms.
Sir M. Doubt not, my lord, they shall be
  well opposed.
Arch. I hope no less, yet needful 'tis to fear;
And, to prevent the worst, Sir Michael, speed:
For if Lord Percy thrive not, ere the king
Dismiss his power, he means to visit us,
For he hath heard of our confederacy,
And 'tis but wisdom to make strong against
  him :
Therefore make haste. I must go write again
To other friends ; and so farewell, Sir Michael.
                              [*Exeunt.*   41

ACT V.

SCENE I. *The* KING'S *camp near Shewsbury.*

Enter the KING, PRINCE OF WALES, LORD
  JOHN OF LANCASTER, EARL OF WESTMORE-
  LAND, SIR WALTER BLUNT, *and* FALSTAFF.

King. How bloodily the sun begins to peer
Above yon busky hill ! the day looks pale

At his distemperature.
Prince.   The southern wind
Doth play the trumpet to his purposes,
And by his hollow whistling in the leaves
Foretells a tempest and a blustering day.
King. Then with the losers let it sympa-
  thize,
For nothing can seem foul to those that win.
                        [*The trumpet sounds.*

Enter WORCESTER *and* VERNON.

How now, my Lord of Worcester ! 'tis not well
That you and I should meet upon such terms
As now we meet. You have deceived our trust
And made us doff our easy robes of peace,
To crush our old limbs in ungentle steel :
This is not well, my lord, this is not well.
What say you to it ? will you again unknit
This churlish knot of all-abhorred war ?
And move in that obedient orb again
Where you did give a fair and natural light,
And be no more an exhaled meteor,
A prodigy of fear and a portent   20
Of broached mischief to the unborn times ?
Wor. Hear me, my liege :
For mine own part, I could be well content
To entertain the lag-end of my life
With quiet hours; for I do protest,
I have not sought the day of this dislike.
King. You have not sought it! how comes
  it then ?
Fal. Rebellion lay in his way, and he found
  it.
Prince. Peace, chewet, peace !
Wor. It pleased your majesty to turn your
  looks   30
Of favor from myself and all our house ;
And yet I must remember you, my lord,
We were the first and dearest of your friends.
For you my staff of office did I break
In Richard's time ; and posted day and night
To meet you on the way, and kiss your hand,
When yet you were in place and in account
Nothing so strong and fortunate as I.
It was myself, my brother and his son,
That brought you home and boldly outdare
The dangers of the time. You swore to us,   41
And you did swear that oath at Doncaster,
That you did nothing purpose 'gainst the state ;
Nor claim no further than your new-fall'n right,
The seat of Gaunt, dukedom of Lancaster :
To this we swore our aid. But in short space
It rain'd down fortune showering on your head;
And such a flood of greatness fell on you,
What with our help, what with the absent king,
What with the injuries of a wanton time,   50
The seeming sufferances that you had borne,
And the contrarious winds that held the king
So long in his unlucky Irish wars
That all in England did repute him dead :
And from this swarm of fair advantages
You took occasion to be quickly woo'd
To gripe the general sway into your hand ;
Forgot your oath to us at Doncaster ;
And being fed by us you used us so
As that ungentle gull, the cuckoo's bird,   60

Useth the sparrow ; did oppress our nest ;
Grew by our feeding to so great a bulk
That even our love durst not come near your
    sight
For fear of swallowing , but with nimble wing
We were enforced, for safety sake, to fly
Out of your sight and raise this present head;
Whereby we stand opposed by such means
As you yourself have forged against yourself
By unkind usage, dangerous countenance,
And violation of all faith and troth   70
Sworn to us in your younger enterprise
    King. These things indeed you have artic-
ulate,
Proclaim'd at market-crosses, read in churches,
To face the garment of rebellion
With some fine color that may please the eye
Of fickle changelings and poor discontents,
Which gape and rub the elbow at the news
Of hurlyburly innovation
And never yet did insurrection want
Such water-colors to impaint his cause ,   80
Nor moody beggars, starving for a time
Of pellmell havoc and confusion
    Prince In both your armies there is many
    a soul
Shall pay full dearly for this encounter,
If once they join in trial   Tell your nephew,
The Prince of Wales doth join with all the
    world
In praise of Henry Percy : by my hopes,
This present enterprise set off his head,
I do not think a braver gentleman,
More active-valiant or more valiant-young,   90
More daring or more bold, is now alive
To grace this latter age with noble deeds
For my part, I may speak it to my shame,
I have a truant been to chivalry ,
And so I hear he doth account me too ;
Yet this before my father's majesty—
I am content that he shall take the odds
Of his great name and estimation,
And will, to save the blood on either side,
Try fortune with him in a single fight   100
    King. And, Prince of Wales, so dare we
    venture thee,
Albeit considerations infinite
Do make against it No, good Worcester, no,
We love our people well , even those we love
That are misled upon your cousin's part ,
And, will they take the offer of our grace,
Both he and they and you, yea, every man
Shall be my friend again and I'll be his :
So tell your cousin, and bring me word
What he will do . but if he will not yield,   110
Rebuke and dread correction wait on us
And they shall do their office So, be gone ,
We will not now be troubled with reply
We offer fair ; take it advisedly
    [*Exeunt Worcester and Vernon*
    Prince. It will not be accepted, on my life
The Douglas and the Hotspur both together
Are confident against the world in arms
    King Hence, therefore, every leader to his
    charge ;
For, on their answer, will we set on them .

And God befriend us, as our cause is just ! 120
    [*Exeunt all but the Prince of Wales and
    Falstaff.*
    Fal Hal, if thou see me down in the
battle and bestride me, so ; 'tis a point of
friendship.
    Prince. Nothing but a colossus can do thee
that friendship. Say thy prayers, and farewell
    Fal. I would 'twere bed-time, Hal, and
all well
    Prince. Why, thou owest God a death
    [*Exit.*
    Fal. 'Tis not due yet , I would be loath to
pay him before his day What need I be so
forward with him that calls not on me ? Well,
'tis no matter , honor pricks me on Yea, but
how if honor prick me off when I come on ?
how then ? Can honor set to a leg ? no . or an
arm ? no or take away the grief of a wound ?
no Honor hath no skill in surgery, then ? no
What is honor ? a word What is in that word
honor ? what is that honor ? air. A trim reckoning ! Who hath it ? he that died o' Wednesday Doth he feel it ? no Doth he hear it ?
no 'Tis insensible, then Yea, to the dead. But
will it not live with the living ? no Why ? detraction will not suffer it Therefore I'll none
of it Honor is a mere scutcheon : and so
ends my catechism [*Exit.*

Scene II. *The rebel camp*

Enter Worcester *and* Vernon.

    Wor. O, no, my nephew must not know,
    Sir Richard,
The liberal and kind offer of the king.
    Ver. 'Twere best he did
    Wor.   Then are we all undone.
It is not possible, it cannot be,
The king should keep his word in loving us ;
He will suspect us still and find a time
To punish this offence in other faults
Suspicion all our lives shall be stuck full of
    eyes ,
For treason is but trusted like the fox,
Who, ne'er so tame, so cherish'd and lock'd
    up,   10
Will have a wild trick of his ancestors
Look how we can, or sad or merrily,
Interpretation will misquote our looks,
And we shall feed like oxen at a stall,
The better cherish'd, still the nearer death.
My nephew's trespass may be well forgot ,
It hath the excuse of youth and heat of blood,
And an adopted name of privilege,
A hair-brain'd Hotspur, govern'd by a spleen:
All his offences live upon my head   20
And on his father's , we did train him on,
And, his corruption being ta'en from us,
We, as the spring of all, shall pay for all.
Therefore, good cousin, let not Harry know,
In any case, the offer of the king
    Ver. Deliver what you will , I'll say 'tis so.
Here comes your cousin.

Enter HOTSPUR *and* DOUGLAS.

Hot. My uncle is return'd :
Deliver up my Lord of Westmoreland.
Uncle, what news ?   30
    Wor. The king will bid you battle pres-
        ently.
    Doug. Defy him by the Lord of Westmore-
        land.
    Hot. Lord Douglas, go you and tell him so.
    Doug. Marry, and shall, and very willingly.
                                        [*Exit.*
    Wor. There is no seeming mercy in the
        king.
    Hot. Did you beg any ? God forbid !
    Wor. I told him gently of our grievances,
Of his oath-breaking ; which he mended thus,
By now forswearing that he is forsworn :
He calls us rebels, traitors ; and will scourge
With haughty arms this hateful name in us. 41

Re-enter DOUGLAS.

    Doug. Arm, gentlemen ; to arms ! for I
        have thrown
A brave defiance in King Henry's teeth,
And Westmoreland, that was engaged, did bear
    it ;
Which cannot choose but bring him quickly on.
    Wor. The Prince of Wales stepp'd forth
        before the king,
And, nephew, challenged you to single fight.
    Hot. O, would the quarrel lay upon our
        heads,
And that no man might draw short breath to-
        day
But I and Harry Monmouth ! Tell me, tell
        me,   50
How show'd his tasking ? seem'd it in con-
        tempt ?
    Ver. No, by my soul ; I never in my life
Did hear a challenge urged more modestly,
Unless a brother should a brother dare
To gentle exercise and proof of arms.
He gave you all the duties of a man ;
Trimm'd up your praises with a princely
        tongue,
Spoke your deservings like a chronicle,
Making you ever better than his praise
By still dispraising praise valued with you; 60
And, which became him like a prince indeed,
He made a blushing cital of himself ;
And chid his truant youth with such a grace
As if he master'd there a double spirit
Of teaching and of learning instantly.
There did he pause: but let me tell the world,
If he outlive the envy of this day,
England did never owe so sweet a hope,
So much misconstrued in his wantonness.
    Hot. Cousin, I think thou art enamored 70
On his follies : never did I hear
Of any prince so wild a libertine.
But be he as he will, yet once ere night
I will embrace him with a soldier's arm,
That he shall shrink under my courtesy.
Arm, arm with speed : and, fellows, soldiers,
        friends,
Better consider what you have to do

Than I, that have not well the gift of tongue,
Can lift your blood up with persuasion.

Enter a Messenger.

    Mess. My lord, here are letters for you. 80
    Hot. I cannot read them now.
O gentlemen, the time of life is short !
To spend that shortness basely were too long,
If life did ride upon a dial's point,
Still ending at the arrival of an hour.
An if we live, we live to tread on kings ;
If die, brave death, when princes die with
        us !
Now, for our consciences, the arms are fair,
When the intent of bearing them is just.

Enter another Messenger.

    Mess. My lord, prepare ; the king comes on
        apace.   90
    Hot. I thank him, that he cuts me from my
        tale,
For I profess not talking ; only this—
Let each man do his best : and here draw I
A sword, whose temper I intend to stain
With the best blood that I can meet withal
In the adventure of this perilous day.
Now, Esperance ! Percy ! and set on.
Sound all the lofty instruments of war,
And by that music let us all embrace ;
For, heaven to earth, some of us never shall
A second time do such a courtesy.   101
        [*The trumpets sound. They embrace, and
                                            exeunt.*

SCENE III. *Plain between the camps.*

The KING *enters with his power. Alarum to
the battle. Then enter* DOUGLAS *and* SIR
WALTER BLUNT.

    Blunt. What is thy name, that in the battle
        thus
Thou crossest me ? what honor dost thou seek
Upon my head ?
    Doug. Know then, my name is Douglas :
And I do haunt thee in the battle thus
Because some tell me that thou art a king.
    Blunt. They tell thee true.
    Doug. The Lord of Stafford dear to-day
        hath bought
Thy likeness, for instead of thee, King Harry,
This sword hath ended him : so shall it thee,
Unless thou yield thee as my prisoner.   10
    Blunt. I was not born a yielder, thou
        proud Scot ;
And thou shalt find a king that will revenge
Lord Stafford's death.
        [*They fight. Douglas kills Blunt.*

Enter HOTSPUR.

    Hot. O Douglas, hadst thou fought at
        Holmedon thus,
I never had triumph'd upon a Scot.
    Doug. All's done, all's won ; here breath-
        less lies the king.
    Hot. Where ?
    Doug. Here.
    Hot. This, Douglas ? no : I know this face
        full well :

A gallant knight he was, his name was Blunt ;
Semblably furnish'd like the king himself. 21
Doug. A fool go with thy soul, whither it
    goes !
A borrow'd title hast thou bought too dear :
Why didst thou tell me that thou wert a king?
Hot. The king hath many marching in his
    coats
Doug. Now, by my sword, I will kill all his
    coats ,
I'll murder all his wardrobe, piece by piece,
Until I meet the king
Hot.   Up, and away !
Our soldiers stand full fairly for the day. 29
                                [*Exeunt.*

Alarum. Enter FALSTAFF, *solus*

Fal. Though I could 'scape shot-free at London, I fear the shot here , here's no scoring
but upon the pate   Soft ! who are you ? Sir
Walter Blunt   there's honor for you ! here's
no vanity ! I am as hot as molten lead, and as
heavy too · God keep lead out of me ! I need
no more weight than mine own bowels   I
have led my ragamuffins where they are peppered . there's not three of my hundred and
fifty left alive , and they are for the town's
end, to beg during life   But who comes
here ?   40

Enter the PRINCE

Prince. What, stand'st thou idle here ? lend
    me thy sword ·
Many a nobleman lies stark and stiff
Under the hoofs of vaunting enemies,
Whose deaths are yet unrevenged . I prithee,
    lend me thy sword
Fal. O Hal, I prithee, give me leave to
breathe awhile   Turk Gregory never did such
deeds in arms as I have done this day.   I have
paid Percy. I have made him sure
Prince He is, indeed and living to kill thee.
I prithee, lend me thy sword   50
Fal. Nay, before God, Hal, if Percy be
alive, thou get'st not my sword , but take my
pistol if thou wilt
Prince Give it me· what, is it in the case ?
Fal Ay, Hal , 'tis hot, 'tis hot , there's
that will sack a city [*The Prince draws it out,
        and finds it to be a bottle of sack*
Prince. What, is it a time to jest and dally
now ? [*He throws the bottle at him   Exit*
Fal Well, if Percy be alive, I'll pierce him
If he do come in my way, so · if he do not, if I
come in his willingly, let him make a carbonado
of me   I like not such grinning honor as Sir
Walter hath · give me life   which if I can
save, so ; if not, honor comes unlooked for, and
there's an end.   [*Exit.*

SCENE IV.   *Another part of the field*

Alarum   Excursions.   Enter the KING, *the*
PRINCE, LORD JOHN OF LANCASTER, *and*
EARL OF WESTMORELAND.

King. I prithee,
Harry, withdraw thyself ; thou bleed'st too
    much.

Lord John of Lancaster, go you with him
Lan. Not I, my lord, unless I did bleed too
Prince. I beseech your majesty, make up,
Lest your retirement do amaze your friends
King. I will do so
My Lord of Westmoreland, lead him to his
    tent.
West. Come, my lord, I'll lead you to your
    tent
Prince Lead me, my lord ? I do not need
    your help .   10
And God forbid a shallow scratch should drive
The Prince of Wales from such a field as this,
Where stain'd nobility lies trodden on,
And rebels' arms triumph in massacres !
Lan. We breathe too long   come, cousin
    Westmoreland,
Our duty this way lies , for God's sake, come.
        [*Exeunt Prince John and Westmoreland.*
Prince. By God, thou hast deceived me,
    Lancaster ,
I did not think thee lord of such a spirit
Before, I loved thee as a brother, John ;
But now, I do respect thee as my soul   20
King I saw him hold Lord Percy at the
    point
With lustier maintenance than I did look for
Of such an ungrown warrior
Prince   O, this boy
Lends mettle to us all !   [*Exit*

Enter DOUGLAS

Doug Another king ! they grow like Hy-
    dra's heads .
I am the Douglas, fatal to all those
That wear those colors on them · what art
    thou,
That counterfeit'st the person of a king ?
King The king himself , who, Douglas,
    grieves at heart
So many of his shadows thou hast met   30
And not the very king   I have two boys
Seek Percy and thyself about the field .
But, seeing thou fall'st on me so luckily,
I will assay thee : so, defend thyself
Doug I fear thou art another counterfeit ;
And yet, in faith, thou bear'st thee like a king:
But mine I am sure thou art. whoe'er thou be,
And thus I win thee [*They fight ; the King
    being in danger, re-enter Prince of Wales*
Prince. Hold up thy head, vile Scot, or thou
    art like
Never to hold it up again ! the spirits   40
Of valiant Shirley, Stafford, Blunt, are in my
    arms :
It is the Prince of Wales that threatens thee ,
Who never promiseth but he means to pay
                [*They fight   Douglas flies*
Cheerly, my lord   how fares your grace ?
Sir Nicholas Gawsey hath for succor sent,
And so hath Clifton   I'll to Clifton straight
King Stay, and breathe awhile ·
Thou hast redeem'd thy lost opinion,
And show'd thou makest some tender of my
    life,
In this fair rescue thou hast brought to me. 50

Prince. O God ! they did me too much in-
jury
That ever said I hearken'd for your death.
If it were so, I might have let alone
The insulting hand of Douglas over you,
Which would have been as speedy in your end
As all the poisonous potions in the world
And saved the treacherous labor of your son
King   Make up to Clifton . I'll to Sir Nich-
olas Gawsey   [*Exit*

Enter HOTSPUR.

Hot. If I mistake not, thou art Harry Mon-
mouth.
Prince   Thou speak'st as if I would deny
my name   60
Hot.   My name is Harry Percy
Prince.   Why, then I see
A very valiant rebel of the name
I am the Prince of Wales ; and think not,
Percy,
To share with me in glory any more ·
Two stars keep not their motion in one sphere;
Nor can one England brook a double reign,
Of Harry Percy and the Prince of Wales
Hot   Nor shall it, Harry ; for the hour is
come
To end the one of us , and would to God
Thy name in arms were now as great as mine!
Prince.   I'll make it greater ere I part from
thee ;   71
And all the budding honors on thy crest
I'll crop, to make a garland for my head.
Hot.   I can no longer brook thy vanities.
[*They fight.*

Enter FALSTAFF.

Fal   Well said, Hal ! to it, Hal ! Nay, you
shall find no boy's play here, I can tell you

Re-enter DOUGLAS , *he fights with* FALSTAFF,
who falls down as if he were dead, and exit
DOUGLAS. HOTSPUR *is wounded, and falls*

Hot.   O, Harry, thou hast robb'd me of my
youth !
I better brook the loss of brittle life
Than those proud titles thou hast won of me ;
They wound my thoughts worse than thy
sword my flesh   80
But thought's the slave of life, and life time's
fool ;
And time, that takes survey of all the world,
Must have a stop. O, I could prophesy,
But that the earthy and cold hand of death
Lies on my tongue : no, Percy, thou art dust
And food for—   [*Dies.*
Prince   For worms, brave Percy . fare thee
well, great heart !
Ill-weaved ambition, how much art thou
shrunk !
When that this body did contain a spirit,
A kingdom for it was too small a bound ;   90
But now two paces of the vilest earth
Is room enough : this earth that bears thee
dead
Bears not alive so stout a gentleman.
If thou wert sensible of courtesy,

I should not make so dear a show of zeal :
But let my favors hide thy mangled face ;
And, even in thy behalf, I'll thank myself
For doing these fair rites of tenderness
Adieu, and take thy praise with thee to heav-
en !
Thy ignominy sleep with thee in the grave, 100
But not remember'd in thy epitaph !
[*He spieth Falstaff on the ground.*
What, old acquaintance ! could not all this
flesh
Keep in a little life ? Poor Jack, farewell !
I could have better spared a better man :
O, I should have a heavy miss of thee,
If I were much in love with vanity !
Death hath not struck so fat a deer to-day,
Though many dearer, in this bloody fray.
Embowell'd will I see thee by and by :
Till then in blood by noble Percy lie. [*Exit.* 110
Fal   [*Rising up*] Embowelled ! if thou em-
bowel me to-day, I'll give you leave to powder
me and eat me too to-morrow. 'Sblood, 'twas
time to counterfeit, or that hot termagant Scot
had paid me scot and lot too. Counterfeit ? I
lie, I am no counterfeit : to die, is to be a
counterfeit, for he is but the counterfeit of a
man who hath not the life of a man : but to
counterfeit dying, when a man thereby liveth,
is to be no counterfeit, but the true and perfect
image of life indeed   The better part of valor
is discretion , in the which better part I have
saved my life. 'Zounds, I am afraid of this
gunpowder Percy, though he be dead · how,
if he should counterfeit too and rise ? by my
faith, I am afraid he would prove the better
counterfeit   Therefore I'll make him sure ;
yea, and I'll swear I killed him. · Why may
not he rise as well as I ?   Nothing confutes me
but eyes, and nobody sees me   Therefore,
sirrah [*stabbing him*], with a new wound in
your thigh, come you along with me.
[*Takes up Hotspur on his back*

Re-enter the PRINCE OF WALES *and* LORD
JOHN OF LANCASTER

Prince.   Come, brother John ; full bravely
hast thou flesh'd
Thy maiden sword
Lan   But, soft ! whom have we here ?
Did you not tell me this fat man was dead ?
Prince.   I did , I saw him dead,
Breathless and bleeding on the ground.   Art
thou alive ?
Or is it fantasy that plays upon our eyesight ?
I prithee, speak ; we will not trust our eyes 139
Without our ears : thou art not what thou
seem'st
Fal.   No, that's certain ; I am not a double
man : but if I be not Jack Falstaff, then am I
a Jack   There is Percy [*throwing the body
down*] : if your father will do me any honor,
so , if not, let him kill the next Percy himself.
I look to be either earl or duke, I can assure
you
Prince.   Why, Percy I killed myself and
saw thee dead.

Fal Didst thou ? Lord, Lord, how this world is given to lying ! I grant you I was down and out of breath , and so was he · but we rose both at an instant and fought a long hour by Shrewsbury clock If I may be believed, so , if not, let them that should reward valor bear the sin upon their own heads I'll take it upon my death, I gave him this wound in the thigh if the man were alive and would deny it, 'zounds, I would make him eat a piece of my sword.

Lan This is the strangest tale that ever I heard.

Prince. This is the strangest fellow, brother John. 159

Come, bring your luggage nobly on your back. For my part, if a lie may do thee grace, I'll gild it with the happiest terms I have

[*A retreat is sounded*

The trumpet sounds retreat ; the day is ours Come, brother, let us to the highest of the field,

To see what friends are living, who are dead

[*Exeunt Prince of Wales and Lancaster.*

Fal. I'll follow, as they say, for reward He that rewards me, God reward him ! If I do grow great, I'll grow less , for I'll purge, and leave sack, and live cleanly as a nobleman should do. [*Exit*

SCENE V. *Another part of the field*

The trumpets sound Enter the KING. PRINCE OF WALES, LORD JOHN OF LANCASTER, EARL OF WESTMORELAND, *with* WORCES-TER *and* VERNON *prisoners*

King Thus ever did rebellion find rebuke. Ill-spirited Worcester ! did not we send grace, Pardon and terms of love to all of you ? And wouldst thou turn our offers contrary ? Misuse the tenor of thy kinsman's trust ? Three knights upon our party slain to-day, A noble earl and many a creature else Had been alive this hour, If like a Christian thou hadst truly borne Betwixt our armies true intelligence, 10

Wor. What I have done my safety urged me to , And I embrace this fortune patiently, Since not to be avoided it falls on me

King. Bear Worcester to the death and Vernon too Other offenders we will pause upon

[*Exeunt Worcester and Vernon, guarded* How goes the field ? [he saw

Prince The noble Scot, Lord Douglas, when The fortune of the day quite turn'd from him, The noble Percy slain, and all his men Upon the foot of fear, fled with the rest , 20 And falling from a hill, he was so bruised That the pursuers took him At my tent The Douglas is , and I beseech your grace I may dispose of him

King. With all my heart

Prince. Then, brother John of Lancaster, to you This honorable bounty shall belong : Go to the Douglas, and deliver him Up to his pleasure, ransomless and free His valor shown upon our crests to-day Hath taught us how to cherish such high deeds 30 Even in the bosom of our adversaries

Lan I thank your grace for this high courtesy, Which I shall give away immediately

King Then this remains, that we divide our power You, son John, and my cousin Westmoreland Towards York shall bend you with your dearest speed, To meet Northumberland and the prelate Scroop, Who, as we hear, are busily in arms : Myself and you, son Harry, will towards Wales, To fight with Glendower and the Earl of March 40 Rebellion in this land shall lose his sway, Meeting the check of such another day . And since this business so fair is done, Let us not leave till all our own be won

[*Exeunt*

KING HENRY IV. PART II.

(WRITTEN ABOUT 1597–98.)

INTRODUCTION.

[See Introduction to Part I.]

DRAMATIS PERSONÆ.

RUMOUR, the Presenter.
KING HENRY the Fourth.
HENRY, PRINCE OF WALES, after- ⎫
    wards King Henry V.,   ⎪
THOMAS, DUKE OF CLARENCE,   ⎬ his
PRINCE JOHN OF LANCASTER,   ⎪ sons.
PRINCE HUMPHREY OF GLOUCESTER, ⎭
EARL OF WARWICK.
EARL OF WESTMORELAND.
EARL OF SURREY.
GOWER.
HARCOURT.
BLUNT.
Lord Chief-Justice of the King's Bench.
A Servant of the Chief-Justice.
EARL OF NORTHUMBERLAND.
SCROOP, Archbishop of York.
LORD MOWBRAY.
LORD HASTINGS.
LORD BARDOLPH.
SIR JOHN COLEVILE.
TRAVERS and MORTON, retainers of Northum-
    berland.

SIR JOHN FALSTAFF.
His Page.
BARDOLPH.
PISTOL.
POINS.
PETO.
SHALLOW, ⎫
SILENCE, ⎬ country justices.
DAVY, Servant to Shallow.
MOULDY, SHADOW, WART, FEEBLE, and
    BULLCALF, recruits.
FANG and SNARE, sheriff's officers.

LADY NORTHUMBERLAND.
LADY PERCY.
MISTRESS QUICKLY, hostess of a tavern in
    Eastcheap.
DOLL TEARSHEET.

Lords   and   Attendants; Porter, Drawers,
    Beadles, Grooms, &c.

A Dancer, speaker of the epilogue.

SCENE : *England.*

INDUCTION.

Warkworth. Before the castle.

Enter Rumour, painted full of tongues

Rum. Open your ears ; for which of you
    will stop
The vent of hearing when loud Rumour speaks?
I, from the orient to the drooping west,
Making the wind my post-horse, still unfold
The acts commenced on this ball of earth :
Upon my tongues continual slanders ride,
The which in every language I pronounce,
Stuffing the ears of men with false reports.
I speak of peace, while covert enmity
Under the smile of safety wounds the world :

And who but Rumour, who but only I,   **11**
Make fearful musters and prepared defence,
Whiles the big year, swoln with some other
    grief,
Is thought with child by the stern tyrant war,
And no such matter ? Rumour is a pipe
Blown by surmises, jealousies, conjectures,
And of so easy and so plain a stop
That the blunt monster with uncounted heads,
The still-discordant wavering multitude,
Can play upon it. But what need I thus   **20**
My well-known body to anatomize
Among my household ? Why is Rumour
    here ?
I run before King Harry's victory ;
Who in a bloody field by Shrewsbury

Hath beaten down young Hotspur and his
　troops,
Quenching the flame of bold rebellion
Even with the rebel's blood　But what mean I
To speak so true at first ?　my office is
To noise abroad that Harry Monmouth fell　　30
Under the wrath of noble Hotspur's sword,
And that the king before the Douglas' rage
Stoop'd his anointed head as low as death
This have I rumor'd through the peasant
　towns
Between that royal field of Shrewsbury
And this worm-eaten hold of ragged stone,
Where Hotspur's father, old Northumberland,
Lies crafty-sick · the posts come tiring on,
And not a man of them brings other news
Than they have learn'd of me. from Rumour's
　tongues
They bring smooth comforts false, worse than
　true wrongs　　　　　　　　　[*Exit.* 40

ACT I.

Scene I. *The same.*

Enter Lord Bardolph.

L. Bard. Who keeps the gate here, ho ?

　　The Porter *opens the gate.*

　　　　　　　Where is the earl ?
Port　What shall I say you are ?
L. Bard.　　　　Tell thou the earl
That the Lord Bardolph doth attend him here
Port.　His lordship is walk'd forth into the
　orchard ,
Please it your honor, knock but at the gate,
And he himself will answer

Enter Northumberland

L. Bard.　　　Here comes the earl
　　　　　　　　　[*Exit Porter.*
North.　What news, Lord Bardolph ? every
　minute now
Should be the father of some stratagem :
The times are wild , contention, like a horse
Full of high feeding, madly hath broke loose
And bears down all before him　　　　11
L. Bard.　　　Noble earl,
I bring you certain news from Shrewsbury.
North.　Good, an God will !
L. Bard.　　　As good as heart can wish
The king is almost wounded to the death ,
And, in the fortune of my lord your son,
Prince Harry slain outright , and both the
　Blunts
Kill'd by the hand of Douglas ; young Prince
　John
And Westmoreland and Stafford fled the field;
And Harry Monmouth's brawn, the hulk Sir
　John,
Is prisoner to your son : O, such a day,　　20
So fought, so follow'd and so fairly won,
Came not till now to dignify the times,
Since Cæsar's fortunes !
　　North.　　　How is this derived ?

Saw you the field ? came you from Shrews-
　bury ?
L. Bard.　I spake with one, my lord, that
　came from thence,
A gentleman well bred and of good name,
That freely render'd me these news for true
　North.　Here comes my servant Travers,
　whom I sent
On Tuesday last to listen after news.

Enter Travers.

L. Bard　My lord, I over-rode him on the
　way ,　　　　　　　　　　　　　　30
And he is furnish'd with no certainties
More than he haply may retail from me
　North.　Now, Travers, what good tidings
　comes with you ?
Tra　My lord, Sir John Umfrevile turn'd
　me back
With joyful tidings , and, being better horsed,
Out-rode me.　After him came spurring hard
A gentleman, almost forspent with speed,
That stopp'd by me to breathe his bloodied
　horse
He ask'd the way to Chester , and of him
I did demand what news from Shrewsbury . 40
He told me that rebellion had bad luck
And that young Harry Percy's spur was cold
With that, he gave his able horse the head,
And bending forward struck his armed heels
Against the panting sides of his poor jade
Up to the rowel-head, and starting so
He seem'd in running to devour the way,
Staying no longer question
　North.　　　Ha ! Again :
Said he young Harry Percy's spur was cold ?
Of Hotspur Coldspur ? that rebellion　　50
Had met ill luck ?
　L. Bard　　　My lord, I'll tell you what ;
If my young lord your son have not the day,
Upon mine honor, for a silken point
I'll give my barony　never talk of it
　North　Why should that gentleman that
　rode by Travers
Give then such instances of loss?
　L. Bard　　　Who, he ?
He was some hilding fellow that had stolen
The horse he rode on, and, upon my life,
Spoke at a venture.　Look, here comes more
　news.

Enter Morton.

　North　Yea, this man's brow, like to a title-
　leaf,　　　　　　　　　　　　　　60
Foretells the nature of a tragic volume :
So looks the strand whereon the imperious
　flood
Hath left a witness'd usurpation.
Say, Morton, didst thou come from Shrews-
　bury ?
　Mor　I ran from Shrewsbury, my noble
　lord ,
Where hateful death put on his ugliest mask
To fright our party
　North　How doth my son and brother?
Thou tremblest ; and the whiteness in thy
　cheek

Is apter than thy tongue to tell thy errand.
Even such a man, so faint, so spiritless,   70
So dull, so dead in look, so woe-begone,
Drew Priam's curtain in the dead of night,
And would have told him half his Troy was
    burnt ;
But Priam found the fire ere he his tongue,
And I my Percy's death ere thou report'st it
This thou wouldst say, ' Your son did thus and
    thus ;
Your brother thus: so fought the noble Doug-
    las '
Stopping my greedy ear with their bold deeds :
But in the end, to stop my ear indeed,
Thou hast a sigh to blow away this praise,   80
Ending with ' Brother, son, and all are dead.'
    Mor.   Douglas is living, and your brother,
    yet ,
But, for my lord your son,—
    North   Why, he is dead.
See what a ready tongue suspicion hath !
He that but fears the thing he would not know
Hath by instinct knowledge from others' eyes
That what he fear'd is chanced.   Yet speak,
    Morton ;
Tell thou an earl his divination lies,
And I will take it as a sweet disgrace
And make thee rich for doing me such wrong
    Mor.   You are too great to be by me gain-
    said ·   91
Your spirit is too true, your fears too certain
    North   Yet, for all this, say not that Percy's
    dead.
I see a strange confession in thine eye ·
Thou shakest thy head and hold'st it fear or sin
To speak a truth.   If he be slain, say so ;
The tongue offends not that reports his death .
And he doth sin that doth belie the dead,
Not he which says the dead is not alive
Yet the first bringer of unwelcome news   100
Hath but a losing office, and his tongue
Sounds ever after as a sullen bell,
Remember'd tolling a departing friend
    L. Bard   I cannot think, my lord, your son
    is dead.
    Mor   I am sorry I should force you to be-
    lieve
That which I would to God I had not seen ,
But these mine eyes saw him in bloody state,
Rendering faint quittance, wearied and out-
    breathed,
To Harry Monmouth ; whose swift wrath beat
    down
The never-daunted Percy to the earth,   110
From whence with life he never more sprung
    up
In few, his death, whose spirit lent a fire
Even to the dullest peasant in his camp,
Being bruited once, took fire and heat away
From the best temper'd courage in his troops ·
For from his metal was his party steel'd ;
Which once in him abated, all the rest
Turn'd on themselves, like dull and heavy
    lead :
And as the thing that's heavy in itself,
Upon enforcement flies with greatest speed,

So did our men, heavy in Hotspur's loss,   121
Lend to this weight such lightness with their
    fear
That arrows fled not swifter toward their aim
Than did our soldiers, aiming at their safety,
Fly from the field.   Then was the noble Wor-
    cester
Too soon ta'en prisoner ; and that furious
    Scot,
The bloody Douglas, whose well-laboring
    sword
Had three times slain the appearance of the
    king,
'Gan vail his stomach and did grace the
    shame
Of those that turn'd their backs, and in his
    flight,   130
Stumbling in fear, was took.   The sum of all
Is that the king hath won, and hath sent out
A speedy power to encounter you, my lord,
Under the conduct of young Lancaster
And Westmoreland.   This is the news at full.
    North.   For this I shall have time enough
    to mourn.
In poison there is physic ; and these news,
Having been well, that would have made me
    sick,
Being sick, have in some measure made me
    well :
And as the wretch, whose fever-weaken'd
    joints,   140
Like strengthless hinges, buckle under life,
Impatient of his fit, breaks like a fire
Out of his keeper's arms, even so my limbs,
Weaken'd with grief, being now enraged with
    grief,
Are thrice themselves   Hence, therefore, thou
    nice crutch !
A scaly gauntlet now with joints of steel
Must glove this hand . and hence, thou sickly
    quoif !
Thou art a guard too wanton for the head
Which princes, flesh'd with conquest, aim t·
    hit
Now bind my brows with iron , and approach
The ragged'st hour that time and spite dare
    bring   151
To frown upon the enraged Northumberland !
Let heaven kiss earth ! now let not Nature's
    hand
Keep the wild flood confined ! let order die !
And let this world no longer be a stage
To feed contention in a lingering act ;
But let one spirit of the first-born Cain
Reign in all bosoms, that, each heart being
    set
On bloody courses, the rude scene may end,
And darkness be the burier of the dead !   160
    Tra   This strained passion doth you wrong,
    my lord
    L. Bard   Sweet earl, divorce not wisdom
    from your honor.
    Mor.   The lives of all your loving complices
Lean on your health ; the which, if you give
    o'er
To stormy passion, must perforce decay.

You cast the event of war, my noble lord,
And summ'd the account of chance, before
    you said
' Let us make head ' It was your presurmise,
That, in the dole of blows, your son might
    drop
You knew he walk'd o'er perils, on an edge,
More likely to fall in than to get o'er ,   171
You were advised his flesh was capable
Of wounds and scars and that his forward
    spirit
Would lift him where most trade of danger
    ranged
Yet did you say ' Go forth ,' and none of this,
Though strongly apprehended, could restrain
The stiff-borne action what hath then be-
    fallen,
Or what hath this bold enterprise brought
    forth,
More than that being which was like to be ?
  L Bard. We all that are engaged to this
    loss   180
Knew that we ventured on such dangerous
    seas
That if we wrought our life 'twas ten to one ,
And yet we ventured, for the gain proposed
Choked the respect of likely peril fear'd ,
And since we are o'erset, venture again
Come, we will all put forth, body and goods
  Mor 'Tis more than time : and, my most
    noble lord,
I hear for certain, and do speak the truth,
The gentle Archbishop of York is up
With well-appointed powers he is a man 190
Who with a double surety binds his follow-
    ers
My lord your son had only but the corpse,
But shadows and the shows of men, to fight ,
For that same word, rebellion, did divide
The action of their bodies from their souls ,
And they did fight with queasiness, constrain'd,
As men drink potions, that their weapons only
Seem'd on our side , but, for their spirits and
    souls,
This word, rebellion, it had froze them up,
As fish are in a pond But now the bishop 200
Turns insurrection to religion
Supposed sincere and holy in his thoughts,
He's followed both with body and with mind,
And doth enlarge his rising with the blood
Of fair King Richard, scraped from Pomfret
    stones ,
Derives from heaven his quarrel and his
    cause ;
Tells them he doth bestride a bleeding land,
Gasping for life under great Bolingbroke ,
And more and less do flock to follow him
  North. I knew of this before ; but, to
    speak truth,   210
This present grief had wiped it from my mind
Go in with me , and counsel every man
The aptest way for safety and revenge
Get posts and letters, and make friends with
    speed :
Never so few, and never yet more need
                           [Exeunt

SCENE II *London. A street.*

Enter FALSTAFF, *with his* Page *bearing his
sword and buckler*

  Fal. Sirrah, you giant, what says the doctor to my water ?
  Page He said, sir, the water itself was a
good healthy water , but, for the party that
owed it, he might have more diseases than he
knew for
  Fal Men of all sorts take a pride to gird
at me . the brain of this foolish-compounded
clay, man, is not able to invent any thing that
tends to laughter, more than I invent or is in-
vented on me I am not only witty in myself,
but the cause that wit is in other men I
do here walk before thee like a sow that hath
overwhelmed all her litter but one If the
prince put thee into my service for any other
reason than to set me off, why then I have no
judgment. Thou whoreson mandrake, thou
art fitter to be worn in my cap than to wait at
my heels I was never manned with an agate
till now but I will inset you neither in gold nor
silver, but in vile apparel, and send you back
again to your master, for a jewel,—the juve-
nal, the prince your master, whose chin is not
yet fledged I will sooner have a beard
grow in the palm of my hand than he shall
get one on his cheek , and yet he will not
stick to say his face is a face-royal God may
finish it when he will, 'tis not a hair amiss
yet he may keep it still at a face-royal, for a
barber shall never earn sixpence out of it ,
and yet he'll be crowing as if he had writ
man ever since his father was a bachelor He
may keep his own grace, but he's almost out
of mine, I can assure him What said Master
Dombledon about the satin for my short cloak
and my slops ?
  Page He said, sir, you should procure him
better assurance than Bardolph he would
not take his band and yours , he liked not the
security
  Fal Let him be damned, like the glutton !
pray God his tongue be hotter ! A whoreson
Achitophel ! a rascally yea-forsooth knave !
to bear a gentleman in hand, and then stand
upon security ! The whoreson smooth-pates
do now wear nothing but high shoes, and
bunches of keys at their girdles , and if a
man is through with them in honest taking
up, then they must stand upon security I
had as lef they would put rat-bane in my
mouth as offer to stop it with security I
looked a' should have sent me two and twenty
yards of satin, as I am a true knight, and he
sends me security Well, he may sleep in security, for he hath the horn of abundance, and
the lightness of his wife shines through it
and yet cannot he see, though he have his own
lanthorn to light him Where's Bardolph ?
  Page He's gone into Smithfield to buy your
worship a horse
  Fal I bought him in Paul's, and he'll buy
me a horse in Smithfield an I could get me

27

but a wife in the stews, I were manned,
horsed, and wived   61

Enter the Lord Chief-Justice and Servant

Page. Sir, here comes the nobleman that
committed the prince for striking him about
Bardolph.

Fal Wait, close , I will not see him

Ch Just What's he that goes there ?

Serv Falstaff, an't please your lordship.

Ch Just He that was in question for the
robbery ?   69

Serv. He, my lord but he hath since done
good service at Shrewsbury , and, as I hear,
is now going with some charge to the Lord
John of Lancaster

Ch Just. What, to York ? Call him back
again.

Serv. Sir John Falstaff !

Fal Boy, tell him I am deaf

Page You must speak louder ; my master
is deaf   79

Ch. Just I am sure he is, to the hearing of
any thing good Go, pluck him by the elbow ,
I must speak with him

Serv Sir John !

Fal What ! a young knave, and begging !
Is there not wars ? is there not employment ?
doth not the king lack subjects ? do not the
rebels need soldiers ? Though it be a shame
to be on any side but one, it is worse shame to
beg than to be on the worst side, were it worse
than the name of rebellion can tell how to
make it   90

Serv You mistake me, sir

Fal. Why, sir, did I say you were an honest
man ? setting my knighthood and my soldiership aside, I had lied in my throat, if I had
said so

Serv I pray you, sir, then set your knighthood and your soldiership aside , and give
me leave to tell you, you lie in your throat, if
you say I am any other than an honest man

Fal I give thee leave to tell me so ! I lay
aside that which grows to me ! If thou get-
test any leave of me, hang me , if thou takest
leave, thou wert better be hanged You hunt
counter hence ! avaunt !

Serv. Sir, my lord would speak with you

Ch Just Sir John Falstaff, a word with you

Fal. My good lord ! God give your lordship good time of day I am glad to see your
lordship abroad I heard say your lordship
was sick I hope your lordship goes abroad by
advice Your lordship, though not clean past
your youth, hath yet some smack of age in
you, some relish of the saltness of time , and
I must humbly beseech your lordship to have
a reverent care of your health.

Ch. Just Sir John, I sent for you before
your expedition to Shrewsbury.

Fal An't please your lordship, I hear his
majesty is returned with some discomfort
from Wales

Ch. Just I talk not of his majesty : you
would not come when I sent for you.   121

Fal. And I hear, moreover, his highness is
fallen into this same whoreson apoplexy

Ch. Just. Well, God mend him ! I pray
you, let me speak with you

Fal This apoplexy is, as I take it, a kind
of lethargy, an't please your lordship , a kind
of sleeping in the blood, a whoreson tingling.

Ch Just What tell you me of it ? be it as
it is   130

Fal. It hath its original from much grief,
from study and perturbation of the brain : I
have read the cause of his effects in Galen :
it is a kind of deafness

Ch. Just I think you are fallen into the
disease , for you hear not what I say to you.

Fal. Very well, my lord, very well · rather, an't please you, it is the disease of not
listening, the malady of not marking, that I
am troubled withal   140

Ch. Just To punish you by the heels would
amend the attention of your ears , and I care
not if I do become your physician

Fal I am as poor as Job, my lord, but not
so patient . your lordship may minister the
potion of imprisonment to me in respect of
poverty , but how should I be your patient to
follow your prescriptions, the wise may make
some dram of a scruple, or indeed a scruple
itself

Ch Just I sent for you, when there were
matters against you for your life, to come
speak with me

Fal. As I was then advised by my learned
counsel in the laws of this land-service, I did
not come

Ch Just Well, the truth is, Sir John, you
live in great infamy

Fal He that buckles him in my belt cannot live in less

Ch. Just Your means are very slender,
and your waste is great.   160

Fal. I would it were otherwise ; I would
my means were greater, and my waist slen-
derer   [prince

Ch Just You have misled the youthful

Fal The young prince hath misled me . I
am the fellow with the great belly, and he my
dog

Ch. Just. Well, I am loath to gall a new-
healed wound : your day's service at Shrewsbury hath a little gilded over your night's exploit on Gad's-hill you may thank the unquiet time for your quiet o'er-posting that action.   171

Fal My lord ?

Ch Just But since all is well, keep it so :
wake not a sleeping wolf.

Fal. To wake a wolf is as bad as to smell a
fox

Ch Just. What ! you are as a candle, the
better part burnt out

Fal A wassail candle, my lord, all tallow :
if I did say of wax, my growth would approve
the truth   181

Ch Just There is not a white hair on your
face but should have his effect of gravity.

Fal. His effect of gravy, gravy, gravy.

Ch. Just. You follow the young prince up and down, like his ill angel

Fal. Not so, my lord, your ill angel is light ; but I hope he that looks upon me will take me without weighing and yet, in some respects, I grant, I cannot go I cannot tell Virtue is of so little regard in these costermonger times that true valor is turned bearherd pregnancy is made a tapster, and hath his quick wit wasted in giving reckonings all the other gifts appertinent to man, as the malice of this age shapes them, are not worth a gooseberry You that are old consider not the capacities of us that are young, you do measure the heat of our livers with the bitterness of your galls · and we that are in the vaward of our youth, I must confess, are wags too   200

Ch. Just. Do you set down your name in the scroll of youth, that are written down old with all the characters of age ? Have you not a moist eye ? a dry hand ? a yellow cheek ? a white beard ? a decreasing leg ? an increasing belly ? is not your voice broken ? your wind short ? your chin double ? your wit single ? and every part about you blasted with antiquity ? and will you yet call yourself young ? Fie, fie, fie, Sir John !

Fal. My lord, I was born about three of the clock in the afternoon, with a white head and something a round belly For my voice, I have lost it with halloing and singing of anthems To approve my youth further, I will not · the truth is, I am only old in judgment and understanding, and he that will caper with me for a thousand marks, let him lend me the money, and have at him ! For the box of the ear that the prince gave you, he gave it like a rude prince, and you took it like a sensible lord I have checked him for it, and the young lion repents, marry, not in ashes and sackcloth, but in new silk and old sack.

Ch. Just. Well, God send the prince a better companion !

Fal. God send the companion a better prince ! I cannot rid my hands of him.

Ch Just. Well, the king hath severed you and Prince Harry. I hear you are going with Lord John of Lancaster against the Archbishop and the Earl of Northumberland.   230

Fal. Yea ; I thank your pretty sweet wit for it But look you pray, all you that kiss my lady Peace at home, that our armies join not in a hot day, for, by the Lord, I take but two shirts out with me, and I mean not to sweat extraordinarily · if it be a hot day, and I brandish any thing but a bottle, I would I might never spit white again There is not a dangerous action can peep out his head but I am thrust upon it : well, I cannot last ever but it was alway yet the trick of our English nation, if they have a good thing, to make it too common. If ye will needs say I am an old man, you should give me rest. I

would to God my name were not so terrible to the enemy as it is I were better to be eaten to death with a rust than to be scoured to nothing with perpetual motion

Ch Just. Well, be honest, be honest, and God bless your expedition !

Fal. Will your lordship lend me a thousand pound to furnish me forth ?   251

Ch Just. Not a penny, not a penny, you are too impatient to bear crosses Fare you well commend me to my cousin Westmoreland   [*Exeunt Chief-Justice and Servant*

Fal. If I do, fillip me with a three-man beetle A man can no more separate age and covetousness than a' can part young limbs and lechery but the gout galls the one, and the pox pinches the other, and so both the degrees prevent my curses Boy !   260

Page. Sir ?

Fal. What money is in my purse ?

Page. Seven groats and two pence

Fal. I can get no remedy against this consumption of the purse borrowing only lingers and lingers it out, but the disease is incurable Go bear this letter to my Lord of Lancaster, this to the prince, this to the Earl of Westmoreland, and this to old Mistress Ursula, whom I have weekly sworn to marry since I perceived the first white hair on my chin About it you know where to find me [*Exit Page*] A pox of this gout ! or, a gout of this pox ! for the one or the other plays the rogue with my great toe. 'Tis no matter if I do halt, I have the wars for my color, and my pension shall seem the more reasonable A good wit will make use of any thing. I will turn diseases to commodity

       [*Exit*

SCENE III. *York. The* ARCHBISHOP'S *palace*

Enter the ARCHBISHOP, *the* LORDS HASTINGS, MOWBRAY, *and* BARDOLPH

Arch Thus have you heard our cause and known our means,
And, my most noble friends, I pray you all,
Speak plainly your opinions of our hopes
And first, lord marshal, what say you to it ?

Mowb I well allow the occasion of our arms,
But gladly would be better satisfied
How in our means we should advance ourselves
To look with forehead bold and big enough
Upon the power and puissance of the king

Hast Our present musters grow upon the file   10
To five and twenty thousand men of choice,
And our supplies live largely in the hope
Of great Northumberland, whose bosom burns
With an incensed fire of injuries

L Bard The question then, Lord Hastings, standeth thus, |sand
Whether our present five and twenty thousand
May hold up head without Northumberland ?

Hast. With him, we may.

L. Bard   Yea, marry, there's the point.
But if without him we be thought too feeble,
My judgment is, we should not step too far
Till we had his assistance by the hand ;   21
For in a theme so bloody-faced as this
Conjecture, expectation, and surmise
Of aids incertain should not be admitted
  Arch   'Tis very true, Lord Bardolph ; for indeed
It was young Hotspur's case at Shrewsbury.
  L Bard   It was, my lord, who lined himself with hope,
Eating the air on promise of supply,
Flattering himself in project of a power
Much smaller than the smallest of his thoughts   30
And so, with great imagination
Proper to madmen, led his powers to death
And winking leap'd into destruction
  Hast   But, by your leave, it never yet did hurt
To lay down likelihoods and forms of hope
  L Bard   †Yes, if this present quality of war,
Indeed the instant action a cause on foot
Lives so in hope as in an early spring
We see the appearing buds ; which to prove fruit,
Hope gives not so much warrant as despair   40
That frosts will bite them. When we mean to build,
We first survey the plot, then draw the model,
And when we see the figure of the house
Then must we rate the cost of the erection ;
Which if we find outweighs ability,
What do we then but draw anew the model
In fewer offices, or at last desist
To build at all ? Much more, in this great work,
Which is almost to pluck a kingdom down
And set another up, should we survey   50
The plot of situation and the model,
Consent upon a sure foundation,
Question surveyors, know our own estate,
How able such a work to undergo,
To weigh against his opposite, or else
We fortify in paper and in figures,
Using the names of men instead of men :
Like one that draws the model of a house
Beyond his power to build it, who, half through,
Gives o'er and leaves his part-created cost   60
A naked subject to the weeping clouds
And waste for churlish winter's tyranny.
  Hast   Grant that our hopes, yet likely of fair birth,   [sess'd
Should be still-born, and that we now pos-
The utmost man of expectation,
I think we are a body strong enough,
Even as we are, to equal with the king.
  L Bard   What, is the king but five and twenty thousand ?
  Hast   To us no more ; nay, not so much, Lord Bardolph
For his divisions, as the times do brawl,   70

Are in three heads : one power against the French,
And one against Glendower, perforce a third
Must take up us : so is the unfirm king
In three divided, and his coffers sound
With hollow poverty and emptiness.
  Arch   That he should draw his several strengths together
And come against us in full puissance,
Need not be dreaded
  Hast   If he should do so,
He leaves his back unarm'd, the French and Welsh
Baying him at the heels   never fear that   80
  L Bard   Who is it like should lead his forces hither ?
  Hast   The Duke of Lancaster and Westmoreland,
Against the Welsh, himself and Harry Monmouth ·
But who is substituted 'gainst the French,
I have no certain notice
  Arch   Let us on,
And publish the occasion of our arms.
The commonwealth is sick of their own choice,
Their over-greedy love hath surfeited
An habitation giddy and unsure
Hath he that buildeth on the vulgar heart   90
O thou fond many, with what loud applause
Didst thou beat heaven with blessing Bolingbroke,   [be !
Before he was what thou wouldst have him
And being now trimm'd in thine own desires,
Thou, beastly feeder, art so full of him,
That thou provokest thyself to cast him up.
So, so, thou common dog, didst thou disgorge
Thy glutton bosom of the royal Richard,
And now thou wouldst eat thy dead vomit up,
And howl'st to find it. What trust is in these times ?   100
They that, when Richard lived, would have him die,
Are now become enamor'd on his grave :
Thou, that threw'st dust upon his goodly head
When through proud London he came sighing on
After the admired heels of Bolingbroke,
Criest now ' O earth, yield us that king again,
And take thou this !' O thoughts of men accursed !
Past and to come seems best ; things present worst
  Mowb   Shall we go draw our numbers and set on ?
  Hast   We are time's subjects, and time bids be gone   [*Exeunt.* 110

ACT II.

SCENE I. *London. A street.*

Enter Hostess, FANG *and his Boy with her, and* SNARE *following.*

Host. Master Fang, have you entered the action?

Fang. It is entered

Host. Where's your yeoman? Is't a lusty yeoman? will a' stand to 't?

Fang. Sirrah, where's Snare?

Host. O Lord, ay! good Master Snare

Snare. Here, here

Fang. Snare, we must arrest Sir John Falstaff   10

Host. Yea, good Master Snare, I have entered him and all.

Snare. It may chance cost some of us our lives, for he will stab

Host. Alas the day! take heed of him, he stabbed me in mine own house, and that most beastly; in good faith, he cares not what mischief he does, if his weapon be out he will foin like any devil, he will spare neither man, woman, nor child   20

Fang. If I can close with him, I care not for his thrust

Host. No, nor I neither; I'll be at your elbow

Fang. An I but fist him once, an a' come but within my vice,—

Host. I am undone by his going, I warrant you, he's an infinitive thing upon my score. Good Master Fang, hold him sure; good Master Snare, let him not 'scape. A' comes continually to Pie-corner—saving your manhoods—to buy a saddle, and he is indited to dinner to the Lubber's-head in Lumbert street, to Master Smooth's the silkman. I pray ye, since my exion is entered and my case so openly known to the world, let him be brought in to his answer. A hundred mark is a long one for a poor lone woman to bear; and I have borne, and borne, and borne, and have been fubbed off, and fubbed off, and fubbed off, from this day to that day, that it is a shame to be thought on. There is no honesty in such dealing, unless a woman should be made an ass and a beast, to bear every knave's wrong. Yonder he comes, and that arrant malmsey-nose knave, Bardolph, with him. Do your offices, do your offices. Master Fang and Master Snare, do me, do me, do me your offices

Enter FALSTAFF, Page, *and* BARDOLPH

Fal. How now! whose mare's dead? what's the matter?

Fang. Sir John, I arrest you at the suit of Mistress Quickly   49

Fal. Away, varlets! Draw. Bardolph cut me off the villain's head, throw the quean in the channel.

Host. Throw me in the channel! I'll throw thee in the channel. Wilt thou? wilt thou? thou bastardly rogue! Murder, murder! Ah, thou honey-suckle villain! wilt thou kill God's officers and the king's? Ah, thou honey-seed rogue! thou art a honey-seed, a man-queller, and a woman-queller

Fal. Keep them off, Bardolph.   60

Fang. A rescue! a rescue!

Host. Good people, bring a rescue or two. Thou wo't wo't thou? thou wo't wo't ta'? do, do, thou rogue! do, thou hemp-seed!

Fal. Away, you scullion! you rampallion! you fustilarian! I'll tickle your catastrophe

Enter the LORD CHIEF-JUSTICE, *and his men*

Ch. Just. What is the matter? keep the peace here, ho!

Host. Good my lord, be good to me. I beseech you, stand to me   70

Ch. Just. How now, Sir John! what are you brawling here?

Doth this become your place, your time and business?

You should have been well on your way to York

Stand from him, fellow: wherefore hang'st upon him?

Host. O most worshipful lord, an't please your grace, I am a poor widow of Eastcheap, and he is arrested at my suit

Ch. Just. For what sum?

Host. It is more than for some, my lord, it if for all, all I have. He hath eaten me out of house and home, he hath put all my substance into that fat belly of his, but I will have some of it out again, or I will ride thee o' nights like the mare

Fal. I think I am as like to ride the mare, if I have any vantage of ground to get up

Ch. Just. How comes this, Sir John? Fie! what man of good temper would endure this tempest of exclamation? Are you not ashamed to enforce a poor widow to so rough a course to come by her own?   90

Fal. What is the gross sum that I owe thee?

Host. Marry, if thou wert an honest man, thyself and the money too. Thou didst swear to me upon a parcel-gilt goblet, sitting in my Dolphin-chamber, at the round table, by a sea-coal fire, upon Wednesday in Wheeson week, when the prince broke thy head for liking his father to a singing-man of Windsor, thou didst swear to me then, as I was washing thy wound, to marry me and make me my lady thy wife. Canst thou deny it? Did not goodwife Keech, the butcher's wife, come in then and call me gossip Quickly? coming in to borrow a mess of vinegar, telling us she had a good dish of prawns, whereby thou didst desire to eat some, whereby I told thee they were ill for a green wound? And didst thou not, when she was gone down stairs, desire me to be no more so familiarly with such poor people, saying that ere long they should call me madam? And didst thou not kiss me and bid me fetch thee thirty shillings? I put thee now to thy book-oath; deny it if thou canst

Fal. My lord, this is a poor mad soul, and she says up and down the town that the eldest son is like you; she hath been in good case, and the truth is, poverty hath distracted her. But for these foolish officers, I beseech you I may have redress against them.

Ch. Just. Sir John, Sir John, I am well acquainted with your manner of wrenching the true cause the false way. It is not a confident brow, nor the throng of words that come with such more than impudent sauciness from you, can thrust me from a level consideration: you have, as it appears to me, practised upon the easy-yielding spirit of this woman, and made her serve your uses both in purse and in person.

Host. Yea, in truth, my lord.

Ch. Just. Pray thee, peace. Pay her the debt you owe her, and unpay the villany you have done her: the one you may do with sterling money, and the other with current repentance.

Fal. My lord, I will not undergo this sneap without reply. You call honorable boldness impudent sauciness : if a man will make courtesy and say nothing, he is virtuous : no, my lord, my humble duty remembered, I will not be your suitor. I say to you, I do desire deliverance from these officers, being upon hasty employment in the king's affairs.   140

Ch. Just. You speak as having power to do wrong : but answer in the effect of your reputation, and satisfy the poor woman.

Fal. Come hither, hostess.

Enter GOWER.

Ch. Just. Now, Master Gower, what news?

Gow. The king, my lord, and Harry Prince of Wales
Are near at hand : the rest the paper tells

Fal. As I am a gentleman.

Host. Faith, you said so before.

Fal. As I am a gentleman. Come, no more words of it.   151

Host. By this heavenly ground I tread on, I must be fain to pawn both my plate and the tapestry of my dining-chambers.

Fal. Glasses, glasses is the only drinking : and for thy walls, a pretty slight drollery, or the story of the Prodigal, or the German hunting in water-work, is worth a thousand of these bed-hangings and these fly-bitten tapestries. Let it be ten pound, if thou canst. Come, an 'twere not for thy humors, there's not a better wench in England. Go, wash thy face, and draw the action. Come, thou must not be in this humor with me; dost not know me ? come, come, I know thou wast set on to this.

Host. Pray thee, Sir John, let it be but twenty nobles : i' faith, I am loath to pawn my plate, so God save me, la !

Fal. Let it alone ; I'll make other shift : you'll be a fool still.   170

Host. Well, you shall have it, though I pawn my gown. I hope you'll come to supper. You'll pay me all together ?

Fal. Will I live ? [*To Bardolph*] Go, with her, with her ; hook on, hook on.

Host. Will you have Doll Tearsheet meet you at supper ?

Fal. No more words ; let's have her.
[*Exeunt Hostess, Bardolph, Officers and Boy.*

Ch. Just. I have heard better news.

Fal. What's the news, my lord ?   180

Ch. Just. Where lay the king last night ?

Gow. At Basingstoke, my lord.

Fal. I hope, my lord, all's well : what is the news, my lord ?

Ch. Just. Come all his forces back ?

Gow. No ; fifteen hundred foot, five hundred horse,
Are marched up to my lord of Lancaster,
Against Northumberland and the Archbishop.

Fal. Comes the king back from Wales, my noble lord ?

Ch. Just. You shall have letters of me presently :   190
Come, go along with me, good Master Gower.

Fal. My lord !

Ch. Just. What's the matter ?

Fal. Master Gower, shall I entreat you with me to dinner ?

Gow. I must wait upon my good lord here; I thank you, good Sir John.

Ch. Just. Sir John, you loiter here too long, being you are to take soldiers up in counties as you go.   200

Fal. Will you sup with me, Master Gower?

Ch. Just. What foolish master taught you these manners, Sir John ?

Fal. Master Gower, if they become me not, he was a fool that taught them me. This is the right fencing grace, my lord ; tap for tap, and so part fair.

Ch. Just. Now the Lord lighten thee ! thou art a great fool.   [*Exeunt.*

SCENE II.   *London. Another street.*

Enter PRINCE HENRY *and* POINS.

Prince. Before God, I am exceeding weary.

Poins. Is't come to that ? I had thought weariness durst not have attached one of so high blood.

Prince. Faith, it does me ; though it discolors the complexion of my greatness to acknowledge it. Doth it not show vilely in me to desire small beer ?

Poins. Why, a prince should not be so loosely studied as to remember so weak a composition.

Prince. Belike then my appetite was not princely got ; for, by my troth, I do now remember the poor creature, small beer. But, indeed, these humble considerations make me out of love with my greatness. What a disgrace is it to me to remember thy name ! or to know thy face to-morrow! or to take note how many pair of silk stockings thou hast, viz. these and those that were thy peach-colored ones! or to bear the inventory of thy shirts, as, one for superfluity, and another for use ! But that the tennis-court-keeper knows better than I ; for it is a low ebb of linen with thee when thou keepest not racket there; as thou hast not done a great while, because the rest of thy low countries have made a shift to eat up thy holland: and God knows, whether those that bawl out

the ruins of thy linen shall inherit his kingdom : but the midwives say the children are
not in the fault ; whereupon the world increases,
and kindreds are mightily strengthened.

Poins. How ill it follows, after you have
labored so hard, you should talk so idly ! Tell
me, how many good young princes would do
so, their fathers being so sick as yours at this
time is ?

Prince. Shall I tell thee one thing, Poins ?

Poins. Yes, faith ; and let it be an excellent
good thing.

Prince. It shall serve among wits of no
higher breeding than thine.

Poins. Go to ; I stand the push of your one
thing that you will tell.   41

Prince. Marry, I tell thee, it is not meet
that I should be sad, now my father is sick :
albeit I could tell thee, as to one it pleases me,
for fault of a better, to call my friend, I could
be sad, and sad indeed too.

Poins. Very hardly upon such a subject.

Prince. By this hand, thou thinkest me as
far in the devil's book as thou and Falstaff for
obduracy and persistency : let the end try the
man. But I tell thee, my heart bleeds inwardly
that my father is so sick : and keeping such vile
company as thou art hath in reason taken from
me all ostentation of sorrow.

Poins. The reason ?

Prince. What wouldst thou think of me, if
I should weep ?

Poins. I would think thee a most princely
hypocrite.   59

Prince. It would be every man's thought ;
and thou art a blessed fellow to think as every
man thinks : never a man's thought in the
world keeps the road-way better than thine :
every man would think me an hypocrite indeed. And what accites your most worshipful
thought to think so ?

Poins. Why, because you have been so lewd
and so much engraffed to Falstaff.

Prince. And to thee.

Poins. By this light, I am well spoke on ;
I can hear it with my own ears : the worst that
they can say of me is that I am a second
brother and that I am a proper fellow of my
hands ; and those two things, I confess, I
cannot help. By the mass, here comes Bardolph.

Enter BARDOLPH *and* Page.

Prince. And the boy that I gave Falstaff :
a' had him from me Christian ; and look, if
the fat villain have not transformed him ape.

Bard. God save your grace !

Prince. And yours, most noble Bardolph !

Bard. Come, you virtuous ass, you bashful
fool, must you be blushing ? wherefore blush
you now ? What a maidenly man-at-arms are
you become ! Is't such a matter to get a pottle-
pot's maidenhead ?

Page. A' calls me e'en now, my lord,
through a red lattice, and I could discern no
part of his face from the window : at last I
spied his eyes, and methought he had made
two holes in the ale-wife's new petticoat and
so peeped through.

Prince. Has not the boy profited ?   90

Bard. Away, you whoreson upright rabbit,
away !

Page. Away, you rascally Althæa's dream,
away !

Prince. Instruct us, boy ; what dream,
boy ?

Page. Marry, my lord, Althæa dreamed
she was delivered of a fire-brand ; and therefore I call him her dream.

Prince. A crown's worth of good interpretation : there 'tis, boy.   100

Poins. O, that this good blossom could be
kept from cankers ! Well, there is sixpence to
preserve thee.

Bard. An you do not make him hanged
among you, the gallows shall have wrong.

Prince. And how doth thy master, Bardolph ?

Bard. Well, my lord. He heard of your
grace's coming to town : there's a letter for
you.

Poins. Delivered with good respect. And
how doth the martlemas, your master ?   110

Bard. In bodily health, sir.

Poins. Marry, the immortal part needs a
physician ; but that moves not him : though
that be sick, it dies not.

Prince. I do allow this wen to be as familiar with me as my dog ; and he holds his
place ; for look you how he writes.

Poins. [*Reads*] ' John Falstaff, knight,'—
every man must know that, as oft as he has
occasion to name himself : even like those that
are kin to the king ; for they never prick their
finger but they say, ' There's some of the
king's blood spilt.' ' How comes that ?' says
he, that takes upon him not to conceive. The
answer is as ready as a borrower's cap, ' I am
the king's poor cousin, sir.'

Prince. Nay, they will be kin to us, or they
will fetch it from Japhet. But to the letter :

Poins. [*Reads*] ' Sir John Falstaff, knight,
to the son of the king, nearest his father, Harry Prince of Wales, greeting.' Why, this is a
certificate.

Prince. Peace !

Poins. [*Reads*] ' I will imitate the honorable Romans in brevity :' he sure means brevity in breath, short-winded. ' I commend me
to thee, I commend thee, and I leave thee. Be
not too familiar with Poins ; for he misuses
thy favors so much, that he swears thou art to
marry his sister Nell. Repent at idle times as
thou mayest ; and so, farewell.   141

    ' Thine, by yea and no, which is as
       much as to say, as thou usest him,
       JACK FALSTAFF with my familiars,
       JOHN with my brothers and sisters,
       and SIR JOHN with all Europe.'

My lord, I'll steep this letter in sack and make
him eat it.

Prince. That's to make him eat twenty of

his words. But do you use me thus, Ned ?
must I marry your sister?   151
  Poins   God send the wench no worse for-
tune ' But I never said so
  Prince   Well, thus we play the fools with
the time, and the spirits of the wise sit in the
clouds and mock us   Is your master here in
London ?
  Bard   Yea, my lord
  Prince   Where sups he ? doth the old boar
feed in the old frank ?   160
  Bard   At the old place, my lord, in East-
cheap
  Prince   What company ?
  Page   Ephesians, my lord, of the old church.
  Prince   Sup any women with him ?
  Page   None, my lord, but old Mistress
Quickly and Mistress Doll Tearsheet
  Prince   What pagan may that be ?
  Page.   A proper gentlewoman, sir, and a
kinswoman of my master's.   170
  Prince   Even such kin as the parish heifers
are to the town bull. Shall we steal upon them,
Ned, at supper?   [low you
  Poins   I am your shadow, my lord , I'll fol-
.   *Prince.*   Sirrah, you boy, and Bardolph, no
word to your master that I am yet come to
town . there's for your silence.
  Bard   I have no tongue, sir
  Page   And for mine, sir, I will govern it   180
  Prince   Fare you well , go. [*Exeunt Bardolph and Page*] This Doll Tearsheet should
be some road.
  Poins   I warrant you, as common as the
way between Saint Alban's and London
  Prince   How might we see Falstaff bestow
himself to-night in his true colors, and not ourselves be seen ?
  Poins   Put on two leathern jerkins and
aprons, and wait upon him at his table as
drawers.   191
  Prince   From a God to a bull ? a heavy
descension ' it was Jove's case   From a prince
to a prentice ? a low transformation' that shall
be mine , for in every thing the purpose must
weigh with the folly.   Follow me, Ned
                     [*Exeunt*

SCENE III   *Warkworth. Before the castle*

Enter NORTHUMBERLAND, LADY NORTHUM-
BERLAND, *and* LADY PERCY

  North.   I pray thee, loving wife, and gentle
    daughter,
Give even way unto my rough affairs :
Put not you on the visage of the times
And be like them to Percy troublesome
  Lady N.   I have given over, I will speak no
    more
Do what you will , your wisdom be your
    guide
  North   Alas, sweet wife, my honor is at
    pawn ,
And, but my going, nothing can redeem it.
  Lady P.   O yet, for God's sake, go not to
    these wars !

The time was, father, that you broke your
    word,   10
When you were more endeared to it than now;
When your own Percy, when my heart's dear
    Harry,
Threw many a northward look to see his
    father
Bring up his powers ; but he did long in vain.
Who then persuaded you to stay at home ?
There were two honors lost, yours and your
    son's
For yours, the God of heaven brighten it !
For his, it stuck upon him as the sun
In the grey vault of heaven, and by his light
Did all the chivalry of England move   20
To do brave acts   he was indeed the glass
Wherein the noble youth did dress themselves:
He had no legs that practised not his gait ,
And speaking thick, which nature made his
    blemish,
Became the accents of the valiant ;
For those that could speak low and tardily
Would turn their own perfection to abuse,
To seem like him   so that in speech, in gait,
In diet, in affections of delight,
In military rules, humors of blood,   30
He was the mark and glass, copy and book,
That fashion'd others   And him, O won-
    drous him '
O miracle of men ! him did you leave,
Second to none, unseconded by you,
To look upon the hideous god of war
In disadvantage , to abide a field
Where nothing but the sound of Hotspur's
    name
Did seem defensible: so you left him.
Never, O never, do his ghost the wrong
To hold your honor more precise and nice   40
With others than with him ' let them alone ·
The marshal and the archbishop are strong:
Had my sweet Harry had but half their num-
    bers,
To-day might I, hanging on Hotspur's neck,
Have talk'd of Monmouth's grave.
  North   Beshrew your heart,
Fair daughter, you do draw my spirits from
    me
With new lamenting ancient oversights.
But I must go and meet with danger there,
Or it will seek me another place
And find me worse provided.
  Lady N   O, fly to Scotland,   50
Till that the nobles and the armed commons
Have of their puissance made a little taste.
  Lady P.   If they get ground and vantage
    of the king,
Then join you with them, like a rib of steel,
To make strength stronger, but, for all our
    loves,
First let them try themselves   So did your
    son ;
He was so suffer'd : so came I a widow;
And never shall have length of life enough
To rain upon remembrance with mine eyes,
That it may grow and sprout as high as
    heaven,   60

For recordation to my noble husband
  North. Come, come, go in with me   'Tis
    with my mind
As with the tide swell'd up unto his height,
That makes a still-stand, running neither way:
Fain would I go to meet the archbishop,
But many thousand reasons hold me back
I will resolve for Scotland   there am I,
Till time and vantage crave my company.
                  [*Exeunt.*

SCENE IV. *London. The Boar's-head Tavern*
in Eastcheap

Enter two DRAWERS

First Draw What the devil hast thou
brought there ? apple-johns ? thou knowest
Sir John cannot endure an apple-john
  Sec. Draw. Mass, thou sayest true The
prince once set a dish of apple-johns before
him, and told him there were five more Sir
Johns, and, putting off his hat, said ' I will now
take my leave of these six dry, round, old,
withered knights ' It angered him to the
heart but he hath forgot that   10
  First Draw Why, then, cover, and set them
down : and see if thou canst find out Sneak's
noise , Mistress Tearsheet would fain hear
some music Dispatch the room where they
supped is too hot , they'll come in straight
  Sec Draw Sirrah, here will be the prince
and Master Poins anon , and they will put on
two of our jerkins and aprons , and Sir John
must not know of it . Bardolph hath brought
word.   20
  First Draw By the mass, here will be old
Utis . it will be an excellent stratagem.
  Sec. Draw. I'll see if I can find out Sneak
                       [*Exit.*

Enter Hostess *and* DOLL TEARSHEET

Host. I' faith, sweetheart, methinks now
you are in an excellent good temperality your
pulsidge beats as extraordinarily as heart
would desire , and your color, I warrant you,
is as red as any rose, in good truth, la ' But,
i' faith, you have drunk too much canaries ,
and that's a marvellous searching wine, and it
perfumes the blood ere one can say ' What's
this ? ' How do you now ?
  Dol Better than I was hem '
  Host. Why, that's well said , a good heart's
worth gold Lo, here comes Sir John.

Enter FALSTAFF

  Fal. [*Singing*] ' When Arthur first in court,'
—Empty the jordan   [*Exit First Drawer*]—
[*Singing*] ' And was a worthy king.' How
now, Mistress Doll '
  Host. Sick of a calm , yea, good faith   40
  Fal So is all her sect , an they be once in
a calm, they are sick.
  Dol You muddy rascal, is that all the
comfort you give me ?
  Fal You make fat rascals, Mistress Doll
  Dol I make them ! gluttony and diseases
make them ; I make them not.

  Fal If the cook help to make the gluttony,
you help to make the diseases, Doll we catch
of you, Doll, we catch of you , grant that, my
poor virtue, grant that   51
  Dol Yea, joy, our chains and our jewels.
  Fal ' Your brooches, pearls, and ouches '
for to serve bravely is to come halting off, you
know to come off the breach with his pike
bent bravely, and to surgery bravely , to
venture upon the charged chambers bravely,—
  Dol Hang yourself, you muddy conger,
hang yourself '   59
  Host. By my troth, this is the old fashion,
you two never meet but you fall to some discord you are both, i good truth, as rheumatic
as two dry toasts , you cannot one bear with
another's confirmities What the good-year !
one must bear, and that must be you you
are the weaker vessel, as they say, the emptier
vessel.
  Dol Can a weak empty vessel bear such a
huge full hogshead ? there's a whole merchant's venture of Bourdeaux stuff in him ,
you have not seen a hulk better stuffed in the
hold Come, I'll be friends with thee, Jack
thou art going to the wars , and whether I
shall ever see thee again or no, there is nobody
cares.

Re-enter First Drawer

  First Draw Sir, Ancient Pistol's below,
and would speak with you
  Dol Hang him, swaggering rascal ' let
him not come hither . it is the foul-mouthed'st
rogue in England
  Host If he swagger, let him not come here.
no, by my faith , I must live among my neighbors I'll no swaggerers I am in good name
and fame with the very best shut the door ,
there comes no swaggerers here I have not
lived all this while, to have swaggering now :
shut the door, I pray you
  Fal Dost thou hear, hostess ?
  Host. Pray ye, pacify yourself, Sir John :
there comes no swaggerers here
  Fal. Dost thou hear ? it is mine ancient
  Host Tilly-fally, Sir John, ne'er tell me
your ancient swaggerer comes not in my doors
I was before Master Tisick, the deputy, t'other
day , and, as he said to me, 'twas no longer
ago than Wednesday last, ' I' good faith,
neighbor Quickly,' says he , Master Dumbe,
our minister, was by then , ' neighbor Quickly,' says he, ' receive those that are civil , for,'
said he, ' you are in an ill name ' now a' said
so, I can tell whereupon , ' for,' says he, ' you
are an honest woman, and well thought on ,
therefore take heed what guests you receive
receive,' says he, ' no swaggering companions ' There comes none here ' you would
bless you to hear what he said no, I'll no
swaggerers
  Fal He's no swaggerer, hostess ; a tame
cheater, i' faith , you may stroke him as
gently as a puppy greyhound he'll not swagger with a Barbary hen, if her feathers turn

back in any show of resistance. Call him up, drawer.   [*Exit First Drawer.*

Host. Cheater, call you him ? I will bar no honest man my house, nor no cheater . but I do not love swaggering, by my troth , I am the worse, when one says swagger: feel, masters, how I shake ; look you, I warrant you.

Dol. So you do, hostess.

Host Do I ? yea, in very truth, do I, an 'twere an aspen leaf . I cannot abide swaggerers.

Enter PISTOL, BARDOLPH, *and* PAGE

Pist. God save you, Sir John !   119

Fal. Welcome, Ancient Pistol Here, Pistol, I charge you with a cup of sack do you discharge upon mine hostess

Pist. I will discharge upon her, Sir John, with two bullets

Fal. She is pistol-proof, sir , you shall hardly offend her.

Host. Come, I'll drink no proofs nor no bullets . I'll drink no more than will do me good, for no man's pleasure, I

Pist. Then to you, Mistress Dorothy , I will charge you   131

Dol. Charge me ! I scorn you, scurvy companion. What ! you poor, base, rascally, cheating, lack-linen mate ' Away, you mouldy rogue, away ' I am meat for your master

Pist. I know you, Mistress Dorothy

Dol Away, you cut-purse rascal ' you filthy bung, away ' by this wine, I'll thrust my knife in your mouldy chaps, an you play the saucy cuttle with me. Away, you bottle-ale rascal ' you basket-hilt stale juggler, you' Since when, I pray you, sir ? God's light, with two points on your shoulder ? much !

Pist. God let me not live, but I will murder your ruff for this

Fal No more, Pistol ; I would not have you go off here . discharge yourself of our company, Pistol

Host. No, Good Captain Pistol , not here, sweet captain   150

Dol Captain ' thou abominable damned cheater, art thou not ashamed to be called captain ? An captains were of my mind, they would truncheon you out, for taking their names upon you before you have earned them You a captain ' you slave, for what ? for tearing a poor whore's ruff in a bawdy-house? He a captain ' hang him, rogue ! he lives upon mouldy stewed prunes and dried cakes. A captain ' God's light, these villains will make the word as odious as the word ' occupy ', which was an excellent good word before it was ill sorted · therefore captains had need look to't

Bard. Pray thee, go down, good ancient.

Fal Hark thee hither, Mistress Doll !

Pist Not I . I tell thee what, Corporal Bardolph I could tear her : I'll be revenged of her

Page. Pray thee, go down.

Pist. I'll see her damned first ; to Pluto s damned lake, by this hand, to the infernal deep, with Erebus and tortures vile also Hold hook and line, say I. Down, down, dogs ! down, faitors ! Have we not Hiren here ?

Host Good Captain Peesel, be quiet , 'tis very late, i' faith : I beseek you now, aggravate your choler.

Pist. These be good humors, indeed ' Shall pack-horses
And hollow pamper'd jades of Asia,
Which cannot go but thirty mile a-day,
Compare with Cæsars, and with Cannibals,
And Trojan Greeks ? nay, rather damn them with   181
King Cerberus ; and let the welkin roar.
Shall we fall foul for toys ?

Host By my troth, captain, these are very bitter words.

Bard Be gone, good ancient : this will grow to a brawl anon

Pist. Die men like dogs ! give crowns like pins ! Have we not Hiren here ?   189

Host. O' my word, captain, there's none such here What the good-year ' do you think I would deny her ? For God's sake, be quiet

Pist. Then feed, and be fat, my fair Calipolis
Come, give's some sack
' Si fortune me tormente, sperato me contento '
Fear we broadsides ? no, let the fiend give fire :
Give me some sack : and, sweetheart, lie thou there.   [*Laying down his sword.*
Come we to full points here ; and are etceteras nothing ?

Fal. Pistol, I would be quiet.

Pist. Sweet knight, I kiss thy neif . what ' we have seen the seven stars.   201

Dol For God's sake, thrust him down stairs . I cannot endure such a fustian rascal.

Pist Thrust him down stairs ! know we not Galloway nags ?

Fal Quoit him down, Bardolph, like a shove-groat shilling · nay, an a' do nothing but speak nothing, a' shall be nothing here

Bard. Come, get you down stairs   209

Pist What ! shall we have incision ? shall we imbrue ? [*Snatching up his sword.*
Then death rock me asleep, abridge my doleful days '
Why, then, let grievous, ghastly, gaping wounds
Untwine the Sisters Three ! Come, Atropos, I say !

Host. Here's goodly stuff toward '

Fal Give me my rapier, boy

Dol. I pray thee, Jack, I pray thee, do not draw.

Fal. Get you down stairs.
  [*Drawing, and driving Pistol out.*

Host. Here's a goodly tumult ! I ll forswear keeping house, afore I'll be in these turrits and frights. So ; murder, I warrant now. Alas, alas! put up your naked weapons, put up your naked weapons.

[*Exeunt Pistol and Bardolph.*

Dol. I pray thee, Jack, be quiet; the rascal's gone. Ah, you whoreson little valiant villain, you! •

Host. Are you not hurt i' the groin? methought a' made a shrewd thrust at your belly.

Re-enter BARDOLPH.

Fal. Have you turned him out o' doors?

Bard. Yea, sir. The rascal's drunk: you have hurt him, sir, i' the shoulder.   231

Fal. A rascal! to brave me!

Dol. Ah, you sweet little rogue, you! Alas, poor ape, how thou sweatest! come, let me wipe thy face; come on, you whoreson chops; ah, rogue! i' faith, I love thee: thou art as valorous as Hector of Troy, worth five of Agamemnon, and ten times better than the Nine Worthies: ah, villain!

Fal. A rascally slave! I will toss the rogue in a blanket.   241

Dol. Do, an thou darest for thy heart: an thou dost, I'll canvass thee between a pair of sheets

Enter Music.

Page. The music is come, sir.

Fal. Let them play. Play, sirs. Sit on my knee, Doll. A rascal bragging slave! the rogue fled from me like quicksilver.

Dol. ' I' faith, and thou followedst him like a cherub. Thou whoreson little tidy Bartholomew boar-pig, when wilt thou leave fighting o' days and foining o' nights, and begin to patch up thine old body for heaven?

Enter, behind, PRINCE HENRY *and* POINS, *disguised.*

Fal. Peace, good Doll! do not speak like a death's-head; do not bid me remember mine end.

Dol. Sirrah, what humor's the prince of?

Fal. A good shallow young fellow: a' would have made a good pantler, a' would ha' chipped bread well.

Dol. They say Poins has a good wit.   260

Fal. He a good wit? hang him, baboon! his wit's as thick as Tewksbury mustard; there's no more conceit in him than is in a mallet.   [then?

Dol. Why does the prince love him so,

Fal. Because their legs are both of a bigness, and a' plays at quoits well, and eats conger and fennel, and drinks off candles' ends for flap-dragons, and rides the wild-mare with the boys, and jumps upon joined-stools, and swears with a good grace, and wears his boots very smooth, like unto the sign of the leg, and breeds no bate with telling of discreet stories; and such other gambol faculties a' has, that show a weak mind and an able body, for the which the prince admits him: for the prince himself is such another; the weight of a hair will turn the scales between their avoirdupois.

Prince. Would not this nave of a wheel have his ears cut off?   279

Poins. Let's beat him before his whore.

Prince. Look, whether the withered elder hath not his poll clawed like a parrot.   281

Poins. Is it not strange that desire should so many years outlive performance?

Fal. Kiss me, Doll.

Prince. Saturn and Venus this year in conjunction! what says the almanac to that?

Poins. And look, whether the fiery Trigon, his man, be not lisping to his master's old tables, his note-book, his counsel-keeper. 290

Fal. Thou dost give me flattering busses.

Dol. By my troth, I kiss thee with a most constant heart.

Fal. I am old, I am old.

Dol. I love thee better than I love e'er a scurvy young boy of them all.

Fal. What stuff wilt have a kirtle of? I shall receive money o' Thursday: shalt have a cap to-morrow. A merry song, come: it grows late; we'll to bed. Thou'lt forget me when I am gone.

Dol. By my troth, thou'lt set me a-weeping, an thou sayest so: prove that ever I dress myself handsome till thy return: well, harken at the end.

Fal. Some sack, Francis.

Prince. } Anon, anon, sir. [*Coming forward.*
Poins. }

Fal. Ha! a bastard son of the king's? And art not thou Poins his brother?

Prince. Why, thou globe of sinful continents, what a life dost thou lead!   310

Fal. A better than thou: I am a gentleman; thou art a drawer.

Prince. Very true, sir; and I come to draw you out by the ears.

Host. O, the Lord preserve thy good grace! by my troth, welcome to London. Now, the Lord bless that sweet face of thine! O Jesu, are you come from Wales?

Fal. Thou whoreson mad compound of majesty, by this light flesh and corrupt blood, thou art welcome.   321

Dol. How, you fat fool! I scorn you.

Poins. My lord, he will drive you out of your revenge and turn all to a merriment, if you take not the heat.

Prince. You whoreson candle-mine, you, how vilely did you speak of me even now before this honest, virtuous, civil gentlewoman!

Host. God's blessing of your good heart! and so she is, by my troth.   330

Fal. Didst thou hear me?

Prince. Yea, and you knew me, as you did when you ran away by Gad's-hill: you knew I was at your back, and spoke it on purpose to try my patience.

Fal. No, no, no; not so; I did not think thou wast within hearing.

Prince. I shall drive you then to confess the wilful abuse; and then I know how to handle you.   [abuse.

Fal. No abuse, Hal, o' mine honor; no

Prince Not to dispraise me, and call me
pantler and bread-chipper and I know not
what ?

Fal. No abuse, Hal.

Poins No abuse ?

Fal. No abuse, Ned, i' the world , honest
Ned, none I dispraised him before the wicked, that the wicked might not fall in love with
him , in which doing, I have done the part of
a careful friend and a true subject, and thy
father is to give me thanks for it. No abuse,
Hal none, Ned, none . no, faith, boys, none.

Prince See now, whether pure fear and
entire cowardice doth not make thee wrong
this virtuous gentlewoman to close with us ?
is she of the wicked ? is thine hostess here of
the wicked ? or is thy boy of the wicked ? or
honest Bardolph, whose zeal burns in his nose,
of the wicked ?

Poins Answer, thou dead elm, answer

Fal The fiend hath pricked down Bardolph irrecoverable , and his face is Lucifer's
privy-kitchen, where he doth nothing but
roast malt-worms For the boy, there is a
good angel about him , but the devil outbids
him too

Prince For the women ?

Fal For one of them, she is in hell already,
and burns poor souls For the other, I owe
her money , and whether she be damned for
that, I know not.

Host No, I warrant you   369

Fal No, I think thou art not , I think thou
art quit for that Marry, there is another
indictment upon thee, for suffering flesh to be
eaten in thy house, contrary to the law , for
the which I think thou wilt howl

Host All victuallers do so , what's a joint
of mutton or two in a whole Lent ?

Prince You, gentlewoman,—

Dol What says your grace ?

Fal His grace says that which his flesh
rebels against   [*Knocking within* 380

Host. Who knocks so loud at door ? Look
to the door there, Francis.

Enter PETO

Prince. Peto, how now ! what news ?

Peto The king your father is at Westminster

And there are twenty weak and wearied posts
Come from the north and, as I came along,
I met and overtook a dozen captains,
Bare-headed, sweating, knocking at the tav-
erns,
And asking every one for Sir John Falstaff

Prince. By heaven, Poins, I feel me much
to blame,   390
So idly to profane the precious time,
When tempest of commotion, like the south
,Borne with black vapor, doth begin to melt
And drop upon our bare unarmed heads.
Give me my sword and cloak. Falstaff, good
night.   [*Exeunt Prince Henry, Poins,*
Peto and Bardolph.

Fal. Now comes in the sweetest morsel of

the night, and we must hence and leave it un-
picked   [*Knocking within.*] More knocking
at the door !

Re-enter BARDOLPH.

How now ! what's the matter ?   400

Bard You must away to court, sir, presently ,
A dozen captains stay at door for you.

Fal [*To the Page*] Pay the musicians, sirrah
Farewell, hostess , farewell, Doll You see,
my good wenches, how men of merit are
sought after . the undeserver may sleep, when
the man of action is called on Farewell, good
wenches : if I be not sent away post, I will
see you again ere I go

Dol I cannot speak , if my heart be not
ready to burst,—well, sweet Jack, have a care
of thyself

Fal Farewell, farewell.

     [*Exeunt Falstaff and Bardolph.*

Host. Well, fare thee well I have known
thee these twenty-nine years, come peascod-
time , but an honester and truer-hearted man,
—well, fare thee well.

Bard [*Within*] Mistress Tearsheet !

Host What's the matter ?

Bard [*Within*] Bid Mistress Tearsheet
come to my master   419

Host. O, run, Doll, run , run, good Doll
come. [*She comes blubbered.*] Yea, will you
come, Doll ?   [*Exeunt.*

ACT III.

SCENE I   *Westminster. The palace.*

Enter the KING *in his nightgown, with a Page.*

King Go call the Earls of Surrey and of
Warwick ;
But, ere they come, bid them o'er-read these
letters,
And well consider of them , make good speed.
     [*Exit Page*
How many thousand of my poorest subjects
Are at this hour asleep ! O sleep, O gentle
sleep,
Nature's soft nurse, how have I frighted thee,
That thou no more wilt weigh my eyelids down
And steep my senses in forgetfulness ?
Why rather, sleep, liest thou in smoky cribs,
Upon uneasy pallets stretching thee   10
And hush'd with buzzing night-flies to thy
slumber,
Than in the perfumed chambers of the great,
Under the canopies of costly state,
And lull'd with sound of sweetest melody ?
O thou dull god, why liest thou with the vile
In loathsome beds, and leavest the kingly couch
A watch-case or a common 'larum-bell ?
Wilt thou upon the high and giddy mast
Seal up the ship-boy's eyes, and rock his brains
In cradle of the rude imperious surge   20
And in the visitation of the winds,
Who take the ruffian billows by the top,

Curling their monstrous heads and hanging
  them
With deafening clamor in the slippery clouds,
That, with the hurly, death itself awakes ?
Canst thou, O partial sleep, give thy repose
To the wet sea-boy in an hour so rude,
And in the calmest and most stillest night,
With all appliances and means to boot,
Deny it to a king ? Then happy low, lie down!
Uneasy lies the head that wears a crown   31

Enter WARWICK *and* SURREY

War Many good morrows to your majesty!
King. Is it good morrow, lords ?
War. 'Tis one o'clock, and past
King Why, then, good morrow to you all,
  my lords
Have you read o'er the letters that I sent you?
War We have, my liege
King Then you perceive the body of our
  kingdom
How foul it is , what rank diseases grow
And with what danger, near the heart of it 40
War It is but as a body yet distemper'd ,
Which to his former strength may be restored
With good advice and little medicine .
My Lord Northumberland will soon be cool'd
King O God ! that one might read the
  book of fate,
And see the revolution of the times
Make mountains level, and the continent,
Weary of solid firmness, melt itself
Into the sea ! and, other times, to see
The beachy girdle of the ocean   50
Too wide for Neptune's hips , how chances
  mock,
And changes fill the cup of alteration
With divers liquors ! O, if this were seen,
The happiest youth, viewing his progress
  through,
What perils past, what crosses to ensue,
Would shut the book, and sit him down and die.
'Tis not ten years gone
Since Richard and Northumberland, great
  friends,
Did feast together, and in two years after
Were they at wars · it is but eight years since 61
This Percy was the man nearest my soul,
Who like a brother toil'd in my affairs
And laid his love and life under my foot,
Yea, for my sake, even to the eyes of Richard
Gave him defiance But which of you was by—
You, cousin Nevil, as I may remember—
  [*To* Warwick.
When Richard, with his eye brimful of tears,
Then check'd and rated by Northumberland,
Did speak these words, now proved a proph-
  ecy ?   69
' Northumberland, thou ladder by the which
My cousin Bolingbroke ascends my throne ;'
Though then, God knows, I had no such intent,
But that necessity so bow'd the state
That I and greatness were compell'd to kiss
' The time shall come,' thus did he follow it,
' The time will come, that foul sin, gathering
  head,

Shall break into corruption ·' so went on,
Foretelling this same time's condition
And the division of our amity
War. There is a history in all men's lives,
Figuring the nature of the times deceased , 81
The which observed, a man may prophesy,
With a near aim, of the main chance of things
As yet not come to life, which in their seeds
And weak beginnings lie intreasured
Such things become the hatch and brood of
  time ,
And by the necessary form of this
King Richard might create a perfect guess
That great Northumberland, then false to him,
Would of that seed grow to a greater falseness;
Which should not find a ground to root upon,
Unless on you
King Are these things then necessities?
Then let us meet them like necessities
And that same word even now cries out on us:
They say the bishop and Northumberland
Are fifty thousand strong
War It cannot be, my lord ;
Rumor doth double, like the voice and echo,
The numbers of the fear'd Please it your
  grace
To go to bed Upon my soul, my lord,
The powers that you already have sent forth
Shall bring this prize in very easily   101
To comfort you the more I have received
A certain instance that Glendower is dead.
Your majesty hath been this fortnight ill,
And these unseason'd hours perforce must add
Unto your sickness
King. I will take your counsel :
And were these inward wars once out of hand,
We would, dear lords, unto the Holy Land.
  [*Exeunt*

SCENE II. *Gloucestershire. Before* JUSTICE
  SHALLOW's *house*

Enter SHALLOW *and* SILENCE, *meeting* ;
  MOULDY, SHADOW, WART, FEEBLE, BULL-
  CALF, *a Servant or two with them*
Shal. Come on, come on, come on, sir ;
give me your hand, sir, give me your hand,
sir: an early stirrer, by the rood ' And how
doth my good cousin Silence ?
Sil Good morrow, good cousin Shallow
Shal And how doth my cousin, your bed-
fellow ? and your fairest daughter and mine,
my god-daughter Ellen ?
Sil. Alas, a black ousel, cousin Shallow ! 9
Shal By yea and nay, sir, I dare say my
cousin William is become a good scholar · he
is at Oxford still, is he not ?
Sil Indeed, sir, to my cost
Shal. A' must, then, to the inns o' court
shortly I was once of Clement's Inn, where
I think they will talk of mad Shallow yet
Sil. You were called ' lusty Shallow ' then,
cousin
Shal. By the mass, I was call'd any thing;
and I would have done any thing indeed too,
and roundly too There was I, and little John
Doit of Staffordshire, and black George Barnes,

and Francis Pickbone, and Will Squele, a Cotswold man , you had not four such swingebucklers in all the inns o' court again : and I may say to you, we knew where the bonarobas were and had the best of them all at commandment. Then was Jack Falstaff, now Sir John, a boy, and page to Thomas Mowbray, Duke of Norfolk.

Sil This Sir John, cousin, that comes hither anon about soldiers?   31

Shal The same Sir John, the very same. I see him break Skogan's head at the court-gate, when a' was a crack not thus high   and the very same day did I fight with one Sampson Stockfish, a fruiterer, behind Gray's Inn   Jesu, Jesu, the mad days that I have spent ! and to see how many of my old acquaintance are dead !

Sil We shall all follow, cousin   39

Shal Certain, 'tis certain , very sure, very sure : death, as the Psalmist saith, is certain to all , all shall die   How a good yoke of bullocks at Stamford fair ?

Sil By my troth, I was not there

Shal Death is certain   Is old Double of your town living yet ?

Sil Dead, sir.

Shal Jesu, Jesu, dead ! a' drew a good bow ; and dead ! a' shot a fine shoot   John a Gaunt loved him well and betted much money on his head   Dead ! a' would have clapped i' the clout at twelve score , and carried you a forehand shaft a fourteen and fourteen and a half, that it would have done a man's heart good to see.   How a score of ewes now ?

Sil Thereafter as they be   a score of good ewes may be worth ten pounds

Shal And is old Double dead ?

Sil Here come two of Sir John Falstaff's men, as I think   60

Enter BARDOLPH and one with him

Bard Good morrow, honest gentlemen · I beseech you, which is Justice Shallow ?

Shal I am Robert Shallow, sir , a poor esquire of this county, and one of the king's justices of the peace · what is your good pleasure with me ?

Bard My captain, sir, commends him to you : 'my captain, Sir John Falstaff, a tall gentleman, by heaven, and a most gallant leader

Shal He greets me well, sir.   I knew him a good backsword man   How doth the good knight ? may I ask how my lady his wife doth ?   71

Bard Sir, pardon , a soldier is better accommodated than with a wife.

Shal It is well said, in faith, sir ; and it is well said indeed too   Better accommodated ! it is good , yea, indeed, is it good phrases are surely, and ever were, very commendable.   Accommodated ! it comes of ' accommodo.' very good , a good phrase.   79

Bard Pardon me, sir ; I have heard the word.   Phrase call you it ? by this good day,

I know not the phrase ; but I will maintain the word with my sword to be a soldier-like word, and a word of exceeding good command, by heaven   Accommodated , that is, when a man is, as they say, accommodated , or when a man is, being, whereby a' may be thought to be accommodated ; which is an excellent thing.

Shal It is very just.   89

Enter FALSTAFF.

Look, here comes good Sir John.   Give me your good hand, give me your worship's good hand · by my troth, you like well and bear your years very well . welcome, good Sir John

Fal I am glad to see you well, good Master Robert Shallow . Master Surecard, as I think?

Shal No, Sir John , it is my cousin Silence, in commission with me

Fal Good Master Silence, it well befits you should be of the peace

Sil Your good worship is welcome.   100

Fal Fie ! this is hot weather, gentlemen. Have you provided me here half a dozen'sufficient men ?

Shal Marry, have we, sir   Will you sit ?

Fal Let me see them, I beseech you

Shal Where's the roll ? where's the roll ? where's the roll ?   Let me see, let me see, let me see   So, so, so, so, so, so, so : yea, marry, sir · Ralph Mouldy !   Let them appear as I call , let them do so, let them do so   Let me see ; where is Mouldy ?   111

Moul Here, an't please you.

Shal What think you, Sir John ? a goodlimbed fellow ; young, strong, and of good friends

Fal Is thy name Mouldy ?

Moul Yea, an't please you

Fal 'Tis the more time thou wert used.

Shal Ha, ha, ha ! most excellent, i' faith ! things that are mouldy lack use · very singular good ! in faith, well said, Sir John, very well said.   120

Fal Prick him.

Moul I was pricked well enough before, an you could have let me alone   my old dame will be undone now for one to do her husbandry and her drudgery : you need not to have pricked me ; there are other men fitter to go out than I

Fal Go to : peace, Mouldy ; you shall go. Mouldy, it is time you were spent

Moul Spent !   129

Shal Peace, fellow, peace ; stand aside · know you where you are ?   For the other, Sir John · let me see.   Simon Shadow !

Fal Yea, marry, let me have him to sit under   he's like to be a cold soldier.

Shal Where's Shadow ?

Shad Here, sir.

Fal Shadow, whose son art thou ?

Shad My mother's son, sir.

Fal Thy mother's son ! like enough, and thy father's shadow: so the son of the female is the shadow of the male: it is often so, indeed ; but much of the father's substance !

Shal. Do you like him, Sir John ?

Fal. Shadow will serve for summer ; prick him, for we have a number of shadows to fill up the muster-book.

Shal. Thomas Wart !

Fal. Where's he ?

Wart. Here, sir.

Fal. Is thy name Wart ?   150

Wart. Yea, sir.

Fal. Thou art a very ragged wart.

Shal. Shall I prick him down, Sir John ?

Fal. It were superfluous ; for his apparel is built upon his back and the whole frame stands upon pins : prick him no more.

Shal. Ha, ha, ha ! you can do it, sir ; you can do it : I commend you well. Francis Feeble !

Fee. Here, sir.

Fal. What trade art thou, Feeble ?   160

Fee. A woman's tailor, sir.

Shal. Shall I prick him, sir ?

Fal. You may : but if he had been a man's tailor, he'ld ha' pricked you. Wilt thou make as many holes in an enemy's battle as thou hast done in a woman's petticoat ?

Fee. I will do my good will, sir ; you can have no more.

Fal. Well said, good woman's tailor ! well said, courageous Feeble ! thou wilt be as valiant as the wrathful dove or most magnanimous mouse. Prick the woman's tailor : well, Master Shallow ; deep, Master Shallow.

Fee. I would Wart might have gone, sir.

Fal. I would thou wert a man's tailor, that thou mightst mend him and make him fit to go. I cannot put him to a private soldier that is the leader of so many thousands : let that suffice, most forcible Feeble.

Fee. It shall suffice, sir.   180

Fal. I am bound to thee, reverend Feeble. Who is next ?

Shal. Peter Bullcalf o' the green !

Fal. Yea, marry, let's see Bullcalf.

Bull. Here, sir.

Fal. 'Fore God, a likely fellow ! Come, prick me Bullcalf till he roar again.

Bull. O Lord ! good my lord captain,—

Fal. What, dost thou roar before thou art picked ?   190

Bull. O Lord, sir ! I am a diseased man.

Fal. What disease hast thou ?

Bull. A whoreson cold, sir, a cough, sir, which I caught with ringing in the king's affairs upon his coronation-day, sir.

Fal. Come, thou shalt go to the wars in a gown ; we will have away thy cold ; and I will take such order that my friends shall ring for thee. Is here all ?   199

Shal. Here is two more called than your number ; you must have but four here, sir : and so, I pray you, go in with me to dinner.

Fal. Come, I will go drink with you, but I cannot tarry dinner. I am glad to see you, by my troth, Master Shallow.

Shal. O, Sir John, do you remember since we lay all night in the windmill in Saint George's field ?

Fal. No more of that, good Master Shallow, no more of that.

Shal. Ha ! 'twas a merry night. And is Jane Nightwork alive ?   211

Fal. She lives, Master Shallow.

Shal. She never could away with me.

Fal. Never, never ; she would always say she could not abide Master Shallow.

Shal. By the mass, I could anger her to the heart. She was then a bona-roba. Doth she hold her own well ?

Fal. Old, old, Master Shallow.   219

Shal. Nay, she must be old ; she cannot choose but be old ; certain she's old ; and had Robin Nightwork by old Nightwork before I came to Clement's Inn.

Sil. That's fifty-five year ago.

Shal. Ha, cousin Silence, that thou hadst seen that that this knight and I have seen ! Ha, Sir John, said I well ?

Fal. We have heard the chimes at midnight, Master Shallow.   229

Shal. That we have, that we have, that we have ; in faith, Sir John, we have : our watchword was ' Hem boys !' Come, let's to dinner; come, let's to dinner : Jesus, the days that we have seen ! Come, come.

[*Exeunt Falstaff and the Justices*

Bull. Good Master Corporate Bardolph, stand my friend ; and here's four Harry ten shillings in French crowns for you. In very truth, sir, I had as lief be hanged, sir, as go : and yet, for mine own part, sir, I do not care ; but rather, because I am unwilling, and, for mine own part, have a desire to stay with my friends ; else, sir, I did not care, for mine own part, so much.

Bard. Go to ; stand aside.

Moul. And, good master corporal captain, for my old dame's sake, stand my friend : she has nobody to do any thing about her when I am gone ; and she is old, and cannot help herself : you shall have forty, sir.   249

Bard. Go to ; stand aside.

Fee. By my troth, I care not ; a man can die but once : we owe God a death : I'll ne'er bear a base mind : an't be my destiny, so ; an't be not, so : no man is too good to serve's prince ; and let it go which way it will, he that dies this year is quit for the next.

Bard. Well said ; thou'rt a good fellow.

Fee. Faith, I'll bear no base mind.

Re-enter FALSTAFF *and the Justices.*

Fal. Come, sir, which men shall I have ?

Shal. Four of which you please.

Bard. Sir, a word with you : I have three pound to free Mouldy and Bullcalf.   261

Fal. Go too ; well.   [have ?

Shal. Come, Sir John, which four will you

Fal. Do you choose for me.

Shal. Marry, then, Mouldy, Bullcalf, Feeble and Shadow.

Fal. Mouldy and Bullcalf for you, Mouldy, stay at home till you are past service : and for your part, Bullcalf, grow till you come unto it . I will none of you   271

Shal. Sir John, Sir John, do not yourself wrong   they are your likeliest men, and I would have you served with the best

Fal. Will you tell me, Master Shallow, how to choose a man ? Care I for the limb, the thewes, the stature, bulk, and big assemblance of a man ! Give me the spirit, Master Shallow Here's Wart , you see what a ragged appearance it is , a' shall charge you and discharge you with the motion of a pewterer's hammer, come off and on swifter than he that gibbets on the brewer's bucket   And this same half-faced fellow, Shadow , give me this man   he presents no mark to the enemy , the foeman may with as great aim level at the edge of a penknife   And for a retreat , how swiftly will this Feeble the woman's tailor run off ' O, give me the spare men, and spare me the great ones.   Put me a caliver into Wart's hand, Bardolph   290

Bard   Hold, Wart, traverse , thus, thus, thus.

Fal   Come, manage me your caliver   So very well   go to   very good, exceeding good O, give me always a little, lean, old, chapt, bald shot.   Well said, i' faith, Wart , thou'rt a good scab   hold, there's a tester for thee

Shal   He is not his craft's master , he doth not do it right   I remember at Mile-end Green, when I lay at Clement's Inn,—I was then Sir Dagonet in Arthur's show,—there was a little quiver fellow, and a' would manage you his piece thus ; and a' would about and about, and come you in and come you in ' rah, tah, tah,' would a' say , ' bounce ' would a' say , and away again would a' go, and again would a' come   I shall ne'er see such a fellow

Fal. These fellows will do well, Master Shallow   God keep you, Master Silence . I will not use many words with you   Fare you well, gentlemen both · I thank you   I must a dozen mile to-night   Bardolph, give the soldiers coats   311

Shal   Sir John, the Lord bless you '   God prosper your affairs '   God send us peace ' At your return visit our house , let our old acquaintance be renewed , peradventure I will with ye to the court

Fal   'Fore God, I would you would, Master Shallow

Shal   Go to ; I have spoke at a word.   God keep you   320

Fal   Fare you well, gentle gentlemen [*Exeunt Justices*] On, Bardolph, lead the men away   [*Exeunt Bardolph, Recruits, &c*] As I return, I will fetch off these justices   I do see the bottom of Justice Shallow. Lord, Lord, how subject we old men are to this vice of lying '   This same starved justice hath done nothing but prate to me of the wildness of his youth, and the feats he hath done about Turnbull Street   and every third word a lie, duer

paid to the hearer than the Turk's tribute.   I do remember him at Clement's Inn like a man made after supper of a cheese-paring   when a' was naked, he was, for all the world, like a forked radish, with a head fantastically carved upon it with a knife . a' was so forlorn, that his dimensions to any thick sight were invincible · a' was the very genius of famine , yet lecherous as a monkey, and the whores called him mandrake· a' came ever in the rearward of the fashion, and sung those tunes to the overscutched huswives that he heard the carmen whistle, and swear they were his fancies or his good-nights   And now is this Vice's dagger become a squire, and talks as familiarly of John a Gaunt as if he had been sworn brother to him , and I'll be sworn a' ne'er saw him but once in the Tilt-yard , and then he burst his head for crowding among the marshal's men   I saw it, and told John a Gaunt he beat his own name ; for you might have thrust him and all his apparel into an eel-skin , the case of a treble hautboy was a mansion for him, a court   and now has he land and beefs. Well, I'll be acquainted with him, if I return ; and it shall go hard but I will make him a philosopher's two stones to me   if the young dace be a bait for the old pike, I see no reason in the law of nature but I may snap at him. Let time shape, and there an end.   [*Exit.*

ACT IV.

SCENE I.   *Yorkshire.   Gaultree Forest.*

Enter the ARCHBISHOP OF YORK, MOWBRAY, HASTINGS, *and others*

Arch   What is this forest call'd ?

Hast   'Tis Gaultree Forest, an't shall please your grace.

Arch   Here stand, my lords ; and send discoverers forth
To know the numbers of our enemies.

Hast   We have sent forth already.

Arch   'Tis well done.
My friends and brethren in these great affairs,
I must acquaint you that I have received
New-dated letters from Northumberland ;
Their cold intent, tenor and substance, thus :
Here doth he wish his person, with such powers
As might hold sortance with his quality,   11
The which he could not levy ; whereupon
He is retired, to ripe his growing fortunes,
To Scotland : and concludes in hearty prayers
That your attempts may overlive the hazard
And fearful meeting of their opposite.

Mowb.   Thus do the hopes we have in him touch ground
And dash themselves to pieces

         Enter a Messenger.

Hast.   Now, what news?

Mess   West of this forest, scarcely off a mile,

In goodly form comes on the enemy .   20
And, by the ground they hide, I judge their
number
Upon or near the rate of thirty thousand
  Mowb   The just proportion that we gave
them out
Let us sway on and face them in the field
  Arch   What well-appointed leader fronts
us here ?

Enter WESTMORELAND

  Mowb   I think it is my Lord of Westmore-
land
  West.   Health and fair greeting from our
general,
The prince, Lord John and Duke of Lancaster
  Arch.   Say on, my Lord of Westmoreland,
in peace
What doth concern your coming ?
  West.   ·   Then, my lord, 30
Unto your grace do I in chief address
The substance of my speech   If that rebel-
lion
Came like itself, in base and abject routs,
Led on by bloody youth, guarded with rags,
And countenanced by boys and beggary,
I say, if damn'd commotion so appear'd,
In his true, native and most proper shape,
You, reverend father, and these noble lords
Had not been here, to dress the ugly form
Of base and bloody insurrection   40
With your fair honors   You, lord arch-
bishop,
Whose see is by a civil peace maintain'd,
Whose beard the silver hand of peace hath
touch'd,   tutor'd,
Whose learning and good letters peace hath
Whose white investments figure innocence,
The dove and very blessed spirit of peace,
Wherefore do you so ill translate yourself
Out of the speech of peace that bears such
grace,
Into the harsh and boisterous tongue of war ,
Turning your books to † graves, your ink to
blood,   50
Your pens to lances and your tongue divine
To a loud trumpet and a point of war ?
  Arch   Wherefore do I this ? so the ques-
tion stands
Briefly to this end   we are all diseased,
And with our surfeiting and wanton hours
Have brought ourselves into a burning fever,
And we must bleed for it , of which disease
Our late king, Richard, being infected, died
But, my most noble Lord of Westmoreland,
I take not on me here as a physician,   60
Nor do I as an enemy to peace
Troop in the throngs of military men ;
But rather show awhile like fearful war,
To diet rank minds sick of happiness
And purge the obstructions which begin to
stop
Our very veins of life   Hear me more plainly
I have in equal balance justly weigh'd
What wrongs our arms may do, what wrongs
we suffer,

And find our griefs heavier than our offences
We see which way the stream of time doth
run,   70
And are enforced from our most quiet there
By the rough torrent of occasion ,
And have the summary of all our griefs,
When time shall serve, to show in articles ,
Which long ere this we offer'd to the king,
And might by no suit gain our audience
When we are wrong'd and would unfold our
griefs,
We are denied access unto his person
Even by those men that most have done us
wrong
The dangers of the days but newly gone,   80
Whose memory is written on the earth
With yet appearing blood, and the examples
Of every minute's instance, present now,
Hath put us in these ill-beseeming arms,
Not to break peace or any branch of it,
But to establish here a peace indeed,
Concurring both in name and quality
  West   When ever yet was your appeal
denied "
Wherein have you been galled by the king ?
What peer hath been suborn'd to grate on you,
That you should seal this lawless bloody book
Of forged rebellion with a seal divine
And consecrate commotion's bitter edge ?
  Arch   † My brother general, the common-
wealth,
To brother born an household cruelty,
I make my quarrel in particular
  West   There is no need of any such re-
dress ,
Or if there were, it not belongs to you
  Mowb   Why not to him in part, and to us
all
That feel the bruises of the days before,   100
And suffer the condition of these times
To lay a heavy and unequal hand
Upon our honors ?
  West   O, my good Lord Mowbray,
Construe the times to their necessities,
And you shall say indeed, it is the time,
And not the king, that doth you injuries
Yet for your part, it not appears to me
Either from the king or in the present time
That you should have an inch of any ground
To build a grief on   were you not restored
To all the Duke of Norfolk's signories,   111
Your noble and right well remember'd father's ?
  Mowb   What thing, in honor, had my father
lost,
That need to be revived and breathed in me ?
The king that loved him, as the state stood
then,
Was force perforce compell'd to banish him
And then that Harry Bolingbroke and he,
Being mounted and both roused in their seats,
Their neighing coursers daring of the spur
Their armed staves in charge, their beavers
down,   120
Then eyes of fire sparkling through sights of
steel
And the loud trumpet blowing them together,

28

Then, then, when there was nothing could
    have stay'd
My father from the breast of Bolingbroke,
O, when the king did throw his warder down,
His own life hung upon the staff he threw ;
Then threw he down himself and all their
    lives
That by indictment and by dint of sword
Have since miscarried under Bolingbroke.
    West. You speak, Lord Mowbray, now you
      know not what.   130
The Earl of Hereford was reputed then
In England the most valiant gentleman :
Who knows on whom fortune would then have
    smiled ?
But if your father had been victor there,
He ne'er had borne it out of Coventry :
For all the country in a general voice
Cried hate upon him ; and all their prayers
    and love
Were set on Hereford, whom they doted on
And bless'd and graced indeed, more than the
    king.
But this is mere digression from my purpose.
Here come I from our princely general   141
To know your griefs ; to tell you from his grace
That he will give you audience ; and wherein
It shall appear that your demands are just,
You shall enjoy them, every thing set off
That might so much as think you enemies.
    Mowb. But he hath forced us to compel this
      offer ;
And it proceeds from policy, not love.
    West. Mowbray, you overween to take it
      so ;
This offer comes from mercy, not from fear :
For, lo ! within a ken our army lies,   151
Upon mine honor, all too confident
To give admittance to a thought of fear.
Our battle is more full of names than yours,
Our men more perfect in the use of arms,
Our armor all as strong, our cause the best ;
Then reason will our heart should be as good :
Say you not then our offer is compell'd.
    Mowb. Well, by my will we shall admit no
      parley.
    West. That argues but the shame of your
      offence :   160
A rotten case abides no handling.
    Hast. Hath the Prince John a full commis-
      sion,
In very ample virtue of his father,
To hear and absolutely to determine
Of what conditions we shall stand upon ?
    West. That is intended in the general's
      name :
I muse you make so slight a question.
    Arch. Then take, my Lord of Westmore-
      land, this schedule,
For this contains our general grievances:
Each several article herein redress'd,   170
All members of our cause, both here and
    hence,
That are insinew'd to this action,
Acquitted by a true substantial form
And present execution of our wills

To us and to our purposes confined,
We come within our awful banks again
And knit our powers to the arm of peace.
    West. This will I show the general. Please
      you, lords,
In sight of both our battles we may meet ; 179
And either end in peace, which God so frame !
Or to the place of difference call the swords
Which must decide it.
    Arch. My lord, we will do so. [*Exit West.*
    Mowb. There is a thing within my bosom
      tells me
That no conditions of our peace can stand.
    Hast. Fear you not that : if we can make
      our peace
Upon such large terms and so absolute
As our conditions shall consist upon,
Our peace shall stand as firm as rocky moun-
    tains.
    Mowb. Yea, but our valuation shall be such
That every slight and false-derived cause, 190
Yea, every idle, nice and wanton reason
Shall to the king taste of this action :
That, were our royal faiths martyrs in love,
We shall be winnow'd with so rough a wind
That even our corn shall seem as light as chaff
And good from bad find no partition.
    Arch. No, no, my lord.   Note this ; the
      king is weary
Of dainty and such picking grievances :
For he hath found to end one doubt by death
Revives two greater in the heirs of life,   200
And therefore will he wipe his tables clean
And keep no tell-tale to his memory
That may repeat and history his loss
To new remembrance ; for full well he knows
He cannot so precisely weed this land
As his misdoubts present occasion :
His foes are so enrooted with his friends
That, plucking to unfix an enemy,
He doth unfasten so and shake a friend :
So that this land, like an offensive wife   210
That hath enraged him on to offer strokes,
As he is striking, holds his infant up
And hangs resolved correction in the arm
That was uprear'd to execution.
    Hast. Besides, the king hath wasted all his
      rods
On late offenders, that he now doth lack
The very instruments of chastisement :
So that his power, like to a fangless lion,
May offer, but not hold.
    Arch.   'Tis very true :
And therefore be assured, my good lord mar-
      shal,   220
If we do now make our atonement well,
Our peace will, like a broken limb united,
Grow stronger for the breaking.
    Mowb.   Be it so.
Here is return'd my Lord of Westmoreland.

    Re-enter WESTMORELAND.

    West. The prince is here at hand : pleaseth
      your lordship
To meet his grace just distance 'tween our
      armies.

Mowb. Your grace of York, in God's name,
then, set forward
Arch Before, and greet his grace   my lord,
we come.   [*Exeunt.*

SCENE II   *Another part of the forest.*

Enter, from one side, MOWBRAY, *attended;
afterwards the* ARCHBISHOP, HASTINGS,
and others from the other side, PRINCE
JOHN OF LANCASTER, *and* WESTMORE-
LAND , Officers, *and others with them*

Lan You are well encounter'd here, my
cousin Mowbray
Good day to you, gentle lord archbishop ,
And so to you, Lord Hastings, and to all
My Lord of York it better show'd with you
When that your flock, assembled by the bell,
Encircled you to hear with reverence
Your exposition on the holy text
Than now to see you here an iron man,
Cheering a rout of rebels with your drum,   9
Turning the word to sword and life to death
That man that sits within a monarch's heart,
And ripens in the sunshine of his favor,
Would he abuse the countenance of the king,
Alack, what mischiefs might he set abrooch
In shadow of such greatness ! With you, lord
bishop,
It is even so. Who hath not heard it spoken
How deep you were within the books of God ?
To us the speaker in his parliament ,
To us the imagined voice of God himself ,
The very opener and intelligencer   20
Between the grace, the sanctities of heaven
And our dull workings O, who shall believe
But you misuse the reverence of your place,
Employ the countenance and grace of heaven,
As a false favorite doth his prince's name,
In deeds dishonorable ? You have ta'en up,
Under the counterfeited zeal of God,
The subjects of his substitute, my father,
And both against the peace of heaven and him
Have here up-swarm'd them.
Arch.   Good my Lord of Lancaster, 30
I am not here against your father's peace ;
But, as I told my lord of Westmoreland,
The time misorder'd doth, in common sense,
Crowd us and crush us to this monstrous form,
To hold our safety up. I sent your grace
The parcels and particulars of our grief,
The which hath been with scorn shoved from
the court,
Whereon this Hydra son of war is born ;
Whose dangerous eyes may well be charm'd
asleep
With grant of our most just and right desires,
And true obedience, of this madness cured,
Stoop tamely to the foot of majesty.
Mowb. If not, we ready are to try our for-
tunes
To the last man.
Hast.   And though we here fall down,
We have supplies to second our attempt .
If they miscarry, theirs shall second them ;
And so success of mischief shall be born

And heir from heir shall hold this quarrel up
Whiles England shall have generation
Lan   You are too shallow, Hastings, much
too shallow,   50
To sound the bottom of the after-times
West Pleaseth your grace to answer them
directly
How far forth you do like these articles
Lan   I like them all, and do allow them
well
And swear here, by the honor of my blood,
My father's purposes have been mistook,
And some about him have too lavishly
Wrested his meaning and authority
My lord, these griefs shall be with speed re-
dress'd ,
Upon my soul, they shall   If this may please
you,   60
Discharge your powers unto their several
counties,
As we will ours   and here between the armies
Let's drink together friendly and embrace,
That all their eyes may bear those tokens
home
Of our restored love and amity
Arch. I take your princely word for these
redresses
Lan. I give it you, and will maintain my
word
And thereupon I drink unto your grace
Hast Go, captain, and deliver to the army
This news of peace   let them have pay, and
part   70
I know it will well please them   Hie thee,
captain   [*Exit Officer*
Arch To you, my noble Lord of Westmore-
land
West I pledge your grace, and, if you knew
what pains
I have bestow'd to breed this present peace,
You would drink freely   but my love to ye
Shall show itself more openly hereafter
Arch I do not doubt you.
West   I am glad of it.
Health to my lord and gentle cousin, Mow-
bray
Mowb You wish me health in very happy
season ;
For I am, on the sudden, something ill   80
Arch. Against ill chances men are ever
merry ,
But heaviness foreruns the good event
West Therefore be merry, coz , since sud-
den sorrow
Serves to say thus, 'some good thing comes
to-morrow.'
Arch Believe me, I am passing light in
spirit
Mowb So much the worse, if your own
rule be true   [*Shouts within.*
Lan. The word of peace is render'd hark,
how they shout '
Mowb This had been cheerful after victory.
Arch. A peace is of the nature of a con-
quest ,
For then both parties nobly are subdued, 90

And neither party loser.

Lan.   Go, my lord,
And let our army be discharged too.
                    [*Exit Westmoreland.*
And, good my lord, so please you, let our
    trains
March by us, that we may peruse the men
We should have coped withal.

Arch.   Go, good Lord Hastings,
And, ere they be dismiss'd, let them march by.
                         [*Exit Hastings.*
Lan. I trust, lords, we shall lie to-night
    together.

                Re-enter WESTMORELAND.

Now, cousin, wherefore stands our army still?
West. The leaders, having charge from you
    to stand,
Will not go off until they hear you speak. 100
Lan. They know their duties.

                Re-enter HASTINGS.

Hast. My lord, our army is dispersed al-
    ready;
Like youthful steers unyoked, they take their
    courses
East, west, north, south; or, like a school
    broke up,
Each hurries toward his home and sporting-
    place.
West. Good tidings, my Lord Hastings;
    for the which
I do arrest thee, traitor, of high treason:
And you, lord archbishop, and you, lord Mow-
    bray,
Of capital treason I attach you both.
Mowb. Is this proceeding just and honor-
    able?   110
West. Is your assembly so?
Arch. Will you thus break your faith?
Lan.   I pawn'd thee none:
I promised you redress of these same griev-
    ances
Whereof you did complain; which, by mine
    honor,
I will perform with a most Christian care.
But for you, rebels, look to taste the due
Meet for rebellion and such acts as yours.
Most shallowly did you these arms commence,
Fondly brought here and foolishly sent hence.
Strike up our drums, pursue the scatter'd
    stray: 120
God, and not we, hath safely fought to-day.
Some guard these traitors to the block of
    death,
Treason's true bed and yielder up of breath.
                         [*Exeunt.*

SCENE III. *Another part of the forest.*

Alarum. Excursions. Enter FALSTAFF
    and COLEVILE, *meeting.*

Fal. What's your name, sir? of what condi-
tion are you, and of what place, I pray?
Cole. I am a knight, sir, and my name is
Colevile of the dale.
Fal. Well, then, Colevile is your name, a

knight is your degree, and your place the dale:
Colevile shall be still your name, a traitor your
degree, and the dungeon your place, a place
deep enough; so shall you be still Colevile of
the dale.   10
Cole. Are not you Sir John Falstaff?
Fal. As good a man as he, sir, whoe'er I
am. Do ye yield, sir? or shall I sweat for
you? If I do sweat, they are the drops of
thy lovers, and they weep for thy death:
therefore rouse up fear and trembling, and do
observance to my mercy.
Cole. I think you are Sir John Falstaff, and
in that thought yield me.   19
Fal. I have a whole school of tongues in
this belly of mine, and not a tongue of them
all speaks any other word but my name. An I
had but a belly of any indifference, I were
simply the most active fellow in Europe: my
womb, my womb, my womb, undoes me.
Here comes our general.

Enter PRINCE JOHN OF LANCASTER, WEST-
    MORELAND, BLUNT, *and others.*

Lan. The heat is past; follow no further
    now:
Call in the powers, good cousin Westmoreland.
                    [*Exit Westmoreland.*
Now, Falstaff, where have you been all this
    while?
When every thing is ended, then you come: 30
These tardy tricks of yours will, on my life,
One time or other break some gallows' back.
Fal. I would be sorry, my lord, but it should
be thus: I never knew yet but rebuke and
check was the reward of valor. Do you think
me a swallow, an arrow, or a bullet? have I,
in my poor and old motion, the expedition of
thought? I have speeded hither with the very
extremest inch of possibility; I have foundered
nine score and odd posts: and here, travel-
tainted as I am, have, in my pure and immac-
ulate valor, taken Sir John Colevile of the dale,
a most furious knight and valorous enemy.
But what of that? he saw me, and yielded;
that I may justly say, with the hook-nosed
fellow of Rome, 'I came, saw, and overcame.'
Lan. It was more of his courtesy than your
deserving.
Fal. I know not: here he is, and here I
yield him: and I beseech your grace, let it be
booked with the rest of this day's deeds; or,
by the Lord, I will have it in a particular ballad else, with mine own picture on the top on't,
Colevile kissing my foot: to the which course
if I be enforced, if you do not all show like gilt
twopences to me, and I in the clear sky of
fame o'ershine you as much as the full moon
doth the cinders of the element, which show
like pins' heads to her, believe not the word of
the noble: therefore let me have right, and let
desert mount.   61
Lan. Thine's too heavy to mount.
Fal. Let it shine, then.
Lan. Thine's too thick to shine.
Fal. Let it do something, my good lord,

that may do me good, and call it what you
wil.
Len. Is thy name Colevile ?
Cole. It is, my lord
Lan. A famous rebel art thou, Colevile
Fal And a famous true subject took him. 70
Cole I am, my lord, but as my betters are
That led me hither , had they been ruled by
    me,
You should have won them dearer than you
    have.
Fal. I know not how they sold themselves·
but thou, like a kind fellow, gavest thyself
away gratis , and I thank thee for thee.

Re-enter WESTMORELAND.

Lan. Now, have you left pursuit ?
West. Retreat is made and execution stay'd.
Lan Send Colevile with his confederates
To York, to present execution .   80
Blunt, lead him hence , and see you guard
    him sure
    [*Exeunt Blunt and others with Colevile.*
And now dispatch we toward the court, my
    lords ·
I hear the king my father is sore sick ·
Our news shall go before us to his majesty,
Which, cousin, you shall bear to comfort him,
And we with sober speed will follow you
    Fal My lord, I beseech you, give me leave
    to go
Through Gloucestershire: and, when you come
    to court,
Stand my good lord, pray, in your good report
    Lan. Fare you well, Falstaff . I, in my con-
    dition,   90
Shall better speak of you than you deserve
    [*Exeunt all but Falstaff*
Fal. I would you had but the wit 'twere
better than your dukedom Good faith, this
same young sober-blooded boy doth not love
me , nor a man cannot make him laugh . but
that's no marvel, he drinks no wine There's
never none of these demure boys come to any
proof for thin drink doth so over-cool their
blood, and making many fish-meals, that they
fall into a kind of male green-sickness , and
then, when they marry, they get wenches
they are generally fools and cowards , which
some of us should be too, but for inflamma-
tion. A good sherris sack hath a two-fold operation in it It ascends me into the brain ,
dries me there all the foolish and dull and
curdy vapors which environ it , makes it apprehensive, quick, forgetive, full of nimble
fiery and delectable shapes , which, delivered
o'er to the voice, the tongue, which is the birth,
becomes excellent wit The second property
of your excellent sherris is, the warming of
the blood ; which, before cold and settled, left
the liver white and pale, which is the badge of
pusillanimity and cowardice , but the sherris
warms it and makes it course from the inwards to the parts extreme : it illumineth the
face, which as a beacon gives warning to all
the rest of this little kingdom, man, to arm ;

and then the vital commoners and inland petty
spirit, muster me all to their captain, the
heart, who, great and puffed up with this ret-
inue, doth any deed of courage , and this valor
comes of sherris So that skill in the weapon
is nothing without sack for that sets it a-work;
and learning a mere hoard of gold kept by a
devil, till sack commences it and sets it in act
and use. Hereof comes it that Prince Harry
is valiant , for the cold blood he did naturally
inherit of his father, he hath, like lean, sterile
and bare land, manured, husbanded and tilled
with excellent endeavor of drinking good and
good store of fertile sherris, that he is become
very hot and valiant It I had a thousand
sons, the first humane principle I would teach
them should be, to forswear thin potations
and to addict themselves to sack.

Enter BARDOLPH.

How now Bardolph ?
    Bard. The army is discharged all and gone
    Fal Let them go I'll through Gloucester-
shire , and there will I visit Master Robert
Shallow, esquire I have him already temper-
ing between my finger and my thumb, and
shortly will I seal with him Come away
               [*Exeunt.*

SCENE IV   *Westminster*   *The Jerusalem*
           Chamber

Enter the KING, *the* PRINCES THOMAS OF
CLARENCE *and* HUMPHREY OF GLOUCES-
TER WARWICK *and others*

King Now, lords, if God doth give suc-
    cessful end
To this debate that bleedeth at our doors,
We will our youth lead on to higher fields
And draw no swords but what are sanctified
Our navy is address'd, our power collected,
Our substitutes in absence well invested.
And every thing lies level to our wish
Only , we want a little personal strength ,
And pause us, till these rebels, now afoot
Come underneath the yoke of government 10
    War Both which we doubt not but your
    majesty
Shall soon enjoy.
    King Humphrey, my son of Gloucester,
Where is the prince your brother ?
    Glou I think he's gone to hunt, my lord,
    at Windsor
    King And how accompanied ?
    Glou.   I do not know, my lord.
    King Is not his brother, Thomas of Clar-
    ence, with him ?
    Glou No, my good lord , he is in presence
    here,
    Cla What would my lord and father ?
    King Nothing but well to thee, Thomas of
    Clarence
How chance thou art not with the prince thy
    brother ?   20
He loves thee, and thou dost neglect him,
    Thomas ,
Thou hast a better place in his affection

Than all thy brothers: cherish it, my boy,
And noble offices thou mayst effect
Of mediation, after I am dead,
Between his greatness and thy other brethren:
Therefore omit him not; blunt not his love,
Nor lose the good advantage of his grace
By seeming cold or careless of his will;
For he is gracious, if he be observed: 30
He hath a tear for pity and a hand
Open as day for melting charity:
Yet notwithstanding, being incensed, he's flint,
As humorous as winter and as sudden
As flaws congealed in the spring of day.
His temper, therefore, must be well observed
Chide him for faults, and do it reverently,
When you perceive his blood inclined to mirth;
But, being moody, give him line and scope,
Till that his passions, like a whale on ground,
Confound themselves with working.   Learn
    this, Thomas,   41
And thou shalt prove a shelter to thy friends,
A hoop of gold to bind thy brothers in,
That the united vessel of their blood,
Mingled with venom of suggestion—
As, force perforce, the age will pour it in—
Shall never leak, though it do work as strong
As aconitum or rash gunpowder.

   Clar.   I shall observe him with all care and
    love.
   King.   Why art thou not at Windsor with
    him, Thomas ?
   Clar.   He is not there to-day; he dines in
    London.
   King.   And how accompanied? canst thou
    tell that?
   Clar.   With Poins, and other his continual
    followers.
   King.   Most subject is the fattest soil to
    weeds ;
And he, the noble image of my youth,
Is overspread with them: therefore my grief
Stretches itself beyond the hour of death:
The blood weeps from my heart when I do
    shape
In forms imaginary the unguided days
And rotten time that you shall look upon   60
When I am sleeping with my ancestors.
For when his headstrong riot hath no curb,
When rage and hot blood are his counsellors,
When means and lavish manners meet to-
    gether,
O, with what wings shall his affection fly
Towards fronting peril and opposed decay !

   War.   My gracious lord, you look beyond
    him quite:
The prince but studies his companions
Like a strange tongue, wherein, to gain the
    language,
'Tis needful that the most immodest word   70
Be look'd upon and learn'd; which once at-
    tain'd,
Your highness knows, come to no further use
But to be known and hated. So, like gross
    terms,
The prince will in the perfectness of time
Cast off his followers ; and their memory

Shall as a pattern or a measure live,
By which his grace must meet the lives of
    others.
Turning past evils to advantages.
   King.   'Tis seldom when the bee doth leave
    her comb
In the dead carrion.

Enter WESTMORELAND.

        Who's here ?   Westmoreland ?   80
   West.   Health to my sovereign, and new hap-
    piness
Added to that that I am to deliver !
Prince John, your son, doth kiss your grace's
    hand:
Mowbray, the Bishop Scoop, Hastings and all
Are brought to the correction of your law ;
There is not now a rebel's sword unsheath'd
But peace puts forth her olive everywhere.
The manner how this action hath been borne
Here at more leisure may your highness read,
With every course in his particular.   90
   King.   O Westmoreland, thou art a summer
    bird,
Which ever in the hunch of winter sings
The lifting up of day.

Enter HARCOURT.

        Look, here's more news.
   Har.   From enemies heaven keep your ma-
    jesty;
And, when they stand against you, may they
    fall
As those that I am come to tell you of !
The Earl Northumberland and the Lord Bar-
    dolph,
With a great power of English and of Scots,
Are by the sheriff of Yorkshire overthrown:
The manner and true order of the fight   100
This packet, please it you, contains at large.
   King.   And wherefore should these good
    news make me sick?
Will fortune never come with both hands full
But write her fair words still in foulest letters?
She either gives a stomach and no food;
Such are the poor in health ; or else a feast
And takes away the stomach ; such are the rich,
That have abundance and enjoy it not.
I should rejoice now at this happy news ;   109
And now my sight fails, and my brain is giddy:
O me ! come near me ; now I am much ill.
   Glou.   Comfort, your majesty !
   Clar.   O my royal father !
   West.   My sovereign lord, cheer up yourself,
    look up.
   War.   Be patient, princes: you do know,
    these fits
Are with his highness very ordinary.
Stand from him, give him air; he'll straight be
    well.
   Clar.   No, no, he cannot long hold out these
    pangs :
The incessant care and labor of his mind
Hath wrought the mure that should confine it
    in

So thin that life looks through and will break
  out
  Glou The people fear me, for they do
  observe
Unfather'd heirs and loathly births of nature
The seasons change their manners, as the
  year
Had found some months asleep and leap'd
  them over
  Clar. The river hath thrice flow'd, no ebb
  between,
And the old folk, time's doting chronicles,
Say it did so a little time before
That our great-grandsire, Edward, sick'd and
  died
  War. Speak lower, princes, for the king
  recovers
  Glou. This apoplexy will certain be his end
  King I pray you, take me up, and bear
  me hence   131
Into some other chamber, softly, pray.

SCENE V. *Another chamber*

The KING *lying on a bed* CLARENCE, GLOU-
CESTER, WARWICK, *and others in attendance.*

  King. Let there be no noise made, my
  gentle friends,
Unless some dull and favorable hand
Will whisper music to my weary spirit.
  Wor. Call for the music in the other room
  King. Set me the crown upon my pillow
  here
  Clar His eye is hollow, and he changes
  much.
  War. Less noise, less noise!

    Enter PRINCE HENRY.

  Prince. Who saw the Duke of Clarence?
  Clar. I am here, brother, full of heaviness
  Prince How now! rain within doors, and
  none abroad!
How doth the king?   10
  Glou Exceeding ill
  Prince. Heard he the good news yet?
Tell it him
  Glou. He alter'd much upon the hearing it
  Prince If he be sick with joy, he'll re-
  cover without physic
  War. Not so much noise, my lords. sweet
  prince, speak low,
The king your father is disposed to sleep.
  Clar. Let us withdraw into the other room.
  War. Will't please your grace to go along
  with us?
  Prince. No; I will sit and watch here by
  the king [*Exeunt all but the Prince* 20
Why doth the crown lie there upon his pillow,
Being so troublesome a bedfellow?
O polish'd perturbation! golden care!
That keep'st the ports of slumber open wide
To many a watchful night! sleep with it now!
Yet not so sound and half so deeply sweet
As he whose brow with homely biggen bound
Snores out the watch of night. O majesty!
When thou dost pinch thy bearer, thou dost
  sit

Like a rich armor worn in heat of day, 30
That scalds with safety. By his gates of
  breath
There lies a downy feather which stirs not·
Did he suspire, that light and weightless down
Perforce must move. My gracious lord! my
  father!
This sleep is sound indeed, this is a sleep
That from this golden rigol hath divorced
So many English kings. Thy due from me
Is tears and heavy sorrows of the blood,
Which nature, love and filial tenderness,
Shall, O dear father, pay thee plenteously 40
My due from thee is this imperial crown,
Which, as immediate from thy place and
  blood,
Derives itself to me. Lo, here it sits,
Which God shall guard. and put the world's
  whole strength
Into one giant arm, it shall not force
This lineal honor from me. this from thee
Will I to mine leave, as 'tis left to me [*Exit.*
  King Warwick! Gloucester! Clarence!

Re-enter WARWICK, GLOUCESTER, CLARENCE,
    and the rest.

  Clar Doth the king call?
  War What would your majesty? How
  fares your grace?   50
  King Why did you leave me here alone,
  my lords?
  Clar We left the prince my brother here,
  my liege,
Who undertook to sit and watch by you
  King The Prince of Wales! Where is
  he? let me see him.
He is not here
  War. This door is open, he is gone this
  way
  Glou He came not through the chamber
  where we stay'd
  King Where is the crown? who took it
  from my pillow?
  War When we withdrew, my liege, we
  left it here
  King The prince hath ta'en it hence. go,
  seek him out   60
Is he so hasty that he doth suppose
My sleep my death?
Find him, my Lord of Warwick, chide him
  hither   [*Exit Warwick.*
This part of his conjoins with my disease,
And helps to end me. See, sons, what things
  you are!
How quickly nature falls into revolt
When gold becomes her object!
For this the foolish over-careful fathers
Have broke their sleep with thoughts, their
  brains with care,
Their bones with industry,   70
For this they have engrossed and piled up
The canker'd heaps of strange-achieved gold;
For this they have been thoughtful to invest
Their sons with arts and martial exercises
When, like the bee, culling from every flower
The virtuous sweets,

Our thighs pack'd with wax, our mouths with
    honey,
We bring it to the hive, and, like the bees,
Are murdered for our pains This bitter taste
Yield his engrossments to the ending father

Re-enter WARWICK.

Now, where is he that will not stay so long
Till his friend sickness hath determined me ?
    War My lord, I found the prince in the
      next room,
Washing with kindly tears his gentle cheeks,
With such a deep demeanor in great sorrow
That tyranny, which never quaff'd but blood,
Would, by beholding him, have wash'd his
    knife
With gentle eye-drops He is coming hither
    King But wherefore did he take away
      the crown ?

Re-enter PRINCE HENRY.

Lo, where he comes. Come hither to me,
    Harry
Depart the chamber, leave us here alone   91
    [*Exeunt Warwick and the rest*
    Prince I never thought to hear you speak
      again   [*thought*
    King Thy wish was father, Harry, to that
I stay too long by thee, I weary thee
Dost thou so hunger for mine empty chair
That thou wilt needs invest thee with my
    honors
Before thy hour be ripe ? O foolish youth !
Thou seek'st the greatness that will overwhelm
    thee
Stay but a little ; for my cloud of dignity
Is held from falling with so weak a wind   100
That it will quickly drop . my day is dim.
Thou hast stolen that which after some few
    hours
Were thine without offence ; and at my death
Thou hast seal'd up my expectation .
Thy life did manifest thou loved'st me not,
And thou wilt have me die assured of it
Thou hidest a thousand daggers in thy
    thoughts,
Which thou hast whetted on thy stony heart,
To stab at half an hour of my life
What ! canst thou not forbear me half an
    hour ?   110
Then get thee gone and dig my grave thyself,
And bid the merry bells ring to thine ear
That thou art crowned, not that I am dead
Let all the tears that should bedew my hearse
Be drops of balm to sanctify thy head
Only compound me with forgotten dust ,
Give that which gave thee life unto the
    worms
Pluck down my officers, break my decrees ,
For now a time is come to mock at form ·
Harry the Fifth is crown'd up, vanity !   120
Down, royal state ! all you sage counsellors,
    hence !
And to the English court assemble now,
From every region, apes of idleness !
Now, neighbor confines, purge you of your
    scum :

Have you a ruffian that will swear, drink,
    dance,
Revel the night, rob, murder, and commit
The oldest sins the newest kind of ways ?
Be happy, he will trouble you no more ,
England shall double gild his treble guilt, 129
England shall give him office, honor, might ,
For the fifth Harry from curb'd license plucks
The muzzle of restraint, and the wild dog
Shall flesh his tooth on every innocent
O my poor kingdom, sick with civil blows !
When that my care could not withhold thy
    riots,
What wilt thou do when riot is thy care ?
O, thou wilt be a wilderness again,
Peopled with wolves, thy old inhabitants !
    Prince. O, pardon me, my liege ! but for
      my tears,
The moist impediments unto my speech,   140
I had forestall'd this dear and deep rebuke
Ere you with grief had spoke and I had heard
The course of it so far There is your crown ,
And He that wears the crown immortally
Long guard it yours ! If I affect it more
Than as your honor and as your renown,
Let me no more from this obedience rise,
Which my most inward true and duteous spirit
Teacheth, this prostrate and exterior bending
God witness with me, when I here came in,
And found no course of breath within your
    majesty,   151
How cold it struck my heart ! If I do feign,
O, let me in my present wildness die
And never live to show the incredulous world
The noble change that I have purposed !
Coming to look on you, thinking you dead,
And dead almost, my liege, to think you were,
I spake unto this crown as having sense,
And thus upbraided it . 'The care on thee de-
    pending
Hath fed upon the body of my father ;   160
Therefore, thou best of gold art worst of gold:
Other, less fine in carat, is more precious,
Preserving life in medicine potable ;
But thou, most fine, most honor'd, most re-
    nown'd,
Hast eat thy bearer up ' Thus, my most
    royal liege,
Accusing it, I put it on my head,
To try with it, as with an enemy
That had before my face murder'd my father,
The quarrel of a true inheritor
But if it did infect my blood with joy,   170
Or swell my thoughts to any strain of pride ;
If any rebel or vain spirit of mine
Did with the least affection of a welcome
Give entertainment to the might of it,
Let God for ever keep it from my head
And make me as the poorest vassal is
That doth with awe and terror kneel to it !
    King. O my son,
God put it in thy mind to take it hence,
That thou mightst win the more thy father's
    love,   180
Pleading so wisely in excuse of it !
Come hither, Harry, sit thou by my bed ;

PRINCE HENRY.   *" There is your crown,*
And He that wears the crown immortally
Long guard it yours!"

KING HENRY IV., PART II., *page* 44?

And hear, I think, the very latest counsel
That ever I shall breathe God knows, my son,
By what by-paths and indirect crook'd ways
 met this crown , and I myself know well
How troublesome it sat upon my head
To thee it shall descend with better quiet,
Better opinion, better confirmation ,
For all the soil of the achievement goes   190
With me into the earth It seem'd in me
But as an honor snatch'd with boisterous hand,
And I had many living to upbraid
My gain of it by their assistances ,
Which daily grew to quarrel and to bloodshed,
Wounding supposed peace all these bold fears
Thou see'st with peril I have answered ,
For all my reign hath been but as a scene
Acting that argument and now my death
Changes the mode , for what in me was pur-
    chased,   200
Falls upon thee in a more fairer sort ,
So thou the garland wear'st successively
Yet, though thou stand'st more sure than I
   could do,
Thou art not firm enough, since griefs are
   green ,
And all my friends, which thou must make
   thy friends,
Have but their stings and teeth newly ta'en
   out ,
By whose fell working I was first advanced
And by whose power I well might lodge a fear
To be again displaced which to avoid,
   cut them off, and had a purpose now   210
To lead out many to the Holy Land,
Lest rest and lying still might make them look
Too near unto my state Therefore, my Harry,
Be it thy course to busy giddy minds
With foreign quarrels , that action, hence
   borne out,
May waste the memory of the former days
More would I, but my lungs are wasted so
That strength of speech is utterly denied me
How I came by the crown, O God forgive ,
And grant it may with thee in true peace live! 221
   Prince. My gracious liege,
You won it, wore it, kept it, gave it me ,
Then plain and right must my possession be
Which I with more than with a common pain
Gainst all the world will rightfully maintain

   Enter LORD JOHN OF LANCASTER.

King Look, look, here comes my John of
   Lancaster
Lan Health, peace, and happiness to my
   royal father!
King. Thou bring'st me happiness and
   peace, son John ;
But health, alack, with youthful wings is flown
From this bare wither'd trunk upon thy sight
My worldly business makes a period.   231
Where is my Lord of Warwick ?
   Prince.   My Lord of Warwick !

   Enter WARWICK, *and others.*

King. Doth any name particular belong
Into the lodging where I first did swoon ?

War 'Tis call'd Jerusalem, my noble lord
King Laud be to God ! even there my life
   must end
It hath been prophesied to me many years,
I should not die but in Jerusalem ,
Which vainly I supposed the Holy Land   239
But bear me to that chamber , there I'll lie ,
In that Jerusalem shall Harry die   [*Exeunt*

ACT V

SCENE I   *Gloucestershire.* SHALLOW'S *house*

Enter SHALLOW, FALSTAFF, BARDOLPH, *and*
   Page

   Shal By cock and pie, sir, you shall not
away to-night What, Davy, I say !
   Fal You must excuse me, Master Robert
Shallow
   Shal I will not excuse you , you shall not
be excused , excuses shall not be admitted ,
there is no excuse shall serve , you shall not
be excused Why, Davy !

   Enter DAVY

   Davy Here, sir   9
   Shal Davy, Davy. Davy, Davy, let me see,
Davy , let me see, Davy , let me see yea,
marry, William cook, bid him come hither Sir
John, you shall not be excused
   Davy Marry, sir, thus , those precepts can-
not be served and, again, sir, shall we sow
the headland with wheat ?
   Shal With red wheat, Davy But for
William cook are there no young pigeons ?
   Davy Yes, sir. Here is now the smith's note
for shoeing and plough-irons   20
   Shal Let it be cast and paid Sir John,
you shall not be excused.
   Davy Now, sir, a new link to the bucket
must need be had and, sir, do you mean to
stop any of William's wages, about the sack he
lost the other day at Hinckley fair ?
   Shal A' shall answer it Some pigeons,
Davy, a couple of short-legged hens, a joint of
mutton, and any pretty little tiny kickshaws,
tell William cook.   30
   Davy. Doth the man of war stay all night,
sir ?
   Shal Yea, Davy I will use him well. a
friend i' the court is better than a penny in
purse Use his men well, Davy , for they are
arrant knaves, and will backbite
   Davy No worse than they are backbitten,
sir ; for they have marvellous foul linen
   Shal Well conceited, Davy about thy
business, Davy   40
   Davy I beseech you, sir, to countenance
William Visor of Woncot against Clement
Perkes of the hill
   Shal. There is many complaints, Davy,
against that Visor that Visor is an arrant
knave, on my knowledge
   Davy. I grant your worship that he is a

knave, sir; but yet, God forbid, sir, but. a
knave should have some countenance at his
friend's request. An honest man, sir, is able to
speak for himself, when a knave is not. I have
served your worship truly, sir, this eight years;
and if I cannot once or twice in a quarter bear
out a knave against an honest man, I have but
a very little credit with your worship. The
knave is mine honest friend, sir; therefore, I
beseech your worship, let him be countenanced.

Shal. Go to; I say he shall have no wrong.
Look about, Davy. [*Exit Davy.*] Where are
you, Sir John? Come, come, come, off with
your boots. Give me your hand, Master Bardolph.

Bard. I am glad to see your worship.

Shal. I thank thee with all my heart, kind
Master Bardolph: and welcome, my tall fellow
[*to the Page*]. Come, sir John.

Fal. I'll follow you, good Master Robert
Shallow. [*Exit Shallow.*] Bardolph, look to
our horses. [*Exeunt Bardolph and Page.*] If
I were sawed into quantities, I should make
four dozen of such bearded hermits' staves as
Master Shallow. It is a wonderful thing to see
the semblable coherence of his men's spirits
and his: they, by observing of him, do bear
themselves like foolish justices; he, by con-
versing with them, is turned into a justice-
like serving-man: their spirits are so married
in conjunction with the participation of society
that they flock together in consent, like so
many wild-geese. If I had a suit to Master
Shallow, I would humor his men with the
imputation of being near their master: if to
his men, I would curry with Master Shallow
that no man could better command his servants.
It is certain that either wise bearing or ignorant carriage is caught, as men take diseases,
one of another: therefore let men take heed of
their company. I will devise matter enough
out of this Shallow to keep Prince Harry in
continual laughter the wearing out of six
fashions, which is four terms, or two actions,
and a' shall laugh without intervallums. O, it is
much that a lie with a slight oath and a jest with
a sad brow will do with a fellow that never
had the ache in his shoulders! O, you shall
see him laugh till his face be like a wet cloak
ill laid up!

Shal. [*Within*] Sir John!

Fal. I come, Master Shallow; I come, Mas-
ter Shallow.	[*Exit.*

SCENE II.	*Westminster. The palace.*

Enter WARWICK *and the* LORD CHIEF-JUSTICE,
meeting.

War. How now, my lord chief-justice!
whither away?

Ch. Just. How doth the king?

War. Exceeding well; his cares are now
all ended.

Ch. Just. I hope, not dead.

War. He's walk'd the way of nature;
And to our purposes he lives no more.

Ch. Just. I would his majesty had call'd
me with him:
The service that I truly did his life
Hath left me open to all injuries.

War. Indeed I think the young king loves
you not.

Ch. Just. I know he doth not, and do arm
myself	10
To welcome the condition of the time,
Which cannot look more hideously upon me
Than I have drawn it in my fantasy.

Enter LANCASTER, CLARENCE, GLOUCESTER,
WESTMORELAND, *and others.*

War. Here come the heavy issue of dead
Harry:
O that the living Harry had the temper
Of him, the worst of these three gentlemen!
How many nobles then should hold their places
That must strike sail to spirits of vile sort!

Ch. Just. O God, I fear all will be over-
turn'd!

Lan. Good morrow, cousin Warwick, good
morrow.	20

Glou. }
Clar. } Good morrow, cousin.

Lan. We meet like men that had forgot to
speak.

War. We do remember; but our argument
Is all too heavy to admit much talk.

Lan. Well, peace be with him that hath
made us heavy!

Ch. Just. Peace be with us, lest we be
heavier!

Glou. O, good my lord, you have lost a
friend indeed;
And I dare swear you borrow not that face
Of seeming sorrow, it is sure your own.

Lan. Though no man be assured what grace
to find,	30
You stand in coldest expectation:
I am the sorrier; would 'twere otherwise.

Clar. Well, you must now speak Sir John
Falstaff fair;
Which swims against your stream of quality.

Ch. Just. Sweet princes, what I did, I did
in honor,
Led by the impartial conduct of my soul:
And never shall you see that I will beg
A ragged and forestall'd remission.
If truth and upright innocency fail me,
I'll to the king my master that is dead,	40
And tell him who hath sent me after him.

War. Here comes the prince.

Enter KING HENRY *the Fifth, attended.*

Ch. Just. Good morrow; and God save
your majesty!

King. This new and gorgeous garment,
majesty,
Sits not so easy on me as you think.
Brothers, you mix your sadness with some
fear:
This is the English, not the Turkish court;
Not Amurath an Amurath succeeds,
But Harry Harry. Yet be sad, good brothers,

For, by my faith, it very well becomes you: 50
Sorrow so royally in you appears
That I will deeply put the fashion on
And wear it in my heart   why, then, be sad ,
But entertain no more of it, good brothers,
Than a joint burden laid upon us all
For me, by heaven, I bid you be assured,
I'll be your father and your brother too ,
Let me but bear your love, I'll bear your cares
Yet weep that Harry's dead , and so will I ,
But Harry lives, that shall convert those tears
By number into hours of happiness   61
Princes   We hope no other from your
    majesty
King   You all look strangely on me : and
    you most ,
You are, I think, assured I love you not
Ch Just   I am assured, if I be measured
    rightly,
Your majesty hath no just cause to hate me
King   No '
How might a prince of my great hopes forget
So great indignities you laid upon me ?
What ' rate, rebuke, and roughly send to
    prison
The immediate heir of England ' Was this
    easy ?
May this be wash'd in Lethe and forgotten ?
Ch Just   I then did use the person of your
    father ,
The image of his power lay then in me
And, in the administration of his law,
Whiles I was busy for the commonwealth,
Your highness pleased to forget my place,
The majesty and power of law and justice,
The image of the king whom I presented,
And struck me in my very seat of judgment ,
Whereon, as an offender to your father,   81
I gave bold way to my authority
And did commit you   If the deed were ill,
Be you contented, wearing now the garland,
To have a son set your decrees at nought,
To pluck down justice from your awful bench,
To trip the course of law and blunt the sword
That guards the peace and safety of your per-
    son ,
Nay, more, to spurn at your most royal image
And mock your workings in a second body. 90
Question your royal thoughts, make the case
    yours ,
Be now the father and propose a son,
Hear your own dignity so much profaned,
See your most dreadful laws so loosely
    slighted,
Behold yourself so by a son disdain'd ,
And then imagine me taking your part
And in your power soft silencing your son
After this cold consideradce, sentence me ,
And, as you are a king, speak in your state
What I have done that misbecame my place,
My person, or my liege's sovereignty.   101
King   You are right, justice, and you
    weigh this well ;
Therefore still bear the balance and the
    sword ·
And I do wish your honours may increase,

Till you do live to see a son of mine
Offend you and obey you, as I did
So shall I live to speak my father's words
' Happy am I, that have a man so bold,
That dares do justice on my proper son ,
And not less happy, having such a son,   110
That would deliver up his greatness so
Into the hands of justice ' You did commit
    me
For which, I do commit into your hand
The unstained sword that you have used to
    bear ,   [same
With this remembrance, that you use the
With the like bold, just and impartial spirit
As you have done 'gainst me   There is my
    hand
You shall be as a father to my youth
My voice shall sound as you do prompt mine
    ear,
And I will stoop and humble my intents   120
To your well-practised wise directions
And, princes all, believe me, I beseech you ;
My father is gone wild into his grave,
For in his tomb he my affections ,
And with his spirit sadly I survive,
To mock the expectation of the world,
To frustrate prophecies and to raze out
Rotten opinion, who hath writ me down
After my seeming   The tide of blood in me
Hath proudly flow'd in vanity till now   130
Now doth it turn and ebb back to the sea,
Where it shall mingle with the state of floods
And flow henceforth in formal majesty
Now call we our high court of parliament
And let us choose such limbs of noble coun-
    sel,
That the great body of our state may go
In equal rank with the best govern'd nation ;
That war, or peace, or both at once, may be
As things acquainted and familiar to us ,
In which you, father, shall have foremost
    hand   140
Our coronation done, we will accite,
As I before remember'd, all our state
And, God consigning to my good intents,
No prince nor peer shall have just cause to
    say,
God shorten Harry's happy life one day '
                                   [*Exeunt.*

SCENE III   *Gloucestershire*   SHALLOW'S
            orchard

Enter FALSTAFF, SHALLOW, SILENCE, DAVY,
    BARDOLPH, *and the Page*

Shal   Nay, you shall see my orchard,
where, in an arbor, we will eat a last year's
pippin of my own graffing, with a dish of car-
aways, and so forth   come, cousin Silence ·
and then to bed
Fal   'Fore God, you have here a goodly
dwelling and a rich
Shal   Barren, barren, barren , beggars all,
beggars all, Sir John many, good an
Spread, Davy , spread, Davy   well said,
Davy.   10

Fal. This Davy serves you for good uses ; he is your serving-man and your husband.

Shal. A good varlet, a good varlet, a very good varlet, Sir John : by the mass, I have drunk too much sack at supper : a good varlet. Now sit down, now sit down : come, cousin.

Sil. Ah, sirrah ! quoth-a, we shall
Do nothing but eat, and make good cheer,   [*Singing.*
And praise God for the merry year ;
When flesh is cheap and females dear,   20
And lusty lads roam here and there
          So merrily,
And ever among so merrily.

Fal. There's a merry heart ! Good Master Silence, I'll give you a health for that anon.

Shal. Give Master Bardolph some wine, Davy.

Davy. Sweet sir, sit ; I'll be with you anon; most sweet sir, sit. Master page, good master page, sit. Proface ! What you want in meat, we'll have in drink : but you must bear ; the heart's all.   [*Exit.*

Shal. Be merry, Master Bardolph ; and,my little soldier there, be merry.

Sil. Be merry, be merry, my wife has all ;   [*Singing.*
For women are shrews, both short and tall:
'Tis merry in hall when beards wag all,
          And welcome merry Shrove-tide.
Be merry, be merry.

Fal. I did not think Master Silence had been a man of this mettle.   41

Sil. Who, I ? I have been merry twice and once ere now.

Re-enter DAVY.

Davy. There's a dish of leather-coats for you.   [*To Bardolph.*

Shal. Davy !

Davy. Your worship ! I'll be with you straight [*to Bardolph*]. A cup of wine, sir ?

Sil. A cup of wine that's brisk and fine,   [*Singing.*
And drink unto the leman mine ;
          And a merry heart lives long-a.   50

Fal. Well said, Master Silence.

Sil. An we shall be merry, now comes in the sweet o' the night.

Fal. Health and long life to you, Master Silence.

Sil. Fill the cup, and let it come ; [*Singing.*
I'll pledge you a mile to the bottom.

Shal. Honest Bardolph, welcome : if thou wantest any thing, and wilt not call, beshrew thy heart. Welcome, my little tiny thief [*to the Page*], and welcome indeed too. I'll drink to Master Bardolph, and to all the cavaleros about London.

Davy. I hope to see London once ere I die.

Bard. An I might see you there, Davy,—

Shal. By the mass, you'll crack a quart together, ha ! will you not, Master Bardolph ?

Bard. Yea, sir, in a pottle-pot.

Shal. By God's liggens, I thank thee : the knave will stick by thee, I can assure thee that. A' will not out ; he is true bred.   71

Bard. And I'll stick by him, sir.

Shal. Why, there spoke a king. Lack nothing : be merry. [*Knocking within.*] Look who's at door there, ho ! who knocks ?   [*Exit Davy.*

Fal. Why, now you have done me right.
          [*To Silence, seeing him take off a bumper.*

Sil. Do me right,   [*Singing.*
          And dub me knight :
               Samingo.
Is't not so ?   80

Fal. 'Tis so.

Sil. Is't so ? Why then, say an old man can do somewhat.

Re-enter DAVY

Davy. An't please your worship, there's one Pistol come from the court with news.

Fal. From the court ! let him come in

Enter PISTOL

How now, Pistol !

Pist. Sir John, God save you !

Fal. What wind blew you hither, Pistol ?

Pist. Not the ill wind which blows no man to good. Sweet knight, thou art now one of the greatest men in this realm.

Sil. By'r lady, I think a' be, but goodman Puff of Barson.

Pist. Puff !
Puff in thy teeth, most recreant coward base!
Sir John, I am thy Pistol and thy friend,
And helter-skelter have I rode to thee,
And tidings do I bring and lucky joys
And golden times and happy news of price

Fal. I pray thee now, deliver them like a man of this world.   101

Pist. A foutre for the world and worldlings base !
I speak of Africa and golden joys.

Fal. O base Assyrian knight, what is thy news ?
Let King Cophetua know the truth thereof.

Sil. And Robin Hood, Scarlet, and John.
                    [*Singing.*

Pist. Shall dunghill curs confront the Helicons ?
And shall good news be baffled ?
Then, Pistol, lay thy head in Furies' lap.   110

Sil. Honest gentleman, I know not your breeding.

Pist. Why then, lament therefore.

Shal. Give me pardon, sir : if, sir, you come with news from the court, I take it there's but two ways, either to utter them, or to conceal them. I am, sir, under the king, in some authority.

Pist. Under which king, Besonian ? speak, or die.

Shal. Under King Harry.

Pist. Harry the Fourth ? or Fifth ?

Shal. Harry the Fourth.

Pist. A foutre for thine office !   120
Sir John, thy tender lambkin now is king ·

Harry the Fifth's the man I speak the
truth
When Pistol lies, do this, and fig me, like
The bragging Spaniard

Fal What, is the old king dead ?

Pist. As nail in door the things I speak
are just

Fal Away, Bardolph ! saddle my horse
Master Robert Shallow, choose what office
thou wilt in the land, 'tis thine Pistol, I will
double-charge thee with dignities. 130

Bard O joyful day !
I would not take a knighthood for my fortune

Pist What ! I do bring good news

Fal Carry Master Silence to bed. Master
Shallow, my Lord Shallow,—be what thou
wilt, I am fortune's steward—get on thy
boots : we'll ride all night O sweet Pistol !
Away, Bardolph ! [*Exit Bard*] Come, Pistol, utter more to me, and withal devise
something to do thyself good Boot, boot,
Master Shallow : I know the young king is
sick for me Let us take any man's horses,
the laws of England are at my commandment Blessed are they that have been my
friends, and woe to my lord chief-justice !

Pist. Let vultures vile seize on his lungs
also !
' Where is the life that late I led ? ' say they
Why, here it is, welcome these pleasant
days ! [*Exeunt.*

Scene IV. *London. A street.*

Enter Beadles, *dragging in* Hostess Quickly *and* Doll Tearsheet

Host. No, thou arrant knave, I would to
God that I might die, that I might have thee
hanged . thou hast drawn my shoulder out of
joint.

First Bead The constables have delivered
her over to me, and she shall have whipping-
cheer enough, I warrant her there hath been
a man or two lately killed about her

Dol Nut-hook, nut-hook, you lie Come
on ; I'll tell thee what, thou damned tripe-
visaged rascal, an the child I now go with do
miscarry, thou wert better thou had'st struck
thy mother, thou paper-faced villain

Host O the Lord, that Sir John were come !
he would make this a bloody day to somebody
But I pray God the fruit of her womb miscarry !

First Bead. If it do, you shall have a dozen
of cushions again, you have but eleven now
Come, I charge you both go with me, for the
man is dead that you and Pistol beat amongst
you

Dol. I'll tell you what, you thin man in a
censer, I will have you as soundly swinged for
this,—you blue-bottle rogue, you filthy fam-
ished correctioner, if you be not swinged, I'll
forswear half-kirtles

First Bead Come, come, you she knight-
errant, come.

Host. O God, that right should thus overcome might ! Well, of sufferance comes ease.

Dol Come, you rogue, come, bring me to
a justice 30

Host Ay, come, you starved blood-hound.

Dol. Goodman death, goodman bones !

Host. Thou atomy, thou !

Dol Come, you thin thing ; come, you
rascal

First Bead Very well. [*Exeunt.*

Scene V *A public place near Westminster Abbey.*

Enter two Grooms, *strewing rushes.*

First Groom More rushes, more rushes

Sec Groom The trumpets have sounded
twice

First Groom 'Twill be two o'clock ere they
come from the coronation dispatch, dispatch.
[*Exeunt.*

Enter Falstaff, Shallow, Pistol, Bardolph, *and* Page

Fal Stand here by me, Master Robert Shallow, I will make the king do you grace I will
leer upon him as a' comes by, and do but mark
the countenance that he will give me

Pist. God bless thy lungs, good knight 9

Fal Come here, Pistol, stand behind me.
O, if I had had time to have made new liveries,
I would have bestowed the thousand pound I
borrowed of you But 'tis no matter, this
poor show doth better this doth infer the zeal
I had to see him

Shal It doth so

Fal It shows my earnestness of affection,—

Shal It doth so

Fal My devotion,—

Shal It doth, if doth, it doth. 20

Fal As it were, to ride day and night; and
not to deliberate, not to remember, not to have
patience to shift me,—

Shal It is best, certain

Fal But to stand stained with travel, and
sweating with desire to see him, thinking of
nothing else, putting all affairs else in oblivion,
as if there were nothing else to be done but to
see him 29

Pist. 'Tis 'semper idem,' for 'obsque hoc
nihil est .' 'tis all in every part

Shal 'Tis so, indeed [liver,

Pist. My knight, I will inflame thy noble
And make thee rage
Thy Doll, and Helen of thy noble thoughts,
Is in base durance and contagious prison ;
Haled thither
By most mechanical and dirty hand :
Rouse up revenge from ebon den with fell
Alecto's snake, 39
For Doll is in Pistol speaks nought but truth

Fal I will deliver her
[*Shouts within, and the trumpets sound*

Pist There roar'd the sea, and trumpet-
clangor sounds

Enter the King *and his train, the* Lord Chief-
Justice *among them*

Fal. God save thy grace, King Hal ! my royal Hal !

Pist. The heavens thee guard and keep, most royal imp of fame !

Fal. God save thee, my sweet boy !

King. My lord chief-justice, speak to that vain man.

Ch. Just. Have you your wits ? know you what 'tis to speak ?

Fal. My king ! my Jove ! I speak to thee, my heart !   50

King. I know thee not, old man : fall to thy prayers ;
How ill white hairs become a fool and jester !
I have long dream'd of such a kind of man,
So surfeit-swell'd, so old and so profane ;
But, being awaked, I do despise my dream.
Make less thy body hence, and more thy grace;
Leave gormandizing; know the grave doth gape
For thee thrice wider than for other men.
Reply not to me with a fool-born jest :
Presume not that I am the thing I was ; 60
For God doth know, so shall the world perceive,
That I have turn'd away my former self ;
So will I those that kept me company.
When thou dost hear I am as I have been,
Approach me, and thou shalt be as thou wast,
The tutor and the feeder of my riots :
Till then, I banish thee, on pain of death,
As I have done the rest of my misleaders,
Not to come near our person by ten mile.
For competence of life I will allow you, 70
That lack of means enforce you not to evil :
And, as we hear you do reform yourselves,
We will, according to your strengths and qualities,   [my lord,
Give you advancement. Be it your charge,
To see perform'd the tenor of our word.
Set on.   [*Exeunt King, &c.*

Fal. Master Shallow, I owe you a thousand pound.

Shal. Yea, marry, Sir John ; which I beseech you to let me have home with me. 80

Fal. That can hardly be, Master Shallow. Do not you grieve at this ; I shall be sent for in private to him : look you, he must seem thus to the world : fear not your advancements ; I will be the man yet that shall make you great.

Shal. I cannot well perceive how, unless you should give me your doublet and stuff me out with straw. I beseech you, good Sir John, let me have five hundred of my thousand.

Fal. Sir, I will be as good as my word : this that you heard was but a color. 91

Shal. A color that I fear you will die in, Sir John.

Fal. Fear no colors: go with me to dinner: come, Lieutenant Pistol ; come, Bardolph: I shall be sent for soon at night.

Re-enter PRINCE JOHN, *the* LORD CHIEF-JUSTICE ; *Officers with them.*

Ch. Just. Go, carry Sir John Falstaff to the Fleet :

Take all his company along with him.

Fal. My lord, my lord,—

Ch. Just. I cannot now speak: I will hear you soon.   100
Take them away.

Pist. Si fortuna me tormenta, spero contenta.
   [*Exeunt all but Prince John and the Chief-Justice.*

Lan. I like this fair proceeding of the king's:
He hath intent his wonted followers
Shall all be very well provided for ;
But all are banish'd till their conversations
Appear more wise and modest to the world.

Ch. Just. And so they are. [my lord.

Lan. The king hath call'd his parliament,

Ch. Just. He hath.   110

Lan. I will lay odds that, ere this year expire,
We bear our civil swords and native fire
As far as France: I heard a bird so sing,
Whose music, to my thinking, pleased the king.
Come, will you hence ? [*Exeunt.*

EPILOGUE.

Spoken by a Dancer.

First my fear ; then my courtesy ; last my speech. My fear is, your displeasure ; my courtesy, my duty ; and my speech, to beg your pardons. If you look for a good speech now, you undo me : for what I have to say is of mine own making; and what indeed I should say will, I doubt, prove mine own marring. But to the purpose, and so to the venture. Be it known to you, as it is very well, I was lately here in the end of a displeasing play, to pray your patience for it and to promise you a better. I meant indeed to pay you with this : which, if like an ill venture it come unluckily home, I break, and you, my gentle creditors, lose. Here I promised you I would be and here I commit my body to your mercies : bate me some and I will pay you some and, as most debtors do, promise you infinitely.

If my tongue cannot entreat you to acquit me, will you command me to use my legs ? and yet that were but light payment, to dance out of your debt. But a good conscience will make any possible satisfaction, and so would I. All the gentlewomen here have forgiven me: if the gentlemen will not, then the gentlemen do not agree with the gentlewomen, which was never seen before in such an assembly.

One word more, I beseech you. If you be not too much cloyed with fat meat, our humble author will continue the story, with Sir John in it, and make you merry with fair Katharine of France : where, for any thing I know, Falstaff shall die of a sweat, unless already a' be killed with your hard opinions ; for Oldcastle died a martyr, and this is not the man. My tongue is weary; when my legs are too, I will bid you good night : and so kneel down before you ; but, indeed, to pray for the queen.

KING HENRY V.

(WRITTEN ABOUT 1599.)

INTRODUCTION.

This play is not mentioned by Meres, and the reference in the chorus of Act V to Essex in Ireland, and in the Prologue to "this wooden O," i.e. the Globe Theatre, built in 1599, make it probable that 1599 was the date of its production. A pirated imperfect quarto appeared in the following year. In this play Shakespeare bade farewell in trumpet tones to the history of England. It was a fitting climax to the great series of works which told of the sorrow and the glory of his country, embodying as it did the purest patriotism of the days of Elizabeth. And as the noblest glories of England are presented in this play, so it presents Shakespeare's ideal of active, practical, heroic manhood. If Hamlet exhibits the dangers and weakness of the contemplative nature, and Prospero, its calm and its conquest, Henry exhibits the utmost greatness which the active nature can attain. He is not an astute politician like his father; Laying put every thing upon a sound substantial basis he need not strain anxious eyes of foresight to discern and provide for contingencies arising out of doubtful deeds; for all that naturally comes within his range he has an unerring eye. A devotion to great objects outside of self fills him with a force of glorious enthusiasm. Hence his religious spirit and his humility or modesty—he feels that the strength he wields comes not from any clever disposition of forces due to his own prudence, but streams into him and through him from his people, his country, his cause, his God. He can be terrible to traitors, and his sternness is without a touch of personal revenge. In the midst of danger he can feel so free from petty heart-eating cares as to enjoy a piece of honest, soldierly mirth. His wooing is as plain, frank, and true as are his acts of piety. He unites around himself in loyal service, the jarring nationalities of his father's time—Englishmen, Scotchmen, Welshmen, Irishmen, all are at Henry's side at Agincourt. Having presented his ideal of English kinghood, Shakespeare could turn aside from history. In this play no character except Henry greatly interested Shakespeare, unless it be the Welsh Fluellen, whom he loves (as Scott loved the Baron of Bradwardine) for his real simplicity underlying his apparatus of learning, and his touching faith in the theory of warfare.

DRAMATIS PERSONÆ.

KING HENRY the Fifth.
DUKE OF GLOUCESTER, }
DUKE OF BEDFORD, } brothers to the King
DUKE OF EXETER, uncle to the King
DUKE OF YORK, cousin to the King
EARLS OF SALISBURY, WESTMORELAND, and WARWICK
ARCHBISHOP OF CANTERBURY.
BISHOP OF ELY
EARL OF CAMBRIDGE
LORD SCROOP
SIR THOMAS GREY.
SIR THOMAS ERPINGHAM, GOWER, FLUELLEN, MACMORRIS, JAMY, officers in King Henry's army.
BATES, COURT, WILLIAMS, soldiers in the same
PISTOL, NYM, BARDOLPH.
BOY
A Herald.

CHARLES the Sixth, King of France.
LEWIS, the Dauphin.
DUKES OF BURGUNDY, ORLEANS, and BOURBON
The Constable of France
RAMBURES and GRANDPRE, French Lords.
Governor of Harfleu
MONTJOY, a French Herald
Ambassadors to the King of England

ISABEL, Queen of France
KATHARINE, daughter to Charles and Isabel
ALICE, a lady attending on her
Hostess of a tavern in Eastcheap, formerly Mistress Quickly, and now married to Pistol

Lords, Ladies, Officers, Soldiers, Citizens, Messengers, and Attendants.
Chorus.

SCENE. England, afterwards France.

(447)

PROLOGUE

Enter Chorus.

Chor. O for a Muse of fire, that would as-
   cend
The brightest heaven of invention,
A kingdom for a stage, princes to act
And monarchs to behold the swelling scene !
Then should the warlike Harry, like himself,
Assume the port of Mars , and at his heels,
Leash'd in like hounds, should famine, sword
   and fire
Crouch for employment But pardon, gentles
   all,
The flat unraised spirits that have dared
On this unworthy scaffold to bring forth   10
So great an object can this cockpit hold
The vasty fields of France ? or may we cram
Within this wooden O the very casques
That did affright the air at Agincourt ?
O, pardon ! since a crooked figure may
Attest in little place a million ;
And let us, ciphers to this great accompt,
On your imaginary forces work
Suppose within the girdle of these walls
Are now confined two mighty monarchies,   20
Whose high upreared and abutting fronts
The perilous narrow ocean parts asunder .
Piece   out   our   imperfections with your
   thoughts ;
Into a thousand parts divide one man,
And make imaginary puissance ,
Think when we talk of horses, that you see
   them
Printing their proud hoofs i' the receiving
   earth ,
For 'tis your thoughts that now must deck our
   kings,
Carry them here and there; jumping o'er
   times,
Turning the accomplishment of many years 30
Into an hour-glass for the which supply,
Admit me Chorus to this history ,
Who prologue-like your humble patience pray,
Gently to hear, kindly to judge, our play.
                            [*Exit.*

ACT I.

SCENE I.   *London.*   *An ante-chamber in the*
   KING's *palace.*

Enter the ARCHBISHOP OF CANTERBURY, *and*
  the BISHOP OF ELY.

Cant. My lord, I'll tell you , that self bill
   is urged,
Which in the eleventh year of the last king's
   reign
Was like, and had indeed against us pass'd,
But that the scambling and unquiet time
Did push it out of farther question.
  Ely But how, my lord, shall we resist it
   now ?
  Cant. It must be thought on. If it pass
   against us,

We lose the better half of our possession ·
For all the temporal lands which men devout
By testament have given to the church   10
Would they strip from us ; being valued thus :
As much as would maintain, to the king's
   honor,
Full fifteen earls and fifteen hundred knights,
Six thousand and two hundred good esquires :
And, to relief of lazars and weak age,
Of indigent faint souls past corporal toil,
A hundred almshouses right well supplied ;
And to the coffers of the king beside,
A thousand pounds by the year . thus runs
   the bill.
  Ely   This would drink deep.
  Cant.   'Twould drink the cup and all.   20
  Ely.   But what prevention ?
  Cant.   The king is full of grace and fair re-
   gard.
  Ely   And a true lover of the holy church.
  Cant   The courses of his youth promised it
   not
The breath no sooner left his father's body,
But that his wildness, mortified in him,
Seem'd to die too , yea, at that very moment
Consideration, like an angel, came
And whipp'd the offending Adam out of him,
Leaving his body as a paradise,   30
To envelop and contain celestial spirits
Never was such a sudden scholar made :
Never came reformation in a flood,
With such a heady currance, scouring faults ;
Nor never Hydra-headed wilfulness
So soon did lose his seat and all at once
As in this king
  Ely   We are blessed in the change.
  Cant   Hear him but reason in divinity,
And all-admiring with an inward wish
You would desire the king were made a
   prelate   40
Hear him debate of commonwealth affairs,
You would say it hath been all in all his
   study
List his discourse of war, and you shall hear
A fearful battle render'd you in music :
Turn him to any cause of policy,
The Gordian knot of it he will unloose,
Familiar as his garter that, when he speaks,
The air, a charter'd libertine, is still,
And the mute wonder lurketh in men's ears,
To steal his sweet and honey'd sentences ;   50
So that the art and practic part of life
Must be the mistress to this theoric :
Which is a wonder how his grace should glean
   it,
Since his addiction was to courses vain.
His companies unletter'd, rude and shallow,
His hours fill'd up with riots, banquets, sports,
And never noted in him any study,
Any retirement, any sequestration
From open haunts and popularity
  Ely.   The strawberry grows underneath the
   nettle   60
And wholesome berries thrive and ripen best
Neighbor'd by fruit of baser quality :
And so the prince obscured his contemplation

Under the veil of wildness , which, no doubt,
Grew like the summer grass, fastest by night,
Unseen, yet crescive in his faculty
  Cant It must be so ; for miracles are
    ceased ,
And therefore we must needs admit the means
How things are perfected
  Ely.   But, my good lord,
How now for mitigation of this bill   70
Urged by the commons ? Doth his majesty
Incline to it, or no ?
  Cant   He seems indifferent,
Or rather swaying more upon our part
Than cherishing the exhibiters against us ;
For I have made an offer to his majesty,
Upon our spiritual convocation
And in regard of causes now in hand,
Which I have open'd to his grace at large,
As touching France, to give a greater sum
Than ever at one time the clergy yet   80
Did to his predecessors part withal
  Ely How did this offer seem received, my
    lord ?
  Cant With good acceptance of his majesty,
Save that there was not time enough to hear,
As I perceived his grace would fain have done,
The severals and unhidden passages
Of his true titles to some certain dukedoms
And generally to the crown and seat of France
Derived from Edward, his great-grandfather
  Ely. What was the impediment that broke
    this off ?   90
  Cant The French ambassador upon that
    instant
Craved audience ; and the hour, I think, is
    come
To give him hearing · is it four o'clock ?
  Ely It is.
  Cant. Then go we in, to know his embassy;
Which I could with a ready guess declare,
Before the Frenchman speak a word of it.
  Ely. I'll wait upon you, and I long to hear
    it.   *[Exeunt.*

SCENE II. *The same. The Presence chamber.*

Enter KING HENRY, GLOUCESTER, BEDFORD,
  EXETER, WARWICK, WESTMORELAND, *and*
  Attendants

  K Hen. Where is my gracious Lord of
    Canterbury ?
  Exe. Not here in presence
  K Hen   Send for him, good uncle.
  West. Shall we call in the ambassador, my
    liege ?
  K. Hen. Not yet, my cousin . we would be
    resolved,
Before we hear him, of some things of weight
That task our thoughts, concerning us and
    France

Enter the ARCHBISHOP OF CANTERBURY, *and*
  the BISHOP OF ELY.

  Cant God and his angels guard your
    sacred throne
And make you long become it !
  K. Hen.   Sure, we thank you.

My learned lord, we pray you to proceed
And justly and religiously unfold   10
Why the law Salique that they have in France
Or should, or should not, bar us in our claim .
And God forbid, my dear and faithful lord,
That you should fashion, wrest, or bow your
    reading,
Or nicely charge your understanding soul
With opening titles miscreate, whose right
Suits not in native colors with the truth ,
For God doth know how many now in health
Shall drop their blood in approbation
Of what your reverence shall incite us to   20
Therefore take heed how you impawn our per-
    son,
How you awake our sleeping sword of war :
We charge you, in the name of God, take heed ;
For never two such kingdoms did contend
Without much fall of blood , whose guiltless
    drops
Are every one a woe, a sore complaint
'Gainst him whose wrong gives edge unto the
    swords
That make such waste in brief mortality.
Under this conjuration, speak, my lord ,
For we will hear, note and believe in heart
That what you speak is in your conscience
    wash'd   31
As pure as sin with baptism
  Cant Then hear me, gracious sovereign,
    and you peers,
That owe yourselves, your lives and services
To this imperial throne There is no bar
To make against your highness' claim to France
But this, which they produce from Pharamond,
' In terram Salicam mulieres ne succedant.'
' No woman shall succeed in Salique land : '
Which Salique land the French unjustly gloze
To be the realm of France, and Pharamond 41
The founder of this law and female bar
Yet their own authors faithfully affirm
That the land Salique is in Germany,
Between the floods of Sala and of Elbe ;
Where Charles the Great, having subdued the
    Saxons,
There left behind and settled certain French ;
Who, holding in disdain the German women
For some dishonest manners of their life,
Establish'd then this law, to wit, no female 50
Should be inheritrix in Salique land .
Which Salique, as I said, 'twixt Elbe and Sala,
Is at this day in Germany call'd Meisen.
Then doth it well appear that Salique law
Was not devised for the realm of France ;
Nor did the French possess the Salique land
Until four hundred one and twenty years
After defunction of King Pharamond,
Idly supposed the founder of this law ;
Who died within the year of our redemption
Four hundred twenty-six , and Charles the
    Great   61
Subdued the Saxons, and did seat the French
Beyond the river Sala, in the year
Eight hundred five Besides, their writers say,
King Pepin, which deposed Childeric,
Did, as heir general, being descended

29

Of Blithild, which was daughter to King Clo-
    thair,
Make claim and title to the crown of France.
Hugh Capet also, who usurped the crown
Of Charles the duke of Lorraine, sole heir
    male   70
Of the true line and stock of Charles the Great,
To find his title with some shows of truth,
Though, in pure truth, it was corrupt and
    naught,
Convey'd himself as heir to the Lady Lingare,
Daughter to Charlemain, who was the son
To Lewis the emperor, and Lewis the son
Of Charles the Great. Also King Lewis the
    Tenth,
Who was sole heir to the usurper Capet,
Could not keep quiet in his conscience,
Wearing the crown of France, till satisfied   80
That fair Queen Isabel, his grandmother,
Was lineal of the Lady Ermengare,
Daughter to Charles the foresaid duke of Lor-
    raine :
By the which marriage the line of Charles the
    Great
Was re-united to the crown of France.
So that, as clear as is the summer's sun,
King Pepin's title and Hugh Capet's claim,
King Lewis his satisfaction, all appear
To hold in right and title of the female :
So do the kings of France unto this day ;   90
Howbeit they would hold up this Salique law
To bar your highness claiming from the female,
And rather choose to hide them in a net
Than amply to imbar their crooked titles
Usurp'd from you and your progenitors.
    K. Hen.   May I with right and conscience
    make this claim ?
    Cant.   The sin upon my head, dread sover-
    eign !
For in the book of Numbers is it writ,
When the man dies, let the inheritance   99
Descend unto the daughter.   Gracious lord,
Stand for your own ; unwind your bloody flag;
Look back into your mighty ancestors :
Go, my dread lord, to your great-grandsire's
    tomb,
From whom you claim ; invoke his warlike
    spirit,
And your great-uncle's, Edward the Black
    Prince,
Who on the French ground play'd a tragedy,
Making defeat on the full power of France,
Whiles his most mighty father on a hill
Stood smiling to behold his lion's whelp
Forage in blood of French nobility.   110
O noble English, that could entertain
With half their forces the full pride of France
And let another half stand laughing by,
All out of work and cold for action !
    Ely.   Awake remembrance of these valiant
    dead
And with your puissant arm renew their feats:
You are their heir ; you sit upon their throne;
The blood and courage that renowned them
Runs in your veins ; and my thrice-puissant
    liege

Is in the very May-morn of his youth,   120
Ripe for exploits and mighty enterprises.
    Exe.   Your brother kings and monarchs of
    the earth
Do all expect that you should rouse yourself,
As did the former lions of your blood.
    West.   They know your grace hath cau:
    and means and might ;
So hath your highness ; never king of England
Had nobles richer and more loyal subjects,
Whose hearts have left their bodies her in
    England
And lie pavilion'd in the fields of France.
    Cant.   O, let their bodies follow, my dear
    liege,   130
With blood and sword and fire to win your
    right ;
In aid whereof we of the spirituulty
Will raise your highness such a mighty sum
As never did the clergy at one time
Bring in to any of your ancestors.
    K. Hen.   We must not only arm to invade
    the French,
But lay down our proportions to defend
Against the Scot, who will make road upon us
With all advantages.
    Cant.   They of those marches, gracious
    sovereign,   140
Shall be a wall sufficient to defend
Our inland from the pilfering borderers.
    K. Hen.   We do not mean the coursing
    snatchers only,
But fear the main intendment of the Scot,
Who hath been still a giddy neighbor to us ;
For you shall read that my great-grandfather
Never went with his forces into France
But that the Scot on his unfurnish'd kingdom
Came pouring, like the tide into a breach,
With ample and brim fulness of his force,   150
Galling the gleaned land with hot assays,
Girding with grievous siege castles and towns;
That England, being empty of defence,
Hath shook and trembled at the ill neighbor-
    hood.
    Cant.   She hath been then more fear'd than
    harm'd, my liege ;
For hear her but exampled by herself :
When all her chivalry hath been in France
And she a mourning widow of her nobles,
She hath herself not only well defended
But taken and impounded as a stray   160
The King of Scots ; whom she did send to
    France,
To fill King Edward's fame with prisoner kings
And make her chronicle as rich with praise
As is the ooze and bottom of the sea
With sunken wreck and sunless treasuries.
    West.   But there's a saying very old and
    true,
    'If that you will France win,
      Then with Scotland first begin :
For once the eagle England being in prey,
To her unguarded nest the weasel Scot   170
Comes sneaking and so sucks her princely eggs,
Playing the mouse in absence of the cat,
To tear and havoc more than she can eat.

Exe. It follows then the cat must stay at
home :
Yet that is but a crush'd necessity,
Since we have locks to safeguard necessaries,
And pretty traps to catch the petty thieves.
While that the armed hand doth fight abroad,
The advised head defends itself at home ,
For government, though high and low and
    lower,   180
Put into parts, doth keep in one consent,
Congreeing in a full and natural close,
Like music.
   Cant.   Therefore doth heaven divide
The state of man in divers functions,
Setting endeavor in continual motion ;
To which is fixed, as an aim or butt,
Obedience · for so work the honey-bees,
Creatures that by a rule in nature teach
The act of order to a peopled kingdom.
They have a king and officers of sorts ,   190
Where some, like magistrates, correct at home,
Others, like merchants, venture trade abroad,
Others, like soldiers, armed in their stings,
Make boot upon the summer's velvet buds,
Which pillage they with merry march bring
    home
To the tent-royal of their emperor ;
Who, busied in his majesty, surveys
The singing masons building roofs of gold,
The civil citizens kneading up the honey,
The poor mechanic porters crowding in   200
Their heavy burdens at his narrow gate,
The sad-eyed justice, with his surly hum,
Delivering o'er to executors pale
The lazy yawning drone. I this infer,
That many things, having full reference
To one consent, may work contrariously
As many arrows, loosed several ways,
Come to one mark , as many ways meet in one
    town ;
As many fresh streams meet in one salt sea ;
As many lines close in the dial's centre ,   210
So may a thousand actions, once afoot,
End in one purpose, and be all well borne
Without defeat. Therefore to France, my
    liege.
Divide your happy England into four ,
Whereof take you one quarter into France,
And you withal shall make all Gallia shake.
If we, with thrice such powers left at home,
Cannot defend our own doors from the dog,
Let us be worried and our nation lose
The name of hardiness and policy   220
   K. Hen. Call in the messengers sent from
    the Dauphin. [*Exeunt some Attendants.*
Now are we well resolved , and, by God's help,
And yours, the noble sinews of our power,
France being ours, we'll bend it to our awe,
Or break it all to pieces : or there we'll sit,
Ruling in large and ample empery
O'er France and all her almost kingly duke-
    doms,
Or lay these bones in an unworthy urn,
Tombless, with no remembrance over them .
Either our history shall with full mouth   230
Speak freely of our acts, or else our grave,

Like Turkish mute, shall have a tongueless
    mouth,
Not worshipp'd with a waxen epitaph.

    Enter Ambassadors of France.

Now are we well prepared to know the pleas-
    ure
Of our fair cousin Dauphin , for we hear
Your greeting is from him, not from the king.
   First Amb. May't please your majesty to
    give us leave
Freely to render what we have in charge ;
Or shall we sparingly show you far off
The Dauphin's meaning and our embassy ?   240
   K Hen. We are no tyrant, but a Christian
    king ,
Unto whose grace our passion is as subject
As are our wretches fetter'd in our prisons ·
Therefore with frank and with uncurbed
    plainness
Tell us the Dauphin's mind
   First Amb   Thus, then, in few.
Your highness, lately sending into France,
Did claim some certain dukedoms, in the right
Of your great predecessor, King Edward the
    Third
In answer of which claim, the prince our master
Says that you savor too much of your youth,
And bids you be advised there's nought in
    France   251
That can be with a nimble galliard won ,
You cannot revel into dukedoms there
He therefore sends you, meeter for your spirit,
This tun of treasure , and, in lieu of this,
Desires you let the dukedoms that you claim
Hear no more of you This the Dauphin
    speaks.
   K. Hen. What treasure, uncle ?
   Exe   Tennis-balls, my liege.
   K Hen. We are glad the Dauphin is so
    pleasant with us ,
His present and your pains we thank you for :
When we have march'd our rackets to these
    balls,   261
We will, in France, by God's grace, play a set
Shall strike his father's crown into the hazard.
Tell him he hath made a match with such a
    wrangler
That all the courts of France will be disturb'd
With chaces And we understand him well,
How he comes o'er us with our wilder days,
Not measuring what use we made of them
We never valued this poor seat of England ,
And therefore, living hence, did give ourself
To barbarous license , as 'tis ever common
That men are merriest when they are from
    home
But tell the Dauphin I will keep my state,
Be like a king and show my sail of greatness
When I do rouse me in my throne of France ·
For that I have laid by my majesty
And plodded like a man for working-days,
But I will rise there with so full a glory
That I will dazzle all the eyes of France,   279
Yea, strike the Dauphin blind to look on us
And tell the pleasant prince this mock of his

Hath turn'd his balls to gun-stones ; and his
   soul
Shall stand sore charged for the wasteful ven-
   geance
That shall fly with them : for many a thou-
   sand widows
Shall this his mock mock out of their dear
   husbands ;
Mock mothers from their sons, mock castles
   down ;
And some are yet ungotten and unborn
That shall have cause to curse the Dauphin's
   scorn.
But this lies all within the will of God,
To whom I do appeal ; and in whose name
Tell you the Dauphin I am coming on,
To venge me as I may and to put forth
My rightful hand in a well-hallow'd cause.
So get you hence in peace ; and tell the
   Dauphin
His jest will savor but of shallow wit,
When thousands weep more than did laugh at
   it.
Convey them with safe conduct. Fare you
   well.   [*Exeunt Ambassadors.*
Exe. This was a merry message.
K. Hen. We hope to make the sender blush
   at it.
Therefore, my lords, omit no happy hour   300
That may give furtherance to our expedition;
For we have now no thought in us but France,
Save those to God, that run before our busi-
   ness.
Therefore let our proportions for these wars
Be soon collected and all things thought upon
That may with reasonable swiftness add
More feathers to our wings ; for, God before,
We'll chide this Dauphin at his father's door.
Therefore let every man now task his thought,
That this fair action may on foot be brought.
                [*Exeunt. Flourish.*

ACT II.

PROLOGUE.

Enter Chorus.

Chor. Now all the youth of England are on
   fire,
And silken dalliance in the wardrobe lies :
Now thrive the armorers, and honor's
   thought
Reigns solely in the breast of every man :
They sell the pasture now to buy the horse,
Following the mirror of all Christian kings,
With winged heels, as English Mercuries.
For now sits Expectation in the air,
And hides a sword from hilts unto the point
With crowns imperial, crowns and coronets,
Promised to Harry and his followers.   11
The French, advised by good intelligence
Of this most dreadful preparation,
Shake in their fear and with pale policy
Seek to divert the English purposes.

O England ! model to thy inward greatness,
Like little body with a mighty heart,
What mightst thou do, that honor would thee
   do,
Were all thy children kind and natural !
But see thy fault ! France hath in thee found
   out   20
A nest of hollow bosoms, which he fills
With treacherous crowns ; and three corrupted
   men,
One, Richard Earl of Cambridge, and the
   second,
Henry Lord Scroop of Masham, and the third,
Sir Thomas Grey, knight, of Northumberland,
Have, for the gilt of France,—O guilt indeed!
Confirm'd conspiracy with fearful France ;
And by their hands this grace of kings must
   die,
If hell and treason hold their promises,
Ere he take ship for France, and in South-
   ampton.   30
Linger your patience on ; †and we'll digest
The abuse of distance ; force a play :
The sum is paid ; the traitors are agreed ;
The king is set from London ; and the scene
Is now transported, gentles, to Southampton ;
There is the playhouse now, there must you
   sit :
And thence to France shall we convey you
   safe,
And bring you back, charming the narrow
   seas
To give you gentle pass ; for, if we may,   39
We'll not offend one stomach with our play.
But, till the king come forth, and not till then,
Unto Southampton do we shift our scene.
                       [*Exit.*

SCENE I. *London. A street.*

Enter Corporal NYM *and* Lieutenant BARDOLPH.

Bard. Well met, Corporal Nym.
Nym. Good morrow, Lieutenant Bardolph.
Bard. What, are Ancient Pistol and you
friends yet ?
Nym. For my part, I care not : I say little ;
but when time shall serve, there shall be smiles;
but that shall be as it may. I dare not fight ;
but I will wink and hold out mine iron : it is
a simple one ; but what though ? it will toast
cheese, and it will endure cold as another
man's sword will : and there's an end.   11
Bard. I will bestow a breakfast to make
you friends ; and we'll be all three sworn
brothers to France : let it be so, good Corporal
Nym.
Nym. Faith, I will live so long as I may,
that's the certain of it ; and when I cannot
live any longer, I will do as I may : that is my
rest, that is the rendezvous of it.
Bard. It is certain, corporal, that he is
married to Nell Quickly : and certainly she
did you wrong ; for you were troth-plight to
her.   21
Nym. I cannot tell : things must be as they

may : men may sleep, and they may have
their throats about them at that time ; and
some say knives have edges It must be as it
may : though patience be a tired mare, yet
she will plod There must be conclusions.
Well, I cannot tell.

Enter Pistol *and* Hostess

Bard. Here comes Ancient Pistol and his
wife good corporal, be patient here. How
now, mine host Pistol '   30
  Pist. Base tike, call'st thou me host ?
Now, by this hand, I swear, I scorn the term ,
Nor shall my Nell keep lodgers
  Host No, by my troth, not long ; for we
cannot lodge and board a dozen or fourteen
gentlewomen that live honestly by the prick
of their needles, but it will be thought we
keep a bawdy house straight [*Nym and
Pistol draw.*] O well a day, Lady, if he be
not drawn now ' we shall see wilful adultery
and murder committed.   40
  Bard. Good lieutenant ! good corporal !
offer nothing here.
  Nym Pish !
  Pist. Pish for thee. Iceland dog ! thou
prick-ear'd cur of Iceland !
  Host Good Corporal Nym, show thy valor,
and put up your sword.
  Nym Will you shog off ? I would have
you solus.
  Pist. 'Solus,' egregious dog ? O viper
vile '   50
The 'solus' in thy most mervailous face ,
The 'solus' in thy teeth, and in thy throat,
And in thy hateful lungs, yea, in thy maw,
perdy,
And, which is worse, within thy nasty mouth!
I do retort the 'solus' in thy bowels '
For I can take, and Pistol's cock is up,
And flashing fire will follow.
  Nym. I am not Barbason ; you cannot
conjure me I have an humor to knock you
indifferently well. If you grow foul with me,
Pistol, I will scour you with my rapier, as I
may, in fair terms : if you would walk off, I
would prick your guts a little, in good terms,
as I may : and that's the humor of it.
  Pist. O braggart vile and damned furious
wight !
The grave doth gape, and doting death is
near ;
Therefore exhale.
  Bard Hear me, hear me what I say : he
that strikes the first stroke, I'll run him up
to the hilts, as I am a soldier   [*Draws.*
  Pist. An oath of mickle might ; and fury
shall abate.   70
Give me thy fist, thy fore-foot to me give :
Thy spirits are most tall.
  Nym. I will cut thy throat, one time or
other, in fair terms : that is the humor of it
  Pist. 'Couple a gorge ''
That is the word. I thee defy again.
O hound of Crete, think'st thou my spouse to
get ?

No ; to the spital go,
And from the powdering tub of infamy
Fetch forth the lazar kite of Cressid's kind, 80
Doll Tearsheet she by name, and her espouse·
I have, and I will hold, the quondam Quickly
For the only she , and —pauca, there's enough
Go to,

Enter the Boy.

  Boy. Mine host Pistol, you must come to
my master, and you, hostess : he is very sick,
and would to bed Good Bardolph, put thy
face between his sheets, and do the office of a
warming-pan Faith, he's very ill.
  Bard Away, you rogue !   90
  Host By my troth, he'll yield the crow a
pudding one of these days The king has
killed his heart Good husband, come home
presently.   [*Exeunt Hostess and Boy
  Bard. Come, shall I make you two friends ?
We must to France together why the devil
should we keep knives to cut one another's
throats ?
  Pist. Let floods o'erswell, and fiends for
food howl on !
  Nym. You'll pay me the eight shillings I
won of you at betting ?
  Pist. Base is the slave that pays   100
  Nym That now I will have : that's the
humor of it
  Pist. As manhood shall compound push
home.   [*They draw
  Bard. By this sword, he that makes the
first thrust, I'll kill him , by this sword, I will
  Pist Sword is an oath, and oaths must
have their course
  Bard. Corporal Nym, an thou wilt be
friends, be friends an thou wilt not, why,
then, be enemies with me too Prithee, put
up
  Nym. I shall have my eight shillings I won
of you at betting ?   111
  Pist. A noble shalt thou have, and present
pay ;
And liquor likewise will I give to thee,
And friendship shall combine, and brother-
hood
I'll live by Nym, and Nym shall live by me ;
Is not this just ? for I shall sutler be
Unto the camp, and profits will accrue.
Give me thy hand
  Nym. I shall have my noble ?
  Pist. In cash most justly paid   120
  Nym. Well, then, that's the humor of't.

Re-enter Hostess.

  Host As ever you came of women, come
in quickly to Sir John Ah, poor heart ! he
is so shaked of a burning quotidian tertian,
that it is most lamentable to behold. Sweet
men, come to him.
  Nym. The king hath run bad humors on
the knight , that's the even of it
  Pist. Nym, thou hast spoke the right ;
His heart is fracted and corroborate   130
  Nym. The king is a good king . but it must

be as it may ; he passes some humors and
careers.

Pist. Let us condole the knight ; for, lamb-
kins we will live.

SCENE II. *Southampton.— A council-chamber.*

Enter EXETER, BEDFORD, *and* WESTMORE-
LAND.

Bed. 'Fore God, his grace is bold, to trust
these traitors.

Exe. They shall be apprehended by and by.

West. How smooth and even they do bear
themselves !
As if allegiance in their bosoms sat,
Crowned with faith and constant loyalty.

Bed. The king hath note of all that they
intend,
By interception which they dream not of.

Exe. Nay, but the man that was his bed-
fellow,
Whom he hath dull'd and cloy'd with gracious
favors,
That he should, for a foreign purse, so sell 10
His sovereign's life to death and treachery.

Trumpets sound. Enter KING HENRY,
SCROOP, CAMBRIDGE, GREY, *and* Attendants.

K. Hen. Now sits the wind fair, and we
will aboard.
My Lord of Cambridge, and my kind Lord of
Masham,
And you, my gentle knight, give me your
thoughts :
Think you not that the powers we bear with
us
Will cut their passage through the force of
France,
Doing the execution and the act
For which we have in head assembled them ?

Scroop. No doubt, my liege, if each man
do his best.

K. Hen. I doubt not that ; since we are
well persuaded   20
We carry not a heart with us from hence
That grows not in a fair consent with ours,
Nor leave not one behind that doth not wish
Success and conquest to attend on us.

Cam. Never was monarch better fear'd and
loved
Than is your majesty : there's not, I think, a
subject
That sits in heart-grief and uneasiness
Under the sweet shade of your government.

Grey. True : those that were your father's
enemies
Have steep'd their galls in honey and do serve
you   30
With hearts create of duty and of zeal.

K. Hen. We therefore have great cause of
thankfulness ;
And shall forget the office of our hand,
Sooner than quittance of desert and merit
According to the weight and worthiness.

Scroop. So service shall with steeled sin-
ews toil,
And labor shall refresh itself with hope,
To do your grace incessant services.

K. Hen. We judge no less. Uncle of Ex-
eter,
Enlarge the man committed yesterday,   40
That rail'd against our person : we consider
It was excess of wine that set him on ;
And on his more advice we pardon him.

Scroop. That's mercy, but too much secu-
rity :
Let him be punish'd, sovereign, lest example
Breed, by his sufferance, more of such a kind.

K. Hen. O, let us yet be merciful.

Cam. So may your highness, and yet punish too.

Grey. Sir,
You show great mercy, if you give him life, 50
After the taste of much correction.

K. Hen. Alas, your too much love and care
of me
Are heavy orisons 'gainst this poor wretch !
If little faults, proceeding on distemper,
Shall not be wink'd at, how shall we stretch
our eye
When capital crimes, chew'd, swallow'd and
digested,   [man,
Appear before us ? We'll yet enlarge that
Though Cambridge, Scroop and Grey, in their
dear care
And tender preservation of our person,
Would have him punished. And now to our
French causes :   60
Who are the late commissioners ?

Cam. I one, my lord :
Your highness bade me ask for it to-day.

Scroop. So did you me, my liege.

Grey. And I, my royal sovereign.

K. Hen. Then, Richard Earl of Cambridge,
there is yours ;
There yours, Lord Scroop of Masham ; and,
sir knight,
Grey of Northumberland, this same is yours :
Read them ; and know, I know your worthi-
ness.
My Lord of Westmoreland, and uncle Exeter,
We will aboard to night. Why, how now,
gentlemen !   71
What see you in those papers that you lose
So much complexion ? Look ye, how they
change !
Their cheeks are paper. Why, what read you
there
That hath so cowarded and chased your blood
Out of appearance ?

Cam. I do confess my fault ;
And do submit me to your highness' mercy.

Grey. } To which we all appeal.
Scroop. }

K. Hen. The mercy that was quick in us
but late,
By your own counsel is suppress'd and kill'd : 80
You must not dare, for shame, to talk of mercy;
For your own reasons turn into your bosoms,
As dogs upon their masters, worrying you.
See you, my princes, and my noble peers,
These English monsters ! My lord of Cam-
bridge here,

You know how apt our love was to accord
To furnish him with all appertinents
Belonging to his honor ; and this man
Hath, for a few light crowns, lightly conspired,
And sworn unto the practices of France,　90
To kill us here in Hampton : to the which
This knight, no less for bounty bound to us
Than Cambridge is, hath likewise sworn.
　　　But, O,
What shall I say to thee, Lord Scroop ? thou
　　cruel,
Ingrateful, savage and inhuman creature !
Thou that didst bear the key of all my coun-
　　sels,
That knew'st the very bottom of my soul,
That almost mightst have coin'd me into gold,
Wouldst thou have practised on me for thy use,
May it be possible, that foreign hire　100
Could out of thee extract one spark of evil
That might annoy my finger ? 'tis so strange,
That, though the truth of it stands off as gross
As black and white, my eye will scarcely
　　see it.
Treason and murder ever kept together,
As two yoke-devils sworn to either's purpose,
Working so grossly in a natural cause,
That admiration did not whoop at them :
But thou, 'gainst all proportion, didst bring in
Wonder to wait on treason and on murder : 110
And whatsoever cunning fiend it was
That wrought upon thee so preposterously
Hath got the voice in hell for excellence :
All other devils that suggest by treasons
Do botch and bungle up damnation
With patches, colors, and with forms being
　　fetch'd
From glistering semblances of piety ;
But he that temper'd thee bade thee stand up,
Gave thee no instance why thou shouldst do
　　treason,
Unless to dub thee with the name of traitor. 120
If that same demon that hath gull'd thee thus
Should with his lion gait walk the whole world,
He might return to vasty Tartar back,
And tell the legions ' I can never win
A soul so easy as that Englishman's.'
O, how hast thou with jealousy infected
The sweetness of affiance ! Show men dutiful?
Why, so didst thou : seem they grave and
　　learned ?
Why, so didst thou : come they of noble fam-
　　ily ?
Why, so didst thou : seem they religious ? 130
Why, so didst thou : or are they spare in diet,
Free from gross passion or of mirth or anger,
Constant in spirit, not swerving with the blood,
Garnish'd and deck'd in modest complement,
Not working with the eye without the ear,
And but in purged judgment trusting neither?
Such and so finely bolted didst thou seem :
And thus thy fall hath left a kind of blot,
To mark the full-fraught man and best indued
With some suspicion. I will weep for thee;140
For this revolt of thine, methinks, is like
Another fall of man. Their faults are open:
Arrest them to the answer of the law ;

And God acquit them of their practices !
　Exe. I arrest thee of high treason, by the
name of Richard Earl of Cambridge.
　I arrest thee of high treason, by the name of
Henry Lord Scroop of Masham.
　I arrest thee of high treason, by the name of
Thomas Grey, knight, of Northumberland. 150
　Scroop. Our purposes God justly hath dis-
　　cover'd ;
And I repent my fault more than my death ;
Which I beseech your highness to forgive,
Although my body pay the price of it.
　Cam. For me, the gold of France did not
　　seduce ;
Although I did admit it as a motive
The sooner to effect what I intended :
But God be thanked for prevention ;
Which I in sufferance heartily will rejoice,
Beseeching God and you to pardon me.　160
　Grey. Never did faithful subject more re-
　　joice
At the discovery of most dangerous treason
Than I do at this hour joy o'er myself.
Prevented from a damned enterprise :
My fault, but not my body, pardon, sovereign.
　K. Hen. God quit you in his mercy ! Hear
　　your sentence.
You have conspired against our royal person,
Join'd with an enemy proclaim'd and from his
　　coffers
Received the golden earnest of our death ;
Wherein you would have sold your king to
　　slaughter,　170
His princes and his peers to servitude,
His subjects to oppression and contempt
And his whole kingdom into desolation.
Touching our person seek we no revenge ;
But we our kingdom's safety must so tender,
Whose ruin you have sought, that to her laws
We do deliver you. Get you therefore hence,
Poor miserable wretches, to your death :
The taste whereof, God of his mercy give　179
You patience to endure, and true repentance
Of all your dear offences ! Bear them hence.
　　　　　[*Exeunt Cambridge, Scroop and Grey,
　　　　　　　　　　　　　　　　guarded.*
Now, lords, for France; the enterprise whereof
Shall be to you, as us, like glorious.
We doubt not of a fair and lucky war,
Since God so graciously hath brought to light
This dangerous treason lurking in our way
To hinder our beginnings. We doubt not now
But every rub is smoothed on our way.
Then forth, dear countrymen : let us deliver
Our puissance into the hand of God,　190
Putting it straight in expedition.
Cheerly to sea ; the signs of war advance :
No king of England, if not king of France.
　　　　　　　　　　　　　　　　　　[*Exeunt.*

SCENE III. *London. Before a tavern.*

Enter PISTOL, HOSTESS, NYM, BARDOLPH, *and*
　　　　　　　Boy.

　Host. Prithee, honey-sweet husband, let
me bring thee to Staines.

Pist. No ; for my manly heart doth yearn.
Bardolph, be blithe : Nym, rouse thy vaunt-
ing veins :
Boy, bristle thy courage up ; for Falstaff he is
dead,
And we must yearn therefore.

Bard. Would I were with him, wheresome'er
he is, either in heaven or in hell !

Host. Nay, sure, he's not in hell : he's in
Arthur's bosom, if ever man went to Arthur's
bosom. A' made a finer end and went away
an it had been any christom child ; a' parted
even just between twelve and one, even at the
turning o' the tide : for after I saw him fumble
with the sheets and play with flowers and smile
upon his fingers' ends, I knew there was but
one way ; for his nose was as sharp as a pen,
and a' babbled of green fields. 'How now, sir
John !' quoth I : 'what, man ! be o' good
cheer.' So a' cried out 'God, God, God !'
three or four times. Now I, to comfort him,
bid him a' should not think of God ; I hoped
there was no need to trouble himself with any
such thoughts yet. So a' bade me lay more
clothes on his feet : I put my hand into the
bed and felt them, and they were as cold as
any stone ; then I felt to his knees, and they
were as cold as any stone, and so upward and
upward, and all was as cold as any stone.

Nym. They say he cried out of sack.

Host. Ay, that a' did.   30

Bard. And of women.

Host. Nay, that a' did not.

Boy. Yes, that a' did ; and said they were
devils incarnate.

Host. A' could never abide carnation ; 'twas
a color he never liked.

Boy. A' said once, the devil would have
him about women.

Host. A' did in some sort, indeed, handle
women ; but then he was rheumatic, and
talked of the whore of Babylon.   41

Boy. Do you not remember, a' saw a flea
stick upon Bardolph's nose, and a' said it was
a black soul burning in hell-fire ?

Bard. Well, the fuel is gone that maintained
that fire : that's all the riches I got in his service.

Nym. Shall we shog ? the king will be
gone from Southampton.

Pist. Come, let's away. My love, give me
thy lips.
Look to my chattels and my movables :   50
Let senses rule ; the word is ' Pitch and Pay:'
Trust none ;
For oaths are straws, men's faiths are wafer-
cakes,
And hold-fast is the only dog, my duck :
Therefore, Caveto be thy counsellor.
Go, clear thy crystals. Yoke-fellows in arms,
Let us to France ; like horse-leeches, my boys,
To suck, to suck, the very blood to suck !

Boy. And that's but unwholesome food they
say.   60

Pist. Touch her soft mouth, and march.

Bard. Farewell, hostess.   [*Kissing her.*

Nym. I cannot kiss, that is the humor of it ;
but, adieu.

Pist. Let housewifery appear : keep close,
I thee command.

Host. Farewell ; adieu.   [*Exeunt.*

SCENE IV. *France. The* KING'S *palace.*

Flourish. Enter the FRENCH KING, *the* DAU-
PHIN, *the* DUKES OF BERRI *and* BRETAGNE,
the CONSTABLE, *and others.*

Fr. King. Thus comes the English with full
power upon us ;
And more than carefully it us concerns
To answer royally in our defences.
Therefore the Dukes of Berri and of Bretagne,
Of Brabant and of Orleans, shall make forth,
And you, Prince Dauphin, with all swift dis-
patch,
To line and new repair our towns of war
With men of courage and with means defend-
ant ;
For England his approaches makes as fierce
As waters to the sucking of a gulf   10
It fits us then to be as provident
As fear may teach us out of late examples
Left by the fatal and neglected English
Upon our fields.

Dau.   My most redoubted father,
It is most meet we arm us 'gainst the foe ;
For peace itself should not so dull a kingdom,
Though war nor no known quarrel were in
question,
But that defences, musters, preparations,
Should be maintain'd, assembled and col-
lected,
As were a war in expectation.   20
Therefore, I say 'tis meet we all go forth
To view the sick and feeble parts of France :
And let us do it with no show of fear ;
No, with no more than if we heard that Eng-
land
Were busied with a Whitsun morris-dance :
For, my good liege, she is so idly king'd,
Her sceptre so fantastically borne
By a vain, giddy, shallow, humorous youth,
That fear attends her not.

Con.   O peace, Prince Dauphin !
You are too much mistaken in this king :   30
Question your grace the late ambassadors,
With what great state he heard their em-
bassy,
How well supplied with noble counsellors,
How modest in exception, and withal
How terrible in constant resolution,
And you shall find his vanities forespent
Were but the outside of the Roman Brutus,
Covering discretion with a coat of folly ;
As gardeners do with ordure hide those roots
That shall first spring and be most delicate. 40

Dau. Well, 'tis not so, my lord high con-
stable ;
But, though we think it so, it is no matter :
In cases of defence 'tis best to weigh
The enemy more mighty than he seems :
So the proportions of defence are fill'd ;

Which of a weak or niggardly projection
Doth, like a miser, spoil his coat with scanting
A little cloth
 Fr. King Think we King Harry strong ,
And, princes, look you strongly arm to meet
 him.
The kindred of him hath been flesh'd upon us,
And he is bred out of that bloody strain 51
That haunted us in our familiar paths .
Witness our too much memorable shame
When Cressy battle fatally was struck,
And all our princes captived by the hand
Of that black name, Edward, Black Prince of
- Wales :
Whiles that his mountain sire, on mountain
 standing,
Up in the air, crown'd with the golden sun,
Saw his heroical seed, and smiled to see him,
Mangle the work of nature and deface 60
The patterns that by God and by French
 fathers
Had twenty years been made This is a stem
Of that victorious stock , and let us fear
The native mightiness and fate of him.

    Enter a Messenger

Mess. Ambassadors from Harry King of
 England
Do crave admittance to your majesty.
 Fr. King We'll give them present audience
Go, and bring them
  [*Exeunt Messenger and certain Lords*
You see this chase is hotly follow'd, friends
 Dau. Turn head, and stop pursuit , for
 coward dogs
Most spend their mouths when what they seem
 to threaten 70
Runs far before them Good my sovereign,
Take up the English short, and let them know
Of what a monarchy you are the head
Self-love, my liege. is not so vile a sin
As self-neglecting

  Re-enter Lords, with Exeter *and train*

 Fr King.   From our brother England ?
 Exe. From him , and thus he greets your
 majesty
He wills you, in the name of God Almighty,
That you divest yourself, and lay apart
The borrow'd glories that by gift of heaven,
By law of nature and of nations, 'long 80
To him and to his heirs ; namely, the crown
And all wide-stretched honors that pertain
By custom and the ordinance of times
Unto the crown of France. That you may
 know
'Tis no sinister nor no awkward claim, [days,
Pick'd from the worm-holes of long-vanish'd
Nor from the dust of old oblivion raked,
He sends you this most memorable line,
In every branch truly demonstrative ,
Willing you overlook this pedigree : 90
And when you find him evenly derived
From his most famed of famous ancestors,
Edward the Third, he bids you then resign
Your crown and kingdom, indirectly held
From him the native and true challenger

 Fr King Or else what follows ?
 Exe Bloody constraint , for if you hide the
 crown
Even in your hearts, there will be rake for it
Therefore in fierce tempest is he coming,
In thunder and in earthquake, like a Jove, 100
That, if requiring fail, he will compel ,
And bids you, in the bowels of the Lord,
Deliver up the crown, and to take mercy
On the poor souls for whom this hungry war
Opens his vasty jaws , and on your head
Turning the widows' tears, the orphans' cries,
The dead men's blood, the pining maidens'
 groans,
For husbands, fathers and betrothed lovers,
That shall be swallow'd in this controversy
This is his claim, his threatening and my mes-
 sage , 110
Unless the Dauphin be in presence here,
To whom expressly I bring greeting too
 Fr King For us, we will consider of this
 further .
To-morrow shall you bear our full intent
Back to our brother England
 Dau   For the Dauphin,
I stand here for him what to him from Eng-
 land ?
 Exe. Scorn and defiance , slight regard,
 contempt,
And any thing that may not misbecome
The mighty sender, doth he prize you at.
Thus says my king , an' if your father's high-
 ness 120
Do not, in grant of all demands at large,
Sweeten the bitter mock you sent his majesty,
He'll call you to so hot an answer of it,
That caves and womby vaultages of France
Shall chide your trespass and return your
 mock
In second accent of his ordnance
 Dau Say, if my father render fair return,
It is against my will ; for I desire
Nothing but odds with England . to that end,
As matching to his youth and vanity, 130
I did present him with the Paris balls
 Exe He'll make your Paris Louvre shake
 for it,
Were it the mistress-court of mighty Europe :
And, be assured, you'll find a difference,
As we his subjects have in wonder found,
Between the promise of his greener days
And these he masters now : now he weighs
 time
Even to the utmost grain that you shall read
In your own losses, if he stay in France
 Fr. King To-morrow shall you know our
 mind at full. 140
 Exe Dispatch us with all speed, lest that
 our king
Come here himself to question our delay ;
For he is footed in this land already
 Fr King You shall be soon dispatch'd with
 fair conditions .
A night is but small breath and little pause
To answer matters of this consequence
       [*Flourish. Exeunt.*

ACT III.

PROLOGUE.

Enter Chorus.

Chor. Thus with imagined wing our swift
    scene flies
In motion of no less celerity
Than that of thought. Suppose that you have
    seen
The well-appointed king at Hampton pier
Embark his royalty ; and his brave fleet
With silken streamers the young Phœbus fan-
    ning :
Play with your fancies, and in them behold
Upon the hempen tackle ship-boys climbing ;
Hear the shrill whistle which doth order give
To sounds confused ; behold the threaden
    sails,   10
Borne with the invisible and creeping wind,
Draw the huge bottoms through the furrow'd
    sea,
Breasting the lofty surge : O, do but think
You stand upon the rivage and behold
A city on the inconstant billows dancing ;
For so appears this fleet majestical,
Holding due course to Harfleur. Follow, fol-
    low :
Grapple your minds to sternage of this navy,
And leave your England, as dead midnight
    still,
Guarded with grandsires, babies and old wo-
    men,
Either past or not arrived to pith and puis-
    sance :
For who is he, whose chin is but enrich'd
With one appearing hair, that will not follow
These cull'd and choice-drawn cavaliers to
    France ?
Work, work your thoughts, and therein see a
    siege ;
Behold the ordnance on their carriages,
With fatal mouths gaping on girded Harfleur.
Suppose the ambassador from the French comes
    back ;
Tells Harry that the king doth offer him
Katharine his daughter, and with her, to
    dowry,   30
Some petty and unprofitable dukedoms.
The offer likes not : and the nimble gunner
With linstock now the devilish cannon touch-
    es,   [*Alarum, and chambers go off.*
And down goes all before them. Still be kind,
And eke out our performance with your mind.
                            [*Exit.*

SCENE I. *France. Before Harfleur.*

Alarum. Enter KING HENRY, EXETER, BED-
FORD, GLOUCESTER, *and* Soldiers, *with scal-
ing-ladders.*

K. Hen. Once more unto the breach, dear
    friends, once more ;
Or close the wall up with our English dead.
In peace there's nothing so becomes a man
As modest stillness and humility :
But when the blast of war blows in our ears,
Then imitate the action of the tiger ;
Stiffen the sinews, summon up the blood,
Disguise fair nature with hard-favor'd rage ;
Then lend the eye a terrible aspect ;
Let it pry through the portage of the head   10
Like the brass cannon ; let the brow o'erwhelm
    it
As fearfully as doth a galled rock
O'erhang and jutty his confounded base,
Swill'd with the wild and wasteful ocean.
Now set the teeth and stretch the nostril wide,
Hold hard the breath and bend up every spirit
To his full height. On, on, you noblest Eng-
    lish,
Whose blood is fet from fathers of war-proof !
Fathers that, like so many Alexanders,
Have in these parts from morn till even fought
And sheathed their swords for lack of argu-
    ment :   21
Dishonor not your mothers ; now attest
That those whom you call'd fathers did beget
    you.
Be copy now to men of grosser blood,
And teach them how to war. And you, good
    yeomen,
Whose limbs were made in England, show us
    here
The mettle of your pasture ; let us swear
That you are worth your breeding ; which I
    doubt not ;
For there is none of you so mean and base,
That hath not noble lustre in your eyes.   30
I see you stand like greyhounds in the slips,
Straining upon the start. The game's afoot :
Follow your spirit, and upon this charge
Cry ' God for Harry, England, and Saint
    George !'
        [*Exeunt. Alarum, and chambers go off.*

SCENE II. *The same.*

Enter NYM, BARDOLPH, PISTOL, *and* BOY.

Bard. On, on, on, on, on ! to the breach, to
    the breach !
Nym. Pray thee, corporal, stay : the knocks
are too hot ; and, for mine own part, I have
not a case of lives : the humor of it is too hot,
that is the very plain-song of it.
Pist. The plain-song is most just ; for hu-
    mors do abound :
Knocks go and come ; God's vassals drop and
    die ;
        And sword and shield,
        In bloody field,
Doth win immortal fame.   10
Boy. Would I were in an alehouse in Lon-
don ! I would give all my fame for a pot of
ale and safety.
Pist. And I :
    If wishes would prevail with me,
    My purpose should not fail with me,
    But thither would I hie.
Boy. As duly, but not as truly,
        As bird doth sing on bough.   20

Enter FLUELLEN.

Flu. Up to the breach, you dogs ! avaunt,
you cullions ! [*Driving them forward*
Pist Be merciful, great duke, to men of
  mould
Abate thy rage, abate thy manly rage,
Abate thy rage, great duke !
Good bawcock, bate thy rage , use lenity,
  sweet chuck '
Nym These be good humors ' your honor
wins bad humors [*Exeunt all but Boy*
Boy As young as I am, I have observed
these three swashers I am boy to them all
three . but all they three, though they would
serve me, could not be man to me , for indeed
three such antics do not amount to a man
For Bardolph, he is white-livered and red-
faced , by the means whereof a' faces it out,
but fights not. For Pistol, he hath a killing
tongue and a quiet sword , by the means
whereof a' breaks words, and keeps whole
weapons For Nym, he hath heard that men
of few words are the best men , and therefore
he scorns to say his prayers, lest a' should be
thought a coward but his few bad words are
matched with as few good deeds , for a' never
broke any man's head but his own, and that
was against a post when he was drunk. They
will steal any thing, and call it purchase
Bardolph stole a lute-case, bore it twelve
leagues, and sold it for three half pence. Nym
and Bardolph are sworn brothers in filching,
and in Calais they stole a fire-shovel I knew
by that piece of service the men would carry
coals. They would have me as familiar with
men's pockets as their gloves or their hand-
kerchers : which makes much against my
manhood, if I should take from another's
pocket to put into mine , for it is plain pock-
eting up of wrongs. I must leave them, and
seek some better service . their villany goes
against my weak stomach, and therefore I
must cast it up [*Exit.*

Re-enter FLUELLEN, GOWER *following*

Gow. Captain Fluellen, you must come
presently to the mines , the Duke of Gloucester would speak with you 60
Flu. To the mines ! tell you the duke, it is
not so good to come to the mines , for, look
you, the mines is not according to the disciplines of the war . the concavities of it is not
sufficient ; for, look you, th' athversary, you
may discuss unto the duke, look you, is digt
himself four yard under the countermines by
Cheshu, I think a' will plow up all, if there is
not better directions
Gow. The Duke of Gloucester, to whom
the order of the siege is given, is altogether
directed by an Irishman, a very valiant gentleman, i' faith
Flu It is Captain Macmorris, is it not ?
Gow. I think it be.
Flu. By Cheshu, he is an ass, as in the
world : I will verify as much in his beard . he
has no more directions in the true disciplines

of the wars, look you, of the Roman disciplines, than is a puppy-dog.

Enter MACMORRIS *and* Captain JAMY.

Gow Here a' comes , and the Scots captain, Captain Jamy, with him 80
Flu Captain Jamy is a marvellous falorous
gentleman, that is certain , and of great expedition and knowledge in th' aunchient wars,
upon my particular knowledge of his directions by Cheshu, he will maintain his argument as well as any military man in the
world, in the disciplines of the pristine wars
of the Romans
Jamy I say gud-day, Captain Fluellen
Flu God-den to your worship, good Captain James 90
Gow. How now, Captain Macmorris ' have
you quit the mines ? have the pioneers given
o'er ?
Mac By Chrish, la ! tish ill done the
work ish give over, the trompet sound the retreat By my hand, I swear, and my father's
soul, the work ish ill done , it ish give over :
I would have blowed up the town, so Chrish
save me, la ! in an hour O, tish ill done,
tish ill done , by my hand, tish ill done ! 99
Flu Captain Macmorris, I beseech you
now, will you voutsafe me, look you, a few
disputations with you, as partly touching or
concerning the disciplines of the war, the Roman wars, in the way of argument, look you,
and friendly communication , partly to satisfy my opinion, and partly for the satisfaction, look you, of my mind, as touching the
direction of the military discipline , that is
the point
Jamy It sall be vary gud, gud feith, gud
captains bath and I sall quit you with gud
leve, as I may pick occasion , that sall I,
marry 111
Mac It is no time to discourse, so Chrish
save me the day is hot, and the weather,
and the wars, and the king, and the dukes
it is no time to discourse The town is be-
seeched, and the trumpet call us to the
breach , and we talk, and, be Chrish, do nothing ' 'tis shame for us all so God sa' me, 'tis
shame to stand still it is shame, by my
hand and there is throats to be cut, and
works to be done , and there ish nothing
done, so Chrish sa' me, la ' 121
Jamy. By the mess, ere theise eyes of mine
take themselves to slomber, ay'll be gud service, or ay'll lig i' the grund for it , ay, or go
to death , and ay'll pay 't as valorously as I
may, that sall I suerly do, that is the breff
and the long. Marry, I wad full fain hear
some question 'tween you twav
Flu Captain Macmorris, I think, look you,
under your correction, there is not many of
your nation— 131
Mac Of my nation ! What ish my nation ?
Ish a villain, and a bastard, and a knave, and
a rascal. What ish my nation ? Who talks
of my nation ?

Flu. Look you, if you take the matter otherwise than is meant, Captain Macmorris, peradventure I shall think you do not use me with that affability as in discretion you ought to use me, look you ; being as good a man as yourself, both in the disciplines of war, and in the derivation of my birth, and in other particularities.

Mac. I do not know you so good a man as myself : so Chrish save me, I will cut off your head.

Gow., Gentlemen both, you will mistake each other.

Jamy. A ! that's a foul fault.
                  [*A parley sounded.*

Gow. The town sounds a parley.   149

Flu. Captain Macmorris, when there is more better opportunity to be required, look you, I will be so bold as to tell you I know the disciplines of war ; and there is an end.
                      [*Exeunt.*

SCENE III. *The same. Before the gates.*

The Governor and some Citizens on the walls ; the English forces below. Enter KING HENRY *and his train.*

K. Hen. How yet resolves the governor of the town ?
This is the latest parle we will admit ;
Therefore to our best mercy give yourselves ;
Or like to men proud of destruction
Defy us to our worst : for, as I am a soldier,
A name that in my thoughts becomes me best,
If I begin the battery once again,
I will not leave the half-achieved Harfleur
Till in her ashes she lie buried.
The gates of mercy shall be all shut up,   10
And the flesh'd soldier, rough and hard of heart,
In liberty of bloody hand shall range
With conscience wide as hell, mowing like grass
Your fresh-fair virgins and your flowering infants.
What is it then to me, if impious war,
Array'd in flames like to the prince of fiends,
Do, with his smirch'd complexion, all fell feats
Enlink'd to waste and desolation ?
What is't to me, when you yourselves are cause,
If your pure maidens fall into the hand   20
Of hot and forcing violation ?
What rein can hold licentious wickedness
When down the hill he holds his fierce career?
We may as bootless spend our vain command
Upon the enraged soldiers in their spoil
As send precepts to the leviathan
To come ashore. Therefore, you men of Harfleur,
Take pity of your town and of your people,
Whiles yet my soldiers are in my command ;
Whiles yet the cool and temperate wind of grace   30
O'erblows the filthy and contagious clouds

Of heady murder, spoil and villany.
If not, why, in a moment look to see
The blind and bloody soldier with foul hand
Defile the locks of your shrill-shrieking daughters ;
Your fathers taken by the silver beards,
And their most reverend heads dash'd to the walls,
Your naked infants spitted upon pikes,
Whiles the mad mothers with their howls confused
Do break the clouds, as did the wives of Jewry   40
At Herod's bloody-hunting slaughtermen.
What say you ? will you yield, and this avoid,
Or, guilty in defence, be thus destroy'd ?

Gov. Our expectation hath this day an end :
The Dauphin, whom of succors we entreated,
Returns us that his powers are yet not ready
To raise so great a siege. Therefore, great king,
We yield our town and lives to thy soft mercy.
Enter our gates ; dispose of us and ours ;
For we no longer are defensible.   50

K. Hen. Open your gates. Come, uncle Exeter,
Go you and enter Harfleur ; there remain,
And fortify it strongly 'gainst the French :
Use mercy to them all. For us, dear uncle,
The winter coming on and sickness growing
Upon our soldiers, we will retire to Calais.
To-night in Harfleur we will be your guest ;
To-morrow for the march are we addrest.
    [*Flourish. The King and his train enter the town.*

SCENE IV. *The* FRENCH KING'S *palace.*

Enter KATHARINE *and* ALICE.

Kath. Alice, tu as été en Angleterre, et tu parles bien le langage.

Alice. Un peu, madame.

Kath. Je te prie, m'enseignez : il faut que j'apprenne à parler. Comment appelez-vous la main en Anglois ?

Alice. La main ? elle est appelée de hand.

Kath. De hand. Et les doigts ?

Alice. Les doigts ? ma foi, j'oublie les doigts ; mais je me souviendrai. Les doigts ? je pense qu'ils sont appelés de fingres ; oui, de fingres.   11

Kath. La main, de hand ; les doigts, de fingres. Je pense que je suis le bon écolier ; j'ai gagné deux mots d'Anglois vitement. Comment appelez-vous les ongles ?

Alice. Les ongles ? nous les appelons de nails.

Kath. De nails. Ecoutez ; dites-moi si je parle bien : de hand, de fingres, et de nails.

Alice. C'est bien dit, madame ; il est fort bon Anglois.   20

Kath. Dites-moi l'Anglois pour le bras.

Alice. De arm, madame.

Kath. Et le coude ?

Alice. De elbow.
Kath. De elbow. Je m'en fais la répétition de tous les mots que vous m'avez appris dès a présent.
Alice Il est trop difficile, madame, comme je pense
Kath Excusez-moi, Alice, écoutez · de hand, de fingres, de nails, de arma, de bilbow 31
Alice. De elbow, madame
Kath. O Seigneur Dieu, je m'en oublie ' de elbow. Comment appelez-vous le col ?
Alice. De neck, madame
Kath. De nick. Et le menton ?
Alice. De chin
Kath De sin Le col, de nick , de menton, de sin. 39
Alice Oui Sauf votre honneur, en vérité, vous prononcez les mots aussi droit que les natifs d'Angleterre
Kath Je ne doute point d'apprendre, par la grace de Dieu, et en peu de temps
Alice. N'avez vous pas dejà oublié ce que je vous ai enseigné ?
Kath Non, je reciterai à vous promptement : de hand, de fingres, de mails,—
Alice De nails, madame
Kath. De nails, de arm, de elbow 50
Alice Sauf votre honneur, de elbow.
Kath Ainsi dis-je , de elbow, de nick, et de sin Comment appelez-vous le pied et la robe ?
Alice. De foot, madame ; et de coun
Kath. De foot et de coun ' O Seigneur Dieu' ce sont mots de son mauvais, corruptible, gros, et impudique, et non pour les dames d'honneur d'user · je voudrais prononcer ces mots devant les seigneurs de France pour tout le monde. Foh' le foot et le coun ' Néanmoins, je reciterai une autre fois ma leçon ensemble de hand, de fingres, de nails, de arm, de elbow, de nick, de sin, de foot, de coun.
Alice. Excellent, madame '
Kath C'est assez pour une fois : allons-nous à dîner [*Exeunt*

SCENE V. *The same*

Enter the KING OF FRANCE, *the* DAUPHIN, *the* DUKE OF BOURBON, *the* CONSTABLE OF FRANCE, *and others*

Fr. King 'Tis certain he hath pass'd the river Somme.
Con And if he be not fought withal, my lord,
Let us not live in France ; let us quit all
And give our vineyards to a barbarous people
Dau O Dieu vivant ! shall a few sprays of us,
The emptying of our fathers' luxury,
Our scions, put in wild and savage stock,
Spirt up so suddenly into the clouds,
And overlook their grafters ?
Bour. Normans, but bastard Normans, Norman bastards ! 10

Mort de ma vie ' if they march along
Unfought withal, but I will sell my dukedom,
To buy a slobbery and a dirty farm
In that nook-shotten isle of Albion
Con Dieu de batailles ' where have they this mettle ?
Is not their climate foggy, raw and dull,
On whom, as in despite, the sun looks pale,
Killing their fruit with frowns ? Can sodden water,
A drench for sur-rein'd jades, their barley-broth, 19
Decoct their cold blood to such valiant heat ?
And shall our quick blood, spirited with wine,
Seem frosty ? O, for honor of our land,
Let us not hang like roping icicles
Upon our houses' thatch, whiles a more frosty people
Sweat drops of gallant youth in our rich fields '
Poor we may call them in their native lords.
Dau By faith and honor,
Our madams mock at us, and plainly say
Our mettle is bred out and they will give
Their bodies to the lust of English youth 30
To new-store France with bastard warriors.
Bour They bid us to the English dancing-schools,
And teach lavoltas high and swift corantos ,
Saying our grace is only in our heels,
And that we are most lofty runaways.
Fr King Where is Montjoy the herald ? speed him hence
Let him greet England with our sharp defiance.
Up, princes ' and, with spirit of honor edged
More sharper than your swords, hie to the field 39
Charles Delabreth, high constable of France ;
You Dukes of Orleans, Bourbon, and of Berri,
Alençon, Brabant, Bar, and Burgundy ;
Jaques Chatillon, Rambures, Vaudemont,
Beaumont, Grandpré, Roussi, and Fauconberg,
Foix, Lestrale, Bouciqualt, and Charolois ,
High dukes, great princes, barons, lords and knights,
For your great seats now quit you of great shames
Bar Harry England, that sweeps through our land
With pennons painted in the blood of Harfleur · Rush on his host, as doth the melted snow 50
Upon the valleys, whose low vassal seat
The Alps doth spit and void his rheum upon :
Go down upon him, you have power enough,
And in a captive chariot into Rouen
Bring him our prisoner
Con This becomes the great.
Sorry am I his numbers are so few,
His soldiers sick and famish'd in their march,
For I am sure, when he shall see our army,
He'll drop his heart into the sink of fear
And for achievement offer us his ransom 60
Fr. King Therefore, lord constable, haste on Montjoy,
And let him say to England that we send

To know what willing ransom he will give.
Prince Dauphin, you shall stay with us in
  Rouen.
Dau. Not so, I do beseech your majesty.
Fr. King. Be patient, for you shall remain
  with us.
Now forth, lord constable and princes all,
And quickly bring us word of England's fall.
                   [*Exeunt.*

SCENE VI. *The English camp in Picardy.*

Enter GOWER *and* FLUELLEN, *meeting.*

Gow. How now, Captain Fluellen! come
you from the bridge?
Flu. I assure you, there is very excellent
services committed at the bridge.
Gow. Is the Duke of Exeter safe?
Flu. The Duke of Exeter is as magnanimous as Agamemnon; and a man that I love
and honor with my soul, and my heart, and
my duty, and my life, and my living, and
my uttermost power: he is not—God be praised
and blessed!—any hurt in the world; but keeps
the bridge most valiantly, with excellent discipline. There is an aunchient lieutenant there
at the pridge, I think in my very conscience he
is as valiant a man as Mark Antony; and he
is a man of no estimation in the world; but I
did see him do as gallant service.
Gow. What do you call him?
Flu. He is called Aunchient Pistol.
Gow. I know him not.   20

Enter PISTOL.

Flu. Here is the man.
Pist. Captain, I thee beseech to do me fa-
  vors:
The Duke of Exeter doth love thee well.
Flu. Ay, I praise God; and I have merited
some love at his hands.
Pist. Bardolph, a soldier, firm and sound
  of heart,
And of buxom valor, hath, by cruel fate,
And giddy Fortune's furious fickle wheel,
That goddess blind,   30
That stands upon the rolling restless stone—
Flu. By your patience, Aunchient Pistol.
Fortune is painted blind, with a muffler afore
her eyes, to signify to you that Fortune is
blind; and she is painted also with a wheel,
to signify to you, which is the moral of it, that
she is turning, and inconstant, and mutability,
and variation: and her foot, look you, is fixed
upon a spherical stone, which rolls, and rolls,
and rolls: in good truth, the poet makes a most
excellent description of it: Fortune is an excellent moral.   40
Pist. Fortune is Bardolph's foe, and frowns
  on him:
For he hath stolen a pax, and hanged must a'
  be:
A damned death!
Let gallows gape for dog; let man go free
And let not hemp his wind-pipe suffocate:
But Exetor hath given the doom of death

For pax of little price.
Therefore, go speak: the duke will hear thy
  voice:
And let not Bardolph's vital thread be cut
With edge of penny cord and vile reproach:
Speak, captain, for his life, and I will thee
  requite.   51
Flu. Aunchient Pistol, I do partly under-
stand your meaning.
Pist. Why then, rejoice therefore.
Flu. Certainly, aunchient, it is not a thing
to rejoice at: for if, look you, he were my
brother, I would desire the duke to use his
good pleasure, and put him to execution; for
discipline ought to be used.
Pist. Die and be damn'd! and figo for thy
  friendship!   60
Flu. It is well.
Pist. The fig of Spain!   [*Exit.*
Flu. Very good.
Gow. Why, this is an arrant counterfeit
rascal; I remember him now; a bawd, a cut-
purse.
Flu. I'll assure you, a' uttered as brave
words at the bridge as you shall see in a summer's day. But it is very well; what he has
spoke to me, that is well, I warrant you, when
time is serve.   69
Gow. Why, 'tis a gull, a fool, a rogue, that
now and then goes to the wars, to grace himself at his return into London under the form
of a soldier. And such fellows are perfect in
the great commanders' names: and they will
learn you by rote where services were done;
at such and such a sconce, at such a breach, at
such a convoy; who came off bravely, who
was shot, who disgraced, what terms the
enemy stood on; and this they con perfectly
in the phrase of war, which they trick up with
new-tuned oaths: and what a beard of the
general's cut and a horrid suit of the camp will
do among foaming bottles and ale-washed
wits, is wonderful to be thought on. But you
must learn to know such slanders of the age,
or else you may be marvellously mistook.
Flu. I tell you what, Captain Gower; I do
perceive he is not the man that he would gladly
make show to the world he is: if I find a hole
in his coat, I will tell him my mind. [*Drum
heard.*] Hark you, the king is coming, and I
must speak with him from the pridge.   91

Drum and colors. Enter KING HENRY,
    GLOUCESTER, *and* Soldiers.

God pless your majesty!
K. Hen. How now, Fluellen! camest thou
  from the bridge?
Flu. Ay, so please your majesty. The
Duke of Exeter has very gallantly maintained
the pridge: the French is gone off, look you;
and there is gallant and most prave passages;
marry, th' athversary was have possession of
the pridge; but he is enforced to retire, and
the Duke of Exeter is master of the pridge: I
can tell your majesty, the duke is a prave
man.   101

K. Hen. What men have you lost, Fluellen?

Flu. The perdition of th' athversary hath been very great, reasonable great : marry, for my part, I think the duke hath lost never a man, but one that is like to be executed for robbing a church, one Bardolph, if your majesty know the man : his face is all bubukles, and whelks, and knobs, and flames o' fire : and his lips blows at his nose, and it is like a coal of fire, sometimes plue and sometimes red ; but his nose is executed and his fire's out.

K. Hen. We would have all such offenders so cut off : and we give express charge, that in our marches through the country, there be nothing compelled from the villages, nothing taken but paid for, none of the French upbraided or abused in disdainful language ; for when lenity and cruelty play for a kingdom, the gentler gamester is the soonest winner.   120

Tucket. Enter MONTJOY.

Mont. You know me by my habit.

K. Hen. Well then I know thee : what shall I know of thee ?

Mont. My master's mind.

K. Hen. Unfold it.

Mont. Thus says my king : Say thou to Harry of England : Though we seemed dead, we did but sleep : advantage is a better soldier than rashness. Tell him we could have rebuked him at Harfleur, but that we thought not good to bruise an injury till it were full ripe : now we speak upon our cue, and our voice is imperial : England shall repent his folly, see his weakness, and admire our sufferance. Bid him therefore consider of his ransom ; which must proportion the losses we have borne, the subjects we have lost, the disgrace we have digested ; which in weight to re-answer, his pettiness would bow under. For our losses, his exchequer is too poor ; for the effusion of our blood, the muster of his kingdom too faint a number ; and for our disgrace, his own person, kneeling at our feet, but a weak and worthless satisfaction. To this add defiance : and tell him, for conclusion, he hath betrayed his followers, whose condemnation is pronounced. So far my king and master ; so much my office.   [quality.

K. Hen. What is thy name? I know thy

Mont. Montjoy.

K. Hen. Thou dost thy office fairly. Turn thee back,

And tell thy king I do not seek him now ; But could be willing to march on to Calais 150 Without impeachment : for, to say the sooth, Though 'tis no wisdom to confess so much Unto an enemy of craft and vantage, My people are with sickness much enfeebled, My numbers lessened, and those few I have Almost no better than so many French ; Who when they were in health, I tell thee, herald,

I thought upon one pair of English legs Did march three Frenchmen. Yet, forgive me, God,   159

That I do brag thus ! This your air of France Hath blown that vice in me ; I must repent. Go therefore, tell thy master here I am ; My ransom is this frail and worthless trunk, My army but a weak and sickly guard ; Yet, God before, tell him we will come on, Though France himself and such another neighbor Stand in our way. There's for thy labor, Montjoy.

Go, bid thy master well advise himself : If we may pass, we will ; if we be hinder'd, We shall your tawny ground with your red blood   170 Discolor : and so, Montjoy, fare you well. The sum of all our answer is but this : We would not seek a battle, as we are ; Nor, as we are, we say we will not shun it : So tell your master.

Mont. I shall deliver so. Thanks to your highness.   [*Exit.*

Glou. I hope they will not come upon us now.

K. Hen. We are in God's hand, brother, not in theirs.

March to the bridge ; it now draws toward night :

Beyond the river we'll encamp ourselves, 180 And on to-morrow, bid them march away.

                                       [*Exeunt.*

SCENE VII. *The French Camp, near Agincourt.*

Enter the CONSTABLE OF France, *the* LORD RAMBURES, ORLEANS, DAUPHIN, *with others.*

Con. Tut ! I have the best armor of the world. Would it were day !

Orl. You have an excellent armor ; but let my horse have his due.

Con. It is the best horse of Europe.

Orl. Will it never be morning ?

Dau. My lord of Orleans, and my lord high constable, you talk of horse and armor ?

Orl. You are as well provided of both as any prince in the world.   10

Dau. What a long night is this ! I will not change my horse with any that treads but on four pasterns. Ca, ha ! he bounds from the earth, as if his entrails were hairs ; le cheval volant, the Pegasus, chez les narines de feu ! When I bestride him, I soar, I am a hawk : he trots the air ; the earth sings when he touches it ; the basest horn of his hoof is more musical than the pipe of Hermes.

Orl. He's of the color of the nutmeg. 20

Dau. And of the heat of the ginger. It is a beast for Perseus : he is pure air and fire ; and the dull elements of earth and water never appear in him, but only in patient stillness while his rider mounts him : he is indeed a horse ; and all other jades you may call beasts.

Con. Indeed, my lord, it is a most absolute and excellent horse.

Dau. It is the prince of palfreys ; his neigh is like the bidding of a monarch and his countenance enforces homage.   31

Orl. No more, cousin.

Dau. Nay, the man hath no wit that cannot, from the rising of the lark to the lodging of the lamb, vary deserved praise on my palfrey : it is a theme as fluent as the sea : turn the sands into eloquent tongues, and my horse is argument for them all : 'tis a subject for a sovereign to reason on, and for a sovereign's sovereign to ride on; and for the world, familiar to us and unknown to lay apart their particular functions and wonder at him. I once writ a sonnet in his praise and began thus : 'Wonder of nature,'—

Orl. I have heard a sonnet begin so to one's mistress.

Dau. Then did they imitate that which I composed to my courser, for my horse is my mistress.

Orl. Your mistress bears well.

Dau. Me well ; which is the prescript praise and perfection of a good and particular mistress.

Con. Nay, for methought yesterday your mistress shrewdly shook your back.

Dau. So perhaps did yours.

Con. Mine was not bridled.

Dau. O then belike she was old and gentle; and you rode, like a kern of Ireland, your French hose off, and in your straight strossers.

Con. You have good judgment in horsemanship.   59

Dau. Be warned by me, then : they that ride so and ride not warily, fall into foul bogs. I had rather have my horse to my mistress.

Con. I had as lief have my mistress a jade.

Dau. I tell thee, constable, my mistress wears his own hair.

Con. I could make as true a boast as that, if I had a sow to my mistress.

Dau. 'Le chien est retourné à son propre vomissement, et la truie lavée au bourbier ;' thou makest use of any thing.   70

Con. Yet do I not use my horse for my mistress, or any such proverb so little kin to the purpose.

Ram. My lord constable, the armor that I saw in your tent to-night, are those stars or suns upon it ?

Con. Stars, my lord.

Dau. Some of them will fall to-morrow, I hope.

Con. And yet my sky shall not want.

Dau. That may be, for you bear a many superfluously, and 'twere more honor some were away.   81

Con. Even as your horse bears your praises ; who would trot as well, were some of your brags dismounted.

Dau. Would I were able to load him with his desert ! Will it never be day ? I will trot to-morrow a mile, and my way shall be paved with English faces.

Con. I will not say so, for fear I should be faced out of my way : but I would it were morning ; for I would fain be about the ears of the English.

Ram. Who will go to hazard with me for twenty prisoners ?

Con. You must first go yourself to hazard, ere you have them.

Dau. 'Tis midnight ; I'll go arm myself.
                                      [*Exit.*

Orl. The Dauphin longs for morning.

Ram. He longs to eat the English.

Con. I think he will eat all he kills.   100

Orl. By the white hand of my lady, he's a gallant prince.

Con. Swear by her foot, that she may tread out the oath.

Orl. He is simply the most active gentleman of France.

Con. Doing is activity ; and he will still be doing.

Orl. He never did harm, that I heard of.

Con. Nor will do none to-morrow : he will keep that good name still.   111

Orl. I know him to be valiant.

Con. I was told that by one that knows him better than you.

Orl. What's he ?

Con. Marry, he told me so himself ; and he said he cared not who knew it.

Orl. He needs not ; it is no hidden virtue in him.   119

Con. By my faith, sir, but it is ; never any body saw it but his lackey : 'tis a hooded valor ; and when it appears, it will bate.

Orl. Ill will never said well.

Con. I will cap that proverb with ' There is flattery in friendship.'

Orl. And I will take up that with ' Give the devil his due.'

Con. Well placed : there stands your friend for the devil : have at the very eye of that proverb with ' A pox of the devil.'   130

Orl. You are the better at proverbs, by how much ' A fool's bolt is soon shot.'

Con. You have shot over.

Orl. 'Tis not the first time you were overshot.

Enter a Messenger.

Mess. My lord high constable, the English lie within fifteen hundred paces of your tents.

Con. Who hath measured the ground ?

Mess. The Lord Grandpré.

Con. A valiant and most expert gentleman. Would it were day ! Alas, poor Harry of England ! he longs not for the dawning as we do.   141

Orl. What a wretched and peevish fellow is this king of England, to mope with his fat-brained followers so far out of his knowledge !

Con. If the English had any apprehension, they would run away.

Orl. That they lack ; for if their heads had any intellectual armor, they could never wear such heavy head-pieces.   149

Ram. That island of England breeds very valiant creatures ; their mastiffs are of unmatchable courage.

Orl. Foolish curs, that run winking into

the mouth of a Russian bear and have their
heads crushed like rotten apples ' You may
as well say, that's a valiant flea that dare eat
his breakfast on the lip of a lion

Con. Just, just, and the men do sympathize with the mastiffs in robustious and
rough coming on, leaving their wits with their
wives and then give them great meals of
beef and iron and steel, they will eat like
wolves and fight like devils

Orl. Ay, but these English are shrewdly
out of beef

Con. Then shall we find to-morrow they
have only stomachs to eat and none to fight
Now is it time to arm come, shall we about
it ?

Orl. It is now two o'clock but, let me
see, by ten
We shall have each a hundred Englishmen
[*Exeunt.*

ACT IV

PROLOGUE

Enter Chorus.

Chor. Now entertain conjecture of a time
When creeping murmur and the poring dark
Fills the wide vessel of the universe
From camp to camp through the foul womb
    of night
The hum of either army stilly sounds,
That the fixed sentinels almost receive
The secret whispers of each other's watch
Fire answers fire, and through their paly
    flames
Each battle sees the other's umber'd face,
Steed threatens steed, in high and boastful
    neighs   10
Piercing the night's dull ear, and from the
    tents
The armorers, accomplishing the knights,
With busy hammers closing rivets up,
Give dreadful note of preparation
The country cocks do crow, the clocks do toll,
And the third hour of drowsy morning name
Proud of their numbers and secure in soul,
The confident and over-lusty French
Do the low-rated English play at dice,
And chide the cripple tardy-gaited night   20
Who, like a foul and ugly witch, doth limp
So tediously away. The poor condemned
    English,
Like sacrifices, by their watchful fires
Sit patiently and inly ruminate
The morning's danger, and their gesture sad
Investing lank-lean cheeks and war-worn coats
Presenteth them unto the gazing moon
So many horrid ghosts O now, who will be-
    hold
The royal captain of this ruin'd band
Walking from watch to watch, from tent to
    tent,   30
Let him cry 'Praise and glory on his head !'
For forth he goes and visits all his host,

Bids them good morrow with a modest smile
And calls them brothers, friends and country-
    men
Upon his royal face there is no note
How dread an army hath enrounded him ,
Nor doth he dedicate one jot of color
Unto the weary and all watched night,
But freshly looks and over-bears attaint
With cheerful semblance and sweet majesty
That every wretch, pining and pale before, 41
Beholding him, plucks comfort from his looks
A largess universal like the sun
His liberal eye doth give to every one,
Thawing cold fear, that mean and gentle all,
Behold, as may unworthiness define,
A little touch of Harry in the night.
And so our scene must to the battle fly ;
Where—O for pity '—we shall much disgrace
With four or five most vile and ragged foils,
Right ill-disposed in brawl ridiculous,   51
The name of Agincourt Yet sit and see,
Minding true things by what their mockeries
    be   [*Exit*

SCENE I *The English camp at Agincourt*

Enter KING HENRY, BEDFORD, *and* GLOU-
CESTER

K Hen Gloucester, 'tis true that we are in
    great danger ,
The greater therefore should our courage be
Good morrow, brother Bedford God Al-
    mighty '
There is some soul of goodness in things evil,
Would men observingly distil it out
For our bad neighbor makes us early stirers,
Which is both healthful and good husbandry
Besides, they are our outward consciences,
And preachers to us all, admonishing
That we should dress us fairly for our end   10
Thus may we gather honey from the weed,
And make a moral of the devil himself

Enter ERPINGHAM

Good morrow, old Sir Thomas Erpingham
A good soft pillow for that good white head
Were better than a churlish turf of France
    Erp Not so, my liege this lodging likes
    me better,
Since I may say ' Now lie I like a king '
    K Hen 'Tis good for men to love their
        present pains
Upon example , so the spirit is eased   19
And when the mind is quicken'd, out of doubt,
The organs, though defunct and dead before,
Break up their drowsy grave and newly move,
With casted slough and fresh legerity
Lend me thy cloak, Sir Thomas Brothers
    both,
Commend me to the princes in our camp ,
Do my good morrow to them, and anon
Desire them all to my pavilion
    Glou We shall, my liege
    Erp Shall I attend your grace ?
    K Hen   No, my good knight ;
Go with my brothers to my lords of England .

30

I and my bosom must debate awhile,   31
And then I would no other company.
   Erp. The Lord in heaven bless thee, noble
     Harry!   [*Exeunt all but King.*
   K. Hen. God-a-mercy, old heart! thou
   speak'st cheerfully.

         Enter PISTOL.

   Pist. Qui va là?
   K. Hen. A friend.
   Pist. Discuss unto me; art thou officer?
Or art thou base, common and popular?
   K. Hen. I am a gentleman of a company.
   Pist. Trail'st thou the puissant pike?   40
   K. Hen. Even so. What are you?
   Pist. As good a gentleman as the emperor.
   K. Hen. Then you are a better than the
   king.
   Pist. The king's a bawcock, and a heart of
   gold,
A lad of life, an imp of fame;
Of parents good, of fist most valiant.
I kiss his dirty shoe, and from heart-string
I love the lovely bully. What is thy name?
   K. Hen. Harry le Roy.
   Pist. Le Roy! a Cornish name: art thou
   of Cornish crew?   50
   K. Hen. No, I am a Welshman.
   Pist. Know'st thou Fluellen?
   K. Hen. Yes.
   Pist. Tell him, I'll knock his leek about
   his pate
Upon Saint Davy's day.
   K. Hen. Do not you wear your dagger in
your cap that day, lest he knock that about
yours.
   Pist. Art thou his friend?
   K. Hen. And his kinsman too.
   Pist. The figo for thee, then!   60
   K. Hen. I thank you: God be with you!
   Pist. My name is Pistol call'd.   [*Exit.*
   K. Hen. It sorts well with your fierceness.

     Enter FLUELLEN *and* GOWER.

   Gow. Captain Fluellen!
   Flu. So! in the name of Jesu Christ, speak
lower. It is the greatest admiration of the
universal world, when the true and aunchient
prerogatifes and laws of the wars is not kept:
if you would take the pains but to examine
the wars of Pompey the Great, you shall find,
I warrant you, that there is no tiddle taddle
nor pibble pabble in Pompey's camp; I warrant you, you shall find the ceremonies of the
wars, and the cares of it, and the forms of it,
and the sobriety of it, and the modesty of it,
to be otherwise.
   Gow. Why, the enemy is loud; you hear
him all night.
   Flu. If the enemy is an ass and a fool and
a prating coxcomb, is it meet, think you, that
we should also, look you, be an ass and a fool
and a prating coxcomb? in your own conscience, now?
   Gow. I will speak lower.
   Flu. I pray you and beseech you that you
will.   [*Exeunt Gower and Fluellen.*

   K. Hen. Though it appear a little out of
   fashion,
There is much care and valor in this Welshman.

Enter three soldiers, JOHN BATES, ALEXAN-
   DER COURT, *and* MICHAEL WILLIAMS.

   Court. Brother John Bates, is not that the
morning which breaks yonder?
   Bates. I think it be: but we have no great
cause to desire the approach of day.   90
   Will. We see yonder the beginning of the
day, but I think we shall never see the end of
it. Who goes there?
   K. Hen. A friend.
   Will. Under what captain serve you?
   K. Hen. Under Sir Thomas Erpingham.
   Will. A good old commander and a most
kind gentleman: I pray you, what thinks he
of our estate?
   K. Hen. Even as men wrecked upon a sand,
that look to be washed off the next tide.   101
   Bates. He hath not told his thought to the
king?
   K. Hen. No; nor it is not meet he should.
For, though I speak it to you, I think the
king is but a man, as I am: the violet smells
to him as it doth to me: the element shows to
him as it doth to me; all his senses have but
human conditions: his ceremonies laid by, in
his nakedness he appears but a man; and
though his affections are higher mounted than
ours, yet, when they stoop, they stoop with
the like wing. Therefore when he sees reason
of fears, as we do, his fears, out of doubt, be
of the same relish as ours are: yet, in reason,
no man should possess him with any appearance of fear, lest he, by showing it, should
dishearten his army.
   Bates. He may show what outward courage
he will; but I believe, as cold a night as 'tis,
he could wish himself in Thames up to the
neck; and so I would he were, and I by him,
at all adventures, so we were quit here.
   K. Hen. By my troth, I will speak my conscience of the king: I think he would not wish
himself any where but where he is.
   Bates. Then I would he were here alone;
so should he be sure to be ransomed, and a
many poor men's lives saved.
   K. Hen. I dare say you love him not so ill,
to wish him here alone, howsoever you speak
this to feel other men's minds: methinks I
could not die any where so contented as in the
king's company; his cause being just and his
quarrel honorable.
   Will. That's more than we know.
   Bates. Ay, or more than we should seek
after; for we know enough, if we know we are
the king's subjects: if his cause be wrong,
our obedience to the king wipes the crime of
it out of us.
   Will. But if the cause be not good, the
king himself hath a heavy reckoning to make,
when all those legs and arms and heads,
chopped off in battle, shall join together at the

latter day and cry all 'We died at such a place,' some swearing, some crying for a surgeon, some upon their wives left poor behind them, some upon the debts they owe, some upon their children rawly left. I am afeard there are few die well that die in a battle, for how can they charitably dispose of any thing, when blood is their argument? Now, if these men do not die well, it will be a black matter for the king that led them to it, whom to disobey were against all proportion of subjection.

K. Hen. So, if a son that is by his father sent about merchandise do sinfully miscarry upon the sea, the imputation of his wickedness, by your rule, should be imposed upon his father that sent him—or if a servant, under his master's command transporting a sum of money, be assailed by robbers and die in many irreconciled iniquities, you may call the business of the master the author of the servant's damnation: but this is not so; the king is not bound to answer the particular endings of his soldiers, the father of his son, nor the master of his servant, for they purpose not their death, when they purpose their services. Besides, there is no king, be his cause never so spotless, if it come to the arbitrement of swords, can try it out with all unspotted soldiers: some peradventure have on them the guilt of premeditated and contrived murder; some, of beguiling virgins with the broken seals of perjury; some, making the wars their bulwark, that have before gored the gentle bosom of peace with pillage and robbery. Now, if these men have defeated the law and outrun native punishment, though they can outstrip men, they have no wings to fly from God: war is his beadle, war is his vengeance; so that here men are punished for beforebreach of the king's laws in now the king's quarrel: where they feared the death, they have borne life away, and where they would be safe, they perish: then if they die unprovided, no more is the king guilty of their damnation than he was before guilty of those impieties for the which they are now visited. Every subject's duty is the king's, but every subject's soul is his own. Therefore should every soldier in the wars do as every sick man in his bed, wash every mote out of his conscience: and dying so, death is to him advantage; or not dying, the time was blessedly lost wherein such preparation was gained: and in him that escapes, it were not sin to think that, making God so free an offer, He let him outlive that day to see His greatness and to teach others how they should prepare.

Will. 'Tis certain, every man that dies ill, the ill upon his own head, the king is not to answer it. 199

Bates. But I do not desire he should answer for me; and yet I determine to fight lustily for him.

K. Hen. I myself heard the king say he would not be ransomed.

Will. Ay, he said so, to make us fight cheerfully: but when our throats are cut, he may be ransomed, and we ne'er the wiser.

K. Hen. If I live to see it, I will never trust his word after.

Will. You pay him then! That's a perilous shot out of an elder-gun, that a poor and private displeasure can do against a monarch! you may as well go about to turn the sun to ice with fanning in his face with a peacock's feather. You'll never trust his word after! come, 'tis a foolish saying.

K. Hen. Your reproof is something too round: I should be angry with you, if the time were convenient.

Will. Let it be a quarrel between us, if you live. 220

K. Hen. I embrace it.

Will. How shall I know thee again?

K. Hen. Give me any gage of thine, and I will wear it in my bonnet: then, if ever thou darest acknowledge it, I will make it my quarrel.

Will. Here's my glove: give me another of thine.

K. Hen. There.

Will. This will I also wear in my cap: if ever thou come to me and say, after to-morrow, 'This is my glove,' by this hand, I will take thee a box on the ear.

K. Hen. If ever I live to see it, I will challenge it.

Will. Thou darest as well be hanged.

K. Hen. Well, I will do it, though I take thee in the king's company.

Will. Keep thy word: fare thee well.

Bates. Be friends, you English fools, be friends: we have French quarrels enow, if you could tell how to reckon. 241

K. Hen. Indeed, the French may lay twenty French crowns to one, they will beat us, for they bear them on their shoulders: but it is no English treason to cut French crowns, and to-morrow the king himself will be a clipper.

[*Exeunt soldiers.*

Upon the king! let us our lives, our souls,
Our debts, our careful wives,
Our children and our sins lay on the king!
We must bear all. O hard condition, 250
Twin-born with greatness, subject to the breath
Of every fool, whose sense no more can feel
But his own wringing! What infinite heart's-ease
Must kings neglect, that private men enjoy!
And what have kings, that privates have not too,
Save ceremony, save general ceremony?
And what art thou, thou idol ceremony?
What kind of god art thou, that suffer'st more
Of mortal griefs than do thy worshippers?
What are thy rents? what are thy comings in?
O ceremony, show me but thy worth! 261
†What is thy soul of adoration?
Art thou aught else but place, degree and form,
Creating awe and fear in other men?

Wherein thou art less happy being fear'd
Than they in fearing.
What drink'st thou oft, instead of homage
    sweet,
But poison'd flattery ? O, be sick, great great-
    ness,
And bid thy ceremony give thee cure !
Think'st thou the fiery fever will go out   270
With titles blown from adulation ?
Will it give place to flexure and low bending ?
Canst thou, when thou command'st the beggar's
    knee,
Command the health of it ? No, thou proud
    dream,
That play'st so subtly with a king's repose ;
I am a king that find thee, and I know
'Tis not the balm, the sceptre and the ball,
The sword, the mace, the crown imperial,
The intertissued robe of gold and pearl,
The farced title running 'fore the king,   280
The throne he sits on, nor the tide of pomp
That beats upon the high shore of this world,
No, not all these, thrice-gorgeous ceremony,
Not all these, laid in bed majestical,
Can sleep so soundly as the wretched slave,
Who with a body fill'd and vacant mind
Gets him to rest, cramm'd with distressful
    bread ;
Never sees horrid night, the child of hell,
But, like a lackey, from the rise to set
Sweats in the eye of Phœbus and all night 290
Sleeps in Elysium ; next day after dawn,
Doth rise and help Hyperion to his horse,
And follows so the ever-running year,
With profitable labor, to his grave :
And, but for ceremony, such a wretch,
Winding up days with toil and nights with
    sleep,
Had the fore-hand and vantage of a king.
The slave, a member of the country's peace,
Enjoys it ; but in gross brain little wots
What watch the king keeps to maintain the
    peace,   300
Whose hours the peasant best advantages.

Enter ERPINGHAM.

Erp. My lord, your nobles, jealous of your
    absence,
Seek through your camp to find you.
K. Hen.   Good old knight,
Collect them all together at my tent :
I'll be before thee.
Erp.   I shall do't, my lord. [*Exit.*
K. Hen. O God of battles ! steal my soldiers'
    hearts ;
Possess them not with fear ; take from them
    now
The sense of reckoning, if the opposed num-
    bers
Pluck their hearts from them. Not to-day, O
    Lord,
O, not to-day, think not upon the fault   310
My father made in compassing the crown !
I Richard's body have interred anew ;
And on it have bestow'd more contrite tears
Than from it issued forced drops of blood ·

Five hundred poor I have in yearly pay,
Who twice a-day their wither'd hands hold up
Toward heaven, to pardon blood ; and I have
    built
Two chantries, where the sad and solemn
    priests
Sing still for Richard's soul. More will I do ;
Though all that I can do is nothing worth, 320
Since that my penitence comes after all,
Imploring pardon.

Enter GLOUCESTER.

Glou. My liege !
K. Hen. My brother Gloucester's voice ?
    Ay ;
I know thy errand, I will go with thee :
The day, my friends and all things stay for
    me.   [*Exeunt.*

SCENE II.   *The French camp.*

Enter the DAUPHIN, ORLEANS, RAMBURES,
    and others.

Orl. The sun doth gild our armor ; up, my
    lords !
Dau. Montez à cheval ! My horse ! varlet !
    laquais ! ha !
Orl. O brave spirit !
Dau. Via ! les eaux et la terre.
Orl. Rien puis ? l'air et la feu.
Dau. Ciel, cousin Orleans.

Enter CONSTABLE.

Now, my lord constable !
Con. Hark, how our steeds for present ser-
    vice neigh !
Dau. Mount them, and make incision in
    their hides,   9
That their hot blood may spin in English eyes,
And dout them with superfluous courage, ha !
Ram. What, will you have them weep our
    horses' blood ?
How shall we, then, behold their natural tears?

Enter Messenger.

Mess. The English are embattled, you
    French peers.
Con. To horse, you gallant princes ! straight
    to horse !
Do but behold yon poor and starved band,
And your fair show shall suck away their
    souls,
Leaving them but the shales and husks of
    men.
There is not work enough for all our hands ;
Scarce blood enough in all their sickly veins 20
To give each naked curtle-axe a stain,
That our French gallants shall to-day draw
    out,
And sheathe for lack of sport : let us but blow
    on them,
The vapor of our valor will o'erturn them.
'Tis positive 'gainst all exceptions, lords,
That our superfluous lackeys and our peasants,
Who in unnecessary action swarm
About our squares of battle, were enow
To purge this field of such a hilding foe,
Though we upon this mountain's basis by   30

Took stand for idle speculation :
But that our honors must not. What's to say ?
A very little little let us do,
And all is done.   Then let the trumpets sound
The tucket sonance and the note to mount ;
For our approach shall so much dare the field
That England shall couch down in fear and
　　yield.

Enter Grandpre.

Grand.　Why do you stay so long, my lords
　　of France ?
You island carrions, desperate of their bones,
Ill-favoredly become the morning field :　　40
Their ragged curtains poorly are let loose,
And our air shakes them passing scornfully :
Big Mars seems bankrupt in their beggar'd
　　host
And faintly through a rusty beaver peeps :
The horsemen sit like fixed candlesticks,
With torch-staves in their hand ; and their
　　poor jades
Lob down their heads, dropping the hides and
　　hips,
The gum down-roping from their pale-dead
　　eyes
And in their pale dull mouths the gimmal bit
Lies foul with chew'd grass, still and motion-
　　less ;　　　　　　　　　　　　　　　　50
And their executors, the knavish crows,
Fly o'er them, all impatient for their hour.
Description cannot suit itself in words
To demonstrate the life of such a battle
In life so lifeless as it shows itself.
　　Con.　They have said their prayers, and
　　　　they stay for death.
　　Dau.　Shall we go send them dinners and
　　　　fresh suits
And give their fasting horses provender,
And after fight with them ?
　　Con.　I stay but for my guidon : to the
　　　　field !　　　　　　　　　　　　　　60
I will the banner from a trumpet take,
And use it for my haste.   Come, come, away !
The sun is high, and we outwear the day.
　　　　　　　　　　　　　　　　　[*Exeunt.*

Scene III.　*The English camp.*

Enter Gloucester, Bedford, Exeter, Er-
　pingham, *with all his host :* Salisbury *and*
　Westmoreland.

　　Glou.　Where is the king ?
　　Bed.　The king himself is rode to view their
　　　battle.
　　West.　Of fighting men they have full three
　　　score thousand.
　　Exe.　There's five to one ; besides, they all
　　　are fresh.
　　Sal.　God's arm strike with us ! 'tis a fear-
　　　ful odds.
God be wi' you, princes all ; I'll to my charge :
If we no more meet till we meet in heaven,
Then, joyfully, my noble Lord of Bedford,
My dear Lord Gloucester, and my good Lord
　　Exeter,
And my kind kinsman, warriors all, adieu !　10

　　Bed.　Farewell, good Salisbury ; and good
　　　luck go with thee !
　　Exe.　Farewell, kind lord ; fight valiantly
　　　to-day :
And yet I do thee wrong to mind thee of it,
For thou art framed of the firm truth of valor.
　　　　　　　　　　　　　　　　[*Exit Salisbury.*
　　Bed.　He is full of valor as of kindness ;
Princely in both.

Enter the King.

　　West.　O that we now had here
But one ten thousand of those men in Eng-
　　land
That do no work to-day !
　　K. Hen.　　　　　What's he that wishes so ?
My cousin Westmoreland ?　No, my fair
　　cousin :
If we are mark'd to die, we are enow　　20
To do our country loss ; and if to live,
The fewer men, the greater share of honor.
God's will ! I pray thee, wish not one man
　　more.
By Jove, I am not covetous for gold,
Nor care I who doth feed upon my cost ;
It yearns me not if men my garments wear ;
Such outward things dwell not in my desires :
But if it be a sin to covet honor,
I am the most offending soul alive.
No, faith, my coz, wish not a man from Eng-
　　land :　　　　　　　　　　　　　　　30
God's peace ! I would not lose so great an
　　honor
As one man more, methinks, would share
　　from me
For the best hope I have.　O, do not wish one
　　more !
Rather proclaim it, Westmoreland, through
　　my host,
That he which hath no stomach to this fight,
Let him depart ; his passport shall be made
And crowns for convoy put into his purse :
We would not die in that man's company
That fears his fellowship to die with us.
This day is called the feast of Crispian :　　40
He that outlives this day, and comes safe home,
Will stand a tip-toe when the day is named,
And rouse him at the name of Crispian.
He that shall live this day, and see old age,
Will yearly on the vigil feast his neighbors,
And say 'To-morrow is Saint Crispian :'
Then will he strip his sleeve and show his
　　scars.
And say 'These wounds I had on Crispin's
　　day.'
Old men forget : yet all shall be forgot,
But he'll remember with advantages　　50
What feats he did that day : then shall our
　　names,
Familiar in his mouth as household words,
Harry the king, Bedford and Exeter,
Warwick and Talbot, Salisbury and Gloucester,
Be in their flowing cups freshly remember'd.
This story shall the good man teach his son ;
And Crispin Crispian shall ne'er go by,
From this day to the ending of the world,

But we in it shall be remember'd ;
We few, we happy few, we band of brothers ;
For he to-day that sheds his blood with me
Shall be my brother ; be he ne'er so vile,
This day shall gentle his condition :
And gentlemen in England now a-bed
Shall think themselves accursed they were not
    here,
And hold their manhoods cheap whiles any
    speaks
That fought with us upon Saint Crispin's day.

    Re-enter SALISBURY.

Sal. My sovereign lord, bestow yourself
    with speed :
The French are bravely in their battles set,
And will with all expedience charge on us. 70
    K. Hen. All things are ready, if our minds
    be so.
West. Perish the man whose mind is back-
    ward now !
    K. Hen. Thou dost not wish more help from
    England, coz ?
West. God's will ! my liege, would you and
    I alone,
Without more help, could fight this royal battle!
    K. Hen. Why, now thou hast unwish'd five
    thousand men ;
Which likes me better than to wish us one.
You know your places : God be with you all !

    Tucket.   *Enter* MONTJOY.

Mont. Once more I come to know of thee,
    King Harry,
If for thy ransom thou wilt now compound, 80
Before thy most assured overthrow :
For certainly thou art so near the gulf,
Thou needs must be englutted. Besides, in
    mercy,
The constable desires thee thou wilt mind
Thy followers of repentance ; that their souls
May make a peaceful and a sweet retire
From off these fields, where, wretches, their
    poor bodies
Must lie and fester.
    K. Hen.   Who hath sent thee now ?
    Mont. The Constable of France.
    K. Hen. I pray thee, bear my former an-
    swer back :   90
Bid them achieve me and then sell my bones.
Good God ! why should they mock poor fellows
    thus ?
The man that once did sell the lion's skin
While the beast lived, was killed with hunting
    him.
A many of our bodies shall no doubt
Find native graves ; upon the which, I trust,
Shall witness live in brass of this day's work :
And those that leave their valiant bones in
    France,
Dying like men, though buried in your dung-
    hills,
They shall be famed ; for there the sun shall
    greet them,   100
And draw their honors reeking up to heaven ;
Leaving their earthly parts to choke your
    clime,

The smell whereof shall breed a plague in
    France.
Mark then abounding valor in our English,
That being dead, like to the bullet's grazing,
Break out into a second course of mischief,
Killing in relapse of mortality.
Let me speak proudly : tell the constable
We are but warriors for the working-day ;
Our gayness and our gilt are all besmirch'd 110
With rainy marching in the painful field ;
There's not a piece of feather in our host—
Good argument, I hope, we will not fly—
And time hath worn us into slovenry :
But, by the mass, our hearts are in the trim ;
And my poor soldiers tell me, yet ere night
They'll be in fresher robes, or they will pluck
The gay new coats o'er the French soldiers'
    heads
And turn them out of service. If they do this,—
As, if God please, they shall,—my ransom then
Will soon be levied. Herald, save thou thy
    labor ;   121
Come thou no more for ransom, gentle herald :
They shall have none, I swear, but these my
    joints ;
Which if they have as I will leave 'em them,
Shall yield them little, tell the constable.
    Mont. I shall, King Harry. And so fare
    thee well :
Thou never shalt hear herald any more. *[Exit.*
    K. Hen. I fear thou 'lt once more come
    again for ransom.

    Enter YORK.

York. My lord, most humbly on my knee I
    beg
The leading of the vaward.   130
    K. Hen. Take it, brave York. Now, sol-
    diers, march away :
And how thou pleasest, God, dispose the day !
    [Exeunt.

    SCENE IV.   *The field of battle.*

Alarum. Excursions. Enter PISTOL, *French
    Soldier, and* Boy.

Pist. Yield, cur !
Fr. Sol. Je pense que vous êtes gentilhomme
de bonne qualité.
Pist. Qualtitie calmie custure me ! Art
thou a gentleman ? what is thy name ? discuss.
Fr. Sol O Seigneur Dieu !
Pist. O, Signieur Dew should be a gentle-
man :
Perpend my words, O Signieur Dew, and
    mark ;
O Signieur Dew, thou diest on point of fox,
Except, O signieur, thou do give to me   10
Egregious ransom.
    Fr. Sol. O, prenez miséricorde ! ayez pitié
de moî !
    Pist. Moy shall not serve ; I will have forty
moys ;
Or I will fetch thy rim out at thy throat
In drops of crimson blood.
    Fr. Sol. Est-il impossible d'échapper la
force de ton bras ?

Pist. Brass, cur !
Thou damned and luxurious mountain goat, 20
Offer'st me brass ?
Fr. Sol. O pardonnez moi !
Pist. Say'st thou me so ? is that a ton of
moys ?
Come hither, boy : ask me this slave in French
What is his name.
Boy. Ecoutez : comment êtes-vous appelé ?
Fr. Sol. Monsieur le Fer.
Boy. He says his name is Master Fer.
Pist. Master Fer ! I'll fer him, and firk him,
and ferret him : discuss the same in French
unto him.	31
Boy. I do not know the French for fer, and
ferret, and tirk.
Pist. Bid him prepare ; for I will cut his
throat.
Fr. Sol. Que dit-il, monsieur ?
Boy. Il me commande de vous dire que vous
faites vous prêt ; car ce soldat ici est disposé
tout à cette heure de couper votre gorge.
Pist. Owy, cuppele gorge, permafoy,
Peasant, unless thou give me crowns, brave
crowns ;	40
Or mangled shalt thou be by this my sword.
Fr. Sol. O, je vous supplie, pour l'amour
de Dieu, me pardonner ! Je suis gentilhomme
de bonne maison : gardez ma vie, et je vous
donnerai deux cents écus.
Pist. What are his words ?
Boy. He prays you to save his life : he is a
gentleman of a good house ; and for his
ransom he will give you two hundred crowns.
Pist. Tell him my fury shall abate, and I
The crowns will take.	51
Fr. Sol. Petit monsieur, que dit-il ?
Boy. Encore qu'il est contre son jurement
de pardonner aucun prisonnier, néanmoins,
pour les écus que vous l'avez promis, il est
content de vous donner la liberté, le franchise-
ment.
Fr. Sol. Sur mes genoux je vous donne
mille remercîmens ; et je m'estime heureux que
je suis tombé entre les mains d'un chevalier,
je pense, le plus brave, vaillant, et très dis-
tingué seigneur d'Angleterre.	61
Pist. Expound unto me, boy.
Boy. He gives you, upon his knees, a thousand thanks ; and he esteems himself happy
that he hath fallen into the hands of one, as
he thinks, the most brave, valorous, and thrice-
worthy signieur of England.
Pist. As I suck blood, I will some mercy
show.
Follow me !	69
Boy. Suivez-vous le grand capitaine. [*Exeunt
Pistol, and French Soldier.*] I did never know
so full a voice issue from so empty a heart :
but the saying is true, ' The empty vessel
makes the greatest sound.' Bardolph and Nym
had ten times more valor than this roaring
devil i' the old play, that every one may pare
his nails with a wooden dagger ; and they are
both hanged ; and so would this be, if he durst
steal any thing adventurously. I must stay

with the lackeys, with the luggage of our camp:
the French might have a good prey of us, if he
knew of it ; for there is none to guard it but
boys.	[*Exit.*

SCENE V.	*Another part of the field.*

Enter CONSTABLE, ORLEANS, BOURBON,
DAUPHIN, *and* RAMBURES.

Con. O diable !
Orl. O seigneur ! le jour est perdu, tout est
perdu !
Dau. Mort de ma vie ! all is confounded,
all !
Reproach and everlasting shame
Sits mocking in our plumes. O méchante for-
tune !
Do not run away.	[*A short alarum.*
Con.	Why, all our ranks are broke.
Dau. O perdurable shame ! let's stab our-
selves.
Be these the wretches that we play'd at dice
for ?
Orl. Is this the king we sent to for his
ransom ?
Bour. Shame and eternal shame, nothing
but shame !	10
Let us die in honor : once more back again ;
And he that will not follow Bourbon now,
Let him go hence, and with his cap in hand,
Like a base pander, hold the chamber-door
Whilst by a slave, no gentler than my dog,
His fairest daughter is contaminated.
Con. Disorder, that hath spoil'd us, friend
us now !
Let us on heaps go offer up our lives.
Orl. We are enow yet living in the field
To smother up the English in our throngs,	20
If any order might be thought upon.
Bour. The devil take order now ! I'll to the
throng :
Let life be short ; else shame will be too long.
[*Exeunt.*

SCENE VI.	*Another part of the field.*

Alarums. Enter KING HENRY *and forces,*
EXETER, *and others.*

K. Hen. Well have we done, thrice valiant
countrymen :
But all's not done ; yet keep the French the
field.
Exe. The Duke of York commends him to
your majesty.
K. Hen. Lives he, good uncle ? thrice within
this hour
I saw him down ; thrice up again and fighting;
From helmet to the spur all blood he was.
Exe. In which array, brave soldier, doth he
lie,
Larding the plain ; and by his bloody side,
Yoke-fellow to his honor-owing wounds,
The noble Earl of Suffolk also lies.	10
Suffolk first died : and York, all haggled over,
Comes to him, where in gore he lay insteep'd,
And takes him by the beard ; kisses the gashes

That bloodily did yawn upon his face ;
And cries aloud ' Tarry, dear cousin Suffolk !
My soul shall thine keep company to heaven ;
Tarry, sweet soul, for mine, then fly abreast,
As in this glorious and well-foughten field
We kept together in our chivalry !'   19
Upon these words I came and cheer'd him up:
He smiled me in the face, raught me his hand,
And, with a feeble gripe, says ' Dear my lord,
Commend my service to my sovereign.'
So did he turn and over Suffolk's neck
He threw his wounded arm and kiss'd his lips ;
And so espoused to death, with blood he seal'd
A testament of noble-ending love.
The pretty and sweet manner of it forced
Those waters from me which I would have
    stopp'd ;
But I had not so much of man in me,   30
And all my mother came into mine eyes
And gave me up to tears.
   K. Hen.   I blame you not ;
For, hearing this, I must perforce compound
With mistful eyes, or they will issue too.
                        [*Alarum.*
But, hark ! what new alarum is this same ?
The French have reinforced their scatter'd
    men :
Then every soldier kill his prisoners :
Give the word through.   [*Exeunt.*

SCENE VII.   *Another part of the field.*

     Enter FLUELLEN *and* GOWER.

Flu. Kill the poys and the luggage ! 'tis expressly against the law of arms: 'tis as arrant a
piece of knavery, mark you now, as can be
offer't ; in your conscience, now, is it not ?
   Gow. 'Tis certain there's not a boy left
alive ; and the cowardly rascals that ran from
the battle ha' done this slaughter : besides,
they have burned and carried away all that
was in the king's tent ; wherefore the king,
most worthily, hath caused every soldier to
cut his prisoner's throat. O, 'tis a gallant
king !   11
   Flu. Ay, he was porn at Monmouth, Captain Gower. What call you the town's name
where Alexander the Pig was born !
   Gow. Alexander the Great.
   Flu. Why, I pray you, is not pig great ? the
pig, or the great, or the mighty, or the huge,
or the magnanimous, are all one reckonings,
save the phrase is a little variations.   19
   Gow. I think Alexander the Great was born
in Macedon ; his father was called Philip of
Macedon, as I take it.
   Flu. I think it is in Macedon where Alexander is porn. I tell you, captain, if you look
in the maps of the 'orld, I warrant you sall
find, in the comparisons between Macedon and
Monmouth, that the situations, look you, is
both alike. There is a river in Macedon ; and
there is also moreover a river in Monmouth :
it is called Wye at Monmouth ; but it is out
of my prains what is the name of the other
river ; but 'tis all one, 'tis alike as my fingers

is to my fingers, and there is salmons in both.
If you mark Alexander's life well, Harry of
Monmouth's life is come after it indifferent
well ; for there is figures in all things. Alexander, God knows, and you know, in his rages,
and his furies, and his wraths, and his cholers,
and his moods, and his displeasures, and his
indignations, and also being a little intoxicates
in his prains, did, in his ales and his angers,
look you, kill his best friend, Cleitus.   41
   Gow. Our king is not like him in that : he
never killed any of his friends.
   Flu. It is not well done, mark you now, to
take the tales out of my mouth, ere it is made
and finished. I speak but in the figures and
comparisons of it : as Alexander killed his
friend Cleitus, being in his ales and his cups ;
so also Harry Monmouth, being in his right
wits and his good judgments, turned away the
fat knight with the great belly-doublet : he
was full of jests, and gipes, and knaveries, and
mocks ; I have forgot his name.
   Gow. Sir John Falstaff.
   Flu. That is he : I'll tell you there is good
men porn at Monmouth.
   Gow. Here comes his majesty.

Alarum. Enter KING HENRY, *and forces,*
WARWICK, GLOUCESTER, EXETER, *and others.*

   K. Hen. I was not angry since I came to
    France
Until this instant. Take a trumpet, herald ;
Ride thou unto the horsemen on yon hill :   60
If they will fight with us, bid them come down,
Or void the field ; they do offend our sight :
If they'll do neither, we will come to them,
And make them skirr away, as swift as stones
Enforced from the old Assyrian slings :
Besides, we'll cut the throats of those we have,
And not a man of them that we shall take
Shall taste our mercy. Go and tell them so.

         Enter MONTJOY.

   Exe. Here comes the herald of the French,
    my liege.
   Glo. His eyes are humbler than they used
    to be.   70
   K. Hen. How now ! what means this,
    herald ? know'st thou not
That I have fined these bones of mine for ran-
    som ?
Comest thou again for ransom ?
   Mont.   No, great king :
I come to thee for charitable license,
That we may wander o'er this bloody field
To look our dead, and then to bury them ;
To sort our nobles from our common men.
For many of our princes—woe the while !—
Lie drown'd and soak'd in mercenary blood ;
So do our vulgar drench their peasant limbs 80
In blood of princes ; and their wounded steeds
Fret fetlock deep in gore and with wild rage
Yerk out their armed heels at their dead mas-
    ters,
Killing them twice. O, give us leave, great
    king,

To view the field in safety and dispose
Of their dead bodies !
  K. Hen.   I tell thee truly, herald,
I know not if the day be ours or no ;
For yet a many of your horsemen peer
And gallop o'er the field
  Mont   The day is yours.
  K. Hen.   Praised be God, and not our
    strength, for it !   90
What is this castle call'd that stands hard by ?
  Mont   They call it Agincourt.
  K. Hen.   Then call we this the field of
    Agincourt,
Fought on the day of Crispin Crispianus.
  Flu   Your grandfather of famous memory,
an't please your majesty, and your great-uncle
Edward the Plack Prince of Wales, as I have
read in the chronicles, fought a most prave
pattle here in France
  K. Hen.   They did, Fluellen   100
  Flu   Your majesty says very true : if your
majesties is remembered of it, the Welshmen
did good service in a garden where leeks did
grow, wearing leeks in their Monmouth caps ;
which, your majesty know, to this hour is an
honorable badge of the service , and I do believe your majesty takes no scorn to wear the
leek upon Saint Tavy's day
  K. Hen.   I wear it for a memorable honor ,
For I am Welsh, you know, good countryman
  Flu.   All the water in Wye cannot wash
your majesty's Welsh plood out of your pody,
I can tell you that   God pless it and preserve
it, as long as it pleases his grace, and his majesty too
  K. Hen.   Thanks, good my countryman
  Flu.   By Jeshu, I am your majesty's coun-
tryman, I care not who know it , I will con-
fess it to all the 'orld I need not to be ashamed
of your majesty, praised be God, so long as
your majesty is an honest man   120
  K. Hen.   God keep me so! Our heralds go
    with him :
Bring me just notice of the numbers dead
On both our parts   Call yonder fellow hither.
    [*Points to Williams. Exeunt Heralds*
                        with Montjoy.
  Exe.   Soldier you must come to the king
  K. Hen.   Soldier, why wearest thou that
glove in thy cap ?
  Will.   An't please your majesty, 'tis the
gage of one that I should fight withal, if he be
alive
  K. Hen.   An Englishman ?   129
  Will.   An't please your majesty, a rascal
that swaggered with me last night , who, if
alive and ever dare to challenge this glove, I
have sworn to take him a box o' th' ear · or if
I can see my glove in his cap, which he swore,
as he was a soldier, he would wear if alive, I
will strike it out soundly.
  K. Hen.   What think you, Captain Fluellen
is it fit this soldier keep his oath ?
  Flu.   He is a craven and a villain else, an't
please your majesty, in my conscience.   140
  K. Hen.   It may be his enemy is a gentleman

of great sort, quite from the answer of his
degree.
  Flu   Though he be as good a gentleman as
the devil is, as Lucifer and Belzebub himself,
it is necessary, look your grace, that he keep
his vow and his oath   if he be perjured, see
you now, his reputation is as arrant a villain
and a Jacksauce, as ever his black shoe trod
upon God's ground and his earth, in my conscience, la !   150
  K. Hen.   Then keep thy vow, sirrah, when
thou meetest the fellow
  Will.   So I will, my liege, as I live
  K. Hen   Who servest thou under ?
  Will.   Under Captain Gower, my liege
  Flu   Gower is a good captain, and is good
knowledge and literatured in the wars
  K. Hen.   Call him hither to me, soldier
  Will.   I will, my liege   [*Exit.*
  K. Hen.   Here, Fluellen ; wear thou this
favor for me and stick it in thy cap · when
Alençon and myself were down together, I
plucked this glove from his helm   if any man
challenge this, he is a friend to Alençon, and
an enemy to our person , if thou encounter
any such, apprehend him, an   thou dost me
love
  Flu   Your grace doo's me as great honors
as can be desired in the hearts of his subjects.
I would fain see the man, that has but two
legs, that shall find himself aggriefed at this
glove , that is all , but I would fain see it
once, an please God of his grace that I might
see
  K. Hen   Knowest thou Gower ?
  Flu   He is my dear friend, an please you
  K. Hen   Pray thee, go seek him, and bring
him to my tent
  Flu.   I will fetch him   [*Exit.*
  K. Hen   My Lord of Warwick, and my
    brother Gloucester.
Follow Fluellen closely at the heels ·
The glove which I have given him for a favor
May haply purchase him a box o' th' ear ;   181
It is the soldier's , I by bargain should
Wear it myself.   Follow, good cousin War-
    wick
If that the soldier strike him, as I judge
By his blunt bearing he will keep his word,
Some sudden mischief may arise of it ,
For I do know Fluellen valiant
And, touched with choler, hot as gunpowder,
And quickly will return an injury
Follow, and see there be no harm between
    them   196
Go you with me, uncle of Exeter   [*Exeunt.*

SCENE VIII   *Before* KING HENRY'S *pavilion.*
      Enter GOWER *and* WILLIAMS.
  Will   I warrant it is to knight you, captain.
          Enter FLUELLEN.
  Flu.   God's will and his pleasure, captain,
I beseech you now, come apace to the king :
there is more good toward you peradventure
than is in your knowledge to dream of,

Will. Sir, know you this glove ?

Flu. Know the glove ! I know the glove is a glove

Will. I know this ; and thus I challenge it.

                [*Strikes him.*

Flu. 'Sblood ! an arrant traitor as any is in the universal world, or in France, or in England !   11

Gow. How now, sir ! you villain !

Will. Do you think I'll be forsworn ?

Flu. Stand away, Captain Gower ; I will give treason his payment into plows, I warrant you.

Will. I am no traitor.

Flu. That's a lie in thy throat. I charge you in his majesty's name, apprehend him : he's a friend of the Duke Alençon's.   19

Enter WARWICK *and* GLOUCESTER.

War. How now, how now ! what's the matter ?

Flu. My Lord of Warwick, here is—praised be God for it !—a most contagious treason come to light, look you, as you shall desire in a summer's day. Here is his majesty.

Enter KING HENRY *and* EXETER.

K. Hen. How now ! what's the matter ?

Flu. My liege, here is a villain and a traitor, that, look your grace, has struck the glove which your majesty is take out of the helmet of Alençon

Will. My liege, this was my glove, here is the fellow of it , and he that I gave it to in change promised to wear it in his cap . I promised to strike him, if he did . I met this man with my glove in his cap, and I have been as good as my word

Flu. Your majesty hear now, saving your majesty's manhood, what an arrant, rascally, beggarly, lousy knave it is . I hope your majesty is pear me testimony and witness, and will avouchment, that this is the glove of Alençon, that your majesty is give me , in your conscience, now ?   40

K. Hen. Give me thy glove, soldier : look, here is the fellow of it

'Twas I, indeed, thou promised'st to strike ; And thou hast given me most bitter terms.

Flu. An please your majesty, let his neck answer for it, if there is any martial law in the world

K. Hen. How canst thou make me satisfaction ?

Will. All offences, my lord, come from the heart : never came any from mine that might offend your majesty.   51

K. Hen. It was ourself thou didst abuse

Will. Your majesty came not like yourself. you appeared to me but as a common man ; witness the night, your garments, your lowliness , and what your highness suffered under that shape, I beseech you take it for your own fault and not mine · for had you been as I took you for, I made no offence ; therefore, I beseech your highness, pardon me.   60

K. Hen. Here, uncle Exeter, fill this glove with crowns,

And give it to this fellow. Keep it, fellow ; And wear it for an honor in thy cap Till I do challenge it. Give him the crowns: And, captain, you must needs be friends with him.

Flu. By this day and this light, the fellow has mettle enough in his belly. Hold, there is twelve pence for you ; and I pray you to serve Got, and keep you out of prawls, and prabbles, and quarrels, and dissensions, and, I warrant you, it is the better for you   71

Will. I will none of your money

Flu. It is with a good will , I can tell you, it will serve you to mend your shoes : come, wherefore should you be so pashful ? your shoes is not so good : 'tis a good silling, I warrant you, or I will change it.

Enter an English *Herald.*

K. Hen. Now, herald, are the dead number'd ?

Her. Here is the number of the slaughter'd French.

K. Hen. What prisoners of good sort are taken, uncle ?   80

Exe. Charles Duke of Orleans, nephew to the king ;

John Duke of Bourbon, and Lord Bouciqualt: Of other lords and barons, knights and squires, Full fifteen hundred, besides common men

K. Hen. This note doth tell me of ten thousand French

That in the field he slain: of princes, in this number,

And nobles bearing banners, there lie dead One hundred twenty six added to these, Of knights, esquires, and gallant gentlemen, 89 Eight thousand and four hundred ; of the which,

Five hundred were but yesterday dubb'd knights :

So that, in these ten thousand they have lost, There are but sixteen hundred mercenaries ; The rest are princes, barons, lords, knights, squires,

And gentlemen of blood and quality. The names of those their nobles that lie dead: Charles Delabreth, high constable of France; Jacques of Chatillon, admiral of France , The master of the cross-bows, Lord Rambures; Great Master of France, the brave Sir Guichard Dolphin,   100

John Duke of Alençon, Anthony Duke of Brabant,

The brother of the Duke of Burgundy, And Edward Duke of Bar . of lusty earls, Grandpré and Roussi, Fauconberg and Foix, Beaumont and Marle, Vaudemont and Lestrale. Here was a royal fellowship of death ! Where is the number of our English dead ?

       [*Herald shews him another paper.*

Edward the Duke of York, the Earl of Suffolk, Sir Richard Ketly, Davy Gam, esquire : None else of name ; and of all other men 110

But five and twenty. O God, thy arm was
    here ;
And not to us, but to thy arm alone,
Ascribe we all ! When, without stratagem,
But in plain shock and even play of battle,
Was ever known so great and little loss
On one part and on the other ? Take it, God,
For it is none but thine !
    Exe.   'Tis wonderful !
    K. Hen. Come, go we in procession to the
    village :
And be it death proclaimed through our host
To boast of this or take the praise from God 120
Which is his only.
    Flu. Is it not lawful, an please your maj-
    esty, to tell how many is killed ?
    K. Hen. Yes, captain ; but with this ac-
    knowledgment,
That God fought for us.
    Flu. Yes, my conscience, he did us great
    good
    K Hen. Do we all holy rites ;
Let there be sung ' Non nobis' and ' Te Deum ;'
The dead with charity enclosed in clay ·
And then to Calais ; and to England then : 130
Where ne'er from France arrived more happy
    men.   [*Exeunt.*

ACT V.

PROLOGUE.

Enter Chorus.

Chor. Vouchsafe to those that have not
    read the story,
That I may prompt them : and of such as have,
I humbly pray them to admit the excuse
Of time, of numbers and due course of things,
Which cannot in their huge and proper life
Be here presented   Now we bear the king
Toward Calais   grant him there ; there seen,
Heave him away upon your winged thoughts
Athwart the sea.   Behold, the English beach
Pales in the flood with men, with wives and
    boys,   10
Whose shouts and claps out-voice the deep-
    mouth'd sea,
Which like a mighty whiffler 'fore the king
Seems to prepare his way. so let him land,
And solemnly see him set on to London.
So swift a pace hath thought that even now
You may imagine him upon Blackheath ;
Where that his lords desire him to have borne
His bruised helmet and his bended sword
Before him through the city. he forbids it, 19
Being free from vainness and self-glorious
    pride ;
Giving full trophy, signal and ostent
Quite from himself to God.   But now behold,
In the quick forge and working-house of
    thought,
How London doth pour out her citizens !
The mayor and all his brethren in best sort,

Like to the senators of the antique Rome,
With the plebeians swarming at their heels,
Go forth and fetch their conquering Cæsar in
As, by a lower but loving likelihood,   29
Were now the general of our gracious empress,
As in good time he may, from Ireland coming,
Bringing rebellion broached on his sword,
How many would the peaceful city quit,
To welcome him ! much more, and much more
    cause,
Did they this Harry.   Now in London place
    him,
As yet the lamentation of the French
Invites the King of England's stay at home ;
The emperor's coming in behalf of France,
To order peace between them , and omit
All the occurrences, whatever chanced,   40
Till Harry's back-return again to France
There must we bring him , and myself have
    play'd
The interim, by remembering you 'tis past
Then brook abridgment, and your eyes ad-
    vance,
After your thoughts, straight back again to
France.   [*Exit*

Scene I.   *France.   The English camp.*

Enter Fluellen *and* Gower.

Gow   Nay, that's right ; but why wear you
your leek to-day ? Saint Davy's day is past
    Flu.   There is occasions and causes why and
wherefore in all things . I will tell you, asse
my friend, Captain Gower   the rascally, scald,
beggarly, lousy, pragging knave, Pistol, which
you and yourself and all the world know to be
no petter than a fellow, look you now, of no
merits, he is come to me and prings me pread
and salt yesterday, look you, and bid me eat
my leek . it was in a place where I could not
breed no contention with him , but I will be
so bold as to wear it in my cap till I see him
once again, and then I will tell him a little
piece of my desires

Enter Pistol.

Gow   Why, here he comes, swelling like a
turkey-cock
    Flu.   'Tis no matter for his swellings nor
his turkey-cocks   God pless you, Aunchient
Pistol ! you scurvy, lousy knave, God pless
    you !
    Pist   Ha ! art thou bedlam ? dost thou
        thirst, base Trojan,   20
To have me fold up Parca's fatal web ?
Hence ' I am qualmish at the smell of leek
    Flu   I peseech you heartily, scurvy, lousy
knave, at my desires, and my requests, and my
petitions, to eat, look you, this leek   because,
look you, you do not love it, nor your affections and your appetites and your disgestions
doo's not agree with it, I would desire you to
eat it
    Pist   Not for Cadwallader and all his goats
    Flu.   There is one goat for you.   30
                            [*Strikes him*]
Will you be so good, scauld knave, as eat it ?

Pist. Base Trojan, thou shalt die.

Flu. You say very true, scauld knave, when God's will is : I will desire you to live in the mean time, and eat your victuals: come, there is sauce for it. [*Strikes him.*] You called me yesterday mountain-squire ; but I will make you to-day a squire of low degree. I pray you, fall to: if you can mock a leek, you can eat a leek. [him. 41

Gow. Enough, captain: you have astonished him.

Flu. I say, I will make him eat some part of my leek, or I will peat his pate four days. Bite, I pray you ; it is good for your green wound and your ploody coxcomb.

Pist. Must I bite ?

Flu. Yes, certainly, and out of doubt and out of question too, and ambiguities.

Pist. By this leek, I will most horribly revenge : I eat and eat, I swear— 50

Flu. Eat, I pray you : will you have some more sauce to your leek ? there is not enough leek to swear by.

Pist. Quiet thy cudgel ; thou dost see I eat.

Flu. Much good do you, scauld knave, heartily. Nay, pray you, throw none away; the skin is good for your broken coxcomb. When you take occasions to see leeks hereafter, I pray you, mock at 'em ; that is all.

Pist. Good. 60

Flu. Ay, leeks is good : hold you, there is a groat to heal your pate.

Pist. Me a groat !

Flu. Yes, verily and in truth, you shall take it ; or I have another leek in my pocket, which you shall eat.

Pist. I take thy groat in earnest of revenge.

Flu. If I owe you any thing, I will pay you in cudgels : you shall be a woodmonger, and buy nothing of me but cudgels. God b' wi' you, and keep you, and heal your pate. 71 [*Exit.*

Pist. All hell shall stir for this.

Gow. Go, go; you are a counterfeit cowardly knave. Will you mock at an ancient tradition, begun upon an honorable respect, and worn as a memorable trophy of predeceased valor and dare not avouch in your deeds any of your words ? I have seen you gleeking and galling at this gentleman twice or thrice. You thought, because he could not speak English in the native garb, he could not therefore handle an English cudgel : you find it otherwise ; and henceforth let a Welsh correction teach you a good English condition. Fare ye well. [*Exit.*

Pist. Doth Fortune play the huswife with me now ?

News have I, that my Nell is dead i' the spital Of malady of France ;

And there my rendezvous is quite cut off.

Old I do wax ; and from my weary limbs Honor is cudgelled. Well, bawd I'll turn, 90 And something lean to cutpurse of quick hand. To England will I steal, and there I'll steal : And patches will I get unto these cudgell'd scars, And swear I got them in the Gallia wars. [*Exit.*

SCENE II. *France. A royal palace.*

Enter, at one door, KING HENRY, EXETER, BEDFORD, GLOUCESTER, WARWICK, WEST-MORELAND, *and other* Lords; *at another, the* FRENCH KING, QUEEN ISABEL, *the* PRINCESS KATHARINE, ALICE *and other* Ladies ; *the* DUKE OF BURGUNDY, *and his train.*

K. Hen. Peace to this meeting, wherefore we are met !

Unto our brother France, and to our sister, Health and fair time of day; joy and good wishes

To our most fair and princely cousin Katharine; And, as a branch and member of this royalty, By whom this great assembly is contrived, We do salute you, Duke of Burgundy; And, princes French, and peers, health to you all !

Fr. King. Right joyous are we to behold your face,

Most worthy brother England ; fairly met: 10 So are you, princes English, every one.

Q. Isa. So happy be the issue, brother England,

Of this good day and of this gracious meeting, As we are now glad to behold your eyes ; Your eyes, which hitherto have borne in them Against the French, that met them in their bent,

The fatal balls of murdering basilisks : The venom of such looks, we fairly hope, Have lost their quality, and that this day Shall change all griefs and quarrels into love.

K. Hen. To cry amen to that, thus we appear. 21

Q. Isa. You English princes all, I do salute you.

Bur. My duty to you both, on equal love, Great Kings of France and England ! That I have labor'd,

With all my wits, my pains and strong endeavors,

To bring your most imperial majesties Unto this bar and royal interview, Your mightiness on both parts best can witness.

Since then my office hath so far prevail'd That, face to face and royal eye to eye, 30 You have congreeted, let it not disgrace me, If I demand, before this royal view, What rub or what impediment there is, Why that the naked, poor and mangled Peace,

Dear nurse of arts, plenties and joyful births, Should not in this best garden of the world Our fertile France, put up her lovely visage ? Alas, she hath from France too long been chased,

And all her husbandry doth lie on heaps, Corrupting in its own fertility. 40 Her vine, the merry cheerer of the heart, Unpruned dies ; her hedges even-pleach'd, Like prisoners wildly overgrown with hair, Put forth disorder'd twigs ; her fallow leas The darnel, hemlock and rank fumitory

Doth root upon, while that the coulter rusts
That should deracinate such savagery ;
The even mead, that erst brought sweetly
     forth
The freckled cowslip, burnet and green clo-
     ver,
Wanting the scythe, all uncorrected, rank,   50
Conceives by idleness and nothing teems
But hateful docks, rough thistles, kecksies,
     burs,
Losing both beauty and utility.
And as our vineyards, fallows, meads and
     hedges,
Defective in their natures, grow to wildness,
Even so our houses and ourselves and chil-
     dren
Have lost, or do not learn for want of time,
The sciences that should become our country;
But grow like savages,—as soldiers will
That nothing do but meditate on blood,—   60
To swearing and stern looks, diffused attire
And every thing that seems unnatural.
Which to reduce into our former favor
You are assembled : and my speech entreats
That I may know the let, why gentle Peace
Should not expel these inconveniences
And bless us with her former qualities.
     K. Hen. If, Duke of Burgundy, you would
          the peace,
Whose want gives growth to the imperfec-
     tions
Which you have cited, you must buy that
     peace   70
With full accord to all our just demands ;
Whose tenors and particular effects
You have enscheduled briefly in your hands.
     Bur. The king hath heard them ; to the
          which as yet
There is no answer made.
     K. Hen.   Well then the peace,
Which you before so urged, lies in his an-
     swer.
     Fr. King. I have but with a cursorary eye
O'erglanced the articles : pleaseth your grace
To appoint some of your council presently
To sit with us once more, with better heed 80
To re-survey them, we will suddenly
Pass our accept and peremptory answer.
     K. Hen. Brother, we shall. Go, uncle Ex-
          eter,
And brother Clarence, and you, brother Glou-
     cester,
Warwick and Huntingdon, go with the king ;
And take with you free power to ratify,
Augment, or alter, as your wisdoms best
Shall see advantageable for our dignity,
Any thing in or out of our demands,
And we'll consign thereto. Will you, fair sis-
     ter,   90
Go with the princes, or stay here with us ?
     Q. Isa. Our gracious brother, I will go with
          them :
Haply a woman's voice may do some good,
When articles too nicely urged be stood on.
     K. Hen. Yet leave our cousin Katharine
          here with us :

She is our capital demand, comprised
Within the fore-rank of our articles.
     Q. Isa. She hath good leave.
          [*Exeunt all except Henry, Katharine
               and Alice.*
     K. Hen. Fair Katharine and most fair,
Will you vouchsafe to teach a soldier terms
Such as will enter at a lady's ear   100
And plead his love-suit to her gentle heart ?
     Kath. Your majesty shall mock at me ; I
cannot speak your England.
     K. Hen. O fair Katharine, if you will love
me soundly with your French heart, I will be
glad to hear you confess it brokenly with your
English tongue. Do you like me, Kate ?
     Kath. Pardonnez-moi, I cannot tell vat is
' like me.'
     K. Hen. An angel is like you, Kate, and
you are like an angel.   111
     Kath. Que dit-il ? que je suis semblable à
les anges ?
     Alice. Oui, vraiment, sauf votre grace,
ainsi dit-il.
     K. Hen. I said so, dear Katharine ; and I
must not blush to affirm it.
     Kath. O bon Dieu ! les langues des hommes
sont pleines de tromperies.
     K. Hen. What says she, fair one ? that the
tongues of men are full of deceits ?   121
     Alice. Oui, dat de tongues of de mans is be
full of deceits : dat is de princess.
     K. Hen. The princess is the better English-
woman. I' faith, Kate, my wooing is fit for
thy understanding : I am glad thou canst
speak no better English ; for, if thou couldst,
thou wouldst find me such a plain king that
thou wouldst think I had sold my farm to
buy my crown. I know no ways to mince it
in love, but directly to say ' I love you :' then
if you urge me farther than to say ' do you in
faith ?' I wear out my suit. Give me your
answer ; i' faith, do : and so clap hands and
a bargain : how say you, lady ?
     Kath. Sauf votre honneur, me understand
vell.
     K. Hen. Marry, if you would put me to
verses or to dance for your sake, Kate, why
you undid me : for the one, I have neither
words nor measure, and for the other, I have
no strength in measure, yet a reasonable
measure in strength. If I could win a lady at
leap-frog, or by vaulting into my saddle with
my armor on my back, under the correction
of bragging be it spoken, I should quickly
leap into a wife. Or if I might buffet for my
love, or bound my horse for her favors, I
could lay on like a butcher and sit like a jack-
an-apes, never off. But, before God, Kate, I
cannot look greenly nor gasp out my eloquence, nor I have no cunning in protestation ; only downright oaths, which I never
use till urged, nor never break for urging. If
thou canst love a fellow of this temper, Kate,
whose face is not worth sun-burning, that
never looks in his glass for love of any thing
he sees there, let thine eye be thy cook. I

speak to thee plain soldier : if thou canst love me for this, take me ; if not, to say to thee that I shall die, is true ; but for thy love, by the Lord, no ; yet I love thee too. And while thou livest, dear Kate, take a fellow of plain and uncoined constancy ; for he perforce must do thee right, because he hath not the gift to woo in other places : for these fellows of infinite tongue, that can rhyme themselves into ladies' favors, they do always reason themselves out again. What ! a speaker is but a prater ; a rhyme is but a ballad. A good leg will fall ; a straight back will stoop ; a black beard will turn white ; a curled pate will grow bald ; a fair face will wither ; a full eye will wax hollow : but a good heart, Kate, is the sun and the moon ; or rather the sun and not the moon ; for it shines bright and never changes, but keeps his course truly. If thou would have such a one, take me ; and take me, take a soldier ; take a soldier, take a king. And what sayest thou then to my love ? speak, my fair, and fairly, I pray thee.

Kath. Is it possible dat I sould love de enemy of France ?   179

K. Hen. No ; it is not possible you should love the enemy of France, Kate : but, in loving me, you should love the friend of France ; for I love France so well that I will not part with a village of it ; I will have it all mine : and, Kate, when France is mine and I am yours, then yours is France and you are mine.

Kath. I cannot tell vat is dat.

K. Hen. No, Kate ? I will tell thee in French ; which I am sure will hang upon my tongue like a new-married wife about her husband's neck, hardly to be shook off. Je quand sur le possession de France, et quand vous avez le possession de moi,—let me see, what then ? Saint Denis be my speed !—donc votre est France et vous êtes mienne. It is as easy for me, Kate, to conquer the kingdom as to speak so much more French : I shall never move thee in French. unless it be to laugh at me.

Kath. Sauf votre honneur, le François que vous parlez, il est meilleur que l'Anglois lequel je parle.   301

K. Hen. No, faith, is't not, Kate : but thy speaking of my tongue, and I thine, most truly-falsely, must needs be granted to be much at one. But, Kate, dost thou understand thus much English, canst thou love me ?

Kath. I cannot tell.

K. Hen. Can any of your neighbors tell, Kate ? I'll ask them. Come, I know thou lovest me : and at night, when you come into your closet, you'll question this gentlewoman about me ; and I know, Kate, you will to her dispraise those parts in me that you love with your heart : but, good Kate, mock me mercifully ; the rather, gentle princess, because I love thee cruelly. If ever thou beest mine, Kate, as I have a saving faith within me tells me thou shalt, I get thee with scambling, and thou must therefore needs prove a good sol-

dier-breeder : shall not thou and I, between Saint Denis and Saint George, compound a boy, half French, half English, that shall go to Constantinople and take the Turk by the beard ? shall we not ? what sayest thou, my fair flower-de-luce ?

Kath. I do not know dat.

K. Hen. No ; 'tis hereafter to know, but now to promise : do but now promise, Kate, you will endeavor for your French part of such a boy ; and for my English moiety take the word of a king and a bachelor. How answer you, la plus belle Katharine du monde, mon très cher et devin déesse ?

Kath. Your majestee ave fausse French enough to deceive de most sage demoiselle dat is en France.

K. Hen. Now, fie upon my false French ! By mine honor, in true English, I love thee, Kate : by which honor I dare not swear thou lovest me ; yet my blood begins to flatter me that thou dost, notwithstanding the poor and untempering effect of my visage. Now, beshrew my father's ambition ! he was thinking of civil wars when he got me : therefore was I created with a stubborn outside, with an aspect of iron, that, when I come to woo ladies, I fright them. But, in faith, Kate, the elder I wax, the better I shall appear : my comfort is, that old age, that ill layer up of beauty, can do no more spoil upon my face : thou hast me, if thou hast me, at the worst ; and thou shalt wear me, if thou wear me, better and better : and therefore tell me, most fair Katharine, will you have me ? Put off your maiden blushes ; avouch the thoughts of your heart with the looks of an empress ; take me by the hand, and say 'Harry of England, I am thine :' which word thou shalt no sooner bless mine ear withal, but I will tell thee aloud 'England is thine, Ireland is thine, France is thine, and Harry Plantagenet is thine ;' who, though I speak it before his face, if he be not fellow with the best king, thou shalt find the best king of good fellows. Come, your answer in broken music ; for thy voice is music and thy English broken ; therefore, queen of all, Katharine, break thy mind to me in broken English ; wilt thou have me?

Kath. Dat is as it sall please de roi mon père.

K. Hen. Nay, it will please him well, Kate ; it shall please him, Kate.

Kath. Den it sall also content me.   370

K. Hen. Upon that I kiss your hand, and I call you my queen.

Kath. Laissez, mon seigneur, laissez, laissez : ma foi, je ne veux point que vous abaisiez votre grandeur en baisant la main d'une de votre seigneurie indigne serviteur ; excusez-moi, je vous supplie, mon très-puissant seigneur.

K. Hen. Then I will kiss your lips, Kate.

Kath. Les dames et demoiselles pour être baisées devant leur noces, il n'est pas la coutume de France.   381

K. Hen. Madam my interpreter, what says she ?

Alice. Dat it is not be de fashion pour les ladies of France,—I cannot tell vat is baiser en Anglish.

K. Hen. To kiss

Alice. Your majesty entendre bettre que moi.

K. Hen. It is not a fashion for the maids in France to kiss before they are married, would she say ?

Alice. Oui, vrament

K. Hen. O Kate, nice customs curtsy to great kings Dear Kate, you and I cannot be confined within the weak list of a country's fashion : we are the makers of manners, Kate, and the liberty that follows our places stops the mouth of all find-faults, as I will do yours, for upholding the nice fashion of your country in denying me a kiss : therefore, patiently and yielding. [*Kissing her*] You have witchcraft in your lips, Kate . there is more eloquence in a sugar touch of them than in the tongues of the French council, and they should sooner persuade Harry of England than a general petition of monarchs. Here comes your father.

Re-enter the FRENCH KING *and his* QUEEN, BURGUNDY, *and other* Lords

Bur God save your majesty ! my royal cousin, teach you our princess English ?

K. Hen. I would have her learn, my fair cousin, how perfectly I love her , and that is good English

Bur. Is she not apt ?

K. Hen. Our tongue is rough, coz, and my condition is not smooth, so that, having neither the voice nor the heart of flattery about me, I cannot so conjure up the spirit of love in her, that he will appear in his true likeness

Bur Pardon the frankness of my mirth, if I answer you for that. If you would conjure in her, you must make a circle , if conjure up love in her in his true likeness, he must appear naked and blind Can you blame her then, being a maid yet rosed over with the virgin crimson of modesty, if she deny the appearance of a naked blind boy in her naked seeing self ? It were, my lord, a hard condition for a maid to consign to

K. Hen. Yet they do wink and yield, as love is blind and enforces.

Bur. They are then excused, my lord, when they see not what they do.   430

K. Hen. Then, good my lord, teach your cousin to consent winking.

Bur. I will wink on her to consent, my lord, if you will teach her to know my meaning: for maids, well summered and warm kept, are like flies at Bartholomew-tide, blind, though they have their eyes ; and then they will endure handling, which before would not abide looking on

K. Hen. This moral ties me over to time and a hot summer ; and so I shall catch the

fly, your cousin, in the latter end and she must be blind too

Bur. As love is, my lord, before it loves

K. Hen. It is so · and you may, some of you, thank love for my blindness, who cannot see many a fair French city for one fair French maid that stands in my way

Fr. King Yes, my lord, you see them perspectively, the cities turned into a maid , for they are all girdled with maiden walls that war hath never entered   450

K. Hen. Shall Kate be my wife ?

Fr. King So please you

K. Hen. I am content , so the maiden cities you talk of may wait on her so the maid that stood in the way for my wish shall show me the way to my will

Fr. King. We have consented to all terms of reason

K. Hen. Is't so, my lords of England ?

West. The king hath granted every article: His daughter first, and then in sequel all,   461 According to their firm proposed natures

Exe. Only he hath not yet subscribed this . Where your majesty demands, that the King of France, having any occasion to write for matter of grant, shall name your highness in this form and with this addition in French, *Notre trescher fils Henri, Roi d'Angleterre, Héritier de France,* and thus in Latin, *Praeclarissimus filius noster Henricus, Rex Angliæ, et Hæres Franciæ.*

Fr. King Nor this I have not, brother, so denied,

But your request shall make me let it pass

K. Hen. I pray you then, in love and dear alliance,

Let that one article rank with the rest ;

And thereupon give me your daughter.

Fr. King. Take her, fair son, and from her blood raise up

Issue to me , that the contending kingdoms

Of France and England, whose very shores look pale

With envy of each other's happiness,

May cease their hatred, and this dear conjunction   480

Plant neighborhood and Christian-like accord

In their sweet bosoms, that never war advance

His bleeding sword 'twixt England and fair France.

All. Amen !

K. Hen. Now, welcome, Kate : and bear me witness all,

That when I kiss her as my sovereign queen.
          [*Flourish*

Q. Isa God, the best maker of all marriages,

Combine your hearts in one, your realms in one !

As man and wife, being two, are one in love,

So be there 'twixt your kingdoms such a spousal,

That never may ill office, or fell jealousy,

Which troubles oft the bed of blessed marriage,

Thrust in between the paction of these king-
    doms,
To make divorce of their incorporate league ;
That English may as French, French English-
    men,
Receive each other.   God speak this Amen !
  All.   Amen !
  K Hen.   Prepare we for our marriage—on
    which day,
My Lord of Burgundy, we'll take your oath,
And all the peers', for surety of our leagues 500
Then shall I swear to Kate, and you to me ;
And may our oaths well kept and prosperous
    be !   [*Sennet. Exeunt*

EPILOGUE.

Enter Chorus.

Chor.   Thus far, with rough and all-unable
pen,

Our bending author hath pursued the story,
In little room confining mighty men,
  Mangling by starts the full course of their
    glory.
Small time, but in that small most greatly
  lived
  This star of England . Fortune made his
    sword ,
By which the world's best garden he achieved,
  And of it left his son imperial lord
Henry the Sixth, in infant bands crown'd King
  Of France and England, did this king suc-
    ceed ;   10
Whose state so many had the managing,
  That they lost France and made his England
    bleed :
Which oft our stage hath shown , and, for
  their sake,
In your fair minds let this acceptance take.
                     [*Exit.*

THE TAMING OF THE SHREW.

(WRITTEN ABOUT 1597.)

INTRODUCTION.

This comedy first appeared in the folio of 1623, but it is in some way closely connected with a play published in 1594, and bearing the almost identical title, *The Taming of A Shrew*. Pope was of the opinion that Shakespeare wrote both plays, but this is hardly plausible. The play in the folio is certainly an enlargement and alteration of the earlier play, and it only remains to ask, was Shakespeare the sole reviser and adapter, or did his task consist of adding and altering certain scenes, so as to render yet more amusing and successful an enlarged version of the play of 1594, already made by some unknown hand? The last seems upon the whole the opinion best supported by the internal evidence. In *The Taming of the Shrew* three parts may be distinguished. (1) The humorous Induction, in which Sly, the drunken tinker, is the chief person; (2) A comedy of character, the Shrew and her tamer, Petruchio, being the hero and heroine; (3) A comedy of intrigue—the story of Bianca and her rival lovers. Now the old play of *A Shrew* contains, in a rude form, the scenes of the Induction and the chief scenes in which Petruchio and Katharina (named by the original writer Ferando and Kate) appear; but nothing in the old play corresponds with the intrigues of Bianca's disguised lovers. It is, however, in the scenes concerned with these intrigues that Shakespeare's hand is least apparent. It may be said that Shakespeare's genius goes in and out with the person of Katharina. We would therefore conjecturally assign the intrigue-comedy to the adapter of the old play, reserving for Shakespeare a title to those scenes—in the main enlarged from the play of *A Shrew*—in which Katharina, Petruchio, and Grumio are speakers. Turning this statement into figures we find that Shakespeare's part in *The Taming of the Shrew* is comprised in the following portions. Induction, Act II, Sc i, L. 169-326, Act III, Sc ii, L. 1-125, and 151-241, Act IV, Sc i ii and iii, Act V, Sc ii, L. 1-180. Such a division, it must be borne in mind, is no more than a conjecture, but it seems to be suggested and fairly indicated by the style of the several parts of the comedy. However this may be, it is clear that Shakespeare cared little for the other characters in comparison with Sly, Katharina, and Petruchio. The play is full of energy and bustling movement, and the characters of Katharina and Petruchio in particular, are firmly and finely drawn, the scenes in which they appear, though infinitely amusing, never quite passing into downright farce. Widely separated dates have been assigned for *The Taming of the Shrew*, from 1594 to 1606. The best portions are in the manner of Shakespeare's comedies of the second period; and attributing the Bianca intrigue-comedy to a writer intermediate between the author of the play of *A Shrew* and Shakespeare, there is no difficulty in supposing that the Shakespeare scenes were written about 1597. Fletcher wrote a humorous continuation of Shakespeare's play, entitled *The Woman's Prize, or the Tamer Tamed*, in which Petruchio reappears.

DRAMATIS PERSONÆ.

A Lord.	TRANIO, } servants to Lucentio.
CHRISTOPHER SLY, a tinker } Persons in	BIONDELLO, }
Hostess, Page, Players, Huntsmen, and Servants. } the Induction	GRUMIO, } servants to Petruchio
	CURTIS, }
	A Pedant
BAPTISTA, a rich gentleman of Padua	
VINCENTIO, an old gentleman of Pisa.	KATHARINA, the shrew, } daughters to Baptista
LUCENTIO, son to Vincentio, in love with Bianca	BIANCA, }
	Widow
PETRUCHIO, a gentleman of Verona, a suitor to Katharina	Tailor, Haberdasher, and Servants attending on Baptista and Petruchio.
GREMIO, } suitors to Bianca.	
HORTENSIO, }	SCENE *Padua, and Petruchio's country house.*

INDUCTION.

SCENE I. *Before an alehouse on a heath.*

Enter HOSTESS *and* SLY.

Sly. I'll pheeze you, in faith.
Host. A pair of stocks, you rogue!
Sly. Ye are a baggage: the Slys are no
rogues; look in the chronicles; we came in
with Richard Conqueror. Therefore paucas
pallabris; let the world slide: sessa!
Host. You will not pay for the glasses you
have burst?.
Sly. No, not a denier. Go by, Jeronimy:
go to thy cold bed, and warm thee.　　　10
Host. I know my remedy; I must go fetch
the third-borough.　　　　　　　　　[*Exit.*
Sly. Third, or fourth, or fifth borough, I'll
answer him by law: I'll not budge an inch,
boy: let him come, and kindly. [*Falls asleep.*
Horns winded.　　*Enter a* Lord *from hunting,*
with his train.

Lord. Huntsman, I charge thee, tender
well my hounds:
†Brach Merriman, the poor cur is emboss'd;
And couple Clowder with the deep-mouth'd
brach.
Saw'st thou not, boy, how Silver made it good
At the hedge-corner, in the coldest fault?　20
I would not lose the dog for twenty pound.
First Hun. Why, Belman is as good as he,
my lord;
He cried upon it at the merest loss
And twice to-day pick'd out the dullest scent:
Trust me, I take him for the better dog.
Lord. Thou art a fool: if Echo were as
fleet,
I would esteem him worth a dozen such.
But sup them well and look unto them all:
To-morrow I intend to hunt again.．
First Hun. I will, my lord.　　　　　30
Lord. What's here? one dead, or drunk?
See, doth he breathe?
Sec. Hun. He breathes, my lord. Were he
not warm'd with ale,
This were a bed but cold to sleep so soundly.
Lord. O monstrous beast! how like a swine
he lies!　　　　　　　　　　　[*image!*
Grim death, how foul and loathsome is thine
Sirs, I will practice on this drunken man.
What think you, if he were convey'd to bed,
Wrapp'd in sweet clothes, rings put upon his
fingers,
A most delicious banquet by his bed,
And brave attendants near him when he
wakes,　　　　　　　　　　　　40
Would not the beggar then forget himself?
First Hun. Believe me, lord, I think he
cannot choose.
Sec. Hun. It would seem strange unto him
when he waked.
Lord. Even as a flattering dream or worth-
less fancy.
Then take him up and manage well the
jest:

Carry him gently to my fairest chamber
And hang it round with all my wanton pic-
tures:
Balm his foul head in warm distilled waters
And burn sweet wood to make the lodging
sweet:
Procure me music ready when he wakes,　50
To make a dulcet and a heavenly sound;
And if he chance to speak, be ready straight
And with a low submissive reverence
Say 'What is it your honor will command?'
Let one attend him with a silver basin
Full of rose-water and bestrew'd with flowers;
Another bear the ewer, the third a diaper,
And say 'Will't please your lordship cool your
hands?'
Some one be ready with a costly suit
And ask him what apparel he will wear;　60
Another tell him of his hounds and horse,
And that his lady mourns at his disease:
Persuade him that he hath been lunatic;
†And when he says he is, say that he dreams,
For he is nothing but a mighty lord.
This do and do it kindly, gentle sirs:
It will be pastime passing excellent,
If it be husbanded with modesty.
First Hun. My lord, I warrant you we will
play our part,
As he shall think by our true diligence　70
He is no less than what we say he is.
Lord. Take him up gently and to bed with
him:
And each one to his office when he wakes.
[*Some bear out* Sly. *A trumpet sounds.*
Sirrah, go see what trumpet 'tis that sounds:
[*Exit Servingman.*
Belike, some noble gentleman that means,
Travelling some journey, to repose him here.

Re-enter Servingman.

How now! who is it?
Serv.　　　　An't please your honor, players
That offer service to your lordship.
Lord. Bid them come near.

Enter Players.

Now, fellows, you are welcome.
Players. We thank your honor.　　　　80
Lord. Do you intend to stay with me to-
night?
A Player. So please your lordship to accept
our duty.
Lord. With all my heart. This fellow I re-
member,
Since once he play'd a farmer's eldest son:
'Twas where you woo'd the gentlewoman so
well:
I have forgot your name; but, sure, that part
Was aptly fitted and naturally perform'd.
A Player. I think 'twas Soto that your
honor means.
Lord. 'Tis very true: thou didst it excel-
lent.
Well, you are come to me in happy time;　90
The rather for I have some sport in hand
Wherein your cunning can assist me much.
There is a lord will hear you play to-night:

But I am doubtful of your modesties ,
Lest over-eyeing of his odd behavior,—
For yet his honor never heard a play—
You break into some merry passion
And so offend him , for I tell you, sirs,
If you should smile he grows impatient.

A Player　Fear not, my lord　we can con-
　　tain ourselves, 100
Were he the veriest antic in the world.

Lord　Go, sirrah, take them to the buttery,
And give them friendly welcome every one
Let them want nothing that my house affords
　　　　　　[*Exit one with the Players*
Sirrah, go you to Bartholomew my page,
And see him dress'd in all suits like a lady
That done, conduct him to the drunkard's
　　chamber ,
And call him 'madam,' do him obeisance
Tell him from me, as he will win my love, 110
He bear himself with honorable action,
Such as he hath observed in noble ladies
Unto their lords, by them accomplished
Such duty to the drunkard let him do
With soft low tongue and lowly courtesy,
And say 'What is't your honor will command,
Wherein your lady and your humble wife
May show her duty and make known her
　　love ?'　　　[*kisses,*
And then with kind embracements, tempting
And with declining head into his bosom, 120
Bid him shed tears, as being overjoy'd
To see her noble lord restored to health,
Who for this seven years hath esteem'd him
No better than a poor and loathsome beggar
And if the boy have not a woman's gift
To rain a shower of commanded tears,
An onion will do well for such a shift,
Which in a napkin being close convey'd
Shall in despite enforce a watery eye
See this dispatch'd with all the haste thou
　　canst
Anon I'll give thee more instructions 130
　　　　　[*Exit a Serving-man*
I know the boy will well usurp the grace,
Voice, gait and action of a gentlewoman
I long to hear him call the drunkard husband,
And how my men will stay themselves
　　from laughter
When they do homage to this simple peasant
I'll in to counsel them , haply my presence
May well abate the over-merry spleen
Which otherwise would grow into extremes
　　　　　　[*Exeunt*

SCENE II　*A bedchamber in the Lord's house.*

*Enter aloft SLY, with Attendants , some with
apparel, others with basin and ewer and
other appurtenances, and Lord*

Sly.　For God's sake, a pot of small ale.
First Serv　Will't please your lordship
　　drink a cup of sack ?
Sec Serv　Will't please your honor taste of
　　these conserves ?
Third Serv　What raiment will your honor
　　wear to-day ?

Sly　I am Christopher Sly , call not me
'honor' nor lordship　I ne'er drunk sack
in my life , and if you give me any conserves,
give me conserves of beef　ne'er ask me what
raiment I'll wear　for I have no more doub-
lets than backs, no more stockings than legs,
nor no more shoes than feet , nay, sometimes
more feet than shoes, or such shoes as my toes
look through the over-leather

Lord　Heaven cease this idle humor in your
　　honor !
O, that a mighty man of such descent,
Of such possessions and so high esteem,
Should be infused with so foul a spirit !

Sly　What would you make me mad ? Am
not I Christopher Sly , old Sly's son of Burton-
heath, by birth a pedlar, by education a card-
maker, by transmutation a bear-herd, and
now by present profession a tinker ? Ask
Marian Hacket the fat ale-wife of Wincot, if
she know me not　if she say I am not fourteen
pence on the score for sheer ale　score me up
for the lyingest knave in Christendom　What !
I am not bestraught　here :—

Third Serv　O, this it is that makes your
　　lady mourn !
Sec Serv　O, this is it that makes your ser-
　　vants droop !

Lord　Hence comes it that your kindred
　　shuns your house, 30
As beaten hence by your strange lunacy
O noble lord, bethink thee of thy birth,
Call home thy ancient thoughts from banish-
　　ment
And banish hence these abject lowly dreams
Look how thy servants do attend on thee,
Each in his office ready at thy beck
Wilt thou have music ? hark ! Apollo plays
　　　　　　[*Music.*
And twenty caged nightingales do sing
Or wilt thou sleep ? we'll have thee to a
　　couch
Softer and sweeter than the lustful bed 40
On purpose trimm'd up for Semiramis
Say thou wilt walk　we will bestrew the
　　ground
Or wilt thou ride ? thy horses shall be trapped,
Their harness studded all with gold and pearl
Dost thou love hawking ? thou hast hawks
　　will soar
Above the morning lark　or wilt thou hunt ?
Thy hounds shall make the welkin answer
　　them
And fetch shrill echoes from the hollow earth

First Serv　Say thou wilt course, thy grey-
　　hounds are as swift
As breathed stags ay fleeter than the roe 50

Sec Serv　Dost thou love pictures ? we will
　　fetch thee straight
Adonis painted by a running brook,
And Cytherea all in sedges hid,
Which seem to move and wanton with her
　　breath
Even as the waving sedges play with wind

Lord　We'll show thee Io as she was a
　　maid,

And how she was beguiled and surprised,
As lively painted as the deed was done.
   Third Serv. Or Daphne roaming through
     a thorny wood,
Scratching her legs that one shall swear she
     bleeds,   60
And at that sight shall sad Apollo weep,
So workmanly the blood and tears are drawn.
   Lord. Thou art a lord, and nothing but a
     lord :
Thou hast a lady far more beautiful
Than any woman in this waning age.
   First Serv. And till the tears that she hath
     shed for thee
Like envious floods o'er-run her lovely face,
She was the fairest creature in the world ;
And yet she is inferior to none.   69
   Sly. Am I a lord ? and have I such a lady?
Or do I dream ? or have I dream'd till now ?
I do not sleep : I see, I hear, I speak ;
I smell sweet savors and I feel soft things :
Upon my life, I am a lord indeed
And not a tinker nor Christophero Sly.
Well, bring our lady hither to our sight ;
And once again, a pot o' the smallest ale.
   Sec. Serv. Will't please your mightiness to
     wash your hands ?
O, how we joy to see your wit restored !
O, that once more you knew but what you
   are !   80
These fifteen years you have been in a dream ;
Or when you waked, so waked as if you slept.
   Sly. These fifteen years ! by my fay, a
     goodly nap.
But did I never speak of all that time ?
   First Serv. O, yes, my lord, but very idle
     words :   [ber,
For though you lay here in this goodly cham-
Yet would you say ye were beaten out of door;
And rail upon the hostess of the house ;
And say you would present her at the leet,
Because she brought stone jugs and no seal'd
     quarts :   90
Sometimes you would call out for Cicely
     Hacket.
   Sly. Ay, the woman's maid of the house.
   Third Serv. Why, sir, you know no house
     nor no such maid,
Nor no such men as you have reckon'd up,
As Stephen Sly and old John Naps of Greece
And Peter Turph and Henry Pimpernell
And twenty more such names and men as
     these
Which never were nor no man ever saw.
   Sly. Now Lord be thanked for my good
     amends !
   All. Amen.   100
   Sly. I thank thee: thou shalt not lose by it.

Enter the Page *as a lady, with attendants.*

   Page. How fares my noble lord ?
   Sly. Marry, I fare well ; for here is cheer
     enough.
Where is my wife ?
   Page. Here, noble lord : what is thy will
     with her ?

   Sly. Are you my wife and will not call me
     husband ?
My men should call me 'lord :' I am your
     goodman.
   Page. My husband and my lord, my lord
     and husband ;
I am your wife in all obedience.
   Sly. I know it well. What must I call her?
   Lord. Madam.   111
   Sly. Al'ce madam, or Joan madam ?
   Lord. 'Madam,' and nothing else : so
     lords call ladies.
   Sly. Madam wife, they say that I have
     dream'd
And slept above some fifteen year or more.
   Page. Ay, and the time seems thirty unto
     me,
Being all this time abandon'd from your bed.
   Sly. 'Tis much. Servants, leave me and
     her alone.
Madam, undress you and come now to bed.
   Page. Thrice noble lord, let me entreat of
     you   120
To pardon me yet for a night or two,
Or, if not so, until the sun be set:
For your physicians have expressly charged,
In peril to incur your former malady,
That I should yet absent me from your bed:
I hope this reason stands for my excuse.
   Sly. Ay, it stands so that I may hardly
tarry so long. But I would be loath to fall into
my dreams again : I will therefore tarry in
despite of the flesh and the blood.   130

Enter a Messenger.

   Mess. Your honor's players, hearing your
     amendment,
Are come to play a pleasant comedy ;
For so your doctors hold it very meet,
Seeing too much sadness hath congeal'd your
     blood,
And melancholy is the nurse of frenzy :
Therefore they thought it good you hear a play
And frame your mind to mirth and merriment.
Which bars a thousand harms and lengthens
     life.
   Sly. Marry, I will, let them play it. Is not
a comonty a Christmas gambold or a tumbling-
trick ?   141
   Page. No, my good lord ; it is more pleas-
     ing stuff.
   Sly. What, household stuff ?
   Page. It is a kind of history.
   Sly. Well, we'll see't. Come, madam wife,
sit by my side and let the world slip: we shall
ne'er be younger.

Flourish.

ACT I.

SCENE I. *Padua. A public place.*

Enter LUCENTIO *and his man* TRANIO.

   Luc. Tranio, since for the great desire I
     had
To see fair Padua, nursery of arts

I am arrived for fruitful Lombardy,
The pleasant garden of great Italy ;
And by my father's love and leave am arm'd
With his good will and thy good company,
My trusty servant, well approved in all,
Here let us breathe and haply institute
A course of learning and ingenious studies
Pisa renown'd for grave citizens   10
Gave me my being and my father first,
A merchant of great traffic through the world,
Vincentio, come of the Bentivolii
Vincentio's son brought up in Florence
It shall become to serve all hopes conceived,
To deck his fortune with his virtuous deeds
And therefore, Tranio, for the time I study,
Virtue and that part of philosophy
Will I apply that treats of happiness
By virtue specially to be achieved   20
Tell me thy mind ; for I have Pisa left
And am to Padua come, as he that leaves
A shallow plash to plunge him in the deep
And with satiety seeks to quench his thirst.
  Tra. Mi perdonato, gentle master mine,
I am in all affected as yourself ;
Glad that you thus continue your resolve
To suck the sweets of sweet philosophy.
Only, good master, while we do admire
This virtue and this moral discipline,   30
Let's be no stoics nor no stocks, I pray ;
Or so devote to Aristotle's checks
As Ovid be an outcast quite abjured
Balk logic with acquaintance that you have
And practise rhetoric in your common talk ;
Music and poesy use to quicken you ;
The mathematics and the metaphysics,
Fall to them as you find your stomach serves
    you ;
No profit grows where is no pleasure ta'en :
In brief, sir, study what you most affect   40
  Luc. Gramercies, Tranio, well dost thou
    advise.
If, Biondello, thou wert come ashore,
We could at once put us in readiness,
And take a lodging fit to entertain
Such friends as time in Padua shall beget
But stay a while : what company is this ?
  Tra. Master, some show to welcome us to
    town

Enter BAPTISTA, KATHARINA, BIANCA, GRE-
  MIO, *and* HORTENSIO. LUCENTIO *and*
  TRANIO *stand by.*

  Bap. Gentlemen, importune me no far-
    ther,
For how I firmly am resolved you know ;
That is, not to bestow my youngest daughter
Before I have a husband for the elder .   51
If either of you both love Katharina,
Because I know you well and love you well,
Leave shall you have to court her at your
    pleasure.
  Gre. [*Aside*] To cart her rather . she's
    too rough for me
There, there, Hortensio, will you any wife ?
  Kath. I pray you, sir, is it your will
To make a stale of me amongst these mates ?

  Hor. Mates, maid ! how mean you that ?
    no mates for you
Unless you were of gentler, milder mould   60
  Kath. I'faith, sir, you shall never need to
    fear
I wis it is not half way to her heart ;
But if it were, doubt not her care should be
To comb your noddle with a three-legg'd stool
And paint your face and use you like a fool
  Hor. From all such devils, good Lord de-
    liver us !
  Gre. And me too, good Lord !
  Tra. Hush, master ! here's some good pas-
    time toward
That wench is stark mad or wonderful fro-
    ward
  Luc. But in the other's silence do I see   70
Maid's mild behavior and sobriety.
Peace, Tranio !
  Tra. Well said, master ; mum ! and gaze
    your fill
  Bap. Gentlemen, that I may soon make
    good
What I have said, Bianca, get you in
And let it not displease thee, good Bianca,
For I will love thee ne'er the less, my girl.
  Kath. A pretty peat ! it is best
Put finger in the eye, an she knew why
  Bian. Sister, content you in my discon-
    tent.   80
Sir, to your pleasure humbly I subscribe
My books and instruments shall be my com-
    pany,
On them to look and practise by myself
  Luc. Hark, Tranio ! thou may'st hear
    Minerva speak
  Hor. Signior Baptista, will you be so
    strange ?
Sorry am I that our good will effects
Bianca's grief
  Gre. Why will you mew her up,
Signior Baptista, for this fiend of hell,
And make her bear the penance of her
    tongue ?
  Bap. Gentlemen, content ye ; I am re-
    solved .   90
Go in, Bianca   [*Exit Bianca*
And for I know she taketh most delight
In music, instruments and poetry,
Schoolmasters will I keep within my house,
Fit to instruct her youth If you Hortensio,
Or Signior Gremio, you, know any such,
Prefer them hither ; for to cunning men
I will be very kind, and liberal
To mine own children in good bringing up ;
And so farewell Katharina, you may stay ;
For I have more to commune with Bianca 101
    [*Exit*
  Kath. Why, and I trust I may go too,
may I not ? What, shall I be appointed hours,
as though, belike, I knew not what to take,
and what to leave, ha ?   [*Exit*
  Gre. You may go to the devil's dam . your
gifts are so good, here's none will hold you
Their love is not so great, Hortensio, but we
may blow our nails together, and fast it fairly

out : our cake's dough on both sides. Farewell : yet, for the love I bear my sweet Bianca, if I can by any means light on a fit man to teach her that wherein she delights, I will wish him to her father.

Hor. So will I, Signior Gremio : but a word, I pray. Though the nature of our quarrel yet never brooked parle, know now, upon advice, it toucheth us both, that we may yet again have access to our fair mistress and be happy rivals in Bianca's love, to labor and effect one thing specially.   .   121

Gre. What's that, I pray ?   [sister.
Hor. Marry, sir, to get a husband for her
Gre. A husband ! a devil.
Hor. I say, a husband.
Gre. I say, a devil. Thinkest thou, Hortensio, though her father be very rich, any man is so very a fool to be married to hell ?

Hor. Tush, Gremio, though it pass your patience and mine to endure her loud alarums, why, man, there be good fellows in the world, an a man could light on them, would take her with all faults, and money enough.

Gre. I cannot tell ; but I had as lief take her dowry with this condition, to be whipped at the high cross every morning.

Hor. Faith, as you say, there's small choice in rotten apples. But come : since this bar in law makes us friends, it shall be so far forth friendly maintained till by helping Baptista's eldest daughter to a husband we set his youngest free for a husband, and then have to't afresh. Sweet Bianca ! Happy man be his dole ! He that runs fastest gets the ring. How say you, Signior Gremio ?

Gre. I am agreed ; and would I had given him the best horse in Padua to begin his wooing that would thoroughly woo her, wed her and bed her and rid the house of her ! Come on. [*Exeunt Gremio and Hortensio.* 150

Tra. I pray, sir, tell me, is it possible That love should of a sudden take such hold ?

Luc. O Tranio, till I found it to be true, I never thought it possible or likely ; But see, while idly I stood looking on, I found the effect of love in idleness : And now in plainness do confess to thee, That art to me as secret and as dear As Anna to the queen of Carthage was, Tranio, I burn, I pine, I perish, Tranio,   160 If I achieve not this young modest girl. Counsel me, Tranio, for I know thou canst ; Assist me, Tranio, for I know thou wilt.

Tra. Master, it is no time to chide you now ;
Affection is not rated from the heart : If love have touch'd you, nought remains but so,
' Redime te captum quam queas minimo.'

Luc. Gramercies, lad, go forward ; this contents :
The rest will comfort, for thy counsel's sound.

Tra. Master, you look'd so longly on the maid,   170
Perhaps you mark'd not what's the pith of all.

Luc. O yes, I saw sweet beauty in her face,
Such as the daughter of Agenor had, That made great Jove to humble him to her hand,
When with his knees he kiss'd the Cretan strand.

Tra. Saw you no more ? mark'd you not how her sister
Began to scold and raise up such a storm That mortal ears might hardly endure the din?

Luc. Tranio, I saw her coral lips to move And with her breath she did perfume the air : Sacred and sweet was all I saw in her.   181

Tra. Nay, then, 'tis time to stir him from his trance.
I pray, awake, sir : if you love the maid, Bend thoughts and wits to achieve her. Thus it stands :
Her eldest sister is so curst and shrewd That till the father rid his hands of her, Master, your love must live a maid at home ; And therefore has he closely mew'd her up, Because she will not be annoy'd with suitors.

Luc. Ah, Tranio, what a cruel father's he! But art thou not advised, he took some care To get her cunning schoolmasters to instruct her ?

Tra. Ay, marry, am I, sir ; and now 'tis plotted.

Luc. I have it, Tranio.

Tra.   Master, for my hand, Both our inventions meet and jump in one.

Luc. Tell me thine first.

Tra.   You will be schoolmaster And undertake the teaching of the maid : That's your device.

Luc.   It is : may it be done ?

Tra. Not possible ; for who shall bear your part,
And be in Padua here Vincentio's son,   200 Keep house and ply his book, welcome his friends,
Visit his countrymen and banquet them ?

Luc. Basta ; content thee, for I have it full.
We have not yet been seen in any house, Nor can we be distinguish'd by our faces For man or master ; then it follows thus ; Thou shalt be master, Tranio, in my stead, Keep house and port and servants, as I should : I will some other be, some Florentine, Some Neapolitan, or meaner man of Pisa. 210 'Tis hatch'd and shall be so : Tranio, at once Uncase thee ; take my color'd hat and cloak : When Biondello comes, he waits on thee ; But I will charm him first to keep his tongue.

Tra. So had you need.
In brief, sir, sith it your pleasure is, And I am tied to be obedient ; For so your father charged me at our parting, ' Be serviceable to my son,' quoth he, Although I think 'twas in another sense ;   220 I am content to be Lucentio, Because so well I love Lucentio.

Luc. Tranio, be so, because Lucentio loves :

And let me be a slave, to achieve that maid
Whose sudden sight hath thrall'd my wounded
    eye
Here comes the rogue

Enter BIONDELLO.

                        Sirrah, where have you been ?
Bion.   Where have I been ' Nay, how
now ' where are you ? Master, has my fellow
Tranio stolen your clothes ? Or you stolen
his ? or both ? pray, what's the news ?   230
Luc   Sirrah, come hither 'tis no time to
    jest,
And therefore frame your manners to the
    time
Your fellow Tranio here, to save my life,
Puts my apparel and my countenance on,
And I for my escape have put on his ,
For in a quarrel since I came ashore
I kill'd a man and fear I was descried :
Wait you on him, I charge you, as becomes,
While I make way from hence to save my
    life
You understand me ?
Bion.   I, sir ' ne'er a whit.   240
Luc   And not a jot of Tranio in your
    mouth
Tranio is changed into Lucentio
Bion.   The better for him would I were
    so too '
Tra   So could I, faith, boy, to have the
    next wish after,
That Lucentio indeed had Baptista's youngest
    daughter
But, sirrah, not for my sake, but your mas-
    ter's, I advise
You use your manners discreetly in all kind
    of companies
When I am alone, why, then I am Tranio ,
But in all places else your master Lucentio
Luc   Tranio, let's go   one thing more
rests, that thyself execute, to make one among
these wooers   if thou ask me why, sufficeth,
my reasons are both good and weighty
                                      [*Exeunt*

The presenters above speak.

First Serv   My lord, you nod , you do not
    mind the play
Sly   Yes, by Saint Anne, do I   A good
matter, surely   comes there any more of it ?
Page.   My lord, 'tis but begun
Sly   'Tis a very excellent piece of work,
madam lady : would 'twere done '   250
                              [*They sit and mark*

SCENE II.   *Padua.   Before* HORTENSIO'S
                house

Enter PETRUCHIO *and his man* GRUMIO

Pet.   Verona, for a while I take my leave,
To see my friends in Padua, but of all
My best beloved and approved friend,
Hortensio, and I trow this is his house
Here, sirrah Grumio; knock, I say
Gru.   Knock, sir ! whom should I knock ?
Is there any man has rebused your worship?

Pet   Villain, I say, knock me here soundly
Gru   Knock you here, sir ' why, sir, what
am I, sir, that I should knock you here, sir ?
Pet   Villain, I say, knock me at this gate
And rap me well, or I'll knock your knave's
    pate
Gru   My master is grown quarrelsome   I
    should knock you first,
And then I know after who comes by the
    worst
Pet   Will it not be ?
Faith, sirrah, an you'll not knock, I'll ring it ;
I'll try how you can sol, fa, and sing it
                        [*He wrings him by the ears*
Gru   Help, masters, help ' my master is
    mad.
Pet   Now, knock when I bid you, sirrah
villain '

Enter HORTENSIO

Hor   How now ' what's the matter ? My
old friend Grumio ' and my good friend
Petruchio '
How do you all at Verona ?
Pet   Signior Hortensio, come you to part
    the fray ?
'Con tutto il cuore, ben trovato,' may I say
Hor   'Alla nostra casa ben venuto, molto
honorato signor mio Petruchio '
Rise, Grumio, rise   we will compound this
    quarrel
Gru   Nay, 'tis no matter, sir, what he
'leges in Latin   If this be not a lawful cause
for me to leave his service, look you, sir, he
bid me knock him and rap him soundly, sir
well, was it fit for a servant to use his master
so, being perhaps, for aught I see, two and
thirty, a pip out ?
Whom would to God I had well knock'd at
    first,
Then had not Grumio come by the worst
Pet   A senseless villain ' Good Hortensio,
I bade the rascal knock upon your gate
And could not get him for my heart to do
    it
Gru   Knock at the gate ' O heavens !
Spake you not these words plain, Sirrah,
knock me here, rap me here, knock me well,
and knock me soundly ? ' And come you now
with, ' knocking at the gate ' ?
Pet   Sirrah, be gone, or talk not, I advise
    you
Hor   Petruchio, patience , I am Grumio's
    pledge
Why, this's a heavy chance 'twixt him and
    you,
Your ancient, trusty, pleasant servant Grumio
And tell me now, sweet friend, what happy
    gale
Blows you to Padua here from old Verona ?
Pet   Such wind as scatters young men
        through the world   56
To seek their fortunes farther than at home
Where small experience grows   But in a few,
Signior Hortensio, thus it stands with me,
Antonio, my father is deceased,

And I have thrust myself into this maze,
Haply to wive and thrive as best I may :
Crowns in my purse I have and goods at home.
And so am come abroad to see the world.
  Hor. Petruchio, shall I then come roundly
    to thee   59
And wish thee to a shrewd ill-favor'd wife ?
Thou'ldst thank me but a little for my coun-
    sel :
And yet I'll promise thee she shall be rich
And very rich : but thou'rt too much my
    friend,
And I'll not wish thee to her.
  Pet. Signior Hortensio, 'twixt such friends
    as we
Few words suffice ; and therefore, if thou
    know
One rich enough to be Petruchio's wife,
As wealth is burden of my wooing dance,
Be she as foul as was Florentius' love,
As old as Sibyl and as curst and shrewd   70
As Socrates' Xanthippe, or a worse,
She moves me not, or not removes, at least,
Affection's edge in me, were she as rough
As are the swelling Adriatic seas :
I come to wive it wealthily in Padua ;
If wealthily, then happily in Padua.
  Gru. Nay, look you, sir, he tells you flatly
what his mind is : why, give him gold enough
and marry him to a puppet or an aglet-baby ;
or an old trot with ne'er a tooth in her head,
though she have as many diseases as two and
fifty horses : why, nothing comes amiss, so
money comes withal.
  Hor. Petruchio, since we are stepp'd thus
    far in,
I will continue that I broach'd in jest.
I can, Petruchio, help thee to a wife
With wealth enough and young and beauteous,
Brought up as best becomes a gentlewoman :
Her only fault, and that is faults enough,
Is that she is intolerable curst
And shrewd and froward, so beyond all meas-
    ure
That, were my state far worser than it is, 91
I would not wed her for a mine of gold.
  Pet. Hortensio, peace ! thou know'st not
    gold's effect :
Tell me her father's name and 'tis enough ;
For I will board her, though she chide as loud
As thunder when the clouds in autumn crack.
  Hor. Her father is Baptista Minola,
An affable and courteous gentleman :
Her name is Katharina Minola,
Renown'd in Padua for her scolding tongue.
  Pet. I know her father, though I know not
    her ;   101
And he knew my deceased father well.
I will not sleep, Hortensio, till I see her ;
And therefore let me be thus bold with you
To give you over at this first encounter,
Unless you will accompany me thither.
  Gru. I pray you, sir, let him go while the
humor lasts. O' my word, an she knew him
as well as I do, she would think scolding
would do little good upon him : she may per-

haps call him half a score knaves or so : why,
that's nothing ; an he begin once, he'll rail in
his rope-tricks. I'll tell you what, sir, an she
stand him but a little, he will throw a figure
in her face and so disfigure her with it that she
shall have no more eyes to see withal than a
cat. You know him not, sir.
  Hor. Tarry, Petruchio, I must go with thee,
For in Baptista's keep my treasure is :
He hath the jewel of my life in hold,
His youngest daughter, beautiful Bianca, 120
And her withholds from me and other more,
Suitors to her and rivals in my love,
Supposing it a thing impossible,
For those defects I have before rehearsed,
That ever Katharina will be woo'd :
Therefore this order hath Baptista ta'en,
That none shall have access unto Bianca
Till Katharine the curst have got a husband.
  Gru. Katharine the curst !
A title for a maid of all titles the worst.   130
  Hor. Now shall my friend Petruchio do me
    grace,
And offer me disguised in sober robes
To old Baptista as a schoolmaster
Well seen in music, to instruct Bianca ;
That so I may, by this device, at least
Have leave and leisure to make love to her
And unsuspected court her by herself.
  Gru. Here's no knavery ! See, to beguile
the old folks, how the young folks lay their
heads together !   140

Enter GREMIO, *and* LUCENTIO *disguised.*

Master, master, look about you : who goes
    there, ha ?
  Hor. Peace, Grumio ! it is the rival of my
    love.
Petruchio, stand by a while.
  Gru. A proper stripling and an amorous !
  Gre. O, very well ; I have perused the note.
Hark you, sir : I'll have them very fairly
    bound :
All books of love, see that at any hand ;
And see you read no other lectures to her :
You understand me : over and beside
Signior Baptista's liberality,   150
I'll mend it with a largess. Take your paper
    too,
And let me have them very well perfumed :
For she is sweeter than perfume itself
To whom they go to. What will you read to
    her ?
  Luc. Whate'er I read to her, I'll plead for
    you
As for my patron, stand you so assured,
As firmly as yourself were still in place :
Yea, and perhaps with more successful words
Than you, unless you were a scholar, sir.
  Gre. O this learning, what a thing it is ! 160
  Gru. O this woodcock, what an ass it is !
  Pet. Peace, sirrah !
  Hor. Grumio, mum ! God save you, Sig-
    nior Gremio.
  Gre. And you are well met, Signior Hor-
    tensio.

Trow you whither I am going ? To Baptista
   Minola
I promised to inquire carefully
About a schoolmaster for the fair Bianca .
And by good fortune I have lighted well
On this young man, for learning and behavior
Fit for her turn, well read in poetry   170
And other books, good ones, I warrant ye.
   Hor. 'Tis well , and I have met a gentle-
      man
Hath promised me to help me to another,
A fine musician to instruct our mistress ,
So shall I no whit be behind in duty
To fair Bianca, so beloved of me
   Gre. Beloved of me ; and that my deeds
      shall prove
   Gru. And that his bags shall prove
   Hor. Gremio, 'tis now no time to vent our
      love :
Listen to me, and if you speak me fair,   180
· I'll tell you news indifferent good for either
Here is a gentleman whom by chance I met,
Upon agreement from us to his liking,
Will undertake to woo curst Katharine,
Yea, and to marry her, if her dowry please.
   Gre. So said, so done, is well.
Hortensio, have you told him all her faults ?
   Pet. I know she is an irksome brawling
      scold :
If that be all, masters, I hear no harm
   Gre No, say'st me so, friend ? What coun-
      try man ?   190
   Pet. Born in Verona, old Antonio's son :
My father dead, my fortune lives for me ,
And I do hope good days and long to see
   Gre. O sir, such a life, with such a wife,
      were strange !
But if you have a stomach, to't i' God's name
You shall have me assisting you in all
But will you woo this wild-cat ?
   Pet   Will I live ?
   Gru. Will he woo her? ay, or I'll hang her.
   Pet. Why came I hither but to that intent ?
Think you a little din can daunt mine ears ? 201
Have I not in my time heard lions roar ?
Have I not heard the sea puff'd up with winds
Rage like an angry boar chafed with sweat ?
Have I not heard great ordnance in the field,
And heaven's artillery thunder in the skies ?
Have I not in a pitched battle heard
Loud 'larums, neighing steeds, and trumpets'
      clang ?
And do you tell me of a woman's tongue,
That gives not half so great a blow to hear
As will a chestnut in a farmer's fire ?   210
Tush, tush ! fear boys with bugs
   Gru.   For he fears none
   Gre Hortensio, hark :
This gentleman is happily arrived,
My mind presumes, for his own good and ours.
   Hor. I promised we would be contributors
And bear his charge of wooing, whatsoe'er
   Gre And so we will, provided that he win
      her.
   Gru. I would I were as sure of a good din-
      ner.

Enter TRANIO *brave, and* BIONDELLO.
   Tra Gentlemen, God save you. If I may
      be bold,
Tell me, I beseech you, which is the readiest
      way
To the house of Signior Baptista Minola ? 221
   Bion. He that has the two fair daughters:
      is't he you mean ?
   Tra. Even he, Biondello
   Gre Hark you, sir , you mean not her to—
   Tra. Perhaps, him and her, sir : what have
      you to do ?
   Pet Not her that chides, sir, at any hand,
      I pray.
   Tra. I love no chiders, sir : Biondello, let s
      away.
   Luc Well begun, Tranio
   Hor.   Sir, a word ere you go,
Are you a suitor to the maid you talk of, yea
      or no ?   230
   Tra. And if I be, sir, is it any offence ?
   Gre. No , if without more words you will
      get you hence.
   Tra. Why, sir, I pray, are not the streets
      as free
For me as for you ?
   Gre.   But so is not she
   Tra For what reason, I beseech you ?
   Gre.   For this reason, if you'll know,
That she's the choice love of Signior Gremio
   Hor. That she's the chosen of Signior Hor-
      tensio
   Tra Softly, my masters ! if you be gentle-
      men,
Do me this right , hear me with patience   240
Baptista is a noble gentleman,
To whom my father is not all unknown ,
And were his daughter fairer than she is,
She may more suitors have and me for one.
Fair Leda's daughter had a thousand wooers ,
Then well one more may fair Bianca have
And so she shall , Lucentio shall make one,
Though Paris came in hope to speed alone
   Gre What ! this gentleman will out-talk
      us all.
   Luc Sir, give him head · I know he'll prove
      a jade
   Pet Hortensio, to what end are all these
      words ?   250
   Hor. Sir, let me be so bold as ask you,
Did you yet ever see Baptista's daughter ?
   Tra. No, sir , but hear I do that he hath
      two,
The one as famous for a scolding tongue
As is the other for beauteous modesty
   Pet. Sir, sir, the first's for me , let her
      go by
   Gre Yea, leave that labor to great Her-
      cules :
And let it be more than Alcides' twelve
   Pet. Sir, understand you this of me in
      sooth:
The youngest daughter whom you hearken for
Her father keeps from all access of suitors, 261
And will not promise her to any man
Until the elder sister first be wed ;

The younger then is free and not before.

Tra. If it be so, sir, that you are the man
Must stead us all and me amongst the rest,
And if you break the ice and do this feat,
Achieve the elder, set the younger free
For our access, whose hap shall be to have her
Will not so graceless be to be ingrate. 270

Hor. Sir, you say well and well you do conceive ;
And since you do profess to be a suitor,
You must, as we do, gratify this gentleman,
To whom we all rest generally beholding.

Tra. Sir, I shall not be slack : in sign whereof,
Please ye we may contrive this afternoon,
And quaff carouses to our mistress' health,
And do as adversaries do in law,
Strive mightily, but eat and drink as friends.

Gru. Bion. O excellent motion ! Fellows, let's be gone. 280

Hor. The motion's good indeed and be it so,
Petruchio, I shall be your ben venuto.

[*Exeunt.*

ACT II.

SCENE I. *Padua. A room in* BAPTISTA'S *house.*

Enter KATHARINA *and* BIANCA.

Bian. Good sister, wrong me not, nor wrong yourself,
To make a bondmaid and a slave of me ;
That I disdain : but for these other gawds,
Unbind my hands, I'll pull them off myself,
Yea, all my raiment, to my petticoat ;
Or what you will command me will I do,
So well I know my duty to my elders.

Kath. Of all thy suitors, here I charge thee, tell
Whom thou lovest best: see thou dissemble not.

Bian. Believe me, sister, of all the men alive 10
I never yet beheld that special face
Which I could fancy more than any other.

Kath. Minion, thou liest. Is't not Hortensio ?

Bian. If you affect him, sister, here I swear
I'll plead for you myself, but you shall have him. [more :

Kath. O then, belike, you fancy riches
You will have Gremio to keep you fair.

Bian. Is it for him you do envy me so ?
Nay then you jest, and now I well perceive
You have but jested with me all this while: 20
I prithee, sister Kate, untie my hands.

Kath. If that be jest, then all the rest was so. [*Strikes her.*

Enter BAPTISTA.

Bap. Why, how now, dame! whence grows this insolence ?
Bianca, stand aside. Poor girl ! she weeps.
Go ply thy needle : meddle not with her.

For shame, thou hilding of a devilish spirit,
Why dost thou wrong her that did ne'er wrong thee ?
When did she cross thee with a bitter word ?

Kath. Her silence flouts me, and I'll be revenged. [*Flies after Bianca.*

Bap. What, in my sight ? Bianca, get thee in. [*Exit Bianca.* 30

Kath. What, will you not suffer me ? Nay, now I see
She is your treasure, she must have a husband
I must dance bare-foot on her wedding day
And for your love to her lead apes in hell.
Talk not to me : I will go sit and weep
Till I can find occasion of revenge. [*Exit.*

Bap. Was ever gentleman thus grieved as I?
But who comes here ?

Enter GREMIO, LUCENTIO *in the habit of a mean man ;* PETRUCHIO, *with* HORTENSIO *as a musician ; and* TRANIO, *with* BIONDELLO *bearing a lute and books.*

Gre. Good morrow, neighbor Baptista.

Bap. Good morrow, neighbor Gremio. God save you, gentlemen ! 41

Pet. And you, good sir ! Pray, have you not a daughter
Call'd Katharina, fair and virtuous ?

Bap. I have a daughter, sir, called Katharina,

Gre. You are too blunt : go to it orderly.

Pet. You wrong me, Signior Gremio : give me leave.
I am a gentleman of Verona, sir,
That, hearing of her beauty and her wit,
Her affability and bashful modesty,
Her wondrous qualities and mild behavior, 50
Am bold to show myself a forward guest
Within your house, to make mine eye the witness
Of that report which I so oft have heard.
And, for an entrance to my entertainment,
I do present you with a man of mine, [*Presenting Hortensio.*
Cunning in music and the mathematics,
To instruct her fully in those sciences,
Whereof I know she is not ignorant :
Accept of him, or else you do me wrong :
His name is Licio, born in Mantua. 60

Bap. You're welcome, sir ; and he, for your good sake.
But for my daughter Katharine, this I know,
She is not for your turn, the more my grief.

Pet. I see you do not mean to part with her,
Or else you like not of my company.

Bap. Mistake me not ; I speak but as I find.
Whence are you, sir ? what may I call your name ?

Pet. Petruchio is my name ; Antonio's son,
A man well known throughout all Italy.

Bap. I know him well : you are welcome for his sake. 70

Gre. Saving your tale, Petruchio, I pray,
Let us, that are poor petitioners, speak too ;
Baccare ! you are marvellous forward.

Pet. O, pardon me, Signior Gremio ; I would fain be doing.

Gre. I doubt it not, sir ; but you will curse
    your wooing.
Neighbor, this is a gift very grateful, I am
sure of it. To express the like kindness, myself,
that have been more kindly beholding to you
than any, freely give unto you this young
scholar [*presenting Lucentio*], that hath been
long studying at Rheims ; as cunning in Greek,
Latin, and other languages, as the other in
music and mathematics : his name is Cambio ;
pray, accept his service.
  Bap. A thousand thanks, Signior Gremio.
Welcome, good Cambio. [*To Tranio*] But,
gentle sir, methinks you walk like a stranger :
may I be so bold to know the cause of your
coming ?
  Tra. Pardon me, sir, the boldness is mine
    own,
That, being a stranger in this city here,   90
Do make myself a suitor to your daughter,
Unto Bianca, fair and virtuous.
Nor is your firm resolve unknown to me,
In the preferment of the eldest sister.
This liberty is all that I request,
That, upon knowledge of my parentage,
I may have welcome 'mongst the rest that woo
And free access and favor as the rest :
And, toward the education of your daughters,
I here bestow a simple instrument,   100
And this small packet of Greek and Latin
    books :
If you accept them, then their worth is great.
  Bap. Lucentio is your name ; of whence, I
    pray ?
  Tra. Of Pisa, sir ; son to Vincentio.
  Bap. A mighty man of Pisa ; by report
I know him well : you are very welcome, sir,
Take you the lute, and you the set of books ;
You shall go see your pupils presently.
Holla, within !

        Enter a Servant.

             Sirrah, lead these gentlemen
To my daughters ; and tell them both,   110
These are their tutors : bid them use them
    well.
  [*Exit Servant, with Lucentio and Hortensio,
                Biondello following.*
We will go walk a little in the orchard,
And then to dinner. You are passing welcome,
And so I pray you all to think yourselves.
  Pet. Signior Baptista, my business asketh
    haste,
And every day I cannot come to woo.
You knew my father well, and in him me,
Left solely heir to all his lands and goods,
Which I have better'd rather than decreased :
Then tell me, if I get your daughter's love, 120
What dowry shall I have with her to wife ?
  Bap. After my death the one half of my
    lands,
And in possession twenty thousand crowns.
  Pet. And, for that dowry, I'll assure her of
Her widowhood, be it that she survive me,
In all my lands and leases whatsoever :
Let specialties be therefore drawn between us,

That covenants may be kept on either hand.
  Bap. Ay, when the special thing is well
    obtain'd,
That is, her love ; for that is all in all.   130
  Pet. Why, that is nothing ; for I tell you
father,
I am as peremptory as she proud-minded ;
And where two raging fires meet together
They do consume the thing that feeds their fury.
Though little fire grows great with little wind,
Yet extreme gusts will blow out fire and all :
So I to her and so she yields to me ;
For I am rough and woo not like a babe.
  Bap. Well mayst thou woo, and happy be
    thy speed !
But be thou arm'd for some unhappy words.
  Pet. Ay, to the proof ; as mountains are for
    winds,   141
That shake not, though they blow perpetually.

  Re-enter HORTENSIO, *with his head broke.*

  Bap. How now, my friend ! why dost thou
    look so pale ?
  Hor. For fear, I promise you, if I look pale.
  Bap. What, will my daughter prove a good
    musician ?
  Hor. I think she'll sooner prove a soldier :
Iron may hold with her, but never lutes.
  Bap. Why, then thou canst not break her
    to the lute ?
  Hor. Why, no ; for she hath broke the
    lute to me.
I did but tell her she mistook her frets,   150
And bow'd her hand to teach her fingering ;
When, with a most impatient devilish spirit,
'Frets, call you these ?' quoth she ; ' I'll fume
    with them :'
And, with that word, she struck me on the
    head,
And through the instrument my pate made
    way ;
And there I stood amazed for a while,
As on a pillory, looking through the lute ;
While she did call me rascal fiddler
And twangling Jack ; with twenty such vile
    terms,
As had she studied to misuse me so.   160
  Pet. Now, by the world, it is a lusty wench ;
I love her ten times more than e'er I did :
O, how I long to have some chat with her !
  Bap. Well, go with me and be not so dis-
    comfited :
Proceed in practice with my younger daughter ;
She's apt to learn and thankful for good turns.
Signior Petruchio, will you go with us,
Or shall I send my daughter Kate to you ?
  Pet. I pray you do. [*Exeunt all but Petru-
    chio.*] I will attend her here,   169
And woo her with some spirit when she comes.
Say that she rail ; why then I'll tell her plain
She sings as sweetly as a nightingale :
Say that she frown ; I'll say she looks as clear
As morning roses newly wash'd with dew :
Say she be mute and will not speak a word ;
Then I'll commend her volubility,
And say she uttereth piercing eloquence :

If she do bid me pack, I'll give her thanks,
As though she bid me stay by her a week :
If she deny to wed, I'll crave the day   180
When I shall ask the banns and when be married.
But here she comes ; and now, Petruchio,
    speak.

          Enter KATHARINA.

Good morrow, Kate ; for that's your name, I
    hear.
  Kath. Well have you heard, but something
    hard of hearing :
They call me Katharine that do talk of me.
  Pet. You lie, in faith ; for you are call'd
    plain Kate,
And bonny Kate and sometimes Kate the curst;
But Kate, the prettiest Kate in Christendom
Kate of Kate Hall, my super-dainty Kate,
For dainties are all Kates, and therefore, Kate,
Take this of me. Kate of my consolation ;   191
Hearing thy mildness prai-ed in every town,
Thy virtues spoke of, and thy beauty sounded,
Yet not so deeply as to thee belongs,
Myself am moved to woo thee for my wife.
  Kath. Moved ! in good time : let him that
    moved you hither
Remove you hence : I knew you at the first
You were a moveable.
  Pet.   Why, what's a moveable?
  Kath. A join'd-stool.
  Pet.   Thou hast hit it : come, sit on me.
  Kath. Asses are made to bear, and so are
    you.
  Pet. Women are made to bear, and so are
    you.
  Kath. No such jade as you, if me you mean.
  Pet. Alas ! good Kate, I will not burden
    thee ;
For, knowing thee to be but young and light—
  Kath. Too light for such a swain as you to
    catch ;
And yet as heavy as my weight should be.
  Pet. Should be ! should—buzz !
  Kath.   Well ta'en, and like a buzzard.
  Pet. O slow-wing'd turtle ! shall a buzzard
    take thee ?
  Kath. Ay, for a turtle, as he takes a buzzard.
  Pet. Come, come, you wasp ; i' faith, you
    are too angry.   210
  Kath. If I be waspish, best beware my sting.
  Pet. My remedy is then, to pluck it out.
  Kath. Ay, if the fool could find it where it
    lies.
  Pet. Who knows not where a wasp does
wear his sting ? In his tail.
  Kath. In his tongue.
  Pet. Whose tongue ?
  Kath. Yours, if you talk of tails : and so
    farewell.
  Pet. What, with my tongue in your tail ?
    nay, come again,
Good Kate ; I am a gentleman.
  Kath. That I'll try. [*She strikes him.* 220
  Pet. I swear I'll cuff you, if you strike again,

  Kath. So may you lose your arms :
If you strike me, you are no gentleman ;
And if no gentleman, why then no arms.
  Pet. A herald, Kate ? O, put me in thy
    books !
  Kath. What is your crest ? a coxcomb ?
  Pet. A combless cock, so Kate will be my
    hen.
  Kath. No cock of mine ; you crow too like
    a craven.
  Pet. Nay, come, Kate, come ; you must not
    look so sour.
  Kath. It is my fashion, when I see a crab.
  Pet. Why, here's no crab ; and therefore
    look not sour.   231
  Kath. There is, there is.
  Pet. Then show it me.
  Kath. Had I a glass, I would.
  Pet. What, you mean my face ?
  Kath. Well aim'd of such a young one.
  Pet. Now, by Saint George, I am too young
    for you.
  Kath. Yet you are wither'd.
  Pet. 'Tis with cares.   240
  Kath. I care not.
  Pet. Nay, hear you, Kate : in sooth you
    scape not so.
  Kath. I chafe you, if I tarry : let me go.
  Pet. No, not a whit : I find you passing
    gentle.
'Twas told me you were rough and coy and
    sullen,
And now I find report a very liar ;
For thou are pleasant, gamesome, passing cour-
    teous,
But slow in speech, yet sweet as spring-time
    flowers :
Thou canst not frown, thou canst not look
    askance,
Nor bite the lip, as angry wenches will,   250
Nor hast thou pleasure to be cross in talk,
But thou with mildness entertain'st thy wooers,
With gentle conference, soft and affable.
Why does the world report that Kate doth
    limp ?
O slanderous world ! Kate like the hazel-twig
Is straight and slender and as brown in hue
As hazel nuts and sweeter than the kernels.
O, let me see thee walk : thou dost not halt.
  Kath. Go, fool, and whom thou keep'st
    command.
  Pet. Did ever Dian so become a grove   260
As Kate this chamber with her princely gait ?
O, be thou Dian, and let her be Kate ;
And then let Kate be chaste and Dian sportful!
  Kath. Where did you study all this goodly
    speech ?
  Pet. It is extempore, from my mother-wit.
  Kath. A witty mother ! witless else her son
  Pet. Am I not wise ?
  Kath. Yes ; keep you warm.
  Pet. Marry, so I mean, sweet Katharine,
    in thy bed :
And therefore, setting all this chat aside,   270
Thus in plain terms: your father hath con-
    sented.

KATHARINE AND PETRUCHIO.

TAMING OF THE SHREW, p. 492

That you shall be my wife ; your dowry 'greed
  on ;
And, will you, nill you, I will marry you.
Now, Kate, I am a husband for your turn ;
For, by this light, whereby I see thy beauty,
Thy beauty, that doth make me like thee well,
Thou must be married to no man but me ;
For I am he am born to tame you Kate,
And bring you from a wild Kate to a Kate
Conformable as other household Kates.   280
Here comes your father : never make denial ;
I must and will have Katharine to my wife.

Re-enter BAPTISTA, GREMIO, *and* TRANIO.

  Bap. Now, Signior Petruchio, how speed
    you with my daughter ?
  Pet. How but well, sir ? how but well ?
It were impossible I should speed amiss.
  Bap. Why, how now, daughter Katharine!
    in your dumps ?   [ise you
  Kath. Call you me daughter ? now, I prom-
You have show'd a tender fatherly regard,
To wish me wed to one half lunatic ;
A mad-cup ruffian and a swearing Jack,   290
That thinks with oaths to face the matter out.
  Pet. Father, 'tis thus : yourself and all the
    world,
That talk'd of her, have talk'd amiss of her :
If she be curst, it is for policy,
For she's not froward, but modest as the dove;
She is not hot, but temperate as the morn ;
For patience she will prove a second Grissel,
And Roman Lucrece for her chastity :
And to conclude, we have 'greed so well to-
    gether,
That upon Sunday is the wedding-day.   300
  Kath. I'll see thee hang'd on Sunday first.
  Gre. Hark, Petruchio ; she says she'll see
    thee hang'd first.
  Tra. Is this your speeding ? nay, then,
    good night our part !
  Pet. Be patient, gentlemen ; I choose her
    for myself :
If she and I be pleased, what's that to you ?
'Tis bargain'd 'twixt us twain, being alone,
That she shall still be curst in company.
I tell you, 'tis incredible to believe
How much she loves me : O, the kindest Kate!
She hung about my neck ; and kiss on kiss
She vied so fast, protesting oath on oath,   311
That in a twink she won me to her love.
O, you are novices ! 'tis a world to see,
How tame, when men and women are alone,
A meacock wretch can make the curstest
    shrew.
Give me thy hand, Kate : I will unto Venice,
To buy apparel 'gainst the wedding-day.
Provide the feast, father, and bid the guests ;
I will be sure my Katharine shall be fine.
  Bap. I know not what to say : but give me
    your hands ;   320
God send you joy, Petruchio! 'tis a match.
  Gre. Tra. Amen, say we : we will be wit-
    nesses.
  Pet. Father, and wife, and gentlemen,
    adieu ;

I will to Venice ; Sunday comes apace :
We will have rings and things and fine array;
And kiss me, Kate, we will be married o'Sun-
    day.
    [*Exeunt Petruchio and Katharina severally.*
  Gre. Was ever match clapp'd up so sud-
    denly ?
  Bap. Faith, gentlemen, now I play a mer-
    chant's part,
And venture madly on a desperate mart.
  Tra. 'Twas a commodity lay fretting by
    you :   330
'Twill bring you gain, or perish on the seas.
  Bap. The gain I seek is, quiet in the match.
  Gre. No doubt but he hath got a quiet
    catch.
But now, Baptista, to your younger daughter:
Now is the day we long have looked for :
I am your neighbor, and was suitor first.
  Tra. And I am one that love Bianca more
Than words can witness, or your thoughts can
    guess.
  Gre. Youngling, thou canst not love so dear
    as I.
  Tra. Greybeard, thy love doth freeze.
  Gre.   But thine doth fry. 340
Skipper, stand back : 'tis age that nourisheth
  Tra. But youth in ladies' eyes that flour-
    isheth.
  Bap. Content you, gentlemen : I will com-
    pound this strife :
'Tis deeds must win the prize ; and he of both
That can assure my daughter greatest dower
Shall have my Bianca's love.
Say, Signior Gremio, what can you assure her?
  Gre. First, as you know, my house within
    the city
Is richly furnished with plate and gold ;
Basins and ewers to lave her dainty hands ;
My hangings all of Tyrian tapestry ;   351
In ivory coffers I have stuff'd my crowns ;
In cypress chests my arras counterpoints,
Costly apparel, tents, and canopies,
Fine linen, Turkey cushions boss'd with pearl
Valance of Venice gold in needlework,
Pewter and brass and all things that belong
To house or housekeeping : then, at my farm
I have a hundred milch-kine to the pail,
Sixscore fat oxen standing in my stalls,   360
And all things answerable to this portion.
Myself am struck in years, I must confess ;
And if I die to-morrow, this is hers,
If whilst I live she will be only mine.
  Tra. That 'only' came well in.   Sir, list
    to me :
I am my father's heir and only son :
If I may have your daughter to my wife,
I'll leave her houses three or four as good,
Within rich Pisa walls, as any one
Old Signior Gremio has in Padua ;   370
Besides two thousand ducats by the year
Of fruitful land, all which shall be her joint-
    ure.
What, have I pinch'd you, Signior Gremio ?
  Gre. Two thousand ducats by the year of
    land !

My land amounts not to so much in all :
That she shall have ; besides an argosy
That now is lying in Marseilles' road.
What, have I choked you with an argosy ?

Tra. Gremio, 'tis known my father hath
    no less
Than three great argosies ; besides two gal-
    liases,   380
And twelve tight galleys : these I will assure
    her,
And twice as much, whate'er thou offer'st
    next.

Gre. Nay, I have offer'd all, I have no
    more ;
And she can have no more than all I have :
If you like me, she shall have me and mine.

Tra. Why, then the maid is mine from all
    the world,
By your firm promise : Gremio is out-vied.

Bap I must confess your offer is the best ;
And, let your father make her the assurance,
She is your own ; else, you must pardon me,
If you should die before him, where's her
    dower ?   391

Tra. That's but a cavil : he is old, I young.

Gre. And may not young men die, as well
    as old ?

Bap. Well, gentlemen,
I am thus resolved : on Sunday next you know
My daughter Katharine is to be married :
Now, on the Sunday following, shall Bianca
Be bride to you, if you make this assurance ;
If not, to Signior Gremio :
And so, I take my leave, and thank you both.

Gre. Adieu, good neighbor.   400
                   [Exit Baptista.
Now I fear thee not : your father were a fool
To give thee all, and in his waning age
Set foot under thy table : tut, a toy !
An old Italian fox is not so kind, my boy.
                          [Exit.

Tra. A vengeance on your crafty wither'd
    hide !
Yet I have faced it with a card of ten.
'Tis in my head to do my master good :
I see no reason but supposed Lucentio
Must get a father, call'd ' supposed Vincentio;'
And that's a wonder : fathers commonly   411
Do get their children ; but in this case of woo-
    ing,
A child shall get a sire, if I fail not of my cun-
    ning.   *[Exit.*

ACT III.

SCENE I. *Padua.* BAPTISTA'S *house.*

Enter LUCENTIO, HORTENSIO, *and* BIANCA.

Luc Fiddler, forbear ; you grow too for-
    ward, sir:
Have you so soon forgot the entertainment
Her sister Katharine welcomed you withal ?

Hor. But, wrangling pedant, this is

The patroness of heavenly harmony :
Then give me leave to have prerogative ;
And when in music we have spent an hour,
Your lecture shall have leisure for as much.

Luc. Preposterous ass, that never read so
    far
To know the cause why music was ordain'd !
Was it not to refresh the mind of man   11
After his studies or his usual pain ?
Then give me leave to read philosophy,
And while I pause, serve in your harmony.

Hor. Sirrah, I will not bear these braves of
    thine.

Bian. Why, gentlemen, you do me double
    wrong,
To strive for that which resteth in my choice :
I am no breeching scholar in the schools ;
I'll not be tied to hours nor 'pointed times,
But learn my lessons as I please myself.   20
And, to cut off all strife, here sit we down :
Take you your instrument, play you the whiles;
His lecture will be done ere you have tuned.

Hor. You'll leave his lecture when I am in
    tune ?

Luc. That will be never : tune your instru-
    ment.

Bian. Where left we last ?

Luc. Here, madam :—
  ' Hic ibat Simois ; hic est Sigeia tellus ;
  Hic steterat Priami regia celsa senis.'

Bian. Construe them.   30

Luc. ' Hic ibat,' as I told you before, ' Simois,' I am Lucentio, ' hic est,' son unto Vincentio of Pisa, ' Sigeia tellus,' disguised thus
to get your love ; ' Hic steterat,' and that
Lucentio that comes a-wooing, ' Priami,' is my
man Tranio, ' regia,' bearing my port, ' celsa
senis,' that we might beguile the old pantaloon.

Hor. Madam, my instrument's in tune.

Bian. Let's hear. O fie ! the treble jars.

Luc. Spit in the hole, man, and tune again.

Bian. Now let me see if I can construe it :
' Hic ibat Simois,' I know you not, ' hic est
Sigeia tellus,' I trust you not ; ' Hic steterat
Priami,' take heed he hear us not, ' regia,'
presume not, ' celsa senis,' despair not.

Hor. Madam, 'tis now in tune.

Luc.   All but the base.

Hor. The base is right ; 'tis the base knave
    that jars.

[Aside] How fiery and forward our pedant is !
Now, for my life, the knave doth court my
    love :
Pedascule, I'll watch you better yet.   50

Bian. In time I may believe, yet I mistrust.

Luc. Mistrust it not : for, sure, Æacides
Was Ajax, call'd so from his grandfather.

Bian. I must believe my master ; else, I
    promise you,
I should be arguing still upon that doubt :
But let it rest. Now, Licio, to you :
Good masters, take it not unkindly, pray,
That I have been thus pleasant with you both.

Hor. You may go walk, and give me leave
    a while :

My lessons make no music in three parts   60
  Luc. Are you so formal, sir? well, I must
    wait,
[*Aside*] And watch withal, for, but I be de-
    ceived,
Our fine musician groweth amorous.
  Hor. Madam, before you touch the instru-
    ment,
To learn the order of my fingering,
I must begin with rudiments of art,
To teach you gamut in a briefer sort,
More pleasant, pithy and effectual,
Than hath been taught by any of my trade:
And there it is in writing, fairly drawn   70
  Bian. Why, I am past my gamut long ago.
  Hor. Yet read the gamut of Hortensio.
  Bian. [*Reads*] "'Gamut' I am, the ground
    of all accord,
  'A re,' to plead Hortensio's passion;
  'B mi,' Bianca, take him for thy lord,
    'C fa ut,' that loves with all affection.
  'D sol re,' one clef, two notes have I:
  'E la mi,' show pity, or I die."
Call you this gamut? tut, I like it not:
Old fashions please me best; I am not so
    nice,
To change true rules for old inventions   81

    Enter a Servant.

  Serv. Mistress, your father prays you leave
    your books
And help to dress your sister's chamber up:
You know to-morrow is the wedding-day.
  Bian. Farewell, sweet masters both, I must
    be gone.   [*Exeunt Bianca and Servant*
  Luc. Faith, mistress, then I have no cause
    to stay.   [*Exit*
  Hor. But I have cause to pry into this pe-
    dant:
Methinks he looks as though he were in love
Yet if thy thoughts, Bianca, be so humble
To cast thy wandering eyes on every stale,   90
Seize thee that list: if once I find thee rang-
    ing,
Hortensio will be quit with thee by changing.
    [*Exit*

SCENE II. *Padua. Before* BAPTISTA'S *house.*

Enter BAPTISTA, GREMIO, TRANIO, KATHA-
  RINA, BIANCA, LUCENTIO, *and* others, attendants

  Bap. [*To Tranio*] Signior Lucentio, this is
    the 'pointed day.
That Katharine and Petruchio should be mar-
    ried,
And yet we hear not of our son-in-law.
What will be said? what mockery will it be,
To want the bridegroom when the priest at-
    tends
To speak the ceremonial rites of marriage!
What says Lucentio to this shame of ours?
  Kath. No shame but mine: I must, forsooth,
    be forced
To give my hand opposed against my heart
Unto a mad-brain rudesby full of spleen: 10

Who woo'd in haste and means to wed at leis-
    ure
I told you, I, he was a frantic fool,
Hiding his bitter jests in blunt behavior:
And, to be noted for a merry man,
He'll woo a thousand, point the day of mar-
    riage,
Make feasts, invite friends, and proclaim the
    banns
Yet never means to wed where he hath woo'd
Now must the world point at poor Katharine,
And say 'Lo there is mad Petruchio's wife,
If it would please him come and marry her!'
  Tra. Patience, good Katharine, and Bap-
    tista too   21
Upon my life Petruchio means but well,
Whatever fortune stays him from his word:
Though he be blunt, I know him passing wise;
Though he be merry, yet withal he's honest
  Kath. Would Katharine had never seen him
    though!
[*Exit weeping, followed by Bianca and others.*
  Bap. Go, girl, I cannot blame thee now to
    weep,
For such an injury would vex a very saint,
Much more a shrew of thy impatient humor.

    Enter BIONDELLO.

  Bion. Master, master! news, old news, and
    such news as you never heard of!   31
  Bap. Is it new and old too? how may that
    be?
  Bion. Why, is it not news, to hear of Petru-
    chio's coming?
  Bap. Is he come?
  Bion. Why, no, sir.
  Bap. What then?
  Bion. He is coming
  Bap. When will he be here?
  Bion. When he stands where I am and sees
    you there   41
  Tra. But say what to thine old news?
  Bion. Why, Petruchio is coming in a new
hat and an old jerkin, a pair of old breeches
thrice turned, a pair of boots that have been
candle-cases, one buckled, another laced, an
old rusty sword ta'en out of the town-armory,
with a broken hilt, and chapeless, with two
broken points: his horse hipped with an old
mothy saddle and stirrups of no kindred; besides, possessed with the glanders and like to
mose in the chine, troubled with the lampass,
infected with the fashions, full of windgalls,
sped with spavins, rayed with the yellows,
past cure of the fives, stark spoiled with the
staggers, begnawn with the bots, swayed in
the back and shoulder-shotten, near-legged
before and with a half-checked bit and a head-
stall of sheep's leather which, being restrained
to keep him from stumbling, hath been often
burst and now repaired with knots, one girth
six times pieced and a woman's crupper of vel-
ure which hath two letters for her name fairly
set down in studs, and here and there pieced
with packthread
  Bap. Who comes with him?

Bion. O, sir, his lackey, for all the world caparisoned like the horse ; with a linen stock on one leg and a kersey boot-hose on the other, gartered with a red and blue list ; an old hat and ' the humor of forty fancies' pricked in't for a feather : a monster, a very monster in apparel, and not like a Christian footboy or a gentleman's lackey.

Tra. 'Tis some odd humor pricks him to this fashion ; Yet oftentimes he goes but mean-apparell'd.

Bap. I am glad he's come, howsoe'er he comes.

Bion. Why, sir, he comes not.

Bap. Didst thou not say he comes ?

Bion. Who ? that Petruchio came ?

Bap. Ay, that Petruchio came. 80

Bion. No, sir ; I say his horse comes, with him on his back.

Bap. Why, that's all one.

Bion. Nay, by Saint Jamy,
I hold you a penny,
A horse and a man
Is more than one,
And yet not many.

Enter PETRUCHIO *and* GRUMIO.

Pet. Come, where be these gallants ? who's at home ?

Bap. You are welcome, sir.

Pet. And yet I come not well. 90

Bap. And yet you halt not.

Tra. Not so well apparell'd As I wish you were.

Pet. Were it better, I should rush in thus. But where is Kate ? where is my lovely bride? How does my father ? Gentles, methinks you frown : And wherefore gaze this goodly company, As if they saw some wondrous monument, Some comet or unusual prodigy ?

Bap. Why, sir, you know this is your wedding-day : First were we sad, fearing you would not come ; 100 Now sadder, that you come so unprovided. Fie, doff this habit, shame to your estate, An eye-sore to our solemn festival !

Tra. And tells us, what occasion of import Hath all so long detain'd you from your wife, And sent you hither so unlike yourself ?

Pet. Tedious it were to tell, and harsh to hear : Sufficeth, I am come to keep my word, Though in some part enforced to digress ; Which, at more leisure, I will so excuse 110 As you shall well be satisfied withal. But where is Kate ? I stay too long from her: The morning wears, 'tis time we were at church.

Tra. See not your bride in these unreverent robes : Go to my chamber; put on clothes of mine.

Pet. Not I, believe me : thus I'll visit her.

Bap. But thus, I trust, you will not marry her.

Pet. Good sooth, even thus ; therefore ha' done with words : To me she's married, not unto my clothes : Could I repair what she will wear in me, 120 As I can change these poor accoutrements, 'Twere well for Kate and better for myself. But what a fool am I to chat with you, When I should bid good morrow to my bride, And seal the title with a lovely kiss !
[*Exeunt Petruchio and Grumio.*

Tra. He hath some meaning in his mad attire : We will persuade him, be it possible, To put on better ere he go to church.

Bap. I'll after him, and see the event of this.
[*Exeunt Baptista, Gremio, and attendants.*

Tra. But to her love concerneth us to add Her father's liking : which to bring to pass, As I before imparted to your worship, I am to get a man,—whate'er he be, It skills not much, we'll fit him to our turn And he shall be Vincentio of Pisa And make assurance here in Padua Of greater sums than I have promised. So shall you quietly enjoy your hope, And marry sweet Bianca with consent.

Luc. Were it not that my fellow-schoolmaster 140 Doth watch Bianca's steps so narrowly, 'Twere good, methinks, to steal our marriage; Which once perform'd, let all the world say no, I'll keep mine own, despite of all the world.

Tra. That by degrees we mean to look into, And watch our vantage in this business : We'll over-reach the greybeard, Gremio, The narrow-prying father, Minola, The quaint musician, amorous Licio ; All for my master's sake, Lucentio. 150

Re-enter GREMIO.

Signior Gremio, came you from the church ?

Gre. As willingly as e'er I came from school.

Tra. And is the bride and bridegroom coming home ?

Gre. A bridegroom say you ? 'tis a groom indeed, A grumbling groom, and that the girl shall find.

Tra. Curster than she ? why, 'tis impossible.

Gre. Why, he's a devil, a devil, a very fiend.

Tra. Why, she's a devil, a devil, the devil's dam.

Gre. Tut, she's a lamb, a dove, a fool to him ! I'll tell you, Sir Lucentio : when the priest 160 Should ask, if Katharine should be his wife, ' Ay, by gogs-wouns,' quoth he ; and swore so loud, That, all-amazed, the priest let fall the book ; And, as he stoop'd again to take it up,

The mad-brain'd bridegroom took him such a
  cuff
' hat down fell priest and book and book and
  priest :
Now take them up,' quoth he, ' if any list.'
  Tra. What said the wench when he rose
  again ?
  Gre. Trembled and shook ; for why, he
  stamp'd and swore,
As if the vicar meant to cozen him. 170
But after many ceremonies done,
He calls for wine : ' A health !' quoth he, as
  if
He had been aboard, carousing to his mates
After a storm ; quaff'd off the muscadel
And threw the sops all in the sexton's face ;
Having no other reason
But that his beard grew thin and hungerly
And seem'd to ask him sops as he was drink-
  ing.
This done, he took the bride about the neck
And kiss'd her lips with such a clamorous
  smack   180
That at the parting all the church did echo :
And I seeing this came thence for very shame ;
And after me, I know, the rout is coming
Such a mad marriage never was before .
Hark, hark ! I hear the minstrels play.
                                    [*Music.*

Re-enter Petruchio, Katharina, Bianca,
Baptista, Hortensio, Grumio, *and* Tran.

  Pet. Gentlemen and friends, I thank you
  for your pains :
I know you think to dine with me to-day,
And have prepared great store of wedding
  cheer ;
But so it is, my haste doth call me hence, 189
And therefore here I mean to take my leave
  Bap. Is't possible you will away to-night ?
  Pet. I must away to-day, before night
  come : '
Make it no wonder ; if you knew my business,
You would entreat me rather go than stay.
And, honest company, I thank you all.
That have beheld me give away myself
To this most patient, sweet and virtuous wife:
Dine with my father, drink a health to me ,
For I must hence ; and farewell to you all.
  Tra. Let us entreat you stay till after din-
  ner.
  Pet. It may not be.
  Gre.   Let me entreat you.
  Pet. It cannot be.
  Kath.   Let me entreat you. 201
  Pet. I am content.
  Kath.   Are you content to stay?
  Pet. I am content you shall entreat me
  stay ;
But yet not stay, entreat me how you can.
  Kath. Now, if you love me, stay.
  Pet.   Grumio, my horse.
  Gru. Ay, sir, they be ready : the oats have
eaten the horses.
  Kath. Nay, then,

Do what thou canst, I will not go to-day ; 210
No, nor to-morrow, not till I please myself
The door is open, sir , there lies your way ;
You may be jogging whiles your boots are
  green ,
For me, I'll not be gone till I please myself :
'Tis like you'll prove a jolly surly groom,
That take it on you at the first so roundly.
  Pet. O Kate, content thee ; prithee, be not
  angry.
  Kath. I will be angry : what hast thou to
  do ?
Father, be quiet , he shall stay my leisure 219
  Gre. Ay, marry, sir, now it begins to work.
  Kath. Gentlemen, forward to the bridal
  dinner :
I see a woman may be made a fool,
If she had not a spirit to resist
  Pet. They shall go forward, Kate, at thy
  command.
Obey the bride, you that attend on her ;
Go to the feast, revel and domineer,
Carouse full measure to her maidenhead,
Be mad and merry, or go hang yourselves:
But for my bonny Kate, she must with me.
Nay, look not big, nor stamp, nor stare, nor
  fret ,   230
I will be master of what is mine own •
She is my goods, my chattels ; she is my
  house,
My household stuff, my field, my barn,
My horse, my ox, my ass, my any thing ;
And here she stands, touch her whoever dare ;
I'll bring mine action on the proudest he
Th' stops my way in Padua. Grumio,
Draw forth thy weapon, we are beset with
  thieves ,
Rescue thy mistress, if thou be a man
Fear not, sweet wench, they shall not touch
  thee, Kate :   240
I'll buckler thee against a million.

                  [*Exeunt Petruchio, Katharina, and Grumio.*
  Bap. Nay, let them go, a couple of quiet
  ones
  Gre. Went they not quickly, I should die
  with laughing
  Tra. Of all mad matches never was the
  like
  Luc. Mistress, what's your opinion of your
  sister ?
  Bian. That, being mad herself, she's madly
  mated.
  Gre. I warrant him, Petruchio is Kated.
  Bap. Neighbors and friends, though bride
  and bridegroom wants
For to supply the place at the table,
You know there wants no junkets at the
  feast.   250
Lucentio, you shall supply the bridegroom's
  place.
And let Bianca take her sister's room.
  Tra. Shall sweet Bianca practise how to
  bride it ?
  Bap. She shall, Lucentio. Come, gentle-
  men, let's go.   ' [*Exeunt.*
                  32

ACT IV.

SCENE I. PETRUCHIO'S *country house.*

Enter GRUMIO.

Gru. Fie, fie on all tired jades, on all mad masters, and all foul ways! Was ever man so beaten? was ever man so rayed? was ever man so weary? I am sent before to make a fire, and they are coming after to warm them. Now, were not I a little pot and soon hot, my very lips might freeze to my teeth, my tongue to the roof of my mouth, my heart in my belly, ere I should come by a fire to thaw me: but I, with blowing the fire, shall warm myself; for, considering the weather, a taller man than I will take cold. Holla, ho! Curtis.

Enter CURTIS.

Curt. Who is that calls so coldly?

Gru. A piece of ice: if thou doubt it, thou mayst slide from my shoulder to my heel with no greater a run but my head and my neck. A fire, good Curtis.

Curt. Is my master and his wife coming, Grumio?

Gru. O, ay, Curtis, ay: and therefore fire, fire; cast on no water.   21

Curt. Is she so hot a shrew as she's reported?

Gru. She was, good Curtis, before this frost: but, thou knowest, winter tames man, woman and beast; for it hath tamed my old master and my new mistress and myself, fellow Curtis.   [no beast.

Curt. Away, you three-inch fool! I am

Gru. Am I but three inches? why, thy horn is a foot; and so long am I at the least. But wilt thou make a fire, or shall I complain on thee to our mistress, whose hand, she being now at hand, thou shalt soon feel, to thy cold comfort, for being slow in thy hot office?

Curt. I prithee, good Grumio, tell me, how goes the world?

Gru. A cold world, Curtis, in every office but thine; and therefore fire: do thy duty, and have thy duty; for my master and mistress are almost frozen to death.   40

Curt. There's fire ready; and therefore, good Grumio, the news.

Gru. Why, 'Jack, boy! ho! boy!' and as much news as will thaw.

Curt. Come, you are so full of cony-catching!

Gru. Why, therefore fire; for I have caught extreme cold. Where's the cook? is supper ready, the house trimmed, rushes strewed, cobwebs swept; the serving-men in their new fustian, their white stockings, and every officer his wedding-garment on? Be the jacks fair within, the jills fair without, the carpets laid, and every thing in order?

Curt. All ready; and therefore, I pray thee, news.

Gru. First, know, my horse is tired; my master and mistress fallen out.

Curt. How?

Gru. Out of their saddles into the dirt; and thereby hangs a tale.   60

Curt. Let's ha't, good Grumio.

Gru. Lend thine ear.

Curt. Here.

Gru. There.   [*Strikes him.*

Curt. This is to feel a tale, not to hear a tale.

Gru. And therefore 'tis called a sensible tale: and this cuff was but to knock at your ear, and beseech listening. Now I begin: Imprimis, we came down a foul hill, my master riding behind my mistress,—   70

Curt. Both of one horse?

Gru. What's that to thee?

Curt. Why, a horse.

Gru. Tell thou the tale: but hadst thou not crossed me, thou shouldst have heard how her horse fell and she under her horse; thou shouldst have heard in how miry a place, how she was bemoiled, how he left her with the horse upon her, how he beat me because her horse stumbled, how she waded through the dirt to pluck him off me, how he swore, how she prayed, that never prayed before, how I cried, how the horses ran away, how her bridle was burst, how I lost my crupper, with many things of worthy memory, which now shall die in oblivion and thou return unexperienced to thy grave.   [than she.

Curt. By this reckoning he is more shrew

Gru. Ay; and that thou and the proudest of you all shall find when he comes home. But what talk I of this? Call forth Nathaniel, Joseph, Nicholas, Philip, Walter, Sugarsop and the rest: let their heads be sleekly combed, their blue coats brushed and their garters of an indifferent knit: let them curtsy with their left legs and not presume to touch a hair of my master's horse-tail till they kiss their hands. Are they all ready?

Curt. They are.

Gru. Call them forth.

Curt. Do you hear, ho? you must meet my master to countenance my mistress.   101

Gru. Why, she hath a face of her own.

Curt. Who knows not that?

Gru. Thou, it seems, that calls for company to countenance her.

Curt. I call them forth to credit her.

Gru. Why, she comes to borrow nothing of them.

Enter four or five Serving-men.

Nath. Welcome home, Grumio!

Phil. How now, Grumio!   110

Jos. What, Grumio!

Nich. Fellow Grumio!

Nath. How now, old lad?

Gru. Welcome, you;—how now, you;—what, you;—fellow, you;—and thus much for greeting. Now, my spruce companions, is all ready, and all things neat?

Nath. All things is ready. How near is our master?   119

Gru. E'en at hand, alighted by this ; and therefore be not—Cock's passion, silence ! I hear my master.

Enter PETRUCHIO *and* KATHARINA.

Pet. Where be these knaves ? What, no man at door
To hold my stirrup nor to take my horse !
Where is Nathaniel, Gregory, Philip ?
All Serv. Here, here, sir , here, sir
Pet Here, sir ! here, sir ! here, sir ! here, sir !
You logger-headed and unpolish'd grooms !
What, no attendance ? no regard ? no duty ?
Where is the foolish knave I sent before ?   130
Gru Here, sir , as foolish as I was before
Pet. You peasant swain ! you whoreson malt-horse drudge !
Did I not bid thee meet me in the park,
And bring along these rascal knaves with thee ?
Gru. Nathaniel's coat, sir, was not fully made,
And Gabriel's pumps were all unpink'd i' the heel ;
There was no link to color Peter's hat,
And Walter's dagger was not come from sheathing
There were none fine but Adam, Ralph, and Gregory ;
The rest were ragged, old, and beggarly ,   140
Yet, as they are, here are they come to meet you
Pet. Go, rascals, go, and fetch my supper in   [*Exeunt Servants*
[*Singing*] Where is the life that late I led—
Where are those—Sit down, Kate, and welcome —
Soud, soud, soud, soud !

Re-enter Servants *with supper.*

Why, when, I say ? Nay, good sweet Kate, be merry.
Off with my boots, you rogues ! you villains, when ?
[*Sings*] It was the friar of orders grey,
    As he forth walked on his way —
Out, you rogue ! you pluck my foot awry   150
Take that, and mend the plucking off the other.   [*Strikes him*
Be merry, Kate. Some water, here , what, ho !
Where's my spaniel Troilus ? Sirrah, get you hence,
And bid my cousin Ferdinand come hither ·
One, Kate, that you must kiss, and be acquainted with.
Where are my slippers ? Shall I have some water ?

Enter one with water.

Come, Kate, and wash, and welcome heartily.
You whoreson villain ! will you let it fall ?   [*Strikes him.*
Kath. Patience, I pray you ; 'twas a fault unwilling.

Pet. A whoreson beetle-headed, flap-ear'd knave !   160
Come, Kate, sit down , I know you have a stomach
Will you give thanks, sweet Kate , or else shall I ?
What's this ? mutton ?
First Serv.   Ay
Pet   Who brought it ?
Peter   I.
Pet 'Tis burnt , and so is all the meat
What dogs are these ! Where is the rascal cook ?
How durst you, villains, bring it from the dresser,
And serve it thus to me that love it not ?
There, take it to you, trenchers, cups, and all ;
    [*Throws the meat, &c. about the stage*
You heedless jolthcads and unmanner'd slaves !
What, do you grumble ? I'll be with you straight   170
Kath I pray you, husband, be not so disquiet
The meat was well, if you were so contented
Pet. I tell thee, Kate, 'twas burnt and dried away ,
And I expressly am forbid to touch it,
For it engenders choler, planteth anger ;
And better 'twere that both of us did fast,
Since, of ourselves, ourselves are choleric,
Than feed it with such over-roasted flesh
Be patient , to-morrow 't shall be mended,
And, for this night, we'll fast for company   180
Come, I will bring thee to thy bridal chamber   [*Exeunt*

Re-enter Servants *severally*

Nath. Peter, didst ever see the like ?
Peter. He kills her in her own humor.

Re-enter CURTIS.

Gru. Where is he ?
Curt In her chamber, making a sermon of continency to her ;
And rails, and swears, and rates, that she, poor soul,
Knows not which way to stand, to look, to speak,
And sits as one new-risen from a dream
Away, away ! for he is coming hither   200
    [*Exeunt*

Re-enter PETRUCHIO

Pet. Thus have I politicly begun my reign,
And 'tis my hope to end successfully.
My falcon now is sharp and passing empty ;
And till she stoop she must not be full-gorged,
For then she never looks upon her lure
Another way I have to man my haggard,
To make her come and know her keeper's call,
That is, to watch her, as we watch these kites
That bate and beat and will not be obedient
She eat no meat to-day, nor none shall eat .
Last night she slept not, nor to-night she shall not,

As with the meat, some undeserved fault
I'll find about the making of the bed ;
And here I'll fling the pillow, there the bolster,
This way the coverlet, another way the sheets :
Ay, and amid this hurly I intend
That all is done in reverend care of her ;
And in conclusion she shall watch all night :
And if she chance to nod I'll rail and brawl
And with the clamor keep her still awake. 220
This is a way to kill a wife with kindness ;
And thus I'll curb her mad and headstrong humor.
He that knows better how to tame a shrew,
Now let him speak : 'tis charity to show.
                                        [*Exit.*

SCENE II. *Padua. Before* BAPTISTA'S *house.*

Enter TRANIO *and* HORTENSIO.

Tra. Is't possible, friend Licio, that Mistress Bianca
Doth fancy any other but Lucentio ?
I tell you, sir, she bears me fair in hand.
Hor. Sir, to satisfy you in what I have said,
Stand by and mark the manner of his teaching.

Enter BIANCA *and* LUCENTIO.

Luc. Now, mistress, profit you in what you read ?
Bian. What, master, read you ? first resolve me that.
Luc. I read that I profess, the Art to Love.
Bian. And may you prove, sir, master of your art !
Luc. While you, sweet dear, prove mistress of my heart !   10
Hor. Quick proceeders, marry ! Now, tell me, I pray,
You that durst swear that your mistress Bianca
Loved none in the world so well as Lucentio.
Tra. O despiteful love ! unconstant womankind !
I tell thee, Licio, this is wonderful.
Hor. Mistake no more : I am not Licio,
Nor a musician, as I seem to be ;
But one that scorn to live in this disguise,
For such a one as leaves a gentleman,
And makes a god of such a cullion :   20
Know, sir, that I am call'd Hortensio.
Tra. Signior Hortensio, I have often heard
Of your entire affection to Bianca ;
And since mine eyes are witness of her lightness,
I will with you, if you be so contented,
Forswear Bianca and her love for ever.
Hor. See, how they kiss and court ! Signior Lucentio,
Here is my hand, and here I firmly vow
Never to woo her more, but do forswear her,
As one unworthy all the former favors   30
That I have fondly flatter'd her withal.
Tra. And here I take the like unfeigned oath,

Never to marry with her though she would entreat :
Fie on her ! see, how beastly she doth court him !
Hor. Would all the world but he had quite forsworn !
For me, that I may surely keep mine oath,
I will be married to a wealthy widow,
Ere three days pass, which hath as long loved me
As I have loved this proud disdainful haggard.
And so farewell, Signior Lucentio.   40
Kindness in women, not their beauteous looks,
Shall win my love : and so I take my leave,
In resolution as I swore before.   [*Exit.*
Tra. Mistress Bianca, bless you with such grace
As 'longeth to a lover's blessed case !
Nay, I have ta'en you napping, gentle love,
And have forsworn you with Hortensio.
Bian. Tranio, you jest : but have you both forsworn me ?
Tra. Mistress, we have.
Luc.   Then we are rid of Licio.
Tra. I' faith, he'll have a lusty widow now,
That shall be woo'd and wedded in a day. 51
Bian. God give him joy !
Tra. Ay, and he'll tame her.
Bian.   He says so, Tranio.
Tra. Faith, he is gone unto the taming-school.
Bian. The taming-school ! what, is there such a place ?
Tra. Ay, mistress, and Petruchio is the master
That teacheth tricks eleven and twenty long,
To tame a shrew and charm her chattering tongue.

Enter BIONDELLO.

Bion. O master, master, I have watch'd so long
That I am dog-weary : but at last I spied   60
†An ancient angel coming down the hill,
Will serve the turn.
Tra.   What is he, Biondello ?
Bion. Master, a mercatante, or a pedant,
I know not what ; but formal in apparel,
In gait and countenance surely like a father.
Luc. And what of him, Tranio ?
Tra. If he be credulous and trust my tale,
I'll make him glad to seem Vincentio,
And give assurance to Baptista Minola,
As if he were the right Vincentio.   70
Take in your love, and then let me alone.
                    [*Exeunt Lucentio and Bianca.*

Enter a Pedant.

Ped. God save you, sir !
Tra.   And you, sir ! you are welcome.
Travel you far on, or are you at the farthest ?
Ped. Sir, at the farthest for a week or two :
But then up farther, and as far as Rome ;
And so to Tripoli, if God lend me life.
Tra. What countryman, I pray ?

Ped.   Of Mantua.
Tra. Of Mantua, sir ? marry, God forbid !
And come to Padua, careless of your life ?
  Ped. My life, sir ! how, I pray ? for that
goes hard.   80
  Tra. 'Tis death for any one in Mantua
To come to Padua. Know you not the cause ?
Your ships are stay'd at Venice, and the
    duke,
For private quarrel 'twixt your duke and him,
Hath publish'd and proclaim'd it openly :
'Tis marvel, but that you are but newly come,
You might have heard it else proclaim'd
    about.
  Ped. Alas ! sir, it is worse for me than so ;
For I have bills for money by exchange
From Florence and must here deliver them. 90
  Tra. Well, sir, to do you courtesy,
This will I do, and this I will advise you :
First, tell me, have you ever been at Pisa ?
  Ped. Ay, sir, in Pisa have I often been,
Pisa renowned for grave citizens.
  Tra. Among them know you one Vin-
    centio ?
  Ped. I know him not, but I have heard of
    him ;
A merchant of incomparable wealth.
  Tra. He is my father, sir ; and, sooth to
    say,   99
In countenance somewhat doth resemble you.
  Bion. [*Aside*] As much as an apple doth
    an oyster, and all one.
  Tra. To save your life in this extremity,
This favor will I do you for his sake ;
And think it not the worst of all your for-
    tunes
That you are like to Sir Vincentio.
His name and credit shall you undertake,
And in my house you shall be friendly lodged :
Look that you take upon you as you should ;
You understand me, sir : so shall you stay
Till you have done your business in the city :
If this be courtesy, sir, accept of it.   111
  Ped. O sir, I do ; and will repute you ever
The patron of my life and liberty.
  Tra. Then go with me to make the matter
    good.
This, by the way, I let you understand ;
My father is here look'd for every day,
To pass assurance of a dower in marriage
'Twixt me and one Baptista's daughter here :
In all these circumstances I'll instruct you :
Go with me to clothe you as becomes you. 120
                           [*Exeunt.*

  Scene III. *A room in* Petruchio's *house.*

    Enter Katharina *and* Grumio.

  Gru. No, no, forsooth ; I dare not for my
    life.
  Kath. The more my wrong, the more his
    spite appears :
What, did he marry me to famish me ?
Beggars, that come unto my father's door,
Upon entreaty have a present alms ;
If not, elsewhere they meet with charity :

But I, who never knew how to entreat,
Nor never needed that I should entreat,
Am starved for meat, giddy for lack of sleep,
With oaths kept waking and with brawling
    fed :   10
And that which spites me more than all these
    wants,
He does it under name of perfect love ;
As who should say, if I should sleep or eat,
'Twere deadly sickness or else present death.
I prithee go and get me some repast ;   •
I care not what, so it be wholesome food.
  Gru. What say you to a neat's foot ?
  Kath. 'Tis passing good : I prithee let me
    have it.
  Gru. I fear it is too choleric a meat.
How say you to a fat tripe finely broil'd ? 20
  Kath. I like it well : good Grumio, fetch
    it me.
  Gru. I cannot tell ; I fear 'tis choleric.
What say you to a piece of beef and mustard?
  Kath. A dish that I do love to feed upon.
  Gru. Ay, but the mustard is too hot a lit-
    tle.
  Kath. Why then, the beef, and let the mus-
    tard rest.
  Gru. Nay then, I will not : you shall have
    the mustard,
Or else you get no beef of Grumio.
  Kath. Then both, or one, or any thing thou
    wilt.
  Gru. Why then, the mustard without the
    beef.   30
  Kath. Go, get thee gone, thou false delud-
    ing slave,   [*Beats him.*
That feed'st me with the very name of meat :
Sorrow on thee and all the pack of you,
That triumph thus upon my misery !
Go, get thee gone, I say.

Enter Petruchio *and* Hortensio *with meat.*

  Pet. How fares my Kate ? What, sweet-
    ing, all amort ?
  Hor. Mistress, what cheer ?
  Kath.   Faith, as cold as can be.
  Pet. Pluck up thy spirits ; look cheerfully
    upon me.
Here, love ; thou see'st how diligent I am 39
To dress thy meat myself and bring it thee :
I am sure, sweet Kate, this kindness merits
    thanks.
What, not a word ? Nay, then thou lovest it
    not ;
And all my pains is sorted to no proof.
Here, take away this dish.
  Kath.   I pray you, let it stand.
  Pet. The poorest service is repaid with
    thanks ;
And so shall mine, before you touch the meat.
  Kath. I thank you, sir.
  Hor. Signior Petruchio, fie ! you are to
    blame.
Come, Mistress Kate, I'll bear you company.
  Pet. [*Aside*] Eat it up all, Hortensio, if
    thou lovest me.   50
Much good do it unto thy gentle heart !

Kate, eat apace : and now, my honey love,
Will we return unto thy father's house
And revel it as bravely as the best,
With silken coats and caps and golden rings,
With ruffs and cuffs and fardingales and
    things ;
With scarfs and fans and double change of
    bravery,
With amber bracelets, beads and all this
    knavery.
What, hast thou dined ? The tailor stays thy
    leisure,   59
To deck thy body with his ruffling treasure.

            Enter Tailor.

Come, tailor, let us see these ornaments ;
Lay forth the gown.

         Enter Haberdasher.

         What news with you, sir ?
Hab.   Here is the cap your worship did
    bespeak.
Pet.   Why, this was moulded on a porrin-
    ger ;
A velvet dish : fie, fie ! 'tis lewd and filthy :
Why, 'tis a cockle or a walnut-shell,
A knack, a toy, a trick, a baby's cap :
Away with it ! come, let me have a bigger.
Kath.   I'll have no bigger : this doth fit the
    time,
And gentlewomen wear such caps as these. 70
Pet.   When you are gentle, you shall have
    one too,
And not till then.
Hor. [*Aside*] That will not be in haste.
Kath.   Why, sir, I trust I may have leave to
    speak ;
And speak I will ; I am no child, no babe :
Your betters have endured me say my mind,
And if you cannot, best you stop your ears.
My tongue will tell the anger of my heart,
Or else my heart concealing it will break,
And rather than it shall, I will be free
Even to the uttermost, as I please, in words.
Pet.   Why, thou say'st true ; it is a paltry
    cap,   81
A custard-coffin, a bauble, a silken pie :
I love thee well, in that thou likest it not.
Kath.   Love me or love me not, I like the
    cap ;
And it I will have, or I will have none.
                [*Exit Haberdasher.*
Pet.   Thy gown ? why, ay : come, tailor,
    let us see't.
O mercy, God ! what masquing stuff is here ?
What's this ? a sleeve ? 'tis like a demi-
    cannon :
What, up and down, carved like an apple-
    tart ?
Here's snip and nip and cut and slish and
    slash,   90
Like to a censer in a barber's shop :
Why, what, i' devil's name, tailor, call'st thou
    this ?
Hor. [*Aside*] I see she's like to have neither
    cap nor gown.

Tai.   You bid me make it orderly and well,
According to the fashion and the time.
Pet.   Marry, and did ; but if you be remem-
    ber'd,
I did not bid you mar it to the time,
Go, hop me over every kennel home,
For you shall hop without my custom, sir : 99
I'll none of it : hence ! make your best of it.
Kath.   I never saw a better-fashion'd gown,
More quaint, more pleasing, nor more com-
    mendable :
Belike you mean to make a puppet of me.
Pet.   Why, true ; he means to make a pup-
    pet of thee.
Tai.   She says your worship means to make
    a puppet of her.
Pet.   O monstrous arrogance ! Thou liest,
thou thread, thou thimble,
Thou yard, three-quarters, half-yard, quarter,
    nail !
Thou flea, thou nit, thou winter-cricket thou !
Braved in mine own house with a skein of
    thread ?
Away, thou rag, thou quantity, thou remnant ;
Or I shall so be-mete thee with thy yard
As thou shalt think on prating whilst thou
    livest !
I tell thee, I, that thou hast marr'd her gown.
Tai.   Your worship is deceived ; the gown
    is made
Just as my master had direction :
Grumio gave order how it should be done.
Gru.   I gave him no order ; I gave him the
    stuff.
Tai.   But how did you desire it should be
    made ?   120
Gru.   Marry, sir, with needle and thread.
Tai.   But did you not request to have it
    cut ?
Gru.   Thou hast faced many things.
Tai.   I have.
Gru.   Face not me : thou hast braved many
men ; brave not me ; I will neither be faced
nor braved. I say unto thee, I bid thy master
cut out the gown ; but I did not bid him cut it
to pieces : ergo, thou liest.
Tai.   Why, here is the note of the fashion
to testify.   131
Pet.   Read it.
Gru.   The note lies in's throat, if he say I
said so.   [gown :'
Tai.   [*Reads*] 'Imprimis, a loose-bodied
Gru.   Master, if ever I said loose-bodied
gown, sew me in the skirts of it, and beat me
to death with a bottom of brown thread : I
said a gown.
Pet.   Proceed.
Tai.   [*Reads*] 'With a small compassed
cape :'   140
Gru.   I confess the cape.
Tai.   [*Reads*] 'With a trunk sleeve :'
Gru.   I confess two sleeves.
Tai.   [*Reads*] 'The sleeves curiously cut.'
Pet.   Ay, there's the villany.
Gru.   Error i' the bill, sir ; error i' the bill.
I commanded the sleeves should be cut out

and sewed up again ; and that I'll prove upon
thee, though thy little finger be armed in a
thimble.

Tai. This is true that I say : an I had thee
in place where, thou shouldst know it.   151

Gru. I am for thee straight : take thou the
bill, give me thy mete-yard, and spare not me.

Hor. God-a-mercy, Grumio ! then he shall
have no odds.

Pet. Well, sir, in brief, the gown is not for
me.   [mistress.

Gru. You are i' the right, sir : 'tis for my

Pet. Go, take it up unto thy master's use.

Gru. Villain, not for thy life : take up my
mistress' gown for thy master's use !   161

Pet. Why, sir, what's your conceit in that ?

Gru. O, sir, the conceit is deeper than you
think for :   [use !
'Take up my mistress' gown to his master's
'O, fie, fie, fie !

Pet. [*Aside*] Hortensio, say thou wilt see
the tailor paid.
Go take it hence ; be gone, and say no more.

Hor. Tailor, I'll pay thee for thy gown to-
morrow :
'Take no unkindness of his hasty words :
Away ! I say ; commend me to thy master. 170
                              [*Exit Tailor.*

Pet. Well, come, my Kate ; we will unto
your father's
Even in these honest mean habiliments :
Our purses shall be proud, our garments poor ;
For 'tis the mind that makes the body rich ;
And as the sun breaks through the darkest
clouds,
So honor peereth in the meanest habit.
What is the jay more precious than the lark,
Because his feathers are more beautiful ?
Or is the adder better than the eel,
Because his painted skin contents the eye ? 180
O, no, good Kate ; neither art thou the worse
For this poor furniture and mean array.
If thou account'st it shame, lay it on me ;
And therefore frolic : we will hence forthwith,
To feast and sport us at thy father's house.
Go, call my men, and let us straight to him ;
And bring our horses unto Long-lane end ;
There will we mount, and thither walk on
foot
Let's see ; I think 'tis now some seven o'clock,
And well we may come there by dinner-time.

Kath. I dare assure you, sir, 'tis almost two ;
And 'twill be supper-time ere you come there.

Pet. It shall be seven ere I go to horse :
Look, what I speak, or do, or think to do,
You are still crossing it. Sirs, let't alone :
I will not go to-day ; and ere I do,
It shall be what o'clock I say it is.

Hor. [*Aside*] Why, so this gallant will command the sun.   [*Exeunt.*

SCENE IV. *Padua. Before* BAPTISTA'S *house.*

Enter TRANIO, *and the* Pedant *dressed like*
VINCENTIO.

Tra. Sir, this is the house : please it you
that I call ?

Ped. Ay, what else ? and but I be deceived
Signior Baptista may remember me,
Near twenty years ago, in Genoa,
Where we were lodgers at the Pegasus.

Tra. 'Tis well ; and hold your own, in any
case,
With such austerity as 'longeth to a father.

Ped. I warrant you.

Enter BIONDELLO.

But, sir, here comes your boy ;
'Twere good he were school'd.

Tra. Fear you not him. Sirrah Biondello,
Now do your duty throughly, I advise you : 11
Imagine 'twere the right Vincentio.

Bion. Tut, fear not me.

Tra. But hast thou done thy errand to
Baptista ?

Bion. I told him that your father was at
Venice,
And that you look'd for him this day in Padua.

Tra. Thou'rt a tall fellow : hold thee that
to drink.
Here comes Baptista : set your countenance,
sir.

Enter BAPTISTA *and* LUCENTIO.

Signior Baptista, you are happily met.
[*To the Pedant*] Sir, this is the gentleman I
told you of :   20
I pray you, stand good father to me now,
Give me Bianca for my patrimony.

Ped. Soft, son !
Sir, by your leave : having come to Padua
To gather in some debts, my son Lucentio
Made me acquainted with a weighty cause
Of love between your daughter and himself :
And, for the good report I hear of you
And for the love he beareth to your daughter
And she to him, to stay him not too long,   30
I am content, in a good father's care,
To have him match'd ; and if you please to
like
No worse than I, upon some agreement
Me shall you find ready and willing
With one consent to have her so bestow'd ;
For curious I cannot be with you,
Signior Baptista, of whom I hear so well.

Bap. Sir, pardon me in what I have to-say :
Your plainness and your shortness please me
well.
Right true it is, your son Lucentio here   40
Doth love my daughter and she loveth him,
Or both dissemble deeply their affections :
And therefore, if you say no more than this,
That like a father you will deal with him
And pass my daughter a sufficient dower,
The match is made, and all is done :
Your son shall have my daughter with con-
sent.

Tra. I thank you, sir. Where then do you
know best
We be affied and such assurance ta'en
As shall with either part's agreement stand ?

Bap. Not in my house, Lucentio · for, you
know,   51

Pitchers have ears, and I have many servants;
Besides, old Gremio is hearkening still ;
And happily we might be interrupted.

  Tra.   Then at my lodging, an it like you:
There doth my father lie ; and there, this night,
We'll pass the business privately and well.
Send for your daughter by your servant here :
My boy shall fetch the scrivener presently.
The worst is this, that, at so slender warning,
You are like to have a thin and slender pittance.   61

  Bap.   It likes me well. Biondello, hie you home,
And bid Bianca make her ready straight ;
And, if you will, tell what hath happened,
Lucentio's father is arrived in Padua,
And how she's like to be Lucentio's wife.

  Bion.   I pray the gods she may with all my heart !

  Tra.   Dally not with the gods, but get thee gone.   [*Exit Bion.*
Signior Baptista, shall I lead the way ?
Welcome ! one mess is like to be your cheer :
Come, sir ; we will better it in Pisa.   71

  Bap.   I follow you.
      [*Exeunt Tranio, Pedant, and Baptista.*

Re-enter BIONDELLO.

  Bion.   Cambio !

  Luc.   What sayest thou, Biondello ?

  Bion.   You saw my master wink and laugh upon you ?

  Luc.   Biondello, what of that ?

  Bion.   Faith, nothing ; but has left me here behind, to expound the meaning or moral of his signs and tokens.   80

  Luc.   I pray thee, moralize them.

  Bion.   Then thus. Baptista is safe, talking with the deceiving father of a deceitful son.

  Luc.   And what of him ?

  Bion.   His daughter is to be brought by you to the supper.

  Luc.   And then ?

  Bion.   The old priest of Saint Luke's church is at your command at all hours.

  Luc.   And what of all this ?   90

  Bion.   I cannot tell ; expect they are busied about a counterfeit assurance : take you assurance of her, ' cum privilegio ad imprimendum solum :' to the church ; take the priest, clerk, and some sufficient honest witnesses :
If this be not that you look for, I have no more to say,
But bid Bianca farewell for ever and a day.

  Luc.   Hearest thou, Biondello ?

  Bion.   I cannot tarry : I knew a wench married in an afternoon as she went to the garden for parsley to stuff a rabbit ; and so may you, sir : and so, adieu, sir. My master hath appointed me to go to Saint Luke's, to bid the priest be ready to come against you come with your appendix.   [*Exit.*

  Luc.   I may, and will, if she be so contented:
She will be pleased ; then wherefore should I doubt ?

Hap what hap may, I'll roundly go about her :
It shall go hard if Cambio go without her.
         [*Exit.*

SCENE V.   *A public road.*

Enter PETRUCHIO, KATHARINA, HORTENSIO,
     and Servants.

  Pet.   Come on, i' God's name ; once more toward our father's.
Good Lord, how bright and goodly shines the moon !

  Kath.   The moon ! the sun : it is not moonlight now.   [bright.

  Pet.   I say it is the moon that shines so

  Kath.   I know it is the sun that shines so bright.   [myself,

  Pet.   Now, by my mother's son, and that's It shall be moon, or star, or what I list,
Or ere I journey to your father's house.
Go on, and fetch our horses back again.
Evermore cross'd and cross'd ; nothing but cross'd !   10

  Hor.   Say as he says, or we shall never go.

  Kath.   Forward, I pray, since we have come so far,
And be it moon, or sun, or what you please :
An if you please to call it a rush-candle,
Henceforth I vow it shall be so for me.

  Pet.   I say it is the moon.

  Kath.   I know it is the moon.

  Pet.   Nay, then you lie : it is the blessed sun.   [sun :

  Kath.   Then, God be bless'd, it is the blessed But sun it is not, when you say it is not ;
And the moon changes even as your mind. 20
What you will have it named, even that it is ;
And so it shall be so for Katharine.

  Hor.   Petruchio, go thy ways ; the field is won.

  Pet.   Well, forward, forward ! thus the bowl should run,
And not unluckily against the bias.
But, soft ! company is coming here.

Enter VINCENTIO.

[*To Vincentio.*] Good morrow, gentle mistress : where away ?
Tell me, sweet Kate, and tell me truly too,
Hast thou beheld a fresher gentlewoman ?
Such war of white and red within her cheeks !
What stars do spangle heaven with such beauty,   31
As those two eyes become that heavenly face ?
Fair lovely maid, once more good day to thee.
Sweet Kate, embrace her for her beauty's sake.

  Hor.   A' will make the man mad, to make a woman of him.

  Kath.   Young budding virgin, fair and fresh and sweet,
Whither away, or where is thy abode ?
Happy the parents of so fair a child ;
Happier the man, whom favorable stars   40
Allot thee for his lovely bed-fellow !

  Pet.   Why, how now, Kate ! I hope thou art not mad :

This is a man, old, wrinkled, faded, wither'd,
And not a maiden, as thou say'st he is.
  Kath. Pardon, old father, my mistaking
    eyes,
That have been so bedazzled with the sun
That every thing I look on seemeth green
Now I perceive thou art a reverend father ;
Pardon, I pray thee, for my mad mistaking
  Pet Do, good old grandsire, and withal
    make known   50
Which way thou travellest : if along with us,
We shall be joyful of thy company.
  Vin Fair sir, and you my merry mistress,
That with your strange encounter much amaz-
    ed me,
My name is call'd Vincentio, my dwelling
  Pisa ;
And bound I am to Padua, there to visit
A son of mine, which long I have not seen.
  Pet. What is his name ?
  Vin.   Lucentio, gentle sir
  Pet Happily met ; the happier for thy son
And now by law, as well as reverend age, 60
I may entitle thee my loving father
The sister to my wife, this gentlewoman,
Thy son by this hath married Wonder not,
Nor be not grieved she is of good esteem,
Her dowry wealthy, and of worthy birth,
Beside, so qualified as may beseem
The spouse of any noble gentleman.
Let me embrace with old Vincentio,
And wander we to see thy honest son,
Who will of thy arrival be full joyous. 70
  Vin. But is this true ? or is it else your
    pleasure,
Like pleasant travellers, to break a jest
Upon the company you overtake ?
  Hor. I do assure thee, father, so it is
  Pet. Come, go along, and see the truth
    hereof,
For our first merriment hath made thee jeal-
    ous   [*Exeunt all but Hortensio*
  Hor. Well, Petruchio, this has put me in
    heart
Have to my widow ! and if she be froward,
Then hast thou taught Hortensio to be un-
    toward.   [*Exit.*

ACT V.

SCENE I. *Padua. Before* LUCENTIO's *house*

GREMIO *discovered. Enter behind* BIONDELLO,
    LUCENTIO, *and* BIANCA

  Bion Softly and swiftly, sir ; for the priest
is ready.
  Luc. I fly, Biondello but they may chance
to need thee at home, therefore leave us
  Bion. Nay, faith, I'll see the church o' your
back ; and then come back to my master's as
soon as I can
    [*Exeunt Lucentio, Bianca, and Biondello*
  Gre. I marvel Cambio comes not all this
while

Enter PETRUCHIO, KATHARINA, VINCENTIO,
    GRUMIO, *with* Attendants.

  Pet. Sir, here's the door, this is Lucentio's
    house
My father's bears more toward the market-
    place,   10
Thither must I, and here I leave you, sir.
  Vin You shall not choose but drink before
    you go
I think I shall command your welcome here,
And, by all likelihood, some cheer is toward
    [*Knocks.*
  Gre They're busy within, you were best
knock louder

Pedant looks out of the window.

  Ped What's he that knocks as he would
beat down the gate ?
  Vin Is Signior Lucentio within, sir ?
  Ped He's within, sir, but not to be spoken
withal
  Vin What if a man bring him a hundred
pound or two, to make merry withal ?
  Ped Keep your hundred pounds to your-
self he shall need none, so long as I live
  Pet Nay, I told you your son was well be-
loved in Padua Do you hear, sir ? To leave
frivolous circumstances, I pray you, tell Signior Lucentio that his father is come from
Pisa, and is here at the door to speak with
him.   30
  Ped Thou liest his father is come from
Padua and here looking out at the window.
  Vin. Art thou his father ?
  Ped Ay, sir, so his mother says, if I may
believe her
  Pet [*To Vincentio*] Why, how now, gentleman ! why, this is flat knavery, to take
upon you another man's name
  Ped Lay hands on the villain I believe
a' means to cozen somebody in this city under
my countenance   41

Re-enter BIONDELLO

  Bion I have seen them in the church together God send 'em good shipping ! But
who is here ? mine old master Vincentio !
now we are undone and brought to nothing
  Vin [*Seeing Biondello*] Come hither, crack-
hemp
  Bion I hope I may choose, sir.
  Vin Come hither, you rogue. What, have
you forgot me ?   50
  Bion Forgot you ! no, sir I could not forget you, for I never saw you before in all my
life
  Vin What, you notorious villain, didst
thou never see thy master's father, Vincentio?
  Bion. What, my old worshipful old master ? yes, marry, sir see where he looks out
of the window
  Vin Is't so, indeed [*Beats Biondello* 60
  Bion Help, help, help ! here's a madman
will murder me   [*Exit.*
  Ped. Help, son ! help, Signior Baptista !
    [*Exit from above*
  Pet Prithee, Kate, let's stand aside and
see the end of this controversy. [*They retire.*

Re-enter Pedant *below;* TRANIO, BAPTISTA,
and Servants.

Tra. Sir, what are you that offer to beat
my servant?

Vin. What am I, sir! nay, what are you,
sir? O immortal gods! O fine villain! A
silken doublet! a velvet hose! a scarlet cloak!
and a copatain hat! O, I am undone! I am
undone! while I play the good husband at
home, my son and my servant spend all at the
university.

Tra. How now! what's the matter?

Bap. What, is the man lunatic?

Tra. Sir, you seem a sober ancient gentleman by your habit, but your words show you
a madman. Why, sir, what 'cerns it you if I
wear pearl and gold? I thank my good father,
I am able to maintain it.   79

Vin. Thy father! O villain! he is a sail-
maker in Bergamo.

Bap. You mistake, sir, you mistake, sir.
Pray, what do you think is his name?

Vin. His name! as if I knew not his name:
I have brought him up ever since he was three
years old, and his name is Tranio.

Ped. Away, away, mad ass! his name is
Lucentio; and he is mine only son, and heir
to the lands of me, Signior Vincentio.   89

Vin. Lucentio! O, he hath murdered his
master! Lay hold on him, I charge you, in
the duke's name. O, my son, my son! Tell
me, thou villain, where is my son Lucentio?

Tra. Call forth an officer.

Enter one with an Officer.

Carry this mad knave to the gaol. Father Baptista, I charge you see that he be forthcoming.

Vin. Carry me to the gaol.

Gre. Stay, officer: he shall not go to prison.

Bap. Talk not, Signior Gremio: I say he
shall go to prison.   100

Gre. Take heed, Signior Baptista, lest you
be cony-catched in this business: I dare swear
this is the right Vincentio.

Ped. Swear, if thou darest.

Gre. Nay, I dare not swear it.

Tra. Then thou wert best say that I am not
Lucentio.   [centio.

Gre. Yes, I know thee to be Signior Lu-

Bap. Away with the dotard! to the gaol
with him!   110

Vin. Thus strangers may be hailed and
abused: O monstrous villain!

Re-enter BIONDELLO, *with* LUCENTIO *and*
BIANCA.

Bion. O! we are spoiled and—yonder he
is: deny him, forswear him, or else we are all
undone.

Luc. [*Kneeling*] Pardon, sweet father.

Vin.   Lives my sweet son?

     [*Exeunt Biondello, Tranio, and Pedant,*
                        as fast as may be.

Bian. Pardon, dear father.

Bap.   How hast thou offended?
Where is Lucentio?

Luc.   Here's Lucentio,
Right son to the right Vincentio;
That have by marriage made thy daughter
    mine,
While counterfeit supposes blear'd thine eyne

Gre. Here's packing, with a witness to deceive us all!

Vin. Where is that damned villain Tranio
That faced and braved me in this matter so?

Bap. Why, tell me, is not this my Cambio?

Bian. Cambio is changed into Lucentio.

Luc. Love wrought these miracles. Bianca's
    love
Made me exchange my state with Tranio,
While he did bear my countenance in the
    town;
And happily I have arrived at the last   130
Unto the wished haven of my bliss.
What Tranio did, myself enforced him to;
Then pardon him, sweet father, for my sake.

Vin. I'll slit the villain's nose, that would
have sent me to the gaol.

Bap. But do you hear, sir? have you married my daughter without asking my good will?

Vin. Fear not, Baptista; we will content
you, go to: but I will in, to be revenged for
this villany.   [*Exit.* 140

Bap. And I, to sound the depth of this
knavery.   [*Exit.*

Luc. Look not pale, Bianca; thy father
will not frown. [*Exeunt Lucentio and Bianca.*

Gre. My cake is dough; but I'll in among
the rest,
Out of hope of all, but my share of the feast.
                         [*Exit.*

Kath. Husband, let's follow, to see the end
of this ado.

Pet. First kiss me, Kate, and we will.

Kath. What, in the midst of the street?

Pet. What, art thou ashamed of me?   150

Kath. No, sir, God forbid; but ashamed
to kiss.

Pet. Why, then let's home again. Come,
sirrah, let's away.

Kath. Nay, I will give thee a kiss: now
pray thee, love, stay.   [*Kate:*

Pet. Is not this well? Come, my sweet
Better once than never, for never too late.
                       [*Exeunt.*

SCENE II. *Padua.* LUCENTIO'S *house.*

Enter BAPTISTA, VINCENTIO, GREMIO, *the*
Pedant, LUCENTIO, BIANCA, PETRUCHIO,
KATHARINA, HORTENSIO, *and* Widow,
TRANIO, BIONDELLO, *and* GRUMIO: *the Ser-
ving-men with* Tranio *bringing in a banquet.*

Luc. At last, though long, our jarring notes
    agree:
And time it is, when raging war is done,
To smile at scapes and perils overblown.
My fair Bianca, bid my father welcome,
While I with self-same kindness welcome
    thine.
Brother Petruchio, sister Katharina,
And thou, Hortensio, with thy loving widow,
Feast with the best, and welcome to my house:

My banquet is to close our stomachs up,
After our great good cheer. Pray you, sit
down ;   10
For now we sit to chat as well as eat

Pet. Nothing but sit and sit, and eat and
eat !

Bap. Padua affords this kindness, son
Petruchio.   [kind.

Pet. Padua affords nothing but what is

Hor. For both our sakes, I would that word
were true.   [widow.

Pet. Now, for my life, Hortensio fears his

Wid. Then never trust me, if I be afeard

Pet. You are very sensible, and yet you
miss my sense .

I mean, Hortensio is afeard of you.

Wid. He that is giddy thinks the world
turns round   20

Pet. Roundly replied.

Kath.   Mistress, how mean you that ?

Wid. I conceive by him.

Pet. Conceives by me ! How likes Hortensio that ?

Hor. My widow says, thus she conceives
her tale.

Pet. Very well mended. Kiss him for that,
good widow

Kath. 'He that is giddy thinks the world
turns round :'

I pray you, tell me what you meant by that

Wid. Your husband, being troubled with a
shrew,

Measures my husband's sorrow by his woe :

And now you know my meaning.   30

Kath. A very mean meaning

Wid.   Right, I mean you

Kath. And I am mean indeed, respecting
you

Pet. To her, Kate !

Hor. To her, widow !

Pet. A hundred marks, my Kate does put .
her down.

Hor. That's my office.

Pet. Spoke like an officer ; ha' to thee, lad !
[*Drinks to Hortensio*

Bap. How likes Gremio these quick-witted
folks ?   [well

Gre. Believe me, sir, they butt together

Bian. Head, and butt ! an hasty-witted
body

Would say your head and butt were head and
horn.

Vin. Ay, mistress bride, hath that awaken'd
you ?

Bian. Ay, but not frighted me ; therefore
I'll sleep again.

Pet. Nay, that you shall not . since you
have begun,

Have at you for a bitter jest or two !

Bian. Am I your bird ? I mean to shift
my bush ;

And then pursue me as you draw your bow.
You are welcome all.
[*Exeunt Bianca, Katharina, and Widow.*

Pet. She hath prevented me. Here, Signior
Tranio.

This bird you aim'd at, though you hit her
not ;   50

Therefore a health to all that shot and miss'd.

Tra. O, sir, Lucentio shpp'd me like his
grey hound,

Which runs himself and catches for his master.

Pet. A good swift simile, but something
currish   [self :

Tra. 'Tis well, sir, that you hunted for your-
'Tis thought your deer does hold you at a bay.

Bap. O ho, Petruchio ! Tranio hits you
now

Luc. I thank thee for that gird, good Tranio.

Hor. Confess, confess, hath he not hit you
here ?

Pet. A' has a little gall'd me, I confess , 60
And, as the jest did glance away from me,
'Tis ten to one it maim'd you two outright

Bap. Now, in good sadness, son Petruchio,
I think thou hast the veriest shrew of all

Pet. Well, I say no : and therefore for assurance

Let's each one send unto his wife ;

And he whose wife is most obedient

To come at first when he doth send for her,

Shall win the wager which we will propose.

Hor. Content. What is the wager ?

Luc.   Twenty crowns.   70

Pet. Twenty crowns !

I'll venture so much of my hawk or hound,

But twenty times so much upon my wife

Luc. A hundred then

Hor.   Content

Pet.   A match ! 'tis done.

Hor. Who shall begin ?

Luc.   That will I.

Go, Biondello, bid your mistress come to me.

Bion. I go   [*Exit.*

Bap. Son, I'll be your half, Bianca comes

Luc. I'll have no halves , I'll bear it all
myself.

Re-enter BIONDELLO.

How now ! what news ?

Bion. Sir, my mistress sends you word
That she is busy and she cannot come

Pet. How ! she is busy and she cannot come!
Is that an answer ?

Gre.   Ay, and a kind one too :
Pray God, sir, your wife send you not a worse.

Pet. I hope, better   [wife

Hor. Sirrah Biondello, go and entreat my
To come to me forthwith.   [*Exit Bion.*

Pet.   O, ho ! entreat her !
Nay, then she must needs come

Hor.   I am afraid, sir,
Do what you can, yours will not be entreated.

Re-enter BIONDELLO.

Now, where's my wife ?   90

Bion. She says you have some goodly jest
in hand :

She will not come · she bids you come to her.

Pet. Worse and worse ; she will not come!
O vile,

Intolerable, not to be endured !

Sirrah Grumio, go to your mistress ;

Say, I command her to come to me.
                                        [Exit Grumio.
Hor. I know her answer.
Pet.   What ?
Hor.   She will not.
Pet. The fouler fortune mine, and there an
     end.
Bap. Now, by my holidame, here comes
     Katharina !

                Re-enter KATHARINA.

Kath. What is your will, sir, that you send
     for me ?   100
Pet. Where is your sister, and Hortensio's
     wife ?
Kath. They sit conferring by the parlor fire.
Pet. Go fetch them hither : if they deny to
     come.   [bands :
Swinge me them soundly forth unto their hus-
Away, I say, and bring them hither straight.
                                        [Exit Katharina.
Luc. Here is a wonder, if you talk of a
     wonder.
Hor. And so it is : I wonder what it bodes.
Pet. Marry, peace it bodes, and love and
     quiet life,
And awful rule and right supremacy;
And, to be short, what not, that's sweet and
     happy ?   110
Bap. Now, fair befal thee, good Petruchio!
The wager thou hast won ; and I will add
Unto their losses twenty thousand crowns ;
Another dowry to another daughter,
For she is changed, as she had never been.
Pet. Nay, I will win my wager better yet
And show more sign of her obedience.
Her new-built virtue and obedience.
See where she comes and brings your froward
     wives
As prisoners to her womanly persuasion.   120

     Re-enter KATHARINA, *with* BIANCA *and*
                     Widow.

Katharina, that cap of yours becomes you not:
Off with that bauble, throw it under-foot.
Wid. Lord, let me never have a cause to sigh,
Till I be brought to such a silly pass !
Bian. Fie ! what a foolish duty call you
     this ?
Luc. I would your duty were as foolish too:
The wisdom of your duty, fair Bianca,
Hath cost me an hundred crowns since supper-
     time.   [duty.
Bian. The more fool you, for laying on my
Pet. Katharine, I charge thee, tell these
     headstrong women   130
What duty they do owe their lords and hus-
     bands.
Wid. Come, come, you're mocking : we
     will have no telling.
Pet. Come on, I say; and first begin with
     her.
Wid. She shall not.
Pet. I say she shall: and first begin with
     her.
Kath. Fie, fie ! unknit that threatening un-
     kind brow,

And dart not scornful glances from those eyes,
To wound thy lord, thy king, thy governor :
It blots thy beauty as frosts do bite the meads,
Confounds thy fame as whirlwinds shake fair
     buds,   140
And in no sense is meet or amiable.
A woman moved is like a fountain troubled,
Muddy, ill-seeming, thick, bereft of beauty;
And while it is so, none so dry or thirsty
Will deign to sip or touch one drop of it.
Thy husband is thy lord, thy life, thy keeper,
Thy head, thy sovereign ; one that cares for
     thee,
And for thy maintenance commits his body
To painful labor both by sea and land,
To watch the night in storms, the day in cold,
Whilst thou liest warm at home, secure and
     safe ;   151
And craves no other tribute at thy hands
But love, fair looks and true obedience ;
Too little payment for so great a debt.
Such duty as the subject owes the prince
Even such a woman oweth to her husband ;
And when she is froward, peevish, sullen, sour,
And not obedient to his honest will,
What is she but a foul contending rebel
And graceless traitor to her loving lord ?   160
I am ashamed that women are so simple
To offer war where they should kneel for peace,
Or seek for rule, supremacy and sway,
When they are bound to serve, love and obey.
Why are our bodies soft and weak and smooth,
Unapt to toil and trouble in the world,
But that our soft conditions and our hearts
Should well agree with our external parts ?
Come, come, you froward and unable worms .
My mind hath been as big as one of yours, 170
My heart as great, my reason haply more,
To bandy word for word and frown for frown;
But now I see our lances are but straws,
Our strength as weak, our weakness past com-
     pare,
That seeming to be most which we indeed least
     are.
Then vail your stomachs, for it is no boot,
And place your hands below your husband's
     foot :
In token of which duty, if he please,
My hand is ready; may it do him ease.
Pet. Why, there's a wench ! Come on, and
     kiss me, Kate.   180
Luc. Well, go thy ways, old lad ; for thou
     shalt ha't.   [toward.
Vin. 'Tis a good hearing when children are
Luc. But a harsh hearing when women are
     froward.
Pet. Come, Kate, we'll to bed.
We three are married, but you two are sped.
[*To Luc.*] 'Twas I won the wager, though you
     hit the white;
And, being a winner, God give you good night
                    [*Exeunt Petruchio and Katharina*
Hor. Now, go thy ways; thou hast tamed
     a curst shrew.
Luc. 'Tis a wonder, by your leave, she
     will be tamed so.   [*Exeunt.*

THE
MERRY WIVES OF WINDSOR.

(WRITTEN ABOUT 1598.)

INTRODUCTION.

This is an offshoot from the comedy of *King Henry IV.*, while *King Henry V.* is the direct continuation of the history. Dennis, in 1702, reports a tradition that this play was written in fourteen days, by order of the Queen ; and Rowe adds : "She was so well pleased with that admirable character of Falstaff, in the two parts of *Henry IV.*, that she commanded him to continue it for one play more, and to show him in love." This may have been the cause why Shakespeare does not fulfill the promiso made in the Epilogue of *Henry IV.*, that Falstaff should re-appear with Henry V. in France ; but, indeed, among the great deeds of the victor of Agincourt there would be small room for a Falstaff. The choice of Windsor as the scene, and the compliments to the owner of Windsor Castle, and to the wearers of the Order of the Garter, suggest that the play was meant especially for Elizabeth and her courtiers. An early sketch of *The Merry Wives* was published in quarto, 1602 ; some touches in the play, as given in the folio, were evidently made after the accession of James I. (1603); the word "council is altered to "king" (Act I., Sc. I., L. 113) ; "these knights will back," exclaims Mrs. Page (Act II., Sc I., L. 52), and the allusion to James's too liberal creation of knights in 1604 was probably appreciated. Some critics have held that the first sketch of *The Merry Wives* was written as early as 1592. A German duke is spoken of by Bardolph as about to visit Windsor, and his gentlemen ride off with nine host of the Garter's horses unpaid for. In the early sketch (Act IV., Sc. v., of the revised play), instead of "cousin-germans," where Evans puns upon the words *cozen* and *German*, occurs the strange "cosen garmombles." Now, Count Frederick of Mömpelgard had visited England and accompanied the Queen to Windsor, Aug. 1592 ; and in the passport which he received for his journey back to the Continent, we read that he shall be furnished with post-horses, and shall pay nothing for the same. Next year the Count became Duke of Wirtemberg, and in 1595 he craved that, in accordance with a promise given, Elizabeth would confer upon him the Order of the Garter, which Elizabeth, on various pretexts, declined. "Garmombles" obviously reverses the true name "Mömpelgard ;" but the inference that the date of the play is 1592, because it refers to the visit of the Germans, is unwarrantable, for such an event would be remembered, and the more so because of the Duke's subsequent unavailing attempt to obtain the honor of the Garter. If we try to make out exact relations between the characters of *The Merry Wives* and the same characters as they appear in the historical plays, we shall fail. The comedy has a certain independence of the histories, and cannot be pieced on to them in any way : the persons are the same and not the same. Mrs. Quickly, servant of Dr. Caius, has a different history from the Mrs. Quickly of the Boar's Head Tavern. Nor is Falstaff conceived in quite the same manner as the Falstaff of *Henry IV.* Here the knight is fatuous, his genius deserts him ; the never-defeated hangs his head before two country dames ; the buck-basket, the drench of Thames water, the blows of Ford's cudgel, are reprisals too coarse upon the most inimitable of jesters. Yet the play is indeed a merry one, with well-contrived incidents and abundance of broad mirth. A country air breathes over the whole ; nowhere else has Shakespeare represented English middle-class life in the country, and he has here done it with a vigorous, healthy pleasure. It is not, however, a poetical play, unless comely English maidenhood, in the person of pretty Anne Page, lend it something of poetry. There is a propriety in the fact that this comedy is written almost wholly in prose. The merry wives are a delightful pair, with "their sly laughing looks, their apple-red cheeks, their brows the lines whereon look more like the work of mirth than of years ;" and Slender, most brainless of youths, most incapable of lovers, is dear for sake of the laugh at him which pretty Anne Page must have when alone. Altogether, if we can accept Falstaff's discomfitures, it is a merry play to laugh at if not to love.

DRAMATIS PERSONÆ.

SIR JOHN FALSTAFF	FORD, } two gentlemen dwelling at Windsor.
FENTON, a gentleman.	PAGE, }
SHALLOW, a country justice.	WILLIAM PAGE, a boy, son to Page.
SLENDER, cousin to Shallow.	SIR HUGH EVANS, a Welsh parson.

DOCTOR CAIUS, a French physician.
Host of the Garter Inn.
BARDOLPH, ⎫
PISTOL, ⎬ sharpers attending on Falstaff.
NYM, ⎭
ROBIN, page to Falstaff.
SIMPLE, servant to Slender.
RUGBY, servant to Doctor Caius.

MISTRESS FORD.
MISTRESS PAGE.
ANNE PAGE, her daughter.
MISTRESS QUICKLY, servant to Doctor Caius.

Servants to Page, Ford, &c.

SCENE : *Windsor, and the neighborhood.*

ACT I.

SCENE I. *Windsor. Before* PAGE'S *house.*

Enter JUSTICE SHALLOW, SLENDER, *and* SIR HUGH EVANS.

Shal. Sir Hugh, persuade me not; I will make a Star-chamber matter of it : if he were twenty Sir John Falstaffs, he shall not abuse Robert Shallow, esquire.

Slen. In the county of Gloucester, justice of peace and ' Coram.'

Shal. Ay, cousin Slender, and ' Custalorum.'

Slen. Ay, and ' Rato-lorum ' too ; and a gentleman born, master parson ; who writes himself ' Armigero,' in any bill, warrant, quittance, or obligation, ' Armigero.'　　11

Shal. Ay, that I do ; and have done any time these three hundred years.

Slen. All his successors gone before him hath done't ; and all his ancestors that come after him may : they may give the dozen white luces in their coat.

Shal. It is an old coat.

Evans. The dozen white louses do become an old coat well ; it agrees well, passant ; it is a familiar beast to man, and signifies love. 21

Shal. The luce is the fresh fish ; the salt fish is an old coat.

Slen. I may quarter, coz.

Shal. You may, by marrying.

Evans. It is marring indeed, if he quarter it.

Shal. Not a whit.

Evans. Yes, py'r lady ; if he has a quarter of your coat, there is but three skirts for yourself, in my simple conjectures : but that is all one. If Sir John Falstaff have committed disparagements unto you, I am of the church, and will be glad to do my benevolence to make atonements and compremises between you.

Shal. The council shall hear it ; it is a riot.

Evans. It is not meet the council hear a riot ; there is no fear of Got in a riot : the council, look you, shall desire to hear the fear of Got, and not to hear a riot ; take your vizaments in that.

Shal. Ha ! o' my life, if I were young again, the sword should end it.　　41

Evans. It is petter that friends is the sword, and end it : and there is also another device in my prain, which peradventure prings goot discretions with it : there is Anne Page, which is daughter to Master Thomas Page, which is pretty virginity.

Slen. Mistress Anne Page ? She has brown hair, and speaks small like a woman.

Evans. It is that fery person for all the orld, as just as you will desire ; and seven hundred pounds of moneys, and gold and silver, is her grandsire upon his death's-bed— Got deliver to a joyful resurrections !—give, when she is able to overtake seventeen years old : it were a goot motion if we leave our pribbles and prabbles, and desire a marriage between Master Abraham and Mistress Anne Page.

Slen. Did her grandsire leave her seven hundred pound ?　　60

Evans. Ay, and her father is make her a petter penny.

Slen. I know the young gentlewoman ; she has good gifts.

Evans. Seven hundred pounds and possibilities is goot gifts.

Shal. Well, let us see honest Master Page. Is Falstaff there ?

Evans. Shall I tell you a lie ? I do despise a liar as I do despise one that is false, or as I despise one that is not true. The knight, Sir John, is there ; and, I beseech you, be ruled by your well-willers. I will peat the door for Master Page.　　　　　[*Knocks.*] What, hoa ! Got pless your house here !

Page. [*Within*] Who's there ?

Enter PAGE.

Evans. Here is Got's plessing, and your friend, and Justice Shallow ; and here young Master Slender, that peradventures shall tell you another tale, if matters grow to your likings.

Page. I am glad to see your worships well. I thank you for my venison, Master Shallow.

Shal. Master Page, I am glad to see you : much good do it your good heart ! I wished your venison better ; it was ill killed. How doth good Mistress Page ?—and I thank you always with my heart, la ! with my heart.

Page. Sir, I thank you.

Shal. Sir, I thank you ; by yea and no, I do.

Page. I am glad to see you, good Master Slender.　　90

Slen. How does your fallow greyhound, sir ? I heard say he was outrun on Cotsall.

Page. It could not be judged, sir.

Slen. You'll not confess, you'll not confess.

Shal. That he will not. 'Tis your fault,
'tis your fault ; 'tis a good dog.

Page. A cur, sir.

Shal. Sir, he's a good dog, and a fair dog:
can there be more said ? he is good and fair.
Is Sir John Falstaff here ? 100

Page. Sir, he is within ; and I would I
could do a good office between you.

Evans. It is spoke as a Christians ought to
speak.

Shal. He hath wronged me, Master Page.

Page. Sir, he doth in some sort confess it.

Shal. If it be confessed, it is not redress'd:
is not that so, Master Page ? He hath wronged
me ; indeed he hath ; at a word, he hath, believe me: Robert Shallow, esquire, saith, he
is wronged. 110

Page. Here comes Sir John.

Enter Sir John Falstaff, Bardolph, Nym,
and Pistol.

Fal. Now, Master Shallow, you'll complain of me to the king ?

Shal. Knight, you have beaten my men,
killed my deer, and broke open my lodge.

Fal. But not kissed your keeper's daughter?

Shal. Tut, a pin ! this shall be answered.

Fal. I will answer it straight ; I have done
all this.
That is now answered.

Shal. The council shall know this. 120

Fal. 'Twere better for you if it were known
in counsel : you'll be laughed at.

Evans. Pauca verba, Sir John ; goot worts.

Fal. Good worts ! good cabbage. Slender,
I broke your head : what matter have you
against me ?

Slen. Marry, sir, I have matter in my head
against you ; and against your coney-catching
rascals, Bardolph, Nym, and Pistol.

Bard. You Banbury cheese ! 130

Slen. Ay, it is no matter.

Pist. How now, Mephostophilus !

Slen. Ay, it is no matter.

Nym. Slice, I say ! pauca, pauca: slice !
that's my humor.

Slen. Where's Simple, my man ? Can you
tell, cousin ?

Evans. Peace, I pray you. Now let us understand. There is three umpires in this matter, as I understand ; that is, Master Page,
fidelicet Master Page ; and there is myself,
fidelicet myself ; and the three party is, lastly
and finally, mine host of the Garter.

Page. We three, to hear it and end it between them.

Evans. Fery goot : I will make a prief of
it in my note-book ; and we will afterwards
ork upon the cause with as great discreetly as
we can.

Fal. Pistol !

Pist. He hears with ears. 150

Evans. The tevil and his tam ! what phrase
is this, 'He hears with ear'? why, it is affec-
tations

Fal. Pistol, did you pick Master Slender's
purse ?

Slen. Ay, by these gloves, did he, or I
would I might never come in mine own great
chamber again else, of seven groats in mill-
sixpences, and two Edward shovel-boards,
that cost me two shilling and two pence a-
piece of Yead Miller, by these gloves. 161

Fal. Is this true, Pistol ?

Evans. No ; it is false, if it is a pick-purse.

Pist. Ha, thou mountain-foreigner ! Sir
John and Master mine,
I combat challenge of this latten bilbo.
Word of denial in thy labras here !
Word of denial : froth and scum, thou liest !

Slen. By these gloves, then, 'twas he.

Nym. Be avised, sir, and pass good humors : I will say ' marry trap' with you, if
you run the nuthook's humor on me ; that is
the very note of it.

Slen. By this hat, then, he in the red face
had it : for though I cannot remember what I
did when you made me drunk, yet I am not
altogether an ass.

Fal. What say you, Scarlet and John ?

Bard. Why, sir, for my part, I say the gentleman had drunk himself out of his five sentences. 180

Evans. It is his five senses : fie, what the
ignorance is !

Bard. And being fap, sir, was, as they say,
cashiered ; and so conclusions passed the
careires.

Slen. Ay, you spake in Latin then too ; but
'tis no matter : I'll ne'er be drunk whilst I live
again, but in honest, civil, godly company, for
this trick : if I be drunk, I'll be drunk with
those that have the fear of God, and not with
drunken knaves. 190

Evans. So Got udge me, that is a virtuous
mind.

Fal. You hear all these matters denied,
gentlemen ; you hear it.

Enter Anne Page, *with wine ;* Mistress
Ford *and* Mistress Page, *following.*

Page. Nay, daughter, carry the wine in ;
we'll drink within. [*Exit Anne Page.*

Slen. O heaven ! this is Mistress Anne
Page.

Page. How now, Mistress Ford !

Fal. Mistress Ford, by my troth, you are
very well met : by your leave, good mistress.
[*Kisses her.* 200

Page. Wife, bid these gentlemen welcome.
Come, we have a hot venison pasty to dinner: come, gentlemen, I hope we shall drink
down all unkindness.

[*Exeunt all except Shal., Slen., and Evans.*

Slen. I had rather than forty shillings I
had my Book of Songs and Sonnets here.

Enter Simple.

How now, Simple ! where have you been ? I
must wait on myself, must I ? You have not
the Book of Riddles about you, have you ?

Sim. Book of Riddles ! why, did you not

lend it to Alice Shortcake upon All-hallow-mas last, a fortnight afore Michaelmas?

Shal. Come, coz; come, coz; we stay for you. A word with you, coz; marry, this, coz: there is, as 'twere, a tender, a kind of tender, made afar off by Sir Hugh here. Do you understand me?

Slen. Ay, sir, you shall find me reasonable; if it be so, I shall do that that is reason.

Shal. Nay, but understand me.

Slen. So I do, sir.   220

Evans. Give ear to his motions, Master Slender: I will description the matter to you, if you be capacity of it.

Slen. Nay, I will do as my cousin Shallow says: I pray you, pardon me; he's a justice of peace in his country, simple though I stand here.

Evans. But that is not the question: the question is concerning your marriage.

Shal. Ay, there's the point, sir.

Evans. Marry, is it; the very point of it; to Mistress Anne Page.   231

Slen. Why, if it be so, I will marry her upon any reasonable demands.

Evans. But can you affection the 'oman? Let us command to know that of your mouth or of your lips; for divers philosophers hold that the lips is parcel of the mouth. Therefore, precisely, can you carry your good will to the maid?   [love her? 240

Shal. Cousin Abraham Slender, can you

Slen. I hope, sir, I will do as it shall become one that would do reason.

Evans. Nay, Got's lords and his ladies! you must speak possitable, if you can carry her your desires towards her.

Shal. That you must. Will you, upon good dowry, marry her?

Slen. I will do a greater thing than that, upon your request, cousin, in any reason.

Shal. Nay, conceive me, conceive me, sweet coz: what I do is to pleasure you, coz. Can you love the maid?

Slen. I will marry her, sir, at your request: but if there be no great love in the beginning, yet heaven may decrease it upon better acquaintance, when we are married and have more occasion to know one another; I hope, upon familiarity will grow more contempt: but if you say, 'Marry her,' I will marry her; that I am freely dissolved, and dissolutely.   260

Evans. It is a fery discretion answer; save the fall is in the ort 'dissolutely:' the ort is, according to our meaning, 'resolutely:' his meaning is good.

Shal. Ay, I think my cousin meant well.

Slen. Ay, or else I would I might be hanged, la!

Shal. Here comes fair Mistress Anne.

Re-enter ANNE PAGE.

Would I were young for your sake, Mistress Anne!

Anne. The dinner is on the table; my father desires your worships' company.   271

Shal. I will wait on him, fair Mistress Anne.

Evans. Od's plessed will! I will not be absence at the grace.

[*Exeunt Shallow and Evans.*

Anne. Will't please your worship to come in, sir?

Slen. No, I thank you, forsooth, heartily; I am very well.

Anne. The dinner attends you, sir.

Slen. I am not a-hungry, I thank you, forsooth. Go, sirrah, for all you are my man, go wait upon my cousin Shallow. [*Exit Simple.*] A justice of peace sometimes may be beholding to his friend for a man. I keep but three men and a boy yet, till my mother be dead: but what though? yet I live like a poor gentleman born.

Anne. I may not go in without your worship: they will not sit till you come.

Slen. I' faith, I'll eat nothing; I thank you as much as though I did.   291

Anne. I pray you, sir, walk in.

Slen. I had rather walk here, I thank you. I bruised my shin th' other day with playing at sword and dagger with a master of fence; three veneys for a dish of stewed prunes; and, by my troth, I cannot abide the smell of hot meat since. Why do your dogs bark so? be there bears i' the town?

Anne. I think there are, sir; I heard them talked of.   301

Slen. I love the sport well; but I shall as soon quarrel at it as any man in England. You are afraid, if you see the bear loose, are you not?

Anne. Ay, indeed, sir.

Slen. That's meat and drink to me, now. I have seen Sackerson loose twenty times, and have taken him by the chain; but, I warrant you, the women have so cried and shrieked at it, that it passed: but women, indeed, cannot abide 'em; they are very ill-favored rough things.

Re-enter PAGE.

Page. Come, gentle Master Slender, come; we stay for you.

Slen. I'll eat nothing, I thank you, sir.

Page. By cock and pie, you shall not choose, sir! come, come.

Slen. Nay, pray you, lead the way.

Page. Come on, sir.

Slen. Mistress Anne, yourself shall go first.

Anne. Not I, sir; pray you, keep on.   321

Slen. Truly, I will not go first; truly, la! I will not do you that wrong.

Anne. I pray you, sir.

Slen. I'll rather be unmannerly than troublesome. You do yourself wrong, indeed, la!

[*Exeunt.*

SCENE II.   *The same*

Enter SIR HUGH EVANS *and* SIMPLE.

Evans. Go your ways, and ask of Doctor Caius' house which is the way: and there dwells one Mistress Quickly, which is in the manner of his nurse, or his dry nurse, or his cook, or his laundry, his washer, and his wringer

Sim. Well, sir

Evans Nay, it is petter yet. Give her this letter, for it is a 'oman that altogether's acquaintance with Mistress Anne Page and the letter is, to desire and require her to solicit your master's desires to Mistress Anne Page I pray you, be gone. I will make an end of my dinner, there's pippins and cheese to come.   [*Exeunt.*

SCENE III *A room in the Garter Inn*

Enter FALSTAFF, HOST, BARDOLPH, NYM, PISTOL, *and* ROBIN.

Fal. Mine host of the Garter!

Host What says my bully-rook? speak scholarly and wisely

Fal Truly, mine host, I must turn away some of my followers

Host. Discard, bully Hercules; cashier let them wag, trot, trot.

Fal. I sit at ten pounds a week

Host. Thou'rt an emperor, Cæsar, Keisar, and Pheezar. I will entertain Bardolph, he shall draw, he shall tap. said I well, bully Hector?

Fal Do so, good mine host

Host I have spoke, let him follow [*To Bard*] Let me see thee froth and lime. I am at a word, follow   [*Exit*

Fal Bardolph, follow him. A tapster is a good trade. an old cloak makes a new jerkin, a withered serving-man a fresh tapster. Go, adieu   20

Bard. It is a life that I have desired. I will thrive.

Pist O base Hungarian wight! wilt thou the spigot wield?   [*Exit Bardolph*

Nym He was gotten in drink. is not the humor conceited?

Fal I am glad I am so acquit of this tinderbox. his thefts were too open, his filching was like an unskilful singer, he kept not time

Nym The good humor is to steal at a minute's rest   31

Pist. 'Convey,' the wise it call. 'Steal!' foh! a fico for the phrase!

Fal Well, sirs, I am almost out at heels.

Pist. Why, then, let kibes ensue

Fal. There is no remedy; I must cony-catch, I must shift.

Pist. Young ravens must have food

Fal Which of you know Ford of this town?

Pist. I ken the wight. he is of substance good   41

Fal My honest lads, I will tell you what I am about

Pist. Two yards, and more

Fal No quips now, Pistol! Indeed, I am in the waist two yards about, but I am now about no waste; I am about thrift. Briefly, I do mean to make love to Ford's wife: I spy

entertainment in her; she discourses, she carves, she gives the leer of invitation. I can construe the action of her familiar style; and the hardest voice of her behavior, to be Englished rightly, is, 'I am Sir John Falstaff's'

Pist He hath studied her will, and translated her will, out of honesty into English

Nym The anchor is deep. will that humor pass?

Fal Now, the report goes she has all the rule of her husband's purse. he hath a legion of angels   60

Pist. As many devils entertain, and 'To her, boy,' say I

Nym The humor rises, it is good. humor me the angels

Fal I have writ me here a letter to her. and here another to Page's wife, who even now gave me good eyes too, examined my parts with most judicious œillades, sometimes the beam of her view gilded my foot, sometimes my portly belly

Pist Then did the sun on dunghill shine

Nym I thank thee for that humor 71

Fal. O, she did so course o'er my exteriors with such a greedy intention, that the appetite of her eye did seem to scorch me up like a burning-glass! Here's another letter to her. she bears the purse too, she is a region in Guiana, all gold and bounty. I will be cheater to them both, and they shall be exchequers to me, they shall be my East and West Indies, and I will trade to them both. Go bear thou this letter to Mistress Page, and thou this to Mistress Ford. we will thrive, lads, we will thrive

Pist Shall I Sir Pandarus of Troy become, And by my side wear steel? then, Lucifer take all!

Nym I will run no base humor here, take the humor-letter. I will keep the havior of reputation

Fal [*To Robin*] Hold, sirrah, bear you these letters tightly, Sail like my pinnace to these golden shores. Rogues, hence, avaunt! vanish like hailstones, go, Trudge, plod away o' the hoof, seek shelter, pack!

Falstaff will learn the humor of the age, French thrift, you rogues, myself and skirted page. [*Exeunt Falstaff and Robin*

Pist Let vultures gripe thy guts! for gourd and fullam holds, And high and low beguiles the rich and poor: Tester I'll have in pouch when thou shalt lack, Base Phrygian Turk!

Nym I have operations which be humors of revenge

Pist Wilt thou revenge?   100

Nym. By welkin and her star!

Pist With wit or steel?

Nym With both the humors, I: I will discuss the humor of this love to Page.

Pist. And I to Ford shall eke unfold How Falstaff, varlet vile,

His dove will prove, his gold will hold,
And his soft couch defile.

Nym. My humor shall not cool : I will incense Page to deal with poison ; I will possess
† him with yellowness, for the revolt of mine
is dangerous : that is my true humor.

Pist. Thou art the Mars of malecontents : I
second thee ; troop on.　　　　[*Exeunt.*

SCENE IV. *A room in* DOCTOR CAIUS'S *house.*

Enter MISTRESS QUICKLY, SIMPLE, *and*
RUGBY.

Quick. What, John Rugby ! I pray thee,
go to the casement, and see if you can see my
master, Master Doctor Caius, coming. If he
do, i' faith, and find any body in the house,
here will be an old abusing of God's patience
and the king's English.

Rug. I'll go watch.

Quick. Go ; and we'll have a posset for't
soon at night, in faith, at the latter end of a
sea-coal fire. [*Exit Rugby.*] An honest, willing, kind fellow, as ever servant shall come
in house withal, and, I warrant you, no tell-
tale nor no breed-bate : his worst fault is,
that he is given to prayer ; he is something
peevish that way : but nobody but has his
fault ; but let that pass. Peter Simple, you
say your name is ?

Sim. Ay, for fault of a better.

Quick. And Master Slender's your master?

Sim. Ay, forsooth.

Quick. Does he not wear a great round
beard, like a glover's paring-knife ?　　21

Sim. No, forsooth : he hath but a little wee
face, with a little yellow beard, a Cain-colored
beard.

Quick. A softly-sprighted man, is he not ?

Sim. Ay, forsooth : but he is as tall a man
of his hands as any is between this and his
head ; he hath fought with a warrener.

Quick. How say you ? O, I should remember him : does he not hold up his head, as it
were, and strut in his gait ?　　31

Sim. Yes, indeed, does he.

Quick. Well, heaven send Anne Page no
worse fortune ! Tell Master Parson Evans I
will do what I can for your master : Anne is a
good girl, and I wish—

Re-enter RUGBY.

Rug. Out, alas ! here comes my master.

Quick. We shall all be shent. Run in here,
good young man ; go into this closet : he will
not stay long. [*Shuts Simple in the closet.*]
What, John Rugby ! John ! what, John, I say !
Go, John, go inquire for my master ; I doubt
he be not well, that he comes not home.　　43
[*Singing*] And down, down, adown-a, &c.

Enter DOCTOR CAIUS.

Caius. Vat is you sing ? I do not like des
toys. Pray you, go and vetch me in my closet
un.boitier vert, a box, a green-a box : do
intend vat I speak ? a green-a box.

Quick. Ay, forsooth ; I'll fetch it you.

[*Aside*] I am glad he went not in himself : if
he had found the young man, he would have
been horn-mad.　　52

Caius. Fe, fe, fe, fe ! ma foi, il fait fort
chaud. Je m'en vais a la cour—la grande
affaire.

Quick. Is it this, sir ?

Caius. Oui ; mette le au mon pocket : de-
peche, quickly. Vere is dat knave Rugby ?

Quick. What, John Rugby ! John !

Rug. Here, sir !

Caius. You are John Rugby, and you are
Jack Rugby. Come, take-a your rapier, and
come after my heel to the court.　　62

Rug. 'Tis ready, sir, here in the porch.

Caius. By my trot, I tarry too long. Od's
me ! Qu'ai-j'oublie ! dere is some simples in
my closet, dat I vill not for the varld I shall
leave behind.

Quick. Ay me, he'll find the young man
there, and be mad !

Caius. O diable, diable ! vat is in my closet?
Villain ! larron ! [*Pulling Simple out.*] Rugby,
my rapier !

Quick. Good master, be content.

Caius. Wherefore shall I be content-a ?

Quick. The young man is an honest man.

Caius. What shall de honest man do in my
closet? dere is no honest man dat shall come
in my closet.

Quick. I beseech you, be not so phlegmatic.
Hear the truth of it : he came of an errand to
me from Parson Hugh.　　81

Caius. Vell.

Sim. Ay, forsooth ; to desire her to—

Quick. Peace, I pray you.　　[tale.

Caius. Peace-a your tongue. Speak-a your

Sim. To desire this honest gentlewoman,
your maid, to speak a good word to Mistress
Anne Page for my master in the way of marriage.

Quick. This is all, indeed, la ! but I'll ne'er
put my finger in the fire, and need not.　　91

Caius. Sir Hugh send-a you ? Rugby, baille
me some paper. Tarry you a little-a while.

[*Writes.*

Quick. [*Aside to Simple.*] I am glad he is
so quiet : if he had been thoroughly moved,
you should have heard him so loud and so
melancholy. But notwithstanding, man, I'll
do you your master what good I can : and the
very yea and the no is, the French doctor, my
master,—I may call him my master, look you,
for I keep his house ; and I wash, wring, brew,
bake, scour, dress meat and drink, make the
beds, and do all myself,—

Sim. [*Aside to Quickly*] 'Tis a great charge
to come under one body's hand.

Quick. [*Aside to Simple*] Are you avised
o' that ? you shall find it a great charge : and
to be up early and down late ; but notwithstanding,—to tell you in your ear ; I would
have no words of it,—my master himself is in
love with Mistress Anne Page : but notwithstanding that, I know Anne's mind,—that's
neither here nor there.

"O, diable, diable! Vat is in my closet? Rugby, my rapier."

Caius. You jack'nape, give-a this letter to Sir Hugh ; by gar, it is a shallenge . I will cut his troat in dee park , and I will teach a scurvy jack-a-nape priest to meddle or make You may be gone , it is not good you tarry here. By gar, I will cut all his two stones , by gar, he shall not have a stone to throw at his dog.

   [*Exit Simple*

Quick Alas, he speaks but for his friend.

Caius. It is no matter-a yet dat do not you tell-a me dat I shall have Anne Page for myself ? By gar, I will kill de Jack priest , and I have appointed mine host of de Jarteer to measure our weapon By gar, I will myself have Anne Page

Quick Sir, the maid loves you, and all shall be well We must give folks leave to prate what, the good-jer '

Caius Rugby, come to the court with me By gar, if I have not Anne Page, I shall turn your head out of my door Follow my heels, Rugby   [*Exeunt Caius and Rugby*

Quick. You shall have An fool s-head of your own No, I know Anne's mind for that never a woman in Windsor knows more of Anne's mind than I do , nor can do more than I do with her. I thank heaven

Fent [*Within*] Who's within there ? ho '

Quick Who's there, I trow ! Come near the house, I pray you   141

Enter Fenton.

Fent How now, good woman ! how dost thou ?

Quick. The better that it pleases your good worship to ask

Fent What news ? how does pretty Mistress Anne ?

Quick In truth, sir, and she is pretty, and honest, and gentle , and one that is your friend, I can tell you that by the way . I praise heaven for it   151

Fent Shall I do any good, thinkest thou ? shall I not lose my suit ?

Quick Troth, sir, all is in his hands above but notwithstanding, Master Fenton, I'll be sworn on a book, she loves you Have not your worship a wart above your eye ?

Fent Yes, marry, have I , what of that ?

Quick Well, thereby hangs a tale good faith, it is such another Nan , but, I detest, an honest maid as ever broke bread we had an hour's talk of that wart I shall never laugh but in that maid's company ' But indeed she is given too much to allicholy and musing: but for you—well, go to.

Fent. Well, I shall see her to-day. Hold, there's money for thee, let me have thy voice in my behalf: if thou seest her before me, commend me.

Quick. Will I? i' faith, that we will; and I will tell your worship more of the wart the next time we have confidence, and of other wooers.

Fent. Well, farewell ; I am in great haste now.

Quick. Farewell to your worship. [*Exit Fenton*] Truly, an honest gentleman : but Anne loves him not , for I know Anne's mind as well as another does. Out upon't ' what have I forgot ?   [*Exit.* 186

ACT II.

Scene I. *Before Page's house*

Enter Mistress Page, with a letter.

Mrs. Page What, have I scaped love-letters in the holiday-time of my beauty, and am I now a subject for them ? Let me see

   [*Reads*

'Ask me no reason why I love you , for though Love use Reason for his physician he admits him not for his counsellor You are not young no more am I , go to then, there's sympathy you are merry, so am I , ha, ha ' then there's more sympathy you love sack, and so do I , would you desire better sympathy ? Let it suffice thee, Mistress Page,—at the least, if the love of soldier can suffice,—that I love thee I will not say, pity me , 'tis not a soldier-like phrase but I say, love me By me,

Thine own true knight,
By day or night,
Or any kind of light,
With all his might
For thee to fight,   John Falstaff'

What a Herod of Jewry is this ' O wicked, wicked world ' One that is well-nigh worn to pieces with age to show himself a young gallant ' What an unweighed behavior hath this Flemish drunkard picked—with the devil's name '—out of my conversation, that he dares in this manner assay me ? Why, he hath not been thrice in my company ' What should I say to him ? I was then frugal of my mirth Heaven forgive me' Why, I'll exhibit a bill in the parliament for the putting down of men How shall I be revenged on him ? for revenged I will be, as sure as his guts are made of puddings

Enter Mistress Ford

Mrs Ford Mistress Page ' trust me, I was going to your house

Mrs Page And, trust me, I was coming to you You look very ill

Mrs Ford Nay, I'll ne'er believe that , I have to show to the contrary.

Mrs Page Faith, but you do, in my mind.

Mrs Ford Well, I do then , yet I say I could show you to the contrary. O Mistress Page, give me some counsel '

Mrs Page What's the matter, woman ?

Mrs Ford O woman, if it were not for one trifling respect, I could come to such honor '

Mrs Page Hang the trifle, woman ' take the honor. What is it ? dispense with trifles; what is it ?

Mrs. Ford. If I would but go to hell for an eternal moment or so, I could be knighted. 50

Mrs. Page. What? thou liest! Sir Alice Ford! These knights will hack; and so thou shouldst not alter the article of thy gentry.

Mrs. Ford. We burn daylight: here, read, read; perceive how I might be knighted. I shall think the worse of fat men, as long as I have an eye to make difference of men's liking: and yet he would not swear; praised women's modesty; and gave such orderly and well-behaved reproof to all uncomeliness, that I would have sworn his disposition would have gone to the truth of his words; but they do no more adhere and keep place together than the Hundredth Psalm to the tune of 'Green Sleeves.' What tempest, I trow, threw this whale, with so many tuns of oil in his belly, ashore at Windsor? How shall I be revenged on him? I think the best way were to entertain him with hope, till the wicked fire of lust have melted him in his own grease. Did you ever hear the like? 70

Mrs. Page. Letter for letter, but that the name of Page and Ford differs! To thy great comfort in this mystery of ill opinions, here's the twin-brother of thy letter: but let thine inherit first; for, I protest, mine never shall. I warrant he hath a thousand of these letters, writ with blank space for different names,— sure, more,—and these are of the second edition: he will print them, out of doubt; for he cares not what he puts into the press, when he would put us two. I had rather be a giantess, and lie under Mount Pelion. Well, I will find you twenty lascivious turtles ere one chaste man.

Mrs. Ford. Why, this is the very same; the very hand, the very words. What doth he think of us?

Mrs. Page. Nay, I know not: it makes me almost ready to wrangle with mine own honesty. I'll entertain myself like one that I am not acquainted withal; for, sure, unless he know some strain in me, that I know not myself, he would never have boarded me in this fury.

Mrs. Ford. 'Boarding,' call you it? I'll be sure to keep him above deck.

Mrs. Page. So will I: if he come under my hatches, I'll never to sea again. Let's be revenged on him: let's appoint him a meeting; give him a show of comfort in his suit and lead him on with a fine-baited delay, till he hath pawned his horses to mine host of the Garter. 100

Mrs. Ford. Nay, I will consent to act any villany against him, that may not sully the chariness of our honesty. O, that my husband saw this letter! it would give eternal food to his jealousy.

Mrs. Page. Why, look where he comes; and my good man too: he's as far from jealousy as I am from giving him cause; and that I hope is an unmeasurable distance.

Mrs. Ford. You are the happier woman. 110

Mrs. Page. Let's consult together against this greasy knight. Come hither. [*They retire.*

Enter FORD *with* PISTOL, *and* PAGE *with* NYM.

Ford. Well, I hope it be not so.

Pist. Hope is a curtal dog in some affairs: Sir John affects thy wife.

Ford. Why, sir, my wife is not young.

Pist. He wooes both high and low, both rich and poor,
Both young and old, one with another, Ford;
He loves the gallimaufry: Ford, perpend.

Ford. Love my wife! · 120

Pist. With liver burning hot. Prevent, or go thou,
Like Sir Actæon he, with Ringwood at thy heels:
O, odious is the name!

Ford. What name, sir?

Pist. The horn, I say. Farewell.
Take heed, have open eye, for thieves do foot by night:
Take heed, ere summer comes or cuckoo-birds do sing.
Away, Sir Corporal Nym!
Believe it, Page; he speaks sense! [*Exit.*

Ford. [*Aside*] I will be patient; I will find out this. 131

Nym. [*To Page*] And this is true; I like not the humor of lying. He hath wronged me in some humors: I should have borne the humored letter to her; but I have a sword and it shall bite upon my necessity. He loves your wife; there's the short and the long. My name is Corporal Nym; I speak and I avouch; 'tis true: my name is Nym and Falstaff loves your wife. Adieu. I love not the humor of bread and cheese, and there's the humor of it. Adieu. 141

Page. 'The humor of it,' quoth a'! here's a fellow frights English out of his wits.

Ford. I will seek out Falstaff.

Page. I never heard such a drawling, affecting rogue.

Ford. If I do find it: well.

Page. I will not believe such a Cataian, though the priest o' the town commended him for a true man. 150

Ford. 'Twas a good sensible fellow: well.

Page. How now, Meg!

· [*Mrs. Page and Mrs. Ford come forward.*

Mrs. Page. Whither go you, George? Hark you.

Mrs. Ford. How now, sweet Frank! why art thou melancholy?

Ford. I melancholy! I am not melancholy. Get you home, go.

Mrs. Ford. Faith, thou hast some crotchets in thy head. Now, will you go, Mistress Page?

Mrs. Page. Have with you. You'll come to dinner, George. [*Aside to Mrs. Ford*] Look who comes yonder: she shall be our messenger to this paltry knight.

Mrs. Ford. [*Aside to Mrs. Page*] Trust me, I thought on her: she'll fit it.

Enter MISTRESS QUICKLY.

Mrs. Page. You are come to see my daughter Anne ?

Quick. Ay, forsooth ; and, I pray, how does good Mistress Anne ?   170

Mrs. Page. Go in with us and see : we have an hour's talk with you.

[*Exeunt Mrs. Page, Mrs. Ford, and Mrs. Quickly.*

Page. How now, Master Ford !

Ford. You heard what this knave told me, did you not ?

Page. Yes : and you heard what the other told me ?

Ford. Do you think there is truth in them ?

Page. Hang 'em, slaves ! I do not think the knight would offer it : but these that accuse him in his intent towards our wives are a yoke of his discarded men ; very rogues, now they be out of service.

Ford. Were they his men ?

Page. Marry, were they.

Ford. I like it never the better for that. Does he lie at the Garter ?

Page. Ay, marry, does he. If he should intend this voyage towards my wife, I would turn her loose to him ; and what he gets more of her than sharp words, let it lie on my head.

Ford. I do not misdoubt my wife ; but I would be loath to turn them together. A man may be too confident : I would have nothing lie on my head : I cannot be thus satisfied.

Page. Look where my ranting host of the Garter comes : there is either liquor in his pate or money in his purse when he looks so merrily.

Enter HOST.

How now, mine host !

Host. How now, bully-rook ! thou'rt a gentleman. Cavaleiro-justice, I say !   201

Enter SHALLOW.

Shal. I follow, mine host, I follow. Good even and twenty, good Master Page ! Master Page, will you go with us ? we have sport in hand.

Host. Tell him, cavaleiro-justice ; tell him, bully-rook.

Shal. Sir, there is a fray to be fought between Sir Hugh the Welsh priest and Caius the French doctor.   210

Ford. Good mine host o' the Garter, a word with you.   [*Drawing him aside.*

Host. What sayest thou, my bully-rook ?

Shal. [*To Page*] Will you go with us to behold it ? My merry host hath had the measuring of their weapons ; and, I think, hath appointed them contrary places ; for, believe me, I hear the parson is no jester. Hark, I will tell you what our sport shall be.

[*They converse apart.*

Host. Hast thou no suit against my knight, my guest-cavaleire ?   221

Ford. None, I protest : but I'll give you a pottle of burnt sack to give me recourse to him and tell him my name is Brook ; only for a jest.

Host. My hand, bully ; thou shalt have egress and regress ;—said I well ?—and thy name shall be Brook. It is a merry knight. Will you go, †An-heires ?

Shal. Have with you, mine host.

Page. I have heard the Frenchman hath good skill in his rapier.   231

Shal. Tut, sir, I could have told you more. In these times you stand on distance, your passes, stoccadoes, and I know not what : 'tis the heart, Master Page ; 'tis here, 'tis here. I have seen the time, with my long sword I would have made you four tall fellows skip like rats.   [wag ?

Host. Here, boys, here, here ! shall we

Page. Have with you. I would rather hear them scold than fight.

[*Exeunt Host, Shal., and Page.*

Ford. Though Page be a secure fool, and stands so firmly on his wife's frailty, yet I cannot put off my opinion so easily : she was in his company at Page's house ; and what they made there, I know not. Well, I will look further into't : and I have a disguise to sound Falstaff. If I find her honest, I lose not my labor ; if she be otherwise, 'tis labor well bestowed.   [*Exit.*

SCENE II. *A room in the Garter Inn.*

Enter FALSTAFF *and* PISTOL.

Fal. I will not lend thee a penny.

Pist. Why, then the world's mine oyster, Which I with sword will open.

Fal. Not a penny. I have been content, sir, you should lay my countenance to pawn : I have grated upon my good friends for three reprieves for you and your coach-fellow Nym ; or else you had looked through the grate, like a gemini of baboons. I am damned in hell for swearing to gentlemen my friends, you were good soldiers and tall fellows ; and when Mistress Bridget lost the handle of her fan, I took't upon mine honor thou hadst it not.

Pist. Didst not thou share ? hadst thou not fifteen pence ?

Fal. Reason, you rogue, reason : thinkest thou I'll endanger my soul gratis ? At a word, hang no more about me, I am no gibbet for you. Go. A short knife and a throng ! To your manor of Pickt-hatch ! Go. You'll not bear a letter for me, you rogue ! you stand upon your honor ! Why, thou unconfinable baseness, it is as much as I can do to keep the terms of my honor precise : I, I, I myself sometimes, leaving the fear of God on the left hand and hiding mine honor in my necessity, am fain to shuffle, to hedge and to lurch ; and yet you, rogue, will ensconce your rags, your cat-a-mountain looks, your red-lattice phrases, and your bold-beating oaths, under the shelter of your honor ! You will not do it, you !   30

Pist. I do relent : what would thou more of man ?

Enter ROBIN.

Rob. Sir, here's a woman would speak with you.
Fal. Let her approach.

Enter MISTRESS QUICKLY.

Quick. Give your worship good morrow.
Fal. Good morrow, good wife.
Quick. Not so, an't please your worship.
Fal. Good maid, then.
Quick. I'll be sworn,
As my mother was, the first hour I was born.
Fal. I do believe the swearer. What with me?   [word or two?
Quick. Shall I vouchsafe your worship a
Fal. Two thousand, fair woman: and I'll vouchsafe thee the hearing.
Quick. There is one Mistress Ford, sir :—I pray, come a little nearer this ways:—I myself dwell with master Doctor Caius,—
Fal. Well, on : Mistress Ford, you say,—
Quick. Your worship says very true : I pray your worship, come a little nearer this ways.
Fal. I warrant thee, nobody hears ; mine own people, mine own people.   51
Quick. Are they so ? God bless them and make them his servants.
Fal. Well, Mistress Ford ; what of her ?
Quick. Why, sir, she's a good creature. Lord, Lord ! your worship's a wanton ! Well, heaven forgive you and all of us. I pray !
Fal. Mistress Ford ; come, Mistress Ford,—
Quick. Marry, this is the short and the long of it ; you have brought her into such a canaries as 'tis wonderful. The best courtier of them all, when the court lay at Windsor, could never have brought her to such a canary. Yet there has been knights, and lords, and gentlemen, with their coaches, I warrant you, coach after coach, letter after letter, gift after gift ; smelling so sweetly, all musk, and so rushling, I warrant you, in silk and gold ; and in such alligant terms ; and in such wine and sugar of the best and the fairest, that would have won any woman's heart ; and, I warrant you, they could never get an eye-wink of her : I had myself twenty angels given me this morning ; but I defy all angels, in any such sort, as they say, but in the way of honesty : and, I warrant you, they could never get her so much as sip on a cup with the proudest of them all : and yet there has been earls, nay, which is more, pensioners ; but, I warrant you, all is one with her.   80
Fal. But what says she to me ? be brief, my good she-Mercury.
Quick. Marry, she hath received your letter, for the which she thanks you a thousand times ; and she gives you to notify that her husband will be absence from his house between ten and eleven.
Fal. Ten and eleven ?
Quick. Ay, forsooth ; and then you may come and see the picture, she says, that you wot of : Master Ford, her husband, will be from home. Alas ! the sweet woman leads an ill

life with him : he's a very jealousy man; she leads a very frampold life with him, good heart.
Fal. Ten and eleven. Woman, commend me to her ; I will not fail her.
Quick. Why, you say well. But I have another messenger to your worship. Mistress Page hath her hearty commendations to you too : and let me tell you in your ear, she's as fartuous a civil modest wife, and one, I tell you, that will not miss you morning nor evening prayer, as any is in Windsor, whoe'er be the other : and she bade me tell your worship that her husband is seldom from home ; but she hopes there will come a time. I never knew a woman so dote upon a man : surely I think you have charms, la ; yes, in truth.
Fal. Not I, I assure thee : setting the attractions of my good parts aside I have no other charms.   111
Quick. Blessing on your heart for't !
Fal. But, I pray thee, tell me this : has Ford's wife and Page's wife acquainted each other how they love me ?
Quick. That were a jest indeed ! they have not so little grace, I hope : that were a trick indeed ! but Mistress Page would desire you to send her your little page, of all loves : her husband has a marvellous infection to the little page ; and truly Master Page is an honest man. Never a wife in Windsor leads a better life than she does : do what she will, say what she will, take all, pay all, go to bed when she list, rise when she list, all is as she will : and truly she deserves it ; for if there be a kind woman in Windsor, she is one. You must send her your page ; no remedy.
Fal. Why, I will.
Quick. Nay, but do so, then : and, look you, he may come and go between you both ; and in any case have a nay-word, that you may know one another's mind, and the boy never need to understand any thing ; for 'tis not good that children should know any wickedness : old folks, you know, have discretion, as they say, and know the world.
Fal. Fare thee well : commend me to them both : there's my purse ; I am yet thy debtor. Boy, go along with this woman. [*Exeunt Mistress Quickly and Robin.*] This news distracts me !
Pist. This punk is one of Cupid's carriers : Clap on more sails ; pursue ; up with your fights :
Give fire : she is my prize, or ocean whelm them all !   [*Exit.*
Fal. Sayest thou so, old Jack? go thy ways ; I'll make more of thy old body than I have done. Will they yet look after thee? Wilt thou, after the expense of so much money, be now a gainer ? Good body, I thank thee. Let them say 'tis grossly done ; so it be fairly done, no matter.

Enter BARDOLPH.

Bard. Sir John, there's one Master Brook

below would fain speak with you, and be acquainted with you, and hath sent your worship a morning's draught of sack.

Fal. Brook is his name?

Bard. Ay, sir

Fal Call him in   [*Exit Bardolph*] Such Brooks are welcome to me, that o'erflow such liquor Ah, ha ! Mistress Ford and Mistress Page have I encompassed you ? go to , via !

Re-enter BARDOLPH, *with* FORD *disguised*

Ford   Bless you, sir !   160

Fal   And you, sir ! Would you speak with me ?

Ford I make bold to press with so little preparation upon you

Fal. You're welcome What's your will ? Give us leave, drawer   [*Exit Bardolph*

Ford. Sir, I am a gentleman that have spent much , my name is Brook

Fal Good Master Brook, I desire more acquaintance of you

Ford Good Sir John, I sue for yours . not to charge you , for I must let you understand I think myself in better plight for a lender than you are the which hath something emboldened me to this unseasoned intrusion , for they say, if money go before, all ways do lie open

Fal Money is a good soldier, sir, and will on

Ford Troth, and I have a bag of money here troubles me . if you will help to bear it, Sir John, take all, or half, for easing me of the carriage

Fal. Sir, I know not how I may deserve to be your porter   181

Ford I will tell you, sir, if you will give me the hearing

Fal Speak, good Master Brook I shall be glad to be your servant

Ford Sir, I hear you are a scholar,—I will be brief with you,—and you have been a man long known to me, though I had never so good means, as desire, to make myself acquainted with you I shall discover a thing to you, wherein I must very much lay open mine own imperfection : but, good Sir John, as you have one eye upon my follies, as you hear them unfolded, turn another into the register of your own , that I may pass with a reproof the easier, sith you yourself know how easy it is to be such an offender.

Fal Very well, sir , proceed

Ford There is a gentlewoman in this town, her husband's name is Ford   ·

Fal Well, sir   200

Ford I have long loved her, and, I protest to you, bestowed much on her , followed her with a doting observance , engrossed opportunities to meet her , fee'd every slight occasion that could but niggardly give me sight of her : not only bought many presents to give her, but have given largely to many to know what she would have given , briefly, I have pursued her as love hath pursued me ,

which hath been on the wing of all occasions. But whatsoever I have merited, either in my mind or in my means, meed, I am sure, I have received none , unless experience be a jewel that I have purchased at an infinite rate, and that hath taught me to say this

'Love like a shadow flies when substance love pursues ,

Pursuing that that flies, and flying what pursues '

Fal Have you received no promise of satisfaction at her hands ?

Ford. Never

Fal. Have you importuned her to such a purpose ?   221

Ford Never.

Fal Of what quality was your love, then ?

Ford. Like a fair house built on another man's ground , so that I have lost my edifice by mistaking the place where I erected it

Fal To what purpose have you unfolded this to me ?

Ford When I have told you that, I have told you all Some say, that though she appear honest to me, yet in other places she enlargeth her mirth so far that there is shrewd construction made of her Now, Sir John, here is the heart of my purpose you are a gentleman of excellent breeding, admirable discourse, of great admittance, authentic in your place and person, generally allowed for your many war-like, court-like, and learned preparations.

Fal O, sir !

Ford. Believe it, for you know it There is money , spend it, spend it, spend more , spend all I have , only give me so much of your time in exchange of it, as to lay an amiable siege to the honesty of this Ford's wife use your art of wooing , win her to consent to you if any man may, you may as soon as any

Fal. Would it apply well to the vehemency of your affection, that I should win what you would enjoy ? Methinks you prescribe to yourself very preposterously   250

Ford. O, understand my drift She dwells so securely on the excellency of her honor, that the folly of my soul dares not present itself she is too bright to be looked against Now, could I come to her with any detection in my hand, my desires had instance and argument to commend themselves I could drive her then from the ward of her purity, her reputation, her marriage-vow, and a thousand other her defences, which now are too too strongly embattled against me What say you to't, Sir John ?

Fal Master Brook, I will first make bold with your money , next, give me your hand and last, as I am a gentleman, you shall, if you will, enjoy Ford's wife

Ford O good sir !

Fal I say you shall

Ford Want no money, Sir John ; you shall want none.

Fal. Want no Mistress Ford, Master Brook; you shall want none. I shall be with her, I may tell you, by her own appointment; even as you came in to me, her assistant or go-between parted from me : I say I shall be with her between ten and eleven ; for at that time the jealous rascally knave her husband will be forth. Cóme you to me at night ; you shall know how I speed.

Ford. I am blest in your acquaintance. Do you know Ford, sir ?   280

Fal. Hang him, poor cuckoldly knave ! I know him not : yet I wrong him to call him poor ; they say the jealous wittolly knave hath masses of money ; for the which his wife seems to me well-favored. I will use her as the key of the cuckoldly rogue's coffer ; and there's my harvest-home.

Ford. I would you knew Ford, sir, that you might avoid him if you saw him.

Fal. Hang him, mechanical salt-butter rogue ! I will stare him out of his wits ; I will awe him with my cudgel : it shall hang like a meteor o'er the cuckold's horns. Master Brook, thou shalt know I will predominate over the peasant, and thou shalt lie with his wife. Come to me soon at night. Ford's a knave, and I will aggravate his style ; thou, Master Brook, shalt know him for knave and cuckold. Come to me soon at night.   [*Exit.*

Ford. What a damned Epicurean rascal is this ! My heart is ready to crack with impatience. Who says this is improvident jealousy ? my wife hath sent to him ; the hour is fixed ; the match is made. Would any man have thought this ? See the hell of having a false woman ! My bed shall be abused, my coffers ransacked, my reputation gnawn at ; and I shall not only receive this villanous wrong, but stand under the adoption of abominable terms, and by him that does me this wrong. Terms ! names ! Amaimon sounds well ; Lucifer, well ; Barbason, well ; yet they are devils' additions, the names of fiends : but Cuckold ! Wittol !—Cuckold ! the devil himself hath not such a name. Page is an ass, a secure ass : he will trust his wife ; he will not be jealous. I will rather trust a Fleming with my butter, Parson Hugh the Welshman with my cheese, an Irishman with my aqua-vitæ bottle, or a thief to walk my ambling gelding, than my wife with herself ; then she plots, then she ruminates, then she devises ; and what they think in their hearts they may effect, they will break their hearts but they will effect. God be praised for my jealousy ! Eleven o'clock the hour. I will prevent this, detect my wife, be revenged on Falstaff, and laugh at Page. I will about it ; better three hours too soon than a minute too late. Fie, fie, fie ! cuckold ! cuckold ! cuckold !   [*Exit.*

SCENE III. *A field near Windsor.*

Enter CAIUS *and* RUGBY

Caius. Jack Rugby

Rug. Sir ?

Caius. Vat is de clock, Jack ?

Rug. 'Tis past the hour, sir. that Sir Hugh promised to meet.

Caius. By gar, he has save his soul, dat he is no come ; he has pray his Pible well, dat he is no come : by gar, Jack Rugby, he is dead already, if he be come.

Rug. He is wise, sir ; he knew your worship would kill him, if he came.   11

Caius. By gar, de herring is no dead so as I vill kill him. Take your rapier, Jack ; I vill tell you how I vill kill him.

Rug. Alas, sir, I cannot fence.

Caius. Villany, take your rapier.

Rug. Forbear ; here's company.

Enter HOST, SHALLOW, SLENDER, *and* PAGE.

Host. Bless thee, bully doctor !

Shal. Save you, Master Doctor Caius !

Page. Now, good master doctor !   20

Slen. Give you good morrow, sir.

Caius. Vat be all you, one, two, tree, four, come for ?

Host. To see thee fight, to see thee foin, to see thee traverse ; to see thee here, to see thee there ; to see thee pass thy punto, thy stock, thy reverse, thy distance, thy montant. Is he dead, my Ethiopian ? is he dead, my Francisco ? ha, bully ! What says my Æsculapius ? my Galen ? my heart of elder ? ha ! is he dead, bully stale ? is he dead ?   31

Caius. By gar, he is de coward Jack priest of de vorld ; he is not show his face.

Host. Thou art a Castalion-King-Urinal. Hector of Greece, my boy !

Caius. I pray you, bear vitness that me have stay six or seven, two, tree hours for him, and he is no come.

Shal. He is the wiser man, master doctor : he is a curer of souls, and you a curer of bodies ; if you should fight, you go against the hair of your professions. Is it not true, Master Page ?

Page. Master Shallow, you have yourself been a great fighter, though now a man of peace.

Shal. Bodykins, Master Page, though I now be old and of the peace, if I see a sword out, my finger itches to make one. Though we are justices and doctors and churchmen, Master Page, we have some salt of our youth in us ; we are the sons of women, Master Page.   51

Page. 'Tis true, Master Shallow.

Shal. It will be found so, Master Page. Master Doctor Caius, I am come to fetch you home. I am sworn of the peace : you have showed yourself a wise physician, and Sir Hugh hath shown himself a wise and patient churchman. You must go with me, master doctor.

Host. Pardon, guest-justice. A word, Mounseur Mockwater.   60

Caius. Mock-vater ! vat is dat ?

Host. Mock-water, in our English tongue, is valor, bully.

Caius. By gar, den, I have as mush mock-
vater as de Englishman   Scurvy jack-dog
priest ! by gar, me vill cut his ears

Host. He will clapper-claw thee tightly,
bully

Caius   Clapper-de-claw ! vat is dat?

Host That is, he will make thee amends   70

Caius. By gar, me do look he shall clapper-
de-claw me , for, by gar, me vill have it

Host And I will provoke him to't, or let
him wag.

Caius Me tank you for dat

Host And, moreover, bully,—but first, master guest, and Master Page, and eke Cavaleiro
Slender, go you through the town to Frogmore.   [*Aside to them.*

Page Sir Hugh is there, is he ?

Host He is there : see what humor he is
in ; and I will bring the doctor about by the
fields   Will it do well ?

Shal. We will do it

Page, Shal , and Slen. Adieu, good master
doctor.   [*Exeunt Page, Shal., and Slen.*

Caius. By gar, me vill kill de priest , for
he speak for a jack-an-ape to Anne Page.

Host Let him die   sheathe thy impatience,
throw cold water on thy choler   go about the
fields with me through Frogmore   I will bring
thee where Mistress Anne Page is, at a farm-
house a-feasting , and thou shalt woo her
Cried I aim" said I well ?

Caius By gar me dank you for dat   by
gar, I love you , and I shall procure-a you de
good guest, de earl, de knight, de lords, de
gentlemen, my patients

Host For the which I will be thy adversary
toward Anne Page   Said I well ?

Caius. By gar, 'tis good , vell said.   100

Host Let us wag, then

Caius. Come at my heels, Jack Rugby.
                 [*Exeunt*

ACT III.

SCENE I. *A field near Frogmore.*

Enter SIR HUGH EVANS and SIMPLE.

Evans. I pray you now, good Master Slender's serving-man, and friend Simple by your
name, which way have you looked for Master
Caius, that calls himself doctor of physic ?

Sim. Marry, sir, the pittie-ward, the park-
ward, every way , old Windsor way, and
every way but the town way.

Evans I most vehemently desire you you
will also look that way.

Sim. I will, sir.   [*Exit.*   10

Evans 'Pless my soul, how full of chollors
I am, and trembling of mind ! I shall be glad
if he have deceived me.   How melancholies I
am ! I will knog his urinals about his knave's
costard when I have good opportunities for the
ork.   'Pless my soul !   [*Sings.*

To shallow rivers, to whose falls
Melodious birds sings madrigals ;
There will we make our peds of roses,
And a thousand fragrant posies   20
To shallow—

Mercy on me ! I have a great dispositions to
cry.   [*Sings.*

Melodious birds sing madrigals—
When as I sat in Pabylon—
And a thousand vagram posies.
To shallow &c.

Re-enter SIMPLE.

Sim. Yonder he is coming, this way, Sir
Hugh.

Evans. He's welcome.   [*Sings.*

To shallow rivers, to whose falls—

Heaven prosper the right ! What weapons is
he ?

Sim. No weapons, sir   There comes my
master, Master Shallow, and another gentleman, from Frogmore, over the stile, this
way.

Evans. Pray you, give me my gown , or
else keep it in your arms.

Enter PAGE, SHALLOW, and SLENDER.

Shal. How now master Parson ! Good
morrow, good Sir Hugh   Keep a gamester
from the dice, and a good student from his
book, and it is wonderful.

Slen. [*Aside*] Ah, sweet Anne Page !   40

Page. 'Save you, good Sir Hugh !

Evans. 'Pless you from his mercy sake, all
of you !

Shal. What, the sword and the word ! do
you study them both, master parson ?

Page. And youthful still ! in your doublet
and hose this raw rheumatic day !

Evans There is reasons and causes for it

Page We are come to you to do a good
office, master parson   50

Evans Fery well : what is it ?

Page Yonder is a most reverend gentleman, who, belike having received wrong by
some person, is at most odds with his own
gravity and patience that ever you saw

Shal. I have lived fourscore years and upward , I never heard a man of his place,
gravity and learning, so wide of his own respect

Evans What is he ?

Page. I think you know him , Master
Doctor Caius, the renowned French physician

Evans Got's will, and his passion of my
heart ! I had as lief you would tell me of a
mess of porridge.

Page Why ?

Evans. He has no more knowledge in Hibo-
crates and Galen,—and he is a knave besides ;
a cowardly knave as you would desires to be
acquainted withal

Page I warrant you, he's the man should
fight with him   71

Slen. [*Aside*] O sweet Anne Page !

Shal. It appears so by his weapons. Keep them asunder : here comes Doctor Caius.

Enter HOST, CAIUS, *and* RUGBY.

Page. Nay, good master parson, keep in your weapon.

Shal. So do you, good master doctor.

Host. Disarm them, and let them question: let them keep their limbs whole and hack our English. 80

Caius. I pray you, let-a me speak a word with your ear. Vherefore vill you not meet-a me ?

Evans [*Aside to Caius*] Pray you, use your patience : in good time.

Caius. By gar, you are de coward, de Jack dog, John ape.

Evans [*Aside to Caius*] Pray you, let us not be laughing-stocks to other men's humors ; I desire you in friendship, and I will one way or other make you amends. [*Aloud*] I will knog your urinals about your knave's coxcomb for missing your meetings and appointments 92

Caius. Diable ! Jack Rugby,—mine host de Jarteer,—have I not stay for him to kill him ? have I not, at de place I did appoint ?

Evans As I am a Christians soul now, look you, this is the place appointed : I'll be judgement by mine host of the Garter.

Host. Peace, I say ! Gallia and Gaul, French and Welsh, soul-curer and body-curer ! 100

Caius. Ay dat is very good ; excellent.

Host. Peace, I say ! hear mine host of the Garter. Am I politic ? am I subtle ? am I a Machiavel ? Shall I lose my doctor ? no ; he gives me the potions and the motions Shall I lose my parson, my priest, my Sir Hugh ? no ; he gives me the proverbs and the no-verbs Give me thy hand, terrestrial , so. Give me thy hand, celestial , so Boys of art, I have deceived you both , I have directed you to wrong places : your hearts are mighty, your skins are whole, and let burnt sack be the issue. Come, lay their swords to pawn. Follow me, lads of peace ; follow, follow, follow.

Shal. Trust me, a mad host Follow, gentlemen, follow.

Slen. [*Aside*] O sweet Anne Page !

[*Exeunt Shal., Slen , Page, and Host.*

Caius. Ha, do I perceive dat? have you make-a de sot of us, ha, ha ?

Evans This is well ; he has made us his vlouting-stog I desire you that we may be friends , and let us knog our brains together to be revenge on this same scall, scurvy, cogging companion, the host of the Garter.

Caius By gar, with all my heart. He promise to bring me where is Anne Page ; by gar, he deceive me too.

Evans. Well, I will smite his noddles Pray you, follow [*Exeunt.*

SCENE II. *A street.*

Enter MISTRESS PAGE *and* ROBIN.

Mrs. Page. Nay, keep your way, little gallant ; you were wont to be a follower, but now you are a leader. Whether had you rather lead mine eyes, or eye your master's heels ?

Rob. I had rather, forsooth, go before you like a man than follow him like a dwarf.

Mrs. Page. O, you are a flattering boy : now I see you'll be a courtier.

Enter FORD.

Ford. Well met, Mistress Page. Whither go you ? 10

Mrs. Page. Truly, sir, to see your wife. Is she at home ?

Ford. Ay ; and as idle as she may hang together, for want of company. I think, if your husbands were dead, you two would marry.

Mrs. Page. Be sure of that,—two other husbands.

Ford. Where had you this pretty weathercock ?

Mrs. Page. I cannot tell what the dickens his name is my husband had him of What do you call your knight's name, sirrah ? 21

Rob. Sir John Falstaff.

Ford. Sir John Falstaff !

Mrs. Page. He, he ; I can never hit on's name. There is such a league between my good man and he ! Is your wife at home indeed ?

Ford. Indeed she is.

Mrs. Page. By your leave, sir : I am sick till I see her. [*Exeunt Mrs. Page and Robin.*

Ford. Has Page any brains ? hath he any eyes ? hath he any thinking ? Sure, they sleep ; he hath no use of them. Why, this boy will carry a letter twenty mile, as easy as a cannon will shoot point-blank twelve score. He pieces out his wife's inclination ; he gives her folly motion and advantage : and now she's going to my wife, and Falstaff's boy with her. A man may hear this shower sing in the wind. And Falstaff's boy with her ! Good plots, they are laid ; and our revolted wives share damnation together. Well ; I will take him, then torture my wife, pluck the borrowed veil of modesty from the so seeming Mistress Page, divulge Page himself for a secure and wilful Actæon , and to these violent proceedings all my neighbors shall cry aim. [*Clock heard.*] The clock gives me my cue, and my assurance bids me search : there I shall find Falstaff I shall be rather praised for this than mocked ; for it is as positive as the earth is firm that Falstaff is there : I will go. 50

Enter PAGE, SHALLOW, SLENDER, HOST, SIR HUGH EVANS, CAIUS, *and* RUGBY.

Shal., Page, &c. Well met, Master Ford.

Ford Trust me, a good knot : I have good cheer at home , and I pray you all go with me.

Shal. I must excuse myself, Master Ford.

Slen. And so must I, sir : we have appointed to dine with Mistress Anne, and I would not break with her for more money than I'll speak of.

Shal. We have lingered about a match be-

tween Anne Page and my cousin Slender, and
this day we shall have our answer.   60
Slen. I hope I have your good will, father
Page.
Page. You have, Master Slender ; I stand
wholly for you : but my wife, master doctor,
is for you altogether.
Caius. Ay, be-gar ; and de maid is love-a
me : my nursh-a Quickly tell me so mush.
Host. What say you to young Master
Fenton ? he capers, he dances, he has eyes of
youth, he writes verses, he speaks holiday, he
smells April and May : he will carry't, he will
carry't ; 'tis in his buttons ; he will carry't. 71
Page. Not by my consent, I promise you.
The gentleman is of no having : he kept company with the wild prince and Poins ; he is of
too high a region ; he knows too much. No,
he shall not knit a knot in his fortunes with the
finger of my substance : if he take her, let him
take her simply ; the wealth I have waits on
my consent, and my consent goes not that way.
Ford. I beseech you heartily, some of you
go home with me to dinner : besides your
cheer, you shall have sport ; I will show you a
monster. Master doctor, you shall go ; so shall
you, Master Page ; and you, Sir Hugh.
Shal. Well, fare you well: we shall have
the freer wooing at Master Page's.
                    [*Exeunt Shal. and Slen.*
Caius. Go home, John Rugby ; I come anon.
                    [*Exit Rugby.*
Host. Farewell, my hearts : I will to my
honest knight Falstaff, and drink canary with
him.   [*Exit.*
Ford. [*Aside*] I think I shall drink in pipe
wine first with him; I'll make him dance.
Will you go, gentles ?
All. Have with you to see this monster.
                    [*Exeunt.*

SCENE III.   *A room in* FORD'S *house.*

Enter MISTRESS FORD *and* MISTRESS PAGE.

Mrs. Ford. What, John ! What, Robert !
Mrs. Page. Quickly, quickly ! is the buck-
basket—
Mrs. Ford. I warrant. What, Robin, I say !

Enter Servants *with a basket.*

Mrs. Page. Come, come, come.
Mrs. Ford. Here, set it down.
Mrs. Page. Give your men the charge ; we
must be brief.
Mrs. Ford. Marry, as I told you before, John
and Robert, be ready here hard by in the brew-
house : and when I suddenly call you, come
forth, and without any pause or staggering
take this basket on your shoulders : that done,
trudge with it in all haste, and carry it among
the whitsters in Datchet-mead, and there
empty it in the muddy ditch close by the
Thames side.
Mrs. Page. You will do it ?
Mrs. Ford. I ha' told them over and over ;
they lack no direction. Be gone, and come

when you are called.   [*Exeunt Servants.* 20
Mrs. Page. Here comes little Robin.

Enter ROBIN.

Mrs. Ford. How now, my eyas-musket !
what news with you ?
Rob. My master, Sir John, is come in at
your back-door, Mistress Ford, and requests
your company.
Mrs. Page. You little Jack-a-Lent, have you
been true to us ?
Rob. Ay, I'll be sworn. My master knows
not of your being here and hath threatened to
put me into everlasting liberty if I tell you of
it ; for he swears he'll turn me away.
Mrs. Page. Thou'rt a good boy : this secrecy
of thine shall be a tailor to thee and shall make
thee a new doublet and hose. I'll go hide me.
Mrs. Ford. Do so. Go tell thy master I am
alone. [*Exit Robin.*] Mistress Page, remember you your cue.
Mrs. Page. I warrant thee ; if I do not act
it, hiss me.   [*Exit.* 41
Mrs. Ford. Go to, then : we'll use this unwholesome humidity, this gross watery pump-
ion ; we'll teach him to know turtles from
jays.

Enter FALSTAFF.

Fal. Have I caught thee, my heavenly
jewel ? Why, now let me die, for I have lived
long enough : this is the period of my ambition : O this blessed hour !
Mrs. Ford. O sweet Sir John !
Fal. Mistress Ford, I cannot cog, I cannot
prate, Mistress Ford. Now shall I sin in my
wish : I would thy husband were dead : I'll
speak it before the best lord ; I would make
thee my lady.
Mrs. Ford. I your lady, Sir John ! alas, I
should be a pitiful lady !
Fal. Let the court of France show me such
another. I see how thine eye would emulate
the diamond : thou hast the right arched
beauty of the brow that becomes the ship-tire,
the tire-valiant, or any tire of Venetian admittance.   61
Mrs. Ford. A plain kerchief, Sir John : my
brows become nothing else ; nor that well
neither.
Fal. By the Lord, thou art a traitor to say
so : thou wouldst make an absolute courtier ;
and the firm fixture of thy foot would give an
excellent motion to thy gait in a semi-circled
farthingale. I see what thou wert, if Fortune
thy foe were not, Nature thy friend. Come,
thou canst not hide it.   71
Mrs. Ford. Believe me, there is no such
thing in me.
Fal. What made me love thee ? let that
persuade thee there's something extraordinary
in thee. Come, I cannot cog and say thou art
this and that, like a many of these lisping
hawthorn-buds, that come like women in
men's apparel, and smell like Bucklersbury in
simple time ; I cannot : but I love thee ; none
but thee : and thou deservest it.   81

Mrs. Ford. Do not betray me, sir. I fear you love Mistress Page.

Fal. Thou mightst as well say I love to walk by the Counter-gate, which is as hateful to me as the reek of a lime-kiln.

Mrs. Ford. Well, heaven knows how I love you ; and you shall one day find it.

Fal. Keep in that mind ; I'll deserve it.

Mrs. Ford. Nay, I must tell you, so you do; or else I could not be in that mind.   91

Rob. [*Within*] Mistress Ford, Mistress Ford ! here's Mistress Page at the door, sweating and blowing and looking wildly, and would needs speak with you presently.

Fal. She shall not see me : I will ensconce me behind the arras.

Mrs. Ford. Pray you, do so : she's a very tattling woman.   [*Falstaff hides himself.*

Re-enter MISTRESS PAGE *and* ROBIN.

What's the matter ? how now !   100

Mrs. Page. O Mistress Ford, what have you done? You're shamed, you're overthrown, you're undone for ever !

Mrs. Ford. What's the matter, good Mistress Page ?

Mrs. Page. O well-a-day, Mistress Ford ! having an honest man to your husband, to give him such cause of suspicion !

Mrs. Ford. What cause of suspicion ?

Mrs. Page. What cause of suspicion ! Out upon you ! how am I mistook in you !   111

Mrs. Ford. Why, alas, what's the matter ?

Mrs. Page. Your husband's coming hither, woman, with all the officers in Windsor, to search for a gentleman that he says is here now in the house by your consent, to take an ill advantage of his absence : you are undone.

Mrs. Ford. 'Tis not so, I hope.

Mrs. Page. Pray heaven it be not so, that you have such a man here ! but 'tis most certain your husband's coming, with half Windsor at his heels, to search for such a one. I come before to tell you. If you know yourself clear, why, I am glad of it ; but if you have a friend here, convey, convey him out. Be not amazed ; call all your senses to you ; defend your reputation, or bid farewell to your good life for ever.

Mrs. Ford. What shall I do ? There is a gentleman my dear friend ; and I fear not mine own shame so much as his peril : I had rather than a thousand pound he were out of the house.

Mrs. Page. For shame ! never stand 'you had rather' and 'you had rather :' your husband's here at hand ; bethink you of some conveyance : in the house you cannot hide him. O, how have you deceived me! Look, here is a basket : if he be of any reasonable stature, he may creep in here ; and throw foul linen upon him, as if it were going to bucking : or—it is whiting-time—send him by your two men to Datchet-mead.   141

Mrs. Ford. He's too big to go in there. What shall I do ?

Fal. [*Coming forward*] Let me see't, let me see't, O, let me see't ! I'll in, I'll in. Follow your friend's counsel. I'll in.

Mrs. Page. What, Sir John Falstaff ! Are these your letters, knight ?

Fal. I love thee. Help me away. Let me creep in here. I'll never—   150
     [*Gets into the basket; they cover him with foul linen.*

Mrs. Page. Help to cover your master, boy. Call your men, Mistress Ford. You dissembling knight!

Mrs. Ford. What, John ! Robert ! John !
     [*Exit Robin.*

Re-enter Servants.

Go take up these clothes here quickly. Where's the cowl-staff? look, how you drumble! Carry them to the laundress in Datchet-mead ; quickly, come.

Enter FORD, PAGE, CAIUS, *and* SIR HUGH EVANS.

Ford. Pray you, come near : if I suspect without cause, why then make sport at me ; then let me be your jest ; I deserve it. How now ! whither bear you this ?

Serv. To the laundress, forsooth.

Mrs. Ford Why, what have you to do whither they bear it ? You were best meddle with buck-washing.

Ford. Buck ! I would I could wash myself of the buck ! Buck, buck, buck ! Ay, buck ; I warrant you, buck ; and of the season too, it shall appear. [*Exeunt servants with the basket.*] Gentlemen, I have dreamed to-night ; I'll tell you my dream. Here, here, here be my keys : ascend my chambers ; search, seek, find out : I'll warrant we'll unkennel the fox. Let me stop this way first. [*Locking the door.*] So, now uncape.

Page. Good Master Ford, be contented: you wrong yourself too much.

Ford. True, Master Page. Up, gentlemen: you shall see sport anon : follow me, gentlemen.   [*Exit.* 180

Evans. This is fery fantastical humors and jealousies.

Caius. By gar, 'tis no the fashion of France; it is not jealous in France.

Page. Nay, follow him, gentlemen ; see the issue of his search.

     [*Exeunt Page, Caius, and Evans.*

Mrs. Page. Is there not a double excellency in this ?

Mrs. Ford. I know not which pleases me better, that my husband is deceived, or Sir John.

Mrs. Page. What a taking was he in when your husband asked who was in the basket ?

Mrs. Ford. I am half afraid he will have need of washing ; so throwing him into the water will do him a benefit.

Mrs. Page. Hang him, dishonest rascal ! I would all of the same strain were in the same distress.

Mrs. Ford. I think my husband hath some

special suspicion of Falstaff's being here , for
I never saw him so gross in his jealousy till
now

Mrs Page I will lay a plot to try that ,
and we will yet have more tricks with Falstaff
his dissolute disease will scarce obey this medicine

Mrs Ford Shall we send that foolish carrion, Mistress Quickly, to him, and excuse his
throwing into the water , and give him another
hope, to betray him to another punishment ?

Mrs Page. We will do it . let him be sent
for to-morrow, eight o'clock, to have amends

Re-enter Ford, Page, Caius, *and* Sir Hugh
Evans

Ford I cannot find him may be the knave
bragged of that he could not compass

Mrs Page [*Aside to Mrs Ford*] Heard you
that ?

Mrs Ford You use me well, Master Ford,
do you ?

Ford Ay, I do so

Mrs Ford Heaven make you better than
your thoughts !

Ford Amen !   220

Mrs Page You do yourself mighty wrong,
Master Ford

Ford Ay, ay , I must bear it

Evans If there be any pody in the house,
and in the chambers, and in the coffers, and in
the presses, heaven forgive my sins at the day
of judgment !

Caius By gar, nor I too there is no bodies

Page Fie, fie, Master Ford ! are you not
ashamed ? What spirit, what devil suggests
this imagination ? I would not ha' your distemper in this kind for the wealth of Windsor
Castle.

Ford 'Tis my fault, Master Page I suffer
for it

Evans You suffer for a pad conscience
your wife is as honest a 'omans as I will desires among five thousand, and five hundred
too

Caius By gar, I see''tis an honest woman

Ford Well, I promised you a dinner Come,
come, walk in the Park I pray you, pardon
me , I will hereafter make known to you why
I have done this Come, wife, come, Mistress
Page I pray you, pardon me, pray heartily,
pardon me

Page Let's go in, gentlemen , but, trust
me, we'll mock him I do invite you to-morrow morning to my house to breakfast after,
we'll a-birding together , I have a fine hawk
for the bush Shall it be so ?

Ford Any thing

Evans. If there is one, I shall make two in
the company   251

Caius If dere be one or two, I shall make-a
the turd

Ford Pray you, go, Master Page

Evans. I pray you now, remembrance to-
morrow on the lousy knave, mine host

Caius Dat is good , by gar, with all my
heart !

Evans A lousy knave, to have his gibes
and his mockeries !   [*Exeunt 260*

SCENE IV *A room in Page's house*
Enter Fenton *and* Anne Page.

Fent I see I cannot get thy father's love ,
Therefore no more turn me to him, sweet Nan

Anne Alas, how then ?

Fent Why, thou must be thyself
He doth object I am too great of birth ,
And that, my state being gall'd with my ex-
pense,
I seek to heal it only by his wealth
Besides these, other bars he lays before me,
My riots past, my wild societies ,
And tells me 'tis a thing impossible
I should love thee but as a property   10

Anne May be he tells you true

Fent No, heaven so speed me in my time
to come !
Albeit I will confess thy father's wealth
Was the first motive that I woo'd thee, Anne
Yet, wooing thee, I found thee of more value
Than stamps in gold or sums in sealed bags ,
And 'tis the very riches of thyself
That now I am at

Anne Gentle Master Fenton,
Yet seek my father's love , still seek it, sir
If opportunity and humblest suit   20
Cannot attain it, why, then,—hark you hither !
[*They converse apart*

Enter Shallow, Slender, *and* Mistress
Quickly

Shal Break their talk, Mistress Quickly
my kinsman shall speak for himself.

Slen I'll make a shaft or a bolt on't . 'slid,
'tis but venturing

Shal Be not dismayed

Slen No, she shall not dismay me . I care
not for that, but that I am afeard

Quick Hark ye , Master Slender would
speak a word with you   30

Anne I come to him [*Aside*] This is my
father's choice
O, what a world of vile ill-favor'd faults
Looks handsome in three hundred pounds
a-year !

Quick And how does good Master Fenton?
Pray you, a word with you

Shal She's coming , to her, coz. O boy,
thou hadst a father !

Slen I had a father, Mistress Anne , my
uncle can tell you good jests of him Pray
you, uncle, tell Mistress Anne the jest, how
my father stole two geese out of a pen, good
uncle   41

Shal Mistress Anne, my cousin loves you.

Slen Ay, that I do , as well as I love any
woman in Gloucestershire.

Shal He will maintain you like a gentlewoman

Slen Ay, that I will, come cut and long-
tail, under the degree of a squire.

Shal He will make you a hundred and fifty
pounds jointure   50
Anne Good Master Shallow, let him woo
for himself
Shal. Marry, I thank you for it ; I thank
you for that good comfort She calls you,
coz I'll leave you
Anne Now, Master Slender,—
Slen Now, good Mistress Anne,—
Anne. What is your will ?
Slen My will ! 'od's heartlings, that's a
pretty jest indeed ! I ne'er made my will yet,
I thank heaven , I am not such a sickly creature, I give heaven praise   62
Anne I mean, Master Slender, what would
you with me ?
Slen Truly, for mine own part, I would
little or nothing with you Your father and
my uncle hath made motions if it be my
luck, so , if not, happy man be his **dole** ! They
can tell you how things go better **than** I can
you may ask your father , here he comes   70

Enter PAGE *and* MISTRESS PAGE.

Page. Now, Master Slender . love him,
    daughter Anne.
Why, how now ! what does Master Fenton
    here ?
You wrong me, sir, thus still to haunt my
    house ·
I told you, sir, my daughter is disposed of
Fent Nay, Master Page, be not impatient
Mrs Page Good Master Fenton, come not
    to my child
Page. She is no match for you
Fent. Sir, will you hear me ?
Page   No, good Master Fenton.
Come, Master Shallow ; come, son Slender, in.
Knowing my mind, you wrong me, Master
    Fenton [*Exeunt Page, Shal., and Slen.*
Quick Speak to Mistress Page.
Fent Good Mistress Page, for that I love
    your daughter
In such a righteous fashion as I do,
Perforce, against all checks, rebukes and
    manners,
I must advance the colors of my love
And not retire let me have your good will.
Anne. Good mother, do not marry me to
    yond fool
Mrs Page I mean it not , I seek you a
    better husband
Quick That's my master, master doctor
Anne Alas, I had rather be set quick i' the
    earth   90
And bowl'd to death with turnips !
Mrs Page Come, trouble not yourself.
Good Master Fenton,
I will not be your friend nor enemy ·
My daughter will I question how she loves
    you,
And as I find her, so am I affected
Till then farewell, sir · she must needs go in ;
Her father will be angry
Fent Farewell, gentle mistress: farewell,
    Nan. [*Exeunt Mrs. Page and Anne.*

Quick. This is my doing, now : ' Nay,'
said I, ' will you cast away your child on a
fool, and a physician ? Look on Master Fenton :' this is my doing
Fent. I thank thee , and I pray thee, once
    to-night
Give my sweet Nan this ring : there's for thy
    pains
Quick Now heaven send thee good fortune ! [*Exit Fenton*] A kind heart he hath :
a woman would run through fire and water
for such a kind heart But yet I would my
master had Mistress Anne , or I would Master
Slender had her ; or, in sooth, I would Master
Fenton had her I will do what I can for them
all three , for so I have promised, and I'll be
as good as my word , but speciously for
Master Fenton Well, I must of another errand
to Sir John Falstaff from my two mistresses .
what a beast am I to slack it !   [*Exit.*

SCENE V. *A room in the Garter Inn.*

Enter FALSTAFF *and* BARDOLPH.

Fal Bardolph, I say,—
Bard Here, sir
Fal. Go fetch me a quart of sack ; put a
toast in't [*Exit Bard*] Have I lived to be
carried in a basket, like a barrow of butcher's
offal, and to be thrown in the Thames ? Well,
if I be served such another trick, I'll have my
brains ta'en out and buttered, and give them
to a dog for a new-year's gift The rogues
slighted me into the river with as little remorse
as they would have drowned a blind bitch's
puppies, fifteen i' the litter and you may know
by my size that I have a kind of alacrity in
sinking , if the bottom were as deep as hell, I
should down. I had been drowned, but that
the shore was shelvy and shallow,—a death
that I abhor , for the water swells a man , and
what a thing should I have been when I had
been swelled ! I should have been a mountain
of mummy.

Re-enter BARDOLPH *with sack.*

Bard Here's Mistress Quickly, sir, to speak
with you.   21
Fal Come, let me pour in some sack to the
Thames water ; for my belly's as cold as if I
had swallowed snowballs for pills to cool the
reins Call her in.
Bard. Come in, woman !

Enter MISTRESS QUICKLY.

Quick. By your leave , I cry you mercy .
give your worship good morrow.
Fal Take away these chalices Go brew
me a pottle of sack finely   30
Bard. With eggs, sir ?
Fal Simple of itself , I'll no pullet-sperm
in my brewage [*Exit Bardolph.*] How now !
Quick. Marry, sir, I come to your worship
from Mistress Ford
Fal. Mistress Ford ! I have had ford

enough ; I was thrown into the ford ; I have my belly full of ford.

Quick. Alas the day ! good heart, that was not her fault : she does so take on with her men ; they mistook their erection. 41

Fal. So did I mine, to build upon a foolish woman's promise.

Quick. Well, she laments, sir, for it, that it would yearn your heart to see it. Her husband goes this morning a-birding ; she desires you once more to come to her between eight and nine : I must carry her word quickly : she'll make you amends, I warrant you.

Fal. Well, I will visit her : tell her so ; and bid her think what a man is : let her consider his frailty, and then judge of my merit. 52

Quick. I will tell her.

Fal. Do so. Between nine and ten, sayest thou ?

Quick. Eight and nine, sir.

Fal. Well, be gone : I will not miss her.

Quick. Peace be with you, sir. [*Exit.*

Fal. I marvel I hear not of Master Brook ; he sent me word to stay within : I like his money well. O, here he comes. 60

Enter FORD.

Ford. Bless you, sir !

Fal. Now, master Brook, you come to know what hath passed between me and Ford's wife ?

Ford. That, indeed, Sir John, is my business.

Fal. Master Brook, I will not lie to you : I was at her house the hour she appointed me.

Ford. And sped you, sir?

Fal. Very ill-favoredly, Master Brook.

Ford. How so, sir ? Did she change her determination ? 70

Fal. No, master Brook ; but the peaking Cornuto her husband, Master Brook, dwelling in a continual 'larum of jealousy, comes me in the instant of our encounter, after we had embraced, kissed, protested, and, as it were, spoke the prologue of our comedy ; and at his heels a rabble of his companions, thither provoked and instigated by his distemper, and, forsooth, to search his house for his wife's love.

Ford. What, while you were there ? 80

Fal. While I was there.

Ford. And did he search for you, and could not find you ?

Fal. You shall hear. As good luck would have it, comes in one Mistress Page ; gives intelligence of Ford's approach ; and, in her invention and Ford's wife's distraction, they conveyed me into a buck-basket.

Ford. A buck-basket !

Fal. By the Lord, a buck-basket ! rammed me in with foul shirts and smocks, socks, foul stockings, greasy napkins ; that, Master Brook, there was the rankest compound of villanous smell that ever offended nostril.

Ford. And how long lay you there ?

Fal. Nay, you shall hear, Master Brook,

what I have suffered to bring this woman to evil for your good. Being thus crammed in the basket, a couple of Ford's knaves, his hinds, were called forth by their mistress to carry me in the name of foul clothes to Datchet-lane: they took me on their shoulders; met the jealous knave their master in the door, who asked them once or twice what they had in their basket : I quaked for fear, lest the lunatic knave would have searched it ; but fate, ordaining he should be a cuckold, held his hand. Well : on went he for a search, and away went I for foul clothes. But mark the sequel, Master Brook : I suffered the pangs of three several deaths ; first, an intolerable fright, to be detected with a jealous rotten bell-wether ; next, to be compassed, like a good bilbo, in the circumference of a peck, hilt to point, heel to head ; and then, to be stopped in, like a strong distillation, with stinking clothes that fretted in their own grease : think of that, — a man of my kidney,—think of that,—that am as subject to heat as butter ; a man of continual dissolution and thaw: it was a miracle to scape suffocation. And in the height of this bath, when I was more than half stewed in grease, like a Dutch dish, to be thrown into the Thames, and cooled, glowing hot, in that surge, like a horse-shoe ; think of that,—hissing hot,—think of that, Master Brook.

Ford. In good sadness, sir, I am sorry that for my sake you have suffered all this. My suit then is desperate ; you'll undertake her no more ?

Fal. Master Brook, I will be thrown into Etna, as I have been into Thames, ere I will leave her thus. Her husband is this morning gone a-birding : I have received from her another embassy of meeting ; 'twixt eight and nine is the hour, Master Brook.

Ford. 'Tis past eight already, sir.

Fal. Is it ? I will then address me to my appointment. Come to me at your convenient leisure, and you shall know how I speed ; and the conclusion shall be crowned with your enjoying her. Adieu. You shall have her, Master Brook ; Master Brook, you shall cuckold Ford. [*Exit.*

Ford. Hum ! ha ! Is this a vision ? Is this a dream ? do I sleep ? Master Ford, awake ! awake, Master Ford ! there's a hole made in your best coat, Master Ford. This 'tis to be married ! this 'tis to have linen and buck-baskets ! Well, I will proclaim myself what I am : I will now take the lecher ; he is at my house ; he cannot 'scape me ; 'tis impossible he should ; he cannot creep into a halfpenny purse, nor into a pepper-box: but, lest the devil that guides him should aid him, I will search impossible places. Though what I am I cannot avoid, yet to be what I would not shall not make me tame : if I have horns to make one mad, let the proverb go with me : I'll be horn-mad. [*Exit.*

ACT IV.

SCENE I. *A street.*

Enter MISTRESS PAGE, MISTRESS QUICKLY, *and* WILLIAM.

Mrs. Page. Is he at Master Ford's already, think'st thou?

* *Quick.* Sure he is by this, or will be presently: but, truly, he is very courageous mad about his throwing into the water. Mistress Ford desires you to come suddenly.

Mrs. Page. I'll be with her by and by; I'll but bring my young man here to school. Look, where his master comes; 'tis a playing-day, I see.

Enter SIR HUGH EVANS.

How now, Sir Hugh! no school to-day? 10

Evans. No; Master Slender is let the boys leave to play.

Quick. Blessing of his heart!

Mrs. Page. Sir Hugh, my husband says my son profits nothing in the world at his book. I pray you, ask him some questions in his accidence. [*head*; come.

Evans. Come hither, William; hold up your

Mrs. Page. Come on, sirrah; hold up your head; answer your master, be not afraid. 20

Evans. William, how many numbers is in nouns?

Will. Two.

Quick. Truly, I thought there had been one number more, because they say, ' 'Od's nouns.'

Evans. Peace your tattlings! What is 'fair,' William?

Will. Pulcher.

Quick. Polecats! there are fairer things than polecats, sure. 30

Evans. You are a very simplicity 'oman: I pray you, peace. What is 'lapis,' William?

Will. A stone.

Evans. And what is 'a stone,' William?

Will. A pebble.

Evans. No, it is 'lapis:' I pray you, remember in your prain.

Will. Lapis.

Evans. That is a good William. What is he, William, that does lend articles? 40

Will. Articles are borrowed of the pronoun, and be thus declined, Singulariter, nominativo, hic, hæc, hoc.

Evans. Nominativo, hig, hag, hog; pray you, mark: genitivo, hujus. Well, what is your accusative case?

Will. Accusativo, hinc.

Evans. I pray you, have your remembrance, child; accusativo, hung, hang, hog.

Quick. 'Hang-hog' is Latin for bacon, I warrant you. 51

Evans. Leave your prabbles, 'oman. What is the focative case, William?

Will. O,—vocativo, O.

Evans. Remember, William; focative is caret.

Quick. And that's a good root.

Evans. 'Oman, forbear.

Mrs. Page. Peace!

Evans. What is your genitive case plural, William? 61

Will. Genitive case!

Evans. Ay.

Will. Genitive,—horum, harum, horum.

Quick. Vengeance of Jenny's case! fie on her! never name her, child, if she be a whore.

Evans. For shame, 'oman.

Quick. You do ill to teach the child such words: he teaches him to hick and to hack, which they'll do fast enough of themselves, and to call 'horum:' fie upon you! 70

Evans. 'Oman, art thou lunatics? hast thou no understandings for thy cases and the numbers of the genders? Thou art as foolish Christian creatures as I would desires.

Mrs. Page. Prithee, hold thy peace.

Evans. Show me now, William, some declensions of your pronouns.

Will. Forsooth, I have forgot.

Evans. It is qui, quæ, quod: if you forget your 'quies,' your 'quæs,' and your 'quods,' you must be preeches. Go your ways, and play; go. [*thought he was.*

Mrs. Page. He is a better scholar than I

Evans. He is a good sprag memory. Farewell, Mistress Page.

Mrs. Page. Adieu, good Sir Hugh.

[*Exit Sir Hugh.*

Get you home, boy. Come, we stay too long.

[*Exeunt*

SCENE II. *A room in* FORD'S *house.*

Enter FALSTAFF *and* MISTRESS FORD.

Fal. Mistress Ford, your sorrow hath eaten up my sufferance. I see you are obsequious in your love, and I profess requital to a hair's breadth; not only, Mistress Ford, in the simple office of love, but in all the accoutrement, complement and ceremony of it. But are you sure of your husband now?

Mrs. Ford. He's a-birding, sweet Sir John.

Mrs. Page. [*Within*] What, ho, gossip Ford! what, ho! 10

Mrs. Ford. Step into the chamber, Sir John.

[*Exit Falstaff.*

Enter MISTRESS PAGE.

Mrs. Page. How now, sweetheart! who's at home besides yourself?

Mrs. Ford. Why, none but mine own people.

Mrs. Page. Indeed!

Mrs. Ford. No, certainly. [*Aside to her*] Speak louder.

Mrs. Page. Truly, I am so glad you have nobody here.

Mrs. Ford. Why? 20

Mrs. Page. Why, woman, your husband is in his old lunes again: he so takes on yonder with my husband; so rails against all married mankind; so curses all Eve's daughters, of what complexion soever; and so buffets himself on the forehead, crying, 'Peer out, peer out!' that any madness I ever yet beheld seemed but tameness, civility and patience, to this his distemper he is in now: I am glad the fat knight is not here.

Mrs. Ford. Why, does he talk of him? 30

Mrs. Page. Of none but him; and swears he was carried out, the last time he searched for him, in a basket; protests to my husband he is now here, and hath drawn him and the rest of their company from their sport, to make another experiment of his suspicion: but I am glad the knight is not here; now he shall see his own foolery.

Mrs. Ford. How near is he, Mistress Page?

Mrs. Page. Hard by; at street end; he will be here anon. 41

Mrs. Ford. I am undone! The knight is here.

Mrs. Page. Why then you are utterly shamed, and he's but a dead man. What a woman are you!—Away with him, away with him! better shame than murder.

Mrs. Ford. Which way should he go? how should I bestow him? Shall I put him into the basket again?

Re-enter FALSTAFF.

Fal. No, I'll come no more i' the basket. May I not go out ere he come? 51

Mrs. Page. Alas, three of Master Ford's brothers watch the door with pistols, that none shall issue out; otherwise you might slip away ere he came. But what make you here?

Fal. What shall I do? I'll creep up into the chimney.

Mrs. Ford. There they always use to discharge their birding-pieces. Creep into the kiln-hole.

Fal. Where is it? 60

Mrs. Ford. He will seek there, on my word. Neither press, coffer, chest, trunk, well, vault, but he hath an abstract for the remembrance of such places, and goes to them by his note: there is no hiding you in the house.

Fal. I'll go out then.

Mrs. Page. If you go out in your own semblance, you die, Sir John. Unless you go out disguised— 69

Mrs. Ford. How might we disguise him?

Mrs. Page. Alas the day, I know not! There is no woman's gown big enough for him; otherwise he might put on a hat, a muffler and a kerchief, and so escape.

Fal. Good hearts, devise something: any extremity rather than a mischief.

Mrs. Ford. My maid's aunt, the fat woman of Brentford, has a gown above.

Mrs. Page. On my word, it will serve him; she's as big as he is: and there's her thrummed hat and her muffler too. Run up, Sir John.

Mrs. Ford. Go, go, sweet Sir John: Mistress Page and I will look some linen for your head.

Mrs. Page. Quick, quick! we'll come dress you straight: put on the gown the while. 81

[*Exit Falstaff.*

Mrs. Ford. I would my husband would meet him in this shape: he cannot abide the old woman of Brentford; he swears she's a witch; forbade her my house and hath threatened to beat her.

Mrs. Page. Heaven guide him to thy husband's cudgel, and the devil guide his cudgel afterwards!

Mrs. Ford. But is my husband coming?

Mrs. Page. Ay, in good sadness, is he; and talks of the basket too, howsoever he hath had intelligence.

Mrs. Ford. We'll try that; for I'll appoint my men to carry the basket again, to meet him at the door with it, as they did last time.

Mrs. Page. Nay, but he'll be here presently: let's go dress him like the witch of Brentford.

Mrs. Ford. I'll first direct my men what they shall do with the basket. Go up; I'll bring linen for him straight. [*Exit.*

Mrs. Page. Hang him, dishonest varlet! we cannot misuse him enough.

We'll leave a proof, by that which we will do,
Wives may be merry, and yet honest too:
We do not act that often jest and laugh;
'Tis old, but true, Still swine eat all the draff. [*Exit.*

Re-enter MISTRESS FORD *with two Servants.*

Mrs. Ford. Go, sirs, take the basket again on your shoulders: your master is hard at door; if he bid you set it down, obey him: quickly, dispatch. [*Exit.*

First Serv. Come, come, take it up.

Sec. Serv. Pray heaven it be not full of knight again.

First Serv. I hope not; I had as lief bear so much lead.

Enter FORD, PAGE, SHALLOW, CAIUS, *and* SIR HUGH EVANS.

Ford. Ay, but if it prove true, Master Page, have you any way then to unfool me again? Set down the basket, villain! Somebody call my wife. Youth in a basket! O you panderly rascals! there's a knot, a ging, a pack, a conspiracy against me: now shall the devil be shamed. What, wife, I say! Come, come forth! Behold what honest clothes you send forth to bleaching!

Page. Why, this passes, Master Ford; you are not to go loose any longer; you must be pinioned.

Evans. Why, this is lunatics! this is mad as a mad dog! 131

Shal. Indeed, Master Ford, this is not well, indeed.

Ford. So say I too, sir.

Re-enter MISTRESS FORD.

Come hither, Mistress Ford; Mistress Ford, the honest woman, the modest wife, the virtuous creature, that hath the jealous fool to her husband! I suspect without cause mistress, do I?

34

Mrs. Ford. Heaven be my witness you do, if you suspect me in any dishonesty.   140
Ford. Well said, brazen-face! hold it out. Come forth, sirrah!
    [*Pulling clothes out of the basket.*
Page. This passes!
Mrs. Ford. Are you not ashamed? let the clothes alone.
Ford. I shall find you anon.
Evans. 'Tis unreasonable! Will you take up your wife's clothes? Come away.
Ford. Empty the basket, I say!
Mrs. Ford. Why, man, why?   150
Ford. Master Page, as I am a man, there was one conveyed out of my house yesterday in this basket; why may not he be there again? In my house I am sure he is: my intelligence is true; my jealousy is reasonable. Pluck me out all the linen.
Mrs. Ford. If you find a man there, he shall die a flea's death.
Page. Here's no man.
Shal. By my fidelity, this is not well, Master Ford; this wrongs you.   161
Evans. Master Ford, you must pray, and not follow the imaginations of your own heart: this is jealousy.
Ford. Well, he's not here I seek for.
Page. No, nor nowhere else but in your brain.
Ford. Help me search my house this one time. If I find not what I seek, show no color for my extremity; let me forever be your table-sport; let them say of me, 'As jealous as Ford, that searched a hollow walnut for his wife's leman.' Satisfy me once more; once more search with me.
Mrs. Ford. What, ho, Mistress Page! come you and the old woman down; my husband will come into the chamber.
Ford. Old woman! what old woman's that?   [Brentford.
Mrs. Ford. Why, it is my maid's aunt of
Ford. A witch, a quean, an old cozening quean! Have I not forbid her my house? She comes of errands, does she? We are simple men; we do not know what's brought to pass under the profession of fortune-telling. She works by charms, by spells, by the figure, and such daubery as this is, beyond our element: we know nothing. Come down, you witch, you hag, you; come down, I say!
Mrs. Ford. Nay, good, sweet husband! Good gentlemen, let him not strike the old woman.   190

Re-enter FALSTAFF *in woman's clothes, and* MISTRESS PAGE.

Mrs. Page. Come, Mother Prat; come, give me your hand.
Ford. I'll prat her. [*Beating him*] Out of my door, you witch, you hag, you baggage, you polecat, you ronyon! out, out! I'll conjure you, I'll fortune-tell you. [*Exit Falstaff.*
Mrs. Page. Are you not ashamed? I think you have killed the poor woman.

Mrs. Ford. Nay, he will do it. 'Tis a goodly credit for you.   200
Ford. Hang her, witch!
Evans. By yea and no, I think the 'oman is a witch indeed: I like not when a 'oman has a great peard; I spy a great peard under his muffler.
Ford. Will you follow, gentlemen? I beseech you, follow; see but the issue of my jealousy: if I cry out thus upon no trail, never trust me when I open again.
Page. Let's obey his humor a little further: come, gentlemen.   211
[*Exeunt Ford, Page, Shal., Caius, and Evans.*
Mrs. Page. Trust me, he beat him most pitifully.
Mrs. Ford. Nay, by the mass, that he did not; he beat him most unpitifully, methought.
Mrs. Page. I'll have the cudgel hallowed and hung o'er the altar; it hath done meritorious service.
Mrs. Ford. What think you? may we, with the warrant of womanhood and the witness of a good conscience, pursue him with any further revenge?   222
Mrs. Page. The spirit of wantonness is, sure, scared out of him: if the devil have him not in fee-simple, with fine and recovery, he will never, I think, in the way of waste, attempt us again.
Mrs. Ford. Shall we tell our husbands how we have served him?
Mrs. Page. Yes, by all means; if it be but to scrape the figures out of your husband's brains. If they can find in their hearts the poor unvirtuous fat knight shall be any further afflicted, we two will still be the ministers.
Mrs. Ford. I'll warrant they'll have him publicly shamed: and methinks there would be no period to the jest, should he not be publicly shamed.
Mrs. Page. Come, to the forge with it then; shape it: I would not have things cool.
    [*Exeunt.*

SCENE III. *A room in the Garter Inn.*

Enter HOST *and* BARDOLPH.

Bard. Sir, the Germans desire to have three of your horses: the duke himself will be to-morrow at court, and they are going to meet him.
Host. What duke should that be comes so secretly? I hear not of him in the court. Let me speak with the gentlemen: they speak English?
Bard. Ay, sir; I'll call them to you.
Host. They shall have my horses; but I'll make them pay; I'll sauce them: they have had my house a week at command; I have turned away my other guests: they must come off; I'll sauce them. Come.   [*Exeunt.*

SCENE IV. *A room in* FORD'S *house.*

Enter PAGE, FORD, MISTRESS PAGE, MISTRESS FORD, *and* SIR HUGH EVANS.

Evans. 'Tis one of the best discretions of a
'oman as ever I did look upon.

Page. And did he send you both these letters at an instant?

Mrs Page. Within a quarter of an hour.

Ford. Pardon me, wife. Henceforth do
what thou wilt,
I rather will suspect the sun with cold
Than thee with wantonness. now doth thy
honor stand,
In him that was of late an heretic,
As firm as faith

Page. 'Tis well, 'tis well, no more 10
Be not as extreme in submission
As in offence
But let our plot go forward let our wives
Yet once again, to make us public sport,
Appoint a meeting with this old fat fellow,
Where we may take him and disgrace him for
it.

Ford. There is no better way than that they
spoke of

Page. How? to send him word they'll meet
him in the park at midnight? Fie, fie! he'll
never come.

Evans. You say he has been thrown in the
rivers and has been grievously beaten as an
old 'oman methinks there should be terrors
in him that he should not come, methinks his
flesh is punished, he shall have no desires

Page. So think I too

Mrs Ford. Devise but how you'll use him
when he comes.
And let us two devise to bring him thither

Mrs Page. There is an old tale goes that
Herne the hunter,
Sometime a keeper here in Windsor forest,
Doth all the winter-time, at still midnight, 30
Walk round about an oak, with great ragg'd
horns,
And there he blasts the tree and takes the
cattle [a chain
And makes milch-kine yield blood and shakes
In a most hideous and dreadful manner
You have heard of such a spirit, and well you
know
The superstitious idle-headed eld
Received and did deliver to our age
This tale of Herne the hunter for a truth

Page. Why, yet there want not many that
do fear
In deep of night to walk by this Herne's oak
But what of this? 41

Mrs Ford. Marry, this is our device,
That Falstaff at that oak shall meet with us

Page. Well, let it not be doubted but he'll
come.
And in this shape when you have brought him
thither,
What shall be done with him? what is your
plot?

Mrs. Page. That likewise have we thought
upon, and thus:
Nan Page my daughter and my little son
And three or four more of their growth we'll
dress

Like urchins, ouphes and fairies, green and
white, 49
With rounds of waxen tapers on their heads,
And rattles in their hands upon a sudden,
As Falstaff, she and I, are newly met,
Let them from forth a sawpit rush at once
With some diffused song upon their sight,
We two in great amazedness will fly
Then let them all encircle him about
And, fairy-like, to-pinch the unclean knight
And ask him why, that hour of fairy revel,
In their so sacred paths he dares to tread
In shape profane

Mrs Ford. And till he tell the truth, 60
Let the supposed fairies pinch him sound
And burn him with their tapers

Mrs Page. The truth being known,
We'll all present ourselves, dis-horn the spirit,
And mock him home to Windsor

Ford. The children must
Be practiced well to this, or they'll ne'er do't

Evans. I will teach the children their behaviors, and I will be like a jack-an-apes also,
to burn the knight with my taber.

Ford. That will be excellent I'll go and
buy them vizards 70

Mrs Page. My Nan shall be the queen of
all the fairies,
Finely attired in a robe of white

Page. That silk will I go buy [*Aside*] And
in that time
Shall Master Slender steal my Nan away
And marry her at Eton Go send to Falstaff
straight.

Ford. Nay, I'll to him again in name of
Brook
He'll tell me all his purpose sure, he'll come

Mrs Page. Fear not you that Go get us
properties
And tricking for our fairies

Evans. Let us about it it is admirable
pleasures and fery honest knaveries 81
      [*Exeunt Page, Ford, and Evans*

Mrs Page. Go, Mistress Ford,
Send quickly to Sir John, to know his mind
      [*Exit Mrs Ford*
I'll to the doctor he hath my good will,
And none but he, to marry with Nan Page
That Slender, though well landed, is an idiot,
And he my husband best of all affects
The doctor is well money'd, and his friends
Potent at court. he, none but he, shall have
her,
Though twenty thousand worthier come to
crave her. [*Exit* 90

    Scene V. *A room in the Garter Inn*

    Enter Host *and* Simple.

Host What wouldst thou have, boor? what,
thick-skin? speak, breathe, discuss, brief,
short, quick, snap

Sim Marry, sir, I come to speak with Sir
John Falstaff from Master Slender

Host There's his chamber, his house, his
castle, his standing-bed and truckle-bed, 'tis

painted about with the story of the Prodigal,
fresh and new. Go knock and call; he'll speak
like an Anthropophaginian unto thee: knock,
I say.　　　　　　　　　　　　　　　　　11
　Sim.　There's an old woman, a fat woman,
gone up into his chamber: I'll be so bold as
stay, sir, till she come down ; I come to speak
with her, indeed.
　Host.　Ha ! a fat woman ! the knight may
be robbed : I'll call.　Bully knight ! bully Sir
John ! speak from thy lungs military: art thou
there ? it is thine host, thine Ephesian, calls.
　Fal.　[*Above*] How now, mine host !　　　20
　Host.　Here's a Bohemian-Tartar tarries the
coming down of thy fat woman.　Let her descend, bully, let her descend ; my chambers
are honorable : fie ! privacy ? fie !

Enter FALSTAFF.

　Fal.　There was, mine host, an old fat woman
even now with me ; but she's gone.
　Sim.　Pray you, sir, was't not the wise
woman of Brentford ?
　Fal.　Ay, marry, was it, mussel-shell: what
would you with her ?　　　　　　　　　　30
　Sim.　My master, sir, Master Slender, sent
to her, seeing her go through the streets, to
know, sir, whether one Nym, sir, that beguiled
him of a chain, had the chain or no.
　Fal.　I spake with the old woman about it.
　Sim.　And what says she, I pray, sir ?
　Fal.　Marry, she says that the very same
man that beguiled Master Slender of his chain
cozened him of it.
　Sim.　I would I could have spoken with the
woman herself ; I had other things to have
spoken with her too from him.　　　　　42
　Fal.　What are they ? let us know.
　Host.　Ay, come ; quick.
　Sim.　I may not conceal them, sir.
　Host.　Conceal them, or thou diest.
　Sim.　Why, sir, they were nothing but about
Mistress Anne Page ; to know if it were my
master's fortune to have her or no.
　Fal.　'Tis, 'tis his fortune.　　　　　　50
　Sim.　What, sir ?
　Fal.　To have her, or no.　Go ; say the
woman told me so.
　Sim.　May I be bold to say so, sir ?
　Fal.　Ay, sir ; like who more bold.
　Sim.　I thank your worship : I shall make
my master glad with these tidings.　　[*Exit.*
　Host.　Thou art clerkly, thou art clerkly, Sir
John.　Was there a wise woman with thee ?
　Fal.　Ay, that there was, mine host ; one
that hath taught me more wit than ever I
learned before in my life ; and I paid nothing
for it neither, but was paid for my learning.

Enter BARDOLPH.

　Bard.　Out, alas, sir! cozenage, mere cozenage !
　Host.　Where be my horses ? speak well of
them, varletto.
　Bard.　Run away with the cozeners ; for so
soon as I came beyond Eton, they threw me

off from behind one of them, in a slough of
mire ; and set spurs and away, like three German devils, three Doctor Faustuses.　　　71
　Host.　They are gone but to meet the duke,
villain : do not say they be fled ; Germans are
honest men.

Enter SIR HUGH EVANS.

　Evans.　Where is mine host ?
　Host.　What is the matter, sir ?
　Evans.　Have a care of your entertainments:
there is a friend of mine come to town, tells me
there is three cozen-germans that has cozened
all the hosts of Readins, of Maidenhead, of
Colebrook, of horses and money.　I tell you
for good will, look you : you are wise and full
of gibes and vlouting-stocks, and 'tis not convenient you should be cozened.　Fare you
well.　　　　　　　　　　　　　　　[*Exit.*

Enter DOCTOR CAIUS.

　Caius.　Vere is mine host de Jarteer ?
　Host.　Here, master doctor, in perplexity
and doubtful dilemma.
　Caius.　I cannot tell vat is dat: but it is
tell-a me dat you make grand preparation for
a duke de Jamany : by my trot, dere is no
duke dat the court is know to come.　I tell you
for good vill : adieu.　　　　　　　[*Exit.*　91
　Host.　Hue and cry, villain, go ! Assist me,
knight.　I am undone ! Fly, run, hue and cry,
villain ! I am undone !
　　　　　　　　　　　　　[*Exeunt Host and Bard.*
　Fal.　I would all the world might be cozened ; for I have been cozened and beaten too.
If it should come to the ear of the court, how
I have been transformed and how my transformation hath been washed and cudgelled,
they would melt me out of my fat drop by drop
and liquor fishermen s boots with me ; I warrant they would whip me with their fine wits
till I were as crest-fallen as a dried pear.　I
never prospered since I forswore myself at
primero.　Well, if my wind were but long
enough to say my prayers, I would repent.

Enter MISTRESS QUICKLY.

Now, whence come you ?
　Quick.　From the two parties, forsooth.
　Fal.　The devil take one party and his dam
the other ! and so they shall be both bestowed.
I have suffered more for their sakes, more
than the villanous inconstancy of man's disposition is able to bear.
　Quick.　And have not they suffered ? Yes,
I warrant ; speciously one of them ; Mistress
Ford, good heart, is beaten black and blue,
that you cannot see a white spot about her.
　Fal.　What tellest thou me of black and
blue ? I was beaten myself into all the colors
of the rainbow ; and I was like to be apprehended for the witch of Brentford: but that
my admirable dexterity of wit, my counterfeiting the action of an old woman, delivered
me, the knave constable had set me i' the
stocks, i' the common stocks, for a witch.
　Quick.　Sir, let me speak with you in your

chamber : you shall hear how things go ; and,
I warrant, to your content. Here is a letter
will say somewhat. Good hearts, what ado
here is to bring you together ! Sure, one of
you does not serve heaven well, that you are
so crossed.   130
   Fal. Come up into my chamber. [*Exeunt.*

SCENE VI. *Another room in the Garter Inn.*

Enter FENTON *and* HOST.

   Host. Master Fenton, talk not to me ; my
mind is heavy : I will give over all.
   Fent. Yet hear me speak. Assist me in my
         purpose,
And, as I am a gentleman, I'll give thee
A hundred pound in gold more than your loss.
   Host. I will hear you, Master Fenton ; and
I will at the least keep your counsel.   [you
   Fent. From time to time I have acquainted
With the dear love I bear to fair Anne Page ;
Who mutually hath answer'd my affection,   10
So far forth as herself might be her chooser,
Even to my wish : I have a letter from her
Of such contents as you will wonder at ;
The mirth whereof so larded with my matter,
That neither singly can be manifested,
Without the show of both ; fat Falstaff
Hath a great scene : the image of the jest
I'll show you here at large. Hark, good mine
      host.
To-night at Herne's oak, just 'twixt twelve
      and one,   19
Must my sweet Nan present the Fairy Queen;
The purpose why, is here : in which disguise,
While other jests are something rank on foot,
Her father hath commanded her to slip
Away with Slender and with him at Eton
Immediately to marry : she hath consented :
Now, sir,
Her mother, ever strong against that match
And firm for Doctor Caius, hath appointed
That he shall likewise shuffle her away,   29
While other sports are tasking of their minds,
And at the deanery, where a priest attends,
Straight marry her : to this her mother's plot
She seemingly obedient likewise hath
Made promise to the doctor. Now, thus it
      rests :
Her father means she shall be all in white,
And in that habit, when Slender sees his time
To take her by the hand and bid her go,
She shall go with him : her mother hath in-
      tended,
The better to denote her to the doctor,
For they must all be mask'd and vizarded, 40
That quaint in green she shall be loose enrobed,
With ribands pendent, flaring 'bout her head;
And when the doctor spies his vantage ripe,
To pinch her by the hand, and, on that token,
The maid hath given consent to go with him.
   Host. Which means she to deceive, father
      or mother ?
   Fent. Both, my good host, to go along with
      me :

And here it rests, that you'll procure the vicar
To stay for me at church 'twixt twelve and one,
And, in the lawful name of marrying,   50
To give our hearts united ceremony.
   Host. Well, husband your device ; I'll to
      the vicar :
Bring you the maid, you shall not lack a priest.
   Fent. So shall I evermore be bound to thee;
Besides, I'll make a present recompense.
                                        [*Exeunt.*

ACT V.

SCENE I. *A room in the Garter Inn.*

Enter FALSTAFF *and* MISTRESS QUICKLY.

   Fal. Prithee, no more prattling ; go. I'll
hold. This is the third time ; I hope good luck
lies in odd numbers. Away ! go. They say
there is divinity in odd numbers, either in
nativity, chance, or death. Away !
   Quick. I'll provide you a chain ; and I'll do
what I can to get you a pair of horns.
   Fal. Away, I say ; time wears : hold up
your head, and mince.   [*Exit Mrs. Quickly.*

Enter FORD.

How now, Master Brook ! Master Brook, the
matter will be known to-night, or never. Be
you in the Park about midnight, at Herne's
oak, and you shall see wonders.
   Ford. Went you not to her yesterday, sir,
as you told me you had appointed ?
   Fal. I went to her, Master Brook, as you
see, like a poor old man : but I came from
her, Master Brook, like a poor old woman.
That same knave Ford, her husband, hath the
finest mad devil of jealousy in him, Master
Brook, that ever governed frenzy. I will tell
you : he beat me grievously, in the shape of a
woman ; for in the shape of man, Master
Brook, I fear not Goliath with a weaver's
beam ; because I know also life is a shuttle.
I am in haste ; go along with me : I'll tell you
all, Master Brook. Since I plucked geese,
played truant and whipped top, I knew not
what 'twas to be beaten till lately. Follow
me : I'll tell you strange things of this knave
Ford, on whom to-night I will be revenged,
and I will deliver his wife into your hand.
Follow. Strange things in hand, Master
Brook ! Follow.   [*Exeunt.*

SCENE II. *Windsor Park.*

Enter PAGE, SHALLOW, *and* SLENDER.

   Page. Come, come ; we'll couch i' the
castle-ditch till we see the light of our fairies.
Remember, son Slender, my daughter.
   Slen. Ay, forsooth ; I have spoke with her
and we have a nay-word how to know one
another : I come to her in white, and cry
'mum ;' she cries 'budget ;' and by that we
know one another.

Shal. That's good too : but what needs either your 'mum' or her 'budget ?' the white will decipher her well enough. It hath struck ten o'clock.

Page. The night is dark ; light and spirits will become it well. Heaven prosper our sport ! No man means evil but the devil, and we shall know him by his horns. Let's away ; follow me.   [*Exeunt.*

SCENE III. *A street leading to the Park.*

Enter MISTRESS PAGE, MISTRESS FORD, *and* DOCTOR CAIUS.

Mrs. Page. Master doctor, my daughter is in green : when you see your time, take her by the hand, away with her to the deanery, and dispatch it quickly. Go before into the Park : we two must go together.

Caius. I know vat I have to do. Adieu.

Mrs. Page. Fare you well, sir. [*Exit Caius.*] My husband will not rejoice so much at the abuse of Falstaff as he will chafe at the doctor's marrying my daughter : but 'tis no matter ; better a little chiding than a great deal of heart-break.   11

Mrs. Ford. Where is Nan now and her troop of fairies, and the Welsh devil Hugh ?

Mrs. Page. They are all couched in a pit hard by Herne's oak, with obscured lights ; which, at the very instant of Falstaff's and our meeting, they will at once display to the night.

Mrs. Ford. That cannot choose but amaze him.

Mrs. Page. If he be not amazed, he will be mocked ; if he be amazed, he will every way be mocked.   21

Mrs. Ford. We'll betray him finely.

Mrs. Page. Against such lewdsters and their lechery Those that betray them do no treachery.

Mrs. Ford. The hour draws on. To the oak, to the oak !   [*Exeunt.*

SCENE IV. *Windsor Park.*

Enter SIR HUGH EVANS, *disguised, with others as Fairies.*

Evans. Trib, trib, fairies ; come ; and remember your parts : be pold, I pray you ; follow me into the pit ; and when I give the watch-'ords, do as I pid you : come, come ; trib, trib   [*Exeunt.*

SCENE V. *Another part of the Park.*

Enter FALSTAFF *disguised as Herne.*

Fal. The Windsor bell hath struck twelve ; the minute draws on. Now, the hot-blooded gods assist me ! Remember, Jove, thou wast a bull for thy Europa ; love set on thy horns. O powerful love ! that, in some respects, makes a beast a man, in some other, a man a beast. You were also, Jupiter, a swan for the love of Leda. O omnipotent Love ! how near the god drew to the complexion of a goose ! A fault done first in the form of a beast. O Jove, a beastly fault ! And then another fault in the semblance of a fowl ; think on't, Jove ; a foul fault ! When gods have hot backs, what shall poor men do ? For me, I am here a Windsor stag ; and the fattest, I think, i' the forest. Send me a cool rut-time, Jove, or who can blame me to piss my tallow ? Who comes here ? my doe ?

Enter MISTRESS FORD *and* MISTRESS PAGE.

Mrs. Ford. Sir John ! art thou there, my deer ? my male deer ?

Fal. My doe with the black scut ! Let the sky rain potatoes ; let it thunder to the tune of Green Sleeves, hail kissing-comfits and snow eringoes ; let there come a tempest of provocation, I will shelter me here.

Mrs. Ford. Mistress Page is come with me, sweetheart.

Fal. Divide me like a bribe buck, each a haunch : I will keep my sides to myself, my shoulders for the fellow of this walk, and my horns I bequeath your husbands. Am I a woodman, ha ? Speak I like Herne the hunter? Why, now is Cupid a child of conscience ; he makes restitution. As I am a true spirit, welcome !   [*Noise within.*

Mrs. Page. Alas, what noise ?

Mrs. Ford. Heaven forgive our sins !

Fal. What should this be ?

Mrs. Ford. }   Away, away ! [*They run off.*
Mrs. Page. }

Fal. I think the devil will not have me damned, lest the oil that's in me should set hell on fire ; he would never else cross me thus.   40

Enter SIR HUGH EVANS, *disguised as before ;* PISTOL, *as Hobgoblin ;* MISTRESS QUICKLY, ANNE PAGE, *and others, as Fairies, with tapers.*

Quick. Fairies, black, grey, green, and white,
You moonshine revellers and shades of night,
You orphan heirs of fixed destiny,
Attend your office and your quality.
Crier Hobgoblin, make the fairy oyes.

Pist. Elves, list your names ; silence, you airy toys.
Cricket, to Windsor chimneys shalt thou leap:
Where fires thou find'st unraked and hearths unswept,
There pinch the maids as blue as bilberry :
Our radiant queen hates sluts and sluttery. 50

Fal. They are fairies ; he that speaks to them shall die :
I'll wink and couch : no man their works must eye.   [*Lies down upon his face.*

Evans. Where's Bede ? Go you, and where you find a maid
That, ere she sleep, has thrice her prayers said,
Raise up the organs of her fantasy ;

Sleep she as sound as careless infancy :
But those as sleep and think not on their sins,
Pinch them, the arms, legs, backs, shoulders,
  sides and shins
  Quick About, about ;
Search Windsor Castle, elves, within and out·
Strew good luck, ouphes, on every sacred
  room .   61
That it may stand till the perpetual doom,
In state as wholesome as in state 'tis fit,
Worthy the owner, and the owner it
The several chairs of order look you scour
With juice of balm and every precious flower.
Each fair instalment, coat, and several crest,
With loyal blazon, evermore be blest !
And nightly, meadow-fairies, look you sing,
Like to the Garter's compass, in a ring :   70
The expressure that it bears, green let it be,
More fertile-fresh than all the field to see ;
And ' Honi soit qui mal y pense' write
In emerald tufts, flowers purple, blue and
  white ;
Let sapphire, pearl and rich embroidery,
Buckled below fair knighthood's bending
  knee :
Fairies use flowers for their charactery.
Away , disperse but till 'tis one o'clock,
Our dance of custom round about the oak
Of Herne the hunter, let us not forget   80
  Evans Pray you, lock hand in hand ; your-
  selves in order set ,
And twenty glow-worms shall our lanterns be,
To guide our measure round about the tree
But, stay ; I smell a man of middle-earth
' *Fal* Heavens defend me from that Welsh
fairy, lest he transform me to a piece of
cheese '
  Pist Vile worm, thou wast o'erlook'd even
  in thy birth
  Quick. With trial-fire touch me his finger-
  end
If he be chaste, the flame will back descend
And turn him to no pain ; but if he start,   90
It is the flesh of a corrupted heart.
  Pist. A trial, come
  Evans.   Come, will this wood take fire ?
    [*They burn him with their tapers.*
  Fal. Oh, Oh, Oh '
  Quick. Corrupt, corrupt, and tainted in
  desire !
About him, fairies ; sing a scornful rhyme ,
And, as you trip, still pinch him to your time.

SONG.

Fie on sinful fantasy !
Fie on lust and luxury !
Lust is but a bloody fire,
Kindled with unchaste desire,   100
Fed in heart, whose flames aspire
As thoughts do blow them, higher and
  higher.
Pinch him, fairies, mutually ;
Pinch him for his villany ;
·Pinch him, and burn him, and turn him about,
Till candles and starlight and moonshine be
  out.

During this song they pinch FALSTAFF. DOC-
TOR CAIUS *comes one way, and steals away
a boy in green;* SLENDER *another way,
and takes off a boy in white ; and* FENTON
comes and steals away Mrs. ANNE PAGE
*A noise of hunting is heard within. All
the Fairies run away* FALSTAFF *pulls
off his buck's head, and rises.*

Enter PAGE, FORD, MISTRESS PAGE, *and*
MISTRESS FORD.

Page Nay, do not fly ; I think we have
watch'd you now .
Will none but Herne the hunter serve your
  turn ?
Mrs Page I pray you, come, hold up the
jest no higher
Now, good Sir John, how like you Windsor
  wives ?   [yokes
†See you these, husband ? do not these fair
Become the forest better than the town ?
Ford. Now, sir, who's a cuckold now ?
Master Brook, Falstaff's a knave, a cuckoldly
knave , here are his horns, Master Brook and,
Master Brook, he hath enjoyed nothing of
Ford's but his buck-basket, his cudgel, and
twenty pounds of money, which must be paid
to Master Brook , his horses are arrested for
it, Master Brook
Mrs. Ford Sir John, we have had ill luck ;
we could never meet I will never take you
for my love again , but I will always count
you my deer
Fal I do begin to perceive that I am made
an ass.
Ford Ay, and an ox too : both the proofs
are extant
Fal. And these are not fairies ? I was three
or four times in the thought they were not
fairies and yet the guiltiness of my mind, the
sudden surprise of my powers, drove the
grossness of the foppery into a received belief,
in despite of the teeth of all rhyme and reason,
that they were fairies See now how wit may
be made a Jack-a-Lent, when 'tis upon ill employment '
Evans Sir John Falstaff, serve Got, and
leave your desires, and fairies will not pinse
you
Ford. Well said, fairy Hugh
Evans. And leave your jealousies too, I
pray you.   140
Ford. I will never mistrust my wife again,
till thou art able to woo her in good English
Fal Have I laid my brain in the sun and
dried it, that it wants matter to prevent so
gross o'erreaching as this ? Am I ridden with
a Welsh goat too ? shall I have a coxcomb of
frize ? 'Tis time I were choked with a piece
of toasted cheese.
Evans Seese is not good to give putter ;
your belly is all putter.
Fal. 'Seese ' and ' putter' ! have I lived
to stand at the taunt of one that makes fritters
of English ? This is enough to be the decay
of lust and late-walking through the realm.

Mrs Page. Why, Sir John, do you think, though we would have thrust virtue out of our hearts by the head and shoulders and have given ourselves without scruple to hell, that ever the devil could have made you our delight ?

Ford. What, a hodge-pudding ? a bag of flax ?

Mrs Page A puffed man ?   160

Page. Old, cold, withered and of intolerable entrails ?

Ford And one that is as slanderous as Satan ?

Page. And as poor as Job ?

Ford And as wicked as his wife ?

Evans. And given to fornications, and to taverns and sack and wine and metheglins, and to drinkings and swearings and starings, pribbles and prabbles ?

Fal. Well, I am your theme you have the start of me ; I am dejected , I am not able to answer the Welsh flannel ; ignorance itself is a plummet o'er me : use me as you will.

Ford. Marry, sir, we'll bring you to Windsor, to one Master Brook, that you have cozened of money, to whom you should have been a pander : over and above that you have suffered, I think to repay that money will be a biting affliction

Page Yet be cheerful, knight : thou shalt eat a posset to-night at my house ; where I will desire thee to laugh at my wife, that now laughs at thee : tell her Master Slender hath married her daughter

Mrs. Page. [*Aside*] Doctors doubt that: if Anne Page be my daughter, she is, by this, Doctor Caius' wife

Enter SLENDER

Slen. Whoa, ho ! ho, father Page !

Page. Son, how now ! how now, son ! have you dispatched ?

Slen Dispatched ! I'll make the best in Gloucestershire know on't ; would I were hanged, la, else.

Page. Of what, son ?

Slen I came yonder at Eton to marry Mistress Anne Page, and she 's a great lubberly boy. If it had not been i' the church, I would have swinged him, or he should have swinged me. If I did not think it had been Anne Page, would I might never stir '—and 'tis a postmaster's boy

Page Upon my life, then, you took the wrong.   201

Slen. What need you tell me that ? I think so, when I took a boy for a girl. If I had been married to him, for all he was in woman's apparel, I would not have had him.

Page Why, this is your own folly. Did not I tell you how you should know my daughter by her garments?

Slen. I went to her in white, and cried ' mum,' and she cried ' budget,' as Anne and I had appointed ; and yet it was not Anne, but a postmaster's boy.

Mrs. Page Good George, be not angry: I knew of your purpose ; turned my daughter into green ; and, indeed, she is now with the doctor at the deanery, and there married.

Enter CAIUS

Caius Vere is Mistress Page ? By gar, I am cozened I ha' married un garçon, a boy; un paysan, by gar, a boy ; it is not Anne Page: by gar, I am cozened.   220

Mrs. Page Why, did you take her in green ?

Caius. Ay, by gar, and 'tis a boy: by gar, I'll raise all Windsor.   [*Exit.*

Ford. This is strange Who hath got the right Anne ?

Page. My heart misgives me: here comes Master Fenton.

Enter FENTON *and* ANNE PAGE.

How now, Master Fenton !

Anne Pardon, good father ! good my mother, pardon !

Page Now, mistress, how chance you went not with Master Slender?   231

Mrs Page. Why went you not with master doctor, maid ?

Fent. You do amaze her . hear the truth of it

You would have married her most shamefully,

Where there was no proportion held in love

The truth is, she and I, long since contracted,

Are now so sure that nothing can dissolve us.

The offence is holy that she hath committed ';

And this deceit loses the name of craft,

Of disobedience, or unduteous title,   240

Since therein she doth evitate and shun

A thousand irreligious cursed hours,

Which forced marriage would have brought upon her.

Ford. Stand not amazed ; here is no remedy :

In love the heavens themselves do guide the state ,

Money buys lands, and wives are sold by fate.

Fal. I am glad, though you have ta'en a special stand to strike at me, that your arrow hath glanced

Page. Well, what remedy ? Fenton, heaven give thee joy !   250

What cannot be eschew'd must be embraced.

Fal. When night-dogs run, all sorts of deer are chased.

Mrs. Page Well, I will muse no further. Master Fenton,

Heaven give you many, many merry days !

Good husband, let us every one go home,

And laugh this sport o'er by a country fire ;

Sir John and all.

Ford.   Let it be so. Sir John,

To Master Brook you yet shall hold your word;

For he to-night shall lie with Mistress Ford. ·

[*Exeunt.*

MUCH ADO ABOUT NOTHING.

INTRODUCTION.

Much Ado About Nothing was entered on the Stationer's register, August 23, 1600, and a well-printed quarto edition appeared in the same year. The play is not mentioned by Meres, who wrote in 1598, and it is probable therefore that it was written at some time in the interval between 1598 and 1600. For the graver portion of the play—the Claudio and Hero story—Shakespeare had an original, perhaps Belleforest's translation in his *Histoires Tragiques* of Bandello's 22nd Novella. The story of Ariodante and Genevra in Ariosto's *Orlando Furioso* (canto v.) is substantially the same This episode had been translated twice into English before Harrington's complete translation of the *Orlando Furioso* appeared in 1591, and it had formed the subject of a play acted before the Queen in 1582-83, the story was also told, in a somewhat altered form, by Spenser (*Faerie Queen*, II, 4) No original has been found for the merrier portion of the play, and Benedick and Beatrice were probably creations of Shakespeare *Much Ado About Nothing* was popular on the stage in Shakespeare's day, and has sustained its reputation. Its variety, ranging from almost burlesque to almost tragedy, and from the euphemistic speech of courtiers to the blundering verbosity of clowns, has contributed to the success of the play The chief persons, Hero and Claudio, Beatrice and Benedick, are contrasted pairs Hero's character is kept subdued and quiet in tone, to throw out the force and color of the character of Beatrice, she is gentle, affectionate, tender, and if playful, playful in a gentle way. If our interest in Hero were made very strong, the pain of her unmerited shame and suffering would be too keen. And Claudio is far from being a lover like Romeo, his wooing is done by proxy, and he does not sink under the anguish of Hero's disgrace and supposed death. Don John, the villain of the piece, is a melancholy egoist, who looks sourly on all the world, and has a special grudge against his brother's young favorite Claudio The chief force of Shakespeare in the play comes out in the characters of Benedick and Beatrice. They have not a touch of misanthropy, nor of sentimentality, but are thoroughly healthy and hearty human creatures, at first a little too much self-pleased, but framed by-and-by to be entirely pleased with one another The thoughts of each from the first are pre-occupied with the other, but neither will put self-esteem to the hazard of a rebuke of making the first advances in love, it only needs, however, that this danger should be removed for the pair to admit the fact that nature has made them over against one another—as their significant names suggest—for man and wife Dogberry and Verges, as well as Beatrice and Benedick, are creations of Shakespeare The blundering watchmen of the time are a source of fun with several Elizabethan playwrights, but Dogberry and goodman Verges are the princes of blundering and incapable officials It is a charming incongruity to find, while Leonato rages and Benedick offers his challenge, that the solemn ass Dogberry is the one to unravel the tangled threads of their fate.

DRAMATIS PERSONÆ.

DON PEDRO, prince of Arragon.
DON JOHN, his bastard brother.
CLAUDIO, a young lord of Florence
BENEDICK, a young lord of Padua.
LEONATO, governor of Messina
ANTONIO, his brother.
BALTHASAR, attendant on Don Pedro.
CONRADE, } followers of Don John.
BORACHIO, }
FRIAR FRANCIS
DOGBERRY, a constable.

VERGES, a headborough.
A Sexton
A Boy

HERO, daughter to Leonato.
BEATRICE, niece to Leonato.
MARGARET } gentlewoman attending o
URSULA, } Hero

Messengers, Watch, Attendants, &c.

SCENE : *Messina*.

(537)

ACT I.

SCENE I. *Before* LEONATO'S *house.*

Enter LEONATO, HERO, *and* BEATRICE, *with a Messenger.*

Leon. I learn in this letter that Don Peter of Arragon comes this night to Messina.

Mess. He is very near by this : he was not three leagues off when I left him.

Leon. How many gentlemen have you lost in this action ?

Mess. But few of any sort, and none of name.

Leon. A victory is twice itself when the achiever brings home full numbers. I find here that Don Peter hath bestowed much honor on a young Florentine called Claudio.

Mess. Much deserved on his part and equally remembered by Don Pedro : he hath borne himself beyond the promise of his age, doing, in the figure of a lamb, the feats of a lion : he hath indeed better bettered expectation than you must expect of me to tell you how.

Leon. He hath an uncle here in Messina will be very much glad of it.

Mess. I have already delivered him letters, and there appears much joy in him ; even so much that joy could not show itself modest enough without a badge of bitterness.

Leon. Did he break out into tears ?

Mess. In great measure.

Leon. A kind overflow of kindness : there are no faces truer than those that are so washed. How much better is it to weep at joy than to joy at weeping !

Beat. I pray you, is Signior Mountanto returned from the wars or no ?   31

Mess. I know none of that name, lady : there was none such in the army of any sort.

Leon. What is he that you ask for, niece ?

Hero. My cousin means Signior Benedick of Padua.

Mess. O, he's returned ; and as pleasant as ever he was.

Beat. He set up his bills here in Messina and challenged Cupid at the flight ; and my uncle's fool, reading the challenge, subscribed for Cupid, and challenged him at the bird-bolt. I pray you, how many hath he killed and eaten in these wars ? But how many hath he killed ? for indeed I promised to eat all of his killing.

Leon. Faith, niece, you tax Signior Benedick too much ; but he'll be meet with you, I doubt it not.

Mess. He hath done good service, lady, in these wars.

Beat. You had musty victual, and he hath holp to eat it : he is a very valiant trencherman ; he hath an excellent stomach.

Mess. And a good soldier too, lady.

Beat. And a good soldier to a lady : but what is he to a lord ?

Mess. A lord to a lord, a man to a man ; stuffed with all honorable virtues.

Beat. It is so, indeed ; he is no less than a stuffed man : but for the stuffing,—well, we are all mortal.   60

Leon. You must not, sir, mistake my niece. There is a kind of merry war betwixt Signior Benedick and her : they never meet but there's a skirmish of wit between them.

Beat. Alas ! he gets nothing by that. In our last conflict four of his five wits went halting off, and now is the whole man governed with one : so that if he have wit enough to keep himself warm, let him bear it for a difference between himself and his horse ; for it is all the wealth that he hath left, to be known a reasonable creature. Who is his companion now ? He hath every month a new sworn brother.

Mess. Is't possible ?

Beat. Very easily possible : he wears his faith but as the fashion of his hat ; it ever changes with the next block.

Mess. I see, lady, the gentleman is not in your books.

Beat. No ; an he were, I would burn my study. But, I pray you, who is his companion? Is there no young squarer now that will make a voyage with him to the devil ?

Mess. He is most in the company of the right noble Claudio.

Beat. O Lord, he will hang upon him like a disease : he is sooner caught than the pestilence, and the taker runs presently mad. God help the noble Claudio ! if he have caught the Benedick, it will cost him a thousand pound ere a' be cured.   90

Mess. I will hold friends with you, lady.

Beat. Do, good friend.

Leon. You will never run mad, niece.

Beat. No, not till a hot January.

Mess. Don Pedro is approached.

Enter DON PEDRO, DON JOHN, CLAUDIO, BENEDICK, *and* BALTHASAR.

D. Pedro. Good Signior Leonato, you are come to meet your trouble : the fashion of the world is to avoid cost, and you encounter cf the

Leon. Never came trouble to my house in the likeness of your grace : for trouble being gone, comfort should remain ; but when you depart from me, sorrow abides and happiness takes his leave.

D. Pedro. You embrace your charge too willingly. I think this is your daughter.

Leon. Her mother hath many times told me so.

Bene. Were you in doubt, sir, that you asked her ?

Leon. Signior Benedick, no ; for then were you a child.

D. Pedro. You have it full, Benedick : we may guess by this what you are, being a man. Truly, the lady fathers herself. Be happy, lady ; for you are like an honorable father.

Bene. If Signior Leonato be her father, she

would not have his head on her shoulders for all Messina, as like him as she is.

Beat. I wonder that you will still be talking, Signior Benedick : nobody marks you.

Bene. What, my dear Lady Disdain ! are you yet living ?   120

Beat. Is it possible disdain should die while she hath such meet food to feed it as Signior Benedick ? Courtesy itself must convert to disdain, if you come in her presence.

Bene. Then is courtesy a turncoat. But it is certain I am loved of all ladies, only you excepted : and I would I could find in my heart that I had not a hard heart ; for, truly, I love none.

Beat. A dear happiness to women : they would else have been troubled with a pernicious suitor. I thank God and my cold blood, I am of your humor for that : I had rather hear my dog bark at a crow than a man swear he loves me.

Bene. God keep your ladyship still in that mind ! so some gentleman or other shall 'scape a predestinate scratched face.

Beat. Scratching could not make it worse, an 'twere such a face as yours were.

Bene. Well, you are a rare parrot-teacher.

Beat. A bird of my tongue is better than a beast of yours.   141

Bene. I would my horse had the speed of your tongue, and so good a continuer. But keep your way, i' God's name ; I have done.

Beat. You always end with a jade's trick : I know you of old.

D. Pedro. That is the sum of all, Leonato. Signior Claudio and Signior Benedick, my dear friend Leonato hath invited you all. I tell him we shall stay here at the least a month ; and he heartily prays some occasion may detain us longer. I dare swear he is no hypocrite, but prays from his heart.

Leon. If you swear, my lord, you shall not be forsworn. [*To Don John*] Let me bid you welcome, my lord : being reconciled to the prince your brother, I owe you all duty.

D. John. I thank you : I am not of many words, but I thank you.

Leon. Please it your grace lead on ?   160

D. Pedro. Your hand, Leonato ; we will go together.

[*Exeunt all except Benedick and Claudio.*

Claud. Benedick, didst thou note the daughter of Signior Leonato ?

Bene. I noted her not ; but I looked on her.

Claud. Is she not a modest young lady ?

Bene. Do you question me, as an honest man should do, for my simple true judgment ; or would you have me speak after my custom, as being a professed tyrant to their sex ? 170

Claud. No ; I pray thee speak in sober judgment.

Bene. Why, i' faith, methinks she's too low for a high praise, too brown for a fair praise and too little for a great praise : only this commendation I can afford her, that were she other

than she is, she were unhandsome ; and being no other but as she is, I do not like her.

Claud. Thou thinkest I am in sport : I pray thee tell me truly how thou likest her.   180

Bene. Would you buy her, that you inquire after her ?

Claud. Can the world buy such a jewel ?

Bene. Yea, and a case to put it into. But speak you this with a sad brow ? or do you play the flouting Jack, to tell us Cupid is a good hare-finder and Vulcan a rare carpenter ? Come, in what key shall a man take you, to go in the song ?

Claud. In mine eye she is the sweetest lady that ever I looked on.   190

Bene. I can see yet without spectacles and I see no such matter : there's her cousin, an she were not possessed with a fury, exceeds her as much in beauty as the first of May doth the last of December. But I hope you have no intent to turn husband, have you ?

Claud. I would scarce trust myself, though I had sworn the contrary, if Hero would be my wife.

Bene. Is't come to this ? In faith, hath not the world one man but he will wear his cap with suspicion ? Shall I never see a bachelor of three-score again ? Go to, i' faith ; an thou wilt needs thrust thy neck into a yoke, wear the print of it and sigh away Sundays. Look ; Don Pedro is returned to seek you.

Re-enter DON PEDRO.

D. Pedro. What secret hath held you here, that you followed not to Leonato's ?

Bene. I would your grace would constrain me to tell.

D. Pedro. I charge thee on thy allegiance.

Bene. You hear, Count Claudio : I can be secret as a dumb man ; I would have you think so ; but, on my allegiance, mark you this, on my allegiance. He is in love. With who ? now that is your grace's part. Mark how short his answer is ;—With Hero, Leonato's short daughter.

Claud. If this were so, so were it uttered.

Bene. Like the old tale, my lord : 'it is not so, nor 'twas not so, but, indeed, God forbid it should be so.'   220

Claud. If my passion change not shortly, God forbid it should be otherwise.

D. Pedro. Amen, if you love her ; for the lady is very well worthy.

Claud. You speak this to fetch me in, my lord.

D. Pedro. By my troth, I speak my thought.   [mine.

Claud. And, in faith, my lord, I spoke

Bene. And by my two faiths and troths, my lord, I spoke mine.

Claud. That I love her, I feel.   230

D. Pedro. That she is worthy, I know.

Bene. That I neither feel how she should be loved nor know how she should be worthy, is the opinion that fire cannot melt out of me : I will die in it at the stake.

D. Pedro. Thou wost ever an obstinate neretic in the despite of beauty.

Claud. And never could maintain his part but in the force of his will.

Bene. That a woman conceived me, I thank her ; that she brought me up, I likewise give her most humble thanks : but that I will have a recheat winded in my forehead, or hang my bugle in an invisible baldrick, all women shall pardon me. Because I will not do 'them the wrong to mistrust any, I will do myself the right to trust none ; and the fine is, for the which I may go the finer, I will live a bachelor.

D. Pedro. I shall see thee, ere I die, look pale with love.   250

Bene. With anger, with sickness, or with hunger, my lord, not with love : prove that ever I lose more blood with love than I will get again with drinking, pick out mine eyes with a ballad-maker's pen and hang me up at the door of a brothel-house for the sign of blind Cupid.

D. Pedro. Well, if ever thou dost fall from this faith, thou wilt prove a notable argument.

Bene. If I do, hang me in a bottle like a cat and shoot at me ; and he that hits me, let him be clapped on the shoulder, and called Adam.   261

D. Pedro. Well, as time shall try :
'In time the savage bull doth bear the yoke.'

Bene. The savage bull may ; but if ever the sensible Benedick bear it, pluck off the bull's horns and set them in my forehead : and let me be vilely painted, and in such great letters as they write 'Here is good horse to hire,' let them signify under my sign 'Here you may see Benedick the married man.' 270

Claud. If this should ever happen, thou wouldst be horn-mad.

D. Pedro. Nay, if Cupid have not spent all his quiver in Venice, thou wilt quake for this shortly.

Bene. I look for an earthquake too, then.

D. Pedro. Well, you will temporize with the hours. In the meantime, good Signior Benedick, repair to Leonato's : commend me to him and tell him I will not fail him at supper ; for indeed he hath made great preparation.   280

Bene. I have almost matter enough in me for such an embassage ; and so I commit you—

Claud. To the tuition of God : From my house, if I had it,—

D. Pedro. The sixth of July : Your loving friend, Benedick.

Bene. Nay, mock not, mock not. The body of your discourse is sometime guarded with fragments, and the guards are but slightly basted on neither : ere you flout old ends any further, examine your conscience : and so I 'eave you.   [*Exit.* 291

Claud. My liege, your highness now may do me good.

D. Pedro. My love is thine to teach : teach it but how,
And thou shalt see how apt it is to learn
Any hard lesson that may do thee good.

Claud. Hath Leonato any son, my lord ?

D. Pedro. No child but Hero ; she's his only heir.
Dost thou affect her, Claudio ?

Claud.   O, my lord,
When you went onward on this ended action,
I look'd upon her with a soldier's eye,   300
That liked, but had a rougher task in hand
Than to drive liking to the name of love :
But now I am return'd and that war-thoughts
Have left their places vacant, in their rooms
Come thronging soft and delicate desires,
All prompting me how fair young Hero is,
Saying, I liked her ere I went to wars.

D. Pedro. Thou wilt be like a lover presently
And tire the hearer with a book of words.
If thou dost love fair Hero, cherish it,   310
And I will break with her and with her father
And thou shalt have her. Was't not to this end
That thou began'st to twist so fine a story ?

Claud. How sweetly you do minister to love,
That know love's grief by his complexion !
But lest my liking might too sudden seem,
I would have salved it with a longer treatise.

D. Pedro. What need the bridge much broader than the flood ?
The fairest grant is the necessity.
Look, what will serve is fit : 'tis once, thou lovest,   320
And I will fit thee with the remedy.
I know we shall have revelling to-night :
I will assume thy part in some disguise
And tell fair Hero I am Claudio,
And in her bosom I'll unclasp my heart
And take her hearing prisoner with the force
And strong encounter of my amorous tale ;
Then after to her father will I break ;
And the conclusion is, she shall be thine.
In practice let us put it presently.   330
                    [*Exeunt.*

SCENE II. *A room in* LEONATO'S *house.*

Enter LEONATO *and* ANTONIO, *meeting.*

Leon. How now, brother ! Where is my cousin, your son ? hath he provided this music ?

Ant. He is very busy about it. But,brother, I can tell you strange news that you yet dreamt not of.

Leon. Are they good ?

Ant. As the event stamps them : but they have a good cover ; they show well outward The prince and Count Claudio, walking in a thick-pleached alley in mine orchard, were thus much overheard by a man of mine : the prince discovered to Claudio that he loved my niece your daughter and meant to acknowledge it this night in a dance ; and if he found her accordant, he meant to take the present time by the top and instantly break with you of it.

Leon. Hath the fellow any wit that told you this?

Ant. A good sharp fellow: I will send for him; and question him yourself. 20

Leon. No, no; we will hold it as a dream till it appear itself: but I will acquaint my daughter withal, that she may be the better prepared for an answer, if peradventure this be true. Go you and tell her of it. [*Enter attendants.*] Cousins, you know what you have to do. O, I cry you mercy, friend; go you with me, and I will use your skill. Good cousin, have a care this busy time. [*Exeunt.*

SCENE III. *The same.*

Enter DON JOHN *and* CONRADE.

Con. What the good-year, my lord! why are you thus out of measure sad?

D. John. There is no measure in the occasion that breeds; therefore the sadness is without limit.

Con. You should hear reason.

D. John. And when I have heard it, what blessing brings it?

Con. If not a present remedy, at least a patient sufferance. 10

D. John. I wonder that thou, being, as thou sayest thou art, born under Saturn, goest about to apply a moral medicine to a mortifying mischief. I cannot hide what I am: I must be sad when I have cause and smile at no man's jests, eat when I have stomach and wait for no man's leisure, sleep when I am drowsy and tend on no man's business, laugh when I am merry and claw no man in his humor.

Con. Yea, but you must not make the full show of this till you may do it without controlment. You have of late stood out against your brother, and he hath ta'en you newly into his grace; where it is impossible you should take true root but by the fair weather that you make yourself: it is needful that you frame the season for your own harvest.

D. John. I had rather be a canker in a hedge than a rose in his grace, and it better fits my blood to be disdained of all than to fashion a carriage to rob love from any: in this, though I cannot be said to be a flattering honest man, it must not be denied but I am a plain-dealing villain. I am trusted with a muzzle and enfranchised with a clog; therefore I have decreed not to sing in my cage. If I had my mouth, I would bite; if I had my liberty, I would do my liking: in the meantime let me be that I am and seek not to alter me.

Con. Can you make no use of your discontent? 40

D. John. I make all use of it, for I use it only.

Who comes here?

Enter BORACHIO.

What news, Borachio?

Bora. I came yonder from a great supper: the prince your brother is royally entertained by Leonato: and I can give you intelligence of an intended marriage.

D. John. Will it serve for any model to build mischief on? What is he for a fool that betroths himself to unquietness? 50

Bora. Marry, it is your brother's right hand.

D. John. Who? the most exquisite Claudio?

Bora. Even he.

D. John. A proper squire! And who, and who? which way looks he?

Bora. Marry, on Hero, the daughter and heir of Leonato.

D. John. A very forward March-chick! How came you to this?

Bora. Being entertained for a perfumer, as I was smoking a musty room, comes me the prince and Claudio, hand in hand, in sad conference: I whipt me behind the arras; and there heard it agreed upon that the prince should woo Hero for himself, and having obtained her, give her to Count Claudio.

D. John. Come, come, let us thither: this may prove food to my displeasure. That young start-up hath all the glory of my overthrow: if I can cross him any way, I bless myself every way. You are both sure, and will assist me? 71

Con. To the death, my lord.

D. John. Let us to the great supper: their cheer is the greater that I am subdued. Would the cook were of my mind! Shall we go prove what's to be done?

Bora. We'll wait upon your lordship.

[*Exeunt.*

ACT II.

SCENE I. *A hall in* LEONATO'S *house.*

Enter LEONATO, ANTONIO, HERO, BEATRICE, *and others.*

Leon. Was not Count John here at supper?

Ant. I saw him not.

Beat. How tartly that gentleman looks! I never can see him but I am heart-burned an hour after.

Hero. He is of a very melancholy disposition.

Beat. He were an excellent man that were made just in the midway between him and Benedick: the one is too like an image and says nothing, and the other too like my lady's eldest son, evermore tattling. 11

Leon. Then half Signior Benedick's tongue in Count John's mouth, and half Count John's melancholy in Signior Benedick's face,—

Beat. With a good leg and a good foot, uncle, and money enough in his purse, such a man would win any woman in the world, if a'. could get her good-will.

Leon. By my troth, niece, thou wilt never get thee a husband, if thou be so shrewd of thy tongue.　21

Ant. In faith, she's too curst.

Beat. Too curst is more than curst : I shall lessen God's sending that way ; for it is said, ' God sends a curst cow short horns ; ' but to a cow too curst he sends none.

Leon. So, by being too curst, God will send you no horns.

Beat. Just, if he send me no husband ; for the which blessing I am at him upon my knees every morning and evening. Lord, I could not endure a husband with a beard on his face : I had rather lie in the woollen.

Leon. You may light on a husband that hath no beard.

Beat. What should I do with him ? dress him in my apparel and make him my waiting-gentlewoman ? He that hath a beard is more than a youth, and he that hath no beard is less than a man : and he that is more than a youth is not for me, and he that is less than a man, I am not for him : therefore, I will even take sixpence in earnest of the bear-ward, and lead his apes into hell.

Leon. Well, then, go you into hell ?

Beat. No, but to the gate ; and there will the devil meet me, like an old cuckold, with horns on his head, and say ' Get you to heaven, Beatrice, get you to heaven ; here's no place for you maids : ' so deliver I up my apes, and away to Saint Peter for the heavens ; he shows me where the bachelors sit, and there live we as merry as the day is long.

Ant. [*To Hero*] Well, niece, I trust you will be ruled by your father.

Beat. Yes, faith ; it is my cousin's duty to make curtsy and say ' Father, as it please you.' But yet for all that, cousin, let him be a handsome fellow, or else make another curtsy and say ' Father, as it please me.'

Leon. Well, niece, I hope to see you one day fitted with a husband.　61

Beat. Not till God make men of some other metal than earth. Would it not grieve a woman to be overmastered with a piece of valiant dust ? to make an account of her life to a clod of wayward marl ? No, uncle, I'll none : Adam's sons are my brethren ; and, truly, I hold it a sin to match in my kindred.

Leon. Daughter, remember what I told you : if the prince do solicit you in that kind, you know your answer.　71

Beat. The fault will be in the music, cousin, if you be not wooed in good time : if the prince be too important, tell him there is measure in every thing and so dance out the answer. For, hear me, Hero : wooing, wedding, and repenting, is as a Scotch jig, a measure, and a cinque pace : the first suit is hot and hasty, like a Scotch jig, and full as fantastical ; the wedding, mannerly-modest, as a measure, full of state and ancientry ; and then comes

repentance and, with his bad legs, falls into the cinque pace faster and faster, till he sink into his grave.

Leon. Cousin, you apprehend passing shrewdly.

Beat. I have a good eye, uncle ; I can see a church by daylight.

Leon. The revellers are entering, brother : make good room.　[*All put on their masks.*

Enter DON PEDRO, CLAUDIO, BENEDICK, BAL-THASAR, DON JOHN, BORACHIO, MAR-GARET, URSULA, *and others, masked.*

D. Pedro. Lady, will you walk about with your friend ?　90

Hero. So you walk softly and look sweetly and say nothing, I am yours for the walk ; and especially when I walk away.

D. Pedro. With me in your company ?

Hero. I may say so, when I please.

D. Pedro. And when please you to say so ?

Hero. When I like your favor ; for God defend the lute should be like the case !

D. Pedro. My visor is Philemon's roof ; within the house is Jove.　100

Hero. Why, then, your visor should be thatched.

D. Pedro. Speak low, if you speak love. ·
　　　　　　　　[*Drawing her aside.*

Balth. Well, I would you did like me.

Marg. So would not I, for your own sake ; for I have many ill-qualities.

Balth. Which is one ?

Marg. I say my prayers aloud.

Balth. I love you the better : the hearers may cry, Amen.　110

Marg. God match me with a good dancer !

Balth. Amen.

Marg. And God keep him out of my sight when the dance is done ! Answer, clerk.

Balth. No more words : the clerk is an-swered.

Urs. I know you well enough ; you are Signior Antonio.

Ant. At a word, I am not.

Urs. I know you by the waggling of your head.　120

Ant. To tell you true, I counterfeit him.

Urs. You could never do him so ill-well, unless you were the very man. Here's his dry hand up and down : you are he, you are he.

Ant. At a word, I am not.

Urs. Come, come, do you think I do not know you by your excellent wit ? can virtue hide itself ? Go to, mum, you are he : graces will appear, and there's an end.

Beat. Will you not tell me who told you so ?

Bene. No, you shall pardon me.　131

Beat. Nor will you not tell me who you are ?

Bene. Not now.

Beat. That I was disdainful, and that I had my good wit out of the ' Hundred Merry Tales : '—well, this was Signior Benedick that said so.

Bene. What's he ?
Beat. I am sure you know him well enough
Bene Not I, believe me
Beat. Did he never make you laugh ? 140
Bene. I pray you, what is he ?
Beat Why, he is the prince's jester a very dull fool , only his gift is in devising impossible slanders none but libertines delight in him , and the commendation is not in his wit, but in his villany , for he both pleases men and angers them, and then they laugh at him and beat him I am sure he is in the fleet · I would he had boarded me
Bene. When I know the gentleman, I'll tell him what you say 151
Beat Do, do ; he'll but break a comparison or two 'on me , which, peradventure not marked or not laughed at, strikes him into melancholy , and then there's a partridge wing saved, for the fool will eat no supper that night [*Music*] We must follow the leaders.
Bene. In every good thing.
Beat Nay, if they lead to any ill, I will leave them at the next turning. 160
    [*Dance. Then exeunt all except Don John, Borachio, and Claudio.*
D. John. Sure my brother is amorous on Hero and hath withdrawn her father to break with him about it The ladies follow her and but one visor remains
Bora. And that is Claudio . I know him by his bearing
D John Are not you Signior Benedick ?
Claud You know me well , I am he.
D. John. Signior, you are very near my brother in his love ; he is enamored on Hero , I pray you, dissuade him from her she is no equal for his birth . you may do the part of an honest man in it
Claud How know you he loves her ?
D John. I heard him swear his affection.
Bora. So did I too ; and he swore he would marry her to-night
D. John Come, let us to the banquet.
    [*Exeunt Don John and Borachio*
Claud. Thus answer I in the name of Benedick,
But hear these ill news with the ears of Claudio. 180
'Tis certain so , the prince wooes for himself.
Friendship is constant in all other things
Save in the office and affairs of love ·
Therefore, all hearts in love use their own tongues ,
Let every eye negotiate for itself
And trust no agent , for beauty is a witch
Against whose charms faith melteth into blood
This is an accident of hourly proof,
Which I mistrusted not Farewell, therefore, Hero !

    Re-enter BENEDICK.

Bene. Count Claudio ? 190
Claud. Yea, the same.
Bene Come, will you go with me ?

Claud Whither ?
Bene Even to the next willow, about your own business, county What fashion will you wear the garland of ? about your neck, like an usurer's chain ? or under your arm, like a lieutenant's scarf ? You must wear it one way, for the prince hath got your Hero
Claud I wish him joy of her 200
Bene Why, that's spoken like an honest drovier so they sell bullocks But did you think the prince would have served you thus ?
Claud I pray you, leave me
Bene Ho ! now you strike like the blind man 'twas the boy that stole your meat, and you'll beat the post
Claud If it will not be, I'll leave you
    [*Exit*
Bene Alas, poor hurt fowl ! now will he creep into sedges But that my Lady Beatrice should know me, and not know me ' The prince's fool ! Ha ? It may be I go under that title because I am merry Yea, but so I am apt to do myself wrong , I am not so reputed it is the base, though bitter, disposition of Beatrice that puts the world into her person, and so gives me out. Well, I'll be revenged as I may.

    Re-enter DON PEDRO

D Pedro Now, signior, where's the count ? did you see him ?
Bene Truth, my lord, I have played the part of Lady Fame I found him here as melancholy as a lodge in a warren I told him, and I think I told him true, that your grace had got the good will of this young lady , and I offered him my company to a willow-tree, either to make him a garland, as being forsaken, or to bind him up a rod, as being worthy to be whipped
D Pedro. To be whipped ' What's his fault ?
Bene. The flat transgression of a schoolboy, who, being overjoyed with finding a birds' nest, shows it his companion, and he steals it
D Pedro Wilt thou make a trust a transgression ? The transgression is in the stealer
Bene Yet it had not been amiss the rod had been made, and the garland too , for the garland he might have worn himself, and the rod he might have bestowed on you, who, as I take it, have stolen his birds' nest
D Pedro I will but teach them to sing, and restore them to the owner. 240
Bene If their singing answer your saying, by my faith, you say honestly
D Pedro. The Lady Beatrice hath a quarrel to you . the gentleman that danced with her told her she is much wronged by you
Bene O, she misused me past the endurance of a block ' an oak but with one green leaf on it would have answered her , my very visor began to assume life and scold with her. She told me, not thinking I had been myself, that I was the prince's jester, that I was duller than a great thaw , huddling jest

upon jest with such impossible conveyance upon me that I stood like a man at a mark, with a whole army shooting at me. She speaks poniards, and every word stabs : if her breath were as terrible as her terminations, there were no living near her ; she would infect to the north star. I would not marry her, though she were endowed with all that Adam had left him before he transgressed : she would have made Hercules have turned spit, yea, and have cleft his club to make the fire too. Come, talk not of her : you shall find her the infernal Ate in good apparel. I would to God some scholar would conjure her ; for certainly, while she is here, a man may live as quiet in hell as in a sanctuary ; and people sin upon purpose, because they would go thither ; so, indeed, all disquiet, horror and perturbation follows her.

D. Pedro. Look, here she comes.   270

Enter CLAUDIO, BEATRICE, HERO, *and* LEONATO.

Bene. Will your grace command me any service to the world's end ? I will go on the slightest errand now to the Antipodes that you can devise to send me on ; I will fetch you a tooth-picker now from the furthest inch of Asia, bring you the length of Prester John's foot, fetch you a hair off the great Cham's beard, do you any embassage to the Pigmies, rather than hold three words' conference with this harpy. You have no employment for me ?

D. Pedro. None, but to desire your good company.

Bene. O God, sir, here's a dish I love not : I cannot endure my Lady Tongue.   [*Exit.*

D. Pedro. Come, lady, come; you have lost the heart of Signior Benedick.

Beat. Indeed, my lord, he lent it me awhile ; and I gave him use for it, a double heart for his single one : marry, once before he won it of me with false dice, therefore your grace may well say I have lost it.   291

D. Pedro. You have put him down, lady, you have put him down.

Beat. So I would not he should do me, my lord, lest I should prove the mother of fools. I have brought Count Claudio, whom you sent me to seek.

D. Pedro. Why, how now, count ! wherefore are you sad ?

Claud. Not sad, my lord.   300

D. Pedro. How then ? sick ?

Claud. Neither, my lord.

Beat. The count is neither sad, nor sick, nor merry, nor well ; but civil count, civil as an orange, and something of that jealous complexion.

D. Pedro. I' faith, lady, I think your blazon to be true ; though, I'll be sworn, if he be so, his conceit is false. Here, Claudio, I have wooed in thy name, and fair Hero is won : I have broke with her father, and his good will obtained : name the day of marriage, and God give thee joy !

Leon. Count, take of me my daughter, and with her my fortunes : his grace hath made the match, and all grace say Amen to it.

Beat. Speak, count, 'tis your cue.

Claud. Silence is the perfectest herald of joy : I were but little happy, if I could say how much. Lady, as you are mine, I am yours : I give away myself for you and dote upon the exchange.   320

Beat. Speak, cousin ; or, if you cannot, stop his mouth with a kiss, and let not him speak neither.   [*heart.*

D. Pedro. In faith, lady, you have a merry

Beat. Yea, my lord ; I thank it, poor fool, it keeps on the windy side of care. My cousin tells him in his ear that he is in her heart.

Claud. And so she doth, cousin.

Beat. Good Lord, for alliance ! Thus goes every one to the world but I, and I am sunburnt ; I may sit in a corner and cry heigh-ho for a husband !

D. Pedro. Lady Beatrice, I will get you one.

Beat. I would rather have one of your father's getting. Hath your grace ne'er a brother like you ? Your father got excellent husbands, if a maid could come by them.

D. Pedro. Will you have me, lady ?

Beat. No, my lord, unless I might have another for working-days : your grace is too costly to wear every day. But, I beseech your grace, pardon me : I was born to speak all mirth and no matter.

D. Pedro. Your silence most offends me, and to be merry best becomes you ; for, out of question, you were born in a merry hour.

Beat. No, sure, my lord, my mother cried ; but then there was a star danced, and under that was I born. Cousins, God give you joy !

Leon. Niece, will you look to those things I told you of ?

Beat. I cry you mercy, uncle. By your grace's pardon.   [*Exit.*

P. Pedro. By my troth, a pleasant-spirited lady.

Leon. There's little of the melancholy element in her, my lord : she is never sad but when she sleeps, and not ever sad then ; for I have heard my daughter say, she hath often dreamed of unhappiness and waked herself with laughing.

D. Pedro. She cannot endure to hear tell of a husband.

Leon. C. by no means : she mocks all her wooers out of suit.

D. Pedro. She were an excellent wife for Benedick.

Leon. O Lord, my lord, if they were but a week married, they would talk themselves mad.

D. Pedro. County Claudio, when mean you to go to church ?   371

Claud. To-morrow, my lord : time goes on crutches till love have all his rites.

Leon. Not till Monday, my dear son, which is hence a just seven-night ; and a time too brief, too, to have all things answer my mind.

D. Pedro. Come, you shake the head at so long a breathing : but, I warrant thee, Claudio, the time shall not go dully by us. I will in the interim undertake one of Hercules' labors ; which is, to bring Signior Benedick and the Lady Beatrice into a mountain of affection the one with the other. I would fain have it a match, and I doubt not but to fashion it, if you three will but minister such assistance as I shall give you direction.

Leon. My lord, I am for you, though it cost me ten nights' watchings.

Claud. And I, my lord.

D. Pedro. And you too, gentle Hero ?

Hero. I will do any modest office, my lord, to help my cousin to a good husband.   391

D. Pedro. And Benedick is not the unhopefullest husband that I know. Thus far can I praise him ; he is of a noble strain, of approved valor and confirmed honesty. I will teach you how to humor your cousin, that she shall fall in love with Benedick ; and I, with your two helps, will so practice on Benedick that, in despite of his quick wit and his queasy stomach, he shall fall in love with Beatrice. If we can do this, Cupid is no longer an archer : his glory shall be ours, for we are the only love-gods. Go in with me, and I will tell you my drift.   [*Exeunt.*

SCENE II. *The same.*

Enter DON JOHN *and* BORACHIO.

D. John. It is so ; the Count Claudio shall marry the daughter of Leonato.

Bora. Yea, my lord ; but I can cross it.

D. John. Any bar, any cross, any impediment will be medicinable to me : I am sick in displeasure to him, and whatsoever comes athwart his affection ranges evenly with mine. How canst thou cross this marriage ?

Bora. Not honestly, my lord ; but so covertly that no dishonesty shall appear in me.

D. John. Show me briefly how.   11

Bora. I think I told your lordship a year since, how much I am in the favor of Margaret, the waiting gentlewoman to Hero.

D. John. I remember.

Bora. I can, at any unseasonable instant of the night, appoint her to look out at her lady's chamber window.

D. John. What life is in that, to be the death of this marriage ?   20

Bora. The poison of that lies in you to temper. Go you to the prince your brother ; spare not to tell him that he hath wronged his honor in marrying the renowned Claudio—whose estimation do you mightily hold up—to a contaminated stale, such a one as Hero.

D. John. What proof shall I make of that?

Bora. Proof enough to misuse the prince, to vex Claudio, to undo Hero and kill Leonato. Look you for any other issue ?   30

D. John. Only to despite them, I will endeavor any thing.

Bora. Go, then ; find me a meet hour to draw Don Pedro and the Count Claudio alone : tell them that you know that Hero loves me ; intend a kind of zeal both to the prince and Claudio, as,—in love of your brother's honor, who hath made this match, and his friend's reputation, who is thus like to be cozened with the semblance of a maid,—that you have discovered thus. They will scarcely believe this without trial : offer them instances ; which shall bear no less likelihood than to see me at her chamber-window, hear me †call Margaret Hero, hear Margaret term me Claudio ; and bring them to see this the very night before the intended wedding,—for in the meantime I will so fashion the matter that Hero shall be absent,—and there shall appear such seeming truth of Hero's disloyalty that jealousy shall be called assurance and all the preparation overthrown.   51

D. John. Grow this to what adverse issue it can, I will put it in practice. Be cunning in the working this, and thy fee is a thousand ducats.

Bora. Be you constant in the accusation, and my cunning shall not shame me.

D. John. I will presently go learn their day of marriage.   [*Exeunt.*

SCENE III. LEONATO'S *orchard.*

Enter BENEDICK.

Bene. Boy !

Enter Boy.

Boy. Signior ?

Bene. In my chamber-window lies a book : bring it hither to me in the orchard.

Boy. I am here already, sir.

Bene. I know that ; but I would have thee hence, and here again. [*Exit Boy.*] I do much wonder that one man, seeing how much another man is a fool when he dedicates his behaviors to love, will, after he hath laughed at such shallow follies in others, become the argument of his own scorn by falling in love : and such a man is Claudio. I have known when there was no music with him but the drum and the fife ; and now had he rather hear the tabor and the pipe : I have known when he would have walked ten mile a-foot to see a good armor ; and now will he lie ten nights awake, carving the fashion of a new doublet. He was wont to speak plain and to the purpose, like an honest man and a soldier ; and now is he turned orthography ; his words are a very fantastical banquet, just so many strange dishes. May I be so converted and see with these eyes ? I cannot tell ; I think not : I will not be sworn but love may transform me to an oyster ; but I'll take my oath on it, till he have made an oyster of me, he shall never make me such a fool. One woman is fair, yet I am well ; another is wise, yet I am well ; another virtuous, yet I am well ; but till all graces be in one woman, one woman shall not come in my grace. Rich she shall

35

be, that's certain; wise, or I'll none; virtuous,
or I'll never cheapen her ; fair, or I'll never
look on her ; mild, or come not near me ; noble, or not I for an angel ; of good discourse,
an excellent musician, and her hair shall be of
what color it please God. Ha! the prince and
Monsieur Love ! I will hide me in the arbor.
　　　　　　　　　　　　　　　　[*Withdraws.*

Enter DON PEDRO, CLAUDIO, *and* LEONATO.

　D. Pedro.　Come, shall we hear this music?
　Claud.　Yea, my good lord.　How still the
　　evening is,　　　　　　　　　　　　40
As hush'd on purpose to grace harmony !
　D. Pedro.　See you where Benedick hath
hid himself ?
　Claud.　O, very well, my lord : the music
　　ended,
We'll fit the kid-fox with a pennyworth.

Enter BALTHASAR *with Music.*

　D. Pedro.　Come, Balthasar, we'll hear that
　　song again.
　Balth.　O, good my lord, tax not so bad a
　　voice
To slander music any more than once.
　D. Pedro.　It is the witness still of excel-
　　lency
To put a strange face on his own perfection.
I pray thee, sing, and let me woo no more. 50
　Balth.　Because you talk of wooing, I will
　　sing ;
Since many a wooer doth commence his suit
To her he thinks not worthy; yet he wooes,
Yet will he swear he loves.
　D. Pedro.　　　　Now, pray thee, come ;
Or, if thou wilt hold longer argument,
Do it in notes.
　Balth.　　　Note this before my notes ;
There's not a note of mine that's worth the
　　noting.
　D. Pedro.　Why, these are very crotchets
　　that he speaks ;
Note, notes, forsooth, and nothing.　　[*Air.*
　Bene.　Now, divine air ! now is his soul
ravished ! Is it not strange that sheeps' guts
should hale souls out of men's bodies ? Well,
a horn for my money, when all's done.　　＼

The Song.

　Balth.　Sigh no more, ladies, sigh no more,
　　　Men were deceivers ever,
　　One foot in sea and one on shore,
　　　To one thing constant never :
　　Then sigh not so, but let them go,
　　　And be you blithe and bonny,
　　Converting all your sounds of woe　70
　　　Into Hey nonny, nonny.

　　Sing no more ditties, sing no moe,
　　　Of dumps so dull and heavy ;
　　The fraud of men was ever so,
　　　Since summer first was leafy
　　Then sigh not so, &c.

　D. Pedro.　By my troth, a good song.
　Balth.　And an ill singer, my lord.

　D. Pedro.　Ha, no, no, faith ; thou singest
well enough for a shift.　　　　　　　80
　Bene.　An he had been a dog that should
have howled thus, they would have hanged
him : and I pray God his bad voice bode no
mischief. I had as lief have heard the night-
raven, come what plague could have come
after it.
　D. Pedro.　Yea, marry, dost thou hear, Balthasar ?　I pray thee, get us some excellent
music ; for to-morrow night we would have it
at the Lady Hero's chamber-window.
　Balth.　The best I can, my lord.　　　90
　D. Pedro.　Do so : farewell. [*Exit Balthasar.*]　Come hither, Leonato.　What was it
you told me of to-day, that your niece Beatrice
was in love with Signior Benedick ?
　Claud.　O, ay : stalk on, stalk on ; the fowl
sits.　I did never think that lady would have
loved any man.
　Leon.　No, nor I neither ; but most wonderful that she should so dote on Signior Benedick, whom she hath in all outward behaviors
seemed ever to abhor.　　　　　　101
　Bene.　Is't possible ?　Sits the wind in that
corner ?
　Leon.　By my troth, my lord, I cannot tell
what to think of it but that she loves him with
an enraged affection : it is past the infinite of
thought.　　　　　　　　　　　　[*feit.*
　D. Pedro.　May be she doth but counter-
　Claud.　Faith, like enough.
　Leon.　O God, counterfeit !　There was
never counterfeit of passion came so near
the life of passion as she discovers it.　111
　D. Pedro.　Why, what effects of passion
shows she ?
　Claud.　Bait the hook well ; this fish will
　Leon.　What effects, my lord ?　She will sit
you, you heard my daughter tell you how. [*bite.*
　Claud.　She did, indeed.
　D. Pedro.　How, how, I pray you ?　You
amaze me : I would have thought her spirit
had been invincible against all assaults of affection.　　　　　　　　　　　　　120
　Leon.　I would have sworn it had, my lord ;
especially against Benedick.
　Bene.　I should think this a gull, but that
the white-bearded fellow speaks it : knavery
cannot, sure, hide himself in such reverence.
　Claud.　He hath ta'en the infection : hold it
up.
　D. Pedro.　Hath she made her affection
known to Benedick ?
　Leon.　No ; and swears she never will :
that's her torment.　　　　　　　130
　Claud.　'Tis true, indeed ; so your daughter
says : 'Shall I,' says she, 'that have so oft encountered him with scorn, write to him that I
love him ? '
　Leon.　This says she now when she is beginning to write to him ; for she'll be up twenty
times a night, and there will she sit in her
smock till she have writ a sheet of paper :
my daughter tells us all.
　Claud.　Now you talk of a sheet of paper, I

remember a pretty jest your daughter told us
of.

Leon.   O, when she had writ it and was
reading it over, she found Benedick and Beatrice between the sheet?

Claud.   That.

Leon.   O, she tore the letter into a thousand
halfpence ; railed at herself, that she should
be so immodest to write to one that she knew
would flout her ; 'I measure him,' says she,
'by my own spirit ; for I should flout him, if
he writ to me ; yea, though I love him, I
should.'   151

Claud.   Then down upon her knees she
falls, weeps, sobs, beats her heart, tears her
hair, prays, curses ; 'O sweet Benedick ! God
give me patience !'

Leon.   She doth indeed ; my daughter says
so : and the ecstasy hath so much overborne
her that my daughter is sometime afeared she
will do a desperate outrage to herself : it is
very true.

D. Pedro.   It were good that Benedick knew
of it by some other, if she will not discover it.

Claud.   To what end ? He would make but
a sport of it and torment the poor lady worse.

D. Pedro.   An he should, it were an alms to
hang him. She's an excellent sweet lady ;
and, out of all suspicion, she is virtuous.

Claud.   And she is exceeding wise.

D. Pedro.   In every thing but in loving Benedick.

Leon.   O, my lord, wisdom and blood combating in so tender a body, we have ten proofs
to one that blood hath the victory. I am sorry
for her, as I have just cause, being her uncle
and her guardian.

D. Pedro.   I would she had bestowed this
dotage on me : I would have daffed all other
respects and made her half myself. I pray
you, tell Benedick of it, and hear what a' will
say.

Leon.   Were it good, think you ?

Claud.   Hero thinks surely she will die ; for
she says she will die, if he love her not, and
she will die, ere she make her love known, and
she will die, if he woo her, rather than she
will bate one breath of her accustomed crossness.

D. Pedro.   She doth well : if she should
make tender of her love, 'tis very possible
he'll scorn it ; for the man, as you know all,
hath a contemptible spirit.

Claud.   He is a very proper man.

D. Pedro.   He hath indeed a good outward
happiness.   191

Claud.   Before God ! and, in my mind, very
wise.

D Pedro.   He doth indeed show some sparks
that are like wit.

Claud.   And I take him to be valiant.

D. Pedro.   As Hector, I assure you : and in
the managing of quarrels you may say he is
wise ; for either he avoids them with great
discretion, or undertakes them with a most
Christian-like fear.   200

Leon.   If he do fear God, a' must necessarily
keep peace : if he break the peace, he ought to
enter into a quarrel with fear and trembling.'

D. Pedro.   And so will he do ; for the man
doth fear God, howsoever it seems not in him
by some large jests he will make. Well, I am
sorry for your niece. Shall we go seek Benedick, and tell him of her love ?

Claud.   Never tell him, my lord : let her
wear it out with good counsel.

Leon.   Nay, that's impossible : she may
wear her heart out first.   210

D. Pedro.   Well, we will hear further of it
by your daughter : let it cool the while. I love
Benedick well ; and I could wish he would
modestly examine himself, to see how much
he is unworthy so good a lady.

Leon.   My lord, will you walk ? dinner is
ready.

Claud.   If he do not dote on her upon this,
I will never trust my expectation.   220

D. Pedro.   Let there be the same net spread
for her ; and that must your daughter and her
gentlewomen carry. The sport will be, when
they hold one an opinion of another's dotage,
and no such matter : that's the scene that I
would see, which will be merely a dumbshow. Let us send her to call him in to dinner.

   [*Exeunt Don Pedro, Claudio, and Leonato.*

Bene.   [*Coming forward*] This can be no
trick : the conference was sadly borne. They
have the truth of this from Hero. They seem
to pity the lady : it seems her affections have
their full bent. Love me ! why, it must be requited. I hear how I am censured : they say
I will bear myself proudly, if I perceive the
love come from her ; they say too that she
will rather die than give any sign of affection.
I did never think to marry : I must not seem
proud : happy are they that hear their detractions and can put them to mending. They say
the lady is fair ; 'tis a truth, I can bear them
witness ; and virtuous ; 'tis so, I cannot reprove it ; and wise, but for loving me ; by my
troth, it is no addition to her wit, nor no great
argument of her folly, for I will be horribly in
love with her. I may chance have some odd
quirks and remnants of wit broken on me, because I have railed so long against marriage :
but doth not the appetite alter ? a man loves
the meat in his youth that he cannot endure
in his age. Shall quips and sentences and
these paper bullets of the brain awe a man
from the career of his humor ? No, the world
must be peopled When I said I would die a
bachelor, I did not think I should live till I
were married. Here comes Beatrice. By
this day ! she's a fair lady : I do spy some
marks of love in her.

Enter BEATRICE.

Beat.   Against my will I am sent to bid you
come in to dinner.

Bene.   Fair Beatrice, I thank you for your
pains.

Beat.   I took no more pains for those thanks

than you take pains to thank me : if it had
been painful, I would not have come.   261
  Bene. You take pleasure then in the message ?
  Beat. Yea, just so much as you may take
upon a knife's point and choke a daw withal.
You have no stomach, signior: fare you well.
                              [Exit.
  Bene. Ha! 'Against my will I am sent to
bid you come in to dinner ;' there's a double
meaning in that. 'I took no more pains for
those thanks than you took pains to thank me:'
that's as much as to say, Any pains that I take
for you is as easy as thanks. If I do not take
pity of her, I am a villain ; if I do not love her,
I am a Jew. I will go get her picture. [*Exit.*

ACT III.

SCENE I. LEONATO'S *garden.*

Enter HERO, MARGARET, *and* URSULA.

  Hero. Good Margaret, run thee to the parlor ;
There shalt thou find my cousin Beatrice
Proposing with the prince and Claudio :
Whisper her ear and tell her, I and Ursula
Walk in the orchard and our whole discourse
Is all of her ; say that thou overheard'st us ;
And bid her steal into the pleached bower,
Where honeysuckles, ripen'd by the sun,
Forbid the sun to enter, like favorites,
Made proud by princes, that advance their
    pride   10
Against that power that bred it : there will she
    hide her,
To listen our purpose. This is thy office ;
Bear thee well in it and leave us alone.
  Marg. I'll make her come, I warrant you,
    presently.   *[Exit.*
  Hero. Now, Ursula, when Beatrice doth
    come,
As we do trace this alley up and down,
Our talk must only be of Benedick.
When I do name him, let it be thy part
To praise him more than ever man did merit :
My talk to thee must be how Benedick   20
Is sick in love with Beatrice. Of this matter
Is little Cupid's crafty arrow made,
That only wounds by hearsay.

    Enter BEATRICE, *behind.*
                       Now begin ;
For look where Beatrice, like a lapwing, runs
Close by the ground, to hear our conference.
  Urs. The pleasant'st angling is to see the
    fish
Cut with her golden oars the silver stream,
And greedily devour the treacherous bait :
So angle we for Beatrice ; who even now
Is couched in the woodbine coverture.   30
Fear you not my part of the dialogue.
  Hero. Then go we near her, that her ear
    lose nothing

Of the false sweet bait that we lay for it.
            [Approaching the bower.
No, truly, Ursula, she is too disdainful ;
I know her spirits are as coy and wild
As haggerds of the rock.
  Urs.   But are you sure
That Benedick loves Beatrice so entirely ?
  Hero. So says the prince and my new-
    trothed lord.
  Urs. And did they bid you tell her of it,
    madam ?
  Hero. They did entreat me to acquaint her
    of it ;   40
But I persuaded them, if they loved Benedick,
To wish him wrestle with affection,
And never to let Beatrice know of it.
  Urs. Why did you so ? Doth not the gentleman
Deserve as full as fortunate a bed
As ever Beatrice shall couch upon ?
  Hero. O god of love! I know he doth deserve
As much as may be yielded to a man :
But Nature never framed a woman's heart
Of prouder stuff than that of Beatrice ;   50
Disdain and scorn ride sparkling in her eyes,
Misprising what they look on, and her wit
Values itself so highly that to her
All matter else seems weak : she cannot love,
Nor take no shape nor project of affection,
She is so self-endeared.
  Urs.   Sure, I think so ;
And therefore certainly it were not good
She knew his love, lest she make sport at it.
  Hero. Why, you speak truth. I never yet
    saw man,
How wise, how noble, young, how rarely featured,   60
But she would spell him backward : if fairfaced,
She would swear the gentleman should be her
    sister ;
If black, why, Nature, drawing of an antique,
Made a foul blot ; if tall, a lance ill-headed ;
If low, an agate very vilely cut ;
If speaking, why, a vane blown with all
    winds ;
If silent, why, a block moved with none.
So turns she every man the wrong side out
And never gives to truth and virtue that
Which simpleness and merit purchaseth.   70
  Urs. Sure, sure, such carping is not commendable.
  Hero. No, not to be so odd and from all
    fashions
As Beatrice is, cannot be commendable :
But who dare tell her so ? If I should speak,
She would mock me into air ; O, she would
    laugh me
Out of myself, press me to death with wit.
Therefore let Benedick, like cover'd fire,
Consume away in sighs, waste inwardly :
It were a better death than die with mocks,
Which is as bad as die with tickling.   80
  Urs. Yet tell her of it : hear what she will
    say.

Hero. No ; rather I will go to Benedick
And counsel him to fight against his passion.
And, truly, I'll devise some honest slanders
To stain my cousin with : one doth not know
How much an ill word may empoison liking.
  Urs. O, do not do your cousin such a
      wrong.
She cannot be so much without true judg-
      ment—
Having so swift and excellent a wit
As she is prized to have—as to refuse   90
So rare a gentleman as Signior Benedick.
  Hero. He is the only man of Italy,
Always excepted my dear Claudio.
  Urs. I pray you, be not angry with me,
      madam,
Speaking my fancy : Signior Benedick,
For shape, for bearing, argument and valor,
Goes foremost in report through Italy.
  Hero. Indeed, he hath an excellent good
      name.
  Urs. His excellence did earn it, ere he had
      it.
When are you married, madam ?   100
  Hero. Why, every day, to-morrow. Come,
      go in :
I'll show thee some attires, and have thy coun-
      sel
Which is the best to furnish me to-morrow.
  Urs. She's limed, I warrant you : we have
      caught her, madam.
  Hero. If it proves so, then loving goes by
      haps :
Some Cupid kills with arrows, some with traps.
      [*Exeunt Hero and Ursula.*
  Beat. [*Coming forward*] What fire is in
      mine ears ? Can this be true ?
Stand I condemn'd for pride and scorn so
      much ?
Contempt, farewell ! and maiden pride, adieu !
No glory lives behind the back of such. 110
And, Benedick, love on ; I will requite thee,
Taming my wild heart to thy loving hand :
If thou dost love, my kindness shall incite thee
To bind our loves up in a holy band ;
For others say thou dost deserve, and I
Believe it better than reportingly.   [*Exit.*

SCENE II. *A room in* LEONATO's *house.*

Enter DON PEDRO, CLAUDIO, BENEDICK, *and*
LEONATO.

  D. Pedro. I do but stay till your marriage
be consummate, and then go I toward Arragon.
  Claud. I'll bring you thither, my lord, if
you'll vouchsafe me.
  D. Pedro. Nay, that would be as great a
soil in the new gloss of your marriage as to
show a child his new coat and forbid him to
wear it. I will only be bold with Benedick for
his company ; for, from the crown of his head
to the sole of his foot, he is all mirth : he hath
twice or thrice cut Cupid's bow-string and the
little hangman dare not shoot at him ; he hath
a heart as sound as a bell and his tongue is

the clapper, for what his heart thinks his tongue
speaks.
  Bene. Gallants, I am not as I have been.
  Leon. So say I : methinks you are sadder.
  Claud. I hope he be in love.
  D. Pedro. Hang him, truant ! there's no
true drop of blood in him, to be truly touched
with love : if he be sad, he wants money. 20
  Bene. I have the toothache.
  D. Pedro. Draw it.
  Bene. Hang it !
  Claud. You must hang it first, and draw it
afterwards.
  D. Pedro. What ! sigh for the toothache ?
  Leon. Where is but a humor or a worm.
  Bene. Well, every one can master a grief
but he that has it.
  Claud. Yet say I, he is in love.   30
  D. Pedro. There is no appearance of fancy
in him, unless it be a fancy that he hath to
strange disguises ; as, to be a Dutchman to-day,
a Frenchman to-morrow, or in the shape of two
countries at once, as, a German from the waist
downward, all slops, and a Spaniard from the
hip upward, no doublet. Unless he have a
fancy to this foolery, as it appears he hath,
he is no fool for fancy, as you would have
it appear he is.
  Claud. If he be not in love with some
woman, there is no believing old signs : a'
brushes his hat o' mornings ; what should that
bode ?   42
  D. Pedro. Hath any man seen him at the
barber's ?
  Claud. No, but the barber's man hath been
seen with him, and the old ornament of his
cheek hath already stuffed tennis-balls.
  Leon. Indeed, he looks younger than he did,
by the loss of a beard.
  D. Pedro. Nay, a' rubs himself with civet :
can you smell him out by that ?   51
  Claud. That's as much as to say, the sweet
youth's in love.
  D. Pedro. The greatest note of it is his
melancholy.
  Claud. And when was he wont to wash his
face ?
  D. Pedro. Yea, or to paint himself ? for the
which, I hear what they say of him.
  Claud. Nay, but his jesting spirit ; which is
now crept into a lute-string and now governed
by stops.
  D. Pedro. Indeed, that tells a heavy tale
for him : conclude, conclude he is in love.
  Claud. Nay, but I know who loves him.
  D. Pedro. That would I know too : I warrant, one that knows him not.
  Claud. Yes, and his ill conditions ; and, in
despite of all, dies for him.
  D. Pedro. She shall be buried with her face
upwards   71
  Bene. Yet is this no charm for the toothache. Old signior, walk aside with me : I
have studied eight or nine wise words to speak
to you, which these hobby-horses must not
hear.   [*Exeunt Benedick and Leonato.*

D. Pedro. For my life, to break with him about Beatrice.

Claud. 'Tis even so. Hero and Margaret have by this played their parts with Beatrice; and then the two bears will not bite one another when they meet. 81

Enter DON JOHN.

D. John. My lord and brother, God save you!

D. Pedro. Good den, brother.

D. John. If your leisure served, I would speak with you.

D. Pedro. In private?

D. John. If it please you : yet Count Claudio may hear; for what I would speak of concerns him.

D. Pedro. What's the matter? 90

D. John. . [*To Claudio*] Means your lordship to be married to-morrow?

D. Pedro. You know he does.

D. John. I know not that, when he knows what I know.

Claud. If there be any impediment, I pray you discover it.

D. John. You may think I love you not : let that appear hereafter, and aim better at me by that I now will manifest. For my brother, I think he holds you well, and in dearness of heart hath holp to effect your ensuing marriage ;—surely suit ill spent and labor ill bestowed.

D. Pedro. Why, what's the matter?

D. John. I came hither to tell you ; and, circumstances shortened, for she has been too long a talking of, the lady is disloyal.

Claud. Who, Hero?

D. Pedro. Even she ; Leonato's Hero, your Hero, every man's Hero. 110

Claud. Disloyal?

D. John. The word is too good to paint out her wickedness ; I could say she were worse : think you of a worse title, and I will fit her to it. Wonder not till further warrant : go but with me to-night, you shall see her chamber-window entered, even the night before her wedding-day : if you love her then, to-morrow wed her ; but it would better fit your honor to change your mind.

Claud. May this be so? 120

D. Pedro. I will not think it.

D. John. If you dare not trust that you see, confess not that you know : if you will follow me, I will show you enough ; and when you have seen more and heard more, proceed accordingly.

Claud. If I see any thing to-night why I should not marry her to-morrow, in the congregation, where I should wed, there will I shame her.

D. Pedro. And, as I wooed for thee to obtain her, I will join with thee to disgrace her.

D. John. I will disparage her no farther till you are my witnesses : bear it coldly but till midnight, and let the issue show itself.

D. Pedro. O day untowardly turned!

Claud. O mischief strangely thwarting!

D. John. O plague right well prevented! so will you say when you have seen the sequel.
[*Exeunt.*

SCENE III. *A street.*

Enter DOGBERRY *and* VERGES *with the Watch.*

Dog. Are you good men and true?

Verg. Yea, or else it were pity but they should suffer salvation, body and soul.

Dog. Nay, that were a punishment too good for them, if they should have any allegiance in them, being chosen for the prince's watch.

Verg. Well, give them their charge, neighbor Dogberry.

Dog. First, who think you the most desartless man to be constable? 10

First Watch. Hugh Otecake, sir, or George Seacole ; for they can write and read.

Dog. Come hither, neighbor Seacole. God hath blessed you with a good name : to be a well-favored man is the gift of fortune ; but to write and read comes by nature.

Sec. Watch. Both which, master constable,—

Dog. You have : I knew it would be your answer. Well, for your favor, sir, why, give God thanks, and make no boast of it ; and for your writing and reading, let that appear when there is no need of such vanity. You are thought here to be the most senseless and fit man for the constable of the watch ; therefore bear you the lantern. This is your charge : you shall comprehend all vagrom men ; you are to bid any man stand, in the prince's name.

Sec. Watch. How if a' will not stand?

Dog. Why, then, take no note of him, but let him go ; and presently call the rest of the watch together and thank God you are rid of a knave.

Verg. If he will not stand when he is bidden, he is none of the prince's subjects.

Dog. True, and they are to meddle with none but the prince's subjects. You shall also make no noise in the streets ; for, for the watch to babble and to talk is most tolerable and not to be endured.

Watch. We will rather sleep than talk : we know what belongs to a watch. 40

Dog. Why, you speak like an ancient and most quiet watchman ; for I cannot see how sleeping should offend : only, have a care that your bills be not stolen. Well, you are to call at all the ale-houses, and bid those that are drunk get them to bed.

Watch. How if they will not?

Dog. Why, then, let them alone till they are sober : if they make you not then the better answer, you may say they are not the men you took them for. 51

Watch. Well, sir.

Dog. If you meet a thief, you may suspect him, by virtue of your office, to be no true man ; and, for such kind of men, the less you meddle or make with them, why the more is for your honesty.

Watch. If we know him to be a thief, shall we not lay hands on him ?

Dog. Truly, by your office, you may , but I think they that touch pitch will be defiled the most peaceable way for you, if you do take a thief, is to let him show himself what he is and steal out of your company.

Verg. You have been always called a merciful man, partner.

Dog. Truly, I would not hang a dog by my will, much more a man who hath any honesty in him

Verg. If you hear a child cry in the night, you must call to the nurse and bid her still it.

Watch. How if the nurse be asleep and will not hear us ?　　　71

Dog. Why, then, depart in peace, and let the child wake her with crying , for the ewe that will not hear her lamb when it baes will never answer a calf when he bleats

Verg. 'Tis very true

Dog. This is the end of the charge :—you, constable, are to present the prince's own person : if you meet the prince in the night, you may stay him　　　81

Verg. Nay, by'r our lady, that I think a' cannot.

Dog. Five shillings to one on t, with any man that knows the statutes, he may stay him : marry, not without the prince be willing , for, indeed, the watch ought to offend no man , and it is an offence to stay a man against his will.

Verg. By'r lady, I think it be so.

Dog. Ha, ha, ha ! Well, masters, good night au there be any matter of weight chances, call up me keep your fellows' counsels and your own ; and good night Come, neighbor

Watch. Well, masters, we hear our charge let us go sit here upon the church-bench till two, and then all to bed

Dog. One word more, honest neighbors. I pray you watch about Signior Leonato's door , for the wedding being there to-morrow, there is a great coil to-night Adieu · be vigitant, I beseech you

[Exeunt Dogberry and Verges.　101

Enter Borachio *and* Conrade

Bora What Conrade !

Watch [*Aside*] Peace ! stir not.

Bora. Conrade, I say !

Con. Here, man ; I am at thy elbow

Bora. Mass, and my elbow itched , I thought there would a scab follow.

Con. I will owe thee an answer for that and now forward with thy tale

Bora Stand thee close, then, under this pent-house, for it drizzles rain ; and I will, like a true drunkard, utter all to thee

Watch. [*Aside*] Some treason, masters yet stand close.

Bora. Therefore know I have earned of Don John a thousand ducats [be so dear ?

Con. Is it possible that any villany should

Bora Thou shouldst rather ask if it were possible any villany should be so rich ; for when rich villains have need of poor ones, poor ones may make what price they will

Con. I wonder at it

Bora That shows thou art unconfirmed. Thou knowest that the fashion of a doublet, or a hat, or a cloak, is nothing to a man.

Con. Yes, it is apparel

Bora. I mean, the fashion.

Con Yes, the fashion is the fashion.

Bora Tush ! I may as well say the fool's the fool But seest thou not what a deformed thief this fashion is ?

Watch. [*Aside*] I know that Deformed ; a' has been a vile thief this seven year , a' goes up and down like a gentleman . I remember his name

Bora. Didst thou not hear somebody ?

Con No , 'twas the vane on the house.

Bora. Seest thou not, I say, what a deformed thief this fashion is ? how giddily a' turns about all the hot bloods between fourteen and five-and-thirty? sometimes fashioning them like Pharaoh's soldiers in the reeky painting, sometime like god Bel's priests in the old church-window, sometime like the shaven Hercules in the smirched worm-eaten tapestry, where his codpiece seems as massy as his club?

Con All this I see ; and I see that the fashion wears out more apparel than the man. But art not thou thyself giddy with the fashion too, that thou hast shifted out of thy tale into telling me of the fashion ?

Bora. Not so, neither but know that I have to-night wooed Margaret, the Lady Hero's gentlewoman, by the name of Hero. she leans me out at her mistress' chamberwindow, bids me a thousand times good night, —I tell this tale vilely —I should first tell thee how the prince, Claudio and my master, planted and placed and possessed by my master Don John, saw afar off in the orchard this amiable encounter　　　161

Con And thought they Margaret was Hero ?

Bora Two of them did, the prince and Claudio ; but the devil my master knew she was Margaret , and partly by his oaths, which first possessed them, partly by the dark night, which did deceive them, but chiefly by my villany, which did confirm any slander that Don John had made, away went Claudio enraged , swore he would meet her, as he was appointed, next morning at the temple, and there, before the whole congregation, shame her with what he saw o'er night and send her home again without a husband.

First Watch. We charge you, in the prince's name, stand !

Sec. Watch Call up the right master constable We have here recovered the most dangerous piece of lechery that ever was known in the commonwealth.　　181

First Watch And one Deformed is one of them : I know him ; a' wears a lock.

Con. Masters, masters,—

Sec. Watch. You'll be made bring Deformed forth, I warrant you.

Con. Masters,—

First Watch. Never speak : we charge you let us obey you to go with us.

Bora. We are like to prove a goodly commodity, being taken up of these men's bills.

Con. A commodity in question, I warrant you. Come, we'll obey you. [*Exeunt.*

SCENE IV. HERO'S *apartment.*

Enter HERO, MARGARET, *and* URSULA.

Hero. Good Ursula, wake my cousin Beatrice, and desire her to rise.

Urs. I will, lady.

Hero. And bid her come hither.

Urs. Well. [*Exit.*

Marg. Troth, I think your other rabato were better.

Hero. No, pray thee, good Meg, I'll wear this.

Marg. By my troth, 's not so good ; and I warrant your cousin will say so.　　　10

Hero. My cousin's a fool, and thou art another : I'll wear none but this.

Marg. I like the new tire within excellently, if the hair were a thought browner ; and your gown's a most rare fashion, i' faith. I saw the Duchess of Milan's gown that they praise so.

Hero O, that exceeds, they say.

Marg. By my troth, 's but a night-gown in respect of yours : cloth o' gold, and cuts, and laced with silver, set with pearls, down sleeves, side sleeves, and skirts, round underborne with a bluish tinsel : but for a fine, quaint, graceful and excellent fashion, yours is worth ten on 't.

Hero. God give me joy to wear it ! for my heart is exceeding heavy.

Marg. 'Twill be heavier soon by the weight of a man.

Hero. Fie upon thee ! art not ashamed ?

Marg. Of what, lady ? of speaking honorably ? Is not marriage honorable in a beggar? Is not your lord honorable without marriage ? I think you would have me say, 'saving your reverence, a husband :' and bad thinking do not wrest true speaking, I'll offend nobody : is there any harm in 'the heavier for a husband'? None, I think; and it be the right husband and the right wife ; otherwise 'tis light, and not heavy : ask my Lady Beatrice else ; here she comes.

Enter BEATRICE.

Hero. Good morrow, coz.

Beat. Good morrow, sweet Hero.　　　40

Hero. Why, how now ? do you speak in the sick tune ?

Beat. I am out of all other tune, methinks.

Marg. Clap's into 'Light o' love ;' that goes without a burden : do you sing it, and I'll dance it.

Beat. Ye light o' love, with your heels ! then,

if your husband have stables enough, you'll see he shall lack no barns.

Marg. O illegitimate construction ! I scorn that with my heels.　　　51

Beat. 'Tis almost five o'clock, cousin ; 'tis time you were ready. By my troth, I am exceeding ill : heigh-ho !

Marg. For a hawk, a horse, or a husband ?

Beat. For the letter that begins them all, H.

Marg. Well, and you be not turned Turk, there's no more sailing by the star.

Beat. What means the fool, trow ?

Marg. Nothing I ; but God send every one their heart's desire !　　　　　　　　　61

Hero. These gloves the count sent me ; they are an excellent perfume.

Beat. I am stuffed, cousin ; I cannot smell.

Marg. A maid, and stuffed ! there's goodly catching of cold.

Beat. O, God help me ! God help me ! how long have you professed apprehension ?

Marg. Even since you left it Doth not my wit become me rarely ?　　　　　　　76

Beat. It is not seen enough, you should wear it in your cap. By my troth, I am sick.

Marg. Get you some of this distilled Carduus Benedictus, and lay it to your heart : it is the only thing for a qualm.

Hero. There thou prickest her with a thistle.

Beat. Benedictus ! why Benedictus? you have some moral in this Benedictus.

Marg. Moral ! no, by my troth, I have no moral meaning ; I meant, plain holy-thistle. You may think perchance that I think you are in love : nay, by'r lady, I am not such a fool to think what I list, nor I list not to think what I can, nor indeed I cannot think, if I would think my heart out of thinking, that you are in love or that you will be in love or that you can be in love. Yet Benedick was such another, and now is he become a man : he swore he would never marry, and yet now, in despite of his heart, he eats his meat without grudging : and how you may be converted I know not, but methinks you look with your eyes as other women do.

Beat. What pace is this that thy tongue keeps ?

Marg. Not a false gallop.

Re-enter URSULA.

Urs. Madam, withdraw: the prince, the count, Signior Benedick, Don John, and all the gallants of the town, are come to fetch you to church.

Hero. Help to dress me, good coz, good Meg, good Ursula. [*Exeunt.*

SCENE V. *Another room in* LEONATO'S *house.*

Enter LEONATO, *with* DOGBERRY *and* VERGES.

Leon. What would you with me, honest neighbor ?

Dog. Marry, sir, I would have some confidence with you that decerns you nearly.

Leon. Brief, I pray you ; for you see it is a busy time with me.

Dog. Marry, this it is, sir.

Verg. Yes, in truth it is, sir.

Leon. What is it, my good friends ?

Dog. Goodman Verges, sir, speaks a little off the matter · an old man, sir, and his wits are not so blunt as, God help, I would desire they were , but in faith, honest as the skin between his brows

Verg. Yes, I thank God I am as honest as any man living that is an old man and no honester than I

Dog Comparisons are odorous · palabras, neighbor Verges.

Leon. Neighbors, you are tedious   20

Dog It pleases your worship to say so, but we are the poor duke's officers , but truly, for mine own part, if I were as tedious as a king, I could find it in my heart to bestow it all of your worship.

Leon All thy tediousness on me, ah ?

Dog Yea, an 'twere a thousand pound more than 'tis ; for I hear as good exclamation on your worship as of any man in the city, and though I be but a poor man, I am glad to hear it   30

Verg. And so am I.

Leon. I would fain know what you have to say

Verg Marry, sir, our watch to-night, excepting your worship's presence, ha' ta'en a couple of as arrant knaves as any in Messina

Dog A good old man, sir , he will be talking : as they say, When the age is in, the wit is out : God help us ' it is a world to see Well said, i' faith, neighbor Verges : well, God's a good man ; an two men ride of a horse, one must ride behind An honest soul, i' faith, sir, by my troth he is, as ever broke bread , but God is to be worshipped , all men are not alike, alas, good neighbor '

Leon. Indeed, neighbor, he comes too short of you.

Dog. Gifts that God gives.

Leon I must leave you

Dog. One word, sir . our watch, sir, have indeed comprehended two aspicious persons, and we would have them this morning examined before your worship

Leon. Take their examination yourself and bring it me : I am now in great haste, as it may appear unto you

Dog. It shall be suffigance.

Leon Drink some wine ere you go : fare you well.

Enter a Messenger.

Mess. My lord, they stay for you to give your daughter to her husband.   60

Leon. I'll wait upon them I am ready
            [*Exeunt Leonato and Messenger*

Dog. Go, good partner, go, get you to Francis Seacole, bid him bring his pen and inkhorn to the gaol : we are now to examination these men.

Verg. And we must do it wisely.

Dog. We will spare for no wit, I warrant you ; here's that shall drive some of them to a non-come only get the learned writer to set down our excommunication and meet me at the gaol.   [*Exeunt*

ACT IV

SCENE I *A church.*

Enter DON PEDRO, DON JOHN, LEONATO, FRIAR FRANCIS, CLAUDIO, BENEDICK, HERO, BEATRICE, *and attendants*

Leon Come, Friar Francis, be brief , only to the plain form of marriage, and you shall recount their particular duties afterwards

Friar. You come hither, my lord, to marry this lady.

Claud No

Leon. To be married to her friar, you come to marry her

Friar Lady, you come hither to be married to this count   10

Hero. I do

Friar If either of you know any inward impediment why you should not be conjoined, I charge you, on your souls, to utter it

Claud Know you any, Hero ?

Hero. None, my lord

Friar Know you any, count ?

Leon I dare make his answer, none

Claud. O, what men dare do ! what men may do ' what men daily do, not knowing what they do '   21

Bene How now ' interjections ? Why, then, some be of laughing, as, ah, ha, he '

Claud Stand thee by, friar Father, by your leave

Will you with free and unconstrained soul
Give me this maid, your daughter ?

Leon As freely, son, as God did give her me

Claud And what have I to give you back, whose worth

May counterpoise this rich and precious gift ?

D Pedro Nothing, unless you render her again   30

Claud Sweet prince, you learn me noble thankfulness

There, Leonato, take her back again :
Give not this rotten orange to your friend ,
She's but the sign and semblance of her honor.
Behold how like a maid she blushes here !
O, what authority and show of truth
Can cunning sin cover itself withal '
Comes not that blood as modest evidence
To witness simple virtue ? Would you not swear,
All you that see her, that she were a maid, 40
By these exterior shows ? But she is none
She knows the heat of a luxurious bed ,
Her blush is guiltiness, not modesty

Leon What do you mean, my lord ?

Claud.   Not to be married,

Not to knit my soul to an approved wanton.

Leon. Dear my lord, if you, in your own proof,
Have vanquish'd the resistance of her youth,
And made defeat of her virginity,—

Claud. I know what you would say: if I have known her,
You will say she did embrace me as a husband,
And so extenuate the 'forehand sin :   51
No, Leonato,
I never tempted her with word too large ;
But, as a brother to his sister, show'd
Bashful sincerity and comely love.

Hero. And seem'd I ever otherwise to you?

Claud. Out on thee ! Seeming ! I will write against it :
You seem to me as Dian in her orb,
As chaste as is the bud ere it be blown ;
But you are more intemperate in your blood
Than Venus, or those pamper'd animals   61
That rage in savage sensuality.

Hero. Is my lord well, that he doth speak so wide ?

Leon. Sweet prince, why speak not you ?

D. Pedro.   What should I speak ?
I stand dishonor'd, that have gone about
To link my dear friend to a common stale.

Leon. Are these things spoken, or do I but dream ?

D. John. Sir, they are spoken, and these things are true.

Bene. This looks not like a nuptial.

Hero.   True ! O God !

Claud. Leonato, stand I here ?   70
Is this the prince ? is this the prince's brother ?
Is this face Hero's ? are our eyes our own ?

Leon. All this is so : but what of this, my lord ?

Claud. Let me but move one question to your daughter ;
And, by that fatherly and kindly power
That you have in her, bid her answer truly.

Leon. I charge thee do so, as thou art my child.

Hero. O, God defend me ! how am I beset !
What kind of catechising call you this ?

Claud. To make you answer truly to your name.   80

Hero. Is it not Hero ?· Who can blot that name
With any just reproach ?

Claud.   Marry, that can Hero;
Hero itself can blot out Hero's virtue.
What man was he talk'd with you yesternight
Out at your window betwixt twelve and one ?
Now, if you are a maid, answer to this.

Hero. I talk'd with no man at that hour, my lord.

D. Pedro. Why, then are you no maiden.
Leonato,
I am sorry you must hear : upon mine honor,
Myself, my brother and this grieved count   90
Did see her, hear her, at that hour last·night
Talk with a ruffian at her chamber-window
Who hath indeed, most like a liberal villain,
Confess'd the vile encounters they have had

A thousand times in secret. ·

D. John. Fie, fie ! they are not to be named, my lord,
Not to be spoke of ;
There is not chastity enough in language
Without offence to utter them. Thus, pretty lady,
I am sorry for thy much misgovernment. 100

Claud. O Hero, what a Hero hadst thou been,
If half thy outward graces had been placed
About thy thoughts and counsels of thy heart!
But fare thee well, most foul, most fair ! farewell,
Thou pure impiety and impious purity.·!
For thee I'll lock up all the gates of love,
And on my eyelids shall conjecture hang,
To turn all beauty into thoughts of harm,
And never shall it more be gracious.

Leon. Hath no man's dagger here a point for me ?   [*Hero swoons.* 110

Beat. Why, how now, cousin ! wherefore sink you down ?

D. John. Come, let us go. These things, come thus to light,
Smother her spirits up.
   [*Exeunt Don Pedro, Don John, and Claudio.*

Bene. How doth the lady ?

Beat.   Dead, I think. Help, uncle !
Hero ! why, Hero ! Uncle ! Signior Benedick ! Friar !   [hand.

Leon. O Fate ! take not away thy heavy
Death is the fairest cover for her shame
That may be wish'd for.

Beat.   How now, cousin Hero !

Friar. Have comfort, lady.

Leon. Dost thou look up ?   120

Friar. Yea, wherefore should she not ?

Leon. Wherefore ! Why, doth not every earthly thing
Cry shame upon her ? Could she here deny
The story that is printed in her blood ?
Do not live, Hero ; do not ope thine eyes:
For, did I think thou wouldst not quickly die,
Thought I thy spirits were stronger than thy shames,
Myself would, on the rearward of reproaches,
Strike at thy life. Grieved I, I had but one ?
Chid I for that at frugal nature's frame ? 130
O, one too much by thee ! Why had I one ?
Why ever wast thou lovely in my eyes ?
Why had I not with charitable hand·
Took up a beggar's issue at my gates,
Who smirch'd thus and mired with infamy,
I might have said ' No part of it is mine ;
This shame derives itself from unknown loins'?
But mine and mine I loved and mine I praised
And mine that I was proud on, mine so much
That I myself was to myself not mine,   140
Valuing of her,—why, she, O, she is fallen
Into a pit of ink, that the wide sea·
Hath drops too few to wash her clean again .
And salt too little which may season give
To her foul-tainted flesh !

Bene.   Sir, sir, be patient.
For my part, I am so attired in wonder,
I know not what to say.

Beat. O, on my soul, my cousin is belied !

Bene. Lady, were you her bedfellow last
night ?

Beat. No, truly not ; although, until last
night,   150
I have this twelvemonth been her bedfellow.

Leon. Confirm'd, confirm'd ! O, that is
stronger made
Which was before barr'd up with ribs of iron !
Would the two princes lie, and Claudio lie,
Who loved her so, that, speaking of her foul-
ness,
Wash'd it with tears ? Hence from her ! let
her die.

Friar. Hear me a little ; for I have only
been
Silent so long and given way unto
†This course of fortune....
By noting of the lady I have mark'd   160
A thousand blushing apparitions
To start into her face, a thousand innocent
shames
In angel whiteness beat away those blushes ;
And in her eye there hath appear'd a fire,
To burn the errors that these princes hold
Against her maiden truth. Call me a fool ;
Trust not my reading nor my observations,
Which with experimental seal doth warrant
The tenor of my book ; trust not my age,
My reverence, calling, nor divinity,   170
If this sweet lady lie not guiltless here
Under some biting error.

Leon.   Friar, it cannot be.
Thou seest that all the grace that she hath left
Is that she will not add to her damnation
A sin of perjury ; she not denies it :
Why seek'st thou then to cover with excuse
That which appears in proper nakedness ?

Friar. Lady, what man is he you are accused of ?

Hero. They know that do accuse me ; I
know none :
If I know more of any man alive   180
Than that which maiden modesty doth war-
rant,
Let all my sins lack mercy! O my father,
Prove you that any man with me conversed
At hours unmeet, or that I yesternight
Maintain'd the change of words with any crea-
ture,
Refuse me, hate me, torture me to death !

Friar. There is some strange misprision in
the princes.   [honor ;

Bene. Two of them have the very bent of
And if their wisdoms be misled in this,
The practice of it lives in John the bastard, 190
Whose spirits toil in frame of villanies.

Leon. I know not. If they speak but truth
of her,
These hands shall tear her; if they wrong her
honor,
The proudest of them shall well hear of it.
Time hath not yet so dried this blood of mine,
Nor age so eat up my invention,
Nor fortune made such havoc of my
means,

Nor my bad life reft me so much of friends,
But they shall find, awaked in such a kind,
Both strength of limb and policy of mind, 200
Ability in means and choice of friends,
To quit me of them throughly.

Friar.   Pause awhile,
And let my counsel sway you in this case.
Your daughter here the princes left for dead :
Let her awhile be secretly kept in,
And publish it that she is dead indeed ;
Maintain a mourning ostentation
And on your family's old monument
Hang mournful epitaphs and do all rites
That appertain unto a burial.   210

Leon. What shall become of this ? what
will this do ?

Friar. Marry, this well carried shall on her
behalf
Change slander to remorse ; that is some
good :
But not for that dream I on this strange
course,
But on this travail look for greater birth.
She dying, as it must so be maintain'd,
Upon the instant that she was accused,
Shall be lamented, pitied and excused
Of every hearer : for it so falls out   219
That what we have we prize not to the worth
Whiles we enjoy it, but being lack'd and lost,
Why, then we rack the value, then we find
The virtue that possession would not show us
Whiles it was ours. So will it fare with
Claudio :
When he shall hear she died upon his words,
The idea of her life shall sweetly creep
Into his study of imagination,
And every lovely organ of her life
Shall come apparell'd in more precious habit,
More moving-delicate and full of life,   230
Into the eye and prospect of his soul,
Than when she lived indeed ; then shall he
mourn,
If ever love had interest in his liver,
And wish he had not so accused her,
No, though he thought his accusation true.
Let this be so, and doubt not but success
Will fashion the event in better shape
Than I can lay it down in likelihood.
But if all aim but this be levell'd false,
The supposition of the lady's death   240
Will quench the wonder of her infamy :
And if it sort not well, you may conceal her,
As best befits her wounded reputation,
In some reclusive and religious life,
Out of all eyes, tongues, minds and injuries.

Bene. Signior Leonato, let the friar advise
you :   [love
And though you know my inwardness and
Is very much unto the prince and Claudio,
Yet, by mine honor, I will deal in this
As secretly and justly as your soul   250
Should with your body.

Leon.   Being that I flow in grief,
The smallest twine may lead me.

Friar. 'Tis well consented : presently
away :

For to strange sores strangely they strain the
cure.
Come, lady, die to live : this wedding-day
Perhaps is but prolong'd : have patience and
endure.
　　　[*Exeunt all but Benedick and Beatrice.*
Bene. Lady Beatrice, have you wept all
this while ?
Beat. Yea, and I will weep a while longer.
Bene. I will not desire that.
Beat. You have no reason ; I do it freely.
Bene. Surely I do believe your fair cousin
is wronged. 261
Beat. Ah, how. much might the man de-
serve of me that would right her !
Bene. Is there any way to show such
friendship ?
Beat. A very even way, but no such friend.
Bene. May a man do it ?
Beat. It is a man's office, but not yours.
Bene. I do love nothing in the world so well
as you : is not that strange ? 270
Beat. As strange as the thing I know not.
It were as possible for me to say I loved
nothing so well as you : but believe me not ;
and yet I lie not ; I confess nothing, nor I deny
nothing. I am sorry for my cousin.
Bene. By my sword, Beatrice, thou lovest me.
Beat. Do not swear, and eat it.
Bene. I will swear by it that you love me ;
and I will make him eat it that says I love not
you.
Beat. Will you not eat your word ? 280
Bene. With no sauce that can be devised to
it. · I protest I love thee.
Beat. Why, then, God forgive me !
Bene. What offence, sweet Beatrice ?
Beat. You have stayed me in a happy hour :
I was about to protest I loved you.
Bene. And do it with all thy heart.
Beat. I love you with so much of my heart
that none is left to protest.
Bene. Come, bid me do any thing for thee.
·*Beat.* Kill Claudio. 291
Bene. Ha ! not for the wide world.
Beat. You kill me to deny it. Farewell.
Bene. Tarry, sweet Beatrice.
Beat. I am gone, though I am here : there
is no love in you : nay, I pray you, let me go.
Bene. Beatrice,—
Beat. In faith, I will go.
Bene. We'll be friends first.
Beat. You dare easier be friends with me
than fight with mine enemy. 301
Bene. Is Claudio thine enemy ?
Beat. Is he not approved in the height a
villain, that hath slandered, scorned, dis-
honored my kinswoman ? O that I were a
man ! What, bear her in hand until they
come to take hands ; and then, with public
accusation, uncovered slander, unmitigated
rancor,—O God, that I were a man ! I would
eat his heart in the market-place.
Bene. Hear me, Beatrice,— 310
Beat. Talk with a man out at a window ! A
proper saying !

Bene. Nay, but, Beatrice,—
Beat. Sweet Hero ! She is wronged, she is
slandered, she is undone.
Bene. Beat—
Beat. Princes and counties ! Surely, a
princely testimony, a goodly count, Count
Comfect ; a sweet gallant, surely ! O that I
were a man for his sake ! or that I had any
friend would be a man for my sake ! But
manhood is melted into courtesies, valor into
compliment, and men are only turned into
tongue, and trim ones too : he is now as valiant as Hercules that only tells a lie and swears
it. I cannot be a man with wishing, therefore
I will die a woman with grieving.
Bene. Tarry, good Beatrice. By this hand,
I love thee.
Beat. Use it for my love some other way
than swearing by it. 330
Bene. Think you in your soul the Count
Claudio hath wronged Hero ?
Beat. Yea, as sure as I have a thought or a
soul.
Bene. Enough, I am engaged ; I will challenge him. I will kiss your hand, and so I
leave you. By this hand, Claudio shall render
me a dear account. As you hear of me, so
think of me. Go, comfort your cousin : I
must say she is dead : and so, farewell.
　　　　　　　　　　　　　　[*Exeunt.*

SCENE II. *A prison.*

Enter DOGBERRY, VERGES, *and* Sexton, *in
gowns; and the* Watch, *with* CONRADE *and*
BORACHIO.

Dog. Is our whole dissembly appeared ?
Verg. O, a stool and a cushion for the sex-
ton.
Sex. Which be the malefactors ?
Dog. Marry, that am I and my partner.
Verg. Nay, that's certain ; we have the ex-
hibition to examine.
Sex. But which are the offenders that are
to be examined ? let them come before master
constable.
Dog. Yea, marry, let them come before me.
What is your name, friend ? 11
Bora. Borachio.
Dog. Pray, write down, Borachio. Yours,
sirrah ?
Con. I am a gentleman, sir, and my name
is Conrade.
·*Dog.* Write down, master gentleman Con-
rade. Masters, do you serve God ?
Con.｝ Yea, sir, we hope.
Bora.｝
Dog. Write down, that they hope they
serve God : and write God first ; for God de-
fend but God should go before such villains !
Masters, it is proved already that you are
little better than false knaves ; and it will go
near to be thought so shortly. How answer
you for yourselves ?
Con. Marry, sir, we say we are none.
Dog. A marvellous witty fellow, I assure
you ; but I will go about with him. Come

you hither, sirrah ; a word in your ear : sir, I
say to you, it is thought you are false knaves.

Bora. Sir, I say to you we are none.

Dog. Well, stand aside. 'Fore God, they
are both in a tale Have you writ down, that
they are none ?

Sex. Master constable, you go not the way
to examine you must call forth the watch
that are their accusers.

Dog. Yea, marry, that's the eftest way Let
the watch come forth. Masters, I charge you,
in the prince's name, accuse these men 40

First Watch. This man said, sir, that Don
John, the prince's brother, was a villain.

Dog. Write down Prince John a villain.
Why, this is flat perjury, to call a prince's
brother villain

Bora Master constable,—

Dog. Pray thee, fellow, peace . I do not
like thy look, I promise thee

Sex. What heard you him say else ?

Sec. Watch. Marry, that he had received a
thousand ducats of Don John for accusing the
Lady Hero wrongfully. 51

Dog. Flat burglary as ever was committed.

Verg. Yea, by mass, that it is.

Sex. What else, fellow ?

First Watch And that Count Claudio did
mean, upon his words, to disgrace Hero before
the whole assembly, and not marry her.

Dog. O villain ! thou wilt be condemned
into everlasting redemption for this.

Sex. What else ? 60

Watch. This is all

Sex. And this is more, masters, than you
can deny. Prince John is this morning secretly stolen away , Hero was in this manner
accused, in this very manner refused, and upon
the grief of this suddenly died Master constable, let these men be bound, and brought to
Leonato's I will go before and show him
their examination [*Exit*

Dog Come, let them be opinioned

Verg. †Let them be in the hands— 70

Con. Off, coxcomb !

Dog. God's my life, where's the sexton ?
let him write down the prince's officer coxcomb. Come, bind them. Thou naughty
varlet ! [ass.

Con. Away ! you are an ass, you are an

Dog Dost thou not suspect my place ? dost
thou not suspect my years ? O that he were
here to write me down an ass ! But, masters,
remember that I am an ass , though it be not
written down, forget not that I am an ass
No, thou villain, thou art full of piety, as
shall be proved upon thee by good witness I
am a wise fellow, and, which is more, an
officer, and, which is more, a householder, and,
which is more, as pretty a piece of flesh as any
is in Messina, and one that knows the law, go
to , and a rich fellow enough, go to , and a
fellow that hath had losses, and one that hath
two gowns and every thing handsome about
him. Bring him away. O that I had been writ
down an ass ! [*Exeunt.* 90

ACT V.

SCENE I *Before* LEONATO'S *house*

Enter LEONATO *and* ANTONIO

Ant If you go on thus, you will kill yourself .

And 'tis not wisdom thus to second grief
Against yourself

Leon I pray thee, cease thy counsel,
Which falls into mine ears as profitless
As water in a sieve give not me counsel ;
Nor let no comforter delight mine ear
But such a one whose wrongs do suit with
 mine
Bring me a father that so loved his child,
Whose joy of her is overwhelm'd like mine,
And bid him speak of patience , 10
Measure his woe the length and breadth of
 mine
And let it answer every strain for strain,
As thus for thus and such a grief for such,
In every lineament, branch, shape, and form :
If such a one will smile and stroke his beard,
†Bid sorrow wag, cry ' hem '' when he should
 groan,
Patch grief with proverbs, make misfortune
 drunk
With candle-wasters , bring him yet to me,
And I of him will gather patience 19
But there is no such man for, brother, men
Can counsel and speak comfort to that grief
Which they themselves not feel, but, tasting it,
Their counsel turns to passion, which before
Would give preceptial medicine to rage,
Fetter strong madness in a silken thread,
Charm ache with air and agony with words :
No, no ; 'tis all men's office to speak patience
To those that wring under the load of sorrow,
But no man's virtue nor sufficiency
To be so moral when he shall endure 30
The like himself. Therefore give me no coun-
 sel
My griefs cry louder than advertisement.

Ant. Therein do men from children nothing differ

Leon I pray thee, peace I will be flesh
 and blood ,
For there was never yet philosopher
That could endure the toothache patiently,
However they have writ the style of gods
And made a push at chance and sufferance.

Ant. Yet bend not all the harm upon yourself ,
Make those that do offend you suffer too 40

Leon There thou speak'st reason: nay, I
 will do so
My soul doth tell me Hero is belied ,
And that shall Claudio know , so shall the
 prince
And all of them that thus dishonor her

Ant Here comes the prince and Claudio
 hastily.

Enter DON PEDRO *and* CLAUDIO.

D. Pedro. Good den, good den.

Claud.   Good day to both of you.
Leon. Hear you, my lords,—
D. Pedro.   We have some haste, Leonato.
Leon. Some haste, my lord! well, fare you
        well, my lord :
Are you so hasty now? well, all is one.
D. Pedro. Nay, do not quarrel with us,
        good old man.   50
Ant. If he could right himself with quar-
        reling,
Some of us would lie low.
Claud.   Who wrongs him?
Leon. Marry, thou dost wrong me ; thou
        dissembler, thou :—
Nay, never lay thy hand upon thy sword ;
I fear thee not.
Claud.   Marry, beshrew my hand,
If it should give your age such cause of fear:
In faith, my hand meant nothing to my sword.
Leon. Tush, tush, man ; never fleer and
        jest at me :
I speak not like a dotard nor a fool,
As under privilege of age to brag   60
What I have done being young, or what would
        do
Were I not old. Know, Claudio, to thy head,
Thou hast so wrong'd mine innocent child and
        me
That I am forced to lay my reverence by
And, with grey hairs and bruise of many days,
Do challenge thee to trial of a man.
I say thou hast belied mine innocent child ;
Thy slander hath gone through and through
        her heart,
And she lies buried with her ancestors ;
O, in a tomb where never scandal slept,   70
Save this of hers, framed by thy villany !
Claud. My villany ?
Leon.   Thine, Claudio ; thine, I say.
D. Pedro. You say not right, old man.
Leon.   My lord, my lord,
I'll prove it on his body, if he dare,
Despite his nice fence and his active practice,
His May of youth and bloom of lustihood.
Claud. Away ! I will not have to do with
        you.
Leon. Canst thou so daff me? Thou hast
        kill'd my child :
If thou kill'st me, boy, thou shalt kill a man.
Ant. He shall kill two of us, and men in-
        deed :   80
But that's no matter ; let him kill one first ;
Win me and wear me ; let him answer me.
Come, follow me, boy ; come, sir boy, come,
        follow me :
Sir boy, I'll whip you from your foining fence ;
Nay, as I am a gentleman, I will.
Leon. Brother,—   [my niece ;
Ant. Content yourself. God knows I loved
And she is dead, slander'd to death by villains,
That dare as well answer a man indeed
As I dare take a serpent by the tongue :   90
Boys, apes, braggarts, Jacks, milksops !
Leon.   Brother Antony,—
Ant. Hold you content. What, man ! I
        know them, yea,

And what they weigh, even to the utmost
        scruple,—
Scambling, out-facing, fashion-monging boys,
That lie and cog and flout, deprave and slander,
Go anticly, show outward hideousness,
And speak off half a dozen dangerous words,
How they might hurt their enemies, if they
        durst ;
And this is all.
Leon. But, brother Antony,—
Ant.   Come, 'tis no matter : 100
Do not you meddle ; let me deal in this,
D. Pedro. Gentlemen both, we will not
        wake your patience.
My heart is sorry for your daughter's death :
But, on my honor, she was charged with noth-
        ing
But what was true and very full of proof.
Leon. My lord, my lord,—
D. Pedro. I will not hear you.
Leon. No? Come, brother ; away ! I will
        be heard.   [for it.
Ant. And shall, or some of us will smart
                [*Exeunt Leonato and Antonio.*
D. Pedro. See, see ; here comes the man
        we went to seek.   110

Enter BENEDICK.

Claud. Now, signior, what news ?
Bene. Good day, my lord.
D. Pedro. Welcome, signior : you are almost come to part almost a fray.
Claud. We had like to have had our two
noses snapped off with two old men without
teeth.
D. Pedro. Leonato and his brother. What
thinkest thou ? Had we fought, I doubt we
should have been too young for them.
Bene. In a false quarrel there is no true
valor. I came to seek you both.   121
Claud. We have been up and down to seek
thee ; for we are high-proof melancholy and
would fain have it beaten away. Wilt thou
use thy wit ?
Bene. It is in my scabbard: shall I draw it ?
D. Pedro. Dost thou wear thy wit by thy
side ?
Claud. Never any did so, though very
many have been beside their wit. I will bid
thee draw, as we do the minstrels ; draw, to
pleasure us.
D. Pedro. As I am an honest man, he looks
pale. Art thou sick, or angry ?   131
Claud. What, courage, man ! What though
care killed a cat, thou hast mettle enough in
thee to kill care.
Bene. Sir, I shall meet your wit in the
career, and you charge it against me. I pray
you choose another subject.
Claud. Nay, then, give him another staff :
this last was broke cross.
D. Pedro. By this light, he changes more
and more : I think he be angry indeed.   141
Claud. If he be, he knows how to turn his
girdle.
Bene. Shall I speak a word in your ear ?

Claud. God bless me from a challenge!

Bene. [*Aside to Claudio.*] You are a villain; I jest not: I will make it good how you dare, with what you dare, and when you dare. Do me right, or I will protest your cowardice. You have killed a sweet lady, and her death shall fall heavy on you. Let me hear from you.   151

Claud. Well, I will meet you, so I may have good cheer.

D. Pedro. What, a feast, a feast?

Claud. I' faith, I thank him; he hath bid me to a calf's head and a capon; the which if I do not carve most curiously, say my knife's naught. Shall I not find a woodcock too?

Bene. Sir, your wit ambles well; it goes easily.

D. Pedro. I'll tell thee how Beatrice praised thy wit the other day. I said, thou hadst a fine wit: 'True,' said she, 'a fine little one.' 'No,' said I, 'a great wit:' 'Right,' says she, 'a great gross one.' 'Nay,' said I, 'a good wit:' 'Just,' said she, 'it hurts nobody.' 'Nay,' said I, 'the gentleman is wise:' 'Certain,' said she, 'a wise gentleman.' 'Nay,' said I, 'he hath the tongues:' 'That I believe,' said she, 'for he swore a thing to me on Monday night, which he forswore on Tuesday morning; there's a double tongue; there's two tongues.' Thus did she, an hour together, trans-shape thy particular virtues: yet at last she concluded with a sigh, thou wast the properest man in Italy.

Claud. For the which she wept heartily and said she cared not.

D. Pedro. Yea, that she did: but yet, for all that, an if she did not hate him deadly, she would love him dearly: the old man's daughter told us all.   180

Claud. All, all; and, moreover, God saw him when he was hid in the garden.

D. Pedro. But when shall we set the savage bull's horns on the sensible Benedick's head?

Claud. Yea, and text underneath, 'Here dwells Benedick the married man'?

Bene. Fare you well, boy: you know my mind. I will leave you now to your gossip-like humor: you break jests as braggarts do their blades, which God be thanked, hurt not. My lord, for your many courtesies I thank you: I must discontinue your company: your brother the bastard is fled from Messina: you have among you killed a sweet and innocent lady. For my Lord Lackbeard there, he and I shall meet: and, till then, peace be with him.   [*Exit.*

D. Pedro. He is in earnest.

Claud. In most profound earnest; and, I'll warrant you, for the love of Beatrice.

D. Pedro. And hath challenged thee. , 200

Claud. Most sincerely.

D. Pedro. What a pretty thing man is when he goes in his doublet and hose and leaves off his wit!

Claud. He is then a giant to an ape: but then is an ape a doctor to such a man.

D. Pedro. But, soft you, let me be: pluck up, my heart, and be sad. Did he not say, my brother was fled?

Enter DOGBERRY, VERGES, *and the* Watch, *with* CONRADE *and* BORACHIO.

Dog. Come you, sir: if justice cannot tame you, she shall ne'er weigh more reasons in her balance: nay, an you be a cursing hypocrite once, you must be looked to.

D. Pedro. How now? two of my brother's men bound! Borachio one!

Claud. Hearken after their offence, my lord.

D. Pedro. Officers, what offence have these men done?

Dog. Marry, sir, they have committed false report; moreover, they have spoken untruths; secondarily, they are slanders; sixth and lastly, they have belied a lady; thirdly, they have verified unjust things; and, to conclude, they are lying knaves.

D. Pedro. First, I ask thee what they have done; thirdly, I ask thee what's their offence; sixth and lastly, why they are committed; and, to conclude, what you lay to their charge.

Claud. Rightly reasoned, and in his own division: and, by my troth, there's one meaning well suited.   231

D. Pedro. Who have you offended, masters, that you are thus bound to your answer? this learned constable is too cunning to be understood: what's your offence?

Bora. Sweet prince, let me go no farther to mine answer: do you hear me, and let this count kill me. I have deceived even your very eyes: what your wisdoms could not discover, these shallow fools have brought to light: who in the night overheard me confessing to this man how Don John your brother incensed me to slander the Lady Hero, how you were brought into the orchard and saw me court Margaret in Hero's garments, how you disgraced her, when you should marry her: my villany they have upon record; which I had rather seal with my death than repeat over to my shame. The lady is dead upon mine and my master's false accusation; and, briefly, I desire nothing but the reward of a villain.

D. Pedro. Runs not this speech like iron through your blood?

Claud. I have drunk poison whiles he uttered it.   [to this?

D. Pedro. But did my brother set thee on?

Bora. Yea, and paid me richly for the practice of it.

D. Pedro. He is composed and framed of treachery:

And fled he is upon this villany.

Claud. Sweet Hero! now thy image doth appear

In the rare semblance that I loved it first.   260

Dog. Come, bring away the plaintiffs: by this time our sexton hath reformed Signior Leonato of the matter: and, masters, do not forget to specify, when time and place shall serve, that I am an ass.

Verg. Here, here comes master Signior Leonato, and the Sexton too.

Re-enter LEONATO *and* ANTONIO, *with the Sexton.*

Leon. Which is the villain? let me see his eyes,
That, when I note another man like him,   270
I may avoid him : which of these is he?

Bora. If you would know your wronger, look on me.

Leon. Art thou the slave that with thy breath hast kill'd
Mine innocent child?

Bora.   Yea, even I alone.

Leon. No, not so, villain ; thou beliest thyself :
Here stand a pair of honorable men ;
A third is fled, that had a hand in it.
I thank you, princes, for my daughter's death:
Record it with your high and worthy deeds :
'Twas bravely done, if you bethink you of it.

Claud. I know not how to pray your patience ;
Yet I must speak. Choose your revenge yourself ;
Impose me to what penance your invention
Can lay upon my sin : yet sinn'd I not
But in mistaking.

D. Pedro.   By my soul, nor I :
And yet, to satisfy this good old man,
I would bend under any heavy weight
That he'll enjoin me to.

Leon. I cannot bid you bid my daughter live ;
That were impossible : but, I pray you both,
Possess the people in Messina here   290
How innocent she died ; and if your love
Can labor ought in sad invention,
Hang her an epitaph upon her tomb
And sing it to her bones, sing it to-night :
To-morrow morning come you to my house,
And since you could not be my son-in-law,
Be yet my nephew : my brother hath a daughter,
Almost the copy of my child that's dead,
And she alone is heir to both of us :
Give her the right you should have given her cousin,   300
And so dies my revenge.

Claud.   O noble sir,
Your over-kindness doth wring tears from me !
I do embrace your offer ; and dispose
For henceforth of poor Claudio.

Leon. To-morrow then I will expect your coming ;
To-night I take my leave. This naughty man
Shall face to face be brought to Margaret,
Who I believe was pack'd in all this wrong,
Hired to it by your brother.

Bora. No, by my soul, she was not,
Nor knew not what she did when she spoke to me,   310
But always hath been just and virtuous
In any thing that I do know by her.

Dog. Moreover,—sir, which indeed is not

under white and black, this plaintiff here, the offender, did call me ass : I beseech you, let it be remembered in his punishment. And also, the watch heard them talk of one Deformed : they say he wears a key in his ear and a lock hanging by it, and borrows money in God's name, the which he hath used so long and never paid that now men grow hard-hearted and will lend nothing for God's sake : pray you, examine him upon that point.

Leon. I thank thee for thy care and honest pains.

Dog. Your worship speaks like a most thankful and reverend youth ; and I praise God for you.

Leon. There's for thy pains.

Dog. God save the foundation !

Leon. Go, I discharge thee of thy prisoner, and I thank thee.

Dog. I leave an arrant knave with your worship ; which I beseech your worship to correct yourself, for the example of others. God keep your worship ! I wish your worship well ; God restore you to health ! I humbly give you leave to depart ; and if a merry meeting may be wished, God prohibit it ! Come, neighbor.   [*Exeunt Dogberry and Verges.*

Leon. Until to-morrow morning, lords, farewell.   [to-morrow.

Ant. Farewell, my lords : we look for you

D. Pedro. We will not fail.

Claud. To-night I'll mourn with Hero.

Leon. [*To the Watch*] Bring you these fellows on. We'll talk with Margaret, How her acquaintance grew with this lewd fellow.   [*Exeunt, severally.*

SCENE II. LEONATO'S *garden.*

Enter BENEDICK *and* MARGARET, *meeting.*

Bene. Pray thee, sweet Mistress Margaret, deserve well at my hands by helping me to the speech of Beatrice.

Marg. Will you then write me a sonnet in praise of my beauty?

Bene. In so high a style, Margaret, that no man living shall come over it ; for, in most comely truth, thou deservest it.

Marg. To have no man come over me ! why, shall I always keep below stairs?   10

Bene. Thy wit is as quick as the greyhound's mouth ; it catches.

Marg. And yours as blunt as the fencer's foils, which hit, but hurt not.

Bene. A most manly wit, Margaret ; it will not hurt a woman : and so, I pray thee, call Beatrice : I give thee the bucklers.

Marg. Give us the swords ; we have bucklers of our own.

Bene. If you use them, Margaret, you must put in the pikes with a vice ; and they are dangerous weapons for maids.

Marg. Well, I will call Beatrice to you, who I think hath legs.

Bene. And therefore will come.

     [*Exit Margaret.*

[*Sings*]   The god of love,
That sits above,
And knows me, and knows me,
How pitiful I deserve,—

I mean in singing ; but in loving, Leander the good swimmer, Troilus the first employer of panders, and a whole bookful of these quondam carpet-mongers, whose names yet run smoothly in the even road of a blank verse, why, they were never so truly turned over and over as my poor self in love. Marry, I cannot show it in rhyme ; I have tried : I can find out no rhyme to 'lady' but 'baby,' an innocent rhyme ; for 'scorn,' 'horn,' a hard rhyme ; for, 'school,' 'fool,' a babbling rhyme ; very ominous endings : no, I was not born under a rhyming planet, nor I cannot woo in festival terms.   41

Enter BEATRICE.

Sweet Beatrice, wouldst thou come when I called thee ?
Beat. Yea, signior, and depart when you bid me.
Bene. O, stay but till then !
Beat. 'Then' is spoken ; fare you well now : and yet, ere I go, let me go with that I came ; which is, with knowing what hath passed between you and Claudio.
Bene. Only foul words ; and thereupon I will kiss thee.   51
Beat. Foul words is but foul wind, and foul wind is but foul breath, and foul breath is noisome ; therefore I will depart unkissed.
Bene. Thou hast frighted the word out of his right sense, so forcible is thy wit. But I must tell thee plainly, Claudio undergoes my challenge ; and either I must shortly hear from him, or I will subscribe him a coward. And, I pray thee now, tell me for which of my bad parts didst thou first fall in love with me ?   61
Beat. For them all together ; which maintained so politic a state of evil that they will not admit any good part to intermingle with them. But for which of my good parts did you first suffer love for me ?
Bene. Suffer love ! a good epithet ! I do suffer love indeed, for I love thee against my will.
Beat. In spite of your heart, I think ; alas, poor heart ! If you spite it for my sake, I will spite it for yours ; for I will never love that which my friend hates.
Bene. Thou and I are too wise to woo peaceably.
Beat. It appears not in this confession : there's not one wise man among twenty that will praise himself.
Bene. An old, an old instance, Beatrice, that lived in the time of good neighbors. If a man do not erect in this age his own tomb ere he dies, he shall live no longer in monument than the bell rings and the widow weeps.
Beat. And how long is that, think you ?
Bene. Question : why, an hour in clamor and a quarter in rheum : therefore is it most expedient for the wise, if Don Worm, his conscience, find no impediment to the contrary, to be the trumpet of his own virtues, as I am to myself. So much for praising myself, who, I myself will bear witness, is praiseworthy : and now tell me, how doth your cousin ?   91
Beat. Very ill.
Bene. And how do you ?
Beat. Very ill too.
Bene. Serve God, love me and mend. There will I leave you too, for here comes one in haste.

Enter URSULA.

Urs. Madam, you must come to your uncle. Yonder's old coil at home : it is proved my Lady Hero hath been falsely accused, the prince and Claudio mightily abused ; and Don John is the author of all, who is fled and gone. Will you come presently ?
Beat. Will you go hear this news, signior ?
Bene. I will live in thy heart, die in thy lap and be buried in thy eyes ; and moreover I will go with thee to thy uncle's.   [*Exeunt.*

SCENE III. *A church.*

Enter DON PEDRO, CLAUDIO, *and three or four with tapers.*

Claud. Is this the monument of Leonato ?
A Lord. It is, my lord.
Claud.   [*Reading out of a scroll*]

Done to death by slanderous tongues
Was the Hero that here lies :
Death, in guerdon of her wrongs,
Gives her fame which never dies.
So the life that died with shame
Lives in death with glorious fame.
Hang thou there upon the tomb,
Praising her when I am dumb.   10
Now, music, sound, and sing your solemn hymn.

SONG.

Pardon, goddess of the night,
Those that slew thy virgin knight ;
For the which, with songs of woe,
Round about her tomb they go.
Midnight, assist our moan ;
Help us to sigh and groan,
Heavily, heavily :
Graves, yawn and yield your dead.
Till death be uttered,   20
Heavily, heavily.

Claud. Now, unto thy bones good night !
Yearly will I do this rite.
D. Pedro. Good morrow, masters ; put your torches out :   [tle day,
The wolves have prey'd : and look, the gen-
Before the wheels of Phœbus, round about
Dapples the drowsy east with spots of grey.
Thanks to you all, and leave us : fare you well.
Claud. Good morrow, masters : each his several way.
D. Pedro. Come, let us hence, and put on other weeds ;   30

36

And then to Leonato's we will go.

Claud. And Hymen now with luckier issue
 speed's
Than this for whom we render'd up this woe.
       [*Exeunt.*

SCENE IV. *A room in* LEONATO's *house.*

Enter LEONATO, ANTONIO, BENEDICK, BEA-
 TRICE, MARGARET, URSULA, FRIAR
 FRANCIS, *and* HERO.

Friar. Did I not tell you she was innocent?

Leon. So are the prince and Claudio, who
 accused her
Upon the error that you heard debated :
But Margaret was in some fault for this,
Although against her will, as it appears
In the true course of all the question.

Ant. Well, I am glad that all things sort so
 well

Bene. And so am I, being else by faith enforced
To call young Claudio to a reckoning for it.

Leon. Well, daughter, and you gentle-
 women all,   10
Withdraw into a chamber by yourselves,
And when I send for you, come hither mask'd.
       [*Exeunt Ladies.*
The prince and Claudio promised by this hour
To visit me. You know your office, brother :
You must be father to your brother's daugh-
 ter,
And give her to young Claudio.

Ant. Which I will do with confirm'd countenance.

Bene. Friar, I must entreat your pains, I
 think.

Friar. To do what, signior?

Bene. To bind me, or undo me ; one of
 them.   20
Signior Leonato, truth it is, good signior,
Your niece regards me with an eye of favor.

Leon. That eye my daughter lent her : 'tis
 most true.

Bene. And I do with an eye of love requite
 her.

Leon. The sight whereof I think you had
 from me,
From Claudio and the prince : but what's your
 will?

Bene. Your answer, sir, is enigmatical :
But, for my will, my will is your good will
May stand with ours, this day to be conjoin'd
In the state of honorable marriage :   30
In which, good friar, I shall desire your help.

Leon. My heart is with your liking.

Friar.   And my help.
Here comes the prince and Claudio.

Enter DON PEDRO *and* CLAUDIO, *and two or
 three others.*

D. Pedro. Good morrow to this fair assembly.

Leon. Good morrow, prince ; good morrow,
 Claudio :
We here attend you. Are you yet determined
To-day to marry with my brother's daughter?

Claud. I'll hold my mind, were she an
 Ethiope.

Leon. Call her forth, brother ; here's the
 friar ready.   [*Exit Antonio.*

D. Pedro. Good morrow, Benedick. Why,
 what's the matter,   40
That you have such a February face,
So full of frost, of storm and cloudiness ?

Claud. I think he thinks upon the savage
 bull.
Tush, fear not, man ; we'll tip thy horns with
 gold
And all Europa shall rejoice at thee,
As once Europa did at lusty Jove,
When he would play the noble beast in love.

Bene. Bull Jove, sir, had an amiable low ;
And some such strange bull leap'd your
 father's cow,
And got a calf in that same noble feat 50
Much like to you, for you have just his bleat.

Claud. For this I owe you : here comes
 other reckonings.

Re-enter ANTONIO, *with the* Ladies *masked.*

Which is the lady I must seize upon ?

Ant. This same is she, and I do give you
 her.

Claud. Why, then she's mine. Sweet, let
 me see your face.

Leon. No, that you shall not, till you take
 her hand
Before this friar and swear to marry her.

Claud. Give me your hand : before this
 holy friar,
I am your husband, if you like of me.

Hero. And when I lived, I was your other
 wife :   [*Unmasking.* 60
And when you loved, you were my other husband.

Claud. Another Hero !

Hero.   Nothing certainer :
One Hero died defiled, but I do live,
And surely as I live, I am a maid.

D. Pedro. The former Hero ! Hero that is
 dead !

Leon. She died, my lord, but whiles her
 slander lived.

Friar. All this amazement can I qualify ;
When after that the holy rites are ended,
I'll tell you largely of fair Hero's death :
Meantime let wonder seem familiar, 70
And to the chapel let us presently.

Bene. Soft and fair, friar. Which is Beatrice ?

Beat. [*Unmasking*] I answer to that name.
 What is your will ?

Bene. Do not you love me ?

Beat.   Why, no ; no more than reason.

Bene. Why, then your uncle and the prince
 and Claudio
Have been deceived ; they swore you did.

Beat. Do not you love me ?

Bene.   Troth, no ; no more than reason.

Beat. Why, then my cousin Margaret and
 Ursula   [did
Are much deceived : for they did swear you

Bene. They swore that you were almost
  sick for me.   80
Beat. They swore that you were well-nigh
  dead for me.
Bene. 'Tis no such matter. Then you do
  not love me?
Beat. No, truly, but in friendly recompense.
Leon. Come, cousin, I am sure you love the
  gentleman.
Claud. And I'll be sworn upon't that he
  loves her;
For here's a paper written in his hand,
A halting sonnet of his own pure brain,
Fashion'd to Beatrice.
Hero.   And here's another
Writ in my cousin's hand, stolen from her
  pocket,
Containing her affection unto Benedick. 90
Bene. A miracle! here's our own hands
against our hearts. Come, I will have thee;
but, by this light, I take thee for pity.
Beat. I would not deny you; but, by this
good day, I yield upon great persuasion; and
partly to save your life, for I was told you
were in a consumption.
Bene. Peace! I will stop your mouth.
              [*Kissing her.*
D. Pedro. How dost thou, Benedick, the
married man?   100
Bene. I'll tell thee what, prince; a college
or wit-crackers cannot flout me out of my
humor. Dost thou think I care for a satire or
an epigram? No: if a man will be beaten
with brains he shall wear nothing handsome

about him. In brief, since I do purpose to
marry, I will think nothing to any purpose
that the world can say against it; and therefore never flout at me for what I have said
against it; for man is a giddy thing, and this
is my conclusion. For thy part, Claudio, I did
think to have beaten thee; but in that thou
art like to be my kinsman, live unbruised and
love my cousin.
Claud. I had well hoped thou wouldst have
denied Beatrice, that I might have cudgelled
thee out of thy single life, to make thee a
double-dealer; which, out of question, thou
wilt be, if my cousin do not look exceedingly
narrowly to thee.
Bene. Come, come, we are friends: let's
have a dance ere we are married, that we may
lighten our own hearts and our wives' heels.
Leon. We'll have dancing afterward.
Bene. First, of my word; therefore play,
music. Prince, thou art sad; get thee a wife,
get thee a wife: there is no staff more reverend than one tipped with horn.

Enter a Messenger.

Mess. My lord, your brother John is ta'en
  in flight,
And brought with armed men back to Mes-
  sina.
Bene. Think not on him till to-morrow:
I'll devise thee brave punishments for him.
Strike up, pipers.   [*Dance.* 131
                [*Exeunt.*

AS YOU LIKE IT.

(WRITTEN ABOUT 1599.)

INTRODUCTION.

As You Like It was entered on the Stationers' register together with Henry V., Much Ado About Nothing, and Jonson's Every Man in His Humour, "to be staied," i.e. not printed; the date is August 4, but the year is not mentioned. The previous entry is dated May 27, 1600, and as the other plays were printed in 1600 and 1601, we infer that the August was that of the year 1600. The comedy is not mentioned by Meres. A line, "Who ever loved that loved not at first sight?" is quoted (Act III., Sc. v., L 82) from Marlowe's Hero and Leander, which was published in 1598. We may set down the following year, 1599, as the probable date of the creation of this charming comedy. The story is taken from Thomas Lodge's prose tale, Rosalynde, Euphues Golden Legacie, first printed in 1590, and a passage in Lodge's dedication probably suggested to Shakespeare the name of his play. Lodge, who wrote this tale on his voyage to the Canaries, founded it in part on the Cook's Tale of Gamelyn, wrongly ascribed to Chaucer, and inserted in some editions as one of the Canterbury Tales. In parts of his work the dramatist follows the story-teller closely, but there are some important differences. The heroic names Orlando, Oliver, and Sir Rowland are due to Shakespeare. It was a thought of Shakespeare to make the rightful and usurping dukes, as in The Tempest, brothers. In Lodge's novel the girl-friends pass in the forest for lady and page, in Shakespeare for brother and sister. Shakespeare omits the incident of Aliena's rescue from robbers by her future husband; love at first sight was natural in Arden, but a band of robbers would have marred the tranquillity of the scene. To Shakespeare we owe the creation of the characters of Jacques, Touchstone, and Audrey. Written perhaps immediately after Henry V., the play presents a striking contrast with that high-pitched historical drama. It is as if Shakespeare's imagination craved repose and refreshment after the life of courts and camps. We are still on French soil, but instead of the sound of the shock of battle at Agincourt, we, hear the waving forest boughs, and the forest streams of Arden, where "they fleet the time carelessly as they did in the Golden World." There is an open-air feeling about this play, as there is about The Merry Wives of Windsor; but in The Merry Wives all the surroundings are English and real, here they belong to a land of romance. For the Renaissance, that age of vast energy, national enterprise, religious strife, and court intrigue, pastoral or idyllic poetry possessed a peculiar charm; the quiet and innocence of a poetical Arcadia was a solace to a life of highly-wrought ambition and aspiration. "Sweet are the uses of adversity," moralizes the banished Duke, and external, material adversity has come to him, to Rosalind, and to Orlando; but if fortune is harsh, nature—both external nature and human character—is sound and sweet, and of real suffering there is none in the play. All that is evil remains in the society which the denizens of the forest have left behind; and both seriously, in the characters of the usurping Duke and Oliver, and playfully, through Touchstone's mockery of court follies, a criticism on what is evil and artificial in society is suggested in contrast with the woodland life. Yet Shakespeare never falls into the conventional, pastoral manner. Orlando is an ideal of youthful strength, beauty, and noble innocence of heart; and Rosalind's bright, tender womanhood seems but to grow more exquisitely feminine in the male attire which she has assumed in self-defence. Her feelings are almost as quick and fine as those of Imogen (she has not, like Imogen, known fear and sorrow), and she uses her wit and bright play of intellect as a protection against her own eager and vivid emotions. Possessed of a delighted consciousness of power to confer happiness, she can dally with disguises, and make what is most serious to her at the same time possess the charm of an exquisite frolic. The melancholy Jacques is a sentimentalist and in some degree a superficial cynic, but he is not a bad-hearted egoist, like Don John; he is a perfectly idle seeker for new sensations and an observer of his own feelings; he is weary of all he has found, and especially professes to despise the artificial society, which yet he never really escapes from as the others do. His wisdom is half foolery, as Touchstone's foolery is half wisdom. Touchstone is the daintiest fool of the comedies, and in comparing him with the clowns of The Comedy of Errors or The Two Gentlemen of Verona, we perceive how Shakespeare's humor has grown in refinement.

DRAMATIS PERSONÆ.

DUKE, living in banishment.
FREDERICK, his brother, an usurper of his dominions.
AMIENS, } lords attending on the banished
JAQUES, } duke.

LE BEAU, a courtier attending upon Frederick.
CHARLES, wrestler to Frederick.
OLIVER, }
JAQUES, } sons of Sir Rowland de Boys.
ORLANDO, }

(564)

ADAM, } servants to Oliver.
DENNIS, }
TOUCHSTONE, a clown.
SIR OLIVER MARTEXT, a vicar.
CORIN, } shepherds.
SILVIUS, }
WILLIAM, a country fellow in love with
  Audrey.
A person representing Hymen.

ROSALIND, daughter to the banished duke.
CELIA, daughter to Frederick.
PHEBE, a shepherdess.
AUDREY a country wench.

Lords, pages, and attendants, &c.

SCENE : *Oliver's house; Duke Frederick's court,
  and the Forest of Arden.*

ACT I.

SCENE I. *Orchard of* OLIVER's *house.*

Enter ORLANDO *and* ADAM.

Orl. †As I remember, Adam, it was upon this fashion bequeathed me by will but poor a thousand crowns, and, as thou sayest, charged my brother, on his blessing, to breed me well : and there begins my sadness. My brother Jaques he keeps at school, and report speaks goldenly of his profit: for my part, he keeps me rustically at home, or, to speak more properly, stays me here at home unkept; for call you that keeping for a gentleman of my birth, that differs not from the stalling of an ox ? His horses are bred better ; for, besides that they are fair with their feeding, they are taught their manage, and to that end riders dearly hired : but I, his brother, gain nothing under him but growth ; for the which his animals on his dunghills are as much bound to him as I. Besides this nothing that he so plentifully gives me, the something that nature gave me his countenance seems to take from me : he lets me feed with his hinds, bars me the place of a brother, and, as much as in him lies, mines my gentility with my education. This is it, Adam, that grieves me ; and the spirit of my father, which I think is within me, begins to mutiny against this servitude : I will no longer endure it, though yet I know no wise remedy how to avoid it.

Adam. Yonder comes my master, your brother.

Orl. Go apart, Adam, and thou shalt hear how he will shake me up. 30

Enter OLIVER.

Oli. Now, sir ! what make you here ?

Orl. Nothing: I am not taught to make any thing.

Oli. What mar you then, sir ?

Orl. Marry, sir, I am helping you to mar that which God made, a poor unworthy brother of yours, with idleness.

Oli. Marry, sir, be better employed, and be naught awhile. 39

Orl. Shall I keep your hogs and eat husks with them ? What prodigal portion have I spent, that I should come to such penury ?

Oli. Know you where your are, sir ?

Orl. O, sir, very well : here in your orchard.

Oli. Know you before whom, sir ?

Orl. Ay, better than him I am before knows me. I know you are my eldest brother ; and, in the gentle condition of blood, you should so know me. The courtesy of nations allows you my better, in that you are the first-born ; but the same tradition takes not away my blood, were there twenty brothers betwixt us : I have as much of my father in me as you ; albeit, I confess, your coming before me is nearer to his reverence.

Oli. What, boy !

Orl. Come, come, elder brother, you are too young in this.

Oli. Wilt thou lay hands on me, villain ?

Orl. I am no villain ; I am the youngest son of Sir Rowland de Boys ; he was my father, and he is thrice a villain that says such a father begot villains. Wert thou not my brother, I would not take this hand from thy throat till this other had pulled out thy tongue for saying so : thou hast railed on thyself.

Adam. Sweet masters, be patient : for your father's remembrance, be at accord.

Oli. Let me go, I say.

Orl. I will not, till I please : you shall hear me. My father charged you in his will to give me good education : you have trained me like a peasant, obscuring and hiding from me all gentleman-like qualities. The spirit of my father grows strong in me, and I will no longer endure it : therefore allow me such exercises as may become a gentleman, or give me the poor allottery my father left me by testament ; with that I will go buy my fortunes.

Oli. And what wilt thou do ? beg, when that is spent ? Well, sir, get you in : I will not long be troubled with you ; you shall have some part of your will : I pray you, leave me.

Orl. I will no further offend you than becomes me for my good.

Oli. Get you with him, you old dog.

Adam. Is 'old dog' my reward ? Most true, I have lost my teeth in your service. God be with my old master ! he would not have spoke such a word.

[*Exeunt Orlando and Adam.*

Oli. Is it even so ? begin you to grow upon me ? I will physic your rankness, and yet give no thousand crowns neither. Holla, Dennis !

Enter DENNIS.

Den. Calls your worship ?

Oli. Was not Charles, the duke's wrestler, here to speak with me?

Den. So please you, he is here at the door and importunes access to you.

Oli. Call him in. [*Exit Dennis.*] 'Twill be a good way; and to-morrow the wrestling is.

Enter CHARLES.

Cha. Good morrow to your worship.   100

Oli. Good Monsieur Charles, what's the new news at the new court?

Cha. There's no news at the court, sir, but the old news: that is, the old duke is banished by his younger brother the new duke; and three or four loving lords have put themselves into voluntary exile with him, whose lands and revenues enrich the new duke; therefore he gives them good leave to wander.

Oli. Can you tell if Rosalind, the duke's daughter, be banished with her father?   111

Cha. O, no; for the duke's daughter, her cousin, so loves her, being ever from their cradles bred together, that she would have followed her exile, or have died to stay behind her. She is at the court, and no less beloved of her uncle than his own daughter; and never two ladies loved as they do.

Oli. Where will the old duke live?

Cha. They say he is already in the forest of Arden, and a many merry men with him; and there they live like the old Robin Hood of England: they say many young gentlemen flock to him every day, and fleet the time carelessly, as they did in the golden world.

Oli. What, you wrestle to-morrow before the new duke?

Cha. Marry, do I, sir; and I came to acquaint you with a matter. I am given, sir, secretly to understand that your younger brother Orlando hath a disposition to come in disguised against me to try a fall. To-morrow, sir, I wrestle for my credit; and he that escapes me without some broken limb shall acquit him well. Your brother is but young and tender; and, for your love, I would be loath to foil him, as I must, for my own honor, if he come in: therefore, out of my love to you, I came hither to acquaint you withal, that either you might stay him from his intendment or brook such disgrace well as he shall run into, in that it is a thing of his own search and altogether against my will.

Oli. Charles, I thank thee for thy love to me, which thou shalt find I will most kindly requite. I had myself notice of my brother's purpose herein and have by underhand means labored to dissuade him from it, but he is resolute. I'll tell thee, Charles: it is the stubbornest young fellow of France, full of ambition, an envious emulator of every man's good parts, a secret and villanous contriver against me his natural brother: therefore use thy discretion; I had as lief thou didst break his neck as his finger. And thou wert best look to't; for if thou dost him any slight disgrace or if he do not mightily grace himself on thee, he will practice against thee by poison, entrap thee by some treacherous device and never leave thee till he hath ta'en thy life by some indirect means or other; for, I assure thee, and almost with tears I speak it, there is not one so young and so villanous this day living. I speak but brotherly of him; but should I anatomize him to thee as he is, I must blush and weep and thou must look pale and wonder.

Cha. I am heartily glad I came hither to you. If he come to-morrow, I'll give him his payment: if ever he go alone again, I'll never wrestle for prize more: and so God keep your worship!

Oli. Farewell, good Charles. [*Exit Charles.*] Now will I stir this gamester: I hope I shall see an end of him; for my soul, yet I know not why, hates nothing more than he. Yet he's gentle, never schooled and yet learned, full of noble device, of all sorts enchantingly beloved, and indeed so much in the heart of the world, and especially of my own people, who best know him, that I am altogether misprised: but it shall not be so, long; this wrestler shall clear all: nothing remains but that I kindle the boy thither; which now I'll go about.   [*Exit.* 180

SCENE II.   *Lawn before the* DUKE's *palace.*

Enter CELIA *and* ROSALIND.

Cel. I pray thee, Rosalind, sweet my coz, be merry.

Ros. Dear Celia, I show more mirth than I am mistress of; and would you yet I were merrier? Unless you could teach me to forget a banished father, you must not learn me how to remember any extraordinary pleasure.

Cel. Herein I see thou lovest me not with the full weight that I love thee. If my uncle, thy banished father, had banished thy uncle, the duke my father, so thou hadst been still with me, I could have taught my love to take thy father for mine: so wouldst thou, if the truth of thy love to me were so righteously tempered as mine is to thee.

Ros. Well, I will forget the condition of my estate, to rejoice in yours.

Cel. You know my father hath no child but I, nor none is like to have: and, truly, when he dies, thou shalt be his heir, for what he hath taken away from thy father perforce, I will render thee again in affection; by mine honor, I will; and when I break that oath, let me turn monster: therefore, my sweet Rose, my dear Rose, be merry.

Ros. From henceforth I will, coz, and devise sports. Let me see; what think you of falling in love?

Cel. Marry, I prithee, do, to make sport withal: but love no man in good earnest; nor no further in sport neither than with safety of a pure blush thou mayst in honor come off again.

Ros. What shall be our sport, then?

ROSALIND AND CELIA.

AS YOU LIKE IT, p. 569

Cel. Let us sit and mock the good house-wife Fortune from her wheel, that her gifts may henceforth be bestowed equally.

Ros. I would we could do so, for her bene-fits are mightily misplaced, and the bountiful blind woman doth most mistake in her gifts to women

Cel. 'Tis true ; for those that she makes fair she scarce makes honest, and those that she makes honest she makes very ill-favoredly.

Ros. Nay, now thou goest from Fortune's office to Nature's Fortune reigns in gifts of the world, not in the lineaments of Nature.

Enter TOUCHSTONE.

Cel. No ? when Nature hath made a fair creature, may she not by Fortune fall into the fire ? Though Nature hath given us wit to flout at Fortune, hath not Fortune sent in this fool to cut off the argument ? 50

Ros. Indeed, there is Fortune too hard for Nature, when Fortune makes Nature's natural the cutter-off of Nature's wit.

Cel. Peradventure this is not Fortune's work neither, but Nature's , who perceiveth our natural wits too dull to reason of such goddesses and hath sent this natural for our whetstone ; for always the dulness of the fool is the whetstone of the wits. How now, wit ! whither wander you ?

Touch. Mistress, you must come away to your father 61

Cel. Were you made the messenger ?

Touch. No, by mine honor, but I was bid to come for you

Ros. Where learned you that oath, fool ?

Touch. Of a certain knight that swore by his honor they were good pancakes and swore by his honor the mustard was naught now I'll stand to it, the pancakes were naught and the mustard was good, and yet was not the knight forsworn 71

Cel. How prove you that, in the great heap of your knowledge ?

Ros. Ay, marry, now unmuzzle your wis-dom

Touch. Stand you both forth now stroke your chins, and swear by your beards that I am a knave

Cel. By our beards, if we had them, thou art

Touch. By my knavery, if I had it, then I were ; but if you swear by that that is not, you are not forsworn : no more was this knight, swearing by his honor, for he never had any ; or if he had, he had sworn it away before ever he saw those pancakes or that mus-tard.

Cel. Prithee, who is't that thou meanest ?

Touch. One that old Frederick, your father, loves.

Cel. My father's love is enough to honor him : enough ! speak no more of him ; you'll be whipped for taxation one of these days. 91

Touch. The more pity, that fools may not speak wisely what wise men do foolishly.

Cel. By my troth, thou sayest true ; for since the little wit that fools have was silenced, the little foolery that wise men have makes a great show. Here comes Monsieur Le Beau.

Ros With his mouth full of news.

Cel. Which he will put on us, as pigeons feed their young 100

Ros Then shall we be news-crammed.

Cel All the better , we shall be the more marketable.

Enter LE BEAU.

Bon jour, Monsieur Le Beau : what's the news ?

Le Beau. Fair princess, you have lost much good sport

Cel Sport ! of what color ?

Le Beau. What color, madam ! how shall I answer you ?

Ros As wit and fortune will. 110

Touch. Or as the Destinies decree.

Cel Well said , that was laid on with a trowel.

Touch. Nay, if I keep not my rank,—

Ros Thou losest thy old smell

Le Beau. You amaze me, ladies I would have told you of good wrestling, which you have lost the sight of

Ros. You tell us the manner of the wrest-ling.

Le Beau. I will tell you the beginning ; and, if it please your ladyships, you may see the end ; for the best is yet to do , and here, where you are, they are coming to perform it

Cel. Well, the beginning, that is dead and buried

Le Beau. There comes an old man and his three sons,—

Cel I could match this beginning with an old tale.

Le Beau Three proper young men, of ex-cellent growth and presence 130

Ros With bills on their necks, 'Be it known unto all men by these presents'

Le Beau The eldest of the three wrestled with Charles, the duke's wrestler ; which Charles in a moment threw him and broke three of his ribs, that there is little hope of life in him ; so he served the second, and so the third. Yonder they lie , the poor old man, their father, making such pitiful dole over them that all the beholders take his part with weeping. 140

Ros Alas !

Touch. But what is the sport, monsieur, that the ladies have lost ?

Le Beau Why, this that I speak of.

Touch. Thus men may grow wiser every day : it is the first time that ever I heard breaking of ribs was sport for ladies.

Cel Or I, I promise thee

Ros. But is there any else longs to see this broken music in his sides ? is there yet another dotes upon rib-breaking ? Shall we see this wrestling, cousin ?

Le Beau. - You must, if you stay here ; for here is the place appointed for the wrestling, and they are ready to perform it.

Cel. Yonder, sure, they are coming: let us now stay and see it.

Flourish. Enter DUKE FREDERICK, Lords, ORLANDO, CHARLES, *and* Attendants.

Duke F. Come on : since the youth will not be entreated, his own peril on his forwardness.

Ros. Is yonder the man ?   160

Le Beau. Even he, madam.

Cel. Alas, he is too young ! yet he looks successfully.

Duke F. How now, daughter and cousin ! are you crept hither to see the wrestling ?

Ros. Ay, my liege, so please you give us leave.

Duke F. You will take little delight in it, I can tell you ; there is such odds in the man. In pity of the challenger's youth I would fain dissuade him, but he will not be entreated. Speak to him, ladies ; see if you can move him.

Cel. Call him hither, good Monsieur Le Beau.

Duke F. Do so : I'll not be by.

Le Beau. Monsieur the challenger, the princesses call for you.

Orl. I attend them with all respect and duty.

Ros. Young man, have you challenged Charles the wrestler ?   179

Orl. No, fair princess ; he is the general challenger : I come but in, as others do, to try with him the strength of my youth.

Cel. Young gentleman, your spirits are too bold for your years. You have seen cruel proof of this man's strength : if you saw yourself with your eyes or knew yourself with your judgment, the fear of your adventure would counsel you to a more equal enterprise. We pray you, for your own sake, to embrace your own safety and give over this attempt.   190

Ros. Do, young sir ; your reputation shall not therefore be misprised : we will make it our suit to the duke that the wrestling might not go forward.

Orl. I beseech you, punish me not with your hard thoughts ; wherein I confess me much guilty, to deny so fair and excellent ladies any thing. But let your fair eyes and gentle wishes go with me to my trial: wherein if I be foiled, there is but one shamed that was never gracious ; if killed, but one dead that was willing to be so : I shall do my friends no wrong, for I have none to lament me, the world no injury, for in it I have nothing ; only in the world I fill up a place, which may be better supplied when I have made it empty.

Ros. The little strength that I have, I would it were with you.

Cel. And mine, to eke out hers.

Ros. Fare you well : pray heaven I be deceived in you!   210

Cel. Your heart's desires be with you !

Cha. Come, where is this young gallant that is so desirous to lie with his mother earth?

Orl. Ready, sir ; but his will hath in it a more modest working.

Duke F. You shall try but one fall.

Cha. No, I warrant your grace, you shall not entreat him to a second, that have so mightily persuaded him from a first.   219

Orl. An you mean to mock me after, you should not have mocked me before : but come your ways.

Ros. Now Hercules be thy speed, young man !

Cel. I would I were invisible, to catch the strong fellow by the leg.   [*They wrestle.*

Ros. O excellent young man !

Cel. If I had a thunderbolt in mine eye, I can tell who should down.

[*Shout. Charles is thrown.*

Duke F. No more, no more.

Orl. Yes, I beseech your grace : I am not yet well breathed.   230

Duke F. How dost thou, Charles ?

Le Beau. He cannot speak, my lord.

Duke F. Bear him away. What is thy name, young man ?

Orl. Orlando, my liege ; the youngest son of Sir Rowland de Boys.

Duke F. I would thou hadst been son to some man else :
The world esteem'd thy father honorable,
But I did find him still mine enemy :
Thou shouldst have better pleased me with this deed,   240
Hadst thou descended from another house.
But fare thee well ; thou art a gallant youth :
I would thou hadst told me of another father.

[*Exeunt Duke Fred., train, and Le Beau.*

Cel. Were I my father, coz, would I do this ?   [son,

Orl. I am more proud to be Sir Rowland's
His youngest son ; and would not change that calling,
To be adopted heir to Frederick.

Ros. My father loved Sir Rowland as his soul,
And all the world was of my father's mind :
Had I before known this young man his son,
I should have given him tears unto entreaties,
Ere he should thus have ventured.   251

Cel.   Gentle cousin,
Let us go thank him and encourage him :
My father's rough and envious disposition
Sticks me at heart. Sir, you have well deserved:
If you do keep your promises in love
But justly, as you have exceeded all promise,
Your mistress shall be happy.

Ros.   Gentleman,

[*Giving him a chain from her neck.*

Wear this for me, one out of suits with fortune,
That could give more, but that her hand lacks means.
Shall we go, coz ?

Cel. Ay. Fare you well, fair gentleman.

Orl. Can I not say, I thank you ? My better parts   261

Are all thrown down, and that which here
    stands up
Is but a quintain, a mere lifeless block.
  Ros. He calls us back : my pride fell with
    my fortunes ;
I'll ask him what he would. Did you call, sir ?
Sir, you have wrestled well and overthrown
More than your enemies.
  Cel.   Will you go, coz ?
  Ros. Have with you. Fare you well.
           [Exeunt Rosalind and Celia.
  Orl. What passion hangs these weights
    upon my tongue ?
I cannot speak to her, yet she urged con-
    ference.
O poor Orlando, thou art overthrown !   271
Or Charles or something weaker masters thee.

Re-enter LE BEAU.

  Le Beau. Good sir, I do in friendship coun-
    sel you
To leave this place. Albeit you have deserved
High commendation, true applause and love,
Yet such is now the duke's condition
That he misconstrues all that you have done.
The duke is humorous ; what he is indeed,
More suits you to conceive than I to speak of.
  Orl. I thank you, sir : and, pray you, tell
    me this ;   280
Which of the two was daughter of the duke
That here was at the wrestling ?
  Le Beau. Neither his daughter, if we judge
    by manners ;
But yet indeed the lesser is his daughter:
The other is daughter to the banish'd duke,
And here detain'd by her usurping uncle,
To keep his daughter company ; whose loves
Are dearer than the natural bond of sisters.
But I can tell you that of late this duke
Hath ta en displeasure 'gainst his gentle niece,
Grounded upon no other argument   291
But that the people praise her for her virtues
And pity her for her good father's sake ;
And, on my life, his malice 'gainst the lady
Will suddenly break forth. Sir, fare you well:
Hereafter, in a better world than this,
I shall desire more love and knowledge of you.
  Orl. I rest much bounden to you : fare you
    well.   *[Exit Le Beau.*
Thus must I from the smoke into the smother;
From tyrant duke unto a tyrant brother : 300
But heavenly Rosalind !   *[Exit.*

SCENE III. *A room in the palace.*

Enter CELIA *and* ROSALIND.

  Cel. Why, cousin ! why, Rosalind ! Cupid
have mercy ! not a word ?
  Ros. Not one to throw at a dog.
  Cel. No, thy words are too precious to be
cast away upon curs ; throw some of them at
me ; come, lame me with reasons.
  Ros. Then there were two cousins laid up ;
when the one should be lamed with reasons
and the other mad without any.
  Cel. But is all this for your father ?   10

  Ros. No, some of it is for my child's father.
O, how full of briers is this working-day world!
  Cel. They are but burs, cousin, thrown
upon thee in holiday foolery : if we walk not
in the trodden paths, our very petticoats will
catch them.
  Ros. I could shake them off my coat : these
burs are in my heart.
  Cel. Hem them away.
  Ros. I would try, if I could cry 'hem' and
have him.   20
  Cel. Come, come, wrestle with thy affections.
  Ros. O, they take the part of a better wrestler than myself !
  Cel. O, a good wish upon you ! you will try
in time, in despite of a fall. But, turning these
jests out of service, let us talk in good earnest:
is it possible, on such a sudden, you should fall
into so strong a liking with old Sir Rowland's
youngest son ?
  Ros. The duke my father loved his father
dearly.   31
  Cel. Doth it therefore ensue that you should
love his son dearly ? By this kind of chase, I
should hate him, for my father hated his father
dearly ; yet I hate not Orlando.
  Ros. No, faith, hate him not, for my sake.
  Cel. Why should I not ? doth he not deserve
well ?
  Ros. Let me love him for that, and do you
love him because I do. Look, here comes the
duke.   41
  Cel. With his eyes full of anger.

Enter DUKE FREDERICK, *with* Lords.

  Duke F. Mistress, dispatch you with your
    safest haste
And get you from our court.
  Ros.   Me, uncle ?
  Duke F.   You, cousin :
Within these ten days if that thou be'st found
So near our public court as twenty miles,
Thou diest for it.
  Ros.   I do beseech your grace,
Let me the knowledge of my fault bear with
    me :
If with myself I hold intelligence
Or have acquaintance with mine own desires,
If that I do not dream or be not frantic,—   51
As I do trust I am not—then, dear uncle,
Never so much as in a thought unborn
Did I offend your highness.
  Duke F.   Thus do all traitors :
If their purgation did consist in words,
They are as innocent as grace itself :
Let it suffice thee that I trust thee not.
  Ros. Yet your mistrust cannot make me a
traitor :
Tell me whereon the likelihood depends.
  Duke F. Thou art thy father's daughter ;
    there's enough.   60
  Ros. So was I when your highness took his
dukedom ;
So was I when your highness banish'd him :
Treason is not inherited, my lord ;

Or, if we did derive it from our friends,
What's that to me ? my father was no traitor :
Then, good my liege, mistake me not so much
To think my poverty is treacherous.
 Cel. Dear sovereign, hear me speak.
 Duke F. Ay, Celia ; we stay'd her for your
    sake,
Else had she with her father ranged along. 70
 Cel. I did not then entreat to have her stay;
It was your pleasure and your own remorse :
I was too young that time to value her ;
But now I know her : if she be a traitor,
Why so am I ; we still have slept together,
Rose at an instant, learn'd, play'd, eat to-
    gether,
And wheresoe'er we went, like Juno's swans,
Still we went coupled and inseparable.
 Duke F. She is too subtle for thee ; and
    her smoothness,
Her very silence and her patience   80
Speak to the people, and they pity her.
Thou art a fool : she robs thee of thy name ;
And thou wilt show more bright and seem
    more virtuous
When she is gone. Then open not thy lips :
Firm and irrevocable is my doom
Which I have pass'd upon her; she is banish'd.
 Cel. Pronounce that sentence then on me,
    my liege :
I cannot live out of her company.
 Duke F. You are a fool. You, niece, pro-
    vide yourself :
If you outstay the time, upon mine honor, 90
And in the greatness of my word, you die.
        [*Exeunt Duke Frederick and Lords.*
 Cel. O my poor Rosalind, whither wilt
    thou go ?
Wilt thou change fathers ? I will give thee
    mine.
I charge thee, be not thou more grieved than I
    am.
 Ros. I have more cause.
 Cel.   Thou hast not, cousin ;
Prithee, be cheerful: know'st thou not, the
    duke
Hath banish'd me, his daughter ?
 Ros.   That he hath not.
 Cel. No, hath not ? Rosalind lacks then the
    love
Which teacheth thee that thou and I am one :
Shall we be sunder'd ? shall we part, sweet
    girl ?   100
No : let my father seek another heir.
Therefore devise with me how we may fly,
Whither to go and what to bear with us ;
And do not seek to take your change upon
    you,
To bear your griefs yourself and leave me out;
For, by this heaven, now at our sorrows pale,
Say what thou canst, I'll go along with thee.
 Ros. Why, whither shall we go ?
 Cel. To seek my uncle in the forest of
    Arden.
 Ros. Alas, what danger will it be to us, 110
Maids as we are, to travel forth so far !
Beauty provoketh thieves sooner than gold.

 Cel. I'll put myself in poor and mean attire
And with a kind of umber smirch my face ;
The like do you : so shall we pass along
And never stir assailants.
 Ros.   Were it not better,
Because that I am more than common tall,
That I did suit me all points like a man ?
A gallant curtle-axe upon my thigh,
A boar-spear in my hand ; and—in my heart
Lie there what hidden woman's fear there
    will—   121
We'll have a swashing and a martial outside,
As many other mannish cowards have
That do outface it with their semblances.
 Cel. What shall I call thee when thou art
    a man ?
 Ros. I'll have no worse a name than Jove's
    own page ;
And therefore look you call me Ganymede.
But what will you be call'd ?
 Cel. Something that hath a reference to my
    state ;
No longer Celia, but Aliena.   130
 Ros. But, cousin, what if we assay'd to steal
The clownish fool out of your father's court ?
Would he not be a comfort to our travel ?
 Cel. He'll go along o'er the wide world
    with me ;
Leave me alone to woo him. Let's away,
And get our jewels and our wealth together,
Devise the fittest time and safest way
To hide us from pursuit that will be made
After my flight. Now go we in content
To liberty and not to banishment. [*Exeunt.* 140

ACT II.

 SCENE I. *The Forest of Arden.*

 Enter DUKE *senior,* AMIENS, *and two or
    three Lords, like foresters.*

 Duke S. Now, my co-mates and brothers in
    exile,
Hath not old custom made this life more sweet
Than that of painted pomp ? Are not these
    woods
More free from peril than the envious court ?
Here feel we but the penalty of Adam,
The seasons' difference, as the icy fang
And churlish chiding of the winter's wind,
Which, when it bites and blows upon my body,
Even till I shrink with cold, I smile and say
' This is no flattery : these are counsellors   10
That feelingly persuade me what I am.'
Sweet are the uses of adversity,
Which, like the toad, ugly and venomous,
Wears yet a precious jewel in his head ;
And this our life exempt from public haunt
Finds tongues in trees, books in the running
    brooks,
Sermons in stones and good in every thing.
I would not change it.
 Ami.   Happy is your grace,
That can translate the stubbornness of fortune
Into so quiet and so sweet a style.   20

Duke S. Come, shall we go and kill us
    venison ?
And yet it irks me the poor dappled fools,
Being native burghers of this desert city,
Should in their own confines with forked heads
Have their round haunches gored.
    First Lord.   Indeed, my lord,
The melancholy Jaques grieves at that,
And, in that kind, swears you do more usurp
Than doth your brother that hath banish'd you.
To-day my Lord of Amiens and myself
Did steal behind him as he lay along   30
Under an oak whose antique root peeps out
Upon the brook that brawls along this wood :
To the which place a poor sequester'd stag,
That from the hunter's aim had ta'en a hurt,
Did come to languish, and indeed, my lord,
The wretched animal heaved forth such groans
That their discharge did stretch his leathern
    coat
Almost to bursting, and the big round tears
Coursed one another down his innocent nose
In piteous chase ; and thus the hairy fool,   40
Much marked of the melancholy Jaques,
Stood on the extremest verge of the swift
    brook,
Augmenting it with tears.
    Duke S.   But what said Jaques ?
Did he not moralize this spectacle ?
    First Lord. O, yes, into a thousand similes.
First, for his weeping into the needless stream ;
' Poor deer,' quoth he ' thou makest a testa-
    ment
As worldlings do, giving thy sum of more
To that which had too much :' then, being
    there alone,
Left and abandon'd of his velvet friends,   50
' 'Tis right :' quoth he ' thus misery doth part
The flux of company :' anon a careless herd,
Full of the pasture, jumps along by him
And never stays to greet him ; ' Ay,' quoth
    Jaques,
' Sweep on, you fat and greasy citizens ;
'Tis just the fashion : wherefore do you look
Upon that poor and broken bankrupt there ? '
Thus most invectively he pierceth through
The body of the country, city, court,
Yea, and of this our life, swearing that we   60
Are mere usurpers, tyrants and what's worse,
To fright the animals and to kill them up
In their assign'd and native dwelling-place.
    Duke S. And did you leave him in this
    contemplation ?
    Sec. Lord. We did, my lord, weeping and
    commenting
Upon the sobbing deer.
    Duke S.   Show me the place :
I love to cope him in these sullen fits,
For then he's full of matter.
    First Lord. I'll bring you to him straight.
                          [*Exeunt.*

       SCENE II.   *A room in the palace.*
     Enter DUKE FREDERICK, *with* Lords.
    Duke F. Can it be possible that no man
    saw them ?

It cannot be : some villains of my court
Are of consent and sufferance in this.
    First Lord. I cannot hear of any that did
    see her.
The ladies, her attendants of her chamber,
Saw her a-bed, and in the morning early
They found the bed untreasured of their mis-
    tress.
    Sec. Lord. My lord, the roynish clown, at
    whom so oft
Your grace was wont to laugh, is also missing.
Hisperia, the princess' gentlewoman,   10
Confesses that she secretly o'erheard
Your daughter and her cousin much commend
The parts and graces of the wrestler
That did but lately foil the sinewy Charles ;
And she believes, wherever they are gone,
That youth is surely in their company.
    Duke F. Send to his brother ; fetch that
    gallant hither ;
If he be absent, bring his brother to me ;
I'll make him find him: do this suddenly,
And let not search and inquisition quail   20
To bring again these foolish runaways.
                          [*Exeunt.*

     SCENE III.   *Before* OLIVER'S *house.*
     Enter ORLANDO *and* ADAM, *meeting.*

    Orl. Who's there ?
    Adam. What, my young master ? O my
    gentle master !
O my sweet master ! O you memory
Of old Sir Rowland ! why, what make you
    here ?
Why are you virtuous ? why do people love
    you ?   [iant ?
And wherefore are you gentle, strong and val-
Why would you be so fond to overcome
The bonny priser of the humorous duke ?
Your praise is come too swiftly home before
    you.
Know you not, master, to some kind of men
Their graces serve them but as enemies ?   11
No more do yours : your virtues, gentle mas-
    ter,
Are sanctified and holy traitors to you.
O, what a world is this, when what is comely
Envenoms him that bears it !
    Orl. Why, what's the matter ?
    Adam.   O unhappy youth !
Come not within these doors ; within this roof
The enemy of all your graces lives :
Your brother—no, no brother ; yet the son—
Yet not the son, I will not call him son   20
Of him I was about to call his father—
Hath heard your praises, and this night he
    means
To burn the lodging where you use to lie
And you within it : if he fail of that,
He will have other means to cut you off.
I overheard him and his practices.
This is no place ; this house is but a butchery:
Abhor it, fear it, do not enter it.
    Orl. Why, whither, Adam, wouldst thou
    have me go ?

Adam. No matter whither, so you come
  not here. 30
Orl. What, wouldst thou have me go and
  beg my food ?
Or with a base and boisterous sword enforce
A thievish living on the common road ?
This I must do, or know not what to do :
Yet this I will not do, do how I can ;
I rather will subject me to the malice
Of a diverted blood and bloody brother.
Adam. But do not so. I have five hundred
  crowns,
The thrifty hire I saved under your father,
Which I did store to be my foster-nurse 40
When service should in my old limbs lie lame
And unregarded age in corners thrown :
Take that, and He that doth the ravens feed,
Yea, providently caters for the sparrow,
Be comfort to my age ! Here is the gold ;
And all this I give you. Let me be your ser-
  vant :
Though I look old, yet I am strong and lusty;
For in my youth I never did apply
Hot and rebellious liquors in my blood, 50
Nor did not with unbashful forehead woo
The means of weakness and debility;
Therefore my age is as a lusty winter,
Frosty, but kindly : let me go with you ;
I'll do the service of a younger man
In all your business and necessities.
Orl. O good old man, how well in thee ap-
  pears
The constant service of the antique world,
When service sweat for duty, not for meed !
Thou art not for the fashion of these times, 60
Where none will sweat but for promotion,
And having that, do choke their service up
Even with the having : it is not so with thee.
But, poor old man, thou prunest a rotten tree,
That cannot so much as a blossom yield
In lieu of all thy pains and husbandry
But come thy ways ; we'll go along together,
And ere we have thy youthful wages spent,
We'll light upon some settled low content.
Adam. Master, go on, and I will follow
  thee,
To the last gasp, with truth and loyalty. 70
From seventeen years till now almost four-
  score
Here lived I, but now live here no more.
At seventeen years many their fortunes seek ;
But at fourscore it is too late a week :
Yet fortune cannot recompense me better
Than to die well and not my master's debtor.
  [*Exeunt.*

SCENE IV. *The Forest of Arden.*

Enter ROSALIND *for* GANYMEDE, CELIA *for*
  ALIENA, *and* TOUCHSTONE.

Ros. O Jupiter, how weary are my spirits !
Touch. I care not for my spirits, if my legs
were not weary.
Ros. I could find in my heart to disgrace
my man's apparel and to cry like a woman ; but
I must comfort the weaker vessel, as doublet

and hose ought to show itself courageous to
petticoat : therefore courage, good Aliena !
Cel. I pray you, bear with me ; I cannot go
no further. 10
Touch. For my part, I had rather bear with
you than bear you ; yet I should bear no cross
if I did bear you, for I think you have no
money in your purse.
Ros. Well, this is the forest of Arden.
Touch. Ay, now am I in Arden ; the more
fool I ; when I was at home, I was in a better
place : but travellers must be content.
Ros. Ay, be so, good Touchstone.

Enter CORIN *and* SILVIUS.

Look you, who comes here ; a young man and
an old in solemn talk. 21
Cor. That is the way to make her scorn you
  still.
Sil. O Corin, that thou knew'st how I do
  love her !
Cor. I partly guess ; for I have loved ere
  now.
Sil. No, Corin, being old, thou canst not
  guess,
Though in thy youth thou wast as a true lover
As ever sigh'd upon a midnight pillow :
But if thy love were ever like to mine—
As sure I think did never man love so—
How many actions most ridiculous 30
Hast thou been drawn to by thy fantasy ?
Cor. Into a thousand that I have forgotten.
Sil. O, thou didst then ne'er love so heartily !
If thou remember'st not the slightest folly
That ever love did make thee run into,
Thou hast not loved :
Or if thou hast not sat as I do now,
Wearying thy hearer in thy mistress' praise,
Thou hast not loved :
Or if thou hast not broke from company 40
Abruptly, as my passion now makes me,
Thou hast not loved.
O Phebe, Phebe, Phebe ! [*Exit.*
Ros. Alas, poor shepherd ! searching of thy
  wound,
I have by hard adventure found mine own.
Touch. And I mine. I remember, when I
was in love I broke my sword upon a stone
and bid him take that for coming a-night to
Jane Smile ; and I remember the kissing of
her batlet and the cow's dugs that her pretty
chopt hands had milked ; and I remember the
wooing of a peascod instead of her, from
whom I took two cods and, giving her them
again, said with weeping tears 'Wear these for
my sake.' We that are true lovers run into
strange capers ; but as all is mortal in nature,
so is all nature in love mortal in folly.
Ros. Thou speakest wiser than thou art
ware of.
Touch. Nay, I shall ne'er be ware of mine
own wit till I break my shins against it. 60
Ros. Jove, Jove ! this shepherd's passion
  Is much upon my fashion.
Touch. And mine ; but it grows something
  stale with me.

Cel. I pray you, one of you question yond
man
If he for gold will give us any food
I faint almost to death
    Touch   Holla, you clown !
    Ros. Peace, fool . he's not thy kinsman
    Cor.   Who calls ?
    Touch. Your betters, sir
    Cor.   Else are they very wretched
    Ros. Peace, I say. Good even to you,
    friend.
    Cor. And to you, gentle sir, and to you all.
    Ros I prithee, shepherd, if that love or
    gold
Can in this desert place buy entertainment,
Bring us where we may rest ourselves and feed
Here's a young maid with travel much op-
    press'd
And faints for succor
    Cor.   Fair sir, I pity her
And wish, for her sake more than for mine
    own,
My fortunes were more able to relieve her ,
But I am shepherd to another man
And do not shear the fleeces that I graze
My master is of churlish disposition   80
And little recks to find the way to heaven
By doing deeds of hospitality
Besides, his cote, his flocks and bounds of
    feed
Are now on sale, and at our sheepcote now,
By reason of his absence, there is nothing
That you will feed on , but what is, come see,
And in my voice most welcome shall you be
    Ros. What is he that shall buy his flock and
    pasture ?
    Cor. That young swain that you saw here
    but erewhile,
That little cares for buying any thing   90
    Ros. I pray thee, if it stand with honesty,
Buy thou the cottage, pasture and the flock,
And thou shalt have to pay for it of us
    Cel. And we will mend thy wages. I like
    this place,
And willingly could waste my time in it
    Cor. Assuredly the thing is to be sold :
Go with me : if you like upon report
The soil, the profit and this kind of life,
I will your very faithful feeder be
And buy it with your gold right suddenly. 100
                         [Exeunt

SCENE V. *The Forest.*

Enter AMIENS, JAQUES, *and others.*

SONG.

Ami. Under the greenwood tree
    Who loves to lie with me,
    And turn his merry note
    Unto the sweet bird's throat,
Come hither, come hither, come hither :
    Here shall he see
    No enemy
But winter and rough weather.

Jaq. More, more, I prithee, more.

Ami It will make you melancholy, Monsieur Jaques
    Jaq. I thank it. More, I prithee, more. I
can suck melancholy out of a song, as a weasel
sucks eggs More, I prithee, more.
    Ami My voice is ragged . I know I cannot
please you
    Jaq I do not desire you to please me, I do
desire you to sing Come, more , another
stanzo. call you 'em stanzos ?
    Ami What you will, Monsieur Jaques 20
    Jaq Nay, I care not for their names , they
owe me nothing Will you sing ?
    Ami More at your request than to please
myself.
    Jaq Well then, if ever I thank any man,
I'll thank you , but that they call compliment
is like the encounter of two dog-apes, and
when a man thanks me heartily, methinks I
have given him a penny and he renders me
the beggarly thanks Come, sing , and you
that will not, hold your tongues
    Ami. Well, I'll end the song Sirs, cover
the while . the duke will drink under this
tree. He hath been all this day to look you
    Jaq And I have been all this day to avoid
him He is too disputable for my company .
I think of as many matters as he, but I give
heaven thanks and make no boast of them
Come, warble, come

SONG

Who doth ambition shun   40
                 [All together here
And loves to live i' the sun,
    Seeking the food he eats
And pleased with what he gets,
Come hither, come hither, come hither
    Here shall he see
    No enemy
But winter and rough weather.

    Jaq I'll give you a verse to this note that
I made yesterday in despite of my invention
    Ami. And I'll sing it   50
    Jaq. Thus it goes —

    If it do come to pass
    That any man turn ass,
    Leaving his wealth and ease,
    A stubborn will to please,
Ducdame, ducdame, ducdame :
    Here shall he see
    Gross fools as he,
    An if he will come to me.

    Ami. What's that ' ducdame' ?   60
    Jaq. 'Tis a Greek invocation, to call fools
into a circle I'll go sleep, if I can; if I cannot,
I'll rail against all the first-born of Egypt
    Ami And I'll go seek the duke · his
banquet is prepared   *[Exeunt severally.*

SCENE VI. *The forest.*

Enter ORLANDO *and* ADAM

    Adam Dear master, I can go no further .
O, I die for food ! Here lie I down, and
measure out my grave. Farewell, kind master.

Orl. Why, how now, Adam! no greater heart in thee ? Live a little ; comfort a little; cheer thyself a little. If this uncouth forest yield any thing savage, I will either be food for it or bring it for food to thee. Thy conceit is nearer death than thy powers. For my sake be comfortable; hold death awhile at the arm's end : I will here be with thee presently ; and if I bring thee not something to eat, I will give thee leave to die : but if thou diest before I come, thou art a mocker of my labor. Well said ! thou lookest cheerly, and I'll be with thee quickly. Yet thou liest in the bleak air : come, I will bear thee to some shelter ; and thou shalt not die for lack of a dinner, if there live any thing in this desert. Cheerly, good Adam !   [*Exeunt.*

SCENE VII. *The forest.*

A table set out. Enter DUKE *senior.* AMIENS, *and* Lords *like* outlaws.

Duke S. I think he be transform'd into a beast ;
For I can no where find him like a man.
First Lord. My lord, he is but even now gone hence :
Here was he merry, hearing of a song.
Duke S. If he, compact of jars, grow musical,
We shall have shortly discord in the spheres.
Go, seek him : tell him I would speak with him.

Enter JAQUES.

First Lord. He saves my labor by his own approach.
Duke S. Why, how now, monsieur! what a life is this,
That your poor friends must woo your company ?   10
What, you look merrily !
Jaq. A fool, a fool ! I met a fool i' the forest,
A motley fool ; a miserable world !
As I do live by food, I met a fool ;
Who laid him down and bask'd him in the sun,
And rail'd on Lady Fortune in good terms,
In good set terms and yet a motley fool.
' Good morrow, fool,' quoth I. ' No, sir,' quoth he,
' Call me not fool till heaven hath sent me fortune : '
And then he drew a dial from his poke,   20
And, looking on it with lack-lustre eye,
Says very wisely, ' It is ten o'clock :
Thus we may see,' quoth he, ' how the world wags :
'Tis but an hour ago since it was nine,
And after one hour more 'twill be eleven ;
And so, from hour to hour, we ripe and ripe,
And then, from hour to hour, we rot and rot ;
And thereby hangs a tale.' When I did hear
The motley fool thus moral on the time,
My lungs began to crow like chanticleer,   30
That fools should be so deep-contemplative,

And I did laugh sans intermission
An hour by his dial. O noble fool !
A worthy fool ! Motley's the only wear.
Duke S. What fool is this ?
Jaq. O worthy fool ! One that hath been a courtier,
And says, if ladies be but young and fair,
They have the gift to know it : and in his brain,
Which is as dry as the remainder biscuit
After a voyage, he hath strange places cramm'd   40
With observation, the which he vents
In mangled forms. O that I were a fool !
I am ambitious for a motley coat.
Duke S. Thou shalt have one.
Jaq.   It is my only suit ;
Provided that you weed your better judgments
Of all opinion that grows rank in them
That I am wise. I must have liberty
Withal, as large a charter as the wind,
To blow on whom I please ; for so fools have;
And they that are most galled with my folly,
They most must laugh. And why, sir, must they so ?   51
The ' why ' is plain as way to parish church :
He that a fool doth very wisely hit
Doth very foolishly, although he smart,
Not to seem senseless of the bob : if not,
The wise man's folly is anatomized
Even by the squandering glances of the fool.
Invest me in my motley ; give me leave
To speak my mind, and I will through and through
Cleanse the foul body of the infected world,
If they will patiently receive my medicine.   61
Duke S. Fie on thee ! I can tell what thou wouldst do.   [good ?
Jaq. What, for a counter, would I do but
Duke S. Most mischievous foul sin, in chiding sin :
For thou thyself hast been a libertine,
As sensual as the brutish sting itself ;
And all the embossed sores and headed evils,
That thou with license of free foot hast caught,
Wouldst thou disgorge into the general world.
Jaq. Why, who cries out on pride,   70
That can therein tax any private party ?
Doth it not flow as hugely as the sea,
†Till that the weary very means do ebb ?
What woman in the city do I name,
When that I say the city-woman bears
The cost of princes on unworthy shoulders ?
Who can come in and say that I mean her,
When such a one as she such is her neighbor?
Or what is he of basest function
That says his bravery is not of my cost,   80
Thinking that I mean him, but therein suits
His folly to the mettle of my speech ?
There then ; how then ? what then ? Let me see wherein
My tongue hath wrong'd him : if it do him right,
Then he hath wrong'd himself ; if he be free,
Why then my taxing like a wild-goose flies,
Unclaim'd of any man. But who comes here?

Enter ORLANDO, *with his sword drawn.*

Orl. Forbear, and eat no more.

Jaq. Why, I have eat none yet.

Orl. Nor shalt not, till necessity be served.

Jaq. Of what kind should this cock come
  of ? 90

Duke S. Art thou thus bolden'd, man, by
thy distress,

Or else a rude despiser of good manners,

That in civility thou seem'st so empty ?

Orl. You touch'd my vein at first : the
thorny point

Of bare distress hath ta'en from me the show

Of smooth civility : yet am I inland bred

And know some nurture. But forbear, I say :

He dies that touches any of this fruit

Till I and my affairs are answered.

Jaq. An you will not be answered with
reason, I must die. 101

Duke S. What would you have ? Your
gentleness shall force

More than your force move us to gentleness.

Orl. I almost die for food ; and let me
have it.

Duke S. Sit down and feed, and welcome
to our table.

Orl. Speak you so gently ? Pardon me, I
pray you :

I thought that all things had been savage
here ;

And therefore put I on the countenance

Of stern commandment. But whate'er you
are

That in this desert inaccessible, 110

Under the shade of melancholy boughs,

Lose and neglect the creeping hours of time ;

If ever you have look'd on better days,

If ever been where bells have knoll'd to church,

If ever sat at any good man's feast,

If ever from your eyelids wiped a tear

And know what 'tis to pity and be pitied,

Let gentleness my strong enforcement be :

In the which hope I blush, and hide my sword.

Duke S. True is it that we have seen
better days, 120

And have with holy bell been knoll'd to
church

And sat at good men's feasts and wiped our
eyes

Of drops that sacred pity hath engender'd ;

And therefore sit you down in gentleness

And take upon command what help we have

That to your wanting may be minister'd.

Orl. Then but forbear your food a little
while,

Whiles, like a doe, I go to find my fawn

And give it food. There is an old poor man,

Who after me hath many a weary step 130

Limp'd in pure love : till he be first sufficed,

Oppress'd with two weak evils, age and
hunger,

I will not touch a bit.

Duke S. Go find him out,

And we will nothing waste till you return.

Orl. I thank ye ; and be blest for your
good comfort ! [*Exit.*

Duke S. Thou seest we are not all alone unhappy :

This wide and universal theatre

Presents more woeful pageants than the scene

Wherein we play in.

Jaq. All the world's a stage,

And all the men and women merely players :

They have their exits and their entrances ;

And one man in his time plays many parts,

His acts being seven ages. At first the infant,

Mewling and puking in the nurse's arms.

And then the whining school-boy, with his
satchel

And shining morning face, creeping like snail

Unwillingly to school. And then the lover,

Sighing like furnace, with a woeful ballad

Made to his mistress' eyebrow. Then a soldier,

Full of strange oaths and bearded like the
pard, 150

Jealous in honor, sudden and quick in quarrel,

Seeking the buble reputation

Even in the cannon's mouth. And then the
justice,

In fair round belly with good capon lined,

With eyes severe and beard of formal cut,

Full of wise saws and modern instances ;

And so he plays his part. The sixth age shifts

Into the lean and slipper'd pantaloon,

With spectacles on nose and pouch on side,

His youthful hose, well saved, a world too
wide 160

For his shrunk shank ; and his big manly
voice,

Turning again toward childish treble, pipes

And whistles in his sound. Last scene of all,

That ends this strange eventful history,

Is second childishness and mere oblivion,

Sans teeth, sans eyes, sans taste, sans every
thing.

Re-enter ORLANDO, *with* ADAM.

Duke S. Welcome. Set down your venerable burthen,

And let him feed.

Orl. I thank you most for him.

Adam. So had you need :

I scarce can speak to thank you for myself.

Duke S. Welcome ; fall to : I will not
trouble you 171

As yet, to question you about your fortunes.

Give us some music ; and, good cousin, sing.

SONG.

Ami. Blow, blow, thou winter wind,
  Thou art not so unkind
    As man's ingratitude ;
  Thy tooth is not so keen,
  Because thou art not seen,
    Although thy breath be rude.

Heigh-ho ! sing, heigh-ho ! unto the green
  holly : 180

Most friendship is feigning, most loving mere
  folly :

  Then, heigh-ho, the holly !
  This life is most jolly.

Freeze, freeze, thou bitter sky,
  That dost not bite so nigh
    As benefits forgot :
Though thou the waters warp,
  Thy sting is not so sharp
    As friend remember'd not.
Heigh-ho ! sing, &c.   190
  Duke S. If that you were the good Sir Row-
    land's son,
As you have whisper'd faithfully you were,
And as mine eye doth his effigies witness
Most truly limn'd and living in your face,
Be truly welcome hither : I am the duke
That loved your father : the residue of your
    fortune,
Go to my cave and tell me. Good old man,
Thou art right welcome as thy master is.
Support him by the arm. Give me your hand,
And let me all your fortunes understand.
                            [*Exeunt.*

ACT III.

SCENE I. *A room in the palace.*

Enter DUKE FREDERICK, Lords, *and* OLIVER.

  Duke F. Not see him since ? Sir, sir, that
    cannot be :
But were I not the better part made mercy,
I should not seek an absent argument
Of my revenge, thou present. But look to it :
Find out thy brother, wheresoe'er he is ;
Seek him with candle ; bring him dead or
    living
Within this twelvemonth, or turn thou no
    more
To seek a living in our territory.
Thy lands and all things that thou dost call
    thine
Worth seizure do we seize into our hands,   10
Till thou canst quit thee by thy brother's
    mouth
Of what we think against thee.
  Oli. O that your highness knew my heart
    in this !
I never loved my brother in my life.
  Duke F. More villain thou. Well, push
    him out of doors ;
And let my officers of such a nature
Make an extent upon his house and lands :
Do this expediently and turn him going.
                            [*Exeunt.*

SCENE II. *The forest.*

Enter ORLANDO, *with a paper.*

  Orl. Hang there, my verse, in witness of my
    love :
And thou, thrice-crowned queen of night,
    survey
With thy chaste eye, from thy pale sphere
    above,
Thy huntress' name that my full life doth
    sway.
O Rosalind ! these trees shall be my books

And in their barks my thoughts I'll charac-
    ter ;
That every eye which in this forest looks
  Shall see thy virtue witness'd every where.
Run, run, Orlando ; carve on every tree
The fair, the chaste and unexpressive she.
                            [*Exit.*

Enter CORIN *and* TOUCHSTONE.

  Cor. And how like you this shepherd's life,
Master Touchstone ?
  Touch. Truly, shepherd, in respect of itself, it is a good life ; but in respect that it is
a shepherd's life, it is naught. In respect that
it is solitary, I like it very well ; but in respect that it is private, it is a very vile life.
Now, in respect it is in the fields, it pleaseth
me well ; but in respect it is not in the court,
it is tedious. As it is a spare life, look you, it
fits my humor well ; but as there is no more
plenty in it, it goes much against my stomach.
Hast any philosophy in thee, shepherd ?
  Cor. No more but that I know the more
one sickens the worse at ease he is ; and that
he that wants money, means and content is
without three good friends ; that the property
of rain is to wet and fire to burn ; that good
pasture makes fat sheep, and that a great
cause of the night is lack of the sun ; that he
that hath learned no wit by nature nor art
may complain of good breeding or comes of a
very dull kindred.
  Touch. Such a one is a natural philosopher.
Wast ever in court, shepherd ?
  Cor. No, truly.
  Touch. Then thou art damned.
  Cor. Nay, I hope.
  Touch. Truly, thou art damned like an ill,
roasted egg, all on one side.   39
  Cor. For not being at court ? Your reason.
  Touch. Why, if thou never wast at court,
thou never sawest good manners ; if thou
never sawest good manners, then thy manners must be wicked ; and wickedness is sin,
and sin is damnation. Thou art in a parlous
state, shepherd.
  Cor. Not a whit, Touchstone : those that
are good manners at the court are as ridiculous in the country as the behavior of the
country is most mockable at the court. You
told me you salute not at the court, but you
kiss your hands : that courtesy would be uncleanly, if courtiers were shepherds.
  Touch. Instance, briefly ; come, instance.
  Cor. Why, we are still handling our ewes,
and their fells, you know, are greasy.
  Touch. Why, do not your courtier's hands
sweat ? and is not the grease of a mutton as
wholesome as the sweat of a man ? Shallow,
shallow. A better instance, I say ; come.
  Cor. Besides, our hands are hard.   60
  Touch. Your lips will feel them the sooner.
Shallow again. A more sounder instance,
come.
  Cor. And they are often tarred over with
the surgery of our sheep : and would you

have us kiss tar ? The courtier's hands are
perfumed with civet.

Touch. Most shallow man ! thou worms-
meat, in respect of a good piece of flesh indeed ! Learn of the wise, and perpend : civet
is of a baser birth than tar, the very uncleanly flux of a cat. Mend the instance,
shepherd.   71

Cor. You have too courtly a wit for me :
I'll rest.

Touch. Wilt thou rest damned ? God help
thee, shallow man ! God make incision in
thee ! thou art raw.

Cor. Sir, I am a true laborer : I earn that I
eat, get that I wear, owe no man hate, envy
no man's happiness, glad of other men's good,
content with my harm, and the greatest of
my pride is to see my ewes graze and my
lambs suck.

Touch. That is another simple sin in you,
to bring the ewes and the rams together and
to offer to get your living by the copulation of
cattle ; to be bawd to a bell-wether, and to
betray a she-lamb of a twelvemonth to a
crooked-pated, old, cuckoldly ram, out of all
reasonable match. If thou beest not damned
for this, the devil himself will have no shepherds ; I cannot see else how thou shouldst
'scape.   90

Cor. Here comes young Master Ganymede,
my new mistress's brother.

Enter ROSALIND, *with a paper, reading.*

Ros. From the east to western Ind,
        No jewel is like Rosalind.
    Her worth, being mounted on the
        wind,
    Through all the world bears Rosalind.
    All the pictures fairest lined
    Are but black to Rosalind.
    Let no fair be kept in mind
    But the fair of Rosalind.   100

Touch. I'll rhyme you so eight years together, dinners and suppers and sleeping-
hours excepted : it is the right butter-
women's rank to market.

Ros. Out, fool !

Touch. For a taste :
    If a hart do lack a hind,
    Let him seek out Rosalind.
    If the cat will after kind,
    So be sure will Rosalind.   110
    Winter garments must be lined,
    So must slender Rosalind.
    They that reap must sheaf and bind ;
    Then to cart with Rosalind.
    Sweetest nut hath sourest rind,
    Such a nut is Rosalind.
    He that sweetest rose will find
    Must find love's prick and Rosalind.
This is the very false gallop of verses : why
do you infect yourself with them ?   120

Ros. Peace, you dull fool ! I found them on
a tree.

Touch. Truly, the tree yields bad fruit.

Ros. I'll graff it with you, and then I shall

graff it with a medlar : then it will be the
earliest fruit i' the country ; for you'll be rotten ere you be half ripe, and that's the right
virtue of the medlar.

Touch. You have said ; but whether wisely
or no, let the forest judge.   130

Enter CELIA, *with a writing.*

Ros. Peace !
Here comes my sister, reading : stand aside.

Cel. [*Reads*]
    Why should this a desert be ?
        For it is unpeopled ? No :
    Tongues I'll hang on every tree,
        That shall civil sayings show :
    Some, how brief the life of man
        Runs his erring pilgrimage,
    That the stretching of a span
        Buckles in his sum of age ;   140
    Some, of violated vows
        'Twixt the souls of friend and friend :
    But upon the fairest boughs,
        Or at every sentence end,
    Will I Rosalinda write,
        Teaching all that read to know
    The quintessence of every sprite
        Heaven would in little show.
    Therefore Heaven Nature charged
        That one body should be fill'd   150
    With all graces wide-enlarged :
        Nature presently distill'd
    Helen's cheek, but not her heart,
        Cleopatra's majesty,
    Atalanta's better part,
        Sad Lucretia's modesty.
    Thus Rosalind of many parts
        By heavenly synod was devised,
    Of many faces, eyes and hearts,
        To have the touches dearest prized.
    Heaven would that she these gifts should
        have,   161
    And I to live and die her slave.

Ros. O most gentle pulpiter ! what tedious
homily of love have you wearied your parish-
ioners withal, and never cried ' Have patience,
good people !'

Cel. How now ! back, friends ! Shepherd,
go off a little. Go with him, sirrah.

Touch. Come, shepherd, let us make an
honorable retreat ; though not with bag and
baggage, yet with scrip and scrippage.   171
                [Exeunt Corin and Touchstone.

Cel. Didst thou hear these verses ?

Ros. O, yes, I heard them all, and more
too ; for some of them had in them more feet
than the verses would bear.

Cel. That's no matter : the feet might bear
the verses.

Ros. Ay, but the feet were lame and could
not bear themselves without the verse and
therefore stood lamely in the verse.   180

Cel. But didst thou hear without wondering how thy name should be hanged and
carved upon these trees ?

Ros. I was seven of the nine days out of
the wonder before you came ; for look here

                        27

what I found on a palm-tree. I was never so be-rhymed since Pythagoras' time, that I was an Irish rat, which I can hardly remember.

Cel. Trow you who hath done this?

Ros. Is it a man? 190

Cel. And a chain, that you once wore, about his neck. Change you color?

Ros. I prithee, who?

Cel. O Lord, Lord! it is a hard matter for friends to meet; but mountains may be removed with earthquakes and so encounter.

Ros. Nay, but who is it?

Cel. Is it possible?

Ros. Nay, I prithee now with most petitionary vehemence, tell me who it is. 200

Cel. O wonderful, wonderful, and most wonderful wonderful! and yet again wonderful, and after that, out of all hooping!

Ros. Good my complexion! dost thou think, though I am caparisoned like a man, I have a doublet and hose in my disposition? One inch of delay more is a South-sea of discovery; I prithee, tell me who is it quickly, and speak apace. I would thou couldst stammer, that thou mightst pour this concealed man out of thy mouth, as wine comes out of a narrow-mouthed bottle, either too much at once, or none at all. I prithee, take the cork out of thy mouth that I may drink thy tidings.

Cel. So you may put a man in your belly.

Ros. Is he of God's making? What manner of man? Is his head worth a hat, or his chin worth a beard?

Cel. Nay, he hath but a little beard.

Ros. Why, God will send more, if the man will be thankful: let me stay the growth of his beard, if thou delay me not the knowledge of his chin.

Cel. It is young Orlando, that tripped up the wrestler's heels and your heart both in an instant.

Ros. Nay, but the devil take mocking: speak, sad brow and true maid.

Cel. I' faith, coz, 'tis he.

Ros. Orlando?

Cel. Orlando. 230

Ros. Alas the day! what shall I do with my doublet and hose? What did he when thou sawest him? What said he? How looked he? Wherein went he? What makes him here? Did he ask for me? Where remains he? How parted he with thee? and when shalt thou see him again? Answer me in one word.

Cel. You must borrow me Gargantua's mouth first: 'tis a word too great for any mouth of this age's size. To say ay and no to these particulars is more than to answer in a catechism. 241

Ros. But doth he know that I am in this forest and in man's apparel? Looks he as freshly as he did the day he wrestled?

Cel. It is as easy to count atomies as to resolve the propositions of a lover; but take a taste of my finding him, and relish it with good observance. I found him under a tree, like a dropped acorn.

Ros. It may well be called Jove's tree, when it drops forth such fruit. 250

Cel. Give me audience, good madam.

Ros. Proceed.

Cel. There lay he, stretched along, like a wounded knight.

Ros. Though it be pity to see such a sight, it well becomes the ground.

Cel. Cry 'holla' to thy tongue, I prithee; it curvets unseasonably. He was furnished like a hunter.

Ros. O, ominous! he comes to kill my heart. 259

Cel. I would sing my song without a burden: thou bringest me out of tune.

Ros. Do you not know I am a woman? when I think, I must speak. Sweet, say on.

Cel. You bring me out. Soft! comes he not here?

Enter ORLANDO *and* JAQUES.

Ros. 'Tis he: slink by, and note him.

Jaq. I thank you for your company; but, good faith, I had as lief have been myself alone. 270

Orl. And so had I; but yet, for fashion sake, I thank you too for your society.

Jaq. God be wi' you: let's meet as little as we can.

Orl. I do desire we may be better strangers.

Jaq. I pray you, mar no more trees with writing love-songs in their barks.

Orl. I pray you, mar no more of my verses with reading them ill-favoredly.

Jaq. Rosalind is your love's name? 280

Orl. Yes, just.

Jaq. I do not like her name.

Orl. There was no thought of pleasing you when she was christened.

Jaq. What stature is she of?

Orl. Just as high as my heart.

Jaq. You are full of pretty answers. Have you not been acquainted with goldsmiths' wives, and conned them out of rings? 289

Orl. Not so; but I answer you right painted cloth, from whence you have studied your questions.

Jaq. You have a nimble wit: I think 'twas made of Atalanta's heels. Will you sit down with me? and we two will rail against our mistress the world and all our misery.

Orl. I will chide no breather in the world but myself, against whom I know most faults.

Jaq. The worst fault you have is to be in love. 300

Orl. 'Tis a fault I will not change for your best virtue. I am weary of you.

Jaq. By my troth, I was seeking for a fool when I found you.

Orl. He is drowned in the brook: look but in, and you shall see him.

Jaq. There I shall see mine own figure.

Orl. Which I take to be either a fool or a cipher.

Jaq. I'll tarry no longer with you : farewell, good Signior Love.   310
Orl. I am glad of your departure : adieu, good Monsieur Melancholy.   [*Exit Jaques.*
Ros. [*Aside to Celia*] I will speak to him, like a saucy lackey and under that habit play the knave with him. Do you hear, forester?
Orl. Very well : what would you ?
Ros. I pray you, what is't o'clock ?
Orl. You should ask me what time o' day : there's no clock in the forest.   319
Ros. Then there is no true lover in the forest ; else sighing every minute and groaning every hour would detect the lazy foot of Time as well as a clock.
Orl. And why not the swift foot of Time ? had not that been as proper ?
Ros. By no means, sir : Time travels in divers paces with divers persons. I'll tell you who Time ambles withal, who Time trots withal, who Time gallops withal and who he stands still withal.
Orl. I prithee, who doth he trot withal.
Ros. Marry, he trots hard with a young maid between the contract of her marriage and the day it is solemnized : if the interim be but a se'nnight, Time's pace is so hard that it seems the length of seven year.
Orl. Who ambles Time withal ?
Ros. With a priest that lacks Latin and a rich man that hath not the gout, for the one sleeps easily because he cannot study, and the other lives merrily because he feels no pain, the one lacking the burden of lean and wasteful learning, the other knowing no burden of heavy tedious penury ; these Time ambles withal.
Orl. Who doth he gallop withal ?
Ros. With a thief to the gallows, for though he go as softly as foot can fall, he thinks himself too soon there.
Orl. Who stays it still withal ?
Ros. With lawyers in the vacation ; for they sleep between term and term and then they perceive not how Time moves.   351
Orl. Where dwell you, pretty youth ?
Ros. With this shepherdess, my sister; here in the skirts of the forest, like fringe upon a petticoat.
Orl. Are you native of this place ?
Ros. As the cony that you see dwell where she is kindled.
Orl. Your accent is something finer than you could purchase in so removed a dwelling.   360
Ros. I have been told so of many : but indeed an old religious uncle of mine taught me to speak, who was in his youth an inland man ; one that knew courtship too well, for there he fell in love. I have heard him read many lectures against it, and I thank God I am not a woman, to be touched with so many giddy offences as he hath generally taxed their whole sex withal.
Orl. Can you remember any of the principal evils that he laid to the charge of women ?   370

Ros. There were none principal ; they were all like one another as half-pence are, every one fault seeming monstrous till his fellow-fault came to match it.
Orl. I prithee, recount some of them.
Ros. No, I will not cast away my physic but on those that are sick. There is a man haunts the forest, that abuses our young plants with carving ' Rosalind ' on their barks; hangs odes upon hawthorns and elegies on brambles, all, forsooth, deifying the name of Rosalind : if I could meet that fancy-monger, I would give him some good counsel, for he seems to have the quotidian of love upon him.
Orl. I am he that is so love-shaked : I pray you tell me your remedy.
Ros. There is none of my uncle's marks upon you : he taught me how to know a man in love ; in which cage of rushes I am sure you are not prisoner.   390
Orl. What were his marks ?
Ros. A lean cheek, which you have not, a blue eye and sunken, which you have not, an unquestionable spirit, which you have not, a beard neglected, which you have not ; but I pardon you for that, for simply your having in beard is a younger brother's revenue : then your hose should be ungartered, your bonnet unbanded, your sleeve unbuttoned, your shoe untied and every thing about you demonstrating a careless desolation ; but you are no such man ; you are rather point-device in your accoutrements as loving yourself than seeming the lover of any other.
Orl. Fair youth, I would I could make thee believe I love.
Ros. Me believe it ! you may as soon make her that you love believe it ; which, I warrant, she is apter to do than to confess she does : that is one of the points in the which women still give the lie to their consciences. But, in good sooth, are you he that hangs the verses on the trees, wherein Rosalind is so admired ?
Orl. I swear to thee, youth, by the white hand of Rosalind, I am that he, that unfortunate he.
Ros. But are you so much in love as your rhymes speak ?
Orl. Neither rhyme nor reason can express how much.   419
Ros. Love is merely a madness, and, I tell you, deserves as well a dark house and a whip as madmen do : and the reason why they are not so punished and cured is, that the lunacy is so ordinary that the whippers are in love too. Yet I profess curing it by counsel.
Orl. Did you ever cure any so ?
Ros. Yes, one, and in this manner. He was to imagine me his love, his mistress ; and I set him every day to woo me : at which time would I, being but a moonish youth, grieve, be effeminate, changeable, longing and liking, proud, fantastical, apish, shallow, inconstant, full of tears, full of smiles, for every passion something and for no passion truly any thing,

as boys and women are for the most part cattle of this color ; would now like him, now loathe him ; then entertain him, then forswear him ; now weep for him, then spit at him ; that I drave my suitor from his mad humor of love to a living humor of madness ; which was, to forswear the full stream of the world, and to live in a nook merely monastic. And thus I cured him ; and this way will I take upon me to wash your liver as clean as a sound sheep's heart, that there shall not be one spot of love in't.

Orl. I would not be cured, youth.

Ros. I would cure you, if you would but call me Rosalind and come every day to my cote and woo me.

Orl. Now, by the faith of my love, I will : tell me where it is.   450

Ros. Go with me to it and I'll show it you : and by the way you shall tell me where in the forest you live. Will you go ?

Orl. With all my heart, good youth.

Ros. Nay, you must call me Rosalind. Come, sister, will you go ?   [*Exeunt.*

SCENE III. *The forest.*

Enter TOUCHSTONE *and* AUDREY ; JAQUES *behind.*

Touch. Come apace, good Audrey : I will fetch up your goats, Audrey. And how, Audrey ? am I the man yet ? doth my simple feature content you ?

Aud. Your features ! Lord warrant us ! what features !

Touch. I am here with thee and thy goats, as the most capricious poet, honest Ovid, was among the Goths.

Jaq. [*Aside*] O knowledge · ill-inhabited, worse than Jove in a thatched house !   11

Touch. When a man's verses cannot be understood, nor a man's good wit seconded with the forward child Understanding, it strikes a man more dead than a great reckoning in a little room. Truly, I would the gods had made thee poetical.

Aud. I do not know what 'poetical' is : is it honest in deed and word ? is it a true thing ?

Touch. No, truly ; for the truest poetry is the most feigning ; and lovers are given to poetry, and what they swear in poetry may be said as lovers they do fein.

Aud. Do you wish then that the gods had made me poetical ?

Touch. I do, truly ; for thou swearest to me thou art honest : now, if thou were a poet, I might have some hope thou didst feign.

Aud. Would you not have me honest ?

Touch. No, truly, unless thou wert hardfavored ; for honesty coupled to beauty is to have honey a sauce to sugar.   31

Jaq. [*Aside*] A material fool !

Aud. Well, I am not fair ; and therefore I pray the gods make me honest.

Touch. Truly, and to cast away honesty upon a foul slut were to put good meat into an unclean dish.

Aud. I am not a slut, though I thank the gods I am foul.   39

Touch. Well, praised be the gods for thy foulness ! sluttishness may come hereafter. But be it as it may be, I will marry thee, and to that end I have been with Sir Oliver Martext, the vicar of the next village, who hath promised to meet me in this place of the forest and to couple us.

Jaq. [*Aside*] I would fain see this meeting.

Aud. Well, the gods give us joy !

Touch. Amen. A man may, if he were of a fearful heart, stagger in this attempt ; for here we have no temple but the wood, no assembly but horn-beasts. But what though ? Courage ! As horns are odious, they are necessary. It is said, 'many a man knows no end of his goods :' right ; many a man has good horns, and knows no end of them. Well, that is the dowry of his wife ; 'tis none of his own getting. Horns ? Even so. Poor men alone ? No, no ; the noblest deer hath them as huge as the rascal. Is the single man therefore blessed ? No : as a walled town is more worthier than a village, so is the forehead of a married man more honorable than the bare brow of a bachelor ; and by how much defence is better than no skill, by so much is a horn more precious than to want. Here comes Sir Oliver.

Enter SIR OLIVER MARTEXT.

Sir Oliver Martext, you are well met : will you dispatch us here under this tree, or shall we go with you to your chapel ?

Sir Oli. Is there none here to give the woman ?

Touch. I will not take her on gift of any man.

Sir Oli. Truly, she must be given, or the marriage is not lawful.   71

Jaq. [*Advancing*] Proceed, proceed : I'll give her.

Touch. Good even, good Master What-ye-call't : how do you, sir ? You are very well met : God 'ild you for your last company : I am very glad to see you : even a toy in hand here, sir : nay, pray be covered.

Jaq. Will you be married, motley ?   79

Touch. As the ox hath his bow, sir, the horse his curb and the falcon her bells, so man hath his desires ; and as pigeons bill, so wedlock would be nibbling.

Jaq. And will you, being a man of your breeding, be married under a bush like a beggar ? Get you to church, and have a good priest that can tell you what marriage is : this fellow will but join you together as they join wainscot ; then one of you will prove a shrunk panel and, like green timber, warp, warp.   90

Touch. [*Aside*] I am not in the mind but I were better to be married of him than of another : for he is not like to marry me well ;

TOUCHSTONE AND AUDREY.

AS YOU LIKE IT. p. 580

and not being well married, it will be a good
excuse for me hereafter to leave my wife.

Jaq Go thou with me, and let me counsel
thee.

Touch Come, sweet Audrey
We must be married, or we must live in baw-
dry.
Farewell, good Master Oliver : not,—   100
    O sweet Oliver,
    O brave Oliver,
  Leave me not behind thee :
but,—
    Wind away,
    Begone, I say,
  I will not to wedding with thee.
  [*Exeunt Jaques, Touchstone and Audrey*
Sir Oli. 'Tis no matter ne er a fantastical
knave of them all shall flout me out of my
calling.   [*Exit.* 109

SCENE IV. *The forest.*

Enter ROSALIND *and* CELIA.

Ros Never talk to me , I will weep

Cel Do, I prithee ; but yet have the grace
to consider that tears do not become a man

Ros. But have I not cause to weep?

Cel As good cause as one would desire ,
therefore weep.

Ros His very hair is of the dissembling
color

Cel. Something browner than Judas's ,
marry, his kisses are Judas's own children. 10

Ros I' faith, his hair is of a good color

Cel. An excellent color · your chestnut was
ever the only color

Ros. And his kissing is as full of sanctity as
the touch of holy bread

Cel. He hath bought a pair of cast lips of
Diana   a nun of winter's sisterhood kisses
not more religiously , the very ice of chastity
is in them

Ros But why did he swear he would come
this morning, and comes not?   21

Cel Nay, certainly, there is no truth in him

Ros. Do you think so?

Cel Yes , I think he is not a pick-purse
nor a horse-stealer, but for his verity in love,
I do think him as concave as a covered goblet
or a worm-eaten nut

Ros. Not true in love ?

Cel Yes, when he is in , but I think he is
not in   30

Ros You have heard him swear downright
he was.

Cel 'Was ' is not 'is ' besides, the oath
of a lover is no stronger than the word of a
tapster ; they are both the confirmer of false
reckonings. He attends here in the forest on
the duke your father

Ros I met the duke yesterday and had
much question with him. he asked me of what
parentage I was , I told him, of as good as he,
so he laughed and let me go. But what talk
we of fathers, when there is such a man as
Orlando ?

Cel. O, that's a brave man ! he writes brave
verses, speaks brave words, swears brave oaths
and breaks them bravely, quite traverse, athwart the heart of his lover , as a puisny tilter,
that spurs his horse but on one side, breaks
his staff like a noble goose but all's brave
that youth mounts and folly guides Who
comes here?

Enter CORIN

Cor. Mistress and master, you have oft in-
quired   50
After the shepherd that complain'd of love,
Who you saw sitting by me on the turf,
Praising the proud disdainful shepherdess
That was his mistress

Cel. Well, and what of him?

Cor If you will see a pageant truly play'd,
Between the pale complexion of true love
And the red glow of scorn and proud disdain,
Go hence a little and I shall conduct you,
If you will mark it.

Ros O, come, let us remove :   60
The sight of lovers feedeth those in love
Bring us to this sight, and you shall say
I'll prove a busy actor in their play   [*Exeunt.*

SCENE V. *Another part of the forest.*

Enter SILVIUS *and* PHEBE

Sil. Sweet Phebe, do not scorn me , do not,
    Phebe ;
Say that you love me not, but say not so
In bitterness The common executioner,
Whose heart the accustom'd sight of death
    makes hard,
Falls not the axe upon the humbled neck
But first begs pardon will you sterner be
Than he that dies and lives by bloody drops?

Enter ROSALIND, CELIA, *and* CORIN, *behind.*

Phe. I would not be thy executioner :
I fly thee, for I would not injure thee
Thou tell'st me there is murder in mine eye ·
'Tis pretty, sure, and very probable,
That eyes, that are the frail'st and softest
    things,
Who shut their coward gates on atomies,
Should be call'd tyrants, butchers, murderers!
Now I do frown on thee with all my heart ;
And if mine eyes can wound, now let them
    kill thee
Now counterfeit to swoon ; why now fall down,
Or if thou canst not, O, for shame, for shame,
Lie not, to say mine eyes are murderers'
Now show the wound mine eye hath made in
    thee   20
Scratch thee but with a pin, and there remains
Some scar of it , lean but upon a rush,
The cicatrice and capable impressure
Thy palm some moment keeps , but now mine
    eyes,
Which I have darted at thee, hurt thee not,
Nor, I am sure, there is no force in eyes

That can do hurt.
　Sil.　　　　　O dear Phebe,
If ever,—as that ever may be near,—
You meet in some fresh cheek the power of
　　fancy,
Then shall you know the wounds invisible　30
That love's keen arrows make.
　Phe.　　　　　　But till that time
Come not thou near me : and when that time
　　comes,
Afflict me with thy mocks, pity me not ;
As till that time I shall not pity thee.
　Ros.　And why, I pray you ?　Who might
　　be your mother,
That you insult, exult, and all at once,
Over the wretched ?　What though you have
　　no beauty,—
As, by my faith, I see no more in you
Than without candle may go dark to bed—
Must you be therefore proud and pitiless ?　40
Why, what means this ?　Why do you look on
　　me ?
I see no more in you than in the ordinary
Of nature's sale-work.　'Od's my little life,
I think she means to tangle my eyes too !
No, faith, proud mistress, hope not after it :
'Tis not your inky brows, your black silk hair,
Your bugle eyeballs, nor your cheek of cream,
That can entame my spirits to your worship.
You foolish shepherd, wherefore do you follow
　　her,
Like foggy south puffing with wind and rain ?
You are a thousand times a properer man
Than she a woman : 'tis such fools as you
That makes the world full of ill-favor'd chil-
　　dren :
'Tis not her glass, but you, that flatters her ;
And out of you she sees herself more proper
Than any of her lineaments can show her.
But, mistress, know yourself : down on your
　　knees,　　　　　　　　　　　　[love :
And thank heaven, fasting, for a good man's
For I must tell you friendly in your ear,
Sell when you can: you are not for all markets:
Cry the man mercy ; love him ; take his offer:
Foul is most foul, being foul to be a scoffer.
So take her to thee, shepherd : fare you well.
　Phe.　Sweet youth, I pray you, chide a year
　　together :
I had rather hear you chide than this man woo.
　Ros.　He's fallen in love with your foulness
and she'll fall in love with my anger.　If it be
so, as fast as she answers thee with frowning
looks, I'll sauce her with bitter words.　Why
look you so upon me ?　　　　　　　　　70
　Phe.　For no ill will I bear you.
　Ros.　I pray you, do not fall in love with me,
For I am falser than vows made in wine :
Besides, I like you not.　If you will know my
　　house,
'Tis at the tuft of olives here hard by.
Will you go, sister ?　Shepherd, ply her hard.
Come, sister.　Shepherdess, look on him better,
And be not proud : though all the world could
　　see,
None could be so abused in sight as he.　　80

Come, to our flock,
　　　　　[*Exeunt Rosalind, Celia and Corin.*
　Phe.　Dead shepherd, now I find thy saw of
　　might,
'Who ever loved that loved not at first sight ?'
　Sil.　Sweet Phebe,—
　Phe.　　　　Ha, what say'st thou, Silvius ?
　Sil.　Sweet Phebe, pity me.
　Phe.　Why, I am sorry for thee, gentle Sil-
　　vius.
　Sil.　Wherever sorrow is, relief would be :
If you do sorrow at my grief in love,
By giving love your sorrow and my grief
Were both extermined.
　Phe.　Thou hast my love : is not that neigh-
　　borly ?　　　　　　　　　　　　90
　Sil.　I would have you.
　Phe.　　　　Why, that were covetousness.
Silvius, the time was that I hated thee,
And yet it is not that I bear thee love ;
But since that thou canst talk of love so well,
Thy company, which erst was irksome to me,
I will endure, and I'll employ thee too :
But do not look for further recompense
Than thine own gladness that thou art em-
　　ploy'd.
　Sil.　So holy and so perfect is my love,
And I in such a poverty of grace,　　　　100
That I shall think it a most plenteous crop
To glean the broken ears after the man
That the main harvest reaps : loose now and
　　then
A scatter'd smile, and that I'll live upon.
　Phe.　Know'st now the youth that spoke to
　　me erewhile ?
　Sil.　Not very well, but I have met him
　　oft ;
And he hath bought the cottage and the
　　bounds
That the old carlot once was master of.
　Phe.　Think not I love him, though I ask
　　for him ;
'Tis but a peevish boy ; yet he talks well ; 110
But what care I for words ? yet words do well
When he that speaks them pleases those that
　　hear.
It is a pretty youth : not very pretty :
But, sure, he's proud, and yet his pride be-
　　comes him :
He'll make a proper man : the best thing in
　　him
Is his complexion ; and faster than his tongue
Did make offence his eye did heal it up.
He is not very tall ; yet for his years he's
　　tall :
His leg is but so so ; and yet 'tis well :
There was a pretty redness in his lip,　　120
A little riper and more lusty red
Than that mix'd in his cheek ; 'twas just the
　　difference
Between the constant red and mingled
　　damask.
There be some women, Silvius, had they
　　mark'd him
In parcels as I did, would have gone near
To fall in love with him ; but, for my part,

I love him not nor hate him not , and yet
I have more cause to hate him than to love
        him :
For what had he to do to chide at me ?
He said mine eyes were black and my hair
        black :   130
And, now I am remember'd, scorn'd at me :
I marvel why I answer'd not again :
But that's all one , omittance is no quittance.
I'll write to him a very taunting letter,
And thou shalt bear it : wilt thou, Silvius?
    Sil   Phebe, with all my heart
    Phe   I'll write it straight ;
The matter 's in my head and in my heart :
I will be bitter with him and passing short.
Go with me, Silvius.   [*Exeunt.*

ACT IV.

SCENE I.   *The forest.*

Enter ROSALIND, CELIA, *and* JAQUES.

Jaq. I prithee, pretty youth, let me be better
acquainted with thee.
    Ros They say you are a melancholy
fellow.
    Jaq I am so ; I do love it better than
laughing
    Ros. Those that are in extremity of either
are abominable fellows and betray themselves
to every modern censure worse than drunkards
    Jaq. Why, 'tis good to be sad and say
nothing.
    Ros Why then, 'tis good to be a post.   9
    Jaq. I have neither the scholar's melan-
choly, which is emulation, nor the musician's,
which is fantastical, nor the courtier's, which
is proud, nor the soldier's, which is ambitious,
nor the lawyer's, which is politic, nor the
lady's, which is nice, nor the lover's, which is
all these · but it is a melancholy of mine own,
compounded of many simples, extracted from
many objects, and indeed the sundry's contemplation of my travels, in which my often
rumination wraps me in a most humorous sadness.   20
    Ros A traveller ' By my faith, you have
great reason to be sad   I fear you have sold
your own lands to see other men's , then, to
have seen much and to have nothing, is to
have rich eyes and poor hands
    Jaq Yes, I have gained my experience
    Ros. And your experience makes you sad ·
I had rather have a fool to make me merry
than experience to make me sad ; and to
travel for it too !

Enter ORLANDO.

    Orl. Good day and happiness, dear Rosa-
lind !
    Jaq. Nay, then, God be wi' you, an you
talk in blank verse.   [*Exit*

    Ros Farewell, Monsieur Traveller . look
you lisp and wear strange suits, disable all the
benefits of your own country, be out of love
with your nativity and almost chide God for
making you that countenance you are, or I
will scarce think you have swam in a gondola.
Why, how now, Orlando ! where have you
been all this while ? You a lover ! An you
serve me such another trick, never come in my
sight more.   41
    Orl My fair Rosalind, I come within an
hour of my promise.
    Ros Break an hour's promise in love ' He
that will divide a minute into a thousand parts
and break but a part of the thousandth part of
a minute in the affairs of love, it may be said
of him that Cupid hath clapped him o' the
shoulder, but I'll warrant him heart-whole
    Orl. Pardon me, dear Rosalind.   50
    Ros. Nay, an you be so tardy, come no
more in my sight . I had as lief be wooed of a
snail.
    Orl. Of a snail ?
    Ros. Ay, of a snail ; for though he comes
slowly, he carries his house on his head ; a
better jointure, I think, than you make a woman · besides he brings his destiny with him.
    Orl. What's that ?
    Ros. Why, horns, which such as you are
fain to be beholding to your wives for : but he
comes armed in his fortune and prevents the
slander of his wife.
    Orl. Virtue is no horn-maker ; and my Rosa-
lind is virtuous.
    Ros. And I am your Rosalind.
    Cel It pleases him to call you so , but he
hath a Rosalind of a better leer than you
    Ros. Come, woo me, woo me, for now I am
in a holiday humor and like enough to consent.
What would you say to me now, an I were
your very very Rosalind ?   71
    Orl. I would kiss before I spoke
    Ros. Nay, you were better speak first, and
when you were gravelled for lack of matter,
you might take occasion to kiss   Very good
orators, when they are out, they will spit , and
for lovers lacking—God warn us !—matter, the
cleanliest shift is to kiss
    Orl. How if the kiss be denied ?
    Ros. Then she puts you to entreaty, and
there begins new matter   81
    Orl Who could be out, being before his be-
loved mistress ?
    Ros Marry, that should you, if I were your
mistress, or I should think my honesty ranker
than my wit
    Orl. What, of my suit ?
    Ros Not out of your apparel, and yet out
of your suit. Am not I your Rosalind ?
    Orl. I take some joy to say you are, because
I would be talking of her.   91
    Ros. Well in her person I say I will not have
you.
    Orl. Then in mine own person I die.
    Ros No, faith, die by attorney. The poor
world is almost six thousand years old, and in

all this time there was not any man died in his own person, videlicit, in a love-cause. Troilus had his brains dashed out with a Grecian club; yet he did what he could to die before, and he is one of the patterns of love. Leander, he would have lived many a fair year, though Hero had turned nun, if it had not been for a hot midsummer night; for, good youth, he went but forth to wash him in the Hellespont and being taken with the cramp was drowned: and the foolish coroners of that age found it was 'Hero of Sestos.' But these are all lies: men have died from time to time and worms have eaten them, but not for love.

Orl. I would not have my right Rosalind of this mind, for, I protest, her frown might kill me.

Ros. By this hand, it will not kill a fly. But come, now I will be your Rosalind in a more coming-on disposition, and ask me what you will. I will grant it.

Orl. Then love me, Rosalind.

Ros. Yes, faith, will I, Fridays and Saturdays and all.

Orl. And wilt thou have me?

Ros. Ay, and twenty such.

Orl. What sayest thou?   120

Ros. Are you not good?

Orl. I hope so.

Ros. Why then, can one desire too much of a good thing? Come, sister, you shall be the priest and marry us. Give me your hand, Orlando. What do you say, sister?

Orl. Pray thee, marry us.

Cel. I cannot say the words.

Ros. You must begin, 'Will you, Orlando—'

Cel. Go to. Will you, Orlando, have to wife this Rosalind?   131

Orl. I will.

Ros. Ay, but when?   [us.

Orl. Why now; as fast as she can marry

Ros. Then you must say 'I take thee, Rosalind, for wife.'

Orl. I take thee, Rosalind, for wife.

Ros. I might ask you for your commission; but I do take thee, Orlando, for my husband: there's a girl goes before the priest; and certainly a woman's thought runs before her actions.   141

Orl. So do all thoughts; they are winged.

Ros. Now tell me how long you would have her after you have possessed her.

Orl. For ever and a day.

Ros. Say 'a day,' without the 'ever.' No, no, Orlando; men are April when they woo, December when they wed: maids are May when they are maids, but the sky changes when they are wives. I will be more jealous of thee than a Barbary cock-pigeon over his hen, more clamorous than a parrot against rain, more new-fangled than an ape, more giddy in my desires than a monkey: I will weep for nothing, like Diana in the fountain, and I will do that when you are disposed to be merry; I will laugh like a hyen, and that when thou art inclined to sleep.

Orl. But will my Rosalind do so?

Ros. By my life, she will do as I do.

Orl. O, but she is wise.   160

Ros. Or else she could not have the wit to do this: the wiser, the waywarder: make the doors upon a woman's wit and it will out at the casement; shut that and 'twill out at the key-hole; stop that, 'twill fly with the smoke out at the chimney.

Orl. A man that had a wife with such a wit, he might say 'Wit, whither wilt?'

Ros. Nay, you might keep that check for it till you met your wife's wit going to your neighbor's bed.   171

Orl. And what wit could wit have to excuse that?

Ros. Marry, to say she came to seek you there. You shall never take her without her answer, unless you take her without her tongue. O, that woman that cannot make her fault her husband's occasion, let her never nurse her child herself, for she will breed it like a fool!

Orl. For these two hours, Rosalind, I will leave thee.   181

Ros. Alas! dear love, I cannot lack thee two hours.

Orl. I must attend the duke at dinner: by two o'clock I will be with thee again.

Ros. Ay, go your ways, go your ways; I knew what you would prove: my friends told me as much, and I thought no less: that flattering tongue of yours won me: 'tis but one cast away, and so, come, death! Two o'clock is your hour?   190

Orl. Ay, sweet Rosalind.

Ros. By my troth, and in good earnest, and so God mend me, and by all pretty oaths that are not dangerous, if you break one jot of your promise or come one minute behind your hour, I will think you the most pathetical break-promise and the most hollow lover and the most unworthy of her you call Rosalind that may be chosen out of the gross band of the unfaithful: therefore beware my censure and keep your promise.   200

Orl. With no less religion than if thou wert indeed my Rosalind: so adieu.

Ros. Well, Time is the old justice that examines all such offenders, and let Time try: adieu.   [*Exit Orlando.*

Cel. You have simply misused our sex in your love-prate: we must have your doublet and hose plucked over your head, and show the world what the bird hath done to her own nest.

Ros. O coz, coz, coz, my pretty little coz, that thou didst know how many fathom deep I am in love! But it cannot be sounded: my affection hath an unknown bottom, like the bay of Portugal.

Cel. Or rather, bottomless, that as fast as you pour affection in, it runs out.

Ros. No, that same wicked bastard of Venus that was begot of thought, conceived of spleen and born of madness, that blind rascally boy that abuses every one's eyes because his own are out, let him be judge how deep I am in love I'll tell thee. Aliena, I cannot be out of the sight of Orlando : I'll go find a shadow and sigh till he come

Cel. And I'll sleep [*Exeunt*

SCENE II. *The forest.*

Enter JAQUES, *Lords, and* Foresters

Jaq. Which is he that killed the deer ?

A Lord Sir, it was I.

Jaq Let's present him to the duke; like a Roman conqueror , and it would do well to set the deer's horns upon his head, for a branch of victory Have you no song, forester, for this purpose ?

For. Yes, sir.

Jaq Sing it : 'tis no matter how it be in tune, so it make noise enough   . 10

SONG.

For What shall he have that kill'd the deer ?
His leather skin and horns to wear.
    Then sing him home ;
        [*The rest shall bear this burden.*
Take thou no scorn to wear the horn ;
It was a crest ere thou wast born :
        Thy father's father wore it,
        And thy father bore it .
The horn, the horn, the lusty horn
Is not a thing to laugh to scorn.
        [*Exeunt.*

SCENE III. *The forest.*

Enter ROSALIND *and* CELIA.

Ros. How say you now ? Is it not past two o'clock ? and here much Orlando '

Cel I warrant you, with pure love and troubled brain, he hath ta'en his bow and arrows and is gone forth to sleep. Look, who comes here.

Enter SILVIUS

Sil. My errand is to you, fair youth ;
My gentle Phebe bid me give you this :
I know not the contents , but, as I guess
By the stern brow and waspish action
Which she did use as she was writing of it, 10
It bears an angry tenor · pardon me :
I am but as a guiltless messenger.

Ros. Patience herself would startle at this letter
And play the swaggerer ; bear this, bear all :
She says I am not fair, that I lack manners ;
She calls me proud, and that she could not love me,
Were man as rare as phœnix 'Od's my will '
Her love is not the hare that I do hunt
Why writes she so to me ? Well, shepherd, well,
This is a letter of you own device   20

Sil No, I protest, I know not the contents : Phebe did write it

Ros.   Come, come, you are a fool

And turn'd into the extremity of love.
I saw her hand : she has a leathern hand,
A free-stone-color'd hand , I verily did think
That her old gloves were on, but 'twas her hands :
She has a huswife's hand , but that's no matter :
I say she never did invent this letter ;
This is a man's invention and his hand.

Sil. Sure, it is hers   30

Ros. Why, 'tis a boisterous and a cruel style,
A style for challengers ; why, she defies me,
Like Turk to Christian : women's gentle brain
Could not drop forth such giant-rude invention,
Such Ethiope words, blacker in their effect
Than in their countenance. Will you hear the letter ?

Sil So please you, for I never heard it yet , Yet heard too much of Phebe's cruelty

Ros She Phebes me : mark how the tyrant writes.   [*Reads*
Art thou god to shepherd turn'd,   40
That a maiden's heart hath burn'd ?

Can a woman rail thus ?

Sil. Call you this railing ?

Ros. [*Reads*]
Why, thy godhead laid apart,
War'st thou with a woman's heart ?

Did you ever hear such railing ?
        Whiles the eye of man did woo me,
        That could do no vengeance to me.
Meaning me a beast.
        If the scorn of your bright eyne   50
        Have power to raise such love in mine,
        Alack, in me what strange effect
        Would they work in mild aspect !
        Whiles you chid me. I did love ;
        How then might your prayers move !
        He that brings this love to thee
        Little knows this love in me ·
        And by him seal up thy mind ;
        Whether that thy youth and kind
        Will the faithful offer take   60
        Of me and all that I can make ;
        Or else by him my love deny,
        And then I'll study how to die.

Sil. Call you this chiding ?

Cel Alas, poor shepherd '

Ros Do you pity him ? no, he deserves no pity. Wilt thou love such a woman ? What, to make thee an instrument and play false strains upon thee ' not to be endured ' Well, go your way to her, for I see love hath made thee a tame snake, and say this to her that if she love me, I charge her to love thee , if she will not, I will never have her unless thou entreat for her. If you be a true lover, hence, and not a word ; for here comes more company.   [*Exit Silvius.*

Enter OLIVER.

Oli. Good morrow, fair ones : pray you, if you know,

Where in the purlieus of this forest stands
A sheep-cote fenced about with olive trees ?
  Cel. West of this place, down in the neigh-
    bor bottom :
The rank of osiers by the murmuring stream
Left on your right hand brings you to the
  place.   81
But at this hour the house doth keep itself ;
There's none within.
  Oli. If that an eye may profit by a tongue,
Then should I know you by description ;
Such garments and such years : 'The boy is
    fair,
Of female favor, and bestows himself
†Like a ripe sister : the woman low
And browner than her brother.' Are not you
The owner of the house I did inquire for ? 90
  Cel. It is no boast, being ask'd, to say we
    are.
  Oli. Orlando doth commend him to you
    both,
And to that youth he calls his Rosalind
He sends this bloody napkin. Are you he ?
  Ros. I am : what must we understand by
    this ?
  Oli. Some of my shame ; if you will know
    of me
What man I am, and how, and why, and
    where
This handkercher was stain'd.
  Cel.   I pray you, tell it.
  Oli. When last the young Orlando parted
    from you
He left a promise to return again   100
Within an hour, and pacing through the for-
    est,
Chewing the food of sweet and bitter fancy,
Lo, what befel ! he threw his eye aside,
And mark what object did present itself :
Under an oak, whose boughs were moss'd
    with age
And high top bald with dry antiquity,
A wretched ragged man, o'ergrown with hair,
Lay sleeping on his back : about his neck
A green and gilded snake had wreathed it-
    self,
Who with her head nimble in threats ap-
    proach'd   110
The opening of his mouth ; but suddenly,
Seeing Orlando, it unlink'd itself,
And with indented glides did slip away
Into a bush : under which bush's shade
A lioness, with udders all drawn dry,
Lay couching, head on ground, with catlike
    watch,
When that the sleeping man should stir ; for
    'tis
The royal disposition of that beast
To prey on nothing that doth seem as dead :
This seen, Orlando did approach the man 120
And found it was his brother, his elder
    brother.
  Cel. O, I have heard him speak of that
    same brother ;
And he did render him the most unnatural
That lived amongst men.

  Oli.   And well he might so do,
For well I know he was unnatural.
  Ros. But, to Orlando : did he leave him
    there,
Food to the suck'd and hungry lioness ?
  Oli. Twice did he turn his back and pur-
    posed so ;
But kindness, nobler ever than revenge,
And nature, stronger than his just occasion,
Made him give battle to the lioness,   131
Who quickly fell before him : in which hurt-
    ling
From miserable slumber I awaked.
  Cel. Are you his brother ?
  Ros.   Was't you he rescued ?
  Cel. Was't you that did so oft contrive to
    kill him ?
  Oli. 'Twas I ; but 'tis not I : I do not shame
To tell you what I was, since my conversion
So sweetly tastes, being the thing I am.
  Ros. But, for the bloody napkin ?
  Oli.   By and by.
When from the first to last betwixt us two 140
Tears our recountments had most kindly
    bathed,
As how I came into that desert place :—
In brief, he led me to the gentle duke,
Who gave me fresh array and entertainment,
Committing me unto my brother's love ;
Who led me instantly unto his cave,
There stripp'd himself, and here upon his arm
The lioness had torn some flesh away,
Which all this while had bled ; and now he
    fainted
And cried, in fainting, upon Rosalind.   150
Brief, I recover'd him, bound up his wound ;
And, after some small space, being strong at
    heart,
He sent me hither, stranger as I am,
To tell this story, that you might excuse
His broken promise, and to give this napkin
Dyed in his blood unto the shepherd youth
That he in sport doth call his Rosalind.
                       [*Rosalind swoons.*
  Cel. Why, how now, Ganymede ! sweet
    Ganymede !
  Oli. Many will swoon when they do look
    on blood.
  Cel. There is more in it. Cousin Gany-
    mede !   160
  Oli. Look, he recovers.
  Ros. I would I were at home.
  Cel.   We'll lead you thither.
I pray you, will you take him by the arm ?
  Oli. Be of good cheer, youth : you a man !
you lack a man's heart.
  Ros. I do so, I confess it. Ah, sirrah, a body
would think this was well counterfeited ! I
pray you, tell your brother how well I coun-
terfeited. Heigh-ho !   169
  Oli. This was not counterfeit : there is too
great testimony in your complexion that it was
a passion of earnest.
  Ros. Counterfeit, I assure you.
  Oli. Well then, take a good heart and
counterfeit to be a man.

As You Like It.

Ros. So I do : but, i' faith, I should have been a woman by right

Cel Come, you look taller and paler : pray you, draw homewards   Good sir, go with us

Oli. That will I, for I must bear answer back   180
How you excuse my brother, Rosalind

Ros I shall devise something   but, I pray you, commend my counterfeiting to him   Will you go ?   [*Exeunt*

ACT V.

SCENE I.   *The forest*

Enter TOUCHSTONE *and* AUDREY.

Touch. We shall find a time, Audrey , patience, gentle Audrey.

Aud Faith, the priest was good enough, for all the old gentleman's saying

Touch A most wicked Sir Oliver, Audrey, a most vile Martext   But, Audrey, there is a youth here in the forest lays claim to you

Aud. Ay, I know who 'tis , he hath no interest in me in the world : here comes the man you mean   10

Touch It is meat and drink to me to see a clown by my truth, we that have good wits have much to answer for , we shall be flouting , we cannot hold

Enter WILLIAM.

Will Good even, Audrey

Aud God ye good even, William.

Will. And good even to you, sir

Touch Good even, gentle friend   Cover thy head, cover thy head , nay, prithee, be covered   How old are you, friend   20

Will Five and twenty, sir

Touch A ripe age   Is thy name William

Will. William, sir.

Touch A fair name   Wast born i' the forest here ?

Will. Ay, sir, I thank God

Touch 'Thank God ,' a good answer   Art rich ?

Will. Faith, sir, so so.

Touch. 'So so' is good, very good, very excellent good ; and yet it is not , it is but so so   Art thou wise ?   31

Will. Ay, sir, I have a pretty wit

Touch Why, thou sayest well   I do now remember a saying, 'The fool doth think he is wise, but the wise man knows himself to be a fool.' The heathen philosopher, when he had a desire to eat a grape, would open his lips when he put it into his mouth , meaning thereby that grapes were made to eat and lips to open   You do love this maid ?   40

Will. I do, sir.

Touch Give me your hand.   Art thou learned ?

Will. No, sir.

Touch Then learn this of me   to have, is to have , for it is a figure in rhetoric that drink, being poured out of a cup into a glass by filling the one doth empty the other , for all your writers do consent that ipse is he   now, you are not ipse, for I am he.

Will Which he, sir ?   50

Touch He, sir, that must marry this woman   Therefore, you clown, abandon,—which is in the vulgar leave,—the society,—which in the boorish is company,—of this female,—which in the common is woman , which together is, abandon the society of this female, or, clown, thou perishest , or, to thy better understanding, diest , or, to wit, I kill thee, make thee away, translate thy life into death, thy liberty into bondage   I will deal in poison with thee, or in bastinado, or in steel , I will bandy with thee in faction , I will o'errun thee with policy , I will kill thee a hundred and fifty ways . therefore tremble, and depart

Aud. Do, good William

Will God rest you merry, sir.   [*Exit.*

Enter CORIN

Cor. Our master and mistress seeks you ; come, away, away '

Touch Trip, Audrey ' trip, Audrey '   I attend, I attend   [*Exeunt.*

SCENE II   *The forest.*

Enter ORLANDO *and* OLIVER

Orl. Is't possible that on so little acquaintance you should like her that but seeing you should love her and loving woo and, wooing, she should grant ? and will you persever to enjoy her

Oli Neither call the giddiness of it in question the poverty of her, the small acquaintance, my sudden wooing, nor her sudden consenting, but say with me, I love Aliena , say with her that she loves me   consent with both that we may enjoy each other   it shall be to your good , for my father's house and all the revenue that was old Sir Rowland's will I estate upon you, and here live and die a shepherd

Orl You have my consent   Let your wedding be to-morrow   thither will I invite the duke and all's contented followers   Go you and prepare Aliena , for look you, here comes my Rosalind

Enter ROSALIND.

Ros. God save you, brother.   20

Oli And you, fair sister   [*Exit.*

Ros O, my dear Orlando, how it grieves me to see thee wear thy heart in a scarf '

Orl It is my arm.

Ros. I thought thy heart had been wounded with the claws of a lion

Orl. Wounded it is, but with the eyes of a lady

Ros Did your brother tell you how I counterfeited to swoon when he showed me your handkercher ?   30

Orl. Ay, and greater wonders than that

Ros. O, I know where you are . nay, 'tis true . there was never any thing so sudden but the fight of two rams and Cæsar's thrasonical brag of ' I came, saw, and overcame ' for your brother and my sister no sooner met but they looked, no sooner looked but they loved, no sooner loved but they sighed, no sooner sighed but they asked one another the reason, no sooner knew the reason but they sought the remedy; and in these degrees have they made a pair of stairs to marriage which they will climb incontinent, or else be incontinent before marriage . they are in the very wrath of love and they will together , clubs cannot part them.

Orl. They shall be married to-morrow, and I will bid the duke to the nuptial But, O, how bitter a thing it is to look into happiness through another man's eyes ! By so much the more shall I to-morrow be at the height of heart-heaviness, by how much I shall think my brother happy in having what he wishes for

Ros. Why then, to-morrow I cannot serve your turn for Rosalind ?

Orl. I can live no longer by thinking.

Ros. I will weary you then no longer with idle talking Know of me then, for now I speak to some purpose, that I know you are a gentleman of good conceit · I speak not this that you should bear a good opinion of my knowledge, insomuch I say I know you are , neither do I labor for a greater esteem than in my in some little measure draw a belief from you, to do yourself good and not to grace me. Believe then, if you please, that I can do strange things · I have, since I was three year old, conversed with a magician, most profound in his art and yet not damnable If you do love Rosalind so near the heart as your gesture cries it out, when your brother marries Aliena, shall you marry her . I know into what straits of fortune she is driven , and it is not impossible to me, if it appear not inconvenient to you, to set her before your eyes to-morrow human as she is and without any danger.

Orl. Speakest thou in sober meanings ?

Ros. By my life, I do ; which I tender dearly, though I say I am a magician Therefore, put you in your best array : bid your friends , for if you will be married to-morrow, you shall, and to Rosalind, if you will.   81

Enter SILVIUS *and* PHEBE.

Look, here comes a lover of mine and a lover of hers

Phe. Youth, you have done me much ungentleness,
To show the letter that I writ to you.

Ros. I care not if I have : it is my study
To seem despiteful and ungentle to you .
You are there followed by a faithful shepherd;
Look upon him, love him ; he worships you

Phe Good shepherd. tell this youth what
'tis to love.

Sil. It is to be all made of sighs and tears ;
And so am I for Phebe   9

Phe. And I for Ganymede,

Orl. And I for Rosalind

Ros And I for no woman.

Sil. It is to be all made of faith and service,
And so am I for Phebe

Phe. And I for Ganymede.

Orl. And I for Rosalind.

Ros. And I for no woman.

Sil. It is to be all made of fantasy,   106
All made of passion and all made of wishes,
All adoration, duty, and observance,
All humbleness, all patience and impatience,
†All purity, all trial, all observance ,
And so am I for Phebe.

Phe. And so am I for Ganymede.

Orl. And so am I for Rosalind

Ros And so am I for no woman

Phe If this be so, why blame you me to
love you ?   110

Sil. If this be so, why blame you me to
love you ?

Orl. If this be so, why blame you me to
love you ?

Ros Who do you speak to, ' Why blame
you me to love you ?'   [hear.

Orl To her that is not here, nor doth not

Ros Pray you, no more of this , 'tis like the howling of Irish wolves against the moon [*To Sil*] I will help you, if I can · [*To Phe.*] I would love you, if I could To-morrow meet me all together, [*To Phe*] I will marry you, if ever I marry woman, and I'll be married to-morrow [*To Orl*] I will satisfy you, if ever I satisfied man, and you shall be married to-morrow · [*To Sil*] I will content you, if what pleases you contents you, and you shall be married to-morrow. [*To Orl*] As you love Rosalind, meet · [*To Sil*] as you love Phebe, meet and as I love no woman, I'll meet. So fare you well I have left you commands 131

Sil I'll not fail, if I live.

Phe. Nor I.

Orl. Nor I.   [*Exeunt.*

SCENE III. *The forest.*

Enter TOUCHSTONE *and* AUDREY.

Touch. To-morrow is the joyful day, Audrey ; to-morrow will we be married

Aud I do desire it with all my heart ; and I hope it is no dishonest desire to desire to be a woman of the world Here comes two of the banished duke's pages

Enter two Pages.

First Page. Well met, honest gentleman

Touch. By my troth, well met. Come it, sit, and a song   9

Sec. Page. We are for you : sit i' the middle

First Page Shall we clap into't roundly, without hawking or spitting or saying we are hoarse, which are the only prologues to a bad voice ?

Sec. Page. I'faith, i'faith ; and both in a tune, like two gipsies on a horse.

SONG.

It was a lover and his lass,
  With a hey, and a ho, and a hey nonino,
That o'er the green corn-field did pass
  In the spring time, the only pretty ring time,
When birds do sing, hey ding a ding, ding : 21
Sweet lovers love the spring.

Between the acres of the rye,
  With a hey, and a ho, and a hey nonino,
These pretty country folks would lie,
  In spring time, &c.

This carol they began that hour,
  With a hey, and a ho, and a hey nonino,
How that a life was but a flower
  In spring time, &c.   30

And therefore take the present time,
  With a hey, and a ho, and a hey nonino ;
For love is crowned with the prime
  In spring time, &c.

Touch. Truly, young gentlemen, though there was no great matter in the ditty, yet the note was very untuneable.

First Page. You are deceived, sir : we kept time, we lost not our time.

Touch. By my troth, yes ; I count it but time lost to hear such a foolish song. God be wi' you ; and God mend your voices ! Come, Audrey.   [*Exeunt.*

SCENE IV. *The forest.*

Enter DUKE senior, AMIENS, JAQUES, OR-LANDO, OLIVER, *and* CELIA.

Duke S. Dost thou believe, Orlando, that the boy
Can do all this that he hath promised ?
  Orl. I sometimes do believe, and sometimes do not ;
‡ As those that fear they hope, and know they fear.

Enter ROSALIND, SILVIUS, *and* PHEBE.

Ros. Patience once more, whiles our com-pact is urged :
You say, if I bring in your Rosalind,
You will bestow her on Orlando here ?
  Duke S. That would I, had I kingdoms to give with her.
  Ros. And you say, you will have her, when I bring her ?
  Orl. That would I, were I of all kingdoms king.   10
  Ros. You say, you'll marry me, if I be will-ing ?
  Phe. That will I, should I die the hour after.
  Ros. But if you do refuse to marry me,
You'll give yourself to this most faithful shepherd ?
  Phe. So is the bargain.

Ros. You say, that you'll have Phebe, if she will ?
  Sil. Though to have her and death were both one thing,
  Ros. I have promised to make all this matter even.
Keep you your word, O duke, to give your daughter ;   19
You yours, Orlando, to receive his daughter :
Keep your word, Phebe, that you'll marry me,
Or else refusing me, to wed this shepherd :
Keep your word, Silvius, that you'll marry her,
If she refuse me : and from hence I go,
To make these doubts all even.
                    [*Exeunt Rosalind and Celia.*
  Duke S. I do remember in this shepherd boy
Some lively touches of my daughter's favor.
  Orl. My lord, the first time that I ever saw him
Methought he was a brother to your daughter:
But, my good lord, this boy is forest-born, 30
And hath been tutor'd in the rudiments
Of many desperate studies by his uncle,
Whom he reports to be a great magician,
Obscured in the circle of this forest.

Enter TOUCHSTONE *and* AUDREY.

  Jaq. There is, sure, another flood toward, and these couples are coming to the ark. Here comes a pair of very strange beasts, which in all tongues are called fools.
  Touch. Salutation and greeting to you all !
  Jaq. Good my lord, bid him welcome : this is the motley-minded gentleman that I have so often met in the forest : he hath been a courtier, he swears.
  Touch. If any man doubt that, let him put me to my purgation. I have trod a measure ; I have flattered a lady ; I have been politic with my friend, smooth with mine enemy ; I have undone three tailors ; I have had four quarrels, and like to have fought one.
  Jaq. And how was that ta'en up ?   50
  Touch. Faith, we met, and found the quarrel was upon the seventh cause.
  Jaq. How seventh cause ? Good my lord, like this fellow.
  Duke S. I like him very well.
  Touch. God 'ild you, sir ; I desire you of the like. I press in here, sir, amongst the rest of the country copulatives, to swear and to forswear : according as marriage binds and blood breaks : a poor virgin, sir, an ill-favored thing, sir, but mine own ; a poor humor of mine, sir, to take that that no man else will : rich honesty dwells like a miser, sir, in a poor house ; as your pearl in your foul oyster.
  Duke S. By my faith, he is very swift and sententious.
  Touch. According to the fool's bolt, sir, and such dulcet diseases.
  Jaq. But, for the seventh cause ; how did you find the quarrel on the seventh cause ? 70
  Touch. Upon a lie seven times removed :—

bear your body more seeming, Audrey :—as thus, sir. I did dislike the cut of a certain courtier's beard : he sent me word, if I said his beard was not cut well, he was in the mind it was : this is called the Retort Courteous. If I sent him word again ' it was not well cut,' he would send me word, he cut it to please himself : this is called the Quip Modest. If again ' it was not well cut,' he disabled my judgment : this is called the Reply Churlish. If again ' it was not well cut,' he would answer, I spake not true : this is called the Reproof-Valiant. If again ' it was not well cut,' he would say, I lied : this is called the Counter-check Quarrelsome . and so to the Lie Circum-stantial and the Lie Direct.

Jaq. And how oft did you say his beard was not well cut ?

Touch I durst go no further than the Lie Circumstantial, nor he durst not **give** me the Lie Direct ; and so we measured **swords** and parted.

Jaq. Can you nominate in order now the degrees of the lie ?

Touch. O sir, we quarrel in print, by the book ; as you have books for good manners : I will name you the degrees. The first, the Retort Courteous ; the second, the Quip Modest ; the third, the Reply Churlish ; the fourth, the Reproof Valiant ; the fifth, the Countercheck Quarrelsome ; the sixth, the Lie with Circumstance ; the seventh, the Lie Direct. All these you may avoid but the Lie Direct ; and you may avoid that too, with an If. I knew when seven justices could not take up a quarrel, but when the parties were met themselves, one of them thought but of an If, as, ' If you said so, then I said so ;' and they shook hands and swore brothers. Your If is the only peace-maker ; much virtue in If.

Jaq. Is not this a rare fellow, my lord ? he's as good at any thing and yet a fool. . 110

Duke S. He uses his folly like a stalking-horse and under the presentation of that he shoots his wit.

Enter HYMEN, ROSALIND, *and* CELIA.

Still Music.

Hym. Then is there mirth in heaven,
        When earthly things made even
          Atone together.
        Good duke, receive thy daughter :
        Hymen from heaven brought her,
          Yea, brought her hither,
        That thou mightst join her hand with
          his
        Whose heart within his bosom is. 121

Ros. [*To duke*] To you I give myself, for I am yours.
[*To Orl.*] To you I give myself, for I am yours.

Duke S. If there be truth in sight, you are my daughter.

Orl. If there be truth in sight, you are my Rosalind.

Phe. If sight and shape be true,
Why then, my love adieu !

Ros. I'll have no father, if you be not he :
I'll have no husband, if you be not he :
Nor ne'er wed woman, if you be not she. 130

Hym. Peace, ho ! I bar confusion :
        'Tis I must make conclusion
          Of these most strange events :
        Here's eight that must take hands
        To join in Hymen's bands,
          If truth holds true contents.
        You and you no cross shall part :
        You and you are heart in heart :
        You to his love must accord,
        Or have a woman to your lord :   140
        You and you are sure together,
        As the winter to foul weather.
        Whiles a wedlock-hymn we sing,
        Feed yourselves with questioning ;
        That reason wonder may diminish,
        How thus we met, and these things finish.

SONG.

Wedding is great Juno's crown :
  O blessed bond of board and bed !
'Tis Hymen peoples every town :
  High wedlock then be honored :   150
Honor, high honor and renown,
To Hymen, god of every town !

Duke S. O my dear niece, welcome thou art to me !
Even daughter, welcome, in no less degree.

Phe. I will not eat my word, now thou art mine ;
Thy faith my fancy to thee doth combine.

Enter JAQUES DE BOYS.

Jaq. de B. Let me have audience for a word or two :
I am the second son of old Sir Rowland,
That bring these tidings to this fair assembly
Duke Frederick, hearing how that every day
Men of great worth resorted to this forest,
Address'd a mighty power ; which were on foot,
In his own conduct, purposely to take
His brother here and put him to the sword :
And to the skirts of this wild wood he came ;
Where meeting with an old religious man,
After some question with him, was converted
Both from his enterprise and from the world ;
His crown bequeathing to his banish'd brother,
And all their lands restored to them again 170
That were with him exiled. This to be true,
I do engage my life.

Duke S.   Welcome, young man ;
Thou offer'st fairly to thy brothers' wedding :
To one his lands withheld, and to the other
A land itself at large, a potent dukedom.
First, in this forest let us do those ends
That here were well begun and well begot :
And after, every of this happy number
That have endured shrewd days and nights with us
Shall share the good of our returned fortune,

According to the measure of their states.   181
Meantime, forget this new-fall'n dignity
And fall into our rustic revelry.
Play, music! And you, brides and bride-
    grooms all,
With measure heap'd in joy, to the measures
    fall.
  Jaq. Sir, by your patience. If I heard you
      rightly,
The duke hath put on a religious life
And thrown into neglect the pompous court?
  Jaq. de B. He hath.
  Jaq. To him will I : out of these conver-
      tites   190
There is much matter to be heard and learn'd.
[*To duke*] You to your former honor I be-
      queath ;
Your patience and your virtue well deserves
      it :
[*To Orl.*] You to a love that your true faith
      doth merit :
[*To Oli.*] You to your land and love and
      great allies :
[*To Sil.*] You to a long and well-deserved
      bed :
[*To Touch.*] And you to wrangling ; for thy
      loving voyage
Is but for two months victuall'd. So, to your
      pleasures :
I am for other than for dancing measures.
  Duke S. Stay, Jaques, stay.   200
  Jaq. To see no pastime I : what you would
      have

I'll stay to know at your abandon'd cave. [*Exit.*
  Duke S. Proceed, proceed : we will begin
      these rites,
As we do trust they'll end, in true delights,
                                          [*A dance.*

EPILOGUE.

  Ros. It is not the fashion to see the lady
the epilogue ; but it is no more unhandsome
than to see the lord the prologue. If it be true
that good wine needs no bush, 'tis true that a
good play needs no epilogue ; yet to good wine
they do use good bushes, and good plays prove
the better by the help of good epilogues. What
a case am I in then, that am neither a good
epilogue nor cannot insinuate with you in the
behalf of a good play ! I am not furnished
like a beggar, therefore to beg will not become
me : my way is to conjure you ; and I'll begin
with the women. I charge you, O women, for
the love you bear to men, to like as much of
this play as please you : and I charge you, O
men, for the love you bear to women—as I
perceive by your simpering, none of you hates
them—that between you and the women the
play may please. If I were a woman I would
kiss as many of you as had beards that
pleased me, complexions that liked me and
breaths that I defied not : and, I am sure, as
many as have good beards or good faces or
sweet breaths will, for my kind offer, when I
make curtsy, bid me farewell.   [*Exeunt.*

TWELFTH NIGHT.

(WRITTEN ABOUT 1600–1601.)

INTRODUCTION.

We learn from Manningham's *Diary* that *Twelfth Night* was acted at the Middle Temple, February 2, 1601–1602. Its date is probably 1600–1601. Manningham writes of the play : "Much like *The Comedy of Errors* or *Menechmi* in Plautus, but most like and neere to that in Italian called *Inganni.*" There are two Italian plays of an earlier date than *Twelfth Night*, entitled *Gl' Inganni* (*The Cheats*), containing incidents in some degree resembling those of Shakespeare's comedy, and in that by Gonzaga, the sister who assumes male attire, producing thereby confusion of identity with her brother, is named Cesare (Shakespeare's Cesario). But a third Italian play, *Gl' Ingannati*, presents a still closer resemblance to *Twelfth Night*, and in its poetical induction, *Il Sacrificio*, occurs the name Malevolti (Malvolio). The story is told in Bandello's novel (ii. 36), and was translated by Belleforest into French, in *Histoires Tragiques*. Whether Shakespeare consulted any Italian source or not, he had doubtless before him the version of the story (from Cinthio's *Hecatomithi*) by Barnabe Rich—the *Historie of Apolonius and Silla* in *Riche His Farewell to Militarie Profession* (1581)—and this, in the main, he followed. The characters of Malvolio, Sir Toby Belch, Sir Andrew Aguecheek, Fabian, the clown Feste, and Maria, with the part they play in the comedy, are creations of Shakespeare. No comedy of Shakespeare's unites such abounding mirth and fine satire, with the charm of a poetical romance. It is the summing up of the several admirable qualities which appear in the joyous comedies, of which it forms the last. An edge is put on the roystering humor of Sir Toby by the sharp waiting-maid wit of Maria, which saves it from becoming an aimless rollicking. Sir Andrew is a Slender grown adult in brainlessness, and who has forgotten that he is not as richly endowed by nature as by fortune. Feste, the clown, is less quaint than Touchstone, but more versatile, less a contemplative fool, and more actively a lover of jest and waggery. Among this abandoned crew of topers and drolls stalks the solemn "yellow-legged stork" Malvolio. His sense of self-importance has diffused itself over all the details of his life, so that the whole of human existence, as he would have it, must become as pompous and as exemplary as the manners of my lady's steward. The cruelty of his deception and disillusion is in proportion to the greatness of his distempered self-esteem. The Duke Orsino is infected with the lover's melancholy, which is fantastical and nice. He nurses his love and dallies with it, and tries to yield up all his consciousness to it, as to a delicious sensation . and therefore his love is not quite earnest or deep. Olivia has not the love-languor of the Duke, but her resolved sorrow for her lost brother, so soon forgotten in a stronger feeling, shows a little of the same unreality of self-conscious emotion which we perceive in the Duke's love ; she is of a nature harmonious and refined, but is too much a child of wealth and ease to win away our chief interest from the heroine of the play· Viola is like a heightened portrait of the Julia of *The Two Gentlemen of Verona*, enriched with lovely color and placed among more poetical surroundings. She has not the pretty sauciness of Rosalind in her disguise, but owns a heart as tender, sweet-natured, and sound-natured as even Rosalind's.

DRAMATIS PERSONÆ.

ORSINO, Duke of Illyria,
SEBASTIAN, brother to Viola.
ANTONIO, a sea captain, friend to Sebastian.
A Sea Captain, friend to Viola
VALENTINE, } gentleman attending on the
CURIO, } Duke.
SIR TOBY BELCH, uncle to Olivia.
SIR ANDREW AGUECHEEK
MALVOLIO, steward to Olivia.

FABIAN,
FESTE, a Clown, } servants to Olivia.
OLIVIA.
VIOLA.
MARIA, Olivia's woman.
Lords, Priests, Sailors, Officers, Musicians, and other Attendants.
SCENE : *A city in Illyria, and the sea-coast near it.*

(502)

ACT I.

Scene I. *The Duke's palace.*

Enter DUKE, CURIO, *and other* Lords ; Musicians *attending.*

Duke. If music be the food of love, play
on ;
Give me excess of it, that, surfeiting,
The appetite may sicken, and so die.
That strain again ! it had a dying fall :
O, it came o'er my ear like the sweet sound,
That breathes upon a bank of violets,
Stealing and giving odor ! Enough , no more :
'Tis not so sweet now as it was before
O spirit of love ! how quick and fresh art thou,
That, notwithstanding thy capacity   10
Receiveth as the sea, nought enters there,
Of what validity and pitch soe'er,
But falls into abatement and low price,
Even in a minute : so full of shapes is fancy
That it alone is high fantastical.
  Cur. Will you go hunt, my lord ?
  Duke.   What, Curio ?
  Cur. The hart.
  Duke. Why, so I do, the noblest that I
have :
O, when mine eyes did see Olivia first,
Methought she purged the air of pestilence !
That instant was I turn'd into a hart ;   21
And my desires, like fell and cruel hounds,
E'er since pursue me.

Enter VALENTINE.

                How now ! what news from her ?
  Val. So please my lord, I might not be ad-
mitted ;
But from her handmaid do return this an-
swer .
The element itself, till seven years' heat,
Shall not behold her face at ample view ,
But, like a cloistress, she will veiled walk
And water once a day her chamber round
With eye-offending brine · all this to season
A brother's dead love, which she would keep
fresh   31
And lasting in her sad remembrance.
  Duke. O, she that hath a heart of that fine
frame
To pay this debt of love but to a brother,
How will she love, when the rich golden shaft
Hath kill'd the flock of all affections else
That live in her , when liver, brain and heart,
These sovereign thrones, are all supplied, and
fill'd
Her sweet perfections with one self king !
Away before me to sweet beds of flowers . 40
Love-thoughts lie rich when canopied with
bowers.   [*Exeunt*

Scene II. *The sea-coast.*

Enter VIOLA, *a Captain, and* Sailors

  Vio. What country, friends, is this ?
  Cap. This is Illyria, lady
  Vio. And what should I do in Illyria ?

My brother he is in Elysium.
Perchance he is not drown'd : what think you,
sailors ?
  Cap. It is perchance that you yourself were
saved.
  Vio. O my poor brother ! and so perchance
may he be.
  Cap. True, madam : and, to comfort you
with chance,
Assure yourself, after our ship did split,
When you and those poor number saved with
you   10
Hung on our driving boat, I saw your brother,
Most provident in peril, bind himself,
Courage and hope both teaching him the prac-
tice,
To a strong mast that lived upon the sea ,
Where, like Arion on the dolphin's back,
I saw him hold acquaintance with the waves
So long as I could see
  Vio. For saying so, there's gold :
Mine own escape unfoldeth to my hope,
Whereto thy speech serves for authority,   20
The like of him. Know'st thou this country ?
  Cap. Ay, madam, well , for I was bred and
born
Not three hours' travel from this very place.
  Vio. Who governs here ?
  Cap. A noble duke, in nature as in name.
  Vio. What is the name ?
  Cap. Orsino.
  Vio. Orsino ! I have heard my father name
him ·
He was a bachelor then.
  Cap. And so is now, or was so very late ,
For but a month ago I went from hence,   31
And then 'twas fresh in murmur,—as, you
know,
What great ones do the less will prattle of,—
That he did seek the love of fair Olivia.
  Vio. What's she ?
  Cap. A virtuous maid, the daughter of a
count
That died some twelvemonth since, then leav-
ing her
In the protection of his son, her brother,
Who shortly also died : for whose dear love,
They say, she hath abjured the company   40
And sight of men
  Vio.   O that I served that lady
And might not be delivered to the world,
Till I had made mine own occasion mellow,
What my estate is !
  Cap.   That were hard to compass ;
Because she will admit no kind of suit,
No, not the duke's
  Vio.   There is a fair behavior in thee, cap-
tain ;
And though that nature with a beauteous wall
Doth oft close in pollution, yet of thee
I will believe thou hast a mind that suits   50
With this thy fair and outward character.
I prithee, and I'll pay thee bounteously,
Conceal me what I am, and be my aid ·
For such disguise as haply shall become
The form of my intent. I'll serve this duke :

Thou shall present me as an eunuch to him :
It may be worth thy pains ; for I can sing
And speak to him in many sorts of music
That will allow me very worth his service.
What else may hap to time I will commit ；60
Only shape thou thy silence to my wit.

Cap. Be you his eunuch, and your mute I'll
be :
When my tongue blabs, then let mine eyes not
see.

Vio. I thank thee : lead me on. [*Exeunt.*

Scene III. Olivia's *house*.

Enter Sir Toby Belch *and* Maria.

Sir To. What a plague means my niece, to
take the death of her brother thus ? I am sure
care's an enemy to life.

Mar. By my troth, Sir Toby, you must come
in earlier o' nights : your cousin, my lady,
takes great exceptions to your ill hours.

Sir To. Why, let her except, before excepted.

Mar. Ay, but you must confine yourself
within the modest limits of order. 9

Sir To. Confine ! I'll confine myself no
finer than I am : these clothes are good enough
to drink in ; and so be these boots too : an
they be not, let them hang themselves in their
own straps.

Mar. That quaffing and drinking will undo
you : I heard my lady talk of it yesterday ;
and of a foolish knight that you brought in one
night here to be her wooer.

Sir To. Who, Sir Andrew Aguecheek ?

Mar. Ay, he.

Sir To. He's as tall a man as any's in Illyria. 20

Mar. What's that to the purpose ?

Sir To. Why, he has three thousand ducats
a year.

Mar. Ay, but he'll have but a year in all
these ducats : he's a very fool and a prodigal.

Sir To. Fie, that you'll say so ! he plays o'
the viol-de-gamboys, and speaks three or four
languages word for word without book, and
hath all the good gifts of nature. 29

Mar. He hath indeed, almost natural : for
besides that he's a fool, he's a great quarreller :
and but that he hath the gift of a coward to
allay the gust he hath in quarrelling, 'tis
thought among the prudent he would quickly
have the gift of a grave.

Sir To. By this hand, they are scoundrels
and subtractors that say so of him. Who are
they ?

Mar. They that add, moreover, he's drunk
nightly in your company. 39

Sir To. With drinking healths to my niece :
I'll drink to her as long as there is a passage
in my throat and drink in Illyria : he's a
coward and a coystrill that will not drink to
my niece till his brains turn o' the toe like a
parish-top. What, wench ! Castiliano vulgo !
for here comes Sir Andrew Agueface.

Enter Sir Andrew Aguecheek.

Sir And. Sir Toby Belch ! how now, Sir
Toby Belch !

Sir To. Sweet sir Andrew !

Sir And. Bless you, fair shrew. 50

Mar. And you too, sir.

Sir To. Accost, Sir Andrew, accost.

Sir And. What's that ?

Sir To. My niece's chambermaid.

Sir And. Good Mistress Accost, I desire
better acquaintance.

Mar. My name is Mary, sir.

Sir And. Good Mistress Mary Accost,—

Sir To. You mistake, knight ; 'accost' is
front her, board her, woo her, assail her. 60

Sir And. By my troth, I would not undertake her in this company. Is that the meaning
of 'accost' ?

Mar. Fare you well, gentlemen.

Sir To. An thou let part so, Sir Andrew,
would thou mightst never draw sword again.

Sir And. An you part so, mistress, I would
I might never draw sword again. Fair lady,
do you think you have fools in hand ?

Mar. Sir, I have not you by the hand. 70

Sir And. Marry, but you shall have ; and
here's my hand.

Mar. Now, sir, 'thought is free :' I pray
you, bring your hand to the buttery-bar and
let it drink.

Sir And. Wherefore, sweet-heart ? what's
your metaphor ?

Mar. It's dry, sir.

Sir And. Why, I think so : I am not such
an ass but I can keep my hand dry. But
what's your jest ? 80

Mar. A dry jest, sir.

Sir And. Are you full of them ?

Mar. Ay, sir, I have them at my fingers'
ends : marry, now I let go your hand, I am
barren. [*Exit.*

Sir To. O knight thou lackest a cup of
canary : when did I see thee so put down ?

Sir And. Never in your life, I think ; unless
you see canary put me down. Methinks sometimes I have no more wit than a Christian or
an ordinary man has : but I am a great eater
of beef and I believe that does harm to my
wit. 91

Sir To. No question.

Sir And. An I thought that, I'ld forswear
it. I'll ride home to-morrow, Sir Toby.

Sir To. Pourquoi, my dear knight ?

Sir And. What is 'pourquoi' ? do or not
do ? I would I had bestowed that time in the
tongues that I have in fencing, dancing and
bear-baiting : O, had I but followed the arts !

Sir To. Then hadst thou had an excellent
head of hair. 101

Sir And. Why, would that have mended
my hair ?

Sir To. Past question ; for thou seest it will
not curl by nature.

Sir And. But it becomes me well enough,
does't not ?

Sir To. Excellent : it hangs like flax on a

distaff ; and I hope to see a housewife take thee between her legs and spin it off.   110

Sir And. Faith, I'll home to-morrow, Sir Toby : your niece will not be seen , or if she be, it's four to one she'll none of me : the count himself here hard by woos her.

Sir To. She'll none o' the count : she'll not match above her degree, neither in estate, years, nor wit ; I have heard her swear't Tut, there's life in't, man

Sir And. I'll stay a month longer. I am a fellow o' the strangest mind i' the world ; I delight in masques and revels sometimes altogether   121

Sir To. Art thou good at these kickshawses, knight ?

Sir And. As any man in Illyria, whatsoever he be, under the degree of my betters ; and yet I will not compare with an old man

Sir To. What is thy excellence in a galliard, knight ?

Sir And. Faith, I can cut a caper.

Sir To. And I can cut the mutton to't.   130

Sir And. And I think I have the back-trick simply as strong as any man in Illyria

Sir To. Wherefore are these things hid ? wherefore have these gifts a curtain before 'em ? are they like to take dust, like Mistress Mall's picture ? why dost thou not go to church in a galliard and come home in a coranto ? My very walk should be a jig ; I would not so much as make water but in a sink-a-pace What dost thou mean? Is it a world to hide virtues in ? I did think, by the excellent constitution of thy leg, it was formed under the star of a galliard.

Sir And. Ay, 'tis strong, and it does indifferent well in a flame-colored stock. Shall we set about some revels ?

Sir To. What shall we do else ? were we not born under Taurus ?

Sir And. Taurus ! That's sides and heart

Sir To. No, sir ; it is legs and thighs Let me see the caper ; ha ! higher : ha, ha ! excellent !   [*Exeunt.* 151

Scene IV. *The* Duke's *palace.*

Enter VALENTINE *and* VIOLA *in man's attire.*

Val. If the duke continue these favors towards you, Cesario, you are like to be much advanced : he hath known you but three days, and already you are no stranger.

Vio. You either fear his humor or my negligence, that you call in question the continuance of his love : is he inconstant, sir, in his favors ?

Val. No, believe me

Vio. I thank you. Here comes the count.

Enter DUKE, CURIO, *and Attendants.*

Duke. Who saw Cesario, ho ?   10

Vio. On your attendance, my lord ; here.

Duke. Stand you a while aloof, Cesario, Thou know'st no less but all ; I have unclasp'd
To thee the book even of my secret soul :

Therefore, good youth, address thy gait unto her ;
Be not denied access, stand at her doors,
And tell them, there thy fixed foot shall grow
Till thou have audience.

Vio.   Sure, my noble lord,
If she be so abandon'd to her sorrow
As it is spoke, she never will admit me.   20

Duke. Be clamorous and leap all civil bounds
Rather than make unprofited return

Vio. Say I do speak with her, my lord, what then ?

Duke. O, then unfold the passion of my love,
Surprise her with discourse of my dear faith :
It shall become thee well to act my woes ;
She will attend it better in thy youth
Than in a nuncio's of more grave aspect.

Vio. I think not so, my lord

Duke.   Dear lad, believe it ;
For they shall yet belie thy happy years,   30
That say thou art a man : Diana's lip
Is not more smooth and rubious ; thy small pipe
Is as the maiden's organ, shrill and sound,
And all is semblative a woman's part.
I know thy constellation is right apt
For this affair. Some four or five attend him ;
All, if you will , for I myself am best
When least in company Prosper well in this,
And thou shalt live as freely as thy lord,
To call his fortunes thine.

Vio.   I'll do my best   40
To woo your lady : [*Aside*] yet, a barful strife :
Whoe'er I woo, myself would be his wife.

[*Exeunt.*

Scene V Olivia's *house.*

Enter MARIA *and* CLOWN.

Mar. Nay, either tell me where thou hast been, or I will not open my lips so wide as a bristle may enter in way of thy excuse : my lady will hang thee for thy absence.

Clo. Let her hang me : he that is well hanged in this world needs to fear no colors.

Mar. Make that good.

Clo. He shall see none to fear.

Mar. A good lenten answer : I can tell thee where that saying was born, of ' I fear no colors.'   10

Clo. Where, good Mistress Mary ?

Mar. In the wars ; and that may you be bold to say in your foolery.

Clo. Well, God give them wisdom that have it ; and those that are fools, let them use their talents.

Mar. Yet you will be hanged for being so long absent ; or, to be turned away, is not that as good as a hanging to you ?   19

Clo. Many a good hanging prevents a bad marriage ; and, for turning away, let summer bear it out.

Mar. You are resolute, then ?

Clo. Not so, neither ; but I am resolved on two points.

Mar. That if one break, the other will hold ; or, if both break, your gaskins fall.

Clo. Apt, in good faith ; very apt. Well, go thy way; if Sir Toby would leave drinking, thou wert as witty a piece of Eve's flesh as any in Illyria.   31

Mar. Peace, you rogue, no more o' that. Here comes my lady : make your excuse wisely, you were best.   [*Exit.*

Clo. Wit, an't be thy will, put me into good fooling ! Those wits, that think they have thee, do very oft prove fools ; and I, that am sure I lack thee, may pass for a wise man : for what says Quinapalus ? 'Better a witty fool, than a foolish wit.'   40

Enter Lady OLIVIA *with* MALVOLIO.

God bless thee, lady !

Oli. Take the fool away.

Clo. Do you not hear, fellows ? Take away the lady.

Oli. Go to, you're a dry fool ; I'll no more of you : besides, you grow dishonest.

Clo. Two faults, madonna, that drink and good counsel will amend : for give the dry fool drink, then is the fool not dry : bid the dishonest man mend himself ; if he mend, he is no longer dishonest ; if he cannot, let the botcher mend him. Any thing that's mended is but patched : virtue that transgresses is but patched with sin ; and sin that amends is but patched with virtue. If that this simple syllogism will serve, so ; if it will not, what remedy ? As there is no true cuckold but calamity, so beauty's a flower. The lady bade take away the fool ; therefore, I say again, take her away.

Oli. Sir, I bade them take away you.   60

Clo. Misprision in the highest degree ! Lady, cucullus non facit monachum ; that's as much to say as I wear not motley in my brain. Good madonna, give me leave to prove you a fool.

Oli. Can you do it ?

Clo. Dexterously, good madonna.

Oli. Make your proof.

Clo. I must catechize you for it, madonna : good my mouse of virtue, answer me.

Oli. Well, sir, for want of other idleness, I'll bide your proof.   71

Clo. Good madonna, why mournest thou ?

Oli. Good fool, for my brother's death.

Clo. I think his soul is in hell, madonna.

Oli. I know his soul is in heaven, fool.

Clo. The more fool, madonna, to mourn for your brother's soul being in heaven. Take away the fool, gentlemen.

Oli. What think you of this fool, Malvolio ? doth he not mend ?   80

Mal. Yes, and shall do till the pangs of death shake him : infirmity, that decays the wise, doth ever make the better fool.

Clo. God send you, sir, a speedy infirmity, for the better increasing your folly ! Sir Toby will be sworn that I am no fox ; but he will not pass his word for two pence that you are no fool.

Oli. How say you to that, Malvolio ?

Mal. I marvel your ladyship takes delight in such a barren rascal : I saw him put down the other day with an ordinary fool that has no more brain than a stone. Look you now, he's out of his guard already ; unless you laugh and minister occasion to him, he is gagged. I protest, I take these wise men, that crow so at these set kind of fools, no better than the fools' zanies.

Oli. Oh, you are sick of self-love, Malvolio, and taste with a distempered appetite. To be generous, guiltless and of free disposition, is to take those things for bird-bolts that you deem cannon-bullets : there is no slander in an allowed fool, though he do nothing but rail ; nor no railing in a known discreet man, though he do nothing but reprove.

Clo. Now Mercury endue thee with leasing, for thou speakest well of fools !

Re-enter MARIA.

Mar. Madam, there is at the gate a young gentleman much desires to speak with you.

Oli. From the Count Orsino, is it ?

Mar. I know not, madam : 'tis a fair young man, and well attended.   111

Oli. Who of my people hold him in delay ?

Mar. Sir Toby, madam, your kinsman.

Oli. Fetch him off, I pray you : he speaks nothing but madman : fie on him ! [*Exit Maria.*] Go you, Malvolio : if it be a suit from the count, I am sick, or not at home ; what you will, to dismiss it. [*Exit Malvolio.*] Now you see, sir, how your fooling grows old, and people dislike it.

Clo. Thou hast spoke for us, madonna, as if thy eldest son should be a fool ; whose skull Jove cram with brains ! for,—here he comes, —one of thy kin has a most weak pia mater.

Enter SIR TOBY.

Oli. By mine honor, half drunk. What is he at the gate, cousin ?

Sir To. A gentleman.

Oli. A gentleman ! what gentleman ?

Sir To. 'Tis a gentleman here—a plague on these pickle-herring ! How now, sot !

Clo. Good Sir Toby !   130

Oli. Cousin, cousin, how have you come so early by this lethargy ?

Sir To. Lechery ! I defy lechery. There's one at the gate.

Oli. Ay, marry, what is he ?

Sir To. Let him be the devil, an he will, I care not : give me faith, say I. Well, it's all one.   [*Exit.*

Oli. What's a drunken man like, fool ?

Clo. Like a drowned man, a fool and a mad man : one draught above heat makes him a fool ; the second mads him ; and a third drowns him.

Oli. Go thou and seek the crowner, and let

him sit o' my coz ; for he's in the third degree of drink. he's drowned : go, look after
him.

Clo. He is but mad yet, madonna ; and the
tool shall look to the madman   [*Exit.*

Re-enter MALVOLIO.

Mal. Madam, yond young fellow swears he
will speak with you. I told him you were
sick ; he takes on him to understand so much,
and therefore comes to speak with you. I told
him you were asleep ; he seems to have a
foreknowledge of that too, and therefore
comes to speak with you. What is to be said
to him, lady? he's fortified against any denial.

Oli. Tell him he shall not speak with me.

Mal. Has been told so ; and he says, he'll
stand at your door like a sheriff's post, and be
the supporter to a bench, but he'll speak with
you.

Oli. What kind o' man is he ?

Mal Why, of mankind   160

Oli. What manner of man ?

Mal. Of very ill manner ; he'll speak with
you, will you or no.

Oli. Of what personage and years is he ?

Mal. Not yet old enough for a man, nor
young enough for a boy ; as a squash is before
'tis a peascod, or a codling when 'tis almost
an apple · 'tis with him in standing water, between boy and man He is very well-favored
and he speaks very shrewishly ; one would
think his mother's milk were scarce out of
him.   171

Oli. Let him approach : call in my gentlewoman

Mal. Gentlewoman, my lady calls.   [*Exit.*

Re-enter MARIA.

Oli. Give me my veil : come, throw it o'er
my face.
We'll once more hear Orsino's embassy.

Enter VIOLA, and Attendants

Vio. The honorable lady of the house,
which is she ?

Oli. Speak to me ; I shall answer for her
Your will ?   180

Vio. Most radiant, exquisite and unmatchable beauty,—I pray you, tell me if this be the
lady of the house, for I never saw her I would
be loath to cast away my speech, for besides
that it is excellently well penned, I have taken
great pains to con it Good beauties, let me
sustain no scorn ; I am very comptible, even
to the least sinister usage

Oli. Whence came you, sir?   189

Vio. I can say little more than I have
studied, and that question's out of my part
Good gentle one, give me modest assurance
if you be the lady of the house, that I may
proceed in my speech.

Oli. Are you a comedian ?

Vio. No, my profound heart : and yet, by
the very fangs of malice I swear, I am not th t
I play. Are you the lady of the house ?

Oli. If I do not usurp myself, I am

Vio. Most certain, if you are she, you do
usurp yourself ; for what is yours to bestow is
not yours to reserve. But this is from my
commission I will on with my speech in your
praise, and then show you the heart of my
message.

Oli. Come to what is important in't : I forgive you the praise.

Vio. Alas, I took great pains to study it,
and 'tis poetical.

Oli. It is the more like to be feigned I
pray you, keep it in I heard you were saucy
at my gates, and allowed your approach rather
to wonder at you than to hear you. If you be
not mad, be gone ; if you have reason, be brief :
'tis not that time of moon with me to make
one in so skipping a dialogue.

Mar Will you hoist sail, sir ? here lies your
way.

Vio. No, good swabber ; I am to hull here
a little longer. Some mollification for your
giant, sweet lady. Tell me your mind : I am
a messenger.   220

Oli. Sure, you have some hideous matter to
deliver, when the courtesy of it is so fearful.
Speak your office.

Vio It alone concerns your ear I bring no
overture of war, no taxation of homage I
hold the olive in my hand ; my words are as
full of peace as matter.

Oli. Yet you began rudely. What are you ?
what would you ?

Vio. The rudeness that hath appeared in
me have I learned from my entertainment
What I am, and what I would, are as secret as
maidenhead, to your ears, divinity, to any
other's, profanation

Oli Give us the place alone : we will be ir
this divinity. [*Exeunt Maria and Attendants*]
Now, sir, what is your text ?

Vio. Most sweet lady,—

Oli. A comfortable doctrine, and much may
be said of it Where lies your text ?   240

Vio In Orsino's bosom.

Oli. In his bosom ! In what chapter of his
bosom ?

Vio To answer by the method, in the first
of his heart

Oli. O, I have read it : it is heresy. Have
you no more to say ?

Vio. Good madam, let me see your face.

Oli Have you any commission from your
lord to negotiate with my face? You are now
out of your text , but we will draw the curtain
and show you the picture. Look you, sir, such
a one I was this present , is't not well done ?
                                      [*Unveiling.*

Vio Excellently done, if God did all

Oli. 'Tis in grain, sir ; 'twill endure wind
and weather.   [*white*

Vio. 'Tis beauty truly blent, whose red and
Nature's own sweet and cunning hand laid on ·
Lady, you are the cruell'st she alive,
If you will lead these graces to the grave 200
And leave the world no copy.

Oli. O, sir, I will not be so hard-hearted ; I will give out divers schedules of my beauty : it shall be inventoried, and every particle and utensil labelled to my will : as, item, two lips, indifferent red ; item, two grey eyes, with lids to them ; item, one neck, one chin, and so forth. Were you sent hither to praise me ?

Vio. I see you what you are, you are too proud ;
But, if you were the devil, you are fair. 270
My lord and master loves you : O, such love
Could be but recompensed, though you were crown'd
The nonpareil of beauty !

Oli.　　　　　　How does he love me ?

Vio. With adorations, fertile tears,
With groans that thunder love, with sighs of fire.

Oli. Your lord does know my mind ; I cannot love him :
Yet I suppose him virtuous, know him noble,
Of great estate, of fresh and stainless youth ;
In voices well divulged, free, learn'd and valiant ;
And in dimension and the shape of nature 280
A gracious person : but yet I cannot love him;
He might have took his answer long ago.

Vio. If I did love you in my master's flame,
With such a suffering, such a deadly life,
In your denial I would find no sense ;
I would not understand it.

Oli.　　　　　　Why, what would you ?

Vio. Make me a willow cabin at your gate,
And call upon my soul within the house ;
Write loyal cantons of contemned love
And sing them loud even in the dead of night : 291
Halloo your name to the reverberate hills
And make the babbling gossip of the air
Cry out ' Olivia ! ' O, you should not rest
Between the elements of air and earth,
But you should pity me !

Oli.　　　　　　You might do much.
What is your parentage ?

Vio. Above my fortunes, yet my state is well :
I am a gentleman.

Oli.　　　　Get you to your lord ;
I cannot love him : let him send no more ;
Unless, perchance, you come to me again, 300
To tell me how he takes it. Fare you well :
I thank you for your pains : spend this for me.

Vio. I am no fee'd post, lady ; keep your purse :
My master, not myself, lacks recompense.
Love make his heart of flint that you shall love ;
And let your fervor, like my master's, be
Placed in contempt ! Farewell, fair cruelty.
　　　　　　　　　　　　　　　　[*Exit.*

Oli. ' What is your parentage ? '
' Above my fortunes, yet my state is well :
I am a gentleman.' I'll be sworn thou art ; 310
Thy tongue, thy face, thy limbs, actions and spirit,
Do give thee five-fold blazon : not too fast :
soft, soft

Unless the master were the man. How now !
Even so quickly may one catch the plague ?
Methinks I feel this youth's perfections
With an invisible and subtle stealth
To creep in at mine eyes. Well, let it be.
What ho, Malvolio !

Re-enter MALVOLIO.

Mal.　　　Here, madam, at your service.

Oli. Run after that same peevish messenger,
The county's man : he left this ring behind him,
Would I or not : tell him I'll none of it. 321
Desire him not to flatter with his lord,
Nor hold him up with hopes ; I am not for him :
If that the youth will come this way to-morrow,
I'll give him reasons for't : hie thee, Malvolio.

Mal. Madam, I will.　　　　　[*Exit.*

Oli. I do I know not what, and fear to find
Mine eye too great a flatterer for my mind.
Fate, show thy force : ourselves we do not owe ;
What is decreed must be, and be this so.
　　　　　　　　　　　　　　　　[*Exit.*

ACT II.

SCENE I. *The sea-coast.*

Enter ANTONIO *and* SEBASTIAN.

Ant. Will you stay no longer ? nor will you not that I go with you ?

Seb. By your patience, no. My stars shine darkly over me : the malignancy of my fate might perhaps distemper yours ; therefore I shall crave of you your leave that I may bear my evils alone : it were a bad recompense for your love, to lay any of them on you.

Ant. Let me yet know of you whither you are bound.　　　　　　　　　　　　　10

Seb. No, sooth, sir : my determinate voyage is mere extravagancy. But I perceive in you so excellent a touch of modesty, that you will not extort from me what I am willing to keep in ; therefore it charges me in manners the rather to express myself. You must know of me then, Antonio, my name is Sebastian, which I called Roderigo. My father was that Sebastian of Messaline, whom I know you have heard of. He left behind him myself and a sister, both born in an hour : if the heavens had been pleased, would we had so ended ! but you, sir, altered that ; for some hour before you took me from the breach of the sea was my sister drowned.

Ant. Alas the day !

Seb. A lady, sir, though it was said she much resembled me, was yet of many accounted beautiful : but, though I could not with such estimable wonder overfar believe that, yet thus far I will boldly publish her : she bore

a mind that envy could not but call fair. She
is drowned already, sir, with salt water, though
I seem to drown her remembrance again with
more.

Ant. Pardon me, sir, your bad entertainment.

Seb. O good Antonio, forgive me your
trouble.

Ant. If you will not murder me for my love,
let me be your servant.

Seb. If you will not undo what you have
done, that is, kill him whom you have recovered, desire it not. Fare ye well at once:
my bosom is full of kindness, and I am yet so
near the manners of my mother, that upon the
least occasion more mine eyes will tell tales of
me. I am bound to the Count Orsino's court:
farewell.   [*Exit.*

Ant. The gentleness of all the gods go with
thee !

I have many enemies in Orsino's court, .
Else would I very shortly see thee there.
But, come what may, I do adore thee so,
That danger shall seem sport, and I will go. 49
          [*Exit.*

SCENE II. *A street.*

Enter VIOLA, MALVOLIO *following.*

Mal. Were not you even now with the
Countess Olivia ?

Vio. Even now, sir ; on a moderate pace I
have since arrived but hither.

Mal. She returns this ring to you, sir : you
might have saved me my pains, to have taken
it away yourself. She adds, moreover, that you
should put your lord into a desperate assurance she will none of him : and one thing more,
that you be never so hardy to come again in his
affairs, unless it be to report your lord's taking of this. Receive it so,

Vio. She took the ring of me: I'll none of it.

Mal. Come, sir, you peevishly threw it to
her ; and her will is, it should be so returned:
if it be worth stooping for, there it lies in your
eye ; if not, be it his that finds it.   [*Exit.*

Vio. I left no ring with her : what means
this lady ?

Fortune forbid my outside have not charm'd
her !

She made good view of me ; indeed, so much,
That sure methought her eyes had lost her
tongue,

For she did speak in starts distractedly.
She loves me, sure; the cunning of her passion
Invites me in this churlish messenger.
None of my lord's ring ! why, he sent her
none.

I am the man : if it be so, as 'tis,
Poor lady, she were better love a dream.
Disguise, I see, thou art a wickedness,
Wherein the pregnant enemy does much.
How easy is it for the proper-false   . 30
In women's waxen hearts to set their forms !
Alas, our frailty is the cause, not we !
For such as we are made of, such we be

How will this fadge ? my master loves her
    dearly ;
And I, poor monster, fond as much on him ;
And she, mistaken, seems to dote on me.
What will become of this ? As I am man,
My state is desperate for my master's love ;
As I am woman,—now alas the day !—
What thriftless sighs shall poor Olivia breathe
O time ! thou must untangle this, not I ;   4
It is too hard a knot for me to untie ! [*Exi*

SCENE III. OLIVIA'S *house.*

Enter SIR TOBY *and* SIR ANDREW.

Sir To. Approach, Sir Andrew: not to be a-
bed after midnight is to be up betimes ; and
' diluculo surgere,' thou know'st,—

Sir And. Nay, my troth, I know not : but
I know, to be up late is to be up late,

Sir To. A false conclusion : I hate it as an
unfilled can. To be up after midnight and to
go to bed then, is early: so that to go to bed
after midnight is to go to bed betimes. Does
not our life consist of the four elements ? 10

Sir And. Faith, so they say; but I think it
rather consists of eating and drinking.

Sir To. Thou'rt a scholar ; let us therefore
eat and drink. Marian, I say! a stoup of wine!

Enter CLOWN.

Sir And. Here comes the fool, i' faith.

Clo. How now, my hearts ! did you never
see the picture of ' we three ' ?

Sir To. Welcome, ass. Now let's have a
catch.

Sir And. By my troth, the fool has an ex
cellent breast. I had rather than forty shillings I had such a leg, and so sweet a breath to
sing, as the fool has. In sooth, thou wast in
very gracious fooling last night, when thou
spokest of Pigrogromitus, of the Vapians pass
ing the equinoctial of Queubus : 'twas very
good, i' faith. I sent thee sixpence for thy
leman : hadst it ?

Clo. I did impeticos thy gratillity; for Mal
volio's nose is no whipstock : my lady has a
white hand, and the Myrmidons are no bottle
ale houses.

Sir And. Excellent ! why, this is the best
fooling, when all is done. Now, a song. 31

Sir To. Come on; there is sixpence for you
let's have a song.

Sir And. There's a testril of me too: if one
knight give a—

Clo. Would you have a love-song, or a song
of good life ?

Sir To. A love-song, a love-song.

Sir And. Ay, ay: I care not for good life.

Clo. [*Sings*]   39

  O mistress mine, where are you roaming ?
  O, stay and hear; your true love's coming,
    That can sing both high and low:
  Trip no further, pretty sweeting ;
  Journeys end in lovers' meeting,
  Every wise man's son doth know

Sir And. Excellent good, i' faith.

Sir To. Good, good.

Clo. [*Sings*]

What is love? 'tis not hereafter;
Present mirth hath present laughter;
What's to come is still unsure:　　50
In delay there lies no plenty,
Then come kiss me, sweet and twenty,
Youth's a stuff will not endure

Sir And. A mellifluous voice, as I am true knight

Sir To. A contagious breath

Sir And. Very sweet and contagious, i' faith

Sir To. To hear by the nose, it is dulcet in contagion. But shall we make the welkin dance indeed? shall we rouse the night-owl in a catch that will draw three souls out of one weaver? shall we do that?

Sir And An you love me, let's do't I am dog at a catch.

Clo. By'r lady, sir, and some dogs will catch well.

Sir And Most certain, Let our catch be, 'Thou knave.'

Clo 'Hold thy peace, thou knave,' knight? I shall be constrained in't to call thee knave, knight.　　　　　70

Sir And. 'Tis not the first time I have constrained one to call me knave * Begin, fool it begins 'Hold thy peace.'

Clo I shall never begin if I hold my peace

Sir And. Good, i' faith　Come, begin.

　　　　　　　　　　　　[*Catch sung.*]

Enter MARIA

Mar. What a caterwauling do you keep here! If my lady have not called up her steward Malvoli and bid him turn you out of doors, never trust me　　　　　79

Sir To My lady's a Cataian, we are politicians, Malvolio's a Peg-a-Ramsey, and 'Three merry men be we' Am not I consanguineous? am I not of her blood? Tillyvally Lady!
　　　　　　　　　　　　　　[*Sings*]
'There dwelt a man in Babylon, lady, lady!'

Clo. Beshrew me, the knight's in admirable fooling.

Sir And Ay, he does well enough if he be disposed, and so do I too: he does it with a better grace, but I do it more natural.

Sir To [*Sings*] 'O, the twelfth day of December,'—　　　　　91

Mar. For the love o' God, peace!

Enter MALVOLIO

Mal. My masters, are you mad? or what are you? Have ye no wit, manners, nor honesty, but to gabble like tinkers at this time of night? Do ye make an alehouse of my lady's house, that ye squeak out your coziers' catches without any mitigation or remorse of voice? Is there no respect of place, persons, nor time in you?

Sir To We did keep time, sir, in our catches. Sneck up!　　　　　101

Mal Sir Toby, I must be round with you. My lady bade me tell you, that, though she harbors you as her kinsman, she's nothing allied to your disorders. If you can separate yourself and your misdemeanors, you are welcome to the house, if not, an it would please you to take leave of her, she is very willing to bid you farewell.

Sir To 'Farewell, dear heart, since I must needs be gone.'　　　　　110

Mar. Nay, good Sir Toby.

Clo. 'His eyes do show his days are almost done.'

Mal Is't even so?

Sir To 'But I will never die.'

Clo. Sir Toby, there you lie.

Mal. This is much credit to you

Sir To 'Shall I bid him go?'

Clo. 'What an if you do?

Sir To. 'Shall I bid him go, and spare not?'

Clo 'O no, no, no, no, you dare not'　121

Sir To. Out o' tune, sir　ye lie, Art any more than a steward? Dost thou think, because thou art virtuous, there shall be no more cakes and ale?

Clo Yes, by Saint Anne, and ginger shall be hot i' the mouth too

Sir To Thou'rt i' the right　Go, sir, rub your chain with crumbs. A stoup of wine, Maria!

Mal. Mistress Mary, if you prized my lady's favor at any thing more than contempt, you would not give means for this uncivil rule: she shall know of it, by this hand.　　　[*Exit.*

Mar. Go shake your ears

Sir And. 'Twere as good a deed as to drink when a man's a-hungry, to challenge him the field, and then to break promise with him and make a fool of him.

Sir To. Do't, knight: I'll write thee a challenge; or I'll deliver thy indignation to him by word of mouth.　　　　　141

Mar. Sweet Sir Toby, be patient for to-night · since the youth of the count's was to-day with my lady, she is much out of quiet For Monsieur Malvolio, let me alone with him if I do not gull him into a nayword, and make him a common recreation, do not think I have wit enough to lie straight in my bed. I know I can do it

Sir To Possess us, possess us; tell us some thing of him.　　　　　150

Mar Marry, sir, sometimes he is a kind of puritan.

Sir And. O, if I thought that, I'd beat him like a dog!

Sir To What for being a puritan? thy exquisite reason, dear knight?

Sir And. I have no exquisite reason for't, but I have reason good enough

Mar. The devil a puritan that he is, or any thing constantly, but a time-pleaser; an affectioned ass, that cons state without book and utters it by great swarths, the best persuaded of himself, so crammed, as he thinks, with excellencies, that it is his grounds of faith that

" Dost thou think, because thou art virtuous,
There shall be no more cakes and ale?"

TWELFTH NIGHT. p. 600

all that look on him love him ; and on that
vice in him will my revenge find notable cause
to work.

Sir To. What wilt thou do ?

Mar. I will drop in his way some obscure
epistles of love ; wherein, by the color of his
beard, the shape of his leg, the manner of his
gait, the expressure of his eye, forehead, and
complexion, he shall find himself most feelingly
personated. I can write very like my lady
your niece : on a forgotten matter we can
hardly make distinction of our hands.

Sir To. Excellent ! I smell a device.

Sir And. I have't in my nose too.

Sir To. He shall think, by the letters that
thou wilt drop, that they come from my niece,
and that she's in love with him.　　　　　180

Mar. My purpose is, indeed, a horse of that
color.

Sir And. And your horse now would make
him an ass.

Mar. Ass, I doubt not.

Sir And. O, 'twill be admirable !

Mar. Sport royal, I warrant you : I know
my physic will work with him. I will plant
you two, and let the fool make a third, where
he shall find the letter : observe his construction of it. For this night, to bed, and dream
on the event. Farewell.　　　　　　　[*Exit.*

Sir To. Good night, Penthesilea.

Sir And. Before me, she's a good wench.

Sir To. She's a beagle, true-bred, and one
that adores me : what o' that ?

Sir And. I was adored once too.

Sir To. Let's to bed, knight. Thou hadst
need send for more money.

Sir And. If I cannot recover your niece, I
am a foul way out.　　　　　　　　　201

Sir To. Send for money, knight : if thou
hast her not i' the end, call me cut.

Sir And. If I do not, never trust me, take
it how you will.

Sir To. Come, come, I'll go burn some sack;
'tis too late to go to bed now : come, knight ;
come, knight.　　　　　　　　　　[*Exeunt.*

SCENE IV. *The Duke's palace.*

Enter DUKE, VIOLA, CURIO, *and others.*

Duke. Give me some music. Now, good
morrow, friends.
Now, good Cesario, but that piece of song,
That old and antique song we heard last night:
Methought it did relieve my passion much,
More than light airs and recollected terms
Of these most brisk and giddy-paced times:
Come, but one verse.

Cur. He is not here, so please your lordship that should sing it.

Duke. Who was it ?　　　　　　　　10

Cur. Feste, the jester, my lord ; a fool that
the lady Olivia's father took much delight in.
He is about the house.

Duke. Seek him out, and play the tune the
while.　　　　　　[*Exit Curio. Music plays.*
Come hither, boy: if ever thou shalt love,

In the sweet pangs of it remember me ;
For such as I am all true lovers are,
Unstaid and skittish in all motions else,
Save in the constant image of the creature
That is beloved. How dost thou like this
tune ?　　　　　　　　　　　　　20

Vio. It gives a very echo to the seat
Where Love is throned.

Duke. Thou dost speak masterly :
My life upon't, young though thou art, thine
eye
Hath stay'd upon some favor that it loves :
Hath it not, boy ?

Vio. A little, by your favor.

Duke. What kind of woman is't ?

Vio. Of your complexion.

Duke. She is not worth thee, then. What
years, i' faith ?

Vio. About your years, my lord.

Duke. Too old, by heaven : let still the
woman take　　　　　　　　　　30
An elder than herself : so wears she to him,
So sways she level in her husband's heart :
For, boy, however we do praise ourselves,
Our fancies are more giddy and unfirm,
More longing, wavering, sooner lost and
worn,
Than women's are.

Vio. I think it well, my lord.

Duke. Then let thy love be younger than
thyself,
Or thy affection cannot hold the bent ;
For women are as roses, whose fair flower
Being once display'd, doth fall that very
hour.　　　　　　　　　　　　40

Vio. And so they are : alas, that they are
so ;
To die, even when they to perfection grow !

Re-enter CURIO *and* CLOWN.

Duke. O, fellow, come, the song we had
last night.
Mark it, Cesario, it is old and plain ;
The spinsters and the knitters in the sun
And the free maids that weave their thread
with bones
Do use to chant it : it is silly sooth,
And dallies with the innocence of love,
Like the old age.

Clo. Are you ready, sir ?　　　　　　50

Duke. Ay ; prithee, sing.　　　　　[*Music.*

SONG.

Clo. Come away, come away, death,
　　And in sad cypress let me be laid
Fly away, fly away, breath ;
　　I am slain by a fair cruel maid.
My shroud of white, stuck all with
yew,
　　O, prepare it !
My part of death, no one so true
　　Did share it.

Not a flower, not a flower sweet,　　　60
　　On my black coffin let there be
strown ;
Not a friend, not a friend greet

My poor corpse, where my bones shall
　　be thrown :
A thousand thousand sighs to save,
　Lay me, O, where
Sad true lover never find my grave,
　To weep there !

Duke. There's for thy pains.

Clo. No pains, sir : I take pleasure in singing, sir.　　　　　　　　　　　　　　70

Duke. I'll pay thy pleasure then.

Clo. Truly, sir, and pleasure will be paid,
one time or another.

Duke. Give me now leave to leave thee.

Clo. Now, the melancholy god protect
thee ; and the tailor make thy doublet of
changeable taffeta, for thy mind is a very
opal. I would have men of such constancy put
to sea, that their business might be every
thing and their intent every where ; for that's
it that always makes a good voyage of nothing. Farewell. 　　　　　　　[*Exit* 81

Duke. Let all the rest give place.
　　　　[*Curio and Attendants retire.*
　　　　Once more, Cesario,
Get thee to yond same sovereign cruelty :
Tell her, my love, more noble than the world,
Prizes not quantity of dirty lands ;
The parts that fortune hath bestow'd upon
　her,
Tell her, I hold as giddily as fortune ;
But 'tis that miracle and queen of gems
That nature pranks her in attracts my soul.

Vio. But if she cannot love you, sir?　90

Duke. I cannot be so answer'd.

Vio. 　　　　　Sooth, but you must.
Say that some lady, as perhaps there is,
Hath for your love as great a pang of heart
As you have for Olivia : you cannot love her;
You tell her so ; must she not then be an-
　swer'd ?

Duke. There is no woman's sides
Can bide the beating of so strong a passion
As love doth give my heart ; no woman's
　heart
So big, to hold so much ; they lack retention
Alas, their love may be call'd appetite,　100
No motion of the liver, but the palate,
That suffer surfeit, cloyment and revolt ;
But mine is all as hungry as the sea,
And can digest as much · make no compare
Between that love a woman can bear me
And that I owe Olivia.

Vio. 　　　　　Ay, but I know——

Duke. What dost thou know ?

Vio. Too well what love women to men
　may owe :
In faith, they are as true of heart as we.
My father had a daughter loved a man,　110
As it might be, perhaps, were I a woman,
I should your lordship.

Duke. 　　　　And what's her history ?

Vio. A blank, my lord. She never told her
　love,
But let concealment, like a worm i' the bud,
Feed on her damask cheek : she pined in
　thought,

And with a green and yellow melancholy
She sat like patience on a monument,
Smiling at grief. Was not this love indeed ?
We men may say more, swear more : but in-
　deed
Our shows are more than will ; for still we
　prove　　　　　　　　　　　　　　120
Much in our vows, but little in our love.

Duke. But died thy sister of her love, my
　boy ?

Vio. I am all the daughters of my father's
　house,
And all the brothers too : and yet I know not.
Sir, shall I to this lady ?

Duke. 　　　　　Ay, that's the theme.
To her in haste ; give her this jewel ; say,
My love can give no place, bide no denay.
　　　　　　　　　　　　　[*Exeunt.*

SCENE V.　OLIVIA'S *garden.*

Enter SIR TOBY, SIR ANDREW, *and* FABIAN.

Sir To. Come thy ways, Signior Fabian.

Fab. Nay, I'll come : if I lose a scruple of
this sport, let me be boiled to death with melancholy.

Sir To. Wouldst thou not be glad to have
the niggardly rascally sheep-biter come by
some notable shame ?

Fab. I would exult, man : you know, he
brought me out o' favor with my lady about
a bear-baiting here.　　　　　　　　10

Sir To. To anger him we'll have the bear
again ; and we will fool him black and blue :
shall we not, Sir Andrew ?

Sir And. An we do not, it is pity of our
lives.

Sir To. Here comes the little villain.

Enter MARIA.

How now, my metal of India !

Mar. Get ye all three into the box-tree :
Malvolio's coming down this walk : he has
been yonder i' the sun practising behavior to
his own shadow this half hour : observe him,
for the love of mockery ; for I know this letter will make a contemplative idiot of him.
Close, in the name of jesting ! Lie thou there
[*throws down a letter*] ; for here comes the
trout that must be caught with tickling.
　　　　　　　　　　　　　　[*Exit.*

Enter MALVOLIO.

Mal. 'Tis but fortune ; all is fortune.
Maria once told me she did affect me : and I
have heard herself come thus near, that
should she fancy, it should be one of my complexion. Besides, she uses me with a more
exalted respect than any one else that follows
her. What should I think on't ?

Sir To. Here's an overweening rogue !

Fab. O, peace ! Contemplation makes a
rare turkey-cock of him : how he jets under
his advanced plumes !

Sir And. 'Slight, I could so beat the rogue!

Sir To. Peace, I say

Mal. To be Count Malvolio · 9

Sir To. Ah, rogue !

Sir And. Pistol him, pistol him.

Sir To. Peace, peace !

Mal. There is example for't ; the lady of the Strachy married the yeoman of the wardrobe.

Sir And. Fie on him, Jezebel !

Fab. O, peace ! now he's deeply in : look how imagination blows him.

Mal. Having been three months married to her, sitting in my state,—   50

Sir To. O, for a stone-bow, to hit him in the eye !

Mal. Calling my officers about me, in my branched velvet gown ; having come from a day-bed, where I have left Olivia sleeping,—

Sir To. Fire and brimstone !

Fab. O, peace, peace !

Mal. And then to have the humor of state ; and after a demure travel of regard, telling them I know my place as I would they should do theirs, to ask for my kinsman Toby,—   61

Sir To. Bolts and shackles !

Fab. O peace, peace, peace ! now, now.

Mal. Seven of my people, with an obedient start, make out for him : I frown the while ; and perchance wind up my watch, or play with my—some rich jewel. Toby approaches ; courtesies there to me,—

Sir To. Shall this fellow live ?

Fab. Though our silence be drawn from us with cars, yet peace.   71

Mal. I extend my hand to him thus, quenching my familiar smile with an austere regard of control,—

Sir To. And does not Toby take you a blow o' the lips then ?

Mal. Saying, ' Cousin Toby, my fortunes having cast me on your niece give me this prerogative of speech,'--

Sir To. What, what ?   80

Mal. ' You must amend your drunkenness.'

Sir To. Out, scab !

Fab. Nay, patience, or we break the sinews of our plot.

Mal. ' Besides, you waste the treasure of your time with a foolish knight,'—

Sir And. That's me, I warrant you.

Mal. ' One Sir Andrew,'—

Sir And. I knew 'twas I : for many do call me fool.   90

Mal. What employment have we here ?

[*Taking up the letter.*

Fab. Now is the woodcock near the gin.

Sir To. O, peace ! and the spirit of humors intimate reading aloud to him !

Mal. By my life, this is my lady's hand : these be her very C's, her U's and her T's ; and thus makes she her great P's. It is, in contempt of question, her hand.

Sir And. Her C's, her U's and her T's : why that ?   100

Mal... [*Reads*] ' To the unknown beloved, this, and my good wishes : '—her very phrases ! By your leave wax. Soft ! and the impres-

sure her Lucrece, with which she uses to seal· 'tis my lady. To whom should this be ?

Fab. This wins him, liver and all.

Mal. [*Reads*]

Jove knows I love :
    But who?
Lips, do not move :
    No man must know.   110

' No man must know.' What follows ? the numbers altered ! ' No man must know :' if this should be thee, Malvolio ?

Sir To. Marry, hang thee, brock !

Mal. [*Reads*]

I may command where I adore ;
    But silence, like a Lucrece knife,
With bloodless stroke my heart doth gore:
    M, O, A, I, doth sway my life.

Fab. A fustian riddle !

Sir To. Excellent wench, say I.   120

Mal. 'M, O, A, I, doth sway my life.' Nay, but first, let me see, let me see, let me see.

Fab. What dish o' poison has she dressed him ?

Sir To. And with what wing the staniel checks at it !

Mal. ' I may command where I adore.' Why, she may command me : I serve her ; she is my lady. Why, this is evident to any formal capacity ; there is no obstruction in this : and the end,—what should that alphabetical position portend ? If I could make that resemble something in me,—Softly ! M, O, A, I,— ·

Sir To. O, ay, make up that : he is now at a cold scent.

Fab. Sowter will cry upon't for all this, though it be as rank as a fox.

Mal. M,—Malvolio ; M,—why, that begins my name.

Fab. Did not I say he would work it out ? the cur is excellent at faults.   140

Mal. M,—but then there is no consonancy in the sequel ; that suffers under probation : A should follow, but O does.

Fab. And O shall end, I hope.

Sir To. Ay, or I'll cudgel him, and make him cry O !

Mal. And then I comes behind.

Fab. Ay, an you had any eye behind you, you might see more detraction at your heels than fortunes before you.   150

Mal. M, O, A, I ; this simulation is not as the former : and yet, to crush this a little, it would bow to me, for every one of these letters are in my name. Soft ! here follows prose.

[*Reads*] ' If this fall into thy hand, revolve. In my stars I am above thee ; but be not afraid of greatness : some are born great, some achieve greatness, and some have greatness thrust upon 'em. Thy Fates open their hands ; let thy blood and spirit embrace them ; and, to inure thyself to what thou art like to be, cast thy humble slough and appear fresh. Be opposite with a kinsman, surly with servants ; let thy tongue tang arguments of state ; put thyself into the trick of singularity ; she thus advises thee that sighs for thee. Remember who commended thy yellow stockings, and wished to see thee ever cross-gartered : I say, remember. Go to, thou art made, if thou desirest to be so ; if not, let me see thee a steward still, the fellow of servants, and not worthy to touch Fortune's fingers. Farewell. She that would alter services with thee,

THE FORTUNATE-UNHAPPY.'

Daylight and champain discovers not more : this is open. 'I will be proud, I will read politic authors, I will baffle Sir Toby, I will wash off gross acquaintance, I will be point-devise the very man. I do not now fool myself, to let imagination jade me ; for every reason excites to this, that my lady loves me. She did commend my yellow stockings of late, she did praise my leg being cross-gartered ; and in this she manifests herself to my love, and with a kind of injunction drives me to these habits of her liking. I thank my stars I am happy. I will be strange, stout, in yellow stockings, and cross-gartered, even with the swiftness of putting on. Jove and my stars be praised ! Here is yet a postscript.

[*Reads*] 'Thou canst not choose but know who I am. If thou entertainest my love, let it appear in thy smiling ; thy smiles become thee well ; therefore in my presence still smile, dear my sweet, I prithee.'

Jove, I thank thee : I will smile ; I will do everything that thou wilt have me.   [*Exit.*

Fab. I will not give my part of this sport for a pension of thousands to be paid from the Sophy.   [device.

Sir To. I could marry this wench for this

Sir And. So could I too.   200

Sir To. And ask no other dowry with her but such another jest.

Sir And. Nor I neither.

Fab. Here comes my noble gull-catcher.

Re-enter MARIA.

Sir To. Wilt thou set thy foot o' my neck ?

Sir And. Or o' mine either ?

Sir To. Shall I play my freedom at tray-trip, and become thy bond-slave ?

Sir And. I' faith, or I either ?   209

Sir To. Why, thou hast put him in such a dream, that when the image of it leaves him he must run mad.

Mar. Nay, but say true ; does it work upon him ?

Sir To. Like aqua-vitæ with a midwife.

Mar. If you will then see the fruits of the sport, mark his first approach before my lady: he will come to her in yellow stockings, and 'tis a color she abhors, and cross-gartered, a fashion she detests ; and he will smile upon her, which will now be so unsuitable to her disposition, being addicted to a melancholy as she is, that it cannot but turn him into a notable contempt. If you will see it, follow me.

Sir To. To the gates of Tartar, thou most excellent devil of wit !

Sir And. I'll make one too.   [*Exeunt.*

ACT III.

SCENE I. OLIVIA'S *garden.*

Enter VIOLA, *and* CLOWN *with a tabor.*

Vio. Save thee, friend, and thy music : dost thou live by thy tabor ?

Clo. No, sir, I live by the church.

Vio. Art thou a churchman ?

Clo. No such matter, sir: I do live by the church ; for I do live at my house, and my house doth stand by the church.

Vio. So thou mayst say, the king lies by a beggar, if a beggar dwell near him ; or, the church stands by thy tabor, if thy tabor stand by the church.   11

Clo. You have said, sir. To see this age ! A sentence is but a cheveril glove to a good wit : how quickly the wrong side may be turned outward !

Vio. Nay, that's certain they that dally nicely with words may quickly make them wanton.

Clo. I would, therefore, my sister had had no name, sir.   20

Vio. Why, man ?

Clo. Why, sir, her name's a word ; and to dally with that word might make my sister wanton. But indeed words are very rascals since bonds disgraced them.

Vio. Thy reason, man ?

Clo. Troth, sir, I can yield you none without words ; and words are grown so false, I am loath to prove reason with them.

Vio. I warrant thou art a merry fellow and carest for nothing.   31

Clo. Not so, sir, I do care for something ; but in my conscience, sir, I do not care for you: if that be to care for nothing, sir, I would it would make you invisible.

Vio. Art not thou the Lady Olivia's fool ?

Clo. No, indeed, sir ; the Lady Olivia has no folly : she will keep no fool, sir, till she be married ; and fools are as like husbands as pilchards are to herrings ; the husband's the bigger : I am indeed not her fool, but her corrupter of words.

Vio. I saw thee late at the Count Orsino's.

Clo. Foolery, sir, does walk about the orb like the sun, it shines every where. I would be sorry, sir, but the fool should be as oft with your master as with my mistress: I think I saw your wisdom there.

Vio. Nay, an thou pass upon me, I'll no more with thee. Hold, there's expenses for thee.

Clo. Now Jove, in his next commodity of hair, send thee a beard !   51

Vio. By my troth, I'll tell thee, I am almost sick for one ; [*Aside*] though I would not have it grow on my chin. Is thy lady within ?

Clo. Would not a pair of these have bred, sir ?   [use.

Vio. Yes, being kept together and put to

Clo. I would play Lord Pandarus of Phrygia, sir, to bring a Cressida to this Troilus.

Vio. I understand you, sir; 'tis well begged.
Clo. The matter, I hope, is not great, sir,
begging but a beggar: Cressida was a beggar.
My lady is within, sir. I will construe to them
whence you come; who you are and what you
would are out of my welkin, I might say 'ele-
ment,' but the word is over-worn. [*Exit.*
Vio. This fellow is wise enough to play the
    fool;
And to do that well craves a kind of wit:
He must observe their mood on whom he jests,
The quality of persons, and the time,   70
And, like the haggard, check at every feather
That comes before his eye. This is a practice
As full of labor as a wise man's art:
For folly that he wisely shows is fit;
But wise men, folly-fall'n, quite taint their wit.

Enter SIR TOBY, *and* SIR ANDREW.

Sir To. Save you, gentleman.
Vio. And you, sir.
Sir And. Dieu vous garde, monsieur.
Vio. Et vous aussi; votre serviteur.
Sir And. I hope, sir, you are; and I am
yours.   81
Sir To. Will you encounter the house? my
niece is desirous you should enter, if your
trade be to her.
Vio. I am bound to your niece, sir; I mean,
she is the list of my voyage.
Sir To. Taste your legs, sir; put them to
motion.
Vio. My legs do better understand me, sir,
than I understand what you mean by bidding
me taste my legs.   91
Sir To. I mean, to go, sir, to enter.
Vio. I will answer you with gait and entrance. But we are prevented.

Enter OLIVIA *and* MARIA.

Most excellent accomplished lady, the hea-
vens rain odors on you!
Sir And. That youth's a rare courtier:
'Rain odors;' well.
Vio. My matter hath no voice, lady, but to
your own most pregnant and vouchsafed ear.
Sir And. 'Odors,' 'pregnant' and 'vouch-
safed:' I'll get 'em all three all ready.
Oli. Let the garden door be shut, and leave
me to my hearing. [*Exeunt Sir Toby, Sir
Andrew, and Maria.*] Give me your hand, sir.
Vio. My duty, madam, and most humble
    service.
Oli. What is your name?
Vio. Cesario is your servant's name, fair
princess.   [world
Oli. My servant, sir! 'Twas never merry
Since lowly feigning was call'd compliment:
You're servant to the Count Orsino, youth.
Vio. And he is yours, and his must needs
be yours:
Your servant's servant is your servant, madam.
Oli. For him, I think not on him: for his
    thoughts,
Would they were blanks, rather than fill'd
    with me!

Vio. Madam, I come to whet your gentle
    thoughts.
On his behalf.
Oli.   O, by your leave, I pray you,
I bade you never speak again of him:
But, would you undertake another suit,
I had rather hear you to solicit that   120
Than music from the spheres.
Vio.   Dear lady,—
Oli. Give me leave, beseech you. I did send,
After the last enchantment you did here,
A ring in chase of you: so did I abuse
Myself, my servant and, I fear me, you:
Under your hard construction must I sit,
To force that on you, in a shameful cunning.
Which you knew none of yours: what might
    you think?
Have you not set mine honor at the stake
And baited it with all the unmuzzled thoughts
That tyrannous heart can think? To one of
    your receiving   131
Enough is shown: a cypress, not a bosom,
Hideth my heart. So, let me hear you speak.
Vio. I pity you.
Oli.   That's a degree to love.
Vio. No, not a grize; for 'tis a vulgar proof
That very oft we pity enemies.
Oli. Why, then, methinks 'tis time to smile
    again.
O world, how apt the poor are to be proud!
If one should be a prey, how much the better
To fall before the lion than the wolf!   140
                 [*Clock strikes.*
The clock upbraids me with the waste of time.
Be not afraid, good youth, I will not have you:
And yet, when wit and youth is come to harvest,
Your wife is alike to reap a proper man:
There lies your way, due west.
Vio. Then westward-ho! Grace and good
    disposition.
Attend your ladyship!
You'll nothing, madam, to my lord by me?
Oli. Stay:
I prithee, tell me what thou thinkest of me.
Vio. That you do think you are not what
    you are.
Oli. If I think so, I think the same of you.
Vio. Then think you right: I am not what
    I am.   [be!
Oli. I would you were as I would have you
Vio. Would it be better, madam, than I am?
I wish it might, for now I am your fool.
Oli. O, what a deal of scorn looks beautiful
In the contempt and anger of his lip!
A murderous guilt shows not itself more soon
Than love that would seem hid: love's night
    is noon.   160
Cesario, by the roses of the spring,
By maidhood, honor, truth and every thing,
I love thee so, that, maugre all thy pride,
Nor wit nor reason can my passion hide.
Do not extort thy reasons from this clause,
For that I woo, thou therefore hast no cause,
But rather reason thus with reason fetter.
Love sought is good, but given unsought is
    better.

Vio. By innocence I swear, and by my
     youth,
I have one heart, one bosom and one truth, 179
And that no woman has ; nor never none
Shall mistress be of it, save I alone.
And so adieu, good madam : never more
Will I my master's tears to you deplore.
     Oli. Yet come again ; for thou perhaps
     mayst move
That heart, which now abhors, to like his love.
                              [*Exeunt.*

SCENE II. OLIVIA'S *house.*

Enter SIR TOBY, SIR ANDREW, *and* FABIAN.

     Sir And. No, faith, I'll not stay a jot
longer.
     Sir To. Thy reason, dear venom, give thy
reason.
     Fab. You must needs yield your reason,
Sir Andrew.
     Sir And. Marry, I saw your niece do more
favors to the count's serving-man than ever
she bestowed upon me ; I saw 't i' the orchard.
     Sir To. Did she see thee the while, old boy?
tell me that.   10
     Sir And. As plain as I see you now.
     Fab. This was a great argument of love in
her toward you.
     Sir And. 'Slight, will you make an ass o'
me ?
     Fab. I will prove it legitimate, sir, upon
the oaths of judgment and reason.
     Sir To. And they have been grand-jury-
men since before Noah was a sailor.
     Fab. She did show favor to the youth in
your sight only to exasperate you, to awake
your dormouse valor, to put fire in your
heart, and brimstone in your liver. You
should then have accosted her ; and with some
excellent jests, fire-new from the mint, you
should have banged the youth into dumbness.
This was looked for at your hand, and this
was balked : the double gilt of this opportunity you let time wash off, and you are now
sailed into the north of my lady's opinion ;
where you will hang like an icicle on a Dutchman's beard, unless you do redeem it by some
laudable attempt either of valor or policy.   31
     Sir And. An't be any way, it must be with
valor ; for policy I hate : I had as lief be a
Brownist as a politician.
     Sir To. Why, then, build me thy fortunes
upon the basis of valor. Challenge me the
count's youth to fight with him ; hurt him in
eleven places : my niece shall take note of it ;
and assure thyself, there is no love-broker in
the world can more prevail in man's commendation with woman than report of valor.   41
     Fab. There is no way but this, Sir Andrew.
     Sir And. Will either of you bear me a chal-
lenge to him ?
     Sir To. Go, write it in a martial hand ; be
curst and brief ; it is no matter how witty, so
it be eloquent and full of invention : taunt
him with the license of ink : if thou thou'st

him some thrice, it shall not be amiss ; and as
many lies as will lie in thy sheet of paper,
although the sheet were big enough for the
bed of Ware in England, set 'em down : go
about it. Let there be gall enough in thy ink,
though thou write with a goose-pen, no matter
about it.
     Sir And. Where shall I find you ?
     Sir To. We'll call thee at the cubiculo : go.
                           [*Exit Sir Andrew.*
     Fab. This is a dear manakin to you, Sir
Toby.
     Sir To. I have been dear to him, lad, some
two thousand strong, or so.
     Fab. We shall have a rare letter from him :
but you'll not deliver't ?   61
     Sir To. Never trust me, then ; and by all
means stir on the youth to an answer. I think
oxen and wainropes cannot hale them together.
For Andrew, if he were opened, and you find
so much blood in his liver as will clog the foot
of a flea, I'll eat the rest of the anatomy.
     Fab. And his opposite, the youth, bears in
his visage no great presage of cruelty.

Enter MARIA

     Sir To. Look, where the youngest wren of
nine comes.   71
     Mar. If you desire the spleen, and will laugh
yourselves into stitches, follow me. Yond gull
Malvolio is turned heathen, a very renegado ;
for there is no Christian, that means to be
saved by believing rightly, can ever believe
such impossible passages of grossness. He's
in yellow stockings.
     Sir To. And cross-gartered ?   79
     Mar. Most villanously ; like a pedant that
keeps a school i' the church. I have dogged
him, like his murderer. He does obey every
point of the letter that I dropped to betray
him : he does smile his face into more lines
than is in the new map with the augmentation
of the Indies : you have not seen such a thing
as 'tis. I can hardly forbear hurling things at
him. I know my lady will strike him : if she
do, he'll smile and take't for a great favor.
     Sir To. Come, bring us, bring us where he
is.   [*Exeunt.* 90

SCENE III. *A street.*

Enter SEBASTIAN *and* ANTONIO.

     Seb. I would not by my will have troubled
         you ;
But, since you make your pleasure of your
         pains,
I will no further chide you.
     Ant. I could not stay behind you : my de-
         sire,
More sharp than filed steel, did spur me forth ;
And not all love to see you, though so much
As might have drawn one to a longer voyage,
But jealousy what might befall your travel,
Being skilless in these parts ; which to a
         stranger,
Unguided and unfriended, often prove   10
Rough and unhospitable : my willing love,

TWELFTH NIGHT.

P. 607

The rather by these arguments of fear,
Set forth in your pursuit.

Seb.　　　　　　　My kind Antonio,
I can no other answer make but thanks,
†And thanks ; and ever.... oft good turns
Are shuffled off with such uncurrent pay :
But, were my worth as is my conscience firm,
You should find better dealing. What's to do?
Shall we go see the reliques of this town ?

Ant.　To-morrow, sir : best first go see your
　　　lodging.　　　　　　　　　　　　20

Seb. · I am not weary, and 'tis long to night:
I pray you, let us satisfy our eyes
With the memorials and the things of fame
That do renown this city.

Ant.　　　　　　　Would you'ld pardon me ;
I do not without danger walk these streets :
Once, in a sea-fight, 'gainst the count his gal-
　　leys
I did some service ; of such note indeed,
That were I ta'en here it would scarce be
　　answer'd.

Seb.　Belike you slew great number of his
　　people.

Ant.　The offence is not of such a bloody
　　nature ;　　　　　　　　　　　　30
Albeit the quality of the time and quarrel
Might well have given us bloody argument.
It might have since been answer'd in repaying
What we took from them ; which, for traffic's
　　sake,
Most of our city did : only myself stood out ;
For which, if I be lapsed in this place,
I shall pay dear.

Seb.　　　　Do not then walk too open.

Ant.　It doth not fit me. Hold, sir, here's
　　my purse.
In the south suburbs, at the Elephant,
Is best to lodge : I will bespeak our diet,　40
Whiles you beguile the time and feed your
　　knowledge
With viewing of the town : there shall you
　　have me.

Seb.　Why I your purse ?　　　　[toy

Ant.　Haply your eye shall light upon some
You have desire to purchase ; and your store,
I think, is not for idle markets, sir.

Seb.　I'll be your purse-bearer and leave you
For an hour.

Ant.　To the Elephant.

Seb.　　　　　　　I do remember. [*Exeunt.*

SCENE IV.　OLIVIA's *garden.*

Enter OLIVIA *and* MARIA.

Oli.　I have sent after him : he says he'll
　　come ;
How shall I feast him ? what bestow of him ?
For youth is bought more oft than begg'd or
　　borrow'd. —
I speak too loud.
Where is Malvolio ? he is sad and civil,
And suits well for a servant with my fortunes :
Where is Malvolio?

Mar.　He's coming, madam ; but in very
strange manner. He is, sure, possessed, madam.

Oli.　Why, what's the matter ? does he rave?

Mar.　No, madam, he does nothing but
smile ; your ladyship were best to have some
guard about you, if he come ; for, sure, the
man is tainted in's wits.

Oli.　Go call him hither. [*Exit Maria.*] I
　　am as mad as he,
If sad and merry madness equal be.

Re-enter MARIA, *with* MALVOLIO.

How now, Malvolio !

Mal.　Sweet lady, ho, ho.

Oli.　Smilest thou ?
I sent for thee upon a sad occasion.　　20

Mal.　Sad, lady ! I could be sad : this does
make some obstruction in the blood, this cross-
gartering ; but what of that ? if it please the
eye of one, it is with me as the very true sonnet is, 'Please one, and please all.'

Oli.　Why, how dost thou, man ? what is
the matter with thee ?

Mal.　Not black in my mind, though yellow
in my legs. It did come to his hands, and commands shall be executed : I think we do know
the sweet Roman hand.　　　　　　31

Oli.　Wilt thou go to bed, Malvolio?

Mal.　To bed ! ay, sweet-heart, and I'll
come to thee.

Oli.　God comfort thee ! Why dost thou
smile so and kiss thy hand so oft ?

Mar.　How do you, Malvolio ?

Mal.　At your request ! yes ; nightingales
answer daws.

Mar.　Why appear you with this ridiculous
boldness before my lady ?　　　　　41

Mal.　'Be not afraid of greatness :' 'twas
well writ.

Oli.　What meanest thou by that, Malvolio?

Mal.　'Some are born great,'—

Oli.　Ha !

Mal.　'Some achieve greatness,'—

Oli.　What sayest thou ?

Mal.　'And some have greatness thrust upon
them.'　　　　　　　　　　　　　50

Oli.　Heaven restore thee !

Mal.　'Remember who commended thy yellow stockings,'—

Oli.　Thy yellow stockings !

Mal.　'And wished to see thee cross-gartered.'

Oli.　Cross-gartered !

Mal.　'Go to, thou art made, if thou desirest
to be so ;'—

Oli.　Am I made ?

Mal.　'If not, let me see thee a servant
still.'　　　　　　　　　　　　　66

Oli.　Why, this is very midsummer madness.

Enter Servant.

Ser.　Madam, the young gentleman of the
Count Orsino's is returned : I could hardly
entreat him back : he attends your ladyship't
pleasure.

Oli.　I'll come to him. [*Exit Servant.*]
Good Maria, let this fellow be looked to.
Where's my cousin Toby ? Let some of my

people have a special care of him : I would not have him miscarry for the half of my dowry.

[*Exeunt Olivia and Maria.*   70

Mal. O, ho ! do you come near me now ? no worse man than Sir Toby to look to me ! This concurs directly with the letter: she sends him on purpose, that I may appear stubborn to him ; for she incites me to that in the letter. 'Cast thy humble slough,' says she ; 'be opposite with a kinsman, surly with servants ; let thy tongue tang with arguments of state ; put thyself into the trick of singularity ;' and consequently sets down the manner how ; as, a sad face, a reverend carriage, a slow tongue, in the habit of some sir of note, and so forth. I have limed her ; but it is Jove's doing, and Jove make me thankful ! And when she went away now, 'Let this fellow be looked to :' fellow ! not Malvolio, nor after my degree, but fellow. Why, every thing adheres together, that no dram of a scruple, no scruple of a scruple, no obstacle, no incredulous or unsafe circumstance—What can be said ? Nothing that can be can come between me and the full prospect of my hopes. Well, Jove, not I, is the doer of this, and he is to be thanked.

Re-enter MARIA, *with* SIR TOBY *and* FABIAN.

Sir To. Which way is he, in the name of sanctity ? If all the devils of hell be drawn in little, and Legion himself possessed him, yet I'll speak to him.

Fab. Here he is, here he is. How is't with you, sir ? how is't with you, man ?

Mal. Go off ; I discard you : let me enjoy my private : go off.   100

Mar. Lo, how hollow the fiend speaks within him ! did not I tell you ? Sir Toby, my lady prays you to have a care of him.

Mal. Ah, ha ! does she so ?

Sir To. Go to, go to ; peace, peace : we must deal gently with him: let me alone. How do you, Malvolio ? how is't with you ? What, man ! defy the devil : consider, he's an enemy to mankind.

Mal. Do you know what you say ?   110

Mar. La you, an you speak ill of the devil, how he takes it at heart ! Pray God, he be not bewitched !

Fab. Carry his water to the wise woman.

Mar. Marry, and it shall be done to-morrow morning, if I live. My lady would not lose him for more than I'll say.

Mal. How now, mistress !

Mar. O Lord !

Sir To. Prithee, hold thy peace ; this is not the way : do you not see you move him? let me alone with him...   122

Fab. No way but gentleness; gently, gently: the fiend is rough,and will not be roughly used.

Sir To. Why, how now, my bawcock ! how dost thou, chuck ?

Mal. Sir !

Sir To. Ay, Biddy, come with me. What, man ! 'tis not for gravity to play at cherry-pit with Satan: hang him, foul collier !   130

Mar. Get him to say his prayers, good Sir Toby, get him to pray.

Mal. My prayers, minx !

Mar. No, I warrant you, he will not hear of godliness.

Mal. Go, hang yourselves all ! you are idle shallow things : I am not of your element : you shall know more hereafter.   [*Exit.*

Sir To. Is't possible ?

Fab. If this were played upon a stage now, I could condemn it as an improbable fiction.

Sir To. His very genius hath taken the infection of the device, man.

Mar. Nay, pursue him now, lest the device take air and taint.

Fab. Why, we shall make him mad indeed.

Mar. The house will be the quieter.

Sir To. Come, we'll have him in a dark room and bound. My niece is already in the belief that he's mad : we may carry it thus, for our pleasure and his penance, till our very pastime, tired out of breath, prompt us to have mercy on him : at which time we will bring the device to the bar and crown thee for a finder of madmen. But see, but see.

Enter SIR ANDREW.

Fab. More matter for a May morning.

Sir And. Here's the challenge, read it . I warrant there's vinegar and pepper in't.

Fab. Is't so saucy ?

Sir And. Ay, is't, I warrant him : do but read.   161

Sir To. Give me.   [*Reads*] ' Youth, whatsoever thou art, thou art but a scurvy fellow.'

Fab. Good, and valiant.

Sir To. [*Reads*] ' Wonder not, nor admire not in thy mind, why I do call thee so, for I will show thee no reason for't.'

Fab. A good note ; that keeps you from the blow of the law.   169

Sir To. [*Reads*] ' Thou comest to the lady Olivia, and in my sight she uses thee kindly : but thou liest in thy throat ; that is not the matter I challenge thee for.'

Fab. Very brief, and to exceeding good sense—less.

Sir To. [*Reads*] ' I will waylay thee going home ; where if it be thy chance to kill me,'—

Fab. Good.

Sir To. [*Reads*] ' Thou killest me like a rogue and a villain.'   180

Fab. Still you keep o' the windy side of the law : good.

Sir To. [*Reads*] ' Fare thee well ; and God have mercy upon one of our souls ! He may have mercy upon mine ; but my hope is better, and so look to thyself. Thy friend, as thou usest him, and thy sworn enemy,   ANDREW AGUECHEEK.' If this letter move him not, his legs cannot : I'll give't him.

Mar. You may have very fit occasion for't : he is now in some commerce with my lady, and will by and by depart.

Sir To. Go, Sir Andrew ; scout me for him

at the corner of the orchard like a bum-baily:
so soon as ever thou seest him, draw ; and, as
thou drawest, swear horrible , for it comes to
pass oft that a terrible oath, with a swaggering
accent sharply twanged off, gives manhood
more approbation than ever proof itself would
have earned him   Away !   200

Sir And.   Nay, let me alone for swearing
                         [*Exit.*

Sir To.   Now will not I deliver his letter ·
for the behavior of the young gentleman gives
him out to be of good capacity and breeding ,
his employment between his lord and my
niece confirms no less · therefore this letter,
being so excellently ignorant, will breed no
terror in the youth . he will find it comes from
a clodpole. But, sir, I will deliver his challenge
by word of mouth; set upon Aguecheek a notable report of valor ; and drive the gentleman,
as I know his youth will aptly receive it, into a
most hideous opinion of his rage, skill, fury
and impetuosity. This will so fright them both
that they will kill one another by the look,
like cockatrices

Re-enter OLIVIA, with VIOLA

Fab   Here he comes with your niece · give
them way till he take leave, and presently after him

Sir To. I will meditate the while upon some
horrid message for a challenge   220
    [*Exeunt Sir Toby, Fabian, and Maria*

Oli   I have said too much unto a heart of
stone
And laid mine honor too unchary out .
There's something in me that reproves my
fault ;
But such a headstrong potent fault it is,
That it but mocks reproof

Vio.   With the same 'havior that your passion bears
Goes on my master's grief.

Oli   Here, wear this jewel for me, 'tis my
picture ;
Refuse it not ; it hath no tongue to vex you ,
And I beseech you come again to-morrow 230
What shall you ask of me that I'll deny,
That honor saved may upon asking give ?

Vio.   Nothing but this , your true love for
my master

Oli.   How with mine honor may I give him
that
Which I have given to you ?

Vio.   I will acquit you.

Oli   Well, come again to-morrow. fare thee
well :
A fiend like thee might bear my soul to hell
                         [*Exit*

Re-enter SIR TOBY and FABIAN

Sir To   Gentleman, God save thee
Vio.   And you, sir.   239

Sir To. That defence thou hast, betake thee
to't : of what nature the wrongs are thou hast
done him, I know not , but thy intercepter,
full of despite, bloody as the hunter, attends

thee at the orchard-end dismount thy tuck
be vare in thy preparation, for thy assailant is
quick, skilful and deadly

Vio.   You mistake, sir ; I am sure no man
hath any quarrel to me my remembrance is
very free and clear from any image of offence
done to any man   250

Sir To   You'll find it otherwise. I assure
you therefore, if you hold your life at any
price, betake you to your guard , for your opposite hath in him what youth, strength, skill
and wrath can furnish man withal

Vio.   I pray you, sir, what is he ?

Sir To   He is knight, dubbed with unhatched
rapier and on carpet consideration , but he is
a devil in private brawl souls and bodies
hath he divorced three , and his incensement
at this moment is so implacable, that satisfaction can be none but by pangs of death and
sepulchre   Hob, nob, is his word , give't or
take't

Vio.   I will return again into the house and
desire some conduct of the lady   I am no
fighter   I have heard of some kind of men
that put quarrels purposely on others, to taste
their valor   belike this is a man of that quirk.

Sir To   Sir, no , his indignation derives itself out of a very competent injury therefore, get you on and give him his desire Back
you shall not to the house, unless you undertake that with me which with as much safety
you might answer him therefore, on, or strip
your sword-stark naked, for meddle you must,
that's certain, or forswear to wear iron about
you

Vio.   This is as uncivil as strange   I beseech you, do me this courteous office, as to
know of the knight what my offence to him
is   it is something of my negligence, nothing
of my purpose

Sir To   I will do so   Signior Fabian, stay
you by this gentleman till my return   [*Exit*

Vio.   Pray you, sir, do you know of this
matter ?

Fab   I know the knight is incensed against
you, even to a mortal arbitrement , but nothing of the circumstance more.

Vio.   I beseech you, what manner of man is
he ?   289

Fab   Nothing of that wonderful promise, to
read him by his form, as you are like to find
him in the proof of his valor   He is, indeed,
sir, the most skilful, bloody and fatal opposite
that you could possibly have found in any part
of Illyria   Will you walk towards him ?   I
will make your peace with him if I can

Vio   I shall be much bound to you for't
I am one that had rather go with sir priest
than sir knight   I care not who knows so
much of my mettle   [*Exeunt* 300

Re-enter SIR TOBY, with SIR ANDREW.

Sir To   Why, man, he's a very devil , I
have not seen such a firago   I had a pass with
him, rapier, scabbard and all, and he gives me
the stuck in with such a mortal motion, that it

                   39

is inevitable ; and on the answer, he pays you
as surely as your feet hit the ground they
step on. They say he has been fencer to the
Sophy.

Sir And. Pox on't, I'll not meddle with
him.

Sir To. Ay, but he will not now be pacified : Fabian can scarce hold him yonder. 310

Sir And. Plague on't, an I thought he had
been valiant and so cunning in fence, I'ld
have seen him damned ere I'ld have challenged him. Let him let the matter slip, and
I'll give him my horse, grey Capilet.

Sir To. I'll make the motion : stand here,
make a good show on't : this shall end without the perdition of souls. [*Aside*] Marry,
I'll ride your horse as well as I ride you. 319

Re-enter FABIAN and VIOLA.

[*To Fab.*] I have his horse to take up the
quarrel : I have persuaded him the youth's a
devil.

Fab. He is as horribly conceited of him ;
and pants and looks pale, as if a bear were at
his heels.

Sir To. [*To Vio.*] There's no remedy, sir ;
he will fight with you for's oath sake : marry,
he hath better bethought him of his quarrel,
and he finds that now scarce to be worth talking
of : therefore draw, for the supportance of his
vow ; he protests he will not hurt you.　330

Vio. [*Aside*] Pray God defend me ! A little
thing would make me tell them how much I
lack of a man.

Fab. Give ground, if you see him furious.

Sir To. Come, Sir Andrew, there's no remedy ; the gentleman will, for his honor's
sake, have one bout with you ; he cannot by
the duello avoid it : but he has promised me,
as he is a gentleman and a soldier, he will not
hurt you. Come on ; to't.　　　　340

Sir And. Pray God, he keep his oath !

Vio. I do assure you, 'tis against my will.
　　　　　　　　　　　　　　[*They draw.*

Enter ANTONIO.

Ant. Put up your sword. If this young
　　gentleman
Have done offence, I take the fault on me :
If you offend him, I for him defy you.

Sir To. You, sir ! why, what are you ?

Ant. One, sir, that for his love dares yet do
　　more
Than you have heard him brag to you he will.

Sir To Nay, if you be an undertaker, I am
for you.　　　　　　　　　　[*They draw.* 350

Enter Officers.

Fab. O good Sir Toby, hold ! here come
the officers.

Sir To. I'll be with you anon.

Vio. Pray, sir, put your sword up, if you
please.

Sir And. Marry, will I, sir ; and, for that
I promised you, I'll be as good as my word :
he will bear you easily and reins well.

First Off. This is the man ; do thy office.

Sec. Off. Antonio, I arrest thee at the suit
of Count Orsino.　　　　　　　　　　361

Ant. You do mistake me, sir.

First Off. No, sir, no jot ; I know your fa-
　　vor well,
Though now you have no sea-cap on your
　　head.
Take him away : he knows I know him well.

Ant. I must obey.　:[*To Vio.*] This comes
　　with seeking you :
But there's no remedy ; I shall answer it.
What will you do, now my necessity
Makes me to ask you for my purse ? It grieves
　　me
Much more for what I cannot do for you　370
Than what befalls myself. You stand amazed ;
But be of comfort.

Sec. Off. Come, sir, away.

Ant. I must entreat of you some of that
　　money.

Vio. What money, sir ?
For the fair kindness you have show'd me
　　here,　　　　　　　　　　　　[trouble,
And, part, being prompted by your present
Out of my lean and low ability
I'll lend you something : my having is not
　　much ;
I'll make division of my present with you :
Hold, there's half my coffer.　　　　381

Ant. Will you deny me now ?
Is't possible that my deserts to you
Can lack persuasion ? Do not tempt my
　　misery,
Lest that it make me so unsound a man
As to upbraid you with those kindnesses
That I have done for you.

Vio. I know of none ;
Nor know I you by voice or any feature :
I hate ingratitude more in a man
Than lying, vainness, babbling, drunkenness,
Or any taint of vice whose strong corruption
Inhabits our frail blood.　　　　　391

Ant. O heavens themselves !

Sec. Off. Come, sir, I pray you, go.

Ant. Let me speak a little. This youth that
　　you see here
I snatch'd one half out of the jaws of death,
Relieved him with such sanctity of love,
And to his image, which methought did prom-
　　ise
Most venerable worth, did I devotion.

First Off. What's that to us ? The time
　　goes by : away !

Ant. But O how vile an idol proves this
　　god
Thou hast, Sebastian, done good feature
　　shame.　　　　　　　　　　400
In nature there's no blemish but the mind ;
None can be call'd deform'd but the unkind :
Virtue is beauty, but the beauteous evil
Are empty trunks o'erflourish'd by the devil.

First Off. The man grows mad : away with
　　him ! Come, come, sir.

Ant. Lead me on.　　[*Exit with Officers.*

Vio. Methinks his words do from such pas-
　　sion fly,

That he believes himself : so do not I.
Prove true, imagination, O, prove true,   409
That I, dear brother, be now ta'en for you !
Sir To. Come hither, knight ; come hither,
Fabian : we'll whisper o'er a couplet or two of
most sage saws.
Vio. He named Sebastian : I my brother
    know
Yet living in my glass ; even such and so
In favor was my brother, and he went
Still in this fashion, color, ornament,
For him I imitate : O, if it prove,
Tempests are kind and salt waves fresh in love.
                    [*Exit.*
Sir To. A very dishonest paltry boy, and
more a coward than a hare : his dishonesty
appears in leaving his friend here in necessity
and denying him ; and for his cowardship, ask
Fabian.
Fab. A coward, a most devout coward, re-
ligious in it.
Sir And. 'Slid, I'll after him again and beat
him.
Sir To. Do ; cuff him soundly, but never
draw thy sword.
Sir And. An I do not,—   [*Exit.* 430
Fab. Come, let's see the event.
Sir To. I dare lay any money 'twill be noth-
ing yet.   [*Exeunt.*

ACT IV.

Scene I. *Before* Olivia's *house.*

Enter Sebastian *and* Clown.

Clo. Will you make me believe that I am
not sent for you ?
Seb. Go to, go to, thou art a foolish fellow:
Let me be clear of thee.
Clo. Well held out, i' faith ! No, I do not
know you ; nor I am not sent to you by my
lady, to bid you come speak with her ; nor
your name is not Master Cesario ; nor this is
not my nose neither. Nothing that is so is so.
Seb. I prithee, vent thy folly somewhere
    else :   11
Thou know'st not me.
Clo. Vent my folly ! he has heard that
word of some great man and now applies it to
a fool. Vent my folly ! I fam afraid this great
lubber, the world, will prove a cockney. I
prithee now, ungird thy strangeness and tell
me what I shall vent to my lady : shall I vent
to her that thou art coming ?
Seb. I prithee, foolish Greek, depart from
    me :
There's money for thee : if you tarry longer,
I shall give worse payment.   21
Clo. By my troth, thou hast an open hand.
These wise men that give fools money get
themselves a good report—after fourteen years'
purchase.

Enter Sir Andrew, Sir Toby, *and* Fabian.

Sir And. Now, sir, have I met you again ?
there's for you.

Seb. Why, there's for thee, and there, and
    there.
Are all the people mad ?
Sir To. Hold, sir, or I'll throw your dagger
o'er the house.   31
Clo. This will I tell my lady straight : I
would not be in some of your coats for two
pence.   [*Exit.*
Sir To. Come on, sir ; hold.
Sir And. Nay, let him alone : I'll go an-
other way to work with him ; I'll have an ac-
tion of battery against him, if there be any law
in Illyria : though I struck him first, yet it's
no matter for that.
Seb. Let go thy hand.   40
Sir To. Come, sir, I will not let you go.
Come, my young soldier, put up your iron:
you are well fleshed ; come on.
Seb. I will be free from thee. What wouldst
    thou now ?
If thou darest tempt me further, draw thy
    sword.
Sir To. What, what ? Nay, then I must
have an ounce or two of this malapert blood
from you.

Enter Olivia.

Oli. Hold, Toby ; on thy life I charge thee,
    hold !
Sir To. Madam !   50
Oli. Will it be ever thus ? Ungracious
    wretch,
Fit for the mountains and the barbarous caves,
Where manners ne'er were preach'd ! out of
    my sight !
Be not offended, dear Cesario.
Rudesby, be gone !
  [*Exeunt* Sir Toby, *Sir Andrew, and Fabian*
              I prithee, gentle friend,
Let thy fair wisdom, not thy passion, sway
In this uncivil and unjust extent
Against thy peace. Go with me to my house,
And hear thou there how many fruitless
    pranks
This ruffian hath botch'd up, that thou thereby
Mayst smile at this : thou shalt not choose but
    go :   61
Do not deny. Beshrew his soul for me,
He started one poor heart of mine in thee.
Seb. What relish is in this ? how runs the
    stream ?
Or I am mad, or else this is a dream :
Let fancy still my sense in Lethe steep ;
If it be thus to dream, still let me sleep !
Oli. Nay, come, I prithee ; would thou 'ldst
    be ruled by me !
Seb. Madam, I will.
Oli.   O, say so, and so be ! [*Exeunt.*

Scene II. Olivia's *house.*

Enter Maria *and* Clown.

Mar. Nay, I prithee, put on this gown and
this beard ; make him believe thou art Sir
Topas the curate : do it quickly ; I'll call Sir
Toby the whilst.   [*Exit.*

Clo. Well, I'll put it on, and I will dissemble myself in't ; and I would I were the first that ever dissembled in such a gown. I am not tall enough to become the function well, nor lean enough to be thought a good student; but to be said an honest man and a good housekeeper goes as fairly as to say a careful man and a great scholar. The competitors enter.

Enter SIR TOBY and MARIA.

Sir To. Jove bless thee, master Parson.

Clo. Bonos dies, Sir Toby : for, as the old hermit of Prague, that never saw pen and ink, very wittily said to a niece of King Gorboduc, 'That that is is ;' so I, being Master Parson, am Master Parson ; for, what is 'that' but 'that,' and 'is' but 'is'?

Sir To. To him, Sir Topas.   20

Clo. What, ho, I say ! peace in this prison !

Sir To. The knave counterfeits well ; a good knave.

Mal. [*Within*] Who calls there ?

Clo. Sir Topas the curate, who comes to visit Malvolio the lunatic.

Mal. Sir Topas, Sir Topas, good Sir Topas, go to my lady.

Clo. Out, hyperbolical fiend ! how vexest thou this man ! talkest thou nothing but of ladies ?   30

Sir To. Well said, Master Parson.

Mal. Sir Topas, never was man thus wronged : good Sir Topas, do not think I am mad ; they have laid me here in hideous darkness.

Clo. Fie, thou dishonest Satan ! I call thee by the most modest terms ; for I am one of those gentle ones that will use the devil himself with courtesy : sayest thou that house is dark ?

Mal. As hell, Sir Topas.   39

Clo. Why it hath bay windows transparent as barricadoes, and the clearstores toward the south north are as lustrous as ebony ; and yet complainest thou of obstruction ?

Mal. I am not mad, Sir Topas : I say to you, this house is dark.

Clo. Madman, thou errest : I say, there is no darkness but ignorance ; in which thou art more puzzled than the Egyptians in their fog.

Mal. I say, this house is as dark as ignorance, though ignorance were as dark as hell ; and I say, there was never man thus abused. I am no more mad than you are : make the trial of it in any constant question.

Clo. What is the opinion of Pythagoras concerning wild fowl ?

Mal. That the soul of our grandam might haply inhabit a bird.

Clo. What thinkest thou of his opinion ?

Mal. I think nobly of the soul, and no way approve his opinion.   60

Clo. Fare thee well. Remain thou still in darkness : thou shalt hold the opinion of Pythagoras ere I will allow of thy wits, and fear to kill a woodcock, lest thou dispossess the soul of thy grandam. Fare thee well.

Mal. Sir Topas, Sir Topas !

Sir To. My most exquisite Sir Topas !

Clo. Nay, I am for all waters.

Mar. Thou mightst have done this without thy beard and gown : he sees thee not.   70

Sir To. To him in thine own voice, and bring me word how thou findest him : I would we were well rid of this knavery. If he may be conveniently delivered, I would he were, for I am now so far in offence with my niece that I cannot pursue with any safety this sport to the upshot. Come by and by to my chamber. · [*Exeunt Sir Toby and Maria.*

Clo. [*Singing*] 'Hey, Robin, jolly Robin,
            Tell me how thy lady does.'

Mal. Fool !   80

Clo. 'My lady is unkind, perdy.'

Mal. Fool !

Clo. 'Alas, why is she so ?'

Mal. Fool, I say !

Clo. 'She loves another'—Who calls, ha ?

Mal. Good fool, as ever thou wilt deserve well at my hand, help me to a candle, and pen, ink and paper : as I am a gentleman, I will live to be thankful to thee for't.

Clo. Master Malvolio ?   90

Mal. Ay, good fool.

Clo. Alas, sir, how fell you besides your five wits ?

Mal. Fool, there was never a man so notoriously abused : I am as well in my wits, fool, as thou art.

Clo. But as well? then you are mad indeed, if you be no better in your wits than a fool.

Mal. They have here propertied me ; keep me in darkness, send ministers to me, asses, and do all they can to face me out of my wits.

Clo. Advise you what you say ; the minister is here. Malvolio, Malvolio, thy wits the heavens restore ! endeavor thyself to sleep, and leave thy vain bibble babble.

Mal. Sir Topas !

Clo. Maintain no words with him, good fellow. Who, I, sir ? not I, sir. God be wi' you, good Sir Topas. Marry, amen. I will, sir, I will.

Mal. Fool, fool, fool, I say !   110

Clo. Alas, sir, be patient. What say you sir ? I am shent for speaking to you.

Mal. Good fool, help me to some light and some paper : I tell thee, I am as well in my wits as any man in Illyria.

Clo. Well-a-day that you were, sir !

Mal. By this hand, I am. Good fool, some ink, paper and light ; and convey what I will set down to my lady : it shall advantage thee more than ever the bearing of letter did.   120

Clo. I will help you to't. But tell me true, are you not mad indeed ? or do you but counterfeit ?

Mal. Believe me, I am not ; I tell thee true.

Clo. Nay, I'll ne'er believe a madman till I see his brains. I will fetch you light and paper and ink.

Mal. Fool, I'll requite it in the highest degree : I prithee, be gone.

Clo. [*Singing*] I am gone, sir,   130
            And anon, sir,

I'll be with you again,
In a trice,
Like to the old Vice,
Your need to sustain ,
Who, with dagger of lath,
In his rage and his wrath,
Cries, ah, ha ! to the devil :
Like a mad lad,
Pare thy nails, dad ,   140
† Adieu, good man devil.   [Exit.

SCENE III. OLIVIA'S garden.

Enter SEBASTIAN.

Seb. This is the air , that is the glorious sun,
This pearl she gave me, I do feel't and see't ,
And though 'tis wonder that enwraps me thus,
Yet 'tis not madness Where's Antonio, then ?
I could not find him at the Elephant
Yet there he was , and there I found this credit,
That he did range the town to seek me out
His counsel now might do me golden service ,
For though my soul disputes well with my
sense,
That this may be some error, but no madness,
Yet doth this accident and flood of fortune
So far exceed all instance, all discourse,
That I am ready to distrust mine eyes
And wrangle with my reason that persuades
me
To any other trust but that I am mad
Or else the lady's mad , yet, if 'twere so,
She could not sway her house, command her
followers,
Take and give back affairs and their dispatch
With such a smooth, discreet and stable bear-
ing   19
As I perceive she does there's something in 't
That is deceiveable. But here the lady comes

Enter OLIVIA and Priest

Ol. Blame not this haste of mine If you
mean well,
Now go with me and with this holy man
Into the chantry by there, before him,
And underneath that consecrated roof,
Plight me the full assurance of your faith ;
That my most jealous and too doubtful soul
May live at peace He shall conceal it
Whiles you are willing it shall come to note
What time we will our celebration keep   30
According to my birth. What do you say ?
Seb. I'll follow this good man, and go with
you ;
And, having sworn truth, ever will be true.
Ol. Then lead the way, good father , and
heavens so shine,
That they may fairly note this act of mine !
                                               [Exeunt.

ACT V

SCENE I. Before OLIVIA'S house.
Enter CLOWN and FABIAN.

Fab. Now, as thou lovest me, let me see
his letter.

Clo. Good Master Fabian, grant me another
request.
Fab. Any thing
Clo Do not desire to see this letter.
Fab This is, to give a dog, and in recom-
pense desire my dog again.

Enter DUKE , VIOLA, CURIO, and Lords

Duke Belong you to the Lady Olivia,
friends ?
Clo Ay, sir , we are some of her trappings
Duke I know thee well how dost thou,
my good fellow ?   11
Clo Truly, sir, the better for my foes and
the worse for my friends
Duke Just the contrary , the better for thy
friends.
Clo No, sir, the worse.
Duke. How can that be ?
Clo Marry sir, they praise me and make
an ass of me , now my foes tell me plainly I
am an ass so that by my foes, sir, I profit in
the knowledge of myself, and by my friends
I am abused so that, conclusions to be as
kisses, if your four negatives make your two
affirmatives, why then, the worse for my
friends and the better for my foes
Duke Why, this is excellent
Clo By my troth, sir, no , though it please
you to be one of my friends
Duke. Thou shalt not be the worse for me .
there's gold   31
Clo But that it would be double-dealing,
sir, I would you could make it another
Duke O, you give me ill counsel
Clo Put your grace in your pocket, sir, for
this once, and let your flesh and blood obey it
Duke Well, I will be so much a sinner, to
be a double-dealer there's another.
Clo Primo, secundo, tertio, is a good play :
and the old saying is, the third pays for all :
the triplex, sir, is a good tripping measure ;
or the bells of Saint Bennet, sir, may put you
in mind , one, two, three
Duke You can fool no more money out of
me at this throw if you will let your lady
know I am here to speak with her, and bring
her along with you, it may awake my bounty
further.
Clo. Marry, sir, lullaby to your bounty till
I come again I go, sir , but I would not have
you to think that my desire of having is the
sin of covetousness but, as you say, sir, let
your bounty take a nap, I will awake it anon.
                                               [Exit.

Vio. Here comes the man, sir, that did
rescue me.

Enter ANTONIO and Officers.

Duke. That face of his I do remember well;
Yet, when I saw it last, it was besmear'd
As black as Vulcan in the smoke of war .
A bawbling vessel was he captain of,
For shallow draught and bulk unprizable ;
With which such scathful grapple did he make
With the most noble bottom of our fleet,   60

That very envy and the tongue of loss
Cried fame and honor on him. What's the
  matter?
First Off. Orsino, this is that Antonio
That took the Phœnix and her fraught from
  Candy ;
And this is he that did the Tiger board,
When your young nephew Titus lost his leg :
Here in the streets, desperate of shame and
  state,
In private brabble did we apprehend him.
  Vio. He did me kindness, sir, drew on my
  side ;
But in conclusion put strange speech upon me :
I know not what 'twas but distraction.   71
  Duke. Notable pirate ! thou salt-water thief!
What foolish boldness brought thee to their
  mercies,
Whom thou, in terms so bloody and so dear,
Hast made thine enemies ?
  Ant.   Orsino, noble sir,
Be pleased that I shake off these names you
  give me :
Antonio never yet was thief or pirate,
Though I confess, on base and ground enough,
Orsino's enemy. A witchcraft drew me hither:
That most ingrateful boy there by your side,
From the rude sea's enraged and foamy mouth
Did I redeem ; a wreck past hope he was :
His life I gave him and did thereto add
My love, without retention or restraint,
All his in dedication ; for his sake
Did I expose myself, pure for his love,
Into the danger of this adverse town ;
Drew to defend him when he was beset :
Where being apprehended, his false cunning,
Not meaning to partake with me in danger, 90
Taught him to face me out of his acquaintance,
And grew a twenty years removed thing
While one would wink ; denied me mine own
  purse,
Which I had recommended to his use
Not half an hour before.
  Vio.   How can this be ?
  Duke. When came he to this town ?
  Ant. To-day, my lord ; and for three
  months before,
No interim, not a minute's vacancy,
Both day and night did we keep company

    Enter OLIVIA *and* Attendants.

  Duke. Here comes the countess : now
  heaven walks on earth.   100
But for thee, fellow ; fellow, thy words are
  madness :
Three months this youth hath tended upon me;
But more of that anon. Take him aside.
  Oli. What would my lord, but that he may
  not have,
Wherein Olivia may seem serviceable ?
Cesario, you do not keep promise with me.
  Vio. Madam !
  Duke. Gracious Olivia,—   [lord,—
  Oli. What do you say, Cesario ? Good my
  Vio. My lord would speak ; my duty hushes
  me,   110

  Oli. If it be aught to the old tune, my lord,
It is as fat and fulsome to mine ear
As howling after music.
  Duke.   Still so cruel ?
  Oli. Still so constant, lord.
  Duke. What, to perverseness ? you uncivil
  lady,
To whose ingrate and unauspicious altars
My soul the faithfull'st offerings hath breathed
  out
That e'er devotion tender'd ! What shall I do ?
  Oli. Even what it please my lord, that
  shall become him.
  Duke. Why should I not, had I the heart
  to do it,   120
Like to the Egyptian thief at point of death,
Kill what I love ?—a savage jealousy
That sometime savors nobly. But hear me
  this :
Since you to non-regardance cast my faith,
And that I partly know the instrument
That screws me from my true place in your
  favor,
Live you the marble-breasted tyrant still ;
But this your minion, whom I know you love,
And whom, by heaven I swear, I tender
  dearly,
Him will I tear out of that cruel eye,   130
Where he sits crowned in his master's spite.
Come, boy, with me ; my thoughts are ripe in
  mischief :
I'll sacrifice the lamb that I do love,
To spite a raven's heart within a dove.
  Vio. And I, most jocund, apt and willingly,
To do you rest, a thousand deaths would die.
  Oli. Where goes Cesario ?
  Vio.   After him I love
More than I love these eyes, more than my
  life,
More, by all mores, than e'er I shall love wife.
If I do feign, you witnesses above   140
Punish my life for tainting of my love !
  Oli. Ay me, detested ! how am I beguiled !
  Vio. Who does beguile you ? who does do
  you wrong ?
  Oli. Hast thou forgot thyself ? is it so long ?
Call forth the holy father.
  Duke.   Come, away !
  Oli. Whither, my lord ? Cesario, husband,
  stay.
  Duke. Husband !
  Oli. Ay, husband : can he that deny ?
  Duke. Her husband, sirrah !
  Vio.   No, my lord, not I.
  Oli. Alas, it is the baseness of thy fear
That makes thee strangle thy propriety :   150
Fear not, Cesario ; take thy fortunes up ;
Be that thou know'st thou art, and then thou
  art
As great as that thou fear'st.

    Enter Priest.

              O, welcome, father !
Father, I charge thee, by thy reverence,
Here to unfold, though lately we intended
To keep in darkness what occasion now

Reveals before 'tis ripe, what thou dost know
Hath newly pass'd between this youth and
    me.
Pries'   A contract of eternal bond of love,
Confirm'd by mutual joinder of your hands,
Attested by the holy close of lips,   161
Strengthen d by interchangement of your
    rings :
And all the ceremony of this compact
Seal'd in my function, by my testimony :
Since when, my watch hath told me, toward
    my grave
I have travell'd but two hours.
    Duke. O thou dissembling cub ! what wilt
        thou be
When time hath sow'd a grizzle on thy case ?
Or will not else thy craft so quickly grow, 169
That thine own trip shall be thine overthrow ?
Farewell, and take her ; but direct thy feet
Where thou and I henceforth may never meet.
    Vio. My lord, I do protest—
    Oli.   O, do not swear .
Hold little faith, though thou hast too much
    fear.

Enter Sir Andrew.

    Sir And. For the love of God, a surgeon !
Send one presently to Sir Toby.
    Oli. What's the matter ?
    Sir And. He has broke my head across and
has given Sir Toby a bloody coxcomb too :
for the love of God, your help ! I had rather
than forty pound I were at home.   181
    Oli. Who has done this, Sir Andrew ?
    Sir And. The count's gentleman, one Ce-
sario : we took him for a coward, but he's the
very devil incarnate.
    Duke. My gentleman, Cesario ?
    Sir And. 'Od's lifelings, here he is ! You
broke my head for nothing ; and that that f
did, I was set on to do't by Sir Toby.
    Vio. Why do you speak to me ? I never
        hurt you :   190
You drew your sword upon me without cause ;
But I bespake you fair, and hurt you not.
    Sir And. If a bloody coxcomb be a hurt,
you have hurt me : I think you set nothing
by a bloody coxcomb.

Enter Sir Toby *and* Clown.

Here comes Sir Toby halting ; you shall hear
more : but if he had not been in drink, he
would have tickled you othergates than he did
    Duke. How now, gentleman ! how is't with
you ?   200
    Sir To. That's all one : has hurt me, and
there's the end on't. Sot, didst see Dick surgeon, sot ?
    Clo. O, he's drunk, Sir Toby, an hour
agone ; his eyes were set at eight i' the morning.
    Sir To. Then he's a rogue, and a passy
measures panyn : I hate a drunken rogue.
    Oli. Away with him ! Who hath made this
havoc with them ?
    Sir And. I'll help you, Sir Toby, because
we'll be dressed together.   211

    Sir To. Will you help ? an ass-head and a
coxcomb and a knave, a thin-faced knave,
a gull !
    Oli. Get him to bed, and let his hurt be
look'd to. [*Exeunt Clown, Fabian, Sir Toby,
                            and Sir Andrew.*

Enter Sebastian.

    Seb. I am sorry, madam, I have hurt your
        kinsman ;
But, had it been the brother of my blood,
I must have done no less with wit and safety.
You throw a strange regard upon me, and by
    that
I do perceive it hath offended you :   220
Pardon me, sweet one, even for the vows
We made each ther but so late ago.
    Duke. One face, one voice, one habit, and
    two persons,
A natural perspective, that is and is not !
    Seb. Antonio, O my dear Antonio !
How have the hours rack'd and tortured me,
Since I have lost thee !
    Ant. Sebastian are you ?
    Seb.   Fear'st thou that, Antonio ?
    Ant. How have you made division of your-
        self ?
An apple, cleft in two, is not more twin   230
Than these two creatures. Which is Sebas-
    tian ?
    Oli. Most wonderful !
    Seb. Do I stand there ? I never had a bro-
        ther ;
Nor can there be that deity in my nature,
Of here and every where. I had a sister,
Whom the blind waves and surges have de-
    vour'd.
Of charity, what kin are you to me ?
What countryman ? what name ? what parent-
    age ?
    Vio. Of Messaline : Sebastian was my
        father ;
Such a Sebastian was my brother too,   240
So went he suited to his watery tomb :
If spirits can assume both form and suit
You come to fright us.
    Seb.   A spirit I am indeed ;
But am in that dimension grossly clad
Which from the womb I did participate.
Were you a woman, as the rest goes even,
I should my tears let fall upon your cheek,
And say 'Thrice-welcome, drowned Viola !'
    Vio. My father had a mole upon his brow
    Seb. And so had mine.   250
    Vio. And died that day when Viola from
        her birth
Had number'd thirteen years.
    Seb. O, that record is lively in my soul !
He finished indeed his mortal act
That day that made my sister thirteen years.
    Vio. If nothing lets to make us happy both
But this my masculine usurp'd attire,
Do not embrace me till each circumstance
Of place, time, fortune, do cohere and jump
That I am Viola : which to confirm,   260
I'll bring you to a captain in this town,

Where lie my maiden weeds, by whose gen-
tle help
I was preserved to serve this noble count
All the occurrence of my fortune since
Hath been between this lady and this lord

Seb. [*To Olivia*] So comes it, lady, you
have been mistook :
But nature to her bias drew in that
You would have been contracted to a maid,
Nor are you therein, by my life, deceived, 269
You are betroth'd both to a maid and man.

Duke Be not amazed, right noble is his
blood
If this be so, as yet the glass seems true,
I shall have share in this most happy wreck
[*To Viola*] Boy, thou hast said to me a thou-
sand times
Thou never shouldst love woman like to me

Vio. And all those sayings will I over-
swear,
And all those swearings keep as true in soul
As doth that orbed continent the fire
That severs day from night

Duke   Give me thy hand,
And let me see thee in thy woman's weeds

Vio. The captain that did bring me first on
shore
Hath my maid's garments. he upon some
action
Is now in durance, at Malvolio's suit,
A gentleman, and follower of my lady's

Oli He shall enlarge him. fetch Malvolio
hither.
And yet, alas, now I remember me,
They say, poor gentleman, he's much distract.

Re-enter CLOWN *with a letter, and* FABIAN,

A most extracting frenzy of mine own
From my remembrance clearly banish'd his,
How does he, sirrah ?   290

Clo. Truly, madam, he holds Belzebub at
the staves's end as well as a man in his case
may do has here writ a letter to you, I
should have given 't you to-day morning, but
as a madman's epistles are no gospels, so it
skills not much when they are delivered

Oli. Open 't, and read it

Clo. Look then to be well edified when the
fool delivers the madman. [*Reads*] ' By the
Lord, madam,' —   300

Oli How now ! art thou mad ?

Clo No, madam, I do but read madness :
an your ladyship will have it as it ought to be,
you must allow Vox

Oli. Prithee, read i' thy right wits

Clo. So I do, madonna, but to read his
right wits is to read thus. therefore perpend,
my princess, and give ear

Oli Read it you, sirrah   [*To Fabian.*

Fab [*Reads*] ' By the Lord, madam, you
wrong me, and the world shall know it
though you have put me into darkness and
given your drunken cousin rule over me, yet
have I the benefit of my senses as well as
your ladyship. I have your own letter that
induced me to the semblance I put on, with

the which I doubt not but to do myself much
right, or you much shame Think of me as
you please I leave my duty a little unthought
of and speak out of my injury

      THE MADLY-USED MALVOLIO '

Oli Did he write this ?   320

Clo Ay, madam

Duke This savors not much of distraction

Oli See him deliver'd, Fabian, bring him
hither   [*Exit Fabian*
My lord, so please you, these things further
thought on,
To think me as well a sister as a wife,
One day shall crown the alliance on 't, so please
you,
Here at my house and at my proper cost

Duke Madam, I am most apt to embrace
your offer.
[*To Viola*] Your master quits you ; and for
your service done him,
So much against the mettle of your sex, 330
So far beneath your soft and tender breeding,
And since you call'd me master for so long,
Here is my hand you shall from this time be
Your master's mistress

Oli   A sister ! you are she,

Re-enter FABIAN, *with* MALVOLIO.

Duke Is this the madman ?

Oli   Ay, my lord, this same
How now, Malvolio !

Mal Madam, you have done me wrong,
Notorious wrong

Oli   'Have I, Malvolio ? No

Mal. Lady, you have Pray you, peruse
that letter.
You must not now deny it is your hand 339
Write from it, if you can, in hand or phrase ;
Or say 'tis not your seal, nor your invention :
You can say none of this well, grant it then
And tell me, in the modesty of honor,
Why you have given me such clear lights of
favor,
Bade me come smiling and cross-garter'd to
you,
To put on yellow stockings and to frown
Upon Sir Toby and the lighter people ;
And, acting this in an obedient hope,
Why have you suffer'd me to be imprison'd,
Kept in a dark house, visited by the priest, 350
And made the most notorious geck and gull
That e'er invention play'd on ? tell me why,

Oli Alas, Malvolio, this is not my writing,
Though, I confess, much like the character :
But out of question 'tis Maria's hand
And now I do bethink me, it was she
First told me thou wast mad, then camest in
smiling,
And in such forms which here were presupposed
Upon thee in the letter Prithee, be content :
This practice hath most shrewdly pass'd upon
thee,   360
But when we know the grounds and authors
of it,
Thou shalt be both the plaintiff and the judge
Of thine own cause.

Fab. Good madam, hear me speak,
And let no quarrel nor no brawl to come
Taint the condition of this present hour,
Which I have wonder'd at In hope it shall not,
Most freely I confess, myself and Toby
Set this device against Malvolio here,
Upon some stubborn and uncourteous parts
We had conceived against him Maria writ
The letter at Sir Toby's great importance , 371
In recompense whereof he hath married her
How with a sportful malice it was follow'd,
May rather pluck on laughter than revenge ;
If that the injuries be justly weigh'd
That have on both sides pass'd

Oli Alas, poor fool, how have they baffled
thee '

Clo Why, 'some are born great, some
achieve greatness, and some have greatness
thrown upon them' I was one, sir, in this
interlude, one Sir Topas, sir , but that's all one
'By the Lord, fool, I am not mad' But do
you remember ? 'Madam, why laugh you at
such a barren rascal ? an you smile not, he's
gagged ' and thus the whirligig of time brings
in his revenges

Mal I'll be revenged on the whole pack of
you [*Exit*.

Oli He hath been most notoriously abused

Duke Pursue him, and entreat him to a
peace .
He hath not told us of the captain yet 390
When that is known and golden time convents,
A solemn combination shall be made

Of our dear souls Meantime, sweet sister,
We will not part from hence Cesario, come ,
For so you shall be, while you are a man ,
But when in other habits you are seen.
Orsino's mistress and his fancy's queen.
[*Exeunt all, except Clown.*

Clo [*Sings*]
When that I was and a little tiny boy,
   With hey, ho, the wind and the rain,
A foolish thing was but a toy, 400
   For the rain it raineth every day.

But when I came to man's estate,
   With hey, ho, &c
'Gainst knaves and thieves men shut their
   gate,
   For the rain, &c.

But when I came, alas ! to wive,
   With hey, ho, &c
By swaggering could I never thrive,
   For the rain, &c.

But when I came unto my beds, 410
   With hey, ho, &c
With toss-pots still had drunken heads,
   For the rain, &c.

A great while ago the world begun,
   With hey, ho, &c
But that's all one, our play is done,
   And we'll strive to please you every day.
      Exit

JULIUS CÆSAR.

(WRITTEN ABOUT 1601.)

INTRODUCTION.

This tragedy was produced as early as 1601, so we infer from a passage in Weaver's *Mirror of Martyrs* (1601) in which reference is made to the speeches of Brutus and Antony. The style of the versification, the diction, the characterization, all bear out the opinion that 1600 or 1601 is the date of *Julius Cæsar*. The historical materials of the play were found by the dramatist in the lives of Cæsar, of Brutus, and of Antony, as given in North's translation of Plutarch. Hints for the speeches of Brutus and Antony seem to have been obtained from Appian's *Civil Wars* (B. II., ch. 137-147) translated into English in 1578. Every thing is wrought out in the play with great care and completeness, it is well planned and well proportioned; there is no tempestuousness of passion, and no artistic mystery. The style is full, but not overburdened with thought or imagery, this is one of the most perfect of Shakespeare's plays, greater tragedies are less perfect, perhaps for the very reason that they try to grasp greater, more terrible, or more piteous themes. In *King Henry V.* Shakespeare had represented a great and heroic man of action. In the serious plays, which come next in chronological order, *Julius Cæsar* and *Hamlet*, the poet represents two men who were forced to act—to act in public affairs, and affairs of life and death—yet who were singularly disqualified for playing the part of men of action. Hamlet cannot act because his moral energy is sapped by a kind of skepticism and sterile despair about life, because his own ideas are more to him than deeds, because his will is diseased. Brutus does act, but he acts as an idealist and theorizer might, with no eye for the actual bearing of facts, and no sense of the true importance of persons. Intellectual loctrines and moral ideas rule the life of Brutus; and his life is most noble, high, and stainless, but his public action is a series of practical mistakes. Yet even while he errs we admire him, for all his errors are those of a pure and lofty spirit. In his wife—Cato's daughter, Portia—Brutus has found one who is equal to and worthy of himself. Shakespeare has shown her as perfectly a woman—sensitive, finely-tempered, tender—yet a woman who by her devotion to moral ideas might stand beside such a father and such a husband. And Brutus, with all his Stoicism, is gentle and tender: he can strike down Cæsar if Cæsar be a tyrant, but he cannot roughly rouse a sleeping boy (Act IV, Sc iii, L 270). Antony is a man of genius, with many splendid and some generous qualities, but self-indulgent, pleasure-loving, and a daring adventurer rather than a great leader of the State. The character of Cæsar is conceived in a curious and almost irritating manner. Shakespeare (as passages in other plays show) was certainly not ignorant of the greatness of one of the world's greatest men. But here it is his weaknesses that are insisted on. He is failing in body and mind, influenced by superstition, yields to flattery, thinks of himself as almost superhuman, has lost some of his insight into character, and his sureness and swiftness of action. Yet the play is rightly named *Julius Cæsar*. His bodily presence is weak, but his spirit rules throughout the play, and rises after his death in all its might, towering over the little band of conspirators, who at length fall before the spirit of Cæsar as it ranges for revenge.

DRAMATIS PERSONÆ.

JULIUS CÆSAR.	
OCTAVIUS CÆSAR,	triumvirs after
MARCUS ANTONIUS,	death of Julius
M ÆMILIUS LEPIDUS,	Cæsar.
CICERO,	
PUBLIUS,	senators
POPILIUS LENA,	
MARCUS BRUTUS,	
CASSIUS,	
CASCA,	
TREBONIUS,	conspirators against
LIGARIUS,	Julius Cæsar.
DECIUS BRUTUS,	
METELLUS CIMBER,	
CINNA,	

FLAVIUS and MARULLUS, tribunes.
ARTEMIDORUS of Cnidos, a teacher of rhetoric
A Soothsayer.

CINNA, a poet. Another Poet.

LUCILIUS,	
TITINIUS,	
MESSALA,	friends to Brutus and
Young CATO,	Cassius.
VOLUMNIUS,	
VARRO,	
CLITUS,	
CLAUDIUS,	
STRATO,	servants to Brutus,
LUCIUS,	
DARDANIUS,	

PINDARUS, servant to Cassius.

CALPURNIA, wife to Cæsar.
PORTIA, wife to Brutus.

Senators, Citizens, Guards, Attendants, &c.

SCENE. *Rome : the neighborhood of Sardis: the neighborhood of Philippi.*

ACT I.

SCENE I. *Rome.   A street.*

Enter FLAVIUS, MARULLUS, *and certain* Commoners.

Flav.   Hence! home, you idle creatures
      get you home :
Is this a holiday? what! know you not,
Being mechanical, you ought not walk
Upon a laboring day without the sign
Of your profession?   Speak, what trade art
      thou ?
First Com.   Why, sir, a carpenter.
Mar.   Where is thy leather apron and thy
      rule ?
What dost thou with thy best apparel on ?
You, sir, what trade are you ?
Sec. Com.   Truly, sir, in respect of a fine
workman, I am but, as you would say, a
      cobbler.   11
Mar.   But what trade art thou?   answer
me directly.
Sec. Com.   A trade, sir, that, I hope, I may
use with a safe conscience ; which is, indeed,
sir, a mender of bad soles.
Mar.   What trade, thou knave ?   thou
naughty knave, what trade ?
Sec. Com.   Nay, I beseech you, sir, be not
out with me : yet, if you be out, sir, I can
mend you.
Mar.   What meanest thou by that ?   mend
me, thou saucy fellow !   21
Sec. Com.   Why, sir, cobble you.
Flav.   Thou art a cobbler, art thou ?
Sec. Com.   Truly, sir, all that I live by is
with the awl : I meddle with no tradesman's
matters, nor women's matters, but with awl.
I am, indeed, sir, a surgeon to old shoes ; when
they are in great danger, I recover them.   As
proper men as ever trod upon neat's leather
have gone upon my handiwork.   30
Flav.   But wherefore art not in thy shop to-
      day ?
Why dost thou lead these men about the
      streets ?
Sec. Com.   Truly, sir, to wear out their
shoes, to get myself into more work.   But,
indeed, sir, we make holiday, to see Cæsar
and to rejoice in his triumph.
Mar.   Wherefore rejoice ?   What conquest
      brings he home ?
What tributaries follow him to Rome,
To grace in captive bonds his chariot-wheels ?
You blocks, you stones, you worse than sense-
      less things !   40
O you hard hearts, you cruel men of Rome,
Knew you not Pompey ?   Many a time and
      oft
Have you climb'd up to walls and battlements,
To towers and windows, yea, to chimney-tops,
Your infants in your arms, and there have sat
The live-long day, with patient expectation,
To see great Pompey pass the streets of Rome:
And when you saw his chariot but appear,
Have you not made an universal shout,

That Tiber trembled underneath her banks, 50
To hear the replication of your sounds
Made in her concave shores ?
And do you now put on your best attire ?
And do you now cull out a holiday ?
And do you now strew flowers in his way
That comes in triumph over Pompey's blood ?
Be gone !
Run to your houses, fall upon your knees,
Pray to the gods to intermit the plague
That needs must light on this ingratitude.   60
      Flav.   Go, go, good countrymen, and, for
      this fault,
Assemble all the poor men of your sort ;
Draw them to Tiber banks, and weep your
      tears
Into the channel, till the lowest stream
Do kiss the most exalted shores of all.
                           [*Exeunt all the Commoners.*
See whether their basest metal be not moved ;
They vanish tongue-tied in their guiltiness.
Go you down that way towards the Capitol ;
This way will I :   disrobe the images,
If you do find them deck'd with ceremonies.
      Mar.   May we do so ?
You know it is the feast of Lupercal.
      Flav.   It is no matter ; let no images
Be hung with Cæsar's trophies.   I'll about,
And drive away the vulgar from the streets :
So do you too, where you perceive them thick.
These growing feathers pluck'd from Cæsar's
      wing
Will make him fly an ordinary pitch,
Who else would soar above the view of men
And keep us all in servile fearfulness.
                                               [*Exeunt.*

SCENE II.   *A public place.*

Flourish.   Enter CÆSAR ; ANTONY, *for the course ;* CALPURNIA, PORTIA, DECIUS, CICERO, BRUTUS, CASSIUS, *and* CASCA ; *a great crowd following, among them a* Soothsayer.

Cæs.   Calpurnia !
Casca.   Peace, ho ! Cæsar speaks.
Cæs.   Calpurnia !
Cal.   Here, my lord.
Cæs.   Stand you directly in Antonius' way,
When he doth run his course.   Antonius !
Ant.   Cæsar, my lord ?
Cæs.   Forget not, in your speed, Antonius,
To touch Calpurnia ; for our elders say,
The barren, touched in this holy chase,
Shake off their sterile curse.
Ant.   I shall remember :
When Cæsar says ' do this,' it is perform'd.   10
Cæs.   Set on ; and leave no ceremony out.
                                              [*Flourish.*
Sooth.   Cæsar !
Cæs.   Ha ! who calls ?
Casca.   Bid every noise be still : peace yet
      again !
Cæs.   Who is it in the press that calls on me?
I hear a tongue, shriller than all the music,
Cry ' Cæsar !' Speak ; Cæsar is turn'd to hear.
Sooth.   Beware the ides of March.

Cæs.   What man is that?
Bru. A soothsayer bids you beware the ides
of March.
Cæs. Set him before me ; let me see his
face.   20
Cas. Fellow, come from the throng ; look
upon Cæsar.
Cæs. What say'st thou to me now ? speak
once again.
Sooth. Beware the ides of March.
Cæs. He is a dreamer ; let us leave him :
pass.   [*Sennet. Exeunt all except
                          Brutus and Cassius.*
Cas. Will you go see the order of the course?
Bru. Not I.
Cas. I pray you, do.
Bru. I am not gamesome: I do lack some
part
Of that quick spirit that is in Antony.
Let me not hinder, Cassius, your desires ;   30
I'll leave you.
Cas. Brutus, I do observe you now of late:
I have not from your eyes that gentleness
And show of love as I was wont to have :
You bear too stubborn and too strange a hand
Over your friend that loves you.
Bru.   Cassius,
Be not deceived : if I have veil'd my look
I turn the trouble of my countenance
Merely upon myself. Vexed I am
Of late with passions of some difference,   40
Conceptions only proper to myself,
Which give some soil perhaps to my beha-
viors ;   [grieved—
But let not therefore my good friends be
Among which number, Cassius, be you one—
Nor construe any further my neglect,
Than that poor Brutus, with himself at war,
Forgets the shows of love to other men.
Cas. Then, Brutus, I have much mistook
your passion ;
By means whereof this breast of mine hath
buried   '   49
Thoughts of great value, worthy cogitations.
Tell me, good Brutus, can you see your face ?
Bru. No, Cassius ; for the eye sees not it-
self,
But by reflection, by some other things.
Cas. 'Tis just :
And it is very much lamented, Brutus,
That you have no such mirrors as will turn
Your hidden worthiness into your eye,
That you might see your shadow. I have
heard,
Where many of the best respect in Rome,
Except immortal Cæsar, speaking of Brutus 60
And groaning underneath this age's yoke,
Have wish'd that noble Brutus had his eyes.
Bru. Into what dangers would you lead me,
Cassius,
That you would have me seek into myself
For that which is not in me ?
Cas. Therefore, good Brutus, be prepared
to hear:
And since you know you cannot see yourself
So well as by reflection, I, your glass,

Will modestly discover to yourself
That of yourself which you yet know not of.
And be not jealous on me, gentle Brutus :   71
Were I a common laugher, or did use
To stale with ordinary oaths my love
To every new protester ; if you know
That I do fawn on men and hug them hard
And after scandal them, or if you know
That I profess myself in banqueting
To all the rout, then hold me dangerous.
                    [*Flourish, and shout*
Bru. What means this shouting ? I do fear,
the people
Choose Cæsar for their king.
Cas.   Ay, do you fear it ? 80
Then must I think you would not have it so.
Bru. I would not, Cassius ; yet I love him
well.
But wherefore do you hold me here so long ?
What is it that you would impart to me ?
If it be aught toward the general good,
Set honor in one eye and death i' the other
And I will look on both indifferently,
For let the gods so speed me as I love
The name of honor more than I fear death.
Cas. I know that virtue to be in you, Bru-
tus,   90
As well as I do know your outward favor.
Well, honor is the subject of my story.
I cannot tell what you and other men
Think of this life ; but, for my single self,
I had as lief not be as live to be
In awe of such a thing as I myself.
I was born free as Cæsar ; so were you :
We both have fed as well, and we can both
Endure the winter's cold as well as he :
For once, upon a raw and gusty day,   100
The troubled Tiber chafing with her shores,
Cæsar said to me ' Darest thou, Cassius, now
Leap in with me into this angry flood,
And swim to yonder point ?' Upon the word,
Accoutred as I was, I plunged in
And bade him follow ; so indeed he did.
The torrent roar'd, and we did buffet it
With lusty sinews, throwing it aside
And stemming it with hearts of controversy ;
But ere we could arrive the point proposed, 110
Cæsar cried ' Help me, Cassius, or I sink !'
I, as Æneas, our great ancestor,
Did from the flames of Troy upon his shoulder
The old Anchises bear, so from the waves of
Tiber
Did I the tired Cæsar. And this man
Is now become a god, and Cassius is
A wretched creature and must bend his body,
If Cæsar carelessly but nod on him.
He had a fever when he was in Spain,
And when the fit was on him, I did mark 120
How he did shake : 'tis true, this god did
shake :
His coward lips did from their color fly,
And that same eye whose bend doth awe the
world
Did lose his lustre : I did hear him groan :
Ay, and that tongue of his that bade the
Romans

Mark him and write his speeches in their
    books,
Alas, it cried 'Give me some drink, Titinius,'
As a sick girl   Ye gods, it doth amaze me
A man of such a feeble temper should
So get the start of the majestic world   130
And bear the palm alone   [*Shout. Flourish*
    Bru   Another general shout !
I do believe that these applauses are
For some new honours that are heap'd on Cæsar
    Cas   Why, man, he doth bestride the nar-
    row world
Like a Colossus, and we petty men
Walk under his huge legs and peep about
To find ourselves dishonorable graves
Men at some time are masters of their fates
The fault, dear Brutus, is not in our stars,   140
But in ourselves, that we are underlings
Brutus and Cæsar   what should be in that
    ' Cæsar ' ?
Why should that name be sounded more than
    yours ?
Write them together, yours is as fair a name ,
Sound them, it doth become the mouth as well,
Weigh them, it is as heavy , conjure with 'em,
Brutus will start a spirit as soon as Cæsar
Now, in the names of all the gods at once,
Upon what meat doth this our Cæsar feed,
That he is grown so great ?   Age, thou art
    shamed !   150
Rome, thou hast lost the breed of noble bloods'
When went there by an age, since the great
    flood,
But it was famed with more than with one
    man ?
When could they say till now, that talk'd of
    Rome,
That her wide walls encompass'd but one man?
Now is it Rome indeed and room enough,
When there is in it but one only man
O, you and I have heard our fathers say,
There was a Brutus once that would have
    brook'd
The eternal devil to keep his state in Rome
As easily as a king   161
    Bru   That you do love me, I am nothing
    jealous ,
What you would work me to, I have some aim .
How I have thought of this and of these times,
I shall recount hereafter ; for this present,
I would not, so with love I might entreat you,
Be any further moved   What you have said
I will consider ; what you have to say
I will with patience hear, and find a time   169
Both meet to hear and answer such high things
Till then, my noble friend, chew upon this
Brutus had rather be a villager
Than to repute himself a son of Rome   ·
Under these hard conditions as this time
Is like to lay upon us
    Cas   I am glad that my weak words
Have struck but thus much show of fire from
    Brutus.   [turning
    Bru   The games are done and Cæsar is re-
    Cas.   As they pass by, pluck Casca by the
    sleeve :

And he will, after his sour fashion, tell you
What hath proceeded worthy note to-day.

    Re-enter CÆSAR and his Train

    Bru   I will do so   But, look you, Cassius,
The angry spot doth glow on Cæsar's brow,
And all the rest look like a chidden train
Calpurnia's cheek is pale ; and Cicero
Looks with such ferret and such fiery eyes
As we have seen him in the Capitol,
Being cross'd in conference by some senators
    Cas   Casca will tell us what the matter is
    Cæs   Antonius !   190
    Ant   Cæsar ?
    Cæs   Let me have men about me that are
    fat ,
Sleek-headed men and such as sleep o' nights
Yond Cassius has a lean and hungry look ,
He thinks too much   such men are dangerous
    Ant   Fear him not, Cæsar , he's not danger-
    ous ,
He is a noble Roman and well given
    Cæs   Would he were fatter ! But I fear
    him not
Yet if my name were liable to fear,
I do not know the man I should avoid   200
So soon as that spare Cassius   He reads much,
He is a great observer and he looks
Quite through the deeds of men   he loves no
    plays,
As thou dost, Antony , he hears no music ,
Seldom he smiles, and smiles in such a sort
As if he mock'd himself and scorn'd his spirit
That could be moved to smile at any thing
Such men as he be never at heart's ease
Whiles they behold a greater than themselves
And therefore are they very dangerous.   210
I rather tell thee what is to be fear'd
Than what I fear ; for always I am Cæsar.
Come on my right hand, for this ear is deaf,
And tell me truly what thou think'st of him
    [*Sennet.   Exeunt Cæsar and all his
    Train, but Casca*
    Casca   You pull'd me by the cloak , would
    you speak with me ?
    Bru   Ay, Casca , tell us what hath chanced
    to-day,
That Cæsar looks so sad
    Casca   Why, you were with him, were
    you not ?
    Bru   I should not then ask Casca what had
    chanced   219
    Casca   Why, there was a crown offered
him   and being offered him, he put it by with
the back of his hand, thus , and then the
people fell a-shouting
    Bru   What was the second noise for ?
    Casca   Why, for that too
    Cas   They shouted thrice   what was the
    last cry for ?
    Casca.   Why, for that too
    Bru   Was the crown offered him thrice ?
    Casca   Ay, marry, was't, and he put it by
thrice, every time gentler than other, and at
every putting-by mine honest neighbors
shouted.

Cas. Who offered him the crown ?

Casca Why, Antony.

Bru. Tell us the manner of it, gentle Casca.

Casca I can as well be hanged as tell the manner of it it was mere foolery , I did not mark it I saw Mark Antony offer him a crown ,—yet 'twas not a crown neither, 'twas one of these coronets ;—and, as I told you, he put it by once · but, for all that, to my thinking, he would fain have had it Then he offered it to him again , then he put it by again· but, to my thinking, he was very loath to lay his fingers off it And then he offered it the third time , he put it the third time by and still as he refused it, the rabblement hooted and clapped their chapped hands and threw up their sweaty night-caps and uttered such a deal of stinking breath because Cæsar refused the crown that it had almost choked Cæsar , for he swounded and fell down at it and for mine own part, I durst not laugh, for fear of opening my lips and receiving the bad air.

Cas. But, soft, I pray you· what, did Cæsar swound ?

Casca He fell down in the market-place, and foamed at mouth, and was speechless

Bru. 'Tis very like . he hath the falling sickness

Cas No, Cæsar hath it not , but you and I And honest Casca, we have the falling sickness.

Casca. I know not what you mean by that ; but, I am sure, Cæsar fell down If the tag-rag people did not clap him and hiss him, according as he pleased and displeased them, as they use to do the players in the theatre, I am no true man

Bru What said he when he came unto himself ?

Casca Marry, before he fell down, when he perceived the common herd was glad he refused the crown, he plucked me ope his doublet and offered them his throat to cut An I had been a man of any occupation, if I would not have taken him at a word, I would I might go to hell among the rogues And so he fell When he came to himself again, he said, If he had done or said any thing amiss he desired their worships to think it was his infirmity. Three or four wenches, where I stood, cried ' Alas, good soul '' and forgave him with all their hearts but there's no heed to be taken of them , if Cæsar had stabbed their mothers, they would have done no less

Bru And after that, he came, thus sad, away ?

Casca Ay. 280

Cas Did Cicero say any thing ?

Casca Ay, he spoke Greek

Cas To what effect ?

Casca Nay, an I tell you that, I'll ne'er look you i' the face again but those that understood him smiled at one another and shook their heads ; but, for mine own part, it was Greek to me. I could tell you more news too .

Marullus and Flavius, for pulling scarfs off Cæsar's images, are put to silence. Fare you well. There was more foolery yet, if I could remember it. 291

Cas. Will you sup with me to-night, Casca ?

Casca. No, I am promised forth

Cas. Will you dine with me to-morrow ?

Casca Ay, if I be alive and your mind hold and your dinner worth the eating.

Cas. Good . I will expect you.

Casca Do so Farewell, both [*Exit.*

Bru What a blunt fellow is this grown to be '

He was quick mettle when he went to school.

Cas. So is he now in execution 301
Of any bold or noble enterprise,
However he puts on this tardy form
This rudeness is a sauce to his good wit,
Which gives men stomach to digest his words
With better appetite.

Bru. And so it is. For this time I will leave you :
To-morrow, if you please to speak with me,
I will come home to you ; or, if you will,
Come home to me, and I will wait for you.

Cas. I will do so : till then, think of the world [*Exit Brutus.* 311
Well, Brutus, thou art noble , yet, I see, .
Thy honorable metal may be wrought
From that it is disposed therefore it is meet
That noble minds keep ever with their likes ;
For who so firm that cannot be seduced ?
Cæsar doth bear me hard , but he loves Brutus
If I were Brutus now and he were Cassius,
He should not humor me I will this night,
In several hands, in at his windows throw,
As if they came from several citizens, 321
Writings all tending to the great opinion
That Rome holds of his name , wherein obscurely
Cæsar's ambition shall be glanced at .
And after this let Cæsar seat him sure ,
For we will shake him, or worse days endure.
[*Exit.*

SCENE III *The same. A street.*

Thunder and lightning Enter from opposite sides, CASCA, *with his sword drawn, and* CICERO

Cic. Good even, Casca brought you Cæsar home ?
Why are you breathless ? and why stare you so ?

Casca. Are not you moved, when all the sway of earth
Shakes like a thing unfirm ? O Cicero,
I have seen tempests, when the scolding winds
Have rived the knotty oaks, and I have seen
The ambitious ocean swell and rage and foam,
To be exalted with the threatening clouds :
But never till to-night, never till now,
Did I go through a tempest dropping fire. 10

Either there is a civil strife in heaven,
Or else the world, too saucy with the gods,
Incenses them to send destruction.

Cic. Why, saw you any thing more won-
    derful?

Casca. A common slave—you know him
    well by sight--
Held up his left hand, which did flame and
    burn
Like twenty torches join'd, and yet his hand,
Not sensible of fire, remain'd un-scorch'd
Besi' s—I ha' not since put up my sword—
Against the Capitol I met a lion,   20
Who glared upon me, and went surly by,
Without annoying me   and there were drawn
Upon a heap a hundred ghastly women,
Transformed with their fear, who swore
    they saw
Men all in fire walk up and down the streets.
And yesterday the bird of night did sit
Even at noon-day upon the market-place,
Hooting and shrieking. When these prodi-
    gies
Do so conjointly meet, let not men say
' These are their reasons, they are natural ,'
For, I believe, they are portentous things   31
Unto the climate that they point upon

Cic. Indeed, it is a strange-disposed time :
But men may construe things after their
    fashion,   [selves
Clean from the purpose of the things them-
Come Cæsar to the Capitol to-morrow ?

Casca. He doth , for he did bid Antonius
Send word to you he would be there to-mor-
    row.

Cic Good night then, Casca · this dis-
    turbed sky
Is not to walk in.

Casca. Farewell, Cicero. [*Exit Cicero.* 40

Enter CASSIUS

Cas. Who's there ?
Casca.   A Roman.
Cas.   Casca, by your voice
Casca. Your ear is good. Cassius, what
    night is this !
Cas. A very pleasing night to honest men
Casca Who ever knew the heavens men-
    nce so ?
Cas. Those that have known the earth so
    full of faults.
For my part, I have walk'd about the streets,
Submitting me unto the perilous night,
And, thus unbraced, Casca, as you see,
Have bared my bosom to the thunder-stone ·
And when the cross blue lightning seem'd to
    open   50
The breast of heaven, I did present myself
Even in the aim and very flash of it.

Casca. But wherefore did you so much
    tempt the heavens ?
It is the part of men to fear and tremble,
When the most mighty gods by tokens send
Such dreadful heralds to astonish us

Cas. You are dull, Casca, and those sparks
    of life

That should be in a Roman you do want,
Or else you use not You look pale and gaze
And put on fear and cast yourself in wonder,
To see the strange impatience of the heavens ·
But if you would consider the true cause
Why all these fires, why all these gliding
    ghosts,
Why birds and beasts from quality and kind,
Why old men fool and children calculate,
Why all these things change from their ordi-
    nance
Their natures and preformed faculties
To monstrous quality,—why, you shall find
That heaven hath infused them with these
    spirits,
To make them instruments of fear and warn
    ing   70
Unto some monstrous state
Now could I, Casca, name to thee a man
Most like this dreadful night,
That thunders, lightens, opens graves, and
    roars
As doth the lion in the Capitol,
A man no mightier than thyself or me
In personal action, yet prodigious grown
And fearful, as these strange eruptions are.

Casca 'Tis Cæsar that you mean , is it not
    Cassius ?   79

Cas Let it be who it is for Romans now
Have thews and limbs like to their ancestors ,
But, woe the while ! our fathers' minds are
    dead,
And we are govern'd with our mothers' spir-
    its ,
Our yoke and sufferance show us womanish

Casca. Indeed, they say the senators to-
    morrow
Mean to establish Cæsar as a king ;
And he shall wear his crown by sea and land,
In every place, save here in Italy.

Cas I know where I will wear this dagger
    then ,
Cassius from bondage will deliver Cassius   90
Therein, ye gods, you make the weak most
    strong ,
Therein, ye gods, you tyrants do defeat ·
Nor stony tower, nor walls of beaten brass,
Nor airless dungeon, nor strong links of iron,
Can be retentive to the strength of spirit ;
But life, being weary of these worldly bars,
Never lacks power to dismiss itself
If I know this, know all the world besides,
That part of tyranny that I do bear
I can shake off at pleasure   [*Thunder still.*

Casca   So can I .   100
So every bondman in his own hand bears
The power to cancel his captivity.

Cas. And why should Cæsar be a tyrant
    then ?
Poor man ! I know he would not be a wolf,
But that he sees the Romans are but sheep :
He were no lion, were not Romans hinds.
Those that with haste will make a mighty fire
Begin it with weak straws : what trash is
    Rome.
What rubbish and what offal, when it serves

For the base matter to illuminate   110
So vile a thing as Cæsar ! But, O grief,
Where hast thou led me ? I perhaps speak
    this
Before a willing bondman ; then I know
My answer must be made   But I am arm'd,
And dangers are to me indifferent
    Casca   You speak to Casca, and to such a
      man
That is no fleering tell-tale   Hold, my hand :
Be factious for redress of all these griefs,
And I will set this foot of mine as far
As who goes farthest.
    Cas.   There's a bargain made   120
Now know you, Casca, I have moved already
Some certain of the noblest-minded Romans
To undergo with me an enterprise
Of honorable-dangerous consequence ;
And I do know, by this, they stay for me
In Pompey's porch . for now, this fearful
    night,
There is no stir or walking in the streets ;
And the complexion of the element
In favor's like the work we have in hand,
Most bloody, fiery, and most terrible   130
    Casca.   Stand close awhile, for here comes
      one in haste.
    Cas   'Tis Cinna , I do know him by his
      gait ;
He is a friend

Enter CINNA.

Cinna, where haste you so ?
    Cin   To find out you   Who's that ? Metel-
      lus Cimber ?
    Cas   No, it is Casca , one incorporate
To our attempts   Am I not stay'd for, Cinna ?
    Cin   I am glad on 't   What a fearful night
      is this !   [sights
There's two or three of us have seen strange
    Cas   Am I not stay'd for ? tell me
    Cin   Yes, you are
O Cassius, if you could   140
But win the noble Brutus to our party—
    Cas   Be you content · good Cinna, take
      this paper,
And look you lay it in the prætor's chair,
Where Brutus may but find it ; and throw
    this
In at his window , set this up with wax
Upon old Brutus' statue . all this done,
Repair to Pompey's porch, where you shall
    find us
Is Decius Brutus and Trebonius there ?
    Cin   All but Metellus Cimber , and he's
      gone   149
To seek you at your house. Well, I will hie,
And so bestow these papers as you bade me
    Cas   That done, repair to Pompey's theatre
                [*Exit Cinna.*
Come, Casca, you and I will yet ere day
See Brutus at his house   three parts of him
Is ours already, and the man entire
Upon the next encounter yields him ours
    Casca.   O, he sits high in all the people's
      hearts :

And that which would appear offence in us,
His countenance, like richest alchemy,
Will change to virtue and to worthiness   160
    Cas   Him and his worth and our great need
      of him
You have right well conceited. Let us go,
For it is after midnight ; and ere day
We will awake him and be sure of him
                [*Exeunt.*

ACT II.

SCENE I   *Rome.   Brutus's orchard.*

Enter BRUTUS.

Bru   What, Lucius, ho !
I cannot, by the progress of the stars,
Give guess how near to day. Lucius, I say !
I would it were my fault to sleep so soundly.
When, Lucius, when ? awake, I say ! what,
    Lucius !

Enter LUCIUS

Luc   Call'd you, my lord ?
Bru.   Get me a taper in my study, Lucius :
When it is lighted, come and call me here
Luc.   I will, my lord.   [*Exit.*
Bru.   It must be by his death : and for my
    part,
I know no personal cause to spurn at him,   11
But for the general. He would be crown'd :
How that might change his nature, there's the
    question
It is the bright day that brings forth the adder;
And that craves wary walking. Crown him ?
    —that —
And then, I grant, we put a sting in him,
That at his will he may do danger with
The abuse of greatness is, when it disjoins
Remorse from power . and, to speak truth of
    Cæsar,   19
I have not known when his affections sway'd
More than his reason   But 'tis a common
    proof,
That lowliness is young ambition's ladder,
Whereto the climber-upward turns his face ;
But when he once attains the upmost round,
He then unto the ladder turns his back,
Looks in the clouds, scorning the base degrees
By which he did ascend   So Cæsar may.
Then, lest he may, prevent. And, since the
    quarrel
Will bear no color for the thing he is,
Fashion it thus , that what he is, augmented,
Would run to these and these extremities : 31
And therefore think him as a serpent's egg
Which, hatch'd, would, as his kind, grow mis-
    chievous,
And kill him in the shell.

Re-enter LUCIUS.

Luc   The taper burneth in your closet, sir.
Searching the window for a flint, I found
This paper, thus seal'd up ; and, I am sure,
It did not lie there when I went to bed.
              [*Gives him the letter.*

Bru. Get you to bed again ; it is not day.
Is not to-morrow, boy, the ides of March ?   40
Luc. I know not, sir
Bru. Look in the calendar, and bring me
    word
Luc. I will, sir   [*Exit*
Bru. The exhalations whizzing in the air
Give so much light that I may read by them
                 [*Opens the letter and reads*
' Brutus, thou sleep'st awake, and see thy-
    self
Shall Rome, &c   Speak, strike, redress !
Brutus, thou sleep'st   aw~ke ''
Such instigations have been often dropp'd
Where I have took them up   50
' Shall Rome, &c ' Thus must I piece it out
Shall Rome stand under one man's awe ?
What, Rome ?
My ancestois did from the streets of Rome
The Tarquin drive, when he was call'd a king
' Speak, strike, redress !' Am I entreated
To speak and strike ? O Rome, I make thee
    promise
If the redress will follow, thou receivest
Thy full petition at the hand of Brutus !

Re-enter Lucius.

Luc. Sir, March is wasted fourteen days
                      [*Knocking within*
Bru. 'Tis good Go to the gate, somebody
    knocks   [*Exit Lucius* 60
Since Cassius first did whet me against Cæsar,
I have not slept
Between the acting of a dreadful thing
And the first motion, all the interim is
Like a phantasma, or a hideous dream
The Genius and the mortal instruments
Are then in council, and the state of man,
Like to a little kingdom, suffers then
The nature of an insurrection

Re-enter Lucius

Luc. Sir, 'tis your brother Cassius at the
    door,
Who doth desire to see you.
Bru.   Is he alone ?   71
Luc. No, sir, there are more with him.
Bru.   Do you know them ?
Luc. No, sir ; their hats are pluck'd about
    their ears,
And half their faces buried in their cloaks,
That by no means I may discover them
By any mark of favor.
Bru.   Let 'em enter [*Exit Lucius*
They are the faction   O conspiracy,
Shamest thou to show thy dangerous brow by
    night,
When evils are most free ? O, then by day
Where wilt thou find a cavern dark enough 80
To mask thy monstrous visage ? Seek none,
    conspiracy ;
Hide it in smiles and affability ?
For if thou path, thy native semblance on,
Not Erebus itself were dim enough
To hide thee from prevention.

Enter the conspirators, Cassius, Casca,
    Decius, Cinna, Metellus Cimber, *and*
    Trebonius
Cas I think we are too bold upon your
    rest .
Good morrow, Brutus, do we trouble you ?
Bru. I have been up this hour, awake all
    night
Know I these men that come along with you ?
Cas. Yes, every man of them, and no man
    here   90
But honors you ; and every one doth wish
You had but that opinion of yourself
Which every noble Roman bears of you
This is Trebonius
Bru.   He is welcome hither.
Cas This, Decius Brutus
Bru   He is welcome too
Cas This, Casca, this, Cinna, and this,
    Metellus Cimber
Bru They are all welcome
What watchful cares do interpose themselves
Betwixt your eyes and night ?
Cas Shall I entreat a word ?   100
               [*Brutus and Cassius whisper.*
Dec Here lies the east   doth not the day
    break here ?
Casca No.
Cin O, pardon, sir, it doth, and yon gray
    lines
That fret the clouds are messengers of day.
Casca You shall confess that you are both
    deceived.
Here, as I point my sword the sun arises,
Which is a great way growing on the south,
Weighing the youthful season of the year
Some two months hence up higher toward the
    north
He first presents his fire, and the high east
Stands, as the Capitol, directly here   111
Bru Give me your hands all over, one by
    one
Cas And let us swear our resolution
Bru No, not an oath   if not the face of
    men,
The sufferance of our souls, the time's abuse,—
If these be motives weak, break off betimes,
And every man hence to his idle bed,
So let high-sighted tyranny range on,
Till each man drop by lottery But if these,
As I am sure they do, be fire enough   120
To kindle cowards and to steel with valor
The melting spirits of women, then, country-
    men,
What need we any spur but our own cause,
To prick us to redress ? what other bond
Than secret Romans, that have spoke the
    word,
And will not palter ? and what other oath
Than honesty to honesty engaged,
That this shall be, or we will fall for it ?
Swear priests and cowards and men cautelous,
Old feeble carrions and such suffering souls
That welcome wrongs ; unto bad causes swear
Such creatures as men doubt ; but do not
    stain

40

The even virtue of our enterprise,
Nor the insuppressive mettle of our spirits,
To think that or our cause or our performance
Did need an oath ; when every drop of blood
That every Roman bears, and nobly bears
Is guilty of a several bastardy,
If he do break the smallest particle
Of any promise that hath pass'd from him.
  Cas.   But what of Cicero ? shall we sound
    him ?   141
I think he will stand very strong with us.
  Casca.   Let us not leave him out.
  Cin.   No, by no means.
  Met.   O, let us have him, for his silver hairs
Will purchase us a good opinion
And buy men's voices to commend our deeds :
It shall be said, his judgment ruled our hands ;
Our youths and wildness shall no whit appear,
But all be buried in his gravity.
  Bru.   O, name him not : let us not break
    with him ;   150
For he will never follow any thing
That other men begin.
  Cas.   Then leave him out.
  Casca.   Indeed he is not fit.
  Dec.   Shall no man else be touch'd but only
    Cæsar ?
  Cas.   Decius, well urged : I think it is not
    meet,
Mark Antony, so well beloved of Cæsar,
Should outlive Cæsar : we shall find of him
A shrewd contriver ; and, you know, his
    means,
If he improve them, may well stretch so far
As to annoy us all : which to prevent,   160
Let Antony and Cæsar fall togather.
  Bru.   Our course will seem too bloody, Caius
    Cassius,
To cut the head off and then hack the limbs,
Like wrath in death and envy afterwards ;
For Antony is but a limb of Cæsar :
Let us be sacrificers, but not butchers, Caius.
We all stand up against the spirit of Cæsar ;
And in the spirit of men there is no blood :
O, that we then could come by Cæsar's spirit,
And not dismember Cæsar ! But, alas, 170
Cæsar must bleed for it ! And, gentle friends,
Let's kill him boldly, but not wrathfully ;
Let's carve him as a dish fit for the gods,
Not hew him as a carcass fit for hounds :
And let our hearts, as subtle masters do,
Stir up their servants to an act of rage,
And after seem to chide 'em. This shall make
Our purpose necessary and not envious :
Which so appearing to the common eyes,
We shall be call'd purgers, not murderers. 180
And for Mark Antony, think not of him ;
For he can do no more than Cæsar's arm
When Cæsar's head is off.
  Cas.   Yet I fear him ;
For in the ingrafted love he bears to Cæsar—
  Bru.   Alas, good Cassius, do not think of
    him :
If he love Cæsar, all that he can do
Is to himself, take thought and die for Cæsar:
And that were much he should ; for he is given

To sports, to wildness and much company.
  Treb.   There is no fear in him ; let him not
    die ;   190
For he will live, and laugh at this hereafter.
                        [*Clock strikes.*
  Bru.   Peace ! count the clock.
  Cas.   The clock hath stricken three.
  Treb.   'Tis time to part.
  Cas.   But it is doubtful yet,
Whether Cæsar will come forth to-day, or no ;
For he is superstitious grown of late,
Quite from the main opinion he held once
Of fantasy, of dreams and ceremonies :
It may be, these apparent prodigies,
The unaccustom'd terror of this night,
And the persuasion of his augurers, 200
May hold him from the Capitol to-day.
  Dec.   Never fear that : if he be so resolved,
I can o'ersway him ; for he loves to hear
That unicorns may be betray'd with trees,
And bears with glasses, elephants with holes,
Lions with toils and men with flatterers ;
But when I tell him he hates flatterers,
He says he does, being then most flattered.
Let me work ;
For I can give his humor the true bent, 210
And I will bring him to the Capitol.
  Cas.   Nay, we will all of us be there to fetch
    him.
  Bru.   By the eighth hour: is that the utter-
    most ?
  Cin.   Be that the uttermost, and fail not
    then.
  Met.   Caius Ligarius doth bear Cæsar hard,
Who rated him for speaking well of Pompey:
I wonder none of you have thought of him.
  Bru.   Now, good Metellus, go along by him :
He loves me well, and I have given him rea-
    sons ;
Send him but hither, and I'll fashion him. 220
  Cas.   The morning comes upon 's : we'll
    leave you, Brutus.
And, friends, disperse yourselves ; but all re-
    member
What you have said, and show yourselves true
    Romans.   [rily ;
  Bru.   Good gentlemen, look fresh and mer-
Let not our looks put on our purposes,
But bear it as our Roman actors do,
With untired spirits and formal constancy:
And so good morrow to you every one.
                  [*Exeunt all but Brutus.*
Boy ! Lucius ! Fast asleep ? It is no matter ;
Enjoy the honey-heavy dew of slumber: 230
Thou hast no figures nor no fantasies,
Which busy care draws in the brains of men
Therefore thou sleep'st so sound.

           Enter PORTIA.

  Por.   Brutus, my lord !
  Bru.   Portia, what mean you ? wherefore
    rise you now ?
It is not for your health thus to commit
Your weak condition to the raw cold morning.
  Por.   Nor for yours neither. You've un-
    gently, Brutus,

BRUTUS AND PORTIA.

Stole from my bed: and yesternight, at sup-
   per,
You suddenly arose, and walk'd about,   239
Musing and sighing, with your arms across,
And when I ask'd you what the matter was,
You stared upon me with ungentle looks,
I urged you further; then you scratch'd your
   head,
And too impatiently stamp'd with your foot,
Yet I insisted, yet you answer'd not,
But, with an angry wafture of your hand,
Gave sign for me to leave you so I did,
Fearing to strengthen that impatience
Which seem'd too much enkindled, and withal
Hoping it was but an effect of humor,   250
Which sometime hath his hour with every
   man
It will not let you eat, nor talk, nor sleep,
And could it work so much upon your shape
As it hath much prevail'd on your condition,
I should not know you, Brutus. Dear my
   lord,
Make me acquainted with your cause of grief
   Bru   I am not well in health, and that is
   all
   Por. Brutus is wise, and, were he not in
   health,
He would embrace the means to come by it
   Bru. Why, so I do Good Portia, go to
   bed   260
   Por   Is Brutus sick? and is it physical
To walk unbraced and suck up the humors
Of the dank morning? What, is Brutus sick,
And will he steal out of his wholesome bed,
To dare the vile contagion of the night
And tempt the rheumy and unpurged air
To add unto his sickness? No, my Brutus,
You have some sick offence within your mind,
Which, by the right and virtue of my place,
I ought to know of and, upon my knees, 270
I charm you, by my once-commended beauty,
By all your vows of love and that great vow
Which did incorporate and make us one,
That you unfold to me, yourself, your half,
Why you are heavy, and what men to-night
Have had resort to you for here have been
Some six or seven, who did hide their faces
Even from darkness
   Bru.   Kneel not, gentle Portia
   Por. I should not need, if you were gentle
   Brutus
Within the bond of marriage, tell me, Brutus,
Is it excepted I should know no secrets 281
That appertain to you? Am I yourself
But, as it were, in sort or limitation,
To keep with you at meals, comfort your bed,
And talk to you sometimes? Dwell I but in
   the suburbs
Of your good pleasure? If it be no more,
Portia is Brutus' harlot, not his wife.
   Bru. You are my true and honorable wife,
As dear to me as are the ruddy drops
That visit my sad heart   290
   Por. If this were true, then should I know
   this secret.
I grant I am a woman; but withal

A woman that Lord Brutus took to wife:
I grant I am a woman, but withal
A woman well-reputed, Cato's daughter,
Think you I am no stronger than my sex,
Being so father'd and so husbanded?
Tell me your counsels, I will not disclose 'em:
I have made strong proof of my constancy,
Giving myself a voluntary wound   300
Here, in the thigh can I bear that with pa-
   tience,
And not my husband's secrets?
   Bru   O ye gods,
Render me worthy of this noble wife!
            [*Knocking within*
Hark, hark! one knocks Portia, go in awhile,
And by and by thy bosom shall partake
The secrets of my heart
All my engagements I will construe to thee,
All the characters of my sad brows
Leave me with haste   [*Exit Portia*] Lucius,
   who's that knocks?

    Re-enter Lucius *with* Ligarius.

   Luc He is a sick man that would speak
   with you   310
   Bru Caius Ligarius, that Metellus spake of.
Boy, stand aside Caius Ligarius! how?
   Lig Vouchsafe good morrow from a feeble
   tongue
   Bru. O, what a time have you chose out,
   brave Caius,
To wear a kerchief! Would you were not
   sick!
   Lig I am not sick, if Brutus have in hand
Any exploit worthy the name of honor
   Bru Such an exploit have I in hand, Li-
   garius,
Had you a healthful ear to hear of it
   Lig By all the gods that Romans bow be-
   fore,   320
I here discard my sickness! Soul of Rome!
Brave son, derived from honorable loins!
Thou, like an exorcist, hast conjured up
My mortified spirit Now bid me run,
And I will strive with things impossible;
Yea, get the better of them What's to do?
   Bru. A piece of work that will make sick
   men whole
   Lig But are not some whole that we must
   make sick?
   Bru. That must we also. What it is, my
   Caius,
I shall unfold to thee, as we are going 330
To whom it must be done.
   Lig.   Set on your foot,
And with a heart new-fired I follow you,
To do I know not what but it sufficeth
That Brutus leads me on
   Bru.   Follow me, then   [*Exeunt.*

      Scene II. *Cæsar's house.*

Thunder and lightning. Enter Cæsar, *in his*
    night-gown.

   Cæs. Nor heaven nor earth have been at
   peace to-night:

Thrice hath Calpurnia in her sleep cried out,
'Help, ho! they murder Cæsar!' Who's with-
    in?

Enter a Servant.

Serv. My lord?
Cæs. Go bid the priests do present sacrifice
And bring me their opinions of success.
Serv. I will, my lord   [*Exit.*

Enter CALPURNIA.

Cal. What mean you, Cæsar? think you
    to walk forth?
You shall not stir out of your house to-day.
    Cæs. Cæsar shall forth: the things that
        threaten'd me   10
Ne'er look'd but on my back, when they shall
    see
The face of Cæsar, they are vanished
    Cal. Cæsar, I never stood on ceremonies,
Yet now they fright me There is one within,
Besides the things that we have heard and
    seen,
Recounts most horrid sights seen by the watch.
A lioness hath whelped in the streets,
And graves have yawn'd, and yielded up their
    dead,
Fierce fiery warriors fought upon the clouds,
In ranks and squadrons and right form of war,
Which drizzled blood upon the Capitol,   21
The noise of battle hurtled in the air,
Horses did neigh, and dying men did groan,
And ghosts did shriek and squeal about the
    streets
O Cæsar! these things are beyond all use,
And I do fear them
    Cæs.   What can be avoided
Whose end is purposed by the mighty gods?
Yet Cæsar shall go forth, for these predictions
Are to the world in general as to Cæsar
    Cal. When beggars die, there are no comets
        seen,   30
The heavens themselves blaze forth the death
    of princes
    Cæs. Cowards die many times before their
        deaths;
The valiant never taste of death but once
Of all the wonders that I yet have heard,
It seems to me most strange that men should
    fear,
Seeing that death, a necessary end,
Will come when it will come
        Re-enter Servant
                What say the augurers?
Serv. They would not have you to stir forth
    to-day.
Plucking the entrails of an offering forth,
They could not find a heart within the beast
    Cæs. The gods do this in shame of coward-
        ice.   41
Cæsar should be a beast without a heart,
If he should stay at home to-day for fear
No, Cæsar shall not: danger knows full well
That Cæsar is more dangerous than he.
We are two lions litter'd in one day,
And I the elder and more terrible:

And Cæsar shall go forth
    Cal.   Alas, my lord,
Your wisdom is consumed in confidence.
Do not go forth to-day: call it my fear   50
That keeps you in the house, and not your
    own.
We'll send Mark Antony to the senate-house:
And he shall say you are not well to-day:
Let me, upon my knee, prevail in this
    Cæs. Mark Antony shall say I am not well;
And, for thy humor, I will stay at home.

Enter DECIUS.

Here's Decius Brutus, he shall tell them so.
    Dec. Cæsar, all hail! good morrow, worthy
        Cæsar:
I come to fetch you to the senate-house.
    Cæs. And you are come in very happy
        time,   60
To bear my greeting to the senators
And tell them that I will not come to-day:
Cannot, is false, and that I dare not, falser:
I will not come to-day: tell them so, Decius
    Cal. Say he is sick.
    Cæs.   Shall Cæsar send a lie?
Have I in conquest stretch'd mine arm so far,
To be afraid to tell graybeards the truth?
Decius, go tell them Cæsar will not come.
    Dec. Most mighty Cæsar, let me know some
        cause,
Lest I be laugh'd at when I tell them so.   70
    Cæs. The cause is in my will: I will not
        come,
That is enough to satisfy the senate
But for your private satisfaction,
Because I love you, I will let you know:
Calpurnia here, my wife, stays me at home:
She dreamt to-night she saw my statua,
Which, like a fountain with an hundred spouts,
Did run pure blood, and many lusty Romans
Came smiling, and did bathe their hands in it:
And these does she apply for warnings, and
    portents,   80
And evils imminent, and on her knee
Hath begg'd that I will stay at home to-day
    Dec. This dream is all amiss interpreted;
It was a vision fair and fortunate:
Your statue spouting blood in many pipes,
In which so many smiling Romans bathed,
Signifies that from you great Rome shall suck
Reviving blood, and that great men shall press
For tinctures, stains relics and cognizance.
This by Calpurnia's dream is signified   90
    Cæs. And this way have you well ex-
        pounded it
    Dec. I have, when you have heard what I
        can say.
And know it now: the senate have concluded
To give this day a crown to mighty Cæsar.
If you shall send them word you will not come,
Their minds may change Besides, it were a
    mock
Apt to be render'd, for some one to say
'Break up the senate till another time,
When Cæsar's wife shall meet with better
    dreams.'

If Cæsar hide himself, shall they not whisper
' Lo, Cæsar is afraid ' ?   101
Pardon me, Cæsar ; for my dear dear love
To your proceeding bids me tell you this ,
And reason to my love is liable
 Cæs. How foolish do your fears seem now,
  Calpurnia !
I am ashamed I did yield to them.
Give me my robe, for I will go

Enter PUBLIUS, BRUTUS, LIGARIUS, METEL-
 LUS, CASCA, TREBONIUS, *and* CINNA

And look where Publius is come to fetch me
 Pub. Good morrow, Cæsar
 Cæs   Welcome, Publius.
What, Brutus, are you stirr'd so early too ?
Good morrow, Casca Caius Ligarius,   111
Cæsar was ne'er so much your enemy
As that same ague which hath made you lean
What is 't o'clock ?
 Bru   Cæsar, 'tis strucken eight
 Cæs. I thank you for your pains and
  courtesy

    Enter ANTONY.

See ' Antony, that revels long o' nights,
Is notwithstanding up Good morrow, Antony.
 Ant. So to most noble Cæsar
 Cæs.   Bid them prepare within.
I am to blame to be thus waited for
Now, Cinna. now, Metellus what, Trebonius !
I have an hour's talk in store for you ,
Remember that you call on me to-day .
Be near me, that I may remember you.
 Treb Cæsar, I will . [*Aside*] and so near
  will I be,
That your best friends shall wish I had been
 further
 Cæs. Good friends, go in, and taste some
  wine with me ;   [gether
And we, like friends, will straightway go to-
 Bru. [*Aside*] That every like is not the
  same, O Cæsar,
The heart of Brutus yearns to think upon '
           [*Exeunt.*

  SCENE III *A street near the Capitol*

  Enter ARTEMIDORUS, *reading a paper*

 Art. ' Cæsar, beware of Brutus , take heed
of Cassius , come not near Casca, have an eye
to Cinna , trust not Trebonius : mark well
Metellus Cimber . Decius Brutus loves thee
not : thou hast wronged Caius Ligarius There
is but one mind in all these men, and it is bent
against Cæsar If thou beest not immortal,
look about you . security gives way to conspiracy. The mighty gods defend thee ! Thy
lover,
        ' ARTEMIDORUS '
Here will I stand till Cæsar pass along,   11
And as a suitor will I give him this
My heart laments that virtue cannot live
Out of the teeth of emulation.
If thou read this, O Cæsar, thou mayst live ,
If not, the Fates with traitors do contrive
            [*Exit.*

  SCENE IV *Another part of the same street,*
    before the house of Brutus.

    Enter PORTIA *and* LUCIUS.

 Por I prithee, boy, run to the senate-house;
Stay not to answer me, but get thee gone .
Why dost thou stay ?
 Luc   To know my errand, madam.
 Por. I would have had thee there, and here
  again,
Ere I can tell thee what thou shouldst **do**
 there
O constancy, be strong upon my side,
Set a huge mountain 'tween my heart and
 tongue !
I have a man's mind, but a woman's might.
How hard it is for women to keep counsel !
Art thou here yet ?
 Luc   Madam, what should I do ? 10
Run to the Capitol, and nothing else ?
And so return to you, and nothing else ?
 Por. Yes, bring me word, boy, if thy lord
  look well,
For he went sickly forth and take good note
What Cæsar doth, what suitors press to him
Hark, boy ' what noise is that ?
 Luc I hear none, madam
 Por.   Prithee, listen well ;
I heard a bustling rumor, like a fray,
And the wind brings it from the Capitol
 Luc. Sooth, madam, I hear nothing.   20

    Enter the Soothsayer

 Por Come hither, fellow . which way hast
  thou been ?
 Sooth. At mine own house, good lady.
 Por. What is 't o'clock ?
 Sooth   About the ninth hour, lady.
 Por Is Cæsar yet gone to the Capitol ?
 Sooth Madam, not yet . I go to take my
  stand,
To see him pass on to the Capitol
 Por. Thou hast some suit to Cæsar, hast thou
  not ?
 Sooth That I have, lady : if it will please
  Cæsar
To be so good to Cæsar as to hear me,
I shall beseech him to befriend himself.   30
 Por Why, know'st thou any harm's in-
  tended towards him ?
 Sooth None that I know will be, much that
  I fear may chance   [row .
Good morrow to you Here the street is nar-
The throng that follows Cæsar at the heels,
Of senators, of prætors, common suitors,
Will crowd a feeble man almost to death :
I'll get me to a place more void, and there
Speak to great Cæsar as he comes along
           [*Exit.*
 Por I must go in Ay me, how weak a
  thing
The heart of woman is ! O Brutus,   40
The heavens speed thee in thine enterprise !
Sure, the boy heard me Brutus hath a suit
That Cæsar will not grant. O, I grow faint.
Run, Lucius, and commend me to my lord ;

Say I am merry : come to me again,
And bring me word what he doth say to thee
         [*Exeunt severally.*

ACT III.

SCENE I. *Rome   Before the Capitol; the
     Senate sitting above.*

A crowd of people, among them ARTEMIDORUS
and the Soothsayer. *Flourish   Enter* CÆSAR,
BRUTUS, CASSIUS, CASCA, DECIUS, METEL-
LUS, TREBONIUS, CINNA, ANTONY, LEPIDUS,
POPILIUS, PUBLIUS, *and others*

Cæs   [*To the Soothsayer*] The ides of March
     are come
Sooth   Ay, Cæsar, but not gone
Art   Hail, Cæsar ! read this schedule
Dec   Trebonius doth desire you to o'er-
     read,
At your best leisure, this his humble suit
Art   O Cæsar, read mine first, for mine's
     a suit
That touches Cæsar nearer : read it, great
     Cæsar
Cæs.   What touches us ourself shall be last
     served
Art   Delay not, Cæsar ; read it instantly,
Cæs   What, is the fellow mad ?
Pub   Sirrah, give place   10
Cas   What, urge you your petitions in the
     street ?
Come to the Capitol.

CÆSAR *goes up to the Senate-House, the rest
     following*

Pop.   I wish your enterprise to-day may
     thrive
Cas   What enterprise, Popilius ?
Pop   Fare you well.
         [*Advances to Cæsar.*
Bru   What said Popilius Lena ?
Cas   He wish'd to day our enterprise might
     thrive
I fear our purpose is discovered
Bru   Look, how he makes to Cæsar ; mark
     him
Cas.   Casca, be sudden, for we fear preven-
     tion.
Brutus, what shall be done ? If this be known,
Cassius or Cæsar never shall turn back,   21
For I will slay myself
Bru   Cassius, be constant ·
Popilius Lena speaks not of our purposes,
For, look, he smiles, and Cæsar doth not change
Cas.   Trebonius knows his time ; for, look
     you, Brutus.
He draws Mark Antony out of the way.
         [*Exeunt Antony and Trebonius.*
Dec.   Where is Metellus Cimber ? Let him
     go,
And presently prefer his suit to Cæsar
Bru.   He is address'd : press near and
     second him.
Cin.   Casca, you are the first that rears
     your hand.   30

Cæs.   Are we all ready ? What is now
     amiss
That Cæsar and his senate must redress ?
Met.   Most high, most mighty, and most
     puissant Cæsar,
Metellus Cimber throws before thy seat
An humble heart,—   [*Kneeling.*
Cæs   I must prevent thee, Cimber.
These couchings and these lowly courtesies
Might fire the blood of ordinary men,
And turn pre-ordinance and first decree
Into the law of children   Be not fond,
To think that Cæsar bears such rebel blood   40
That will be thaw'd from the true quality
With that which melteth fools, I mean, sweet
     words,
Low-crooked court'sies and base spaniel-
     fawning
Thy brother by decree is banished .
If thou dost bend and pray and fawn for him,
I spurn thee like a cur out of my way.
Know, Cæsar doth not wrong, nor without
     cause
Will he be satisfied.
Met   Is there no voice more worthy than
     my own
To sound more sweetly in great Cæsar's ear
For the repealing of my banish'd brother ?   51
Bru.   I kiss thy hand, but not in flattery,
     Cæsar ,
Desiring thee that Publius Cimber may
Have an immediate freedom of repeal
Cæs   What, Brutus !
Cas   Pardon, Cæsar , Cæsar, pardon :
As low as to thy foot doth Cassius fall,
To beg enfranchisement for Publius Cimber
Cæs   I could be well moved, if I were as you:
If I could pray to move, prayers would move
     me .
But I am constant as the northern star,   60
Of whose true-fix'd and resting quality
There is no fellow in the firmament
The skies are painted with unnumber'd sparks,
They are all fire and every one doth shine,
But there's but one in all doth hold his place.
So in the world , 'tis furnish'd well with men,
And men are flesh and blood, and apprehen-
     sive ;
Yet in the number I do know but one
That unassailable holds on his rank,
Unshaked of motion   and that I am he,   70
Let me a little show it, even in this ,
That I was constant Cimber should be ban-
     ish'd,
And constant do remain to keep him so.
Cin.   O Cæsar,—
Cæs   Hence ! wilt thou lift up Olympus ?
Dec   Great Cæsar,—
Cæs   Doth not Brutus bootless kneel ?
Casca.   Speak, hands, for me !
     [*Casca first, then the other Conspirators,*
     and Marcus Brutus stab Cæsar.
Cæs.   Et tu, Brute ! Then fall, Cæsar
            [*Dies*
Cin.   Liberty ! Freedom ! Tyranny is
     dead !

Run hence, proclaim, cry it about the streets.
Cas.   Some to the common pulpits, and cry
   out   80
' Liberty, freedom, and enfranchisement !'
Bru. People and senators, be not affrighted;
Fly not ; stand still : ambition's debt is paid.
Casca. Go to the pulpit, Brutus.
Dec.   And Cassius too.
Bru. Where's Publius ?
Cin. Here, quite confounded with this
   mutiny.
Met. Stand fast together, lest some friend
   of Cæsar's
Should chance—
Bru. Talk not of standing. Publius, good
   cheer ;
There is no harm intended to your person, 90
Nor to no Roman else : so tell them, Publius.
Cas. And leave us, Publius , lest that the
   people,   [chief.
Rushing on us, should do your age some mis-
Bru. Do so : and let no man abide this
   deed,
But we the doers.

Re-enter TREBONIUS.

Cas.   Where is Antony ?
Tre. Fled to his house amazed :
Men, wives and children stare, cry out and
   run
As it were doomsday.
Bru. Fates, we will know your pleasures :
That we shall die, we know ; 'tis but the time
And drawing days out, that men stand upon.
Cas. Why, he that cuts off twenty years of
   life   101
Cuts off so many years of fearing death.
Bru. Grant that, and then is death a bene-
   fit :
So are we Cæsar's friends, that have abridged
His time of fearing death. Stoop, Romans,
   stoop,
And let us bathe our hands in Cæsar's blood
Up to the elbows, and besmear our swords :
Then walk we forth, even to the market-place,
And, waving our red weapons o'er our heads,
Let's all cry ' Peace, freedom and liberty !'
Cas. Stoop, then, and wash. How many
   ages hence   111
Shall this our lofty scene be acted over
In states unborn and accents yet unknown !
Bru. How many times shall Cæsar bleed
   in sport,
That now on Pompey's basis lies along
No worthier than the dust !
Cas.   So oft as that shall be,
So often shall the knot of us be call'd
The men that gave their country liberty.
Dec. What, shall we forth ?
Cas.   Ay, every man away :
Brutus shall lead ; and we will grace his heels
With the most boldest and best hearts of
   Rome.   121

Enter a Servant.

Bru. Soft ! who comes here ? A friend of
   Antony's.

Serv. Thus, Brutus, did my master bid me
   kneel :
Thus did Mark Antony bid me fall down ;
And, being prostrate, thus he bade me say :
Brutus is noble, wise, valiant, and honest ;
Cæsar was mighty, bold, royal, and loving :
Say I love Brutus, and I honor him ;
Say I fear'd Cæsar, honor'd him and loved
   him.
If Brutus will vouchsafe that Antony   130
May safely come to him, and be resolved
How Cæsar hath deserved to lie in death,
Mark Antony shall not love Cæsar dead
So well as Brutus living ; but will follow
The fortunes and affairs of noble Brutus
Through the hazards of this untrod state
With all true faith. So says my master An-
   tony.
Bru. Thy master is a wise and valiant Ro-
   man ;
I never thought him worse.
Tell him, so please him come unto this place,
He shall be satisfied ; and, by my honor, 141
Depart untouch'd.
Serv.   I'll fetch him presently. [*Exit.*
Bru. I know that we shall have him well
   to friend.
Cas. I wish we may : but yet have I a
   mind
That fears him much ; and my misgiving
   still
Falls shrewdly to the purpose.
Bru. But here comes Antony.

Re-enter ANTONY.

                     Welcome, Mark Antony.
Ant. O mighty Cæsar ! dost thou lie so
   low ?
Are all thy conquests, glories, triumphs, spoils,
Shrunk to this little measure ? Fare thee well.
I know not, gentlemen, what you intend,   151
Who else must be let blood, who else is rank :
If I myself, there is no hour so fit
As Cæsar's death hour, nor no instrument
Of half that worth as those your swords, made
   rich
With the most noble blood of all this world.
I do beseech ye, if you bear me hard,
Now, whilst your purpled hands do reek and
   smoke,
Fulfil your pleasure. Live a thousand years,
I shall not find myself so apt to die :   160
No place will please me so, no mean of death,
As here by Cæsar, and by you cut off,
The choice and master spirits of this age.
Bru. O Antony, beg not your death of us.
Though now we must appear bloody and
   cruel,
As, by our hands and this our present act,
You see we do, yet see you but our hands
And this the bleeding business they have
   done :
Our hearts you see not ; they are pitiful ;
And pity to the general wrong of Rome— 170
As fire drives out fire, so pity pity—
Hath done this deed on Cæsar. For your part,

To you our swords have leaden points, Mark
   Antony :
†Our arms, in strength of malice, and our
   hearts
Of brothers' temper, do receive you in
With all kind love, good thoughts, and rever-
   ence.
  Cas. Your voice shall be as strong as any
   man's
In the disposing of new dignities.
  Bru. Only be patient till we have appeased
The multitude, beside themselves with fear,
And then we will deliver you the cause,   181
Why I, that did love Cæsar when I struck him,
Have thus proceeded.
  Ant.   I doubt not of your wisdom.
Let each man render me his bloody hand :
First, Marcus Brutus, will I shake with you ;
Next, Caius Cassius, do I take your hand ;
Now, Decius Brutus, yours : now yours, Me-
   tellus ;
Yours, Cinna ; and, my valiant Casca, yours ;
Though last, not least in love, yours, good
   Trebonius.
Gentlemen all,—alas, what shall I say ?   190
My credit now stands on such slippery ground,
That one of two bad ways you must conceit
   me,
Either a coward or a flatterer.
That I did love thee, Cæsar, O, 'tis true :
If then thy spirit look upon us now,
Shall it not grieve thee dearer than thy death,
To see thy Antony making his peace,
Shaking the bloody fingers of thy foes,
Most noble ! in the presence of thy corse ?
Had I as many eyes as thou hast wounds, 200
Weeping as fast as they stream forth thy
   blood,
It would become me better than to close
In terms of friendship with thine enemies.
Pardon me, Julius ! Here wast thou bay'd,
   brave hart ;
Here didst thou fall ; and here thy hunters
   stand,
Sign'd in thy spoil, and crimson'd in thy lethe.
O world, thou wast the forest to this hart ;
And this, indeed, O world, the heart of thee.
How like a deer, strucken by many princes,
Dost thou here lie ?   210
  Cas. Mark Antony,—
  Ant.   Pardon me, Caius Cassius :
The enemies of Cæsar shall say this ;
Then, in a friend, it is cold modesty.
  Cas. I blame you not for praising Cæsar so;
But what compact mean you to have with us?
Will you be prick'd in number of our friends ;
Or shall we on, and not depend on you ?
  Ant. Therefore I took your hands, but was,
   indeed,
Sway'd from the point, by looking down on
   Cæsar.   219
Friends am I with you all and love you all,
Upon this hope, that you shall give me reasons
Why and wherein Cæsar was dangerous.
  Bru. Or else were this a savage spectacle :
Our reasons are so full of good regard

That were you, Antony, the son of Cæsar,
You should be satisfied.
  Ant.   That's all I seek :
And am moreover suitor that I may
Produce his body to the market-place ;
And in the pulpit, as becomes a friend,
Speak in the order of his funeral.   230
  Bru. You shall, Mark Antony.
  Cas.   Brutus, a word with you.
[*Aside to Bru.*] You know not what you do :
   do not consent
That Antony speak in his funeral :
Know you how much the people may be
   moved
By that which he will utter ?
  Bru.   By your pardon ;
I will myself into the pulpit first,
And show the reason of our Cæsar's death :
What Antony shall speak, I will protest
He speaks by leave and by permission,
And that we are contented Cæsar shall   240
Have all true rites and lawful ceremonies.
It shall advantage more than do us wrong.
  Cas. I know not what may fall ; I like it
   not.
  Bru. Mark Antony, here, take you Cæsar's
   body.
You shall not in your funeral speech blame
   us,
But speak all good you can devise of Cæsar,
And say you do't by our permission ;
Else shall you not have any hand at all
About his funeral : and you shall speak
In the same pulpit whereto I am going,   250
After my speech is ended.
  Ant.   Be it so ;
I do desire no more.
  Bru. Prepare the body then, and follow us.
              [*Exeunt all but Antony.*
  Ant. O, pardon me, thou bleeding piece of
   earth,
That I am meek and gentle with these butch-
   ers !
Thou art the ruins of the noblest man
That ever lived in the tide of times.
Woe to the hand that shed this costly blood !
Over thy wounds now do I prophesy,—
Which, like dumb mouths, do ope their ruby
   lips,   260
To beg the voice and utterance of my tongue—
A curse shall light upon the limbs of men ;
Domestic fury and fierce civil strife
Shall cumber all the parts of Italy ;
Blood and destruction shall be so in use
And dreadful objects so familiar
That mothers shall but smile when they be-
   hold
Their infants quarter'd with the hands of
   war ;
All pity choked with custom of fell deeds :
And Cæsar's spirit, ranging for revenge,   270
With Ate by his side come hot from hell,
Shall in these confines with a monarch's voice
Cry 'Havoc,' and let slip the dogs of war ;
That this foul deed shall smell above the earth
With carrion men, groaning for burial.

Enter a Servant

You serve Octavius Cæsar, do you not ?
　Serv. I do, Mark Antony.
　Ant. Cæsar did write for him to come to
Rome
　Serv He did receive his letters, and is
coming,
And bid me say to you by word of mouth—
O Cæsar !— 　　　　　　*[Seeing the body* 281
　Ant Thy heart is big, get thee apart and
weep
Passion, I see, is catching , for mine eyes,
Seeing those beads of sorrow stand in thine,
Began to water Is thy master coming ?
　Serv He lies to-night within seven leagues
of Rome
　Ant Post back with speed, and tell him
what hath chanced
Here is a mourning Rome, a dangerous Rome,
No Rome of safety for Octavius yet ; 　　289
Hie hence, and tell him so. Yet, stay awhile;
Thou shalt not back till I have borne this corse
Into the market-place there shall I try,
In my oration, how the people take
The cruel issue of these bloody men ,
According to the which, thou shalt discourse
To young Octavius of the state of things
Lend me your hand
　　　　　　　[Exeunt with Cæsar's body

SCENE II. *The Forum.*

Enter BRUTUS *and* CASSIUS, *and a throng
of* Citizens

　Citizens We will be satisfied , let us be
satisfied
　Bru. Then follow me, and give me audi-
ence, friends
Cassius, go you into the other street,
And part the numbers
Those that will hear me speak, let 'em stay
here ,
Those that will follow Cassius, go with him ,
And public reasons shall be rendered
Of Cæsar's death
　First Cit I will hear Brutus speak
　Sec. Cit. I will hear Cassius , and compare
their reasons,
When severally we hear them rendered 　10
　　　*[Exit Cassius, with some of the Citizens
　　　　　　Brutus goes into the pulpit*
　Third Cit The noble Brutus is ascended .
silence !
　Bru. Be patient till the last.
Romans, countrymen, and lovers ! hear me for
my cause, and be silent, that you may hear
believe me for mine honor, and have respect
to mine honor, that you may believe ' censure
me in your wisdom, and awake your senses,
that you may the better judge If there be any
in this assembly, any dear friend of Cæsar's,
to him I say, that Brutus' love to Cæsar was
no less than his If then that friend demand
why Brutus rose against Cæsar, this is my
answer:—Not that I loved Cæsar less, but that
I loved Rome more. Had you rather Cæsar

were living and die all slaves, than that Cæsar
were dead, to live all free men ? As Cæsar
loved me, I weep for him , as he was fortunate, I rejoice at it, as he was valiant, I honor
him . but, as he was ambitious, I slew him
There is tears for his love, joy for his fortune,
honor for his valor, and death for his ambition
Who is here so base that would be a bondman?
If any, speak, for him have I offended Who
is here so rude that would not be a Roman ?
If any, speak, for him have I offended Who
is here so vile that will not love his country ?
If any, speak, for him have I offended I pause
for a reply
　All. None, Brutus, none
　Bru. Then none have I offended I have
done no more to Cæsar than you shall do to
Brutus The question of his death is enrolled
in the Capitol, his glory not extenuated, wherein he was worthy, nor his offences enforced,
for which he suffered death

Enter ANTONY *and others, with* CÆSAR's *body.*

Here comes his body, mourned by Mark Antony who, though he had no hand in his death,
shall receive the benefit of his dying, a place
in the commonwealth, as which of you shall
not ? With this I depart,—that, as I slew my
best lover for the good of Rome, I have the
same dagger for myself, when it shall please
my country to need my death.
　All. Live, Brutus ! live, live !
　First Cit Bring him with triumph home
unto his house
　Sec Cit Give him a statue with his ances-
tors
　Third Cit Let him be Cæsar
　Fourth Cit. 　　　　Cæsar's better parts
Shall be crown'd in Brutus
　First Cit. We'll bring him to his house
With shouts and clamors.
　Bru 　　　　　My countrymen,—
　Sec Cit. Peace, silence ! Brutus speaks.
　First Cit 　　　　　　Peace, ho !
　Bru Good countrymen, let me depart alone,
And, for my sake, stay here with Antony 　61
Do grace to Cæsar's corpse, and grace his
speech
Tending to Cæsar's glories , which Mark An-
tony,
By our permission is allow'd to make.
I do entreat you, not a man depart,
Save I alone, till Antony have spoke　*[Exit.*
　First Cit. Stay, ho ! and let us hear Mark
Antony.
　Third Cit Let him go up into the public
chair ,
We'll hear him Noble Antony, go up.
　Ant For Brutus' sake, I am beholding to
you 　　　　*[Goes into the pulpit* 70
　Fourth Cit. What does he say of Brutus ?
　Third Cit He says, for Brutus' sake,
He finds himself beholding to us all
　Fourth Cit 'Twere best he speak no harm
of Brutus here
　First Cit This Cæsar was a tyrant.

Third Cit.   Nay, that's certain·
We are blest that Rome is rid of him
     Sec. Cit. Peace ! let us hear what Antony
     can say
     Ant You gentle Romans,—
     Citizens   Peace, ho ! let us hear him
     Ant Friends, Romans, countrymen, lend
     me your ears ;
I come to bury Cæsar, not to praise him
The evil that men do lives after them ,   80
The good is oft interred with their bones ;
So let it be with Cæsar The noble Brutus
Hath told you Cæsar was ambitious :
If it were so, it was a grievous fault,
And grievously hath Cæsar answer'd it
Here, under leave of Brutus and the rest—
For Brutus is an honorable man ,
So are they all, all honorable men—
Come I to speak in Cæsar's funeral
He was my friend, faithful and just to me 90
But Brutus says he was ambitious ,
And Brutus is an honorable man.
He hath brought many captives home to Rome,
Whose ransoms did the general coffers fill :
Did this in Cæsar seem ambitious ?
When that the poor have cried, Cæsar hath
     wept
Ambition should be made of sterner stuff .
Yet Brutus says he was ambitious ,
And Brutus is an honorable man
You all did see that on the Lupercal   100
I thrice presented him a kingly crown,
Which he did thrice refuse was this ambition?
Yet Brutus says he was ambitious ;
And, sure, he is an honorable man
I speak not to disprove what Brutus spoke,
But here I am to speak what I do know
You all did. love him once, not without cause:
What cause withholds you then, to mourn for
     him ?
O judgment ! thou art fled to brutish beasts,
And men have lost their reason Bear with
     me ,   110
My heart is in the coffin there with Cæsar,
And I must pause till it come back to me
     First Cit. Methinks there is much reason
     in his sayings
     Sec. Cit. If thou consider rightly of the
     matter,
Cæsar has had great wrong.
     Third Cit.   Has he, masters ?
I fear there will a worse come in his place
     Fourth Cit Mark'd ye his words ? He
     would not take the crown ;
Therefore 'tis certain he was not ambitious
     First Cit. If it be found so, some will dear
     abide it
     Sec. Cit Poor soul ! his eyes are red as fire
     with weeping.   120
     Third Cit. There's not a nobler man in
     Rome than Antony.
     Fourth Cit. Now mark him, he begins
     again to speak.   [might
     Ant. But yesterday the word of Cæsar
Have stood against the world ; now lies he
     there,

And none so poor to do him reverence.
O masters, if I were disposed to stir
Your hearts and minds to mutiny and rage,
I should do Brutus wrong, and Cassius wrong,
Who, you all know, are honorable men .
I will not do them wrong ; I rather choose 130
To wrong the dead, to wrong myself and you,
Than I will wrong such honorable men
But here's a parchment with the seal of Cæsar;
I found it in his closet, 'tis his will .
Let but the commons hear this testament—
Which, pardon me, I do not mean to read—
And they would go and kiss dead Cæsar's
     wounds
And dip their napkins in his sacred blood,
Yea, beg a hair of him for memory,
And, dying, mention it within their wills, 140
Bequeathing it as a rich legacy
Unto their issue
     Fourth Cit We'll hear the will : read it,
     Mark Antony.
     All. The will, the will ! we will hear Cæsar's
     will.
     Ant Have patience, gentle friends, I must
     not read it ;
It is not meet you know how Cæsar loved you.
You are not wood, you are not stones, but men;
And, being men, hearing the will of Cæsar,
It will inflame you, it will make you mad: 149
'Tis good you know not that you are his heirs;
For, if you should, O, what would come of it!
     Fourth Cit Read the will : we'll hear it,
     Antony,
You shall read us the will, Cæsar's will.
     Ant Will you be patient ? will you stay
     awhile ?
I have o'ershot myself to tell you of it :
I fear I wrong the honorable men
Whose daggers have stabb'd Cæsar ; I do fear
     it
     Fourth Cit They were traitors : honorable
     men !
     All The will ! the testament !
     Sec. Cit They were villains, murderers
the will ! read the will.   160
     Ant You will compel me, then, to read the
     will ?
Then make a ring about the corpse of Cæsar,
And let me show you him that made the will.
Shall I descend ? and will you give me leave ?
     Several Cit Come down.
     Sec. Cit Descend.
     Third Cit. You shall have leave.
                              [*Antony comes down.*
     Fourth Cit. A ring ; stand round.
     First Cit Stand from the hearse, stand
     from the body.
     Sec. Cit. Room for Antony, most noble An-
     tony   170
     Ant. Nay, press not so upon me; stand far
     off
     Several Cit. Stand back ; room , bear back.
     Ant If you have tears, prepare to shed
     them now.
You all do know this mantle : I remember
The first time ever Cæsar put it on ;

'Twas on a summer's evening, in his tent,
That day he overcame the Nervii :
Look, in this place ran Cassius' dagger through:
See what a rent the envious Casca made :
Through this the well-beloved Brutus stabb'd;
And as he pluck'd his cursed steel away,   181
Mark how the blood of Cæsar follow'd it,
As rushing out of doors, to be resolved
If Brutus so unkindly knock'd, or no,
For Brutus, as you know, was Cæsar's angel:
Judge, O you gods, how dearly Cæsar loved
   him !
This was the most unkindest cut of all ;
For when the noble Cæsar saw him stab,
Ingratitude, more strong than traitors' arms,
Quite vanquish'd him : then burst his mighty
   heart,   190
And, in his mantle muffling up his face,
Even at the base of Pompey's statue,
Which all the while ran blood, great Cæsar
   fell.
O, what a fall was there, my countrymen
Then I, and you, and all of us fell down,
Whilst bloody treason flourish'd over us
O, now you weep, and, I perceive, you feel
The dint of pity : these are gracious drops.
Kind souls, what, weep you when you but be-
   hold
Our Cæsar's vesture wounded ?   Look you
   here,   200
Here is himself, marr'd, as you see, with trai-
   tors

First Cit   O piteous spectacle !
Sec. Cit   O noble Cæsar !
Third Cit   O woful day !
Fourth Cit.   O traitors, villains !
First Cit   O most bloody sight !
Sec. Cit   We will be revenged.
All   Revenge !   About !   Seek !   Burn !
Fire !   Kill !   Slay !   Let not a traitor live !
Ant.   Stay, countrymen   210
First Cit.   Peace there ! hear the noble An-
   tony.
Sec. Cit   We'll hear him, we'll follow him,
we'll die with him.
Ant.   Good friends, sweet friends, let me
   not stir you up
To such a sudden flood of mutiny.
They that have done this deed are honorable :
What private griefs they have, alas, I know
   not,
That made them do it they are wise and
   honorable,
And will, no doubt, with reasons answer you.
I come not, friends, to steal away your hearts :
I am no orator, as Brutus is ;   221
But, as you know me all, a plain blunt man,
That love my friend, and that they know full
   well
That gave me public leave to speak of him
For I have neither wit, nor words, nor worth,
Action, nor utterance, nor the power of speech,
To stir men's blood. I only speak right on,
I tell you that which you yourselves do know ;
Show you sweet Cæsar's wounds, poor poor
   dumb mouths,

And bid them speak for me : but were I Bru-
   tus,   230
And Brutus Antony, there were an Antony
Would ruffle up your spirits and put a tongue
In every wound of Cæsar that should move
The stones of Rome to rise and mutiny.
All.   We'll mutiny.
First Cit.   We'll burn the house of Brutus.
Third Cit   Away, then I come, seek the con-
   spirators
Ant.   Yet hear me, countrymen ; yet hear
   me speak.
All.   Peace, ho ! Hear Antony.   Most noble
   Antony !
Ant.   Why, friends, you go to do you know
   not what :   240
Wherein hath Cæsar thus deserved your loves?
Alas, you know not. I must tell you, then.
You have forgot the will I told you of.
All.   Most true.   The will !   Let's stay and
   hear the will.
Ant.   Here is the will, and under Cæsar's
   seal.
To every Roman citizen he gives,
To every several man, seventy-five drachmas.
Sec. Cit.   Most noble Cæsar I We'll revenge
   his death
Third Cit.   O royal Cæsar !
Ant.   Hear me with patience.   250
All.   Peace, ho !   [walks,
Ant   Moreover, he hath left you all his
His private arbors and new-planted orchards,
On this side Tiber, he hath left them you,
And to your heirs for ever, common pleasures,
To walk abroad, and recreate yourselves
Here was a Cæsar ! when comes such another ?
First Cit.   Never, never. Come, away, away!
We'll burn his body in the holy place,
And with the brands fire the traitors' houses.
Take up the body.   261
Sec. Cit.   Go fetch fire.
Third Cit   Pluck down benches.
Fourth Cit.   Pluck down forms, windows,
   any thing [*Exeunt Citizens with the body.*
Ant   Now let it work   Mischief, thou art
   afoot,
Take thou what course thou wilt !

   Enter a Servant
      How now, fellow
Serv.   Sir, Octavius is already come to Rome.
Ant.   Where is he ?
Serv.   He and Lepidus are at Cæsar's house.
Ant   And thither will I straight to visit him:
He comes upon a wish   Fortune is merry,   271
And in this mood will give us any thing
Serv   I heard him say, Brutus and Cassius
Are rid like madmen through the gates of
   Rome   [people
Ant   Belike they had some notice of the
How I had moved them.   Bring me to Octa-
   vius.   [*Exeunt.*

Scene III.   *A street.*
   Enter Cinna *the poet*

Cin.   I dreamt to-night that I did feast with
Cæsar,

And things unlucky charge my fantasy : .
I have no will to wander forth of doors,
Yet something leads me forth.

Enter Citizens.

First Cit. What is your name ?
Sec. Cit. Whither are you going ?
Third Cit. Where do you dwell ?
Fourth Cit. Are you a married man or a
bachelor ?
Sec. Cit. Answer every man directly.   10
First Cit. Ay, and briefly.
Fourth Cit. Ay, and wisely.
Third Cit. Ay, and truly, you were best.
Cin. What is my name ? Whither am I
going ? Where do I dwell ? Am I a married
man or a bachelor ? Then, to answer every
man directly and briefly, wisely and truly :
wisely I say, I am a bachelor.
Sec. Cit. That's as much as to say, they are
fools that marry : you'll bear me a bang for
that, I fear. Proceed ; directly.   21
Cin. Directly, I am going to Cæsar's funeral.
First Cit. As a friend or an enemy ?
Cin. As a friend.
Sec. Cit. That matter is answered directly.
Fourth Cit. For your dwelling,—briefly.
Cin. Briefly, I dwell by the Capitol.
Third Cit. Your name, sir, truly.
Cin. Truly, my name is Cinna.
First Cit. Tear him to pieces ; he's a con-
spirator.   31
Cin. I am Cinna the poet, I am Cinna the
poet.
Fourth Cit. Tear him for his bad verses, tear
him for his bad verses.
Cin. I am not Cinna the conspirator.
Fourth Cit. It is no matter, his name's
Cinna ; pluck but his name out of his heart,
and turn him going.
Third Cit. Tear him, tear him ! Come,
brands, ho ! fire-brands : to Brutus', to Cas-
sius' ; burn all : some to Decius' house, and
some to Casca's ; some to Ligarius' : away, go!
[*Exeunt.*

ACT IV.

SCENE I. *A house in Rome.*

ANTONY, OCTAVIUS, *and* LEPIDUS, *seated at a
table.*

Ant. These many, then, shall die ; their
names are prick'd.
Oct. Your brother too must die ; consent
you, Lepidus ?
Lep. I do consent,—
Oct. Prick him down, Antony.
Lep. Upon condition Publius shall not live,
Who is your sister's son, Mark Antony.
Ant. He shall not live ; look, with a spot I
damn him.
But, Lepidus, go you to Cæsar's house ;
Fetch the will hither, and we shall determine
How to cut off some charge in legacies.

Lep. What, shall I find you here?   10
Oct. Or here, or at the Capitol.
[*Exit Lepidus*
Ant. This is a slight unmeritable man,
Meet to be sent on errands : is it fit,
The three-fold world divided, he should stand
One of the three to share it ?
Oct. So you thought him;
And took his voice who should be prick'd to
die,
In our black sentence and proscription.
Ant. Octavius, I have seen more days than
you :
And though we lay these honors on this man,
To ease ourselves of divers slanderous loads, 20
He shall but bear them as the ass bears gold,
To groan and sweat under the business,
Either led or driven, as we point the way ;
And having brought our treasure where we
will,
Then take we down his load, and turn him off,
Like to the empty ass, to shake his ears,
And graze in commons.
Oct. You may do your will
But he's a tried and valiant soldier.
Ant. So is my horse, Octavius ; and for
that
I do appoint him store of provender :   30
It is a creature that I teach to fight,
To wind, to stop, to run directly on,
His corporal motion govern'd by my spirit.
And, in some taste, is Lepidus but so ;
He must be taught and train'd and bid go
forth ;
A barren-spirited fellow ; one that feeds
On abjects, orts and imitations,
Which, out of use and staled by other men,
Begin his fashion : do not talk of him,
But as a property. And now, Octavius,   40
Listen great things :—Brutus and Cassius
Are levying powers : we must straight make
head :
Therefore let our alliance be combined,
†Our best friends made, our means stretch'd ;
And let us presently go sit in council,
How covert matters may be best disclosed,
And open perils surest answered.
Oct. Let us do so : for we are at the stake,
And bay'd about with many enemies ;
And some that smile have in their hearts, I
fear,   50
Millions of mischiefs. [*Exeunt.*

SCENE II. *Camp near Sardis. Before Brutus's
tent.*

Drum. Enter BRUTUS, LUCILIUS, LUCIUS, *and
Soldiers ;* TITINIUS *and* PINDARUS *meeting
them.*

Bru. Stand, ho !
Lucil. Give the word, ho ! and stand.
Bru. What now, Lucilius ! is Cassius near ?
Lucil. He is at hand ; and Pindarus is come
To do you salutation from his master.
Bru. He greets me well. Your master,
Pindarus,

In his own change, or by ill officers,
Hath given me some worthy cause to wish
Things done, undone : but, if he be at hand,
I shall be satisfied
  Pin   I do not doubt   10
But that my noble master will appear
Such as he is, full of regard and honor
  Bru. He is not doubted A word, Lucilius ,
How he received you, let me be resolved
  Lucil With courtesy and with respect
    enough ,
But not with such familiar instances,
Nor with such free and friendly conference,
As he hath used of old
  Bru.   Thou hast described
A hot friend cooling ever note, Lucilius,
When love begins to sicken and decay,   20
It useth an enforced ceremony.
There are no tricks in plain and simple faith ,
But hollow men, like horses hot at hand,
Make gallant show and promise of their mettle;
But when they should endure the bloody spur,
They fall their crests, and, like deceitful jades,
Sink in the trial Comes his army on ?
  Lucil They mean this night in Sardis to be
    quarter'd ,
The greater part, the horse in general,
Are come with Cassius
  Bru   Hark ! he is arrived 30
            [*Low march within.*
March gently on to meet him.

    Enter CASSIUS *and his powers.*

  Cas. Stand, ho !
  Bru. Stand, ho ! Speak the word along.
  First Sol Stand !
  Sec Sol Stand !
  Third Sol Stand !
  Cas. Most noble brother, you have done
    me wrong.   [enemies ?
  Bru. Judge me, you gods ! wrong I mine
And, if not so, how should I wrong a brother ?
  Cas Brutus, this sober form of yours hides
    wrongs ;   40
And when you do them—
  Bru.   Cassius, be content ,
Speak your griefs softly : I do know you well.
Before the eyes of both our armies here, [us,
Which should perceive nothing but love from
Let us not wrangle : bid them move away ,
Then in my tent, Cassius, enlarge your griefs,
And I will give you audience
  Cas.   Pindarus,
Bid our commanders lead their charges off
A little from this ground
  Bru. Lucilius, do you the like , and let no
    man   50
Come to our tent till we have done our confer-
    ence.
Let Lucius and Titinius guard our door
              [*Exeunt.*

    SCENE III. *Brutus's tent*

    Enter BRUTUS *and* CASSIUS.

  Cas. That you have wrong'd me doth ap-
    pear in this :

You have condemn'd and noted Lucius Pella
For taking bribes here of the Sardians ,
Wherein my letters, praying on his side,
Because I knew the man, were slighted off
  Bru You wronged yourself to write in
    such a case
  Cas In such a time as this it is not meet
That every nice offence should bear his com-
    ment
  Bru Let me tell you, Cassius, you yourself
Are much condemn'd to have an itching palm ,
To sell and mart your offices for gold   11
To undeservers.
  Cas   I an itching palm !
You know that you are Brutus that speak this,
Or, by the gods, this speech were else your last.
  Bru The name of Cassius honors this
    corruption,
And chastisement doth therefore hide his head,
  Cas Chastisement !
  Bru Remember March, the ides of March
    remember .
Did not great Julius bleed for justice' sake ?
What villain touch'd his body, that did stab,
And not for justice ? What, shall one of us,
That struck the foremost man of all this world
But for supporting robbers, shall we now
Contaminate our fingers with base bribes,
And sell the mighty space of our large honors
For so much trash as may be grasped thus ?
I had rather be a dog, and bay the moon,
Than such a Roman
  Cas.   Brutus, bay not me ;
I'll not endure it you forget yourself,
To hedge me in , I am a soldier, I,   30
Older in practice, abler than yourself
To make conditions
  Bru   Go to , you are not, Cassius.
  Cas. I am
  Bru. I say you are not
  Cas Urge me no more, I shall forget my-
    self ,
Have mind upon your health, tempt me no
    further.
  Bru Away, slight man !
  Cas. Is't possible ?
  Bru   Hear me, for I will speak.
Must I give way and room to your rash
    choler ?
Shall I be frighted when a madman stares ? 40
  Cas. O ye gods, ye gods ! must I endure
    all this ?
  Bru. All this ! ay, more fret till your
    proud heart break ,
Go show your slaves how choleric you are.
And make your bondmen tremble. Must I
    budge ?
Must I observe you ? must I stand and crouch
Under your testy humor ? By the gods,
You shall digest the venom of your spleen,
Though it do split you ; for, from this day
    forth,
I'll use you for my mirth, yea, for my laughter,
When you are waspish.
  Cas   Is it come to this ? 50
  Bru. You say you are a better soldier ;

Let it appear so ; make your vaunting true,
And it shall please me well : for mine own
    part,
I shall be glad to learn of noble men.
    Cas. You wrong me every way ; you wrong
    me, Brutus ;
I said, an elder soldier, not a better :
Did I say ' better ' ?
    Bru.   If you did, I care not.
    Cas. When Cæsar lived, he durst not thus
    have moved me.
    Bru. Peace, peace ! you durst not so have
    tempted him.
    Cas. I durst not !   .   60
    Bru. No.
    Cas. What, durst not tempt him !
    Bru.   For your life you durst not.
    Cas. Do not presume too much upon my
    love ;
I may do that I shall be sorry for.
    Bru. You have done that you should be
    sorry for.
There is no terror, Cassius, in your threats,
For I am arm'd so strong in honesty
That they pass by me as the idle wind,
Which I respect not. I did send to you
For certain sums of gold, which you denied
    me :   70
For I can raise no money by vile means :
By heaven, I had rather coin my heart,
And drop my blood for drachmas, than to
    wring   [trash
From the hard hands of peasants their vile
By any indirection : I did send
To you for gold to pay my legions,
Which you denied me: was that done like
    Cassius ?
Should I have answer'd Caius Cassius so ?
When Marcus Brutus grows so covetous,   79
To lock such rascal counters from his friends,
Be ready, gods, with all your thunderbolts ;
Dash him to pieces !
    Cas.   I denied you not.
    Bru. You did.
    Cas. I did not : he was but a fool that
    brought
My answer back.   Brutus hath rived my
    heart :
A friend should bear his friend's infirmities,
But Brutus makes mine greater than they are.
    Bru. I do not, till you practice them on
    me.
    Cas. You love me not.
    Bru.   I do not like your faults.
    Cas. A friendly eye could never see such
    faults.   90
    Bru. A flatterer's would not, though they
    do appear
As huge as high Olympus.
    Cas. Come, Antony, and young Octavius,
    come,
Revenge yourselves alone on Cassius,
For Cassius is aweary of the world ;
Hated by one he loves ; braved by his brother;
Check'd like a bondman ; all his faults ob-
    served,

Set in a note-book, learn'd, and conn'd by
    rote,
To cast into my teeth.   O, I could weep
My spirit from mine eyes !   There is my
    dagger,   100
And here my naked breast ; within, a heart
Dearer than Plutus' mine, richer than gold :
If that thou be'st a Roman, take it forth ;
I, that denied thee gold, will give my heart :
Strike, as thou didst at Cæsar ; for, I know,
When thou didst hate him worst, thou lovedst
    him better
Than ever thou lovedst Cassius.
    Bru.   Sheathe your dagger :
Be angry when you will, it shall have scope ;
Do what you will, dishonor shall be humor.
O Cassius, you are yoked with a lamb   110
That carries anger as the flint bears fire ;
Who, much enforced, shows a hasty spark,
And straight is cold again.
    Cas.   Hath Cassius lived
To be but mirth and laughter to his Brutus,
When grief, and blood ill-temper'd, vexeth
    him ?
    Bru. When I spoke that, I was ill-temper'd
    too.
    Cas. Do you confess so much ?   Give me
    your hand.
    Bru. And my heart too.
    Cas.   O Brutus !   120
    Bru.   What's the matter ?
    Cas. Have not you love enough to bear
    with me,
When that rash humor which my mother gave
    me
Makes me forgetful ?
    Bru. Yes, Cassius ; and, from henceforth,
When you are over-earnest with your Brutus,
He'll think your mother chides, and leave you
    so.
    Poet. [*Within*] Let me go in to see the
    generals ;
There is some grudge between 'em, 'tis not
    meet
They be alone.
    Lucil. [*Within*] You shall not come to
    them.
    Poet. [*Within*] Nothing but death shall
    stay me.

Enter Poet, *followed by* LUCILIUS, TITINIUS,
        and LUCIUS.

    Cas. How now ! what's the matter ?
    Poet. For shame, you generals ! what do
    you mean ?   130
Love, and be friends, as two such men should
    be ;
For I have seen more years, I'm sure, than ye.
    Cas. Ha, ha ! how vilely doth this cynic
    rhyme !
    Bru. Get you hence, sirrah ; saucy fellow,
    hence !
    Cas. Bear with him, Brutus ; 'tis his
    fashion.
    Bru. I'll know his humor, when he knows
    his time :

What should the wars do with these jigging
   fools ?
Companion, hence !
Cas.   Away, away, be gone !
                        [*Exit Poet.*
  Bru. Lucilius and Titinius, bid the com-
   manders
Prepare to lodge their companies to-night 140
  Cas. And come yourselves, and bring
   Messala with you
Immediately to us.
        [*Exeunt Lucilius and Titinius.*
  Bru. Lucius, a bowl of wine ! [*Exit Lucius.*
  Cas. I did not think you could have been
   so angry.
  Bru. O Cassius, I am sick of many griefs.
  Cas. Of your philosophy you make no use,
If you give place to accidental evils.
  Bru. No man bears sorrow better. Portia
   is dead.
  Cas. Ha ! Portia !
  Bru. She is dead.
  Cas. How 'scaped I killing when I cross'd
   you so ?   150
O insupportable and touching loss !
Upon what sickness ?
  Bru.   Impatient of my absence,
And grief that young Octavius with Mark
   Antony
Have made themselves so strong :—for with
   her death
That tidings came;—with this she fell distract,
And, her attendants absent, swallow'd fire.
  Cas. And died so ?
  Bru.   Even so.
  Cas.   O ye immortal gods !

Re-enter LUCIUS, *with wine and taper.*

  Bru. Speak no more of her. Give me a
   bowl of wine.
In this I bury all unkindness, Cassius.
  Cas. My heart is thirsty for that noble
   pledge.   160
Fill, Lucius, till the wine o'erswell the cup ;
I cannot drink too much of Brutus' love.
  Bru. Come in, Titinius !   [*Exit Lucius.*

Re-enter TITINIUS, *with* MESSALA.

          Welcome, good Messala.
Now sit we close about this taper here,
And call in question our necessities.
  Cas. Portia, art thou gone ?
  Bru.   No more, I pray you.
Messala, I have here received letters,
That young Octavius and Mark Antony
Come down upon us with a mighty power,
Bending their expedition toward Philippi. 170
  Mes. Myself have letters of the selfsame
   tenor.
  Bru. With what addition ?
  Mes. That by proscription and bills of out-
   lawry,
Octavius, Antony, and Lepidus,
Have put to death an hundred senators.
  Bru. Therein our letters do not well agree;
Mine speak of seventy senators that died

By their proscriptions, Cicero being one.
  Cas. Cicero one !
  Mes.   Cicero is dead,
And by that order of proscription.   180
Had you your letters from your wife, my lord ?
  Bru. No, Messala.
  Mes. Nor nothing in your letters writ of
   her ?
  Bru. Nothing, Messala.
  Mes.   That, methinks, is strange.
  Bru. Why ask you ? hear you aught of
   her in yours ?
  Mes. No, my lord.
  Bru. Now, as you are a Roman, tell me
   true.
  Mes. Then like a Roman bear the truth I
   tell :   [her.
For certain she is dead, and by strange man-
  Bru. Why, farewell, Portia. We must die,
   Messala :   190
With meditating that she must die once,
I have the patience to endure it now.
  Mes. Even so great men great losses should
   endure.
  Cas. I have as much of this in art as you,
But yet my nature could not bear it so.
  Bru. Well, to our work alive. What do
   you think ?
Of marching to Philippi presently ?
  Cas. I do not think it good.
  Bru.   Your reason ?
  Cas.   This it is :
'Tis better that the enemy seek us :
So shall he waste his means, weary his sol-
   diers,   200
Doing himself offence ; whilst we, lying still,
Are full of rest, defence, and nimbleness.
  Bru. Good reasons must, of force, give
   place to better.
The people 'twixt Philippi and this ground
Do stand but in a forced affection ;
For they have grudged us contribution :
The enemy, marching along by them,
By them shall make a fuller number up,
Come on refresh'd, new-added, and encour-
   aged ;
From which advantage shall we cut him off,
If at Philippi we do face him there,   211
These people at our back.
  Cas.   Hear me, good brother.
  Bru. Under your pardon. You must note
   beside,
That we have tried the utmost of our friends,
Our legions are brim-full, our cause is ripe :
The enemy increaseth every day ;
We, at the height, are ready to decline.
There is a tide in the affairs of men,
Which, taken at the flood, leads on to fortune;
Omitted, all the voyage of their life   200
Is bound in shallows and in miseries.
On such a full sea are we now afloat ;
And we must take the current when it serves,
Or lose our ventures.
  Cas.   Then, with your will, go on ;
We'll along ourselves, and meet them at
   Philippi.

Bru. The deep of night is crept upon our
talk,
And nature must obey necessity ;
Which we will niggard with a little rest
There is no more to say ?
Cas　　　　　　　No more.　Good night ·
Early to-morrow will we rise, and hence　230
Bru　Lucius ! [*Enter Lucius*] My gown
[*Exit Lucius.*] Farewell, good Messala .
Good night, Titinius　Noble, noble Cassius,
Good night, and good repose
Cas　　　　　O my dear brother !
This was an ill beginning of the night
Never come such division 'tween our souls !
Let it not, Brutus.
　Bru.　　　　　Every thing is well.
Cas　Good night, my lord
Bru.　　　　Good night, good brother
Tit. Mess　Good night, Lord Brutus
Bru.　　　　Farewell, every one
　　　　　　　　　[*Exeunt all but Brutus*

Re-enter LUCIUS, *with the gown*

Give me the gown　Where is thy instrument ?
Luc　Here in the tent
Bru.　What, thou speak'st drowsily ? 240
Poor knave, I blame thee not , thou art o'er-
　watch'd
Call Claudius and some other of my men
I'll have them sleep on cushions in my tent.
Luc　Varro and Claudius !

Enter VARRO *and* CLAUDIUS

Var.　Calls my lord ?
Bru.　I pray you, sirs, lie in my tent and
　sleep ;
It may be I shall raise you by and by
On business to my brother Cassius
Var.　So please you, we will stand and
　watch your pleasure.
Bru　I will not have it so : lie down, good
　sirs ;　　　　　　　　　　　250
It may be I shall otherwise bethink me
Look, Lucius, here's the book I sought for so ;
I put it in the pocket of my gown
　　　　　　　　[*Var and Clau lie down.*
Luc.　I was sure your lordship did not give
　it me
Bru.　Bear with me, good boy, I am much
　forgetful.
Canst thou hold up thy heavy eyes awhile,
And touch thy instrument a strain or two ?
Luc.　Ay, my lord, an't please you
Bru.　　　　　It does, my boy :
I trouble thee too much, but thou art willing
Luc.　It is my duty, sir　　　　　260
Bru.　I should not urge thy duty past thy
　might ,
I know young bloods look for a time of rest.
Luc.　I have slept, my lord, already
Bru.　It was well done ; and thou shalt
　sleep again ,
I will not hold thee long . if I do live,
I will be good to thee.　[*Music, and a song.*
This is a sleepy tune.　O murderous slumber,
Lay'st thou thy leaden mace upon my boy,

That plays thee music ?　Gentle knave, good
　night ;　　　　　　　　　　269
I will not do thee so much wrong to wake thee :
If thou dost nod, thou break'st thy instrument ;
I'll take it from thee , and, good boy, good
　night.
Let me see, let me see ; is not the leaf turn'd
　down
Where I left reading ?　Here it is, I think.

Enter the Ghost of CÆSAR.

How ill this taper burns !　Ha ! who comes
　here ?
I think it 's the weakness of mine eyes
That shapes this monstrous apparition.
It comes upon me　Art thou any thing ?
Art thou some god, some angel, or some devil,
That makest my blood cold and my hair to
　stare ?　　　　　　　　　　280
Speak to me what thou art
　Ghost.　Thy evil spirit, Brutus.
　Bru　Why comest thou ?
　Ghost　To tell thee thou shalt see me at
　　Philippi.
　Bru.　Well ; then I shall see thee again ?
　Ghost　Ay, at Philippi
　Bru.　Why, I will see thee at Philippi, then.
　　　　　　　　　　[*Exit Ghost.*
Now I have taken heart thou vanishest :
Ill spirit, I would hold more talk with thee
Boy, Lucius ! Varro ! Claudius ! Sirs, awake !
Claudius !　　　　　　　　　291
　Luc.　The strings, my lord, are false.
　Bru　He thinks he still is at his instrument.
Lucius, awake !
　Luc　My lord ?
　Bru.　Didst thou dream, Lucius, that thou
　　so criedst out ?
　Luc.　My lord, I do not know that I did cry.
　Bru.　Yes, that thou didst · didst thou see
　　any thing ?
　Luc　Nothing, my lord
　Bru　Sleep again, Lucius　Sirrah Clau-
　　dius !　　　　　　　　　300
[*To Var*] Fellow thou, awake !
　Var　My lord ?
　Clau.　My lord ?
　Bru.　Why did you so cry out, sirs, in your
　　sleep ?
　Var. Clau.　Did we, my lord ?
　Bru.　　　　Ay · saw you any thing ?
　Var.　No, my lord, I saw nothing.
　Clau.　　　　Nor I, my lord.
　Bru.　Go and commend me to my brother
　　Cassius ;
Bid him set on his powers betimes before,
And we will follow
　Var. Clau.　　It shall be done, my lord. 308
　　　　　　　　　　[*Exeunt.*

ACT V.

SCENE I.　*The plains of Philippi.*

Enter OCTAVIUS, ANTONY, *and their* army.

Oct.　Now, Antony, our hopes are answered

You said the enemy would not come down,
But keep the hills and upper regions ;
It proves not so . their battles are at hand ;
They mean to warn us at Philippi here,
Answering before we do demand of them
  Ant. Tut, I am in their bosoms, and I know
Wherefore they do it . they could be content
To visit other places ; and come down
With fearful bravery, thinking by this face 10
To fasten in our thoughts that they have cour-
    age ;
But 'tis not so.

    Enter a Messenger.
  Mess.   Prepare you, generals :
The enemy comes on in gallant show ;
Their bloody sign of battle is hung out,
And something to be done immediately.
  Ant. Octavius, lead your battle softly on,
Upon the left hand of the even field
  Oct Upon the right hand I ; keep thou the
    left
  Ant Why do you cross me in this exigent ?
  Oct. I do not cross you , but I will do so
                  [*March.* 20
Drum. Enter BRUTUS, CASSIUS, *and their*
  Army ; LUCILIUS, TITINIUS, MESSALA, *and*
  others.
  Bru. They stand. and would have parley
  Cas Stand fast, Titinius . we must out and
    talk.
  Oct Mark Antony, shall we give sign of
    battle ?
  Ant. No, Cæsar, we will answer on their
    charge.
Make forth , the generals would have some
    words
  Oct Stir not until the signal.
  Bru. Words before blows is it so, country-
    men ?
  Oct. Not that we love words better, as you
    do.
  Bru. Good words are better than bad
    strokes, Octavius.
  Ant. In your bad strokes, Brutus, you give
    good words :   30
Witness the hole you made in Cæsar's heart,
Crying 'Long live ! hail, Cæsar !'
  Cas   Antony,
The posture of your blows are yet unknown ;
But for your words, they rob the Hybla bees,
And leave them honeyless
  Ant   Not stingless too.
  Bru. O, yes, and soundless too ,
For you have stol'n their buzzing, Antony,
And very wisely threat before you sting
  Ant. Villains, you did not so, when your
    vile daggers
Hack'd one another in the sides of Cæsar · 40
You show'd your teeth like apes, and fawn'd
  like hounds,
And bow'd like bondmen, kissing Cæsar's feet,
Whilst damned Casca, like a cur, behind
Struck Cæsar on the neck. O you flatterers !
  Cas. Flatterers ! Now, Brutus, thank your-
    self ·

This tongue had not offended so to-day,
It Cassius might have ruled.
  Oct Come, come, the cause : if arguing
    make us sweat,
The proof of it will turn to redder drops.
Look ;   50
I draw a sword against conspirators ,
When think you that the sword goes up again?
Never, till Cæsar's three and thirty wounds
Be well avenged , or till another Cæsar
Have added slaughter to the sword of traitors
  Bru Cæsar, thou canst not die by traitors'
    hands,
Unless thou bring'st them with thee
  Oct   So I hope ,
I was not born to die on Brutus' sword
  Bru. O, if thou wert the noblest of thy
    strain,
Young man, thou couldst not die more honor-
    able   60
  Cas A peevish schoolboy, worthless of such
    honor,
Join'd with a masker and a reveller !
  Ant. Old Cassius still !
  Oct   Come, Antony, away !
Defiance. traitors, hurl we in your teeth
If you dare fight to-day, come to the field ;
If not, when you have stomachs
    [*Exeunt Octavius, Antony, and their army*
  Cas. Why, now, blow wind, swell billow
    and swim bark !
The storm is up, and all is on the hazard
  Bru Ho, Lucilius ! hark, a word with you.
  Lucil.   [*Standing forth*] My lord ?
      [*Brutus and Lucilius converse apart.*
  Cas. Messala !
  Mess [*Standing forth*] What says my gen-
    eral ?   70
  Cas Messala,
This is my birth-day ; as this very day
Was Cassius born Give me thy hand, Mes-
    sala .
Be thou my witness that against my will,
As Pompey was, am I compell'd to set
Upon one battle all our liberties.
You know that I held Epicurus strong
And his opinion · now I change my mind,
And partly credit things that do presage.
Coming from Sardis, on our former ensign 80
Two mighty eagles fell, and there they perch'd,
Gorging and feeding from our soldiers' hands ;
Who to Philippi here consorted us ·
This morning are they fled away and gone ;
And in their steads do ravens, crows and kites,
Fly o'er our heads and downward look on us,
As we were sickly prey then shadows seem
A canopy most fatal, under which
Our army lies, ready to give up the ghost.
  Mes Believe not so
  Cas.   I but believe it partly ; 90
For I am fresh of spirit and resolved
To meet all perils very constantly.
  Bru. Even so, Lucilius.
  Cas.   Now, most noble Brutus,
The gods to-day stand friendly, that we may,
Lovers in peace. lead on our days to age !

41

But since the affairs of men rest still incertain,
Let's reason with the worst that may befall.
If we do lose this battle, then is this
The very last time we shall speak together :
What are you then determined to do ?   100
   Bru. Even by the rule of that philosophy
By which I did blame Cato for the death
Which he did give himself, I know not how,
But I do find it cowardly and vile,
For fear of what might fall, so to prevent
The time of life : arming myself with patience
To stay the providence of some high powers
That govern us below.
   Cas.   Then, if we lose this battle,
You are contented to be led in triumph
Thorough the streets of Rome ?   110
   Bru. No, Cassius, no : think not, thou noble
     Roman,
That ever Brutus will go bound to Rome ;
He bears too great a mind. But this same day
Must end that work the ides of March begun ;
And whether we shall meet again I know not.
Therefore our everlasting farewell take :
For ever, and for ever, farewell, Cassius !
If we do meet again, why, we shall smile ;
If not, why then, this parting was well made.
   Cas. For ever, and for ever, farewell, Brutus!
If we do meet again, we'll smile indeed ;   121
If not, 'tis true this parting was well made.
   Bru. Why, then, lead on. O, that a man
     might know
The end of this day's business ere it come !
But it sufficeth that the day will end,
And then the end is known. Come, ho ! away !
                  [*Exeunt.*

SCENE II.   *The same. The field of battle.*

Alarum. Enter BRUTUS *and* MESSALA.

   Bru. Ride, ride, Messala, ride, and give these
     bills
Unto the legions on the other side.
                  [*Loud alarum.*
Let them set on at once ; for I perceive
But cold demeanor in Octavius' wing,
And sudden push gives them the overthrow.
Ride, ride, Messala : let them all come down.
                  [*Exeunt.*

SCENE III.   *Another part of the field.*

Alarums. Enter CASSIUS *and* TITINIUS.

   Cas. O, look, Titinius, look, the villains fly!
Myself have to mine own turn'd enemy :
This ensign here of mine was turning back ;
I slew the coward, and did take it from him.
   Tit. O Cassius, Brutus gave the word too
     early ;
Who, having some advantage on Octavius,
Took it too eagerly : his soldiers fell to spoil,
Whilst we by Antony are all enclosed.

Enter PINDARUS.

   Pin. Fly further off, my lord, fly further
     off ;
Mark Antony is in your tents, my lord :   10
Fly, therefore, noble Cassius, fly far off.

   Cas. This hill is far enough. Look, look,
     Titinius ;
Are those my tents where I perceive the fire ?
   Tit. They are, my lord.
   Cas.   Titinius, if thou lovest me,
Mount thou my horse, and hide thy spurs in
     him,
Till he have brought thee up to yonder troops,
And here again ; that I may rest assured
Whether yond troops are friend or enemy.
   Tit. I will be here again, even with a
     thought.   [*Exit.*   19
   Cas. Go, Pindarus, get higher on that hill ;
My sight was ever thick ; regard Titinius,
And tell me what thou notest about the field.
              [*Pindarus ascends the hill.*
This day I breathed first : time is come round,
And where I did begin, there shall I end ;
My life is run his compass. Sirrah, what
     news ?
   Pin. [*Above*] O my lord !
   Cas. What news ?
   Pin. [*Above*] Titinius is enclosed round
     about
With horsemen, that make to him on the spur;
Yet he spurs on. Now they are almost on
     him.   30
Now, Titinius ! Now some light. O, he lights
     too.   [for joy.
He's ta'en. [*Shout.*] And, hark ! they shout
   Cas. Come down, behold no more.
O, coward that I am, to live so long,
To see my best friend ta'en before my face !

PINDARUS *descends.*

Come hither, sirrah :
In Parthia did I take thee prisoner ;
And then I swore thee, saving of thy life,
That whatsoever I did bid thee do,
Thou shouldst attempt it. Come now, keep
     thine oath ;   40
Now be a freeman : and with this good sword,
That ran through Cæsar's bowels, search this
     bosom.
Stand not to answer : here, take thou the
     hilts ;
And, when my face is cover'd, as 'tis now,
Guide thou the sword. [*Pindarus stabs him.*]
     Cæsar, thou art revenged,
Even with the sword that kill'd thee.   [*Dies.*
   Pin. So, I am free ; yet would not so have
     been,
Durst I have done my will. O Cassius,
Far from this country Pindarus shall run,
Where never Roman shall take note of him. 50
                  [*Exit.*

Re-enter TITINIUS *with* MESSALA.

   Mes. It is but change, Titinius ; for Octa-
     vius
Is overthrown by noble Brutus' power,
As Cassius' legions are by Antony.
   Tit. These tidings will well comfort
     Cassius.
   Mes. Where did you leave him ?
   Tit.   All disconsolate,
With Pindarus his bondman, on this hill.

Mes. Is not that he that lies upon the ground ?
Tit. He lies not like the living. O my heart !
Mes. Is not that he ?
Tit.   No, this was he, Messala,
But Cassius is no more. O setting sun, 60
As in thy red rays thou dost sink to-night,
So in his red blood Cassius' day is set ;
The sun of Rome is set ! Our day is gone ;
Clouds, dews, and dangers come ; our deeds are done !
Mistrust of my success hath done this deed.
Mes. Mistrust of good success hath done this deed.
O hateful error, melancholy's child,
Why dost thou show to the apt thoughts of men   [ceived.
The things that are not ? O error, soon con-
Thou never comest unto a happy birth, 70
But kill'st the mother that engender'd thee !
Tit. What, Pindarus ! where art thou, Pindarus ?
Mes. Seek him, Titinius, whilst I go to meet
The noble Brutus, thrusting this report
Into his ears ; I may say, thrusting it ;
For piercing steel and darts envenomed
Shall be as welcome to the ears of Brutus
As tidings of this sight.
Tit.   Hie you, Messala,
And I will seek for Pindarus the while.
[*Exit Messala.*
Why didst thou send me forth, brave Cassius ?
Did I not meet thy friends ? and did not they
Put on my brows this wreath of victory,
And bid me give it thee ? Didst thou not hear their shouts ?
Alas, thou hast misconstrued every thing !
But, hold thee, take this garland on thy brow ;
Thy Brutus bid me give it thee, and I
Will do his bidding. Brutus, come apace,
And see how I regarded Caius Cassius.
By your leave, gods :—this is a Roman's part :
Come ; Cassius' sword, and find Titinius' heart.   [*Kills himself.* 90

Alarum. Re-enter MESSALA, *with* BRUTUS, *young* CATO, STRATO, VOLUMNIUS, *and* LUCILIUS.

Bru. Where, where, Messala, doth his body lie ?
Mes. Lo, yonder, and Titinius mourning it
Bru. Titinius' face is upward.
Cato.   He is slain.
Bru. O Julius Cæsar, thou art mighty yet !
Thy spirit walks abroad, and turns our swords
In our own proper entrails. [*Low alarums.*
Cato.   Brave Titinius !
Look, whether he have not crown'd dead Cassius !
Bru. Are yet two Romans living such as these ?
The last of all the Romans, fare thee well !
It is impossible that ever Rome 100

Should breed thy fellow. Friends, I owe more tears
To this dead man than you shall see me pay.
I shall find time, Cassius, I shall find time.
Come, therefore, and to Thasos send his body :
His funerals shall not be in our camp,
Lest it discomfort us. Lucilius, come ;
And come, young Cato ; let us to the field.
Labeo and Flavius, set our battles on :
'Tis three o'clock ; and, Romans, yet ere night
We shall try fortune in a second fight.
[*Exeunt.*

SCENE IV. *Another part of the field.*

Alarum. Enter fighting, Soldiers *of both armies ; then* BRUTUS, *young* CATO, LUCILIUS, *and others.*

Bru. Yet, countrymen, O, yet hold up your heads !
Cato. What bastard doth not ? Who will go with me ?
I will proclaim my name about the field :
I am the son of Marcus Cato, ho !
A foe to tyrants, and my country's friend ;
I am the son of Marcus Cato, ho !
Bru. And I am Brutus, Marcus Brutus, I ;
Brutus, my country's friend ; know me for Brutus !   [*Exit.*
Lucil. O young and noble Cato, art thou down ?
Why, now thou diest as bravely as Titinius ;
And mayst be honor'd, being Cato's son. 11
First Sold. Yield, or thou diest.
Lucil.   Only I yield to die :
There is so much that thou wilt kill me straight ;   [*Offering money.*
Kill Brutus, and be honor'd in his death.
First Sold. We must not. A noble prisoner !
Sec. Sold. Room, ho ! Tell Antony, Brutus is ta'en.   [the general.
First Sold. I'll tell the news. Here comes

Enter ANTONY.

Brutus is ta'en, Brutus is ta'en, my lord.
Ant. Where is he ?
Lucil. Safe, Antony ; Brutus is safe enough :
I dare assure thee that no enemy 21
Shall ever take alive the noble Brutus :
The gods defend him from so great a shame !
When you do find him, or alive or dead,
He will be found like Brutus, like himself.
Ant. This is not Brutus, friend ; but, I assure you,
A prize no less in worth : keep this man safe ;
Give him all kindness : I had rather have
Such men my friends than enemies. Go on,
And see whether Brutus be alive or dead ; 30
And bring us word unto Octavius' tent
How every thing is chanced.   [*Exeunt.*

SCENE V. *Another part of the field.*

Enter BRUTUS, DARDANIUS, CLITUS, STRATO, *and* VOLUMNIUS.

Bru. Come, poor remains of friends, rest on this rock.

Cli. Statilius show'd the torch-light, but,
　my lord,
He came not back · he is or ta'en or slain
Bru. Sit thee down, Clitus . slaying is the
　word ,
It is a deed in fashion. Hark thee, Clitus.
　　　　　　　　　　　　[*Whispers*
Cli What, I, my lord ? No, not for all the
　world
Bru Peace then ! no words.
Cli. 　　　　　　I'll rather kill myself.
Bru Hark thee, Dardanius　　[*Whispers*
Dar. 　　　　Shall I do such a deed ?
Cli. O Dardanius !
Dar O Clitus !　　　　　　　　　10
Cli. What ill request did Brutus make to
　thee ?
Dar. To kill him, Clitus Look, he
　meditates.
Cli Now is that noble vessel full of grief,
That it runs over even at his eyes.
Bru. Come hither, good Volumnius , list
　a word.
Vol. What says my lord ?
Bru 　　　　　Why, this, Volumnius :
The ghost of Cæsar hath appear'd to me
Two several times by night ; at Sardis once,
And, this last night, here in Philippi fields :
I know my hour is come.
Vol. 　　　　　Not so, my lord. 20
Bru Nay, I am sure it is, Volumnius.
Thou seest the world, Volumnius, how it goes,
Our enemies have beat us to the pit
　　　　　　　　　[*Low alarums*
It is more worthy to leap in ourselves,
Than tarry till they push us. Good Volum-
　nius,
Thou know'st that we two went to school to-
　gether .
Even for that our love of old, I prithee,
Hold thou my sword-hilts, whilst I run on it
Vol. That's not an office for a friend, my
　lord　　　　　　[*Alarum still.*
Cli Fly, fly, my lord ; there is no tarrying
　here. 　　　　　　　　　　30
Bru. Farewell to you ; and you ; and you,
　Volumnius
Strato thou hast been all this while asleep ;
Farewell to thee too, Strato　Countrymen,
My heart doth joy that yet in all my life
I found no man but he was true to me.
I shall have glory by this losing day
More than Octavius and Mark Antony
By this vile conquest shall attain unto
So fare you well at once ; for Brutus' tongue
Hath almost ended his life's history · 　40
Night hangs upon mine eyes ; my bones
　would rest,

That have but labor'd to attain this hour.
　　[*Alarum. Cry within,* ' Fly, fly, fly !'
Cli Fly, my lord, fly.
Bru. 　　　　Hence ! I will follow
　[*Exeunt Clitus, Dardanius, and Volumnius*
I prithee, Strato, stay thou by thy lord :
Thou art a fellow of a good respect ;
Thy life hath had some smatch of honor in it :
Hold then my sword, and turn away thy face,
While I do run upon it　Wilt thou, Strato ?
Stra Give me your hand first. Fare you
　well, my lord.
Bru. Farewell, good Strato. [*Runs on his
　sword*] Cæsar, now be still : 　　　50
I kill'd not thee with half so good a will.
　　　　　　　　　　　　　[*Dies.*

Alarum. Retreat Enter OCTAVIUS, ANTONY,
　MESSALA, LUCILIUS, *and the army.*

Oct What man is that ?
Mes My master's man. Strato, where is
　thy master ?
Stra Free from the bondage you are in,
　Messala :
The conquerors can but make a fire of him ;
For Brutus only overcame himself,
And no man else hath honor by his death.
Lucil So Brutus should be found　I thank
　thee, Brutus,
That thou hast proved Lucilius' saying true
Oct. All that served Brutus, I will entertain
　them. 　　　　　　　　　60
Fellow, wilt thou bestow thy time with me ?
Stra. Ay, if Messala will prefer me to you.
Oct. Do so, good Messala.
Mes How died my master Strato ?
Stra I held the sword, and he did run on
　it.
Mes. Octavius, then take him to follow
　thee,
That did the latest service to my master
Ant This was the noblest Roman of them
　all :
All the conspirators save only he
Did that they did in envy of great Cæsar ; 70
He only, in a general honest thought
And common good to all, made one of them.
His life was gentle, and the elements
So mix'd in him that Nature might stand up
And say to all the world ' This was a man !'
Oct According to his virtue let us use him,
With all respect and rites of burial.
Within my tent his bones to-night shall lie,
Most like a soldier, order'd honorably.
So call the field to rest ; and let's away, 　80
To part the glories of this happy day.
　　　　　　　　　　　　[*Exeunt.*

HAMLET,

(WRITTEN ABOUT 1602.)

INTRODUCTION.

Hamlet represents the mid period of the growth of Shakespeare's genius, when comedy and history ceased to be adequate for the expression of his deeper thoughts and sadder feelings about life, and when he was just entering upon his great series of tragic writings. In July, 1602, the printer Roberts entered in the Stationers' register, "The Revenge of Hamlet, Prince of Denmark, as y* latelie was acted by the Lord Chamberlain his servantes," and in the next year the play was printed. The true relation of this first quarto of *Hamlet* to the second quarto, published in 1604—"newly imprinted, and enlarged to almost as much againe as it was"—is a matter in dispute. It is believed by some critics that the quarto of 1603 is merely an imperfect report of the play as we find it in the edition of the year after; but there are some material differences which cannot thus be explained. In the earlier quarto, instead of Polonius and Reynaldo, we find the names Corambis and Montano, the order of certain scenes varies from that of the later quarto, "the madness of Hamlet is much more pronounced, and the Queen's innocence of her husband's murder much more explicitly stated." We are forced to believe either that the earlier quarto contains portions of an old play by some other writer than Shakespeare—an opinion adopted on apparently insufficient grounds by some recent editor—or that it represents imperfectly Shakespeare's first draught of the play, and that the difference between it and the second quarto is due to Shakespeare's revision of his own work. This last opinion seems to be the true one, but the value of any comparison between the two quartos, with a view to understand Shakespeare's manner of rehandling his work, is greatly diminished by the fact that numerous gaps of the imperfect report given in the earlier quarto seem to have been filled in by a stupid stage hack. That an old play on the subject of Hamlet existed there can be no doubt, it is referred to in 1589 (perhaps in 1587) by Nash, in his *Epistle* prefixed to Greene's *Menaphon*, and again in 1596 by Lodge (*Wit's Miserie and the World's Madnesse*), where he alludes to "the vizard of the Ghost which cried so miserably at the Theator, like an oister wife, 'Hamlet, revenge'." A German play on the subject of Hamlet exists which is supposed to have been acted by English players in Germany in 1603, the name Corambus appears in it, and it is possible that portions of the old pre-Shakespearean drama are contained in the German *Hamlet*. The old play may have been one of the bloody tragedies of revenge among which we find *Titus Andronicus* and *The Spanish Tragedy*, and it would be characteristic of Shakespeare that he should refine the motives and spirit of the drama, so as to make the duty of vengeance laid upon Hamlet a painful burden which he is hardly able to support. Besides the old play of Hamlet, Shakespeare had probably before him the prose *Hystorie of Hamblet* (though no edition exists earlier than 1608), translated from Belleforest's *Histoires Tragiques*. The story had been told some hundreds of years previously in the *Historia Danica* of Saxo Grammaticus (about 1180–1208). The Hamlet of the *Hystorie*, after a fierce revenge, becomes King of Denmark, marries two wives, and finally dies in battle.

No play of Shakespeare's has had a higher power of interesting spectators and readers, and none has given rise to a greater variety of conflicting interpretations. It has been rightly named a tragedy of thought, and in this respect, as well as others, takes its place beside *Julius Cæsar*. Neither Brutus nor Hamlet is the victim of an overmastering passion as are the chief persons of the later tragedies—e.g. Othello, Macbeth, Coriolanus. The burden of a terrible duty is laid upon each of them, and neither is fitted for bearing such a burden. Brutus is disqualified for action by his moral idealism, his student-like habits, his capacity for dealing with abstractions rather than with men and things. Hamlet is disqualified for action by his excess of the reflective tendency, and by his unstable will, which alternates between complete inactivity and fits of excited energy. Naturally sensitive, he receives a painful shock from the hasty second marriage of his mother, already the springs of faith and joy in his nature are embittered, then follows the terrible discovery of his father's murder, with the injunction laid upon him to revenge the crime, upon this again follow the repulses which he receives from Ophelia. A deep melancholy lays hold of his spirit, and all of life grows dark and sad to his vision. Although hating his father's murderer, he has little heart to push on his revenge. He is aware that he is suspected and surrounded by spies. Partly to baffle them, partly to create a veil behind which to seclude his true self, partly because his whole moral nature is indeed deeply disordered, he assumes the part of one whose wits have gone astray. Except for one loyal friend, he is alone among enemies or supposed traitors. Ophelia he regards as no more loyal or honest to him than his mother had been to her dead husband. The ascertainment of Claudius's guilt by means of the play still leaves him incapable of the last decisive act of vengeance. Not so, however, with the king, who now recognizing his foe in Hamlet, does not delay to despatch him to a bloody death in England. But there is in Hamlet a terrible power of sudden and desperate action. From the melancholy which broods over him after the burial of Ophelia he rouses himself to the play of swords with Laertes, and at the last, with strength which leaps up before its final extinction, he accomplishes the punishment of the malefactor. Horatio, with his fortitude, his self-possession, his strong equanimity is a contrast to the Prince. And Laertes, who takes violent measures at the shortest notice to revenge *his* father's murder, is in another way a contrast; but Laertes is the young gallant of the period, and his capacity for action arises in part from the absence of those moral checks of which Hamlet is sensible. Polonius is owner of the shallow wisdom of this world, and exhibits this grotesquely while now on the brink of dotage, he sees, but cannot see through Hamlet's ironical mockery of him. Ophelia is tender, sensitive, affectionate, but the reverse of heroic, she fails Hamlet in his need, and then in her turn becoming the sufferer, gives way under the pressure of her afflictions. We do not honor, we only commiserate her.

(645)

DRAMATIS PERSONÆ.

CLAUDIUS, king of Denmark.
HAMLET, son to the late, and nephew to the present king.
POLONIUS, lord chamberlain.
HORATIO, friend to Hamlet.
LAERTES, son to Polonius.
VOLTIMAND,
CORNELIUS,
ROSENCRANTZ,   } courtiers.
GUILDENSTERN,
OSRIC,
A Gentleman,
A Priest.
MARCELLUS, } officers.
BERNARDO,
FRANCISCO, a soldier.

REYNALDO, servant to Polonius.
Players.
Two Clowns, grave-diggers.
FORTINBRAS, prince of Norway.
A Captain.
English Ambassadors.

GERTRUDE, queen of Denmark, and mother to Hamlet.
OPHELIA, daughter to Polonius.

Lords, Ladies, Officers, Soldiers, Sailors, Messengers, and other Attendants.

Ghost of Hamlet's Father.

SCENE : *Denmark.*

ACT I.

SCENE I. *Elsinore. A platform before the castle.*

FRANCISCO *at his post. Enter to him* BERNARDO.

Ber. Who's there?
Fran. Nay, answer me : stand, and unfold yourself.
Ber. Long live the king !
Fran. Bernardo ?
Ber. He.
Fran. You come most carefully upon your hour.
Ber. 'Tis now struck twelve ; get thee to bed, Francisco.
Fran. For this relief much thanks : 'tis bitter cold,
And I am sick at heart.
Ber. Have you had quiet guard ?
Fran. Not a mouse stirring.   10
Ber. Well, good night.
If you do meet Horatio and Marcellus,
The rivals of my watch, bid them make haste.
Fran. I think I hear them. Stand, ho !
Who's there ?

Enter HORATIO *and* MARCELLUS

Hor. Friends to this ground.
Mar.   And liegemen to the Dane.
Fran. Give you good night.
Mar.   O, farewell, honest soldier:
Who hath relieved you?
Fran.   Bernardo has my place.
Give you good night.   [*Exit.*
Mar.   Holla ! Bernardo !
Ber.   Say,
What, is Horatio there ?
Hor.   A piece of him.
Ber. Welcome, Horatio : welcome, good Marcellus.   20
Mar. What, has this thing appear'd again to-night ?
Ber. I have seen nothing.

Mar. Horatio says 'tis but our fantasy,
And will not let belief take hold of him
Touching this dreaded sight, twice seen of us :
Therefore I have entreated him along
With us to watch the minutes of this night ;
That if again this apparition come,
He may approve our eyes and speak to it.
Hor. Tush, tush, 'twill not appear.
Ber.   Sit down awhile ;   30
And let us once again assail your ears,
That are so fortified against our story
What we have two nights seen.
Hor.   Well, sit we down,
And let us hear Bernardo speak of this.
Ber. Last night of all,
When yond same star that's westward from the pole
Had made his course to illume that part of heaven
Where now it burns, Marcellus and myself,
The bell then beating one,—

Enter Ghost.

Mar. Peace, break thee off ; look, where it comes again !   40
Ber. In the same figure, like the king that's dead.
Mar. Thou art a scholar ; speak to it, Horatio.
Ber. Looks it not like the king ? mark it, Horatio.
Hor. Most like : it harrows me with fear and wonder.
Ber. It would be spoke to.
Mar.   Question it, Horatio.
Hor. What art thou that usurp'st this time of night,
Together with that fair and warlike form
In which the majesty of buried Denmark
Did sometimes march ? by heaven I charge thee, speak !
Mar. It is offended.
Ber.   See, it stalks away !   50
Hor. Stay ! speak, speak ! I charge thee, speak !   [*Exit Ghost.*

Mar. 'Tis gone, and will not answer.

Ber. How now, Horatio! you tremble and look pale :

Is not this something more than fantasy ?

What think you on't ?

Hor. Before my God, I might not this believe

Without the sensible and true avouch

Of mine own eyes.

Mar.   Is it not like the king ?

Hor. As thou art to thyself :

Such was the very armor he had on   60

When he the ambitious Norway combated ;

So frown'd he once, when, in an angry parle,

He smote the sledded Polacks on the ice.

'Tis strange.

Mar. Thus twice before, and jump at this dead hour,

With martial stalk hath he gone by our watch.

Hor. In what particular thought to work I know not ;

But in the gross and scope of my opinion,

This bodes some strange eruption to our state.

Mar Good now, sit down, and tell me, he that knows,   70

Why this same strict and most observant watch

So nightly toils the subject of the land,

And why such daily cast of brazen cannon,

And foreign mart for implements of war ;

Why such impress of shipwrights, whose sore task

Does not divide the Sunday from the week ;

What might be toward, that this sweaty haste

Doth make the night joint-laborer with the day :

Who is't that can inform me ?

Hor.   That can I ;

At least, the whisper goes so. Our last king,

Whose image even but now appear'd to us,   81

Was, as you know, by Fortinbras of Norway,

Thereto prick'd on by a most emulate pride,

Dared to the combat ; in which our valiant Hamlet—

For so this side of our known world esteem'd him—

Did slay this Fortinbras ; who by a seal'd compact,

Well ratified by law and heraldry,

Did forfeit, with his life, all those his lands

Which he stood seized of, to the conqueror :

Against the which, a moiety competent   90

Was gaged by our king ; which had return'd

To the inheritance of Fortinbras,

Had he been vanquisher ; as, by the same covenant,

And carriage of the article design'd,

His fell to Hamlet. Now, sir, young Fortinbras,

Of unimproved mettle hot and full,

Hath in the skirts of Norway here and there

Shark'd up a list of lawless resolutes,

For food and diet, to some enterprise

That hath a stomach in't ; which is no other—   101

As it doth well appear unto our state—

But to recover of us, by strong hand

And terms compulsatory, those foresaid lands

So by his father lost : and this, I take it,

Is the main motive of our preparations,

The source of this our watch and the chief head

Of this post-haste and romage in the land.

Ber. I think it be no other but e'en so :

Well may it sort that this portentous figure

Comes armed through our watch ; so like the king   110

That was and is the question of these wars.

Hor. A mote it is to trouble the mind's eye.

In the most high and palmy state of Rome,

A little ere the mightiest Julius fell,

The graves stood tenantless and the sheeted dead

Did squeak and gibber in the Roman streets :

†As stars with trains of fire and dews of blood,

Disasters in the sun ; and the moist star

Upon whose influence Neptune's empire stands

Was sick almost to doomsday with eclipse : 120

And even the like precurse of fierce events,

As harbingers preceding still the fates

And prologue to the omen coming on,

Have heaven and earth together demonstrated

Unto our climatures and countrymen.—

But soft, behold ! lo, where it comes again !

Re-enter Ghost.

I'll cross it, though it blast me. Stay, illusion!

If thou hast any sound, or use of voice,

Speak to me :

If there be any good thing to be done,   130

That may to thee do ease and grace to me,

Speak to me :   [*Cock crows.*

If thou art privy to thy country's fate,

Which, happily, foreknowing may avoid,

O, speak !

Or if thou hast uphoarded in thy life

Extorted treasure in the womb of earth,

For which, they say, you spirits oft walk in death,

Speak of it : stay, and speak ! Stop it, Marcellus.

Mar. Shall I strike at it with my partisan ?

Hor. Do, if it will not stand.   141

Ber.   'Tis here !

Hor.   'Tis here !

Mar. 'Tis gone !   [*Exit Ghost.*

We do it wrong, being so majestical,

To offer it the show of violence ;

For it is, as the air, invulnerable,

And our vain blows malicious mockery.

Ber. It was about to speak, when the cock crew.

Hor. And then it started like a guilty thing

Upon a fearful summons. I have heard,

The cock, that is the trumpet to the morn,   150

Doth with his lofty and shrill-sounding throat

Awake the god of day ; and, at his warning,

Whether in sea or fire, in earth or air,

The extravagant and erring spirit hies

To his confine : and of the truth herein

This present object made probation.

Mar. It faded on the crowing of the cock.

Some say that ever 'gainst that season comes

Wherein our Saviour's birth is celebrated,   159

The bird of dawning singeth all night long :

And then, they say, no spirit dares stir abroad;
The nights are wholesome ; then no planets
    strike,
No fairy takes, nor witch hath power to charm,
So hallow'd and so gracious is the time.
    Hor. So have I heard and do in part be-
    lieve it.
But, look, the morn, in russet mantle clad,
Walks o'er the dew of you high eastward hill:
Break we our watch up; and by my advice,
Let us impart what we have seen to-night
Unto young Hamlet ; for, upon my life,   170
This spirit, dumb to us, will speak to him.
Do you consent we shall acquaint him with it,
As needful in our loves, fitting our duty ?
    Mar. Let's do't, I pray ; and I this morn-
    ing know
Where we shall find him most conveniently.
                                    [*Exeunt.*

SCENE II.   *A room of state in the castle.*

Enter the KING, QUEEN, HAMLET, POLONIUS,
    LAERTES, VOLTIMAND, CORNELIUS, Lords,
    and Attendants.

    King. Though yet of Hamlet our dear bro-
    ther's death
The memory be green, and that it us befitted
To bear our hearts in grief and our whole
    kingdom,
To be contracted in one brow of woe,
Yet so far hath discretion fought with nature
That we with wisest sorrow think on him,
Together with remembrance of ourselves,
Therefore our sometime sister, now our queen,
The imperial jointress to this warlike state
Have we, as 'twere with a defeated joy,—   10
With an auspicious and a dropping eye,
With mirth in funeral and with dirge in mar-
    riage,
In equal scale weighing delight and dole,—
Taken to wife : nor have we herein barr'd
Your better wisdoms, which have freely gone
With this affair along.   For all, our thanks.
Now follows, that you know, young Fortinbras,
Holding a weak supposal of our worth,
Or thinking by our late dear brother's death
Our state to be disjoint and out of frame,   20
Colleagued with the dream of his advantage,
He hath not fail'd to pester us with message,
Importing the surrender of those lands
Lost by his father, with all bonds of law,
To our most valiant brother. So much for him.
Now for ourself and for this time of meeting :
Thus much the business is : we have here writ
To Norway, uncle of young Fortinbras,—
Who, impotent and bed-rid, scarcely hears
Of this his nephew's purpose,—to suppress 30
His further gait herein ; in that the levies,
The lists and full proportions, are all made
Out of his subject : and we here dispatch
You, good Cornelius, and you, Voltimand,
For bearers of this greeting to old Norway
Giving to you no further personal power
To business with the king, more than the scope
Of these delated articles allow,

Farewell, and let your haste commend your
    duty.
    Cor. ⎱ In that and all things will we show
    Vol. ⎰   our duty.   40
    King. We doubt it nothing : heartily fare-
    well.
            [*Exeunt Voltimand and Cornelius.*
And now, Laertes, what's the news with you?
You told us of some suit ; what is't, Laertes ?
You cannot speak of reason to the Dane,
And loose your voice : what wouldst thou beg,
    Laertes,
That shall not be my offer, not thy asking ?
The head is not more native to the heart,
The hand more instrumental to the mouth,
Than is the throne of Denmark to thy father.
What wouldst thou have, Laertes ?
    Laer.   My dread lord,   50
Your leave and favor to return to France ;
From whence though willingly I came to Den-
    mark,
To show my duty in your coronation,
Yet now, I must confess, that duty done,
My thoughts and wishes bend again toward
    France
And bow them to your gracious leave and
    pardon.
    King. Have you your father's leave ? What
    says Polonius ?
    Pol. He hath, my lord, wrung from me my
    slow leave
By laborsome petition, and at last
Upon his will I seal'd my hard consent :   60
I do beseech you, give him leave to go.
    King. Take thy fair hour, Laertes ; time be
    thine,
And thy best graces spend it at thy will !
But now, my cousin Hamlet, and my son,—
    Ham. [*Aside*] A little more than kin, and
    less than kind.
    King. How is it that the clouds still hang
    on you ?
    Ham. Not so, my lord ; I am too much i'
    the sun.
    Queen. Good Hamlet, cast thy nighted color
    off,
And let thine eye look like a friend on Den-
    mark.
Do not for ever with thy vailed lids   70
Seek for thy noble father in the dust :
Thou know'st 'tis common ; all that lives must
    die,
Passing through nature to eternity.
    Ham. Ay, madam, it is common.
    Queen.   If it be,
Why seems it so particular with thee ?
    Ham. Seems, madam ! nay it is ; I know
    not 'seems.'
'Tis not alone my inky cloak, good mother,
Nor customary suits of solemn black,
Nor windy suspiration of forced breath,
No, nor the fruitful river in the eye,   80
Nor the dejected 'havior of the visage,
Together with all forms, moods, shapes of
    grief,
That can denote me truly : these indeed seem,

For they are actions that a man might play :
But I have that within which passeth show ;
These but the trappings and the suits of woe.
   King.   'Tis sweet and commendable in your
     nature, Hamlet;
To give these mourning duties to your father :
But, you must know, your father lost a father ;
That father lost, lost his, and the survivor
   bound'   90
In filial obligation for some term
To do obsequious sorrow : but to persever
In obstinate condolement is a course
Of impious stubbornness ; 'tis unmanly grief ;
It shows a will most incorrect to heaven,
A heart unfortified, a mind impatient,
An understanding simple and unschool'd :
For what we know must be and is as common
As any the most vulgar thing to sense,
Why should we in our peevish opposition 100
Take it to heart ? Fie ! 'tis a fault to heaven,
A fault against the dead, a fault to nature,
To reason most absurd : whose common theme
Is death of fathers, and who still hath cried,
From the first corse till he that died to-day,
'This must be so.' We pray you, throw to
   earth
This unprevailing woe, and think of us
As of a father : for let the world take note,
You are the most immediate to our throne ;
And with no less nobility of love   110
Than that which dearest father bears his son,
Do I impart toward you. For your intent
In going back to school in Wittenburg,
It is most retrograde to our desire :
And we beseech you, bend you to remain
Here, in the cheer and comfort of our eye,
Our chiefest courtier, cousin, and our son.
   Queen.   Let not thy mother lose her prayers,
     Hamlet:
I pray thee, stay with us ; go not to Wittenberg.
   Ham.   I shall in all my best obey you,
     madam
   King.   Why, 'tis a loving and a fair reply :
Be as ourself in Denmark. Madam, come ;
This gentle and unforced accord of Hamlet
Sits smiling to my heart : in grace whereof,
No jocund health that Denmark drinks to-day,
But the great cannon to the clouds shall tell,
And the king's rouse the heavens shall bruit
   again,
Re-speaking earthly thunder. Come away.
                [*Exeunt all but Hamlet.*
   Ham.   O, that this too too solid flesh would
     melt,
Thaw and resolve itself into a dew !   130
Or that the Everlasting had not fix'd
His canon 'gainst self-slaughter ! O God! God!
How weary, stale, flat and unprofitable,
Seem to me all the uses of this world !
Fie on't ! ah fie ! 'tis an unweeded garden,
That grows to seed ; things rank and gross in
   nature
Possess it merely. That it should come to this!,
But two months dead : nay, not so much, not
   two :
So excellent a king ; that was, to this,   139

Hyperion to a satyr ; so loving to my mother
That he might not beteem the winds of heaven
Visit her face too roughly. Heaven and earth!
Must I remember ? why, she would hang on
   him,
As if increase of appetite had grown
By what it fed on : and yet, within a month—
Let me not think on't—Frailty, thy name is
   woman !—
A little month, or ere those shoes were old
With which she follow'd my poor father's
   body,
Like Niobe, all tears :—why she, even she—
O God ! a beast, that wants discourse of rea-
   son,   150
Would have mourn'd longer—married with my
   uncle,
My father's brother, but no more like my father
Than I to Hercules : within a month :
Ere yet the salt of most unrighteous tears
Had left the flushing in her galled eyes,
She married. O, most wicked speed, to post
With such dexterity to incestuous sheets !
It is not nor it cannot come to good :
But break, my heart ; for I must hold my
   tongue.

Enter Horatio, Marcellus, *and* Bernardo,

   Hor.   Hail to your lordship !
   Ham.   I am glad to see you well: 160
Horatio,—or I do forget myself.
   Hor.   The same, my lord, and your poor
     servant ever.
   Ham.   Sir, my good friend ; I'll change that
     name with you :   [tio ?
And what make you from Wittenberg, Hora-
Marcellus ?
   Mar.   My good lord—
   Ham.   I am very glad to see you. Good
     even, sir.
But what, in faith, make you from Wittenberg?
   Hor.   A truant disposition, good my lord.
   Ham.   I would not hear your enemy say so,
Nor shall you do mine ear that violence, 171
To make it truster of your own report
Against yourself : I know you are no truant
But what is your affair in Elsinore ?
We'll teach you to drink deep ere you depart.
   Hor.   My lord, I came to see your father's
     funeral.
   Ham.   I pray thee, do not mock me, fellow-
     student ;
I think it was to see my mother's wedding.
   Hor.   Indeed, my lord, it follow'd hard upon.
   Ham.   Thrift, thrift, Horatio ! the funeral
     baked meats   180
Did coldly furnish forth the marriage tables.
Would I had met my dearest foe in heaven
Or ever I had seen that day, Horatio !
My father !—methinks I see my father.
   Hor.   Where, my lord ?
   Ham.   In my mind's eye, Horatio.
   Hor.   I saw him once ; he was a goodly
     king.
   Ham.   He was a man, take him for all in all,
I shall not look upon his like again.

Hor.   My lord, I think I saw him yester-
    night.

Ham.   Saw ? who ?   190

Hor. My lord, the king your father.

Ham.   The king my father !

Hor. Season your admiration for awhile
With an attent ear, till I may deliver,
Upon the witness of these gentlemen,
This marvel to you.

Ham.   For God's love, let me hear.

Hor. Two nights together had these gen-
    tlemen,
Marcellus and Bernardo, on their watch,
In the dead vast and middle of the night,
Been thus encounter'd. A figure like your
    father,
Armed at point exactly, cap-a-pe,   200
Appears before them, and with solemn march
Goes slow and stately by them : thrice he
    walk'd
By their oppress'd and fear-surprised eyes,
Within his truncheon's length , whilst they,
    distilled
Almost to jelly with the act of fear.
Stand dumb and speak not to him   This to me
In dreadful secrecy impart they did ,
And I with them the third night kept the
    watch ,
Where, as they had deliver'd, both in time,
Form of the thing, each word made true and
    good,   210
The apparition comes : I knew your father ;
These hands are not more like

Ham.   But where was this ?

Mar. My lord, upon the platform where we
    watch'd

Ham Did you not speak to it ?

Hor.   My lord, I did ;
But answer made it none · yet once methought
It lifted up its head and did address
Itself to motion, like as it would speak ;
But even then the morning cock crew loud,
And at the sound it shrunk in haste away,
And vanish'd from our sight

Ham.   'Tis very strange 220

Hor. As I do live, my honor'd lord, 'tis
    true ;
And we did think it writ down in our duty
To let you know of it

Ham. Indeed, indeed, sirs, but this troubles
    me
Hold you the watch to-night ?

Mar. }
Ber }   We do, my lord.

Ham Arm'd, say you ?

Mar. }
Ber } Arm'd, my lord.

Ham. From top to toe ?

Mar. }
Ber }   My lord, from head to foot.

Ham. Then saw you not his face ?

Hor. O, yes, my lord ; he wore his beaver
    up.   230

Ham. What, look'd he frowningly ?

Hor. A countenance more in sorrow than
    in anger.

Ham. Pale or red ?

Hor. Nay, very pale.

Ham.   And fix'd his eyes upon you ?

Hor Most constantly.

Ham.   I would I had been there.

Hor. It would have much amazed you

Ham. Very like, very like., Stay'd it long ?

Hor. While one with moderate haste might
    tell a hundred.

Mar. }
Ber. } Longer, longer.

Hor Not when I saw't

Ham.   His beard was grizzled,—no ? 240

Hor. It was, as I have seen it in his life,
A sable silver'd.

Ham   I will watch to-night ;
Perchance 'twill walk again.

Hor.   I warrant it will.

Ham. If it assume my noble father's per-
    son,
I'll speak to it, though hell itself should gape
And bid me hold my peace 'I pray you all,
If you have hitherto conceal'd this sight,
Let it be tenable in your silence still ;
And whatsoever else shall hap to-night,
Give it an understanding, but no tongue: 250
I will requite your loves So, fare you well :
Upon the platform, 'twixt eleven and twelve,
I'll visit you.

All.   Our duty to your honor.

Ham Your loves, as mine to you fare-
    well.   [*Exeunt all but Hamlet.*
My father's spirit in arms ! all is not well ;
I doubt some foul play : would the night
    were come !
Till then sit still, my soul : foul deeds will
    rise,
Though all the earth o'erwhelm them, to
    men's eyes.   [*Exit.*

SCENE III. *A room in Polonius' house.*

Enter LAERTES *and* OPHELIA.

Laer. My necessaries are embark'd : fare-
    well :
And, sister, as the winds give benefit
And convoy is assistant, do not sleep,
But let me hear from you.

Oph   Do you doubt that ?

Laer. For Hamlet and the trifling of his
    favor,
Hold it a fashion and a toy in blood,
A violet in the youth of primy nature,
Forward, not permanent, sweet, not lasting,
The perfume and suppliance of a minute ;
No more.

Oph. No more but so ?

Laer.   Think it no more : 10
For nature, crescent, does not grow alone
In thews and bulk, but, as this temple waxes,
The inward service of the mind and soul
Grows wide withal. Perhaps he loves you
    now,
And now no soil nor cautel doth besmirch
The virtue of his will : but you must fear,
His greatness weigh'd, his will is not his own;

For he himself is subject to his birth :
He may not, as unvalued persons do,
Carve for himself ; for on his choice depends
The safety and health of this whole state ;   21
And therefore must his choice be circum-
    scribed
Unto the voice and yielding of that body
Whereof he is the head.   Then if he says he
    loves you,
It fits your wisdom so far to believe it
As he in his particular act and place
May give his saying deed ; which is no fur-
    ther
Than the main voice of Denmark goes withal.
Then weigh what loss your honor may sus-
    tain,
If with too credent ear you list his songs,   30
Or lose your heart, or your chaste treasure
    open
To his unmaster'd importunity.
Fear it, Ophelia, fear it, my dear sister,
And keep you in the rear of your affection,
Out of the shot and danger of desire.
The chariest maid is prodigal enough,
If she unmask her beauty to the moon :
Virtue itself 'scapes not calumnious strokes :
The canker galls the infants of the spring,
Too oft before their buttons be disclosed,   40
And in the morn and liquid dew of youth
Contagious blastments are most imminent.
Be wary then ; best safety lies in fear :
Youth to itself rebels, though none else near.
    Oph.   I shall the effect of this good lesson
      keep,
As watchman to my heart.   But, good my
      brother,
Do not, as some ungracious pastors do,
Show me the steep and thorny way to heav-
    en ;
Whiles, like a puff'd and reckless libertine,
Himself the primrose path of dalliance treads,
And recks not his own rede.   51
    Laer.   —O, fear me not.
I stay too long : but here my father comes.

                 Enter POLONIUS.

A double blessing is a double grace ;
Occasion smiles upon a second leave.
    Pol.   Yet here, Laertes ! aboard, aboard,
      for shame !
The wind sits in the shoulder of your sail,
And you are stay'd for.   There ; my blessing
    with thee !
And these few precepts in thy memory
See thou character.   Give thy thoughts no
    tongue,
Nor any unproportioned thought his act.   60
Be thou familiar, but by no means vulgar.
Those friends thou hast, and their adoption
    tried,
Grapple them to thy soul with hoops of steel ;
But do not dull thy palm with entertainment
Of each new-hatch'd, unfledged comrade. Be-
    ware
Of entrance to a quarrel, but being in,
Bear't that the opposed may beware of thee.

Give every man thy ear, but few thy voice ;
Take each man's censure, but reserve thy
      judgment.
Costly thy habit as thy purse can buy,   70
But not express'd in fancy ; rich, not gaudy ;
For the apparel oft proclaims the man,
And they in France of the best rank and sta-
    tion
†Are of a most select and generous chief in
    that.
Neither a borrower nor a lender be ;
For loan oft loses both itself and friend,
And borrowing dulls the edge of husbandry.
This above all : to thine ownself be true,
And it must follow, as the night the day,
Thou canst not then be false to any man.   80
Farewell : my blessing season this in thee !
    Laer.   Most humbly do I take my leave, my
      lord.
    Pol.   The time invites you ; go ; your serv-
      ants tend.
    Laer.   Farewell, Ophelia ; and remember
      well
What I have said to you.
    Oph.   'Tis in my memory lock'd,
And you yourself shall keep the key of it.
    Laer.   Farewell.   [*Exit.*
    Pol.   What is 't, Ophelia, he hath said to
      you ?
    Oph.   So please you, something touching
      the Lord Hamlet.
    Pol.   Marry, well bethought :   90
'Tis told me, he hath very oft of late
Given private time to you ; and you yourself
Have of your audience been most free and
    bounteous :
If it be so, as so 'tis put on me,
And that in way of caution, I must tell you,
You do not understand yourself so clearly
As it behoves my daughter and your honor.
What is between you ? give me up the truth.
    Oph.   He hath, my lord, of late made many
      tenders
Of his affection to me.   100
    Pol.   Affection ! pooh ! you speak like a
      green girl,
Unsifted in such perilous circumstance.
Do you believe his tenders, as you call them ?
    Oph.   I do not know, my lord, what I should
      think.
    Pol.   Marry, I'll teach you : think yourself
      a baby ;
That you have ta'en these tenders for true
      pay,
Which are not sterling.   Tender yourself
      more dearly ;
Or—not to crack the wind of the poor phrase,
Running it thus—you'll tender me a fool.
    Oph.   My lord, he hath importuned me
      with love   110
In honorable fashion.
    Pol.   Ay, fashion you may call it ; go to, go
      to.
    Oph.   And hath given countenance to his
      speech, my lord,
With almost all the holy vows of heaven.

Pol. Ay, springes to catch woodcocks. I do
　　know,
When the blood burns, how prodigal the soul
Lends the tongue vows : these blazes, daugh-
　　ter,
Giving more light than heat, extinct in both,
Even in their promise, as it is a-making,
You must not take for fire.　From this time
Be somewhat scanter of your maiden pres-
　　ence ;　　　　　　　　　　　　　　121
Set your entreatments at a higher rate
Than a command to parley.　For Lord Ham-
　　let,
Believe so much in him, that he is young
And with a larger tether may he walk
Than may be given you : in few, Ophelia,
Do not believe his vows ; for they are brokers,
Not of that dye which their investments show,
But mere implorators of unholy suits,
Breathing like sanctified and pious bawds,
The better to beguile.　This is for all :　131
I would, not, in plain terms, from this time
　　forth,
Have you so slander any moment leisure,
As to give words or talk with the Lord Ham-
　　let.
Look to't, I charge you : come your ways.
Oph. I shall obey, my lord.　　　[*Exeunt.*

SCENE IV.　*The platform.*

Enter HAMLET, HORATIO, *and* MARCELLUS.

Ham. The air bites shrewdly ; it is very
　　cold.
Hor. It is a nipping and an eager air.
Ham. What hour now ?
Hor.　　　　　　I think it lacks of twelve.
Ham. No, it is struck.
Hor. Indeed ? I heard it not: then it draws
　　near the season
Wherein the spirit held his wont to walk.
　　[*A flourish of trumpets, and ordnance
　　　　　　　　　shot off, within.*
What does this mean, my lord ?
Ham.　　The king doth wake to-night and
　　takes his rouse,
Keeps wassail, and the swaggering up-spring
　　reels ;
And, as he drains his draughts of Rhenish
　　down,　　　　　　　　　　　　　10
The kettle-drum and trumpet thus bray out
The triumph of his pledge.
Hor.　　　　　　Is it a custom ?
Ham. Ay, marry, is't :
But to my mind, though I am native here
And to the manner born, it is a custom
More honor'd in the breach than the observ-
　　ance.
This heavy-headed revel east and west
Makes us traduced and tax'd of other nations:
They clepe us drunkards, and with swinish
　　phrase
Soil our addition ; and indeed it takes　　20
From our achievements, though perform'd at
　　height,
The pith and marrow of our attribute.

So, oft it chances in particular men,
That for some vicious mole of nature in them,
As, in their birth—wherein they are not
　　guilty,
Since nature cannot choose his origin—
By the o'ergrowth of some complexion,
Oft breaking down the pales and forts of rea-
　　son,
Or by some habit that too much o'er-leavens
The form of plausive manners, that these
　　men,　　　　　　　　　　　　　　30
Carrying, I say, the stamp of one defect,
Being nature's livery, or fortune's star,—
Their virtues else—be they as pure as grace,
As infinite as man may undergo—
Shall in the general censure take corruption
From that particular fault : the dram of teale
Doth all the noble substance †of a doubt
To his own scandal.
Hor.　　　　　Look, my lord, it comes !

Enter Ghost.

Ham. Angels and ministers of grace de-
　　fend us !
Be thou a spirit of health or goblin damn'd,
Bring with thee airs from heaven or blasts
　　from hell,　　　　　　　　　　　41
Be thy intents wicked or charitable,
Thou comest in such a questionable shape
That I will speak to thee : I'll call thee Ham-
　　let,
King, father, royal Dane : O, answer me !
Let me not burst in ignorance ; but tell
Why thy canonized bones, hearsed in death,
Have burst their cerements ; why the sepul-
　　chre,
Wherein we saw thee quietly inurn'd,
Hath oped his ponderous and marble jaws, 50
To cast thee up again.　What may this mean,
That thou, dead corse, again in complete steel
Revisit'st thus the glimpses of the moon,
Making night hideous ; and we fools of nature
So horridly to shake our disposition
With thoughts beyond the reaches of our
　　souls ?
Say, why is this ? wherefore ? what should
　　we do ?　　　　[*Ghost beckons Hamlet.*
Hor. It beckons you to go away with it,
As if it some impartment did desire
To you alone.
Mar. Look, with what courteous action 60
It waves you to a more removed ground :
But do not go with it.
Hor.　　　　　No, by no means.
Ham. It will not speak ; then I will follow
　　it.
Hor. Do not, my lord.
Ham.　　Why, what should be the fear ?
I do not set my life at a pin's fee ;
And for my soul, what can it do to that,
Being a thing immortal as itself ?
It waves me forth again : I'll follow it.
Hor. What if it tempt you toward the flood,
　　my lord,
Or to the dreadful summit of the cliff　　70
That beetles o'er his base into the sea,

And there assume some other horrible form,
Which might deprive your sovereignty of
　　reason
And draw you into madness ? think of it :
The very place puts toys of desperation,
Without more motive, into every brain
That looks so many fathoms to the sea
And hears it roar beneath.

Ham.　　　　　　It waves me still.
Go on ; I'll follow thee.

Mar.　You shall not go, my lord.

Ham.　　　　　Hold off your hands.　80

Hor.　Be ruled ; you shall not go.

Ham.　　　　　My fate cries out,
And makes each petty artery in this body
As hardy as the Nemean lion's nerve.
Still am I call'd. Unhand me, gentlemen.
By heaven, I'll make a ghost of him that lets
　　me !
I say, away ! Go on ; I'll follow thee.
　　　　　　[*Exeunt Ghost and Hamlet.*

Hor.　He waxes desperate with imagination.

Mar.　Let's follow ; 'tis not fit thus to obey
　　him.

Hor.　Have after. To what issue will this
　　come ?

Mar.　Something is rotten in the state of
　　Denmark.　　　　　　　　　90

Hor.　Heaven will direct it.

Mar.　　　Nay, let's follow him.　[*Exeunt.*

SCENE V.　*Another part of the platform.*

Enter GHOST *and* HAMLET.

Ham.　Where wilt thou lead me ? speak ;
　　I'll go no further.

Ghost.　Mark me.

Ham.　　　I will.

Ghost.　　　My hour is almost come,
When I to sulphurous and tormenting flames
Must render up myself.

Ham.　　　　Alas, poor ghost !

Ghost.　Pity me not, but lend thy serious
　　hearing
To what I shall unfold.

Ham.　　　Speak ; I am bound to hear.

Ghost.　So art thou to revenge, when thou
　　shalt hear.

Ham.　What ?

Ghost.　I am thy father's spirit,
Doom'd for a certain term to walk the night,
And for the day confined to fast in fires,　11
Till the foul crimes done in my days of nature
Are burnt and purged away. But that I am
　　forbid
To tell the secrets of my prison-house,
I could a tale unfold whose lightest word
Would harrow up thy soul, freeze thy young
　　blood,
Make thy two eyes, like stars, start from their
　　spheres,
Thy knotted and combined locks to part
And each particular hair to stand on end,
Like quills upon the fretful porpentine :　20
But this eternal blazon must not be
To ears of flesh and blood. List, list, O, list !

If thou didst ever thy dear father love—

Ham.　O God !

Ghost.　Revenge his foul and most unnatural
　　murder.

Ham.　Murder !

Ghost.　Murder most foul, as in the best it
　　is ;
But this most foul, strange and unnatural.

Ham.　Haste me to know't, that I, with
　　wings as swift
As meditation or the thoughts of love,　30
May sweep to my revenge.

Ghost.　　　I find thee apt ;
And duller shouldst thou be than the fat weed
That roots itself in ease on Lethe wharf,
Wouldst thou not stir in this. Now, Hamlet,
　　hear :
'Tis given out that, sleeping in my orchard,
A serpent stung me ; so the whole ear of Den-
　　mark
Is by a forged process of my death
Rankly abused : but know, thou noble youth,
The serpent that did sting thy father's life
Now wears his crown.

Ham.　　　O my prophetic soul ! 40
My uncle !

Ghost.　Ay, that incestuous, that adulterate
　　beast,
With witchcraft of his wit, with traitorous
　　gifts,—
O wicked wit and gifts, that have the power
So to seduce !—won to his shameful lust
The will of my most seeming-virtuous queen :
O Hamlet, what a falling-off was there !
From me, whose love was of that dignity
That it went hand in hand even with the vow
I made to her in marriage, and to decline　50
Upon a wretch whose natural gifts were poor
To those of mine !
But virtue, as it never will be moved,
Though lewdness court it in a shape of heaven,
So lust, though to a radiant angel link'd,
Will sate itself in a celestial bed,
And prey on garbage.
But, soft ! methinks I scent the morning air ;
Brief let me be. Sleeping within my orchard,
My custom always of the afternoon,　　60
Upon my secure hour thy uncle stole,
With juice of cursed hebenon in a vial,
And in the porches of my ears did pour
The leperous distilment ; whose effect
Holds such an enmity with blood of man
That swift as quicksilver it courses through
The natural gates and alleys of the body,
And with a sudden vigor it doth posset
And curd, like eager droppings into milk,
The thin and wholesome blood : so did it mine;
And a most instant tetter bark'd about,　71
Most lazar-like, with vile and loathsome crust,
All my smooth body.
Thus was I, sleeping, by a brother's hand
Of life, of crown, of queen, at once dispatch'd:
Cut off even in the blossoms of my sin,
Unhousel'd, disappointed, unanel'd,
No reckoning made, but sent to my account
With all my imperfections on my head:

O, horrible ! O, horrible ! most horrible ! 80
If thou hast nature in thee, bear it not ;
Let not the royal bed of Denmark be
A couch for luxury and damned incest.
But, howsoever thou pursuest this act,
Taint not thy mind, nor let thy soul contrive
Against thy mother aught : leave her to heaven
And to those thorns that in her bosom lodge,
To prick and sting her. Fare thee well at
    once !
The glow-worm shows the matin to be near,
And 'gins to pale his uneffectual fire :   90
Adieu, adieu ! Hamlet, remember me. [*Exit.*
    Ham. O all you host of heaven ! O earth !
    what else ?
And shall I couple hell ? O, fie ! Hold, hold,
    my heart ;
And you, my sinews, grow not instant old,
But bear me stiffly up. Remember thee !
Ay, thou poor ghost, while memory holds a
    seat
In this distracted globe. Remember thee !
Yea, from the table of my memory
I'll wipe away all trivial fond records,
All saws of books, all forms, all pressures past,
That youth and observation copied there ; 101
And thy commandment all alone shall live
Within the book and volume of my brain,
Unmix'd with baser matter : yes, by heaven !
O most pernicious woman !
O villain, villain, smiling, damned villain !
My tables,—meet it is I set it down,
That one may smile, and smile, and be a vil-
    lain ;
At least I'm sure it may be so in Denmark :
                              [*Writing.*
So, uncle, there you are. Now to my word ;
It is ' Adieu, adieu ! remember me.'   111
I have sworn 't.
    Mar. }
    Hor. } [*Within*] My lord, my lord,—
    Mar.   [*Within*] Lord Hamlet,—
    Hor.   [*Within*] Heaven secure him !
    Ham. So be-it-!
    Hor. [*Within*] Hillo, ho, ho, my lord !
    Ham. Hillo, ho, ho, boy ! come, bird, come.

Enter HORATIO *and* MARCELLUS.

    Mar. How is't, my noble lord ?
    Hor.   What news, my lord ?
    Ham. O, wonderful !
    Hor.   Good my lord, tell it.
    Ham. No ; you'll reveal it.
    Hor. Not I, my lord, by heaven.
    Mar.   Nor I, my lord. 120
    Ham. How say you, then ; would heart of
    man once think it ?
But you'll be secret ?
    Hor. }
    Mar. }   Ay, by heaven, my lord.
    Ham. There's ne'er a villain dwelling in
    all Denmark
But he's an arrant knave.
    Hor. There needs no ghost, my lord, come
    from the grave
To tell us this.

    Ham.   Why, right ; you are i' the right ;
And so, without more circumstance at all,
I hold it fit that we shake hands and part ;
You, as your business and desire shall point you;
For every man has business and desire,   130
Such as it is ; and for mine own poor part,
Look you, I'll go pray.
    Hor. These are but wild and whirling words,
    my lord.
    Ham. I'm sorry they offend you, heartily ;
Yes, 'faith heartily.
    Hor.   There's no offence, my lord.
    Ham. Yes, by Saint Patrick, but there is,
    Horatio,
And much offence too. Touching this vision
    here,
It is an honest ghost, that let me tell you :
For your desire to know what is between us,
O'ermaster 't as you may. And now, good
    friends,   140
As you are friends, scholars and soldiers,
Give me one poor request.
    Hor. What is't, my lord ? we will.
    Ham. Never make known what you have
    seen to-night.
    Hor. }
    Mar. } My lord, we will not.
    Ham.   Nay, but swear 't.
    Hor.   In faith,
My lord, not I.
    Mar.   Nor I, my lord, in faith.
    Ham. Upon my sword.
    Mar. We have sworn, my lord, already.
    Ham. Indeed, upon my sword, indeed.
    Ghost. [*Beneath*] Swear.
    Ham. Ah, ha, boy ! say'st thou so ? art
    thou there, truepenny ?   150
Come on—you hear this fellow in the cellarage—
Consent to swear.
    Hor.   Propose the oath, my lord.
    Ham. Never to speak of this that you have
    seen,
Swear by my sword.
    Ghost. [*Beneath*] Swear.
    Ham. Hic et ubique ? then we'll shift our
    ground.
Come hither, gentlemen,
And lay your hands again upon my sword :
Never to speak of this that you have heard,
Swear by my sword.   160
    Ghost. [*Beneath*] Swear.
    Ham. Well said, old mole ! canst work i'
    the earth so fast ?
A worthy pioner ! Once more remove, good
    friends.
    Hor. O day and night, but this is wondrous
    strange !
    Ham. And therefore as a stranger give it
    welcome.
There are more things in heaven and earth,
    Horatio,
Than are dreamt of in your philosophy.
But come ;
Here, as before, never, so help you mercy,
How strange or odd soe'er I bear myself, 170
As I perchance hereafter shall think meet

To put an antic disposition on,
That you, at such times seeing me, never shall,
With arms encumber'd thus, or this head-
    shake,
Or by pronouncing of some doubtful phrase,
As ' Well, well, we know,' or ' We could, an
    if we would,'
Or ' If we list to speak,' or ' There be, an if
    they might,'
Or such ambiguous giving out, to note
That you know aught of me: this not to do,
So grace and mercy at your most need help
    you,   180
Swear.
  Ghost. [*Beneath*] Swear.
  Ham. Rest, rest, perturbed spirit ! [*They
    swear.*] So, gentlemen,
With all my love I do commend me to you :
And what so poor a man as Hamlet is
May do, to express his love and friending to
    you,
God willing, shall not lack. Let us go in to-
    gether ;
And still your fingers on your lips, I pray.
The time is out of joint : O cursed spite,
That ever I was born to set it right !
Nay, come, let's go together. [*Exeunt.* 190

ACT II.

  Scene I. *A room in Polonius' house.*

   Enter POLONIUS *and* REYNALDO.

  Pol. Give him this money and these notes,
    Reynaldo.
  Rey. I will, my lord.
  Pol. You shall do marvellous, wisely, good
    Reynaldo,
Before you visit him, to make inquire
Of his behavior.
  Rey.   My lord, I did intend it.
  Pol. Marry, well said ; very well said.
    Look you, sir,
Inquire me first what Danskers are in Paris ;
And how, and who, what means, and where
    they keep,
What company, at what expense ; and finding
By this encompassment and drift of question
That they do know my son, come you more
    nearer   11
Than your particular demands will touch it :
Take you, as 'twere, some distant knowledge
    of him ;
As thus, ' I know his father and his friends,
And in part him :' do you mark this, Rey-
    naldo ?
  Rey. Ay, very well, my lord.
  Pol. ' And in part him ; but' you may say
    ' not well :
But, if 't be he I mean, he's very wild ;
Addicted so and so :' and there put on him
What forgeries you please ; marry, none so
    rank   20
As may dishonor him ; take heed of that ;
But, sir, such wanton, wild and usual slips

As are companions noted and most known
To youth and liberty.
  Rey.   As gaming, my lord.
  Pol. Ay, or drinking, fencing, swearing,
    quarrelling,
Drabbing : you may go so far.
  Rey. My lord, that would dishonor him.
  Pol. 'Faith, no ; as you may season it in
    the charge
You must not put another scandal on him,
That he is open to incontinency ;   30
That's not my meaning: but breathe his faults
    so quaintly
That they may seem the taints of liberty,
The flash and outbreak of a fiery mind,
A savageness in unreclaimed blood,
Of general assault.
  Rey.   But, my good lord,—
  Pol. Wherefore should you do this ?
  Rey.   Ay, my lord,
I would know that.
  Pol.   Marry, sir, here's my drift;
And, I believe, it is a fetch of wit:
You laying these slight sullies on my son,
As 'twere a thing a little soil'd i' the working,
Mark you,   41
Your party in converse, him you would sound,
Having ever seen in the prenominate crimes
The youth you breathe of guilty, be assured
He closes with you in this consequence ;
' Good sir,' or so, or ' friend,' or ' gentleman,'
According to the phrase or the addition
Of man and country.
  Rey.   Very good, my lord.
  Pol. And then, sir, does he this—he does—
what was I about to say ? By the mass, I was
about to say something : where did I leave ?
  Rey. At ' closes in the consequence,' at
' friend or so,' and ' gentleman.'
  Pol. At ' closes in the consequence,' ay,
    marry ;
He closes thus : ' I know the gentleman ;
I saw him yesterday, or t' other day,
Or then, or then ; with such, or such ; and, as
    you say,
There was a' gaming ; there o'ertook in's
    rouse ;
There falling out at tennis :' or perchance,
' I saw him enter such a house of sale,'   60
Videlicet, a brothel, or so forth.
See you now ;
Your bait of falsehood takes this carp of truth:
And thus do we of wisdom and of reach,
With windlasses and with assays of bias,
By indirections find directions out :
So by my former lecture and advice,
Shall you my son. You have me, have you
    not ?
  Rey. My lord, I have.
  Pol.   God be wi' you ; fare you well.
  Rey. Good my lord !   70
  Pol. Observe his inclination in yourself.
  Rey. I shall, my lord.
  Pol. And let him ply his music.
  Rey.   Well, my lord.
  Pol. Farewell.   [*Exit Reynaldo.*

Enter OPHELIA.

How now, Ophelia ! what's the matter ?

Oph. O, my lord, my lord, I have been so
　　affrighted !

Pol. With what, i' the name of God ?

Oph. My lord, as I was sewing in my
　　closet,
Lord Hamlet, with his doublet all unbraced ;
No hat upon his head ; his stockings foul'd,
Ungarter'd, and down-gyved to his ancle ; 80
Pale as his shirt ; his knees knocking each
　　other ;
And with a look so piteous in purport
As if he had been loosed out of hell
To speak of horrors,—he comes before me.

Pol. Mad for thy love ?

Oph. 　　　　　　My lord, I do not know ;
But truly, I do fear it.

Pol. 　　　　　　What said he ?

Oph. He took me by the wrist and held me
　　hard ;
Then goes he to the length of all his arm ;
And, with his other hand thus o'er his brow,
He falls to such perusal of my face　　　90
As he would draw it. Long stay'd he so ;
At last, a little shaking of mine arm
And thrice his head thus waving up and down,
He raised a sigh so piteous and profound
As it did seem to shatter all his bulk
And end his being : that done, he lets me go :
And, with his head over his shoulder turn'd,
He seem'd to find his way without his eyes ;
For out o'doors he went without their helps,
And, to the last, bended their light on me. 100

Pol. Come, go with me : I will go seek
　　the king.
This is the very ecstasy of love,
Whose violent property fordoes itself
And leads the will to desperate undertakings
As oft as any passion under heaven
That does afflict our natures. I am sorry.
What, have you given him any hard words of
　　late ?　　　　　　　　[command,

Oph. No, my good lord, but, as you did
I did repel his letters and denied
His access to me.

Pol. 　　　　That hath made him mad. 110
I am sorry that with better heed and judg-
　　ment　　　　　　　　　　[fie,
I had not quoted him : I fear'd he did but tri-
And meant to wreck thee ; but, beshrew my
　　jealousy !
By heaven, it is as proper to our age
To cast beyond ourselves in our opinions
As it is common for the younger sort
To lack discretion. Come, go we to the king :
This must be known ; which, being kept close,
　　might move
More grief to hide than hate to utter love.
　　　　　　　　　　　　　　　　[*Exeunt.*

SCENE II. *A room in the castle.*

Enter KING, QUEEN, ROSENCRANTZ, GUILD-
ENSTERN, *and* Attendants.

King. Welcome, dear Rosencrantz and
　　Guildenstern !

Moreover that we much did long to see you,
The need we have to use you did provoke
Our hasty sending. Something have you heard
Of Hamlet's transformation ; so call it,
Sith nor the exterior nor the inward man
Resembles that it was. What it should be,
More than his father's death, that thus hath
　　put him
So much from the understanding of himself,
I cannot dream of : I entreat you both, 10
That, being of so young days brought up with
　　him,
And sith so neighbor'd to his youth and ha-
　　vior,
That you vouchsafe your rest here in our court
Some little time : so by your companies
To draw him on to pleasures, and to gather,
So much as from occasion you may glean,
Whether aught, to us unknown, afflicts him
　　thus,
That, open'd, lies within our remedy.

Queen. Good gentlemen, he hath much
　　talk'd of you ;
And sure I am two men there are not living
To whom he more adheres. If it will please
　　you　　　　　　　　　　　　21
To show us so much gentry and good will
As to expend your time with us awhile,
For the supply and profit of our hope,
Your visitation shall receive such thanks
As fits a king's remembrance.

Ros. 　　　　　　Both your majesties
Might, by the sovereign power you have of us,
Put your dread pleasures more into command
Than to entreaty.

Guil. 　　　　But we both obey,
And here give up ourselves, in the full bent
To lay our service freely at your feet,　31
To be commanded.

King. Thanks, Rosencrantz and gentle
　　Guildenstern.

Queen. Thanks, Guildenstern and gentle
　　Rosencrantz :
And I beseech you instantly to visit　—
My too much changed son. Go, some of you,
And bring these gentlemen where Hamlet is.

Guil. Heavens make our presence and our
　　practices
Pleasant and helpful to him !

Queen. 　　　　　　　Ay, amen !
　　[*Exeunt Rosencrantz, Guildenstern, and
　　　　　　　　　　some Attendants.*

Enter POLONIUS.

Pol. The ambassadors from Norway, my
　　good lord,　　　　　　　　40
Are joyfully return'd.

King. Thou still hast been the father of
　　good news.

Pol. Have I, my lord ? I assure my good
　　liege,
I hold my duty, as I hold my soul,
Both to my God and to my gracious king :
And I do think, or else this brain of mine
Hunts not the trail of policy so sure
As it hath used to do, that I have found

The very cause of Hamlet's lunacy.

King. O, speak of that ; that do I long to
  hear.   50

Pol. Give first admittance to the ambassadors ;

My news shall be the fruit to that great feast.

King. Thyself do grace to them, and bring
  them in.   *[Exit Polonius.*

He tells me, my dear Gertrude, he hath found
The head and source of all your son's distemper.

Queen. I doubt it is no other but the main;
His father's death, and our o'erhasty marriage.

King. Well, we shall sift him.

Re-enter POLONIUS, *with* VOLTIMAND *and
      Cornelius.*

          Welcome, my good friends !

Say, Voltimand, what from our brother Norway ?

Volt. Most fair return of greetings and
  desires.   60

Upon our first, he sent out to suppress
His nephew's levies ; which to him appear'd
To be a preparation 'gainst the Polack ;
But, better look'd into, he truly found
It was against your highness : whereat grieved,
That so his sickness, age and impotence
Was falsely borne in hand, sends out arrests
On Fortinbras ; which he, in brief, obeys ;
Receives rebuke from Norway, and in fine
Makes vow before his uncle never more 70
To give the assay of arms against your majesty.
Whereon old Norway, overcome with joy,
Gives him three thousand crowns in annual fee,
And his commission to employ those soldiers,
So levied as before, against the Polack :
With an entreaty, herein further shown,
               [Giving a paper.
That it might please you to give quiet pass
Through your dominions for this enterprise,
On such regards of safety and allowance
As therein are set down.

King.   It likes us well ; 80
And at our more consider'd time we'll read,
Answer, and think upon this business.
Meantime we thank you for your well-took
  labor :
Go to your rest ; at night we'll feast together :
Most welcome home !
         [Exeunt Voltimand and Cornelius.

Pol.   This business is well ended.
My liege, and madam, to expostulate
What majesty should be, what duty is,
Why day is day, night night, and time is time,
Were nothing but to waste night, day and time.
Therefore, since brevity is the soul of wit,⎰ 90
And tediousness the limbs and outward flour-
  ishes,
I will be brief : your noble son is mad :
Mad call I it ; for, to define true madness,
What is't but to be nothing else but mad ?
But let that go.

Queen.   More matter, with less art.

Pol. Madam, I swear I use no art at all.

That he is mad, 'tis true : 'tis true 'tis pity ;
And pity 'tis 'tis true : a foolish figure ;
But farewell it, for I will use no art.
Mad let us grant him, then : and now remains
That we find out the cause of this effect, 101
Or rather say, the cause of this defect,
For this effect defective comes by cause :
Thus it remains, and the remainder thus.
Perpend.
I have a daughter—have while she is mine—
Who, in her duty and obedience, mark,
Hath given me this : now gather, and surmise.
                  [Reads.
'To the celestial and my soul's idol, the most
beautified Ophelia,'—   110
That's an ill phrase, a vile phrase ; 'beautified'
is a vile phrase : but you shall hear. Thus :
                  [Reads.
' In her excellent white bosom, these, &c.'

Queen. Came this from Hamlet to her ?

Pol. Good madam, stay awhile ; I will be
  faithful.   *[Reads.*
  ' Doubt thou the stars are fire ;
    Doubt that the sun doth move ;
  Doubt truth to be a liar ;
    But never doubt I love.   119
' O dear Ophelia, I am ill at these numbers ;
I have not art to reckon my groans : but that
I love thee best, O most best, believe it. Adieu.
  ' Thine evermore, most dear lady, whilst
      this machine is to him, HAMLET.'
This, in obedience, hath my daughter shown
  me,
And more above, hath his solicitings,
As they fell out by time, by means and place,
All given to mine ear.

King.   But how hath she
Received his love ?

Pol.   What do you think of me ?

King. As of a man faithful and honorable.

Pol. I would fain prove so. But what might
  you think,   131
When I had seen this hot love on the wing—
As I perceived it, I must tell you that,
Before my daughter told me—what might you,
Or my dear majesty your queen here, think,
If I had play'd the desk or table-book,
Or given my heart a winking, mute and dumb,
Or look'd upon this love with idle sight ;
What might you think ? No, I went round to
  work,
And my young mistress thus I did bespeak :
'Lord Hamlet is a prince, out of thy star ; 141
This must not be :' and then I precepts gave
  her,
That she should lock herself from his resort,
Admit no messengers, receive no tokens.
Which done, she took the fruits of my advice ;
And he, repulsed—a short tale to make—
Fell into a sadness, then into a fast,
Thence to a watch, thence into a weakness,
Thence to a lightness, and, by this declension,
Into the madness wherein now he raves, 150
And all we mourn for.

King.   Do you think 'tis this ?

Queen. It may be, very likely.
                42

Pol. Hath there been such a time—I'd fain
know that—
That I have positively said '*'Tis so,*'
When it proved otherwise ?
King.　　　　　　Not that I know
Pol [*Pointing to his head and shoulder*]
Take this from this, if this be otherwise.
If circumstances lead me, I will find
Where truth is hid, though it were hid indeed
Within the centre
King.　　　How may we try it further ?
Pol. You know, sometimes he walks four
hours together　　　　　　　　　　160
Here in the lobby
Queen　　' So he does indeed.
Pol At such a time I'll loose my daughter
to him
Be you and I behind an arras then ;
Mark the encounter : if he love her not
And be not from his reason fall'n thereon,
Let me be no assistant for a state,
But keep a farm and carters.
King　　　　　We will try it
Queen But, look, where sadly the poor
wretch comes reading
Pol Away, I do beseech you, both away ·
I'll board him presently.
　　　[*Exeunt King, Queen, and Attendants.*

　　　Enter HAMLET, *reading*

　　　　　　O, give me leave :　170
How does my good Lord Hamlet ?
Ham Well, God-a-mercy.
Pol. Do you know me, my lord ?
Ham. Excellent well ; you are a fishmonger.
Pol Not I, my lord.
Ham Then I would you were so honest a
man.
Pol Honest, my lord !
Ham. Ay, sir ; to be honest, as this world
goes, is to be one man picked out of ten thousand
Pol That's very true, my lord　　　180
Ham For if the sun breed maggots in a
dead dog, being a god kissing carrion,—Have
you a daughter?
Pol. I have, my lord
Ham Let her not walk i' the sun · conception is a blessing . but not as your daughter
may conceive Friend, look to 't
Pol. [*Aside*] How say you by that ? Still
harping on my daughter : yet he knew me
not at first ; he said I was a fishmonger he
is far gone, far gone : and truly in my youth
I suffered much extremity for love ; very near
this I'll speak to him again What do you
read, my lord ?
Ham. Words, words, words.
Pol. What is the matter, my lord ?
Ham Between who?
Pol I mean, the matter that you read, my
lord.
Ham. Slanders, sir for the satirical rogue
says here that old men have grey beards, that
their faces are wrinkled, their eyes purging
thick amber and plum-tree gum and that they

have a plentiful lack of wit, together with
most weak hams . all which, sir, though I
most powerfully and potently believe, yet I
hold it not honesty to have it thus set down,
for yourself, sir, should be old as I am, if like
a crab you could go backward.
Pol. [*Aside*] Though this be madness, yet
there is method in 't Will you walk out of
the air, my lord ?
Ham Into my grave　　　　　　　210
Pol Indeed, that is out o' the air　[*Aside*]
How pregnant sometimes his replies are ! a
happiness that often madness hits on, which
reason and sanity could not so prosperously be
delivered of. I will leave him, and suddenly
contrive the means of meeting between him
and my daughter.—My honorable lord, I will
most humbly take my leave of you.
Ham You cannot, sir, take from me any
thing that I will more willingly part withal :
except my life, except my life, except my life.
Pol Fare you well, my lord.
Ham These tedious old fools !

　　Enter ROSENCRANTZ *and* GUILDENSTERN.

Pol. You go to seek the Lord Hamlet ;
there he is.
Ros. [*To Polonius*] God save you, sir !
　　　　　　　　　[*Exit Polonius.*
Guil. My honored lord !
Ros My most dear lord !
Ham My excellent good friends! How dost
thou, Guildenstern ? Ah, Rosencrantz ! Good
lads, how do ye both ?　　　　　230
Ros. As the indifferent children of the earth.
Guil. Happy, in that we are not over-happy ;
On fortune's cap we are not the very button. ,
Ham. Nor the soles of her shoe ?
Ros Neither, my lord
Ham Then you live about her waist, or in
the middle of her favors ?
Guil. 'Faith, her privates we.
Ham. In the secret parts of fortune ? O,
most true , she is a strumpet. What's the news ?
Ros None, my lord, but that the world's
grown honest　　　　　　　　241
Ham. Then is doomsday near · but your ·
news is not true Let me question more in
particular what have you, my good friends,
deserved at the hands of fortune, that she sends
you to prison hither ?
Guil Prison, my lord !
Ham. Denmark's a prison.
Ros Then is the world one　　　　250
Ham A goodly one ; in which there are
many confines, wards and dungeons, Denmark
being one o' the worst.
Ros We think not so, my lord
Ham. · Why, then, 'tis none to you , for
there is nothing either good or bad, but thinking makes it so : to me it is a prison.
Ros. Why then, your ambition makes it one,
'tis too narrow for your mind　　　259
Ham. O God, I could be bounded in a nutshell and count myself a king of infinite space,
were it not that I have bad dreams.

Guil. Which dreams indeed are ambition, for the very substance of the ambitious is merely the shadow of a dream.

Ham. A dream itself is but a shadow.

Ros. Truly, and I hold ambition of so airy and light a quality that it is but a shadow's shadow.

Ham. Then are our beggars bodies, and our monarchs and outstretched heroes the beggars' shadows. Shall we to the court ? for, by my fay, I cannot reason.

Ros. } We'll wait upon you.
Guil. }

Ham. No such matter : I will not sort you with the rest of my servants, for, to speak to you like an honest man, I am most dreadfully attended. But, in the beaten way of friendship, what make you at Elsinore ?

Ros. To visit you, my lord ; no other occasion.

Ham. Beggar that I am, I am even poor in thanks ; but I thank you : and sure, dear friends, my thanks are too dear a halfpenny. Were you not sent for ? Is it your own inclining ? Is it a free visitation ? Come, deal justly with me : come, come ; nay, speak.

Guil. What should we say, my lord ?

Ham. Why, any thing, but to the purpose. You were sent for ; and there is a kind of confession in your looks which your modesties have not craft enough to color : I know the good king and queen have sent for you. 291

Ros. To what end, my lord ?

Ham. That you must teach me. But let me conjure you, by the rights of our fellowship, by the consonancy of our youth, by the obligation of our ever-preserved love, and by what more dear a better proposer could charge you withal, be even and direct with me, whether you were sent for, or no ?

Ros. [*Aside to Guil.*] What say you ? 300

Ham. [*Aside*] Nay, then, I have an eye of you.—If you love me, hold not off.

Guil. My lord, we were sent for.

Ham. I will tell you why ; so shall my anticipation prevent your discovery, and your secrecy to the king and queen moult no feather. I have of late—but wherefore I know not—lost all my mirth, forgone all custom of exercises ; and indeed it goes so heavily with my disposition that this goodly frame, the earth, seems to me a sterile promontory, this most excellent canopy, the air, look you, this brave o'erhanging firmament, this majestical roof fretted with golden fire, why, it appears no other thing to me than a foul and pestilent congregation of vapors. What a piece of work is a man ! how noble in reason ! how infinite in faculty ! in form and moving how express and admirable ! in action how like an angel ! in apprehension how like a god ! the beauty of the world ! the paragon of animals ! And yet, to me, what is this quintessence of dust ? man delights not me : no, nor woman neither, though by your smiling you seem to say so.

Ros. My lord, there was no such stuff in my thoughts.

Ham. Why did you laugh then, when I said ' man delights not me ' ?

Ros. To think, my lord, if you delight not in man, what lenten entertainment the players shall receive from you : we coted them on the way ; and hither are they coming, to offer you service.

Ham. He that plays the king shall be welcome ; his majesty shall have tribute of me ; the adventurous knight shall use his foil and target ; the lover shall not sigh gratis ; the humorous man shall end his part in peace ; the clown shall make those laugh whose lungs are tickled o' the sere ; and the lady shall say her mind freely, or the blank verse shall halt for't. What players are they ? 340

Ros. Even those you were wont to take delight in, the tragedians of the city.

Ham. How chances it they travel ? their residence, both in reputation and profit, was better both ways.

Ros. I think their inhibition comes by the means of the late innovation.

Ham. Do they hold the same estimation they did when I was in the city ? are they so followed ? 350

Ros. No, indeed, are they not.

Ham. How comes it ? do they grow rusty?

Ros. Nay, their endeavor keeps in the wonted pace : but there is, sir, an aery of children, little eyases, that cry out on the top of question, and are most tyrannically clapped for't : these are now the fashion, and so berattle the common stages—so they call them—that many wearing rapiers are afraid of goosequills and dare scarce come thither. 360

Ham. What, are they children ? who maintains 'em ? how are they escoted ? Will they pursue the quality no longer than they can sing ? will they not say afterwards, if they should grow themselves to common players—as it is most like, if their means are no better—their writers do them wrong, to make them exclaim against their own succession ?

Ros. 'Faith, there has been much to do on both sides ; and the nation holds it no sin to tarre them to controversy : there was, for a while, no money bid for argument, unless the poet and the player went to cuffs in the question.

Ham. Is't possible ?

Guil. O, there has been much throwing about of brains.

Ham. Do the boys carry it away ?

Ros. Ay, that they do, my lord ; Hercules and his load too. 379

Ham. It is not very strange ; for mine uncle is king of Denmark, and those that would make mows at him while my father lived, give twenty, forty, fifty, an hundred ducats a-piece for his picture in little. 'Sblood, there is something in this more than natural, if philosophy could find it out.

[*Flourish of trumpets within.*

Guil. There are the players.

Ham. Gentlemen, you are welcome to Elsinore. Your hands, come then: the appurtenance of welcome is fashion and ceremony: let me comply with you in this garb, lest my extent to the players, which, I tell you, must show fairly outward should more appear like entertainment than yours. You are welcome: but my uncle-father and aunt-mother are deceived.

Guil. In what, my dear lord?

Ham. I am but mad north-north-west: when the wind is southerly I know a hawk from a handsaw.

Enter POLONIUS.

Pol. Well be with you, gentlemen!

Ham. Hark you, Guildenstern; and you too: at each ear a hearer: that great baby you see there is not yet out of his swaddling-clouts.

Ros. Happily he's the second time come to them; for they say an old man is twice a child.

Ham. I will prophesy he comes to tell me of the players; mark it. You say right, sir: o'Monday morning; 'twas so indeed.

Pol. My lord, I have news to tell you.

Ham. My lord, I have news to tell you. When Roscius was an actor in Rome,—   410

Pol. The actors are come hither, my lord.

Ham. Buz, buz!

Pol. Upon mine honor,—

Ham. Then came each actor on his ass,—

Pol. The best actors in the world, either for tragedy, comedy, history, pastoral, pastoral-comical, historical-pastoral, tragical-historical, tragical-comical-historical-pastoral, scene individable, or poem unlimited: Seneca cannot be too heavy, nor Plautus too light. For the law of writ and the liberty, these are the only men.   421

Ham. O Jephthah, judge of Israel, what a treasure hadst thou!

Pol. What a treasure had he, my lord?

Ham. Why,

    'One fair daughter and no more,
    The which he loved passing well.'

Pol. [*Aside*] Still on my daughter.

Ham. Am I not i' the right, old Jephthah?

Pol. If you call me Jephthah, my lord, I have a daughter that I love passing well. 431

Ham. Nay, that follows not.

Pol. What follows, then, my lord?

Ham. Why,

     'As by lot, God wot,'
and then, you know,
  'It came to pass, as most like it was,'—
the first row of the pious chanson will show you more; for look, where my abridgement comes.

Enter four or five Players.

You are welcome, masters; welcome, all. I am glad to see thee well. Welcome, good friends. O, my old friend! thy face is valanced since I saw thee last: comest thou to beard me in Denmark? What, my young lady and mistress! By'r lady, your ladyship is nearer to heaven than when I saw you last, by the altitude of a chopine. Pray God, your voice, like a piece of uncurrent gold, be not cracked within the ring. Masters, you are all welcome. We'll e'en to't like French falconers, fly at any thing we see: we'll have a speech straight: come, give us a taste of your quality; come, a passionate speech.

First Play. What speech, my lord?

Ham. I heard thee speak me a speech once, but it was never acted; or, if it was, not above once; for the play, I remember, pleased not the million; 'twas caviare to the general: but it was—as I received it, and others, whose judgments in such matters cried in the top of mine—an excellent play, well digested in the scenes, set down with as much modesty as cunning. I remember, one said there were no sallets in the lines to make the matter savory, nor no matter in the phrase that might indict the author of affectation; but called it an honest method, as wholesome as sweet, and by very much more handsome than fine. One speech in it I chiefly loved: 'twas Æneas' tale to Dido; and thereabout of it especially, where he speaks of Priam's slaughter: if it live in your memory, begin at this line: let me see, let me see—   471

'The rugged Pyrrhus, like the Hyrcanian beast,'—

it is not so:—it begins with Pyrrhus:—

'The rugged Pyrrhus, he whose sable arms,
Black as his purpose, did the night resemble
When he lay couched in the ominous horse,
Hath now this dread and black complexion smear'd
With heraldry more dismal; head to foot
Now is he total gules; horridly trick'd
With blood of fathers, mothers, daughters, sons,
Baked and impasted with the parching streets,
That lend a tyrannous and damned light
To their lord's murder: roasted in wrath and fire,
And thus o'er-sized with coagulate gore,
With eyes like carbuncles, the hellish Pyrrhus
Old grandsire Priam seeks.'

So, proceed you.

Pol. 'Fore God, my lord, well spoken, with good accent and good discretion.

First Play.   'Anon he finds him
Striking too short at Greeks; his antique sword,
Rebellious to his arm, lies where it falls,
Repugnant to command: unequal match'd,
Pyrrhus at Priam drives; in rage strikes wide;
But with the whiff and wind of his fell sword
The unnerved father falls. Then senseless Ilium,
Seeming to feel this blow, with flaming top

Stoops to his base, and with a hideous crash
Takes prisoner Pyrrhus' ear: for, lo! his
  sword,
Which was declining on the milky head 500
Of reverend Priam, seem'd i' the air to
  stick:
So, as a painted tyrant, Pyrrhus stood,
And like a neutral to his will and matter,
Did nothing
But, as we often see, against some storm,
A silence in the heavens, the rack stand still,
The bold winds speechless and the orb be-
  low
As hush as death, anon the dreadful thunder
Doth rend the region, so, after Pyrrhus'
  pause,   509
Aroused vengeance sets him new a-work;
And never did the Cyclops' hammers fall
On Mars's armor forged for proof eterne
With less remorse than Pyrrhus' bleeding
  sword
Now falls on Priam.
Out, out, thou strumpet, Fortune! All you
  gods,
In general synod, take away her power;
Break all the spokes and fellies from her
  wheel,
And bowl the round nave down the hill of
  heaven,
As low as to the fiends!'
Pol This is too long.   520
Ham. It shall to the barber's, with your
beard Prithee, say on he's for a jig or a
tale of bawdry, or he sleeps: say on: come to
Hecuba.
First Play. 'But who, O. who had seen the
mobled queen—'
Ham. 'The mobled queen?'
Pol That's good; 'mobled queen' is good.
First Play 'Run barefoot up and down,
  threatening the flames
With bisson rheum; a clout upon that head
Where late the diadem stood, and for a robe,
About her lank and all o'er-teemed loins,
A blanket, in the alarm of fear caught up;
Who this had seen, with tongue in venom
  steep'd,
'Gainst Fortune's state would treason have
  pronounced:
But if the gods themselves did see her then
When she saw Pyrrhus make malicious
  sport
In mincing with his sword her husband's
  limbs,
The instant burst of clamor that she made,
Unless things mortal move them not at all,
Would have made milch the burning eyes of
  heaven,   540
And passion in the gods.'
Pol. Look, whether he has not turned his
color and has tears in's eyes. Pray you, no
more.
Ham. 'Tis well; I'll have thee speak out
the rest soon. Good my lord, will you see the
players well bestowed? Do you hear, let them
be well used; for they are the abstract and

brief chronicles of the time: after your death
you were better have a bad epitaph than their
ill report while you live   551
Pol. My lord, I will use them according to
their desert.
Ham. God's bodykins, man, much better:
use every man after his desert, and who
should 'scape whipping? Use them after your
own honor and dignity: the less they deserve,
the more merit is in your bounty. Take them
in
Pol. Come, sirs   559
Ham. Follow him, friends: we'll hear a
play to-morrow. [*Exit Polonius with all
the Players but the First*] Dost thou hear
me, old friend, can you play the Murder of
Gonzago?
First Pla Ay, my lord.
Ham. We'll ha't to-morrow night You
could, for a need, study a speech of some dozen
or sixteen lines, which I would set down and
insert in't, could you not?
First Play Ay, my lord.   569
Ham. Very well Follow that lord; and
look you mock him not [*Exit First Player.*]
My good friends, I'll leave you till night you
are welcome to Elsinore.
Ros Good my lord!
Ham. Ay, so, God be wi' ye: [*Exeunt
Rosencrantz and Guildenstern*] Now I am
  alone
O, what a rogue and peasant slave am I!
Is it not monstrous that this player here,
But in a fiction, in a dream of passion,
Could force his soul so to his own conceit
That from her working all his visage wann'd,
Tears in his eyes, distraction in's aspect, 581
A broken voice, and his whole function suiting
With forms to his conceit? and all for nothing!
For Hecuba!
What's Hecuba to him, or he to Hecuba,
That he should weep for her? What would
  he do,
Had he the motive and the cue for passion
That I have? He would drown the stage with
  tears
And cleave the general ear with horrid speech,
Make mad the guilty and appal the free,   590
Confound the ignorant, and amaze indeed
The very faculties of eyes and ears.
Yet I,
A dull and muddy-mettled rascal, peak,
Like John-a-dreams, unpregnant of my cause,
And can say nothing, no, not for a king,
Upon whose property and most dear life
A damn'd defeat was made Am I a coward?
Who calls me villain? breaks my pate across?
Plucks off my beard, and blows it in my face?
Tweaks me by the nose? gives me the lie i'
  the throat,   600
As deep as to the lungs? who does me this?
Ha!
'Swounds, I should take it · for it cannot be
But I am pigeon-liver'd and lack gall
To make oppression bitter, or ere this
I should have fatted all the region kites

With this slave's offal : bloody, bawdy villain!
Remorseless, treacherous, lecherous, kindless
     villain !
O, vengeance !   610
(Why, what an ass am I !   This is most brave,
That I, the son of a dear father murder'd,
Prompted to my revenge by heaven and hell,
Must, like a whore, unpack my heart with
     words,
And fall a-cursing, like a very drab,
A scullion !
Fie upon't! foh ! About, my brain ! I have
     heard
That guilty creatures sitting at a play
Have by the very cunning of the scene
Been struck so to the soul that presently   620
They have proclaim'd their malefactions ;
For murder, though it have no tongue, will
     speak
With most miraculous organ. I'll have these
     players
Play something like the murder of my father
Before mine uncle: I'll observe his looks ;
I'll tent him to the quick: if he but blench,
I know my course. The spirit that I have seen
May be the devil : and the devil hath power
To assume a pleasing shape ; yea, and perhaps   630
As he is very potent with such spirits,
Abuses me to damn me: I'll have grounds
More relative than this : the play 's the thing
Wherein I'll catch the conscience of the king.
                          [Exit.

ACT III.

SCENE I. *A room in the castle.*

Enter KING, QUEEN, POLONIUS, OPHELIA,
    ROSENCRANTZ, *and* GUILDENSTERN.

    King. And can you, by no drift of circum-
     stance,
Get from him why he puts on this confusion,
Grating so harshly all his days of quiet
With turbulent and dangerous lunacy ?
    Ros. He does confess he feels himself dis-
     tracted ;
But from what cause he will by no means
     speak.
    Guil. Nor do we find him forward to be
     sounded,
But, with a crafty madness, keeps aloof,
When we would bring him on to some confes-
     sion
Of his true state.
    Queen.   Did he receive you well ?   10
    Ros. Most like a gentleman.
    Guil. But with much forcing of his dispo-
     sition.
    Ros. Niggard of question ; but. of our de-
     mands,
Most free in his reply.
    Queen.   Did you assay him
To any pastime ?

    Ros. Madam, it so fell out, that certain
     players   [him ;
We o'er-raught on the way: of these we told
And there did seem in him a kind of joy
To hear of it : they are about the court,
And, as I think, they have already order   20
This night to play before him.
    Pol.   'Tis most true:
And he beseech'd me to entreat your majesties
To hear and see the matter.
    King. With all my heart ; and it doth much
     content me
To hear him so inclined.
Good gentlemen, give him a further edge,
And drive his purpose on to these delights.
    Ros. We shall, my lord.
        [*Exeunt Rosencrantz and Guildenstern.*
    King.   Sweet Gertrude, leave us too;
For we have closely sent for Hamlet hither,
That he, as 'twere by accident, may here   30
Affront Ophelia :
Her father and myself, lawful espials,
Will so bestow ourselves that, seeing, unseen,
We may of their encounter frankly judge,
And gather by him, as he is behaved,
If 't be the affliction of his love or no
That thus he suffers for.
    Queen.   I shall obey you.
And for your part, Ophelia, I do wish
That your good beauties be the happy cause
Of Hamlet's wildness: so shall I hope your
     virtues   40
Will bring him to his wonted way again,
To both your honors.
    Oph. Madam, I wish it may. [*Exit Queen.*
    Pol. Ophelia, walk you here. Gracious, so
     please you,
We will bestow ourselves. [*To Ophelia*] Read
     on this book ;
That show of such an exercise may color
Your loneliness. We are oft to blame in this,—
'Tis too much proved—that with devotion's
     visage
And pious action we do sugar o'er
The devil himself.
    King. [*Aside.*] O, 'tis too true!
How smart a lash that speech doth give my
     conscience !   50
The harlot's cheek, beautied with plastering
     art,
Is not more ugly to the thing that helps it
Than is my deed to my most painted word:
O heavy burthen !
    Pol. I hear him coming: let's withdraw,
     my lord. [*Exeunt King and Polonius*

Enter HAMLET.

    Ham. To be, or not to be: that is the
     question ;
Whether 'tis nobler in the mind to suffer
The slings and arrows of outrageous fortune,
Or to take arms against a sea of troubles,
And by opposing end them ? To die: to sleep;
No more ; and by a sleep to say we end   61
The heart-ache and the thousand natural
     shocks

That flesh is heir to, 'tis a consummation
Devoutly to be wish'd. To die, to sleep;
To sleep : perchance to dream: ay, there's
    the rub ;
For in that sleep of death what dreams may
    come
When we have shuffled off this mortal coil,
Must give us pause : there's the respect
That makes calamity of so long life ;
For who would bear the whips and scorns of
    time,   70
The oppressor's wrong, the proud man's con-
    tumely,
The pangs of despised love, the law's delay,
The insolence of office and the spurns
That patient merit of the unworthy takes,
When he himself might his quietus make
With a bare bodkin ? who would fardels bear,
To grunt and sweat under a weary life,
But that the dread of something after death,
The undiscover'd country from whose bourn
No traveller returns, puzzles the will   80
And makes us rather bear those ills we have
Than fly to others that we know not of ?
Thus conscience does make cowards of us all ;
And thus the native hue of resolution
Is sicklied o'er with the pale cast of thought,
And enterprises of great pith and moment
With this regard their currents turn awry,
And lose the name of action.—Soft you now!
The fair Ophelia ! Nymph, in thy orisons
Be all my sins remember'd.
    Oph.   Good my lord, 90
How does your honor for this many a day ?
    Ham. I humbly thank you ; well, well,
    well.
    Oph. My lord, I have remembrances of
    yours,
That I have longed long to re-deliver ;
I pray you, now receive them.
    Ham.   No, not I ;
I never gave you aught.
    Oph. My honor'd lord, you know right well
    you did ;
And, with them, words of so sweet breath com-
    posed
As made the things more rich: their perfume
    lost,
Take these again ; for to the noble mind 100
Rich gifts wax poor when givers prove unkind.
There, my lord.
    Ham. Ha, ha ! are you honest ?
    Oph. My lord ?
    Ham. Are you fair ?
    Oph. What means your lordship ?
    Ham. That if you be honest and fair, your
honesty should admit no discourse to your
beauty.
    Oph. Could beauty, my lord, have better
commerce than with honesty ?   110
    Ham. Ay, truly; for the power of beauty
will sooner transform honesty from what it is
to a bawd than the force of honesty can translate beauty into his likeness : this was sometime a paradox, but now the time gives it
proof. I did love you once.

    Oph. Indeed, my lord, you made me believe
so.
    Ham. You should not have believed me;
for virtue cannot so inoculate our old stock
but we shall relish of it : I loved you not. 120
    Oph. I was the more deceived.
    Ham. Get thee to a nunnery: why wouldst
thou be a breeder of sinners ? I am myself
indifferent honest ; but yet I could accuse me
of such things that it were better my mother
had not borne me : I am very proud, revenge-
ful, ambitious, with more offences at my beck
than I have thoughts to put them in, imagination to give them shape, or time to act them
in. What should such fellows as I do crawling
between earth and heaven ? We are arrant
knaves, all ; believe none of us. Go thy ways
to a nunnery. Where's your father ?
    Oph. At home, my lord.
    Ham. Let the doors be shut upon him, that
he may play the fool no where but in's own
house. Farewell.
    Oph. O, help him, you sweet heavens !
    Ham. If thou dost marry, I'll give thee this
plague for thy dowry : be thou as chaste as ice,
as pure as snow, thou shalt not escape calumny.
Get thee to a nunnery, go : farewell. Or, if
thou wilt needs marry, marry a fool ; for wise
men know well enough what monsters you
make of them. To a nunnery, go, and quickly
too. Farewell.
    Oph. O heavenly powers, restore him !
    Ham. I have heard of your paintings too,
well enough; God has given you one face, and
you make yourselves another: you jig, you
amble, and you lisp, and nick-name God's creatures, and make your wantonness your ignorance. Go to, I'll no more on't ; it hath made
me mad. I say, we will have no more marriages : those that are married already, all but
one, shall live; the rest shall keep as they are.
To a nunnery, go.   *[Exit.*
    Oph. O, what a noble mind is here o'er-
    thrown !
The courtier's, soldier's, scholar's, eye, tongue,
    sword ;
The expectancy and rose of the fair state, 160
The glass of fashion and the mould of form,
The observed of all observers, quite, quite
    down !
And I, of ladies most deject and wretched,
That suck'd the honey of his music vows,
Now see that noble and most sovereign reason,
Like sweet bells jangled, out of tune and harsh;
That unmatch'd form and feature of blown
    youth
Blasted with ecstasy : O, woe is me,
To have seen what I have seen, see what I see!

    Re-enter KING *and* POLONIUS.

    King. Love ! his affections do not that way
    tend ;   170
Nor what he spake, though it lack'd form a
    little,
Was not like madness. There's something in
    his soul,

O'er which his melancholy sits on brood ;
And I do doubt the hatch and the disclose
Will be some danger : which for to prevent,
I have in quick determination
Thus set it down : he shall with speed to Eng-
    land,
For the demand of our neglected tribute :
Haply the seas and countries different
With variable objects shall expel   180
This something-settled matter in his heart,
Whereon his brains still beating puts him thus
From fashion of himself. What think you on't?
  Pol. It shall do well : but yet do I believe
The origin and commencement of his grief
Sprung from neglected love. How now, Ophe-
    lia !
You need not tell us what Lord Hamlet said ;
We heard it all. My lord, do as you please ;
But, if you hold it fit, after the play   189
Let his queen mother all alone entreat him
To show his grief : let her be round with him;
And I'll be placed, so please you, in the ear
Of all their conference. If she find him not,
To England send him, or confine him where
Your wisdom best shall think.
  King.   It shall be so :
Madness in great ones must not unwatch'd go.
          [*Exeunt.*

  SCENE II. *A hall in the castle.*

  Enter HAMLET *and* Players.

  Ham. Speak the speech, I pray you, as I
pronounced it to you, trippingly on the tongue:
but if you mouth it, as many of your players
do, I had as lief the town-crier spoke my lines.
Nor do not saw the air too much with your
hand, thus, but use all gently ; for in the very
torrent, tempest, and, as I may say, the whirl-
wind of passion, you must acquire and beget a
temperance that may give it smoothness. O,
it offends me to the soul to hear a robustious
periwig-pated fellow tear a passion to tatters,
to very rags, to split the ears of the ground-
lings, who for the most part are capable of
nothing but inexplicable dumb-shows and
noise : I would have such a fellow whipped
for o'erdoing Termagant ; it out-herods Herod :
pray you, avoid it.
  First Play. I warrant your honor.
  Ham. Be not too tame neither, but let your
own discretion be your tutor : suit the action
to the word, the word to the action ; with this
special observance, that you o'erstep not the
modesty of nature : for any thing so overdone
is from the purpose of playing, whose end,
both at the first and now, was and is, to hold,
as 'twere, the mirror up to nature ; to show
virtue her own feature, scorn her own image,
and the very age and body of the time his form
and pressure. Now this overdone, or come
tardy off, though it make the unskilful laugh,
cannot but make the judicious grieve ; the
censure of the which one must in your allowance o'erweigh a whole theatre of others. O,
there be players that I have seen play, and

heard others praise, and that highly, not to
speak it profanely, that, neither having the
accent of Christians nor the gait of Christian,
pagan, nor man, have so strutted and bellowed
that I have thought some of nature's journey-
men had made men and not made them well,
they imitated humanity so abominably.
  First Play. I hope we have reformed that
indifferently with us, sir.   41
  Ham. O, reform it altogether. And let
those that play your clowns speak no more
than is set down for them ; for there be of
them that will themselves laugh, to set on
some quantity of barren spectators to laugh
too ; though, in the mean time, some necessary
question of the play be then to be considered :
that's villanous, and shows a most pitiful
ambition in the fool that uses it. Go, make
you ready.   [*Exeunt Players.*

  Enter POLONIUS, ROSENCRANTZ, *and* GUILD-
      ENSTERN.

How now, my lord ! will the king hear this
piece of work ?
  Pol. And the queen too, and that presently.
  Ham. Bid the players make haste. [*Exit
Polonius.*] Will you two help to hasten them ?
  Ros. }
  Guil. } We will, my lord.

    [*Exeunt Rosencrantz and Guildenstern.*
  Ham. What ho ! Horatio !

    Enter HORATIO

  Hor. Here, sweet lord, at your service.
  Ham. Horatio, thou art e'en as just a man
As e'er my conversation coped withal, 60
  Hor. O, my dear lord,—
  Ham.   Nay, do not think I flatter ;
For what advancement may I hope from thee
That no revenue hast but thy good spirits,
To feed and clothe thee ? Why should the
    poor be flatter'd ?
No, let the candied tongue lick absurd pomp,
And crook the pregnant hinges of the knee
Where thrift may follow fawning. Dost thou
    hear ?
Since my dear soul was mistress of her choice
And could of men distinguish, her election 69
Hath seal'd thee for herself ; for thou hast been
As one, in suffering all, that suffers nothing,
A man that fortune's buffets and rewards
Hast ta'en with equal thanks : and blest are
    those
Whose blood and judgment are so well com-
    mingled,
That they are not a pipe for fortune's finger
To sound what stop she please. Give me that
    man
That is not passion's slave, and I will wear him
In my heart's core, ay, in my heart of heart,
As I do thee.—Something too much of this.—
There is a play to-night before the king ; 80
One scene of it comes near the circumstance
Which I have told thee of my father's death :
I prithee, when thou seest that act afoot,
Even with the very comment of thy soul

Observe mine uncle : if his occulted guilt
Do not itself unkennel in one speech,
It is a damned ghost that we have seen,
And my imaginations are as foul
As Vulcan's stithy   Give him heedful note ;
For I mine eyes will rivet to his face,   90
And after we will both our judgments join
In censure of his seeming
   Hor.   Well, my lord ·
If he steal aught the whilst this play is playing,
And 'scape detecting, I will pay the theft.
   Ham   They are coming to the play , I must
be idle
Get you a place.

Danish march.   A flourish   Enter KING,
QUEEN, POLONIUS, OPHELIA, ROSENCRANTZ,
GUILDENSTERN, *and others*

   King   How fares our cousin Hamlet ?
   Ham.   Excellent. i' faith, of the chameleon's
dish . I eat the air, promise-crammed . you
cannot feed capons so   100
   King.   I have nothing with this answer,
Hamlet , these words are not mine
   Ham   No, nor mine now   [*To Polonius*]
My lord, you played once i' the university,
you say ?
   Pol   That did I, my lord , and was ac-
counted a good actor.
   Ham   What did you enact ?
   Pol.   I did enact Julius Cæsar : I was killed
i' the Capitol ; Brutus killed me   110
   Ham.   It was a brute part of him to kill so
capital a calf there   Be the players ready ?
   Ros   Ay, my lord , they stay upon your
patience
   Queen.   Come hither, my dear Hamlet, sit
by me
   Ham.   No, good mother, here's metal more
attractive ·
   Pol.   [*To the King*] O, ho ! do you mark
that ?
   Ham.   Lady, shall I lie in your lap ?
            [*Lying down at Ophelia's feet*
   Oph.   No, my lord·   120
   Ham.   I mean, my head upon your lap ?
   Oph.   Ay, my lord
   Ham.   Do you think I meant country mat-
ters ?
   Oph.   I think nothing, my lord.
   Ham   That's a fair thought to lie between
maids' legs.
   Oph.   What is, my lord ?
   Ham.   Nothing——
   Oph.   You are merry, my lord.
   Ham.   Who, I ?
   Oph.   Ay, my lord   130
   Ham.   O God, your only jig-maker. What
should a man do but be merry ? for, look you,
how cheerfully my mother looks, and my father
died within these two hours.
   Oph.   Nay, 'tis twice two months, my lord
   Ham   ·So long ? Nay then, let the devil
wear black, for I'll have a suit of sables. O
heavens ! die two months ago, and not forgot-
ten yet ? Then there's hope a great man's

memory may outlive his life half a year : but,
by'r lady, he must build churches, then , or
else shall he suffer not thinking on, with the
hobby-horse, whose epitaph is ' For, O, for, O,
the hobby-horse is forgot '

Hautboys play   The dumb-show enters.

*Enter a King and a Queen very lovingly ; the
Queen embracing him, and he her. She
kneels, and makes show of protestation unto
him   He takes her up, and declines his head
upon her neck . lays him down upon a bank
of flowers she, seeing him asleep, leaves
him   Anon comes in a fellow, takes off his
crown, kisses it, and pours poison in the
King's ears, and exit   The Queen returns ;
finds the King dead, and makes passionate
action   The Poisoner, with some two or three
Mutes, comes in again, seeming to lament
with her   The dead body is carried away
The Poisoner wooes the Queen with gifts .
she seems loath and unwilling awhile, but in
the end accepts his love   [Exeunt.*
   Oph   What means this, my lord ?
   Ham   Marry, this is miching mallecho ; it
means mischief
   Oph   Belike this show imports the argument of the play   150

Enter Prologue.

   Ham   We shall know by this fellow · the
players cannot keep counsel , they'll tell all.
   Oph   Will he tell us what this show meant?
   Ham   Ay, or any show that you'll show
him   be not you ashamed to show, he'll not
shame to tell you what it means
   Oph   You are naught, you are naught · I'll
mark the play.
   Pro.   For us, and for our tragedy,
Here stooping to your clemency,   160
     We beg your hearing patiently [*Exit.*
   Ham   Is this a prologue, or the posy of a
·ring ?
   Oph   'Tis brief, my lord.
   Ham   As woman's love

Enter two Players, King *and* Queen.

   P King   Full thirty times hath Phœbus'
cart gone round
Neptune's salt wash and Tellus' orbed ground,
And thirty dozen moons with borrow'd sheen
About the world have times twelve thirties
been,
Since love our hearts and Hymen did our
hands
Unite commutual in most sacred bands. 170
   P. Queen   So many journeys may the
sun and moon
Make us again count o'er ere love be done !
But, woe is me, you are so sick of late,
So far from cheer and from your former
state,
That I distrust you   Yet, though I distrust,
Discomfort you, my lord, it nothing must :
For women's fear and love holds quantity ;
In neither aught, or in extremity

Now, what my love is, proof hath made you
    know ;
And as my love is sized, my fear is so : 180
Where love is great, the littlest doubts are
    fear ;
Where little fears grow great, great love
    grows there.
    P. King.   'Faith, I must leave thee, love,
    and shortly too ;
My operant powers their functions leave to
    do:
And thou shalt live in this fair world be-
    hind,
Honor'd, beloved ; and haply one as kind
For husband shalt thou—
    P. Queen.   O, confound the rest !
Such love must needs be treason in my
    breast:
In second husband let me be accurst ! 189
None wed the second but who kill'd the first.
    Ham. [*Aside*] Wormwood, wormwood.
    P. Queen. The instances that second mar-
    riage move
Are base respects of thrift, but none of love:
A second time I kill my husband dead,
When second husband kisses me in bed.
    P. King.   I do believe you think what
    now you speak ;
But what we do determine oft we break.
Purpose is but the slave to memory,
Of violent birth, but poor validity ;
Which now, like fruit unripe, sticks on the
    tree ;   200
But fall, unshaken, when they mellow be.
Most necessary 'tis that we forget
To pay ourselves what to ourselves is debt :
What to ourselves in passion we propose,
The passion ending, doth the purpose lose.
The violence of either grief or joy
Their own enactures with themselves de-
    stroy:
Where joy most revels, grief doth most la-
    ment ;
Grief joys, joy grieves, on slender accident.
This world is not for aye, nor 'tis not strange
That even our loves should with our for-
    tunes change ;
For 'tis a question left us yet to prove,
Whether love lead fortune, or else fortune
    love.
The great man down, you mark his favorite
    flies ;
The poor advanced makes friends of ene-
    mies.
And hitherto doth love on fortune tend ;
For who not needs shall never lack a friend,
And who in want a hollow friend doth try,
Directly seasons him his enemy.
But, orderly to end where I begun,   220
Our wills and fates do so contrary run
That our devices still are overthrown ;
Our thoughts are ours, their ends none of
    our own :
So think thou wilt no second husband wed ;
But die thy thoughts when thy first lord is
    dead

    P. Queen. Nor earth to me give food, nor
    heaven light !
Sport and repose lock from me day and
    night !
To desperation turn my trust and hope !
An anchor's cheer in prison be my scope !
Each opposite that blanks the face of joy 230
Meet what I would have well and it destroy!
Both here and hence pursue me lasting
    strife,
If, once a widow, ever I be wife !
    Ham.   If she should break it now !
    P. King.   'Tis deeply sworn. Sweet, leave
    me here awhile ;
My spirits grow dull, and fain I would be-
    guile
The tedious day with sleep.   [*Sleeps.*
    P. Queen.   Sleep rock thy brain ;
And never come mischance between us
    twain !   [*Exit.*
    Ham. Madam, how like you this play ? 239
    Queen. The lady protests too much, me-
    thinks.
    Ham. O, but she'll keep her word.
    King. Have you heard the argument ? Is
there no offence in 't ?
    Ham. No, no, they do but jest, poison in
jest ; no offence i' the world.
    King. What do you call the play ?
    Ham. The Mouse-trap. Marry, how ? Tro-
pically. This play is the image of a murder
done in Vienna : Gonzago is the duke's name;
his wife, Baptista : you shall see anon ; 'tis a
knavish piece of work : but what o' that ?
your majesty and we that have free souls, it
touches us not : let the galled jade wince, our
withers are unwrung.

             Enter LUCIANUS.

This is one Lucianus, nephew to the king.
    Oph. You are as good as a chorus, my lord.
    Ham. I could interpret between you and
your love, if I could see the puppets dallying.
    Oph. You are keen, my lord, you are keen.
    Ham. It would cost you a groaning to take
off my edge.   260
    Oph. Still better, and worse.
    Ham. So you must take your husbands. Be-
gin, murderer; pox, leave thy damnable faces,
and begin. Come : 'the croaking raven doth
bellow for revenge.'
    Luc. Thoughts black, hands apt, drugs
    fit, and time agreeing ;
Confederate season, else no creature seeing ;
Thou mixture rank, of midnight weeds col-
    lected,
With Hecate's ban thrice blasted, thrice in-
    fected,
Thy natural magic and dire property,   270
On wholesome life usurp immediately.
    [*Pours the poison into the sleeper's ears.*
    Ham. He poisons him i' the garden for's
estate. His name's Gonzago : the story is extant, and writ in choice Italian : you shall see
anon how the murderer gets the love of Gon-
zago's wife.

Oph. The king rises.
Ham. What, frighted with false fire !
Queen. How fares my lord ?
Pol. Give o'er the play.
King. Give me some light,: away !   280
All. Lights, lights, lights !
   [*Exeunt all but Hamlet and Horatio.*
Ham. Why, let the stricken deer go weep,
   The hart ungalled play ;
   For some must watch, while some
      must sleep :
   So runs the world away.
Would not this, sir, and a forest of feathers—
if the rest of my fortunes turn Turk with me—
with two Provincial roses on my razed shoes,
get me a fellowship in a cry of players, sir ?
Hor. Half a share.   290
Ham. A whole one, I.
   For thou dost know, O Damon dear,
    This realm dismantled was
   Of Jove himself ; and now reigns here
    A very, very—pajock.
Hor. You might have rhymed.
Ham. O good Horatio, I'll take the ghost's
word for a thousand pound. Didst perceive ?
Hor. Very well, my lord.
Ham. Upon the talk of the poisoning ?   300
Hor. I did very well note him.
Ham. Ah, ha ! Come, some music ! come,
the recorders !
   For if the king like not the comedy,
   Why then, belike, he likes it not, perdy.
Come, some music !

Re-enter Rosencrantz *and* Guildenstern.

Guil. Good my lord, vouchsafe me a word
with you.
Ham. Sir, a whole history.
Guil. The king, sir,—   310
Ham. Ay, sir, what of him ?
Guil. Is in his retirement marvellous dis-
tempered.
Ham. With drink, sir ?
Guil. No, my lord, rather with choler.
Ham. Your wisdom should show itself more
richer to signify this to his doctor : for, for
me to put him to his purgation would perhaps
plunge him into far more choler.   319
Guil. Good my lord, put your discourse
into some frame and start not so wildly from
my affair.
Ham. I am tame, sir : pronounce.
Guil. The queen, your mother, in most great
affliction of spirit, hath sent me to you.
Ham. You are welcome.
Guil. Nay, good my lord, this courtesy is
not of the right breed. If it shall please you
to make me a wholesome answer, I will do
your mother's commandment : if not, your
pardon and my return shall be the end of my
business.   330
Ham. Sir, I cannot.
Guil. What, my lord ?
Ham. Make you a wholesome answer; my
wit's diseased : but, sir, such answer as I can
make, you shall command ; or, rather, as you

say, my mother : therefore no more, but to
the matter : my mother, you say,—
Ros. Then thus she says ; your behavior
hath struck her into amazement and admiration.   339
Ham. O wonderful son, that can so astonish a mother ! But is there no sequel at the
heels of this mother's admiration ? Impart.
Ros. She desires to speak with you in her
closet, ere you go to bed.
Ham. We shall obey, were she ten times
our mother. Have you any further trade with
us ?
Ros. My lord, you once did love me.
Ham. So I do still, by these pickers and
stealers.   349
Ros. Good my lord, what is your cause of
distemper ? you do, surely, bar the door upon
your own liberty, if you deny your griefs to
your friend.
Ham. Sir, I lack advancement.
Ros. How can that be, when you have the
voice of the king himself for your succession
in Denmark ?
Ham. Ay, but sir, 'While the grass grows,'—
the proverb is something musty.   359

   Re-enter Players *with recorders.*

O, the recorders ! let me see one. To with-
draw with you :—why do you go about to recover the wind of me, as if you would drive
me into a toil ?
Guil. O, my lord, if my duty be too bold,
my love is too unmannerly.
Ham. I do not well understand that. Will
you play upon this pipe ?
Guil. My lord, I cannot.
Ham. I pray you.
Guil. Believe me, I cannot.
Ham. I do beseech you.   370
Guil. I know no touch of it, my lord.
Ham. 'Tis as easy as lying: govern these
ventages with your fingers and thumb, give it
breath with your mouth, and it will discourse
most eloquent music. Look you, these are the
stops.
Guil. But these cannot I command to any
utterance of harmony ; I have not the skill.
Ham. Why, look you now, how unworthy
a thing you make of me ! You would play
upon me ; you would seem to know my stops ;
you would pluck out the heart of my mystery;
you would sound me from my lowest note to
the top of my compass : and there is much
music, excellent voice, in this little organ; yet
cannot you make it speak. 'Sblood, do you
think I am easier to oe played on than a pipe?
Call me what instrument you will, though
you can fret me, yet you cannot play upon
me.

   Enter Polonius.

God bless you, sir !   390
Pol. My lord, the queen would speak with
you, and presently.
Ham. Do you see yonder cloud that's almost in shape of a camel ?

Pol By the mass, and 'tis like a camel, indeed.

Ham. Methinks it is like a weasel.

Pol It is backed like a weasel

Ham. Or like a whale?

Pol Very like a whale.   399

Ham. Then I will come to my mother by
and by   They fool me to the top of my bent.
I will come by and by

Pol. I will say so

Ham. By and by is easily said. [*Exit Polonius*] Leave me, friends.

                              [*Exeunt all but Hamlet.*

'Tis now the very witching time of night,
When churchyards yawn and hell itself
    breathes out
Contagion to this world · now could I drink
    hot blood,
And do such bitter business as the day
Would quake to look on.   Soft! now to my
    mother   410
O heart, lose not thy nature, let not ever
The soul of Nero enter this firm bosom
Let me be cruel, not unnatural :
I will speak daggers to her, but use none ;
My tongue and soul in this be hypocrites,
How in my words soever she be shent,
To give them seals never, my soul, consent !
                                              [*Exit.*

Scene III.   *A room in the castle.*

Enter King, Rosencrantz, *and*
Guildenstern

King. I like him not, nor stands it safe with
    us
To let his madness range.   Therefore prepare
    you ;
I your commission will forthwith dispatch,
And he to England shall along with you :
The terms of our estate may not endure
Hazard so dangerous as doth hourly grow
Out of his lunacies

Guil   We will ourselves provide
Most holy and religious fear it is
To keep those many many bodies safe
That live and feed upon your majesty.   10

Ros. The single and peculiar life is bound,
With all the strength and armor of the mind,
To keep itself from noyance ; but much more
That spirit upon whose weal depend and rest
The lives of many   The cease of majesty
Dies not alone ; but, like a gulf, doth draw
What's near it with it   it is a massy wheel,
Fix'd on the summit of the highest mount,
To whose huge spokes ten thousand lesser
    things
Are mortised and adjoin'd ; which, when it
    falls,   20
Each small annexment, petty consequence,
Attends the boisterous ruin   Never alone
Did the king sigh, but with a general groan.

King Arm you, I pray you, to this speedy
    voyage,
For we will fetters put upon this fear,
Which now goes too free-footed.

Ros. }
Guil }   We will haste us.

            [*Exeunt Rosencrantz and Guildenstern.*
                    Enter Polonius.

Pol. My lord, he's going to his mother's
    closet .
Behind the arras I'll convey myself,
To hear the process, I'll warrant she'll tax
    him home :
And, as you said, and wisely was it said,   30
'Tis meet that some more audience than a
    mother,   [hear
Since nature makes them partial, should o'er-
The speech, of vantage.   Fare you well, my
    liege :
I'll call upon you ere you go to bed,
And tell you what I know.

King.   Thanks, dear my lord
                                    [*Exit Polonius*
O, my offence is rank, it smells to heaven ;
It hath the primal eldest curse upon't,
A brother's murder   Pray can I not,
Though inclination be as sharp as will :   39
My stronger guilt defeats my strong intent ;
And, like a man to double business bound,
I stand in pause where I shall first begin,
And both neglect   What if this cursed hand
Were thicker than itself with brother's blood,
Is there not rain enough in the sweet heavens
To wash it white as snow ?   Whereto serves
    mercy
But to confront the visage of offence ?
And what's in prayer but this two-fold force,
To be forestalled ere we come to fall,   49
Or pardon'd being down ?   Then I'll look up ;
My fault is past   But, O, what form of prayer
Can serve my turn ?   'Forgive me my foul
    murder' ?
That cannot be ; since I am still possess'd
Of those effects for which I did the murder.
My crown, mine own ambition and my queen.
May one be pardon'd and retain the offence ?
In the corrupted currents of this world
Offence's gilded hand may shove by justice,
And oft 'tis seen the wicked prize itself
Buys out the law · but 'tis not so above ;   60
There is no shuffling, there the action lies
In his true nature, and we ourselves com-
    pell'd,
Even to the teeth and forehead of our faults, ·
To give in evidence.   What then ?   what
    rests ?
Try what repentance can ; what can it not ?
Yet what can it when one can not repent ?
O wretched state !   O bosom black as death !
O limed soul, that, struggling to be free,
Art more engaged !   Help, angels !   Make
    assay !
Bow, stubborn knees ; and, heart with strings
    of steel,   70
Be soft as sinews of the new-born babe !
All may be well.   [*Retires and kneels.*
                    Enter Hamlet.

Ham. Now might I do it pat, now he is
    praying ;

And now I'll do't. And so he goes to heaven;
And so am I revenged. That would be
    scann'd :
A villain kills my father ; and for that,
I, his sole son, do this same villain send
To heaven.
O, this is hire and salary, not revenge.
He took my father grossly, full of bread ; 80
With all his crimes broad blown, as flush as
    May ;
And how his audit stands who knows save
    heaven ?
But in our circumstance and course of
    thought,
'Tis heavy with him : and am I then revenged,
To take him in the purging of his soul,
When he is fit and season'd for his passage ?
No !
Up, sword ; and know thou a more horrid
    hent :
When he is drunk asleep, or in his rage,
Or in the incestuous pleasure of his bed ; 90
At gaming, swearing, or about some act
That has no relish of salvation in't ;
Then trip him, that his heels may kick at
    heaven,
And that his soul may be as damn'd and
    black
As hell, whereto it goes. My mother stays :
This physic but prolongs thy sickly days.
                                        [*Exit.*
King. [*Rising*] My words fly up, my
    thoughts remain below :
Words without thoughts never to heaven go.
                                        [*Exit.*

SCENE IV.   *The Queen's closet.*

Enter QUEEN *and* POLONIUS.

Pol. He will come straight. Look you lay
    home to him :
Tell him his pranks have been too broad to
    bear with,
And that your grace hath screen'd and stood
    between
Much heat and him. I'll sconce me even here.
Pray you, be round with him.
Ham. [*Within*] Mother, mother, mother !
Queen.   I'll warrant you,
Fear me not : withdraw, I hear him coming.
    [*Polonius hides behind the arras.*

Enter HAMLET.

Ham. Now, mother, what's the matter ?
Queen. Hamlet, thou hast thy father much
    offended.
Ham. Mother, you have my father much
    offended.   10
Queen. Come, come, you answer with an
    idle tongue.
Ham. Go, go, you question with a wicked
    tongue.
Queen. Why, how now, Hamlet !
Ham.   What's the matter now ?
Queen. Have you forgot me ?
Ham.   No, by the rood, not so :

You are the queen, your husband's brother's
    wife ;
And—would it were not so !—you are my
    mother.
Queen. Nay, then, I'll set those to you
    that can speak.
Ham. Come, come, and sit you down ; you
    shall not budge ;
You go not till I set you up a glass
Where you may see the inmost part of you. 20
Queen. What wilt thou do ? thou wilt not
    murder me ?
Help, help, ho !
Pol. [*Behind*] What, ho ! help, help, help !
Ham. [*Drawing*] How now ! a rat ? Dead,
    for a ducat, dead !
                [*Makes a pass through the arras.*
Pol. [*Behind*] O, I am slain !
                                    [*Falls and dies.*
Queen. O me, what hast thou done ?
Ham.   Nay, I know not :
Is it the king ?
Queen. O, what a rash and bloody deed is
    this !
Ham. A bloody deed ! almost as bad, good
    mother,
As kill a king, and marry with his brother.
Queen. As kill a king !
Ham.   Ay, lady, 'twas my word. 30
    [*Lifts up the arras and discovers Polonius.*
Thou wretched, rash, intruding fool, fare-
    well !
I took thee for thy better : take thy fortune ;
Thou find'st to be too busy is some danger.
Leave wringing of your hands : peace ! sit
    you down,
And let me wring your heart ; for so I shall,
If it be made of penetrable stuff,
If damned custom have not brass'd it so
That it is proof and bulwark against sense.
Queen. What have I done, that thou darest
    wag thy tongue
In noise so rude against me ?
Ham.   Such an act   40
That blurs the grace and blush of modesty,
Calls virtue hypocrite, takes off the rose
From the fair forehead of an innocent love
And sets a blister there, makes marriage-
    vows
As false as dicers' oaths : O, such a deed
As from the body of contraction plucks
The very soul, and sweet religion makes
A rhapsody of words : heaven's face doth
    glow :
Yea, this solidity and compound mass,
With tristful visage, as against the doom, 50
Is thought-sick at the act.
Queen.   Ay me, what act,
That roars so loud, and thunders in the in-
    dex ?
Ham. Look here, upon this picture, and on
    this,
The counterfeit presentment of two brothers.
See, what a grace was seated on this brow ;
Hyperion's curls ; the front of Jove himself ;
An eye like Mars, to threaten and command ;

A station like the herald Mercury
New-lighted on a heaven-kissing hill ;
A combination and a form indeed,   60
Where every god did seem to set his seal,
To give the world assurance of a man .
This was your husband. Look you now, what
    follows
Here is your husband ; like a mildew'd ear,
Blasting his wholesome brother. Have you
    eyes ?
Could you on this fair mountain leave to feed,
And batten on this moor ? Ha ! have you
    eyes ?
You cannot call it love , for at your age
The hey-day in the blood is tame, it's humble,
And waits upon the judgment and what
    judgment   70
Would step from this to this ? Sense, sure,
    you have,
Else could you not have motion ; but sure,
    that sense
Is apoplex'd ; for madness would not err,
Nor sense to ecstasy was ne'er so thrall'd
But it reserved some quantity of choice,
To serve in such a difference. What devil
    was't
That thus hath cozen'd you at hoodman-
    blind ?
Eyes without feeling, feeling without sight,
Ears without hands or eyes, smelling sans all,
Or but a sickly part of one true sense   80
Could not so mope
O shame ! where is thy blush ? Rebellious
    hell,
If thou canst mutine in a matron's bones,
To flaming youth let virtue be as wax,
And melt in her own fire . proclaim no shame
When the compulsive ardor gives the charge,
Since frost itself as actively doth burn
And reason panders will
    Queen   O Hamlet, speak no more .
Thou turn'st mine eyes into my very soul ,
And there I see such black and grained spots
As will not leave their tinct   91
    Ham   Nay, but to live
In the rank sweat of an enseamed bed,
Stew'd in corruption, honeying and making
    love
Over the nasty sty,—
    Queen.   O, speak to me no more ;
These words, like daggers, enter in mine
    ears ;
No more, sweet Hamlet !
    Ham   A murderer and a villain ;
A slave that is not twentieth part the tithe
Of your precedent lord , a vice of kings ;
A cutpurse of the empire and the rule,
That from a shelf the precious diadem stole,
And put it in his pocket !   101
    Queen   No more !
    Ham   A king of shreds and patches,—

Enter Ghost.

Save me, and hover o'er me with your wings,
You heavenly guards ! What would your
    gracious figure ?

    Queen. Alas, he's mad !
    Ham Do you not come your tardy son to
    chide,
That, lapsed in time and passion, lets go by
The important acting of your dread com-
    mand ?
O, say !
    Ghost Do not forget : this visitation   110
Is but to whet thy almost blunted purpose
But, look, amazement on thy mother sits :
O, step between her and her fighting soul :
Conceit in weakest bodies strongest works :
Speak to her, Hamlet
    Ham   How is it with you, lady ?
    Queen Alas, how is't with you,
That you do bend your eye on vacancy
And with the incorporal air do hold dis-
    course ?
Forth at your eyes your spirits wildly peep ;
And, as the sleeping soldiers in the alarm, 120
Your bedded hair, like life in excrements,
Starts up, and stands on end O gentle son,
Upon the heat and flame of thy distemper
Sprinkle cool patience. Whereon do you
    look ?
    Ham. On him, on him ! Look you, how
    pale he glares !
His form and cause conjoin'd, preaching to
    stones,
Would make them capable. Do not look upon
    me ;
Lest with this piteous action you convert
My stern effects then what I have to do
Will want true color ; tears perchance for
    blood   130
    Queen To whom do you speak this ?
    Ham Do you see nothing there ?
    Queen. Nothing at all ; yet all that is I see
    Ham. Nor did you nothing hear ?
    Queen. No, nothing but ourselves.
    Ham. Why, look you there ! look, how it
    steals away !
My father, in his habit as he lived !
Look, where he goes, even now, out at the
    portal !   [*Exit Ghost*
    Queen This is the very coinage of your
    brain :
This bodiless creation ecstasy
Is very cunning in
    Ham.   Ecstasy !
My pulse, as yours, doth temperately keep
    time,   140
And makes as healthful music . it is not mad-
    ness
That I have utter'd : bring me to the test,
And I the matter will re-word , which mad-
    ness
Would gambol from. Mother, for love of
    grace,
Lay not that flattering unction to your soul,
That not your trespass, but my madness
    speaks
It will but skin and film the ulcerous place,
Whilst rank corruption, mining all within,
Infects unseen. Confess yourself to heaven ;
Repent what's past ; avoid what is to come ;

And do not spread the compost on the weeds,
To make them ranker. Forgive me this my
    virtue ;
For in the fatness of these pursy times
Virtue itself of vice must pardon beg,
Yea, curb and woo for leave to do him good.
    Queen. O Hamlet, thou hast cleft my heart
        in twain.
    Ham. O, throw away the worser part of it,
And live the purer with the other half.
Good night : but go not to mine uncle's bed ;
Assume a virtue, if you have it not.   160
That monster, custom, who all sense doth eat,
†Of habits devil, is angel yet in this,
That to the use of actions fair and good
He likewise gives a frock or livery,
That aptly is put on. Refrain to-night,
And that shall lend a kind of easiness
To the next abstinence : the next more easy ;
For use almost can change the stamp of nature,
†And either....the devil, or throw him out
With wondrous potency. Once more, good
        night :   170
And when you are desirous to be bless'd,
I'll blessing beg of you. For this same lord,
                    [*Pointing to Polonius.*
I do repent : but heaven hath pleased it so,
To punish me with this and this with me,
That I must be their scourge and minister.
I will bestow him, and will answer well
The death I gave him. So, again, good night.
I must be cruel, only to be kind :
Thus bad begins and worse remains behind.
One word more, good lady.
    Queen.   What shall I do ?   180
    Ham. Not this, by no means, that I bid
        you do :
Let the bloat king tempt you again to bed ;
Pinch wanton on your cheek ; call you his
        mouse ;
And let him, for a pair of reechy kisses,
Or paddling in your neck with his damn'd
        fingers,
Make you to ravel all this matter out,
That I essentially am not in madness,
But mad in craft. 'Twere good you let him
        know ;
For who, that's but a queen, fair, sober, wise,
Would from a paddock, from a bat, a gib,   190
Such dear concernings hide ? who would do
        so ?
No, in despite of sense and secrecy,
Unpeg the basket on the house's top,
Let the birds fly, and, like the famous ape,
To try conclusions, in the basket creep,
And break your own neck down.
    Queen. Be thou assured, if words be made
        of breath,
And breath of life, I have no life to breathe
What thou hast said to me.
    Ham. I must to England ; you know that ?
    Queen.   Alack, 200
I had forgot : 'tis so concluded on.
    Ham. There's letters seal'd : and my two
        schoolfellows,
Whom I will trust as I will adders fang'd,

They bear the mandate ; they must sweep my
        way,
And marshal me to knavery. Let it work ;
For 'tis the sport to have the engineer
Hoist with his own petar : and 't shall go hard
But I will delve one yard below their mines,
And blow them at the moon : O, 'tis most
        sweet,
When in one line two crafts directly meet. 210
This man shall set me packing :
I'll lug the guts into the neighbor room.
Mother, good night. Indeed this counsellor
Is now most still, most secret and most grave,
Who was in life a foolish prating knave.
Come, sir, to draw toward an end with you.
Good night, mother.
            [*Exeunt severally ; Hamlet dragging
                        in Polonius.*

ACT IV.

SCENE I. *A room in the castle.*
Enter KING, QUEEN, ROSENCRANTZ, *and*
        GUILDENSTERN.

    King. There's matter in these sighs, these
        profound heaves :
You must translate : 'tis fit we understand
        them.
Where is your son ?
    Queen. Bestow this place on us a little
        while.
        [*Exeunt Rosencrantz and Guildenstern.*
Ah, my good lord, what have I seen to-night !
    King. What, Gertrude ? How does Ham-
        let ?
    Queen. Mad as the sea and wind, when
        both contend
Which is the mightier : in his lawless fit,
Behind the arras hearing something stir,
Whips out his rapier, cries, 'A rat, a rat !'
And, in this brainish apprehension, kills   11
The unseen good old man.
    King.   O heavy deed !
It had been so with us, had we been there :
His liberty is full of threats to all ;
To you yourself, to us, to every one.
Alas, how shall this bloody deed be answer'd?
It will be laid to us, whose providence
Should have kept short, restrain'd and out of
        haunt,
This mad young man : but so much was our
        love,
We would not understand what was most fit ;
But, like the owner of a foul disease,   21
To keep it from divulging, let it feed
Even on the pith of life. Where is he gone ?
    Queen. To draw apart the body he hath
        kill'd :
O'er whom his very madness, like some ore
Among a mineral of metals base,
Shows itself pure ; he weeps for what is done.
    King. O Gertrude, come away !
The sun no sooner shall the mountains touch,
But we will ship him hence : and this vile
        deed   30

We must, with all our majesty and skill,
Both countenance and excuse. Ho, Guildenstern !

Re-enter ROSENCRANTZ *and* GUILDENSTERN.

Friends both, go join you with some further
   aid :
Hamlet in madness hath Polonius slain,
And from his mother's closet hath he dragg'd
   him :
Go seek him out ; speak fair, and bring the
   body
Into the chapel   I pray you, haste in this
            [*Exeunt Rosencrantz and Guildenstern*
Come, Gertrude, we'll call up our wisest
   friends ;
And let them know, both what we mean to do,
†And what's untimely done   40
Whose whisper o'er the world's diameter,
As level as the cannon to his blank,
Transports his poison'd shot, may miss our
   name,
And hit the woundless air. O, come away !
My soul is full of discord and dismay.
                     [*Exeunt.*

   SCENE II.   *Another room in the castle*

            Enter HAMLET.

Ham.   Safely stowed.
Ros }
Guil } [*Within*] Hamlet ! Lord Hamlet !
Ham.   What noise? who calls on Hamlet ?
O, here they come.

Enter ROSENCRANTZ *and* GUILDENSTERN.

Ros   What have you done, my lord, with
   the dead body ?
Ham   Compounded it with dust, whereto
   'tis kin
Ros   Tell us where 'tis, that we may take
   it thence
And bear it to the chapel
Ham   Do not believe it.
Ros.   Believe what ?   10
Ham.   That I can keep your counsel and
not mine own   Besides, to be demanded of a
sponge ! what replication should be made by
the son of a king ?
Ros.   Take you me for a sponge, my lord ?
Ham.   Ay, sir, that soaks up the king's
countenance, his rewards, his authorities But
such officers do the king best service in the
end : he keeps them, like an ape, in the corner
of his jaw, first mouthed, to be last swallowed:
when he needs what you have gleaned, it is
but squeezing you, and, sponge, you shall be
dry again.
Ros   I understand you not, my lord.
Ham   I am glad of it : a knavish speech
sleeps in a foolish ear
Ros.   My lord, you must tell us where the
body is, and go with us to the king.
Ham.   The body is with the king, but the
king is not with the body. The king is a
thing—   30

Guil.   A thing, my lord !
Ham: Of nothing . bring me to him. Hide
fox, and all after.   [*Exeunt.*

   SCENE III.   *Another room in the castle.*

         Enter KING, *attended.*

King.   I have sent to seek him, and to find
   the body.
How dangerous is it that this man goes loose !
Yet must not we put the strong law on him :
He's loved of the distracted multitude,
Who like not in their judgment, but their
   eyes ;
And where 'tis so, the offender's scourge is
   weigh'd,
But never the offence. To bear all smooth
   and even,
This sudden sending him away must seem
Deliberate pause   diseases desperate grown
By desperate appliance are relieved,   10
Or not at all.

         Enter ROSENCRANTZ.

         How now ! what hath befall'n ?
Ros.   Where the dead body is bestow'd, my
   lord,
We cannot get from him
King.   But where is he ?
Ros.   Without, my lord ; guarded, to know
   your pleasure.
King.   Bring him before us.
Ros.   Ho, Guildenstern ! bring in my lord.

   Enter HAMLET *and* GUILDENSTERN.

King   Now, Hamlet, where's Polonius ?
Ham.   At supper.
King.   'At supper ' where ?   •   19
Ham   Not where he eats, but where he is
eaten : a certain convocation of politic worms
are e'en at him. Your worm is your only emperor for diet   we fat all creatures else to fat
us, and we fat ourselves for maggots • your
fat king and your lean beggar is but variable
service, two dishes, but to one table: that's the
end.
King.   Alas, alas '
Ham.   A man may fish with the worm that
hath eat of a king, and eat of the fish that
hath fed of that worm   30
King.   What dost you mean by this ?
Ham.   Nothing but to show you how a king
may go a progress through the guts of a
beggar.
King.   Where is Polonius ?
Ham.   In heaven , send hither to see : if
your messenger find him not there, seek him
i' the other place yourself. But indeed, if you
find him not within this month, you shall nose
him as you go up the stairs into the lobby.
King.   Go seek him there   40
                     [*To some Attendants.*
Ham.   He will stay till ye come.
                     [*Exeunt Attendants.*
King.   Hamlet, this deed, for thine especial
   safety,—
Which we do tender, as we dearly grieve

For that which thou hast done,—must send
    thee hence
With fiery quickness : therefore prepare thy-
    self ;
The bark is ready, and the wind at help,
The associates tend, and every thing is bent
For England.
Ham.   For England !
King.   Ay, Hamlet.
Ham.   Good.
King. So is it, if thou knew'st our purposes.
Ham. I see a cherub that sees them. But,
come ; for England ! Farewell, dear mother.
King. Thy loving father, Hamlet.
Ham. My mother : father and mother is
man and wife ; man and wife is one flesh ;
and so, my mother. Come, for England !
                          [Exit.

King. Follow him at foot ; tempt him with
    speed abroad ;
Delay it not ; I'll have him hence to-night:
Away ! for every thing is seal'd and done
That else leans on the affair : pray you, make
    haste.
    [Exeunt Rosencrantz and Guildenstern.
And, England, if my love thou hold'st at
    aught—
As my great power thereof may give thee
    sense,
Since yet thy cicatrice looks raw and red
After the Danish sword, and thy free awe
Pays homage to us—thou mayst not coldly set
Our sovereign process ; which imports at full,
By letters congruing to that effect,
The present death of Hamlet. Do it, England;
For like the hectic in my blood he rages,
And thou must cure me : till I know 'tis done,
Howe'er my haps, my joys were ne'er begun.
                        [Exit. 70

SCENE IV. *A plain in Denmark.*

Enter FORTINBRAS, *a* Captain, *and* Soldiers,
    marching.

For. Go, captain, from me greet the Danish
    king ;
Tell him that, by his license, Fortinbras
Craves the conveyance of a promised march
Over his kingdom. You know the rendezvous.
If that his majesty would aught with us,
We shall express our duty in his eye ;
And let him know so.
Cap.   I will do't, my lord.
For. Go softly on.
        [Exeunt Fortinbras and Soldiers.

Enter HAMLET, ROSENCRANTZ, GUILDEN-
    STERN, *and others.*

Ham. Good sir, whose powers are these ?
Cap. They are of Norway, sir.   10
Ham. How purposed, sir, I pray you ?
Cap. Against some part of Poland.
Ham. Who commands them, sir ?
Cap. The nephews to old Norway, Fortin-
    bras.
Ham. Goes it against the main of Poland,
    sir,

Or for some frontier ?
Cap. Truly to speak, and with no addition,
We go to gain a little patch of ground
That hath in it no profit but the name.
To pay five ducats, five, I would not farm it ;
Nor will it yield to Norway or the Pole   21
A ranker rate, should it be sold in fee.
Ham. Why, then the Polack never will
    defend it.
Cap. Yes, it is already garrison'd.
Ham. Two thousand souls and twenty thou-
    sand ducats
Will not debate the question of this straw :
This is the imposthume of much wealth and
    peace,
That inward breaks, and shows no cause with-
    out
Why the man dies. I humbly thank you, sir.
Cap. God be wi' you, sir.   *[Exit.*
Ros.   Wil't please you go, my lord ? 30
Ham. I'll be with you straight. Go a little
    before.   *[Exeunt all except Hamlet.*
How all occasions do inform against me,
And spur my dull revenge ! What is a man,
If his chief good and market of his time
Be but to sleep and feed ? a beast, no more.
Sure, he that made us with such large dis-
    course,
Looking before and after, gave us not
That capability and god-like reason
To fust in us unused. Now, whether it be
Bestial oblivion, or some craven scruple   40
Of thinking too precisely on the event,
A thought which, quarter'd, hath but one part
    wisdom
And ever three parts coward, I do not know
Why yet I live to say ' This thing's to do ;'
Sith I have cause and will and strength and
    means
To do't. Examples gross as earth exhort me :
Witness this army of such mass and charge
Led by a delicate and tender prince,
Whose spirit with divine ambition puff'd
Makes mouths at the invisible event,   50
Exposing what is mortal and unsure
To all that fortune, death and danger dare,
Even for an egg-shell. Rightly to be great
Is not to stir without great argument,
But greatly to find quarrel in a straw
When honor's at the stake. How stand I then,
That have a father kill'd, a mother stain'd,
Excitements of my reason and my blood,
And let all sleep ? while to my shame, I see
The imminent death of twenty thousand men,
That, for a fantasy and trick of fame,   61
Go to their graves like beds, fight for a plot
Whereon the numbers cannot try the cause,
Which is not tomb enough and continent
To hide the slain ? O, from this time forth,
My thoughts be bloody, or be nothing worth !
                          [Exit.

SCENE V. *Elsinore. A room in the castle.*

Enter QUEEN, HORATIO, *and a* Gentleman.

Queen. I will not speak with her.
                          43

Gent. She is importunate, indeed distract :
Her mood will needs be pitied.
Queen.   What would she have ?
Gent. She speaks much of her father ; says
   she hears
There's tricks i' the world ; and hems, and
   beats her heart ;
Spurns enviously at straws ; speaks things in
   doubt,
That carry but half sense : her speech is noth-
   ing,
Yet the unshaped use of it doth move
The hearers to collection ; they aim at it,
And botch the words up fit to their own
   thoughts ;   10
Which, as her winks, and nods, and gestures
   yield them,
Indeed would make one think there might be
   thought,
Though nothing sure, yet much unhappily.
Hor. 'Twere good she were spoken with ;
   for she may strew
Dangerous conjectures in ill-breeding minds.
Queen. Let her come in. [*Exit Horatio.*
To my sick soul, as sin's true nature is,
Each toy seems prologue to some great amiss :
So full of artless jealousy is guilt,
It spills itself in fearing to be spilt.   20

   Re-enter HORATIO, *with* OPHELIA.

Oph. Where is the beauteous majesty of
   Denmark ?
Queen. How now, Ophelia !
Oph. [*Sings*] How should I your true love
   know
     From another one?
   By his cockle hat and staff,
     And his sandal shoon.
Queen. Alas, sweet lady, what imports this
   song ?
Oph. Say you ? nay, pray you, mark.
[*Sings*] He is dead and gone, lady,
     He is dead and gone ;   30
   At his head a grass-green turf,
     At his heels a stone.
Queen. Nay, but, Ophelia,—
Oph. Pray you, mark.
[*Sings*] White his shroud as the mountain
   snow,—

   Enter KING.

Queen. Alas, look here, my lord.
Oph. [*Sings*] Larded with sweet flowers ;
   Which bewept to the grave did go
     With true-love showers.
King. How do you, pretty lady ?   40
Oph. Well, God 'ild you ! They say the owl
was a baker's daughter. Lord, we know what
we are, but know not what we may be. God
be at your table !
King. Conceit upon her father.
Oph. Pray you, let's have no words of this ;
but when they ask you what it means, say you
this :
[*Sings.*] To-morrow is Saint Valentine's day,
   All in the morning betime,

And I a maid at your window,   50
   To be your Valentine.
Then up he rose, and donn'd his clothes,
   And dupp'd the chamber-door ;
Let in the maid, that out a maid
   Never departed more.
King. Pretty Ophelia !
Oph. Indeed, la, without an oath, I'll make
   an end on't :
[*Sings*] By Gis and by Saint Charity,
   Alack, and fie for shame !
Young men will do't, if they come to't ;
   By cock, they are to blame.   61
Quoth she, before you tumbled me,
   You promised me to wed.
So would I ha' done, by yonder sun,
   An thou hadst not come to my bed.
King. How long hath she been thus ?
Oph. I hope all will be well. We must be
patient : but I cannot choose but weep, to think
they should lay him i' the cold ground. My
brother shall know of it : and so I thank you
for your good counsel. Come, my coach !
Good night, ladies ; good night, sweet ladies ;
good night, good night.   [*Exit.*
King. Follow her close ; give her good
   watch,
I pray you.   [*Exit Horatio.*
O, this is the poison of deep grief ; it springs
All from her father's death. O Gertrude,
   Gertrude,   [spies,
When sorrows come, they come not single
But in battalions. First, her father slain ;
Next, your son gone ; and he most violent
   author   80
Of his own just remove : the people muddied,
Thick and unwholesome in their thoughts and
   whispers,
For good Polonius' death ; and we have done
   but greenly,
In hugger-mugger to inter him : poor Ophelia
Divided from herself and her fair judgment,
Without the which we are pictures, or mere
   beasts :
Last, and as much containing as all these,
Her brother is in secret come from France ;
Feeds on his wonder, keeps himself in clouds,
And wants not buzzers to infect his ear   90
With pestilent speeches of his father's death
Wherein necessity, of matter beggar'd,
Will nothing stick our person to arraign
In ear and ear. O my dear Gertrude, this,
Like to a murdering-piece, in many places
Gives me superfluous death. [*A noise within.*
Queen.   Alack, what noise is this ?
King. Where are my Switzers ? Let them
   guard the door.

   Enter another Gentleman.

What is the matter ?
   Gent.   Save yourself, my lord :
The ocean, overpeering of his list,
Eats not the flats with more impetuous haste
Than young Laertes, in a riotous head,   100
O'erbears your officers. The rabble call him
   lord ;

And, as the world were now but to begin,
Antiquity forgot, custom not known,
The ratifiers and props of every word,
They cry 'Choose we . Laertes shall be king;'
Caps, hands, and tongues, applaud it to the
      clouds :
'Laertes shall be king, Laertes king!'
      Queen. How cheerfully on the false trail
            they cry !
O, this is counter, you false Danish dogs ! 110
King. The doors are broke [*Noise within.*

Enter LAERTES, *armed*, *Danes following.*

Laer. Where is this king ? Sirs, stand you
      all without
Danes. No, let's come in.
Laer.   I pray you, give me leave.
Danes. We will, we will
                  [*They retire without the door*
Laer. I thank you : keep the door. O thou
      vile king,
Give me my father !
      Queen.   Calmly, good Laertes
Laer. That drop of blood that's calm pro-
      claims me bastard,
Cries cuckold to my father, brands the harlot
Even here, between the chaste unsmirched
      brow
Of my true mother
      King   What is the cause, Laertes, 120
That thy rebellion looks so giant-like ?
Let him go, Gertrude , do not fear our person :
There's such divinity doth hedge a king,
That treason can but peep to what it would,
Acts little of his will   Tell me, Laertes,
Why thou art thus incensed. Let him go,
      Gertrude.
Speak, man.
      Laer. Where is my father ?
      King   Dead.
      Queen.   But not by him.
King. Let him demand his fill.
      Laer. How came he dead ? I'll not be jug-
            gled with :   130
To hell, allegiance ! vows, to the blackest
      devil !
Conscience and grace, to the profoundest pit !
I dare damnation. To this point I stand,
That both the worlds I give to negligence,
Let come what comes ; only I'll be revenged
Most thoroughly for my father.
      King.   Who shall stay you ?
Laer. My will, not all the world :
And for my means, I'll husband them so well,
They shall go far with little.
      King.   Good Laertes,
If you desire to know the certainty   140
Of your dear father's death, is't writ in your
      revenge,
That, swoopstake, you will draw both friend
      and foe,
Winner and loser ?
      Laer. None but his enemies.
King.   Will you know them then ?
Laer. To his good friends thus wide I'll ope
      my arms ;

And like the kind life-rendering pelican,
Repast them with my blood
      King   Why, now you speak
Like a good child and a true gentleman
That I am guiltless of your father's death,
And am most sensible in grief for it,   150
It shall as level to your judgment pierce
As day does to your eye
      Danes [*Within*] Let her come in.
      Laer. How now ' what noise is that ?

                  Re-enter OPHELIA.

O heat, dry up my brains ' tears seven times
      salt,
Burn out the sense and virtue of mine eye !
By heaven, thy madness shall be paid by
      weight,
Till our scale turn the beam   O rose of May!
Dear maid, kind sister sweet Ophelia !
O heavens ' is't possible, a young maid's wits
Should be as mortal as an old man's life ? 160
Nature is fine in love, and where 'tis fine,
It sends some precious instance of itself
After the thing it loves.
      Oph. [*Sings*]
            They bore him barefaced on the bier;
            Hey non nonny, nonny, hey nonny,
            And in his grave rain'd many a tear—
Fare you well, my dove !
      Laer. Hadst thou thy wits, and didst per-
            suade revenge,
It could not move thus
      Oph. [*Sings*] You must sing a-down a-down
            An you call him a-down-a   171
O, how the wheel becomes it ' It is the false
steward, that stole his master's daughter.
      Laer. This nothing's more than matter
      Oph There's rosemary, that's for remem-
brance ; pray, love, remember . and there is
pansies, that's for thoughts
      Laer. A document in madness, thoughts
and remembrance fitted.   179
      Oph There's fennel for you, and colum-
bines · there's rue for you ; and here's some
for me : we may call it herb-grace o' Sundays.
O, you must wear your rue with a difference.
There's a daisy · I would give you some violets,
but they withered all when my father died:
they say he made a good end,—
            [*Sings*] For bonny sweet Robin is all my
      joy   [itself,
Laer Thought and affliction, passion, hell
She turns to favor and to prettiness.
      Oph. [*Sings*] And will he not come again ?
            And will he not come again ?
            No, no, he is dead,
            Go to thy death-bed :
            He never will come again.

            His beard was as white as snow,
            All flaxen was his poll :
            He is gone, he is gone
            And we cast away moan :
            God ha' mercy on his soul !

And of all Christian souls, I pray God. God
be wi' ye.   [*Exit.* 200

Laer. Do you see this, O God?

King. Laertes, I must commune with your grief,

Or you deny me right. Go but apart,

Make choice of whom your wisest friends you will.   [me :

And they shall hear and judge 'twixt you and

If by direct or by collateral hand

They find us touch'd, we will our kingdom give,

Our crown, our life, and all that we call ours,

To you in satisfaction ; but if not,

Be you content to lend your patience to us,

And we shall jointly labor with your soul 211

To give it due content.

Laer.   Let this be so ;

His means of death, his obscure funeral—

No trophy, sword, nor hatchment o'er his bones,

No noble rite nor formal ostentation—

Cry to be heard, as 'twere from heaven to earth,

That I must call't in question.

King.   So you shall ;

And where the offence is let the great axe fall.

I pray you, go with me.   [*Exeunt.*

SCENE VI. *Another room in the castle.*

Enter HORATIO *and a* Servant.

Hor. What are they that would speak with me ?

Serv. Sailors, sir: they say they have letters for you.

Hor. Let them come in.   [*Exit Servant.*

I do not know from what part of the world

I should be greeted, if not from Lord Hamlet.

Enter Sailors.

First Sail. God bless you, sir.

Hor. Let him bless thee too.

First Sail. He shall, sir, an't please him. There's a letter for you, sir; it comes from the ambassador that was bound for England ; if your name be Horatio, as I am let to know it is.   11

Hor. [*Reads*] 'Horatio, when thou shalt have overlooked this, give these fellows some means to the king : they have letters for him. Ere we were two days old at sea, a pirate of very warlike appointment gave us chase. Finding ourselves too slow of sail, we put on a compelled valor, and in the grapple I boarded them : on the instant they got clear of our ship ; so I alone became their prisoner. They have dealt with me like thieves of mercy: but they knew what they did; I am to do a good turn for them. Let the king have the letters I have sent ; and repair thou to me with as much speed as thou wouldst fly death. I have words to speak in thine ear will make thee dumb ; yet are they much too light for the bore of the matter. These good fellows will bring thee where I am. Rosencrantz and Guildenstern hold their course for England : of them I have much to tell thee. Farewell.   30

'He that thou knowest thine, HAMLET.'

Come, I will make you way for these your letters ;

And do't the speedier, that you may direct me

To him from whom you brought them.

         [*Exeunt.*

SCENE VII. *Another room in the castle.*

Enter KING *and* LAERTES.

King. Now must your conscience my acquaintance seal,

And you must put me in your heart for friend,

Sith you have heard, and with a knowing ear,

That he which hath your noble father slain

Pursued my life.

Laer.   It well appears : but tell me

Why you proceeded not against these feats,

So crimeful and so capital in nature,

As by your safety, wisdom, all things else,

You mainly were stirr'd up.

King.   O, for two special reasons ;

Which may to you, perhaps, seem much unsinew'd,   10

But yet to me they are strong. The queen his mother

Lives almost by his looks ; and for myself—

My virtue or my plague, be it either which—

She's so conjunctive to my life and soul,

That, as the star moves not but in his sphere,

I could not but by her. The other motive,

Why to a public count I might not go,

Is the great love the general gender bear him;

Who, dipping all his faults in their affection,

Would, like the spring that turneth wood to stone,

Convert his gyves to graces; so that my arrows,

Too slightly timber'd for so loud a wind,

Would have reverted to my bow again,

And not where I had aim'd them.

Laer. And so have I a noble father lost ;

A sister driven into desperate terms,

Whose worth, if praises may go back again,

Stood challenger on mount of all the age

For her perfections: but my revenge will come.

King. Break not your sleeps for that : you must not think   30

That we are made of stuff so flat and dull

That we can let our beard be shook with danger

And think it pastime. You shortly shall hear more :

I loved your father, and we love ourself :

And that, I hope, will teach you to imagine—

Enter a Messenger.

How now ! what news ?

Mess.   Letters, my lord, from Hamlet :

This to your majesty; this to the queen.

King. From Hamlet ! who brought them ?

Mess. Sailors, my lord, they say ; I saw them not :

They were given me by Claudio ; he received them   40

Of him that brought them.

King.   Laertes, you shall hear them.

Leave us.   [*Exit Messenger.*

[*Reads*] 'High and mighty, You shall know
I am set naked on your kingdom　To-morrow
shall I beg leave to see your kingly eyes. when
I shall, first asking your pardon thereunto, re-
count the occasion of my sudden and more
strange return　'HAMLET.'
What should this mean ? Are all the rest
　come back ?　　　　　　　　　　　　50
Or is it some abuse, and no such thing ?
　Laer　Know you the hand ?
　King　'Tis Hamlet's character　'Naked!'
And in a postscript here, he says 'alone.'
Can you advise me ?
　Laer. I'm lost in it, my lord　But let him
　come ,
It warms th　　　sickness in my heart,
That I shall live and tell him to his teeth,
'Thus didest thou '
　King　　　　　If it be so, Laertes—
As how should it be so ? how otherwise ?—
Will you be ruled by me ?
　Laer　　　　　　Ay, my lord ,　60
So you will not o'errule me to a peace
　King. To thine own peace　If he be now
　return'd,
As checking at his voyage, and that he means
No more to undertake it, I will work him
To an exploit, now ripe in my device,
Under the which he shall not choose but fall
And for his death no wind of blame shall
　breathe,
But even his mother shall uncharge the prac-
　tice
And call it accident.
　Laer　My lord, I will be ruled ,
The rather, if you could devise it so　　70
That I might be the organ.
　King　　　It falls right
You have been talk'd of since your travel
　much,
And that in Hamlet's hearing, for a quality
Wherein, they say, you shine your sum of
　parts
Did not together pluck such envy from him
As did that one, and that, in my regard,
Of the unworthiest siege.
　Laer.　　What part is that, my lord ?
　King. A very riband in the cap of youth,
Yet needful too ; for youth no less becomes
The light and careless livery that it wears　80
Than settled age his sables and his weeds,
Importing health and graveness.　Two months
　since,
Here was a gentleman of Normandy —
I've seen myself, and served against, the
　French,
And they can well on horseback . but this gal-
　lant
Had witchcraft in t ; he grew unto his seat ,
And to such wondrous doing brought his horse,
As he had been incorpsed and demi-natured
With the brave beast . so far he topp'd my
　thought,
That I, in forgery of shapes and tricks,　90
Come short of what he did
　Laer.　　　　A Norman was't ?

　King　A Norman
　Laer. Upon my life, Lamond.
　King　　　　　The very same.
　Laer　I know him well . he is the brooch
　indeed
And gem of all the nation
　King.　He made confession of you,
And gave you such a masterly report
For art and exercise in your defence
And for your rapier most especially,
That he cried out, 'twould be a sight indeed,
If one could match you　the scrimers of their
　nation,　　　　　　　　　　　101
He swore, had had neither motion, guard, nor
　eye,
If you opposed them　Sir, this report of his
Did Hamlet so envenom with his envy
That he could nothing do but wish and beg
Your sudden coming o'er, to play with him
Now, out of this,—
　Laer　　　　What out of this, my lord ?
　King　Laertes, was your father dear to
　you ?
Or are you like the painting of a sorrow,
A face without a heart ?
　Laer　　　Why ask you this ? 110
　King　Not that I think you did not love
　your father ,
But that I know love is begun by time ,
And that I see, in passages of proof,
Time qualifies the spark and fire of it.
There lives within the very flame of love
A kind of wick or snuff that will abate it ;
And nothing is at a like goodness still ,
For goodness, growing to a plurisy,
Dies in his own too much . that we would do,
We should do when we would ; for this 'would'
　changes　　　　　　　　　　　120
And hath abatements and delays as many
As there are tongues, are hands, are acci-
　dents,
And then this 'should' is like a spendthrift
　sigh,
That hurts by easing. But, to the quick o' the
　ulcer :—
Hamlet comes back : what would you under-
　take,
To show yourself your father's son in deed
More than in words ?
　Laer　　　To cut his throat i' the church
　King. No place, indeed, should murder
　sanctuarize ;
Revenge should have no bounds. But, good
　Laertes,
Will you do this, keep close within your cham-
　ber　　　　　　　　　　　　130
Hamlet return'd shall know you are come
　home
We'll put on those shall praise your excellence
And set a double varnish on the fame
The Frenchman gave you, bring you in fine to-
　gether
And wager on your heads　he, being remiss,
Most generous and free from all contriving,
Will not peruse the foils , so that, with ease,
Or with a little shuffling, you may choose

A sword unbated, and in a pass of practice
Requite him for your father
Laer　　　　　　I will do't ·　　140
And, for that purpose, I'll anoint my sword,
I bought an unction of a mountebank,
So mortal that, but dip a knife in it,
Where it draws blood no cataplasm so rare,
Collected from all simples that have virtue
Under the moon, can save the thing from death
That is but scratch'd withal I'll touch my
　　point
With this contagion, that, if I gall him slightly,
It may be death.
King.　　　Let's further think of this ;
Weigh what convenience both of time and
　　means　　　　　　　　150
May fit us to our shape · if this should fail,
And that our drift look through our bad per-
　　formance,
'Twere better not assay'd : therefore this pro-
　　ject
Should have a back or second, that might hold,
If this should blast in proof Soft ' let me see:
We'll make a solemn wager on your cunnings
I ha't.
When in your motion you are hot and dry—
As make your bouts more violent to that end—
And that he calls for drink, I'll have prepared
　　him　　　　　　　　160
A chalice for the nonce, whereon but sipping,
If he by chance escape your venom'd stuck,
Our purpose may hold there.

Enter QUEEN.

　　　　　How now, sweet queen '
Queen　One woe doth tread upon another's
　　heel,
So fast they follow , your sister's drown'd,
　　Laertes
Laer　Drown'd ! O, where ?
Queen　There is a willow grows aslant a
　　brook,
That shows his hoar leaves in the glassy
　　stream ,
There with fantastic garlands did she come
Of crow-flowers, nettles, daisies, and long pur-
　　ples　　　　　　　170
That liberal shepherds give a grosser name,
But our cold maids do dead men's fingers call
　· them :
There, on the pendent boughs her coronet
　　weeds
Clambering to hang, an envious sliver broke ;
When down her weedy trophies and herself
Fell in the weeping brook. Her clothes spread
　　wide ,
And, mermaid-like, awhile they bore her up :
Which time she chanted snatches of old tunes,
As one incapable of her own distress,
Or like a creature native and indued　　180
Unto that element : but long it could not be
Till that her garments, heavy with their drink,
'Pull'd the poor wretch from her melodious lay
To muddy death.
Laer.　　Alas, then, she is drown'd ?
Queen.　Drown'd, drown'd.

Laer.　Too much of water hast thou, poor
　　Ophelia,
And therefore I forbid my tears : but yet
It is our trick ; nature her custom holds,
Let shame say what it will : when these are
　　gone,　　　　　　189
The woman will be out.　Adieu, my lord ·
I have a speech of fire, that fain would blaze,
But that this folly douts it　　　　[*Exit*
King　　　　　Let's follow, Gertrude ,
How much I had to do to calm his rage !
Now fear I this will give it start again ;
Therefore let's follow.　　　　[*Exeunt*

ACT V.

SCENE I.　*A churchyard.*

Enter two Clowns, *with spades, &c.*

First Clo.　Is she to be buried in Christian
burial that wilfully seeks her own salvation ?
　Sec Clo　I tell thee she is . and therefore
make her grave straight · the crowner hath
sat on her, and finds it Christian burial
　First Clo.　How can that be, unless she
drowned herself in her own defence ?
　Sec. Clo.　Why, 'tis found so.
　First Clo　It must be 'se offendendo ;' it
cannot be else.　For here lies the point : if I
drown myself wittingly, it argues an act · and
an act hath three branches: it is, to act, to do,
to perform　argal, she drowned herself wittingly.
　Sec Clo.　Nay, but hear you, goodman
delver,—
　First Clo　Give me leave. Here lies the
water , good　here stands the man , good : if
the man go to this water, and drown himself,
it is, will he, nill he, he goes,—mark you that :
but if the water come to him and drown him,
he drowns not himself · argal, he that is not
guilty of his own death shortens not his own
life. ·
　Sec Clo　But is this law, ?
　First Clo　Ay, marry, is't , crowner's quest
law.
　Sec. Clo.　Will you ha' the truth on't ? If
this had not been a gentlewoman, she should
have been buried out o' Christian burial
　First Clo　Why, there thou say'st　and the
more pity that great folk should have countenance in this world to drown or hang themselves, more than their even Christian　Come,
my spade.　There is no ancient gentleman but
gardeners, ditchers, and grave-makers . they
hold up Adam's profession
　Sec Clo　Was he a gentleman ?
　First Clo.　He was the first that ever bore
arms.
　Sec. Clo.　Why, he had none.　　30
　First Clo　What, art a heathen ? How dost
thou understand the Scripture ? The Scripture says ' Adam digged ' could he dig without arms ? I'll put another question to thee .

If thou answerest me not to the purpose, confess thyself—

Sec. Clo. Go to.

First Clo. What is he that builds stronger than either the mason, the shipwright, or the carpenter ?

Sec. Clo. The gallows-maker ; for that frame outlives a thousand tenants. 50

First Clo. I like thy wit well, in good faith the gallows does well , but how does it well ? it does well to those that do ill now thou dost ill to say the gallows is built stronger than the church: argal, the gallows may do well to thee. To't again, come

Sec. Clo. 'Who builds stronger than a mason, a shipwright, or a carpenter ?'

First Clo Ay, tell me that, and unyoke

Sec. Clo. Marry, now I can tell. 60

First Clo. To't

Sec. Clo. Mass, I cannot tell.

Enter HAMLET *and* HORATIO, *at a distance.*

First Clo. Cudgel thy brains no more about it, for your dull ass will not mend his pace with beating , and, when you are asked this question next, say 'a grave-maker .' the houses that he makes last till doomsday. Go, get thee to †Yaughan fetch me a stoup of liquor. [*Exit Sec Clown.*

[*He digs and sings.*

In youth, when I did love, did love,
Methought it was very sweet, 70
To contract, O, the time, for, ah, my behove,
O, methought, there was nothing meet

Ham Has this fellow no feeling of his business, that he sings at grave-making ?

Hor. Custom hath made it in him a property of easiness.

Ham 'Tis e'en so · the hand of little employment hath the daintier sense

First Clo. [*Sings*]
But age, with his stealing steps,
Hath claw'd me in his clutch, 80
And hath shipped me intil the land,
As if I had never been such.

[*Throws up a skull.*

Ham. That skull had a tongue in it, and could sing once · how the knave jowls it to the ground, as if it were Cain's jaw-bone, that did the first murder ! It might be the pate of a politician, which this ass now o'er-reaches · one that would circumvent God, might it not ?

Hor. It might, my lord. 89

Ham. Or of a courtier; which could say 'Good morrow, sweet lord ! How dost thou, good lord?' This might be my lord such-a-one, that praised my lord such-a-one's horse, when he meant to beg it ; might it not ?

Hor. Ay, my lord.

Ham. Why, e'en so: and now my Lady Worm's ; chapless, and knocked about the mazzard with a sexton's spade. here's fine revolution, an we had the trick to see't. Did these bones cost no more the breeding, but to play at loggats with 'em ? mine ache to think on't. 101

First Clo. [*Sings*]
A pick-axe, and a spade, a spade,
For and a shrouding sheet :
O, a pit of clay for to be made
For such a guest is meet.

[*Throws up another skull.*

Ham There's another . why may not that be the skull of a lawyer ? Where be his quiddities now, his quillets, his cases, his tenures, and his tricks ? why does he suffer this rude knave now to knock him about the sconce with a dirty shovel, and will not tell him of his action of battery ? Hum ! This fellow might be in's time a great buyer of land, with his statutes, his recognizances, his fines, his double vouchers, his recoveries . is this the fine of his fines, and the recovery of his recoveries, to have his fine pate full of fine dirt ? will his vouchers vouch him no more of his purchases, and double ones too, than the length and breadth of a pair of indentures ? The very conveyances of his lands will hardly lie in this box , and must the inheritor himself have no more, ha ?

Hor. Not a jot more, my lord

Ham Is not parchment made of sheep-skins ?

Hor Ay, my lord, and of calf-skins too

Ham They are sheep and calves which seek out assurance in that I will speak to this fellow. Whose grave's this, sirrah ?

First Clo. Mine, sir

[*Sings*] O, a pit of clay for to be made
For such a guest is meet 130

Ham. I think it be thine, indeed , for thou liest in 't

First Clo You lie out on't, sir, and therefore it is not yours : for my part, I do not lie in't, and yet it is mine

Ham Thou dost lie in't, to be in't and say it is thine : 'tis for the dead, not for the quick ; therefore thou liest

First Clo 'Tis a quick lie, sir ; 'twill away again, from me to you. 140

Ham What man dost thou dig it for ?

First Clo For no man, sir

Ham. What woman, then ?

First Clo For none, neither.

Ham. Who is to be buried in't ?

First Clo One that was a woman, sir ; but, rest her soul, she's dead

Ham How absolute the knave is ! we must speak by the card, or equivocation will undo us By the Lord, Horatio, these three years I have taken a note of it , the age is grown so picked that the toe of the peasant comes so near the heel of the courtier, he galls his kibe. How long hast thou been a grave-maker ?

First Clo Of all the days i' the year, I came to't that day that our last king Hamlet overcame Fortinbras

Ham How long is that since ?

First Clo Cannot you tell that ? every fool can tell that it was the very day that young Hamlet was born ; he that is mad, and sent into England,

Ham Ay, marry, why was he sent into England ?

First Clo. Why, because he was mad : he shall recover his wits there ; or, if he do not, it's no great matter there.

Ham. Why ?

First Clo. 'Twill not be seen in him there ; there the men are as mad as he. 170

Ham. How came he mad ?

First Clo. Very strangely, they say.

Ham. How strangely ?

First Clo. Faith, e'en with losing his wits.

Ham. Upon what ground ?

First Clo. Why, here in Denmark : I have been sexton here, man and boy, thirty years

Ham. How long will a man lie i' the earth ere he rot ? • 179

First Clo. I' faith, if he be not rotten before he die—as we have many pocky corses now-a-days, that will scarce hold the laying in—he will last you some eight year or nine year : a tanner will last you nine year.

Ham. Why he more than another ?

First Clo Why, sir, his hide is so tanned with his trade, that he will keep out water a great while ; and your water is a sore decayer of your whoreson dead body. Here s a skull now ; this skull has lain in the earth three and twenty years 191

Ham. Whose was it ?

First Clo. A whoreson mad fellow's it was . whose do you think it was ?

Ham Nay, I know not

First Clo. A pestilence on him for a mad rogue ! a' poured a flagon of Rhenish on my head once. This same skull, sir, was Yorick's skull, the king's jester

Ham. This ? 200

First Clo E'en that.

Ham. Let me see [*Takes the skull.*] Alas, poor Yorick ! I knew him, Horatio a fellow of infinite jest, of most excellent fancy . he hath borne me on his back a thousand times , and now, how abhorred in my imagination it is ! my gorge rises at it. Here hung those lips that I have kissed I know not how oft Where be your gibes now ? your gambols ? your songs ? your flashes of merriment, that were wont to set the table on a roar ? Not one now, to mock your own grinning ? quite chap-fallen ? Now get you to my lady's chamber, and tell her, let her paint an inch thick, to this favor she must come ; make her laugh at that. Prithee, Horatio, tell me one thing

Hor. What's that, my lord ?

Ham. Dost thou think Alexander looked o' this fashion i' the earth ?

Hor. E'en so. 220

Ham. And smelt so ? pah !

[*Puts down the skull.*

Hor. E'en so, my lord.

Ham. To what base uses we may return, Horatio ! Why may not imagination trace the noble dust of Alexander, till he find it stopping a bung-hole ? [*consider so.*

Hor. 'Twere to consider too curiously, to

Ham. No, faith, not a jot ; but to follow him thither with modesty enough, and likelihood to lead it : as thus : Alexander died, Alexander was buried, Alexander returneth into dust ; the dust is earth ; of earth we make loam , and why of that loam, whereto he was converted, might they not stop a beer-barrel ?
Imperious Cæsar, dead and turn'd to clay,
Might stop a hole to keep the wind away :
O, that that earth, which kept the world in awe,
Should patch a wall to expel the winter's flaw !
But soft ! but soft ! aside : here comes the king.

Enter Priest, &c in procession; the Corpse of OPHELIA, LAERTES *and* Mourners *following;* KING, QUEEN, *their trains, &c.*

The queen, the courtiers : who is this they follow ?
And with such maimed rites ? This doth betoken
The corse they follow did with desperate hand
Fordo its own life • 'twas of some estate.
Couch we awhile, and mark.

[*Retiring with Horatio.*

Laer What ceremony else ?

Ham. That is Laertes,
A very noble youth : mark.

Laer What ceremony else ?

First Priest. Her obsequies have been as far enlarged
As we have warrantise : her death was doubtful ; 250
And, but that great command o'ersways the order,
She should in ground unsanctified have lodged
Till the last trumpet: for charitable prayers,
Shards, flints and pebbles should be thrown on her ;
Yet here she is allow'd her virgin crants,
Her maiden strewments and the bringing home
Of bell and burial

Laer Must there no more be done ?

First Priest. No more be done :
We should profane the service of the dead
To sing a requiem and such rest to her 260
As to peace-parted souls.

Laer. Lay her i' the earth :
And from her fair and unpolluted flesh
May violets spring ! I tell thee, churlish priest,
A ministering angel shall my sister be,
When thou liest howling.

Ham. What, the fair Ophelia !

Queen. Sweets to the sweet : farewell !

[*Scattering flowers.*

I hoped thou shouldst have been my Hamlet's wife ;
I thought thy bride-bed to have deck'd, sweet maid,
And not have strew'd thy grave.

Laer. O, treble woe
Fall ten times treble on that cursed head, 270
Whose wicked deed thy most ingenious sense
Deprived thee of ! Hold off the earth awhile,

"Alas! Poor Yorick, I knew him well."

Till I have caught her once more in mine arms:
[*Leaps into the grave.*
Now pile your dust upon the quick and dead,
Till of this flat a mountain you have made,
To o'ertop old Pelion, or the skyish head
Of blue Olympus.
Ham. [*Advancing*] What is he whose grief
Bears such an emphasis? whose phrase of
   sorrow
Conjures the wandering stars, and makes them
   stand
Like wonder-wounded hearers? This is I, 280
Hamlet the Dane. [*Leaps into the grave.*
Laer.   The devil take thy soul!
[*Grappling with him.*
Ham. Thou pray'st not well.
I prithee, take thy fingers from my throat;
For, though I am not splenitive and rash,
Yet have I something in me dangerous,
Which let thy wiseness fear: hold off thy hand
King. Pluck them asunder.
Queen.   Hamlet, Hamlet!
All. Gentlemen,—
Hor.   Good my lord, be quiet.
[*The Attendants part them, and they
come out of the grave.*
Ham. Why I will fight with him upon this
   theme
Until my eyelids will no longer wag. 290
Queen. O my son, what theme?
Ham. I loved Ophelia: forty thousand
   brothers
Could not, with all their quantity of love,
Make up my sum. What wilt thou do for her?
King. O, he is mad, Laertes.
Queen. For love of God, forbear him.
Ham. 'Swounds, show me what thou'lt do:
Woo't weep? woo't fight? woo't fast? woo't
   tear thyself?
Woo't drink up eisel? eat a crocodile?
I'll do't. Dost thou come here to whine? 300
To outface me with leaping in her grave?
Be buried quick with her, and so will I:
And, if thou prate of mountains, let them
   throw
Millions of acres on us, till our ground,
Singeing his pate against the burning zone,
Make Ossa like a wart! Nay, an thou'lt
   mouth,
I'll rant as well as thou.
Queen.   This is mere madness:
And thus awhile the fit will work on him;
Anon, as patient as the female dove,
When that her golden couplets are disclosed,
His silence will sit drooping.
Ham.   Hear you, sir;
What is the reason that you use me thus?
I loved you ever: but it is no matter;
Let Hercules himself do what he may,
The cat will mew and dog will have his day.
[*Exit.*
King. I pray you, good Horatio, wait upon
   him.   [*Exit Horatio.*
[*To Laertes*] Strengthen your patience in our
   last night's speech;
We'll put the matter to the present push.

Good Gertrude, set some watch over your son.
This grave shall have a living monument: 320
An hour of quiet shortly shall we see;
Till then, in patience our proceeding be
[*Exeunt*

SCENE II. *A hall in the castle.*

Enter HAMLET *and* HORATIO.

Ham. So much for this, sir: now shall you
   see the other;
You do remember all the circumstance?
Hor. Remember it, my lord?
Ham. Sir, in my heart there was a kind of
   fighting,
That would not let me sleep: methought I lay
Worse than the mutines in the bilboes. Rashly,
And praised be rashness for it, let us know,
Our indiscretion sometimes serves us well,
When our deep plots do pall: and that should
   teach us
There's a divinity that shapes our ends, 10
Rough-hew them how we will,—
Hor.   That is most certain.
Ham. Up from my cabin,
My sea-gown scarf'd about me, in the dark
Groped I to find out them; had my desire,
Finger'd their packet, and in fine withdrew
To mine own room again; making so bold,
My fears forgetting manners, to unseal
Their grand commission; where I found, Ho-
   ratio,—
O royal knavery!—an exact command,
Larded with many several sorts of reasons 20
Importing Denmark's health and England's too,
With, ho! such bugs and goblins in my life,
That, on the supervise, no leisure bated,
No, not to stay the grinding of the axe,
My head should be struck off.
Hor.   Is't possible?
Ham. Here's the commission: read it at
   more leisure.
But wilt thou hear me how I did proceed?
Hor. I beseech you.
Ham. Being thus be-netted round with vil-
   lanies,—
Ere I could make a prologue to my brains, 30
They had begun the play—I sat me down,
Devised a new commission, wrote it fair:
I once did hold it, as our statists do,
A baseness to write fair and labor'd much
How to forget that learning, but, sir, now
It did me yeoman's service: wilt thou know
The effect of what I wrote?
Hor.   Ay, good my lord.
Ham. An earnest conjuration from the
   king,
As England was his faithful tributary,
As love between them like the palm might
   flourish,   40
As peace should still her wheaten garland
   wear
And stand a comma 'tween their amities,
And many such-like 'As'es of great charge,
That, on the view and knowing of these con-
   tents,

Without debatement further, more or less,
He should the bearers put to sudden death,
Not shriving-time allow'd.

Hor.   How was this seal'd?

Ham. Why, even in that was heaven or-
dinant.
I had my father's signet in my purse,
Which was the model of that Danish seal; 50
Folded the writ up in form of the other,
Subscribed it, gave't the impression, placed it
safely,
The changeling never known. Now, the next
· day   [quent
Was our sea-fight; and what to this was se-
Thou know'st already.

Hor.· So Guildenstern and Rosencrantz go
to't.

Ham. Why, man, they did make love to
this employment;
They are not near my conscience; their de-
feat
Does by their own insinuation grow.
'Tis dangerous when the baser nature comes
Between the pass and fell incensed points 61
Of mighty opposites.

Hor.   Why, what a king is this!

Ham. Does it not, think'st thee, stand me
now upon—
He that hath kill'd my king and whored my
mother,
Popp'd in between the election and my hopes,
Thrown out his angle for my proper life,
And with such cozenage—is't not perfect con-
science,
To quit him with this arm? and is't not to be
damn'd,
To let this canker of our nature come
In further evil?   70

Hor. It must be shortly known to him
from England
What is the issue of the business there.

Ham. It will be short: the interim is mine;
And a man's life's no more than to say 'One.'
But I am very sorry, good Horatio,
That to Laertes I forgot myself;
For, by the image of my cause, I see
The portraiture of his: I'll court his favors
But, sure, the bravery of his grief did put me
Into a towering passion.

Hor.   Peace! who comes here? 80

Enter OSRIC.

Osr. Your lordship is right welcome back
to Denmark.

Ham. I humbly thank you, sir. Dost know
this water-fly?

Hor. No, my good lord.

Ham. Thy state is the more gracious; for
'tis a vice to know him. He hath much land,
and fertile: let a beast be lord of beasts, and
his crib shall stand at the king's mess: 'tis a
chough; but, as I say, spacious in the possession of dirt.   90

Osr. Sweet lord, if your lordship were at
leisure, I should impart a thing to you from
his majesty.

Ham. I will receive it, sir, with all diligence of spirit. Put your bonnet to his right
use; 'tis for the head.

Osr. I thank your lordship, it is very hot.·

Ham. No, believe me, 'tis very cold; the
wind is northerly.   99

Osr. It is indifferent cold, my lord, indeed.

Ham. But yet methinks it is very sultry
and hot for my complexion.

Osr. Exceedingly, my lord; it is very sultry,—as 'twere,—I cannot tell how. But, my
lord, his majesty bade me signify to you that
he has laid a great wager on your head: sir,
this is the matter,—

Ham. I beseech you, remember—
[*Hamlet moves him to put on his hat.*

Osr. Nay, good my lord; for mine ease, in
good faith. Sir, here is newly come to court
Laertes; believe me, an absolute gentleman,
full of most excellent differences, of very soft
society and great showing: indeed, to speak
feelingly of him, he is the card or calendar of
gentry, for you shall find in him the continent of what part a gentleman would see. ·

Ham. Sir, his definement suffers no perdition in you; though, I know, to divide him
inventorially would dizzy the arithmetic of
memory, and yet but yaw neither, in respect of his quick sail. a But, in the verity of
extolment, I take him to be a soul of great
article; and his infusion of such dearth and
rareness, as, to make true diction of him, his
semblable is his mirror; and who else would
trace him, his umbrage, nothing more.

Osr. Your lordship speaks most infallibly
of him.

Ham. The concernancy, sir? why do we
wrap the gentleman in our more rawer
breath?

Osr. Sir?   130

Hor. Is't not possible to understand in another tongue? You will do't, sir, really.

Ham. What imports the nomination of
this gentleman?

Osr. Of Laertes?

Hor. His purse is empty already; all's
golden words are spent.

Ham. Of him, sir.

Osr. I know you are not ignorant—

Ham. I would you did, sir; yet, in faith,
if you did, it would not much approve me.
Well, sir.

Osr. You are not ignorant of what excellence Laertes is—

Ham. I dare not confess that. lest I should
compare with him in excellence; but, to
know a man well, were to know himself.

Osr. I mean, sir, for his weapon; but in
the imputation laid on him by them, in his
meed he's unfellowed.   150

Ham. What's his weapon?

Osr. Rapier and dagger.

Ham. That's two of his weapons: but,
well.

Osr. The king, sir, hath wagered with him
six Barbary horses: against the which he has

Imponed, as I take it, six French rapiers and poniards, with their assigns, as girdle, hangers, and so : three of the carriages, in faith, are very dear to fancy, very responsive to the hilts, most delicate carriages, and of very liberal conceit.

Ham. What call you the carriages?

Hor. I knew you must be edified by the margent ere you had done.

Osr. The carriages, sir, are the hangers.

Ham. The phrase would be more german to the matter, if we could carry cannon by our sides : I would it might be hangers till then. But, on : six Barbary horses against six French swords, their assigns, and three liberal-conceited carriages ; that's the French bet against the Danish. Why is this 'imponed,' as you call it?   171

Osr. The king, sir, hath laid, that in a dozen passes between yourself and him, he shall not exceed you three hits : he hath laid on twelve for nine ; and it would come to immediate trial, if your lordship would vouchsafe the answer.

Ham. How if I answer 'no'?

Osr. I mean, my lord, the opposition of your person in trial.   179

Ham. Sir, will walk here in the hall : if it please his majesty, 'tis the breathing time of day with me ; let the foils be brought, the gentleman willing, and the king hold his purpose, I will win for him an I can ; if not, I will gain nothing but my shame and the odd hits.

Osr. Shall I re-deliver you e'en so?

Ham. To this effect, sir; after what flourish your nature will.

Osr. I commend my duty to your lordship.

Ham. Yours, yours. [*Exit Osric.*] He does well to commend it to himself; there are no tongues else for's turn.

Hor. This lapwing runs away with the shell on his head.

Ham. He did comply with his dug, before he sucked it. Thus has he—and many more of the same bevy that I know the drossy age dotes on—only got the tune of the time and outward habit of encounter ; a kind of yesty collection, which carries them through and through the most †fond· and winnowed opinions ; and do but blow them to their trial, the bubbles are out.

Enter a Lord.

Lord. My lord, his majesty commended him to you by young Osric, who brings back to him, that you attend him in the hall : he sends to know if your pleasure hold to play with Laertes, or that you will take longer time.

Ham. I am constant to my purposes : they follow the king's pleasure : if his fitness speaks, mine is ready ; now or whensoever, provided I be so able as now.   211

Lord. The king and queen and all are coming down.

Ham. In happy time.

Lord. The queen desires you to use some gentle entertainment to Laertes before you fall to play.

Ham. She well instructs me. [*Exit Lord.*

Hor. You will lose this wager, my lord.

Ham. I do not think so : since he went into France, I have been in continual practice : I shall win at the odds. But thou wouldst not think how ill all's here about my heart : but it is no matter.

Hor. Nay, good my lord,—

Ham. It is but foolery ; but it is such a kind of gain-giving, as would perhaps trouble a woman.

Hor. If your mind dislike any thing, obey it : I will forestal their repair hither, and say you are not fit.   229

Ham. Not a whit, we defy augury : there's a special providence in the fall of a sparrow. If it be now, 'tis not to come ; if it be not to come, it will be now ; if it be not now, yet it will come : the readiness is all : since no man has aught of what he leaves, what is't to leave betimes?

Enter KING, QUEEN, LAERTES, Lords, OSRIC, *and* Attendants *with foils, &c.*

King. Come, Hamlet, come, and take this hand from me.

[*The King puts Laertes' hand into Hamlet's.*

Ham. Give me your pardon, sir : I've done you wrong ;
But pardon't, as you are a gentleman.
This presence knows,
And you must needs have heard, how I am punish'd   240
With sore distraction. What I have done,
That might your nature, honor and exception
Roughly awake, I here proclaim was madness.
Was't Hamlet wrong'd Laertes? Never Hamlet :
If Hamlet from himself be ta'en away,
And when he's not himself does wrong Laertes,
Then Hamlet does it not, Hamlet denies it.
Who does it, then? His madness : if't be so,
Hamlet is of the faction that is wrong'd ;
His madness is poor Hamlet's enemy.   250
Sir, in this audience,
Let my disclaiming from a purposed evil
Free me so far in your most generous thoughts,
That I have shot mine arrow o'er the house,
And hurt my brother.

Laer.   I am satisfied in nature,
Whose motive, in this case, should stir me most
To my revenge : but in my terms of honor
I stand aloof ; and will no reconcilement,
Till by some elder masters, of known honor,
I have a voice and precedent of peace,   262
To keep my name ungored. But till that time,
I do receive your offer'd love like love,

And will not wrong it.

Ham.   I embrace it freely ;
And will this brother's wager frankly play.
Give us the foils. Come on.

Laer.   Come, one for me.

Ham. I'll be your foil, Laertes : in mine
     ignorance
Your skill shall, like a star i' the darkest
     night,
Stick fiery off indeed.

Laer.   You mock me, sir.

Ham. No, by this hand.

King. Give them the foils, young Osric.
     Cousin Hamlet,   · 270
You know the wager ?

Ham. ·   Very well, my lord ;
Your grace hath laid the odds o' the weaker
     side.

King. I do not fear it ; I have seen you
     both :
But since he is better'd, we have therefore
     odds.

Laer. This is too heavy, let me see another.

Ham. This likes me well. These foils have
     all a length ?   [*They prepare to play.*

Osr. Ay, my good lord.

King. Set me the stoups of wine upon that
     table.
If Hamlet give the first or second hit,
Or quit in answer of the third exchange,   280
Let all the battlements their ordnance fire ;
The king shall drink to Hamlet's better breath;
And in the cup an union shall he throw,
Richer than that which four successive kings
In Denmark's crown have worn. Give me the
     cups ;
And let the kettle to the trumpet speak,   ·
The trumpet to the cannoneer without,
The cannons to the heavens, the heavens to
     earth,
' Now the king drinks to Hamlet.' Come, be-
     gin ;
And you, the judges, bear a wary eye.   290

Ham. Come on, sir.

Laer.   Come, my lord.   [*They play.*

Ham.   One.

Laer.   No.

Ham.   Judgment.

Osr. A hit, a very palpable hit.

Laer.   Well ; again.

King. Stay ; give me drink. Hamlet, this
     pearl is thine ;
Here's to thy health.

     [*Trumpets sound, and cannon shot off*
                         within.
           Give him the cup.

Ham. I'll play this bout first ; set it by
     awhile.
Come. [*They play.*] Another hit ; what say
     you ?

Laer. A touch, a touch, I do confess.

King. Our son shall win.

Queen.   He's fat, and scant of breath.
Here, Hamlet, take my napkin, rub thy
     brows ;
The queen carouses to thy fortune, Hamlet.

Ham. Good madam !   301

·*King.*   Gertrude, do not drink.

Queen. I will, my lord ; I pray you, pardon
     me.

King. [*Aside*] It is the poison'd cup : it is
     too late.

Ham. I dare not drink yet, madam ; by
     and by.

Queen. Come, let me wipe thy face.

Laer. My lord, I'll hit him now.

King.   I do not think't.

Laer. [*Aside*] And yet 'tis almost 'gainst
     my conscience.

Ham. Come, for the third, Laertes : you
     but dally ;
I pray you, pass with your best violence ;
I am afeard you make a wanton of me.   310

Laer. Say you so ? come on.   [*They play.*

Osr. Nothing, neither way.

Laer. Have at you now !
[*Laertes wounds Hamlet ; then in scuffling,
     they change rapiers, and Hamlet wounds
     Laertes.*

King. Part them ; they are incensed.

Ham. Nay, come, again. [*The Queen falls.*

Osr.   Look to the queen there, ho !

Hor. They bleed on both sides. How is it,
     my lord ?

Osr. How is't, Laertes ?

Laer. Why, as a woodcock to mine own
     springe, Osric :
I am justly kill'd with mine own treachery.

Ham. How does the queen ?

King.   She swounds to see them bleed.

Queen. No, no, the drink, the drink,—O
     my dear Hamlet,—   320
The drink, the drink ! I am poison'd.   [*Dies.*

Ham. O villany ! Ho ! let the door be
     lock'd :
Treachery ! Seek it out.

Laer. It is here, Hamlet : Hamlet, thou
     art slain ;
No medicine in the world can do thee good ;
In thee there is not half an hour of life ; · ·
The treacherous instrument is in thy hand,
Unbated and envenom'd : the foul practice
Hath turn'd itself on me ; lo, here I lie,   329
Never to rise again : thy mother's poison'd :
I can no more : the king, the king's to blame.

Ham. The point !—envenom'd too !
Then, venom, to thy work. [*Stabs the King.*

All. Treason ! treason !

King. O, yet defend me, friends ; I am but
     hurt.

Ham. Here, thou incestuous, murderous,
     damned Dane,
Drink off this potion. Is thy union here ?
Follow my mother.   [*King dies.*

Laer.   He is justly served ;
It is a poison temper'd by himself.   339
Exchange forgiveness with me, noble Hamlet :
Mine and my father's death come not upon
     thee,
Nor thine on me.   [*Dies.*

Ham. Heaven make thee free of it ! I fol-
     low thee.

HAMLET.

                    " Horatio, I am dead:
Thou livest: report me and my cause aright
To the unsatisfied."

                                           HAMLET, p 685

I am dead, Horatio. Wretched queen, adieu !
You that look.pale and tremble at this chance,
That are but mutes or audience to this act,
Had I but time—as this fell sergeant, death,
Is strict in his arrest—O, I could tell you—
But let it be. Horatio, I am .dead ;
Thou livest ; report me and my cause aright
To the unsatisfied.
    Hor.   Never believe it :   351
I am more an antique Roman than a Dane :
Here's yet some liquor left.
    Ham.   As thou'rt a man,
Give me the cup : let go ; by heaven, I'll
    have't.
O good Horatio, what a wounded name,
Things standing thus unknown, shall live be-
    hind me !
If thou didst ever hold me in thy heart
Absent thee from felicity awhile,
And in this harsh world draw thy breath in
    pain,
To tell my story.
        [*March afar off, and shot within.*
    What warlike noise is this ?   360
    Osr. Young Fortinbras, with conquest come
    from Poland,
To the ambassadors of England gives
This warlike volley.
    Ham.   O, I die, Horatio ;
The potent poison quite o'er-crows my spirit :
I cannot live to hear the news from England ;
But I do prophesy the election lights
On Fortinbras : he has my dying voice ;
So tell him, with the occurrents, more and
    less,
Which have solicited. The rest is silence.
                     [*Dies.*
    Hor. Now cracks a noble heart. Good
    night, sweet prince :   370
And flights of angels sing thee to thy rest !)
Why does the drum come hither ?
                  [*March within.*

Enter FORTINBRAS, *the* English Ambassadors,
            and others.

    Fort. Where is this sight ?
    Hor.   What is it ye would see ?
If aught of woe or wonder, cease your search.
    Fort. This quarry cries on havoc. O proud
    death,
What feast is toward in thine eternal cell,
That thou so many princes at a shot

So bloodily hast struck ?
    First Amb.   The sight is dismal ;
And our affairs from England come too late :
The ears are senseless that should give us
    hearing,
To tell him his commandment is fulfill'd, 381
That Rosencrantz and Guildenstern are dead :
Where should we have our thanks ?
    Hor.   Not from his mouth,
Had it the ability of life to thank you :
He never gave commandment for their death.
But since, so jump upon this bloody question,
You from the Polack wars, and you from Eng-
    land,
Are here arrived, give order that these bodies
High on a stage be placed to the view ;   389
And let me speak to the yet unknowing world
How these things came about: so shall you
    hear
Of carnal, bloody, and unnatural acts,
Of accidental judgments, casual slaughters,
Of deaths put on by cunning and forced cause,
And, in this upshot, purposes mistook
Fall'n on the inventors' heads : all this can I
Truly deliver.
    Fort.   Let us haste to hear it,
And call the noblest to the audience.
For me, with sorrow I embrace my fortune :
I have some rights of memory in this kingdom,
Which now to claim my vantage doth invite
    me.
    Hor. Of that I shall have also cause to
    speak,
And from his mouth whose voice will draw on
    more ;
But let this same be presently perform'd,
Even while men's minds are wild ; lest more
    mischance
On plots and errors, happen.
    Fort.   Let four captains
Bear Hamlet, like a soldier, to the stage ;
For he was likely, had he been put on,
To have proved most royally : and, for his
    passage,
The soldiers' music and the rites of war   410
Speak loudly for him.
Take up the bodies : such a sight as this
Becomes the field, but here shows much amiss.
Go, bid the soldiers shoot.
        [*A dead march. Exeunt, bearing off the
        dead bodies ; after which a peal of ord-
        nance is shot off.*

ALL'S WELL THAT ENDS WELL.

(WRITTEN ABOUT 1602.)

INTRODUCTION.

Among the plays of Shakespeare mentioned by Meres in his *Palladis Tamia* (1598) occurs the name of *Love's Labour's Won.* This has been identified by some critics with *The Taming of the Shrew* and by others with *Much Ado About Nothing*, but the weight of authority inclines to the opinion that under this title Meres spoke of the play known to us as *All's Well that Ends Well.* It seems not improbable that *All's Well*, as we possess it in the First Folio—and no earlier edition exists—is a rehandling, very thoroughly carried out, of an earlier version of this comedy. Coleridge believed that two styles were discernible in it, and there is certainly a larger proportion of rhyming lines in it than in any other play written after the year 1600. It is, however, far from certain that any portion of the play is of early origin, and assigning conjecturally the date about 1602 as that of the completion of the whole, we may view it as belonging to the later group of the second cycle of Shakespeare's comedies, not so early, therefore, as *Twelfth Night* or *As You Like It*, and certainly earlier than *Measure for Measure.* The story of Helena and Bertram was found by Shakespeare in Paynter's *Palace of Pleasure* (1566), Paynter having translated it from the *Decameron* of Boccacio (Novel 9, Third day). Shakespeare added the characters of the Countess, Lafeu, Parolles, and the Clown. What interested the poet's imagination in Boccacio's story was evidently the position and person of the heroine. In Boccacio, Giletta, the physician's daughter, is inferior in rank to the young Count, Beltramo, but she is rich. Shakespeare's Helena is of humbler birth than his Bertram, and she is also poor. Yet poor, and comparatively low-born, she aspires to be the young Count's wife, she pursues him to Paris, and wins him against his will. To show Helena thus reversing in a measure the ordinary relations of man and woman, and yet to show her neither self-seeking nor unwomanly, was the task which the dramatist attempted. On the one hand he insists much on Bertram's youth, and gives him the faults and vices of youth, making the reader or spectator of the play feel that his hero has great need of such a finely-tempered, right-willed and loyal nature to stand by his side as that of Helena. On the other hand he shows us Helena's enthusiastic attachment to Bertram, her fears and cares on his behalf, her adhesion to him rather than to herself, when her husband seems to set their interests in opposition to one another, until we come to feel that the imperious need which makes Helena overstep social conventions is the need of perfect service to the man she loves. Bertram's beauty and courage must bear part of the blame for Helena's loving him better than he deserves. With the youthful desire for independence which makes him break away from her, she can intelligently sympathize. In the last Act she appears—when he has entangled himself in falsehood and shame—to save him, and rescue him from his baser self. We feel that when he has at last really found Helena, he is safe, and all ends well. Parolles, the incarnation of bragging meanness, is the counterfoil of Helena—she, the doer of virtuous deeds; he, the utterer of vain and swelling words; she, all brave womanliness; he, too cowardly for manhood. Parolles has been compared to Falstaff, but they ought rather to be contrasted; for Sir John is a man of genius, with real wit and power of fascination, and no ridicule can destroy him, but the exposure of Parolles makes him dwindle into his native pitifulness. The Countess is a charming creation of Shakespeare; in no play, unless it be some of his latest romantic dramas, is old age made more beautiful and dignified.

DRAMATIS PERSONÆ.

KING OF FRANCE.
DUKE OF FLORENCE.
BERTRAM, Count of Rousillon.
LAFEU, an old lord.
PAROLLES, a follower of Bertram.
Steward, } servants to the Countess of
Clown, } Rousillon.
A Page.
COUNTESS OF ROUSILLON, mother to Bertram.
HELENA, a gentlewoman protected by the Countess.

An old Widow of Florence.
DIANA, daughter to the Widow.
VIOLENTA, } neighbors and friends to the
MARIANA, } Widow.

Lords, Officers, Soldiers, &c., French and Florentine.

. SCENE : *Rousillon ; Paris; Florence; Marseilles.*

ACT I.

Scene I. *Rousillon. The* Count's *palace.*

Enter Bertram, *the* Countess of Rousillon, Helena, *and* Lafeu, *all in black.*

Count. In delivering my son from me, I bury a second husband.

Ber. And I in going, madam, weep o'er my father's death anew : but I must attend his majesty's command to whom I am now in ward, evermore in subjection.

Laf. You shall find of the king a husband, madam ; you, sir, a father · he that so generally is at all times good must of necessity hold his virtue to you ; whose worthiness would stir it up where it wanted rather than lack it where there is such abundance.

Count. What hope is there of his majesty's amendment ?

Laf. He hath abandoned his physicians, madam ; under whose practices he hath persecuted time with hope, and finds no other advantage in the process but only the losing of hope by time

Count This young gentlewoman had a father,—O, that 'had' ! how sad a passage 'tis !—whose skill was almost as great as his honesty ; had it stretched so far, would have made nature immortal, and death should have play for lack of work Would, for the king's sake, he were living ! I think it would be the death of the king's disease.

Laf. How called you the man you speak of, madam ?

Count He was famous, sir, in his profession, and it was his great right to be so Gerard de Narbon 31

Laf. He was excellent indeed, madam . the king very lately spoke of him admiringly and mourningly : he was skilful enough to have lived still, if knowledge could be set up against mortality.

Ber. What is it, my good lord, the king languishes of ?

Laf. A fistula, my lord.

Ber. I heard not of it before.

Laf. I would it were not notorious Was this gentlewoman the daughter of Gerard de Narbon ?

Count His sole child, my lord, and bequeathed to my overlooking I have those hopes of her good that her education promises, her dispositions she inherits, which makes fair gifts fairer ; for where an unclean mind carries virtuous qualities, there commendations go with pity; they are virtues and traitors too, in her they are the better for their simpleness, she derives her honesty and achieves her goodness.

Laf. Your commendations, madam, get from her tears.

Count. 'Tis the best brine a maiden can season her praise in. The remembrance of her father never approaches her heart but the tyranny of her sorrows takes all livelihood from her cheek. No more of this, Helena ; go to, no more , lest it be rather thought you affect a sorrow than have it. 61

Hel. I do affect a sorrow indeed, but I have it too.

Laf. Moderate lamentation is the right of the dead, excessive grief the enemy to the living.

Count If the living be enemy to the grief, the excess makes it soon mortal

Ber Madam, I desire your holy wishes.

Laf How understand we that ?

Count. Be thou blest, Bertram, and succeed thy father 70
In manners, as in shape ! thy blood and virtue Contend for empire in thee, and thy goodness Share with thy birthright ! Love all, trust a few,
Do wrong to none . be able for thine enemy Rather in power than use, and keep thy friend [fence,
Under thy own life's key : be check'd for silence, But never tax'd for speech What heaven more will, [down,
That thee may furnish and my prayers pluck Fall on thy head ! Farewell, my lord ,
'Tis an unseason'd courtier, good my lord, 80 Advise him

Laf He cannot want the best That shall attend his love

Count. Heaven bless him ! Farewell, Bertram [*Exit.*

Ber. [*To Helena*] the best wishes that can be forged in your thoughts be servants to you ! Be comfortable to my mother, your mistress and make much of her

Laf. Farewell, pretty lady : you must hold the credit of your father.

[*Exeunt Bertram and Lafeu.*

Hel. O, were that all ! I think not on my father ; 90
And these great tears grace his remembrance more
Than those I shed for him What was he like ? I have forgot him : my imagination Carries no favour in't but Bertram's I am undone there is no living, none,
If Bertram be away 'Twere all one That I should love a bright particular star And think to wed it, he is so above me :
In his bright radiance and collateral light Must I be comforted. not in his sphere 100 The ambition in my love thus plagues itself . The hind that would be mated by the lion Must die for love. 'Twas pretty, though a plague,
To see him every hour ; to sit and draw His arched brows, his hawking eye, his curls, In our heart's table . heart too capable Of every line and trick of his sweet favor : But now he's gone, and my idolatrous fancy Must sanctify his reliques. Who comes here ?

Enter PAROLLES.

[*Aside*] One that goes with him : I love him for his sake ; 110

And yet I know him a notorious liar,
Think him a great way fool, solely a coward;
Yet these fixed evils sit so fit in him,
That they take place, when virtue's steely
   bones
†Look bleak i' the cold wind : withal, full oft
   we see
Cold wisdom waiting on superfluous folly.

Par. Save you, fair queen !
Hel. And you, monarch !
Par. No.
Hel. And no.   120
Par. Are you meditating on virginity ?
Hel. Ay. You have some stain of soldier
in you : let me ask you a question. Man is
enemy to virginity; how may we barricado it
against him ?
Par. Keep him out.
Hel. But he assails; and our virginity,
though valiant, in the defence yet is weak :
unfold to us some warlike resistance.
Par. There is none: man, sitting down
before you, will undermine you and blow you
up.   130
Hel. Bless our poor virginity from under-
miners and blowers up ! Is there no military
policy, how virgins might blow up men ?
Par. Virginity being blown down, man will
quicklier be blown up : marry, in blowing him
down again, with the breach yourselves made,
you lose your city. It is not politic in the
commonwealth of nature to preserve virginity.
Loss of virginity is rational increase and there
was never virgin got till virginity was first
lost. That you were made of is metal to make
virgins. Virginity by being once lost may be
ten times found; by being ever kept, it is ever
lost : 'tis too cold a companion; away with 't !
Hel. I will stand for 't a little, though therefore I die a virgin.
Par. There's little can be said in 't; 'tis
against the rule of nature. To speak on the
part of virginity, is to accuse your mothers;
which is most infallible disobedience. He that
hangs himself is a virgin : virginity murders
itself and should be buried in highways out of
all sanctified limit, as a desperate offendress
against nature. Virginity breeds mites, much
like a cheese; consumes itself to the very
paring, and so dies with feeding his own
stomach. Besides, virginity is peevish, proud,
idle, made of self-love, which is the most inhibited sin in the canon. Keep it not; you
cannot choose but loose by't : out with 't !
within ten year it will make itself ten, which
is a goodly increase; and the principal itself
not much the worse : away with 't !
Hel. How might one do, sir, to lose it to
her own liking ?
Par. Let me see : marry, ill, to like him
that ne'er it likes. 'Tis a commodity will
lose the gloss with lying; the longer kept, the
less worth : off with 't while 'tis vendible;
answer the time of request. Virginity, like an
old courtier, wears her cap out of fashion :
richly suited, but insuitable : just like the

brooch and the tooth-pick, which wear not
now. Your date is better in your pie and
your porridge than in your cheek; and your
virginity, your old virginity, is like one of our
French withered pears, it looks ill, it eats drily;
marry, 'tis a withered pear; it was formerly
better; marry, yet 'tis a withered pear : will
you anything with it ?
Hel. †Not my virginity yet....
There shall your master have a thousand loves,
A mother and a mistress and a friend,   181
A phœnix, captain and an enemy,
A guide a goddess, and a sovereign,
A counsellor, a traitress, and a dear;
His humble ambition, proud humility,
His jarring concord, and his discord dulcet,
His faith, his sweet disaster; with a world
Of pretty, fond, adoptions christendoms,
That blinking Cupid gossips. Now shall he—
I know not what he shall. God send him well!
The court's a learning place, and he is one—
Par. What one, i' faith ?
Hel. That I wish well. 'Tis pity—
Par. What's pity ?
Hel. That wishing well had not a body in't,
Which might be felt; that we, the poorer born,
Whose baser stars do shut us up in wishes,
Might with effects of them follow our friends,
And show what we alone must think, which
   never
Return us thanks.   200

Enter Page.

Page. Monsieur Parolles, my lord calls for
   you.   *Exit.*
Par. Little Helen, farewell; if I can re-
member thee, I will think of thee at court.
Hel. Monsieur Parolles, you were born
under a charitable star.
Par. Under Mars, I.
Hel. I especially think, under Mars.
Par. Why under Mars ?
Hel. The wars have so kept you under that
you must needs be born under Mars.   210
Par. When he was predominant.
Hel. When he was retrograde, I think,
rather.
Par. Why think you so ?   [fight.
Hel. You go so much backward when you
Par. That's for advantage.
Hel. So is running away, when fear pro-
poses the safety; but the composition that
your valor and fear makes in you is a virtue
of a good wing, and I like the wear well. 219
Par. I am so full of businesses, I cannot
answer thee acutely. I will return perfect
courtier; in the which, my instruction shall
serve to naturalize thee, so thou wilt be capable of a courtier's counsel and understand what
advice shall thrust upon thee; else thou diest
in thine unthankfulness, and thine ignorance
makes thee away : farewell. When thou hast
leisure, say thy prayers; when thou hast
none, remember thy friends; get thee a good
husband, and use him as he uses thee; so,
farewell.   [*Exit.* 230

Hel. Our remedies oft in ourselves do lie,
Which we ascribe to heaven : the fated sky
Gives us free scope, only doth backward pull
Our slow designs when we ourselves are dull.
What power is it which mounts my love so high,
That makes me see, and cannot feed mine eye ?
†The mightiest space in fortune nature brings
To join like likes and kiss like native things.
Impossible be strange attempts to those
That weigh their pains in sense and do suppose   240
†What hath been cannot be : who ever strove
So show her merit, that did miss her love ?
The king's disease—my project may deceive me,
But my intents are fix'd and will not leave me.
                                                [*Exit.*

SCENE II. *Paris. The* KING'S *palace.*

Flourish of cornets. Enter the KING OF
FRANCE, *with letters, and divers Attendants.*

King. The Florentines and Senoys are by the ears ;
Have fought with equal fortune and continue
A braving war.
  First Lord. So 'tis reported, sir.
  King. Nay, 'tis most credible ; we here receive it
A certainty, vouch'd from our cousin Austria,
With caution that the Florentine will move us
For speedy aid ; wherein our dearest friend
Prejudicates the business and would seem
To have us make denial.
  First Lord.   His love and wisdom,
Approved so to your majesty, may plead   10
For amplest credence.
  King.   He hath arm'd our answer,
And Florence is denied before he comes :
Yet, for our gentlemen that mean to see
The Tuscan service, freely have they leave
To stand on either part.
  Sec. Lord.   It well may serve
A nursery to our gentry, who are sick
For breathing and exploit.
  King.   What's he comes here ?

Enter BERTRAM, LAFEU, *and* PAROLLES.

  First Lord. It is the Count Rousillon, my good lord,
Young Bertram.
  King. Youth, thou bear'st thy father's face ;   20
Frank nature, rather curious than in haste,
Hath well composed thee. Thy father's moral parts
Mayst thou inherit too ! Welcome to Paris.
  Ber. My thanks and duty are your majesty's.
  King. I would I had that corporal soundness now,
As when thy father and myself in friendship
First tried our soldiership ! He did look far
Into the service of the time and was
Discipled of the bravest : he lasted long ;

But on us both did haggish age steal on
And wore us out of act. It much repairs me
To talk of your good father. In his youth   31
He had the wit which I can well observe
To-day in our young lords ; but they may jest
Till their own scorn return to them unnoted
Ere they can hide their levity in honor ;
†So like a courtier, contempt nor bitterness
Were in his pride or sharpness ; if they were,
His equal had awaked them, and his honor,
Clock to itself, knew the true minute when
Exception bid him speak, and at this time   40
His tongue obey'd his hand : who were below him
He used as creatures of another place
And bow'd his eminent top to their low ranks,
Making them proud of his humility,
†In their poor praise he humbled. Such a man
Might be a copy to these younger times ;
Which, follow'd well, would demonstrate them now
But goers backward.
  Ber.   His good remembrance, sir,
Lies richer in your thoughts than on his tomb ;
So in approof lives not his epitaph   50
As in your royal speech.
  King. Would I were with him ! He would always say—
Methinks I hear him now ; his plausive words
He scatter'd not in ears, but grafted them,
To grow there and to bear,—' Let me not live,'—
This his good melancholy oft began,
On the catastrophe and heel of pastime,
When it was out,—' Let me not live,' quoth he,
' After my flame lacks oil, to be the snuff   59
Of younger spirits, whose apprehensive senses
All but new things disdain ; whose judgments are   [stancies
Mere fathers of their garments ; whose constancies
Expire before their fashions. This he wish'd ;
I after him do after him wish too,
Since I nor wax nor honey can bring home,
I quickly were dissolved from my hive,
To give some laborers room.
  Sec. Lord.   You are loved, sir :
They that least lend it you shall lack you first.
  King. I fill a place, I know't. How long is't, count,
Since the physician at your father's died ?   70
He was much famed.
  Ber.   Some six months since, my lord.
  King. If he were living, I would try him yet.
Lend me an arm ; the rest have worn me out
With several applications ; nature and sickness
Debate it at their leisure. Welcome, count ;
My son's no dearer.
  Ber.   Thank your majesty.
                                [*Exeunt. Flourish.*

SCENE III. *Rousillon. The* COUNT'S *palace.*

Enter COUNTESS, *Steward, and* Clown.

  Count. I will now hear ; what say you of this gentlewoman ?

44

Stew. Madam, the care I have had to even your content, I wish might be found in the calendar of my past endeavors; for then we wound our modesty and make foul the clearness of our deservings, when of ourselves we publish them.

Count. What does this knave here? Get you gone, sirrah: the complaints I have heard of you I do not all believe: 'tis my slowness that I do not; for I know you lack not folly to commit them, and have ability enough to make such knaveries yours.

Clo. 'Tis not unknown to you, madam, I am a poor fellow.

Count. Well, sir.

Clo. No, madam, 'tis not so well that I am poor, though many of the rich are damned: but, if I may have your ladyship's good will to go to the world, Isbel the woman and I will do as we may.   21

Count. Wilt thou needs be a beggar?

Clo. I do beg your good will in this case.

Count. In what case?

Clo. In Isbel's case and mine own. Service is no heritage: and I think I shall never have the blessing of God till I have issue o' my body; for they say barnes are blessings.   [marry.

Count. Tell me thy reason why thou wilt

Clo. My poor body, madam, requires it: I am driven on by the flesh; and he must needs go that the devil drives.

Count. Is this all your worship's reason?

Clo. Faith, madam, I have other holy reasons, such as they are.

Count. May the world know them?

Clo. I have been, madam, a wicked creature, as you and all flesh and blood are; and, indeed, I do marry that I may repent.

Count. Thy marriage, sooner than thy wickedness.   41

Clo. I am out o' friends, madam; and I hope to have friends for my wife's sake.

Count. Such friends are thine enemies, knave.

Clo. You're shallow, madam, in great friends; for the knaves come to do that for me which I am a weary of. He that ears my land spares my team and gives me leave to in the crop; if I be his cuckold, he's my drudge: he that comforts my wife is the cherisher of my flesh and blood; he that cherishes my flesh and blood loves my flesh and blood; he that loves my flesh and blood is my friend: ergo, he that kisses my wife is my friend. If men could be contented to be what they are, there were no fear in marriage; for young Charbon the Puritan and old Poysam the Papist, howsome'er their hearts are severed in religion, their heads are both one; they may joul horns together, like any deer i' the herd.

Count. Wilt thou ever be a foul-mouthed and calumnious knave?   61

Clo. A prophet I, madam; and I speak the truth the next way:

For I the ballad will repeat,
Which men full true shall find;

Your marriage comes by destiny,
Your cuckoo sings by kind.

Count. Get you gone, sir; I'll talk with you more anon.

Stew. May it please you, madam, that he bid Helen come to you: of her I am to speak.

Count. Sirrah, tell my gentlewoman I would speak with her; Helen, I mean.

Clo. Was this fair face the cause, quoth she,
Why the Grecians sacked Troy?
Fond done, done fond,
Was this King Priam's joy?
With that she sighed as she stood,
With that she sighed as she stood,
And gave this sentence then;   80
Among nine bad if one be good,
Among nine bad if one be good,
There's yet one good in ten.

Count. What, one good in ten? you corrupt the song, sirrah.

Clo. One good woman in ten, madam; which is a purifying o' the song: would God would serve the world so all the year! we'ld find no fault with the tithe-woman, if I were the parson. One in ten, quoth a'! An we might have a good woman born but one every blazing star, or at an earthquake, 'twould mend the lottery well: a man may draw his heart out, ere a' pluck one.

Count. You'll be gone, sir knave, and do as I command you.

Clo. That man should be at woman's command, and yet no hurt done! Though honesty be no puritan, yet it will do no hurt; it will wear the surplice of humility over the black gown of a big heart. I am going, forsooth: the business is for Helen to come hither. [*Exit.*

Count. Well, now.

Stew. I know, madam, you love your gentlewoman entirely.

Count. Faith, I do: her father bequeathed her to me; and she herself, without other advantage, may lawfully make title to as much love as she finds: there is more owing her than is paid; and more shall be paid her than she'll demand.

Stew. Madam, I was very late more near her than I think she wished me: alone she was, and did communicate to herself her own words to her own ears; she thought, I dare vow for her, they touched not any stranger sense. Her matter was, she loved your son: Fortune, she said, was no goddess, that had put such difference betwixt their two estates; Love no god, that would not extend his might, only where qualities were level; Dian no queen of virgins, that would suffer her poor knight surprised, without rescue in the first assault or ransom afterward. This she delivered in the most bitter touch of sorrow that e'er I heard virgin exclaim in: which I held my duty speedily to acquaint you withal; sithence, in the loss that may happen, it concerns you something to know it.

Count. You have discharged this honestly;

keep it to yourself : many likelihoods informed
me of this before, which hung so tottering in
the balance that I could neither believe nor
misdoubt. Pray you, leave me still this in
your bosom , and I thank you for your honest
care ; I will speak with you further anon.
                                [*Exit Steward.*

Enter HELENA.

Even so it was with me when I was young ·
If ever we are nature's, these are ours , this
     thorn
Doth to our rose of youth rightly belong ;
Our blood to us, this to our blood is born ;
It is the show and seal of nature's truth,
Where love's strong passion is impress'd in
     youth .
By our remembrances of days foregone,   140
†Such were our faults, or then we thought
     them none
Her eye is sick on't : I observe her now.
Hel. What is your pleasure, madam ?
Count   You know, Helen,
I am a mother to you
Hel. Mine honorable mistress
Count   Nay, a mother ·
Why not a mother ? When I said ' a mother,'
Methought you saw a serpent : what's in
     ' mother,'
That you start at it ? I say, I am your mother,
And put you in the catalogue of those
That were enwombed mine 'tis often seen 150
Adoption strives with nature and choice breeds
A native slip to us from foreign seeds
You ne'er oppress'd me with a mother's groan,
Yet I express to you a mother's care .
God's mercy, maiden ! does it curd thy blood
To say I am thy mother ? What's the matter,
That this distemper'd messenger of wet,
The many-color'd Iris, rounds thine eye ?
Why ? that you are my daughter ?
Hel.   That I am not.
Count. I say, I am your mother.
Hel.   Pardon, madam ; 160
The Count Rousillon cannot be my brother :
I am from humble, he from honor'd name ,
No noble upon my parents, his all noble :
My master, my dear lord he is , and I
His servant live, and will his vassal die ·
He must not be my brother.
Count   Nor I your mother ?
Hel. You are my mother, madam ; would
     you were,—   [ther,—
So that my lord your son were not my bro-
Indeed my mother ! or were you both our
     mothers,
I care no more for than I do for heaven,   170
So I were not his sister. Can't no other,
But, I your daughter, he must be my brother ?
Count. Yes, Helen, you might be my
     daughter-in-law :
God shield you mean it not ! daughter and
     mother
So strive upon your pulse. What, pale again?
My fear hath catch'd your fondness : now I

The mystery of your loneliness, and find
Your salt tears' head . now to all sense 'tis
     gross
You love my son , invention is ashamed,
Against the proclamation of thy passion, 180
To say thou do-t not   therefore tell me true ,
But tell me then, 'tis so , for, look, thy cheeks
Confess it, th' one to th' other , and thine eyes
See it so grossly shown in thy behaviors
That in their kind they speak it   only sin
And hellish obstinacy tie thy tongue,
That truth should be suspected. Speak, is't
     so ?
If it be so, you have wound a goodly clew ;
If it be not, forswear't howe'er, I charge
     thee,
As heaven shall work in me for thine avail,
Tell me truly.   191
Hel.   Good madam, pardon me !
Count. Do you love my son ?
Hel.   Your pardon, noble mistress !
Count. Love you my son ?
Hel.   Do not you love him, madam ?
Count. Go not about , my love hath in t a
     bond,
Whereof the world takes note : come, come,
     disclose
The state of your affection , for your passions
Have to the full appeach'd
Hel.   Then, I confess,
Here on my knee, before high heaven and you,
That before you, and next unto high heaven,
I love your son.   200
My friends were poor, but honest ; so's my
     love
Be not offended , for it hurts not him
That he is loved of me   I follow him not
By any token of presumptuous suit ,
Nor would I have him till I do deserve him ;
Yet never know how that desert should be
I know I love in vain, strive against hope
Yet in this captious and intenible sieve
I still pour in the waters of my love
And lack not to lose still   thus, Indian-like,
Religious in mine error, I adore   211
The sun, that looks upon his worshipper,
But knows of him no more   My dearest
     madam,
Let not your hate encounter with my love
For loving where you do   but if yourself,
Whose aged honor cites a virtuous youth,
Did ever in so true a flame of liking
Wish chastely and love dearly, that your Dian
Was both herself and love   O, then, give pity
To her, whose state is such that cannot choose
But lend and give where she is sure to lose ,
That seeks not to find that her search implies,
But riddle-like lives sweetly where she dies !
Count Had you not lately an intent,— speak
     truly,—
To go to Paris ?
Hel.   Madam, I had
Count.   Wherefore ? tell true.
Hel. I will tell truth, by grace itself I swear.
You know my father left me some prescrip-
     tions

Of rare and proved effects, such as his reading
And manifest experience had collected
For general sovereignty; and that he will'd me
In heedfull'st reservation to bestow them, 231
As notes whose faculties inclusive were
More than they were in note : amongst the
   rest,
There is a remedy, approved, set down,
To cure the desperate languishings whereof
The king is render'd lost.
  Count.   This was your motive
For Paris, was it ? speak.
  Hel. My lord your son made me to think of
   this ;
Else Paris and the medicine and the king
Had from the conversation of my thoughts
Haply been absent then. 241
  Count.   But think you, Helen,
If you should tender your supposed aid,
He would receive it ? he and his physicians
Are of a mind ; he, that they cannot help him,
They, that they cannot help : how shall they
   credit
A poor unlearned virgin, when the schools,
Embowell'd of their doctrine, have left off
The danger to itself ?
  Hel.   There's something in't,
More than my father's skill, which was the
   greatest
Of his profession, that his good receipt 250
Shall for my legacy be sanctified
By the luckiest stars in heaven : and, would
   your honor
But give me leave to try success, I'ld venture
The well-lost life of mine on his grace's cure
By such a day and hour.
  Count.   Dost thou believe't ?
  Hel. Ay, madam, knowingly.
  Count. Why, Helen, thou shalt have my
  leave and love,
Means and attendants and my loving greetings
To those of mine in court : I'll stay at home
And pray God's blessing into thy attempt : 260
Be gone to-morrow ; and be sure of this,
What I can help thee to thou shalt not miss.
                      [Exeunt.

ACT II.

SCENE I. *Paris. The* KING's *palace.*

Flourish of cornets. Enter the KING, *attended
with divers young* Lords *taking leave for the
Florentine war* ; BERTRAM, *and* PAROLLES.

  King. Farewell, young lords ; these war-
  like principles
Do not throw from you : and you, my lords,
  farewell :
Share the advice betwixt you ; if both gain,
  all
The gift doth stretch itself as 'tis received,
And is enough for both.
  First Lord.   'Tis our hope, sir,
After well enter'd soldiers, to return
And find your grace in health.

  King. No, no; it cannot be ; and yet my
  heart
Will not confess he owes the malady
That doth my life besiege. Farewell, young
  lords ; 10
Whether I live or die, be you the sons
Of worthy Frenchmen : let higher Italy,—
†Those bated that inherit but the fall
Of the last monarchy,—see that you come
Not to woo honor, but to wed it ; when
The bravest questant shrinks, find what you
  seek,
That fame may cry you loud : I say, farewell.
  Sec. Lord. Health, at your bidding, serve
  your majesty !
  King. Those girls of Italy, take heed of
  them :
They say, our French lack language to deny,
If they demand : beware of being captives, 21
Before you serve.
  Both.   Our hearts receive your warnings.
  King. Farewell. Come hither to me.
                  [Exit, attended.
  First Lord. O my sweet lord, that you will
  stay behind us !
  Par. 'Tis not his fault, the spark.
  Sec. Lord.   O, 'tis brave wars !
  Par. Most admirable : I have seen those
  wars.   [with
  Ber. I am commanded here, and kept a coil
' Too young ' and ' the next year ' and ' 'tis too
  early.'
  Par. An thy mind stand to't, boy, steal
  away bravely.
  Ber. I shall stay here the forehorse to a
  smock, 30
Creaking my shoes on the plain masonry,
Till honor be bought up and no sword worn.
But one to dance with ! By heaven, I'll steal
  away.
  First Lord. There's honor in the theft,
  Par.   Commit it, count.
  Sec. Lord. I am your accessary ; and so,
  farewell.
  Ber. I grow to you, and our parting is a tor-
  tured body.
  First Lord. Farewell, captain.
  Sec. Lord. Sweet Monsieur Parolles !
  Par. Noble heroes, my sword and yours are
kin. Good sparks and lustrous, a word, good
metals : you shall find in the regiment of the
Spinii one Captain Spurio, with his cicatrice,
an emblem of war, here on his sinister cheek ;
it was this very sword entrenched it : say to
him, I live ; and observe his reports for me.
  First Lord. We shall, noble captain.
                [Exeunt Lords.
  Par. Mars dote on you for his novices !
what will ye do ?
  Ber. Stay : the king.   50
  Re-enter KING. BERTRAM *and* PAROLLES
             retire.

  Par. [*To* Ber.] Use a more spacious ceremony to the noble lords ; you have restrained
yourself within the list of too cold an adieu ;

be more expressive to them · for they wear
themselves in the cap of the time, there do
muster true gait, eat, speak, and move under
the influence of the most received star , and
though the devil lead the measure, such are to
be followed . after them, and take a more
dilated farewell

Ber . And I will do so.   60
Par Worthy fellows ; and like to prove
most sinewy sword-men

       [*Exeunt Bertram and Parolles.*

       Enter LAFEU.

Laf. [*Kneeling*] Pardon, my lord, for me
and for my tidings
King. I'll fee thee to stand up
Laf. Then here's a man stands, that has
brought his pardon
I would you had kneel'd, my lord, to ask me
mercy,
And that at my bidding you could so stand up.
King I would I had , so I had broke thy
pate,
And ask'd thee mercy for't
Laf. Good faith, across · but, my good lord
'tis thus ;   70
Will you be cured of your infirmity ?
King. No.
Laf. O, will you eat no grapes, my royal
fox ?
Yes, but you will my noble grapes, an if
My royal fox could reach them . I have seen a
medicine
That's able to breathe life into a stone,
Quicken a rock, and make you dance canary
With spritely fire and motion , whose simple
touch,
Is powerful to araise King Pepin, nay,
To give great Charlemain a pen in's hand.   80
And write to her a love-line
King,   What 'her' is this ?
Laf. Why, Doctor She · my lord, there's one
arrived
If you will see her : now, by my faith and
honor,
If seriously I may convey my thoughts
In this my light deliverance, I have spoke
With one that, in her sex, her years, profes-
sion,
Wisdom and constancy, hath amazed me more
Than I dare blame my weakness . will you see
her,
For that is her demand, and know her business?
That done, laugh well at me
King   Now, good Lafeu, 90
Bring in the admiration , that we with thee
May spend our wonder too, or take off thine
By wondering how thou took'st it
Laf.   Nay, I'll fit you,
And not be all day neither.   [*Exit.*
King. Thus he his special nothing ever pro-
logues.

     Re-enter LAFEU, *with* HELENA

Laf. Nay, come your ways.
King,   This haste hath wings indeed,

Laf Nay, come your ways.
This is his majesty ; say your mind to him :
A traitor you do look like , but such traitors
His majesty seldom fears . I am Cressid's un-
cle,   100
That dare leave two together ; fare you well
       [*Exit*
King Now, fair one, does your business
follow us ?
Hel Ay, my good lord.
Gerard de Narbon was my father ;
In what he did profess, well found
King   I knew him
Hel The rather will I spare my praises
towards him .
Knowing him is enough On's bed of death
Many receipts he gave me chiefly on,
Which, as the dearest issue of his practice,
And of his old experience the only darling, 110
He bade me store up, as a triple eye,
Safer than mine own two, more dear , I have so;
And hearing your high majesty is touch'd
With that malignant cause wherein the honor
Of my dear father's gift stands chief in power,
I come to tender it and my appliance
With all bound humbleness
King   We thank you, maiden ,
But may not be so credulous of cure,
When our most learned doctors leave vs and
The congregated college have concluded   120
That laboring art can never ransom nature
From her inaudible estate , I say we must not
So stain our judgment, or corrupt our hope,
To prostitute our past-cure malady
To empirics, or to dissever so
Our great self and our credit, to esteem
A senseless help when help past sense we deem.
Hel My duty then shall pay me for my
pains
I will no more enforce mine office on you ,
Humbly entreating from your royal thoughts
A modest one, to bear me back again   131
King I cannot give thee less, to be call'd
grateful :
Thou thought'st to help me , and such thanks
I give
As one near death to those that wish him live·
But what at full I know, thou know'st no part,
I knowing all my peril, thou no art
Hel. What I can do can do no hurt to try,
Since you set up your rest 'gainst remedy.
He that of greatest works is finisher
Oft does them by the weakest minister :   140
So holy writ in babes hath judgment shown,
When judges have been babes ; great floods
have flown
From simple sources, and great seas have
dried
When miracles have by the greatest been denied.
Oft expectation fails and most oft there
Where most it promises, and oft it hits
Where hope is coldest and despair most fits
King I must not hear thee ; fare thee well,
kind maid ,
Thy pains not used must by thyself be paid ·
Proffers not took reap thanks for their reward,

Hel Inspired merit so by breath is barr'd :
It is not so with Him that all things knows
As 'tis with us that square our guess by shows;
But most it is presumption in us when
The help of heaven we count the act of men.
Dear sir, to my endeavors give consent ;
Of heaven, not me, make an experiment.
I am not an impostor that proclaim
Myself against the level of mine aim ;
But know I think and think I know most sure
My art is not past power nor you past cure

King Art thou so confident ? within what
   space
Hopest thou my cure ?

Hel.   The great'st grace lending grace
Ere twice the horses of the sun shall bring
Their fiery torcher his diurnal ring,
Ere twice in murk and occidental damp
Moist Hesperus hath quench'd his sleepy lamp,
Or four and twenty times the pilot's glass
Hath told the thievish minutes how they pass,
What is infirm from your sound parts shall fly,
Health shall live free and sickness freely die

King   Upon thy certainly and confidence
What darest thou venture ?

Hel   Tax of impudence,
A strumpet's boldness, a divulged shame
Traduced by odious ballads my maiden's
   name
Sear'd otherwise , nay, worse—if worse—ex-
   tended
With vilest torture let my life be ended

King Methinks in thee some blessed spirit
   doth speak
His powerful sound within an organ weak
And what impossibility would slay   180
In common sense, sense saves another way
Thy life is dear , for all that life can rate
Worth name of life in thee hath estimate,
Youth, beauty, wisdom, courage, all
That happiness and prime can happy call :
Thou this to hazard needs must intimate
Skill infinite or monstrous desperate
Sweet practiser, thy physic I will try,
That ministers thine own death if I die.

Hel. If I break time, or flinch in property
Of what I spoke, unpitied let me die,
And well deserved : not helping, death's my
   fee ;
But, if I help, what do you promise me ?

King. Make thy demand

Hel   But will you make it even ?

King Ay, by my sceptre and my hopes of
   heaven

Hel. Then shalt thou give me with thy
   kingly hand
What husband in thy power I will command :
Exempted be from me the arrogance
To choose from forth the royal blood of France,
My low and humble name to propagate   200
With any branch or image of thy state ;
But such a one, thy vassal, whom I know
Is free for me to ask, thee to bestow

King Here is my hand ; the premises observed,
Thy will by my performance shall be served ;

So make the choice of thy own time, for I,
Thy resolved patient, on thee still rely.
More should I question thee, and more I must,
Though more to know could not be more to
   trust,
From whence thou camest, how tended on :
   but rest   216
Unquestion'd welcome and undoubted blest
Give me some help here, ho ! If thou proceed
As high as word, my deed shall match thy
   meed.   [*Flourish Exeunt.*

SCENE II   *Rousillon.* The COUNT'S *palace.*

Enter COUNTESS *and* CLOWN

Count. Come on, sir ; I shall now put you
to the height of your breeding

Clo I will show myself highly fed and
lowly taught . I know my business is but to
the court

Count. To the court ! why, what place
make you special, when you put off that with
such contempt ? But to the court '

Clo Truly, madam, if God have lent a man
any manners, he may easily put it off at court
he that cannot make a leg, put off's cap, kiss
his hand and say nothing, has neither leg,
hands, lip, nor cap , and indeed such a fellow,
to say precisely, were not for the court , but
for me, I have an answer will serve all men

Count Marry, that's a bountiful answer
that fits all questions.

Col. It is like a barber's chair that fits all
buttocks, the pin-buttock, the quatch-buttock,
the brawn buttock, or any buttock.

Count Will your answer serve fit to all
questions ?   21

Clo As fit as ten groats is for the hand of
an attorney, as your French crown for your
taffeta punk, as Tib's rush for Tom's fore-
finger, as a pancake for Shrove Tuesday, a
morris for May-day, as the nail to his hole, the
cuckold to his horn, as a scolding queen to a
wrangling knave, as the nun's lip to the friar's
mouth, nay, as the pudding to his skin.

Count. Have you, I say, an answer of such
fitness for all questions ?   31

Clo. From below your duke to beneath
your constable, it will fit any question

Count. It must be an answer of most monstrous size that must fit all demands.

Clo But a trifle neither, in good faith, if
the learned should speak truth of it : here it
is, and all that belongs to't Ask me if I am
a courtier : it shall do you no harm to learn

Count. To be young again, if we could I
will be a fool in question, hoping to be the
wiser by your answer I pray you, sir, are
you a courtier ?

Clo. O Lord, sir ! There's a simple putting
off. More, more, a hundred of them

Count Sir, I am a poor friend of yours,
that loves you   [me.

Clo. O Lord, sir ' Thick, thick, spare not

Count I think, sir, you can eat none of
this homely meat.

Clo. O Lord, sir! Nay, put me to't, I war-
rant you.   51
Count. You were lately whipped, sir, as I
think.
Clo. O Lord, sir! spare not me.
Count. Do you cry, 'O Lord, sir!' at your
whipping, and 'spare not me?' Indeed your
'O Lord, sir!' is very sequent to your whip-
ping: you would answer very well to a whip-
ping, if you were but bound to't.
Clo. I ne'er had worse luck in my life in
my 'O Lord, sir!' I see things may serve
long, but not serve ever.   61
Count. I play the noble housewife with the
time,
To entertain't so merrily with a fool.
Clo. O Lord, sir! why, there't serves well
again.
Count. An end, sir; to your business.
Give Helen this,
And urge her to a present answer back:
Commend me to my kinsmen and my son:
This is not much.
Clo. Not much commendation to them.   70
Count. Not much employment for you:
you understand me?
Clo. Most fruitfully: I am there before my
legs.
Count. Haste you again. [*Exeunt severally.*

SCENE III. *Paris. The* KING's *palace.*

Enter BERTRAM, LAFEU, *and* PAROLLES.

Laf. They say miracles are past; and we
have our philosophical persons, to make mod-
ern and familiar, things supernatural and
causeless. Hence is it that we make trifles of
terrors, ensconcing ourselves into seeming
knowledge, when we should submit ourselves
to an unknown fear.
Par. Why, 'tis the rarest argument of won-
der that hath shot out in our latter times.
Ber. And so 'tis.
Laf. To be relinquish'd of the artists,— 10
Par. So I say.
Laf. Both of Galen and Paracelsus.
Par. So I say.
Laf. Of all the learned and authentic fel-
lows,—
Par. Right; so I say.
Laf. That gave him out incurable,—
Par. Why, there 'tis; so say I too.
Laf. Not to be helped,—
Par. Right; as 'twere, a man assured of a—
Laf. Uncertain life, and sure death.   20
Par. Just, you say well; so would I have
said.
Laf. I may truly say, it is a novelty to the
world.
Par. It is, indeed: if you will have it in
showing, you shall read it in—what do you
call there?
Laf. A showing of a heavenly effect in an
earthly actor.
Par. That's it; I would have said the very
same.   30

Laf. Why, your dolphin is not lustier:
'fore me, I speak in respect—
Par. Nay, 'tis strange, 'tis very strange,
that is the brief and the tedious of it; and
he's of a most facinerious spirit that will not
acknowledge it to be the—
Laf. Very hand of heaven.
Par. Ay, so I say.
Laf. In a most weak—[*pausing*] and debile
minister, great power, great transcendence:
which should, indeed, give us a further use to
be made the better, whilst I have a tooth in
my head: why, he's able to lead her a coranto.
Par. Mort du vinaigre! is not this Helen?
Laf. 'Fore God, I think so.   51
King. Go, call before me all the lords in
court.
Sit, my preserver, by thy patient's side;
And with this healthful hand, whose banish'd
sense
Thou hast repeal'd, a second time receive
The confirmation of my promised gift,
Which but attends thy naming.

Enter three or four Lords.

Fair maid, send forth thine eye: this youthful
parcel
Of noble bachelors stand at my bestowing,
O'er whom both sovereign power and father's
voice   60
I have to use: thy frank election make;
Thou hast power to choose, and they none to
forsake.
Hel. To each of you one fair and virtuous
mistress
Fall, when Love please! marry, to each, but
one!
Laf. I'd give bay Curtal and his furniture,
My mouth no more were broken than those
boys',
And writ as little beard.
King.   Peruse them well:
Not one of those but had a noble father.
Hel. Gentlemen,
Heaven hath through me restored the king to
health.   70
All. We understand it, and thank heaven
for you.
Hel. I am a simple maid, and therein weal-
thiest,
That I protest I simply am a maid.
Please it your majesty, I have done already:
The blushes in my cheeks thus whisper me,
'We blush that thou shouldst choose; but, be
refused,
Let the white death sit on thy cheek for ever;
We'll ne'er come there again.'
King.   Make choice; and, see,

Who shuns thy love shuns all his love in me.
Hel Now, Dian, from thy altar do I fly, 80
And to imperial Love, that god most high,
Do my sighs stream   Sir, will you hear my
        suit ?
First Lord   And grant it
Hel.   Thanks, sir , all the
    rest is mute
Laf   I had rather be in this choice than
throw ames-ace for my life
Hel   The honor, sir, that flames in your fair
        eyes,
Before I speak, too threateningly replies
Love make your fortunes twenty times above
Her that so wishes and her humble love '
See Lord   No better, if you please
Hel   My wish receive, 90
Which great Love grant ' and so, I take my
        leave.
Laf   Do all they deny her ?   An they were
sons of mine, I'd have them whipped , or I
would send them to the Turk, to make eunuchs
of.
Hel   Be not afraid that I your hand should
        take ,
I'll never do you wrong for your own sake
Blessing upon your vows ' and in your bed
Find fairer fortune, if you ever wed '
Laf   These boys are boys of ice, they'll
none have her   sure, they are bastards to the
English , the French ne'er got 'em   101
Hel   You are too young, too happy, and
    too good,
To make yourself a son out of my blood
Fourth Lord   Fair one, I think not so
Laf   There's one grape yet , I am sure thy
father drunk wine   but if thou be'st not an
ass, I am a youth of fourteen , I have known
thee already
Hel   [*To Bertram*] I dare not say I take
    you , but I give
Me and my service, ever whilst I live,   110
Into your guiding power   Thus is the man.
King.   Why, then, young Bertram, take her;
    she's thy wife.
Ber   My wife, my liege ' I shall beseech
    your highness,
In such a business give me leave to use
The help of mine own eyes
King   Know'st thou not, Bertram,
What she has done for me ?
Ber.   Yes, my good lord ,
But never hope to know why I should marry
    her
King   Thou know'st she has raised me
    from my sickly bed
Ber   But follows it, my lord, to bring me
    down
Must answer for your raising ? I know her
    well   120
She had her breeding at my father's charge
A poor physician's daughter my wife ' Disdain
Rather corrupt me ever '
King   'Tis only title thou disdain'st in her,
    the which
I can build up   Strange is it that our bloods, .

Of color, weight, and heat, pour'd all together,
Would quite confound distinction, yet stand off
In differences so mighty.   If she be
All that is virtuous, save what thou dislikest,
A poor physician's daughter, thou dislikest 130
Of virtue for the name , but do not so :
From lowest place when virtuous things pro-
        ceed,
The place is dignified by the doer's deed :
Where great additions swell's, and virtue none,
It is a dropsied honor.   Good alone
Is good without a name.   Vileness is so :
The property by what it is should go,
Not by the title.   She is young, wise, fair ;
In these to nature she's immediate heir,
And these breed honor · that is honor's scorn,
Which challenges itself as honor's born   141
And is not like the sire · honors thrive,
When rather from our acts we them derive
Than our foregoers · the mere word's a slave
Debosh'd on every tomb, on every grave
A lying trophy, and as oft is dumb
Where dust and damn'd oblivion is the tomb
Of honor'd bones indeed.   What should be
        said ?
If thou canst like this creature as a maid,
I can create the rest   virtue and she   150
Is her own dower , honor and wealth from
    me
Ber   I cannot love her, nor will strive to
        do't
King   Thou wrong'st thyself, if thou shouldst
    strive to choose
Hel   That you are well restored, my lord,
    I'm glad :
Let the rest go
King   My honor's at the stake , which to
    defeat,
I must produce my power.   Here, take her
    hand,
Proud scornful boy, unworthy this good gift ;
That dost in vile misprision shackle up   ＼
My love and her desert, that canst not dream,
We, poising us in her detective scale,   161
Shall weigh thee to the beam ; that wilt not
    know,
It is in us to plant thine honor where
We please to have it grow.   Check thy con-
    tempt ·
Obey our will, which travails in thy good :
Believe not thy disdain, but presently
Do thine own fortunes that obedient right
Which both thy duty owes and our power
    claims ;
Or I will throw thee from my care for ever
Into the staggers and the careless lapse   170
Of youth and ignorance , both my revenge
    and hate
Loosing upon thee, in the name of justice, .
Without all terms of pity   Speak , thine an-
    swer   [mit
Ber   Pardon, my gracious lord ; for I sub-
My fancy to your eyes · when I consider
What great creation and what dole of honor
Flies where you bid it, I find that she, which
    late

Was in my nobler thoughts most base, is now
The praised of the king; who, so ennobled,
Is as 'twere born so.

King.   Take her by the hand, 180
And tell her she is thine: to whom I promise
A counterpoise, if not to thy estate
A balance more replete.

Ber.   I take her hand.

King. Good fortune and the favor of the
king
Smile upon this contract; whose ceremony
Shall seem expedient on the now-born brief,
And be perform'd to-night: the solemn feast
Shall more attend upon the coming space,
Expecting absent friends. As thou lov'st her,
Thy love's to me religious; else, does err   190

[*Exeunt all but Lafeu and Parolles.*

Laf. [*Advancing*] Do you hear, monsieur? a
word with you.

Par. Your pleasure, sir?

Laf. Your lord and master did well to
make his recantation.

Par. Recantation! My lord! my master!

Laf. Ay; is it not a language I speak?

Par. A most harsh one, and not to be understood without bloody succeeding. My
master!   200

Laf. Are you companion to the Count Rousillon?

Par. To any count, to all counts, to what
is man.

Laf. To what is count's man: count's master is of another style.

Par. You are too old, sir, let it satisfy
you; you are too old.

Laf. I must tell thee, sirrah, I write man;
to which title age cannot bring thee.   210

Par. What I dare too well do, I dare not
do.

Laf. I did think thee, for two ordinaries,
to be a pretty wise fellow; thou didst make
tolerable vent of thy travel; it might pass;
yet the scarfs and the bannerets about thee did
manifoldly dissuade me from believing thee
a vessel of too great a burthen. I have now
found thee; when I lose thee again, I care
not; yet art thou good for nothing but taking
up; and that thou't scarce worth.

Par. Hadst thou not the privilege of antiquity upon thee,—   221

Laf. Do not plunge thyself too far in anger,
lest thou hasten thy trial; which if—Lord
have mercy on thee for a hen! So, my good
window of lattice, fare thee well; thy casement I need not open, for I look through thee.
Give me thy hand.

Par. My lord, you give me most egregious
indignity.

Laf. Ay, with all my heart; and thou art
worthy of it.   231

Par. I have not, my lord, deserved it.

Laf. Yes, good faith, every dram of it; and
I will not bate thee a scruple.

Par. Well, I shall be wiser.

Laf. Even as soon as thou canst, for thou
hast to pull at a smack o' the contrary. If

ever thou be'st bound in thy scarf and beaten,
thou shalt find what it is to be proud of thy
bondage. I have a desire to hold my acquaintance with thee; or rather my knowledge, that
I may say in the default, he is a man I know.

Par. My lord, you do me most insupportable vexation.

Laf. I would it were hell-pains for thy sake,
and my poor doing eternal: for doing I am
past; as I will by thee, in what motion age
will give me leave.   [*Exit.*

Par. Well, thou hast a son shall take this
disgrace off me; scurvy, old, filthy, scurvy
lord! Well, I must be patient; there is no
fettering of authority. I'll beat him, by my
life, if I can meet him with any convenience,
an he were double and double a lord. I'll
have no more pity of his age than I would
of— I'll beat him, an if I could but meet him
again.

Re-enter LAFEU.

Laf. Sirrah, your lord and master's married; there's news for you: you have a new
mistress.

Par. I most unfeignedly beseech your lordship to make some reservation of your
wrongs: he is my good lord; whom I serve
above is my master.

Laf. Who? God?

Par. Ay, sir.

Laf. The devil it is that's thy master. Why
dost thou garter up thy arms o' this fashion?
dost make hose of thy sleeves? do other servants so? Thou wert best set thy lower part
where thy nose stands. By mine honor, if I
were but two hours younger, I'd beat thee:
methinks, thou art a general offence, and
every man should beat thee. I think thou
wast created for men to breathe themselves
upon thee.

Par. This is hard and undeserved measure,
my lord.

Laf. Go to, sir; you were beaten in Italy
for picking a kernel out of a pomegranate;
you are a vagabond and no true traveller: you
are more saucy with lords and honorable per-
sonages than the commission of your birth
and virtue gives you heraldry. You are not
worth another word, else I'ld call you knave.
I leave you.   [*Exit.* 281

Par. Good, very good; it is so then: good,
very good; let it be concealed awhile.

Re-enter BERTRAM.

Ber. Undone, and forfeited to cares for
ever!

Par. What's the matter, sweet-heart?

Ber. Although before the solemn priest I
have sworn,
I will not bed her.

Par. What, what, sweet-heart?

Ber. O my Parolles, they have married
me!
I'll to the Tuscan wars, and never bed her.   290

Par. France is a dog-hole, and it no more
merits

The tread of a man's foot : to the wars !

Ber. There's letters from my mother : what the import is, I know not yet.

Par. Ay, that would be known. To the wars, my boy, to the wars !
He wears his honor in a box unseen,
That hugs his kicky-wicky here at home,
Spending his manly marrow in her arms,
Which should sustain the bound and high curvet
Of Mars's fiery steed. To other regions   300
France is a stable ; we that dwell in't jades ;
Therefore, to the war !

Ber. It shall be so : I'll send her to my house,
Acquaint my mother with my hate to her,
And wherefore I am fled ; write to the king
That which I durst not speak ; his present gift
Shall furnish me to those Italian fields,
Where noble fellows strike : war is no strife
To the dark house and the detested wife.

Par. Will this capriccio hold in thee ? art sure ?   310

Ber. Go with me to my chamber, and advise me.
I'll send her straight away : to-morrow
I'll to the wars, she to her single sorrow.

Par. Why, these balls bound ; there's noise in it. 'Tis hard :
A young man married is a man that's marr'd :
Therefore away, and leave her bravely ; go :
The king has done you wrong : but, hush, 'tis so.   [*Exeunt.*

SCENE IV. *Paris. The* KING's *palace.*

Enter HELENA *and* CLOWN.

Hel. My mother greets me kindly ; is she well?

Clo. She is not well ; but yet she has her health : she's very merry ; but yet she is not well : but thanks be given, she's very well and wants nothing i' the world ; but yet she is not well.

Hel. If she be very well, what does she ail, that she's not very well ?

Clo. Truly, she's very well indeed, but for two things.

Hel. What two things?   10

Clo. One, that she's not in heaven, whither God send her quickly ! the other that she's in earth, from whence God send her quickly !

Enter PAROLLES.

Par. Bless you, my fortunate lady .

Hel. I hope, sir, I have your good will to have mine own good fortunes.

Par. You had my prayers to lead them on ; and to keep them on, have them still. O, my knave, how does my old lady ?

Clo. So that you had her wrinkles and I her money, I would she did as you say.   21

Par. Why, I say nothing.

Clo. Marry, you are the wiser man ; for many a man's tongue shakes out his master's undoing : to say nothing, to do nothing, to know nothing, and to have nothing, is to be a great part of your title ; which is within a very little of nothing.

Par. Away ! thou'rt a knave.

Clo. You should have said, sir, before a knave thou'rt a knave ; that's, before me thou'rt a knave : this had been truth, sir.   31

Par. Go to, thou art a witty fool ; I have found thee.

Clo. Did you find me in yourself, sir ? or were you taught to find me ? The search, sir, was profitable ; and much fool may you find in you, even to the world's pleasure and the increase of laughter.

Par. A good knave, i' faith, and well fed. Madam, my lord will go away to-night ;   40
A very serious business calls on him.
The great prerogative and rite of love,
Which, as your due, time claims, he does acknowledge ;
But puts it off to a compell'd restraint ;
Whose want, and whose delay, is strew'd with sweets,
Which they distil now in the curbed time,
To make the coming hour o'erflow with joy
And pleasure drown the brim.

Hel.   What's his will else ?

Par. That you will take your instant leave o' the king,
And make this haste as your own good proceeding,   50
Strengthen'd with what apology you think
May make it probable need.

Hel.   What more commands he ?

Par. That, having this obtain'd, you presently
Attend his further pleasure.

Hel. In every thing I wait upon his will.

Par. I shall report it so,

Hel.   I pray you.   [*Exit Parolles.*]
Come, sirrah.   [*Exeunt.*

SCENE V. *Paris. The* KING's *palace.*

Enter LAFEU *and* BERTRAM.

Laf. But I hope your lordship thinks not him a soldier.

Ber. Yes, my lord, and of very valiant approof.

Laf. You have it from his own deliverance.

Ber. And by other warranted testimony.

Laf. Then my dial goes not true : I took this lark for a bunting.

Ber. I do assure you, my lord, he is very great in knowledge and accordingly valiant.

Laf. I have then sinned against his experience and transgressed against his valor ; and my state that way is dangerous, since I cannot yet find in my heart to repent. Here he comes : I pray you, make us friends ; I will pursue the amity.

Enter PAROLLES.

Par. [*To Bertram*] These things shall be done, sir.

HELENA AND THE CLOWN.

ALL'S WELL THAT ENDS WELL, p. 698

Laf. Pray you, sir, who's his tailor?

Par. Sir?

Laf O, I know him well, I, sir, he, sir, 's a good workman, a very good tailor.   21

Ber [*Aside to Par*] Is she gone to the king?

Par. She is.

Ber. Will she away to-night?

Par. As you'll have her

Ber. I have writ my letters, casketed my treasure,

Given order for our horses, and to-night,

When I should take possession of the bride,

End ere I do begin.   29

Laf A good traveller is something at the latter end of a dinner, but one that lies three thirds and uses a known truth to pass a thousand nothings with, should be once heard and thrice beaten God save you, captain

Ber. Is there any unkindness between my lord and you, monsieur?

Par. I know not how I have deserved to run into my lord's displeasure

Laf You have made shift to run into 't, boots and spurs and all, like him that leaped into the custard, and out of it you'll run again, rather than suffer question for your residence

Ber. It may be you have mistaken him, my lord.

Laf. And shall do so ever, though I took him at 's prayers Fare you well, my lord, and believe this of me, there can be no kernel in this light nut, the soul of this man in his clothes Trust him not in matter of heavy consequence, I have kept of them tame, and know their natures Farewell, monsieur I have spoken better of you than you have or will to deserve at my hand, but we must do good against evil   [*Exit.*

Par. An idle lord, I swear.

Ber. I think so.

Par. Why, do you not know him?

Ber Yes, I do know him well, and common speech

Gives him a worthy pass Here comes my clog.

Enter HELENA.

Hel. I have, sir, as I was commanded from you,

Spoke with the king and have procured his leave   60

For present parting, only he desires

Some private speech with you

Ber I shall obey his will

You must not marvel, Helen, at my course,

Which holds not color with the time, nor does

The ministration and required office

On my particular Prepared I was not

For such a business, therefore am I found

So much unsettled. this drives me to entreat you

That presently you take your way for home,

And rather muse than ask why I entreat you,

For my respects are better than they seem   71

And my appointments have in them a need

Greater than shows itself at the first view

To you that know them not This to my mother   [*Giving a letter.*

'Twill be two days ere I shall see you, so

I leave you to your wisdom

Hel Sir, I can nothing say,

But that I am your most obedient servant.

Ber Come, come, no more of that

Hel And ever shall

With true observance seek to eke out that

Wherein toward me my homely stars have fail'd

To equal my great fortune

Ber Let that go   81

My haste is very great farewell, hie home

Hel Pray, sir, your pardon

Ber Well, what would you say?

Hel I am not worthy of the wealth I owe,

Nor dare I say 'tis mine, and yet it is,

But, like a timorous thief, most fain would steal

What law does vouch mine own

Ber. What would you have?

Hel Something, and scarce so much nothing, indeed

I would not tell you what I would, my lord Faith, yes,   90

Strangers and foes do sunder, and not kiss

Ber I pray you, stay not, but in haste to horse

Hel I shall not break your bidding, good my lord

Ber. Where are my other men, monsieur? Farewell   [*Exit Helena*

Go thou toward home, where I will never come

Whilst I can shake my sword or hear the drum

Away, and for our flight

Par Bravely, coragio!

    [*Exeunt*

ACT III

SCENE I. *Florence The* DUKE's *palace.*

Flourish Enter the DUKE *of Florence, attended, the two Frenchmen, with a troop of soldiers*

Duke So that from point to point now have you heard

The fundamental reasons of this war,

Whose great decision hath much blood let forth

And more thirsts after.

First Lord Holy seems the quarrel

Upon your grace's part, black and fearful

On the opposer

Duke Therefore we marvel much our cousin France

Would in so just a business shut his bosom

Against our borrowing prayers

Sec Lord Good my lord,

The reasons of our state I cannot yield,   10

But like a common and an outward man,

That the great figure of a council frames
By self-unable motion · therefore dare not
Say what I think of it, since I have found
Myself in my incertain grounds to fail
As often as I guess'd
　Duke　　　　　　Be it his pleasure
　First Lord　But I am sure the younger of
　　　our nature,
That surfeit on their ease, will day by day
Come here for physic
　Duke　　　　　　Welcome shall they be ,
And all the honors that can fly from us　　20
Shall on them settle　You know your places
　　well ,
When better fall, for your avails they fell ·
To-morrow to the field　[*Flourish Exeunt.*

SCENE II.　*Rousillon The* COUNT'S *palace*

Enter COUNTESS *and* CLOWN

　Count　It hath happened all as I would
have had it, save that he comes not along with
her
　Clo　By my troth, I take my young lord to
be a very melancholy man
　Count　By what observance, I pray you?
　Clo.　Why, he will look upon his boot and
sing , mend the ruff and sing , ask questions
and sing , pick his teeth and sing　I know a
man that had this trick of melancholy sold a
goodly manor for a song　　　　　　　10
　Count　Let me see what he writes, and
when he means to come　　[*Opening a letter.*
　Clo　I have no mind to Isbel since I was at
court　our old ling and our Isbels o' the country are nothing like your old ling and your
Isbels o' the court　the brains of my Cupid's
knocked out, and I begin to love, as an old
man loves money, with no stomach
　Count　What have we here ?
　Clo　E'en that you have there　[*Exit*　20
　Count [*Reads*]　I have sent you a daughter-
in-law　she hath recovered the king, and undone me　I have wedded her, not bedded her ,
and sworn to make the 'not' eternal. You
shall hear I am run away　know it before the
report come　If there be breadth enough in
the world, I will hold a long distance　My duty
to you,　　　　　　　Your unfortunate son,
　　　　　　　　　　　　　　　　BERTRAM
This is not well, rash and unbridled boy,　　30
To fly the favors of so good a king ,
To pluck his indignation on thy head
By the misprising of a maid too virtuous
For the contempt of empire

Re-enter CLOWN.

　Clo.　O madam, yonder is heavy news within between two soldiers and my young lady !
　Count　What is the matter ?
　Clo　Nay, there is some comfort in the
news, some comfort , your son will not be
killed so soon as I thought he would　　40
　Count　Why should he be killed ?
　Clo　So say I, madam, if he run away, as I
hear he does ; the danger is in standing to't ;

that's the loss of men, though it be the getting
of children　Here they come will tell you
more . for my part, I only hear your son was
run away.　　　　　　　　　　　[*Exit.*

Enter HELENA, *and two Gentlemen.*

　First Gent　Save you, good madam
　Hel　Madam, my lord is gone, for ever
gone.
　Sec. Gent　Do not say so
　Count　Think upon patience.　Pray you,
　gentlemen,　　　　　　　　　　　50
I have felt so many quirks of joy and grief,
That the first face of neither, on the start,
Can woman me unto't . where is my son, I
　pray you ?
　Sec. Gent　Madam, he's gone to serve the
　duke of Florence
We met him thitherward , for thence we came,
And, after some dispatch in hand at court,
Thither we bend again
　Hel　Look on his letter, madam , here's
　my passport
[*Reads*]　When thou canst get the ring upon
my finger which never shall come off, and
show me a child begotten of thy body that I
am father to, then call me husband . but in
such a ' then ' I write a ' never.'
This is a dreadful sentence
　Count　Brought you this letter, gentlemen ?
　First Gent.　　　　　　　　Ay, madam ;
And for the contents' sake are sorry for our
　pains
　Count　I prithee, lady, have a better cheer ;
If thou engrossest all the griefs are thine,
Thou robb'st me of a moiety : he was my son ;
But I do wash his name out of my blood,　　70
And thou art all my child　Towards Florence
　is he ?
　Sec Gent　Ay, madam
　Count　　　　　　　　And to be a soldier ?
　Sec Gent.　Such is his noble purpose ; and,
　believe 't,
The duke will lay upon him all the honor
That good convenience claims
　Count　　　　　　　Return you thither ?
　First Gent.　Ay, madam, with the swiftest
　wing of speed.
　Hel. [*Reads*]　Till I have no wife I have no-
　thing in France.
'Tis bitter.
　Count　Find you that there ?
　Hel　　　　　　　　Ay, madam
　First Gent　'Tis but the boldness of his
hand, haply, which his heart was not consent-
ing to　　　　　　　　　　　　　80
　Count　Nothing in France, until he have
　no wife !
There's nothing here that is too good for him
But only she , and she deserves a lord
That twenty such rude boys might tend upon
And call her hourly mistress　Who was with
him ?
　First Gent.　A servant only, and a gentle-
　man
Which I have sometime known.

Count. Parolles, was it not?
First Gent. Ay, my good lady, he
Count A very tainted fellow, and full of
wickedness
My son corrupts a well-derived nature   90
With his inducement.
First Gent Indeed, good lady,
The fellow has a deal of that too much,
Which holds him much to have
Count. You're welcome, gentlemen
I will entreat you, when you see my son,
To tell him that his sword can never win
The honor that he loses more I'll entreat you
Written to bear along
Sec Gent. We serve you, madam,
In that and all your worthiest affairs
Count Not so, but as we change our cour-
tesies.   100
Will you draw near !
  [*Exeunt Countess and Gentlemen*
Hel. 'Till I have no wife, I have nothing
in France '
Nothing in France, until he has no wife !
Thou shalt have none, Rousillon, none in
France ,
Then hast thou all again Poor lord ! is't I
That chase thee from thy country and expose
Those tender limbs of thine to the event
Of the none-sparing war ? and is it I
That drive thee from the sportive court,
where thou
Wast shot at with fair eyes, to be the mark
Of smoky muskets ? O you leaden messen-
gers,   111
That ride upon the violent speed of fire,
†Fly with false aim , move the still-peering
air,   [lord.
That sings with piercing , do not touch my
Whoever shoots at him, I set him there ,
Whoever charges on his forward breast,
I am the caitiff that do hold him to't ,
And, though I kill him not, I am the cause
His death was so effected Letter 'twere
I met the ravin lion when he roar'd   120
With sharp constraint of hunger , better
'twere
That all the miseries which nature owes
Were mine at once. No, come thou home,
Rousillon,
Whence honor but of danger wins a scar,
As oft it loses all . I will be gone ,
My being here it is that hold thee hence
Shall I stay here to do't ? no, no, although
The air of paradise did fan the house
And angels officed all I will be gone,
That pitiful rumor may report my flight,   130
To consolate thine ear. Come, night , end,
day '
For with the dark, poor thief, I'll steal away
      [*Exit.*

SCENE III. *Florence. Before the* DUKE'S
palace.

Flourish. Enter the DUKE *of Florence,* BER-
TRAM, PAROLLES, *Soldiers, Drum, and*
Trumpets.

Duke The general of our horse thou art ,
and we,
Great in our hope, lay our best love and cre
dence
Upon thy promising fortune
Ber Sir, it is
A charge too heavy for my strength, but yet
We'll strive to bear it for your worthy sake
To the extreme edge of hazard
Duke Then go thou forth ;
And fortune play upon thy prosperous helm,
As thy auspicious mistress '
Ber. This very day,
Great Mars, I put myself into thy file .
Make me but like my thoughts, and I shall
prove   10
A lover of thy drum, hater of love [*Exeunt.*

SCENE IV. *Rousillon The* COUNT'S *palace.*

Enter COUNTESS *and* Steward

Count Alas ' and would you take the let-
ter of her ?
Might you not know she would do as she has
done,
By sending me a letter ? Read it again.
Stew. [*Reads*]
I am Saint Jaques' pilgrim, thither gone :
Ambitious love hath so in me offended,
That barefoot plod I the cold ground upon,
With sainted vow my faults to have
amended
Write, write, that from the bloody course of
war
My dearest master, your dear son, may
hie
Bless him at home in peace, whilst I from far
His name with zealous fervor sanctify .   11
His taken labors bid him me forgive ,
I, his despiteful Juno, sent him forth
From courtly friends, with camping foes to
live,
Where death and danger dogs the heels of
worth .
He is too good and fair for death and me
Whom I myself embrace, to set him free.
Count. Ah, what sharp stings are in her
mildest words '
Rinaldo, you did never lack advice so much,
As letting her pass so had I spoke with her,
I could have well diverted her intents,   21
Which thus she hath prevented
Stew Pardon me, madam
If I had given you this at over-night,
She might have been o'erta en , and yet she
writes,
Pursuit would be but vain
Count What angel shall
Bless this unworthy husband ? he cannot
thrive,
Unless her prayers, whom heaven delights to
hear
And loves to grant, reprieve him from the
wrath
Of greatest justice Write, write, Rinaldo,
To this unworthy husband of his wife ;   30

Let every word weigh heavy of her worth
That he does weigh too light : my greatest
    grief,
Though little he do feel it, set down sharply.
Dispatch the most convenient messenger :
When haply he shall hear that she is gone,
He will return ; and hope I may that she,
Hearing so much, will speed her foot again,
Led hither by pure love : which of them both
Is dearest to me, I have no skill in sense
To make distinction : provide this messen-
    ger :   40
My heart is heavy and mine age is weak ;
Grief would have tears, and sorrow bids me
    speak.   [*Exeunt.*

SCENE V. *Florence. Without the walls. A
tucket afar off.*

Enter an old Widow *of Florence,* DIANA, VIO-
LENTA, *and* MARIANA, *with other* Citizens.

Wid. Nay, come ; for if they do approach
the city, we shall lose all the sight.

Dia. They say the French count has done
most honorable service.

Wid. It is reported that he has taken their
greatest commander ; and that with his own
hand he slew the duke's brother. [*Tucket.*]
We have lost our labor ; they are gone a contrary way : hark ! you may know by their
trumpets.   9

Mar. Come, let's return again, and suffice
ourselves with the report of it. Well, Diana,
take heed of this French earl : the honor of a
maid is her name ; and no legacy is so rich as
honesty.

Wid. I have told my neighbor how you
have been solicited by a gentleman his companion.

Mar. I know that knave ; hang him ! one
Parolles : a filthy officer he is in those sug-
gestions for the young earl. Beware of them,
Diana ; their promises, enticements, oaths,
tokens, and all these engines of lust, are not
the things they go under : many a maid hath
been seduced by them ; and the misery is, example, that so terrible shows in the wreck of
maidenhood, cannot for all that dissuade succession, but that they are limed with the
twigs that threaten them. I hope I need not
to advise you further ; but I hope your own
grace will keep you where you are, though
there were no further danger known but the
modesty which is so lost.   30

Dia. You shall not need to fear me.

Wid. I hope so.

Enter HELENA, *disguised like a Pilgrim.*

Look, here comes a pilgrim : I know she
will lie at my house ; thither they send one
another : I'll question her. God save you,
pilgrim ! whither are you bound ?

Hel. To Saint Jaques le Grand.
Where do the palmers lodge, I do beseech
    you ?

Wid. At the Saint Francis here beside the
port.

Hel. Is this the way ?   40

Wid. Ay, marry, is't. [*A march afar.*
Hark you ! they come this way.
If you will tarry, holy pilgrim,
But till the troops come by,
I will conduct you where you shall be lodged;
The rather, for I think I know your hostess
As ample as myself.

Hel.   Is it yourself ?

Wid. If you shall please so, pilgrim.

Hel. I thank you, and will stay upon your
    leisure.

Wid. You came, I think, from France ?

Hel.   I did so.

Wid. Here you shall see a countryman of
    yours   50
That has done worthy service.

Hel.   His name, I pray you.

Dia. The Count Rousillon : know you such
    a one ?

Hel. But by the ear, that hears most nobly
    of him :
His face I know not.

Dia.   Whatsome'er he is,
He's bravely taken here. He stole from
    France,
As 'tis reported, for the king had married him
Against his liking : think you it is so ?

Hel. Ay, surely, mere the truth : I know
    his lady.

Dia. There is a gentleman that serves the
    count
Reports but coarsely of her.

Hel.   What's his name ? 60

Dia. Monsieur Parolles.

Hel.   O, I believe with him,
In argument of praise, or to the worth
Of the great count himself, she is too mean
To have her name repeated : all her deserv-
    ing
Is a reserved honesty, and that
I have not heard examined.

Dia.   Alas, poor lady !
'Tis a hard bondage to become the wife
Of a detesting lord.

Wid. I warrant, good creature, whereso-
e'er she is,
Her heart weighs sadly : this young maid
    might do her   70
A shrewd turn, if she pleased.

Hel.   How do you mean ?
May be the amorous count solicits her
In the unlawful purpose.

Wid.   He does indeed :
And brokes with all that can in such a suit
Corrupt the tender honor of a maid :
But she is arm'd for him and keeps her guard
In honestest defence.

Mar.   The gods forbid else !

Wid. So, now they come :

    Drum and Colors.

Enter BERTRAM, PAROLLES, *and the whole
    army.*

That is Antonio, the duke's eldest son ;
That, Escalus.

Hel   Which is the Frenchman ?
Dia.   He , 80
That with the plume . 'tis a most gallant fellow
I would he loved his wife if he were honester
He were much goodlier is't not a handsome gentleman ?
Hel I like him well
Dia 'Tis pity he is not honest · yond's that same knave
That leads him to these places were I his lady,
I would poison that vile rascal
Hel   Which is he ?
Dia. That jack-an-apes with scarfs why is he melancholy ?
Hel. Perchance he's hurt i' the battle 90
Par Lose our drum ! well
Mar He's shrewdly vexed at something . look, he has spied us
Wid Marry, hang you !
Mar And your courtesy, for a ring-carrier ! [*Exeunt Bertram, Parolles, and army*
Wid The troop is past Come, pilgrim, I will bring you
Where you shall host of enjoin'd penitents
There's four or five, to great Saint Jaques bound,
Already at my house
Hel.   I humbly thank you
Please it this matron and this gentle maid 100
To eat with us to-night, the charge and thanking
Shall be for me , and, to requite you further,
I will bestow some precepts of this virgin
Worthy the note
Both. We'll take your offer kindly
                  [*Exeunt.*

Scene VI. *Camp before Florence*

Enter BERTRAM *and the two French* Lords.

Sec. Lord. Nay, good my lord, put him to't, let him have his way
First Lord If your lordship find him not a hilding, hold me no more in your respect
Sec Lord On my life, my lord, a bubble
Ber. Do you think I am so far deceived in him ?
Sec. Lord. Believe it, my lord, in mine own direct knowledge, without any malice, but to speak of him as my kinsman, he's a most notable coward, an infinite and endless liar, an hourly promise-breaker, the owner of no one good quality worthy your lordship's entertainment
First Lord. It were fit you knew him , lest, reposing too far in his virtue, which he hath not, he might at some great and trusty business in a main danger fail you
Ber. I would I knew in what particular action to try him 19
First Lord. None better than to let him fetch off his drum, which you hear him so confidently undertake to do.

Sec Lord. I, with a troop of Florentines, will suddenly surprise him , such I will have, whom I am sure he knows not from the enemy · we will bind and hoodwink him so, that he shall suppose no other but that he is carried into the leaguer of the adversaries, when we bring him to our own tents Be but your lordship present at his examination if he do not, for the promise of his life and in the highest compulsion of base fear, offer to betray you and deliver all the intelligence in his power against you, and that with the divine forfeit of his soul upon oath, never trust my judgment in any thing
First Lord O, for the love of laughter, let him fetch his drum , he says he has a stratagem for't when your lordship sees the bottom of his success in't, and to what metal this counterfeit lump of ore will be melted, if you give him not John Drum's entertainment, your inclining cannot be removed Here he comes.

Enter PAROLLES

Sec Lord [*Aside to Ber*] O, for the love of laughter, hinder not the design let him fetch off his drum in any hand.
Ber How now, monsieur ! this drum sticks sorely in your disposition
First Lord A pox on't, let it go , 'tis but a drum 49
Par. 'But a drum'! is't 'but a drum'? A drum so lost ! There was excellent command, —to charge in with our horse upon our own wings, and to rend our own soldiers !
First Lord That was not to be blamed in the command of the service it was a disaster of war that Cæsar himself could not have prevented, if he had been there to command
Ber Well, we cannot greatly condemn our success some dishonor we had in the loss of that drum , but it is not to be recovered 60
Par. It might have been recovered
Ber It might , but it is not now
Par It is to be recovered · but that the merit of service is seldom attributed to the true and exact performer, I would have that drum or another, or 'hic jacet.'
Ber Why, if you have a stomach, to't, monsieur if you think your mystery in stratagem can bring this instrument of honor again into his native quarter, be magnanimous in the enterprise and go on , I will grace the attempt for a worthy exploit if you speed well in it, the duke shall both speak of it, and extend to you what further becomes his greatness, even to the utmost syllable of your worthiness [*der take it.*
Par By the hand of a soldier, I will undertake it.
Ber. But you must not now slumber in it
Par I'll about it this evening and I will presently pen down my dilemmas, encourage myself in my certainty, put myself into my mortal preparation , and by midnight look to hear further from me
Ber May I be bold to acquaint his grace you are gone about it ?

Par. I know not what the success will be,
my lord, but the attempt I vow
Ber I know thou'rt valiant, and, to the
possibility of thy soldiership, will subscribe
for thee. Farewell. 90
Par. I love not many words 　[*Exit*
Sec Lord No more than a fish loves water.
Is not this a strange fellow, my lord, that so
confidently seems to undertake this business,
which he knows is not to be done, damns
himself to do and dares better be damned than
to do't?
First Lord You do not know him, my
lord, as we do. certain it is that he will steal
himself into a man's favor and for a week
escape a great deal of discoveries, but when
you find him out, you have him ever after 101
Ber. Why, do you think he will make no
deed at all of this that so seriously he does address himself unto?
Sec. Lord None in the world, but return
with an invention and clap upon you two or
three probable lies but we have almost embossed him; you shall see his fall to-night,
for indeed he is not for your lordship's respect. 109
First Lord We'll make you some sport
with the fox ere we case him He was first
smoked by the old lord Lafeu. when his disguise and he is parted, tell me what a sprat
you shall find him; which you shall see this
very night
Sec Lord. I must go look my twigs he
shall be caught
Ber Your brother he shall go along with
, me
Sec Lord As't please your lordship I'll
leave you. 　[*Exit*
Ber. Now will I lead you to the house, and
show you
The lass I spoke of.
First Lord But you say she's honest
Ber That's all the fault I spoke with her
but once 120
And found her wondrous cold, but I sent to
her,
By this same coxcomb that we have i' the
wind,
Tokens and letters which she did re-send,
And this is all I have done. She's a fair
creature:
Will you go see her?
First Lord. With all my heart, my lord
　[*Exeunt*

SCENE VII *Florence The Widow's house.*

Enter HELENA and Widow.

Hel If you misdoubt me that I am not she,
I know not how I shall assure you further,
But I shall lose the grounds I work upon.
Wid. Though my estate be fallen, I was
well born,
Nothing acquainted with these businesses;
And would not put my reputation now
In any staining act.

Hel. 　　　Nor would I wish you.
First, give me trust, the count he is my hus-
band,
And what to your sworn counsel I have spoken
Is so from word to word, and then you can-
not, 10
By the good aid that I of you shall borrow,
Err in bestowing it
Wid 　　　I should believe you:
For you have show'd me that which well ap-
proves
You're great in fortune
Hel 　　　Take this purse of gold,
And let me buy your friendly help thus far,
Which I will over-pay and pay again
When I have found it 　The count he wooes
your daughter.
Lays down his wanton siege before her
beauty,
Resolved to carry her · let her in fine consent,
As we'll direct her how 'tis best to bear it 20
Now his important blood will nought deny
That she'll demand a ring the county wears,
That downward hath succeeded in his house
From son to son, some four or five descents ·
Since the first father wore it. this ring he
holds
In most rich choice, yet in his idle fire,
To buy his will, it would not seem too dear
Howe'er repented after
Wid 　　　Now I see
The bottom of your purpose.
Hel You see it lawful, then : it is no more,
But that your daughter, ere she seems as
won, 31
Desires this ring, appoints him an encounter;
In fine, delivers me to fill the time,
Herself most chastely absent after this,
To marry her, I'll add three thousand crowns
To what is passed already
Wid 　　　I have yielded :
Instruct my daughter how she shall persever,
That time and place with this deceit so lawful
May prove coherent Every night he comes
With musics of all sorts and songs composed
To her unworthiness · it nothing steads us 41
To chide him from our eaves ; for he persists
As if his life lay on't
Hel 　　　Why then to-night
Let us assay our plot, which, if it speed,
Is wicked meaning in a lawful deed
And lawful meaning in a lawful time,
Where both not sin, and yet a sinful fact :
But let's about it. 　　　[*Exeunt.*

ACT IV.

SCENE I. *Without the Florentine camp.*

*Enter Second French Lord, with five or six
other Soldiers in ambush.*

Sec Lord. He can come no other way but
by this hedge-corner. When you sally upon
him, speak what terrible language you will :
though you understand it not yourselves, no

ALL'S WELL THAT ENDS WELL.

P. 705

matter, for we must not seem to understand
him, unless some one among us whom we
must produce for an interpreter.

First Sold. Good captain, let me be the interpreter.

Sec. Lord. Art not acquainted with him?
knows he not thy voice?   11

First Sold. No, sir, I warrant you.

Sec. Lord. But what linsey-woolsey hast
thou to speak to us again?

First Sold. E'en such as you speak to me.

Sec. Lord. He must think us some band of
strangers i' the adversary's entertainment.
Now he hath a smack of all neighboring languages, therefore we must every one be a man
of his own fancy, not to know what we speak
one to another; so we seem to know, is to
know straight our purpose choughs' language,
gabble enough, and good enough. As for you,
interpreter, you must seem very politic. But
couch, ho! here he comes, to beguile two
hours in a sleep, and then to return and swear
the lies he forges.

Enter PAROLLES

Par. Ten o'clock: within these three hours
'twill be time enough to go home. What
shall I say I have done? It must be a very
plausive invention that carries it: they begin
to smoke me, and disgraces have of late
knocked too often at my door. I find my
tongue is too foolhardy, but my heart hath
the fear of Mars before it and of his creatures,
not daring the reports of my tongue.

Sec. Lord. This is the first truth that e'er
thine own tongue was guilty of.

Par. What the devil should move me to
undertake the recovery of this drum, being
not ignorant of the impossibility, and knowing I had no such purpose? I must give myself some hurts, and say I got them in exploit:
yet slight ones will not carry it, they will
say, 'Came you off with so little?' and great
ones I dare not give. Wherefore, what's the
instance? Tongue, I must put you into a but-
ter-woman's mouth and buy myself another
of Bajazet's mule, if you prattle me into these
perils.

Sec. Lord. Is it possible he should know
what he is, and be that he is?   49

Par. I would the cutting of my garments
would serve the turn, or the breaking of my
Spanish sword.

Sec. Lord. We cannot afford you so.

Par. Or the baring of my beard, and to say
it was in stratagem.

Sec. Lord. 'Twould not do.

Par. Or to drown my clothes, and say I
was stripped.

Sec. Lord. Hardly serve.

Par. Though I swore I leaped from the
window of the citadel   61

Sec. Lord. How deep?

Par. Thirty fathom.

Sec. Lord. Three great oaths would scarce
make that be believed.

Par. I would I had any drum of the enemy's: I would swear I recovered it.

Sec. Lord. You shall hear one anon.

Par. A drum now of the enemy's,—
    [*Alarum within*

Sec. Lord. Throca movousus, cargo, cargo,
cargo   71

All. Cargo, cargo, cargo, villiando par
corbo, cargo.

Par. O, ransom, ransom! do not hide
mine eyes.   [*They seize and blindfold him.*

First Sold. Boskos thromuldo boskos.

Par. I know you are the Muskos' regiment
And I shall lose my life for want of language;
If there be here German, or Dane, low Dutch,
Italian, or French, let him speak to me, I'll
Discover that which shall undo the Florentine.

First Sold. Boskos vauvado. I understand
thee, and can speak thy tongue. Kerelybonto,
sir, betake thee to thy faith, for seventeen
poniards are at thy bosom.

Par. O!

First Sold. O, pray, pray, pray! Manka
revania dulche.

Sec. Lord. Oscorbidulchos volivorco.

First Sold. The general is content to spare
thee yet,
And, hoodwink'd as thou art, will lead thee
on   90
To gather from thee haply thou mayst inform
Something to save thy life.

Par.   O, let me live!
And all the secrets of our camp I'll show,
Their force, their purposes; nay, I'll speak
that
Which you will wonder at.

First Sold.   But wilt thou faithfully?

Par. If I do not, damn me.

First Sold. Acordo linta.
Come on, thou art granted space.
    [*Exit, with Parolles guarded. A short
        alarum within.*

Sec. Lord. Go, tell the Count Rousillon,
and my brother,
We have caught the woodcock, and will keep
him muffled   100
Till we do hear from them.

Sec. Sold.   Captain, I will.

Sec. Lord. A' will betray us all unto ourselves:
Inform on that.

Sec. Sold. So I will, sir.

Sec. Lord. Till then I'll keep him dark and
safely lock'd.   [*Exeunt.*

SCENE II. *Florence. The Widow's house.*

Enter BERTRAM *and* DIANA.

Ber. They told me that your name was
Fontibell.

Dia. No, my good lord, Diana.

Ber.   Titled goddess!
And worth it, with addition! But, fair soul,
In your fine frame hath love no quality?
If the quick fire of youth light not your mind,

15

You are no maiden, but a monument :
When you are dead, you should be such a one
As you are now, for you are cold and stern ;
And now you should be as your mother was
When your sweet self was got.　　　　　10
　Dia. She then was honest.
　Ber.　　　　　　So should you be.
　Dia.　　　　　　　　　No :
My mother did but duty ; such, my lord,
As you owe to your wife.
　Ber.　　　　No more o' that ;
I prithee, do not strive against my vows :
I was compell'd to her ; but I love thee
By love's own sweet constraint, and will for
　　ever
Do thee all rights of service.
　Dia.　　　　Ay, so you serve us
Till we serve you ; but when you have our
　roses,
You barely leave our thorns to prick ourselves
And mock us with our bareness.
　Ber.　　　　How have I sworn !　20
　Dia. 'Tis not the many oaths that makes
　the truth,
But the plain single vow that is vow'd true.
What is not holy, that we swear not by,
But take the High'st to witness : then, pray
　you, tell me,
If I should swear by God's great attributes,
I loved you dearly, would you believe my
　oaths,
When I did love you ill ? This has no hold-
　ing,
To swear by him whom I protest to love,
That I will work against him : therefore your
　oaths
Are words and poor conditions, but unseal'd,
At least in my opinion.　　　　　31
　Ber.　　　　Change it, change it ;
Be not so holy-cruel : love is holy ;
And my integrity ne'er knew the crafts
That you do charge men with.　Stand no more
　off,
But give thyself unto my sick desires,
Who then recover : say thou art mine, and
　ever
My love as it begins shall so persever.
　Dia. ·†I see that men make ropes in such a
　scarre
That we'll forsake ourselves.　Give me that
　ring.
　Ber. I'll lend it thee, my dear ; but have no
　power　　　　　　　　　　　　40
To give it from me.
　Dia.　　　Will you not, my lord ?
　Ber. It is an honor 'longing to our house,
Bequeathed down from many ancestors ;
Which were the greatest obloquy i' the world
In me to lose.
　Dia.　　Mine honor's such a ring :
My chastity's the jewel of our house,
Bequeathed down from many ancestors ;
Which were the greatest obloquy i' the world
In me to lose : thus your own proper wisdom
Brings in the champion Honor on my part, 50
Against your vain assault.

　Ber. ·　　　Here, take my ring :
My house, mine honor, yea, my life, be thine,
And I'll be bid by thee.
　Dia. When midnight comes, knock at my
　chamber-window :
I'll order take my mother shall not hear.
Now will I charge you in the band of truth,
When you have conquer'd my yet maiden bed,
Remain there but an hour, nor speak to me :
My reasons are most strong ; and you shall
　know them
When back again this ring shall be deliver'd :
And on your finger in the night I'll put　　61
Another ring, that what in time proceeds
May token to the future our past deeds.
Adieu, till then ; then, fail not.　You have won
A wife of me, though there my hope be done.
　Ber. A heaven on earth I have won by
　wooing thee.　　　　　　　　[*Exit.*
　Dia. For which live long to thank both
　heaven and me !
You may so in the end.
My mother told me just how he would woo,
As if she sat in 's heart ; she says all men　70
Have the like oaths : he had sworn to marry
　me
When his wife's dead ; therefore I'll lie with
　him
When I am buried.　Since Frenchmen are so
　braid,
Marry that will, I live and die a maid :
Only in this disguise I think't no sin
To cozen him that would unjustly win.　[*Exit.*

　　　SCENE III.　*The Florentine camp.*

Enter the two French Lords and some two or
　　　three Soldiers.

　First Lord. You have not given him his
mother's letter ?
　Sec. Lord. I have delivered it an hour since :
there is something in't that stings his nature ;
for on the reading it he changed almost into
another man.
　First Lord. He has much worthy blame
laid upon him for shaking off so good a wife
and so sweet a lady.　　　　　　　　9
　Sec. Lord. Especially he hath incurred the
everlasting displeasure of the king, who had
even tuned his bounty to sing happiness to
him.　I will tell you a thing, but you shall let
it dwell darkly with you.
　First Lord. When you have spoken it, 'tis
dead, and I am the grave of it.
　Sec. Lord. He hath perverted a young gentlewoman here in Florence, of a most chaste
renown ; and this night he fleshes his will in
the spoil of her honor : he hath given her his
monumental ring, and thinks himself made in
the unchaste composition.
　First Lord. Now, God delay our rebellion !
as we are ourselves, what things are we !
　Sec. Lord. Merely our own traitors.　And
as in the common course of all treasons, we
still see them reveal themselves, till they
attain to their abhorred ends, so he that in this

action contrives against his own nobility, in
his proper stream o'erflows himself   30

First Lord Is it not meant damnable in us,
to be trumpeters of our unlawful intents ? We
shall not then have his company to-night ?

Sec Lord Not till after midnight , for he
is dieted to his hour

First Lord That approaches apace ; I
would gladly have him see his company anatomized, that he might take a measure of his
own judgments, wherein so curiously he had
set this counterfeit   40

Sec Lord We will not meddle with him
till he come ; for his presence must be the
whip of the other

First Lord. In the mean time, what hear
you of these wars ?

Sec Lord I hear there is an overture of
peace

First Lord Nay, I assure you, a peace concluded

Sec Lord What will Count Rousillon do
then ? will he travel higher, or return again
into France ?   51

First Lord I perceive, by this demand,
you are not altogether of his council

Sec Lord Let it be forbid, sir , so should
I be a great deal of his act

First Lord Sir, his wife some two months
since fled from his house her pretence is a pilgrimage to Saint Jaques le Grand , which holy
undertaking with most austere sanctimony
she accomplished , and, there residing, the
tenderness of her nature became as a prey to
her grief , in fine, made a groan of her last
breath, and now she sings in heaven

Sec Lord How is this justified ?

First Lord The stronger part of it by her
own letters, which makes her story true, even
to the point of her death her death itself,
which could not be her office to say is come,
was faithfully confirmed by the rector of the
place   60

Sec Lord Hath the count all this intelligence ?

First Lord. Ay, and the particular confirmations, point from point, so to the full arming
of the verity

Sec Lord I am heartily sorry that he'll be
glad of this.

First Lord How mightily sometimes we
make us comforts of our losses !

Sec Lord And how mightily some other
times we drown our gain in tears ! The great
dignity that his valor hath here acquired for
him shall at home be encountered with a
shame as ample

First Lord The web of our life is of a
mingled yarn, good and ill together our virtues would be proud, if our faults whipped
them not ; and our crimes would despair, if
they were not cherished by our virtues

Enter a Messenger.

How now ' where's your master?

Serv. He met the duke in the street, sir, of
whom he hath taken a solemn leave his lordship will next morning for France The duke
hath offered him letters of commendations to
the king

Sec Lord. They shall be no more than
needful there, if they were more than they can
commend.

First Lord They cannot be too sweet for
the king's tartness Here's his lordship now.

Enter Bertram

How now, my lord ' is't not after midnight ?

Ber I have to-night dispatched sixteen
businesses, a month's length a-piece, by an
abstract of success I have congied with the
duke, done my adieu with his nearest , buried
a wife, mourned for her , writ to my lady
mother I am returning , entertained my convoy , and between these main parcels of dispatch effected many nicer needs , the last was
the greatest. but that I have not ended yet

Sec. Lord If the business be of any difficulty, and this morning your departure hence,
it requires haste of your lordship   109

Ber I mean, the business is not ended, as
fearing to hear of it hereafter But shall we
have this dialogue between the fool and the
soldier ? Come, bring forth this counterfeit
module, he has deceived me, like a double-
meaning prophesier

Sec Lord Bring him forth has sat i' the
stocks all night, poor gallant knave

Ber No matter , his heels have deserved
it, in usurping his spurs so long How does he
carry himself ?   120

Sec Lord I have told your lordship already,
the stocks carry him But to answer you as
you would be understood he weeps like a
wench that had shed her milk he hath confessed himself to Morgan, whom he supposes
to be a friar, from the time of his remembrance
to this very instant disaster of his setting i' the
stocks ' and what think you he hath confessed'?

Ber. Nothing of me, has a' ?   129

Sec Lord His confession is taken, and it
shall be read to his face if your 'lordship be
in't, as I believe you are, you must have the
patience to hear it

Enter Parolles guarded, and First Soldier.

Ber A plague upon him ' muffled ! he can
say nothing of me hush, hush '

First Lord Hoodman comes ' Portotarta-
rosa.

First Sold He calls for the tortures what
will you say without em ?

Par. I will confess what I know without
constraint if ye pinch me like a pasty, I can
say no more   141

First Sold. Bosko chimurcho.

First Lord Boblibindo chicurmurco,

First Sold You are a merciful general
Our general bids you answer to what I shall
ask you out of a note.

Par And truly, as I hope to live

First Sold [*Reads*] 'First demand of him

how many horse the duke is strong.' What
say you to that ?   150

Par. Five or six thousand , but very weak
and unserviceable the troops are all scattered,
and the commanders very poor rogues, upon
my reputation and credit and as I hope to live.

First Sold Shall I set down your answer so?

Par Do I'll take the sacrament on't, how
and which way you will

Ber. All's one to him. What a past-saving
slave is this '   159

First Lord You're deceived, my lord this
is Monsieur Parolles, the gallant militarist,—
that was his own phrase,—that had the whole
theoric of war in the knot of his scarf, and the
practice in the chape of his dagger

Sec Lord I will never trust a man again
for keeping his sword clean, nor believe he
can have every thing in him by wearing his
apparel neatly

First Sold Well, that's set down   169

Par Five or six thousand horse, I said,—I
will say true,—or thereabouts, set down, for
I'll speak truth

First Lord He's very near the truth in
this

Ber But I con him no thanks for't, in the
nature he delivers it

Par Poor rogues, I pray you, say

First Sold Well, that's set down.

Par I humbly thank you, sir a truth's a
truth, the rogues are marvellous poor   179

First Sold [*Reads*] 'Demand of him, of
what strength they are a-foot ' What say you
to that ?

Par By my troth, sir, if I were to live this
present hour, I will tell true Let me see
Spurio, a hundred and fifty , Sebastian, so
many, Corambus, so many , Jaques, so many,
Guiltian, Cosmo, Lodowick, and Gratii, two
hundred and fifty each , mine own company,
Chitopher, Vaumond, Bentii, two hundred and
fifty each . so that the muster-file, rotten and
sound, upon my life, amounts not to fifteen
thousand poll , half of the which dare not
shake the snow from off their cassocks, lest
they shake themselves to pieces

Ber What shall be done to him ?

First Lord Nothing, but let him have
thanks. Demand of him my condition, and
what credit I have with the duke

First Sold Well, that's set down [*Reads*]
'You shall demand of him, whether one Captain Dumain be i' the camp, a Frenchman,
what his reputation is with the duke ; what
his valor, honesty, and expertness in wars , or
whether he thinks it were not possible, with
well-weighing sums of gold, to corrupt him to
a revolt ' What say you to this ? what do
you know of it ?

Par I beseech you, let me answer to the
particular of the inter'gatories · demand them
singly

First Sold. Do you know this captain
Dumain ?   210

Par. I know him: a' was a botcher's 'pren-

tice in Paris, from whence he was whipped for
getting the shrieve's fool with child,—a dumb
innocent, that could not say him nay.

Ber Nay, by your leave, hold your hands;
though I know his brains are forfeit to the
next tile that falls

First Sold Well, is this captain in the duke
of Florence's camp ?   219

Par Upon my knowledge, he is, and lousy.

First Lord. Nay, look not so upon me ; we
shall hear of your lordship anon

First Sold What is his reputation with the
duke ?

Par. The duke knows him for no other but
a poor officer of mine , and writ to me this
other day to turn him out o' the band I think
I have his letter in my pocket

First Sold Marry, we'll search   229

Par In good sadness, I do not know, either
it is there, or it is upon a file with the duke's
other letters in my tent

First Sold Here 'tis , here's a paper . shall
I read it to you ?

Par. I do not know if it be it or no

Ber Our interpreter does it well.

First Lord Excellently.

First Sold [*Reads*] 'Dian, the count's a
fool, and full of gold,'—

Par That is not the duke's letter, sir . that
is an advertisement to a proper maid in Florence, one Diana, to take heed of the allure-
ment of one Count Rousillon, a foolish idle
boy, but for all that very ruttish I pray you,
sir, put it up again

First Sold Nay, I'll read it first, by your
favor

Par. My meaning in't, I protest, was very
honest in the behalf of the maid ; for I knew
the young count to be a dangerous and lascivious boy, who is a whale to virginity and
devours up all the fry it finds   250

Ber Damnable both-sides rogue !

First Sold. [*Reads*] 'When he swears oaths,
bid him drop gold, and take it ,

After he scores, he never pays the score :
Half won is match well made , match, and
well make it ;

He ne'er pays after-debts, take it before ,
And say a soldier, Dian, told thee this,
Men are to mell with, boys are not to kiss :
For count of this, the count's a fool, I know it,
Who pays before, but not when he does owe it.'
Thine, as he vowed to thee in thine ear,   260
           PAROLLES '

Ber. He shall be whipped through the army
with this rhyme in's forehead

Sec Lord. This is your devoted friend, sir,
the manifold linguist and the armipotent
soldier.

Ber. I could endure any thing before but a
cat, and now he's a cat to me.

First Sold I perceive, sir, by the general's
looks, we shall be fain to hang you.   269

Par My life, sir, in any case not that I
am afraid to die , but that, my offences being
many, I would repent out the remainder of

nature . let me live, sir, in a dungeon, i' the
stocks, or any where, so I may live

First Sold We'll see what may be done,
so you confess freely, therefore, once more to
this Captain Dumain you have answered to
his reputation with the duke and to his valor .
what is his honesty ?   279

Par He will steal, sir, an egg out of a
cloister . for rapes and ravishments he parallels Nessus he professes not keeping of oaths,
in breaking 'em he is stronger than Hercules
he will lie, sir, with such volubility, that you
would think truth were a fool drunkenness
is his best virtue, for he will be swine-drunk ,
and in his sleep he does little harm, save to
his bed-clothes about him , but they know his
conditions and lay him in straw I have but
little more to say, sir, of his honesty he has
every thing that an honest man should not
have , what an honest man should have, he
has nothing

First Lord I begin to love him for this

Ber. For this description of thine honesty?
A pox upon him for me, he's more and more a
cat

First Sold What say you to his expertness
in war ?

Par . Faith, sir, he has led the drum before
the English tragedians, to belie him, I will not,
and more of his soldiership I know not , except, in that country he had the honor to be
the officer at a place there called Mile-end, to
instruct for the doubling of files I would do
the man what honor I can, but of this I am
not certain

First Lord. He hath out-villamed villany so
far, that the rarity redeems him

Ber. A pox on him, he's a cat still

First Sold His qualities being at this poor
price, I need not to ask you if gold will corrupt
him to revolt   310

Par Sir, for a quart d'écu he will sell the
fee-simple of his salvation, the inheritance of
it , and cut the entail from all remainders, and
a perpetual succession for it perpetually.

First Sold What's his brother, the other
Captain Dumain ?

Sec Lord. Why does he ask him of me ?

First Sold What's he ?

Par E'en a crow o' the same nest , not
altogether so great as the first in goodness, but
greater a great deal in evil he excels his
brother for a coward , yet his brother is reputed
one of the best that is . in a retreat he outruns
any lackey , marry, in coming on he has the
cramp

First Sold If your life be saved, will you
undertake to betray the Florentine ?

Par Ay, and the captain of his horse,
Count Rousillon

First Sold I'll whisper with the general,
and know his pleasure   330

Par [*Aside*] I'll no more drumming , a
plague of all drums ! Only to seem to deserve
well, and to beguile the supposition of that
lascivious young boy the count, have I run

into this danger Yet who would have suspected an ambush where I was taken ?

First Sold There is no remedy, sir, but
you must die the general says, you that have
so traitorously discovered the secrets of your
army and made such pestiferous reports of
men very nobly held, can serve the world for
no honest use , therefore you must die Come,
headsman, off with his head   [my death !

Par O I ord, sir, let me live, or let me see

First Lord That shall you, and take your
leave of all your friends   [*Unblinding him.*
So, look about you know you any here ?

Ber Good morrow, noble captain   349

Sec Lord God bless you, Captain Parolles.

First Lord God save you, noble captain

Sec Lord. Captain, what greeting will you
to my Lord Lafeu ? I am for France

First Lord Good captain, will you give me
a copy of the sonnet you writ to Diana in behalf of the Count Rousillon ? an I were not a
very coward, I'ld compel it of you but tare
you well   [*Exeunt Bertram and Lords*

First Sold. You are undone, captain, all
but your scarf , that has a knot on't yet   359

Par Who cannot be crushed with a plot ?

First Sold If you could find out a country
where but women were that had received so
much shame, you might begin an impudent
nation. Fare ye well, sir , I am for France
too . we shall speak of you there
                                   [*Exit with Soldiers*

Par. Yet am I thankful if my heart were
                                                great,
'Twould burst at this Captain I'll be no more,
But I will eat and drink, and sleep as soft
As captain shall simply the thing I am
Shall make me live Who knows himself a
                              braggart,   370
Let him fear this, for it will come to pass
That every braggart shall be found an ass
Rust, sword ! cool, blushes ! and, Parolles, live
Safest in shame ! being fool'd, by foolery
                              thrive !
There's place and means for every man alive
I'll after them.   [*Exit*

SCENE IV.   *Florence.   The Widow's house*

Enter HELENA, *Widow, and* DIANA

Hel. That you may well perceive I have not
                              wrong'd you,
One of the greatest in the Christian world
Shall be my surety , 'fore whose throne 'tis
                              needful,
Ere I can perfect mine intents, to kneel .
Time was, I did him a desired office,
Dear almost as his life , which gratitude
Through flinty Tartar's bosom would peep
                              forth,
And answer, thanks I duly am inform'd
His grace is at Marseilles , to which place
We have convenient convoy. You must know,
I am supposed dead the army breaking,   11
My husband hies him home ; where, heaven
                              aiding

And by the leave of my good lord the king,
We'll be before our welcome.
  Wid.   Gentle madam,
You never had a servant to whose trust
Your business was more welcome.
  Hel.   Nor you, mistress,
Ever a friend whose thoughts more truly labour
To recompense your love doubt not but *heaven*
Hath brought me up to be your daughter's
  dower,
As it hath fated her to be my motive   20
And helper to a husband But, O strange men!
That can such sweet use make of what they
  hate,
When saucy trusting of the cozen'd thoughts
Defiles the pitchy night so lust doth play
With what it loathes for that which is away
But more of this hereafter You, Diana,
Under my poor instructions yet must suffer
Something in my behalf
  Dia   Let death and honesty
Go with your impositions, I am yours
Upon your will to suffer.
  Hel.   Yet, I pray you   30
But with the word the time will bring on sum-
  mer,
When briers shall have leaves as well as
  thorns,
And be as sweet as sharp. We must away ,
Our wagon is prepared, and time revives us
ALL'S WELL THAT ENDS WELL still the fine's
  the clown ;
Whate'er the course, the end is the renown
                      [Exeunt

SCENE V   *Rousillon The* COUNT'S *palace*

Enter COUNTESS, LAFEU, *and* CLOWN.

  Laf No, no, no, your son was misled with
a snipt-taffeta fellow there, whose villanous
saffron would have made all the unbaked and
doughy youth of a nation in his color your
daughter-in-law had been alive at this hour,
and your son here at home, more advanced by
the king than by that red-tailed humble-bee I
speak of.
  Count I would I had not known him , it
was the death of the most virtuous gentlewoman that ever nature had praise for
creating If she had partaken of my flesh,
and cost me the dearest groans of a mother, I
could not have owed her a more rooted love
  Laf. 'Twas a good lady, 'twas a good lady '
we may pick a thousand salads ere we light on
such another herb
  Clo Indeed, sir, she was the sweet marjo-
ram of the salad, or rather, the herb of grace
  Laf. They are not herbs, you knave , they
are nose-herbs   20
  Clo. I am no great Nebuchadnezzar, sir ; I
have not much skill in grass.
  Laf Whether dost thou profess thyself, a
knave or a fool ?
  Clo. A fool, sir, at a woman's service, and a
knave at a man's
  Laf. Your distinction ?

  Clo I would cozen the man of his wife and
do his service.
  Laf So you were a knave at his service,
indeed   31
  Clo And I would give his wife my bauble,
sir, to do her service.
  Laf I will subscribe for thee, thou art
both knave and fool.
  Clo. At your service.
  Laf. No, no, no.
  Clo Why, sir, if I cannot serve you, I can
serve as great a prince as you are.
  Laf. Who's that ? a Frenchman ?   40
  Clo Faith, sir, a' has an English name ,
but his fisnomy is more hotter in France than
there.
  Laf. What prince is that ?
  Clo. The black prince, sir ; alias, the
prince of darkness , alias, the devil.
  Laf Hold thee, there's my purse · I give
thee not this to suggest thee from thy master
thou talkest of , serve him still
  Clo I am a woodland fellow, sir, that
always loved a great fire , and the master I
speak of ever keeps a good fire. But, sure, he
is the prince of the world , let his nobility remain in's court. I am for the house with the
narrow gate, which I take to be too little for
pomp to enter some that humble themselves
may , but the many will be too chill and
tender, and they'll be for the flowery way that
leads to the broad gate and the great fire
  Laf. Go thy ways, I begin to be aweary of
thee, and I tell thee so before, because I would
not fall out with thee Go thy ways let my
horses be well looked to, without any tricks
  Clo. If I put any tricks upon 'em, sir, they
shall be jades' tricks , which are their own
right by the law of nature   *[Exit.*
  Laf. A shrewd knave and an unhappy
  Count. So he is My lord that's gone made
himself much sport out of him by his authority he remains here, which he thinks is a
patent for his sauciness , and, indeed, he has
no pace, but runs where he will   71
  Laf I like him well , 'tis not amiss And
I was about to tell you, since I heard of the
good lady's death and that my lord your son
was upon his return home, I moved the king
my master to speak in the behalf of my daughter ; which, in the minority of them both, his
majesty, out of a self-gracious remembrance,
did first propose his highness hath promised
me to do it . and, to stop up the displeasure
he hath conceived against your son, there is
no fitter matter. How does your ladyship
like it ?
  Count. With very much content, my lord ,
and I wish it happily effected
  Laf. His highness comes post from Marseilles, of as able body as when he numbered
thirty : he will be here to-morrow, or I am de
ceived by him that in such intelligence hath
seldom failed.
  Count. It rejoices me, that I hope I shall
see him ere I die. I have letters that my son

will be here to-night I shall beseech your
lordship to remain with me till they meet together
Laf   Madam, I was thinking with what
manners I might safely be admitted.
Count   You need but plead your honorable
privilege
Laf.   Lady, of that I have made a bold
charter , but I thank my God it holds yet.

Re-enter CLOWN

Clo   O madam, yonder's my lord your son
with a patch of velvet on's face whether
there be a scar under't or no, the velvet
knows , but 'tis a goodly patch of velvet his
left cheek is a cheek of two pile and a half, but
his right cheek is worn bare.
Laf   A scar nobly got, or a noble scar, is a
good livery of honor ; so belike is that.
Clo   But it is your carbonadoed face
Laf.   Let us go see your son, I pray you · I
long to talk with the young noble soldier 109
Clo   Faith there's a dozen of 'em, with
delicate fine hats and most courteous feathers,
which bow the head and nod at every man
                                             [*Exeunt.*

ACT V.

SCENE I. *Marseilles   A street.*

Enter HELENA, Widow, *and* DIANA, *with two*
Attendants

Hel.   But this exceeding posting day and
    night
Must wear your spirits low ; we cannot help
    it ·
But since you have made the days and nights
    as one,
To wear your gentle limbs in my affairs,
Be bold you do so grow in my requital
As nothing can unroot you   In happy time ,

Enter a Gentleman

This man may help me to his majesty's ear,
If he would spend his power. God save you,
    sir
Gent.   And you
Hel   Sir, I have seen you in the court of
    France   10
Gent   I have been sometimes there
Hel.   I do presume, sir, that you are not
    fallen
From the report that goes upon your good-
    ness ,
And therefore, goaded with most sharp occa-
    sions,
Which lay nice manners by, I put you to
The use of your own virtues, for the which
I shall continue thankful
Gent   What's your will ?
Hel.   That it will please you
To give this poor petition to the king,
And aid me with that store of power you
    have   20
To come into his presence.

Gent.   The king's not here.
Hel   Not here, sir !
Gent   Not, indeed :
He hence removed last night and with more
    haste
Than is his use
Wid.   Lord, how we lose our pains !
Hel.   ALL'S WELL THAT ENDS WELL yet,
Though time seem so adverse and means un-
    fit
I do beseech you, whither is he gone ?
Gent.   Marry, as I take it, to Rousillon ;
Whither I am going
Hel.   I do beseech you, sir,
Since you are like to see the king before me,
Commend the paper to his gracious hand, 31
Which I presume shall render you no blame
But rather make you thank your pains for it.
I will come after you with what good speed
Our means will make us means
Gent.   This I'll do for you
Hel   And you shall find yourself to be well
    thank'd,
Whate'er falls more.   We must to horse
    again
Go, go, provide.   [*Exeunt.*

SCENE II. *Rousillon.   Before the* COUNT'S
palace.

Enter CLOWN, *and* PAROLLES, *following*

Par.   Good Monsieur Lavache, give my
Lord Lafeu this letter : I have ere now, sir,
been better known to you, when I have held
familiarity with fresher clothes , but I am
now, sir, muddied in fortune's mood, and
smell somewhat strong of her strong displeasure
Clo   Truly, fortune's displeasure is but
sluttish, if it smell so strongly as thou speakest of I will henceforth eat no fish of fortune's buttering Prithee, allow the wind. 10
Par.   Nay, you need not to stop your nose,
sir , I spake but by a metaphor
Clo   Indeed, sir, if your metaphor stink, I
will stop my nose , or against any man's metaphor. Prithee, get thee further.
Par.   Pray you, sir, deliver me this paper
Clo   Foh ! prithee, stand away . a paper
from fortune's close-stool to give to a nobleman ' Look, here he comes himself.   19

Enter LAFEU

Here is a purr of fortune's, sir, or of fortune's
cat,—but not a musk-cat,—that has fallen into the unclean fishpond of her displeasure,
and, as he says, is muddied withal pray you,
sir, use the carp as you may ; for he looks
like a poor, decayed, ingenious foolish, rascally knave I do pity his distress in my
similes of comfort and leave him to your lordship   [*Exit*
Par.   My lord, I am a man whom fortune
hath cruelly scratched   29
Laf   And what would you have me to do ?
'Tis too late to pare her nails now. Wherein
have you played the knave with fortune. that

she should scratch you, who of herself is a
good lady and would not have knaves thrive
long under her ? There's a quart d'écu for
you : let the justices make you and fortune
friends I am for other business

Par. I beseech your honor to hear me one
single word.

Laf You beg a single penny more . come,
you shall ha't ; save your word　　　　　40

Par My name, my good lord, is Parolles

Laf You beg more than 'word,' then
Cox my passion ! give me your hand How
does your drum ?

Par O my good lord, you were the first
that found me !

Laf Was I, in sooth ? and I was the first
that lost thee

Par It lies in you, my lord, to bring me in
some grace, for you did bring me out　　50

Laf Out upon thee, knave ! dost thou put
upon me at once both the office of God and
the devil ? One brings thee in grace and the
other brings thee out [*Trumpets sound*] The
king's coming , I know by his trumpets
Sirrah, inquire further after me ; I had talk of
you last night though you are a fool and a
knave, you shall eat , go to, follow

Par. I praise God for you.　　　[*Exeunt*

SCENE III　*Rousillon The* COUNT'S *palace*

Flourish. Enter KING, COUNTESS, LAFEU,
the two French *Lords, with* Attendants

King We lost a jewel of her , and our
esteem
Was made much poorer by it but your son,
As mad in folly, lack'd the sense to know
Her estimation home

Count.　　　'Tis past, my liege ;
And I beseech your majesty to make it
Natural rebellion, done i' the blaze of youth ;
When oil and fire, too strong for reason's
force,
O'erbears it and burns on

King　　　　My honor'd lady,
I have forgiven and forgotten all ,
Though my revenges were high bent upon
him,
And watch'd the time to shoot

Laf　　　　This I must say,　11
But first I beg my pardon, the young lord
Did to his majesty, his mother and his lady
Offence of mighty note , but to himself
The greatest wrong of all. He lost a wife
Whose beauty did astonish the survey
Of richest eyes, whose words all ears took
captive,
Whose dear perfection hearts that scorn'd to
serve
Humbly call'd mistress

King　　　　Praising what is lost
Makes the remembrance dear Well, call him
hither ;　　　　　　　20
We are reconciled, and the first view shall
kill
All repetition : let him not ask our pardon

The nature of his great offence is dead,
And deeper than oblivion we do bury
The incensing relics of it let him approach,
A stranger, no offender , and inform him
So 'tis our will he should

Gent.　　　I shall, my liege. [*Exit.*
King What says he to your daughter ?
have you spoke ?

Laf. All that he is hath reference to your
highness

King Then shall we have a match. I have
letters sent me　　　　　　30
That set him high in fame

　　　　Enter BERTRAM.

Laf　　　He looks well on't
King I am not a day of season,
For thou mayst see a sunshine and a hail
In me at once but to the brightest beams
Distracted clouds give way , so stand thou
forth ,
The time is fair again.

Ber.　　　My high-repeated blames,
Dear sovereign, pardon to me.

King　　　　All is whole ;
Not one word more of the consumed time.
Let's take the instant by the forward top ;
For we are old, and on our quick'st decrees 40
The inaudible and noiseless foot of Time
Steals ere we can effect them. You remember
The daughter of this lord ?

Ber Admiringly, my liege, at first
I stuck my choice upon her, ere my heart
Durst make too bold a herald of my tongue
Where the impression of mine eye infixing,
Contempt his scornful perspective did lend
me,
Which warp'd the line of every other favor ;
Scorn'd a fair color, or express'd it stolen , 50
Extended or contracted all proportions
To a most hideous object : thence it came
That she whom all men praised and whom
myself,
Since I have lost, have loved, was in mine eye
The dust that did offend it

King　　　　Well excused :
That thou didst love her, strikes some scores
away
From the great compt . but love that comes
too late,
Like a remorseful pardon slowly carried,
To the great sender turns a sour offence,
Crying, ' That's good that's gone ' Our rash
faults　　　　　　　60
Make trivial price of serious things we have,
Not knowing them until we know their grave:
Oft our displeasures, to ourselves unjust,
Destroy our friends and after weep their dust·
†Our own love waking cries to see what's
done,
While shame full late sleeps out the after-
noon.
Be this sweet Helen's knell, and now forget
her.
Send forth your amorous token for fair Maud-
lin :

The main consents are had, and here we'll
    stay
To see our widower's second marriage-day. 70
Count. Which better than the first, O dear
    heaven, bless!
Or, ere they meet, in me, O nature, cesse!
Laf. Come on, my son, in whom my
    house's name
Must be digested, give a favor from you
To sprinkle in the spirits of my daughter,
That she may quickly come [*Bertram gives
    a ring*] By my old beard,
And every hair that's on't, Helen, that's
    dead,
Was a sweet creature such a ring as this,
The last that e'er I took her leave at court,
I saw upon her finger
    Ber.   Hers it was not   80
King Now, pray you, let me see it; for
    mine eye,
While I was speaking, oft was fasten'd to't.
This ring was mine, and, when I gave it
    Helen,
I bade her, if her fortunes ever stood
Necessitied to help, that by this token
I would relieve her Had you that craft, to
    reave her
Of what should stead her most?
    Ber.   My gracious sovereign,
Howe'er it pleases you to take it so,
The ring was never hers
    Count   Son, on my life,
I have seen her wear it, and she reckon'd it
At her life's rate   91
    Laf.   I am sure I saw her wear it
Ber You are deceived, my lord, she nev-
    er saw it   [me,
In Florence was it from a casement thrown
Wrapp'd in a paper, which contain'd the name
Of her that threw it. noble she was, and
    thought
I stood engaged but when I had subscribed
To mine own fortune and inform'd her fully
I could not answer in that course of honor
As she had made the overture, she ceased
In heavy satisfaction and would never   100
Receive the ring again
    King.   Plutus himself,
That knows the tinct and multiplying medi-
    cine,
Hath not in nature's mystery more science
Than I have in this ring. 'twas mine, 'twas
    Helen's,
Whoever gave it you. Then, if you know
That you are well acquainted with yourself,
Confess 'twas hers, and by what rough en-
    forcement
You got it from her: she call'd the saints to
    surety
That she would never put it from her finger,
Unless she gave it to yourself in bed,   110
Where you have never come, or sent it us
Upon her great disaster
    Ber.   She never saw it.
King. Thou speak'st it falsely, as I love
    mine honor;

And makest conjectural fears to come into
    me
Which I would fain shut out. If it should
    prove   [so,—
That thou art so inhuman,—'twill not prove
And yet I know not: thou didst hate her
    deadly,
And she is dead; which nothing, but to close
Her eyes myself, could win me to believe,
More than to see this ring. Take him away.
                [*Guards seize Bertram.*
My fore-past proofs, howe'er the matter fall,
Shall tax my fears of little vanity,
Having vainly fear'd too little. Away with
    him!
We'll sift this matter further.
    Ber.   If you shall prove
This ring was ever hers, you shall as easy
Prove that I husbanded her bed in Florence,
Where yet she never was.   [*Exit, guarded.*
King. I am wrapp'd in dismal thinkings.

        Enter a Gentleman.

Gent.   Gracious sovereign,
Whether I have been to blame or no, I know
    not:
Here's a petition from a Florentine,   130
Who hath for four or five removes come short
To tender it herself. I undertook it,
Vanquish'd thereto by the fair grace and
    speech
Of the poor supplant, who by this I know
Is here attending: her business looks in her
With an importing visage, and she told me,
In a sweet verbal brief, it did concern
Your highness with herself
    King [*Reads*] Upon his many protestations
to marry me when his wife was dead, I blush
to say it, he won me. Now is the Count Rou-
sillon a widower: his vows are forfeited to
me, and my honor's paid to him. He stole
from Florence, taking no leave, and I follow
him to his country for justice. grant it me, O
king! in you it best lies; otherwise a seducer
flourishes, and a poor maid is undone
               DIANA CAPILET.
Laf. I will buy me a son-in-law in a fair,
and toll for this I'll none of him.
King. The heavens have thought well on
    thee, Lafeu,   150
To bring forth this discovery. Seek these
    suitors:
Go speedily and bring again the count.
I am afeard the life of Helen, lady,
Was foully snatch'd
    Count.   Now, justice on the doers!

        Re-enter BERTRAM, *guarded.*

King. I wonder, sir, sith wives are mon-
    sters to you,
And that you fly them as you swear them
    lordship,
Yet you desire to marry.

      Enter Widow and DIANA.

                What woman's that?
Dia. I am, my lord, a wretched Florentine,

Derived from the ancient Capulet :
My suit, as I do understand, you know,   160
And therefore know how far I may be pitied
Wid   I am her mother, sir, whose age and
honor
Both suffer under this complaint we bring,
And both shall cease, without your remedy
King   Come hither, count , do you know
these women ?
Ber   My lord, I neither can nor will deny
But that I know them : do they charge me
further ?
Dia   Why do you look so strange upon
your wife ?
Ber.   She's none of mine, my lord
Dia   If you shall marry,
You give away this hand, and that is mine ;
You give away heaven's vows, and those are
mine ;   171
You give away myself, which is known mine,
For I by vow am so embodied yours,
That she which marries you must marry me,
Either both or none
Laf.   Your reputation comes too short for
my daughter ; you are no husband for her.
Ber.   My lord, this is a fond and desperate
creature,
Whom sometime I have laugh'd with · let
your highness   179
Lay a more noble thought upon mine honor
Than for to think that I would sink it here
King   Sir, for my thoughts, you have them
ill to friend
Till your deeds gain them . fairer prove your
honor
Than in my thought it lies
Dia   Good my lord,'
Ask him upon his oath, if he does think
He had not my virginity
King   What say'st thou to her ?
Ber.   She's impudent, my lord,
And was a common gamester to the camp
Dia   He does me wrong, my lord , if I were
so,
He might have bought me at a common price
Do not believe him. O, behold this ring,
Whose high respect and rich validity
Did lack a parallel , yet for all that
He gave it to a commoner o' the camp,
If I be one.
Count.   He blushes, and 'tis it :
Of six preceding ancestors, that gem,
Conferr'd by testament to the sequent issue,
Hath it been owed and worn This is his
wife ,
That ring's a thousand proofs.
King.   Methought you said
You saw one here in court could witness it
Dia   I did, my lord, but loath am to pro-
duce   201
So bad an instrument : his name's Parolles
Laf.   I saw the man to-day, if man he be
King.   Find him, and bring him hither.
                     [*Exit an Attendant*.
Ber.   What of him ?
He's quoted for a most perfidious slave,

With all the spots o' the world tax'd and de-
bosh'd ;
Whose nature sickens but to speak a truth.
Am I or that or this for what he'll utter,
That will speak any thing ?
King.   She hath that ring of yours
Ber.   I think she has · certain it is I liked
her,   210
And boarded her i' the wanton way of youth :
She knew her distance and did angle for me,
Madding my eagerness with her restraint,
As all impediments in fancy's course
Are motives of more fancy ; and, in fine,
Her infinite cunning, with her modern grace,
Subdued me to her rate she got the ring ;
And I had that which any inferior might
At market-price have bought
Dia   I must be patient :
You, that have turn'd off a first so noble
wife,   220
May justly diet me   I pray you yet ,
Since you lack virtue, I will lose a husband ;
Send for your ring, I will return it home,
And give me mine again.
Ber   I have it not
King.   What ring was yours, I pray you ?
Dia.   Sir, much like
The same upon your finger
King.   Know you this ring ? this ring was
his of late   [abed
Dia.   And this was it I gave him, being
King   The story then goes false, you threw
it him
Out of a casement.
Dia   I have spoke the truth. 230

Enter PAROLLES.

Ber.   My lord, I do confess the ring was
hers
King.   You boggle shrewdly, every feather
starts you
Is this the man you speak of ?
Dia.   Ay, my lord
King.   Tell me, sirrah, but tell me true, I
charge you,
Not fearing the displeasure of your master,
Which on your just proceeding I'll keep off,
By him and by this woman here what know
you ?
Par   So please your majesty, my master
hath been an honorable gentleman : tricks he
hath had in him, which gentlemen have. 240
King.   Come, come, to the purpose : did he
love this woman ?
Par.   Faith, sir, he did love her ; but how?
King.   How, I pray you ?
Par.   He did love her, sir, as a gentleman
loves a woman.
King.   How is that ?
Par.   He loved her, sir, and loved her not.
King.   As thou art a knave, and no knave.
What an equivocal companion is this !   250
Par.   I am a poor man, and at your majesty's
command
Laf.   He's a good drum, my lord, but a
naughty orator.

Dia. Do you know he promised me marriage?

Par. Faith, I know more than I'll speak.

King. But wilt thou not speak all thou knowest?

Par. Yes, so please your majesty. I did go between them, as I said: but more than that, he loved her: for indeed he was mad for her, and talked of Satan and of Limbo and of Furies and I know not what: yet I was in that credit with them at that time that I knew of their going to bed, and of other motions, as promising her marriage, and things which would derive me ill will to speak of; therefore I will not speak what I know.

King. Thou hast spoken all already, unless thou canst say they are married: but thou art too fine in thy evidence; therefore stand aside. This ring, you say, was yours? 271

Dia.   Ay, my good lord.

King. Where did you buy it? or who gave it you?

Dia. It was not given me, nor I did not buy it.

King. Who lent it you?

Dia.   It was not lent me neither.

King. Where did you find it, then?

Dia.   I found it not.

King. If it were yours by none of all these ways,

How could you give it him?

Dia.   I never gave it him.

Laf. This woman's an easy glove, my lord; she goes off and on at pleasure.

King. This ring was mine; I gave it his first wife. 280

Dia. It might be yours or hers, for aught I know.

King. Take her away; I do not like her now;

To prison with her: and away with him. Unless thou tell'st me where thou hadst this ring,

Thou diest within this hour.

Dia.   I'll never tell you.

King. Take her away.

Dia.   I'll put in bail, my liege.

King. I think thee now some common customer.

Dia. By Jove, if ever I knew man, 'twas you.

King. Wherefore hast thou accused him all this while?

Dia. Because he's guilty, and he is not guilty: 290

He knows I am no maid, and he'll swear to't; I'll swear I am a maid, and he knows not. Great king, I am no strumpet, by my life; I am either maid, or else this old man's wife.

King. She does abuse our ears: to prison with her.

Dia. Good mother, fetch my bail. Stay, royal sir: [*Exit Widow.*

The jeweller that owes the ring is sent for, And he shall surety me. But for this lord, Who hath abused me, as he knows himself,

Though yet he never harm'd me, here I quit him: 300

He knows himself my bed he hath defiled; And at that time he got his wife with child: Dead though she be, she feels her young one kick:

So there's my riddle: one that's dead is quick: And now behold the meaning.

Re-enter Widow, *with* HELENA.

King.   Is there no exorcist Beguiles the truer office of mine eyes? Is't real that I see?

Hel.   No, my good lord; 'Tis but the shadow of a wife you see, The name and not the thing.

Ber.   Both, both. O, pardon!

Hel. O my good lord, when I was like this maid, 310

I found you wondrous kind. There is your ring;

And, look you, here's your letter; this it says: 'When from my finger you can get this ring And are by me with child,' &c. This is done: Will you be mine, now you are doubly won?

Ber. If she, my liege, can make me know this clearly,

I'll love her dearly, ever, ever dearly.

Hel. If it appear not plain and prove untrue,

Deadly divorce step between me and you! O my dear mother, do I see you living? 320

Laf. Mine eyes smell onions; I shall weep anon:

[*To* Parolles] Good Tom Drum, lend me a handkercher: so,

I thank thee: wait on me home, I'll make sport with thee:

Let thy courtesies alone, they are scurvy ones.

King. Let us from point to point this story know,

To make the even truth in pleasure flow.

[*To Diana*] If thou be'st yet a fresh uncropped flower,

Choose thou thy husband, and I'll pay thy dower;

For I can guess that by thy honest aid Thou keep'st a wife herself, thyself a maid. Of that and all the progress, more or less, 331 Resolvedly more leisure shall express: All yet seems well; and if it end so meet, The bitter past, more welcome is the sweet.

                       [*Flourish.*

EPILOGUE.

King. The king's a beggar, now the play is done:

All is well ended, if this suit be won, That you express content; which we will pay, With strife to please you, day exceeding day: Ours be your patience then, and yours our parts;

Your gentle hands lend us, and take our hearts.   · [*Exeunt.* 340

MEASURE FOR MEASURE.

(WRITTEN ABOUT 1603.)

INTRODUCTION.

This is one of the darkest and most painful of the comedies of Shakespeare, but its darkness is lit by the central figure of Isabella, with her white passion of purity and of indignation against sin. The play deals with deep things of our humanity—with righteousness and charity, with self-deceit, and moral weakness and strength, even with life and death themselves. All that is soft, melodious, romantic, has disappeared from the style; it shows a fearless vigor, penetrating imagination, and much intellectual force and boldness. Its date is uncertain. Two passages (Act I, Sc 1, L 68-73, and Act II, Sc iv, L 24-29) have been conjectured to contain 'a courtly apology for King James I 's stately and ungracious demeanor on his entry into England," and possibly the revival in 1604 of a statute which punished with death any divorced person who married again while his or her former husband or wife was living, may have added point to one chief incident in the play. Shakespeare took the story from Whetstone's play *Promos and Cassandra* (1578), and the prose telling of the tale by the same author in his *Heptameron of Civil Discourses* (1582). Whetstone's original was a story in the *Hecatomithi* of Giraldi Cinthio. Shakespeare alters some of the incidents, making the Duke present in disguise throughout, preserving the honor of the heroine, and introducing the character of Mariana to take her wifely place by Angelo as a substitute for Isabella. *Measure for Measure*, like *The Merchant of Venice*, is remarkable for its great pleading scenes, and to Portia's ardor and intellectual force Isabella adds a noble severity of character, a devotion to an ideal of rectitude and purity, and a religious enthusiasm. In Vienna, "where corruption boils and bubbles," appears this figure of virginal strength and uprightness; at the last she is to preside over the sinful city and perhaps to save it. She is almost "a thing ensky'd and sainted," yet she returns from the cloister to the world, there to fill her place as wife and Duchess. Angelo, at the outset, though he must be conscious of the wrong he has done to his betrothed, is more self-deceived than a deceiver. He does not know his own heart, and is severe against others in his imagined superiority to every possible temptation. A terrible abyss is opened to him in the evil passion of his own nature. The unmasking of the self-deceiver is not here, as in the happy comedies, a piece of the mirth of the play; it is painful and stern. The Duke acts throughout as a kind of overruling providence; he has the wisdom of the serpent, which he uses for good ends, and he looks through life with a steady gaze, which results in a justice and even tenderness towards others. Claudio is made chiefly to be saved by his sister, but he has a grace of youth and a clinging enjoyment of life and love, which interest us in him sufficiently for pity if not for admiration. The minor characters possess each his characteristic texture, but are less important individually than as representatives of the wide-spread social corruption and degradation which surround the chief characters, and form the soil on which they move and the air they breathe. "We never throughout the play get into the free open joyous atmosphere, so invigorating in other works of Shakespeare, the oppressive gloom of the prison, the foul breath of the house of shame, are only exchanged for the chilly damp of conventual walls, or the oppressive retirement of the monastery."

DRAMATIS PERSONÆ.

VINCENTIO, the Duke.
ANGELO, Deputy.
ESCALUS, an ancient Lord.
CLAUDIO, a young gentleman.
LUCIO, a fantastic.
Two other gentlemen
PROVOST
THOMAS, } two friars.
PETER, }
A Justice.
VARRIUS
ELBOW, a simple constable.
FROTH, a foolish gentleman.

POMPEY, servant to Mistress Overdone.
ABHORSON, an executioner.
BARNARDINE, a dissolute prisoner.

ISABELLA, sister to Claudio.
MARIANA, betrothed to Angelo.
JULIET, beloved of Claudio.
FRANCISCA, a nun
MISTRESS OVERDONE, a bawd.

Lords, Officers, Citizens, Boy, and Attendants.

SCENE : *Vienna.*

ACT I.

Scene I. *An apartment in the* Duke's *palace.*

Enter Duke, Escalus, Lords *and Attendants.*

Duke. Escalus.

Escal. My lord.

Duke. Of government the properties to
 unfold,   [course ;
Would seem in me to affect speech and dis-
Since I am put to know that your own science
Exceeds, in that, the lists of all advice
My strength can give you : then no more re-
 mains,
†But that to your sufficiency........
....as your worth is able,
And let them work. The nature of our people,
Our city's institutions, and the terms 11
For common justice, you're as pregnant in
As art and practice hath enriched any
That we remember. There is our commission,
From which we would not have you warp.
  Call hither,
I say, bid come before us Angelo.
      [*Exit an Attendant.*
What figure of us think you he will bear ?
For you must know, we have with special soul
Elected him our absence to supply,
Lent him our terror, dress'd him with our love,
And given his deputation all the organs 21
Of our own power : what think you of it ?

Escal. If any in Vienna be of worth
To undergo such ample grace and honor,
It is Lord Angelo.

Duke.   Look where he comes.

Enter Angelo.

Ang. Always obedient to your grace's will,
I come to know your pleasure.

Duke.   Angelo,
There is a kind of character in thy life,
That to the observer doth thy history
Fully unfold. Thyself and thy belongings 30
Are not thine own so proper as to waste
Thyself upon thy virtues, they on thee.
Heaven doth with us as we with torches do,
Not light them for themselves ; for if our vir-
 tues
Did go forth of us, 'twere all alike
As if we had them not. Spirits are not finely
 touch'd
But to fine issues, nor Nature never lends
The smallest scruple of her excellence
But, like a thrifty goddess, she determines
Herself the glory of a creditor,   40
Both thanks and use. But I do bend my speech
To one that can my part in him advertise ;
Hold therefore, Angelo :—
In our remove be thou at full ourself ;
Mortality and mercy in Vienna
Live in thy tongue and heart : old Escalus,
Though first in question, is thy secondary.
Take thy commission.

Ang.   Now, good my lord,
Let there be some more test made of my metal,
Before so noble and so great a figure 50
Be stamp'd upon it.

Duke.   No more evasion :
We have with a leaven'd and prepared choice
Proceeded to you ; therefore take your honors.
Our haste from hence is of so quick condition
That it prefers itself and leaves unquestion'd
Matters of needful value. We shall write to you,
As time and our concernings shall importune,
How it goes with us, and do look to know
What doth befall you here. So, fare you well:
To the hopeful execution do I leave you 60
Of your commissions.

Ang.   Yet give leave, my lord,
That we may bring you something on the way.

Duke. My haste may not admit it ;
Nor need you, on mine honor, have to do
With any scruple ; your scope is as mine own
So to enforce or qualify the laws
As to your soul seems good. Give me your
 hand :
I'll privily away. I love the people,
But do not like to stage me to their eyes :
Though it do well, I do not relish well 70
Their loud applause and Aves vehement ;
Nor do I think the man of safe discretion
That does affect it. Once more, fare you well.

Ang. The heavens give safety to your purposes !

Escal. Lead forth and bring you back in
 happiness !

Duke. I thank you. Fare you well. [*Exit.*

Escal. I shall desire you, sir, to give me
 leave   [cerns me
To have free speech with you ; and it con-
To look into the bottom of my place :
A power I have, but of what strength and
 nature   80
I am not yet instructed.

Ang. 'Tis so with me. Let us withdraw
 together,
And we may soon our satisfaction have
Touching that point.

Escal. I'll wait upon your honor. [*Exeunt.*

Scene II. *A street.*

Enter Lucio *and two Gentlemen.*

Lucio. If the duke with the other dukes
come not to composition with the King of Hungary, why then all the dukes fall upon the king.

First Gent. Heaven grant us its peace, but
not the King of Hungary's !

Sec. Gent. Amen.

Lucio. Thou concludest like the sanctimo-
nious pirate, that went to sea with the Ten
Commandments, but scraped one out of the
table.

Sec. Gent. 'Thou shalt not steal' ? 10

Lucio. Ay, that he razed.

First Gent. Why, 'twas a commandment to
command the captain and all the rest from
their functions : they put forth to steal. There's
not a soldier of us all, that, in the thanksgiving
before meat, do relish the petition well that
prays for peace.

Sec. Gent. I never heard any soldier dislike

Lucio I believe thee ; for I think thou
never wast where grace was said   20
Sec Gent No ? a dozen times at least.
First Gent. What, in metre ?
Lucio In any proportion or in any language
First Gent I think, or in any religion.
Lucio Ay, why not ? Grace is grace, de-
spite of all controversy as, for example, thou
thyself art a wicked villain despite of all grace
First Gent Well, there went but a pair of
shears between us
Lucio I grant ; as there may between the
lists and the velvet Thou art the list   31
First Gent. And thou the velvet thou art
good velvet, thou'rt a three-piled piece, I warrant thee · I had as lief be a list of an English
kersey as be piled, as thou art piled, for a
French velvet Do I speak feelingly now ?
Lucio I think thou dost , and, indeed, with
most painful feeling of thy speech : I will, out
of thine own confession, learn to begin thy
health , but, whilst I live, forget to drink after
thee   40
First Gent I think I have done myself
wrong, have I not ?
Sec. Gent. Yes, that thou hast, whether
thou art tainted or free
Lucio Behold, behold, where Madam
Mitigation comes ! I have purchased as many
diseases under her roof as come to—
Sec Gent. To what, I pray ?
Lucio. Judge.
Sec Gent To three thousand dolors a year
First Gent Ay, and more.   51
Lucio A French crown more
First Gent. Thou art always figuring
diseases in me , but thou art full of error ; I
am sound
Lucio Nay not as one would say, healthy ,
but so sound as things that are hollow thy
bones are hollow ; impiety has made a feast of
thee.

Enter MISTRESS OVERDONE

First Gent How now ! which of your hips
has the most profound sciatica ?
Mrs Ov. Well, well , there's one yonder arrested and carried to prison was worth five
thousand of you all
Sec Gent Who's that, I pray thee ?
Mrs Ov. Marry, sir, that's Claudio, Signior
Claudio
First Gent Claudio to prison ? 'tis not so
Mrs Ov. Nay, but I know 'tis so · I saw
him arrested, saw him carried away ; and,
which is more, within these three days his
head to be chopped off.   70
Lucio But, after all this fooling, I would
not have it so Art thou sure of this ?
Mrs Ov I am too sure of it and it is for
getting Madam Julietta with child
Lucio Believe me, this may be . he promised to meet me two hours since, and he was
ever precise in promise-keeping
Sec. Gent Besides, you know, it draws something near to the speech we had to such a purpose

First Gent. But, most of all, agreeing with
the proclamation.   81
Lucio. Away ! let's go learn the truth of it.
     [*Exeunt Lucio and Gentlemen.*
Mrs Ov Thus, what with the war, what
with the sweat, what with the gallows and
what with poverty, I am custom-shrunk.

Enter POMPEY.

How now ! what's the news with you ?
Pom Yonder man is carried to prison.
Mrs Ov. Well , what has he done ?
Pom. A woman
Mrs Ov But what's his offence ?   90
Pom Groping for trouts in a peculiar river.
Mrs. Ov. What, is there a maid with child
by him ?
Pom No, but there's a woman with maid
by him. You have not heard of the proclama-
tion, have you ?
Mrs Ov What proclamation, man ?
Pom All houses in the suburbs of Vienna
must be plucked down
Mrs Ov And what shall become of those
in the city ?   101
Pom They shall stand for seed : they had
gone down too, but that a wise burgher put in
for them
Mrs Ov But shall all our houses of resort
in the suburbs be pulled down ?
Pom To the ground, mistress
Mrs Ov. Why, here's a change indeed in the
commonwealth ! What shall become of me ?
Pom Come , fear you not . good counsellors lack no clients · though you change your
place, you need not change your trade , I'll be
your tapster still. Courage ! there will be pity
taken on you you that have worn your eyes
almost out in the service, you will be considered.
Mrs Ov. What's to do here, Thomas tapster ? let's withdraw
Pom Here comes Signior Claudio, led by
the provost to prison , and there's Madam
Juliet   [*Exeunt.*

Enter PROVOST, CLAUDIO, JULIET, *and*
Officers

Claud. Fellow, why dost thou show me
thus to the world ?   120
Bear me to prison, where I am committed.
Prov. I do it not in evil disposition,
But from Lord Angelo by special charge.
Claud Thus can the demigod Authority
Make us pay down for our offence by weight
The words of heaven , on whom it will, it will;
On whom it will not. so , yet still 'tis just

Re-enter LUCIO *and two* Gentlemen.

Lucio. Why, how now, Claudio ! whence
comes this restraint ?
Claud. From too much liberty, my Lucio,
liberty :
As surfeit is the father of much fast,   130
So every scope by the immoderate use
Turns to restraint Our natures do pursue,
Like rats that ravin down their proper bane,

A thirsty evil , and when we drink we die.

Lucio If I could speak so wisely under an arrest, I would send for certain of my creditors . and yet, to say the truth, I had as lief have the foppery of freedom as the morality of imprisonment What's thy offence, Claudio ?

Claud What but to speak of would offend again   140

Lucio What, is't murder?

Claud No

Lucio Lechery ?

Claud. Call it so

Prov Away, sir ' you must go.

Claud One word, good friend Lucio, a word with you

Lucio A hundred, if they'll do you any good

Is lechery so look'd after ?

Claud Thus stands it with me upon a true contract

I got possession of Julietta's bed ·   150
You know the lady , she is fast my wife,
Save that we do the denunciation lack
Of outward order this we came not to,
Only for propagation of a dower
Remaining in the coffer of her friends,
From whom we thought it meet to hide our love
Till time had made them for us But it chances
The stealth of our most mutual entertainment
With character too gross is writ on Juliet

Lucio With child, perhaps ?

Claud   Unhappily, even so   160
And the new deputy now for the duke—
Whether it be the fault and glimpse of newness,
Or whether that the body public be
A horse whereon the governor doth ride,
Who, newly in the seat, that it may know
He can command, lets it straight feel the spur ,
Whether the tyranny be in his place,
Or in his eminence that fills it up,
I stagger in —but this new governor
Awakes me all the enrolled penalties   170
Which have, like unscour'd armor, hung by the wall
So long that nineteen zodiacs have gone round
And none of them been worn, and, for a name,
Now puts the drowsy and neglected act
Freshly on me 'tis surely for a name

Lucio. I warrant it is and thy head stands so tickle on thy shoulders that a milkmaid, if she be in love, may sigh it off Send after the duke and appeal to him

Claud I have done so, but he's not to be found.   180

I prithee, Lucio, do me this kind service
This day my sister should the cloister enter
And there receive her approbation .
Acquaint her with the danger of my state
Implore her, in my voice, that she make friends
To the strict deputy ; bid herself assay him :
I have great hope in that ; for in her youth
There is a prone and speechless dialect,

Such as move men; beside, she hath prosperous art
When she will play with reason and discourse,
And well she can persuade   191

Lucio. I pray she may , as well for the encouragement of the like, which else would stand under grievous imposition, as for the enjoying of thy life, who I would be sorry should be thus foolishly lost at a game of ticktack I'll to her

Claud I thank you, good friend Lucio

Lucio Within two hours

Claud   Come, officer, away'
                                   [*Exeunt.*

SCENE III   *A monastery.*

Enter Duke *and* FRIAR THOMAS

Duke. No, holy father , throw away that thought ,
Believe not that the dribbling dart of love
Can pierce a complete bosom. Why I desire thee
To give me secret harbor, hath a purpose
More grave and wrinkled than the aims and ends
Of burning youth

Fri. T   May your grace speak of it .

Duke My holy sir, none better knows than you
How I have ever loved the life removed
And held in idle price to haunt assemblies
Where youth, and cost, and witless bravery keeps   10
I have deliver'd to Lord Angelo,
A man of structure and firm abstinence,
My absolute power and place here in Vienna,
And he supposes me travell'd to Poland ,
For so I have strew'd it in the common ear,
And so it is received Now, pious sir,
You will demand of me why I do this ?

Fri T Gladly, my lord

Duke We have strict statutes and most biting laws,
The needful bits and curbs to headstrong weeds,   20
Which for this nineteen years we have let slip,
Even like an o'ergrown lion in a cave,
That goes not out to prey Now, as fond fathers,
Having bound up the threatening twigs of birch,
Only to stick it in their children's sight
For terror, not to use, in time the rod
Becomes more mock'd than fear'd , so our decrees,
Dead to infliction, to themselves are dead ;
And liberty plucks justice by the nose ,
The baby beats the nurse, and quite athwart
Goes all decorum.   31

Fri. T.   It rested in your grace
To unloose this tied-up justice when you pleased :
And it in you more dreadful would **have** seem'd
Than in Lord Angel**o**

Duke.   I do fear, too dreadful .
Sith 'twas my fault to give the people scope,
'Twould be my tyranny to strike and gall them
For what I bid them do for we bid this be done,
When evil deeds have their permissive pass
And not the punishment Therefore indeed, my father,
I have on Angelo imposed the office ,   40
Who may, in the ambush of my name, strike home,
†And yet my nature never in the fight
To do in slander And to behold his sway,
I will, as 'twere a brother of your order,
Visit both prince and people · therefore, I prithee,
Supply me with the habit and instruct me
How I may formally in person bear me
Like a true friar. More reasons for this action
At our more leisure shall I render you ,
Only, this one : Lord Angelo is precise ,   50
Stands at a guard with envy , scarce confesses
That his blood flows, or that his appetite
Is more to bread than stone . hence shall we see,
If power change purpose, what our seemers be
                         [*Exeunt*

SCENE IV. *A nunnery.*

Enter ISABELLA *and* FRANCISCA

Isab   And have you nuns no farther privileges ?
Fran   Are not these large enough ?
Isab.   Yes, truly, I speak not as desiring more ;
But rather wishing a more strict restraint
Upon the sisterhood, the votarists of Saint Clare
Lucio [*Within*] Ho ! Peace be in this place!
Isab   Who's that which calls ?
Fran   It is a man's voice Gentle Isabella,
Turn you the key, and know his business of him ,
You may, I may not , you are yet unsworn
When you have vow'd, you must not speak with men   10
But in the presence of the prioress
Then, if you speak, you must not show your face,
Or, if you show your face, you must not speak.
He calls again , I pray you, answer him [*Exit*
Isab   Peace and prosperity ! Who is't that calls ?

Enter LUCIO

Lucio   Hail, virgin, if you be, as those cheek-roses
Proclaim you are no less ! Can you so stead me
As bring me to the sight of Isabella,
A novice of this place and the fair sister
To her unhappy brother Claudio ?   20
Isab.   Why ' her unhappy brother' ? let me ask,
The rather for I now must make you know
I am that Isabella and his sister.

Lucio   Gentle and fair, your brother kindly greets you .
Not to be weary with you, he's in prison.
Isab.   Woe me ! for what ?
Lucio   For that which, if myself might be his judge,
He should receive his punishment in thanks :
He hath got his friend with child
Isab   Sir, make me not your story.
Lucio   It is true   30
I would not—though 'tis my familiar sin
With maids to seem the lapwing and to jest,
Tongue far from heart—play with all virgins so ·
I hold you as a thing ensky'd and sainted,
By your renouncement an immortal spirit,
And to be talk'd with in sincerity,
As with a saint
Isab   You do blaspheme the good in mocking me
Lucio   Do not believe it Fewness and truth, 'tis thus
Your brother and his lover have embraced :
As those that feed grow full, as blossoming time   41
That from the seedness the bare fallow brings
To teeming foison, even so her plenteous womb
Expresseth his full tilth and husbandry
Isab   Some one with child by him ? My cousin Juliet ?
Lucio   Is she your cousin ?
Isab   Adoptedly , as school-maids change their names
By vain though apt affection
Lucio.   She it is.
Isab   O, let him marry her
Lucio   This is the point.
The duke is very strangely gone from hence ;
Bore many gentlemen, myself being one,   51
In hand and hope of action . but we do learn
By those that know the very nerves of state,
His givings-out were of an infinite distance
From his true-meant design Upon his place,
And with full line of his authority,
Governs Lord Angelo, a man whose blood
Is very snow-broth ; one who never feels
The wanton stings and motions of the sense,
But doth rebate and blunt his natural edge   60
With profits of the mind, study and fast.
He—to give fear to use and liberty,
Which have for long run by the hideous law,
As mice by lions—hath pick'd out an act,
Under whose heavy sense your brother's life
Falls into forfeit . he arrests him on it ,
And follows close the rigor of the statute,
To make him an example All hope is gone,
Unless you have the grace by your fair prayer
To soften Angelo · and that's my pith of business   70
'Twixt you and your poor brother
Isab   Doth he so seek his life ?
Lucio.   Has censured him
Already , and, as I hear, the provost hath
A warrant for his execution.
Isab.   Alas ! what poor ability's in me
To do him good ?

Lucio.   Assay the power you have.
Isab. My power ? Alas, I doubt—
Lucio   Our doubts are traitors
And make us lose the good we oft might win
By fearing to attempt Go to Lord Angelo,
And let him learn to know, when maidens sue,
Men give like gods , but when they weep and
        kneel,
All their petitions are as freely theirs
As they themselves would owe them.
Isab   I'll see what I can do
Lucio.   But speedily.
Isab I will about it straight ;
No longer staying but to give the mother
Notice of my affair. I humbly thank you'
Commend me to my brother soon at night
I'll send him certain word of my success
Lucio. I take my leave of you.
Isab.   Good sir, adieu   90
                          [*Exeunt.*

ACT II

SCENE I.   *A hall in* ANGELO'S *house*

Enter ANGELO, ESCALUS, *and a Justice.* Provost, Officers, *and other* Attendants, *behind.*

Ang   We must not make a scarecrow of the
        law,
Setting it up to fear the birds of prey,
And let it keep one shape, till custom make it
Their perch and not their terror
Escal.   Ay, but yet
Let us be keen, and rather cut a little,
Than fall, and bruise to death. Alas, this gen-
        tleman,
Whom I would save, had a most noble father'
Let but your honor know,
Whom I believe to be most strait in virtue,
That, in the working of your own affections,
Had time cohered with place or place with
        wishing,   11
Or that the resolute acting of your blood
Could have attain'd the effect of your own
        purpose,
Whether you had not sometime in your life
Err'd in this point which now you censure
        him,
And pull'd the law upon you.
Ang. 'Tis one thing to be tempted, Escalus,
Another thing to fall I not deny,
Tho jury, passing on the prisoner's life,
May in the sworn twelve have a thief or two
Guiltier than him they try What's open made
        to justice,   21
†That justice seizes . what know the laws
That thieves do pass on thieves ? 'Tis very
        pregnant,
The jewel that we find, we stoop and take 't
Because we see it ; but what we do not see
We tread upon, and never think of it.
You may not so extenuate his offence
For I have had such faults ; but rather tell
        me,
When I, that censure him, do so offend,

Let mine own judgment pattern out my death,
And nothing come in partial Sir, he must
        die.
Escal Be it as your wisdom will
Ang   Where is the provost ?
Prov. Here, if it like your honor
Ang   See that Claudio
Be executed by nine to-morrow morning
Bring him his confessor, let him be prepared ,
For that's the utmost of his pilgrimage
                          [*Exit Provost.*
Escal. [*Aside*] Well, heaven forgive him !
        and forgive us all '
Some rise by sin, and some by virtue fall .
†Some run from brakes of ice, and answer
        none :
And some condemned for a fault alone.   40

Enter ELBOW, *and* Officers *with* FROTH *and*
POMPEY

Elb Come, bring them away if these be
good people in a commonweal that do nothing
but use their abuses in common houses, I know
no law ' bring them away.
Ang How now, sir ' What's your name ?
and what's the matter ?
Elb If it please your honor, I am the poor
duke's constable and my name is Elbow I do
lean upon justice, sir, and do bring in here
before your good honor two notorious benefactors.   50
Ang. Benefactors ? Well , what benefactors are they ? are they not malefactors ?
Elb If it please your honor, I know not
well what they are . but precise villains they
are, that I am sure of , and void of all profanation in the world that good Christians ought
to have
Escal This comes off well , here's a wise
officer.
Ang Go to what quality are they of ?
Elbow is your name ? why dost thou not speak,
Elbow ?   60
Pom He cannot, sir , he's out at elbow.
Ang. What are you, sir ?
Elb He, sir ' a tapster, sir , parcel-bawd ;
one that serves a bad woman ; whose house,
sir, was, as they say, plucked down in the
suburbs ; and now she professes a hot-house,
which, I think, is a very ill house too
Escal. How know you that ?
Elb. My wife, sir, whom I detest before
heaven and your honor,—   70
Escal How ? thy wife?
Elb Ay, sir , whom, I thank heaven, is
an honest woman,—
Escal. Dost thou detest her therefore ?
Elb. I say, sir, I will detest myself also, as
well as she, that this house, if it be not a
bawd's house, it is pity of her life, for it is
a naughty house
Escal. How dost thou know that, constable ?
Elb. Marry, sir, by my wife , who, if she
had been a woman cardinally given, might
have been accused in fornication. adultery.
and all uncleanliness there.

48

Escal. By the woman's means?

Elb. Ay, sir, by Mistress Overdone's means: but as she spit in his face, so she defied him

Pom. Sir, if it please your honor, this is not so

Elb Prove it before these varlets here, thou honorable man ; prove it.

Escal. Do you hear how he misplaces ? 90

Pom Sir, she came in great with child ; and longing, saving your honor's reverence, for stewed prunes ; sir, we had but two in the house, which at that very distant time stood, as it were, in a fruit-dish, a dish of some three-pence ; your honors have seen such dishes ; they are not China dishes, but very good dishes,—　　　　　　　　　　　[sir

Escal. Go to, go to : no matter for the dish,

Pom No, indeed, sir, not of a pin ; you are therein in the right . but to the point As I say, this Mistress Elbow, being, as I say, with child, and being great-bellied, and longing, as I said, for prunes , and having but two in the dish, as I said, Master Froth here, this very man, having eaten the rest, as I said, and, as I say, paying for them very honestly ; for, as you know, Master Froth, I could not give you three-pence again

Froth. No, indeed

Pom. Very well ; you being then, if you be remembered, cracking the stones of the foresaid prunes,—　　　　　　　　　　　111

Froth. Ay, so I did indeed

Pom Why, very well , I telling you then, if you be remembered, that such a one and such a one were past cure of the thing you wot of, unless they kept very good diet, as I told you,—

Froth. All this is true.

Pom Why, very well, then,—

Escal. Come, you are a tedious fool : to the purpose What was done to Elbow's wife, that he hath cause to complain of ? Come me to what was done to her

Pom. Sir, your honor cannot come to that yet

Escal. No, sir, nor I mean it not.

Pom. Sir, but you shall come to it, by your honor's leave And, I beseech you, look into Master Froth here, sir , a man of fourscore pound a year ; whose father died at Hallowmas . was't not at Hallowmas, Master Froth ?

Froth All-hallond eve　　　　　　　130

Pom Why, very well ; I hope here be truths. He, sir, sitting, as I say, in a lower chair, sir ; 'twas in the Bunch of Grapes, where indeed you have a delight to sit, have you not ?

Froth. I have so ; because it is an open room and good for winter

Pom Why, very well, then ; I hope here be truths

Ang. This will last out a night in Russia, When nights are longest there : I'll take my leave,　　　　　　　　　　　140

And leave you to the hearing of the cause ; Hoping you'll find good cause to whip them all.

Escal. I think no less. Good morrow to your lordship.　　　　　　[*Exit Angelo.*

Now, sir, come on what was done to Elbow's wife, once more ?

Pom. Once, sir ? there was nothing done to her once

Elb. I beseech you, sir, ask him what this man did to my wife

Pom. I beseech your honor, ask me　　150

Escal Well, sir ; what did this gentleman to her ?

Pom. I beseech you, sir, look in this gentleman's face. Good Master Froth, look upon his honor , 'tis for a good purpose. Doth your honor mark his face ?

Escal Ay, sir, very well

Pom. Nay, I beseech you, mark it well.

Escal. Well, I do so.

Pom. Doth your honor see any harm in his face ?　　　　　　　　　　　160

Escal. Why, no

Pom I'll be supposed upon a book, his face is the worst thing about him. Good, then ; if his face be the worst thing about him, how could Master Froth do the constable's wife any harm ? I would know that of your honor

Escal He's in the right Constable, what say you to it ?

Elb First, an it like you, the house is a respected house , next, this is a respected fellow , and his mistress is a respected woman.

Pom By this hand, sir, his wife is a more respected person than any of us all.

Elb Varlet, thou liest , thou liest, wicked varlet ! the time has yet to come that she was ever respected with man, woman, or child.

Pom Sir, she was respected with him before he married with her.

Escal. Which is the wiser here ? Justice or Iniquity ? Is this true ?　　　　　181

Elb O thou caitiff! O thou varlet ! O thou wicked Hannibal ! I respected with her before I was married to her ! If ever I was respected with her, or she with me, let not your worship think me the poor duke's officer. Prove this, thou wicked Hannibal, or I'll have mine action of battery on thee

Escal. If he took you a box o' the ear, you might have your action of slander too 190

Elb Marry, I thank your good worship for it. What is't your worship's pleasure I shall do with this wicked caitiff ?

Escal. Truly, officer, because he hath some offences in him that thou wouldst discover if thou couldst, let him continue in his courses till thou knowest what they are.

Elb Marry, I thank your worship for it. Thou seest, thou wicked varlet, now, what's come upon thee : thou art to continue now, thou varlet ; thou art to continue.　　201

Escal. Where were you born, friend ?

Froth. Here in Vienna, sir.

Escal. Are you of fourscore pounds a
year ?
Froth Yes, an't please you, sir
Escal. So. What trade are you of, sir ?
Pom. A tapster , a poor widow's tapster
Escal. Your mistress' name ?
Pom Mistress Overdone
Escal Hath she had any more than one
husband ?   211
Pom Nine, sir , Overdone by the last
Escal. Nine ' Come hither to me, Master
Froth Master Froth, I would not have you
acquainted with tapsters . they will draw you,
Master Froth, and you will hang them. Get
you gone, and let me hear no more of you
Froth I thank you worship. For mine
own part, I never come into any room in a
tap-house, but I am drawn in   220
Escal Well, no more of it, Master Froth
farewell *[Exit Froth]* Come you hither to
me, Master tapster What's your name,
Master tapster ?
Pom Pompey
Escal What else ?
Pom Bum, sir.
Escal Troth, and your bum is the greatest
thing about you , so that in the beastliest
sense you are Pompey the Great Pompey,
you are partly a bawd, Pompey, howsoever
you color it in being a tapster, are you not ?
come, tell me true . it shall be the better for
you
Pom. Truly, sir, I am a 'poor fellow that
would live.
Escal. How would you live, Pompey ? by
being a bawd ? What do you think of the
trade, Pompey ? is it a lawful trade ?
Pom. If the law would allow it, sir
Escal But the law will not allow it, Pompey , nor it shall not be allowed in Vienna 241
Pom Does your worship mean to geld and
splay all the youth of the city ?
Escal. No, Pompey.
Pom. Truly, sir, in my poor opinion, they
will to't then. If your worship will take order for the drabs and the knaves, you need
not to fear the bawds
Escal There are pretty orders beginning, I
can tell you : it is but heading and hanging.
Pom If you head and hang all that offend
that way but for ten year together, you'll be
glad to give out a commission for more heads
if this law hold in Vienna ten year, I'll rent
the fairest house in it after three-pence a bay .
if you live to see this come to pass, say Pompey told you so.
Escal. Thank you, good Pompey ; and, in
requital of your prophecy, hark you I advise
you, let me not find you before me again upon
any complaint whatsoever , no, not for dwelling where you do : if I do, Pompey, I shall
beat you to your tent, and prove a shrewd
Cæsar to you ; in plain dealing, Pompey, I
shall have you whipt : so, for this time, Pompey, fare you well.
Pom. I thank your worship for your good

counsel *[Aside]* but I shall follow it as the
flesh and fortune shall better determine.
Whip me ? No, no , let carman whip his jade.
The valiant heart is not whipt out of his trade
      [Exit. 270
Escal Come hither to me, Master Elbow ;
come hither, Master constable How long
have you been in this place of constable ?
Elb Seven year and a half, sir
Escal I thought, by your readiness in the
office, you had continued in it some time You
say, seven years together ?
Elb And a half, sir.
Escal Alas, it hath been great pains to you
They do you wrong to put you so oft upon 't :
are there not men in your ward sufficient to
serve it ?
Elb Faith, sir, few of any wit in such
matters · as they are chosen, they are glad to
choose me for them , I do it for some piece of
money, and go through with all
Escal Look you bring me in the names of
some six or seven, the most sufficient of your
parish.
Elb To your worship's house, sir ?
Escal To my house Fare you well
       [Exit Elbow
What's o'clock, think you ?   280
Just Eleven, sir
Escal. I pray you home to dinner with me
Just. I humbly thank you.
Escal. It grieves me for the death of
    Claudio ;
But there's no remedy
Just Lord Angelo is severe
Escal   It is but needful .
Mercy is not itself, that oft looks so ,
Pardon is still the nurse of second woe :
But yet,—poor Claudio ! There is no remedy
Come, sir.   *[Exeunt.* 290

  SCENE II *Another room in the same.*

    Enter PROVOST *and a Servant.*

Serv He's hearing of a cause, he will
    come straight
I'll tell him of you
Prov   Pray you, do. *[Exit Servant]*
    I'll know
His pleasure . may be he will relent Alas,
He hath but as offended in a dream !
All sects, all ages smack of this vice , and he
To die for 't !

      Enter ANGELO.

Ang. Now, what's the matter, provost ?
Prov. Is it your will Claudio shall die to-
    morrow ?
Ang Did not I tell thee yea ? hadst thou
    not order ?
Why dost thou ask again ?
Prov   Lest I might be too rash :
Under your good correction, I have seen, 10
When, after execution. judgment hath
Repented o'er his doom.
Ang. ·   **Go to ;** let that be mine :

Do you your office, or give up your place,
And you shall well be spared
 Prov.   I crave your honor's pardon.
What shall be done, sir, with the groaning
  Juliet ?
She's very near her hour.
 Ang.   Dispose of her
To some more fitter place, and that with speed.

Re-enter Servant.

 Serv Here is the sister of the man con-
  demn'd
Desires access to you.
 Ang   Hath he a sister ?
 Prov Ay, my good lord ; a very virtuous
  maid,   20
And to be shortly of a sisterhood,
If not already
 Ang.   Well, let her be admitted
          [*Exit Servant*
See you the fornicatress be removed :
Let her have needful, but not lavish, means ;
There shall be order for't.

Enter ISABELLA *and* LUCIO

 Prov.   God save your honor !
 Ang Stay a little while [*To Isab*] You're
welcome : what's your will ?
 Isab I am a woeful suitor to your honor,
Please but your honor hear me
 Ang.   Well , what's your suit ?
 Isab There is a vice that most I do abhor,
And most desire should meet the blow of jus-
  tice ;
For which I would not plead, but that I must,
For which I must not plead, but that I am
At war 'twixt will and will not
 Ang.   Will ; the matter ?
 Isab I have a brother is condemn'd to die·
I do beseech you, let it be his fault,
And not my brother
 Prov [*Aside*] Heaven give thee moving
  graces !
 Ang Condemn the fault and not the actor
of it ?
Why, every fault's condemn'd ere it be done :
Mine were the very cipher of a function,
To fine the faults whose fine stands in record,
And let go by the actor.   41
 Isab O just but severe law !
I had a brother, then Heaven keep your
  honor !
 Lucio. [*Aside to Isab*] Give't not o'er so :
  to him again, entreat him ;
Kneel down before him, hang upon his gown:
You are too cold : if you should need a pin,
You could not with more tame a tongue desire
  it :
To him, I say !
 Isab Must he needs die ?
 Ang.   Maiden, no remedy
 Isab Yes , I do think that you might' par-
  don him,
And neither heaven nor man grieve at the
  mercy.
 Ang. I will not do't.

 Isab.   But can you, if you would ? 51
 Ang. Look, what I will not, that I cannot
  do.
 Isab. But might you do't, and do the world
  no wrong,
If so your heart were touch'd with that re-
  morse
As mine is to him ?
 Ang   He's sentenced , 'tis too late.
 Lucio. [*Aside to Isab.*] You are too cold.
 Isab. Too late ? why, no , I, that do speak
  a word,
May call it back again Well, believe this,
No ceremony that to great ones 'longs,
Not the king's crown, nor the deputed sword,
The marshal's truncheon, nor the judge's
  robe, ·   61
Become them with one half so good a grace
As mercy does.
If he had been as you and you as he,
You would have slipt like him ; but he, like
  you,
Would not have been so stern.
 Ang   Pray you, be gone.
 Isab I would to heaven I had your po-
  tency,
And you were Isabel ! should it then be thus ?
No , I would tell what 'twere to be a judge,
And what a prisoner
 Lucio. [*Aside to Isab.*] Ay, touch him ;
  there's the vein   70
 Ang. Your brother is a forfeit of the law,
And you but waste your words.
 Isab.   Alas, alas !
Why, all the souls that were were forfeit
  once ;
And He that might the vantage best have
  took
Found out the remedy How would you be,
If He, which is the top of judgment, should
But judge you as you are ? O, think on
  that ,
And mercy then will breathe within your lips,
Like man new made.
 Ang   Be you content, fair maid !
It is the law, not I condemn your brother 80
Were he my kinsman, brother, or my son, ,
It should be thus with him . he must die to-
  morrow.
 Isab. To-morrow ! O, that's sudden ! Spare
  him, spare him !
He's not prepared for death. Even for our
  kitchens
We kill the fowl of season : shall we serve
  heaven
With less respect than we do minister
To our gross selves ? Good, good my lord,
  bethink you ;
Who is it that hath died for this offence ?
There's many have committed it
 Lucio. [*Aside to Isab*] Ay, well said.
 Ang The law hath not been dead, though
  it hath slept .   90
Those many had not dared to do that evil,
If the first that did the edict infringe
Had answer'd for his deed . now 'tis awake

Takes note of what is done ; and, like a
      prophet,
Looks in a glass, that shows what future evils,
Either new, or by remissness new-conceived,
And so in progress to be hatch'd and born,
Are now to have no successive degrees,
But, ere they live, to end.
  Isab.   Yet show some pity.
  Ang. I show it most of all when I show
      justice ,   100
For then I pity those I do not know,
Which a dismiss'd offence would after gall ;
And do him right that, answering one foul
      wrong,
Lives not to act another. Be satisfied ;
Your brother dies to-morrow ; be content.
  Isab. So you must be the first that gives
      this sentence,
And he, that suffers O, it is excellent
To have a giant's strength , but it is tyran-
      nous
To use it like a giant
  Lucio   [*Aside to Isab*] That's well said.
  Isab Could great men thunder   110
As Jove himself does, Jove would ne'er be
      quiet,
For every pelting, petty officer
Would use his heaven for thunder ;
Nothing but thunder ! Merciful Heaven,
Thou rather with thy sharp and sulphurous
      bolt
Split'st the unwedgeable and gnarled oak
Than the soft myrtle · but man, proud man,
Drest in a little brief authority,
Most ignorant of what he's most assured,
His glassy essence, like an angry ape,   120
Plays such fantastic tricks before high heaven
As make the angels weep , who, with our
      spleens,
Would all themselves laugh mortal.
  Lucio   [*Aside to Isab*] O, to him, to him,
      wench ! he will relent ;
He's coming ; I perceive 't.
  Prov.   [*Aside*] Pray heaven she win him !
  Isab. We cannot weigh our brother with
      ourself :
Great men may jest with saints ; 'tis wit in
      them,
But in the less foul profanation.
  Lucio. Thou'rt i' the right, girl ; more o'
      that
  Isab. That in the captain's but a choleric
      word,   130
Which in the soldier is flat blasphemy.
  Lucio. [*Aside to Isab*] Art avised o' that ?
      more on 't.
  Ang. Why do you put these sayings upon
      me ?
  Isab. Because authority, though it err like
      others,
Hath yet a kind of medicine in itself,
That skins the vice o' the top Go to your
      bosom ;
Knock there, and ask your heart what it
      doth know ,
That's like my brother's fault : if it confess

A natural guiltiness such as is his,
Let it not sound a thought upon your tongue
Against my brother's life.
  Ang.   [*Aside*] She speaks, and 'tis
Such sense, that my sense breeds with it Fare
      you well.
  Isab Gentle my lord, turn back.
  Ang I will bethink me : come again to-
      morrow.
  Isab. Hark how I'll bribe you : good my
      lord, turn back
  Ang How ! bribe me ?
  Isab Ay, with such gifts that heaven shall
      share with you
  Lucio. [*Aside to Isab*] You had marr'd all
      else
  Isab Not with fond shekels of the tested
      gold,
Or stones whose rates are either rich or poor
As fancy values them , but with true prayers
That shall be up at heaven and enter there
Ere sun-rise, prayers from preserved souls,
From fasting maids whose minds are dedicate
To nothing temporal
  Ang   Well , come to me to-morrow.
  Lucio. [*Aside to Isab*] Go to , 'tis well ,
      away !
  Isab Heaven keep your honor safe !
  Ang.   [*Aside*] Amen :
For I am that way going to temptation,
Where prayers cross
  Isab   At what hour to-morrow
Shall I attend your lordship ?
  Ang.   At any time 'fore noon 160
  Isab 'Save your honor !
            [*Exeunt Isabella, Lucio, and Provost*
  Ang.   From thee, even from thy virtue ·
What's this, what's this ? Is this her fault or
      mine ?
The tempter or the tempted, who sins most ?
      Ha !
Not she · nor doth she tempt . but it is I
That, lying by the violet in the sun,
Do as the carrion does, not as the flower,
Corrupt with virtuous season. Can it be
That modesty may more betray our sense
Than woman's lightness ? Having waste
      ground enough,   170
Shall we desire to raze the sanctuary
And pitch our evils there ? O, fie, fie, fie !
What dost thou, or what art thou, Angelo ?
Dost thou desire her foully for those things
That make her good ? O, let her brother
      live !
Thieves for their robbery have authority
When judges steal themselves. What, do I
      love her,
That I desire to hear her speak again,
And feast upon her eyes ? What is't I dream
      on ?
O cunning enemy, that, to catch a saint, 180
With saints dost bait thy hook ! Most dan-
      gerous
Is that temptation that doth goad us on
To sin in loving virtue , never could the
      strumpet,

With all her double vigor, art and nature,
Once stir my temper ; but this virtuous maid
Subdues me quite　Ever till now,
When men were fond, I smiled and wonder'd
　　how.　　　　　　　　　　　[*Exit.*

SCENE III. *A room in a prison.*

Enter, severally, DUKE *disguised as a friar,*
　and PROVOST.

Duke. Hail to you, provost ! so I think you
　are.
Prov. I am the provost　What's your will,
　good friar ?
Duke　Bound by my charity and my blest
　order,
I come to visit the afflicted spirits
Here in the prison. Do me the common right
To let me see them and to make me know
The nature of their crimes, that I may minister
To them accordingly.
Prov. I would do more than that, if more
　were needful.

Enter JULIET.

Look, here comes one : a gentlewoman of
　mine,　　　　　　　　　　　　　　10
Who, falling in the flaws of her own youth,
Hath blister'd her report · she is with child ;
And he that got it, sentenced ; a young man
More fit to do another such offence
Than die for this.
Duke.　When must he die ?
Prov　.　　　As I do think, to-morrow.
I have provided for you . stay awhile,
　　　　　　　　　　　　[*To Juliet*
And you shall be conducted.
　Duke. Repent you, fair one, of the sin you
　　carry ?
Jul.　I do ; and bear the shame most pa-
　tiently.　　　　　　　　　　　　20
Duke. · I'll teach you how you shall arraign
　your conscience,
And try your penitence, if it be sound,
Or hollowly put on
Jul.　　　　I'll gladly learn.
　Duke. Love you the man that wrong'd
　　you ?
Jul.　Yes, as I love the woman that wrong'd
　him
　Duke. So then it seems your most offence-
　　ful act
Was mutually committed ?
Jul　　　Mutually
　Duke　Then was your sin of heavier kind
　than his
Jul　I do confess it, and repent it, father.
Duke. 'Tis meet so, daughter　but lest you
·　do repent,　　　　　　　　　　　30
As that the sin hath brought you to this
· shame,
Which sorrow is always towards ourselves,
　not heaven,
Showing we would not spare heaven as we
　love it,
But as we stand in fear.—

Jul.　I do repent me, as it is an evil,
And take the shame with joy
　Duke.　　　　　There rest.
Your partner as I hear, must die to-morrow,
And I am going with instruction to him.
Grace go with you, Benedicite !　　　[*Exit.*
Jul.　Must die to-morrow ! O injurious love,
That respites me a life, whose very comfort
Is still a dying horror !
Prov.　　　'Tis pity of him. [*Exeunt.*

SCENE IV. *A room in* ANGELO'S *house.*

Enter ANGELO.

Ang. When I would pray and think, I think
　and pray
To several subjects. Heaven hath my empty
　words ;
Whilst my invention, hearing not my tongue,
Anchors on Isabel . Heaven in my mouth,
As if I did but only chew his name ;
And in my heart the strong and swelling evil
Of my conception. The state, whereon I
　studied,
Is like a good thing, being often read,
Grown fear'd and tedious ; yea, my gravity,
Wherein—let no man hear me—I take pride,
Could I with boot change for an idle plume, 11
Which the air beats for vain　O place, O form,
How often dost thou with thy case, thy habit,
Wrench awe from fools and tie the wiser souls
To thy false seeming !　Blood, thou art blood
Let's write good angel on the devil's horn :
'Tis not the devil's crest

Enter a Servant.

　　　　　How now·?·who's there ?
Serv. One Isabel, a sister, desires access to
you.
Ang.　Teach her the way. [*Exit Serv.*]　O
　heavens !
Why does my blood thus muster to my heart,
Making both it unable for itself,　　　21
And dispossessing all my other parts
Of necessary fitness ?
So play the foolish throngs with one that
　swoons ;
Come all to help him, and so stop the air
By which he should revive : and even so
The general, subject to a well-wish'd king,
Quit their own part, and in obsequious fond-
　ness
Crowd to his presence, where their untaught
　love
Must needs appear offence.

Enter ISABELLA.

　　　　　How now, fair maid ?　30
Isab　I am come to know your pleasure.
Ang.　That you might know it, would much
　better please me
Than to demand what 'tis.　Your brother can-
　not live.
Isab　Even so　Heaven keep your honor !
Ang　Yet may he live awhile ; and, it may
　be,
As long as you or I : yet he must die.

Isab. Under your sentence ?
Ang. Yea.
Isab. When, I beseech you ? that in his re-
prieve,
Longer or shorter, he may be so fitted 40
That his soul sicken not
  Ang Ha ! fie, these filthy vices ! It were
  as good
To pardon him that hath from nature stolen
A man already made, as to remit
Their saucy sweetness that do coin heaven's
  image
In stamps that are forbid · 'tis all as easy
Falsely to take away a life true made
As to put metal in restrained means
To make a false one
  Isab. 'Tis set down so in heaven, but not
  in earth 50
  Ang Say you so ? then I shall pose you
  quickly.
Which had you rather, that the most just law
Now took your brother's life , or, to redeem
  him,
Give up your body to such sweet uncleanness
· As she that he hath stain'd ?
  Isab. Sir, believe this,
I had rather give my body than my soul
  Ang I talk not of your soul · our compell'd
  sins
Stand more for number than for accompt
  Isab. How say you ?
  Ang. Nay, I'll not warrant that , for I can
  speak
Against the thing I say. Answer to this : 60
I, now the voice of the recorded law,
Pronounce a sentence on your brother's life .
Might there not be a charity in sin
To save this brother's life ?
  Isab Please you to do't,
I'll take it as a peril to my soul
It is no sin at all, but charity.
  Ang Pleased you to do't at peril of your
  soul,
Were equal poise of sin and charity.
  Isab That I do beg his life, if it be sin,
Heaven let me bear it ! you granting of my
  suit,
If that be sin, I'll make it my morn prayer 71
To have it added to the faults of mine,
And nothing of your answer.
  Ang Nay, but hear me.
Your sense pursues not mine : either you are
  ignorant,
Or seem so craftily ; and that's not good.
  Isab. Let me be ignorant, and in nothing
  good,
But graciously to know I am no better.
  Ang. Thus wisdom wishes to appear most
  bright
When it doth tax itself , as these black masks
Proclaim an enshield beauty ten times louder
Than beauty could, display'd But mark me ;
To be received plain, I'll speak more gross :
Your brother is to die.
  Isab. So.
  Ang. And his offence is so, as it appears,

Accountant to the law upon that pain.
  Isab True.
  Ang. Admit no other way to save his life,—
As I subscribe not that, nor any other,
But in the loss of question,—that you, his sis-
  ter, 90
Finding yourself desired of such a person,
Whose credit with the judge, or own great
  place,
Could fetch your brother from the manacles
Of the all-building law ; and that there were
No earthly mean to save him, but that either
You must lay down the treasures of your body
To this supposed, or else to let him suffer ,
What would you do ?
  Isab. As much for my poor brother as my-
  self 100
That is, were I under the terms of death,
The impression of keen whips I'ld wear as
  rubies,
And strip myself to death, as to a bed
That longing have been sick for, ere I'ld yield
My body up to shame
  Ang Then must your brother die.
  Isab. And 'twere the cheaper way :
Better it were a brother died at once,
Than that a sister, by redeeming him,
Should die for ever.
  Ang Were not you then as cruel as the
  sentence
That you have slander'd so ? 110
  Isab Ignomy in ransom and free pardon
Are of two houses : lawful mercy
Is nothing kin to foul redemption.
  Ang You seem'd of late to make the law
  a tyrant ,
And rather proved the sliding of your brother
A merriment than a vice
  Isab. O, pardon me, my lord ; it oft falls
  out,
To have what we would have, we speak not
  what we mean
I something do excuse the thing I hate,
For his advantage that I dearly love 120
  Ang. We are all frail
  Isab Else let my brother die,
If not a feodary, but only he
Owe and succeed thy weakness.
  Ang. Nay, women are frail too.
  Isab. Ay, as the glasses where they view
  themselves ;
Which are as easy broke as they make forms.
Women ! Help Heaven ! men their creation
  mar
In profiting by them. Nay, call us ten times
  frail ;
For we are soft as our complexions are,
And credulous to false prints.
  Ang. I think it well : 130
And from this testimony of your own sex,—
Since I suppose we are made to be no stronger
Than faults may shake our frames,—let me
  be bold ;
I do arrest your words Be that you are,
That is, a woman ; if you be more, you're
  none ;

If you be one, as you are well express'd
By all external warrants, show it now,
By putting on the destined livery.   [lord,
    Isab I have no tongue but one : gentle my
Let me entreat you speak the former lan-
    guage   140
    Ang Plainly conceive, I love you.
    Isab My brother did love Juliet,
And you tell me that he shall die for it.
    Ang. He shall not, Isabel, if you give me
        love
    Isab I know your virtue hath a license in't,
Which seems a little fouler than it is,
To pluck on others
    Ang   Believe me, on mine honor,
My words express my purpose.   [lieved,
    Isab. Ha ! little honor to be much be-
And most pernicious purpose !   Seeming,
    seeming !   150
I will proclaim thee, Angelo ; look for't ·
Sign me a present pardon for my brother,
Or with an outstretch'd throat I'll tell the
        world aloud
What man thou art
    Ang.   Who will believe thee, Isabel ?
My unsoil'd name, the austereness of my life,
My vouch against you, and my place i' the
        state,
Will so your accusation overweigh,
That you shall stifle in your own report
And smell of calumny   I have begun,
And now I give my sensual race the rein · 160
Fit thy consent to my sharp appetite ,
Lay by all nicety and prolixious blushes,
That banish what they sue for , redeem thy
        brother
By yielding up thy body to my will ;
Or else he must not only die the death,
But thy unkindness shall his death draw out
To lingering sufferance. Answer me to-mor-
        row,
Or, by the affection that now guides me most,
I'll prove a tyrant to him. As for you,
Say what you can, my false o'erweighs your
        true.   [*Exit* 170
    Isab. To whom should I complain ? Did I
        tell this,
Who would believe me ? O perilous mouths,
That bear in them one and the self-same
        tongue,
Either of condemnation or approof ;
Bidding the law make court'sy to their will
Hooking both right and wrong to the appetite,
To follow as it draws ! I'll to my brother .
Though he hath fallen by prompture of the
        blood,
Yet hath he in him such a mind of honor,
That, had he twenty heads to tender down 180
On twenty bloody blocks, he'ld yield them up,
Before his sister should her body stoop
To such abhorr'd pollution
Then, Isabel, live chaste, and, brother, die :
More than our brother is our chastity.
I'll tell him yet of Angelo's request,
And fit his mind to death, for his soul's rest.
                                    [*Exit.*

ACT III.

SCENE I   *A room in the prison.*

Enter DUKE *disguised as before,* CLAUDIO,
    and PROVOST

    Duke. So then you hope of pardon from
        Lord Angelo ?
    Claud The miserable have no other medi-
        cine
But only hope
I've hope to live, and am prepared to die.
    Duke Be absolute for death ; either death
        or life
Shall thereby be the sweeter. Reason thus
    with life :
If I do lose thee, I do lose a thing
That none but fools would keep . a breath thou
    art,
Servile to all the skyey influences,   9
That dost this habitation, where thou keep'st,
Hourly afflict · merely, thou art death's fool ;
For him thou labor'st by thy flight to shun
And yet runn'st toward him still. Thou art
    not noble ,
For all the accommodations that thou bear'st
Are nursed by baseness. Thou'rt by no means
    valiant ;
For thou dost fear the soft and tender fork
Of a poor worm. Thy best of rest is sleep,
And that thou oft provokest , yet grossly
    fear'st
Thy death, which is no more   Thou art not
    thyself ;   19
For thou exist'st on many a thousand grains
That issue out of dust   Happy thou art not ;
For what thou hast not, still thou strivest to
    get,
And what thou hast, forget'st. · Thou art not
    certain ;
For thy complexion shifts to strange effects,
After the moon   If thou art rich, thou'rt
    poor ;
For, like an ass whose back with ingots bows,
Thou bear'st thy heavy riches but a journey,
And death unloads thee, Friend hast thou
    none ;
For thine own bowels, which do call thee sire,
The mere effusion of thy proper loins,   30
Do curse the gout, serpigo, and the rheum,
For ending thee no sooner. Thou hast nor
    youth nor age
But, as it were, an after-dinner's sleep,
Dreaming on both , for all thy blessed youth
Becomes as aged, and doth beg the alms
Of palsied eld , and when thou art old and
    rich,
Thou hast neither heat, affection, limb, nor
    beauty,
To make thy riches pleasant. What's yet in
    this
That bears the name of life ? Yet in this life
Lie hid moe thousand deaths : yet death we
    fear,
That makes these odds all even.   41
    Claud.   I humbly thank you.

To sue to live, I find I seek to die ;
And, seeking death, find life let it come on
  Isab. [*Within*] What, ho! Peace here ,
  grace and good company !
  Prov. Who's there ? come in· the wish
  deserves a welcome
  Duke. Dear sir, ere long I'll visit you
  again
  Claud. Most holy sir, I thank you.

Enter ISABELLA.

  Isab. My business is a word or two with
  Claudio
  Prov And very welcome Look, signior,
  here's your sister
  Duke. Provost, a word with you   50
  Prov. As many as you please
  Duke Bring me to hear them speak, where
I may be concealed
      [*Exeunt Duke and Provost.*
  Claud Now, sister, what's the comfort ?
  Isab.   Why,
As all comforts are , most good, most good in-
  deed
Lord Angelo, having affairs to heaven,
Intends you for his swift ambassador,
Where you shall be an everlasting leiger
Therefore your best appointment make with
  speed ,   60
To-morrow you set on
  Claud.   Is there no remedy ?
  Isab None, but such remedy as, to save
  a head,
To cleave a heart in twain
  Claud   But is there any ?
  Isab. Yes, brother, you may live
There is a devilish mercy in the judge,
If you'll implore it that will free your life,
But fetter you till death
  Claud   Perpetual durance?
  Isab Ay, just, perpetual durance, a re-
  straint,
Though all the world's vastidity you had.
To a determined scope
  Claud   But in what nature ? 70
  Isab In such a one as, you consenting to't,
Would bark your honor from that trunk you
  bear,
And leave you naked
  Claud.   Let me know the point
  Isab O, I do fear thee, Claudio, and I
  quake,
Lest thou a feverous life shouldst entertain,
And six or seven winters more respect
Than a perpetual honor Darest thou die ?
The sense of death is most in apprehension ;
And the poor beetle, that we tread upon,
In corporal sufferance finds a pang as great 80
As when a giant dies
  Claud   Why give you me this shame ?
Think you I can a resolution fetch
From flowery tenderness ? If I must die
I will encounter darkness as a bride,
And hug it in mine arms.
  Isab There spake my brother ; there my
    father's grave

Did utter forth a voice. Yes, thou must die :
Thou art too noble to conserve a life
In base appliances This outward-sainted
  deputy,
Whose settled visage and deliberate word 90
Nips youth i' the head and follies doth em-
  mew
As falcon doth the fowl, is yet a devil ;
His filth within being cast, he would appear
A pond as deep as hell
  Claud   The prenzie Angelo !
  Isab O, 'tis the cunning livery of hell,
The damned'st body to invest and cover
In prenzie guards! Dost thou think, Claudio?
If I would yield him my virginity,
Thou mightst be freed
  Claud.   O heavens ! it cannot be
  Isab. Yes, he would give 't thee, from this
    rank offence, 100
So to offend him still This night's the time
That I should do what I abhor to name,
Or else thou diest to-morrow.
  Claud   Thou shalt not do't.
  Isab. O, were it but my life,
I'ld throw it down for your deliverance
As frankly as a pin
  Claud   Thanks, dear Isabel.
  Isab. Be ready, Claudio, for your death
    to-morrow
  Claud Yes Has he affections in him,
That thus can make him bite the law by the
  nose,
When he would force it? Sure, it is no sin, 110
Or of the deadly seven, it is the least
  Isab Which is the least?
  Claud If it were damnable, he being so
  wise,
Why would he for the momentary trick
Be perdurably fined ? O Isabel !
  Isab What says my brother ?
  Claud   Death is a fearful thing.
  Isab And shamed life a hateful
  Claud Ay, but to die, and go we know not
  where ,
To lie in cold obstruction and to rot ,
This sensible warm motion to become 120
A kneaded clod , and the delighted spirit
To bathe in fiery floods, or to reside
In thrilling region of thick-ribbed ice ,
To be imprison'd in the viewless winds,
And blown with restless violence round about
The pendent world , or to be worse than
  worst
Of those that lawless and uncertain thought
Imagine howling 'tis too horrible !
The weariest and most loathed worldly life
That age, ache, penury and imprisonment 130
Can lay on nature is a paradise
To what we fear of death.
  Isab. Alas, alas !
  Claud   Sweet sister, let me live:
What sin you do to save a brother's life,
Nature dispenses with the deed so far
That it becomes a virtue
  Isab.   O you beast !
O faithless coward ! O dishonest wretch !

Wilt thou be made a man out of my vice ?
Is't not a kind of incest, to take life
From thine own sister's shame ? What should
   I think ?   140
Heaven shield my mother play'd my father
   fair !
For such a warped slip of wilderness
Ne'er issued from his blood. Take my de-
   fiance !
Die, perish ! Might but my bending down
Reprieve thee from thy fate, it should pro-
   ceed :
I'll pray a thousand prayers for thy death,
No word to save thee.
   Claud.   Nay, hear me, Isabel.
   Isab.   O, fie, fie, fie !
Thy sin's not accidental, but a trade.
Mercy to thee would prove itself a bawd : 150
'Tis best thou diest quickly.
   Claud.   O hear me, Isabella !

            Re-enter Duke.

   Duke.   Vouchsafe a word, young sister, but
one word.
   Isab.   What is your will ?
   Duke.   Might you dispense with your leisure, I would by and by have some speech with
you : the satisfaction I would require is likewise your own benefit.
   Isab.   I have no superfluous leisure; my stay
must be stolen out of other affairs ; but I will
attend you awhile.   [*Walks apart.*
   Duke.   Son, I have overheard what hath
passed between you and your sister. Angelo
had never the purpose to corrupt her ; only he
hath made an essay of her virtue to practise
his judgment with the disposition of natures:
she, having the truth of honor in her, hath
made him that gracious denial which he is
most glad to receive. I am confessor to Angelo, and I know this to be true ; therefore
prepare yourself to death : do not satisfy
your resolution with hopes that are fallible :
to-morrow you must die ; go to your knees
and make ready.
   Claud.   Let me ask my sister pardon. I am
so out of love with life that I will sue to be rid
of it.
   Duke.   Hold you there : farewell.   [*Exit
Claudio.*]   Provost, a word with you !

            Re-enter Provost.

   Prov.   What's your will, father ?
   Duke.   That now you are come, you will be
gone. Leave me awhile with the maid : my
mind promises with my habit no loss shall
touch her by my company.
   Prov.   In good time.
   [*Exit Provost. Isabella comes forward.*
   Duke.   The hand that hath made you fair
hath made you good : the goodness that is
cheap in beauty makes beauty brief in goodness ; but grace, being the soul of your complexion, shall keep the body of it ever fair.
The assault that Angelo hath made to you,
fortune hath conveyed to my understanding ;
and, but that frailty hath examples for his

falling, I should wonder at Angelo. How will
you do to content this substitute, and to save
your brother ?
   Isab.   I am now going to resolve him: I had
rather my brother die by the law than my son
should be unlawfully born. But, O, how much
is the good duke deceived in Angelo ! If ever
he return and I can speak to him, I will open
my lips in vain, or discover his government.
   Duke.   That shall not be much amiss : yet,
as the matter now stands, he will avoid your
accusation ; he made trial of you only. Therefore fasten your ear on my advisings : to the
love I have in doing good a remedy presents
itself. I do make myself believe that you
may most uprighteously do a poor wronged
lady a merited benefit ; redeem your brother
from the angry law; do no stain to your own
gracious person ; and much please the absent
duke, if peradventure he shall ever return to
have hearing of this business.   211
   Isab.   Let me hear you speak farther. I
have spirit to do anything that appears not
foul in the truth of my spirit.
   Duke.   Virtue is bold, and goodness never
fearful. Have you not heard speak of Mariana, the sister of Frederick the great soldier
who miscarried at sea ?
   Isab.   I have heard of the lady, and good
words went with her name.   220
   Duke.   She should this Angelo have married ; was affianced to her by oath, and the
nuptial appointed : between which time of the
contract and limit of the solemnity, her brother
Frederick was wrecked at sea, having in that
perished vessel the dowry of his sister. But
mark how heavily this befell to the poor gentlewoman : there she lost a noble and renowned
brother, in his love toward her ever most kind
and natural ; with him, the portion and sinew
of her fortune, her marriage-dowry ; with
both, her combinate husband, this well-seeming
Angelo.
   Isab.   Can this be so ? did Angelo so leave
her ?
   Duke.   Left her in her tears, and dried not one
of them with his comfort ; swallowed his vows
whole, pretending in her discoveries of dishonor : in few, bestowed her on her own
lamentation, which she yet wears for his sake;
and he, a marble to her tears, is washed with
them, but relents not.
   Isab.   What a merit were it in death to take
this poor maid from the world ! What corruption in this life, that it will let this man
live ! But how out of this can she avail ?
   Duke.   It is a rupture that you may easily
heal : and the cure of it not only saves your
brother, but keeps you from dishonor in doing
it.
   Isab.   Show me how, good father.
   Duke.   This forenamed maid hath yet in
her the continuance of her first affection: his
unjust unkindness, that in all reason should
have quenched her love, hath, like an impediment in the current, made it more violent and

unruly. Go you to Angelo; answer his requiring with a plausible obedience; agree with his demands to the point, only refer yourself to this advantage, first, that your stay with him may not be long, that the time may have all shadow and silence in it, and the place answer to convenience. This being granted in course,—and now follows all,—we shall advise this wronged maid to stead up your appointment, go in your place, if the encounter acknowledge itself hereafter, it may compel him to her recompense and here, by this, is your brother saved, your honor untainted, the poor Mariana advantaged, and the corrupt deputy scaled. The maid will I frame and make fit for his attempt. If you think well to carry this as you may, the doubleness of the benefit defends the deceit from reproof. What think you of it?

Isab. The image of it gives me content already, and I trust it will grow to a most prosperous perfection.

Duke. It lies much in your holding up. Haste you speedily to Angelo; if for this night he entreat you to his bed, give him promise of satisfaction. I will presently to Saint Luke's: there, at the moated grange, resides this dejected Mariana. At that place call upon me, and dispatch with Angelo, that it may be quickly.

Isab. I thank you for this comfort. Fare you well, good father. [*Exeunt severally.* 281

SCENE II. *The street before the prison.*

Enter, on one side, DUKE *disguised as before, on the other,* ELBOW, *and Officers with* POMPEY.

Elb. Nay, if there be no remedy for it, but that you will needs buy and sell men and women like beasts, we shall have all the world drink brown and white bastard.

Duke. O heavens! what stuff is here?

Pom. 'Twas never merry world since, of two usuries, the merriest was put down, and the worser allowed by order of law a furred gown to keep him warm, and furred with fox and lamb-skins too, to signify, that craft, being richer than innocency, stands for the facing.   11

Elb. Come your way, sir. 'Bless you, good father friar.

Duke. And you, good brother father. What offence hath this man made you, sir?

Elb. Marry, sir, he hath offended the law: and, sir, we take him to be a thief too, sir, for we have found upon him, sir, a strange picklock, which we have sent to the deputy.

Duke. Fie, sirrah! a bawd, a wicked bawd! The evil that thou causest to be done,   21
That is thy means to live. Do thou but think
What 'tis to cram a maw or clothe a back
From such a filthy vice: say to thyself,
From their abominable and beastly touches
I drink, I eat, array myself, and live.
Canst thou believe thy living is a life,
So stinkingly depending? Go mend, go mend.

Pom. Indeed, it does stink in some sort, sir; but yet, sir, I would prove—   30

Duke. Nay, if the devil have given thee proofs for sin,
Thou wilt prove his. Take him to prison, officer:
Correction and instruction must both work
Ere this rude beast will profit.

Elb. He must before the deputy, sir; he has given him warning: the deputy cannot abide a whoremaster: if he be a whoremonger, and comes before him, he were as good go a mile on his errand.

Duke. That we were all, as some would seem to be,   40
From our faults, as faults from seeming, free!

Elb. His neck will come to your waist,—a cord, sir.

Pom. I spy comfort, I cry bail. Here's a gentleman and a friend of mine.

Enter LUCIO

Lucio. How now, noble Pompey! What, at the wheels of Cæsar? art thou led in triumph? What, is there none of Pygmalion's images, newly made woman, to be had now, for putting the hand in the pocket and extracting it clutched? What reply, ha? What sayest thou to this tune, matter and method? Is't not drowned i' the last rain, ha? What sayest thou, Trot? Is the world as it was, man? Which is the way? Is it sad, and few words? or how? The trick of it?

Duke. Still thus, and thus, still worse!

Lucio. How doth my dear morsel, thy mistress? Procures she still, ha?

Pom. Troth, sir, she hath eaten up all her beef, and she is herself in the tub.

Lucio. Why, 'tis good, it is the right of it, it must be so: ever your fresh whore and your powdered bawd: an unshunned consequence; it must be so. Art going to prison, Pompey?

Pom. Yes, faith, sir.

Lucio. Why, 'tis not amiss, Pompey. Farewell go, say I sent thee thither. For debt, Pompey? or how?

Elb. For being a bawd, for being a bawd.

Lucio. Well, then, imprison him: if imprisonment be the due of a bawd, why, 'tis his right: bawd is he doubtless, and of antiquity too, bawd-born. Farewell, good Pompey. Commend me to the prison, Pompey: you will turn good husband now, Pompey; you will keep the house.

Pom. I hope, sir, your good worship will be my bail.

Lucio. No, indeed, will I not, Pompey; it is not the wear. I will pray, Pompey, to increase your bondage: if you take it not patiently, why, your mettle is the more. Adieu, trusty Pompey. 'Bless you, friar.   81

Duke. And you.

Lucio. Does Bridget paint still, Pompey, ha?

Elb. Come your ways, sir; come.

Pom. You will not bail me, then, sir ?

Lucio Then, Pompey, nor now What news abroad, friar ? what news ?

Elb. Come your ways, sir, come

Lucio Go to kennel, Pompey, go. [*Exeunt Elbow, Pompey and Officers.*] What news, friar, of the duke ?   91

Duke I know none Can you tell me of any ?

Lucio. Some say he is with the Emperor of Russia ; other some, he is in Rome. but where is he, think you ?

Duke I know not where; but wheresoever, I wish him well.

Lucio It was a mad fantastical trick of him to steal from the state, and usurp the beggary he was never born to. Lord Angelo dukes it well in his absence ; he puts transgression to 't.   101

Duke. He does well in 't

Lucio. A little more lenity to lechery would do no harm in him . something too crabbed that way, friar.   [must cure it

Duke It is too general a vice, and severity

Lucio. Yes, in good sooth, the vice is of a great kindred ; it is well allied but it is impossible to extirp it quite, friar, till eating and drinking be put down, They say this Angelo was not made by man and woman after this downright way of creation · is it true, think you ?

Duke. How should he be made, then ?

Lucio Some report a sea-maid spawned him ; some, that he was begot between two stock-fishes. But it is certain that when he makes water his urine is congealed ice ; that I know to be true : † and he is a motion generative ; that's infallible.   [apace

Duke You are pleasant, sir, and speak

Lucio Why, what a ruthless thing is this in him, for the rebellion of a codpiece to take away the life of a man ! Would the duke that is absent have done this ? Ere he would have hanged a man for the getting a hundred bastards, he would have paid for the nursing a thousand · he had some feeling of the sport he knew the service, and that instructed him to mercy.

Duke I never heard the absent duke much detected for women ‗he was not inclined that way.

Lucio. O, sir, you are deceived   131

Duke 'Tis not possible. '

Lucio. Who, not the duke ? yes, your beggar of fifty, and his use was to put a ducat in her clack-dish. the duke had crotchets in him He would be drunk too ; that let me inform you

Duke. You do him wrong, surely.

Lucio. Sir, I was an inward of his. A shy fellow was the duke and I believe I know the cause of his withdrawing.   140

Duke What, I prithee, might be the cause ?

Lucio. No, pardon ; 'tis a secret must be locked within the teeth and the lips : but this

I can let you understand, the greater file of the subject held the duke to be wise

Duke. Wise ! why, no question but he was.

Lucio. A very superficial, ignorant, unweighing fellow.

Duke. Either this is envy in you, folly, or mistaking · the very stream of his life and the business he hath helmed must upon a warranted need give him a better proclamation. Let him be but testimonied in his own bringings-forth, and he shall appear to the envious a scholar, a statesman and a soldier Therefore you speak unskilfully , or if your knowledge be more it is much darkened in your malice

Lucio Sir, I know him, and I love him,

Duke Love talks with better knowledge, and knowledge with dearer love.   160

Lucio Come, sir, I know what I know.

Duke. I can hardly believe that, since you know not what you speak But, if ever the duke return as our prayers are he may, let me desire you to make your answer before him If it be honest you have spoke, you have courage to maintain it: I am bound to call upon you , and, I pray you, your name ?

Lucio Sir, my name is Lucio ; well known to the duke   170

Duke. He shall know you better, sir, if I may live to report you.

Lucio. I fear you not.

Duke. O, you hope the duke will return no more , or you imagine me too unhurtful an opposite But indeed I can do you little harm; you 'll forswear this again

Lucio I'll be hanged first : thou art deceived in me, friar. But no more of this Canst thou tell if Claudio die to-morrow or no ?   180

Duke. Why should he die, sir ?

Lucio. Why ? For filling a bottle with a tundish I would the duke we talk of were returned again : the ungenitured agent will unpeople the province with continency . sparrows must not build in his house-eaves, because they are lecherous. The duke yet would have dark deeds darkly answered , he would never bring them to light : would he were returned ! Marry, this Claudio is condemned for untrussing Farewell, good friar: I prithee, pray for me. The duke, I say to thee again, would eat mutton on Fridays. He's not past it yet, and I say to thee, he would mouth with a beggar, though she smelt brown bread and garlic say that I said so. Farewell.   [*Exit.*

Duke. No might nor greatness in mortality Can censure 'scape ; back-wounding calumny The whitest virtue strikes What king so strong

Can tie the gall up in the slanderous tongue ? But who comes here ?   ⁻ 200

Enter Escalus, Provost, *and* Officers *with* Mistress Overdone

Escal. Go ; away with her to prison .

Mrs. Ov. Good my lord, be good to me, your honor is accounted a merciful man ; good my lord

Escal. Double and treble admonition, and still forfeit in the same kind ! This would make mercy swear and play the tyrant

Prov A bawd of eleven years' continuance, may it please your honor

Mrs Ov. My lord, this is one Lucio's information against me Mistress Kate Keepdown was with child by him in the duke's time, he promised her marriage his child is a year and a quarter old, come Philip and Jacob : I have kept it myself ; and see how he goes about to abuse me !

Escal. That fellow is a fellow of much license : let him be called before us　Away with her to prison ! Go to, no more words. [*Exeunt Officers with Mistress Ov*] Provost, my brother Angelo will not be altered, Claudio must die to-morrow. let him be furnished with divines, and have all charitable preparation. If my brother wrought by my pity, it should not be so with him.

Prov. So please you, this friar hath been with him, and advised him for the entertainment of death

Escal. Good even, good father

Duke. Bliss and goodness on you !

Escal. Of whence are you ?

Duke. Not of this country, though my chance is now　　　　　　　　　　　260
To use it for my time　I am a brother
Of gracious order, late come from the See
In special business from his holiness

Escal. What news abroad i' the world ?

Duke. None, but that there is so great a fever on goodness, that the dissolution of it must cure it　novelty is only in request, and it is as dangerous to be aged in any kind of course, as it is virtuous to be constant in any undertaking　There is scarce truth enough alive to make societies secure ; but security enough to make fellowships accurst　much upon this riddle runs the wisdom of the world This news is old enough, yet it is every day's news. I pray you, sir, of what disposition was the duke ?

Escal One that, above all other strifes, contended especially to know himself

Duke What pleasure was he given to ?

Escal Rather rejoicing to see another merry, than merry at any thing which professed to make him rejoice . a gentleman of all temperance. But leave we him to his events, with a prayer they may prove prosperous ; and let me desire to know how you find Claudio prepared　I am made to understand that you have lent him visitation

Duke. He professes to have received no sinister measure from his judge, but most willingly humbles himself to the determination of justice · yet had he framed to himself, by the instruction of his frailty, many deceiving promises of life, which I by my good leisure

have discredited to him, and now is he resolved to die.

Escal. You have paid the heavens your function, and the prisoner the very debt of your calling. I have labored for the poor gentleman to the extremest shore of my modesty . but my brother justice have I found so severe, that he hath forced me to tell him he is indeed Justice.

Duke If his own life answer the straitness of his proceeding, it shall become him well, wherein if he chance to fail, he hath sentenced himself

Escal I am going to visit the prisoner. Fare you well

Duke Peace be with you !
　　　　　[*Exeunt Esculus and Provost.*
He who the sword of heaven will bear
Should be as holy as severe ;
Pattern in himself to know,
†Grace to stand, and virtue go ;
More nor less to others paying
Than by self-offences weighing　　　　　　280
Shame to him whose cruel striking
Kills for faults of his own liking !
Twice treble shame on Angelo,
To weed my vice and let his grow !
O, what may man within him hide,
Though angel on the outward side !
†How may likeness made in crimes,
Making practice on the times,
To draw with idle spiders' strings
Most ponderous and substantial things !　290
Craft against vice I must apply .
With Angelo to-night shall lie
His old betrothed but despised ;
† So disguise shall, by the disguised,
Pay with falsehood false exacting,
And perform an old contracting.　　　　[*Exit.*

ACT IV.

SCENE I. *The moated grange at* ST LUKE'S
　　　　Enter MARIANA *and a* BOY.

BOY *sings.*

Take, O, take those lips away,
　That so sweetly were forsworn ;
And those eyes, the break of day,
　Lights that do mislead the morn :
But my kisses bring again, bring again .
Seals of love, but sealed in vain, sealed in
　vain.

Mari Break off thy song, and haste thee quick away :
Here comes a man of comfort, whose advice
Hath often still'd my brawling discontent.
　　　　　　　　　　　　[*Exit Boy.*

Enter DUKE *disguised as before.*

I cry you mercy, sir, and well could wish　10
You had not found me here so musical :
Let me excuse me, and believe me so,
My mirth it much displeased, but pleased my
　woe

Duke. 'Tis good ; though music oft hath
　　such a charm
To make bad good, and good provoke to harm.
I pray you, tell me, hath any body inquired
　for me here to-day ? much upon this time
have I promised here to meet.
　Mari. You have not been inquired after : I
have sat here all day. 　　　　　　　　　20

Enter ISABELLA.

　Duke. I do constantly believe you. The
time is come even now. I shall crave your
forbearance a little : may be I will call upon
you anon, for some advantage to yourself.
　Mari. I am always bound to you. 　[*Exit.*
　Duke. Very well met, and well come.
What is the news from this good deputy ?
　Isab. He hath a garden circummured with
　brick,
Whose western side is with a vineyard back'd ;
And to that vineyard is a planched gate, 　30
That makes his opening with this bigger key :
This other doth command a little door
Which from the vineyard to the garden leads ;
There have I made my promise
Upon the heavy middle of the night
To call upon him.
　Duke. 　　　But shall you on your knowledge
　find this way ?
　Isab. I have ta'en a due and wary note
　upon't :
With whispering and most guilty diligence,
In action all of precept, he did show me 　40
The way twice o'er.
　Duke. 　　　Are there no other tokens
Between you 'greed concerning her observ-
　ance ?
　Isab. No, none, but only a repair i' the
　dark ;
And that I have possess'd him my most stay
Can be but brief ; for I have made him know
I have a servant comes with me along,
That stays upon me, whose persuasion is
I come about my brother.
　Duke. 　　　'Tis well borne up.
I have not yet made known to Mariana
A word of this. What, ho ! within ! come
　forth ! 　　　　　　　　　　　　　50

Re-enter MARIANA.

I pray you, be acquainted with this maid ;
She comes to do you good.
　Isab. 　　　　　I do desire the like.
　Duke. Do you persuade yourself that I re-
　spect you ?
　Mari. Good friar, I know you do, and have
　found it.
　Duke. Take, then, this your companion by
　the hand,
Who hath a story ready for your ear.
I shall attend your leisure : but make haste ;
The vaporous night approaches.
　Mari. Will't please you walk aside ?
　　　　　　[*Exeunt Mariana and Isabella.*
　Duke. O place and greatness ! millions of
　false eyes 　　　　　　　　　　60

Are stuck upon thee : volumes of report
Run with these false and most contrarious
　quests
Upon thy doings : thousand escapes of wit
Make thee the father of their idle dreams,
And rack thee in their fancies.

Re-enter MARIANA *and* ISABELLA.

　　　　　　　　Welcome, how agreed ?
　Isab. She 'll take the enterprise upon her,
　father,
If you advise it.
　Duke. 　　　It is not my consent,
But my entreaty too.
　Isab. 　　　　　Little have you to say
When you depart from him, but, soft and
　low,
' Remember now my brother.'
　Mari. 　　　　　　Fear me not. 70
　Duke. Nor, gentle-daughter, fear you not
　at all.
He is your husband on a pre-contract :
To bring you thus together, 'tis no sin,
Sith that the justice of your title to him
Doth flourish the deceit. Come, let us go :
Our corn 's to reap, for yet our tithe's to sow.
　　　　　　　　　　　　　[*Exeunt.*

SCENE II.　*A room in the prison.*

Enter PROVOST *and* POMPEY.

　Prov. Come hither, sirrah. Can you cut
off a man's head ?
　Pom. If the man be a bachelor, sir, I can ;
but if he be a married man, he's his wife's
head, and I can never cut off a woman's head.
　Prov. Come, sir, leave me your snatches,
and yield me a direct answer. To-morrow
morning are to die Claudio and Barnardine.
Here is in our prison a common executioner,
who in his office lacks a helper : if you will
take it on you to assist him, it shall redeem
you from your gyves ; if not, you shall have
your full time of imprisonment and your deliverance with an unpitied whipping, for you
have been a notorious bawd.
　Pom. Sir, I have been an unlawful bawd
time out of mind ; but yet I will be content to
be a lawful hangman. I would be glad to receive some instruction from my fellow partner.
　Prov. What, ho ! Abhorson ! Where's Abhorson, there ? 　　　　　　　　21

Enter ABHORSON.

　Abhor. Do you call, sir ?
　Prov. Sirrah, here's a fellow will help you
to-morrow in your execution. If you think it
meet, compound with him by the year, and
let him abide here with you ; if not, use him
for the present and dismiss him. He cannot
plead his estimation with you ; he hath been
a bawd.
　Abhor. A bawd, sir ? fie upon him ! he
will discredit our mystery. 　　　　30
　Prov. Go to, sir ; you weigh equally ; a
feather will turn the scale. 　　　　[*Exit.*

Pom. Pray, sir, by your good favor,—for surely, sir, a good favor you have, but that you have a hanging look,—do you call, sir, your occupation a mystery?

Abhor. Ay, sir ; a mystery.

Pom. Painting, sir, I have heard say, is a mystery ; and your whores, sir, being members of my occupation, using painting, do prove my occupation a mystery : but what mystery there should be in hanging, if I should be hanged, I cannot imagine.

Abhor. Sir, it is a mystery.

Pom. Proof?

Abhor. Every true man's apparel fits your thief : if it be too little for your thief, your true man thinks it big enough ; if it be too big for your thief, your thief thinks it little enough : so every true man's apparel fits your thief.   50

Re-enter PROVOST.

Prov. Are you agreed?

Pom. Sir, I will serve him ; for I do find your hangman is a more penitent trade than your bawd ; he doth oftener ask forgiveness.

Prov. You, sirrah, provide your block and your axe to-morrow four o'clock.

Abhor. Come on, bawd ; I will instruct thee in my trade ; follow.

Pom. I do desire to learn, sir : and I hope, if you have occasion to use me for your own turn, you shall find me yare ; for truly, sir, for your kindness I owe you a good turn.

Prov. Call hither Barnardine and Claudio :
    [*Exeunt Pompey and Abhorson.*
The one has my pity ; not a jot the other, Being a murderer, though he were my brother.

Enter CLAUDIO.

Look, here's the warrant, Claudio, for thy death :
'Tis now dead midnight, and by eight to-morrow
Thou must be made immortal. Where's Barnardine?

Claud. As fast lock'd up in sleep as guiltless labor
When it lies starkly in the traveller's bones :
He will not wake.   71

Prov.   Who can do good on him?

Well, go, prepare yourself. [*Knocking within.*]
    But, hark, what noise?

Heaven give your spirits comfort! [*Exit Claudio.*] By and by,
I hope it is some pardon or reprieve
For the most gentle Claudio.

Enter DUKE *disguised as before.*

        Welcome, father.

Duke. The best and wholesomest spirits of the night
Envelope you, good Provost! Who call'd here of late?

Prov. None, since the curfew rung.

Duke. Not Isabel?

Prov.   No.

Duke.   They will, then, ere't be long.

Prov. What comfort is for Claudio?   80

Duke. There's some in hope.

Prov.   It is a bitter deputy.

Duke. Not so, not so ; his life is parallel'd
Even with the stroke and line of his great justice :
He doth with holy abstinence subdue
That in himself which he spurs on his power
To qualify in others : were he meal'd with that
Which he corrects, then were he tyrannous ;
But this being so, he's just. [*Knocking within.*
        Now are they come.
        [*Exit Provost.*
This is a gentle provost : seldom when
The steeled gaoler is the friend of men. .
        [*Knocking within.* 90
How now! what noise? That spirit's possessed with haste
That wounds the unsisting postern with these strokes.

Re-enter PROVOST.

Prov. There he must stay until the officer
Arise to let him in : he is call'd up.

Duke. Have you no countermand for Claudio yet,
But he must die to-morrow?

Prov.   None, sir, none.

Duke. As near the dawning, provost, as it is,
You shall hear more ere morning.

Prov.   Happily
You something know ; yet I believe there comes
No countermand ; no such example have we:
Besides, upon the very siege of justice   101
Lord Angelo hath to the public ear
Profess'd the contrary.

Enter a MESSENGER.

        This is his lordship's man.

Duke. And here comes Claudio's pardon.

Mes. [*Giving a paper.*] My lord hath sent you this note ; and by me this further charge, that you swerve not from the smallest article of it, neither in time, matter, or other circumstance. Good morrow ; for, as I take it, it is almost day.

Prov. I shall obey him. [*Exit Messenger.*

Duke. [*Aside*] This is his pardon, purchased by such sin
For which the pardoner himself is in.
Hence hath offence his quick celerity,
When it is borne in high authority :
When vice makes mercy, mercy's so extended,
That for the fault's love is the offender friended.
Now, sir, what news?

Prov. I told you. Lord Angelo, belike thinking me remiss in mine office, awakens me with this unwonted putting-on ; methinks strangely, for he hath not used it before.   121

Duke. Pray you, let's hear.

Prov. [*Reads*]

' Whatsoever you may hear to the contrary, let Claudio be executed by four of the clock ; and in the afternoon Barnardine : for my better satisfaction, let me have Claudio's head sent me by five. Let this be duly performed ; with a thought that more depends on it than we must yet deliver. Thus fail not to do your office, as you will answer it at your peril.' 130 What say you to this, sir ?.

Duke. What is that Barnardine who is to be executed in the afternoon ?

Prov. A Bohemian born, but here nursed up and bred ; one that is a prisoner nine years old.

Duke. How came it that the absent duke had not either delivered him to his liberty or executed him ? I have heard it was ever his manner to do so.

Prov. His friends still wrought reprieves for him : and, indeed, his fact, till now in the government of Lord Angelo, came not to an undoubtful proof.

Duke. It is now apparent ?

Prov. Most manifest, and not denied by himself.

Duke. Hath he borne himself penitently in prison ? how seems he to be touched ?

Prov. A man that apprehends death no more dreadfully but as a drunken sleep ; careless, reckless, and fearless of what's past, present, or to come ; insensible of mortality, and desperately mortal.

Duke. He wants advice.

Prov. He will hear none : he hath evermore had the liberty of the prison ; give him leave to escape hence, he would not : drunk many times a day, if not many days entirely drunk. We have very oft awaked him, as if to carry him to execution, and showed him a seeming warrant for it : it hath not moved him at all. 161

Duke. More of him anon. There is written in your brow, provost, honesty and constancy : if I read it not truly, my ancient skill beguiles me ; but, in the boldness of my cunning, I will lay myself in hazard. Claudio, whom here you have warrant to execute, is no greater forfeit to the law than Angelo who hath sentenced him. To make you understand this in a manifested effect, I crave but four days' respite ; for the which you are to do me both a present and a dangerous courtesy.

Prov. Pray, sir, in what ?

Duke. In the delaying death.

Prov. Alack, how may I do it, having the hour limited, and an express command, under penalty, to deliver his head in the view of Angelo ? I may make my case as Claudio's, to cross this in the smallest.

Duke. By the vow of mine order I warrant you, if my instructions may be your guide. Let this Barnardine be this morning executed, and his head borne to Angelo.

Prov. Angelo hath seen them both, and will discover the favor.

Duke. O, death's a great disguiser ; and you may add to it. Shave the head, and tie the beard ; and say it was the desire of the penitent to be so bared before his death : you know the course is common. If any thing fall to you upon this, more than thanks and good fortune, by the saint whom I profess, I will plead against it with my life.

Prov. Pardon me, good father ; it is against my oath. [the deputy ?

Duke. Were you sworn to the duke, or to

Prov. To him, and to his substitutes.

Duke. You will think you have made no offence, if the duke avouch the justice of your dealing ? 201

Prov. But what likelihood is in that ?

Duke. Not a resemblance, but a certainty. Yet since I see you fearful, that neither my coat, integrity, nor persuasion can with ease attempt you, I will go further than I meant, to pluck all fears out of you. Look you, sir, here is the hand and seal of the duke : you know the character, I doubt not ; and the signet is not strange to you.

Prov. I know them both. 210

Duke. The contents of this is the return of the duke : you shall anon over-read it at your pleasure ; where you shall find, within these two days he will be here. This is a thing that Angelo knows not ; for he this very day receives letters of strange tenor ; perchance of the duke's death ; perchance entering into some monastery ; but, by chance, nothing of what is writ. Look, the unfolding star calls up the shepherd. Put not yourself into amazement how these things should be : all difficulties are but easy when they are known. Call your executioner, and off with Barnardine's head : I will give him a present shrift and advise him for a better place. Yet you are amazed ; but this shall absolutely resolve you. Come away ; it is almost clear dawn.

                     [*Exeunt.*

SCENE III. *Another room in the same.*

Enter POMPEY.

Pom. I am as well acquainted here as I was in our house of profession : one would think it were Mistress Overdone's own house, for here be many of her old customers. First, here's young Master Rash ; he's in for a commodity of brown paper and old ginger, ninescore and seventeen pounds ; of which he made five marks, ready money : marry, then ginger was not much in request, for the old women were all dead. Then is there here one Master Caper, at the suit of Master Three-pile the mercer, for some four suits of peach-colored satin, which now peaches him a beggar. Then have we here young Dizy, and young Master Deep-vow, and Master Copperspur, and Master Starve-lackey the rapier and dagger man, and young Drop-heir that killed lusty Pudding, and Master Forthlight the tilter, and brave Master Shooty the great trav-

eller, and wild Half-can that stabbed Pots,
and a think, forty more ; all great doers in
our trade, and are now ' for the Lord's sake '

Enter ABHORSON.

Abhor. Sirrah, bring Barnardine hither.
Pom. Master Barnardine ! you must rise
and be hanged, Master Barnardine !
Abhor. What, ho, Barnardine !
Bar. [*Within*] A pox o' your throats ! Who
makes that noise there ? What are you ?
Pom Your friends, sir, the hangman You
must be so good, sir, to rise and be put to death
Bar. [*Within*] Away, you rogue, away ! I
am sleepy.   31
Abhor. Tell him he must awake, and that
quickly too.
Pom. Pray, Master Barnardine, awake till
you are executed, and sleep afterwards
Abhor. Go in to him, and fetch him out
Pom. He is coming, sir, he is coming ; I
hear his straw rustle.
Abhor. Is the axe upon the block, sirrah ?
Pom. Very ready, sir.   40

Enter BARNARDINE

Bar. How now, Abhorson ? what's the
news with you ?
Abhor. Truly, sir, I would desire you to
clap into your prayers, for, look you, the
warrant's come
Bar. You rogue, I have been drinking all
night, I am not fitted for 't
Pom O, the better, sir, for he that drinks
all night, and is hanged betimes in the morning, may sleep the sounder all the next day
Abhor. Look you, sir ; here comes your
ghostly father · do we jest now, think you ?

Enter DUKE disguised as before

Duke Sir, induced by my charity, and
hearing how hastily you are to depart, I am
come to advise you, comfort you and pray with
you.
Bar Friar, not I : I have been drinking
hard all night, and I will have more time to
prepare me, or they shall beat out my brains
with billets : I will not consent to die this day,
that's certain
Duke. O, sir, you must : and therefore I
   beseech you   60
Look forward on the journey you shall go.
Bar. I swear I will not die to-day for any
man's persuasion
Duke. But hear you
Bar. Not a word · if you have any thing to
say to me, come to my ward, for thence will
not I to-day.   [*Exit.*
Duke. Unfit to live or die O gravel heart !
After him, fellows ; bring him to the block
     [*Exeunt Abhorson and Pompey*

Re-enter PROVOST.

Prov. Now, sir, how do you find the prisoner ?   70
Duke. A creature unprepared, unmeet for
death ;

And to transport him in the mind he is -
Were damnable
  Prov. Here in the prison, father,
There died this morning of a cruel fever
One Ragozine, a most notorious pirate,
A man of Claudio's years, his beard and head
Just of his color What if we do omit
This reprobate till he were well inclined,
And satisfy the deputy with the visage
Of Ragozine, more like to Claudio ?   8
  Duke O, 'tis an accident that heaven pro-
    vides !
Dispatch it presently, the hour draws on
Prefix'd by Angelo see this be done,
And sent according to command, whiles I
Persuade this rude wretch willingly to die.
  Prov. This shall be done, good father, pres-
ently.
But Barnardine must die this afternoon :
And how shall we continue Claudio,
To save me from the danger that might come
If he were known alive ?
  Duke.   Let this be done   90
Put them in secret holds, both Barnardine and
    Claudio
Ere twice the sun hath made his journal greet-
    ing
To the under generation, you shall find
Your safety manifested
  Prov I am your free dependant
  Duke Quick, dispatch, and send the head
    to Angelo   [*Exit Provost.*
Now will I write letters to Angelo,—
The provost, he shall bear them,—whose con-
    tents
Shall witness to him I am near at home,
And that, by great injunctions, I am bound 100
To enter publicly · him I'll desire
To meet me at the consecrated fount
A league below the city, and from thence,
By cold gradation and well-balanced form,
We shall proceed with Angelo.

Re-enter PROVOST.

  Prov Here is the head, I'll carry it myself.
  Duke Convenient is it Make a swift return;
For I would commune with you of such things
That want no ear but yours
  Prov   I'll make all speed   [*Exit.*
  Isab [*Within*] Peace ho, be here !   110
  Duke The tongue of Isabel She's come to
    know
If yet her brother's pardon be come hither :
But I will keep her ignorant of her good,
To make her heavenly comforts of despair,
When it is least expected

Enter ISABELLA.

  Isab   Ho, by your leave !
  Duke Good morning to you, fair and gra-
    cious daughter.
  Isab The better, given me by so holy a man.
Hath yet the deputy sent my brother's pardon?
  Duke He hath released him, Isabel, from
    the world
His head is off and sent to Angelo.   120

Isab. Nay, but it is not so.

Duke. It is no other : show your wisdom,
    daughter,
In your close patience.

Isab. O, I will to him and pluck out his
    eyes !

Duke. You shall not be admitted to his sight.

Isab. Unhappy Claudio ! wretched Isabel !
Injurious world ! most damned Angelo !

Duke. This nor hurts him nor profits you a
    jot ;
Forbear it therefore ; give your cause to
    heaven.
Mark what I say, which you shall find   130
By every syllable a faithful verity :
The duke comes home to-morrow ; nay, dry
    your eyes ;
One of our convent and his confessor,
Gives me this instance : already he hath carried
Notice to Escalus and Angelo,
Who do prepare to meet him at the gates,
There to give up their power. If you can, pace
    your wisdom
In that good path that I would wish it go,
And you shall have your bosom on this wretch,
Grace of the duke, revenges to your heart, 140
And general honor.

Isab.   I am directed by you.

Duke. This letter, then, to Friar Peter give;
'Tis that he sent me of the duke's return :
Say, by this token, I desire his company
At Mariana's house to-night. Her cause and
    yours
I'll perfect him withal, and he shall bring you
Before the duke, and to the head of Angelo
Accuse him home and home. For my poor self,
I am combined by a sacred vow
And shall be absent. Wend you with this
    letter :
Command these fretting waters from your eyes
With a light heart ; trust not my holy order,
If I pervert your course. Who's here ?

Enter LUCIO.

Lucio. Good even. Friar, where's the
provost ?

Duke. Not within, sir.

Lucio. O pretty Isabella, I am pale at mine
heart to see thine eyes so red : thou must be
patient. I am fain to dine and sup with water
and bran ; I dare not for my head fill my
belly ; one fruitful meal would set me to 't.
But they say the duke will be here to-morrow.
By my troth, Isabel, I loved thy brother : if
the old fantastical duke of dark corners had
been at home, he had lived.   [*Exit Isabella.*

Duke. Sir, the duke is marvellous little beholding to your reports ; but the best is, he
lives not in them.

Lucio. Friar, thou knowest not the duke so
well as I do : he's a better woodman than thou
takest him for.   171

Duke. Well, you'll answer this one day.
Fare ye well.

Lucio. Nay, tarry ; I'll go along with thee :
I can tell thee pretty tales of the duke.

Duke. You have told me too many of him
already, sir, if they be true ; if not true, none
were enough.

Lucio. I was once before him for getting a
wench with child.   180

Duke. Did you such a thing ?

Lucio. Yes, marry, did I : but I was fain to
forswear it ; they would else have married me
to the rotten medlar.

Duke. Sir, your company is fairer than
honest. Rest you well.

Lucio. By my troth, I'll go with thee to the
lane's end : if bawdy talk offend you, we'll
have very little of it. Nay, friar, I am a kind
of burr ; I shall stick.   [*Exeunt.* 190

SCENE IV. *A room in* ANGELO'S *house.*

Enter ANGELO *and* ESCALUS.

Escal. Every letter he hath writ hath dis-
vouched other.

Ang. In most uneven and distracted manner.
His actions show much like to madness : pray
heaven his wisdom be not tainted ! And why
meet him at the gates, and redeliver our authorities there ?

Escal. I guess not.

Ang. And why should we proclaim it in an
hour before his entering, that if any crave
redress of injustice, they should exhibit their
petitions in the street ?

Escal. He shows his reason for that : to
have a dispatch of complaints, and to deliver
us from devices hereafter, which shall then
have no power to stand against us.

Ang. Well, I beseech you, let it be proclaimed betimes i' the morn ; I'll call you at
your house : give notice to such men of sort
and suit as are to meet him.   20

Escal. I shall, sir. Fare you well.

Ang. Good night.   [*Exit Escalus.*
This deed unshapes me quite, makes me un-
    pregnant
And dull to all proceedings. A deflower'd
    maid !
And by an eminent body that enforced
The law against it ! But that her tender
    shame
Will not proclaim against her maiden loss,
How might she tongue me ! Yet reason dares
    her no ;
For my authority bears of a credent bulk,
That no particular scandal once can touch 30
But it confounds the breather. He should
    have lived,   [sense,
Save that his riotous youth, with dangerous
Might in the times to come have ta'en revenge,
By so receiving a dishonor'd life
With ransom of such shame. Would yet he
    had lived !
Alack, when once our grace we have forgot,
Nothing goes right : we would, and we would
    not.   [*Exit.*

SCENE V. *Fields without the town.*

Enter DUKE *in his own habit, and* FRIAR
    PETER

Duke. These letters at fit time deliver me :
                         [*Giving letters.*
The provost knows our purpose and our plot
The matter being afoot, keep your instruction,
And hold you ever to our special drift ;
Though sometimes you do blench from this to
    that,
As cause doth minister. Go call at Flavius'
    house,
And tell him where I stay : give the like
    notice
To Valentinus, Rowland, and to Crassus,
And bid them bring the trumpets to the gate ;
But send me Flavius first.
   Fri. P. It shall be speeded well. [*Exit.* 10

Enter VARRIUS.

  Duke. I thank thee, Varrius ; thou hast
made good haste :
Come, we will walk. There's other of our
    friends
Will greet us here anon, my gentle Varrius.
                         [*Exeunt.*

SCENE VI. *Street near the city gate.*

Enter ISABELLA *and* MARIANA.

 Isab. To speak so indirectly I am loath :
I would say the truth ; but to accuse him so,
That is your part : yet I am advised to do it ;
He says, to veil full purpose.
 Mari.   Be ruled by him.
 Isab. Besides, he tells me that, if perad-
    venture
He speak against me on the adverse side,
I should not think it strange ; for 'tis a physic
That's bitter to sweet end.
 Mari. I would Friar Peter—
 Isab.   O, peace ! the friar is come.

Enter FRIAR PETER.

 Fri. P. Come, I have found you out a
    stand most fit,   10
Where you may have such vantage on the
    duke,
He shall not pass you. Twice have the
    trumpets sounded ;
The generous and gravest citizens
Have hent the gates, and very near upon
The duke is entering : therefore, hence, away !
                        [*Exeunt.*

ACT V.

SCENE I. *The city gate.*

MARIANA *veiled,* ISABELLA, *and* FRIAR PETER,
  at their stand. Enter DUKE, VARRIUS,
  LORDS, ANGELO, ESCALUS, LUCIO, PROVOST,
  OFFICERS, *and* CITIZENS, *at several doors.*

 Duke. My very worthy cousin, fairly met !
Our old and faithful friend, we are glad to
    see you.
 Ang. }
 Escal. } Happy return be to your royal grace!

 Duke. Many and hearty thankings to you
    both
We have made inquiry of you ; and we hear
Such goodness of your justice, that our soul
Cannot but yield you forth to public thanks,
Forerunning more requital.
 Ang.   You make my bonds still greater.
 Duke. O, your desert speaks loud ; and I
    should wrong it,
To lock it in the wards of covert bosom,   10
When it deserves, with characters of brass,
A forted residence 'gainst the tooth of time
And razure of oblivion. Give me your hand,
And let the subject see, to make them know
That outward courtesies would fain proclaim
Favors that keep within. Come, Escalus,
You must walk by us on our other hand ;
And good supporters are you.

FRIAR PETER *and* ISABELLA *come forward.*

 Fri. P. Now is your time : speak loud and
    kneel before him.
 Isab. Justice, O royal duke ! Vail your re-
    gard   20
Upon a wrong'd, I would fain have said, a
    maid !
O worthy prince, dishonor not your eye
By throwing it on any other object
Till you have heard me in my true complaint
And given me justice, justice, justice, justice !
 Duke. Relate your wrongs ; in what ? by
    whom ? be brief.
Here is Lord Angelo shall give you justice :
Reveal yourself to him.
 Isab.   O worthy duke,
You bid me seek redemption of the devil :
Hear me yourself ; for that which I must
    speak   30
Must either punish me, not being believed,
Or wring redress from you. Hear me, O hear
    me, here !
 Ang. My lord, her wits, I fear me, are not
    firm :
She hath been a suitor to me for her brother
Cut off by course of justice,—
 Isab.   By course of justice !
 Ang. And she will speak most bitterly and
    strange.
 Isab. Most strange, but yet most truly,
    will I speak :
That Angelo's forsworn ; is it not strange ?
That Angelo's a murderer ; is 't not strange ?
That Angelo is an adulterous thief,   40
An hypocrite, a virgin-violator ;
Is it not strange and strange ?
 Duke.   Nay, it is ten times strange.
 Isab. It is not truer he is Angelo
Than this is all as true as it is strange :
Nay, it is ten times true ; for truth is truth
To the end of reckoning.
 Duke.   Away with her ! Poor soul,
She speaks this in the infirmity of sense.
 Isab. O prince, I conjure thee, as thou be-
    lievest
There is another comfort than this world,
That thou neglect me not, with that opinion

That I am touch'd with madness ! Make not
    impossible   51
That which but seems unlike : 'tis not im-
    possible
But one, the wicked'st caitiff on the ground,
May seem as shy, as grave, as just, as ab-
    solute
As Angelo ; even so may Angelo,
In all his dressings, characts, titles, forms,
Be an arch-villain ; believe it, royal prince :
If he be less, he's nothing ; but he's more,
Had I more name for badness.
    Duke.   By mine honesty,
If she be mad,—as I believe no other,—   60
Her madness hath the oddest frame of sense,
Such a dependency of thing on thing,
As e'er I heard in madness.
    Isab.   O gracious duke,
Harp not on that, nor do not banish reason
For inequality ; but let your reason serve
To make the truth appear where it seems hid,
And hide the false seems true.
    Duke.   Many that are not mad
Have, sure, more lack of reason. What would
    you say ?
    Isab. I am the sister of one Claudio,
Condemn'd upon the act of fornication   70
To lose his head ; condemn'd by Angelo :
I, in probation of a sisterhood,
Was sent to by my brother ; one Lucio
As then the messenger,—
    Lucio.   That's I, an't like your grace:
I came to her from Claudio, and desired her
To try her gracious fortune with Lord Angelo
For her poor brother's pardon.
    Isab.   That's he indeed.
    Duke. You were not bid to speak.
    Lucio.   No, my good lord ;
Nor wish'd to hold my peace.
    Duke.   I wish you now, then ;
Pray you, take note of it : and when you have
A business for yourself, pray heaven you then
Be perfect.
    Lucio. I warrant your honor.
    Duke. The warrant 's for yourself ; take
    heed to't.
    Isab. This gentleman told somewhat of my
    tale,—
    Lucio. Right.
    Duke. It may be right ; but you are i' the
    wrong
To speak before your time. Proceed.
    Isab.   I went
To this pernicious caitiff deputy,—
    Duke. That's somewhat madly spoken.
    Isab.   Pardon it;
The phrase is to the matter.   90
    Duke. Mended again. The matter ; pro-
    ceed.   [by,
    Isab. In brief, to set the needless process
How I persuaded, how I pray'd, and kneel'd,
How he refell'd me, and how I replied,—
For this was of much length,—the vile con-
    clusion
I now begin with grief and shame to utter :
He would not, but by gift of my chaste body

To his concupiscible intemperate lust,
Release my brother ; and, after much debate-
    ment,
My sisterly remorse confutes mine honor,   100
And I did yield to him : but the next morn be-
    times,
His purpose surfeiting, he sends a warrant
For my poor brother's head.
    Duke.   This is most likely !
    Isab. O, that it were as like as it is true !
    Duke. By heaven, fond wretch, thou
    know'st not what thou speak'st,
Or else thou art suborn'd against his honor
In hateful practice. First, his integrity
Stands without blemish. Next, it imports no
    reason
That with such vehemency he should pursue
Faults proper to himself : if he had so
    offended,   [self
He would have weigh'd thy brother by him-
And not have cut him off. Some one hath set
    you on :
Confess the truth, and say by whose advice
Thou camest here to complain.
    Isab.   And is this all ?
Then, O you blessed ministers above,
Keep me in patience, and with ripen'd time
Unfold the evil which is here wrapt up
In countenance ! Heaven shield your grace
    from woe,
As I, thus wrong'd, hence unbelieved go !
    Duke. I know you'ld fain be gone. An
    officer !   120
To prison with her ! Shall we thus permit
A blasting and a scandalous breath to fall
On him so near us ? This needs must be a
    practice.
Who knew of your intent and coming hither ?
    Isab. One that I would were here, Friar
    Lodowick.
    Duke. A ghostly father, belike. Who knows
    that Lodowick ?   [friar ;
    Lucio. My lord, I know him ; 'tis a meddling
I do not like the man : had he been lay, my
    lord,   [grace
For certain words he spake against your
In your retirement, I had swinged him
    soundly.   130
    Duke. Words against me ! this is a good
    friar, belike !
And to set on this wretched woman here
Against our substitute ! Let this friar be
    found.
    Lucio. But yesternight, my lord, she and
    that friar,
I saw them at the prison : a saucy friar,
A very scurvy fellow.
    Fri. P. Blessed be your royal grace !
I have stood by, my lord, and I have heard
Your royal ear abused. First, hath this woman
Most wrongfully accused your substitute,   140
Who is as free from touch or soil with her
As she from one ungot.
    Duke.   We did believe no less.
Know you that Friar Lodowick that she speaks
    of?

Fri. P. I know him for a man divine and
holy ; ·
Not scurvy, nor a temporary meddler,
As he's reported by this gentleman ,
And, on my trust, a man that never yet
Did, as he vouches, misreport your grace
  Lucio. My lord, most villanously , believe
it.
  Fri P. Well, he in time may come to clear
himself ,   150
But at this instant he is sick, my lord,
Of a strange fever Upon his mere request,
Being come to knowledge that there was com-
plaint
Intended 'gainst Lord Angelo, came I hither,
To speak, as from his mouth, what he doth
know
Is true and false , and what he with his oath
And all probation will make up full clear,
Whensoever he's convented. First, for this
woman,
To justify this worthy nobleman,
So vulgarly and personally accused,   160
Her shall you hear disproved to her eyes,
Till she herself confess it
  Duke.   Good friar, let's hear it
     [*Isabella is carried off guarded , and
       Mariana comes forward*
Do you not smile at this, Lord Angelo ?
O heaven, the vanity of wretched fools !
Give us some seats Come, cousin Angelo ;
In this I'll be impartial , be you judge
Of your own cause. Is this the witness, friar ?
First, let her show her face, and after speak
  Mari. Pardon, my lord , I will not show my
face
Until my husband bid me.   170
  Duke. What, are you married ?
  Mari. No, my lord
  Duke. Are you a maid ?
  Mari. No, my lord
  Duke. A widow, then?
  Mari. Neither, my lord
  Duke. Why, you are nothing then : neither
maid, widow, nor wife !
  Lucio. My lord, she may be a punk ; for
many of them are neither maid, widow, nor
wife.   180
  Duke. Silence that fellow : I would he had
some cause
To prattle for himself
  Lucio. Well, my lord.
  Mari. My lord, I do confess I ne'er was
married ,
And I confess besides I am no maid
I have known my husband ; yet my husband
Knows not that ever he knew me
  Lucio He was drunk then, my lord : it can
be no better.
  Duke. For the benefit of silence, would
thou wert so too !   191
  Lucio. Well, my lord.
  Duke. This is no witness for Lord Angelo.
  Mari. Now I come to't, my lord :
She that accuses him of fornication,
In self-same manner doth accuse my husband.

And charges him, my lord, with such a time
When I'll depose I had him in mine arms
With all the effect of love
  Ang Charges she more than me ?
  Mari   Not that I know. 200
  Duke No ? you say your husband
  Mari. Why, just, my lord, and that is An-
gelo,   [body,
Who thinks he knows that he ne'er knew my
But knows he thinks that he knows Isabel's
  Ang. This is a strange abuse Let's see
thy face
  Mari My husband bids me , now I will
unmask.   [*Unveiling*
This is that face, thou cruel Angelo,
Which once thou sworest was worth the look-
ing on ,
This is the hand which, with a vow'd contract,
Was fast belock'd in thine , this is the body
That took away the match from Isabel, 211
And did supply thee at thy garden-house
In her imagined person
  Duke.   Know you this woman ?
  Lucio Carnally, she says
  Duke   Sirrah, no more !
  Lucio Enough, my lord
  Ang My lord, I must confess I know this
woman   [marriage
And five years since there was some speech of
Betwixt myself and her , which was broke off,
Partly for that her promised proportions
Came short of composition, but in chief 220
For that her reputation was disvalued
In levity . since which time of five years
I never spake with her, saw her, nor heard
from her,
Upon my faith and honor.
  Mari   Noble prince,
As there comes light from heaven and words
from breath,
As there is sense in truth and truth in virtue,
I am affianced this man's wife as strongly
As words could make up vows and, my good
lord,
But Tuesday night last gone in's garden-house
He knew me as a wife As this is true, 230
Let me in safety raise me from my knees ,
Or else for ever be confixed here,
A marble monument !
  Ang   I did but smile till now:
Now, good my lord, give me the scope of jus-
tice ;
My patience here is touch'd I do perceive
These poor informal women are no more
But instruments of some more mightier mem-
ber
That sets them on : let me have way, my lord,
To find this practice out
  Duke.   Ay, with my heart ;
And punish them to your height of pleasure.
Thou foolish friar, and thou pernicious woman,
Compact with her that's gone, think'st thou
thy oaths,
Though they would swear down each partic-
ular saint,
Were testimonies against his worth and credit

That's seal'd in approbation ?   You, Lord Es-
   calus,
Sit with my cousin ; lend him your kind pains
To find out this abuse, whence 'tis derived.
There is another friar that set them on ;
Let him be sent for.
   Fri. P.   Would he were here, my lord ! for
   he indeed   250
Hath set the women on to this complaint :
Your provost knows the place where he abides
And he may fetch him.
   Duke.   Go do it instantly.   [*Exit Provost.*
And you, my noble and well-warranted cousin,
Whom it concerns to hear this matter forth,
Do with your injuries as seems you best,
In any chastisement : I for a while will leave
   you ;
But stir not you till you have well determined
Upon these slanderers.
   Escal.   My lord, we'll do it throughly.   260
                       [*Exit Duke.*
Signior Lucio, did not you say you knew that
Friar Lodowick to be a dishonest person ?
   Lucio.   'Cucullus non facit monachum :'
honest in nothing but in his clothes ; and one
that hath spoke most villanous speeches of the
duke.
   Escal.   We shall entreat you to abide here
till he come and enforce them against him :
we shall find this friar a notable fellow.
   Lucio.   As any in Vienna, on my word.
   Escal.   Call that same Isabel here once
again : I would speak with her.
              [*Exit an Attendant.*]
Pray you, my lord, give me leave to question;
you shall see how I'll handle her.
   Lucio.   Not better than he, by her own report.
   Escal.   Say you ?
   Lucio.   Marry, sir, I think, if you handled
her privately, she would sooner confess : per-
chance, publicly, she'll be ashamed.
   Escal.   I will go darkly to work with her.
   Lucio.   That's the way; for women are light
at midnight.   281

Re-enter OFFICERS *with* ISABELLA ; *and*
   PROVOST *with the* DUKE *in his friar's habit.*

   Escal.   Come on, mistress : here's a gentle-
woman denies all that you have said.
   Lucio.   My lord, here comes the rascal I
spoke of ; here with the provost.
   Escal.   In very good time: speak not you
to him till we call upon you.
   Lucio.   Mum.
   Escal.   Come, sir : did you set these women
on to slander Lord Angelo ? they have con-
fessed you did   291
   Duke.   'Tis false.
   Escal.   How ! know you where you are ?
   Duke.   Respect to your great place ! and let
   the devil
Be sometime honor'd for his burning throne !
Where is the duke ? 'tis he should hear me
   speak.   [*you speak* :
   Escal.   The duke's in us ; and we will hear

Look you speak justly.
   Duke.   Boldly, at least.   But, O, poor souls,
Come you to seek the lamb here of the fox ?
Good night to your redress ! Is the duke gone ?
Then is your cause gone too.   The duke's un-
   just,
Thus to retort your manifest appeal,
And put your trial in the villain's mouth
Which here you come to accuse.
   Lucio.   This is the rascal ; this is he I spoke
   of.   [low'd friar,
   Escal.   Why, thou unreverend and unhal-
Is't not enough thou hast suborn'd these
   women
To accuse this worthy man, but, in foul mouth
And in the witness of his proper ear,   310
To call him villain ? and then to glance from
   him
To the duke himself, to tax him with injustice?
Take him hence ; to the rack with him ! We'll
   touse you
Joint by joint, but we will know his purpose.
What, 'unjust' !
   Duke.   Be not so hot ; the duke
Dare no more stretch this finger of mine than he
Dare rack his own : his subject am I not,
Nor here provincial.   My business in this state
Made me a looker on here in Vienna,   319
Where I have seen corruption boil and bubble
Till it o'er-run the stew ; laws for all faults,
But faults so countenanced, that the strong
   statutes
Stand like the forfeits in a barber's shop,
As much in mock as mark.
   Escal.   Slander to the state ! Away with
him to prison !
   Ang.   What can you vouch against him,
   Signior Lucio ?
Is this the man that you did tell us of ?
   Lucio.   'Tis he, my lord. Come hither, good-
man baldpate : do you know me ?
   Duke.   I remember you, sir, by the sound
of your voice : I met you at the prison, in the
absence of the duke.
   Lucio.   O, did you so ? And do you remem-
ber what you said of the duke ?
   Duke.   Most notedly, sir.
   Lucio.   Do you so, sir ? And was the duke
a fleshmonger, a fool, and a coward, as you
then reported him to be ?
   Duke.   You must, sir, change persons with
me, ere you make that my report ; you, indeed, spoke so of him ; and much more, much
worse.   341
   Lucio.   O thou damnable fellow ! Did not
I pluck thee by the nose for thy speeches ?
   Duke.   I protest I love the duke as I love
myself.
   Ang.   Hark, how the villain would close
now, after his treasonable abuses !
   Escal.   Such a fellow is not to be talked
withal.   Away with him to prison ! Where is
the provost ?   Away with him to prison ! lay
bolts enough upon him : let him speak no
more.   Away with those giglots too, and with
the other confederate companion !

Duke [*To Provost.*] Stay, sir ; stay awhile
Ang   What, resists he ? Help him, Lucio.
Lucio. Come, sir ; come, sir ; come. sir ;
foh, sir ! Why, you bald-pated, lying rascal,
you must be hooded, must you ? Show your
knave's visage, with a pox to you ! show your
sheep-biting face, and be hanged an hour !
Will't not off ?   360
        [*Pulls off the friar's hood, and discovers
                                             the Duke*
Duke Thou art the first knave that e'er
made-t a duke
First, provost, let me bail these gentle three
[*To Lucio*] Sneak not away, sir ; for the friar
             and you
Must have a word anon   Lay hold on him.
Lucio This may prove worse than hanging.
Duke. [*To Escalus*] What you have spoke
I pardon . sit you down .
We'll borrow place of him   [*To Angelo*] Sir,
             by your leave
Hast thou or word, or wit, or impudence,
That yet can do thee office ? If thou hast,
Rely upon it till my tale be heard,   370
And hold no longer out
        Ang.   O my dread lord,
I should be guiltier than my guiltiness,
To think I can be undiscernible,
When I perceive your grace, like power divine,
Hath look'd upon my passes. Then, good
             prince,
No longer session hold upon my shame,
But let my trial be mine own confession .
Immediate sentence then and sequent death
Is all the grace I beg
        Duke.   Come hither, Mariana.
Say, wast thou e'er contracted to this woman?
Ang I was, my lord.   381
Duke. Go take her hence, and marry her
instantly.
Do you the office, friar , which consummate,
Return him here again. Go with him, provost
        [*Exeunt Angelo, Mariana, Friar Peter
                                    and Provost.*
Escal. My lord, I am more amazed at his
dishonor
Than at the strangeness of it.
        Duke.   Come hither, Isabel.
Your friar is now your prince . as I was then
Advertising and holy to your business,
Not changing heart with habit, I am still
Attorney'd at your service.
        Isab   O, give me pardon, 390
That I, your vassal, have employ'd and pain'd,
Your unknown sovereignty '
        Duke.   You are pardon'd, Isabel :
And now, dear maid, be you as free to us.
Your brother's death, I know, sits at your heart;
And you may marvel why I obscured myself,
Laboring to save his life, and would not rather
Make rash remonstrance of my hidden power
Than let him so be lost. O most kind maid,
It was the swift celerity of his death,
Which I did think with slower foot came on,
That brain'd my purpose. But, peace be with
             him !   401

That life is better life, past fearing, death,
Than that which lives to fear ? make it your
             comfort,
So happy is your brother.
        Isab.   I do, my lord.

Re-enter Angelo, Mariana, Friar Peter,
             and Provost.

Duke. For this new-married man approach-
             ing here,
Whose salt imagination yet hath wrong'd
Your well defended honor, you must pardon
For Mariana's sake . but as he adjudged your
             brother,—
Being criminal, in double violation
Of sacred chastity and of promise-breach 410
Thereon dependent, for your brother's life,—
The very mercy of the law cries out
Most audible, even from his proper tongue,
'An Angelo for Claudio, death for death !'
Haste still pays haste, and leisure answers.
             leisure ,
Like doth quit like, and MEASURE still FOR
             MEASURE
Then, Angelo, thy fault's thus manifested ;
Which, though thou wouldst deny, denies thee
             vantage.
We do condemn thee to the very block
Where Claudio stoop'd to death, and with like
             haste   420
Away with him '
        Mari.   O my most gracious lord,
I hope you will not mock me with a husband.
Duke. It is your husband mock'd you with .
             a husband
Consenting to the safeguard of your honor,
I thought your marriage fit ; else imputation,
For that he knew you, might reproach your
             life   [sessions,
And choke your good to come : for his pos-
Although by confiscation they are ours,
We do instate and widow you withal,
To buy you a better husband
        Mari   O my dear lord, 430.
I crave no other, nor no better man.
        Duke. Never crave him , we are definitive.
Mari. Gentle my liege,—   [*Kneeling.*
Duke   You do but lose your labor.
Away with him to death ! [*To Lucio*] Now,
             sir, to you   [my part.
Mari O my good lord ' Sweet Isabel, take
Lend me your knees, and all my life to come
I'll lend you all my life to do you service
Duke. Against all sense you do importune
             her :
Should she kneel down in mercy of this fact;
Her brother's ghost his paved bed would
             break,
And take her hence in horror.
Mari   Isabel,   441
Sweet Isabel, do yet but kneel by me ;
Hold up your hands, say nothing ; I'll speak.
             all.
They say, best men are moulded out of faults ;.
And, for the most, become much more the bet-
             ter

For being a little bad : so may my husband.
O Isabel, will you not lend a knee ?
Duke.   He dies for Claudio's death.
Isab.   Most bounteous sir, [*Kneeling.*
Look, if it please you, on this man condemn'd,
As if my brother lived : I partly think   450
A due sincerity govern'd his deeds,
Till he did look on me : since it is so,
Let him not die.   My brother had but justice,
In that he did the thing for which he died :
For Angelo,
His act did not o'ertake his bad intent,
And must be buried but as an intent
That perish'd by the way : thoughts are no
     subjects ;
Intents but merely thoughts.
Mari.   Merely, my lord.
Duke.   Your suit's unprofitable ; stand up,
     I say.   460
I have bethought me of another fault.
Provost, how came it Claudio was beheaded
At an unusual hour ?
Prov.   It was commanded so.
Duke. Had you a special warrant for the
     deed ?   [message.
Prov. No, my good lord ; it was by private
Duke. For which I do discharge you of
     your office :
Give up your keys.
Prov.   Pardon me, noble lord :
I thought it was a fault, but knew it not ;
Yet did repent me, after more advice ; ·
For testimony whereof, one in the prison, 470
That should by private order else have died,
I have reserved alive.
Duke.   What's he ?
Prov.   His name is Barnardine.
Duke. I would thou hadst done so by
     Claudio.
Go fetch him hither ; let me look upon him.
                   [*Exit Provost.*
Escal. I am sorry, one so learned and so
     wise
As you, Lord Angelo, have still appear'd,
Should slip so grossly, both in the heat of blood,
And lack of temper'd judgment afterward.
Ang. I am sorry that such sorrow I procure :
And so deep sticks it in my penitent heart 480
That I crave death more willingly than mercy ;
'Tis my deserving, and I do entreat it.

Re-enter PROVOST, *with* BARNARDINE,
     CLAUDIO *muffled, and* JULIET.

Duke.   Which is that Barnardine ?
Prov.   This, my lord.
Duke.   There was a friar told me of this
     man.
Sirrah, thou art said to have a stubborn soul,
That apprehends no further than this world,
And squarest thy life according.   Thou'rt con-
     demn'd :
But, for those earthly faults, I quit them all ;
And pray thee take this mercy to provide 489
For better times to come.   Friar, advise him ;
I leave him to your hand.   What muffled fel-
     low's that ?

Prov. This is another prisoner that I saved,
Who should have died when Claudio lost his
     head ;
As like almost to Claudio as himself.
                 [*Unmuffles Claudio.*
Duke. [*To Isabella*] If he be like your
     brother, for his sake
Is he pardon'd ; and, for your lovely sake,
Give me your hand and say you will be mine.
He is my brother too : but fitter time for that.
By this Lord Angelo perceives he's safe ;
Methinks I see a quickening in his eye. · 500
Well, Angelo, your evil quits you well :
Look that you love your wife ; her worth
     worth yours.
I find an apt remission in myself ;
And yet here's one in place I cannot pardon.
[*To Lucio*] You, sirrah, that knew me for a
     fool, a coward,
One all of luxury, an ass, a madman ;
Wherein have I so deserved of you,
That you extol me thus ?
Lucio. 'Faith, my lord, I spoke it but ac-
cording to the trick.   If you will hang me for it,
you may ; but I had rather it would please you
I might be whipt.
Duke.   Whipt first, sir, and hanged after.
Proclaim it, provost, round about the city,
Is any woman wrong'd by this lewd fellow,
As I have heard him swear himself there's
     one
Whom he begot with child, let her appear,
And he shall marry her : the nuptial finish'd,
Let him be whipt and hang'd.
Lucio. I beseech your highness, do not
marry me to a whore.   Your highness said
even now, I made you a duke : good my lord,
do not recompense me in making me a cuckold.
Duke.   Upon mine honor, thou shalt marry
     her.
Thy slanders I forgive ; and therewithal
Remit thy other forfeits.   Take him to prison;
And see our pleasure herein executed.
Lucio. Marrying a punk, my lord, is press-
ing to death, whipping, and hanging.
Duke. Slandering a prince deserves it. 530
              [*Exeunt Officers with Lucio.*
She, Claudio, that you wrong'd, look you re-
     store.
Joy to you, Mariana ! Love her, Angelo :
I have confess'd her and I know her virtue.
Thanks, good friend Escalus, for thy much
     goodness:
There's more behind that is more gratulate.
Thanks, provost, for thy care and secrecy :
We shall employ thee in a worthier place.
Forgive him, Angelo, that brought you home
The head of Ragozine for Claudio's :
The offence pardons itself.   Dear Isabel,   540
I have a motion much imports your good ;
Whereto if you'll a willing ear incline,
What's mine is yours and what is yours is
     mine.
So, bring us to our palace ; where we'll show
What's yet behind, that's meet you all should
     know.   [*Exeunt.*

TROILUS AND CRESSIDA.

(WRITTEN ABOUT 1603 ?)

INTRODUCTION.

This play appeared in two quarto editions in the year 1609; on the title-page of the earlier of the two it is stated to have been acted at the Globe, the later contains a singular preface in which the play is spoken of as "never stal'd with the stage, never clapper-clawed with the palmes of the vulgar," and as having been published against the will of "the grand possessors." Perhaps the play was printed at first for the use of the theatre, with the intention of being published after having been represented, and the printers, against the known wishes of the proprietors of Shakespeare's manuscript, anticipated the first representation and issued the quarto with the attractive announcement that it was an absolute novelty. The editors of the folio, after having decided that *Troilus and Cressida* should follow *Romeo and Juliet* among the tragedies, changed their minds, apparently uncertain how the play should be classed, and placed it between the Histories and Tragedies, this led to the cancelling of a leaf, and the filling up of a blank space left by the alteration, with the Prologue to *Troilus and Cressida*—a prologue which is believed by several critics not to have come from Shakespeare's hand. There is extreme uncertainty with respect to the date of the play. Dekker and Chettle were engaged in 1599 upon a play on this subject, and, from an entry in the Stationers' register, February 7, 1602—1603, it appears that a *Troilus and Cressida* had been acted by Shakespeare's company, the Lord Chamberlain's Servants. Was this Shakespeare's play? We are thrown back upon internal evidence to decide this question, and the internal evidence is itself of a conflicting kind, and has led to opposite conclusions. The massive worldly wisdom of Ulysses argues, it is supposed, in favor of a late date, and the general tone of the play has been compared with that of *Timon of Athens*. The fact that it does not contain a single weak ending, and only six light endings, is, however, almost decisive evidence against our placing it after either *Timon* or *Macbeth*, and the other metrical characteristics are considered, by the most careful student of this class of evidence in the case of the present play (Hertzberg), to point to a date about 1603. Other authorities place it as late as 1608 or 1609, while a third theory (that of Verplanck and Grant White) attempts to solve the difficulties by supposing that it was first written in 1603, and revised and enlarged shortly before the publication of the quarto. Parts of the play—notably the last battle of Hector—appear not to be by Shakespeare. The interpretation of the play itself is as difficult as the ascertainment of the external facts of its history. With what intention, and in what spirit did Shakespeare write this strange comedy? All the Greek heroes who fought against Troy are pitilessly exposed to ridicule, Helen and Cressida are light, sensual, and heartless, for whose sake it seems infatuated folly to strike a blow, Troilus is an enthusiastic young fool, and even Hector, though valiant and generous, spends his life in a cause which he knows to be unprofitable, if not evil. All this is seen and said by Thersites, whose mind is made up of the scum of the foulness of human life. But can Shakespeare's view of things have been the same as that of Thersites? The central theme, the young love and faith of Troilus given to one who was false and fickle, and his discovery of his error, lends its color to the whole play. It is the comedy of disillusion. And as Troilus passed through the illusion of his first love for woman, so by middle life the world itself often appears like one that has not kept her promises, and who is a poor deceiver. We come to see the seamy side of life, and from this mood of disillusion it is a deliverance to pass on even to a dark and tragic view of life, to which beauty and virtue reappear, even though human weakness or human vice may do them bitter wrong. Now such a mood of contemptuous depreciation of life may have come over Shakespeare, and spoilt him, at that time, for a writer of comedy. But for Isabella we should find the coming on of this mood in *Measure for Measure*, there is perhaps a touch of it in *Hamlet*. At this time *Troilus and Cressida* may have been written, and soon afterwards Shakespeare, rousing himself to a deeper inquest into things, may have passed on to his great series of tragedies. The materials for *Troilus and Cressida* were found by Shakespeare in Chaucer's *Troilus and Creseide*, Caxton's translation from the French, *Recuyles, or Destruction of Troy*, and perhaps also Lydgate's *Troye Boke*.

DRAMATIS PERSONÆ.

PRIAM, king of Troy.
HECTOR,
TROILUS,
PARIS, } his sons.
DEIPHOBUS,
HELENUS,

MARGARELON, a bastard son of Priam.
ÆNEAS,
ANTENOR, } Trojan commanders.
CALCHAS, a Trojan priest, taking part with the Greeks.
PANDARUS, uncle to Cressida.

(745)

AGAMEMNON, the Grecian general.
MENELAUS, his brother.
ACHILLES,
AJAX,
ULYSSES,
NESTOR, } Grecian princes.
DIOMEDES,
PATROCLUS,
THERSITES, a deformed and scurrilous Grecian.
ALEXANDER, servant to Cressida.
Servant to Troilus.

Servant to Paris.
Servant to Diomedes.

HELEN, wife to Menelaus.
ANDROMACHE, wife to Hector.
CASSANDRA, daughter to Priam, a prophetess.
CRESSIDA, daughter to Calchas.

Trojan and Greek Soldiers, and Attendants.

SCENE : *Troy, and the Grecian camp before it.*

PROLOGUE.

IN Troy, there lies the scene. From isles of
    Greece
The princes orgulous, their high blood chafed,
Have to the port of Athens sent their ships,
Fraught with the ministers and instruments
Of cruel war : sixty and nine, that wore
Their crownets regal, from the Athenian bay
Put forth toward Phrygia ; and their vow is
    made
To ransack Troy, within whose strong im-
    mures
The ravish'd Helen, Menelaus' queen,
With wanton Paris sleeps ; and that's the
    quarrel.   10
To Tenedos they come ;
And the deep-drawing barks do there disgorge
Their warlike fraughtage : now on Dardan
    plains
The fresh and yet unbruised Greeks do pitch
Their brave pavilions : Priam's six-gated city,
Dardan, and Tymbria, Helias, Chetas, Troien,
And Antenorides, with massy staples
And corresponsive and fulfilling bolts,
Sperr up the sons of Troy.
Now expectation, tickling skittish spirits,   20
On one and other side, Trojan and Greek,
Sets all on hazard : and hither am I come
A prologue arm'd, but not in confidence
Of author's pen or actor's voice, but suited
In like conditions as our argument,
To tell you, fair beholders, that our play
Leaps o'er the vaunt and firstlings of those
    broils,
Beginning in the middle, starting thence away
To what may be digested in a play.   29
Like or find fault ; do as your pleasures are :
Now good or bad, 'tis but the chance of war.

ACT I.

SCENE I. *Troy. Before Priam's palace.*

Enter TROILUS *armed, and* PANDARUS.

Tro. Call here my varlet ; I'll unarm
    again :
Why should I war without the walls of Troy,
That find such cruel battle here within ?
Each Trojan that is master of his heart,
Let him to field ; Troilus, alas ! hath none.

Pan. Will this gear ne'er be mended ?
Tro. The Greeks are strong and skilful to
    their strength,
Fierce to their skill and to their fierceness
    valiant ;
But I am weaker than a woman's tear,
Tamer than sleep, fonder than ignorance,   10
Less valiant than the virgin in the night
And skilless as unpractised infancy.
Pan. Well, I have told you enough of this :
for my part, I'll not meddle nor make no fur-
ther. He that will have a cake out of the wheat
must needs tarry the grinding.
Tro. Have I not tarried ?
Pan. Ay, the grinding ; but you must tarry
    the bolting.
Tro. Have I not tarried ?
Pan. Ay, the bolting, but you must tarry
    the leavening.   20
Tro. Still have I tarried.
Pan. Ay, to the leavening ; but here's yet
in the word 'hereafter' the kneading, the
making of the cake, the heating of the oven
and the baking ; nay, you must stay the cool-
ing too, or you may chance to burn your lips.
Tro. Patience herself, what goddess e'er
    she be,
Doth lesser blench at sufferance than I do.
At Priam's royal table do I sit ;
And when fair Cressid comes into my
    thoughts,—   30
So, traitor ! 'When she comes !' When is she
    thence ?
Pan. Well, she looked yesternight fairer
than ever I saw her look, or any woman else.
Tro. I was about to tell thee :—when my
    heart,
As wedged with a sigh, would rive in twain,
Lest Hector or my father should perceive me,
I have, as when the sun doth light a storm,
Buried this sigh in wrinkle of a smile :
But sorrow, that is couch'd in seeming glad-
    ness,
Is like that mirth fate turns to sudden sad-
    ness.   40
Pan. An her hair were not somewhat
darker than Helen's—well, go to—there were
no more comparison between the women ;
but, for my part, she is my kinswoman ; I
would not, as they term it, praise her : but I
would somebody had heard her talk yester-

day, as I did: I will not dispraise your sister
Cassandra's wit; but—

Tro. O Pandarus ! I tell thee, Pandarus,—
When I do tell thee, there my hopes lie
drown'd,
Reply not in how many fathoms deep   50
They lie indrench'd: I tell thee I am mad
In Cressid's love . thou answer'st 'she is
fair ,'
Pour'st in the open ulcer of my heart
Her eyes, her hair, her cheek, her gait, her
voice,
Handlest in thy discourse, O, that her hand,
In whose comparison all whites are ink,
Writing their own reproach, to whose soft
seizure
The cygnet's down is harsh and spirit of sense
Hard as the palm of ploughman · this thou
tell'st me,
As true thou tell'st me, when I say I love
her ,   60
But, saying thus, instead of oil and balm,
Thou lay'st in every gash that love hath given
me
The knife that made it.

Pan. I speak no more than truth.

Tro. Thou dost not speak so much.

Pan Faith, I'll not meddle in't. Let her be
as she is: if she be fair, 'tis the better for
her ; an she be not, she has the mends in her
own hands.

Tro. Good Pandarus, how now, Pandarus !

Pan. I have had my labor for my travail ,
ill-thought on of her and ill-thought on of
you ; gone between and between, but small
thanks for my labor.

Tro What, art thou angry, Pandarus ?
what, with me ?

Pan. Because she's kin to me, therefore
she's not so fair as Helen : an she were not
kin to me, she would be as fair on Friday as
Helen is on Sunday. But what care I ? I care
not an she were a black-a-moor ; 'tis all one
to me.   80

Tro. Say I she is not fair ?

Pan. I do not care whether you do or no
She's a fool to stay behind her father , let her
to the Greeks ; and so I'll tell her the next
time I see her : for my part, I'll meddle nor
make no more i' the matter.

Tro. Pandarus,—

Pan. Not I.

Tro. Sweet Pandarus,—

Pan. Pray you, speak no more to me : I
will leave all as I found it, and there an end.

[*Exit Pandarus. An alarum.* 91

Tro. Peace, you ungracious clamors ! peace,
rude sounds !
Fools on both sides ! Helen must needs be
fair,
When with your blood you daily paint her
thus.
I cannot fight upon this argument ;
It is too starved a subject for my sword.
But Pandarus,—O gods, how do you plague
me !

I cannot come to Cressid but by Pandar ;
And he's as tetchy to be woo'd to woo,
As she is stubborn-chaste against all suit. 100
Tell me, Apollo, for thy Daphne's love,
What Cressid is, what Pandar, and what we ?
Her bed is India , there she lies, a pearl :
Between our Ilium and where she resides,
Let it be call'd the wild and wandering flood,
Ourself the merchant, and this sailing Pandar
Our doubtful hope, our convoy and our bark.

Alarum   Enter ÆNEAS

Æne How now, Prince Troilus ! wherefore not afield ?

Tro Because not there this woman's an-
swer sorts,
For womanish it is to be from thence   110
What news, Æneas, from the field to-day ?

Æne That Paris is returned home and
hurt.

Tro By whom, Æneas ?

Æne. Troilus, by Menelaus.

Tro. Let Paris bleed , 'tis but a scar to
scorn ;
Paris is gored with Menelaus' horn [*Alarum.*

Æne. Hark, what good sport is out of
town to-day !

Tro Better at home, if 'would I might'
were ' may '
But to the sport abroad : are you bound
thither ?

Æne. In all swift haste.

Tro.   Come, go we then together.

[*Exeunt.*

SCENE II. *The same. A street.*

Enter CRESSIDA *and* ALEXANDER.

Cres Who were those went by ?

Alex.   Queen Hecuba and Helen.

Cres. And whither go they ?

Alex   Up to the eastern tower,
Whose height commands as subject all the
vale,
To see the battle. Hector, whose patience
Is, as a virtue, fix'd, to-day was moved .
He chid Andromache and struck his armorer,
And, like as there were husbandry in war,
Before the sun rose he was harness'd light,
And to the field goes he , where every flower
Did, as a prophet, weep what it foresaw   10
In Hector's wrath

Cres   What was his cause of anger ?

Alex. The noise goes, this there is among
the Greeks
A lord of Trojan blood, nephew to Hector ;
They call him Ajax.

Cres.   Good ; and what of him ?

Alex. They say he is a very man per se,
And stands alone.

Cres. So do all men, unless they are drunk,
sick, or have no legs.

Alex. This man, lady, hath robbed many
beasts of their particular additions ; he is as
valiant as the lion, churlish as the bear, slow
as the elephant : a man into whom nature
hath so crowded humors that his valor is

crushed into folly, his folly sauced with discretion there is no man hath a virtue that he hath not a glimpse of, nor any man an attaint but he carries some stain of it. he is melancholy without cause, and merry against the hair · he hath the joints of every thing, but everything so out of joint that he is a gouty Briareus, many hands and no use, or purblind Argus, all eyes and no sight   31

Cres But how should this man, that makes me smile, make Hector angry?

Alex. They say he yesterday coped Hector in the battle and struck him down, the disdain and shame whereof hath ever since kept Hector fasting and waking.

Cres. Who comes here?

Alex. Madam, your uncle Pandarus.

Enter PANDARUS.

Cres. Hector's a gallant man   40

Alex. As may be in the world, lady.

Pan. What's that? what's that?

Cres. Good morrow, uncle Pandarus.

Pan. Good morrow, cousin Cressid . what do you talk of? Good morrow, Alexander. How do you, cousin? When were you at Ilium?

Cres. This morning, uncle.

Pan What were you talking of when I came? Was Hector armed and gone ere ye came to Ilium? Helen was not up, was she?

Cres. Hector was gone, but Helen was not up

Pan. Even so. Hector was stirring early

Cres That were we talking of, and of his anger.

Pan. Was he angry?

Cres. So he says here.

Pan. True, he was so I know the cause too : he'll lay about him to-day, I can tell them that : and there's Troilus will not come far behind him ; let them take heed of Troilus, I can tell them that too.   61

Cres. What, is he angry too?

Pan. Who, Troilus? Troilus is the better man of the two

Cres. O Jupiter! there's no comparison

Pan What, not between Troilus and Hector? Do you know a man if you see him?

Cres. Ay, if I ever saw him before and knew him.

Pan Well, I say Troilus is Troilus.   70

Cres. Then you say as I say, for, I am sure, he is not Hector.

Pan. No, nor Hector is not Troilus in some degrees.

Cres. 'Tis just to each of them ; he is himself.

Pan. Himself! Alas, poor Troilus! I would he were.

Cres. So he is.

Pan. Condition, I had gone barefoot to India.   80

Cres. He is not Hector

Pan. Himself! no, he's not himself : would a' were himself! Well, the gods are above ;

time must friend or end : well, Troilus, well : I would my heart were in her body. No, Hector is not a better man than Troilus.

Cres. Excuse me.

Pan He is elder.

Cres Pardon me, pardon me.   89

Pan Th' other's not come to't ; you shall tell me another tale, when th' other's come to't. Hector shall not have his wit this year.

Cres He shall not need it, if he have his own.

Pan. Nor his qualities.

Cres. No matter.

Pan Nor his beauty

Cres. 'Twould not become him ; his own's better.

Pan. You have no judgment, niece : Helen herself swore th' other day, that Troilus, for a brown favor—for so 'tis, I must confess,—not brown neither,—

Cres. No, but brown

Pan 'Faith, to say truth, brown and not brown.

Cres. To say the truth, true and not true

Pan. She praised his complexion above Paris.

Cres. Why, Paris hath color enough.

Pan So he has.   109

Cres Then Troilus should have too much : if she praised him above, his complexion is higher than his , he having color enough, and the other higher, is too flaming a praise for a good complexion I had as lief Helen's golden tongue had commended Troilus for a copper nose

Pan I swear to you, I think Helen loves him better than Paris

Cres Then she's a merry Greek indeed.

Pan Nay, I am sure she does. She came to him th' other day into the compassed window,—and, you know, he has not past three or four hairs on his chin,—

Cres. Indeed, a tapster's arithmetic may soon bring his particulars therein to a total

Pan. Why, he is very young : and yet will he, within three pound, lift as much as his brother Hector

Cres Is he so young a man and so old a lifter?   129

Pan But to prove to you that Helen loves him : she came and puts me her white hand to his cloven chin—

Cres Juno have mercy! how came it cloven?

Pan Why, you know, 'tis dimpled : I think his smiling becomes him better than any man in all Phrygia.

Cres. O, he smiles valiantly.

Pan Does he not?

Cres. O yes, an 'twere a cloud in autumn.

Pan. Why, go to, then : but to prove to you that Helen loves Troilus,—   141

Cres. Troilus will stand to the proof, if you'll prove it so.

Pan. Troilus! why, he esteems her no more than I esteem an addle egg.

Cres. If you love an addle egg as well as you love an idle head, you would eat chickens i' the shell

Pan. I cannot choose but laugh, to think how she tickled his chin · indeed, she has a marvellous white hand, I must needs confess,— 151

Cres. Without the rack

Pan And she takes upon her to spy a white hair on his chin

Cres Alas, poor chin ! many a wart is richer.

Pan. But there was such laughing ! Queen Hecuba laughed that her eyes ran o'er.

Cres. With mill-stones

Pan. And Cassandra laughed.

Cres But there was more temperate fire under the pot of her eyes . did her eyes run o'er too ? 161

Pan. And Hector laughed

Cres. At what was all this laughing ?

Pan. Marry, at the white hair that Helen spied on Troilus' chin

Cres An't had been a green hair, I should have laughed too

Pan They laughed not so much at the hair as at his pretty answer.

Cres. What was his answer ? 170

Pan. Quoth she, ' Here's but two and fifty hairs on your chin, and one of them is white.'

Cres. This is her question.

Pan. That's true , make no question of that. ' Two and fifty hairs,' quoth he, 'and one white : that white hair is my father, and all the rest are his sons ' ' Jupiter !' quoth she, which of these hairs is Paris, my husband ?' 'The forked one,' quoth he,' pluck't out, and give it him.' But there was such laughing ! and Helen so blushed, and Paris so chafed, and all the rest so laughed, that it passed

Cres. So let it now ; for it has been a great while going by.

Pan. Well, cousin, I told you a thing yesterday , think on't.

Cres. So I do

Pan. I'll be sworn 'tis true , he will weep you, an 'twere a man born in April 189

Cres And I'll spring in his tears, an 'twere a nettle against May.

[*A retreat sounded.*

Pan. Hark ! they are coming from the field : shall we stand up here, and see them as they pass toward Ilium ? good niece, do, sweet niece Cressida.

Cres. At your pleasure.

Pan. Here, here, here's an excellent place ; here we may see most bravely : I'll tell you them all by their names as they pass by ; but mark Troilus above the rest. 200

Cres. Speak not so loud

ÆNEAS *passes.*

Pan. That's Æneas: is not that a brave man ? he's one of the flowers of Troy, I can tell you : but mark Troilus ; you shall see anon.

ANTENOR *passes.*

Cres. Who's that ?

Pan. That's Antenor : he has a shrewd wit, I can tell you , and he's a man good enough : he's one o' the soundest judgments in Troy, whosoever, and a proper man of person When comes Troilus? I'll show you Troilus anon if he see me, you shall see him nod at me

Cres. Will he give you the nod ?

Pan You shall see.

Cres. If he do, the rich shall have more.

HECTOR *passes.*

Pan That's Hector, that, that, look you, that , there's a fellow ' Go thy way, Hector ! There's a brave man, niece O brave Hector ' Look how he looks ' there's a countenance ! is't not a brave man ?

Cres O, a brave man ' 220

Pan. Is a' not ? it does a man's heart good Look you what hacks are on his helmet' look you yonder, do you see ? look you there there's no jesting , there's laying on, take't off who will, as they say · there be hacks !

Cres. Be those with swords ?

Pan. Swords ' any thing, he cares not ; an the devil come to him, it's all one by God's lid, it does one's heart good. Yonder comes Paris, yonder comes Paris. 230

PARIS *passes.*

Look ye yonder, niece , is't not a gallant man too, is't not ? Why, this is brave now. Who said he came hurt home to-day ? he's not hurt · why, this will do Helen's heart good now, ha ! Would I could see Troilus now ! You shall see Troilus anon

HELENUS *passes.*

Cres. Who's that ?

Pan That's Helenus I marvel where Troilus is That's Helenus I think he went not forth to-day. That's Helenus. 240

Cres Can Helenus fight, uncle ?

Pan Helenus ? no Yes, he'll fight indifferent well. I marvel where Troilus is. Hark ! do you not hear the people cry ' Troilus '? Helenus is a priest

Cres. What sneaking fellow comes yonder ?

TROILUS *passes.*

Pan. Where ? yonder ? that's Deiphobus. 'Tis Troilus ! there's a man, niece ! Hem ! Brave Troilus ' the prince of chivalry !

Cres Peace, for shame, peace ! 250

Pan. Mark him , note him. O brave Troilus ' Look well upon him, niece : look you how his sword is bloodied, and his helm more hacked than Hector's, and how he looks, and how he goes ' O admirable youth ! he ne'er saw three and twenty. Go thy way, Troilus, go thy way ' Had I a sister were a grace, or a daughter a goddess, he should take his choice. O admirable man ! Paris ?

Paris is dirt to him ; and, I warrant, Helen, to
change, would give an eye to boot.   260
  Cres. Here come more.

              Forces pass.

  Pan. Asses, fools, dolts! chaff and bran,
chaff and bran! porridge after meat! I
could live and die i' the eyes of Troilus.
Ne'er look, ne'er look : the eagles are gone :
crows and daws, crows and daws! I had
rather be such a man as Troilus than Agamemnon and all Greece.

  Cres. There is among the Greeks Achilles,
a better man than Troilus.   269

  Pan. Achilles! a drayman, a porter, a very
camel.

  Cres. Well, well.

  Pan. ' Well, well! ' Why, have you any
discretion ? have you any eyes ? Do you
know what a man is ? Is not birth, beauty,
good shape, discourse, manhood, learning,
gentleness, virtue, youth, liberality, and such
like, the spice and salt that season a man ?

  Cres. Ay, a minced man : and then to be
baked with no date in the pie, for then the
man's date's out.   281

  Pan. You are such a woman! one knows
not at what ward you lie.

  Cres. Upon my back, to defend my belly ;
upon my wit, to defend my wiles ; upon my
secrecy, to defend mine honesty ; my mask, to
defend my beauty ; and you, to defend all
these : and at all these wards I lie, at a thousand watches.

  Pan. Say one of your watches.   290

  Cres. Nay, I'll watch you for that ; and
that's one of the chiefest of them too : if I
cannot ward what I would not have hit, I can
watch you for telling how I took the blow ;
unless it swell past hiding, and then it's past
watching.

  Pan. You are such another!

        Enter TROILUS'S Boy.

  Boy. Sir, my lord would instantly speak
with you.

  Pan. Where ?

  Boy. At your own house ; there he unarms
him.   300

  Pan. Good boy, tell him I come. [*Exit boy.*]
I doubt he be hurt. Fare ye well, good niece.

  Cres. Adieu, uncle.

  Pan. I'll be with you, niece, by and by.

  Cres. To bring, uncle ?

  Pan. Ay, a token from Troilus.

  Cres. By the same token, you are a bawd.

              [*Exit Pandarus.*
Words, vows, gifts, tears, and love's full
  sacrifice,
He offers in another's enterprise :
But more in Troilus thousand fold I see   310
Than in the glass of Pandar's praise may be ;
Yet hold I off. Women are angels, wooing :
Things won are done ; joy's soul lies in the
  doing.   [*not this :*
That she beloved knows nought that knows
Men prize the thing ungain'd more than it is :

That she was never yet that ever knew
Love got so sweet as when desire did sue.
Therefore this maxim out of love I teach :
Achievement is command ; ungain'd, beseech :
Then though my heart's content firm love
  doth bear,   320
Nothing of that shall from mine eyes appear.
                [*Exeunt*

SCENE III. *The Grecian camp. Before
      Agamemnon's tent.*

Sennet. Enter AGAMEMNON, NESTOR, ULYS-
  SES, MENELAUS, *and others.*

  Agam. Princes,
What grief hath set the jaundice on your
  cheeks ?
The ample proposition that hope makes
In all designs begun on earth below
Fails in the promised largeness : checks and
  disasters
Grow in the veins of actions highest rear'd,
As knots, by the conflux of meeting sap,
Infect the sound pine and divert his grain
Tortive and errant from his course of growth.
Nor, princes, is it matter new to us   10
That we come short of our suppose so far
That after seven years' siege yet Troy walls
  stand ;
Sith every action that hath gone before,
Whereof we have record, trial did draw
Bias and thwart, not answering the aim,
And that unbodied figure of the thought
That gave't surmised shape. Why then, you
  princes,
Do you with cheeks abashed behold our
  works,
And call them shames ? which are indeed
  nought else
But the protractive trials of great Jove   20
To find persistive constancy in men :
The fineness of which metal is not found
In fortune's love ; for then the bold and
  coward,
The wise and fool, the artist and unread,
The hard and soft seem all affined and kin :
But, in the wind and tempest of her frown,
Distinction, with a broad and powerful fan,
Puffing at all, winnows the light away ;
And what hath mass or matter, by itself
Lies rich in virtue and unmingled.   30

  Nest. With due observance of thy godlike
  seat,
Great Agamemnon, Nestor shall apply
Thy latest words. In the reproof of chance
Lies the true proof of men : the sea being
  smooth,
How many shallow bauble boats dare sail
Upon her patient breast, making their way
With those of nobler bulk!
But let the ruffian Boreas once enrage
The gentle Thetis, and anon behold
The strong-ribb'd bark through liquid moun-
  tains cut,   40
Bounding between the two moist elements,
Like Perseus' horse : where's then the saucy
  boat

Whose weak untimber'd sides but even now
Co-rivall'd greatness ? Either to harbor fled,
Or made a toast for Neptune. Even so
Doth valor's show and valor's worth divide
In storms of fortune ; for in her ray and
　brightness
The herd hath more annoyance by the breeze
Than by the tiger ; but when the splitting
　wind
Makes flexible the knees of knotted oaks, 50
And flies fled under shade, why, then the
　thing of courage
As roused with rage with rage doth sympa-
　thize,
And with an accent tuned in selfsame key
Retorts to chiding fortune
　　Ulyss　　　　　　　Agamemnon,
Thou great commander, nerve and bone of
　Greece,
Heart of our numbers, soul and only spirit,
In whom the tempers and the minds of all
Should be shut up, hear what Ulysses speaks
Besides the applause and approbation
To which, [*To Agamemnon*] most mighty for
　thy place and sway,　　　　　　　　60
[*To Nestor*] And thou most reverend for thy
　stretch'd-out life
I give to both your speeches, which were such
As Agamemnon and the hand of Greece
Should hold up high in brass, and such again
As venerable Nestor, hatch'd in silver,
Should with a bond of air, strong as the axle-
　tree
On which heaven rides, knit all the Greekish
　ears
To his experienced tongue, yet let it please
　both,
Thou great, and wise, to hear Ulysses speak.
　　Agam　Speak, prince of Ithaca, and be't
　of less expect　　　　　　　　　　　70
That matter needless, of importless burden,
Divide thy lips, than we are confident,
When rank Thersites opes his mastic jaws,
We shall hear music, wit and oracle
　　Ulyss　Troy, yet upon his basis, had been
　down,
And the great Hector's sword had lack'd a
　master,
But for these instances.
The specialty of rule hath been neglected .
And, look, how many Grecian tents do stand
Hollow upon this plain, so many hollow fac-
　tions　　　　　　　　　　　　　　80
When that the general is not like the hive
To whom the foragers shall all repair,
What honey is expected ? Degree being viz-
　arded,
The unworthiest shows as fairly in the mask.
The heavens themselves, the planets and this
　centre
Observe degree, priority and place,
Insisture, course, proportion, season, form,
Office and custom, in all line of order ;
And therefore is the glorious planet Sol
In noble eminence enthroned and sphered　90
Amidst the other ; whose medicinable eye

Corrects the ill aspects of planets evil,
And posts, like the commandment of a king,
Sans check to good and bad　but when the
　planets
In evil mixture to disorder wander,
What plagues and what portents ! what mu-
　tiny !
What raging of the sea ! shaking of earth !
Commotion in the winds ! frights, changes,
　horrors,
Divert and crack, rend and deracinat
The unity and married calm of states　　100
Quite from their fixure ! O, when degree is
　shaked,
Which is the ladder to all high designs,
Then enterprise is sick ! How could commu-
　nities,
Degrees in schools and brotherhoods in cities,
Peaceful commerce from dividable shores,
The primogenitive and due of birth,
Prerogative of age, crowns, sceptres, laurels,
But by degree, stand in authentic place ?
Take but degree away, untune that string,
And, hark, what discord follows ! each thing
　meets　　　　　　　　　　　　　110
In mere oppugnancy　the bounded waters
Should lift their bosoms higher than the
　shores
And make a sop of all this solid globe :
Strength should be lord of imbecility,
And the rude son should strike his father
　dead .
Force should be right , or rather, right and
　wrong,
Between whose endless jar justice resides,
Should lose their names, and so should justice
　too
Then every thing includes itself in power,
Power into will, will into appetite ,　　120
And appetite, an universal wolf,
So doubly seconded with will and power,
Must make perforce an universal prey,
And last eat up himself　Great Agamemnon,
This chaos, when degree is suffocate,
Follows the choking
And this neglection of degree it is
That by a pace goes backward, with a pur-
　pose
It hath to climb　The general's disdain'd
By him one step below, he by the next,　130
That next by him beneath , so every step,
Exampled by the first pace that is sick
Of his superior, grows to an envious fever
Of pale and bloodless emulation .
And 'tis this fever that keeps Troy on foot,
Not her own sinews　To end a tale of length,
Troy in our weakness stands, not in her
　strength　　　　　　　　　　[cover'd
　　Nest.　Most wisely hath Ulysses here dis-
The fever whereof all our power is sick.
　　Agam　The nature of the sickness found,
　Ulysses,　　　　　　　　　　　　140
What is the remedy ?
　　Ulyss　The great Achilles, whom opinion
　crowns
The sinew and the forehand of our host,

Having his ear full of his airy fame,
Grows dainty of his worth, and in his tent
Lies mocking our designs : with him Patro-
clus
Upon a lazy bed the livelong day
Breaks scurril jests,
And with ridiculous and awkward action,
Which, slanderer, he imitation calls, 150
He pageants us. Sometime, great Agamem-
non,
Thy topless deputation he puts on,
And, like a strutting player, whose conceit
Lies in his hamstring, and doth think it rich
To hear the wooden dialogue and sound
'Twixt his stretch'd footing and the scaffold-
age,—
Such to-be-pitied and o'er-wrested seeming
He acts thy greatness in : and when he speaks,
'Tis like a chime a-mending ; with terms un-
squared,
Which, from the tongue of roaring Typhon
dropp'd, 160
Would seem hyperboles. At this fusty stuff
The large Achilles, on his press'd bed lolling,
From his deep chest laughs out a loud ap-
plause ;
Cries 'Excellent ! 'tis Agamemnon just.
Now play me Nestor'; hem, and stroke thy
beard,
As he being drest to some oration.'
That's done, as near as the extremest ends
Of parallels, as like as Vulcan and his wife :
Yet god Achilles still cries 'Excellent !
'Tis Nestor right. Now play him me, Patro-
clus, 170
Arming to answer in a night alarm.'
And then, forsooth, the faint defects of age
Must be the scene of mirth ; to cough and
spit,
And, with a palsy-fumbling on his gorget,
Shake in and out the rivet : and at this sport
Sir Valor dies ; cries 'O, enough, Patroclus ;
Or give me ribs of steel ! I shall split all
In pleasure of my spleen.' And in this fash-
ion,
All our abilities, gifts, natures, shapes,
Severals and generals of grace exact, 180
Achievements, plots, orders, preventions,
Excitements to the field, or speech for truce,
Success or loss, what is or is not, serves
As stuff for these two to make paradoxes.
Nest. And in the imitation of these twain—
Who, as Ulysses says, opinion crowns
With an imperial voice—many are infect.
Ajax is grown self-will'd, and bears his head
In such a rein, in full as proud a place
As broad Achilles ; keeps his tent like him ;
Makes factious feasts ; rails on our state of
war, 191
Bold as an oracle, and sets Thersites,
A slave whose gall coins slanders like a mint,
To match us in comparisons with dirt,
To weaken and discredit our exposure,
How rank soever rounded in with danger.
Ulyss. They tax our policy, and call it
cowardice,

Count wisdom as no member of the war,
Forestall prescience, and esteem no act 199
But that of hand : the still and mental parts,
That do contrive how many hands shall strike,
When fitness calls them on, and know by
measure
Of their observant toil the enemies' weight,—
Why, this hath not a finger's dignity :
They call this bed-work, mappery, closet-war;
So that the ram that batters down the wall,
For the great swing and rudeness of his poise,
They place before his hand that made the en-
gine,
Or those that with the fineness of their souls
By reason guide his execution. 210
Nest. Let this be granted, and Achilles'
horse
Makes many Thetis' sons. [A tucket.
Agam. What trumpet ? look, Menelaus.
Men. From Troy.

Enter ÆNEAS.

Agam. What would you 'fore our tent ?
Æne. Is this great Agamemnon's tent, I
pray you ?
Agam. Even this.
Æne. May one, that is a herald and a
prince,
Do a fair message to his kingly ears ?
Agam. With surety stronger than Achilles'
arm 220
'Fore all the Greekish heads, which with one
voice
Call Agamemnon head and general
Æne. Fair leave and large security. How
may
A stranger to those most imperial looks
Know them from eyes of other mortals ?
Agam. How !
Æne. Ay ;
I ask, that I might waken reverence,
And bid the cheek be ready with a blush
Modest as morning when she coldly eyes
The youthful Phœbus : 230
Which is that god in office, guiding men ?
Which is the high and mighty Agamemnon ?
Agam. This Trojan scorns us ; or the men
of Troy
Are ceremonious courtiers.
Æne. Courtiers as free, as debonair, un-
arm'd,
As bending angels ; that's their fame in
[peace :
But when they would seem soldiers, they have
galls,
Good arms, strong joints, true swords ; and,
Jove's accord,
Nothing so full of heart. But peace, Æneas,
Peace, Trojan ; lay thy finger on thy lips ! 240
The worthiness of praise distains his worth,
If that the praised himself bring the praise
forth :
But what the repining enemy commends,
That breath fame blows ; that praise, sole
pure, transcends.
Agam. Sir, you of Troy, call you yourself
Æneas ?

Æne.   Ay, Greek, that is my name.
Agam.   What's your affair, I pray you?
Æne.   Sir, pardon; 'tis for Agamemnon's
   ears.
Agam.   He hears naught privately that
   comes from Troy.
Æne.   Nor I from Troy come not to whisper
   him: 250
I bring a trumpet to awake his ear,
To set his sense on the attentive bent,
And then to speak.
   Agam.   Speak frankly as the wind;
It is not Agamemnon's sleeping hour:
That thou shalt know. Trojan, he is awake,
He tells thee so himself.
   Æne.   Trumpet, blow loud,
Send thy brass voice through all these lazy
   tents;
And every Greek of mettle, let him know,
What Troy means fairly shall be spoke aloud.
         [*Trumpet sounds.*
We have, great Agamemnon, here in Troy 260
A prince call'd Hector,—Priam is his father,—
Who in this dull and long-continued truce
Is rusty grown: he bade me take a trumpet,
And to this purpose speak. Kings, princes,
   lords!
If there be one among the fair'st of Greece
That holds his honor higher than his ease,
That seeks his praise more than he fears his
   peril,
That knows his valor, and knows not his fear,
That loves his mistress more than in confes-
   sion,
With truant vows to her own lips he loves,
And dare avow her beauty and her worth 271
In other arms than hers,—to him this chal-
   lenge.
Hector, in view of Trojans and of Greeks,
Shall make it good, or do his best to do it,
He hath a lady, wiser, fairer, truer,
Than ever Greek did compass in his arms,
And will to-morrow with his trumpet call
Midway between your tents and walls of Troy,
To rouse a Grecian that is true in love:
If any come, Hector shall honor him;   280
If none, he'll say in Troy when he retires,
The Grecian dames are sunburnt and not
   worth
The splinter of a lance. Even so much.
   Agam.   This shall be told our lovers, Lord
     Æneas;
If none of them have soul in such a kind,
We left them all at home: but we are soldiers;
And may that soldier a mere recreant prove,
That means not, hath not, or is not in love!
If then one is, or hath, or means to be,
That one meets Hector; if none else, I am he.
   Nest.   Tell him of Nestor, one that was a
   man   291
When Hector's grandsire suck'd: he is old
   now;
But if there be not in our Grecian host
One noble man that hath one spark of fire,
To answer for his love, tell him from me
I'll hide my silver beard in a gold beaver

And in my vantbrace put this wither'd brawn,
And meeting him will tell him that my lady
Was fairer than his grandam and as chaste
As may be in the world: his youth in flood,
I'll prove this truth with my three drops of
   blood.   301
   Æne.   Now heavens forbid such scarcity of
   youth!
   Ulyss.   Amen.
   Agam.   Fair Lord Æneas, let me touch your
   hand;
To our pavilion shall I lead you, sir.
Achilles shall have word of this intent;
So shall each lord of Greece, from tent to
   tent:
Yourself shall feast with us before you go
And find the welcome of a noble foe.
     [*Exeunt all but Ulysses and Nestor.*
   Ulys.   Nestor!   310
   Nest.   What says Ulysses?
   Ulyss.   I have a young conception in my
   brain;
Be you my time to bring it to some shape.
   Nest.   What is't?
   Ulyss.   This 'tis:
Blunt wedges rive hard knots: the seeded
   pride
That hath to this maturity blown up
In rank Achilles must or now be cropp'd,
Or, shedding, breed a nursery of like evil,
To overbulk us all.
   Nest.   Well, and how?   320
   Ulyss.   This challenge that the gallant Hec-
   tor sends,
However it is spread in general name,
Relates in purpose only to Achilles.
   Nest.   The purpose is perspicuous even as
   substance,
Whose grossness little characters sum up:
And, in the publication, make no strain,
But that Achilles, were his brain as barren
As banks of Libya,—though, Apollo knows,
'Tis dry enough,—will, with great speed of
   judgment,
Ay, with celerity, find Hector's purpose   330
Pointing on him.
   Ulyss.   And wake him to the answer, think
   you?
   Nest.   Yes, 'tis most meet: whom may you
   else oppose,
That can from Hector bring his honor off,
If not Achilles? Though't be a sportful com-
   bat,
Yet in the trial much opinion dwells;
For here the Trojans taste our dear'st repute
With their finest palate: and trust to me,
   Ulysses,
Our imputation shall be oddly poised
In this wild action; for the success,   340
Although particular, shall give a scantling
Of good or bad unto the general;
And in such indexes, although small pricks
To their subsequent volumes, there is seen
The baby figure of the giant mass
Of things to come at large. It is supposed
He that meets Hector issues from our choice

                   48

And choice, being mutual act of all our souls,
Makes merit her election, and doth boil,
As 'twere from us all, a man distill'd   350
Out of our virtues ; who miscarrying,
What heart receives from hence the conquer-
   ing part,
To steel a strong opinion to themselves ?
Which entertain'd, limbs are his instruments,
In no less working than are swords and bows
Directive by the limbs.
  Ulyss. Give pardon to my speech :
Therefore 'tis meet Achilles meet not Hector.
Let us, like merchants, show our foulest wares,
And think, perchance, they'll sell ; if not, 360
The lustre of the better yet to show,
Shall show the better. Do not consent
That ever Hector and Achilles meet ;
For both our honor and our shame in this
Are dogg'd with two strange followers.
  Nest. I see them not with my old eyes :
   what are they ?
  Ulyss. What glory our Achilles shares from
   Hector,
Were he not proud, we all should share with
   him :
But he already is too insolent ;
And we were better parch in Afric sun   370
Than in the pride and salt scorn of his eyes,
Should he 'scape Hector fair : if he were foil'd,
Why then, we did our main opinion crush
In taint of our best man. No, make a lottery;
And, by device, let blockish Ajax draw
The sort to fight with Hector : among ourselves
Give him allowance for the better man ;
For that will physic the great Myrmidon
Who broils in loud applause, and make him
   fall
His crest that prouder than blue Iris bends.
If the dull brainless Ajax come safe off,   381
We'll dress him up in voices : if he fail,
Yet go we under our opinion still
That we have better men. But, hit or miss,
Our project's life this shape of sense assumes :
Ajax employ'd plucks down Achilles' plumes.
  Nest. Ulysses,
Now I begin to relish thy advice ;
And I will give a taste of it forthwith
To Agamemnon : go we to him straight.   390
Two curs shall tame each other : pride alone
Must tarre the mastiffs on, as 'twere their
   bone.   [*Exeunt.*

ACT II.

SCENE I. *A part of the Grecian camp.*

Enter AJAX *and* THERSITES.

  Ajax. Thersites !
  Ther. Agamemnon, how if he had boils ?
full, all over, generally ?
  Ajax. Thersites !
  Ther. And those boils did run ? say so : did
not the general run then ? were not that a
botchy core ?
  Ajax. Dog !

  Ther. Then would come some matter from
him ; I see none now.   10
  Ajax. Thou bitch-wolf's son, canst thou
not hear ? [*Beating him*] Feel, then.
  Ther. The plague of Greece upon thee, thou
mongrel beef-witted lord !
  Ajax. Speak then, thou vinewedst leaven,
speak : I will beat thee into handsomeness.
  Ther. I shall sooner rail thee into wit and
holiness : but, I think, thy horse will sooner
con an oration than thou learn a prayer without book. Thou canst strike, canst thou ? a
red murrain o' thy jade's tricks !   21
  Ajax. Toadstool, learn me the proclamation.
  Ther. Dost thou think I have no sense, thou
strikest me thus ?
  Ajax. The proclamation !
  Ther. Thou art proclaimed a fool, I think.
  Ajax. Do not, porpentine, do not : my
fingers itch.
  Ther. I would thou didst itch from head to
foot and I had the scratching of thee ; I would
make thee the loathsomest scab in Greece.
When thou art forth in the incursions, thou
strikest as slow as another.
  Ajax. I say, the proclamation !
  Ther. Thou grumblest and railest every
hour on Achilles, and thou art as full of envy
at his greatness as Cerberus is at Proserpina's
beauty, ay, that thou barkest at him.
  Ajax. Mistress Thersites !
  Ther. Thou shouldest strike him.   40
  Ajax. Cobloaf !
  Ther. He would pun thee into shivers with
his fist, as a sailor breaks a biscuit.
  Ajax. [*Beating him*] You whoreson cur !
  Ther. Do, do.
  Ajax. Thou stool for a witch !
  Ther. Ay, do, do ; thou sodden-witted lord !
thou hast no more brain than I have in mine
elbows ; an assinego may tutor thee : thou
scurvy-valiant ass ! thou art here but to thrash
Trojans ; and thou art bought and sold among
those of any wit, like a barbarian slave. If
thou use to beat me, I will begin at thy heel,
and tell what thou art by inches, thou thing of
no bowels, thou !
  Ajax. You dog !
  Ther. You scurvy lord !
  Ajax. [*Beating him*] You cur !
  Ther. Mars his idiot ! do, rudeness ; do,
camel ; do, do.   59

Enter ACHILLES *and* PATROCLUS.

  Achil. Why, how now, Ajax ! wherefore
do you thus ? How now, Thersites ! what's
the matter, man ?
  Ther. You see him there, do you ?
  Achil. Ay ; what's the matter ?
  Ther. Nay, look upon him.
  Achil. So I do : what's the matter ?
  Ther. Nay, but regard him well.
  Achil. 'Well !' why, I do so.
  Ther. But yet you look not well upon him ;
for whosoever you take him to be, he is Ajax.

Achil. I know that, fool. 71
Ther. Ay, but that fool knows not himself
Ajax Therefore I beat thee.
Ther. Lo, lo, lo, lo, what modicums of wit
he utters ! his evasions have ears thus long I
have bobbed his brain more than he has beat
my bones I will buy nine sparrows for a
penny, and his pia mater is not worth the
ninth part of a sparrow This lord, Achilles,
Ajax, who wears his wit in his belly and his
guts in his head, I'll tell you what I say of
him. 81
Achil. What ?
Ther. I say, this Ajax—
[*Ajax offers to beat him.*
Achil. Nay, good Ajax.
Ther. Has not so much wit—
Achil. Nay, I must hold you.
Ther. As will stop the eye of Helen's needle,
for whom he comes to fight.
Achil. Peace, fool !
Ther I would have peace and quietness,
but the fool will not he there that he : look
you there.
Ajax. O thou damned cur ' I shall—
Achil Will you set your wit to a fool's ?
Ther. No, I warrant you , for a fool's will
shame it.
Pat   Good words, Thersites
Achil. What's the quarrel ?
Ajax. I bade the vile owl go learn me the
tenor of the proclamation, and he rails upon
me 100
Ther. I serve thee not.
Ajax Well, go to, go to
Ther. I serve here voluntarily.
Achil Your last service was sufferance,
'twas not voluntary no man is beaten volun-
tary' Ajax was here the voluntary, and you
as under an impress
Ther. E'en so , a great deal of your wit,
too, lies in your sinews, or else there be liars
Hector shall have a great catch, if he knock
out either of your brains : a' were as good
crack a fusty nut with no kernel
Achil. What, with me too, Thersites ?
Ther There's Ulysses and old Nestor,
whose wit was mouldy ere your grandsires
had nails on their toes, yoke you like
draughtoxen and make you plough up the
wars
Achil What, what?
Ther. Yes, good sooth : to, Achilles ! to,
Ajax ! to ' 120
Ajax. I shall cut out your tongue.
Ther. 'Tis no matter, I shall speak as much
as thou afterwards
Patr. No more words, Thersites , peace '
Ther. I will hold my peace when Achilles'
brach bids me, shall I ?
Achil. There's for you, Patroclus
Ther. I will see you hanged, like clotpoles,
ere I come any more to your tents I will keep
where there is wit stirring and leave the faction
of fools. [*Exit.*
Patr. A good riddance.

Achil Marry, this, sir, is proclaim'd through
all our host
That Hector, by the fifth hour of the sun,
Will with a trumpet 'twixt our tents and Troy
To-morrow morning call some knight to arms
That hath a stomach , and such a one that
dare
Maintain—I know not what . 'tis trash Fare-
well
Ajax Farewell Who shall answer him ?
Achil I know not 'tis put to lottery; other-
wise 140
He knew his man.
Ajax. O, meaning you I will go learn
more of it. [*Exeunt.*

SCENE II. *Troy. A room in Priam's palace.*

Enter PRIAM, HECTOR, TROILUS, PARIS, *and*
HELENUS.

Pri. After so many hours, lives. speeches
spent,
Thus once again says Nestor from the Greeks:
' Deliver Helen, and all damage else—
As honor, loss of time, travail, expense,
Wounds, friends, and what else dear that is
consumed
In hot digestion of this cormorant war—
Shall be struck off.' Hector, what say you
to 't ?
Hect. Though no man lesser fears the
Greeks than I
As far as toucheth my particular,
Yet, dread Priam, 10
There is no lady of more softer bowels,
More spongy to suck in the sense of fear
More ready to cry out ' Who knows what fol-
lows ? '
Than Hector is the wound of peace is surety,
Surety secure , but modest doubt is call'd
The beacon of the wise, the tent that searches
To the bottom of the worst Let Helen go
Since the first sword was drawn about this
question,
Every tithe soul, 'mongst many thousand
dismes,
Hath been as dear as Helen , I mean, of ours·
If we have lost so many tenths of ours,
To guard a thing not ours nor worth to us,
Had it our name, the value of one ten,
What merit s in that reason which denies
The yielding of her up ?
Tro. Fie, fie, my brother !
Weigh you the worth and honor of a king ·
So great as our dread father in a scale
Of common ounces ? will you with counters
sum
The past proportion of his infinite ?
And buckle in a waist most fathomless 30
With spans and inches so diminutive
As fears and reasons ? fie, for godly shame !
Hel No marvel, though you bite so snarp
at reasons,
You are so empty of them Should not our
father
Bear the great sway of his affairs with reasons,

Because your speech hath none that tells him
　　so ?
　Tro. You are for dreams and slumbers,
　　brother priest ;
You fur your gloves with reason. Here are
　　your reasons :
You know an enemy intends you harm ,
You know a sword employ'd is perilous,　　40
And reason flies the object of all harm :
Who marvels then, when Helenus beholds
A Grecian and his sword, if he do set
The very wings of reason to his heels
And fly like chidden Mercury from Jove,
Or like a star disorb'd ? Nay, if we talk of
　　reason,
Let's shut our gates and sleep: manhood and
　　honor.
Should have hare-hearts, would they but fat
　　their thoughts
With this cramm'd reason : reason and respect
Make livers pale and lustihood deject.　　50
　Hect. Brother, she is not worth what she
　　doth cost
The holding.
　Tro. What is aught, but as 'tis valued ?
　Hect. But value dwells not in particular
　　will ;
It holds his estimate and dignity
As well wherein 'tis precious of itself
As in the prizer . 'tis mad idolatry
To make the service greater than the god ,
And the will dotes that is attributive
To what infectiously itself affects,
Without some image of the affected merit.　60
　Tro. I take to-day a wife, and my election
Is led on in the conduct of my will ;
My will enkindled by mine eyes and ears,
Two traded pilots 'twixt the dangerous shores
Of will and judgment : how may I avoid,
Although my will distaste what it elected,
The wife I chose ? there can be no evasion
To blench from this and to stand firm by
　　honor :
We turn not back the silks upon the merchant,
When we have soil'd them, nor the remainder
　　viands　　　　　　　　　　　　　　70
We do not throw in unrespective sieve,
Because we now are full. It was thought
　　meet
Paris should do some vengeance on the
　　Greeks :
Your breath of full consent bellied his sails ;
The seas and winds, old wranglers, took a
　　truce　　　　　　　　　　　　　　[sired,
And did him service : he touch'd the ports de-
And for an old aunt whom the Greeks held
　　captive,
He brought a Grecian queen, whose youth and
　　freshness　　　　　　　　　　　　[ling.
Wrinkles Apollo's, and makes stale the morn-
Why keep we her ? the Grecians keep our
　　aunt :　　　　　　　　　　　　　80
Is she worth keeping ? why, she is a pearl,
Whose price hath launch'd above a thousand
　　ships,
And turn'd crown'd kings to merchants.

If you'll avouch 'twas wisdom Paris went—
As you must needs, for you all cried 'Go, go,'—
If you'll confess he brought home noble prize—
As you must needs, for you all clapp'd your
　　hands
And cried ' Inestimable ! '—why do you now
The issue of your proper wisdoms rate,
And do a deed that fortune never did,　　90
Beggar the estimation which you prized
Richer than sea and land ? O, theft most base,
That we have stol'n what we do fear to keep !
But, thieves, unworthy of a thing so stol'n,
That in their country did them that disgrace,
We fear to warrant in our native place !
　Cas. [*Within*] Cry, Trojans, cry !
　Pri.　　What noise ? what shriek is this?
　Tro. 'Tis our mad sister, I do know her
　　voice.
　Cas. [*Within*] Cry, Trojans !
　Hect. It is Cassandra.　　　　　　100

Enter CASSANDRA, *raving.*

　Cas. Cry, Trojans, cry ! lend me ten thou-
　　sand eyes,
And I will fill them with prophetic tears.
　Hect. Peace, sister, peace !
　Cas. Virgins and boys, mid-age and wrin-
　　kled eld,
Soft infancy, that nothing canst but cry,
Add to my clamors ! let us pay betimes
A moiety of that mass of moan to come.
Cry, Trojans, cry ! practice your eyes with
　　tears !
Troy must not be, nor goodly Ilion stand ;
Our firebrand brother, Paris, burns us all.　110
Cry, Trojans, cry ! a Helen and a woe :
Cry, cry ! Troy burns, or else let Helen go.
　　　　　　　　　　　　　　　[*Exit.*
　Hect. Now, youthful Troilus, do not these
　　high strains
Of divination in our sister work
Some touches of remorse ? or is your blood
So madly hot that no discourse of reason,
Nor fear of bad success in a bad cause.
Can qualify the same ?
　Tro.　　　　Why, brother Hector,
We may not think the justness of each act
Such and no other than event doth form it,
Nor once deject the courage of our minds,　121
Because Cassandra's mad : her brain-sick rap-
　　tures
Cannot distaste the goodness of a quarrel
Which hath our several honors all engaged
To make it gracious. For my private part,
I am no more touch'd than all Priam's sons :
And Jove forbid there should be done amongst
　　us
Such things as might offend the weakest spleen
To fight for and maintain !
　Par. Else might the world convince of levity
As well my undertakings as your counsels :
But I attest the gods, your full consent
Gave wings to my propension and cut off
All fears attending on so dire a project.
For what, alas, can these my single arms ?
What propugnation is in one man's valor,

To stand the push and enmity of those
This quarrel would excite ? Yet, I protest,
Were I alone to pass the difficulties
And had as ample power as I have will,   140
Paris should ne'er retract what he hath done,
Nor faint in the pursuit.
    Pri.   Paris, you speak
Like one besotted on your sweet delights :
You have the honey still, but these the gall ;
So to be valiant is no praise at all.
    Par. Sir, I propose not merely to myself
The pleasures such a beauty brings with it ;
But I would have the soil of her fair rape
Wiped off, in honorable keeping her.
What treason were it to the ransack'd queen,
Disgrace to your great worths and shame to
    me,   151
Now to deliver her possession up
On terms of base compulsion ! Can it be
That so degenerate a strain as this
Should once set footing in your generous
    bosoms ?
There's not the meanest spirit on our party
Without a heart to dare or sword to draw
When Helen is defended, nor none so noble
Whose life were ill bestow'd or death unfamed
Where Helen is the subject ; then, I say,   160
Well may we fight for her whom we know
    well,
The world's large spaces cannot paralle'.
    Hect. Paris and Troilus, you have both said
    well,
And on the cause and question now in hand
Have glozed, but superficially : not much
Unlike young men, whom Aristotle thought
Unfit to hear moral philosophy :
The reasons you allege do more conduce
To the hot passion of distemper'd blood
Than to make up a free determination   170
'Twixt right and wrong, for pleasure and re-
    venge
Have ears more deaf than adders to the voice
Of any true decision. Nature craves
All dues be render'd to their owners : now,
What nearer debt in all humanity
Than wife is to the husband ? If this law
Of nature be corrupted through affection,
And that great minds, of partial indulgence
To their benumbed wills, resist the same,
There is a law in each well-order'd nation 180
To curb those raging appetites that are
Most disobedient and refractory.
If Helen then be wife to Sparta's king,
As it is known she is, these moral laws
Of nature and of nations speak aloud
To have her back return'd : thus to persist
In doing wrong extenuates not wrong,
But makes it much more heavy. Hector's
    opinion
Is this in way of truth ; yet ne'ertheless,
My spritely brethren, I propend to you   190
In resolution to keep Helen still,
For 'tis a cause that hath no mean dependance
Upon our joint and several dignities.
    Tro. Why, there you touch'd the life of
    our design ;

Were it not glory that we more affected
Than the performance of our heaving spleens,
I would not wish a drop of Trojan blood
Spent more in her defence. But, worthy Hec-
    tor,
She is a theme of honor and renown,
A spur to valiant and magnanimous deeds,
Whose present courage may beat down our
    foes,   201
And fame in time to come canonize us ;
For, I presume, brave Hector would not lose
So rich advantage of a promised glory
As smiles upon the forehead of this action
For the wide world's revenue.
    Hect.   I am yours,
You valiant offspring of great Priamus.
I have a roisting challenge sent amongst
The dull and factious nobles of the Greeks
Will strike amazement to their drowsy spirits:
I was advertised their great general slept, 211
Whilst emulation in the army crept :
This, I presume, will wake him. [*Exeunt.*

    SCENE III. *The Grecian camp. Before
        Achilles' tent.*

    Enter THERSITES, *solus.*

    Ther. How now, Thersites ! what, lost in
the labyrinth of thy fury ! Shall the elephant
Ajax carry it thus ? he beats me, and I rail at
him : O, worthy satisfaction ! would it were
otherwise ; that I could bent him, whilst he
railed at me. 'Sfoot, I'll learn to conjure and
raise devils, but I'll see some issue of my spite-
ful execrations. Then there's Achilles, a rare
enginer ! If Troy be not taken till these two
undermine it, the walls will stand till they fall
of themselves. O thou great thunder-darter
of Olympus, forget that thou art Jove, the king
of gods, and, Mercury, lose all the serpentine
craft of thy caduceus, if ye take not that little
little less than little wit from them that they
have ! which short-armed ignorance itself
knows is so abundant scarce, it will not in cir-
cumvention deliver a fly from a spider, without drawing their massy irons and cutting the
web. After this, the vengeance on the whole
camp ! or rather, the bone-ache ! for that, methinks, is the curse dependant on those that
war for a placket. I have said my prayers and
devil Envy say Amen. What ho ! my Lord
Achilles !

    Enter PATROCLUS.

    Patr. Who's there ? Thersites ! Good Ther-
sites, come in and rail.
    Ther. If I could have remembered a gilt
counterfeit, thou wouldst not have slipped out
of my contemplation : but it is no matter ; thyself upon thyself ! The common curse of
mankind, folly and ignorance, be thine in great
revenue ! heaven bless thee from a tutor, and
discipline come not near thee ! Let thy blood
be thy direction till thy death ! then if she
that lays thee out says thou art a fair corse,
I'll be sworn and sworn upon't she never

shrouded any but lazars.   Amen.   Where's Achilles ?

Patr.   What, art thou devout ? wast thou in prayer ?

Ther.   Ay : the heavens hear me !   40

Enter ACHILLES.

Achil.   Who's there ?

Patr.   Thersites, my lord.

Achil.   Where, where?   Art_thou come ? why, my cheese, my digestion, why hast thou not served thyself in to my table so many meals ? Come, what's Agamemnon ?

Ther.   Thy commander, Achilles.   Then tell me, Patroclus, what's Achilles ?

Patr.   Thy lord, Thersites : then tell me, I pray thee, what's thyself ?   ·   50

Ther.   Thy knower, Patroclus : then tell me, Patroclus, what art thou ?

Patr.   Thou mayst tell that knowest.

Achil.   O, tell, tell.

Ther.   I'll decline the whole question. Agamemnon commands Achilles ; Achilles is my lord ; I am Patroclus' knower, and Patroclus is a fool.

Patr.   You rascal !

Ther.   Peace, fool ! I have not done.   60

Achil.   He is a privileged man. Proceed, Thersites.

Ther.   Agamemnon is a fool ; Achilles is a fool ; Thersites is a fool, and, as aforesaid, Patroclus is a fool.

Achil.   Derive this ; come.

Ther.   Agamemnon is a fool to offer to command Achilles ; Achilles is a fool to be commanded of Agamemnon ; Thersites is a fool to serve such a fool, and Patroclus is a fool positive.   70

Patr.   Why am I a fool ?

Ther.   Make that demand of the prover. It suffices me thou art. Look you, who comes here ?

Achil.   Patroclus, I'll speak with nobody. Come in with me, Thersites.   [*Exit.*

Ther.   Here is such patchery, such juggling and such knavery ! all the argument is a cuckold and a whore ; a good quarrel to draw emulous factions and bleed to death upon. Now, the dry serpigo on the subject ! and war and lechery confound all !   [*Exit.*

Enter AGAMEMNON, ULYSSES, NESTOR, DIOMEDES, *and* AJAX.

Agam.   Where is Achilles ?

Patr.   Within his tent ; but ill disposed, my lord.

Agam.   ,Let it be known to him that we are here.

He shent our messengers ; and we lay by Our appertainments, visiting of him : Let him be told so ; lest perchance he think We dare not move the question of our place, Or know not what we are.   ·   90

Patr.   I shall say so to him. [*Exit.*

Ulyss.   We saw him at the opening of his tent :

He is not sick.

Ajax.   Yes, lion-sick, sick of proud heart : you may call it melancholy, if you will favor the man ; but, by my head, 'tis pride : but why, why ? let him show us the cause. A word, my lord.   [*Takes Agamemnon aside.*

Nest.   What moves Ajax thus to bay at him ?

Ulyss.   Achilles hath inveigled his fool from him.   100

Nest.   Who, Thersites ?

Ulyss.   He.

Nest.   Then will Ajax lack matter, if he have lost his argument.

Ulyss.   No, you see, he is his argument that has his argument, Achilles.

Nest.   All the better ; their fraction is more our wish than their faction : but it was a strong composure a fool could disunite.   109

Ulyss.   The amity that wisdom knits not, folly may easily untie. Here comes Patroclus.

Re-enter PATROCLUS

Nest.   No Achilles with him.

Ulyss.   The elephant hath joints, but none for courtesy : his legs are legs for necessity, not for flexure.

Patr.   Achilles bids me say, he is much sorry,   ,[ure

If any thing more than your sport and pleas-
Did move your greatness and this noble state
To call upon him ; he hopes it is no other
But for your health and your digestion sake,
And after-dinner's breath.   121

Agam.   Hear you, Patroclus :
We are too well acquainted with these answers :
But his evasion, wing'd thus swift with scorn,
Cannot outfly our apprehensions.
Much attribute he hath, and much the reason
Why we ascribe it to him ; yet all his virtues,
Not virtuously on his own part beheld,
Do in our eyes begin to lose their gloss,
Yea, like fair fruit in an unwholesome dish,
Are like to rot untasted. Go and tell him, 130
We come to speak with him ; and you shall not sin,
If you do say we think him over-proud
And under-honest, in self-assumption greater
Than in the note of judgment ; and worthier than himself
Here tend the savage strangeness he puts on,
Disguise the holy strength of their command,
And underwrite in an observing kind
His humorous predominance ; yea, watch
His pettish lunes, his ebbs, his flows, as if 139
The passage and whole carriage of this action
Rode on his tide. Go tell him this, and add,
That if he overhold his price so much,
We'll none of him ; but let him, like an engine
Not portable, lie under this report :
' Bring action hither, this cannot go to war :
A stirring dwarf we do allowance give
Before a sleeping giant.' Tell him so.

Patr.   I shall ; and bring his answer presently.   [*Exit.*

Agam　In second voice we'll not be satis-
fied ;
We come to speak with him　Ulysses, enter
you.　　　　　　　　　　[*Exit Ulysses.* 150
Ajax.　What is he more than another ?
Agam　No more than what he thinks he is.
Ajax　Is he so much ?　Do you not think
he thinks himself a better man than I am ?
Agam.　No question.
Ajax　Will you subscribe his thought, and
say he is ?
Agam　No, noble Ajax ; you are as strong,
as valiant, as wise, no less noble, much more
gentle, and altogether more tractable.　　160
Ajax.　Why should a man be proud ?　How
doth pride grow ?　I know not what pride is.
Agam　Your mind is the clearer, Ajax, and
your virtues the fairer.　He that is proud eats
up himself　pride is his own glass, his own
trumpet, his own chronicle , and whatever
praises itself but in the deed, devours the deed
in the praise.
Ajax　I do hate a proud man, as I hate the
engendering of toads　　　　　　　　　170
Nest　Yet he loves himself : is 't not
strange ?　　　　　　　　　　　　　[*Aside.*

Re-enter ULYSSES

Ulyss.　Achilles will not to the field to-
morrow.
Agam.　What's his excuse ?
Ulyss　　　　　　　He doth rely on none,
But carries on the stream of his dispose
Without observance or respect of any,
In will peculiar and in self-admission
Agam　Why will he not upon our fair re-
quest
Untent his person and share the air with us ?
Ulyss.　Things small as nothing, for re-
quest's sake only,
He makes important　possess'd he is with
greatness,　　　　　　　　　　　　180
And speaks not to himself but with a pride
That quarrels at self-breath　imagined worth
Holds in his blood such swoln and hot dis-
course
That 'twixt his mental and his active parts
Kingdom'd Achilles in commotion rages
And batters down himself ·　what should I
say ?
He is so plaguy proud that the death-tokens
of it
Cry ' No recovery '
Agam　　　　　Let Ajax go to him
Dear lord, go you and greet him in his tent
'Tis said he holds you well, and will be led 190
At your request a little from himself
Ulyss.　O Agamemnon, let it not be so !
We'll consecrate the steps that Ajax makes
When they go from Achilles .　shall the proud
lord
That bastes his arrogance with his own seam
And never suffers matter of the world
Enter his thoughts, save such as do revolve
And ruminate himself, shall he be worshipp'd
Of that we hold an idol more than he ?　199

No, this thrice worthy and right valiant lord
Must not so stale his palm, nobly acquired ,
Nor, by my will, assubjugate his merit,
As amply titled as Achilles is,
By going to Achilles .
That were to enlard his fat already pride'
And add more coals to Cancer when he burns
With entertaining great Hyperion
This lord go to him !　Jupiter forbid,
And say in thunder ' Achilles go to him.'
Nest.　[*Aside to Dio.*]　O, this is well ; he
rubs the vein of him.　　　　　　　210
Dio　[*Aside to Nest*]　And how his silence
drinks up this applause '
Ajax　If I go to him, with my armed fist
I'll pash him o'er the face
Agam.　O, no, you shall not go
Ajax　An a' be proud with me, I'll pheeze
his pride
Let me go to him
Ulyss　Not for the worth that hangs upon
our quarrel.
Ajax.　A paltry, insolent fellow '
Nest　How he describes himself '
Ajax　Can he not be sociable ?　　220
Ulyss　The raven chides blackness.
Ajax　I'll let his humor- blood
Agam.　He will be the physician that should
be the patient
Ajax　An all men were o' my mind,—
Ulyss　Wit would be out of fashion.
Ajax　A' should not bear it so, a' should
eat swords first　shall pride carry it ?
Nest　An 'twould, you'ld carry half.
Ulyss　A' would have ten shares　　230
Ajax　I will knead him , I'll make him
supple
Nest　He's not yet through warm : force
him with praises . pour in, pour in , his am-
bition is dry
Ulyss　[*To Agam*]　My lord, you feed too
much on this dislike
Nest　Our noble general, do not do so.
Dio.　You must prepare to fight without
Achilles
Ulyss　Why, 'tis this naming of him does
him harm
Here is a man—but 'tis before his face ,　240
I will be silent
Nest　　　　　Wherefore should you so ?
He is not emulous, as Achilles is
Ulyss　Know the whole world, he is as
valiant
Ajax.　A whoreson dog, that shall palter
thus with us !
Would he were a Trojan !
Nest　What a vice were it in Ajax now,—
Ulyss　If he were proud,—
Dio.　Or covetous of praise,—
Ulyss　Ay, or surly borne,—
Dio.　Or strange, or self-affected !　250
Ulyss　Thank the heavens, lord, thou art
of sweet composure ;
Praise him that got thee, she that gave thee
suck :
Famed be thy tutor, and thy parts of nature

Thrice famed, beyond all erudition :
But he that disciplined thy arms to fight,
Let Mars divide eternity in twain,
And give him half : and, for thy vigor,
Bull-bearing Milo his addition yield
To sinewy Ajax. I will not praise thy wisdom,
Which, like a bourn, a pale, a shore, confines
Thy spacious and dilated parts : here's Nes-
     tor ;   261
Instructed by the antiquary times,
He must, he is, he cannot but be wise :
But pardon, father Nestor, were your days
As green as Ajax' and your brain so temper'd,
You should not have the eminence of him,
But be as Ajax.

Ajax.   Shall I call you father ?
Nest. Ay, my good son.
Dio.   Be ruled by him, Lord Ajax.
Ulyss. There is no tarrying here ; the hart
     Achilles
Keeps thicket. Please it our great general
To call together all his state of war ;   271
Fresh kings are come to Troy : to-morrow
We must with all our main of power stand
     fast :
And here's a lord,—come knights from east to
     west,
And cull their flower, Ajax shall cope the
     best.

Agam. Go we to council. Let Achilles
     sleep :
Light boats sail swift, though greater hulks
     draw deep.   [*Exeunt.*

ACT III.

SCENE I. *Troy. Priam's palace.*

Enter a Servant *and* PANDARUS.

Pan. Friend, you ! pray you, a word: do
not you follow the young Lord Paris ?
Serv. Ay, sir, when he goes before me.
Pan. You depend upon him, I mean ?
Serv. Sir, I do depend upon the lord.
Pan. You depend upon a noble gentleman;
I must needs praise him.
Serv. The lord be praised !
Pan. You know me, do you not ?
Serv. Faith, sir, superficially.   10
Pan. Friend, knows me better ; I am the
Lord Pandarus.
Serv. I hope I shall know your honor
better.
Pan. I do desire it.
Serv. You are in the state of grace.
Pan. Grace ! not so, friend : honor and
lordship are my titles. [*Music within.*] What
music is this ?
Serv. I do but partly know, sir : it is music
in parts.   20
Pan. Know you the musicians ?
Serv. Wholly, sir.
Pan. Who play they to ?
Serv. To the hearers, sir.

Pan. At whose pleasure, friend ?
Serv. At mine, sir, and theirs that love music.
Pan. Command, I mean, friend.
Serv. Who shall I command, sir ?
Pan. Friend, we understand not one another : I am too courtly and thou art too cun
ning. At whose request do these men play ?
Serv. That's to 't indeed, sir : marry, sir,
at the request of Paris my lord, who's there in
person ; with him, the mortal Venus, the
heart-blood of beauty, love's invisible soul,—
Pan. Who, my cousin Cressida ?
Serv. No, sir, Helen : could you not find
out that by her attributes ?
Pan. It should seem, fellow, that thou hast
not seen the Lady Cressida. I come to speak
with Paris from the Prince Troilus : I will
make a complimental assault upon him, for my
business seethes.
Serv. Sodden business ! there's a stewed
phrase indeed !

Enter PARIS *and* HELEN, *attended.*

Pan. Fair be to you, my lord, and to all this
fair company ! fair desires, in all fair measure,
fairly guide them ! especially to you, fair
queen ! fair thoughts be your fair pillow !   49
Helen. Dear lord, you are full of fair words.
Pan. You speak your fair pleasure, sweet
queen. Fair prince, here is good broken
music.
Par. You have broke it, cousin : and by
my life, you shall make it whole again ; you
shall piece it out with a piece of your performance. Nell, he is full of harmony.
Pan. Truly, lady, no.
Helen. O, sir,—
Pan. Rude, in sooth ; in good sooth, very
rude.   60
Par. Well said, my lord ! well, you say so
in fits.
Pan. I have business to my lord, dear queen.
My lord, will you vouchsafe me a word ?
Helen. Nay, this shall not hedge us out : we'll
hear you sing, certainly.
Pan. Well, sweet queen, you are pleasant
with me. But, marry, thus, my lord ; my
dear lord and most esteemed friend, your brother Troilus,—   70
Helen. My Lord Pandarus ; honey-sweet
lord,—
Pan. Go to, sweet queen, go to :—commends
himself most affectionately to you,—
Helen. You shall not bob us out of our melody : if you do, our melancholy upon your
head !
Pan. Sweet queen, sweet queen ! that's a
sweet queen, i' faith.
Helen. And to make a sweet lady sad is a
sour offence.   80
Pan. Nay, that shall not serve your turn ;
that shall not, in truth, la. Nay, I care not
for such words ; no, no. And, my lord, he
desires you, that if the king call for him at
supper, you will make his excuse.
Helen. My Lord Pandarus,—

Pan. What says my sweet queen, my very
very sweet queen?

Par What exploit's in hand? where sups
he to-night? 90

Helen. Nay, but, my lord,—

Pan What says my sweet queen? My
cousin will fall out with you. You must not
know where he sups

Pan I'll lay my life, with my disposer Cressida.

Pan No, no, no such matter, you are wide
come, your disposer is sick

Par. Well, I'll make excuse

Pan. Ay, good my lord Why should you
say Cressida? no, your poor disposer's sick.

Par. I say.

Pan. You spy! what do you spy? Come,
give me an instrument Now, sweet queen.

Helen Why, this is kindly done

Pan My niece is horribly in love with a
thing you have, sweet queen.

Helen She shall have it, my lord, if it be
not my lord Paris

Pan He! no, she'll none of him, they two
are twain 111

Helen. Falling in, after falling out, may
make them three

Pan Come, come, I'll hear no more of this,
I'll sing you a song now.

Helen. Ay, ay, prithee now. By my troth,
sweet lord, thou hast a fine forehead

Pan Ay, you may, you may.

Helen. Let thy song be love this love will
undo us all O Cupid, Cupid, Cupid! 120

Pan. Love! ay, that it shall, i' faith.

Par. Ay, good now, love, love, nothing but
love

Pan In good troth, it begins so [*Sings*
Love, love, nothing but love, still more!
For, O, love's bow
Shoots buck and doe:
The shaft confounds,
Not that it wounds,
But tickles still the sore 130
These lovers cry Oh! oh! they die!
Yet that which seems the wound to kill,
Doth turn oh! oh! to ha! ha! he!
So dying love lives still
Oh! oh! a while, but ha! ha! ha!
Oh! oh! groans out for ha! ha! ha!
Heigh-ho!

Helen. In love, i' faith, to the very tip of
the nose. 139

Par. He eats nothing but doves, love, and
that breeds hot blood, and hot blood begets
hot thoughts, and hot thoughts beget hot deeds,
and hot deeds is love.

Pan. Is this the generation of love? hot
blood, hot thoughts, and hot deeds? Why,
they are vipers: is love a generation of vipers?
Sweet lord, who's a-field to-day?

Par Hector, Deiphobus, Helenus, Antenor,
and all the gallantry of Troy I would fain
have armed to-day, but my Nell would not
have it so How chance my brother Troilus
went not? 151

Helen He hangs the lip at something . you
know all, Lord Pandarus.

Pan Not I, honey-sweet queen. I long to
hear how they sped to-day. You'll remember
your brother's excuse?

Par To a hair

Pan. Farewell, sweet queen.

Helen Commend me to your niece

Pan I will, sweet queen [*Exit* 160
[*A retreat sounded.*

Par They're come from field : let us to
Priam's hall,
To greet the warriors. Sweet Helen, I must
woo you
To help unarm our Hector his stubborn
buckles,
With these your white enchanting fingers
touch'd,
Shall more obey than to the edge of steel
Or force of Greekish sinews, you shall do
more
Than all the island kings,—disarm great
Hector

Helen. 'Twill make us proud to be his
servant, Paris,
Yea, what he shall receive of us in duty
Gives us more palm in beauty than we have,
Yea, overshines ourself. 171

Par. Sweet, above thought I love thee.
[*Exeunt*

SCENE II *The same. Pandarus' orchard.*

Enter PANDARUS *and* TROILUS' BOY, *meeting.*

Pan. How now! where's thy master? at
my cousin Cressida's?

Boy No, sir; he stays for you to conduct
him thither

Pan. O, here he comes.

Enter TROILUS.

How now, how now!

Tro Sirrah, walk off. [*Exit Boy.*

Pan Have you seen my cousin?

Tro. No, Pandarus I stalk about her door,
Like a strange soul upon the Stygian banks 10
Staying for waftage O, be thou my Charon,
And give me swift transportance to those fields
Where I may wallow in the lily-beds
Proposed for the deserver! O gentle Pandarus,
From Cupid's shoulder pluck his painted wings
And fly with me to Cressid!

Pan. Walk here i' the orchard, I'll bring
her straight. [*Exit.*

Tro I am giddy; expectation whirls me
round 20
The imaginary relish is so sweet
That it enchants my sense · what will it be,
When that the watery palate tastes indeed
Love's thrice repured nectar? death, I fear me,
Swooning destruction, or some joy too fine,
Too subtle-potent, tuned too sharp in sweetness,
For the capacity of my ruder powers:
I fear it much, and I do fear besides,
That I shall lose distinction in my joys;

As doth a battle, when they charge on heaps
The enemy flying.   -   30

Re-enter PANDARUS.

Pan. She's making her ready, she'll come
straight: you must be witty now. She does
so blush, and fetches her wind so short, as if
she were frayed with a sprite: I'll fetch her.
It is the prettiest villain she fetches her
breath as short as a new-ta'en sparrow   [*Exit*
Tro Even such a passion doth embrace
  my bosom.
My heart beats thicker than a feverous pulse;
And all my powers do their bestowing lose,
Like vassalage at unawares encountering   40
The eye of majesty.

Re-enter PANDARUS *with* CRESSIDA.

Pan. Come, come, what need you blush?
shame's a baby. Here she is now. swear the
oaths now to her that you have sworn to me
What, are you gone again? you must be
watched ere you be made tame, must you?
Come your ways, come your ways, an you
draw backward, we'll put you i' the fills Why
do you not speak to her? Come, draw this
curtain, and let's see your picture Alas the
day, how loath you are to offend daylight! an
'twere dark, you'ld close sooner So, so, rub
on, and kiss the mistress How now! a kiss in
fee-farm! build there, carpenter, the air is
sweet Nay, you shall fight your hearts out
ere I part you The falcon as the tercel, for
all the ducks i' the river   go to, go to
Tro. You have bereft me of all words, lady.
Pan. Words pay no debts, give her deeds:
but she'll bereave you o' the deeds too, if she
call your activity in question What, billing
again? Here's 'In witness whereof the parties interchangeably'—Come in, come in: I'll
go get a fire   [*Exit*
Cres. Will you walk in, my lord?
Tro. O Cressida, how often have I wished
me thus!
Cres. Wished, my lord! The gods grant,—
O my lord!
Tro. What should they grant? what makes
this pretty abruption? What too curious dreg
espies my sweet lady in the fountain of our
love?
Cres More dregs than water, if my fears
have eyes
Tro. Fears make devils of cherubins, they
never see truly.
Cres Blind fear, that seeing reason leads,
finds safer footing than blind reason stumbling
without fear: to fear the worst oft cures the
worse.   79
Tro. O, let my lady apprehend no fear:
in all Cupid's pageant there is presented no
monster.
Cres. Nor nothing monstrous neither?
Tro. Nothing, but our undertakings, when
we vow to weep seas, live in fire, eat rocks,
tame tigers, thinking it harder for our mistress to devise imposition enough than for us
to undergo any difficulty imposed. This is the

monstruosity in love, lady, that the will is
infinite and the execution confined, that the
desire is boundless and the act a slave to limit.
Cres. They say all lovers swear more performance than they are able and yet reserve
an ability that they never perform, vowing
more than the perfection of ten and discharg-
ing less than the tenth part of one They that
have the voice of lions and the act of hares, are
they not monsters?
Tro. Are there such? such are not we.
praise us as we are tasted, allow us as we
prove, our head shall go bare till merit crown
it no perfection in reversion shall have a
praise in present: we will not name desert
before his birth, and, being born, his addition
shall be humble Few words to fair faith:
Troilus shall be such to Cressid as what envy
can say worst shall be a mock for his truth,
and what truth can speak truest not truer than
Troilus.
Cres. Will you walk in, my lord?

Re-enter PANDARUS.

Pan. What, blushing still? have you not
done talking yet?   109
Cres Well, uncle, what folly I commit, I
dedicate to you.
Pan. I thank you for that: if my lord get
a boy of you, you'll give him me Be true to
my lord: if he flinch, chide me for it.
Tro You know now your hostages, your
uncle's word and my firm faith
Pan Nay, I'll give my word for her too:
our kindred, though they be long ere they are
wooed, they are constant being won they are
burs, I can tell you, they'll stick where they
are thrown.
Cres Boldness comes to me now, and brings
  me heart   . 121
Prince Troilus, I have loved you night and day
For many weary months.
Tro Why was my Cressid then so hard to
  win?
Cres Hard to seem won. but I was won,
  my lord,
With the first glance that ever—pardon me—
If I confess much, you will play the tyrant
I love you now, but not, till now, so much
But I might master it in faith, I lie;   129
My thoughts were like unbridled children,
  grown
Too headstrong for their mother. See, we
  fools!
Why have I blabb'd? who shall be true to us,
When we are so unsecret to ourselves?
But, though I loved you well, I woo'd you not;
And yet, good faith, I wish'd myself a man,
Or that we women had men's privilege
Of speaking first. Sweet, bid me hold my
  tongue,
For in this rapture I shall surely speak
The thing I shall repent. See, see, your
  silence,
Cunning in dumbness, from my weakness
  draws

My very soul of counsel ! stop my mouth 141
 Tro. And shall, albeit sweet music issues
 thence
 Pan. Pretty, i' faith.
 Cres. My lord, I do beseech you, pardon
me ;
'Twas not my purpose, thus to beg a kiss :
I am ashamed O heavens ! what have I done ?
For this time will I take my leave, my lord.
 Tro. Your leave, sweet Cressid !
 Pan. Leave ! an you take leave till to-
morrow morning,—   150
 Cres. Pray you, content you
 Tro.   What offends you, lady ?
 Cres. Sir, mine own company
 Tro.   You cannot shun
Yourself.
 Cres. Let me go and try .
I have a kind of self resides with you ;
But an unkind self, that itself will leave,
To be another's fool I would be gone
Where is my wit ? I know not what I speak
 Tro. Well know they what they speak that
 speak so wisely.
 Cres Perchance, my lord, I show more
 craft than love ,   160
And fell so roundly to a large confession,
To angle for your thoughts but you are wise,
Or else you love not, for to be wise and love
Exceed's man's might , that dwells with gods
 above
 Tro O that I thought it could be in a
 woman—
As, if it can, I will presume in you—
To feed for aye her lamp and flames of love ,
To keep her constancy in plight and youth,
Outliving beauty's outward, with a mind 169
That doth renew swifter than blood decays !
Or that persuasion could but thus convince me,
That my integrity and truth to you
Might be affronted with the match and weight
Of such a winnow'd purity in love ,
How were I then uplifted ! but, alas !
I am as true as truth's simplicity
And simpler than the infancy of truth.
 Cres In that I'll war with you
 Tro.   O virtuous fight,
When right with right wars who shall be most
 right !   179
True swains in love shall in the world to come
Approve their truths by Troilus : when their
 rhymes,
Full of protest, of oath and big compare,
Want similes, truth tired with iteration,
As true as steel, as plantage to the moon,
As sun to day, as turtle to her mate,
As iron to adamant, as earth to the centre,
Yet, after all comparisons of truth,
As truth's authentic author to be cited,
' As true as Troilus ' shall crown up the verse,
And sanctify the numbers.
 Cres.   Prophet may you be ! 190
If I be false, or swerve a hair from truth,
When time is old and hath forgot itself,
When waterdrops have worn the stones of
 Troy,

And blind oblivion swallow'd cities up,
And mighty states characterless are grated
To dusty nothing, yet let memory,
From false to false, among false maids in love,
Upbraid my falsehood ! when they've said
 ' as false
As air, as water, wind, or sandy earth,
As fox to lamb, as wolf to heifer's calf, 200
Pard to the hind, or stepdame to her son,'
' Yea,' let them say, to stick the heart of false-
 hood,
' As false as Cressid '
 Pan Go to, a bargain made : seal it, seal it;
I'll be the witness Here I hold your hand,
here my cousin's If ever you prove false one
to another, since I have taken such pains to
bring you together, let all pitiful goers-be-
tween be called to the world's end after my
name , call them all Pandars, let all constant
men be Troiluses, all false women Cressids,
and all brokers-between Pandars ! say, amen.
 Tro Amen
 Cres Amen
 Pan Amen Whereupon I will show you
a chamber with a bed , which bed, because it
shall not speak of your pretty encounters,
press it to death away !
And Cupid grant all tongue-tied maidens here
Bed, chamber, Pandar to provide this gear !
         [Exeunt. 221

SCENE III. *The Grecian camp. Before
    Achilles' tent*

Enter AGAMEMNON, ULYSSES, DIOMEDES,
 NESTOR, AJAX, MENELAUS, *and* CALCHAS

 Cal Now, princes, for the service I have
 done you,
The advantage of the time prompts me aloud
To call for recompense Appear it to your
 mind
†That, through the sight I bear in things to ·
 love,
I have abandon'd Troy, left my possession,
Incurr'd a traitor's name , exposed myself,
From certain and possess'd conveniences,
To doubtful fortunes , sequestering from me
 all
That time, acquaintance, custom and condition
Made tame and most familiar to my nature,
And here, to do you service, am become 11
As new into the world, strange, unacquainted
I do beseech you, as in way of taste,
To give me now a little benefit,
Out of those many register'd in promise,
Which, you say, live to come in my behalf
 Agam What wouldst thou of us, Trojan ?
 make demand.
 Cal. You have a Trojan prisoner, call'd
 Antenor.
Yesterday took : Troy holds him very dear.
Oft have you—often have you thanks there-
 fore—   20
Desired my Cressid in right great exchange,
Whom Troy hath still denied . but this An-
 tenor,

I know, is such a wrest in their affairs
That their negotiations all must slack,
Wanting his manage ; and they will almost
Give us a prince of blood, a son of Priam,
In change of him : let him be sent, great prin-
   ces,
And he shall buy my daughter ; and her pres-
   ence
Shall quite strike off all service I have done,
In most accepted pain.

Agam.   Let Diomedes bear him, 30
And bring us Cressid hither : Calchas shall
   have
What he requests of us. Good Diomed,
Furnish you fairly for this interchange :
Withal bring word if Hector will to-morrow
Be answer'd in his challenge : Ajax is ready.

Dio. This shall I undertake ; and 'tis a
   burden
Which I am proud to bear.

                [Exeunt Diomedes and Calchas.

Enter ACHILLES *and* PATROCLUS, *before their
tent.*

Ulyss. Achilles stands i' the entrance of
   his tent :
Please it our general to pass strangely by him,
As if he were forgot ; and, princes all,   40
Lay negligent and loose regard upon him :
I will come last. 'Tis like he'll question me
Why such unplausive eyes are bent on him :
If so, I have derision medicinable,
To use between your strangeness and his pride,
Which his own will shall have desire to drink :
It may be good : pride hath no other glass
To show itself but pride, for supple knees
Feed arrogance and are the proud man's fees.

Agam. We'll execute your purpose, and
   put on   50
A form of strangeness as we pass along :
So do each lord, and either greet him not,
Or else disdainfully, which shall shake him
   more
Than if not look'd on. I will lead the way.

Achil. What, comes the general to speak
   with me ?
You know my mind, I'll fight no more 'gainst
   Troy.

Agam. What says Achilles ? would he
   aught with us ?

Nest. Would you, my lord, aught with the
   general ?

Achil. No.

Nest. Nothing, my lord.   60

Agam. The better.

         [Exeunt Agamemnon and Nestor.

Achil. Good day, good day.

Men. How do you ? how do you ?   [*Exit.*

Achil. What, does the cuckold scorn me ?

Ajax. How now, Patroclus !

Achil. Good morrow, Ajax.

Ajax. Ha ?

Achil. Good morrow.

Ajax. Ay, and good next day too. [*Exit.*

Achil. What mean these fellows ? Know
they not Achilles ?   70

Patr. They pass by strangely : they were
   used to bend,
To send their smiles before them to Achilles ;
To come as humbly as they used to creep
To holy altars.

Achil.   What, am I poor of late ?
'Tis certain, greatness, once fall'n out with
   fortune,
Must fall out with men too : what the declined
   is
He shall as soon read in the eyes of others
As feel in his own fall ; for men, like butter-
   flies,
Show not their mealy wings but to the sum-
   mer,
And not a man, for being simply man,   80
Hath any honor, but honor for those honors
That are without him, as place, riches, favor,
Prizes of accident as oft as merit :
Which when they fall, as being slippery stand-
   ers,
The love that lean'd on them as slippery too,
Do one pluck down another and together
Die in the fall. But 'tis not so with me :
Fortune and I are friends : I do enjoy
At ample point all that I did possess,
Save these men's looks ; who do, methinks,
   find out   90
Something not worth in me such rich behold-
   ing
As they have often given. Here is Ulysses ;
I'll interrupt his reading.
How now Ulysses !

Ulyss.   Now, great Thetis' son !

Achil. What are you reading ?

Ulyss.   A strange fellow here
Writes me : 'That man, how dearly ever
   parted,
How much in having, or without or in,
Cannot make boast to have that which he hath,
Nor feels not what he owes, but by reflection ;
As when his virtues shining upon others   100
Heat them and they retort that heat again
To the first giver.'

Achil.   This is not strange, Ulysses.
The beauty that is borne here in the face
The bearer knows not, but commends itself
To others' eyes ; nor doth the eye itself,
That most pure spirit of sense, behold itself,
Not going from itself ; but eye to eye opposed
Salutes each other with each other's form ;
For speculation turns not to itself,
Till it hath travell'd and is mirror'd there 110
Where it may see itself. This is not strange
at all.

Ulyss. I do not strain at the position,—
It is familiar,—but at the author's drift ;
Who, in his circumstance, expressly proves
That no man is the lord of any thing,
Though in and of him there be much consist-
   ing,
Till he communicate his parts to others ;
Nor doth he of himself know them for aught
Till he behold them form'd in the applause
Where they're extended ; who, like an arch,
   reverberates   120

The voice again, or, like a gate of steel
Fronting the sun, receives and renders back
His figure and his heat. I was much wrapt in
    this ;
And apprehended here immediately
The unknown Ajax.
Heavens, what a man is there ! a very horse,
That has he knows not what. Nature, what
    things there are
Most abject in regard and dear in use !
What things again most dear in the esteem
And poor in worth ! Now shall we see to-
    morrow—   130
An act that very chance doth throw upon
    him—
Ajax renown'd. O heavens, what some men
    do,
While some men leave to do !
How some men creep in skittish fortune's
    hall,
Whiles others play the idiots in her eyes !
How one man eats into another's pride,
While pride is fasting in his wantonness !
To see these Grecian lords !—why, even al-
    ready
They clap the lubber Ajax on the shoulder,
As if his foot were on brave Hector's breast
And great Troy shrieking.   141
    Achil. I do believe it ; for they pass'd by
    me
As misers do by beggars, neither gave to me
Good word nor look : what, are my deeds
    forgot ?
    Ulyss. Time hath, my lord, a wallet at his
    back,
Wherein he puts alms for oblivion,
A great-sized monster of ingratitudes :
Those scraps are good deeds past ; which are
    devour'd
As fast as they are made, forgot as soon
As done : perseverance, dear my lord,   150
Keeps honor bright : to have done is to hang
Quite out of fashion, like a rusty mail
In monumental mockery. Take the instant
    way ;
For honor travels in a strait so narrow,
Where one but goes abreast : keep then the
    path ;
For emulation hath a thousand sons
That one by one pursue : if you give way,
Or hedge aside from the direct forthright,
Like to an enter'd tide, they all rush by
And leave you hindmost ;   160
Or, like a gallant horse fall'n in first rank,
Lie there for pavement to the abject rear,
O'er-run and trampled on : then what they do
    in present,
Though less than yours in past, must o'ertop
    yours ;
For time is like a fashionable host
That slightly shakes his parting guest by the
    hand,   [fly,
And with his arms outstretch'd, as he would
Grasps in the comer : welcome ever smiles,
And farewell goes out sighing. O, let not
    virtue seek

Remuneration for the thing it was ;   170
For beauty, wit,
High birth, vigor of bone, desert in service,
Love, friendship, charity, are subjects all
To envious and calumniating time.
One touch of nature makes the whole world
    kin,
That all with one consent praise new-born
    gawds,
Though they are made and moulded of things
    past,
And give to dust that is a little gilt
More laud than gilt o'er-dusted.
The present eye praises the present object :
Then marvel not, thou great and complete
    man,   181
That all the Greeks begin to worship Ajax ;
Since things in motion sooner catch the eye
Than what not stirs. The cry went once on
    thee,
And still it might, and yet it may again,
If thou wouldst not entomb thyself alive
And case thy reputation in thy tent ;
Whose glorious deeds, but in these fields of
    late,
Made emulous missions 'mongst the gods
    themselves
And drave great Mars to faction.
    Achil.   Of this my privacy 190
I have strong reasons.
    Ulyss.   But 'gainst your privacy
The reasons are more potent and heroical :
'Tis known, Achilles, that you are in love
With one of Priam's daughters.
    Achil.   Ha ! known !
    Ulyss. Is that a wonder ?
The providence that's in a watchful state
Knows almost every grain of Plutus' gold,
Finds bottom in the uncomprehensive deeps,
Keeps place with thought and almost, like the
    gods,
Does thoughts unveil in their dumb cradles.
There is a mystery—with whom relation 201
Durst never meddle—in the soul of state ;
Which hath an operation more divine
Than breath or pen can give expressure to :
All the commerce that you have had with
    Troy
As perfectly is ours as yours, my lord ;
And better would it fit Achilles much
To throw down Hector than Polyxena :
But it must grieve young Pyrrhus now at
    home,   210
When fame shall in our islands sound her
    trump,
And all the Greekish girls shall tripping sing,
' Great Hector's sister did Achilles win,
But our great Ajax bravely beat down him.'
Farewell, my lord : I as your lover speak ;
The fool slides o'er the ice that you should
    break.   [*Exit.*
    Patr. To this effect, Achilles, have I moved
    you :
A woman impudent and mannish grown
Is not more loathed than an effeminate man
In time of action. I stand condemn'd for this ;

They think my little stomach to the war   220
And your great love to me restrains you thus:
Sweet, rouse yourself ; and the weak wanton
  Cupid
Shall from your neck unloose his amorous
  fold,
And, like a dew-drop from the lion's mane,
Be shook to air.

Achil.   Shall Ajax fight with Hector ?
Patr. Ay, and perhaps receive much honor
  by him.
Achil. I see my reputation is at stake ;
My fame is shrewdly gored.

Patr.   O, then, beware ;
Those wounds heal ill that men do give them-
  selves :
Omission to do what is necessary   230
Seals a commission to a blank of danger ;
And danger, like an ague, subtly taints
Even then when we sit idly in the sun.

Achil. Go call Thersites hither, sweet Patro-
  clus :
I'll send the fool to Ajax and desire him
To invite the Trojan lords after the combat
To see us here unarm'd : I have a woman's
  longing,
An appetite that I am sick withal,
To see great Hector in his weeds of peace,
To talk with him and to behold his visage,
Even to my full of view.   241

Enter THERSITES.

A labor saved !

Ther. A wonder !
Achil. What ?
Ther. Ajax goes up and down the field,
asking for himself.
Achil. How so ?
Ther. He must fight singly to-morrow with
Hector, and is so prophetically proud of an
heroical cudgelling that he raves in saying
nothing.
Achil. How can that be ?   250
Ther. Why, he stalks up and down like a
peacock,—a stride and a stand : ruminates
like an hostess that hath no arithmetic but her
brain to set down her reckoning : bites his lip
with a politic regard, as who should say
'There were wit in this head, an 'twould
out;' and so there is, but it lies as coldly in
him as fire in a flint, which will not show
without knocking. The man's undone forever ; for if Hector break not his neck i' the
combat, he'll break 't himself in vain-glory.
He knows not me: I said ' Good morrow,
Ajax;' and he replies ' Thanks, Agamemnon.'
What think you of this man that takes me for
the general ? He's grown a very land-fish,
languageless, a monster. A plague of opinion !
a man may wear it on both sides, like a leather
jerkin.

Achil. Thou must be my ambassador to
him, Thersites.
Ther. Who, I ? why, he'll answer nobody ;
he professes not answering : speaking is for
beggars ; he wears his tongue in 's arms. I

will put on his presence : let Patroclus make
demands to me, you shall see the pageant of
Ajax.

Achil. To him, Patroclus ; tell him I humbly desire the valiant Ajax to invite the most
valorous Hector to come unarmed to my tent,
and to procure safe-conduct for his person of
the magnanimous and most illustrious six-or
seven-times-honored captain-general of the
Grecian army, Agamemnon, et cetera. Do
this.   280

Patr. Jove bless great Ajax !
Ther. Hum !
Patr. I come from the worthy Achilles,—
Ther. Ha !
Patr. Who most humbly desires you to
invite Hector to his tent,—
Ther. Hum !
Patr. And to procure safe-conduct from
Agamemnon.
Ther. Agamemnon !   290
Patr. Ay, my lord.
Ther. Ha !
Patr. What say you to 't ?
Ther. God b' wi' you, with all my heart.
Patr. Your answer, sir.
Ther. If to-morrow be a fair day, by eleven
o'clock it will go one way or other : how-
soever, he shall pay for me ere he has me.
Patr. Your answer, sir.
Ther. Fare you well, with all my heart.
Achil. Why, but he is not in this tune, is
he ?   301
Ther. No, but he's out o' tune thus. What
music will be in him when Hector has knocked
out his brains, I know not ; but, I am sure,
none, unless the fiddler Apollo get his sinews
to make catlings on.
Achil. Come, thou shalt bear a letter to
him straight.
Ther. Let me bear another to his horse ;
for that's the more capable creature.   310
Achil. My mind is troubled, like a fountain
  stirr'd ;
And I myself see not the bottom of it.
            [*Exeunt Achilles and Patroclus.*
Ther. Would the fountain of your mind
were clear again, that I might water an ass at
it ! I had rather be a tick in a sheep than
such a valiant ignorance.   *Exit.*

ACT IV.

SCENE I. *Troy. A street.*

Enter, from one side, ÆNEAS, *and* Servant
  with a torch ; *from the other,* PARIS, DEI-
  PHOBUS, ANTENOR, DIOMEDES, *and others,*
  with torches.

Par. See, ho ! who is that there ?
Dei.   It is the Lord Æneas.
Æne. Is the prince there in person ?
Had I so good occasion to lie long
As you, Prince Paris, nothing but heavenly
  business

Should rob my bed-mate of my company
  Dio. That's my mind too. Good morrow,
    Lord Æneas
  Par. A valiant Greek, Æneas,—take his
    hand,—
Witness the process of your speech, wherein
You told how Diomed, a whole week by days,
Did haunt you in the field
  Æne   Health to you, valiant sir, 10
During all question of the gentle truce ,
But when I meet you on arm'd, as black defiance
As heart can think or courage execute
  Dio. The one and other Diomed embraces
Our bloods are now in calm , and, so long,
    health !
But when contention and occasion meet,
By Jove, I'll play the hunter for thy life
With all my force, pursuit and policy.
  Æne And thou shalt hunt a lion, that will
    fly
With his face backward   In humane gentle-
    ness,   20
Welcome to Troy ' now, by Anchises' life,
Welcome, indeed ' By Venus' hand I swear,
No man alive can love in such a sort
The thing he means to kill more excellently
  Dio   We sympathize   Jove, let Æneas
    live,
If to my sword his fate be not the glory,
A thousand complete courses of the sun '
But, in mine emulous honor, let him die,
With every joint a wound, and that to-mor-
    row '
  Æne. We know each other well   30
  Dio   We do , and long to know each other
    worse
  Par   This is the most despiteful gentle
    greeting,
The noblest hateful love, that e'er I heard of.
What business, lord, so early ?
  Æne I was sent for to the king ; but why,
    I know not
  Par His purpose meets you · 'twas to
    bring this Greek
To Calchas' house, and there to render him,
For the enfreed Antenor, the fair Cressid
Let's have your company, or, if you please,
Haste there before us   I constantly do
    think—   40
Or rather, call my thought a certain knowl-
    edge—
My brother Troilus lodges there to-night :
Rouse him and give him note of our ap-
    proach,
With the whole quality wherefore I fear
We shall be much unwelcome
  Æne.   That I assure you
Troilus had rather Troy were borne to Greece
Than Cressid borne from Troy
  Par.   There is no help ;
The bitter disposition of the time
Will have it so   On, lord , we'll follow you
  Æne. Good morrow, all   50
                    [*Exit with Servant*
  Par. And tell me, noble Diomed, faith, tell
    me true,

Even in the soul of sound good-fellowship,
Who, in your thoughts, merits fair Helen
    best,
Myself or Menelaus ?
  Dio   Both alike ·
He merits well to have her, that doth seek
    her,
Not making any scruple of her soilure,
With such a hell of pain and world of charge,
And you as well to keep her, that defend her,
Not palating the taste of her dishonor,
With such a costly loss of wealth and friends:
He, like a puling cuckold, would drink up 61
The lees and dregs of a flat tamed piece ,
You, like a lecher, out of whorish loins
Are pleased to breed out your inheritors :
Both merits poised, each weighs nor less nor
    more ,   ·
But he as he, the heavier for a whore
  Par. You are too bitter to your country-
    woman
  Dio. She's bitter to her country : hear me,
    Paris
For every false drop in her bawdy veins
A Grecian's life hath sunk , for every scruple
Of her contaminated carrion weight,   71
A Trojan hath been slain   since she could
    speak,
She hath not given so many good words
    breath
As for her Greeks and Trojans suffer'd death.
  Par   Fair Diomed, you do as chapmen do,
Dispraise the thing that you desire to buy :
But we in silence hold this virtue well,
We'll but commend what we intend to sell.
Here lies our way   [*Exeunt.*

  SCENE II.   *The same. Court of Pandarus'*
               house.

    Enter TROILUS *and* CRESSIDA

  Tro Dear, trouble not yourself . the morn
    is cold.
  Cres   Then, sweet my lord, I'll call mine
    uncle down ,
He shall unbolt the gates
  Tro   Trouble him not ;
To bed, to bed · sleep kill those pretty eyes,
And give as soft attachment to thy senses
As infants' empty of all thought !
  Cres.   Good morrow, then.
  Tro I prithee now, to bed.
  Cres.   Are you a-weary of me ?
  Tro O Cressida ' but that the busy day,
Waked by the lark, hath roused the ribald
    crows,
And dreaming night will hide our joys no
    longer,
I would not from thee.
  Cres   Night hath been too brief.
  Tro. Beshrew the witch ! with venomous
    wights she stays
As tediously as hell, but flies the grasps of
    love
With wings more momentary-swift than
    thought.

You will catch cold, and curse me.

Cres.　　　　　　　　　　Prithee, tarry :
You men will never tarry.
O foolish Cressid ! I might have still held off,
And then you would have tarried. Hark !
　　there's one up.
Pan. [*Within*] What, 's all the doors open
　　here ?
Tro. It is your uncle.　　　　　　　　20
Cres. A pestilence on him ! now will he be
　　mocking :
I shall have such a life !

Enter PANDARUS.

Pan. How now, how now ! how go maid-
en-heads ? Here, you maid ! where's my
cousin Cressid ?
Cres. Go hang yourself, you naughty mock-
　　ing uncle !
You bring me to do, and then you flout me
　　too.
Pan. To do what ? to do what ? let her
say what : what have I brought you to do ?
Cres. Come, come, beshrew your heart !
　　you'll ne'er be good,　　　　　　　30
Nor suffer others.
Pan. Ha, ha ! Alas, poor wretch ! ah, poor
capocchia ! hast not slept to-night ? would he
not, a naughty man, let it sleep ? a bugbear
take him !
Cres. Did not I tell you ? Would he were
　　knock'd i' the head ! [*Knocking within.*
Who's that at door ? good uncle, go and see.
My lord, come you again into my chamber :
You smile and mock me, as if I meant
　　naughtily.
Tro. Ha, ha !　　　　　　　　39
Cres. Come, you are deceived, I think of
　　no such thing. [*Knocking within.*
How earnestly they knock ! Pray you, come
　　in :
I would not for half Troy have you seen here.
　　　　　　[*Exeunt Troilus and Cressida.*
Pan. Who's there ? what's the matter ?
will you beat down the door ? How now !
what's the matter ?

Enter ÆNEAS.

Æne. Good morrow, lord, good morrow.
Pan. Who's there ? my Lord Æneas ! By
　　my troth,
I knew you not : what news with you so
　　early ?
Æne. Is not Prince Troilus here ?
Pan. Here ! what should he do here ?　50
Æne. Come, he is here, my lord ; do not
　　deny him :
It doth import him much to speak with me.
Pan. Is he here, say you ? 'tis more than
I know, I'll be sworn : for my own part, I
came in late. What should he do here ?
Æne. Who !—nay, then : come, come,
you'll do him wrong ere you're ware : you'll
be so true to him, to be false to him : do not
you know of him, but yet go fetch him hither ; go.

Re-enter TROILUS.

Tro. How now ! what's the matter ?　60
Æne. My lord, I scarce have leisure to
　　salute you,
My matter is so rash : there is at hand
Paris your brother, and Deiphobus,
The Grecian Diomed, and our Antenor
Deliver'd to us ; and for him forthwith,
Ere the first sacrifice, within this hour,
We must give up to Diomedes' hand
The Lady Cressida.
Tro.　　　　　　　Is it so concluded ?
Æne. By Priam and the general state of
　　Troy :
They are at hand and ready to effect it.　70
Tro. How my achievements mock me !
I will go meet them : and, my Lord Æneas,
We met by chance ; you did not find me here.
Æne. Good, good, my lord ; the secrets of
　　nature
Have not more gift in taciturnity.
　　　　　　[*Exeunt Troilus and Æneas.*
Pan. Is't possible ? no sooner got but lost ?
The devil take Antenor ! the young prince
will go mad : a plague upon Antenor ! I
would they had broke 's neck !

Re-enter CRESSIDA.

Cres. How now ! what's the matter ? who
was here ?　　　　　　　　81
Pan. Ah, ah !
Cres. Why sigh you so profoundly ? where's
my lord ? gone ! Tell me, sweet uncle,
what's the matter ?
Pan. Would I were as deep under the
earth as I am above !
Cres. O the gods ! what's the matter ?
Pan. Prithee, get thee in : would thou
hadst ne'er been born ! I knew thou wouldst
be his death. O, poor gentleman ! A plague
upon Antenor !
Cres. Good uncle, I beseech you, on my
knees I beseech you, what's the matter ?
Pan. Thou must be gone, wench, thou
must be gone ; thou art changed for Antenor : thou must to thy father, and be gone
from Troilus : 'twill be his death ; 'twill be
his bane ; he cannot bear it.
Cres. O you immortal gods ! I will not go.
Pan. Thou must.　　　　　　　101
Cres. I will not, uncle : I have forgot my
　　father ;
I know no touch of consanguinity ;
No kin, no love, no blood, no soul so near me
As the sweet Troilus. O you gods divine !
Make Cressid's name the very crown of false-
　　hood,
If ever she leave Troilus ! Time, force, and
　　death,
Do to this body what extremes you can ;
But the strong base and building of my love
Is as the very centre of the earth,　　110
Drawing all things to it. I'll go in and
　　weep,—
Pan. Do, do.

Cres Tear my bright hair and scratch my
  praised cheeks,
Crack my clear voice with sobs and break my
  heart
With sounding Troilus. I will not go from
  Troy.   [*Exeunt.*

SCENE III. *The same Street before Pan-*
   darus' house.

Enter PARIS, TROILUS, ÆNEAS, DEIPHOBUS,
  ANTENOR, *and* DIOMEDES.

 Par. It is great morning, and the hour
  prefix'd
Of her delivery to this valiant Greek
Comes fast upon. Good my brother Troilus,
Tell you the lady what she is to do,
And haste her to the purpose
  Tro.   Walk into her house ;
I'll bring her to the Grecian presently .
And to his hand when I deliver her,
Think it an altar, and thy brother Troilus
A priest there offering to it his own heart
         [*Exit.*
 Par. I know what 'tis to love ,
And would, as I shall pity, I could help !
Please you walk in, my lords. [*Exeunt.*

SCENE IV. *The same. Pandarus' house.*

Enter PANDARUS *and* CRESSIDA

 Pan Be moderate, be moderate
 Cres Why tell you me of moderation ?
The grief is fine, full, perfect, that I taste,
And violenteth in a sense as strong
As that which causeth it how can I moder-
  ate it ?
If I could temporize with my affection,
Or brew it to a weak and colder palate,
The like allayment could I give my grief .
My love admits no qualifying dross ,
No more my grief, in such a precious loss. 10
 Pan Here, here, here he comes
    Enter TROILUS
 Ah, sweet ducks !
 Cres O Troilus ! Troilus ! [*Embracing him.*
 Pan. What a pair of spectacles is here' Let
me embrace too 'O heart,' as the goodly
saying is,
  '—— O heart, heavy heart,
  Why sigh'st thou without breaking ? '
where he answers again,
  'Because thou canst not ease thy smart 20
  By friendship nor by speaking '
There was never a truer rhyme Let us cast
away nothing, for we may live to have need
of such a verse we see it, we see it How
now, lambs ?
 Tro. Cressid, I love thee in so strain'd a
  purity,
That the bless'd gods, as angry with my
  fancy,
More bright in zeal than the devotion which
Cold lips blow to their deities, take thee from
  me
 Cres. Have the gods envy ? 30

 Pan Ay, ay, ay, ay , 'tis too plain a case
 Cres And is it true that I must go from
  Troy ?
 Tro A hateful truth
 Cres   What, and from Troilus too ?
 Tro From Troy and Troilus
 Cres.   Is it possible ?
 Tro. And suddenly ; where injury of
  chance
Puts back leave-taking, justles roughly by
All time of pause, rudely beguiles our lips
Of all rejoindure, forcibly prevents
Our lock'd embrasures, strangles our dear
  vows   39
Even in the birth of our own laboring breath
We two, that with so many thousand sighs
Did buy each other, must poorly sell our-
  selves
With the rude brevity and discharge of one.
Injurious time now with a robber's haste
Crams his rich thievery up, he knows not how:
As many farewells as be stars in heaven,
With distinct breath and consign'd kisses to
  them,
He fumbles up into a lose adieu,
And scants us with a single famish'd kiss,
Distasted with the salt of broken tears 50
 Æne [*Within*] My lord, is the lady ready?
 Tro Hark ' you are call'd . some say the
  Genius so
Cries ' come ' to him that instantly must die
Bid them have patience , she shall come anon
 Pan. Where are my tears ? rain, to lay this
wind, or my heart will be blown up by the
root   [*Exit.*
 Cres I must then to the Grecians ?
 Tro   No remedy.
 Cres A woful Cressid 'mongst the merry
  Greeks !
When shall we see again ?
 Tro. Hear me, my love be thou but true
  of heart,—   60
 Cres. I true ! how now ' what wicked deem
  is this ?
 Tro Nay, we must use expostulation kindly,
For it is parting from us
I speak not ' be thou true ' as fearing thee,
For I will throw my glove to Death himself,
That there's no maculation in thy heart .
But ' be thou true,' say I, to fashion in
My sequent protestation , be thou true,
And I will see thee
 Cres O, you shall be exposed, my lord, to
  dangers   70
As infinite as imminent ' but I'll be true.
 Tro And I'll grow friend with danger
  Wear this sleeve   [see you ?
 Cres. And you this glove When shall I
 Tro I will corrupt the Grecian sentinels,
To give thee nightly visitation.
But yet be true
 Cres   O heavens ! ' be true' again '
 Tro. Hear while I speak it, love
The Grecian youths are full of quality ,
They're loving, well composed with gifts of
  nature,

Flowing and swelling o'er with arts and ex-
　ercise :　　　　　　　　　　　　　　80
How novelty may move, and parts with per-
　son,
Alas, a kind of godly jealousy—
Which, I beseech you, call a virtuous sin—
Makes me afeard.

　Cres.　　　　O heavens ! you love me not.
　Tro.　Die I a villain, then !
In this I do not call your faith in question
So mainly as my merit : I cannot sing,
Nor heel the high lavolt, nor sweeten talk,
Nor play at subtle games ; fair virtues all,
To which the Grecians are most prompt and
　pregnant :　　　　　　　　　　　　90
But I can tell that in each grace of these
There lurks a still and dumb-discoursive devil
That tempts most cunningly : but be not
　tempted.

　Cres.　Do you think I will ?
　Tro.　No.
But something may be done that we will not :
And sometimes we are devils to ourselves,
When we will tempt the frailty of our powers,
Presuming on their changeful potency.

　Æne. [*Within*] Nay, good my lord,—
　Tro.　　　Come, kiss ; and let us part. 100
　Par. [*Within*] Brother Troilus !
　Tro.　　　Good brother, come you hither ;
And bring Æneas and the Grecian with you.
　Cres.　My lord, will you be true ?
　Tro.　Who, I ? alas, it is my vice, my fault :
Whiles others fish with craft for great opinion,
I with great truth catch mere simplicity ;
Whilst some with cunning gild their copper
　crowns,
With truth and plainness I do wear mine bare.
Fear not my truth : the moral of my wit　109
Is ' plain and true ;' there's all the reach of it.

Enter ÆNEAS, PARIS, ANTENOR, DEIPHOBUS,
　and DIOMEDES.

Welcome, Sir Diomed ! here is the lady
Which for Antenor we deliver you :
At the port, lord, I'll give her to thy hand,
And by the way possess thee what she is.
Entreat her fair ; and, by my soul, fair Greek,
If e'er thou stand at mercy of my sword,
Name Cressid, and thy life shall be as safe
As Priam is in Ilion.

　Dio.　　　　Fair Lady Cressid,
So please you, save the thanks this prince
　expects :
The lustre in your eye, heaven in your cheek,
Pleads your fair usage ; and to Diomed　121
You shall be mistress, and command him
　wholly.　　　　　　　　　　[teously,
　Tro.　Grecian, thou dost not use me cour-
To shame the zeal of my petition to thee
In praising her : I tell thee, lord of Greece,
She is as far high-soaring o'er thy praises
As thou unworthy to be call'd her servant.
I charge thee use her well, even for my charge;
For, by the dreadful Pluto, if thou dost not,
Though the great bulk Achilles be thy guard,
I'll cut thy throat.　　　　　　　　131

　Dio.　O, be not moved, Prince Troilus :
Let me be privileged by my place and message,
To be a speaker free ; when I am hence,
I'll answer to my lust : and know you, lord,
I'll nothing do on charge : to her own worth
She shall be prized ; but that you say ' be't so,'
I'll speak it in my spirit and honor, ' no.'
　Tro.　Come, to the port. I'll tell thee, Dio-
　med,
This brave shall oft make thee to hide thy
　head.　　　　　　　　　　　　　　139
Lady, give me your hand, and, as we walk,
To our own selves bend we our needful talk.
　[*Exeunt Troilus, Cressida, and Diomedes.*
　　　　　　　　　　　[*Trumpet within.*
　Par.　Hark ! Hector's trumpet.
　Æne.　　How have we spent this morning !
The prince must think me tardy and remiss,
That swore to ride before him to the field.
　Par.　'Tis Troilus' fault: come, come, to
　field with him.
　Dei.　Let us make ready straight.
　Æne.　Yea, with a bridegroom's fresh
　alacrity,
Let us address to tend on Hector's heels :—
The glory of our Troy doth this day lie
On his fair worth and single chivalry.　150
　　　　　　　　　　　　　　[*Exeunt.*

SCENE V.　*The Grecian camp.　Lists set out.*

Enter AJAX, *armed* ; AGAMEMNON, ACHIL-
LES, PATROCLUS, MENELAUS, ULYSSES,
NESTOR, *and others.*

　Agam.　Here art thou in appointment fresh
　and fair,
Anticipating time with starting courage.
Give with thy trumpet a loud note to Troy,
Thou dreadful Ajax ; that the appalled air
May pierce the head of the great combatant
And hale him hither.
　Ajax.　　Thou, trumpet, there's my purse.
Now crack thy lungs, and split thy brazen
　pipe :
Blow, villain, till thy sphered bias cheek
Outswell the colic of puff'd Aquilon :
Come, stretch thy chest, and let thy eyes spout
　blood ;　　　　　　　　　　　　10
Thou blow'st for Hector.　[*Trumpet sounds.*
　Ulyss.　No trumpet answers.
　Achil.　　　'Tis but early days.
　Agam.　Is not yond Diomed, with Calchas'
　daughter ?
　Ulyss.　'Tis he, I ken the manner of his
　gait ;
He rises on the toe : that spirit of his
In aspiration lifts him from the earth.

Enter DIOMEDES, *with* CRESSIDA.

　Agam.　Is this the Lady Cressid ?
　Dio.　　　　　　　Even she.
　Agam.　Most dearly welcome to the Greeks,
　sweet lady.
　Nest.　Our general doth salute you with a
　kiss.
　Ulyss.　Yet is the kindness but particular ;

'Twere better she were kiss'd in general   21
Nest   And very courtly counsel I'll begin
So much for Nestor.
   Achil   I'll take that winter from your lips,
       fair lady
Achilles bids you welcome
   Men   I had good argument for kissing
       once
   Pat.   But that's no argument for kissing
       now.
For this popp'd Paris in his hardiment,
And parted thus you and your argument
   Ulyss   O deadly gall, and theme of all our
       scorns!   30
For which we lose our heads to gild his horns.
   Pat   The first was Menelaus' kiss this,
       mine
Patroclus kisses you
   Men   O, this is trim
   Pat   Paris and I kiss evermore for him
   Men   I'll have my kiss, sir. Lady, by your
       leave
   Cres   In kissing, do you render or receive?
   Pat   Both take and give
   Cres   I'll make my match to live,
The kiss you take is better than you give,
Therefore no kiss
   Men   I'll give you boot, I'll give you three
       for one   40
   Cres.   You're an odd man, give even or give
       none.
   Men   An odd man, lady ' every man is odd
   Cres   No, Paris is not, for you know 'tis
       true,
That you are odd, and he is even with you
   Men   You fillip me o' the head
   Cres.   No, I'll be sworn
   Ulyss.   It were no match, your nail against
       his horn
May I, sweet lady, beg a kiss of you?
   Cres   You may
   Ulyss   I do desire it
   Cres.   Why, beg, then
   Ulyss   Why then for Venus' sake, give me
       a kiss,
When Helen is a maid again, and his.   50
   Cres.   I am your debtor, claim it when 'tis
       due.
   Ulyss   Never's my day, and then a kiss of
       you.
   Dio.   Lady, a word   I'll bring you to your
       father.   [*Exit with Cressida.*
   Nest.   A woman of quick sense
   Ulyss.   Fie, fie upon her !
There's language in her eye, her cheek, her lip,
Nay, her foot speaks, her wanton spirits look
       out
At every joint and motive of her body
O, these encounterers, so glib of tongue,
That give accosting welcome ere it comes,
And wide unclasp the tables of their thoughts
To every ticklish reader ! set them down   61
For sluttish spoils of opportunity
And daughters of the game   [*Trumpet within*
   All.   The Trojans' trumpet
   Agam.   Yonder comes the troop.

Enter Hector, *armed*, Æneas, Troilus, *and
   other Trojans, with* Attendants

   Æne   Hail, all you state of Greece ' what
       shall be done
To him that victory commands ? or do you
       purpose
A victor shall be known ? will you the knights
Shall to the edge of all extremity
Pursue each other, or shall be divided
By any voice or order of the field ?   70
Hector bade ask
   Agam   Which way would Hector have it?
   Æne   He cares not, he'll obey conditions
   Achil   'Tis done like Hector, but securely
       done,
A little proudly, and great deal misprizing
The knight opposed
   Æne   If not Achilles, sir,
What is your name ?
   Achil   If not Achilles, nothing
   Æne   Therefore Achilles, but, whate'er
       know this
In the extremity of great and little,
Valor and pride excel themselves in Hector,
The one almost as infinite as all,   80
The other blank as nothing   Weigh him well,
And that which looks like pride is courtesy
This Ajax is half made of Hector's blood.
In love whereof, half Hector stays at home ;
Half heart, half hand, half Hector comes to
       seek
This blended knight, half Trojan and half
       Greek
   Achil   A maiden battle, then ? O, I per-
       ceive you

Re-enter Diomedes.

   Agam   Here is Sir Diomed Go, gentle
       knight,
Stand by our Ajax as you and Lord Æneas
Consent upon the order of their fight,   90
So be it, either to the uttermost,
Or else a breath the combatants being kin
Half stints their strife before their strokes be-
       gin   [*Ajax and Hector enter the lists.*
   Ulyss   They are opposed already
   Agam   What Trojan is that same that looks
       so heavy ?
   Ulyss.   The youngest son of Priam, a true
       knight,
Not yet mature, yet matchless, firm of word,
Speaking in deeds and deedless in his tongue,
Not soon provoked nor being provoked soon
       calm'd ·
His heart and hand both open and both free,
For what he has he gives, what thinks he
       shows ;   101
Yet gives he not till judgment guide his
       bounty,
Nor dignifies an impure thought with breath ;
Manly as Hector, but more dangerous :
For Hector in his blaze of wrath subscribes
To tender objects, but he in heat of action
Is more vindicative than jealous love ·
They call him Troilus, and on him erect

A second hope, as fairly built as Hector.
Thus says Æneas ; one that knows the youth
Even to his inches, and with private soul 111
Did in great Ilion thus translate him to me.
        [*Alarum. Hector and Ajax fight.*
   Agam.   They are in action.
   Nest.   Now, Ajax, hold thine own !
   Tro.   Hector, thou sleep'st ;
Awake thee !
   Agam.   His blows are well disposed: there,
     Ajax !
   Dio.   You must no more.   [*Trumpets cease.*
   Æne.   Princes, enough, so please you.
   Ajax.   I am not warm yet ; let us fight
     again.
   Dio.   As Hector pleases.
   Hect.   Why, then will I no more :
Thou art, great lord, my father's sister's son,
A cousin-german to great Priam's seed ; 121
The obligation of our blood forbids
A gory emulation 'twixt us twain :
Were thy commixtion Greek and Trojan so
That thou couldst say 'This hand is Grecian
     all,
And this is Trojan ; the sinews of this leg
All Greek, and this all Troy ; my mother's
     blood
Runs on the dexter cheek, and this sinister
Bounds in my father's ;' by Jove multipotent,
Thou shouldst not bear from me a Greekish
     member   130
Wherein my sword had not impressure made
Of our rank feud : but the just gods gainsay
That any drop thou borrow'dst from thy
     mother,
My sacred aunt, should by my mortal sword
Be drain'd ! Let me embrace thee, Ajax :
By him that thunders, thou hast lusty arms ;
Hector would have them fall upon him thus :
Cousin, all honor to thee !
   Ajax.   I thank thee, Hector :
Thou art too gentle and too free a man :
I came to kill thee, cousin, and bear hence 140
A great addition earned in thy death.
   Hect.   Not Neoptolemus so mirable,
On whose bright crest Fame with her loud'st
     O yes
Cries ' This is he,' could promise to himself
A thought of added honor torn from Hector.
   Æne.   There is expectance here from both
     the sides,
What further you will do.
   Hect.   We'll answer it ;
The issue is embracement : Ajax, farewell.
   Ajax.   If I might in entreaties find success—
As seld I have the chance—I would desire 150
My famous cousin to our Grecian tents.
   Dio.   'Tis Agamemnon's wish, and great
     Achilles
Doth long to see unarm'd the valiant Hector.
   Hect.   Æneas, call my brother Troilus to
     me,
And signify this loving interview
To the expecters of our Trojan part ;
Desire them home. Give me thy hand, my
     cousin ;

I will go eat with thee and see your knights.
   Ajax.   Great Agamemnon comes to meet us
     here.
   Hect.   The worthiest of them tell me name
     by name ;   160
But for Achilles, mine own searching eyes
Shall find him by is large and portly size.
   Agam.   Worthy of arms ! as welcome as to
     one
That would be rid of such an enemy ;
But that's no welcome : understand more clear,
What's past and what's to come is strew'd
     with husks
And formless ruin of oblivion ;
But in this extant moment, faith and troth,
Strain'd purely from all hollow bias-drawing,
Bids thee, with most divine integrity,   170
From heart of very heart, great Hector, wel-
     come.
   Hect.   I thank thee, most imperious Aga-
     memnon.
   Agam.   [*To Troilus*] My well-famed lord
     of Troy, no less to you.
   Men.   Let me confirm my princely brother's
     greeting :
You brace of warlike brothers, welcome hither.
   Hect.   Who must we answer ?
   Æne.   The noble Menelaus.
   Hect.   O, you, my lord ? by Mars his gaunt-
     let, thanks !
Mock not, that I affect the untraded oath ;
Your quondam wife swears still by Venus'-
     glove :
She's well, but bade me not commend her to
     you.   180
   Men.   Name her not now, sir ; she's a deadly
     theme.
   Hect.   O, pardon ; I offend.
   Nest.   I have, thou gallant Trojan, seen thee
     oft
Laboring for destiny make cruel way
Through ranks of Greekish youth, and I have
     seen thee,
As hot as Perseus, spur thy Phrygian steed,
Despising many forfeits and subduements,
When thou hast hung thy advanced sword i'
     the air,
Not letting it decline on the declined,
That I have said to some my standers by 190
' Lo, Jupiter is yonder, dealing life !'
And I have seen thee pause and take thy
     breath,
When that a ring of Greeks have hemm'd thee
     in,
Like an Olympian wrestling : this have I seen;
But this thy countenance, still lock'd in steel,
I never saw till now. I knew thy grandsire,
And once fought with him : he was a soldier
     good ;
But, by great Mars, the captain of us all,
Never like thee. Let an old man embrace
     thee ;
And, worthy warrior, welcome to our tents.
   Æne.   'Tis the old Nestor.   201
   Hect.   Let me embrace thee, good old chron-
     icle,

That hast so long walk'd hand in hand with
  time .
Most reverend Nestor, I am glad to clasp thee
  Nest I would my arms could match thee in
    contention,
As they contend with thee in courtesy.
  Hect. I would they could
  Nest. Ha '
By this white beard, I'd fight with thee to-
  morrow
Well, welcome, welcome !—I have seen the
  time   210
  Ulyss I wonder now how yonder city
  stands
When we have here her base and pillar by us
  Hect I know your favor, Lord Ulysses,
  well
Ah, sir, there's many a Greek and Trojan
  dead,
Since first I saw yourself and Diomed
In Ilion, on your Greekish embassy
  Ulyss Sir, I foretold you then what would
  ensue :
My prophecy is but half his journey yet;
For yonder walls, that pertly front your town,
Yond towers, whose wanton tops do buss the
  clouds,   220
Must kiss their own feet
  Hect.   I must not believe you .
There they stand yet, and modestly I think,
The fall of every Phrygian stone will cost
A drop of Grecian blood the end crowns all,
And that old common arbitrator, Time,
Will one day end it
  Ulyss. So to him we leave it
Most gentle and most valiant Hector, wel-
  come .
After the general, I beseech you next
To feast with me and see me at my tent.
  Achil. I shall forestall thee, Lord Ulysses,
  thou !   230
Now, Hector, I have fed mine eyes on thee ,
I have with exact view perused thee, Hector,
And quoted joint by joint
  Hect.   Is this Achilles ?
  Achil. I am Achilles
  Hect. Stand fair, I pray thee . let me look
  on thee.
  Achil. Behold thy fill
  Hect.   Nay, I have done already
  Achil. Thou art too brief I will the second
  time.
As I would buy thee, view thee limb by limb
  Hect O, like a book of sport thou'lt read
  me o'er ,
But there's more in me than thou under-
  stand'st   240
Why dost thou so oppress me with thine eye ?
  Achil Tell me, you heavens, in which part
  of his body
Shall I destroy him ? whether there, or there,
  or there ?
That I may give the local wound a name
And make distinct the very breach whereout
Hector's great spirit flew : answer me,
  heavens ! .

  Hect It would discredit the blest gods,
  proud man,
To answer such a question · stand again :
Think'st thou to catch my life so pleasantly
As to prenominate in nice conjecture   250
Where thou wilt hit me dead ?
  Achil.   I tell thee, yea.
  Hect. Wert thou an oracle to tell me so,
I'ld not believe thee Henceforth guard thee
  well ,
For I'll not kill thee there, nor there, nor
  there .
But, by the forge that stithied Mars his helm,
I'll kill thee every where, yea, o'er and o'er.
You wisest Grecians, pardon me this brag ,
His insolence draws folly from my lips ,
But I'll endeavor deeds to match these words,
Or may I never—
  Ajax Do not chafe thee, cousin · 260
And you, Achilles, let these threats alone,
Till accident on purpose bring you to't
You may have every day enough of Hector,
If you have stomach , the general state, I fear,
Can scarce entreat you to be odd with him
  Hect I pray you, let us see you in the
  field
We have had pelting wars, since you refused
The Grecians' cause
  Achil   Dost thou entreat me, Hector ?
To-morrow do I meet thee, fell as death ,
To-night all friends
  Hect   Thy hand upon that match 270
  Agam First, all you peers of Greece, go to
  my tent ,
There in the full convive we : afterwards,
As Hector's leisure and your bounties shall
Concur together, severally entreat him.
Beat loud the tabourines, let the trumpets
  blow,
That this great soldier may his welcome know.
    [*Exeunt all except Troilus and Ulysses*
  Tro. My Lord Ulysses, tell me, I beseech
  you,
In what place of the field doth Calchas keep ?
  Ulyss. At Menelaus' tent, most princely
  Troilus   279
There Diomed doth feast with him to-night ;
Who neither looks upon the heaven nor earth,
But gives all gaze and bent of amorous view
On the fair Cressid
  Tro Shall I, sweet lord, be bound to you
  so much,
After we part from Agamemnon's tent,
To bring me thither ?
  Ulyss. You shall command me, sir.
As gentle tell me, of what honor was
This Cressida in Troy ? Had she no lover
  there
That wails her absence ?
  Tro O, sir, to such as boasting show their
  scars   290
A mock is due Will you walk on, my lord ?
She was beloved, she loved , she is, and
  doth .
But still sweet love is food for fortune's tooth
    [*Exeunt*

ACT V.

SCENE I. *The Grecian camp. Before Achilles'
tent.*

Enter ACHILLES *and* PATROCLUS.

Achil. I'll heat his blood with Greekish
wine to-night,
Which with my scimitar I'll cool to-morrow.
Patroclus, let us feast him to the height.
   Patr. Here comes Thersites.

Enter THERSITES.

Achil.   How now, thou core of envy !
Thou crusty batch of nature, what's the news ?
   Ther. Why, thou picture of what thou
seemest, and idol of idiot worshippers, here's
a letter for thee.
   Achil. From whence, fragment?
   Ther. Why, thou full dish of fool, from
Troy.   10
   Patr. Who keeps the tent now ?
   Ther. The surgeon's box, or the patient's
wound.
   Patr. Well said, adversity ! and what need
these tricks ?
   Ther. Prithee, be silent, boy ; I profit not
by thy talk : thou art thought to be Achilles'
male varlet.
   Patr. Male varlet, you rogue ! what's
that ?
   Ther. Why, his masculine whore. Now,
the rotten diseases of the south, the guts-grip-
ing, ruptures, catarrhs, loads o' gravel i'
the back, lethargies, cold palsies, raw eyes,
dirt-rotten livers, wheezing lungs, bladders
full of imposthume, sciaticas, limekilns i' the
palm, incurable bone-ache, and the rivelled
fee-simple of the tetter, take and take again
such preposterous discoveries !
   Patr. Why thou damnable box of envy,
thou, what meanest thou to curse thus ?   30
   Ther. Do I curse thee ?
   Patr. Why, no, you ruinous butt, you
whoreson indistinguishable cur, no.
   Ther. No ! why art thou then exasperate,
thou idle immaterial skein of sleave-silk, thou
green sarcenet flap for a sore eye, thou tassel
of a prodigal's purse, thou ? Ah, how the
poor world is pestered with such waterflies,
diminutives of nature !
   Patr. Out, gall !   40
   Ther. Finch-egg !
   Achil. My sweet Patroclus, I am thwarted
quite
From my great purpose in to-morrow's battle.
Here is a letter from Queen Hecuba,
A token from her daughter, my fair love,
Both taxing me and gaging me to keep
An oath that I have sworn. I will not break it:
Fall Greeks ; fail fame ; honor or go or stay ;
My major vow lies here, this I'll obey.
Come, come, Thersites, help to trim my tent :
This night in banqueting must all be spent. 51
Away, Patroclus !
                   [*Exeunt Achilles and Patroclus.*
   Ther. With too much blood and too little

brain, these two may run mad ; but, if with
too much brain and too little blood they do.
I'll be a curer of madmen. Here's Agamemnon, an honest fellow enough and one that
loves quails ; but he has not so much brain
as earwax : and the goodly transformation
of Jupiter there, his brother, the bull,—the
primitive statue, and oblique memorial of
cuckolds ; a thrifty shoeing-horn in a chain,
hanging at his brother's leg,—to what form
but that he is, should wit larded with malice
and malice forced with wit turn him to ? To
an ass, were nothing ; he is both ass and ox :
to an ox, were nothing ; he is both ox and ass.
To be a dog, a mule, a cat, a fitchew, a toad,
a lizard, an owl, a puttock, or a herring without a roe, I would not care ; but to be Menelaus, I would conspire against destiny. Ask
me not what I would be, if I were not Thersites ; for I care not to be the louse of a lazar,
so I were not Menelaus ! Hey-day ! spirit
and fires !

Enter HECTOR, TROILUS, AJAX, AGAMEMNON,
ULYSSES, NESTOR, MENELAUS, *and* DIO-
MEDES, *with lights.*

   Agam. We go wrong, we go wrong.
   Ajax.   No, yonder 'tis ;
There, where we see the lights.
   Hect.   I trouble you.
   Ajax. No, not a whit.
   Ulyss.   Here comes himself to guide you.

Re-enter ACHILLES.

   Achil. Welcome, brave Hector ; welcome,
princes all.
   Agam. So now, fair prince of Troy, I bid
good night.
Ajax commands the guard to tend on you.
   Hect. Thanks and good night to the
Greeks' general.   80
   Men. Good night, my lord.
   Hect. Good night, sweet lord Menelaus.
   Ther. Sweet draught : ' sweet' quoth 'a !
sweet sink, sweet sewer.
   Achil. Good night and welcome. both at
once, to those
That go or tarry.
   Agam. Good night.
          [*Exeunt Agamemnon and Menelaus.*
   Achil. Old Nestor tarries ; and you, too,
Diomed,
Keep Hector company an hour or two.
   Dio. I cannot, lord ; I have important bus-
iness,
The tide whereof is now. Good night, great
Hector.   90
   Hect. Give me your hand.
   Ulyss. [*Aside to Troilus*] Follow his torch ;
he goes to Calchas' tent :
I'll keep you company.
   Tro.   Sweet sir, you honor me.
   Hect. And so, good night.
          [*Exit Diomedes ; Ulysses and Troilus
                                following.*
   Achil.   Come, come, enter my tent.
   [*Exeunt Achilles, Hector, Ajax, and Nestor.*

Ther That same Diomed's a false-hearted rogue, a most unjust knave , I will no more trust him when he leers than I will a serpent when he hisses . he will spend his mouth, and promise, like Brabbler the hound , but when he performs, astronomers foretell it , it is prodigious, there will come some change , the sun borrows of the moon, when Diomed keeps his word. I will rather leave to see Hector, than not to dog him they say he keeps a Trojan drab, and uses the traitor Calchas' tent I'll after Nothing but lechery ! all incontinent varlets ! [*Exit.*

SCENE II *The same Before Calchas' tent.*
Enter DIOMEDES

Dio What, are you up here, ho ? speak.
Cal [*Within*] Who calls ?
Dio. Diomed Calchas, I think. Where's your daughter ?
Cal [*Within*] She comes to you.

Enter TROILUS *and* ULYSSES, *at a distance;*
after them, THERSITES

Ulyss Stand where the torch may not discover us.

Enter CRESSIDA

Tro. Cressid comes forth to him
Dio How now, my charge !
Cres Now, my sweet guardian ! Hark, a word with you. [*Whispers*
Tro. Yea, so familiar !
Ulyss She will sing any man at first sight
Ther And any man may sing her, if he can take her cliff ; she's noted 11
Dio. Will you remember ?
Cres Remember ! yes
Dio Nay, but do, then ;
And let your mind be coupled with your words
Tro. What should she remember ?
Ulyss. List.
Cres Sweet honey Greek, tempt me no more to folly.
Ther. Roguery !
Dio. Nay, then,— 20
Cres. I'll tell you what,—
Dio Foh, foh ! come, tell a pin . you are forsworn.
Cres. In faith, I cannot . what would you have me do ?
Ther. A juggling trick, — to be secretly open
Dio What did you swear you would bestow on me ?
Cres I prithee, do not hold me to mine oath ;
Bid me do any thing but that, sweet Greek
Dio. Good night
Tro Hold, patience !
Ulyss How now, Trojan ! 30
Cres. Diomed,—
Dio. No, no, good night : I'll be your fool no more
Tro. Thy better must.

Cres Hark, one word in your ear.
Tro O plague and madness !
Ulyss You are moved, prince ; let us depart, I pray you,
Lest your displeasure should enlarge itself
To wrathful terms this place is dangerous ,
The time right deadly , I beseech you, go
Tro Behold, I pray you ! 39
Ulyss. Nay, good my lord, go off .
You flow to great distraction , come, my lord
Tro I pray thee, stay.
Ulyss You have not patience , come
Tro I pray you, stay , by hell and all hell's torments,
I will not speak a word !
Dio. And so, good night.
Cres Nay, but you part in anger
Tro Doth that grieve thee ?
O wither'd truth !
Ulyss Why, how now, lord !
Tro By Jove,
I will be patient.
Cres Guardian !—why, Greek !
Dio. Foh, foh ! adieu , you palter
Cres. In faith, I do not . come hither once again
Ulyss You shake, my lord, at something: will you go ? 50
You will break out
Tro. She strokes his cheek !
Ulyss Come, come
Tro. Nay, stay , by Jove, I will not speak a word
There is between my will and all offences
A guard of patience stay a little while
Ther How the devil Luxury, with his fat rump and potato-finger, tickles these together ! Fry, lechery, fry !
Dio But will you, then ?
Cres In faith, I will, la , never trust me else
Dio Give me some token for the surety of it. 60
Cres. I'll fetch you one [*Exit.*
Ulyss You have sworn patience
Tro Fear me not, sweet lord ;
I will not be myself, nor have cognition
Of what I feel I am all patience

Re-enter CRESSIDA

Ther. Now the pledge , now, now, now!
Cres. Here, Diomed, keep this sleeve.
Tro O beauty ! where is thy faith ?
Ulyss My lord,—
Tro. I will be patient outwardly I will
Cres You look upon that sleeve , behold it well.
He loved me—O false wench !—Give't me again 70
Dio Whose was't ?
Cres It is no matter, now I have't again.
I will not meet with you to-morrow night
I prithee, Diomed, visit me no more
Ther Now she sharpens : well said, whetstone !
Dio. I shall have it

Cres.　　　　　　What, this?
Dio.　　　　　　　　　　　　Ay, that.
Cres.　O, all you gods! O pretty, pretty
　　pledge!
Thy master now lies thinking in his bed
Of thee and me, and sighs, and takes my glove,
And gives memorial dainty kisses to it,　　80
As I kiss thee. Nay, do not snatch it from me;
He that takes that doth take my heart withal.
Dio.　I had your heart before, this follows it.
Tro.　I did swear patience.
Cres.　You shall not have it, Diomed; faith,
　　you shall not ;
I'll give you something else.
Dio.　I will have this : whose was it?
Cres.　　　　　　　　It is no matter.
Dio.　Come, tell me whose it was.
Cres.　'Twas one's that loved me better
　　than you will.
But, now you have it, take it.
Dio.　　　　　　Whose was it?　90
Cres.　Bv all Diana's waiting-women yond,
And by herself, I will not tell you whose.
Dio.　To-morrow will I wear it on my helm,
And grieve his spirit that dares not challenge it.
Tro.　Wert thou the devil, and worest it
　　on thy horn,
It should be challenged.
Cres.　Well, well, 'tis done, 'tis past : and
　　yet it is not ;
I will not keep my word.
Dio.　　　　　Why, then, farewell;
Thou never shalt mock Diomed again.
Cres.　You shall not go : one cannot speak a
　　word,　　100
But it straight starts you.
Dio.　　　　　I do not like this fooling.
Ther.　Nor I, by Pluto: but that that likes
not you pleases me best.
Dio.　What, shall I come? the hour?
Cres.　Ay, come :—O Jove!—do come :—I
　　shall be plagued.
Dio.　Farewell till then.
Cres.　　　　　Good night : I prithee, come.
　　　　　　　　　　　　　[*Exit Diomedes.*
Troilus, farewell! one eye yet looks on thee;
But with my heart the other eye doth see.
Ah, poor our sex! this fault in us I find,
The error of our eye directs our mind :　110
What error leads must err; O, then conclude
Minds sway'd by eyes are full of turpitude.
　　　　　　　　　　　　　　　[*Exit.*
Ther.　A proof of strength she could not
　　publish more,
Unless she said ' My mind is now turn'd whore.'
Ulyss.　All's done, my lord.
Tro.　　　　.　　　　It is.
Ulyss.　　　　Why stay we, then?
Tro.　To make a recordation to my soul
Of every syllable that here was spoke.
But if I tell how these two did co-act,
Shall I not lie in publishing a truth?
Sith yet there is a credence in my heart,　120
An esperance so obstinately strong,
That doth invert the attest of eyes and ears,
As if those organs had deceptious functions,

Created only to calumniate.
Was Cressid here?
Ulyss.　　　　　　I cannot conjure, Trojan.
Tro.　She was not, sure.
Ulyss.　　　　　　　　Most sure she was.
Tro.　Why, my negation hath no taste of
　　madness.
Ulyss.　Nor mine, my lord : Cressid was
　　here but now.
Tro.　Let it not be believed for womanhood!
Think, we had mothers ; do not give advan-
　　tage　　　　　　　　　　　　　　　130
To stubborn critics, apt, without a theme,
For depravation, to square the general sex
By Cressid's rule : rather think this not Cres-
　　sid.
Ulyss.　What hath she done, prince, that
　　can soil our mothers?
Tro.　Nothing at all, unless that this were
　　she.
Ther.　Will he swagger himself out on 's
　　own eyes?
Tro.　This she? no, this is Diomed's Cres
　　sida :
If beauty have a soul, this is not she ;
If souls guide vows, if vows be sanctimonies,
If sanctimony be the gods' delight,　　140
If there be rule in unity itself,
This is not she. O madness of discourse,
That cause sets up with and against itself!
Bi-fold authority! where reason can revolt
Without perdition, and loss assume all reason
Without revolt : this is, and is not, Cressid.
Within my soul there doth conduce a fight
Of this strange nature that a thing inseparate
Divides more wider than the sky and earth,
And yet the spacious breadth of this division
Admits no orifex for a point as subtle　151
As Ariachne's broken woof to enter.
Instance, O instance! strong as Pluto's gates:
Cressid is mine, tied with the bonds of heaven:
Instance, O instance! strong as heaven itself;
The bonds of heaven are slipp'd, dissolved,
　　and loosed ;
And with another knot, five-finger-tied,
The fractions of her faith, orts of her love,
The fragments, scraps, the bits and greasy
　　relics　　　　　　　　　　　　　　159
Of her o'er-eaten faith, are bound to Diomed.
Ulyss.　May worthy Troilus be half attach'd
With that which here his passion doth ex-
　　press?
Tro.　Ay, Greek; and that shall be divulged
　　well
In characters as red as Mars his heart
Inflamed with Venus : never did young man
　　fancy
With so eternal and so fix'd a soul.
Hark, Greek : as much as I do Cressid love,
So much by weight hate I her Diomed :
That sleeve is mine that he'll bear on his helm;
Were it a casque composed by Vulcan's skill,
My sword should bite it : not the dreadful
　　spout　　　　　　　　　　　　　　171
Which shipmen do the hurricano call,
Constringed in mass by the almighty sun,

Shall dizzy with more clamor Neptune's ear
In his descent than shall my prompted sword
Falling on Diomed
 Ther He'll tickle it for his concupy.
 Tro O Cressid ! O false Cressid ! false,
false, false !
Let all untruths stand by thy stained name,
And they'll seem glorious
 Ulyss   O, contain yourself ,
Your passion draws ears hither.   181

   Enter ÆNEAS.

 Æne I have been seeking you this hour,
 my lord
Hector, by this, is arming him in Troy,
Ajax, your guard, stays to conduct you home
 Tro Have with you, prince My courteous
 lord, adieu
Farewell, revolted fair ! and, Diomed,
Stand fast, and wear a castle on thy head !
 Ulyss. I'll bring you to the gates
 Tro Accept distracted thanks
   [*Exeunt Troilus, Æneas, and Ulysses*
 Ther. Would I could meet that rogue Diomed ! I would croak like a raven, I would
bode, I would bode Patroclus will give me
any thing for the intelligence of this whore
the parrot will not do more for an almond than
he for a commodious drab Lechery, lechery,
still, wars and lechery, nothing else holds
fashion a burning devil take them ! [*Exit*

Scene III. *Troy. Before Priam's palace.*

  Enter Hector *and* Andromache

 And. When was my lord so much urgently
 temper'd,
To stop his ears against admonishment ?
Unarm, unarm, and do not fight to-day.
 Hect You train me to offend you , get you
 in :
By all the everlasting gods, I'll go !
 And My dreams will, sure, prove ominous
 to the day
 Hect. No more, I say.

   Enter Cassandra.

 Cas Where is my brother Hector ?
 And. Here, sister ; arm'd, and bloody in
 intent.
Consort with me in loud and dear petition, 9
Pursue we him on knees , for I have dream'd
Of bloody turbulence, and this whole night
Hath nothing been but shapes and forms of
 slaughter
 Cas. O, 'tis true
 Hect. Ho ! bid my trumpet sound !
 Cas No notes of sally, for the heavens,
 sweet brother.
 Hect. Be gone, I say: the gods have heard
 me swear.
 Cas. The gods are deaf to hot and peevish
 vows :
They are polluted offerings, more abhorr'd
Than spotted livers in the sacrifice
 And. O, be persuaded ! do not count it
 holy

To hurt by being just : it is as lawful, 20
For we would give much, to use violent thefts,
And rob in the behalf of charity.
 Cas It is the purpose that makes strong
 the vow ,
But vows to every purpose must not hold :
Unarm, sweet Hector.
 Hect   Hold you still, I say,
Mine honor keeps the weather of my fate .
Life every man holds dear , but the brave man
Holds honor far more precious-dear than life

   Enter Troilus

How now, young man ! mean'st thou to fight
 to-day ?
 And Cassandra, call my father to persuade
   [*Exit Cassandra.* 30
 Hect No, faith, young Troilus , doff thy
 harness, youth ;
I am to-day i' the vein of chivalry
Let grow thy sinews till their knots be strong
And tempt not yet the brushes of the war
Unarm thee, go, and doubt thou not, brave
 boy,
I'll stand to-day for thee and me and Troy
 Tro Brother, you have a vice of mercy in
 you,
Which better fits a lion than a man
 Hect What vice is that, good Troilus ?
 chide me for it
 Tro When many times the captive Grecian
 falls, 40
Even in the fan and wind of your fair sword,
You bid them rise, and live.
 Hect. O, 'tis fair play
 Tro Fool's play, by heaven, Hector.
 Hect How now ! how now !
 Tro For the love of all the gods,
Let's leave the hermit pity with our mothers,
And when we have our armors buckled on,
The venom'd vengeance ride upon our swords,
Spur them to ruthful work, rein them from
 ruth
 Hect Fie, savage, fie !
 Tro Hector, then 'tis wars
 Hect. Troilus, I would not have you fight
 to-day. 50
 Tro. Who should withhold me ?
Not fate, obedience, nor the hand of Mars
Beckoning with fiery truncheon my retire ;
Not Priamus and Hecuba on knees,
Their eyes o'ergalled with recourse of tears ;
Nor you, my brother, with your true sword
 drawn,
Opposed to hinder me, should stop my way,
But by my ruin

   Re-enter Cassandra, *with* Priam

 Cas Lay hold upon him, Priam, hold him
 fast
He is thy crutch ; now if thou lose thy stay,
Thou on him leaning, and all Troy on thee, 61
Fall all together
 Pri. Come, Hector, come, go back
Thy wife hath dream'd ; thy mother hath had
 visions ;

Cassandra doth foresee ; and I myself
Am like a prophet suddenly enrapt
To tell thee that this day is ominous:
Therefore, come back.
    Hect.   Æneas is a-field ;
And I do stand engaged to many Greeks,
Even in the faith of valor, to appear
This morning to them,
    Pri.   Ay, but thou shalt not go.
    Hect.   I must not break my faith.   71
You know me dutiful : therefore, dear sir,
Let me not shame respect ; but give me leave
To take that course by your consent and voice,
Which you do here forbid me, royal Priam.
    Cas.   O Priam, yield not to him !
    And.   Do not, dear father.
    Hect.   Andromache, I am offended with you:
Upon the love you bear me, get you in.
                     [*Exit Andromache.*
    Tro.   This foolish, dreaming, superstitious
       girl
Makes all these bodements.
    Cas.   O, farewell, dear Hector !
Look, how thou diest ! look, how thy eye turns
       pale !   81
Look, how thy wounds do bleed at many vents!
Hark, how Troy roars ! how Hecuba cries out!
How poor Andromache shrills her dolors
       forth !
Behold, distraction, frenzy and amazement,
Like witless antics, one another meet,
And all cry, Hector ! Hector's dead ! O Hec-
       tor !
    Tro.   Away ! away !
    Cas.   Farewell: yet, soft ! Hector, I take
       my leave :
Thou dost thyself and all our Troy deceive.
                          [*Exit.*
    Hect.   You are amazed, my liege, at her ex-
       claim :   91
Go in and cheer the town : we'll forth and
       fight,
Do deeds worth praise and tell you them at
       night.
    Pri.   Farewell: the gods with safety stand
       about thee !
[*Exeunt severally Priam and Hector. Alarums.*
    Tro.   They are at it, hark ! Proud Diomed,
       believe,
I come to lose my arm, or win my sleeve.

            Enter PANDARUS.

    Pan.   Do you hear, my lord ? do you hear?
    Tro.   What now ?
    Pan.   Here's a letter come from yond poor
girl.
    Tro.   Let me read.   100
    Pan.   A whoreson tisick, a whoreson rascally
tisick so troubles me, and the foolish fortune of
this girl; and what one thing, what another, that
I shall leave you one o' these days: and I have a
rheum in mine eyes too, and such an ache in my
bones that, unless a man were cursed, I cannot
tell what to think on 't. What says she there?
    Tro.   Words, words, mere words, no matter
       from the heart :

The effect doth operate another way.   105
                  [*Tearing the letter.*
Go, wind, to wind, there turn and change to-
       gether.
My love with words and errors still she feeds;
But edifies another with her deeds.
                  [*Exeunt severally*

SCENE IV.   *Plains between Troy and the Gre-*
            cian camp.

    Alarums : excursions. Enter THERSITES.

    Ther.   Now they are clapper-clawing one
another ; I'll go look on. That dissembling
abominable varlet, Diomed, has got that same
scurvy doting foolish young knave's sleeve of
Troy there in his helm : I would fain see them
meet ; that that same young Trojan ass, that
loves the whore there, might send that Greekish whore-masterly villain, with the sleeve,
back to the dissembling luxurious drab, of a
sleeveless errand. O' the t'other side, the
policy of those crafty swearing rascals, that
stale old mouse-eaten dry cheese, Nestor, and
that same dog-fox, Ulysses, is not proved
worthy a blackberry : they set me up, in
policy, that mongrel cur, Ajax, against that
dog of as bad a kind, Achilles : and now is
the cur Ajax prouder than the cur Achilles,
and will not arm to-day ; whereupon the Grecians begin to proclaim barbarism, and policy
grows into an ill opinion. Soft ! here comes
sleeve, and t'other.

     Enter DIOMEDES, TROILUS *following.*

    Tro.   Fly not ; for shouldst thou take the
       river Styx,   20
I would swim after.
    Dio.   Thou dost miscall retire :
I do not fly, but advantageous care
Withdrew me from the odds of multitude :
Have at thee !
    Ther.   Hold thy whore, Grecian !—now for
thy whore, Trojan !—now the sleeve, now the
sleeve !
       [*Exeunt Troilus and Diomedes, fighting.*
                Enter HECTOR.

    Hect.   What art thou, Greek ? art thou for
Hector's match ?
Art thou of blood and honor ?
    Ther.   No, no, I am a rascal ; a scurvy rail-
ing knave : a very filthy rogue.   31
    Hect.   I do believe thee : live.   [*Exit.*
    Ther.   God-a-mercy, that thou wilt believe
me ; but a plague break thy neck for frighting
me ! What's become of the wenching rogues ?
I think they have swallowed one another : I
would laugh at that miracle : yet, in a sort,
lechery eats itself. I'll seek them !   [*Exit.*

    SCENE V.   *Another part of the pleins.*

     Enter DIOMEDES *and a Servant.*

    Dio.   Go, go, my servant, take thou Troilus'
horse :
Present the fair steed to my lady Cressid :

Fellow, commend my service to her beauty ,
Tell her I have chastised the amorous Trojan,
And am her knight by proof.
   Serv   I go, my lord [*Exit*

Enter AGAMEMNON

Agam Renew, renew ' The fierce Poly-
    damas
Hath beat down Menon bastard Margarelon
Hath Doreus prisoner,
And stands colossus-wise, waving his beam,
Upon the pashed corses of the kings   10
Epistrophus and Cedius Polyxenes is slain,
Amphimachus and Thoas deadly hurt,
Patroclus ta'en or slain, and Palamedes
Sore hurt and bruised the dreadful Sagittary
Appals our numbers haste we, Diomed,
To reinforcement, or we perish all

Enter NESTOR

Nest. Go, bear Patroclus' body to Achilles,
And bid the snail-paced Ajax arm for shame.
There is a thousand Hectors in the field
Now here he fights on Galathe his horse,   20
And there lacks work , anon he's there afoot,
And there they fly or die, like scaled sculls
Before the belching whale then is he yonder,
And there the strawy Greeks, ripe for his edge,
Fall down before him, like the mower's swath
Here, there, and every where, he leaves and
    takes,
Dexterity so obeying appetite
That what he will he does, and does so much
That proof is call'd impossibility

Enter ULYSSES.

Ulyss. O, courage, courage, princes ' great
    Achilles   30
Is arming, weeping, cursing, vowing ven-
    geance
Patroclus' wounds have roused his drowsy
    blood,
Together with his mangled Myrmidons,
That noseless, handless, hack'd and chipp'd,
    come to him,
Crying on Hector Ajax hath lost a friend
And foams at mouth, and he is arm'd and at it,
Roaring for Troilus, who hath done to-day
Mad and fantastic execution,
Engaging and redeeming of himself
With such a careless force and forceless care
As if that luck, in very spite of cunning,   41
Bade him win all

Enter AJAX.

Ajax. Troilus ! thou coward Troilus ! [*Exit*
Dio.   Ay, there, there
Nest. So, so, we draw together.

Enter ACHILLES.

Achil   Where is this Hector ?
Come, come, thou boy-queller, show thy face;
Know what it is to meet Achilles angry .
Hector ' where's Hector ? I will none but
    Hector.   [*Exeunt.*

SCENE VI. *Another part of the plains.*

Enter AJAX

Ajax Troilus, thou coward Troilus, show
    thy head '

Enter DIOMEDES

Dio Troilus, I say ' where's Troilus ?
Ajax   What wouldst thou ?
Dio I would correct him
Ajax Were I the general, thou shouldst
    have my office
Ere that correction Troilus, I say ' what,
    Troilus '

Enter TROILUS

Tro O traitor Diomed ' turn thy false face,
    thou traitor,
And pay thy life thou owest me for my horse '
Dio Ha, art thou there ?
Ajax I'll fight with him alone stand,
    Diomed   9
Dio He is my prize , I will not look upon
Tro Come, both you cogging Greeks ,
    have at you both ' [*Exeunt, fighting.*

Enter HECTOR

Hect. Yea, Troilus ? O, well fought, my
    youngest brother '

Enter ACHILLES

Achil Now do I see thee, ha ' have at thee,
    Hector '
Hect Pause, if thou wilt
Achil. I do disdain thy courtesy, proud
    Trojan
Be happy that my arms are out of use .
My rest and negligence befriends thee now,
But thou anon shalt hear of me again ,
Till when, go seek thy fortune   [*Exit.*
Hect   Fare thee well . 19
I would have been much more a fresher man,
Had I expected thee How now, my brother !

Re-enter TROILUS

Tro Ajax hath ta'en Æneas ' shall it be ?
No, by the flame of yonder glorious heaven,
He shall not carry him I'll be ta'en too,
Or bring him off fate, hear me what I say '
I reck not though I end my life to-day. [*Exit*

Enter one in sumptuous armor.

Hect Stand, stand, thou Greek , thou art
    a goodly mark .
No ? wilt thou not ? I like thy armor well ,
I'll frush it and unlock the rivets all,
But I'll be master of it wilt thou not, beast,
    abide ?   30
Why, then fly on, I'll hunt thee for thy hide
                      [*Exeunt*

SCENE VII. *Another part of the plains.*

Enter ACHILLES, *with* Myrmidons

Achil Come here about me, you my Myr-
    midons ;

Mark what I say. Attend me where I wheel :
Strike not a stroke, but keep yourselves in
　　breath :
And when I have the bloody Hector found,
Empale him with your weapons round about ;
In fellest manner execute your aims.
Follow me, sirs, and my proceedings eye :
It is decreed Hector the great must die.
　　　　　　　　　　　　　　[*Exeunt.*

Enter MENELAUS *and* PARIS, *fighting : then*
　　　　　　　　THERSITES.

Ther. The cuckold and the cuckold-maker
are at it. Now, bull ! now, dog ! 'Loo, Paris,
'loo ! now my double-henned sparrow ! 'loo,
Paris, 'loo ! The bull has the game : ware
horns, ho !　　[*Exeunt Paris and Menelaus.*

　　　　Enter MARGARELON.

Mar. Turn, slave, and fight.
Ther. What art thou ?
Mar. A bastard son of Priam's.
Ther. I am a bastard too ; I love bastards :
I am a bastard begot, bastard instructed, bastard in mind, bastard in valor, in every thing
illegitimate. One bear will not bite another,
and wherefore should one bastard ? Take
heed, the quarrel's most ominous to us : if the
son of a whore fight for a whore, he tempts
judgment : farewell, bastard.　　[*Exit.*
Mar. The devil take thee, coward ! [*Exit.*

SCENE VIII. *Another part of the plains.*

　　　　Enter HECTOR.

Hect. Most putrefied core, so fair without,
Thy goodly armor thus hath cost thy life.
Now is my day's work done ; I'll take good
　　breath :
Rest, sword ; thou hast thy fill of blood and
　　death.
　[*Puts off his helmet and hangs his shield
　　　　　　　　　　　　behind him.*

　Enter ACHILLES *and* Myrmidons.

Achil. Look, Hector, how the sun begins to
　　set ;
How ugly night comes breathing at his heels :
Even with the vail and darking of the sun,
To close the day up, Hector's life is done.
Hect. I am unarm'd ; forego this vantage,
　　Greek.
Achil. Strike, fellows, strike ; this is the
　　man I seek.　　　　[*Hector falls.* 10
So, Ilion, fall thou next ! now, Troy, sink
　　down !
Here lies thy heart, thy sinews, and thy bone.
On, Myrmidons, and cry you all amain,
' Achilles hath the mighty Hector slain.'
　　　　　　　　　　[*A retreat sounded.*
Hark ! a retire upon our Grecian part.
Myr. The Trojan trumpets sound the like,
　　my lord.
Achil. The dragon wing of night o'er-
　　spreads the earth,
And, stickler-like, the armies separates.

My half-supp'd sword, that frankly would
　　have fed,
Pleased with this dainty bait, thus goes to bed.
　　　　　　　　　　[*Sheathes his sword.*
Come, tie his body to my horse's tail ;
Along the field I will the Trojan trail. [*Exeunt.*

SCENE IX. *Another part of the plains.*

Enter AGAMEMNON, AJAX, MENELAUS, NES-
　TOR, DIOMEDES, *and others, marching.
Shouts within.*

Agam. Hark ! hark ! what shout is that ?
Nest. Peace, drums !
[*Within*] Achilles ! Achilles ! Hector's slain !
　　Achilles.
Dio. The bruit is, Hector's slain, and by
　　Achilles.
Ajax. If it be so, yet bragless let it be ;
Great Hector was a man as good as he.
Agam. March patiently along : let one be
　　sent
To pray Achilles see us at our tent.
If in his death the gods have us befriended,　9
Great Troy is ours, and our sharp wars are
　　ended.　　　　　[*Exeunt, marching.*

SCENE X. *Another part of the plains.*

　　Enter ÆNEAS *and* Trojans

Æne. Stand, ho ! yet are we masters of the
　　field ;
Never go home ; here starve we out the night.

　　　　Enter TROILUS.

Tro. Hector is slain.
All.　　　　Hector ! the gods forbid !
Tro. He's dead ; and at the murderer's
　　horse's tail,
In beastly sort, dragg'd through the shameful
　　field.
Frown on, you heavens, effect your rage with
　　speed !
Sit, gods, upon your thrones, and smile at
　　Troy !
I say, at once let your brief plagues be mercy,
And linger not our sure destructions on !
Æne. My lord, you do discomfort all the
　　host.　　　　　　　　　　　　　　1C
Tro. You understand me not that tell me so :
I do not speak of flight, of fear, of death,
But dare all imminence that gods and men
Address their dangers in. Hector is gone :
Who shall tell Priam so, or Hecuba ?
Let him that will a screech-owl aye be call'd,
Go in to Troy, and say there, Hector's dead :
There is a word will Priam turn to stone ;
Make wells and Niobes of the maids and wives,
Cold statues of the youth, and, in a word,　20
Scare Troy out of itself. But, march away :
Hector is dead ; there is no more to say.
Stay yet. You vile abominable tents,
Thus proudly pight upon our Phrygian plains,
Let Titan rise as early as he dare,
I'll through and through you ! and, thou great-
　　sized coward,
No space of earth shall sunder our two hates :

I'll haunt thee like a wicked conscience still,
That mouldeth goblins swift as frenzy's
    thoughts
Strike a free march to Troy! with comfort go
Hope of revenge shall hide our inward woe. 31
                              [*Exeunt Æneas and Trojans*

As TROILUS *is going out, enter, from the other
    side,* PANDARUS.

Pan   But hear you, hear you!
Tro   Hence, broker-lackey! ignomy and
    shame
Pursue thy life, and live aye with thy name!
                              [*Exit.*
Pan   A goodly medicine for my aching
bones! O world! world! world! thus is the
poor agent despised! O traitors and bawds,
how earnestly are you set a-work, and how ill
requited! why should our endeavor be so
loved and the performance so loathed? what

verse for it? what instance for it? Let me
see·   41
    Full merrily the humble-bee doth sing,
    Till he hath lost his honey and his sting;
    And being once subdued in armed tail,
    Sweet honey and sweet notes together fail
Good traders in the flesh, set this in your
    painted cloths.
As many as be here of pander's hall,
Your eyes, half out, weep out at Pandar's fall,
Or if you cannot weep, yet give some groans,
Though not for me, yet for your aching bones.
Brethren and sisters of the hold-door trade,
Some two months hence my will shall here be
    made
It should be now, but that my fear is this,
Some galled goose of Winchester would hiss:
Till then I'll sweat and seek about for eases,
And at that time bequeathe you my diseases
                              [*Exit*

OTHELLO.

(WRITTEN ABOUT 1604.)

INTRODUCTION.

Othello is the only play which appeared in quarto (in 1622) in the interval between Shakespeare's death and the publication of the first folio. We have no means, except by internal evidence, of ascertaining the date at which the play was written. Upon the strength of a supposed allusion to the armorial bearings of the new order of Baronets, instituted in 1611 (Act III, Sc. iv. L. 46–47), the play has been referred to a year not earlier than 1611, but the metrical tests confirm the impression produced by the general character and spirit of the tragedy, that it cannot belong to the same period as *The Tempest, Cymbeline,* and *The Winter's Tale*. It is evidently one of the group of tragedies of passion which includes *Macbeth* and *Lear*. The year 1604 has been accepted by several critics as a not improbable date for *Othello*. The original of the story is found in Cinthio's *Hecatomithi*, but it has been in a marvellous manner elevated and re-created by Shakespeare. Coleridge has justly said that the agonized doubt which lays hold of the Moor is not the jealousy of a man of naturally jealous temper, and he contrasts Othello with Leontes in *The Winter's Tale*, and Leonatus in *Cymbeline*. A mean watchfulness or prying suspicion is the last thing that Othello could be guilty of. He is of a free and noble nature, naturally trustful, with a kind of grand innocence, retaining some of his barbaric simpleness of soul in midst of the subtle and astute politicians of Venice. He is great in simple heroic action, but unversed in the complex affairs of life, and a stranger to the malignant deceits of the debased Italian character. Nothing is more chivalrous, more romantic, than the love of Othello and Desdemona. The beautiful Italian girl is fascinated by the real strength and grandeur, and the tender protectiveness of the Moor. He is charmed by the sweetness, the sympathy, the gentle disposition, the gracious womanliness of Desdemona. But neither quite rightly knows the other, there is none of that perfect equality and perfect knowledge between them which unite so flawlessly Brutus and Portia. There is no character in Shakespeare's plays so full of serpentine power and serpentine poison as Iago. He is envious of Cassio, and suspects that the Moor may have wronged his honor, but his malignancy is out of all proportion to even its alleged motives. Cassio, notwithstanding his moral weaknesses, is a chivalrous nature, possessed by enthusiastic admiration of his great general and the beautiful lady who is his wife. But Iago can see neither human virtue nor greatness. All things to him are common and unclean, and he is content that they should be so. He is not the sly, sneaking, and too manifest villain of some of the actors of his part. He is "honest Iago," and passes for a rough yet shrewd critic of life, who is himself frank and candid. To ensnare the nobly guileless Othello was, therefore, no impossible task. Shakespeare does not allow Iago to triumph; his end is wretched as his life has been. And Othello restored to love through such tragic calamity, dies once more reunited to his wife, and loyal, in spite of all his wrongs, to the city of his adoption. It is he who has sinned, and not she who was dearer to him than himself, and of his own wrongs and griefs he can make a sudden end.

DRAMATIS PERSONÆ.

DUKE OF VENICE.
BRABANTIO, senator.
Other Senators.
GRATIANO, brother to Brabantio.
LODOVICO, kinsman to Brabantio.
OTHELLO, a noble Moor in the service of the Venetian state.
CASSIO, his lieutenant.
IAGO, his ancient.
RODERIGO, a Venetian gentleman.
MONTANO. Othello's predecessor in the government of Cyprus.

Clown, servant to Othello.

DESDEMONA, daughter to Brabantio and wife to Othello.
EMILIA, wife to Iago.
BIANCA, mistress to Cassio.

Sailor, Messenger, Herald Officers, Gentlemen, Musicians, and Attendants.

SCENE. *Venice a Sea-port in Cyprus.*

ACT I.

SCENE I *Venice. A street.*

Enter RODERIGO *and* IAGO.

Rod. Tush ! never tell me ; I take it much
unkindly
That thou, Iago, who hast had my purse
As if the strings were thine, shouldst know of
this
Iago. 'Sblood, but you will not hear me :
If ever I did dream of such a matter,
Abhor me
Rod. Thou told'st me thou didst hold him
in thy hate.
Iago. Despise me, if I do not Three great
ones of the city,
In personal suit to make me his lieutenant,
Off-capp'd to him : and, by the faith of man,
I know my price, I am worth no worse a
place :   11
But he, as loving his own pride and purposes,
Evades them, with a bombast circumstance
Horribly stuff'd with epithets of war ;
And, in conclusion,
Nonsuits my mediators ; for, ' Certes,' says
he,
' I have already chose my officer.'
And what was he ?
Forsooth, a great arithmetician,
One Michael Cassio, a Florentine,   20
†A fellow almost damn'd in a fair wife ;
That never set a squadron in the field,
Nor the division of a battle knows
More than a spinster ; unless the bookish
theoric,
Wherein the toged consuls can propose
As masterly as he : mere prattle, without
practice.
Is all his soldiership. But he, sir, had the
election.
And I, of whom his eyes had seen the proof
At Rhodes, at Cyprus and on other grounds
Christian and heathen, must be be-lee'd and
calm'd   30
By debitor and creditor : this counter-caster,
He, in good time, must his lieutenant be,
And I—God bless the mark !—his Moorship's
ancient
Rod. By heaven, I rather would have been
his hangman.
Iago. Why, there's no remedy ; 'tis the
curse of service,
Preferment goes by letter and affection,
And not by old gradation, where each second
Stood heir to the first. Now, sir, be judge
yourself,
Whether I in any just term am affined
To love the Moor.
Rod.   I would not follow him then 40
Iago. O, sir, content you ;
I follow him to serve my turn upon him :
We cannot all be masters, nor all masters
Cannot be truly follow'd You shall mark
Many a duteous and knee-crooking knave,
That, doting on his own obsequious bondage,

Wears out his time, much like his master's
ass,
For nought but provender, and when he's
old, cashier'd :
Whip me such honest knaves. Others there
are
Who, trimm'd in forms and visages of duty,
Keep yet their hearts attending on them-
selves,   51
And, throwing but shows of service on their
lords,
Do well thrive by them and when they have
lined their coats
Do themselves homage : these fellows have
some soul ,
And such a one do I profess myself. For, sir,
It is as sure as you are Roderigo,
Were I the Moor, I would not be Iago :
In following him, I follow but myself ;
Heaven is my judge, not I for love and duty,
But seeming so, for my peculiar end   60
For when my outward action doth demon-
strate
The native act and figure of my heart
In compliment extern, 'tis not long after
But I will wear my heart upon my sleeve
For daws to peck at I am not what I am
Rod. What a full fortune does the thick-
lips owe,
If he can carry't thus !
Iago.   Call up her father,
Rouse him : make after him, poison his de-
light,
Proclaim him in the streets ; incense her kins-
men,
And, though he in a fertile climate dwell, 70
Plague him with flies . though that his joy
be joy,
Yet throw such changes of vexation on't,
As it may lose some color.
Rod. Here is her father's house ; I'll call
aloud
Iago. Do, with like timorous accent and
dire yell
As when, by night and negligence, the fire
Is spied in populous cities.
Rod. What, ho, Brabantio ! Signior Bra-
bantio, ho !
Iago. Awake ! what, ho, Brabantio !
thieves ! thieves ! thieves !
Look to your house, your daughter and your
bags !   80
Thieves ! thieves !

BRABANTIO *appears above, at a window.*

Bra. What is the reason of this terrible
summons ?
What is the matter there ?
Rod. Signior, is all your family within ?
Iago. Are your doors lock'd ?
Bra.   Why, wherefore ask you this ?
Iago. 'Zounds, sir, you're robb'd ; for
shame, put on your gown ;
Your heart is burst, you have lost half your
soul ,
Even now, now, very now, an old black ram

Is tupping your white ewe. Arise, arise ;
Awake the snorting citizens with the bell, 90
Or else the devil will made a grandsire of
　　you :
Arise, I say.
　　Bra.　　　　What, have you lost your wits ?
　　Rod.　Most reverend signior, do you know
　　　my voice ?
　　Bra.　Not I : what are you ?
　　Rod.　My name is Roderigo.
　　Bra.　　　　　　　The worser welcome :
I have charged thee not to haunt about my
　　doors :
In honest plainness thou hast heard me say
My daughter is not for thee ; and now, in
　　madness,
Being full of supper and distempering
　　draughts,
Upon malicious bravery, dost thou come 100
To start my quiet.
　　Rod.　Sir, sir, sir,—
　　Bra.　　　　　But thou must needs be sure
My spirit and my place have in them power
To make this bitter to thee.
　　Rod.　　　　　　　Patience, good sir.
　　Bra.　What tell'st thou me of robbing ?
　　this is Venice ;
My house is not a grange.
　　Rod.　　　　　　Most grave Brabantio,
In simple and pure soul I come to you.
　　Iago.　'Zounds, sir, you are one of those
that will not serve God, if the devil bid you.
Because we come to do you service and you
think we are ruffians, you'll have your daugh-
ter covered with a Barbary horse ; you'll
have your nephews neigh to you ; you'll have
coursers for cousins and gennets for germans.
　　Bra.　What profane wretch art thou ?
　　Iago.　I am one, sir, that comes· to tell you
your daughter and the Moor are now making
the beast with two backs.
　　Bra.　Thou art a villain.
　　Iago.　　　　　　You are—a senator.
　　Bra.　This thou shalt answer ; I know thee,
　　Roderigo.　　　　　　　　　　　　120
　　Rod.　Sir, I will answer any thing. But, I
　　beseech you,
If 't be your pleasure and most wise consent,
As partly I find it is, that your fair daughter,
At this odd-even and dull watch o' the night,
Transported, with no worse nor better guard
But with a knave of common hire, a gon-
　　dolier,
To the gross clasps of a lascivious Moor,—
If this be known to you and your allowance,
We then have done you bold and saucy
　　wrongs ;
But if you know not this, my manners tell
　　me　　　　　　　　　　　　　　　130
We have your wrong rebuke. Do not believe
That, from the sense of all civility,
I thus would play and trifle with your rever-
　　ence :
Your daughter, if you have not given her
　　leave,
I say again, hath made a gross revolt ·

Tying her duty, beauty, wit and fortunes
In an extravagant and wheeling stranger
Of here and every where. Straight satisfy
　　yourself :
If she be in her chamber or your house,
Let loose on me the justice of the state　140
For thus deluding you.
　　Bra.　　　　　　Strike on the tinder, ho !
Give me a taper ! call up all my people !
This accident is not unlike my dream :
Belief of it oppresses me already.
Light, I say ! light !　　　　　[*Exit above.*
　　Iago.　　　　Farewell ; for I must leave you:
It seems not meet, nor wholesome to my
　　place,
To be produced—as, if I stay, I shall—
Against the Moor : for, I do know, the state,
However this may gall him with some check,
Cannot with safety cast him, for he's em-
　　bark'd　　　　　　　　　　　　150
With such loud reason to the Cyprus wars,
Which even now stand in act, that, for their
　　souls,
Another of his fathom they have none,
To lead their business : in which regard,
Though I do hate him as I do hell-pains,
Yet, for necessity of present life,
I must show out a flag and sign of love,
Which is indeed but sign. That you shall
　　surely find him,
Lead to the Sagittary the raised search ;
And there will I be with him. So, farewell.
　　　　　　　　　　　　　　　　[*Exit.* 160

Enter, below, BRABANTIO, *and* Servants *with*
　　　　　　　　torches.

　　Bra.　It is too true an evil : gone she is ;
And what's to come of my despised time
Is nought but bitterness. Now, Roderigo,
Where didst thou see her ? O unhappy girl !
With the Moor, say'st thou ? Who would be
　　a father !
How didst thou know 'twas she ? O, she de-
　　ceives me
Past thought ! What said she to you ? Get
　　more tapers :
Raise all my kindred. Are they married,
　　think you ?
　　Rod.　Truly, I think they are. · ·
　　Bra.　O heaven ! How got she out ? O
　　treason of the blood !　　　　　　170
Fathers, from hence trust not your daugh-
　　ters' minds
By what you see them act. Is there not
　　charms
By which the property of youth and maidhood
May be abused ? Have you not read, Rod-
　　erigo,
Of some such thing ?
　　Rod.　　　　　Yes, sir, I have indeed.
　　Bra.　Call up my brother. O; would you
　　had had her !
Some one way, some another. Do you know
Where we may apprehend her and the Moor ?
　　Rod.　I think I can discover him, if you
　　please

To get good guard and go along with me. 180
Bra. Pray you, lead on. At every house
   I'll call ;
I may command at most. Get weapons, ho !
And raise some special officers of night.
On, good Roderigo : I'll deserve your pains.
                       [Exeunt.

SCENE II. *Another street.*

Enter OTHELLO, IAGO, *and* Attendants *with torches.*

Iago. Though in the trade of war I have
   slain men,
Yet do I hold it very stuff o' the conscience
To do no contrived murder : I lack iniquity
Sometimes to do me service : nine or ten
   times
I had thought to have yerk'd him here under
   the ribs.
  Oth. 'Tis better as it is.
  Iago.   Nay, but he prated,
And spoke such scurvy and provoking terms
Against your honor
That, with the little godliness I have,
I did full hard forbear him. But, I pray you,
   sir,   10
Are you fast married ? Be assured of this,
That the magnifico is much beloved,
And hath in his effect a voice potential
As double as the duke's : he will divorce you;
Or put upon you what restraint and griev-
   ance
The law, with all his might to enforce it on,
Will give him cable.
  Oth.   Let him do his spite :
My services which I have done the signiory
Shall out-tongue his complaints. 'Tis yet to
   know,—   19
Which, when I know that boasting is an honor,
I shall promulgate—I fetch my life and being
From men of royal siege, and my demerits
May speak unbonneted to as proud a fortune
As this that I have reach'd : for know, Iago,
But that I love the gentle Desdemona,
I would not my unhoused free condition
Put into circumscription and confine
For the sea's worth. But, look ! what lights
   come yond ?
  Iago. Those are the raised father and his
   friends :
You were best go in.
  Oth.   Not I : I must be found : 30
My parts, my title and my perfect soul
Shall manifest me rightly. Is it they ?
  Iago. By Janus, I think no.

Enter CASSIO, *and certain* Officers *with torches.*
  Oth. The servants of the duke, and my
   lieutenant.
The goodness of the night upon you, friends !
What is the news ?
  Cas.   The duke does greet you, general,
And he requires your haste-post-haste appear-
   ance,
Even on the instant.
  Oth.   What is the matter, think you ?

Cas. Something from Cyprus, as I may
   divine :
It is a business of some heat : the galleys   46
Have sent a dozen sequent messengers
This very night at one another's heels,
And many of the consuls, raised and met,
Are at the duke's already : you have been
   hotly call'd for ;
When, being not at your lodging to be found,
The senate hath sent about three several
   quests
To search you out.
  Oth.   'Tis well I am found by you.
I will but spend a word here in the house,
And go with you.   *[Exit.*
  Cas.   Ancient, what makes he here ?
  Iago. 'Faith, he to-night hath boarded a
   land carack :   56
If it prove lawful prize, he's made for ever.
  Cas. I do not understand.
  Iago.   He's married.
  Cas.   To who ?

Re-enter OTHELLO.

  Iago. Mary, to—Come, captain, will you
   go ?
  Oth.   Have with you.
  Cas. Here comes another troop to seek for
   you.
  Iago. It is Brabantio. General, be advised;
He comes to bad intent.

Enter BRABANTIO, RODERIGO, *and* Officers
    with torches and weapons.

  Oth.   Holla ! stand there !
  Rod. Signior, it is the Moor.
  Bra.   Down with him, thief !
             [They draw on both sides.
  Iago. You, Roderigo ! come, sir, I am for
   you.
  Oth. Keep up your bright swords, for the
   dew will rust them.
Good signior, you shall more command with
   years   60
Than with your weapons.
  Bra. O thou foul thief, where hast thou
   stow'd my daughter ?
Damn'd as thou art, thou hast enchanted her;
For I'll refer me to all things of sense,
If she in chains of magic were not bound,
Whether a maid so tender, fair and happy,
So opposite to marriage that she shunn'd
The wealthy curled darlings of our nation,
Would ever have, to incur a general mock,
Run from her guardage to the sooty bosom 70
Of such a thing as thou, to fear, not to delight
Judge me the world, if 'tis not gross in sense
That thou hast practised on her with foul
   charms,
Abused her delicate youth with drugs or
   minerals
That weaken motion : I'll have 't disputed on;
'Tis probable and palpable to thinking.
I therefore apprehend and do attach thee
For an abuser of the world, a practiser
Of arts inhibited and out of warrant.
                        80

Lay hold upon him : if he do resist, 80
Subdue him at his peril.
Oth. Hold your hands,
Both you of my inclining, and the rest:
Were it my cue to fight, I should have known it
Without a prompter. Where will you that I go
To answer this your charge?
Bra. To prison, till fit time
Of law and course of direct session
Call thee to answer.
Oth. What if I do obey?
How may the duke be therewith satisfied,
Whose messengers are here about my side,
Upon some present business of the state 90
To bring me to him?
First Off. 'Tis true, most worthy signior,
The duke's in council, and your noble self,
I am sure, is sent for.
Bra. How ! the duke in council !
In this time of the night ! Bring him away :
Mine's not an idle cause : the duke himself,
Or any of my brothers of the state,
Cannot but feel this wrong as 'twere their own ;
For if such actions may have passage free,
Bond-slaves and pagans shall our statesmen
be. [*Exeunt.*

SCENE III. *A council-chamber*

The DUKE *and Senators sitting at a table ;*
Officers *attending.*

Duke. There is no composition in these news
That gives them credit.
First Sen. Indeed, they are disproportion'd;
My letters say a hundred and seven galleys.
Duke. And mine, a hundred and forty.
Sec. Sen. And mine, two hundred
But though they jump not on a just account,—
As in these cases, where the aim reports,
'Tis oft with difference—yet do they all confirm
A Turkish fleet, and bearing up to Cyprus.
Duke. Nay, it is possible enough to judgment :
I do not so secure me in the error, 10
But the main article I do approve
In fearful sense.
Sailor. [*Within*] What, ho ! what, ho !
what, ho !
First Off. A messenger from the galleys
Enter a Sailor.

Duke. Now, what's the business?
Sail. The Turkish preparation makes for Rhodes ;
So was I bid report here to the state
By Signior Angelo.
Duke. How say you by this change?
First Sen. This cannot be,
By no assay of reason : 'tis a pageant,
To keep us in false gaze. When we consider
The importance of Cyprus to the Turk, 20

And let ourselves again but understand,
That as it more concerns the Turk than Rhodes,
So may he with more facile question bear it,
For that it stands not in such warlike brace,
But altogether lacks the abilities
That Rhodes is dress'd in, if we make thought of this,
We must not think the Turk is so unskilful
To leave that latest which concerns him first,
Neglecting an attempt of ease and gain,
To wake and wage a danger profitless. 35
Duke. Nay, in all confidence, he's not for Rhodes.
First Off. Here is more news.

Enter a Messenger.

Mess. The Ottomites, reverend and gracious,
Steering with due course towards the isle of Rhodes,
Have there injointed them with an after fleet.
First Sen. Ay, so I thought. How many, as you guess?
Mess. Of thirty sail : and now they do restem
Their backward course, bearing with frank appearance
Their purposes toward Cyprus. Signior Montano,
Your trusty and most valiant servitor, 40
With his free duty recommends you thus,
And prays you to believe him.
Duke. 'Tis certain, then, for Cyprus.
Marcus Luccicos, is not he in town?
First Sen. He's now in Florence.
Duke. Write from us to him ; post-post-haste dispatch.
First Sen. Here comes Brabantio and the valiant Moor.

Enter BRABANTIO, OTHELLO, IAGO,
RODERIGO, *and* Officers

Duke. Valiant Othello, we must straight employ you
Against the general enemy Ottoman.
[*To Brabantio*] I did not see you ; welcome, gentle signior ; 50
We lack'd your counsel and your help tonight.
Bra. So did I yours. Good your grace, pardon me ;
Neither my place nor aught I heard of business
Hath raised me from my bed, nor doth the general care
Take hold on me, for my particular grief
Is of so flood-gate and o'erbearing nature
That it engluts and swallows other sorrows
And it is still itself.
Duke. Why, what's the matter?
Bra. My daughter ! O, my daughter !
Duke and Sen. Dead?
Bra. Ay, to me ;
She is abused, stol'n from me, and corrupted
By spells and medicines bought of mountebanks ; 61
For nature so preposterously to err,

Being not deficient, blind, or lame of sense,
Sans witchcraft could not.
   Duke. Whoe'er he be that in this foul pro-
     ceeding
Hath thus beguiled your daughter of herself
And you of her, the bloody book of law
You shall yourself read in the bitter letter
After your own sense, yea, though our proper
    son
Stood in your action.
   Bra.   Humbly I thank your grace. 70
Here is the man, this Moor, whom now, it
   seems,
Your special mandate for the state-affairs
Hath hither brought.
   Duke and Sen.   We are very sorry for't.
   Duke. [*To Othello*] What, in your own
   part, can you say to this?
   Bra. Nothing, but this is so.
   Oth. Most potent, grave, and reverend sig-
   niors,
My very noble and approved good masters,
That I have ta'en away this old man's daugh-
   ter,
It is most true; true, I have married her:
The very head and front of my offending 80
Hath this extent, no more. Rude am I in my
   speech,
And little bless'd with the soft phrase of peace:
For since these arms of mine had seven years'
   pith,   [used
Till now some nine moons wasted, they have
Their dearest action in the tented field,
And little of this great world can I speak,
More than pertains to feats of broil and battle,
And therefore little shall I grace my cause
In speaking for myself. Yet, by your gra-
   cious patience,
I will a round unvarnish'd tale deliver 90
Of my whole course of love; what drugs,
What charms,
What conjuration and what mighty magic,
For such proceeding I am charged withal,
I won his daughter.
   Bra.   A maiden never bold;
Of spirit so still and quiet, that her motion
Blush'd at herself; and she, in spite of nature,
Of years, of country, credit, every thing,
To fall in love with what she fear'd to look on!
It is a judgment maim'd and most imperfect
That will confess perfection so could err 100
Against all rules of nature, and must be driven
To find out practices of cunning hell,
Why this should be. I therefore vouch again
That with some mixtures powerful o'er the
   blood,
Or with some dram conjured to this effect,
He wrought upon her.
   Duke.   To vouch this, is no proof,
Without more wider and more overt test
Than these thin habits and poor likelihoods
Of modern seeming do prefer against him.
   First Sen. But, Othello, speak: 110
Did you by indirect and forced courses
Subdue and poison this young maid's affec-
   tions?

Or came it by request and such fair question
As soul to soul affordeth?
   Oth.   I do beseech you,
Send for the lady to the Sagittary,
And let her speak of me before her father:
If you do find me foul in her report,
The trust, the office I do hold of you,
Not only take away, but let your sentence
Even fall upon my life.
   Duke.   Fetch Desdemona hither. 120
   Oth. Ancient, conduct them: you best
   know the place. [*Exeunt Iago and At-
             tendants.*
And, till she come, as truly as to heaven
I do confess the vices of my blood,
So justly to your grave ears I'll present
How I did thrive in this fair lady's love,
And she in mine.
   Duke. Say it, Othello.
   Oth. Her father loved me; oft invited me
Still question'd me the story of my life,
From year to year, the battles, sieges, fortunes
That I have pass'd.   131
I ran it through, even from my boyish days,
To the very moment that he bade me tell it;
Wherein I spake of most disastrous chances,
Of moving accidents by flood and field,
Of hair-breadth scapes i' the imminent deadly
   breach,
Of being taken by the insolent foe
And sold to slavery, of my redemption thence
And portance in my travels' history:
Wherein of antres vast and deserts idle, 140
Rough quarries, rocks and hills whose heads
   touch heaven,
It was my hint to speak,—such was the pro-
   cess;
And of the Cannibals that each other eat,
The Anthropophagi and men whose heads
Do grow beneath their shoulders. This to hear
Would Desdemona seriously incline:
But still the house-affairs would draw her
   thence:
Which ever as she could with haste dispatch,
She'ld come again, and with a greedy ear
Devour up my discourse: which I observing,
Took once a pliant hour, and found good
   means   151
To draw from her a prayer of earnest heart
That I would all my pilgrimage dilate,
Whereof by parcels she had something heard,
But not intentively: I did consent,
And often did beguile her of her tears,
When I did speak of some distressful stroke
That my youth suffer'd. My story being done,
She gave me for my pains a world of sighs:
She swore, in faith, 'twas strange, 'twas pas-
   sing strange,   160
'Twas pitiful, 'twas wondrous pitiful:
She wish'd she had not heard it, yet she wish'd
That heaven had made her such a man: she
   thank'd me,
And bade me, if I had a friend that loved her,
I should but teach him how to tell my story,
And that would woo her. Upon this hint I
   spake:

She loved me for the dangers I had pass'd,
And I loved her that she did pity them
This only is the witchcraft I have used :
Here comes the lady let her witness it.   170

Enter DESDEMONA, IAGO, *and* Attendants.

Duke   I think this tale would win my
     daughter too.
Good Brabantio,
Take up this mangled matter at the best :
Men do their broken weapons rather use
Than their bare hands
    Bra.   I pray you, hear her speak :
If she confess that she was half the wooer,
Destruction on my head, if my bad blame
Light on the man ! Come hither, gentle mis-
    tress !
Do you perceive in all this noble company
Where most you owe obedience ?
    Des.   My noble father, 180
I do perceive here a divided duty
To you I am bound for life and education ,
My life and education both do learn me
How to respect you ; you are the lord of duty;
I am hitherto your daughter . but here's my
    husband,
And so much duty as my mother show'd
To you, preferring you before her father.
So much I challenge that I may profess
Due to the Moor my lord
    Bra   God be wi' you ! I have done.
Please it your grace, on to the state-affairs
I had rather to adopt a child than get it   191
Come hither, Moor
I here do give thee that with all my heart
Which, but thou hast already, with all my
    heart
I would keep from thee For your sake, jewel,
I am glad at soul I have no other child .
For thy escape would teach me tyranny,
To hang clogs on them I have done, my lord.
    Duke.   Let me speak like yourself, and lay
    a sentence,   199
Which, as a grise or step, may help these lovers
Into your favor.
When remedies are past, the griefs are ended
By seeing the worst, which late on hopes de-
    pended
To mourn a mischief that is past and gone
Is the next way to draw new mischief on.
What cannot be preserved when fortune takes
Patience her injury a mockery makes
The robb'd that smiles steals something from
    the thief ;
He robs himself that spends a bootless grief.
    Bra   So let the Turk of Cyprus us beguile,
We lose it not, so long as we can smile   211
He bears the sentence well that nothing bears
But the free comfort which from thence he
    hears,
But he bears both the sentence and the sorrow
That, to pay grief, must of poor patience bor-
    row.
These sentences, to sugar, or to gall,
Being strong on both sides, are equivocal :
But words are words ; I never yet did hear

That the bruised heart was pierced through
    the ear
I humbly beseech you, proceed to the affairs
    of state   220
    Duke.   The Turk with a most mighty prep-
aration makes for Cyprus. Othello, the fortitude of the place is best known to you , and
though we have there a substitute of most
allowed sufficiency, yet opinion, a sovereign
mistress of effects, throws a more safer voice
on you. you must therefore be content to
slubber the gloss of your new fortunes with
this more stubborn and boisterous expedition.
    Oth.   The tyrant custom, most grave sena-
    tors,   230
Hath made the flinty and steel couch of war
My thrice-driven bed of down : I do agnize
A natural and prompt alacrity
I find in hardness, and do undertake
These present wars against the Ottomites.
Most humbly therefore bending to your state,
I crave fit disposition for my wife,
Due reference of place and exhibition,
With such accommodation and besort
As levels with her breeding.
    Duke.   If you please,   240
Be't at her father's.
    Bra.   I'll not have it so.
    Oth.   Nor I
    Des   Nor I ; I would not there reside
To put my father in impatient thoughts
By being in his eye. Most gracious duke,
To my unfolding lend your prosperous ear ;
And let me find a charter in your voice,
To assist my simpleness.
    Duke.   What would you, Desdemona ?
    Des   That I did love the Moor to live with
    him,   249
My downright violence and storm of fortunes
May trumpet to the world: my heart's subdued
Even to the very quality of my lord :
I saw Othello's visage in his mind,
And to his honor and his valiant parts
Did I my soul and fortunes consecrate
So that, dear lords, it I be left behind,
A moth of peace, and he go to the war,
The rites for which I love him are bereft me,
And I a heavy interim shall support
By his dear absence. Let me go with him.   260
    Oth   Let her have your voices.
Vouch with me, heaven, I therefore beg it not,
To please the palate of my appetite,
Nor to comply with heat—the young affects
In me defunct—and proper satisfaction,
But to be free and bounteous to her mind :
And heaven defend your good souls, that you
    think
I will your serious and great business scant
For she is with me : no, when light-wing'd toys
Of feather'd Cupid seal with wanton dullness
My speculative and officed instruments,   271
That my disports corrupt and taint my busi-
    ness,
Let housewives make a skillet of my helm,
And all indign and base adversities
Make head against my estimation !

Duke. Be it as you shall privately determine,
Either for her stay or going · the affair cries h'aste,
And speed must answer it.
    First Sen. You must away to-night.
    Oth.   With all my heart.
    Duke. At nine i' the morning here we'll
    meet again.   280
Othello, leave some officer behind,
And he shall our commission bring to you :
With such things else of quality and respect
As doth import you.
    Oth.   So please your grace, my ancient ;
A man he is of honesty and trust :
To his conveyance I assign my wife,
With what else needful your good grace shall think
To be sent after me.
    Duke.   Let it be so.
Good night to every one. [*To Brab.*] And, noble signior,
If virtue no delighted beauty lack,   290
Your son-in-law is far more fair than black.
    First Sen. Adieu, brave Moor; use Desdemona well.
    Bra. Look to her, Moor, if thou hast eyes to see :
She has deceived her father, and may thee.
    [*Exeunt Duke, Senators, Officers, &c.*
    Oth. My life upon her faith ! Honest Iago,
My Desdemona must I leave to thee :
I prithee, let thy wife attend on her :
And bring them after in the best advantage.
Come, Desdemona : I have but an hour
Of love, of worldly matters and direction,   300
To spend with thee : we must obey the time.
    [*Exeunt Othello and Desdemona.*
    Rod. Iago,—
    Iago. What say'st thou, noble heart ?
    Rod. What will I do, thinkest thou ?
    Iago. Why, go to bed, and sleep.
    Rod. I will incontinently drown myself.
    Iago. If thou dost, I shall never love thee after. Why, thou silly gentleman !
    Rod. It is silliness to live when to live is torment ; and then have we a prescription to die when death is our physician.   311
    Iago. O villanous ! I have looked upon the world for four times seven years ; and since I could distinguish betwixt a benefit and an injury, I never found man that knew how to love himself. Ere I would say, I would drown myself for the love of a guinea-hen, I would change my humanity with a baboon.
    Rod. What should I do ? I confess it is my shame to be so fond ; but it is not in my virtue to amend it.   321
    Iago. Virtue ! a fig ! 'tis in ourselves that we are thus or thus. Our bodies are our gardens, to the which our wills are gardeners : so that if we will plant nettles, or sow lettuce, set hyssop and weed up thyme, supply it with one gender of herbs, or distract it with many, either to have it sterile with idleness, or manured with industry, why, the power and cor-

rigible authority of this lies in our wills. If the balance of our lives had not one scale of reason to poise another of sensuality, the blood and baseness of our natures would conduct us to most preposterous conclusions : but we have reason to cool our raging motions, our carnal stings, our unbitted lusts, whereof I take this that you call love to be a sect or scion.
    Rod. It cannot be.
    Iago. It is merely a lust of the blood and a permission of the will. Come, be a man. Drown thyself ! drown cats and blind puppies. I have professed me thy friend and I confess me knit to thy deserving with cables of perdurable toughness ; I could never better stead thee than now. Put money in thy purse; follow thou the wars; defeat thy favor with an usurped beard ; I say, put money in thy purse. It cannot be that Desdemona should long continue her love to the Moor,—put money in thy purse,—nor he his to her : it was a violent commencement, and thou shalt see an answerable sequestration :—put but money in thy purse. These Moors are changeable in their wills:—fill thy purse with money: —the food that to him now is as luscious as locusts, shall be to him shortly as bitter as coloquintida. She must change for youth : when she is sated with his body, she will find the error of her choice : she must have change, she must : therefore put money in thy purse. If thou wilt needs damn thyself, do it a more delicate way than drowning. Make all the money thou canst : if sanctimony and a frail vow betwixt an erring barbarian and a supersubtle Venetian be not too hard for my wits and all the tribe of hell, thou shalt enjoy her ; therefore make money. A pox of drowning thyself ! it is clean out of the way : seek thou rather to be hanged in compassing thy joy than to be drowned and go without her.
    Rod. Wilt thou be fast to my hopes, if I depend on the issue ?   370
    Iago. Thou art sure of me :—go, make money :—I have told thee often, and I re-tell thee again and again, I hate the Moor : my cause is hearted ; thine hath no less reason. Let us be conjunctive in our revenge against him : if thou canst cuckold him, thou dost thyself a pleasure, me a sport. There are many events in the womb of time which will be delivered. Traverse ! go, provide thy money. We will have more of this to-morrow. Adieu.
    Rod. Where shall we meet i' the morning ?   381
    Iago. At my lodging.
    Rod. I'll be with thee betimes.
    Iago. Go to ; farewell. Do you hear, Roderigo ?
    Rod. What say you ?
    Iago. No more of drowning, do you hear ?
    Rod. I am changed : I'll go sell all my land.   [*Exit.*
    Iago. Thus do I ever make my fool my purse :   [fane,
For I mine own gain'd knowledge should pro-

If I would time expend with such a snipe,
But for my sport and profit. I hate the Moor :
And it is thought abroad, that 'twixt my
　　sheets
He has done my office : I know not if't be
　　true ;
But I, for mere suspicion in that kind,
Will do as if for surety. He holds me well ;
The better shall my purpose work on him.
Cassio's a proper man : let me see now :
To get his place and to plume up my will　399
In double knavery—How, how ? Let's see :—
After some time, to abuse Othello's ear
That he is too familiar with his wife.
He hath a person and a smooth dispose
To be suspected, framed to make women
　　false.
The Moor is of a free and open nature,
That thinks men honest that but seem to be
　　so,
And will as tenderly be led by the nose
As asses are.
I have't. It is engender'd. Hell and night
Must bring this monstrous birth to the world's
　　light.　　　　　　　　　　　[*Exit.*　410

ACT II.

SCENE I. *A Sea-port in Cyprus. An open
place near the quay.*

Enter MONTANO *and two* Gentlemen.

　Mon. What from the cape can you discern
at sea ?
　First Gent. Nothing at all : it is a high-
wrought flood ;
I cannot, 'twixt the heaven and the main,
Descry a sail.
　Mon. Methinks the wind hath spoke aloud
at land ;
A fuller blast ne'er shook our battlements :
If it hath ruffian'd so upon the sea,
What ribs of oak, when mountains melt on
　them,
Can hold the mortise ? What shall we hear of
　this ?
　Sec. Gent. A segregation of the Turkish
　fleet :　　　　　　　　　　　　　　　　10
For do but stand upon the foaming shore,
The chidden billow seems to pelt the clouds ;
The wind-shaked surge, with high and mon-
strous mane,
Seems to cast water on the burning bear,
And quench the guards of the ever-fixed pole :
I never did like molestation view
On the enchafed flood.
　Mon.　　　　　　If that the Turkish fleet
Be not enshelter'd and embay'd, they are
　drown'd :
It is impossible they bear it out.

Enter a third Gentleman.

　Third Gent. News, lads ! our wars are
　done.　　　　　　　　　　　　　　20
The desperate tempest hath so bang'd the
Turks,

That their designment halts : a noble ship of
　Venice
Hath seen a grievous wreck and sufferance
On most part of their fleet.
　Mon. How ! is this true ?
　Third Gent.　　　　　The ship is here put in,
A Veronesa ; Michael Cassio,
Lieutenant to the warlike Moor Othello,
Is come on shore : the Moor himself at sea,
And is in full commission here for Cyprus.
　Mon. I am glad on't ; 'tis a worthy gov-
ernor.　　　　　　　　　　　　　　30
　Third Gent. But this same Cassio, though
　he speak of comfort
Touching the Turkish loss, yet he looks sadly,
And prays the Moor be safe ; for they were
　parted
With foul and violent tempest.
　Mon.　　　　　　Pray heavens he be ;
For I have served him, and the man com-
mands
Like a full soldier. Let's to the seaside, ho !
As well to see the vessel that's come in
As to throw out our eyes for brave Othello,
Even till we make the main and the aerial
　blue
An indistinct regard.
　Third Gent.　　　Come, let's do so :　　40
For every minute is expectancy
Of more arrivance.

Enter CASSIO.

　Cas. Thanks, you the valiant of this war-
like isle,
That so approve the Moor ! O, let the heavens
Give him defence against the elements,
For I have lost him on a dangerous sea.
　Mon. Is he well shipp'd ?
　Cas. His bark is stoutly timber'd, and his
　pilot
Of very expert and approved allowance ;
Therefore my hopes, not surfeited to death,
Stand in bold cure.　　　　　　　　51
　　　[*A cry within* ' A sail, a sail, a sail !'

Enter a fourth Gentleman.

　Cas. What noise ?
　Fourth Gent. The town is empty ; on the
　brow o' the sea
Stand ranks of people, and they cry ' A sail !'
　Cas. My hopes do shape him for the gover-
nor.　　　　　　　　　　　[*Guns heard.*
　Sec. Gent. They do discharge their shot of
　courtesy :
Our friends at least.
　Cas.　　　　I pray you, sir, go forth,
And give us truth who 'tis that is arrived.
　Sec. Gent. I shall.　　　　　　　[*Exit.*
　Mon. But, good lieutenant, is your general
　wived ?　　　　　　　　　　　　60
　Cas. Most fortunately : he hath achieved a
　maid
That paragons description and wild fame ;
One that excels the quirks of blazoning pens,
And in the essential vesture of creation
Does tire the ingener.

Re-enter second Gentleman.

How now ! who has put in ?

Sec. Gent. 'Tis one Iago, ancient to the general

Cas Has had most favorable and happy speed

Tempests themselves, high seas, and howling winds,

The gutter'd rocks and congregated sands,—

Traitors ensteep'd to clog the guiltless keel,—

As having sense of beauty, do omit   71

Their mortal natures, letting go safely by

The divine Desdemona.

Mon.   What is she ?

Cas She that I spake of, our great captain's captain,

Left in the conduct of the bold Iago,

Whose footing here anticipates our thoughts

A se'nnight's speed   Great Jove, Othello guard,

And swell his sail with thine own powerful breath,

That he may bless this bay with his tall ship,

Make love's quick pants in Desdemona's arms,   80

Give renew'd fire to our extincted spirits

And bring all Cyprus comfort !

Enter Desdemona, Emilia, Iago, Roderigo, *and* Attendants

O, behold,

The riches of the ship is come on shore !

Ye men of Cyprus, let her have your knees.

Hail to thee, lady ! and the grace of heaven,

Before, behind thee, and on every hand,

Enwheel thee round !

Des   I thank you, valiant Cassio.

What tidings can you tell me of my lord ?

Cas   He is not yet arrived · nor know I aught

But that he's well and will be shortly here   90

Des   O, but I fear—How lost you company ?

Cas.   The great contention of the sea and skies

Parted our fellowship—But, hark ! a sail

[*Within* 'A sail, a sail !'   *Guns heard.*

Sec. Gen.   They give their greeting to the citadel,

This likewise is a friend.

Cas.   See for the news.   [*Exit gentlemen.*

Good ancient, you are welcome   [*To Emilia*]

Welcome, mistress.

Let it not gall your patience, good Iago,

That I extend my manners, 'tis my breeding

That gives me this bold show of courtesy 100

[*Kissing her.*

Iago.   Sir, would she give you so much of her lips

As of her tongue she oft bestows on me,

You'ld have enough.

Des.   Alas, she has no speech.

Iago.   In faith, too much,

I find it still, when I have list to sleep.

Marry, before your ladyship, I grant,

She puts her tongue a little in her heart,

And chides with thinking.

Emil   You have little cause to say so.

Iago.   Come on, come on, you are pictures out of doors,   110

Bells in your parlors, wild-cats in your kitchens,

Saints in your injuries, devils being offended.

Players in your housewifery, and housewives in your beds

Des.   O, fie upon thee, slanderer !

Iago   Nay, it is true, or else I am a Turk :

You rise to play and go to bed to work

Emil.   You shall not write my praise.

Iago.   No, let me not

Des   What wouldst thou write of me, if thou shouldst praise me ?

Iago   O gentle lady, do not put me to't ,

For I am nothing, if not critical   120

Des   Come on, assay. There's one gone to the harbor ?

Iago.   Ay, madam.

Des   I am not merry ; but I do beguile

The thing I am, by seeming otherwise.

Come, how wouldst thou praise me ?

Iago   I am about it , but indeed my invention

Comes from my pate as birdlime does from frize ;

It plucks out brains and all : but my Muse labors,

And thus she is deliver'd

If she be fair and wise, fairness and wit,   130

The one's for use, the other useth it

Des   Well praised ! How if she be black and witty ?

Iago.   If she be black, and thereto have a wit,

She'll find a white that shall her blackness fit

Des   Worse and worse.

Emil.   How if fair and foolish ?

Iago.   She never yet was foolish that was fair,

For even her folly help'd her to an heir.

Des   These are old fond paradoxes to make

fools laugh i' the alehouse. What miserable

praise hast thou for her that's foul and foolish ?   141

Iago   There's none so foul and foolish thereunto,

But does foul pranks which fair and wise ones do

Des   O heavy ignorance ! thou praisest the worst best   But what praise couldst thou bestow on a deserving woman indeed, one that, in the authority of her merit did justly put on the vouch of very malice itself ?

Iago   She that was ever fair and never proud,

Had tongue at will and yet was never loud, 150

Never lack'd gold and yet went never gay,

Fled from her wish and yet said 'Now I may,'

She that being anger'd, her revenge being nigh,

Bade her wrong stay and her displeasure fly,

She that in wisdom never was so frail

To change the cod's head for the salmon's tail,

She that could think and ne'er disclose her
mind,
See suitors following and not look behind,
She was a wight, if ever such wight were,—
　Des.　To do what?　　　　　　　　　160
　Iago　To suckle fools and chronicle small
beer
　Des.　O most lame and impotent conclusion'
Do not learn of him, Emilia, though he be thy
husband. How say you, Cassio? is he not a
most profane and liberal counsellor?
　Cas　He speaks home, madam you may
relish him more in the soldier than in the
scholar.
　Iago.　[*Aside*] He takes her by the palm.
ay, well said, whisper : with as little a web as
this will I ensnare as great a fly as Cassio Ay,
smile upon her, do ; I will give thee in thine
own courtship. You say true ; 'tis so, indeed.
if such tricks as these strip you out of your
lieutenantry, it had been better you had not
kissed your three fingers so oft, which now
again you are most apt to play the sir in Very
good , well kissed ! an excellent courtesy'
'tis so, indeed Yet again your fingers to your
lips ? would they were clyster-pipes for your
sake ! [*Trumpet within.*] The Moor ! I know
his trumpet　　　　　　　　　　　180
　Cas　'Tis truly so
　Des　Let's meet him and receive him
　Cas.　Lo, where he comes !

Enter OTHELLO *and* Attendants.

　Oth　O my fair warrior '
　Des.　　　　　　My dear Othello !
　Oth　It gives me wonder great as my con-
tent
To see you here before me O my soul's joy !
If after every tempest come such calms,
May the winds blow till they have waken'd
death !
And let the laboring bark climb hills of seas
Olympus-high and duck again as low　　190
As hell's from heaven' If it were now to die,
'Twere now to be most happy , for, I fear,
My soul hath her content so absolute
That not another comfort like to this
Succeeds in unknown fate
　Des.　　　　　The heavens forbid
But that our loves and comforts should in-
crease,
Even as our days do grow !
　Oth　　　　　Amen to that, sweet powers !
I cannot speak enough of this content ;
It stops me here ; it is too much of joy :
And this, and this, the greatest discords be
　　　　　　　　[*Kissing her.* 200
That e'er our hearts shall make '
　Iago [*Aside*] O, you are well tuned now !
But I'll set down the pegs that make this
music,
As honest as I am
　Oth.　　　　Come, let us to the castle.
News, friends , our wars are done, the Turks
are drown'd.
How does my old acquaintance of this isle ?

Honey, you shall be well desired in Cyprus ;
I have found great love amongst them. O my
sweet,
I prattle out of fashion, and I dote
In mine own comforts. I prithee, good Iago,
Go to the bay and disembark my coffers :　210
Bring thou the master to the citadel ;
He is a good one, and his worthiness
Does challenge much respect. Come, Desde-
mona,
Once more, well met at Cyprus.
[*Exeunt Othello, Desdemona, and Attendants.*
　Iago.　Do thou meet me presently at the
harbor. Come hither If thou be'st valiant,—
as, they say, base men being in love have then
a nobility in their natures more than is native
to them,—list me The lieutenant to-night
watches on the court of guard —first, I must
tell thee this—Desdemona is directly in love
with him　　　　　　　　　　　221
　Rod　With him ' why, 'tis not possible.
　Iago.　Lay thy finger thus, and let thy soul
be instructed. Mark me with what violence
she first loved the Moor, but for bragging and
telling her fantastical lies : and will she love
him still for prating ? let not thy discreet
heart think it Her eye must be fed ; and
what delight shall she have to look on the
devil ? When the blood is made dull with
the act of sport, there should be, again to inflame it and to give satiety a fresh appetite,
loveliness in favor, sympathy in years,
manners and beauties ; all which the Moor is
defective in : now for want of these required
conveniences, her delicate tenderness will find
itself abused, begin to heave the gorge, dis-
relish and abhor the Moor ; very nature will
instruct her in it and compel her to some second
choice. Now, sir, this granted,—as it is a
most pregnant and unforced position—who
stands so eminent in the degree of this fortune
as Cassio does? a knave very voluble ; no
further conscionable than in putting on the
mere form of civil and humane seeming, for
the better compassing of his salt and most
hidden loose affection? why, none , why,
none : a slipper and subtle knave, a finder of
occasions, that has an eye can stamp and
counterfeit advantages, though true advantage never present itself ; a devilish knave
Besides, the knave is handsome, young, and
hath all those requisites in him that folly and
green minds look after. a pestilent complete
knave ; and the woman hath found him already.
　Rod　I cannot believe that in her , she's
full of most blessed condition
　Iago.　Blessed fig's-end ! the wine she drinks
is made of grapes : if she had been blessed,
she would never have loved the Moor. Blessed
pudding ' Didst thou not see her paddle with
the palm of his hand ? didst not mark that?
　Rod.　Yes, that I did ; but that was but
courtesy
　Iago.　Lechery, by this hand ; an index and .
obscure prologue to the history of lust and

foul thoughts. They met so near with their lips that their breaths embraced together Villanous thoughts, Roderigo ! when these mutualities so marshal the way, hard at hand comes the master and main exercise, the incorporate conclusion, Pish ! But, sir, be you ruled by me : I have brought you from Venice. Watch you to-night , for the command, I'll lay't upon you. Cassio knows you not I'll not be far from you : do you find some occasion to anger Cassio, either by speaking too loud, or tainting his discipline ; or from what other course you please, which the time shall more favorably minister.

Rod. Well.

Iago. Sir, he is rash and very sudden in choler, and haply may strike at you . provoke him, that he may , for even out of that will I cause these of Cyprus to mutiny ; whose qualification shall come into no true taste again but by the displanting of Cassio. So shall you have a shorter journey to your desires by the means I shall then have to prefer them , and the impediment most profitably removed, without the which there were no expectation of our prosperity.

Rod. I will do this, if I can bring it to any opportunity.   290

Iago. I warrant thee. Meet me by and by at the citadel : I must fetch his necessaries ashore. Farewell.

Rod. Adieu.   [*Exit.*

Iago. That Cassio loves her, I do well believe it ;
That she loves him, 'tis apt and of great credit :
The Moor, howbeit that I endure him not,
Is of a constant, loving, noble nature,
And I dare think he'll prove to Desdemona
A most dear husband.   Now, I do love her too ,   300
Not out of absolute lust, though peradventure
I stand accountant for as great a sin,
But partly led to diet my revenge,
For that I do suspect the lusty Moor
Hath leap'd into my seat , the thought whereof
Doth, like a poisonous mineral, gnaw my inwards ;
And nothing can or shall content my soul
Till I am even'd with him, wife for wife,
Or failing so, yet that I put the Moor
At least into a jealousy so strong   310
That judgment cannot cure.   Which thing to do,
If this poor trash of Venice, whom I trash
For his quick hunting, stand the putting on,
I'll have our Michael Cassio on the hip,
Abuse him to the Moor in the rank garb—
For I fear Cassio with my night-cap too—
Make the Moor thank me, love me and reward me,
For making him egregiously an ass
And practising upon his peace and quiet   319
Even to madness.   'Tis here, but yet confused
Knavery's plain face is never seen till used
[*Exit.*

SCENE II. *A street.*

Enter a Herald *with a proclamation;* People *following.*

Her. It is Othello's pleasure, our noble and valiant general, that, upon certain tidings now arrived, importing the mere perdition of the Turkish fleet, every man put himself into triumph , some to dance, some to make bonfires, each man to what sport and revels his addiction leads him : for, besides these beneficial news, it is the celebration of his nuptial   So much was his pleasure should be proclaimed All offices are open, and there is full liberty of feasting from this present hour of five till the bell have told eleven   Heaven bless the isle of Cyprus and our noble general Othello !
[*Exeunt.*

SCENE III.   *A hall in the castle.*

Enter OTHELLO, DESDEMONA, CASSIO, *and* Attendants.

Oth   Good Michael, look you to the guard to-night ·
Let's teach ourselves that honorable stop,
Not to outsport discretion.

Cas   Iago hath direction what to do ;
But, notwithstanding, with my personal eye
Will I look to't

Oth.   Iago is most honest.
Michael, good night : to-morrow with your earliest
Let me have speech with you. [*To Desdemona*]
Come, my dear love,
The purchase made, the fruits are to ensue ;
That profit 's yet to come 'tween me and you.
Good night   11
[*Exeunt Othello, Desdemona, and Attendants.*

Enter IAGO.

Cas. Welcome, Iago , we must to the watch

Iago   Not this hour, lieutenant ; 'tis not yet ten o' the clock.   Our general cast us thus early for the love of his Desdemona , who let us not therefore blame   he hath not yet made wanton the night with her , and she is sport for Jove.

Cas   She's a most exquisite lady

Iago.   And, I'll warrant her, full of game

Cas.   Indeed, she's a most fresh and delicate creature.   21

Iago.   What an eye she has ! methinks it sounds a parley of provocation

Cas.   An inviting eye ; and yet methinks right modest

Iago.   And when she speaks, is it not an alarum to love ?

Cas   She is indeed perfection

Iago.   Well, happiness to their sheets ! Come, lieutenant, I have a stoup of wine ; and here without are a brace of Cyprus gallants that would fain have a measure to the health of black Othello

Cas   Not to-night, good Iago   I have very poor and unhappy brains for drinking : I could

well wish courtesy would invent some other
custom of entertainment.

Iago. O, they are our friends; but one cup.
I'll drink for you   39

Cas. I have drunk but one cup to-night,
and that was craftily qualified too, and, behold,
what innovation it makes here : I am unfortunate in the infirmity, and dare not task my
weakness with any more.

Iago What, man ! 'tis a night of revels :
the gallants desire it

Cas Where are they ?

Iago. Here at the door ; I pray you, call
them in

Cas. I'll do't , but it dislikes me   [*Exit.*

Iago If I can fasten but one cup upon him,
With that which he hath drunk to-night al-
ready,   51
He'll be as full of quarrel and offence
As my young mistress' dog. Now, my sick
           fool Roderigo,
Whom love hath turn'd almost the wrong side
           out,
To Desdemona hath to-night caroused
Potations pottle-deep , and he's to watch .
Three lads of Cyprus, noble swelling spirits,
That hold their honors in a wary distance,
The very elements of this warlike isle,
Have I to-night fluster d with flowing cups, 60
And they watch too. Now, 'mongst this flock
           of drunkards,
Am I to put our Cassio in some action
That may offend the isle.—But here they come.
If consequence do but approve my dream,
My boat sails freely, both with wind and
           stream.

Re-enter CASSIO ; *with him* MONTANO *and*
Gentlemen , *servants following with wine.*

Cas 'Fore God, they have given me a rouse
already.

Mon Good faith, a little one , not past a
pint, as I am a soldier.

Iago Some wine, ho !   70
[*Sings*]   And let me the canakin clink, clink :
           And let me the canakin clink :
           A soldier's a man ,
           A life's but a span ;
           Why, then, let a soldier drink.
Some wine, boys !

Cas 'Fore God, an excellent song.

Iago. I learned it in England, where, in-
deed, they are most potent in potting : your
Dane, your German, and your swag-bellied
Hollander—Drink, ho !—are nothing to your
English   81

Cas Is your Englishman so expert in his
drinking ?

Iago Why, he drinks you, with facility,
your Dane dead drunk ; he sweats not to overthrow your Almain ; he gives your Hollander
a vomit, ere the next pottle can be filled.

Cas To the health of our general !

Mon. I am for it, lieutenant ; and I'll do
you justice   90

Iago. O sweet England !

King Stephen was a worthy peer,
   His breeches cost him but a crown ,
He held them sixpence all too dear,
   With that he call'd the tailor lown.
He was a wight of high renown,
   And thou art but of low degree :
'Tis pride that pulls the country down ;
   Then take thine auld cloak about thee.
Some wine, ho !   100

Cas Why, this is a more exquisite song
than the other.

Iago Will you hear't again ?

Cas No , for I hold him to be unworthy of
his place that does those things   Well, God's
above all ; and there be souls must be saved,
and there be souls must not be saved

Iago It's true, good lieutenant

Cas For mine own part,—no offence to the
general, nor any man of quality,—I hope to be
saved   111

Iago And so do I too, lieutenant.

Cas. Ay, but, by your leave, not before me;
the lieutenant is to be saved before the ancient.
Let's have no more of this, let's to our affairs—
Forgive us our sins '—Gentlemen, let's look to
our business   Do not think, gentlemen, I am
drunk   this is my ancient, this is my right
hand, and this is my left . I am not drunk
now , I can stand well enough, and speak well
enough.   120

All. Excellent well.

Cas Why, very well then ; you must not
think then that I am drunk   [*Exit*

Mon To the platform, masters , come, let's
set the watch.

Iago You see this fellow that is gone be-
fore ,
He is a soldier fit to stand by Cæsar
And give direction   and do but see his vice ;
'Tis to his virtue a just equinox,
The one as long as the other   'tis pity of him
I fear the trust Othello puts him in,   131
On some odd time of his infirmity,
Will shake this island

Mon.   But is he often thus ?

Iago 'Tis evermore the prologue to his
           sleep :
He'll watch the horologe a double set,
If drink rock not his cradle.

Mon   It were well
The general were put in mind of it
Perhaps he sees it not , or his good nature
Prizes the virtue that appears in Cassio,   139
And looks not on his evils . is not this true ?

Enter RODERIGO.

Iago. [*Aside to him*] How now, Roderigo !
I pray you, after the lieutenant , go
                              [*Exit Roderigo.*

Mon And 'tis great pity that the noble
           Moor
Should hazard such a place as his own second
With one of an ingraft infirmity :
It were an honest action to say
So to the Moor

Iago.   Not I, for this fair island :

I do love Cassio well ; and would do much
To cure him of this evil—But, hark ! what
noise ?

[Cry within : 'Help ! help !'

Re-enter CASSIO, *driving in* RODERIGO.

Cas You rogue ! you rascal !
Mon 　　　　What's the matter, lieutenant ?
Cas A knave teach me my duty !　　　　151
I'll beat the knave into a twiggen bottle
Rod. Beat me !
Cas 　　　　Dost thou prate, rogue ?
　　　　　　　　[Striking Roderigo.
Mon. 　　　　Nay, good lieutenant,
　　　　　　　　[Staying him.
I pray you, sir, hold your hand
Cas 　　　　Let me go, sir,
Or I'll knock you o'er the mazzard
Mon 　　　　Come, come, you're drunk
Cas Drunk !　　　　*[They fight*
Iago [*Aside to Roderigo*] Away, I say , go
out, and cry a mutiny. [*Exit Roderigo.*
Nay, good lieutenant,—alas, gentlemen ,—
Help, ho !—Lieutenant,—sir,—Montano,—sir ,
Help, masters'—Here's a goodly watch indeed!
　　　　　　　　[*Bell rings*
Who's that which rings the bell ?—Diablo, ho!
The town will rise　God's will, lieutenant,
hold !
You will be shamed for ever

Re-enter OTHELLO *and* Attendants

Oth. 　　　　What is the matter here ?
Mon 'Zounds, I bleed still , I am hurt to
the death　　　　*[Faints*
Oth. Hold, for your lives !
Iago Hold, ho ! Lieutenant,—sir,—Mon-
tano,—gentlemen,—
Have you forgot all sense of place and duty ?
Hold ! the general speaks to you, hold, hold,
for shame !
Oth. Why, how now, ho ! from whence
ariseth this ?
Are we turn'd Turks, and to ourselves do that
Which heaven hath forbid the Ottomites ? 171
For Christian shame, put by this barbarous
brawl
He that stirs next to carve for his own rage
Holds his soul light , he dies upon his motion.
Silence that dreadful bell　it frights the isle
From her propriety. What is the matter, mas-
ters ?
Honest Iago, that look'st dead with grieving,
Speak, who began this ? on thy love, I charge
thee
Iago I do not know　friends all but now,
even now,　　　　179
In quarter, and in terms like bride and groom
Devesting them for bed , and then, but now—
As if some planet had unwitted men—
Swords out, and tilting one at other's breast,
In opposition bloody　I cannot speak
Any beginning to this peevish odds ;
And would in action glorious I had lost
Those legs that brought me to a part of it !
Oth. How comes it, Michael, you are thus
forgot ?

Cas. I pray you, pardon me ; I cannot speak.
Oth. Worthy Montano, you were wont be
civil ,　　　　190
The gravity and stillness of your youth
The world hath noted, and your name is great
In mouths of wisest censure . what's the mat-
ter,
That you unlace your reputation thus
And spend your rich opinion for the name
Of a night-brawler ? give me answer to it.
Mon Worthy Othello, I am hurt to danger:
Your officer, Iago, can inform you,—
While I spare speech, which something now
offends me,—
Of all that I do know . nor know I aught　200
By me that's said or done amiss this night .
Unless self-charity be sometimes a vice,
And to defend ourselves it be a sin
When violence assails us
Oth 　　　　Now, by heaven,
My blood begins my safer guides to rule ,
And passion, having my best judgment collied,
Assays to lead the way　if I once stir,
Or do but lift this arm, the best of you
Shall sink in my rebuke. Give me to know
How this foul rout began, who set it on , 210
And he that is approved in this offence,
Though he had twinn'd with me, both at a
birth,
Shall lose me　What ! in a town of war,
Yet wild, the people's hearts brimful of fear,
To manage private and domestic quarrel,
In night, and on the court and guard of safety!
'Tis monstrous　Iago, who began't ?
Mon If partially affined, or leagued in office,
Thou 'ost deliver more or less than truth,
Thou art no soldier
Iago 　　　　Touch me not so near : 220
I had rather have this tongue cut from my
mouth
Than it should do offence to Michael Cassio;
Yet, I persuade myself, to speak the truth
Shall nothing wrong him. Thus it is, general.
Montano and myself being in speech,
There comes a fellow crying out for help
And Cassio following him with determined
sword,
To execute upon him　Sir, this gentleman
Steps in to Cassio, and entreats his pause .
Myself the crying fellow did pursue,　230
Lest by his clamor—as it so fell out—
The town might fall in fright　he, swift of
foot,
Outran my purpose , and I return'd the rather
For that I heard the clink and fall of swords,
And Cassio high in oath ; which till to-night
I ne'er might say before. When I came back—
For this was brief—I found them close together,
At blow and thrust ; even as again they were
When you yourself did part them
More of this matter cannot I report ·　240
But men are men : the best sometimes forget:
Though Cassio did some little wrong to him,
As men in rage strike those that wish them
best.
Yet surely Cassio, I believe, received

From him that fled some strange indignity,
Which patience could not pass.

Oth.   I know, Iago,
Thy honesty and love doth mince this matter,
Making it light to Cassio. Cassio, I love thee ;
But never more be officer of mine.

Re-enter DESDEMONA, *attended.*

Look, if my gentle love be not raised up !   250
I'll make thee an example.

Des.   What's the matter ?
Oth.   All's well now, sweeting ; come away
        to bed.   [geon :
Sir, for your hurts, myself will be your sur-
Lead him off.   [*To Montano, who is led off.*
Iago, look with care about the town,
And silence those whom this vile brawl dis-
        tracted.
Come, Desdemona : 'tis the soldiers' life
To have their balmy slumbers waked with
        strife. [*Exeunt all but Iago and Cassio.*
Iago.   What, are you hurt, lieutenant ?
Cas.   Ay, past all surgery.   260
Iago.   Marry, heaven forbid !
Cas.   Reputation, reputation, reputation ! O,
I have lost my reputation ! I have lost the im-
mortal part of myself, and what remains is
bestial. My reputation, Iago, my reputation !
Iago.   As I am an honest man, I thought
you had received some bodily wound ; there
is more sense in that than in reputation.
Reputation is an idle and most false imposition : oft got without merit, and lost without
deserving : you have lost no reputation at all,
unless you repute yourself such a loser.
What, man ! there are ways to recover the
general again : you are but now cast in his
mood, a punishment more in policy than in
malice , even so as one would beat his of-
fenceless dog to affright an imperious lion :
sue to him again, and he's yours.
Cas.   I will rather sue to be despised than
to deceive so good a commander with so
slight, so drunken, and so indiscreet an officer. Drunk ? and speak parrot ? and squab-
ble ? swagger ? swear ? and discourse fustian with one's own shadow ? O thou invisi-
-ble spirit of wine, if thou hast no name to be
known by, let us call thee devil !
Iago.   What was he that you followed with
your sword ? What had he done to you ?
Cas.   I know not.
Iago.   Is't possible ?
Cas.   I remember a mass of things, but
nothing distinctly ; a quarrel, but nothing
wherefore. O God, that men should put an
enemy in their mouths to steal away their
brains ! that we should, with joy, pleasance,
revel and applause, transform ourselves into
beasts !
Iago.   Why, but you are now well enough :
how came you thus recovered ?
Cas.   It hath pleased the devil drunkenness
to give place to the devil wrath ; one unper-
fectness shows me another, to make me
frankly despise myself.   300

Iago.   Come, you are too severe a moraler :
as the time, the place, and the condition of
this country stands, I could heartily wish this
had not befallen ; but, since it is as it is,
mend it for your own good.
Cas.   I will ask him for my place again ;
he shall tell me I am a drunkard ! Had I as
many mouths as Hydra, such an answer
would stop them all. To be now a sensible
man, by and by a fool, and presently a beast!
O strange ! Every inordinate cup is unblessed
and the ingredient is a devil.
Iago.   Come, come, good wine is a good
familiar creature, if it be well used : exclaim
no more against it. And, good lieutenant, I
think you think I love you.
Cas.   I have well approved it, sir. I drunk !
Iago.   You or any man living may be drunk
at a time, man. I'll tell you what you shall
do. Our general's wife is now the general : I
may say so in this respect, for that he hath
devoted and given up himself to the contemplation, mark, and denotement of her parts
and graces : confess yourself freely to her ;
importune her help to put you in your place
again : she is of so free, so kind, so apt, so
blessed a disposition, she holds it a vice in
her goodness not to do more than she is re-
quested : this broken joint between you and
her husband entreat her to splinter ; and, my
fortunes against any lay worth naming, this
crack of your love shall grow stronger than it
was before.   331
Cas.   You advise me well.
Iago.   I protest, in the sincerity of love and
honest kindness.
Cas.   I think it freely ; and betimes in the
morning I will beseech the virtuous Desdemona to undertake for me : I am desperate of
my fortunes if they check me here.
Iago.   You are in the right. Good night,
lieutenant ; I must to the watch.   340
Cas.   Good night, honest Iago.   [*Exit.*
Iago.   And what's he then that says I play
        the villain ?
When this advice is free I give and honest,
Probal to thinking and indeed the course
To win the Moor again ? For 'tis most easy
The inclining Desdemona to subdue
In any honest suit : she's framed as fruitful
As the free elements. And then for her
To win the Moor—were't to renounce his
        baptism,
All seals and symbols of redeemed sin,   350
His soul is so enfetter'd to her love,
That she may make, unmake, do what she
        list,
Even as her appetite shall play the god
With his weak function. How am I then a
        villain
To counsel Cassio to this parallel course,
Directly to his good ? Divinity of hell !
When devils will the blackest sins put on,
They do suggest at first with heavenly shows,
As I do now : for whiles this honest fool
Plies Desdemona to repair his fortunes   360

And she for him pleads strongly to the Moor,
I'll pour this pestilence into his ear,
That she repeals him for her body's lust ;
And by how much she strives to do him good,
She shall undo her credit with the Moor
So will I turn her virtue into pitch,
And out of her own goodness make the net
That shall enmesh them all

Re-enter RODERIGO.

How now, Roderigo !
Rod I do follow here in the chase, not like
a hound that hunts, but one that fills up the
cry My money is almost spent , I have been
to-night exceedingly well cudgelled ; and I
think the issue will be, I shall have so much
experience for my pains, and so, with no
money at all and a little more wit, return
again to Venice
Iago How poor are they that have not pa-
tience !
What wound did ever heal but by degrees ?
Thou know'st we work by wit, and not by
witchcraft ;
And wit depends on dilatory time
Does't not go well ? Cassio hath beaten thee,
And thou, by that small hurt, hast cashier'd
Cassio : 381
Though other things grow fair against the
sun,
Yet fruits that blossom first will first be ripe :
Content thyself awhile. By the mass, 'tis
morning ,
Pleasure and action make the hours seem
short
Retire thee , go where thou art billeted :
Away, I say , thou shalt know more here-
after
Nay, get thee gone [*Exit Roderigo.*] Two
things are to be done
My wife must move for Cassio to her mis-
tress ,
I'll set her on , 390
Myself the while to draw the Moor apart,
And bring him jump when he may Cassio
find
Soliciting his wife ay, that's the way :
Dull not device by coldness and delay. [*Exit.*]

ACT III

SCENE I. *Before the castle.*

Enter CASSIO *and some* MUSICIANS.

Cas. Masters, play here , I will content
your pains ;
Something that's brief ; and bid ' Good morrow, general ' [*Music.*]

Enter Clown.

Clo. Why, masters, have your instruments
been in Naples, that they speak i' the nose
thus ?
First Mus. How, sir, how !

Clo. Are these, I pray you, wind-instru-
ments ?
First Mus Ay, marry, are they, sir.
Clo. O, thereby hangs a tail
First Mus. Whereby hangs a tale, sir ? 9
Clo. Marry, sir, by many a wind-instru-
ment that I know. But, masters, here's
money for you : and the general so likes
your music, that he desires you, for love's
sake, to make no more noise with it
First Mus Well, sir, we will not
Clo. If you have any music that may not
be heard, to't again but, as they say, to
hear music the general does not greatly care.
First Mus We have none such, sir
Clo. Then put up your pipes in your bag,
for I'll away . go , vanish into air ; away ! 21
[*Exeunt Musicians.*]
Cas. Dost thou hear, my honest friend ?
Clo No, I hear not your honest friend , I
hear you.
Cas. Prithee, keep up thy quillets There's
a poor piece of gold for thee : if the gentlewoman that attends the general's wife be
stirring, tell her there's one Cassio entreats
her a little favor of speech wilt thou do this"
Clo. She is stirring, sir : if she will stir
hither, I shall seem to notify unto her. 31
Cas. Do, good my friend. [*Exit Clown.*]

Enter IAGO.

In happy time, Iago.
Iago. You have not been a-bed, then ?
Cas Why, no ; the day had broke
Before we parted I have made bold, Iago,
To send in to your wife my suit to her
Is, that she will to virtuous Desdemona
Procure me some access
Iago I'll send her to you presently ;
And I'll devise a mean to draw the Moor
Out of the way, that your converse and busi-
ness
May be more free. 41
Cas I humbly thank you for't [*Exit Iago*]
I never knew
A Florentine more kind and honest.

Enter EMILIA.

Emil. Good morrow, good lieutenant : I
am sorry
For your displeasure ; but all will sure be
well.
The general and his wife are talking of it ;
And she speaks for you stoutly the Moor
replies,
That he you hurt is of great fame in Cyprus,
And great affinity, and that in wholesome
wisdom
He might not but refuse you; but he protests
he loves you 50
And needs no other suitor but his likings
To take the safest occasion by the front
To bring you in again.
Cas Yet, I beseech you,
If you think fit, or that it may be done,
Give me advantage of some brief discourse

With Desdemona alone

Emil   Pray you, come in ;
I will bestow you where you shall have time
To speak your bosom freely
Cas   I am much bound to you   [*Exeunt.*

SCENE II.   *A room in the castle*

Enter OTHELLO, IAGO, *and Gentlemen.*

Oth   These letters give, Iago, to the pilot ,
And by him do my duties to the senate ·
That done, I will be walking on the works ,
Repair there to me
Iago.   Well, my good lord, I'll do't
Oth   This fortification, gentlemen, shall we
see't ?
Gent.   We'll wait upon your lordship
                             [*Exeunt*

SCENE III.   *The garden of the castle*

Enter DESDEMONA, CASSIO, *and* EMILIA.

Des   Be thou assured, good Cassio, I will
do
All my abilities in thy behalf.
Emil.   Good madam, do . I warrant it
grieves my husband,
As if the case were his
Des   O, that's an honest fellow   Do not
doubt, Cassio,
But I will have my lord and you again
As friendly as you were.
Cas   Bounteous madam,
Whatever shall become of Michael Cassio,
He's never any thing but your true servant
Des   I know't , I thank you   You do love
my lord .   10
You have known him long , and be you well
assured
He shall in strangeness stand no further off
Than in a politic distance
Cas   Ay, but, lady,
That policy may either last so long,
Or feed upon such nice and waterish diet,
Or breed itself so out of circumstance,
That, I being absent and my place supplied,
My general will forget my love and service.
Des   Do not doubt that , before Emilia
here
I give thee warrant of thy place   assure thee,
If I do vow a friendship, I'll perform it   21
To the last article : my lord shall never rest ,
I'll watch him tame and talk him out of pa-
tience ,
His bed shall seem a school, his board a
shrift ;
I'll intermingle every thing he does
With Cassio's suit : therefore be merry, Cas-
sio ,
For thy solicitor shall rather die
Than give thy cause away.
Emil.   Madam, here comes my lord
Cas   Madam, I'll take my leave.   30
Des   Why, stay, and hear me speak
Cas   Madam, not now . I am very ill at
ease,

Unfit for mine own purposes
Des   Well, do your discretion   [*Exit Cassio.*

Enter OTHELLO *and* IAGO.

Iago.   Ha ! I like not that
Oth   What dost thou say ?
Iago   Nothing, my lord   or it—I know not
what
Oth.   Was not that Cassio parted from my
wife ?
Iago   Cassio, my lord ! No, sure, I cannot
think it,
That he would steal away so guilty-like,
Seeing you coming
Oth.   I do believe 'twas he.   40
Des   How now, my lord !
I have been talking with a suitor here,
A man that languishes in your displeasure.
Oth.   Who is't you mean ?
Des.   Why, your lieutenant, Cassio.   Good
my lord,
If I have any grace or power to move you,
His present reconciliation take ,
For if he be not one that truly loves you,
That errs in ignorance and not in cunning,
I have no judgment in an honest face :   50
I prithee, call him back
Oth   Went he hence now ?
Des   Ay, sooth , so humbled
That he hath left part of his grief with me,
To suffer with him   Good love, call him back.
Oth.   Not now, sweet Desdemona , some
other time
Des   But shall't be shortly ?
Oth.   The sooner, sweet, for you.
Des   Shall't be to-night at supper ?
Oth   No, not to-night.
Des   To-morrow dinner, then ?
Oth.   I shall not dine at home ;
I meet the captains at the citadel
Des.   Why, then, to-morrow night ; or Tues-
day morn ;   60
On Tuesday noon, or night ; on Wednesday
morn ·
I prithee, name the time, but let it not
Exceed three days : in faith, he's penitent ;
And yet his trespass, in our common reason—
Save that, they say, the wars must make ex-
amples .
Out of their best—is not almost a fault
To incur a private check. When shall he
come ?
Tell me, Othello . I wonder in my soul,
What you would ask me, that I should deny,
Or stand so mammering on. What ! Michael
     Cassio,   70
That came a-wooing with you, and so many a
time,
When I have spoke of you dispraisingly,
Hath ta'en your part , to have so much to do
To bring him in ! Trust me, I could do much,—
Oth.   Prithee, no more · let him come when
he will ;
I will deny thee nothing.
Des   Why, this is not a boon ;
'Tis as I should entreat you wear your gloves,

CASSIO AND DESDEMONA.

OTHELLO, p. 708

Or feed .on nourishing dishes, or keep you
　　warm,
Or sue to you to do a peculiar profit
To your own person : nay, when I have a suit
Wherein I mean to touch your love indeed, 87
It shall be full of poise and difficult weight
And fearful to be granted.

Oth.　　　　　　I will deny thee nothing .
Whereon, I do beseech thee, grant me this,
To leave me but a little to myself.

Des.　Shall I deny you ? no : farewell, my
　　lord.

Oth.　Farewell, my Desdemona: I'll come
　　to thee straight.

Des.　Emilia, come.　Be as your fancies
　　teach you ;
Whate'er you be, I am obedient.
　　　　　　[*Exeunt Desdemona and Emilia.*

Oth.　Excellent wretch ! Perdition catch
　　my soul,　　　　　　　　　　　96
But I do love thee ! and when I love thee not,
Chaos is come again.

Iago.　My noble lord,—

Oth.　　　　　What dost thou say, Iago ?

Iago.　Did Michael Cassio, when you woo'd
　　my lady,
Know of your love ?

Oth.　He did, from first to last: why dost
　　thou ask ?

Iago.　But for a satisfaction of my thought ;
No further harm.

Oth.　　　　Why of thy thought, Iago ?

Iago.　I did not think he had been acquaint-
　　ed with her.

Oth.　O, yes ; and went between us very oft.

Iago.　Indeed !　　　　　　　　　101

Oth.　Indeed ! ay, indeed : discern'st thou
　　aught in that ?
Is he not honest ?

Iago.　　　　Honest, my lord !

Oth.　　　　　Honest ! ay, honest.

Iago.　My lord, for aught I know.

Oth.　What dost thou think ?

Iago.　　　　　Think, my lord !

Oth.　　　　　　Think my lord !
By heaven, he echoes me,
As if there were some monster in his thought
Too hideous to be shown.　Thou dost mean
　　something :
I heard thee say even now, thou likedst not
　　that,
When Cassio left my wife : what didst not
　　like ?　　　　　　　　　　　　110
And when I told thee he was of my counsel
In my whole course of wooing, thou criedst
　　' Indeed !'　　　　　　[gether,
And didst contract and purse thy brow to-
As if thou then hadst shut up in thy brain
Some horrible conceit : if thou dost love me,
Show me thy thought.

Iago.　My lord, you know I love you.

Oth.　　　　　I think thou dost ;
And, for I know thou 'rt full of love and hon-
　　esty,
And weigh'st thy words before thou givest
　　them breath,

Therefore these stops of thine fright me the
　　more :　　　　　　　　　　　120
For such things in a false disloyal knave
Are tricks of custom, but in a man that's just
They are close delations, working from the
　　heart
That passion cannot rule.

Iago.　　　　　　For Michael Cassio,
I dare be sworn I think that he is honest.

Oth.　I think so too.

Iago.　　　Men should be what they seem ;
Or those that be not, would they might seem
　　none !

Oth.　Certain, men should be what they
　　seem.

Iago.　Why, then, I think Cassio's an honest
　　man.

Oth.　Nay, yet there's more in this :　130
I prithee, speak to me as to thy thinkings,
As thou dost ruminate, and give thy worst of
　　thoughts
The worst of words.

Iago.　　　　Good my lord, pardon me :
Though I am bound to every act of duty,
I am not bound to that all slaves are free to.
Utter my thoughts ? Why, say they are vile
　　and false ;
As where's that palace whereinto foul things
Sometimes intrude not ? who has a breast so
　　pure,
But some uncleanly apprehensions
Keep leets and law-days and in session sit 140
With meditations lawful ?

Oth.　Thou dost conspire against thy friend,
　　Iago,　　　　　　　　[his ear
If thou but think'st him wrong'd and makest
A stranger to thy thoughts.

Iago.　　　　　I do beseech you—
Though I perchance am vicious in my guess,
As, I confess, it is my nature's plague
To spy into abuses, and oft my jealousy
Shapes faults that are not—that your wisdom
　　yet,
From one that so imperfectly conceits,
Would take no notice, nor build yourself a
　　trouble　　　　　　　　　　150
Out of his scattering and unsure observance.
It were not for your quiet nor your good,
Nor for my manhood, honesty, or wisdom,
To let you know my thoughts.

Oth.　　　　What dost thou mean ?

Iago.　Good name in man and woman, dear
　　my lord,
Is the immediate jewel of their souls :
Who steals my purse steals trash ; 'tis some-
　　thing, nothing ;
'Twas mine, 'tis his, and has been slave to
　　thousands ;
But that filches from me my good name
Robs me of that which not enriches him　160
And makes me poor indeed.

Oth.　By heaven, I'll know thy thoughts.

Iago.　You cannot, if my heart were in your
　　hand ;
Nor shall not, whilst 'tis in my custody.

Oth.　Ha !

Iago   O, beware, my lord, of jealousy ;
It is the green-eyed monster which doth mock
The meat it feeds on ; that cuckold lives in bliss
Who, certain of his fate, loves not his wronger,
But, O, what damned minutes tells he o'er
Who dotes, yet doubts, suspects, yet strongly
  loves !   170
Oth.   O misery !
Iago   Poor and content is rich and rich
  enough,
But riches fineless is as poor as winter
To him that ever fears he shall be poor.
Good heaven, the souls of all my tribe defend
From jealousy !
Oth.   Why, why is this ?
Think'st thou I'ld make a life of jealousy,
To follow still the changes of the moon
With fresh suspicions ? No, to be once in
  doubt
Is once to be resolved : exchange me for a goat,
When I shall turn the business of my soul 181
To such exsufflicate and blown surmises,
Matching thy inference   'Tis not to make me
  jealous   [pany,
To say my wife is fair, feeds well, loves com-
Is free of speech, sings, plays and dances well ,
Where virtue is, these are more virtuous :
Nor from mine own weak merits will I draw
The smallest fear or doubt of her revolt ,
For she had eyes, and chose me   No, Iago ;
I'll see before I doubt , when I doubt, prove ,
And on the proof, there is no more but this,—
Away at once with love or jealousy !
Iago   I am glad of it , for now I shall have
  reason
To show the love and duty that I bear you
With franker spirit therefore, as I am bound,
Receive it from me   I speak not yet of proof.
Look to your wife , observe her well with
  Cassio ;
Wear your eye thus, not jealous nor secure
I would not have your free and noble nature,
Out of self-bounty, be abused , look to't . 200
I know our country disposition well ,
In Venice they do let heaven see the pranks
They dare not show their husbands , their best
  conscience
Is not to leave 't undone, but keep't unknown
  Oth   Dost thou say so ?
Iago   She did deceive her father, marrying
  you ;
And when she seem'd to shake and fear your
  looks,
She loved them most
  Oth.   And so she did.
  Iago   Why, go to then ;
She that, so young, could give out such a
  seeming,
To seal her father's eyes up close as oak—210
He thought 'twas witchcraft—but I am much
  to blame ,
I humbly do beseech you of your pardon
For too much loving you.
  Oth.   I am bound to thee for ever.
  Iago.   I see this hath a little dash'd your
  spirits.

Oth.   Not a jot, not a jot.
Iago.   I' faith, I fear it has.
I hope you will consider what is spoke
Comes from my love. But I do see you're
  moved .
I am to pray you not to strain my speech
To grosser issues nor to larger reach
Than to suspicion.   220
  Oth.   I will not
  Iago.   Should you do so, my lord,
My speech should fall into such vile success
As my thoughts aim not at Cassio's my worthy
  friend—
My lord, I see you're moved.
  Oth.   No, not much moved :
I do not think but Desdemona's honest
  Iago   Long live she so ! and long live you
  to think so !
  Oth   And yet, how nature erring from it-
  self,—
  Iago   Ay, there's the point. as—to be bold
  with you—
Not to affect many proposed matches   229
Of her own clime, complexion, and degree,
Whereto we see in all things nature tends—
Foh ! one may smell in such a will most rank,
Foul disproportion, thoughts unnatural.
But pardon me , I do not in position
Distinctly speak of her , though I may fear
Her will, recoiling to her better judgment,
May fall to match you with her country forms
And happily repent
  Oth.   Farewell, farewell ·
If more thou dost perceive, let me know more;
Set on thy wife to observe   leave me, Iago.
  Iago.   [Going] My lord, I take my leave.
  Oth   Why did I marry ? This honest crea-
  ture doubtless
Sees and knows more, much more, than he
  unfolds
  Iago [Returning] My lord, I would I might
  entreat your honor
To scan this thing no further, leave it to time:
Though it be fit that Cassio have his place,
For sure, he fills it up with great ability,
Yet, if you please to hold him off awhile,
You shall by that perceive him and his means:
Note, if your lady strain his entertainment
With any strong or vehement importunity, 251
Much will be seen in that.   In the mean time,
Let me be thought too busy in my fears—
As worthy cause I have to fear I am—
And hold her free, I do beseech your honor.
  Oth.   Fear not my government.
  Iago.   I once more take my leave.   [Exit
  Oth.   This fellow's of exceeding honesty,
And knows all qualities, with a learned spirit,
Of human dealings. If I do prove her hag-
  gard,   260
Though that her jesses were my dear heart-
  strings,
I'ld whistle her off and let her down the wind
To prey at fortune. Haply, for I am black
And have not those soft parts of conversation
That chamberers have, or for I am declined
Into the vale of years,—yet that's not much—

She's goue   I am abused ; and my relief
Must be to loathe her.   O curse of marriage,
That we can call these delicate creatures ours,
And not their appetites ! I had rather be a
   toad,   270
And live upon the vapor of a dungeon,
Than keep a corner in the thing I love
For others' uses.   Yet, 'tis the plague of great
   ones ;
Prerogatived are they less than the base ;
'Tis destiny unshunnable, like death ·
Even then this forked plague is fated to us
When we do quicken.   Desdemona comes :

   Re-enter DESDEMONA *and* EMILIA.

If she be false, O, then heaven mocks itself !
I'll not believe 't.
  Des.   How now, my dear Othello !
Your dinner, and the generous islanders   280
By you invited, do attend your presence.
  Oth. I am to blame
  Des.   Why do you speak so faintly?
Are you not well ?
  Oth. I have a pain upon my forehead here.
  Des. 'Faith, that's with watching , 'twill
   away again :
Let me but bind it hard, within this hour
It will be well
  Oth.   Your napkin is too little :
   [*He puts the handkerchief from him ; and
                  it drops.*
Let it alone   Come, I'll go in with you
  Des. I am very sorry that you are not well
   [*Exeunt Othello and Desdemona.*
  Emil. I am glad I have found this napkin:
This was her first remembrance from the Moor:
My wayward husband hath a hundred times
Woo'd me to steal it , but she so loves the
   token,
For he conjured her she should ever keep it,
That she reserves it evermore about her
To kiss and talk to   I'll have the work ta'en
   out,
And give 't Iago : what he will do with it
Heaven knows, not I ,
I nothing but to please his fantasy.

   Re-enter IAGO

  Iago How now ' what do you here alone ?
  Emil. Do not you chide ; I have a thing for
   you   301
  Iago A thing for me ? it is a common
   thing—
  Emil. Ha !
  Iago To have a foolish wife.
  Emil O, is that all ? What will you give
   me now
For the same handkerchief ?
  Iago.   What handkerchief ?
  Emil What handkerchief ?
Why, that the Moor first gave to Desdemona,
That which so often you did bid me steal.
  Iago Hast stol'n it from her ?   310
  Emil. No, 'faith , she let it drop by negli-
   gence,
And, to the advantage, I, being here, took 't up.

Look, here it is.
  Iago.   A good wench ; give it me.
  Emil. What will you do with t, that you
   have been so earnest
To have me filch it ?
  Iago. [*Snatching it*] Why, what's that to
   you ?
  Emil. If it be not for some purpose of im-
   port,
Give 't me again : poor lady, she'll run mad
When she shall lack it.
  Iago. Be not acknown on 't ; I have use
   for it
Go, leave me   [*Exit Emilia.* 320
I will in Cassio's lodging lose this napkin,
And let him find it.   Trifles light as air
Are to the jealous confirmations strong
As proofs of holy writ , this may do something.
The Moor already changes with my poison :
Dangerous conceits are, in their natures, poi-
   sons,
Which at the first are scarce found to distaste,
But with a little act upon the blood,
Burn like the mines of sulphur.   I did say so:
Look, where he comes '

   Re-enter OTHELLO.

          Not poppy, nor mandragora, 330
Nor all the drowsy syrups of the world,
Shall ever medicine thee to that sweet sleep
Which thou owedst yesterday.
  Oth.   Ha ' ha ' false to me ?
  Iago. Why, how now, general! no more of
   that
  Oth. Avaunt ' be gone ' thou hast set me
   on the rack
I swear 'tis better to be much abused
Than but to know 't a little
  Iago   How now, my lord !
  Oth What sense had I of her stol'n hours
   of lust ?
I saw 't not, thought it not, it harm'd not me.
I slept the next night well, was free and merry,
I found not Cassio's kisses on her lips.   341
He that is robb'd, not wanting what is stol'n,
Let him not know 't, and he's not robb'd at all.
  Iago I am sorry to hear this
  Oth I had been happy, if the general camp,
Pioners and all, had tasted her sweet body,
So I had nothing known.   O, now, for ever
Farewell the tranquil mind ' farewell content!
Farewell the plumed troop, and the big wars,
That make ambition virtue ' O, farewell ' 350
Farewell the neighing steed, and the shrill
   trump,
The spirit-stirring drum, the ear-piercing fife,
The royal banner, and all quality,
Pride, pomp and circumstance of glorious war!
And O you mortal engines, whose rude throats
The immortal Jove's dead clamors counterfeit,
Farewell ! Othello's occupation 's gone !
  Iago Is 't possible, my lord ?
  Oth. Villain, be sure thou prove my love a
   whore,
Be sure of it ; give me the ocular proof : 360
Or by the worth of man's eternal soul,

Thou hadst been better have been born a dog
Than answer my waked wrath !
 Iago.   Is't come to this ?
 Oth. Make me to see't ; or, at the least, so
  prove it,
That the probation bear no hinge nor loop
To hang a doubt on ; or woe upon thy life !
 Iago. My noble lord,—
 Oth. If thou dost slander her and torture
 me,
Never pray more ; abandon all remorse ;
On horror's head horrors accumulate ; 370
Do deeds to make heaven weep, all earth
 amazed ;
For nothing canst thou to damnation add
Greater than that.
 Iago.   O grace ! O heaven forgive me!
Are you a man ? have you a soul or sense ?
God be wi' you ; take mine office. O wretched
 fool,
That livest to make thine honesty a vice !
O monstrous world ! Take note, take note, O
 world,
To be direct and honest is not safe.
I thank you for this profit ; and from hence
I'll love no friend, sith love breeds such offence.
 Oth. Nay, stay : thou shouldst be honest.
 Iago. I should be wise, for honesty's a fool
And loses that it works for.
 Oth.   By the world,
I think my wife be honest and think she is not;
I think that thou art just and think thou art
 not.
I'll have some proof. Her name, that was as
 fresh
As Dian's visage, is now begrimed and black
As mine own face. If there be cords, or knives,
Poison, or fire, or suffocating streams,
I'll not endure it. Would I were satisfied ! 390
 Iago. I see, sir, you are eaten up with pas-
 sion :
I do repent me that I put it to you.
You would be satisfied ?
 Oth.   Would ! nay, I will.
 Iago. And may : but, how ? how satisfied,
 my lord ?
Would you, the supervisor, grossly gape on—
Behold her topp'd ?
 Oth.   Death and damnation ! O !
 Iago. It were a tedious difficulty, I think,
To bring them to that prospect : damn them
 then,
If ever mortal eyes do see them bolster
More than their own ! What then ? how then?
What shall I say ? Where's satisfaction ? 401
It is impossible you should see this,
Were they as prime as goats, as hot as mon-
 keys,
As salt as wolves in pride, and fools as gross
As ignorance made drunk. But yet, I say,
If imputation and strong circumstances,
Which lead directly to the door of truth,
Will give you satisfaction, you may have 't.
 Oth. Give me a living reason she's disloyal.
 Iago. I do not like the office :   410
But, sith I am enter'd in this cause so far,

Prick'd to 't by foolish honesty and love,
I will go on. I lay with Cassio lately ;
And, being troubled with a raging tooth,
I could not sleep.
There are a kind of men so loose of soul,
That in their sleeps will mutter their affairs :
One of this kind is Cassio :
In sleep I heard him say ' Sweet Desdemona,
Let us be wary, let us hide our loves ; ' 420
And then, sir, would he gripe and wring my
 hand,
Cry ' O sweet creature ! ' and then kiss me
 hard,
As if he pluck'd up kisses by the roots
That grew upon my lips : then laid his leg
Over my thigh, and sigh'd, and kiss'd ; and
 then
Cried ' Cursed fate that gave thee to the
 Moor ! '
 Oth. O monstrous ! monstrous !
 Iago.   Nay, this was but his dream.
 Oth. But this denoted a foregone con-
 clusion :
'Tis a shrewd doubt, though it be but a dream.
 Iago. And this may help to thicken other
 proofs   430
That do demonstrate thinly.
 Oth.   I'll tear her all to pieces.
 Iago. Nay, but be wise : yet we see noth-
 ing done ;
She may be honest yet. Tell me but this,
Have you not sometimes seen a handkerchief
Spotted with strawberries in your wife's hand?
 Oth. I gave her such a one ; 'twas my first
 gift.
 Iago. I know not that ; but such a hand-
 kerchief—
I am sure it was your wife's—did I to-day
See Cassio wipe his beard with.
 Oth.   If it be that,—
 Iago. If it be that, or any that was hers, 440
It speaks against her with the other proofs.
 Oth. O, that the slave had forty thousand
 lives !
One is too poor, too weak for my revenge.
Now do I see 'tis true. Look here, Iago ;
All my fond love thus do I blow to heaven.
'Tis gone.
Arise, black vengeance, from thy hollow cell !
Yield up, O love, thy crown and hearted throne
To tyrannous hate ! Swell, bosom, with thy
 fraught,
For 'tis of aspics' tongues !
 Iago.   Yet be content. 450
 Oth. O, blood, blood, blood !
 Iago. Patience, I say ; your mind perhaps
 may change.
 Oth. Never, Iago. Like to the Pontic sea,
Whose icy current and compulsive course
Ne'er feels retiring ebb, but keeps due on
To the Propontic and the Hellespont,
Even so my bloody thoughts, with violent
 pace,
Shall ne'er look back, ne'er ebb to humble
 love,
Till that a capable and wide revenge.

Swallow them up. Now, by yond marble
  heaven,   460
[*Kneels*] In the due reverence of a sacred vow
I here engage my words
  Iago   Do not rise yet
[*Kneels*] Witness, you ever-burning lights
  above,
You elements that clip us round about,
Witness that here Iago doth give up
The execution of his wit, hands, heart,
To wrong'd Othello's service ' Let him com-
  mand,
And to obey shall be in me remorse,
What bloody business ever.   [*They rise.*
  Oth.   I greet thy love,
Not with vain thanks, but with acceptance
  bounteous,   470
And will upon the instant put thee to't
Within these three days let me hear thee say
That Cassio's not alive
  Iago   My friend is dead , 'tis done at your
    request :
But let her live
  Oth.   Damn her, lewd minx ' O, damn her !
Come, go with me apart , I will withdraw,
To furnish me with some swift means of death
For the fair devil   Now art thou my lieuten-
  ant
  Iago.   I am your own for ever.   [*Exeunt*

Scene IV. *Before the castle*

Enter Desdemona, Emilia, *and* Clown

  Des.   Do you know, sirrah, where Lieuten-
ant Cassio lies ?
  Clo   I dare not say he lies any where.
  Des   Why, man ?
  Clo   He's a soldier, and for one to say a
soldier lies, is stabbing.
  Des.   Go to ' where lodges he ?
  Clo   To tell you where he lodges, is to tell
you where I lie.
  Des   Can any thing be made of this ?   10
  Clo.   I know not where he lodges and for
me to devise a lodging and say he lies here or
he lies there, were to lie in mine own throat
  Des   Can you inquire him out, and be edi-
fied by report ?
  Clo   I will catechize the world for him ;
that is, make questions, and by them answer
  Des   Seek him, bid him come hither . tell
him I have moved my lord on his behalf, and
hope all will be well.   20
  Clo   To do this is within the compass of
man's wit · and therefore I will attempt the
doing it   [*Exit.*
  Des   Where should I lose that handker-
chief, Emilia ?
  Emil   I know not, madam
  Des   Believe me, I had rather have lost my
    purse
Full of crusadoes · and, but my noble Moor
Is true of mind and made of no such base-
  ness
As jealous creatures are, it were enough
To put him to ill thinking.

  Emil   Is he not jealous ?
  Des.   Who, he ? I think the sun where he
    was born   30
Drew all such humors from him
  Emil   Look, where he comes.
  Des   I will not leave him now till Cassio
Be call'd to him.

Enter Othello.

            How is't with you, my lord ?
  Oth.   Well, my good lady [*Aside*] O, hard-
    ness to dissemble '—
How do you, Desdemona ?
  Des   Well, my good lord
  Oth.   Give me your hand this hand is
    moist, my lady.
  Des   It yet hath felt no age nor known no
    sorrow
  Oth   This argues fruitfulness and liberal
    heart   [quires
Hot, hot, and moist this hand of yours re-
A sequester from liberty, fasting and prayer,
Much castigation, exercise devout ,   41
For here's a young and sweating devil here,
That commonly rebels 'tis a good hand,
A frank one,
  Des   You may indeed say so ,
For twas that hand that gave away my heart.
  Oth   A liberal hand the hearts of old gave
    hands
But our new heraldry is hands not hearts
  Des   I cannot speak of this Come now,
    your promise
  Oth.   What promise chuck ?
  Des   I have sent to bid Cassio come speak
    with you   50
  Oth.   I have a salt and sorry rheum offends
    me .
Lend me thy handkerchief
  Des   Here, my lord.
  Oth.   That which I gave you
  Des.   I have it not about me.
  Oth.   Not ?
  Des   No, indeed, my lord
  Oth.   That is a fault
That handkerchief
Did an Egyptian to my mother give ·
She was a charmer, and could almost read
The thoughts of people she told her, while
    she kept it,
'Twould make her amiable and subdue my
    father
Entirely to her love, but if she lost it   60
Or made a gift of it, my father's eye
Should hold her loathed and his spirits should
    hunt
After new fancies · she, dying, gave it me ;
And bid me, when my fate would have me
    wive,
To give it her I did so · and take heed on't ;
Make it a darling like your precious eye ,
To lose 't or give 't away were such perdition
As nothing else could match
  Des.   Is 't possible ?
  Oth.   'Tis true : there's magic in the web of
    it ;

A sibyl, that had number'd in the world   70
The sun to course two hundred compasses,
In her prophetic fury sew'd the work ;
The worms were hallow'd that did breed the
        silk ,
And it was dyed in mummy which the skilful
Conserved of maidens' hearts
    Des   Indeed ! is't true ?
    Oth. Most veritable , therefore look to 't
        well
    Des. Then would to God that I had never
        seen 't !
    Oth. Ha ! wherefore ?
    Des Why do you speak so startingly and
        rash ?
    Oth Is 't lost ? is 't gone ? speak, is it out
        o' the way ?   80
    Des. Heaven bless us !
    Oth Say you ?
    Des It is not lost ; but what an if it were ?
    Oth How !
    Des. I say, it is not lost
    Oth.   Fetch 't, let me see 't
    Des Why, so I can, sir, but I will not now
This is a trick to put me from my suit .
Pray you, let Cassio be received again
    Oth Fetch me the handkerchief . my mind
        misgives
    Des Come, come ;   90
You'll never meet a more sufficient man
    Oth The handkerchief !
    Des.   I pray, talk me of Cassio
    Oth The handkerchief !
    Des.   A man that all his time
Hath founded his good fortunes on your love,
Shared dangers with you,—
    Oth The handkerchief !
    Des In sooth, you are to blame
    Oth Away !   [*Exit*
    Emil. Is not this man jealous ?
    Des I ne'er saw this before   100
Sure, there's some wonder in this handker-
        chief
I am most unhappy in the loss of it
    Emil 'Tis not a year or two shows us a
        man ·
They are all but stomachs, and we all but
        food ,
To eat us hungerly, and when they are full,
They belch us Look you, Cassio and my
        husband !

Enter CASSIO and IAGO

    Iago There is no other way ; 'tis she must
        do 't
And, lo, the happiness! go, and importune her.
    Des. How now, good Cassio! what 's the
        news with you ?
    Cas Madam, my former suit : I do beseech
        you   110
That by your virtuous means I may again
Exist, and be a member of his love
Whom I with all the office of my heart
Entirely honor · I would not be delay'd.
If my offence be of such mortal kind
That nor my service past, nor present sorrows,

Nor purposed merit in futurity,
Can ransom me into his love again,
But to know so must be my benefit ;
So shall I clothe me in a forced content,   120
And shut myself up in some other course,
To fortune's alms
    Des   Alas, thrice-gentle Cassio !
My advocation is not now in tune ;
My lord is not my lord , nor should I know
        him,
Were he in favor as in humor alter'd
So help me every spirit sanctified,
As I have spoken for you all my best
And stood within the blank of his displeasure
For my free speech ! you must awhile be
        patient ·
What I can do I will ; and more I will   130
Than for myself I dare let that suffice you.
    Iago Is my lord angry ?
    Emil.   He went hence but now,
And certainly in strange unquietness.
    Iago Can he be angry ? I have seen the
        cannon,
When it hath blown his ranks into the air,
And, like the devil, from his very arm
Puff'd his own brother —and can he be angry?
Something of moment then I will go meet
        him
There's matter in 't indeed, if he be angry.
    Des. I prithee, do so.   [*Exit Iago*
                Something, sure, of state,   140
Either from Venice, or some unhatch'd prac-
        tice
Made demonstrable here in Cyprus to him,
Hath puddled his clear spirit . and in such
        cases
Men's natures wrangle with inferior things,
Though great ones are their object 'Tis even
        so ,
For let our finger ache, and it indues
Our other healthful members even to that
        sense
Of pain . nay, we must think men are not gods,
Nor of them look for such observances
As fit the bridal. Beshrew me much, Emilia,
I was, unhandsome warrior as I am,   151
Arraigning his unkindness with my soul ;
But now I find I had suborn'd the witness,
And he's indicted falsely.
    Emil. Pray heaven it be state-matters, as
        you think,
And no conception nor no jealous toy
Concerning you
    Des. Alas the day ! I never gave him cause.
    Emil But jealous souls will not be answer'd
        so ,
They are not ever jealous for the cause,   160
But jealous for they are jealous . 'tis a mon-
        ster
Begot upon itself, born on itself.
    Des. Heaven keep that monster from
        Othello's mind !
    Emil Lady, amen
    Des. I will go seek him. Cassio, walk here-
        about ·
If I do find him fit, I'll move your suit

And seek to effect it to my uttermost
　Cas　I humbly thank your ladyship
　　　　　[*Exeunt Desdemona and Emilia.*

　　　　　Enter BIANCA

　Bian.　Save you, friend Cassio !
　Cas.　　　　What make you from home ?
How is it with you, my most fair Bianca ? 170
I' faith, sweet love, I was coming to your
　house
　Bian　And I was going to your lodging,
　　Cassio
What, keep a week away ? seven days and
　nights ?　　　　　　　　[hours,
Eight score eight hours ? and lovers' absent
More tedious than the dial eight score times ?
O weary reckoning !
　Cas　　　　　Pardon me, Bianca :
I have this while with leaden thoughts been
　press'd
But I shall, in a more continuate time,
Strike off this score of absence　Sweet Bianca,
　　[*Giving her Desdemona's handkerchief*
Take me this work out
　Bian.　O Cassio, whence came this ? 180
This is some token from a newer friend .
To the felt absence now I feel a cause ·
Is 't come to this ?　Well, well.
　Cas　　　　　Go to, woman !
Throw your vile guesses in the devil's teeth,
From whence you have them　You are jealous
　now
That this is from some mistress, some remem-
　brance .
No, in good troth, Bianca
　Bian.　　　Why, whose is it ?
　Cas.　I know not, sweet . I found it in my
　　chamber.
I like the work well · ere it be demanded—
As like enough it will—I'ld have it copied　190
Take it, and do 't , and leave me for this time
　Bian.　Leave you ! wherefore ?
　Cas.　I do attend here on the general ,
And think it no addition, nor my wish,
To have him see me woman'd
　Bian.　　　Why, I pray you ?
　Cas　Not that I love you not.
　Bian.　　　　But that you do not love me
I pray you, bring me on the way a little,
And say if I shall see you soon at night
　Cas.　'Tis but a little way that I can bring
　　you ;
For I attend here · but I'll see you soon　200
　Bian.　'Tis very good ; I must be circum-
　　stanced.　　　　　　　[*Exeunt.*

　　　　　ACT IV.

　SCENE I.　*Cyprus.　Before the castle.*

　　　Enter OTHELLO *and* IAGO.

　Iago　Will you think so ?
　Oth.　　　　Think so, Iago !
　Iago.　　　　　　　What,
To kiss in private ?
　Oth.　　　　An unauthorized kiss.

　Iago.　Or to be naked with her friend in bed
An hour or more, not meaning any harm ?
　Oth　Naked in bed, Iago, and not mean
　　harm !
It is hypocrisy against the devil :
They that mean virtuously, and yet do so,
The devil their virtue tempts, and they tempt
　heaven
　Iago　So they do nothing, 'tis a venial slip
But if I give my wife a handkerchief,—　10
　Oth　What then ?
　Iago　Why, then, 'tis hers, my lord , and,
　　being hers,
She may, I think, bestow't on any man
　Oth　She is protectress of her honor too ·
May she give that ?
　Iago　Her honor is an essence that's not
　　seen ,
They have it very oft that have it not
But, for the handkerchief,—
　Oth　By heaven, I would most gladly have
　　forgot it
Thou said'st—O, it comes o'er my memory, 20
As doth the raven o'er the infected house,
Boding to all—he had my handkerchief
　Iago　Ay, what of that ?
　Oth.　　　　That's not so good now
　Iago.　　　　　　　What,
If I had said I had seen him do you wrong ?
Or heard him say,—as knaves be such abroad,
Who having, by their own importunate suit,
Or voluntary dotage of some mistress,
Convinced or supplied them, cannot choose
But they must blab—
　Oth　　　　Hath he said any thing ?
　Iago　He hath, my lord , but be you well
　　assured,　　　　　　　30
No more than he'll unswear
　Oth　　　　What hath he said ?
　Iago　'Faith, that he did—I know not what
　　he did
　Oth　What ? what ?
　Iago　Lie—
　Oth　　　With her ; what you will.
　Iago　With her, on her ; what you will.
　Oth　Lie with her ! lie on her ! We say he
on her, when they belie her　Lie with her !
that's fulsome.—Handkerchief—confessions—
handkerchief !—To confess, and be hanged for
his labor ,—first, to be hanged, and then to
confess—I tremble at it　Nature would not
invest herself in such shadowing passion with-
out some instruction　It is not words that
shake me thus　Pish ! Noses, ears, and lips.
—Is't possible ?—Confess—handkerchief !—O
devil !　　　　　[*Falls in a trance.*
　Iago　Work on,
My medicine, work !　Thus credulous fools
　are caught ,
And many worthy and chaste dames even thus,
All guiltless, meet reproach.　What, ho ! my
　lord !
My lord, I say ! Othello !

　　　　　Enter CASSIO.

　　　　　How now, Cassio !

Cas. What's the matter? 50
Iago My lord is fall'n into an epilepsy .
This is his second fit ; he had one yesterday.
Cas. Rub him about the temples.
Iago No, forbear ;
The lethargy must have his quiet course .
If not, he foams at mouth and by and by
Breaks out to savage madness Look, he stirs ·
Do you withdraw yourself a little while,
He will recover straight when he is gone,
I would on great occasion speak with you 59
[*Exit Cassio*
How is it, general? have you not hurt your
head ?
Oth Dost thou mock me ?
Iago. I mock you ! no, by heaven
Would you would bear your fortune like a man !
Oth. A horned man's a monster and a beast.
Iago. There's many a beast then in a popu-
lous city,
And many a civil monster
Oth Did he confess it ?
Iago. Good sir, be a man ;
Think every bearded fellow that's but yoked
May draw with you there's millions now alive
That nightly lie in those unproper beds
Which they dare swear peculiar your case is
better 70
O, 'tis the spite of hell, the fiend's arch-mock,
To lip a wanton in a secure couch,
And to suppose her chaste! No, let me know;
And knowing what I am, I know what she
shall be
Oth O, thou art wise , 'tis certain
Iago Stand you awhile apart ;
Confine yourself but in a patient list
Whilst you were here o'erwhelmed with your
grief—
A passion most unsuiting such a man—
Cassio came hither · I shifted him away,
And laid good 'scuse upon your ecstasy, 80
Bade him anon return and here speak with me,
The which he promised Do but encave your-
self, [scorns,
And mark the fleers, the gibes, and notable
That dwell in every region of his face ,
For I will make him tell the tale anew,
Where, how, how oft, how long ago, and when
He hath, and is again to cope your wife .
I say, but mark his gesture. Marry, patience,
Or I shall say you are all in all in spleen,
And nothing of a man
Oth Dost thou hear, Iago ? 90
I will be found most cunning in my patience ,
But--dost thou hear ?--most bloody.
Iago That's not amiss ;
But yet keep time in all. Will you withdraw?
[*Othello retires*
Now will I question Cassio of Bianca,
A housewife that by selling her desires
Buys herself bread and clothes it is a creature
That dotes on Cassio , as 'tis the strumpet's
plague
To beguile many and be beguiled by one :
He, when he hears of her, cannot refrain 99
From the excess of laughter. Here he comes:

Re-enter CASSIO.

As he shall smile, Othello shall go mad ;
And his unbookish jealousy must construe
Poor Cassio's smiles, gestures and light be-
havior,
Quite in the wrong How do you now, lieu-
tenant ?
Cas. The worser that you give me the ad-
dition
Whose want even kills me.
Iago. Ply Desdemona well, and you are
sure on't
[*Speaking lower*] Now, if this suit lay in
Bianca's power,
How quickly should you speed !
Cas. Alas, poor caitiff !
Oth Look, how he laughs already ! 110
Iago I never knew woman love man so.
Cas. Alas, poor rogue ! I think, i' faith, she
loves me.
Oth. Now he denies it faintly, and laughs
it out
Iago Do you hear, Cassio ?
Oth. Now he importunes him
To tell it o'er go to , well said, well said
Iago She gives it out that you shall marry
her
Do you intend it ?
Cas. Ha, ha, ha ! 120
Oth Do you triumph, Roman ? do you
triumph ?
Cas I marry her ! what? a customer ! Pri-
thee, bear some charity to my wit : do not
think it so unwholesome Ha, ha, ha !
Oth So, so, so, so · they laugh that win.
Iago 'Faith, the cry goes that you shall
marry her.
Cas Prithee, say true
Iago. I am a very villain else
Oth Have you scored me ? Well 130
Cas. This is the monkey's own giving out :
she is persuaded I will marry her, out of her
own love and flattery, not out of my promise.
Oth Iago beckons me , now he begins the
story.
Cas She was here even now ; she haunts
me in every place I was the other day talk-
ing on the sea-bank with certain Venetians ;
and thither comes the bauble, and, by this hand,
she falls me thus about my neck— 140
Oth. Crying 'O dear Cassio !' as it were .
his gesture imports it.
Cas. So hangs, and lolls, and weeps upon
me ; so hales, and pulls me ha, ha, ha !
Oth. Now he tells how she plucked him to
my chamber. O, I see that nose of yours, but
not that dog I shall throw it to.
Cas Well, I must leave her company.
Iago. Before me ! look, where she comes.
Cas 'Tis such another fitchew ! marry, a
perfumed one. 151

Enter BIANCA.

What do you mean by this haunting of me ?
Bian. Let the devil and his dam haunt you
What did you mean by that same handker-

chief you gave me even now ? I was a fine fool
to take it. I must take out the work ?—A
likely piece of work, that you should find it in
your chamber, and not know who left it there !
This is some minx's token, and I must take out
the work ? There ; give it your hobby-horse:
wheresoever you had it, I'll take out no work
on 'it.   161
 Cas. How now, my sweet Bianca ! how
now ! how now !   [kerchief !
 Oth. By heaven, that should be my hand-
 Bian. An you'll come to supper to-night,
you may ; an you will not, come when you are
next prepared for.   [*Exit.*
 Iago. After her, after her.
 Cas. 'Faith, I must ; she'll rail in the street
else.   171
 Iago. Will you sup there ?
 Cas. 'Faith, I intend so.
 Iago. Well, I may chance to see you ; for I
would very fain speak with you.
 Cas. Prithee, come ; will you ?
 Iago. Go to ; say no more. [*Exit Cassio.*
 Oth. [*Advancing*] How shall I murder him,
Iago ?
 Iago. Did you perceive how he laughed at
his vice ?   181
 Oth. O Iago !
 Iago. And did you see the handkerchief ?
 Oth. Was that mine ?
 Iago. Yours by this hand : and to see how
he prizes the foolish woman your wife ! she
gave it him, and he hath given it his whore.
 Oth. I would have him nine years a-killing.
A fine woman ! a fair woman ! a sweet woman !
 Iago. Nay, you must forget that.   190
 Oth. Ay, let her rot, and perish, and be
damned to-night ; for she shall not live : no,
my heart is turned to stone ; I strike it, and it
hurts my hand. O, the world hath not a
sweeter creature : she might lie by an emperor's side and command him tasks.
 Iago. Nay, that's not your way.
 Oth. Hang her ! I do but say what she is :
so delicate with her needle : an admirable
musician : O ! she will sing the savageness out
of a bear : of so high and plenteous wit and
invention :—   201
 Iago. She's the worse for all this.
 Oth. O, a thousand thousand times : and
then, of so gentle a condition !
 Iago. Ay, too gentle.
 Oth. Nay, that's certain : but yet the pity
of it, Iago ! O Iago, the pity of it, Iago !
 Iago. If you are so fond over her iniquity,
give her patent to offend ; for, if it touch not
you, it comes near nobody.   210
 Oth. I will chop her into messes : cuckold
me !
 Iago. O, 'tis foul in her.
 Oth. With mine officer !
 Iago. That's fouler.
 Oth. Get me some poison, Iago ; this night:
I'll not expostulate with her, lest her body and
beauty unprovide my mind again : this night,
Iago   219

 Iago. Do it not with poison, strangle her in
her bed, even the bed she hath contaminated.
 Oth. Good, good : the justice of it pleases :
very good.
 Iago. And for Cassio, let me be his under-
taker : you shall hear more by midnight.
 Oth. Excellent good. [*A trumpet within.*]
   What trumpet is that same ?
 Iago. Something from Venice, sure. 'Tis
   Lodovico
Come from the duke : and, see, your wife is
  with him.

Enter Lodovico, Desdemona, *and* Attend-
     ants.

 Lod. Save you, worthy general !
 Oth.   With all my heart, sir.
 Lod. The duke and senators of Venice greet
  you.   [*Gives him a letter.*
 Oth. I kiss the instrument of their pleasures.
    [*Opens the letter, and reads.*
 Des. And what's the news, good cousin
  Lodovico ?
 Iago. I am very glad to see you, signior ;
Welcome to Cyprus.
 Lod. I thank you. How does Lieutenant
  Cassio ?
 Iago. Lives, sir.
 Des. Cousin, there's fall'n between him and
  my lord
An unkind breach : but you shall make all
  well.
 Oth. Are you sure of that ?
 Des. My lord ?
 Oth. [*Reads*] 'This fail you not to do, as
you will—'   240
 Lod. He did not call ; he's busy in the
  paper.
Is there division 'twixt my lord and Cassio ?
 Des. A most unhappy one : I would do
  much
To atone them, for the love I bear to Cassio.
 Oth. Fire and brimstone !
 Des.   My lord ?
 Oth.   Are you wise ?
 Des. What, is he angry ?
 Lod.   May be the letter moved him ;
For, as I think, they do command him home,
Deputing Cassio in his government.
 Des. Trust me, I am glad on't.
 Oth.   Indeed !
 Des.   My lord ?
 Oth. I am glad to see you mad.
 Des.   Why, sweet Othello,— 250
 Oth. [*Striking her*] Devil !
 Des. I have not deserved this.
 Lod. My lord, this would not be believed
  in Venice,
Though I should swear I saw't : 'tis very
  much :
Make her amends ; she weeps.
 Oth.   O devil, devil !
If that the earth could teem with woman's tears,
Each drop she falls would prove a crocodile.
Out of my sight !
 Des. I will not stay to offend you. [*Going*

Lod. Truly, an obedient lady :
I do beseech your lordship, call her back　260
Oth. Mistress !
Des.　　　　　My lord ?
Oth.　　　　What would you with her, sir ?
Lod. Who, I, my lord ?
Oth. Ay , you did wish that I would make
　　her turn ·
Sir, she can turn, and turn, and yet go on
And turn again , and she can weep, sir, weep ,
And she's obedient, as you say, obedient,
Very obedient　Proceed you in your tears
Concerning this, sir,—O well-painted pas-
　　sion !—
I am commanded home. Get you away ,
I'll send for you anon　Sir, I obey the man-
　　date,　　　　　　　　　　　　　270
And will return to Venice　Hence, avaunt !
　　　　　　　　　　　[*Exit Desdemona*
Cassio shall have my place　And, sir, to-
　　night,
I do entreat that we may sup together
You are welcome, sir, to Cyprus—Goats and
　　monkeys !　　　　　　[*Exit*
Lod. Is this the noble Moor whom our full
　　senate
Call all in all sufficient ?　Is this the nature
Whom passion could not shake ? whose solid
　　virtue
The shot of accident, nor dart of chance,
Could neither graze nor pierce ?
Iago.　　　　　He is much changed
Lod. Are his wits safe ? is he not light of
　　brain ?　　　　　　　　　　　280
Iago. He's that he is · I may not breathe
　　my censure
What he might be　if what he might he is
　　not,
I would to heaven he were !
Lod.　　　　　What, strike his wife !
Iago. 'Faith, that was not so well , yet
　　would I knew
That stroke would prove the worst !
Lod.　　　　　Is it his use ?
Or did the letters work upon his blood,
And new-create this fault ?
Iago.　　　　　Alas, alas !
It is not honesty in me to speak
What I have seen and known　You shall ob-
　　serve him,
And his own courses will denote him so　290
That I may save my speech · do but go after,
And mark how he continues
Lod. I am sorry that I am deceived in him
　　　　　　　　　　　　　　[*Exeunt*

SCENE II　*A room in the castle.*

Enter OTHELLO *and* EMILIA.

Oth. You have seen nothing then ?
Emil Nor ever heard, nor ever did sus-
　　pect
Oth. Yes, you have seen Cassio and she
　　together
Emil But then I saw no harm. and then I
　　heard

Each syllable that breath made up between
　　them.
Oth. What, did they never whisper ?
Emil　　　　　　Never, my lord.
Oth. Nor send you out o' the way ?
Emil. Never
Oth. To fetch her fan, her gloves, her mask,
　　nor nothing ?
Emil Never, my lord.　　　　　　10
Oth. That's strange
Emil I durst, my lord, to wager she is
　　honest,
Lay down my soul at stake : if you think
　　other,
Remove your thought ; it doth abuse your
　　bosom.
If any wretch have put this in your head,
Let heaven requite it with the serpent's curse !
For, if she be not honest, chaste, and true,
There's no man happy ; the purest of their
　　wives
Is foul as slander.
Oth.　　　Bid her come hither · go
　　　　　　　　　　　[*Exit Emilia.*
She says enough , yet she's a simple bawd　20
That cannot say as much. This is a subtle
　　whore,
A closet lock and key of villanous secrets :
And yet she'll kneel and pray , I have seen
　　her do 't

Enter DESDEMONA *with* EMILIA.

Des My lord, what is your will ?
Oth.　　　Pray, chuck, come hither.
Des. What is your pleasure ?
Oth.　　　　Let me see your eyes ;
Look in my face.
Des.　　　What horrible fancy 's this ?
Oth [*To Emilia*] Some of your function,
　　mistress ;
Leave procreants alone and shut the door ;
Cough, or cry ' hem,' if any body come :
Your mystery, your mystery . nay, dispatch.
　　　　　　　　　　　[*Exit Emilia*　30
Des Upon my knees, what doth your
　　speech import ?
I understand a fury in your words.
But not the words
Oth Why, what art thou ?
Des　　　Your wife, my lord ; your true
And loyal wife
Oth.　　　Come, swear it, damn thyself ;
Lest, being like one of heaven, the devils
　　themselves
Should fear to seize thee : therefore be double
　　damn'd :
Swear thou art honest
Des.　　　Heaven doth truly know it.
Oth. Heaven truly knows that thou art false
　　as hell.
Des. To whom, my lord ? with whom ?
　　how am I false ?　　　　　　40
Oth. O Desdemona ! away ! away ! away !
Des. Alas the heavy day ! · Why do you
　　weep ?
Am I the motive of these tears, my lord ?

DESDEMONA. *"Upon my knees, what doth your speech import?"*

OTHELLO, p. 808

If haply you my father do suspect
An instrument of this your calling back,
Lay not your blame on me , if you have lost
  him,
Why, I have lost him too
    Oth   Had it pleased heaven
To try me with affliction , had they rain'd
All kinds of sores and shames on my bare
  head
Steep'd me in poverty to the very lips,   50
Given to captivity me and my utmost hopes,
I should have found in some place of my soul
A drop of patience , but, alas, to make me
†A fixed figure for the time of scorn
To point his slow unmoving finger at !
Yet could I bear that too , well, very well
But there, where I have garner'd up my heart,
Where either I must live, or bear no life ,
The fountain from the which my current runs,
Or else dries up , to be discarded thence ! 60
Or keep it as a cistern for foul toads
To knot and gender in ! Turn thy complexion
  there,
Patience, thou young and rose-lipp'd cheru-
  bin,—
Ay, there, look grim as hell !
    Des   I hope my noble lord esteems me
    honest
    Oth O, ay , as summer flies are in the
    shambles,
That quicken even with blowing O thou
  weed,
Who art so lovely fair and smell'st so sweet
That the sense aches at thee, would thou hadst
  ne'er been born !
    Des   Alas, what ignorant sin have I com-
    mitted ?   70
    Oth Was this fair paper, this most goodly
    book,   [putted !
Made to write ' whore ' upon ? What com-
Committed ! O thou public commoner !
I should make very forges of my cheeks,
That would to cinders burn up modesty,
Did I but speak thy deeds What committed!
Heaven stops the nose at it and the moon
  winks,
The bawdy wind that kisses all it meets
Is hush'd within the hollow mine of earth,
And will not hear it What committed !   80
Impudent strumpet !
    Des   By heaven, you do me wrong
    Oth Are you not a strumpet ?
    Des   No, as I am a Christian
If to preserve this vessel for my lord
From any other foul unlawful touch
Be not to be a strumpet, I am none
    Oth What, not a whore ?
    Des   No, as I shall be saved.
    Oth Is't possible ?
    Des   O, heaven forgive us !
    Oth   I cry you mercy, then .
I took you for that cunning whore of Venice
That married with Othello. [*Raising his voice*]
  You, mistress,   90
That have the office opposite to Saint Peter,
And keep the gate of hell !

            You, you, ay, you !
We have done our course ; there's money for
  your pains
I pray you, turn the key and keep our counsel.
                  [*Exit*
    Emil Alas, what does this gentleman con-
    ceive ?
How do you, madam ? how do you, my good
  lady ?
    Des   'Faith half asleep
    Emil Good madam, what's the matter
    with my lord ?
    Des   With who ?
    Emil Why, with my lord, madam.   100
    Des   Who is thy lord ?
    Emil   He that is yours, sweet lady.
    Des   I have none , do not talk to me,
    Emilia ;
I cannot weep , nor answer have I none,
But what should go by water Prithee, to-
  night
Lay on my bed my wedding sheets remem-
  ber ,
And call thy husband hither
    Emil   Here's a change indeed ! [*Exit.*
    Des 'Tis meet I should be used so, very
    meet.
How have I been behaved, that he might
  stick
The small'st opinion on my least misuse ?

    Iago What is your pleasure, madam ?
    How is't with you ?   110
    Des   I cannot tell. Those that do teach
    young babes
Do it with gentle means and easy tasks :
He might have chid me so , for, in good faith,
I am a child to chiding
    Iago   What's the matter, lady ?
    Emil Alas, Iago, my lord hath so bewhored
    her
Thrown such despite and heavy terms upon
  her,
As true hearts cannot bear
    Des   Am I that name, Iago ?
    Iago   What name, fair lady ?
    Des Such as she says my lord did say I
    was
    Emil He call'd her whore a beggar in his
    drink   120
Could not have laid such terms upon his callat.
    Iago Why did he so ?
    Des   I do not know , I am sure I am none
    such
    Iago Do not weep, do not weep. Alas the
    day !
    Emil Hath she forsook so many noble
    matches,
Her father and her country and her friends,
To be call'd whore ? would it not make one
  weep ?
    Des   It is my wretched fortune
    Iago   Beshrew him for't !

How comes this trick upon him?

Des. Nay, heaven doth know.

Emil. I will be hang'd, if some eternal villain, 130
Some busy and insinuating rogue,
Some cogging, cozening slave, to get some office,
Have not devised this slander; I'll be hang'd else. [possible

Iago Fie, there is no such man, it is impossible

Des If any such there be, heaven pardon him!

Emil A halter pardon him! and hell gnaw his bones!
Why should he call her whore? who keeps her company?
What place? what time? what form? what likelihood? [knave,
The Moor's abused by some most villanous
Some base notorious knave, some scurvy fellow 140
O heaven, that such companions thou'ldst unfold,
And put in every honest hand a whip
To lash the rascals naked through the world
Even from the east to the west!

Iago Speak within door

Emil O, fie upon them! Some such squire he was
That turn'd your wit the seamy side without,
And made you to suspect me with the Moor

Iago You are a fool, go to.

Des O good Iago,
What shall I do to win my lord again?
Good friend, go to him, for, by this light of heaven, 150
I know not how I lost him Here I kneel ·
If e'er my will did trespass 'gainst his love,
Either in discourse of thought or actual deed,
Or that mine eyes, mine ears, or any sense,
Delighted them in any other form,
Or that I do not yet, and ever did,
And ever will—though he do shake me off
To beggarly divorcement—love him dearly,
Comfort forswear me! Unkindness may do much,
And his unkindness may defeat my life, 160
But never taint my love I cannot say 'whore '
It does abhor me now I speak the word,
To do the act that might the addition earn
Not the world's mass of vanity could make me

Iago I pray you, be content, 'tis but his humor :
The business of the state does him offence,
And he does chide with you

Des. If 'twere no other,—

Iago 'Tis but so, I warrant
[*Trumpets within*
Hark, how these instruments summon to supper!
The messengers of Venice stay the meat, 170
Go in, and weep not, all things shall be well
[*Exeunt Desdemona and Emilia.*

Enter RODERIGO.

How now, Roderigo!

Rod I do not find that thou dealest justly with me.

Iago. What in the contrary?

Rod. Every day thou daffest me with some device, Iago, and rather, as it seems to me now, keepest from me all conveniency than suppliest me with the least advantage of hope. I will indeed no longer endure it, nor am I yet persuaded to put up in peace what already I have foolishly suffered

Iago Will you hear me, Roderigo?

Rod. 'Faith, I have heard too much, for your words and performances are no kin together.

Iago. You charge me most unjustly

Rod. With no ight but truth I have wasted myself out of my means The jewels you have had from me to deliver to Desdemona would half have corrupted a votarist you have told me she hath received them and returned me expectations and comforts of sudden respect and acquaintance, but I find none

Iago Well; go to; very well

Rod Very well! go to! I cannot go to, man, nor 'tis not very well nay, I think it is scurvy, and begin to find myself fobbed in it.

Iago Very well.

Rod. I tell you 'tis not very well. I will make myself known to Desdemona : if she will return me my jewels, I will give over my suit and repent my unlawful solicitation, if not, assure yourself I will seek satisfaction of you

Iago You have said now

Rod Ay, and said nothing but what I protest intendment of doing

Iago Why, now I see there's mettle in thee, and even from this instant to build on thee a better opinion than ever before. Give me thy hand, Roderigo thou hast taken against me a most just exception, but yet, I protest, I have dealt most directly in thy affair.

Rod It hath not appeared

Iago I grant indeed it hath not appeared, and your suspicion is not without wit and judgment. But Roderigo, if thou hast that in thee indeed which I have greater reason to believe now than ever, I mean purpose, courage and valor, this night show it if thou the next night following enjoy not Desdemona, take me from this world with treachery and devise engines for my life

Rod Well what is it? is it within reason and compass?

Iago Sir, there is especial commission come from Venice to depute Cassio in Othello's place

Rod Is that true? why, then Othello and Desdemona return again to Venice

Iago. O, no; he goes into Mauritania and takes away with him the fair Desdemona, unless his abode be lingered here by some accident wherein none can be so determinate as the removing of Cassio.

Rod How do you mean, removing of him?

Iago Why, by making him uncapable of Othello's place; knocking out his brains.

Rod. And that you would have me to do?

Iago Ay, if you dare do yourself a profit and a right. He sups to-night with a harlotry, and thither will I go to him he knows not yet of his honourable fortune. If you will watch his going thence, which I will fashion to fall out between twelve and one, you may take him at your pleasure I will be near to second your attempt, and he shall fall between us. Come, stand not amazed at it, but go along with me ; I will show you such a necessity in his death that you shall think yourself bound to put it on him It is now high suppertime, and the night grows to waste about it

Rod. I will hear further reason for this.

Iago. And you shall be satisfied [*Exeunt.*

SCENE III. *Another room in the castle.*

Enter OTHELLO, LODOVICO, DESDEMONA, EMILIA, *and* Attendants

Lod. I do beseech you, sir, trouble yourself no further

Oth O, pardon me . 'twill do me good to walk.

Lod. Madam, good night , I humbly thank your ladyship

Des Your honor is most welcome

Oth   Will you walk, sir ?
O,—Desdemona,—

Des. My lord ?

Oth. Get you to bed on the instant ; I will be returned forthwith dismiss your attendant there : look it be done

Des. I will, my lord   10
[*Exeunt Othello, Lodovico, and Attendants*

Emil How goes it now ? he looks gentler than he did

Des He says he will return incontinent :
He hath commanded me to go to bed,
And bade me to dismiss you

Emil   Dismiss me !

Des It was his bidding . therefore, good Emilia,
Give me my nightly wearing, and adieu .
We must not now displease him

Emil. I would you had never seen him !

Des So would not I my love doth so approve him,
That even his stubbornness, his checks, his frowns,— .   20
Prithee, unpin me,—have grace and favor in them

Emil I have laid those sheets you bade me on the bed.

Des. All's one. Good faith, how foolish are our minds !
If I do die before thee, prithee, shroud me
In one of those same sheets

Emil   Come, come, you talk.

Des. My mother had a maid call'd Barbara·
She was in love, and he she loved proved mad
And did forsake her : she had a song of ' willow ;'
An old thing 'twas, but it express'd her fortune,
And she died singing it : that song to-night

Will not go from my mind ; I have much to do,
But to go hang my head all at one side,
And sing it like poor Barbara. Prithee, dispatch

Emil. Shall I go fetch your night-gown ?

Des   No, unpin me here-
This Lodovico is a proper man

Emil A very handsome man.

Des He speaks well

Emil I know a lady in Venice would have walked barefoot to Palestine for a touch of his nether lip.   44

Des [*Singing*] The poor soul sat sighing by a sycamore tree,
Sing all a green willow
Her hand on her bosom, her head on her knee,
Sing willow, willow, willow :
The fresh streams ran by her, and murmur'd her moans ,
Sing willow, willow, willow :
Her salt tears fell from her, and soften'd the stones ,—
Lay by these —
[*Singing*] Sing willow, willow, willow ;
Prithee, hie thee , he'll come anon —   50
[*Singing*] Sing all a green willow must be my garland.
Let nobody blame him his scorn I approve,—
Nay, that's not next —Hark ! who is't that knocks ?

Emil. It's the wind

Des. [*Singing*] I call'd my love false love ;
but what said he then ?
Sing willow, willow, willow :
If I court moe women, you'll couch with moe men —   [itch ,
So, get thee gone , good night Mine eyes do
Doth that bode weeping ?

Emil   'Tis neither here nor there

Des I have heard it said so. O, these men, these men !   60
Dost thou in conscience think,—tell me, Emilia,—
That there be women do abuse their husbands
In such gross kind ?

Emil There be some such, no question

Des Wouldst thou do such a deed for all the world ?

Emil. Why, would not you ?

Des   No. by this heavenly light !

Emil Nor I neither by this heavenly light,
I might do't as well i' the dark

Des Wouldst thou do such a deed for all the world ?

Emil The world's a huge thing it is a great price
For a small vice.

Des. In troth, I think thou wouldst not 70

Emil In trot, I think I should , and undo't when I had done Marry, I would not do such a thing for a joint-ring, nor for measures of lawn, nor for gowns, petticoats, nor caps, nor any petty exhibition , but, for the whole world,—why, who would not make her husband a cuckold to make him a monarch ? I should venture purgatory for't.

Des. Beshrew me, if I would do such a
        wrong
For the whole world.   79
  Emil. Why the wrong is but a wrong i' the
world : and having the world for your labor,
'tis a wrong in your own world, and you
might quickly make it right.
  Des. I do not think there is any such wo-
man,
  Emil. Yes, a dozen ; and as many to the
vantage as would store the world they played
for.
But I do think it is their husbands' faults
If wives do fall : say that they slack their du-
ties,
And pour our treasures into foreign laps,
Or else break out in peevish jealousies,   90
Throwing restraint upon us ; or say they strike
        us,
Or scant our former having in despite ;
Why, we have galls, and though we have some
        grace,
Yet have we some revenge. Let husbands know
Their wives have sense like them : they see
        and smell
And have their palates both for sweet and sour,
As husbands have. What is it that they do
When they change us for others ? Is it sport ?
I think it is : and doth affection breed it ?
I think it doth : is't frailty that thus errs ? 100
It is so too : and have not we affections,
Desires for sport, and frailty, as men have ?
Then let them use us well : else let them know,
The ills we do, their ills instruct us so.
  Des. Good night, good night : heaven me
        such uses send,
Not to pick bad from bad, but by bad mend !
                                     [*Exeunt.*

ACT V.

SCENE I. *Cyprus. A street.*

Enter IAGO *and* RODERIGO.

Iago. Here, stand behind this bulk ; straight
        will he come :
Wear thy good rapier bare, and put it home :
Quick, quick ; fear nothing ; I'll be at thy
        elbow :
It makes us, or it mars us ; think on that,
And fix most firm thy resolution.
  Rod. Be near at hand ; I may miscarry in't.
  Iago. Here, at thy hand : be bold, and take
        thy stand.   [*Retires.*
  Rod. I have no great devotion to the deed ;
And yet he hath given me satisfying reasons :
'Tis but a man gone. Forth, my sword : he
        dies.   10
  Iago. I have rubb'd this young quat almost
        to the sense,
And he grows angry. Now, whether he kill
        Cassio,
Or Cassio him, or each do kill the other,
Every way makes my gain : live Roderigo,
He calls me to a restitution large

Of gold and jewels that I bobb'd from him,
As gifts to Desdemona ;
It must not be : if Cassio do remain,
He hath a daily beauty in his life
That makes me ugly ; and, besides, the Moor
May unfold me to him ; there stand I in much
        peril :   21
No, he must die. But so : I hear him coming.

Enter CASSIO.

Rod. I know his gait, 'tis he.—Villain, thou
        diest !   [*Makes a pass at Cassio.*
  Cas. That thrust had been mine enemy in-
        deed,
But that my coat is better than thou know'st :
I will make proof of thine.
              [*Draws, and wounds Roderigo.*
  Rod.   O, I am slain !
  [*Iago from behind wounds Cassio in th·
                                   leg, and exi*
  Cas. I am maim'd for ever. Help, ho !
        murder ! murder !   [*Falls.*

Enter OTHELLO.

Oth. The voice of Cassio : Iago keeps his
        word.
  Rod. O, villain that I am !
  Oth.   It is even so.
  Cas. O, help, ho ! light ! a surgeon !   30
  Oth. 'Tis he :—O brave Iago, honest and
        just,
That hast such noble sense of thy friend's
        wrong !
Thou teachest me. Minion, your dear lies
        dead,
And your unblest fate hies : strumpet, I come.
Forth of my heart those charms, thine eyes,
        are blotted ;
Thy bed, lust-stain'd, shall with lust's blood
        be spotted.   [*Exit.*

Enter LODOVICO *and* GRATIANO.

Cas. What, ho ! no watch ? no passage ?
        murder ! murder !
  Gra. 'Tis some mischance ; the cry is very
        direful.
  Cas. O, help !
  Lod. Hark !   40
  Rod. O wretched villain !
  Lod. Two or three groan : it is a heavy
        night :
These may be counterfeits : let's think't un-
        safe
To come in to the cry without more help.
  Rod. Nobody come ? then shall I bleed to
        death.
  Lod. Hark !

Re-enter IAGO, *with a light.*

Gra. Here's one comes in his shirt, with
        light and weapons.
  Iago. Who's there ? whose noise is this
        that cries on murder ?
  Lod. We do not know.
  Iago.   Did not you hear a cry ?
  Cas. Here, here ! for heaven's sake, help
        me !

Iago   What's the matter ? 50
Gra   This is Othello's ancient, as I take it.
Lod.   The same indeed , a very valiant fel-
 low
Iago   What are you here that cry so griev-
 ously ?
Cas.   Iago ? O, I am spoil'd, undone by
 villains !
Give me some help
Iago   O me, lieutenant ! what villains have
 done this ?
Cas.   I think that one of them is hereabout,
And cannot make away.
Iago   O treacherous villains !
What are you there ? come in, and give some
 help.   [*To Lodovico and Gratiano*
Rod.   O, help me here !   60
Cas   That's one of them.
Iago.   O murderous slave ' O villain '
                        [*Stabs Roderigo.*
Rod.   O damn'd Iago ' O inhuman dog '
Iago.   Kill men i' the dark '—Where be
 these bloody thieves ?—
How silent is this town '—Ho ' murder '
 murder !—
What may you be ? are you of good or evil ?
Lod.   As you shall prove us, praise us
Iago   Signior Lodovico ?
Lod   He, sir.
Iago.   I cry you mercy Here's Cassio hurt
 by villains
Gra   Cassio '   70
Iago.   How is't, brother '
Cas   My leg is cut in two
Iago   Marry, heaven forbid '
Light, gentlemen ; I'll bind it with my shirt.

Enter BIANCA.

Bian.   What is the matter, ho ? who is't
 that cried ?
Iago.   Who is't that cried '
Bian   O my dear Cassio ' my sweet Cassio!
O Cassio, Cassio, Cassio '
Iago   O notable strumpet ! Cassio, may
 you suspect
Who they should be that have thus mangled
 you ?
Cas.   No.   80
Gra.   I am sorry to find you thus : I have
 been to seek you
Iago.   Lend me a garter So O, for a chair,
To bear him easily hence '
Bian.   Alas, he faints ! O Cassio, Cassio,
 Cassio !
Iago.   Gentlemen all, I do suspect this trash
To be a party in this injury.
Patience awhile, good Cassio Come, come ;
Lend me a light Know we this face or no ?
Alas my friend and my dear countryman
Roderigo ! no .—yes, sure '—O heaven ! Rod-
 erigo   90
Gra.   What, of Venice ?
Iago.   Even he, sir ; did you know him ?
Gra   Know him ! ay
Iago   Signior Gratiano ? I cry you gentle
 pardon ;

These bloody accidents must excuse my man-
 ners,
That so neglected you.
Gra   I am glad to see you.
Iago   How do you, Cassio ? O, a chair, a
 chair '
Gra   Roderigo '
Iago   He, he, 'tis he [*A chair brought in.*]
 O, that's well said , the chair
Some good man bear him carefully from hence ,
I'll fetch the general's surgeon [*To Bianca*]
 For you, mistress,   100
Save you your labor He that lies slain here,
 Cassio,   [you ?
Was my dear friend what malice was between
Cas   None in the world , nor do I know
 the man
Iago   [*To Bian*] What, look you pale ? O,
 bear him out o' the air
          [*Cassio and Roderigo are borne off.*
Stay you, good gentlemen Look you pale,
 mistress ?
Do you perceive the gastness of her eye ?
Nay, if you stare, we shall hear more anon
Behold her well , I pray you, look upon her
Do you see, gentlemen ? nay, guiltiness will
 speak,
Though tongues were out of use   110

Enter EMILIA

Emil.   'Las, what's the matter ? what's the
 matter, husband ?
Iago.   Cassio hath here been set on in the
 dark
By Roderigo and fellows that are scaped :
He's almost slain, and Roderigo dead.
Emil   Alas, good gentleman ' alas, good
 Cassio !
Iago   This is the fruit of whoring Prithee,
 Emilia,
Go know of Cassio where he supp'd to-night
[*To Bianca*] What, do you shake at that ?
Bian   He supp'd at my house , but I there-
 fore shake not
Iago.   O, did he so ? I charge you, go with
 me.   120
Emil   Fie, fie upon thee, strumpet '
Bian.   I am no strumpet , but of life as
 honest
As you that thus abuse me
Emil.   As I ' foh ! fie upon thee !
Iago   Kind gentlemen, let's go see poor
 Cassio dress'd
Come, mistress, you must tell's another tale
Emilia, run you to the citadel,
And tell my lord and lady what hath happ'd.
Will you go on? I pray. [*Aside*] This is the
 night
That either makes me or fordoes me quite.
                        [*Exeunt.*

SCENE II. *A bedchamber in the castle :* DES-
DEMONA *in bed asleep , a light burning*
          Enter OTHELLO.

Oth.   It is the cause, it is the cause, my
 soul,—

Let me not name it to you, you chaste stars !—
It is the cause   Yet I'll not shed her blood ;
Nor scar that whiter skin of hers than snow,
And smooth as monumental alabaster.
Yet she must die, else she'll betray more men.
Put out the light, and then put out the light
If I quench thee, thou flaming minister,
I can again thy former light restore,   9
Should I repent me   but once put out thy light,
Thou cunning'st pattern of excelling nature,
I know not where is that Promethean heat
That can thy light relume.   When I have
      pluck'd the rose,
I cannot give it vital growth again,
It must needs wither . I'll smell it on the tree
                              [Kissing her
Ah, balmy breath, that dost almost persuade
Justice to break her sword !   One more, one
      more
Be thus when thou art dead, and I will kill
      thee,
And love thee after   One more, and this the
      last .
So sweet was ne'er so fatal   I must weep, 20
But they are cruel tears   this sorrow's heav-
      enly ,
It strikes where it doth love   She wakes
   Des.   Who's there ? Othello ?
   Oth   Ay, Desdemona
   Des   Will you come to bed, my lord ?
   Oth   Have you pray'd to-night, Desdemona?
   Des   Ay, my lord
   Oth   If you bethink yourself of any crime
Unreconciled as yet to heaven and grace,
Solicit for it straight
   Des   Alas, my lord, what do you mean by
      that ?
   Oth.   Well, do it, and be brief , I will walk
      by   30
I would not kill thy unprepared spirit ;
No; heaven forfend ' I would not kill thy soul.
   Des   Talk you of killing ?
   Oth   Ay, I do
   Des   Then heaven
Have mercy on me '
   Oth   Amen, with all my heart '
   Des   If you say so, I hope you will not kill
      me
   Oth   Hum '
   Des   And yet I fear you ; for you are fatal
      then
When your eyes roll so : why I should fear I
      know not,
Since guiltiness I know not ; but yet I feel I
      fear
   Oth   Think on thy sins
   Des   They are loves I bear to you. 40
   Oth   Ay, and for that thou diest
   Des   That death's unnatural that kills for
      loving
Alas, why gnaw you so your nether lip ?
Some bloody passion shakes your very frame·
These are portents ; but yet I hope, I hope,
They do not point on me
   Oth.   Peace, and be still !
   Des.   I will so.   What's the matter ?

   Oth.   That handkerchief which I so loved
      and gave thee
Thou gavest to Cassio.
   Des   No, by my life and soul !
Send for the man, and ask him.
   Oth   Sweet soul, take heed, 50
Take heed of perjury ; thou art on thy death-
      bed
   Des.   Ay, but not yet to die
   Oth   Yes, presently :
Therefore confess thee freely of thy sin ,
For to deny each article with oath
Cannot remove nor choke the strong concep-
      tion
That I do groan withal   Thou art to die.
   Des   Then Lord have mercy on me !
   Oth   I say, amen.
   Des   And have you mercy too ! I never did
Offend you in my life , never loved Cassio
But with such general warranty of heaven 60
As I might love , I never gave him token.
   Oth   By heaven, I saw my handkerchief
      in's hand
O perjured woman ' thou dost stone my
      heart,
And makest me call what I intend to do
A murder, which I thought a sacrifice
I saw the handkerchief
   Des   He found it then ;
I never gave it him · send for him hither ,
Let him confess a truth
   Oth   He hath confess'd.
   Des   What, my lord ?
   Oth   That he hath used thee
   Des   How ? unlawfully ?
   Oth.   Ay. 70
   Des.   He will not say so
   Oth   No, his mouth is stopp'd ;
Honest Iago hath ta'en order for't
   Des   O ' my fear interprets . what, is he
      dead ?
   Oth   Had all his hairs been lives, my great
      revenge
Had stomach for them all
   Des.   Alas ' he is betray'd and I undone
   Oth.   Out, strumpet ! weep'st thou for him
      to my face ?   [not !
   Des   O, banish me, my lord, but kill me
   Oth   Down, strumpet !
   Des.   Kill me to-morrow . let me live to-
      night !   80
   Oth.   Nay, if you strive,—
   Des.   But half an hour !
   Oth   Being done, there is no pause.
   Des   But while I say one prayer !
   Oth.   It is too late.
                              [He stifles her.
   Emil   [Within]   My lord, my lord ! what,
      ho ! my lord, my lord !
   Oth   What noise is this ?   Not dead ? not
      yet quite dead ?
I that am cruel am yet merciful ;
I would not have thee linger in thy pain :
So, so
   Emil.   [Within]   What, ho ! my lord, my
      lord !

Oth.   Who's there?

Emil. [*Within*] O, good my lord, I would
    speak a word with you!   90
Oth   Yes: 'tis Emilia. By and by. She's
    dead
'Tis like she comes to speak of Cassio's
    death.—
The noise was here Ha! no more moving?
Still as the grave Shall she come in? were t
    good'—
I think she stirs again —no What's best to
    do?
If she come in, she'll sure speak to my wife •
My wife! my wife! what wife? I have no
    wife
O, insupportable! O heavy hour!
Methinks it should be now a huge eclipse
Of sun and moon, and that the affrighted
    globe
Should yawn at alteration.
Emil   [*Within*] I do beseech you 101
That I may speak with you, O, good my lord!
Oth I had forgot thee O, come in, Emilia,
Soft, by and by Let me the curtains draw
Where art thou?   [*Unlocks the door*

    Enter EMILIA.

    What's the matter with thee now?
Emil. O, my good lord, yonder's foul mur-
    ders done!
Oth What, now?
Emil. But now, my lord.
Oth It is the very error of the moon;
She comes more nearer earth than she was
    wont,   110
And makes men mad.
Emil   Cassio, my lord, hath kill'd a young
    Venetian
Call'd Roderigo
Oth   Roderigo kill'd!
And Cassio kill'd!
Emil   No, Cassio is not kill'd
Oth Not Cassio kill'd! then murder's out
    of tune,
And sweet revenge grows harsh
Des. O, falsely, falsely murder'd!
Emil   Alas, what cry is that?
Oth That! what?
Emil Out, and alas! that was my lady's
    voice   119
Help! help, ho! help! O lady, speak again!
Sweet Desdemona! O sweet mistress, speak!
Des A guiltless death I die
Emil O, who hath done this deed?
Des Nobody, I myself Farewell:
Commend me to my kind lord. O, farewell!
     [*Dies*
Oth Why, how should she be murder'd?
Emil   Alas, who knows?
Oth You heard her say herself, it was not I.
Emil She said so I must needs report the
    truth.
Oth She's, like a liar, gone to burning hell.
'Twas I that kill'd her.
Emil   O, the more angel she, 130
And you the blacker devil!

Oth. She turn'd to folly, and she was a
    whore.
Emil. Thou dost belie her, and thou art a
    devil.
Oth She was false as water
Emil   Thou art rash as fire, to say
That she was false O, she was heavenly
    true!   [else
Oth Cassio did top her ark thy husband
O, I were damn'd beneath all depth in hell,
But that I did proceed upon just grounds
To this extremity Thy husband knew it all
Emil My husband!   140
Oth Thy husband
Emil That she was false to wedlock?
Oth Ay, with Cassio Nay, had she been
    true,
If heaven would make me such another world
Of one entire and perfect chrysolite,
I'd not have sold her for it
Emil My husband!
Oth Ay, 'twas he that told me first
An honest man he is, and hates the slime
That sticks on filthy deeds
Emil   My husband!
Oth What needs this iteration, woman? I
    say thy husband
Emil O mistress, villany hath made mocks
    with love,   150
My husband say that she was false!
Oth   He, woman;
I say thy husband dost understand the
    word?
My friend, thy husband, honest, honest Iago
Emil If he say so, may his pernicious soul
Rot half a grain a day! he lies to the heart
She was too fond of her most filthy bargain.
Oth Ha!
Emil Do thy worst •
This deed of thine is no more worthy heaven
Than thou wast worthy her   161
Oth   Peace, you were best
Emil Thou hast not half that power to do
    me harm
As I have to be hurt O gull! O dolt!
As ignorant as dirt! thou hast done a deed—
I care not for thy sword, I'll make thee
    known,
Though I lost twenty lives—Help! help, ho!
    help!
The Moor hath kill'd my mistress! Murder!
    murder!

    Enter MONTANO, GRATIANO, IAGO, *and*
    others.

Mon What is the matter? How now, gen-
    eral!
Emil O, are you come, Iago? you have
    done well,
That men must lay their murders on your
    neck   170
Gra What is the matter?
Emil Disprove this villain, if thou be'st a
    man
He says thou told'st him that his wife was
    false •

I know thou didst not, thou'rt not such a villain :
Speak, for my heart is full

Iago. I told him what I thought, and told
no more
Than what he found himself was apt and
true.

Emil. But did you ever tell him she was
false ?

Iago I did.

Emil. You told a lie ; an odious, damned
lie ;   180
Upon my soul, a lie, a wicked lie.
She false with Cassio '—did you say with
Cassio ?

Iago. With Cassio, mistress Go to, charm
your tongue.

Emil I will not charm my tongue ; I am
bound to speak :
My mistress here lies murder'd in her bed,—

All O heavens forfend !

Emil. And your reports have set the murder on

Oth. Nay, stare not, masters : it is true,
indeed

Gra 'Tis a strange truth.

Mon. O monstrous act!

Emil Villany, villany, villany ! 190
I think upon't, I think . I smell't: O villany'—
I thought so then : — I'll kill myself for
grief —
O villany, villany !

Iago. What, are you mad ? I charge you,
get you home

Emil. Good gentlemen, let me have leave
to speak :
'Tis proper I obey him, but not now.
Perchance, Iago, I will ne'er go home

Oth O'! O ! O '   [*He falls on the bed.*

Emil. Nay, lay thee down and roar ;
For thou hast kill'd the sweetest innocent
That e'er did lift up eye

Oth. [*Rising*] O, she was foul ! 200
I scarce did know you, uncle : there lies your
niece,
Whose breath, indeed, these hands have newly stopp'd .
I know this act shows horrible and grim.

Gra. Poor Desdemona ! I am glad thy
father's dead :
Thy match was mortal to him, and pure grief
Shore his old thread in twain : did he live
now,
This sight would make him do a desperate
turn,
Yea, curse his better angel from his side,
And fall to reprobation.

Oth. 'Tis pitiful ; but yet Iago knows 210
That she with Cassio hath the act of shame
A thousand times committed , Cassio confess'd it :
And she did gratify his amorous works
With that recognizance and pledge of love
Which I first gave her ; I saw it in his hand :
It was a handkerchief, an antique token
My father gave my mother.

Emil. O heaven ' O heavenly powers !

Iago. Come, hold your peace.

Emil.   'Twill out, 'twill out : I peace !
No, I will speak as liberal as the north : 220
Let heaven and men and devils, let them all,
All, all, cry shame against me, yet I'll speak

Iago. Be wise, and get you home.

Emil.   I will not
    [*Iago offers to stab Emilia.*

Gra   Fie!
Your sword upon a woman ?

Emil O thou dull Moor ' that handker
chief thou speak'st of
I found by fortune and did give my husband;
For often, with a solemn earnestness,
More than indeed belong'd to such a trifle,
He begg'd of me to steal it.

Iago.   Villanous whore !

Emil She give it Cassio ! no, alas ! I found
it,   230
And I did give't my husband

Iago   Filth, thou liest !

Emil. By heaven, I do not, I do not, gentlemen.
O murderous coxcomb ! what should such a
fool
Do with so good a woman ?

Oth   Are there no stones in heaven
But what serve for the thunder ?—Precious
villian !
    [*He runs at Iago . Iago, from behind,
         stabs Emilia, and exit.*

Gra The woman falls , sure, he hath kill'd
his wife.

Emil Ay, ay : O, lay me by my mistress'
side.

Gra. He's gone, but his wife's kill'd.

Mon 'Tis a notorious villain. Take you this
weapon,
Which I have here recover'd from the Moor :
Come, guard the door without ; let him not
pass,   241
But kill him rather. I'll after that same villain,
For 'tis a damned slave.
    [*Exeunt Montano and Gratiano.*

Oth   I am not valiant neither,
But every puny whipster gets my sword :
But why should honor outlive honesty ?
Let it go all

Emil.   What did thy song bode, lady ?
Hark, canst thou hear me ? I will play the
swan,
And die in music. [*Singing*] Willow, willow,
willow,—
Moor, she was chaste ; she loved thee, cruel
Moor ;
So come my soul to bliss, as I speak true; 250
So speaking as I think, I die, I die.   [*Dies.*

Oth. I have another weapon in this chamber ;
It is a sword of Spain, the ice-brook's temper :—
O, here it is. Uncle, I must come forth.

Gra. [*Within*] If thou attempt it, it will
cost thee dear :

Thou hast no weapon, and perforce must suf-
    fer.
Oth. Look in upon me then and speak with
    me,
Or, naked as I am, I will assault thee.

Re-enter GRATIANO.

Gra. What is the matter?
Oth.   Behold, I have a weapon;
A better never did itself sustain   260
Upon a soldier's thigh: I have seen the day,
That, with this little arm and this good sword,
I have made my way through more impedi-
    ments
Than twenty times your stop: but, O vain
    boast!
Who can control his fate? 'tis not so now.
Be not afraid, though you do see me weap-
    on'd;
Here is my journey's end, here is my butt,
And very sea-mark of my utmost sail.
Do you go back dismay'd? 'tis a lost fear;
Man but a rush against Othello's breast,   270
And he retires. Where should Othello go?
Now, how dost thou look now? O ill-starr'd
    wench!
Pale as thy smock! when we shall meet at
    compt,
This look of thine will hurl my soul from
    heaven,
And fiends will snatch at it. Cold, cold, my
    girl!
Even like thy chastity. O cursed slave!
Whip me, ye devils,
From the possession of this heavenly sight!
Blow me about in winds! roast me in sul-
    phur!
Wash me in steep-down gulfs of liquid fire!
O Desdemona! Desdemona! dead!   281
Oh! Oh! Oh!

Enter LODOVICO, MONTANO, CASSIO *carried in
a chair, and* Officers *with* IAGO, *prisoner.*

Lod. Where is this rash and most unfor-
    tunate man?
Oth. That's he that was Othello: here I
    am.
Lod. Where is that viper? bring the villain
    forth.
Oth. I look down towards his feet; but that's
    a fable.
If that thou be'st a devil, I cannot kill thee.
                        [*Wounds* Iago.
Lod. Wrench his sword from him.
Iago.   I bleed, sir; but not kill'd.
Oth. I am not sorry neither: I'ld have thee
    live;
For, in my sense, 'tis happiness to die.   200
Lod. O thou Othello, thou wert once so
    good,
Fall'n in the practice of a damned slave,
What shall be said to thee?
Oth.   Why, any thing:
An honorable murderer, if you will;
For nought I did in hate, but all in honor,

Lod. This wretch hath part confess'd his
    villany:
Did you and he consent in Cassio's death?
Oth. Ay.
Cas. Dear general, I never gave you cause.
Oth. I do believe it, and I ask your pardon.
Will you, I pray, demand that demi-devil 301
Why he hath thus ensnared my soul and
    body?
Iago. Demand me nothing: what you know,
    you know:
From this time forth I never will speak word.
Lod. What, not to pray?
Gra.   Torments will ope your lips.
Oth. Well, thou dost best.
Lod. Sir, you shall understand what hath
    befall'n,
Which, as I think, you know not. Here is a
    letter
Found in the pocket of the slain Roderigo;
And here another: the one of them imports
The death of Cassio to be undertook   311
By Roderigo.
Oth. O villain!
Cas.   Most heathenish and most gross!
Lod. Now here's another discontented
    paper,
Found in his pocket too; and this, it seems,
Roderigo meant to have sent this damned vil-
    lain;
But that belike Iago in the interim
Came in and satisfied him.
Oth.   O the pernicious caitiff!
How came you, Cassio, by that handkerchief
That was my wife's?
Cas.   I found it in my chamber: 320
And he himself confess'd but even now
That there he dropp'd it for a special purpose
Which wrought to his desire.
Oth.   O fool! fool! fool!
Cas. There is besides in Roderigo's letter,
How he upbraids Iago, that he made him
Brave me upon the watch; whereon it came
That I was cast: and even but now he spake,
After long seeming dead, Iago hurt him,
Iago set him on.
Lod. You must forsake this room, and go
    with us: 330
Your power and your command is taken off,
And Cassio rules in Cyprus. For this slave,
If there be any cunning cruelty
That can torment him much and hold him
    long,
It shall be his. You shall close prisoner rest,
Till that the nature of your fault be known
To the Venetian state. Come, bring him
    away.
Oth. Soft you; a word or two before you
    go.
I have done the state some service, and they
    know't.
No more of that. I pray you, in your letters,
When you shall these unlucky deeds relate,
Speak of me as I am; nothing extenuate,
Nor set down aught in malice: then must you
    speak

                                           52

Of one that loved not wisely but too well ;
Of one not easily jealous, but being wrought
Perplex'd in the extreme; of one whose
  hand,
Like the base Indian, threw a pearl away
Richer than all his tribe ; of one whose sub-
  dued eyes,
Albeit unused to the melting mood,
Drop tears as fast as the Arabian trees   350
Their medicinal gum   Set you down this ;
And say besides, that in Aleppo once,
Where a malignant and a turban'd Turk
Beat a Venetian and traduced the state,
I took by the throat the circumcised dog
And smote him, thus.   [*Stabs himself.*
  Lod.   O bloody period !
  Gra.   All that's spoke is marr'd.
  Oth.   I kiss'd thee ere I kill'd thee : no way
    but this ;

Killing myself, to die upon a kiss.
              [*Falls on the bed, and dies.*
  Cas. This did I fear, but thought he had no
        weapon ;   360
For he was great of heart.
  Lod.   [*To Iago*] O Spartan dog,
More fell than anguish, hunger, or the sea !
Look on the tragic loading of this bed ;
This is thy work : the object poisons sight ;
Let it be hid.   Gratiano, keep the house,
And seize upon the fortunes of the Moor,
For they succeed on you. To you, lord gover-
        nor,
Remains the censure of this hellish villain ;
The time, the place, the torture : O, enforce
        it !
Myself will straight aboard : and to the state
This heavy act with heavy heart relate.   371
                                      [*Exeunt.*

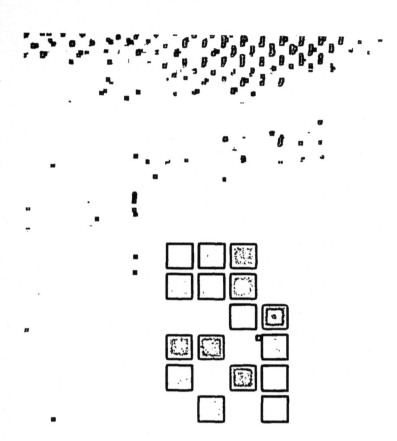